TABLE OF THE INCOMPLETE ELLIPTIC INTEGRAL OF THE THIRD KIND

A TABLE OF THE INCOMPLETE ELLIPTIC INTEGRAL OF THE THIRD KIND

By

R. G. Selfridge

and

J. E. Maxfield

Research Department

U. S. Naval Ordnance Test Station, INYOKERN, CALIF.

RESEARCH DEPT.

DOVER PUBLICATIONS, INC.

NEW YORK

1958

U. S. NAVAL ORDNANCE TEST STATION
(An Activity of the Bureau of Ordnance)

W. W. HOLLISTER, CAPT., USN
Commander

WM. B. MCLEAN, PH.D.
Technical Director

Released Within the Department of Defense

as

NAVORD REPORT 5643
NOTS 1870

Library of Congress Catalog Card Number 58-59927

Printed in the United States of America

FOREWORD

The tables included in this book were computed to solve a specific problem. It was found that the surface area of certain geometrical bodies could be expressed only in terms of the incomplete elliptic integral of the third and lower kinds. A search of the literature was made, which determined that complete values for the integral of the third kind were not available, and it was therefore decided to compute such a table.

This table will be of greatest use to physicists, engineers, and applied mathematicians who work in the fields of fluid dynamics, heat flow, and related topics. The integral appears in the solution of problems dealing with the motion of the spherical pendulum and related mechanisms, in problems of magnetic potentials due to circular current or of the gravitational potential of a uniform circular disk, and in certain kinds of seismological work.

Formerly, rough approximations or individual values calculated with considerable effort had to serve. It is hoped that the users of this table will find it useful and that the onus of the incomplete elliptic integral of the third kind has been permanently lifted.

The actual computation of this table was performed in 1956 and early in 1957 on an IBM Type 704 Calculator; the greatest difficulty was encountered not in constructing the table but in obtaining satisfactory checking.

The introductory pages have been reviewed for technical accuracy by L. E. Ward, Jr. and D. E. Zilmer; the tables have not been reviewed, as an echo-checking procedure described in the Introduction was used to ensure complete printing, and the computation was verified with a check integral at the completion of each value of α.

JOHN H. SHENK
Head, Research Department

Released under
the authority of:

WM. B. MC LEAN
Technical Director

ACKNOWLEDGMENT

The table was computed to aid in the solutions of a problem proposed by K. H. Bischel and his colleagues. Support and encouragement toward completion and publication were freely given by H. E. Tillitt and J. H. Shenk of the Research Department. Mr. Emlen Littell and other personnel of the Technical Information Department of the Station assisted the authors in editing, in negotiation, and in the mechanics of book publishing.

CONTENTS

INTRODUCTION

ELLIPTIC INTEGRALS OF THE THIRD KIND

The elliptic integral of the third kind is given by the formulas

$$\Pi(\phi, \alpha^2, k) = \int_0^{\phi} \frac{d\theta}{(1 - \alpha^2 \sin^2\theta)\sqrt{1 - k^2 \sin^2\theta}}$$

$$= \int_0^{y} \frac{dt}{(1 - \alpha^2 t^2)\sqrt{(1 - t^2)(1 - k^2 t^2)}}$$

where $y = \sin\phi$, $t = \sin\theta$, $\alpha^2 \neq 1$, $\alpha^2 \neq k^2$.

If $\phi = \pi/2$ ($y = 1$), the integral is said to be complete and one writes $\Pi(\pi/2, \alpha^2, k) = \Pi(\alpha^2, k)$.

There are two important reference sources for elliptic integrals of the third kind.[1,2] The second of these is a compendium of available tables, and errors for many of them; the first contains some tables and a large supply of useful formulas.

For certain values of α^2 the elliptic integral can be reduced to combinations of Theta and Jacobian Zeta functions of real arguments. Hence, it can be evaluated with available tables (the formulas are listed in the appropriate section). These 'hyperbolic' cases occur if $\alpha^2 > 1$ or $0 < \alpha^2 < k^2$. For the remaining or 'circular' cases, the arguments of the Theta and Zeta functions are complex. This table considers the range $\alpha^2 < 1$, which introduces some excess only for the range $0 < \alpha^2 < k^2$.

In all cases the complete integral can be reduced to com-

[1] Byrd, P. F. and M. D. Friedman. *Handbook of Elliptic Integrals for Engineers and Physicists*. Berlin, Springer, 1954.

[2] Fletcher, Alan. "Guide to Tables of Elliptic Functions," *Math. Tables*, Vol. 3 (1948–1949), pp. 229–281.

binations of integrals of the first and second kind; Fletcher lists the few tables available.[2]

The following sections list some formulas,[3] showing the relations that may be established between the different elliptic integrals.

Complete Integrals

Complete integrals may be given using Heuman's Lambda function [4]

$$\Lambda_0(\beta, k) = \frac{2}{\pi}\left[EF(\beta, k') + KE(\beta, k') - KF(\beta, k')\right]$$

or the Jacobian Zeta function[5]

$$Z(\beta, k) = E(\beta, k) - EF(\beta, k)/K$$

where

$k'^2 + k^2 = 1, \quad E = E(\pi/2, k), \quad K = F(\pi/2, k).$
$E(\beta, k)$ is the elliptic integral of the second kind.
$F(\beta, k)$ is the elliptic integral of the first kind.

CASE I. $\alpha^2 < 0$

$$\phi = \sin^{-1}\sqrt{\frac{\alpha^2}{\alpha^2 - k^2}} \qquad \beta = \sin^{-1}\frac{1}{\sqrt{1-\alpha^2}}$$

$$\Pi(\alpha^2, k) = \frac{k^2 K}{k^2 - \alpha^2} - \frac{\pi}{2}\frac{\alpha^2 \Lambda_0(\phi, k)}{\sqrt{\alpha^2(1-\alpha^2)(\alpha^2 - k^2)}}$$

$$\Pi(-k, k) = \frac{1}{4(1+k)}\left[\pi + 2(1+k)K\right]$$

$$\Pi(\alpha^2, k) = \frac{K}{1-\alpha^2} + \frac{\pi}{2}\frac{\alpha^2[\Lambda_0(\beta, k) - 1]}{\sqrt{\alpha^2(1-\alpha^2)(\alpha^2 - k^2)}}$$

[3] Byrd and Friedman, *op. cit.*, p. 600.

[4] *Ibid.*, pp. 344–349. See also C. Heuman. "Tables of Complete Elliptic Integrals," *J. Math. Phys.*, Vol. 19–20 (1940–1941), pp. 127–206.

[5] *Ibid.*, pp. 336-343.

CASE II. $k^2 < \alpha^2 < 1$

$$\theta = \sin^{-1} \sqrt{\frac{1-\alpha^2}{1-k^2}} \qquad \xi = \sin^{-1} \sqrt{\frac{\alpha^2 - k^2}{\alpha^2(1-k^2)}}$$

$$\Pi(\alpha^2, k) = K + \frac{\pi}{2} \frac{\alpha[1-\Lambda_0(\theta, k)]}{\sqrt{(\alpha^2-k^2)(1-\alpha^2)}}$$

$$\Pi(k^2, k) = E/1 - k^2$$

$$\Pi(k, k) = \frac{1}{4(1-k)} [\pi + 2(1-k)k]$$

$$\Pi(\alpha^2, k) = \frac{\pi}{2} \frac{\alpha\Lambda_0(\xi, k)}{\sqrt{(\alpha^2-k^2)(1-\alpha^2)}}$$

CASE III. $0<\alpha^2<k^2$

$$\beta = \sin^{-1}(\alpha/k)$$

$$\Pi(\alpha^2, k) = K + \frac{\alpha K Z(\beta, k)}{\sqrt{(1-\alpha^2)(k^2-\alpha^2)}}$$

$$\Pi(k^2, k) = E/(1-k^2)$$

CASE IV. $\alpha^2>1$

$$\beta = \sin^{-1}(1/\alpha)$$

$$\Pi(\alpha^2, k) = -\frac{\alpha K Z(\beta, k)}{\sqrt{(\alpha^2-1)(\alpha^2-k^2)}}$$

For complex parameter α^2, certain cases may be reduced to combinations of real parameters.[6]

Incomplete Integrals

The formulas for incomplete integrals are far more complicated, and involve Theta functions. For this reason only the formulas for the hyperbolic cases are given.

$$v = \pi F(\phi, k)/2K \qquad \omega(\gamma) = \pi F(\gamma, k)/2K$$

$$p = \pi K'/2K = \pi K(k')/2K \qquad q = e^{-2p}$$

[6] Byrd and Friedman, *op. cit.*, pp. 231-232.

CASE I. $\alpha^2>1$

$$A=\sin^{-1}(1/\alpha)$$

$$\theta_1(v)=2\sum_{m=1}^{\infty}(-1)^{m-1}q^{(m-1/2)^2}\sin(2m-1)v$$

$$\Omega_4=\frac{1}{2}\ln\frac{\theta_1[\omega(A)+v]}{\theta_1[\omega(A)-v]}=\frac{1}{2}\ln\frac{\sin[\omega(A)+v]}{\sin[\omega(A)-v]}$$

$$+\sum_{m=1}^{\infty}q^m\frac{\sin 2mv\sin 2m\omega(A)}{m\sinh 2mp}$$

$$\Pi(\phi,\alpha^2,k)=-\frac{\alpha[F(\phi,k)Z(A,k)-\Omega_4]}{\sqrt{(\alpha^2-1)(\alpha^2-k^2)}}$$

$$\Pi(\phi,1,k)=\frac{1}{k'^2}[k'^2F(\phi,k)-E(\phi,k)$$

$$+\sqrt{1-k^2\sin^2\phi}\tan\phi]$$

CASE II. $0<\alpha^2<k^2$

$$\beta=\sin^{-1}(\alpha/k)\qquad\theta_0(v)=1+2\sum_{m=1}^{\infty}(-1)^m q^{m^2}\cos 2mv$$

$$\Omega_3=\frac{1}{2}\ln\frac{\theta_0[v+\omega(\beta)]}{\theta_0[v-\omega(\beta)]}=\sum_{m=1}^{\infty}\frac{\sin 2m\omega(\beta)\sin 2mv}{m\sinh 2mp}$$

$$\Pi(\phi,\alpha^2,k)=F(\phi,k)+\frac{\alpha[F(\phi,k)Z(\beta,k)-\Omega_3]}{\sqrt{(1-\alpha^2)(k^2-\alpha^2)}}$$

$$\Pi(\phi,k^2,k)=\frac{1}{k'^2}\left[E(\phi,k)-k^2\frac{\sin\phi\cos\phi}{\sqrt{1-k^2\sin^2\phi}}\right]$$

Differential Equations

The third elliptic integral also satisfies the following equation:

$$k^2k'^2(k^2-\alpha^2)\frac{\partial^3\Pi}{\partial k^3}+k(\alpha^2+4k^2+3\alpha^2k^2-8k^4)\frac{\partial^2\Pi}{\partial k^2}$$

$$+(2k^2-\alpha^2-13k^4)\frac{\partial\Pi}{\partial k}-3k^3\Pi=-\frac{3k^3\sin\phi\cos\phi}{\sqrt{(1-k^2\sin^2\phi)^5}}$$

If $\phi=\pi/2$, the right side of this equation conveniently vanishes. This equation supplied a very useful check on the computations.

Addition Formula

There is one other relation of considerable importance, in that it enables one to consider only the case of $|\alpha^2|\leqq 1$.

$$\Pi(\phi,\alpha^2,k)+\Pi(\phi,k^2/\alpha^2,k)=F(\phi,k)$$

$$+\sqrt{\frac{\alpha^2}{(1-\alpha^2)(\alpha^2-k^2)}}\tan^{-1}\sqrt{\frac{(1-\alpha^2)(\alpha^2-k^2)}{\alpha^2(1-k^2\sin^2\phi)}}\tan\phi$$

METHOD OF COMPUTATION AND CHECKING

These tables were produced on an IBM Type 704 Calculator, using a simple Simpson's Rule method of integration. The results of integration were stored for each .01 radian, and printed out in groups of ten lines at a time. In order to compensate for accumulated roundoff in the angle, every .1 radian was fed in from a separate list, adjusting the mesh size for one integration, so that at no point is the angle in error by more than 10^{-7}.

The method of printing is naturally of concern, since a large amount of error can occur here. Printing was handled by the computer using a method known as echo-checking. With this process, the type wheels are set as ordered, and then an independent pulse is returned to the computer, indicating what symbol has been printed. A comparison of the return, or echo, with the initial command ensures that what was printed is what was desired. After being printed by the computer, the tabulation was reproduced by the photolithographic process, so that there should be no variation between the initial printing and the final result.

There still remained the problem of checking the computation. This was handled in the following way: Computation proceeded by Simpson's Rule with a mesh size of about .0025 until $\phi = 1.57$. At this point the mesh size was changed so that the next point was computed with $\phi = \pi/2$, yielding all the complete integrals. An entirely different method was then used for obtaining the complete integral, and this has been printed as the last line of each group in the table. Comparison between these lines gives a very excellent indication of the upper limit of the error. There are possible roundoff errors in both the table and the independent check but it seems entirely reasonable that if there is a check for the first n places then the first $n - 1$ places are correct. Furthermore, since the value for $\phi = \pi/2$ was based on all the prior computations for smaller angles, if there is a check at $\pi/2$ the prior computations should have at least the same accuracy.

With the argument as outlined, no attempt has been made to proof or check the printed sheets in any way other than by a comparison of the resultant complete integrals.

Computation of the Check Integral

The complete integral was computed by using the differential equation given earlier, integrating from 0 to K_{15}. For values of $\alpha^2 < 0$ no problems were encountered. For values of $\alpha^2 > 0$ there is the problem of a singularity at $k = \alpha$. This was handled by integrating from 0 to the largest k_i less than α, and then starting again at $k = \alpha$.

Integration was handled by Gill's version of the Runge-Kutta fourth-order method.[7] The necessary starting values are given by the following formulas:

[7] Gill, "A Process for the Step-by-Step Integration of Differential Equations in an Automatic Digital Computing Machine," *Proc. Camb. Phil. Soc.*, Vol. 47 (1951), pp. 96–108.

$k=0$

$$\Pi = \pi/2\sqrt{1-\alpha^2}$$

$$\frac{\partial \Pi}{\partial k} = 0$$

$$\partial^2\Pi/\partial k^2 = \frac{\pi}{2\alpha^2}\left(\frac{1}{\sqrt{1-\alpha^2}} - 1\right)$$

$$\frac{\partial^3 \Pi}{\partial k^3} = 0$$

$E = E(\pi/2, \alpha)$ and $F = F(\pi/2, \alpha)$ are complete integrals of the second and first kinds, respectively.

$k=\alpha$

$$\Pi = E/1-\alpha^2$$

$$\partial\Pi/\partial k = \frac{1}{3\alpha(1-\alpha^2)^2}\left[E + \alpha^2 E - (1-\alpha^2)F\right]$$

$$\frac{\partial^2\Pi}{\partial k^2} = \frac{1}{5\alpha(1-\alpha^2)}\left[3\alpha\Pi - (1-13\alpha^2)\frac{\partial\Pi}{\partial k}\right]$$

$$= \frac{E}{15\alpha^2(1-\alpha^2)^3}(4\alpha^4 + 21\alpha^2 - 1)$$

$$+ \frac{F}{15\alpha^2(1-\alpha^2)^2}(1-13\alpha^2)$$

$$\partial^3\Pi/\partial k^3 = \frac{E}{105(1-\alpha^2)^4\alpha^3}(36\alpha^6 + 618\alpha^4 + 72\alpha^2 - 6)$$

$$+ \frac{F}{105(1-\alpha^2)^3\alpha^3}(6 - 69\alpha^2 - 297\alpha^4).$$

USE OF THE TABLE

This table is given primarily as a function of α^2. For each value of α^2 fifteen values of k are tabulated for $k = \sin\theta$, $\theta = .1(.1)1.5$, and angular values of $\phi = 0(.01)1.57$ and $\phi = \pi/2$. The last line of each group is a duplicate computation of the complete integral, which serves as a check on the computation. If the two values given for the complete integral agree to n places, this can be considered to give an accurate table to within ± 2 in the nth place. To allow for the slight inaccuracies in angles, and accumulated roundoff, the safest estimate is probably that the values given are correct to $n - 1$ places if the two complete integrals agree to n places.

It will be noticed that certain fractional values print with a sequence of 9's (e.g., .099999 for .1). The particular program used for printing does not make any attempt at rounding off; hence any error that produces a number very slightly less than desired, will produce a sequence of 9's. In all cases, however, the angular values are correct to within 5 in the seventh place.

The table has been printed, for each α, in groups of three. Each group yields a full set of angular values, on four facing pages, for five of the fifteen possible values of k. The entire table is ordered in increasing sequence on α^2, starting at $\alpha^2 = -1.00$.

For values of $\alpha^2 < -1$, one must use the relation given as an addition formula, which yields the value of $\Pi(\phi, \alpha^2, k)$ as a function of $\Pi(\phi, k^2/\alpha^2, k)$. Since large negative values of α^2 will depend on the values for small negative α^2, more values than might be expected are given for $-.1 < \alpha^2 < 0$.

The one missing α^2, namely $\alpha^2 = 0$, is given by $\Pi(\phi, 0, k) = F(\phi, k)$.

TABLE OF THE INCOMPLETE ELLIPTIC INTEGRAL OF THE THIRD KIND

$\alpha =$ -1.000000

Θ	K VALUES				
	.009966711	.039469502	.087332193	.151646642	.229848846
.0000000	.000000	.000000	.000000	.000000	.000000
.0100000	.009999	.009999	.009999	.009999	.009999
.0200000	.019997	.019997	.019997	.019997	.019997
.0300000	.029991	.029991	.029991	.029991	.029992
.0400000	.039978	.039979	.039979	.039980	.039981
.0500000	.049958	.049959	.049960	.049961	.049963
.0600000	.059928	.059929	.059931	.059933	.059936
.0700000	.069886	.069888	.069891	.069894	.069899
.0800000	.079831	.079833	.079837	.079843	.079849
.0900000	.089759	.089763	.089769	.089776	.089786
.1000000	.099670	.099675	.099683	.099694	.099707
.1100000	.109562	.109569	.109579	.109593	.109611
.1200000	.119433	.119441	.119455	.119473	.119496
.1300000	.129281	.129291	.129309	.129332	.129360
.1400000	.139103	.139117	.139138	.139167	.139203
.1500000	.148900	.148916	.148943	.148978	.149022
.1600000	.158668	.158688	.158720	.158763	.158816
.1700000	.168407	.168430	.168469	.168520	.168583
.1800000	.178114	.178142	.178187	.178248	.178323
.1900000	.187788	.187821	.187874	.187946	.188033
.2000000	.197428	.197466	.197528	.197612	.197713
.2100000	.207032	.207076	.207148	.207244	.207361
.2200000	.216599	.216649	.216731	.216842	.216977
.2300000	.226127	.226184	.226278	.226404	.226557
.2400000	.235615	.235680	.235786	.235929	.236103
.2500000	.245062	.245136	.245255	.245415	.245611
.2600000	.254467	.254549	.254683	.254863	.255083
.2700000	.263828	.263920	.264069	.264270	.264515
.2800000	.273145	.273247	.273412	.273636	.273909
.2900000	.282416	.282529	.282712	.282959	.283261
.3000000	.291640	.291764	.291967	.292239	.292573
.3100000	.300817	.300954	.301176	.301475	.301842
.3200000	.309946	.310095	.310338	.310667	.311069
.3300000	.319025	.319188	.319454	.319812	.320252
.3400000	.328054	.328232	.328521	.328912	.329390
.3500000	.337033	.337226	.337540	.337964	.338484
.3600000	.345961	.346169	.346509	.346969	.347533
.3700000	.354836	.355062	.355429	.355926	.356535
.3800000	.363659	.363902	.364298	.364834	.365492
.3900000	.372429	.372690	.373117	.373693	.374401

$\alpha = -1.000000$

Θ	K VALUES				
	.009966711	.039469502	.087332193	.151646642	.229848846
.4000000	.381146	.381426	.381884	.382503	.383264
.4100000	.389809	.390109	.390599	.391263	.392078
.4200000	.398417	.398738	.399262	.399973	.400845
.4300000	.406971	.407314	.407873	.408632	.409564
.4400000	.415471	.415836	.416432	.417240	.418235
.4500000	.423915	.424304	.424938	.425798	.426857
.4600000	.432305	.432717	.433391	.434305	.435431
.4700000	.440639	.441076	.441791	.442761	.443956
.4800000	.448918	.449381	.450138	.451165	.452433
.4900000	.457141	.457631	.458431	.459519	.460861
.5000000	.465309	.465826	.466672	.467821	.469240
.5100000	.473422	.473967	.474859	.476072	.477570
.5200000	.481480	.482054	.482993	.484272	.485852
.5300000	.489482	.490086	.491075	.492421	.494086
.5400000	.497429	.498064	.499103	.500519	.502271
.5500000	.505321	.505988	.507079	.508567	.510408
.5600000	.513159	.513858	.515003	.516563	.518497
.5700000	.520942	.521674	.522874	.524510	.526538
.5800000	.528671	.529437	.530693	.532407	.534533
.5900000	.536346	.537147	.538460	.540254	.542479
.6000000	.543967	.544804	.546176	.548051	.550379
.6100000	.551535	.552409	.553841	.555799	.558233
.6200000	.559050	.559961	.561455	.563499	.566040
.6300000	.566513	.567461	.569019	.571150	.573801
.6400000	.573923	.574911	.576533	.578753	.581517
.6500000	.581282	.582309	.583996	.586308	.589188
.6600000	.588589	.589656	.591411	.593816	.596814
.6700000	.595845	.596954	.598777	.601277	.604396
.6800000	.603051	.604201	.606095	.608691	.611933
.6899999	.610206	.611400	.613364	.616060	.619428
.7000000	.617313	.618550	.620587	.623383	.626880
.7100000	.624370	.625652	.627762	.630661	.634289
.7200000	.631379	.632706	.634891	.637895	.641656
.7300000	.638340	.639712	.641974	.645084	.648982
.7400000	.645253	.646672	.649012	.652230	.656267
.7500000	.652120	.653586	.656004	.659333	.663511
.7600000	.658941	.660455	.662953	.666394	.670716
.7700000	.665715	.667278	.669858	.673412	.677881
.7800000	.672445	.674057	.676719	.680390	.685007
.7899999	.679130	.680793	.683538	.687326	.692095

$\alpha =$ -1.000000

Θ	K VALUES				
	.009966711	.039469502	.087332193	.151646642	.229848846
.8000000	.685771	.687485	.690315	.694222	.699145
.8100000	.692369	.694134	.697050	.701079	.706157
.8200000	.698924	.700741	.703744	.707896	.713133
.8300000	.705437	.707307	.710399	.714674	.720073
.8400000	.711909	.713831	.717013	.721415	.726978
.8500000	.718339	.720316	.723588	.728118	.733847
.8600000	.724729	.726761	.730125	.734784	.740682
.8700000	.731080	.733166	.736623	.741414	.747483
.8799999	.737391	.739534	.743084	.748009	.754251
.8899999	.743664	.745863	.749509	.754568	.760986
.9000000	.749899	.752155	.755897	.761092	.767688
.9100000	.756097	.758411	.762250	.767583	.774359
.9200000	.762258	.764630	.768567	.774040	.780999
.9300000	.768384	.770815	.774851	.780464	.787609
.9400000	.774473	.776964	.781100	.786857	.794188
.9500000	.780529	.783079	.787316	.793217	.800738
.9600000	.786550	.789161	.793500	.799547	.807260
.9699999	.792537	.795209	.799652	.805845	.813753
.9799999	.798492	.801226	.805772	.812114	.820218
.9899999	.804415	.807210	.811862	.818354	.826656
1.0000000	.810306	.813164	.817921	.824565	.833067
1.0100000	.816166	.819087	.823951	.830748	.839453
1.0200000	.821995	.824980	.829952	.836903	.845813
1.0300000	.827795	.830844	.835924	.843031	.852147
1.0400000	.833565	.836679	.841868	.849132	.858458
1.0500000	.839307	.842485	.847785	.855208	.864744
1.0600000	.845021	.848265	.853676	.861258	.871007
1.0699999	.850708	.854017	.859540	.867283	.877248
1.0799999	.856368	.859743	.865379	.873284	.883466
1.0899999	.862002	.865444	.871192	.879262	.889662
1.1000000	.867610	.871119	.876982	.885216	.895837
1.1100000	.873193	.876770	.882747	.891147	.901991
1.1200000	.878752	.882396	.888490	.897057	.908125
1.1300000	.884287	.888000	.894209	.902944	.914239
1.1400000	.889798	.893580	.899906	.908811	.920333
1.1500000	.895288	.899138	.905582	.914658	.926409
1.1600000	.900755	.904674	.911237	.920484	.932467
1.1700000	.906200	.910189	.916871	.926291	.938507
1.1800000	.911625	.915684	.922485	.932079	.944530
1.1899999	.917029	.921159	.928080	.937848	.950536

$\alpha = -1.000000$

Θ	K VALUES				
	.009966711	.039469502	.087332193	.151646642	.229848846
1.2000000	.922413	.926614	.933656	.943600	.956526
1.2100000	.927778	.932050	.939213	.949335	.962500
1.2200000	.933125	.937467	.944753	.955052	.968458
1.2300000	.938453	.942867	.950276	.960753	.974402
1.2400000	.943764	.948250	.955781	.966438	.980331
1.2500000	.949057	.953616	.961271	.972108	.986247
1.2599999	.954334	.958965	.966745	.977763	.992148
1.2699999	.959596	.964299	.972203	.983404	.998037
1.2799999	.964842	.969618	.977647	.989031	1.003913
1.2899999	.970073	.974922	.983077	.994644	1.009778
1.3000000	.975289	.980213	.988493	1.000245	1.015630
1.3100000	.980492	.985489	.993896	1.005833	1.021471
1.3200000	.985682	.990753	.999286	1.011409	1.027302
1.3300000	.990859	.996004	1.004665	1.016974	1.033122
1.3400000	.996023	1.001243	1.010031	1.022528	1.038932
1.3500000	1.001176	1.006470	1.015387	1.028071	1.044733
1.3600000	1.006318	1.011686	1.020732	1.033605	1.050524
1.3700000	1.011449	1.016893	1.026066	1.039128	1.056308
1.3799999	1.016571	1.022089	1.031391	1.044643	1.062082
1.3899999	1.021682	1.027275	1.036707	1.050149	1.067849
1.4000000	1.026784	1.032453	1.042015	1.055647	1.073609
1.4100000	1.031878	1.037622	1.047314	1.061137	1.079362
1.4200000	1.036964	1.042784	1.052605	1.066620	1.085108
1.4300000	1.042042	1.047937	1.057890	1.072096	1.090849
1.4400000	1.047113	1.053084	1.063167	1.077566	1.096583
1.4500000	1.052178	1.058225	1.068439	1.083030	1.102312
1.4600000	1.057236	1.063360	1.073704	1.088488	1.108037
1.4700000	1.062289	1.068489	1.078964	1.093942	1.113757
1.4800000	1.067337	1.073613	1.084220	1.099391	1.119473
1.4900000	1.072381	1.078733	1.089471	1.104836	1.125185
1.5000000	1.077420	1.083848	1.094719	1.110277	1.130894
1.5100000	1.082456	1.088961	1.099963	1.115715	1.136600
1.5200000	1.087489	1.094070	1.105204	1.121151	1.142304
1.5300000	1.092519	1.099177	1.110442	1.126584	1.148005
1.5400000	1.097548	1.104282	1.115679	1.132015	1.153705
1.5500000	1.102574	1.109385	1.120915	1.137445	1.159404
1.5600000	1.107600	1.114487	1.126149	1.142875	1.165102
1.5699999	1.112625	1.119589	1.131383	1.148303	1.170800
1.5707963	1.113026	1.119995	1.131800	1.148735	1.171253
1.5707963	1.113025	1.119995	1.131799	1.148735	1.171253

$\alpha =$ -1.000000

Θ	K VALUES				
	.318821117	.415016431	.514599755	.613601043	.708073407
.0000000	.000000	.000000	.000000	.000000	.000000
.0100000	.009999	.009999	.009999	.009999	.009999
.0200000	.019997	.019997	.019998	.019998	.019998
.0300000	.029992	.029992	.029993	.029993	.029994
.0400000	.039982	.039983	.039984	.039985	.039986
.0500000	.049965	.049967	.049969	.049971	.049973
.0600000	.059939	.059943	.059946	.059950	.059953
.0700000	.069904	.069909	.069915	.069921	.069926
.0800000	.079857	.079865	.079873	.079882	.079890
.0900000	.089797	.089808	.089820	.089832	.089844
.1000000	.099722	.099738	.099754	.099771	.099786
.1100000	.109630	.109651	.109673	.109695	.109716
.1200000	.119521	.119549	.119577	.119605	.119633
.1300000	.129392	.129427	.129464	.129500	.129534
.1400000	.139243	.139287	.139332	.139377	.139420
.1500000	.149071	.149125	.149180	.149236	.149288
.1600000	.158876	.158940	.159008	.159075	.159139
.1700000	.168655	.168733	.168813	.168894	.168971
.1800000	.178408	.178500	.178596	.178691	.178782
.1900000	.188133	.188241	.188354	.188466	.188573
.2000000	.197829	.197955	.198086	.198217	.198342
.2100000	.207496	.207641	.207792	.207943	.208088
.2200000	.217130	.217297	.217471	.217644	.217810
.2300000	.226733	.226923	.227121	.227319	.227509
.2400000	.236301	.236517	.236742	.236967	.237182
.2500000	.245836	.246079	.246333	.246586	.246829
.2600000	.255334	.255608	.255892	.256177	.256450
.2700000	.264796	.265102	.265420	.265738	.266044
.2800000	.274221	.274561	.274915	.275270	.275611
.2900000	.283607	.283984	.284377	.284770	.285149
.3000000	.292955	.293371	.293805	.294240	.294658
.3100000	.302262	.302720	.303198	.303677	.304139
.3200000	.311529	.312032	.312556	.313083	.313590
.3300000	.320755	.321305	.321879	.322455	.323011
.3400000	.329939	.330539	.331165	.331795	.332402
.3500000	.339081	.339733	.340415	.341101	.341763
.3600000	.348180	.348888	.349628	.350374	.351093
.3700000	.357236	.358002	.358804	.359612	.360392
.3800000	.366248	.367075	.367942	.368816	.369660
.3900000	.375216	.376107	.377043	.377986	.378898

$\alpha =$ -1.000000

Θ	K VALUES				
	.318821117	.415016431	.514599755	.613601043	.708073407
.4000000	.384139	.385098	.386105	.387121	.388104
.4100000	.393018	.394047	.395129	.396221	.397279
.4200000	.401851	.402955	.404115	.405287	.406423
.4300000	.410640	.411820	.413062	.414318	.415536
.4400000	.419383	.420643	.421971	.423314	.424618
.4500000	.428080	.429425	.430841	.432276	.433670
.4600000	.436732	.438163	.439673	.441203	.442690
.4700000	.445339	.446860	.448466	.450095	.451681
.4800000	.453899	.455514	.457221	.458953	.460641
.4900000	.462414	.464127	.465937	.467777	.469572
.5000000	.470883	.472697	.474616	.476567	.478473
.5100000	.479307	.481225	.483256	.485324	.487344
.5200000	.487685	.489711	.491859	.494047	.496187
.5300000	.496018	.498156	.500424	.502737	.505002
.5400000	.504306	.506559	.508951	.511394	.513788
.5500000	.512549	.514921	.517442	.520019	.522548
.5600000	.520747	.523241	.525896	.528612	.531280
.5700000	.528900	.531522	.534314	.537174	.539985
.5800000	.537010	.539761	.542695	.545704	.548665
.5900000	.545075	.547961	.551041	.554203	.557319
.6000000	.553097	.556121	.559352	.562673	.565949
.6100000	.561075	.564242	.567628	.571113	.574554
.6200000	.569011	.572323	.575870	.579523	.583136
.6300000	.576903	.580366	.584077	.587905	.591695
.6400000	.584754	.588371	.592252	.596259	.600232
.6500000	.592563	.596338	.600393	.604585	.608747
.6600000	.600330	.604267	.608502	.612884	.617241
.6700000	.608057	.612160	.616578	.621157	.625716
.6800000	.615743	.620017	.624624	.629405	.634171
.6899999	.623389	.627837	.632638	.637627	.642607
.7000000	.630996	.635622	.640622	.645825	.651026
.7100000	.638563	.643373	.648577	.653999	.659427
.7200000	.646092	.651088	.656502	.662150	.667813
.7300000	.653582	.658770	.664398	.670278	.676183
.7400000	.661035	.666419	.672266	.678385	.684538
.7500000	.668451	.674035	.680107	.686470	.692880
.7600000	.675830	.681618	.687921	.694535	.701208
.7700000	.683174	.689170	.695708	.702580	.709525
.7800000	.690481	.696691	.703470	.710607	.717831
.7899999	.697754	.704181	.711207	.718615	.726126

$\alpha =$ -1.000000

Θ	K VALUES				
	.318821117	.415016431	.514599755	.613601043	.708073407
.8000000	.704993	.711641	.718919	.726605	.734412
.8100000	.712197	.719071	.726608	.734578	.742689
.8200000	.719368	.726473	.734273	.742536	.750958
.8300000	.726506	.733846	.741915	.750477	.759221
.8400000	.733613	.741191	.749536	.758404	.767478
.8500000	.740687	.748509	.757135	.766317	.775730
.8600000	.747730	.755801	.764713	.774217	.783978
.8700000	.754743	.763066	.772271	.782104	.792223
.8799999	.761725	.770306	.779809	.789979	.800466
.8899999	.768679	.777521	.787329	.797843	.808707
.9000000	.775603	.784711	.794830	.805697	.816948
.9100000	.782499	.791878	.802313	.813540	.825189
.9200000	.789367	.799021	.809779	.821375	.833432
.9300000	.796208	.806141	.817229	.829201	.841677
.9400000	.803022	.813240	.824662	.837020	.849925
.9500000	.809810	.820316	.832080	.844832	.858178
.9600000	.816572	.827372	.839483	.852637	.866435
.9699999	.823309	.834407	.846872	.860437	.874699
.9799999	.830022	.841421	.854247	.868232	.882969
.9899999	.836710	.848417	.861609	.876022	.891247
1.0000000	.843375	.855393	.868959	.883809	.899533
1.0100000	.850018	.862351	.876296	.891593	.907829
1.0200000	.856637	.869291	.883622	.899374	.916135
1.0300000	.863235	.876214	.890937	.907154	.924452
1.0400000	.869811	.883119	.898241	.914932	.932781
1.0500000	.876367	.890008	.905536	.922710	.941123
1.0600000	.882902	.896881	.912821	.930487	.949478
1.0699999	.889417	.903739	.920097	.938265	.957847
1.0799999	.895913	.910581	.927364	.946045	.966232
1.0899999	.902390	.917409	.934623	.953825	.974632
1.1000000	.908848	.924223	.941875	.961608	.983048
1.1100000	.915289	.931024	.949119	.969394	.991482
1.1200000	.921712	.937811	.956357	.977182	.999934
1.1300000	.928118	.944585	.963589	.984974	1.008404
1.1400000	.934508	.951347	.970814	.992770	1.016893
1.1500000	.940881	.958097	.978034	1.000571	1.025401
1.1600000	.947239	.964836	.985249	1.008376	1.033930
1.1700000	.953582	.971564	.992460	1.016186	1.042480
1.1800000	.959910	.978280	.999666	1.024002	1.051050
1.1899999	.966224	.984987	1.006867	1.031824	1.059643

$\alpha =$ -1.000000

Θ	K VALUES				
	.318821117	.415016431	.514599755	.613601043	.708073407
1.2000000	.972524	.991684	1.014065	1.039652	1.068257
1.2100000	.978811	.998371	1.021260	1.047486	1.076894
1.2200000	.985085	1.005049	1.028452	1.055327	1.085554
1.2300000	.991346	1.011718	1.035640	1.063175	1.094236
1.2400000	.997595	1.018379	1.042827	1.071030	1.102942
1.2500000	1.003832	1.025032	1.050011	1.078892	1.111671
1.2599999	1.010059	1.031677	1.057193	1.086762	1.120424
1.2699999	1.016274	1.038314	1.064373	1.094640	1.129201
1.2799999	1.022479	1.044945	1.071552	1.102525	1.138001
1.2899999	1.028673	1.051568	1.078729	1.110419	1.146825
1.3000000	1.034858	1.058186	1.085905	1.118320	1.155673
1.3100000	1.041034	1.064797	1.093081	1.126229	1.164544
1.3200000	1.047201	1.071402	1.100255	1.134146	1.173438
1.3300000	1.053359	1.078001	1.107429	1.142070	1.182356
1.3400000	1.059509	1.084596	1.114602	1.150003	1.191296
1.3500000	1.065651	1.091185	1.121775	1.157944	1.200259
1.3600000	1.071786	1.097769	1.128948	1.165892	1.209244
1.3700000	1.077914	1.104349	1.136121	1.173847	1.218250
1.3799999	1.084035	1.110925	1.143293	1.181810	1.227277
1.3899999	1.090150	1.117497	1.150466	1.189780	1.236325
1.4000000	1.096258	1.124065	1.157639	1.197757	1.245392
1.4100000	1.102361	1.130629	1.164811	1.205741	1.254479
1.4200000	1.108459	1.137190	1.171985	1.213732	1.263584
1.4300000	1.114552	1.143748	1.179158	1.221728	1.272706
1.4400000	1.120640	1.150304	1.186332	1.229731	1.281844
1.4500000	1.126724	1.156856	1.193505	1.237738	1.290999
1.4600000	1.132804	1.163407	1.200680	1.245752	1.300168
1.4700000	1.138880	1.169955	1.207854	1.253770	1.309350
1.4800000	1.144953	1.176501	1.215029	1.261792	1.318545
1.4900000	1.151023	1.183045	1.222204	1.269819	1.327752
1.5000000	1.157091	1.189588	1.229380	1.277849	1.336969
1.5100000	1.163156	1.196130	1.236556	1.285883	1.346194
1.5200000	1.169219	1.202670	1.243732	1.293919	1.355428
1.5300000	1.175280	1.209209	1.250908	1.301958	1.364668
1.5400000	1.181341	1.215748	1.258084	1.309998	1.373914
1.5500000	1.187400	1.222286	1.265261	1.318040	1.383164
1.5600000	1.193458	1.228823	1.272437	1.326083	1.392416
1.5699999	1.199517	1.235361	1.279614	1.334127	1.401670
1.5707963	1.199999	1.235881	1.280185	1.334767	1.402407
1.5707963	1.199999	1.235881	1.280185	1.334767	1.402406

$\alpha =$ -1.000000

Θ	K VALUES				
	.794250555	.868696860	.928444378	.971111163	.994996249
.0000000	.000000	.000000	.000000	.000000	.000000
.0100000	.009999	.009999	.009999	.009999	.009999
.0200000	.019998	.019998	.019998	.019998	.019998
.0300000	.029994	.029994	.029995	.029995	.029995
.0400000	.039987	.039987	.039988	.039989	.039989
.0500000	.049974	.049976	.049977	.049978	.049979
.0600000	.059956	.059959	.059961	.059963	.059964
.0700000	.069931	.069935	.069939	.069941	.069942
.0800000	.079897	.079904	.079909	.079912	.079914
.0900000	.089854	.089863	.089871	.089876	.089879
.1000000	.099801	.099813	.099823	.099830	.099834
.1100000	.109735	.109752	.109765	.109775	.109780
.1200000	.119657	.119679	.119696	.119708	.119715
.1300000	.129566	.129593	.129615	.129630	.129639
.1400000	.139459	.139493	.139520	.139540	.139551
.1500000	.149337	.149379	.149412	.149436	.149450
.1600000	.159198	.159249	.159289	.159319	.159335
.1700000	.169041	.169102	.169151	.169186	.169206
.1800000	.178866	.178938	.178996	.179038	.179061
.1900000	.188671	.188756	.188824	.188873	.188901
.2000000	.198456	.198555	.198635	.198692	.198724
.2100000	.208220	.208335	.208427	.208493	.208530
.2200000	.217963	.218095	.218201	.218277	.218319
.2300000	.227683	.227833	.227955	.228041	.228090
.2400000	.237379	.237551	.237688	.237787	.237843
.2500000	.247052	.247246	.247402	.247513	.247576
.2600000	.256701	.256919	.257094	.257220	.257290
.2700000	.266325	.266569	.266765	.266906	.266985
.2800000	.275924	.276195	.276415	.276572	.276660
.2900000	.285496	.285798	.286042	.286217	.286315
.3000000	.295043	.295377	.295647	.295841	.295950
.3100000	.304563	.304932	.305230	.305444	.305564
.3200000	.314056	.314462	.314790	.315026	.315158
.3300000	.323522	.323968	.324328	.324586	.324731
.3400000	.332961	.333448	.333842	.334125	.334284
.3500000	.342372	.342904	.343334	.343643	.343816
.3600000	.351756	.352335	.352803	.353139	.353328
.3700000	.361112	.361740	.362249	.362615	.362820
.3800000	.370440	.371121	.371673	.372069	.372292
.3900000	.379740	.380477	.381074	.381503	.381745

$\alpha =$ -1.000000

Θ	K VALUES				
	.794250555	.868696860	.928444378	.971111163	.994996249
.4000000	.389013	.389808	.390452	.390916	.391177
.4100000	.398258	.399114	.399809	.400309	.400591
.4200000	.407475	.408396	.409144	.409683	.409986
.4300000	.416665	.417654	.418458	.419037	.419363
.4400000	.425828	.426888	.427750	.428372	.428722
.4500000	.434963	.436099	.437022	.437688	.438064
.4600000	.444072	.445286	.446274	.446987	.447389
.4700000	.453155	.454451	.455506	.456268	.456698
.4800000	.462212	.463593	.464719	.465532	.465991
.4900000	.471243	.472714	.473913	.474781	.475270
.5000000	.480248	.481813	.483090	.484014	.484535
.5100000	.489229	.490892	.492250	.493232	.493787
.5200000	.498186	.499950	.501392	.502437	.503027
.5300000	.507119	.508990	.510520	.511629	.512256
.5400000	.516029	.518010	.519632	.520808	.521474
.5500000	.524916	.527012	.528730	.529977	.530682
.5600000	.533781	.535998	.537815	.539135	.539882
.5700000	.542625	.544966	.546888	.548284	.549075
.5800000	.551448	.553919	.555949	.557426	.558262
.5900000	.560251	.562857	.565000	.566560	.567444
.6000000	.569035	.571781	.574041	.575688	.576622
.6100000	.577800	.580692	.583075	.584812	.585797
.6200000	.586548	.589591	.592101	.593932	.594971
.6300000	.595279	.598478	.601120	.603050	.604146
.6400000	.603993	.607356	.610135	.612167	.613322
.6500000	.612692	.616224	.619146	.621284	.622501
.6600000	.621377	.625084	.628155	.630404	.631684
.6700000	.630048	.633937	.637163	.639527	.640873
.6800000	.638707	.642784	.646170	.648655	.650070
.6899999	.647354	.651627	.655179	.657789	.659277
.7000000	.655991	.660466	.664192	.666931	.668494
.7100000	.664617	.669302	.673208	.676083	.677725
.7200000	.673235	.678137	.682230	.685246	.686969
.7300000	.681846	.686973	.691259	.694422	.696231
.7400000	.690449	.695809	.700298	.703613	.705511
.7500000	.699047	.704649	.709346	.712820	.714811
.7600000	.707641	.713492	.718407	.722046	.724134
.7700000	.716230	.722341	.727482	.731293	.733481
.7800000	.724818	.731197	.736572	.740562	.742855
.7899999	.733404	.740060	.745679	.749856	.752259

$\alpha =$ -1.000000

Θ	K VALUES				
	.794250555	.868696860	.928444378	.971111163	.994996249
.8000000	.741990	.748934	.754805	.759177	.761694
.8100000	.750577	.757819	.763952	.768526	.771163
.8200000	.759166	.766716	.773122	.777907	.780668
.8300000	.767759	.775627	.782317	.787322	.790213
.8400000	.776355	.784554	.791538	.796772	.799799
.8500000	.784958	.793498	.800788	.806261	.809430
.8600000	.793567	.802462	.810070	.815791	.819108
.8700000	.802185	.811445	.819384	.825364	.828837
.8799999	.810812	.820451	.828733	.834984	.838619
.8899999	.819449	.829481	.838120	.844654	.848458
.9000000	.828099	.838537	.847547	.854375	.858358
.9100000	.836761	.847620	.857016	.864152	.868320
.9200000	.845438	.856732	.866529	.873987	.878350
.9300000	.854130	.865876	.876090	.883884	.888451
.9400000	.862839	.875052	.885701	.893846	.898627
.9500000	.871566	.884263	.895364	.903876	.908882
.9600000	.880313	.893510	.905083	.913979	.919220
.9699999	.889080	.902796	.914859	.924157	.929646
.9799999	.897870	.912123	.924696	.934415	.940165
.9899999	.906682	.921492	.934597	.944756	.950780
1.0000000	.915520	.930906	.944565	.955186	.961498
1.0100000	.924383	.940366	.954603	.965708	.972323
1.0200000	.933273	.949875	.964714	.976326	.983261
1.0300000	.942192	.959435	.974902	.987046	.994319
1.0400000	.951141	.969048	.985169	.997873	1.005501
1.0500000	.960121	.978716	.995520	1.008811	1.016815
1.0600000	.969133	.988440	1.005958	1.019867	1.028268
1.0699999	.978179	.998225	1.016487	1.031045	1.039866
1.0799999	.987260	1.008071	1.027110	1.042351	1.051618
1.0899999	.996376	1.017980	1.037832	1.053792	1.063530
1.1000000	1.005530	1.027956	1.048656	1.065374	1.075613
1.1100000	1.014722	1.038000	1.059586	1.077103	1.087874
1.1200000	1.023954	1.048114	1.070627	1.088987	1.100323
1.1300000	1.033227	1.058302	1.081783	1.101033	1.112970
1.1400000	1.042541	1.068564	1.093058	1.113248	1.125826
1.1500000	1.051899	1.078903	1.104458	1.125641	1.138903
1.1600000	1.061300	1.089322	1.115985	1.138220	1.152212
1.1700000	1.070747	1.099823	1.127647	1.150993	1.165766
1.1800000	1.080239	1.110407	1.139446	1.163971	1.179580
1.1899999	1.089778	1.121078	1.151389	1.177163	1.193669

$\alpha =$ -1.000000

Θ	K VALUES				
	.794250555	.868696860	.928444378	.971111163	.994996249
1.2000000	1.099364	1.131836	1.163479	1.190579	1.208048
1.2100000	1.108999	1.142685	1.175723	1.204229	1.222734
1.2200000	1.118684	1.153626	1.188125	1.218126	1.237746
1.2300000	1.128417	1.164661	1.200691	1.232281	1.253105
1.2400000	1.138202	1.175791	1.213426	1.246707	1.268830
1.2500000	1.148037	1.187019	1.226335	1.261416	1.284947
1.2599999	1.157923	1.198347	1.239423	1.276423	1.301480
1.2699999	1.167861	1.209774	1.252696	1.291741	1.318458
1.2799999	1.177851	1.221304	1.266159	1.307387	1.335909
1.2899999	1.187892	1.232937	1.279817	1.323375	1.353866
1.3000000	1.197986	1.244674	1.293675	1.339722	1.372367
1.3100000	1.208132	1.256516	1.307738	1.356446	1.391451
1.3200000	1.218329	1.268464	1.322009	1.373565	1.411159
1.3300000	1.228577	1.280517	1.336495	1.391096	1.431542
1.3400000	1.238876	1.292677	1.351198	1.409060	1.452652
1.3500000	1.249225	1.304942	1.366122	1.427475	1.474547
1.3600000	1.259624	1.317312	1.381270	1.446363	1.497294
1.3700000	1.270072	1.329786	1.396644	1.465742	1.520966
1.3799999	1.280567	1.342364	1.412247	1.485635	1.545644
1.3899999	1.291108	1.355043	1.428078	1.506060	1.571420
1.4000000	1.301695	1.367823	1.444139	1.527038	1.598398
1.4100000	1.312325	1.380699	1.460428	1.548587	1.626694
1.4200000	1.322997	1.393671	1.476943	1.570724	1.656439
1.4300000	1.333710	1.406734	1.493680	1.593463	1.687783
1.4400000	1.344461	1.419886	1.510636	1.616818	1.720893
1.4500000	1.355248	1.433121	1.527804	1.640796	1.755958
1.4600000	1.366070	1.446437	1.545176	1.665401	1.793192
1.4700000	1.376924	1.459827	1.562744	1.690630	1.832830
1.4800000	1.387807	1.473288	1.580497	1.716474	1.875133
1.4900000	1.398717	1.486812	1.598422	1.742915	1.920376
1.5000000	1.409651	1.500395	1.616506	1.769927	1.968842
1.5100000	1.420607	1.514029	1.634734	1.797472	2.020797
1.5200000	1.431581	1.527709	1.653087	1.825504	2.076450
1.5300000	1.442571	1.541427	1.671548	1.853964	2.135893
1.5400000	1.453574	1.555176	1.690097	1.882783	2.199020
1.5500000	1.464586	1.568948	1.708714	1.911883	2.265438
1.5600000	1.475605	1.582737	1.727377	1.941178	2.334393
1.5699999	1.486628	1.596534	1.746064	1.970575	2.404787
1.5707963	1.487506	1.597633	1.747553	1.972918	2.410416
1.5707963	1.487505	1.597632	1.747552	1.972916	2.410415

$\alpha = -.949999$

Θ	K VALUES				
	.009966711	.039469502	.087332193	.151646642	.229848846
.0000000	.000000	.000000	.000000	.000000	.000000
.0100000	.009999	.009999	.009999	.009999	.009999
.0200000	.019997	.019997	.019997	.019997	.019997
.0300000	.029991	.029991	.029991	.029992	.029992
.0400000	.039979	.039980	.039980	.039981	.039982
.0500000	.049960	.049961	.049962	.049963	.049965
.0600000	.059932	.059933	.059934	.059937	.059940
.0700000	.069892	.069894	.069896	.069900	.069904
.0800000	.079839	.079842	.079846	.079851	.079858
.0900000	.089771	.089775	.089781	.089788	.089798
.1000000	.099687	.099692	.099700	.099710	.099723
.1100000	.109584	.109591	.109601	.109615	.109632
.1200000	.119461	.119470	.119483	.119502	.119524
.1300000	.129316	.129327	.129344	.129368	.129396
.1400000	.139148	.139161	.139183	.139212	.139247
.1500000	.148954	.148971	.148997	.149033	.149076
.1600000	.158734	.158754	.158786	.158829	.158882
.1700000	.168485	.168509	.168548	.168599	.168662
.1800000	.178207	.178235	.178280	.178342	.178416
.1900000	.187897	.187930	.187983	.188055	.188143
.2000000	.197554	.197593	.197655	.197738	.197840
.2100000	.207178	.207222	.207293	.207390	.207507
.2200000	.216765	.216816	.216898	.217009	.217143
.2300000	.226316	.226374	.226467	.226593	.226747
.2400000	.235829	.235894	.236000	.236143	.236317
.2500000	.245302	.245376	.245495	.245656	.245852
.2600000	.254735	.254817	.254951	.255132	.255352
.2700000	.264126	.264218	.264368	.264569	.264815
.2800000	.273475	.273577	.273743	.273967	.274241
.2900000	.282780	.282893	.283077	.283325	.283628
.3000000	.292041	.292165	.292368	.292641	.292976
.3100000	.301256	.301393	.301615	.301916	.302283
.3200000	.310425	.310574	.310818	.311147	.311550
.3300000	.319546	.319710	.319976	.320336	.320776
.3400000	.328620	.328798	.329088	.329480	.329960
.3500000	.337645	.337838	.338153	.338579	.339101
.3600000	.346621	.346830	.347171	.347633	.348198
.3700000	.355546	.355773	.356141	.356640	.357252
.3800000	.364422	.364666	.365063	.365601	.366261
.3900000	.373247	.373509	.373937	.374516	.375226

$\alpha = -.949999$

θ	K VALUES				
	.009966711	.039469502	.087332193	.151646642	.229848846
.4000000	.382020	.382301	.382761	.383382	.384146
.4100000	.390741	.391043	.391535	.392202	.393021
.4200000	.399410	.399733	.400259	.400973	.401849
.4300000	.408027	.408371	.408933	.409695	.410632
.4400000	.416591	.416958	.417557	.418369	.419369
.4500000	.425102	.425493	.426130	.426995	.428059
.4600000	.433560	.433975	.434652	.435571	.436703
.4700000	.441965	.442404	.443123	.444098	.445300
.4800000	.450316	.450781	.451542	.452576	.453850
.4900000	.458613	.459106	.459911	.461004	.462354
.5000000	.466857	.467377	.468228	.469384	.470811
.5100000	.475048	.475596	.476493	.477714	.479221
.5200000	.483185	.483762	.484708	.485995	.487585
.5300000	.491268	.491876	.492871	.494226	.495902
.5400000	.499298	.499937	.500984	.502409	.504172
.5500000	.507275	.507946	.509045	.510542	.512396
.5600000	.515199	.515902	.517055	.518627	.520574
.5700000	.523069	.523807	.525015	.526663	.528707
.5800000	.530887	.531659	.532925	.534651	.536793
.5900000	.538653	.539460	.540784	.542591	.544834
.6000000	.546367	.547210	.548593	.550483	.552829
.6100000	.554028	.554909	.556353	.558327	.560780
.6200000	.561638	.562556	.564063	.566123	.568686
.6300000	.569197	.570154	.571724	.573873	.576547
.6400000	.576705	.577701	.579337	.581576	.584365
.6500000	.584163	.585199	.586901	.589233	.592139
.6600000	.591570	.592647	.594418	.596844	.599869
.6700000	.598928	.600047	.601887	.604409	.607557
.6800000	.606236	.607398	.609308	.611929	.615202
.6899999	.613496	.614701	.616684	.619405	.622806
.7000000	.620707	.621956	.624012	.626836	.630367
.7100000	.627870	.629164	.631295	.634223	.637888
.7200000	.634986	.636326	.638533	.641567	.645367
.7300000	.642055	.643441	.645726	.648868	.652807
.7400000	.649077	.650511	.652875	.656127	.660206
.7500000	.656054	.657536	.659979	.663344	.667566
.7600000	.662985	.664516	.667041	.670519	.674888
.7700000	.669871	.671451	.674059	.677653	.682171
.7800000	.676714	.678344	.681035	.684747	.689416
.7899999	.683512	.685193	.687970	.691801	.696624

$\alpha = -.949999$

Θ	K VALUES				
	.009966711	.039469502	.087332193	.151646642	.229848846
.8000000	.690267	.692000	.694863	.698815	.703795
.8100000	.696980	.698765	.701715	.705791	.710930
.8200000	.703650	.705488	.708528	.712728	.718029
.8300000	.710279	.712171	.715300	.719628	.725093
.8400000	.716868	.718814	.722034	.726490	.732122
.8500000	.723415	.725417	.728729	.733316	.739116
.8600000	.729924	.731980	.735387	.740105	.746078
.8700000	.736393	.738506	.742007	.746859	.753006
.8799999	.742823	.744993	.748590	.753578	.759901
.8899999	.749216	.751444	.755137	.760262	.766765
.9000000	.755571	.757857	.761648	.766912	.773597
.9100000	.761890	.764235	.768125	.773529	.780398
.9200000	.768172	.770576	.774567	.780114	.787168
.9300000	.774419	.776883	.780975	.786666	.793909
.9400000	.780631	.783156	.787349	.793186	.800620
.9500000	.786809	.789395	.793691	.799675	.807303
.9600000	.792953	.795600	.800001	.806134	.813957
.9699999	.799064	.801774	.806280	.812562	.820584
.9799999	.805142	.807915	.812527	.818961	.827183
.9899999	.811189	.814025	.818744	.825331	.833756
1.0000000	.817204	.820104	.824931	.831673	.840302
1.0100000	.823188	.826152	.831089	.837987	.846824
1.0200000	.829142	.832172	.837218	.844274	.853319
1.0300000	.835067	.838162	.843319	.850534	.859791
1.0400000	.840963	.844123	.849392	.856768	.866238
1.0500000	.846831	.850057	.855439	.862976	.872662
1.0600000	.852670	.855964	.861459	.869160	.879063
1.0699999	.858483	.861844	.867453	.875319	.885442
1.0799999	.864269	.867698	.873422	.881453	.891798
1.0899999	.870029	.873526	.879366	.887565	.898133
1.1000000	.875764	.879329	.885286	.893653	.904448
1.1100000	.881474	.885108	.891183	.899720	.910741
1.1200000	.887160	.890863	.897056	.905764	.917015
1.1300000	.892822	.896595	.902907	.911787	.923270
1.1400000	.898460	.902304	.908736	.917789	.929505
1.1500000	.904077	.907991	.914543	.923771	.935722
1.1600000	.909671	.913656	.920329	.929733	.941921
1.1700000	.915244	.919301	.926096	.935676	.948103
1.1800000	.920796	.924925	.931842	.941600	.954267
1.1899999	.926328	.930529	.937569	.947506	.960415

$\alpha = -\ .949999$

θ	K VALUES				
	.009966711	.039469502	.087332193	.151646642	.229848846
1.2000000	.931841	.936113	.943277	.953395	.966547
1.2100000	.937334	.941679	.948967	.959266	.972664
1.2200000	.942808	.947227	.954640	.965120	.978765
1.2300000	.948264	.952756	.960295	.970958	.984851
1.2400000	.953703	.958269	.965934	.976781	.990924
1.2500000	.959125	.963765	.971556	.982588	.996982
1.2599999	.964531	.969244	.977163	.988381	1.003028
1.2699999	.969920	.974708	.982755	.994159	1.009060
1.2799999	.975295	.980157	.988332	.999923	1.015080
1.2899999	.980654	.985592	.993895	1.005675	1.021088
1.3000000	.985999	.991012	.999444	1.011413	1.027085
1.3100000	.991331	.996419	1.004981	1.017140	1.033070
1.3200000	.996649	1.001813	1.010505	1.022854	1.039045
1.3300000	1.001954	1.007194	1.016017	1.028557	1.045010
1.3400000	1.007248	1.012564	1.021517	1.034249	1.050965
1.3500000	1.012529	1.017922	1.027006	1.039931	1.056910
1.3600000	1.017800	1.023269	1.032485	1.045602	1.062847
1.3700000	1.023060	1.028605	1.037953	1.051265	1.068775
1.3799999	1.028309	1.033932	1.043412	1.056918	1.074695
1.3899999	1.033550	1.039249	1.048862	1.062563	1.080607
1.4000000	1.038781	1.044558	1.054303	[illegible]	1.086513
1.4100000	1.044003	1.049858	1.059736	[illegible]	1.092411
1.4200000	1.049218	1.055150	1.065162	[illegible]	1.098303
1.4300000	1.054425	1.060434	1.070580	[illegible]	1.104188
1.4400000	1.059625	1.065712	1.075992	[illegible]	1.110069
1.4500000	1.064818	1.070983	1.081397	1.096276	1.115944
1.4600000	1.070005	1.076249	1.086797	1.101874	[illegible]
1.4700000	1.075187	1.081508	1.092191	1.107466	[illegible]
1.4800000	1.080364	1.086763	1.097581	1.113055	[illegible]
1.4900000	1.085536	1.092014	1.102966	1.118639	[illegible]
1.5000000	1.090705	1.097261	1.108348	1.124219	[illegible]
1.5100000	1.095869	1.102504	1.113726	1.129796	[illegible]
1.5200000	1.101031	1.107744	1.119101	1.135371	[illegible]
1.5300000	1.106190	1.112981	1.124474	1.140943	[illegible]
1.5400000	1.111347	1.118217	1.129845	1.146514	[illegible]
1.5500000	1.116503	1.123451	1.135215	1.152083	[illegible]
1.5600000	1.121658	1.128684	1.140583	1.157652	[illegible]
1.5699999	1.126812	1.133917	1.145951	1.163219	[illegible]
1.5707963	1.127222	1.134334	1.146379	1.163663	[illegible]
1.5707963	1.127222	1.134333	1.146378	1.163662	[illegible]

$\alpha = -\ .949999$

Θ	K VALUES				
	.318821117	.415016431	.514599755	.613601043	.708073407
.0000000	.000000	.000000	.000000	.000000	.000000
.0100000	.009999	.009999	.009999	.009999	.009999
.0200000	.019997	.019998	.019998	.019998	.019998
.0300000	.029992	.029993	.029993	.029994	.029994
.0400000	.039983	.039984	.039985	.039986	.039987
.0500000	.049967	.049969	.049971	.049973	.049975
.0600000	.059943	.059946	.059950	.059953	.059957
.0700000	.069909	.069915	.069921	.069926	.069932
.0800000	.079865	.079873	.079882	.079890	.079898
.0900000	.089809	.089820	.089832	.089844	.089856
.1000000	.099738	.099754	.099771	.099787	.099803
.1100000	.109652	.109673	.109695	.109717	.109738
.1200000	.119549	.119577	.119605	.119634	.119661
.1300000	.129428	.129463	.129499	.129536	.129570
.1400000	.139288	.139331	.139376	.139421	.139464
.1500000	.149126	.149179	.149235	.149290	.149343
.1600000	.158942	.159007	.159074	.159141	.159205
.1700000	.168734	.168812	.168892	.168973	.169050
.1800000	.178501	.178594	.178689	.178785	.178876
.1900000	.188243	.188351	.188463	.188575	.188683
.2000000	[illegible]	.198082	.198213	.198344	.198469
.2100000	[illegible]	.207787	.207939	.208090	.208235
.2200000	[illegible]	.217465	.217639	.217812	.217979
.2300000	[illegible]	.227113	.227312	.227510	.227700
.2400000	[illegible]	.236732	.236957	.237182	.237398
.2500000	.246077	.246321	.246575	.246829	.247072
.2600000	.255604	.255878	.256163	.256448	.256722
.2700000	.265096	.265402	.265721	.266041	.266347
.2800000	.274554	.274894	.275249	.275605	.275946
.2900000	.283974	.284352	.284746	.285140	.285520
.3000000	.293358	.293775	.294211	.294647	.295066
.3100000	.302705	.303164	.303643	.304124	.304586
.3200000	.312012	.312516	.313042	.313570	.314079
.3300000	.321281	.321832	.322408	.322987	.323544
.3400000	.330510	.331112	.331740	.332372	.332981
.3500000	.339699	.340353	.341038	.341726	.342390
.3600000	.348848	.349558	.350301	.351049	.351770
.3700000	.357955	.358723	.359529	.360339	.361122
.3800000	.367020	.367851	.368721	.369598	.370446
.3900000	.376044	.376939	.377878	.378825	.379741

$\alpha = -\ .949999$

Θ	K VALUES				
	.318821117	.415016431	.514599755	.613601043	.708073407
.4000000	.385025	.385988	.386999	.388019	.389007
.4100000	.393964	.394998	.396085	.397181	.398244
.4200000	.402860	.403968	.405134	.406311	.407452
.4300000	.411713	.412899	.414146	.415408	.416632
.4400000	.420522	.421789	.423123	.424473	.425783
.4500000	.429288	.430639	.432063	.433505	.434906
.4600000	.438011	.439449	.440967	.442504	.444000
.4700000	.446690	.448219	.449834	.451472	.453066
.4800000	.455325	.456949	.458665	.460407	.462105
.4900000	.463916	.465639	.467460	.469311	.471116
.5000000	.472464	.474289	.476219	.478183	.480100
.5100000	.480969	.482898	.484942	.487023	.489056
.5200000	.489430	.491468	.493630	.495832	.497986
.5300000	.497847	.499999	.502282	.504610	.506890
.5400000	.506221	.508489	.510898	.513358	.515769
.5500000	.514552	.516941	.519480	.522075	.524621
.5600000	.522840	.525353	.528027	.530762	.533449
.5700000	.531086	.533726	.536539	.539420	.542253
.5800000	.539289	.542061	.545018	.548049	.551033
.5900000	.547449	.550358	.553462	.556649	.559790
.6000000	.555568	.558616	.561874	.565221	.568524
.6100000	.563645	.566837	.570252	.573765	.577235
.6200000	.571681	.575021	.578598	.582282	.585926
.6300000	.579676	.583168	.586912	.590772	.594595
.6400000	.587630	.591278	.595194	.599236	.603245
.6500000	.595544	.599352	.603444	.607674	.611874
.6600000	.603418	.607391	.611664	.616088	.620485
.6700000	.611253	.615394	.619854	.624476	.629078
.6800000	.619048	.623362	.628014	.632841	.637653
.6899999	.626805	.631296	.636144	.641183	.646212
.7000000	.634524	.639196	.644246	.649501	.654755
.7100000	.642205	.647063	.652320	.657798	.663283
.7200000	.649848	.654897	.660366	.666073	.671796
.7300000	.657455	.662698	.668385	.674328	.680296
.7400000	.665025	.670467	.676377	.682562	.688783
.7500000	.672560	.678204	.684343	.690777	.697258
.7600000	.680059	.685911	.692284	.698973	.705722
.7700000	.687523	.693587	.700200	.707151	.714176
.7800000	.694953	.701233	.708091	.715311	.722620
.7899999	.702349	.708850	.715959	.723454	.731056

$\alpha = -.949999$

Θ	K VALUES				
	.318821117	.415016431	.514599755	.613601043	.708073407
.8000000	.709712	.716438	.723804	.731582	.739484
.8100000	.717041	.723998	.731626	.739694	.747905
.8200000	.724339	.731530	.739426	.747792	.756320
.8300000	.731605	.739035	.747205	.755875	.764730
.8400000	.738839	.746513	.754963	.763945	.773136
.8500000	.746042	.753964	.762701	.772002	.781539
.8600000	.753216	.761391	.770419	.780048	.789939
.8700000	.760360	.768792	.778118	.788082	.798338
.8799999	.767474	.776168	.785799	.796106	.806737
.8899999	.774560	.783521	.793462	.804120	.815135
.9000000	.781618	.790850	.801108	.812125	.823535
.9100000	.788648	.798156	.808737	.820122	.831937
.9200000	.795651	.805440	.816349	.828111	.840342
.9300000	.802628	.812701	.823947	.836093	.848751
.9400000	.809578	.819942	.831529	.844068	.857164
.9500000	.816503	.827162	.839097	.852038	.865584
.9600000	.823404	.834361	.846652	.860002	.874010
.9699999	.830280	.841541	.854193	.867963	.882443
.9799999	.837131	.848701	.861721	.875919	.890885
.9899999	.843960	.855843	.869237	.883872	.899336
1.0000000	.850766	.862966	.876741	.891823	.907797
1.0100000	.857549	.870072	.884235	.899773	.916269
1.0200000	.864310	.877161	.891717	.907720	.924753
1.0300000	.871050	.884232	.899190	.915668	.933249
1.0400000	.877769	.891288	.906653	.923615	.941759
1.0500000	.884468	.898328	.914107	.931563	.950283
1.0600000	.891147	.905352	.921552	.939512	.958822
1.0699999	.897807	.912362	.928989	.947462	.967377
1.0799999	.904447	.919357	.936418	.955415	.975948
1.0899999	.911070	.926338	.943841	.963370	.984537
1.1000000	.917674	.933306	.951256	.971329	.993143
1.1100000	.924261	.940260	.958665	.979291	1.001769
1.1200000	.930830	.947202	.966068	.987257	1.010413
1.1300000	.937384	.954132	.973465	.995228	1.019077
1.1400000	.943921	.961050	.980858	1.003204	1.027762
1.1500000	.950442	.967957	.988245	1.011185	1.036468
1.1600000	.956948	.974853	.995629	1.019172	1.045196
1.1700000	.963440	.981738	1.003008	1.027166	1.053946
1.1800000	.969917	.988613	1.010383	1.035165	1.062718
1.1899999	.976380	.995478	1.017755	1.043172	1.071514

$\alpha = -$ .949999

Θ	K VALUES				
	.318821117	.415016431	.514599755	.613601043	.708073407
1.2000000	.982829	1.002334	1.025124	1.051186	1.080333
1.2100000	.989266	1.009180	1.032490	1.059207	1.089176
1.2200000	.995690	1.016018	1.039854	1.067236	1.098043
1.2300000	1.002102	1.022848	1.047216	1.075272	1.106934
1.2400000	1.008502	1.029670	1.054575	1.083317	1.115850
1.2500000	1.014890	1.036483	1.061933	1.091370	1.124791
1.2599999	1.021268	1.043290	1.069290	1.099431	1.133756
1.2699999	1.027635	1.050089	1.076645	1.107501	1.142747
1.2799999	1.033991	1.056882	1.084000	1.115579	1.151763
1.2899999	1.040338	1.063668	1.091353	1.123666	1.160803
1.3000000	1.046675	1.070449	1.098707	1.131762	1.169869
1.3100000	1.053004	1.077223	1.106059	1.139866	1.178959
1.3200000	1.059323	1.083992	1.113411	1.147979	1.188074
1.3300000	1.065634	1.090755	1.120763	1.156101	1.197213
1.3400000	1.071938	1.097514	1.128115	1.164231	1.206376
1.3500000	1.078233	1.104267	1.135467	1.172370	1.215562
1.3600000	1.084522	1.111017	1.142820	1.180517	1.224772
1.3700000	1.090803	1.117762	1.150172	1.188672	1.234004
1.3799999	1.097078	1.124503	1.157525	1.196835	1.243258
1.3899999	1.103347	1.131240	1.164878	1.205006	1.252534
1.4000000	1.109609	1.137974	1.172232	1.213184	1.261830
1.4100000	1.115867	1.144704	1.179586	1.221370	1.271146
1.4200000	1.122119	1.151431	1.186941	1.229563	1.280482
1.4300000	1.128366	1.158156	1.194296	1.237762	1.289835
1.4400000	1.134609	1.164877	1.201652	1.245968	1.299206
1.4500000	1.140847	1.171597	1.209008	1.254179	1.308593
1.4600000	1.147082	1.178314	1.216365	1.262396	1.317995
1.4700000	1.153313	1.185029	1.223723	1.270619	1.327412
1.4800000	1.159541	1.191742	1.231081	1.278846	1.336842
1.4900000	1.165766	1.198454	1.238439	1.287078	1.346284
1.5000000	1.171989	1.205164	1.245798	1.295313	1.355736
1.5100000	1.178209	1.211873	1.253157	1.303552	1.365198
1.5200000	1.184428	1.218580	1.260517	1.311794	1.374668
1.5300000	1.190645	1.225287	1.267877	1.320039	1.384145
1.5400000	1.196860	1.231993	1.275237	1.328286	1.393627
1.5500000	1.203075	1.238699	1.282598	1.336534	1.403114
1.5600000	1.209288	1.245404	1.289958	1.344783	1.412604
1.5699999	1.215502	1.252109	1.297319	1.353033	1.422095
1.5707963	1.215997	1.252643	1.297905	1.353690	1.422851
1.5707963	1.215996	1.252642	1.297905	1.353689	1.422850

$\alpha = -.949999$

Θ	K VALUES				
	.794250555	.868696860	.928444378	.971111163	.994996249
.0000000	.000000	.000000	.000000	.000000	.000000
.0100000	.009999	.009999	.009999	.009999	.009999
.0200000	.019998	.019998	.019998	.019998	.019998
.0300000	.029995	.029995	.029995	.029995	.029995
.0400000	.039988	.039989	.039989	.039990	.039990
.0500000	.049977	.049978	.049979	.049980	.049981
.0600000	.059960	.059963	.059965	.059966	.059967
.0700000	.069937	.069941	.069944	.069947	.069948
.0800000	.079906	.079912	.079917	.079921	.079923
.0900000	.089866	.089875	.089883	.089888	.089891
.1000000	.099817	.099829	.099839	.099847	.099851
.1100000	.109757	.109774	.109787	.109796	.109802
.1200000	.119686	.119707	.119724	.119737	.119744
.1300000	.129602	.129629	.129651	.129666	.129675
.1400000	.139504	.139538	.139565	.139585	.139596
.1500000	.149392	.149434	.149467	.149491	.149505
.1600000	.159264	.159315	.159356	.159385	.159401
.1700000	.169120	.169181	.169230	.169265	.169285
.1800000	.178960	.179032	.179090	.179132	.179155
.1900000	.188781	.188866	.188934	.188983	.189011
.2000000	.198584	.198683	.198763	.198820	.198852
.2100000	.208367	.208482	.208575	.208641	.208678
.2200000	.218131	.218263	.218369	.218445	.218488
.2300000	.227874	.228025	.228146	.228233	.228282
.2400000	.237596	.237767	.237905	.238004	.238060
.2500000	.247296	.247490	.247646	.247758	.247820
.2600000	.256973	.257191	.257367	.257493	.257564
.2700000	.266628	.266873	.267070	.267211	.267290
.2800000	.276260	.276532	.276752	.276910	.276998
.2900000	.285868	.286171	.286415	.286590	.286688
.3000000	.295452	.295787	.296058	.296252	.296361
.3100000	.305011	.305381	.305680	.305895	.306015
.3200000	.314546	.314954	.315282	.315518	.315651
.3300000	.324057	.324503	.324864	.325123	.325269
.3400000	.333542	.334030	.334425	.334709	.334869
.3500000	.343001	.343535	.343966	.344276	.344450
.3600000	.352436	.353017	.353486	.353824	.354014
.3700000	.361845	.362476	.362986	.363353	.363560
.3800000	.371229	.371912	.372466	.372864	.373088
.3900000	.380587	.381326	.381925	.382356	.382599

$\alpha = -\ .949999$

Θ	K VALUES				
	.794250555	.868696860	.928444378	.971111163	.994996249
.4000000	.389919	.390718	.391365	.391831	.392093
.4100000	.399227	.400087	.400785	.401287	.401570
.4200000	.408509	.409434	.410186	.410727	.411032
.4300000	.417766	.418760	.419567	.420149	.420477
.4400000	.426998	.428064	.428930	.429555	.429907
.4500000	.436206	.437347	.438275	.438945	.439322
.4600000	.445390	.446610	.447603	.448319	.448724
.4700000	.454549	.455852	.456913	.457679	.458111
.4800000	.463685	.465074	.466206	.467024	.467486
.4900000	.472797	.474277	.475483	.476356	.476848
.5000000	.481886	.483461	.484745	.485675	.486200
.5100000	.490953	.492626	.493993	.494982	.495540
.5200000	.499998	.501774	.503226	.504277	.504871
.5300000	.509022	.510905	.512445	.513562	.514193
.5400000	.518025	.520019	.521653	.522837	.523507
.5500000	.527007	.529118	.530848	.532104	.532814
.5600000	.535969	.538202	.540033	.541363	.542116
.5700000	.544913	.547272	.549208	.550615	.551412
.5800000	.553838	.556328	.558374	.559862	.560705
.5900000	.562745	.565371	.567532	.569104	.569995
.6000000	.571635	.574403	.576683	.578343	.579284
.6100000	.580509	.583425	.585827	.587579	.588573
.6200000	.589367	.592436	.594967	.596815	.597863
.6300000	.598210	.601438	.604104	.606050	.607156
.6400000	.607040	.610433	.613238	.615288	.616453
.6500000	.615856	.619420	.622370	.624528	.625755
.6600000	.624660	.628402	.631502	.633773	.635065
.6700000	.633453	.637379	.640636	.643023	.644383
.6800000	.642235	.646352	.649772	.652281	.653711
.6899999	.651007	.655323	.658911	.661547	.663051
.7000000	.659771	.664292	.668056	.670824	.672404
.7100000	.668527	.673261	.677208	.680113	.681773
.7200000	.677277	.682231	.686368	.689416	.691159
.7300000	.686020	.691203	.695537	.698735	.700564
.7400000	.694760	.700179	.704718	.708070	.709990
.7500000	.703495	.709160	.713911	.717425	.719439
.7600000	.712228	.718147	.723119	.726801	.728913
.7700000	.720959	.727142	.732343	.736200	.738415
.7800000	.729690	.736145	.741585	.745624	.747945
.7899999	.738422	.745159	.750847	.755076	.757508

$\alpha =$ - .949999

θ	K VALUES				
	.794250555	.868696860	.928444378	.971111163	.994996249
.8000000	.747155	.754185	.760130	.764556	.767105
.8100000	.755892	.763224	.769436	.774069	.776739
.8200000	.764632	.772278	.778767	.783615	.786412
.8300000	.773378	.781348	.788126	.793197	.796127
.8400000	.782130	.790437	.797514	.802818	.805886
.8500000	.790889	.799544	.806933	.812480	.815693
.8600000	.799658	.808673	.816386	.822186	.825550
.8700000	.808437	.817825	.825874	.831939	.835460
.8799999	.817226	.827001	.835400	.841740	.845427
.8899999	.826029	.836203	.844966	.851594	.855454
.9000000	.834845	.845434	.854574	.861503	.865544
.9100000	.843676	.854694	.864228	.871471	.875701
.9200000	.852523	.863985	.873929	.881499	.885928
.9300000	.861388	.873310	.883679	.891593	.896230
.9400000	.870271	.882670	.893483	.901754	.906610
.9500000	.879175	.892067	.903341	.911987	.917072
.9600000	.888100	.901503	.913258	.922296	.927621
.9699999	.897048	.910981	.923236	.932683	.938262
.9799999	.906020	.920501	.933277	.943154	.948998
.9899999	.915017	.930066	.943385	.953712	.959836
1.0000000	.924041	.939678	.953563	.964361	.970779
1.0100000	.933092	.949340	.963814	.975107	.981835
1.0200000	.942173	.959052	.974142	.985953	.993007
1.0300000	.951284	.968818	.984549	.996904	1.004303
1.0400000	.960428	.978639	.995040	1.007966	1.015728
1.0500000	.969604	.988518	1.005617	1.019143	1.027290
1.0600000	.978814	.998457	1.016285	1.030442	1.038995
1.0699999	.988060	1.008458	1.027047	1.041867	1.050850
1.0799999	.997343	1.018524	1.037907	1.053426	1.062863
1.0899999	1.006665	1.028656	1.048869	1.065123	1.075043
1.1000000	1.016025	1.038857	1.059937	1.076967	1.087398
1.1100000	1.025426	1.049129	1.071115	1.088962	1.099938
1.1200000	1.034869	1.059474	1.082408	1.101117	1.112671
1.1300000	1.044354	1.069895	1.093820	1.113440	1.125608
1.1400000	1.053884	1.080394	1.105356	1.125937	1.138761
1.1500000	1.063458	1.090973	1.117020	1.138617	1.152141
1.1600000	1.073079	1.101635	1.128816	1.151489	1.165760
1.1700000	1.082746	1.112382	1.140751	1.164562	1.179632
1.1800000	1.092462	1.123215	1.152828	1.177845	1.193772
1.1899999	1.102226	1.134138	1.165053	1.191349	1.208193

$\alpha = -.949999$

θ	K VALUES				
	.794250555	.868696860	.928444378	.971111163	.994996249
1.2000000	1.112041	1.145152	1.177430	1.205083	1.222913
1.2100000	1.121905	1.156260	1.189966	1.219059	1.237950
1.2200000	1.131821	1.167462	1.202666	1.233289	1.253322
1.2300000	1.141789	1.178762	1.215534	1.247784	1.269049
1.2400000	1.151810	1.190161	1.228576	1.262558	1.285154
1.2500000	1.161883	1.201662	1.241797	1.277624	1.301662
1.2599999	1.172010	1.213264	1.255204	1.292995	1.318597
1.2699999	1.182190	1.224971	1.268800	1.308687	1.335988
1.2799999	1.192424	1.236783	1.282593	1.324716	1.353866
1.2899999	1.202712	1.248702	1.296586	1.341096	1.372265
1.3000000	1.213055	1.260728	1.310785	1.357847	1.391222
1.3100000	1.223451	1.272862	1.325195	1.374984	1.410776
1.3200000	1.233900	1.285106	1.339821	1.392526	1.430973
1.3300000	1.244403	1.297459	1.354666	1.410493	1.451862
1.3400000	1.254959	1.309921	1.369735	1.428904	1.473498
1.3500000	1.265567	1.322492	1.385032	1.447779	1.495940
1.3600000	1.276226	1.335171	1.400559	1.467139	1.519256
1.3700000	1.286935	1.347959	1.416319	1.487005	1.543521
1.3799999	1.297694	1.360853	1.432313	1.507397	1.568819
1.3899999	1.308501	1.373851	1.448544	1.528337	1.595245
1.4000000	1.319355	1.386953	1.465010	1.549844	1.622903
1.4100000	1.330254	1.400156	1.481710	1.571938	1.651915
1.4200000	1.341196	1.413456	1.498643	1.594635	1.682413
1.4300000	1.352181	1.426850	1.515805	1.617952	1.714552
1.4400000	1.363205	1.440336	1.533191	1.641900	1.748503
1.4500000	1.374266	1.453908	1.550796	1.666488	1.784460
1.4600000	1.385364	1.467562	1.568610	1.691719	1.822642
1.4700000	1.396494	1.481294	1.586626	1.717591	1.863290
1.4800000	1.407655	1.495098	1.604832	1.744094	1.906672
1.4900000	1.418843	1.508968	1.623216	1.771211	1.953071
1.5000000	1.430057	1.522898	1.641762	1.798913	2.002777
1.5100000	1.441293	1.536881	1.660456	1.827163	2.056061
1.5200000	1.452549	1.550911	1.679279	1.855913	2.113138
1.5300000	1.463820	1.564980	1.698213	1.885102	2.174104
1.5400000	1.475105	1.579082	1.717237	1.914659	2.238849
1.5500000	1.486400	1.593207	1.736331	1.944505	2.306969
1.5600000	1.497701	1.607349	1.755473	1.974551	2.377692
1.5699999	1.509006	1.621500	1.774639	2.004702	2.449891
1.5707963	1.509906	1.622627	1.776166	2.007105	2.455664
1.5707963	1.509906	1.622626	1.776165	2.007103	2.455663

$\alpha =$ -.899999

Θ	K VALUES				
	.009966711	.039469502	.087332193	.151646642	.229848846
.0000000	.000000	.000000	.000000	.000000	.000000
.0100000	.009999	.009999	.009999	.009999	.009999
.0200000	.019997	.019997	.019997	.019997	.019997
.0300000	.029991	.029992	.029992	.029992	.029992
.0400000	.039980	.039981	.039981	.039982	.039983
.0500000	.049962	.049963	.049964	.049965	.049967
.0600000	.059935	.059936	.059938	.059940	.059943
.0700000	.069898	.069899	.069902	.069906	.069910
.0800000	.079848	.079850	.079854	.079860	.079866
.0900000	.089783	.089787	.089793	.089800	.089810
.1000000	.099703	.099708	.099716	.099727	.099740
.1100000	.109606	.109612	.109623	.109637	.109654
.1200000	.119489	.119498	.119511	.119530	.119552
.1300000	.129352	.129363	.129380	.129403	.129432
.1400000	.139193	.139206	.139227	.139257	.139292
.1500000	.149009	.149025	.149052	.149088	.149131
.1600000	.158800	.158820	.158852	.158895	.158948
.1700000	.168564	.168588	.168627	.168678	.168741
.1800000	.178300	.178328	.178374	.178435	.178510
.1900000	.188006	.188039	.188093	.188164	.188252
.2000000	.197681	.197719	.197782	.197865	.197967
.2100000	.207324	.207368	.207439	.207536	.207654
.2200000	.216932	.216983	.217065	.217176	.217311
.2300000	.226506	.226563	.226657	.226783	.226937
.2400000	.236043	.236108	.236214	.236357	.236532
.2500000	.245543	.245616	.245736	.245897	.246094
.2600000	.255004	.255087	.255221	.255401	.255622
.2700000	.264426	.264518	.264668	.264869	.265116
.2800000	.273807	.273909	.274075	.274300	.274574
.2900000	.283146	.283260	.283444	.283692	.283996
.3000000	.292443	.292568	.292771	.293045	.293380
.3100000	.301697	.301834	.302057	.302358	.302727
.3200000	.310906	.311056	.311301	.311631	.312035
.3300000	.320070	.320234	.320501	.320862	.321304
.3400000	.329188	.329367	.329658	.330051	.330533
.3500000	.338260	.338454	.338770	.339197	.339721
.3600000	.347285	.347495	.347837	.348300	.348868
.3700000	.356262	.356489	.356859	.357360	.357973
.3800000	.365190	.365435	.365834	.366374	.367037
.3900000	.374070	.374334	.374763	.375344	.376058

$\alpha =$ -.899999

Θ	K VALUES				
	.009966711	.039469502	.087332193	.151646642	.229848846
.4000000	.382901	.383184	.383645	.384269	.385036
.4100000	.391682	.391985	.392479	.393148	.393971
.4200000	.400412	.400736	.401265	.401982	.402862
.4300000	.409093	.409439	.410003	.410769	.411710
.4400000	.417722	.418091	.418693	.419509	.420513
.4500000	.426301	.426693	.427334	.428203	.429273
.4600000	.434828	.435245	.435926	.436849	.437987
.4700000	.443304	.443746	.444469	.445449	.446658
.4800000	.451729	.452197	.452962	.454002	.455283
.4900000	.460102	.460597	.461407	.462507	.463864
.5000000	.468423	.468946	.469802	.470965	.472401
.5100000	.476693	.477245	.478147	.479375	.480892
.5200000	.484911	.485492	.486444	.487739	.489339
.5300000	.493077	.493689	.494691	.496055	.497741
.5400000	.501192	.501835	.502888	.504323	.506099
.5500000	.509255	.509930	.511037	.512545	.514412
.5600000	.517266	.517975	.519136	.520719	.522681
.5700000	.525227	.525970	.527187	.528847	.530906
.5800000	.533136	.533914	.535189	.536928	.539086
.5900000	.540995	.541808	.543142	.544963	.547223
.6000000	.548803	.549653	.551047	.552951	.555317
.6100000	.556561	.557448	.558904	.560894	.563367
.6200000	.564268	.565194	.566713	.568790	.571374
.6300000	.571926	.572890	.574474	.576641	.579339
.6400000	.579534	.580539	.582189	.584448	.587261
.6500000	.587093	.588139	.589856	.592209	.595140
.6600000	.594604	.595690	.597477	.599925	.602979
.6700000	.602066	.603195	.605052	.607598	.610775
.6800000	.609479	.610652	.612581	.615227	.618531
.6899999	.616846	.618062	.620065	.622812	.626246
.7000000	.624165	.625427	.627503	.630355	.633921
.7100000	.631437	.632745	.634897	.637855	.641556
.7200000	.638663	.640017	.642247	.645312	.649152
.7300000	.645844	.647245	.649553	.652728	.656708
.7400000	.652979	.654428	.656816	.660103	.664226
.7500000	.660069	.661566	.664036	.667437	.671706
.7600000	.667114	.668662	.671214	.674731	.679148
.7700000	.674116	.675714	.678350	.681985	.686553
.7800000	.681074	.682723	.685445	.689199	.693922
.7899999	.687990	.689690	.692499	.696374	.701254

$\alpha =$ -.899999

Θ	K VALUES				
	.009966711	.039469502	.087332193	.151646642	.229848846
.8000000	.694863	.696616	.699512	.703512	.708550
.8100000	.701695	.703501	.706486	.710611	.715811
.8200000	.708485	.710345	.713421	.717672	.723038
.8300000	.715234	.717149	.720316	.724697	.730230
.8400000	.721943	.723914	.727174	.731686	.737388
.8500000	.728613	.730639	.733994	.738638	.744513
.8600000	.735244	.737327	.740776	.745555	.751605
.8700000	.741836	.743977	.747522	.752438	.758665
.8799999	.748390	.750589	.754232	.759286	.765693
.8899999	.754908	.757165	.760907	.766100	.772690
.9000000	.761388	.763704	.767546	.772881	.779656
.9100000	.767832	.770208	.774151	.779630	.786593
.9200000	.774240	.776678	.780723	.786346	.793499
.9300000	.780614	.783112	.787260	.793031	.800376
.9400000	.786953	.789513	.793766	.799685	.807225
.9500000	.793258	.795881	.800239	.806308	.814045
.9600000	.799530	.802216	.806680	.812901	.820838
.9699999	.805769	.808519	.813090	.819464	.827604
.9799999	.811977	.814790	.819470	.825999	.834343
.9899999	.818152	.821030	.825820	.832505	.841056
1.0000000	.824297	.827240	.832140	.838984	.847744
1.0100000	.830411	.833420	.838431	.845435	.854407
1.0200000	.836496	.839571	.844695	.851859	.861045
1.0300000	.842551	.845693	.850930	.858257	.867659
1.0400000	.848578	.851787	.857138	.864630	.874249
1.0500000	.854577	.857854	.863320	.870977	.880817
1.0600000	.860548	.863893	.869476	.877299	.887362
1.0699999	.866492	.869907	.875606	.883598	.893885
1.0799999	.872410	.875894	.881711	.889872	.900387
1.0899999	.878302	.881856	.887791	.896124	.906867
1.1000000	.884170	.887793	.893848	.902353	.913327
1.1100000	.890012	.893706	.899881	.908560	.919767
1.1200000	.895831	.899596	.905892	.914746	.926187
1.1300000	.901626	.905462	.911880	.920910	.932589
1.1400000	.907398	.911306	.917846	.927054	.938971
1.1500000	.913147	.917128	.923792	.933178	.945336
1.1600000	.918875	.922929	.929716	.939282	.951683
1.1700000	.924582	.928709	.935621	.945368	.958013
1.1800000	.930268	.934468	.941506	.951435	.964326
1.1899999	.935934	.940208	.947371	.957484	.970623

$\alpha =$ -.899999

θ	K VALUES				
	.009966711	.039469502	.087332193	.151646642	.229848846
1.2000000	.941580	.945928	.953218	.963516	.976904
1.2100000	.947207	.951630	.959048	.969530	.983170
1.2200000	.952816	.957313	.964859	.975528	.989421
1.2300000	.958407	.962979	.970654	.981510	.995657
1.2400000	.963980	.968628	.976432	.987477	1.001880
1.2500000	.969537	.974260	.982194	.993428	1.008089
1.2599999	.975077	.979877	.987940	.999365	1.014285
1.2699999	.980601	.985477	.993672	1.005288	1.020468
1.2799999	.986110	.991063	.999389	1.011197	1.026639
1.2899999	.991605	.996634	1.005092	1.017093	1.032798
1.3000000	.997085	1.002192	1.010782	1.022976	1.038946
1.3100000	1.002551	1.007735	1.016458	1.028848	1.045084
1.3200000	1.008005	1.013266	1.022123	1.034707	1.051210
1.3300000	1.013445	1.018785	1.027775	1.040555	1.057327
1.3400000	1.018874	1.024291	1.033416	1.046393	1.063434
1.3500000	1.024291	1.029786	1.039045	1.052220	1.069532
1.3600000	1.029696	1.035271	1.044665	1.058037	1.075620
1.3700000	1.035092	1.040745	1.050274	1.063845	1.081701
1.3799999	1.040477	1.046209	1.055873	1.069644	1.087774
1.3899999	1.045852	1.051663	1.061464	1.075435	1.093839
1.4000000	1.051219	1.057109	1.067046	1.081217	1.099897
1.4100000	1.056577	1.062546	1.072620	1.086992	1.105948
1.4200000	1.061927	1.067976	1.078187	1.092760	1.111993
1.4300000	1.067269	1.073398	1.083746	1.098521	1.118032
1.4400000	1.072605	1.078813	1.089298	1.104276	1.124065
1.4500000	1.077934	1.084222	1.094845	1.110025	1.130093
1.4600000	1.083257	1.089625	1.100386	1.115769	1.136117
1.4700000	1.088574	1.095022	1.105921	1.121508	1.142136
1.4800000	1.093886	1.100415	1.111452	1.127242	1.148151
1.4900000	1.099194	1.105803	1.116979	1.132973	1.154163
1.5000000	1.104498	1.111187	1.122501	1.138699	1.160172
1.5100000	1.109799	1.116568	1.128021	1.144423	1.166177
1.5200000	1.115096	1.121946	1.133537	1.150144	1.172181
1.5300000	1.120391	1.127321	1.139051	1.155863	1.178182
1.5400000	1.125683	1.132695	1.144564	1.161580	1.184182
1.5500000	1.130975	1.138067	1.150074	1.167296	1.190181
1.5600000	1.136265	1.143437	1.155584	1.173011	1.196179
1.5699999	1.141555	1.148808	1.161094	1.178725	1.202176
1.5707963	1.141976	1.149235	1.161532	1.179180	1.202654
1.5707963	1.141975	1.149235	1.161532	1.179180	1.202653

$\alpha =$ -.899999

Θ	K VALUES				
	.318821117	.415016431	.514599755	.613601043	.708073407
.0000000	.000000	.000000	.000000	.000000	.000000
.0100000	.009999	.009999	.009999	.009999	.009999
.0200000	.019998	.019998	.019998	.019998	.019998
.0300000	.029993	.029993	.029994	.029994	.029995
.0400000	.039984	.039985	.039986	.039987	.039988
.0500000	.049969	.049971	.049973	.049975	.049977
.0600000	.059946	.059950	.059953	.059957	.059960
.0700000	.069915	.069921	.069926	.069932	.069937
.0800000	.079874	.079882	.079890	.079899	.079907
.0900000	.089821	.089832	.089844	.089856	.089868
.1000000	.099755	.099770	.099787	.099803	.099819
.1100000	.109674	.109695	.109717	.109739	.109760
.1200000	.119578	.119605	.119634	.119662	.119689
.1300000	.129464	.129499	.129535	.129571	.129606
.1400000	.139332	.139376	.139421	.139466	.139509
.1500000	.149181	.149234	.149290	.149345	.149398
.1600000	.159008	.159073	.159140	.159208	.159272
.1700000	.168813	.168891	.168972	.169052	.169129
.1800000	.178595	.178687	.178783	.178878	.178970
.1900000	.188352	.188460	.188573	.188685	.188793
.2000000	.198084	.198210	.198341	.198472	.198597
.2100000	.207788	.207934	.208086	.208237	.208382
.2200000	.217465	.217633	.217807	.217981	.218147
.2300000	.227113	.227304	.227503	.227701	.227892
.2400000	.236731	.236948	.237173	.237399	.237615
.2500000	.246319	.246563	.246818	.247072	.247316
.2600000	.255875	.256149	.256435	.256721	.256995
.2700000	.265398	.265705	.266024	.266344	.266651
.2800000	.274888	.275229	.275585	.275941	.276283
.2900000	.284343	.284722	.285117	.285512	.285892
.3000000	.293764	.294182	.294618	.295056	.295476
.3100000	.303149	.303610	.304090	.304572	.305036
.3200000	.312498	.313003	.313531	.314060	.314570
.3300000	.321810	.322363	.322941	.323521	.324079
.3400000	.331085	.331688	.332319	.332952	.333563
.3500000	.340322	.340978	.341665	.342355	.343021
.3600000	.349520	.350232	.350978	.351728	.352453
.3700000	.358679	.359450	.360259	.361072	.361858
.3800000	.367799	.368632	.369506	.370386	.371237
.3900000	.376879	.377778	.378721	.379671	.380590

$\alpha =$ -.899999

Θ	K VALUES				
	.318821117	.415016431	.514599755	.613601043	.708073407
.4000000	.385919	.386886	.387901	.388925	.389917
.4100000	.394918	.395957	.397048	.398150	.399217
.4200000	.403877	.404991	.406161	.407344	.408491
.4300000	.412795	.413987	.415241	.416508	.417738
.4400000	.421672	.422945	.424286	.425642	.426959
.4500000	.430508	.431866	.433297	.434746	.436154
.4600000	.439302	.440748	.442274	.443820	.445323
.4700000	.448055	.449593	.451217	.452864	.454467
.4800000	.456766	.458400	.460126	.461878	.463585
.4900000	.465436	.467169	.469001	.470862	.472678
.5000000	.474064	.475899	.477842	.479817	.481746
.5100000	.482651	.484592	.486649	.488743	.490789
.5200000	.491196	.493248	.495423	.497640	.499808
.5300000	.499699	.501865	.504163	.506508	.508803
.5400000	.508162	.510445	.512871	.515348	.517775
.5500000	.516583	.518988	.521545	.524159	.526724
.5600000	.524963	.527494	.530187	.532943	.535650
.5700000	.533302	.535963	.538797	.541699	.544554
.5800000	.541601	.544395	.547374	.550429	.553436
.5900000	.549859	.552791	.555920	.559132	.562298
.6000000	.558078	.561151	.564434	.567809	.571139
.6100000	.566256	.569475	.572918	.576460	.579959
.6200000	.574395	.577763	.581370	.585086	.588761
.6300000	.582494	.586017	.589793	.593687	.597544
.6400000	.590555	.594235	.598185	.602264	.606309
.6500000	.598576	.602419	.606549	.610818	.615056
.6600000	.606560	.610570	.614883	.619348	.623787
.6700000	.614506	.618686	.623189	.627855	.632502
.6800000	.622414	.626770	.631466	.636341	.641201
.6899999	.630285	.634820	.639717	.644805	.649886
.7000000	.638119	.642839	.647940	.653249	.658556
.7100000	.645917	.650825	.656137	.661672	.667214
.7200000	.653679	.658780	.664307	.670075	.675859
.7300000	.661406	.666704	.672453	.678460	.684493
.7400000	.669097	.674598	.680573	.686826	.693116
.7500000	.676754	.682461	.688668	.695174	.701729
.7600000	.684377	.690295	.696740	.703505	.710332
.7700000	.691966	.698100	.704789	.711820	.718928
.7800000	.699522	.705876	.712814	.720119	.727515
.7899999	.707046	.713624	.720818	.728403	.736097

$\alpha =$ -.899999

Θ	K VALUES				
	.318821117	.415016431	.514599755	.613601043	.708073407
.8000000	.714537	.721345	.728799	.736673	.744672
.8100000	.721997	.729038	.736760	.744928	.753242
.8200000	.729425	.736705	.744700	.753171	.761808
.8300000	.736823	.744346	.752620	.761401	.770371
.8400000	.744190	.751962	.760521	.769619	.778932
.8500000	.751528	.759552	.768402	.777827	.787491
.8600000	.758836	.767118	.776266	.786024	.796049
.8700000	.766116	.774660	.784112	.794211	.804608
.8799999	.773367	.782178	.791940	.802390	.813168
.8899999	.780591	.789674	.799752	.810560	.821730
.9000000	.787787	.797147	.807548	.818722	.830295
.9100000	.794957	.804598	.815329	.826877	.838864
.9200000	.802101	.812028	.823095	.835027	.847437
.9300000	.809219	.819437	.830846	.843170	.856016
.9400000	.816312	.826826	.838583	.851309	.864602
.9500000	.823380	.834195	.846308	.859443	.873195
.9600000	.830424	.841544	.854019	.867573	.881797
.9699999	.837444	.848875	.861719	.875701	.890407
.9799999	.844441	.856187	.869406	.883826	.899028
.9899999	.851415	.863481	.877083	.891949	.907660
1.0000000	.858368	.870758	.884749	.900071	.916303
1.0100000	.865298	.878018	.892405	.908193	.924959
1.0200000	.872208	.885261	.900051	.916315	.933628
1.0300000	.879096	.892489	.907689	.924437	.942312
1.0400000	.885964	.899701	.915317	.932561	.951011
1.0500000	.892813	.906898	.922938	.940686	.959725
1.0600000	.899642	.914081	.930551	.948814	.968456
1.0699999	.906453	.921249	.938156	.956945	.977205
1.0799999	.913245	.928404	.945755	.965079	.985972
1.0899999	.920019	.935545	.953347	.973217	.994758
1.1000000	.926776	.942674	.960934	.981359	1.003563
1.1100000	.933515	.949790	.968515	.989506	1.012388
1.1200000	.940239	.956894	.976091	.997658	1.021235
1.1300000	.946946	.963987	.983662	1.005817	1.030103
1.1400000	.953637	.971068	.991229	1.013981	1.038993
1.1500000	.960313	.978139	.998792	1.022152	1.047906
1.1600000	.966975	.985199	1.006352	1.030329	1.056842
1.1700000	.973622	.992250	1.013908	1.038514	1.065801
1.1800000	.980255	.999290	1.021461	1.046707	1.074785
1.1899999	.986875	1.006322	1.029011	1.054907	1.083794

$\alpha =$ -.899999

Θ	K VALUES				
	.318821117	.415016431	.514599755	.613601043	.708073407
1.2000000	.993481	1.013344	1.036560	1.063116	1.092827
1.2100000	1.000075	1.020358	1.044106	1.071333	1.101886
1.2200000	1.006657	1.027364	1.051650	1.079559	1.110970
1.2300000	1.013227	1.034362	1.059193	1.087794	1.120081
1.2400000	1.019785	1.041352	1.066735	1.096037	1.129217
1.2500000	1.026332	1.048335	1.074276	1.104290	1.138380
1.2599999	1.032868	1.055311	1.081816	1.112552	1.147569
1.2699999	1.039394	1.062280	1.089355	1.120824	1.156784
1.2799999	1.045910	1.069244	1.096894	1.129105	1.166026
1.2899999	1.052417	1.076201	1.104433	1.137395	1.175294
1.3000000	1.058914	1.083152	1.111971	1.145695	1.184589
1.3100000	1.065403	1.090098	1.119510	1.154005	1.193909
1.3200000	1.071883	1.097039	1.127049	1.162324	1.203256
1.3300000	1.078355	1.103975	1.134588	1.170653	1.212628
1.3400000	1.084819	1.110906	1.142128	1.178991	1.222024
1.3500000	1.091276	1.117832	1.149668	1.187338	1.231446
1.3600000	1.097726	1.124755	1.157209	1.195694	1.240892
1.3700000	1.104169	1.131673	1.164751	1.204059	1.250362
1.3799999	1.110605	1.138588	1.172293	1.212432	1.259855
1.3899999	1.117036	1.145499	1.179837	1.220814	1.269370
1.4000000	1.123461	1.152407	1.187381	1.229204	1.278907
1.4100000	1.129881	1.159312	1.194926	1.237602	1.288465
1.4200000	1.136295	1.166214	1.202471	1.246008	1.298042
1.4300000	1.142705	1.173114	1.210018	1.254420	1.307639
1.4400000	1.149110	1.180011	1.217566	1.262840	1.317254
1.4500000	1.155512	1.186905	1.225114	1.271266	1.326886
1.4600000	1.161909	1.193798	1.232663	1.279698	1.336534
1.4700000	1.168304	1.200689	1.240213	1.288135	1.346197
1.4800000	1.174695	1.207578	1.247764	1.296578	1.355874
1.4900000	1.181083	1.214465	1.255315	1.305025	1.365563
1.5000000	1.187469	1.221351	1.262867	1.313477	1.375264
1.5100000	1.193852	1.228236	1.270420	1.321932	1.384974
1.5200000	1.200234	1.235120	1.277973	1.330391	1.394693
1.5300000	1.206614	1.242003	1.285526	1.338852	1.404419
1.5400000	1.212993	1.248886	1.293080	1.347316	1.414151
1.5500000	1.219371	1.255767	1.300634	1.355781	1.423887
1.5600000	1.225749	1.262649	1.308188	1.364247	1.433626
1.5699999	1.232126	1.269530	1.315743	1.372714	1.443367
1.5707963	1.232634	1.270078	1.316344	1.373388	1.444143
1.5707963	1.232633	1.270078	1.316344	1.373388	1.444142

$\alpha =$ -.899999

Θ	K VALUES				
	.794250555	.868696860	.928444378	.971111163	.994996249
.0000000	.000000	.000000	.000000	.000000	.000000
.0100000	.009999	.009999	.009999	.009999	.009999
.0200000	.019998	.019998	.019998	.019998	.019998
.0300000	.029995	.029995	.029996	.029996	.029996
.0400000	.039989	.039990	.039990	.039991	.039991
.0500000	.049979	.049980	.049981	.049982	.049983
.0600000	.059963	.059966	.059968	.059970	.059971
.0700000	.069942	.069947	.069950	.069952	.069954
.0800000	.079914	.079921	.079926	.079929	.079931
.0900000	.089878	.089887	.089895	.089900	.089903
.1000000	.099834	.099846	.099856	.099863	.099867
.1100000	.109779	.109796	.109809	.109818	.109824
.1200000	.119714	.119736	.119753	.119765	.119772
.1300000	.129638	.129665	.129687	.129702	.129711
.1400000	.139549	.139583	.139610	.139630	.139641
.1500000	.149447	.149488	.149522	.149546	.149560
.1600000	.159331	.159381	.159422	.159451	.159468
.1700000	.169200	.169261	.169310	.169345	.169365
.1800000	.179054	.179126	.179184	.179226	.179249
.1900000	.188891	.188976	.189045	.189094	.189121
.2000000	.198712	.198811	.198891	.198948	.198980
.2100000	.208515	.208630	.208722	.208789	.208826
.2200000	.218300	.218432	.218538	.218615	.218657
.2300000	.228066	.228217	.228339	.228426	.228475
.2400000	.237813	.237985	.238123	.238222	.238278
.2500000	.247540	.247734	.247891	.248003	.248066
.2600000	.257247	.257465	.257641	.257768	.257838
.2700000	.266933	.267178	.267375	.267516	.267596
.2800000	.276598	.276871	.277091	.277249	.277338
.2900000	.286241	.286545	.286790	.286965	.287064
.3000000	.295863	.296199	.296470	.296665	.296774
.3100000	.305462	.305833	.306133	.306348	.306468
.3200000	.315039	.315448	.315777	.316014	.316147
.3300000	.324594	.325042	.325404	.325664	.325810
.3400000	.334126	.334616	.335012	.335297	.335457
.3500000	.343635	.344170	.344602	.344913	.345088
.3600000	.353120	.353703	.354175	.354513	.354704
.3700000	.362583	.363216	.363729	.364097	.364304
.3800000	.372023	.372709	.373265	.373665	.373890
.3900000	.381440	.382182	.382784	.383217	.383460

$\alpha =$ -.899999

Θ	K VALUES				
	.794250555	.868696860	.928444378	.971111163	.994996249
.4000000	.390833	.391635	.392285	.392753	.393016
.4100000	.400204	.401068	.401769	.402274	.402558
.4200000	.409552	.410482	.411236	.411780	.412086
.4300000	.418878	.419876	.420687	.421272	.421601
.4400000	.428181	.429252	.430122	.430750	.431104
.4500000	.437461	.438608	.439541	.440214	.440594
.4600000	.446720	.447947	.448945	.449666	.450072
.4700000	.455958	.457268	.458335	.459105	.459540
.4800000	.465174	.466571	.467710	.468533	.468997
.4900000	.474369	.475857	.477071	.477949	.478445
.5000000	.483544	.485128	.486420	.487356	.487884
.5100000	.492698	.494382	.495757	.496752	.497314
.5200000	.501833	.503621	.505082	.506140	.506738
.5300000	.510949	.512845	.514396	.515520	.516156
.5400000	.520047	.522056	.523700	.524893	.525568
.5500000	.529126	.531253	.532995	.534260	.534976
.5600000	.538188	.540438	.542282	.543622	.544380
.5700000	.547234	.549610	.551562	.552980	.553783
.5800000	.556263	.558772	.560835	.562334	.563184
.5900000	.565276	.567924	.570102	.571687	.572586
.6000000	.574276	.577067	.579365	.581039	.581988
.6100000	.583260	.586201	.588624	.590391	.591394
.6200000	.592232	.595328	.597881	.599745	.600803
.6300000	.601191	.604448	.607137	.609101	.610217
.6400000	.610139	.613562	.616393	.618462	.619638
.6500000	.619075	.622673	.625650	.627828	.629068
.6600000	.628001	.631779	.634909	.637202	.638506
.6700000	.636919	.640883	.644172	.646583	.647956
.6800000	.645828	.649986	.653440	.655975	.657419
.6899999	.654729	.659089	.662715	.665378	.666897
.7000000	.663624	.668192	.671997	.674794	.676390
.7100000	.672514	.677298	.681288	.684224	.685902
.7200000	.681399	.686407	.690589	.693671	.695433
.7300000	.690280	.695521	.699903	.703136	.704986
.7400000	.699159	.704641	.709231	.712622	.714563
.7500000	.708037	.713767	.718574	.722129	.724166
.7600000	.716914	.722903	.727934	.731659	.733796
.7700000	.725792	.732048	.737312	.741216	.743457
.7800000	.734671	.741205	.746711	.750800	.753150
.7899999	.743553	.750374	.756132	.760414	.762877

$\alpha =$ -.899999

Θ	K VALUES				
	.794250555	.868696860	.928444378	.971111163	.994996249
.8000000	.752439	.759557	.765577	.770060	.772642
.8100000	.761330	.768757	.775048	.779741	.782446
.8200000	.770227	.777973	.784547	.789458	.792293
.8300000	.779132	.787208	.794076	.799215	.802184
.8400000	.788045	.796463	.803636	.809012	.812122
.8500000	.796967	.805740	.813231	.818854	.822112
.8600000	.805901	.815041	.822861	.828743	.832154
.8700000	.814846	.824367	.832530	.838681	.842253
.8799999	.823805	.833719	.842239	.848672	.852412
.8899999	.832779	.843101	.851991	.858717	.862634
.9000000	.841768	.852513	.861789	.868821	.872923
.9100000	.850775	.861957	.871634	.878987	.883282
.9200000	.859800	.871435	.881530	.889216	.893714
.9300000	.868844	.880948	.891478	.899514	.904224
.9400000	.877909	.890500	.901482	.909884	.914817
.9500000	.886997	.900091	.911544	.920328	.925495
.9600000	.896108	.909724	.921667	.930851	.936264
.9699999	.905244	.919400	.931854	.941457	.947128
.9799999	.914406	.929122	.942108	.952149	.958092
.9899999	.923595	.938891	.952432	.962933	.969161
1.0000000	.932813	.948711	.962830	.973812	.980340
1.0100000	.942061	.958582	.973303	.984790	.991635
1.0200000	.951341	.968507	.983857	.995873	1.003052
1.0300000	.960653	.978488	.994494	1.007066	1.014597
1.0400000	.969999	.988527	1.005217	1.018374	1.026276
1.0500000	.979380	.998627	1.016031	1.029801	1.038096
1.0600000	.988798	1.008790	1.026939	1.041354	1.050064
1.0699999	.998254	1.019018	1.037944	1.053038	1.062188
1.0799999	1.007748	1.029312	1.049052	1.064860	1.074475
1.0899999	1.017283	1.039677	1.060266	1.076826	1.086935
1.1000000	1.026860	1.050113	1.071589	1.088943	1.099575
1.1100000	1.036479	1.060624	1.083027	1.101217	1.112406
1.1200000	1.046143	1.071211	1.094584	1.113656	1.125436
1.1300000	1.055851	1.081877	1.106264	1.126268	1.138678
1.1400000	1.065605	1.092624	1.118072	1.139060	1.152141
1.1500000	1.075407	1.103454	1.130013	1.152042	1.165839
1.1600000	1.085257	1.114371	1.142091	1.165221	1.179783
1.1700000	1.095157	1.125375	1.154312	1.178607	1.193988
1.1800000	1.105106	1.136470	1.166680	1.192211	1.208468
1.1899999	1.115107	1.147657	1.179201	1.206041	1.223239

$\alpha =$ -.899999

Θ	K VALUES				
	.794250555	.868696860	.928444378	.971111163	.994996249
1.2000000	1.125160	1.158939	1.191880	1.220110	1.238317
1.2100000	1.135266	1.170318	1.204722	1.234428	1.253721
1.2200000	1.145426	1.181795	1.217733	1.249006	1.269470
1.2300000	1.155639	1.193373	1.230917	1.263859	1.285585
1.2400000	1.165907	1.205055	1.244282	1.278998	1.302088
1.2500000	1.176231	1.216840	1.257832	1.294437	1.319005
1.2599999	1.186610	1.228732	1.271572	1.310192	1.336362
1.2699999	1.197044	1.240731	1.285509	1.326276	1.354188
1.2799999	1.207535	1.252840	1.299648	1.342707	1.372515
1.2899999	1.218083	1.265058	1.313993	1.359500	1.391377
1.3000000	1.228686	1.277388	1.328551	1.376673	1.410812
1.3100000	1.239345	1.289830	1.343326	1.394244	1.430862
1.3200000	1.250061	1.302385	1.358323	1.412232	1.451572
1.3300000	1.260831	1.315052	1.373546	1.430657	1.472993
1.3400000	1.271656	1.327832	1.389000	1.449538	1.495181
1.3500000	1.282535	1.340725	1.404688	1.468896	1.518198
1.3600000	1.293468	1.353730	1.420614	1.488753	1.542113
1.3700000	1.304453	1.366847	1.436780	1.509130	1.567002
1.3799999	1.315489	1.380073	1.453187	1.530048	1.592952
1.3899999	1.326575	1.393408	1.469836	1.551529	1.620061
1.4000000	1.337710	1.406849	1.486728	1.573593	1.648435
1.4100000	1.348892	1.420393	1.503862	1.596259	1.678199
1.4200000	1.360119	1.434039	1.521235	1.619546	1.709490
1.4300000	1.371389	1.447782	1.538843	1.643470	1.742465
1.4400000	1.382700	1.461619	1.556683	1.668042	1.777300
1.4500000	1.394051	1.475545	1.574746	1.693271	1.814196
1.4600000	1.405438	1.489557	1.593027	1.719162	1.853375
1.4700000	1.416859	1.503648	1.611514	1.745711	1.895088
1.4800000	1.428312	1.517813	1.630197	1.772908	1.939606
1.4900000	1.439794	1.532046	1.649062	1.800735	1.987221
1.5000000	1.451302	1.546342	1.668095	1.829165	2.038231
1.5100000	1.462833	1.560692	1.687279	1.858157	2.092914
1.5200000	1.474384	1.575091	1.706597	1.887661	2.151490
1.5300000	1.485952	1.589530	1.726029	1.917617	2.214058
1.5400000	1.497534	1.604002	1.745554	1.947952	2.280506
1.5500000	1.509126	1.618499	1.765150	1.978583	2.350418
1.5600000	1.520724	1.633013	1.784795	2.009420	2.423003
1.5699999	1.532327	1.647536	1.804465	2.040364	2.497101
1.5707963	1.533251	1.648693	1.806032	2.042830	2.503026
1.5707963	1.533250	1.648692	1.806031	2.042829	2.503025

$\alpha = - .849999$

θ	K VALUES				
	.009966711	.039469502	.087332193	.151646642	.229848846
.0000000	.000000	.000000	.000000	.000000	.000000
.0100000	.009999	.009999	.009999	.009999	.009999
.0200000	.019997	.019997	.019997	.019997	.019998
.0300000	.029992	.029992	.029992	.029993	.029993
.0400000	.039982	.039982	.039982	.039983	.039984
.0500000	.049964	.049965	.049966	.049967	.049969
.0600000	.059939	.059940	.059942	.059944	.059947
.0700000	.069903	.069905	.069908	.069911	.069916
.0800000	.079856	.079858	.079863	.079868	.079875
.0900000	.089795	.089799	.089805	.089813	.089822
.1000000	.099720	.099725	.099733	.099743	.099756
.1100000	.109628	.109634	.109645	.109659	.109676
.1200000	.119518	.119526	.119540	.119558	.119580
.1300000	.129388	.129399	.129416	.129439	.129468
.1400000	.139237	.139251	.139272	.139301	.139337
.1500000	.149064	.149080	.149107	.149142	.149186
.1600000	.158866	.158886	.158918	.158962	.159014
.1700000	.168643	.168667	.168706	.168757	.168820
.1800000	.178394	.178422	.178467	.178529	.178603
.1900000	.188116	.188149	.188202	.188274	.188362
.2000000	.197808	.197846	.197909	.197992	.198094
.2100000	.207470	.207514	.207586	.207683	.207800
.2200000	.217099	.217150	.217233	.217343	.217479
.2300000	.226696	.226754	.226847	.226974	.227128
.2400000	.236258	.236323	.236430	.236573	.236748
.2500000	.245784	.245858	.245978	.246139	.246336
.2600000	.255274	.255357	.255491	.255672	.255893
.2700000	.264727	.264819	.264969	.265171	.265418
.2800000	.274140	.274243	.274409	.274634	.274909
.2900000	.283514	.283628	.283812	.284061	.284365
.3000000	.292848	.292973	.293176	.293451	.293787
.3100000	.302140	.302277	.302501	.302803	.303173
.3200000	.311390	.311541	.311786	.312117	.312522
.3300000	.320597	.320762	.321029	.321391	.321834
.3400000	.329761	.329940	.330232	.330626	.331109
.3500000	.338880	.339074	.339391	.339820	.340345
.3600000	.347954	.348165	.348508	.348973	.349542
.3700000	.356982	.357210	.357582	.358084	.358700
.3800000	.365965	.366210	.366611	.367153	.367818
.3900000	.374900	.375165	.375596	.376180	.376896

$\alpha =$ - •849999

Θ	K VALUES				
	•009966711	•039469502	•087332193	•151646642	•229848846
•4000000	•383789	•384073	•384536	•385163	•385933
•4100000	•392630	•392934	•393431	•394103	•394929
•4200000	•401423	•401749	•402280	•402999	•403884
•4300000	•410168	•410515	•411083	•411852	•412797
•4400000	•418864	•419235	•419839	•420660	•421669
•4500000	•427511	•427906	•428549	•429423	•430498
•4600000	•436110	•436528	•437213	•438141	•439285
•4700000	•444658	•445103	•445829	•446815	•448030
•4800000	•453158	•453629	•454398	•455443	•456732
•4900000	•461608	•462106	•462920	•464027	•465392
•5000000	•470008	•470534	•471395	•472565	•474009
•5100000	•478358	•478913	•479822	•481057	•482584
•5200000	•486659	•487244	•488201	•489505	•491115
•5300000	•494909	•495525	•496534	•497907	•499605
•5400000	•503110	•503758	•504819	•506263	•508051
•5500000	•511262	•511942	•513056	•514575	•516455
•5600000	•519363	•520077	•521247	•522841	•524817
•5700000	•527416	•528164	•529390	•531063	•533136
•5800000	•535418	•536202	•537486	•539239	•541414
•5900000	•543372	•544192	•545536	•547371	•549649
•6000000	•551277	•552134	•553539	•555459	•557843
•6100000	•559133	•560028	•561495	•563502	•565995
•6200000	•566941	•567874	•569406	•571501	•574106
•6300000	•574700	•575673	•577270	•579456	•582176
•6400000	•582411	•583424	•585089	•587368	•590206
•6500000	•590075	•591129	•592863	•595236	•598195
•6600000	•597691	•598788	•600591	•603062	•606143
•6700000	•605260	•606400	•608275	•610845	•614052
•6800000	•612783	•613967	•615914	•618585	•621922
•6899999	•620259	•621488	•623510	•626284	•629752
•7000000	•627690	•628964	•631061	•633941	•637544
•7100000	•635075	•636395	•638570	•641557	•645297
•7200000	•642415	•643782	•646035	•649132	•653012
•7300000	•649710	•651125	•653458	•656667	•660689
•7400000	•656961	•658425	•660839	•664162	•668330
•7500000	•664168	•665682	•668179	•671617	•675933
•7600000	•671332	•672896	•675477	•679033	•683500
•7700000	•678453	•680068	•682735	•686410	•691031
•7800000	•685531	•687199	•689952	•693750	•698527
•7899999	•692568	•694288	•697130	•701051	•705988

$\alpha = -.849999$

θ	K VALUES				
	.009966711	.039469502	.087332193	.151646642	.229848846
.8000000	.699564	.701337	.704268	.708315	.713414
.8100000	.706518	.708346	.711367	.715542	.720806
.8200000	.713432	.715315	.718429	.722732	.728164
.8300000	.720307	.722245	.725452	.729887	.735489
.8400000	.727141	.729136	.732438	.737007	.742781
.8500000	.733938	.735990	.739387	.744091	.750041
.8600000	.740696	.742805	.746300	.751141	.757270
.8700000	.747416	.749584	.753177	.758157	.764467
.8799999	.754099	.756326	.760018	.765139	.771633
.8899999	.760745	.763032	.766825	.772089	.778769
.9000000	.767355	.769703	.773598	.779006	.785875
.9100000	.773930	.776339	.780337	.785891	.792951
.9200000	.780470	.782941	.787042	.792745	.799999
.9300000	.786975	.789509	.793716	.799568	.807019
.9400000	.793446	.796043	.800356	.806361	.814010
.9500000	.799885	.802545	.806966	.813123	.820975
.9600000	.806290	.809015	.813544	.819857	.827912
.9699999	.812663	.815453	.820092	.826561	.834823
.9799999	.819005	.821860	.826610	.833237	.841708
.9899999	.825315	.828236	.833098	.839886	.848568
1.0000000	.831595	.834583	.839558	.846507	.855403
1.0100000	.837845	.840900	.845989	.853101	.862213
1.0200000	.844066	.847189	.852392	.859669	.869000
1.0300000	.850257	.853449	.858768	.866211	.875763
1.0400000	.856421	.859681	.865117	.872728	.882503
1.0500000	.862557	.865886	.871440	.879220	.889221
1.0600000	.868666	.872065	.877737	.885688	.895916
1.0699999	.874748	.878218	.884010	.892133	.902591
1.0799999	.880804	.884345	.890257	.898554	.909244
1.0899999	.886835	.890447	.896480	.904952	.915877
1.1000000	.892840	.896524	.902680	.911329	.922489
1.1100000	.898822	.902578	.908857	.917683	.929082
1.1200000	.904779	.908608	.915011	.924017	.935656
1.1300000	.910714	.914616	.921144	.930330	.942212
1.1400000	.916626	.920601	.927255	.936622	.948749
1.1500000	.922515	.926565	.933344	.942895	.955268
1.1600000	.928383	.932507	.939414	.949149	.961770
1.1700000	.934230	.938429	.945463	.955384	.968256
1.1800000	.940057	.944331	.951494	.961601	.974725
1.1899999	.945863	.950213	.957505	.967800	.981178

$\alpha = -$ .849999

Θ	K VALUES				
	.009966711	.039469502	.087332193	.151646642	.229848846
1.2000000	.951650	.956076	.963498	.973982	.987616
1.2100000	.957418	.961920	.969473	.980147	.994038
1.2200000	.963168	.967747	.975431	.986296	1.000446
1.2300000	.968900	.973556	.981371	.992429	1.006840
1.2400000	.974615	.979348	.987296	.998547	1.013221
1.2500000	.980313	.985124	.993205	1.004650	1.019588
1.2599999	.985994	.990883	.999098	1.010738	1.025942
1.2699999	.991660	.996628	1.004977	1.016813	1.032284
1.2799999	.997311	1.002357	1.010841	1.022874	1.038614
1.2899999	1.002947	1.008072	1.016691	1.028922	1.044932
1.3000000	1.008570	1.013773	1.022528	1.034958	1.051240
1.3100000	1.014178	1.019461	1.028353	1.040982	1.057536
1.3200000	1.019774	1.025136	1.034164	1.046994	1.063822
1.3300000	1.025356	1.030799	1.039964	1.052995	1.070099
1.3400000	1.030927	1.036450	1.045753	1.058986	1.076366
1.3500000	1.036486	1.042090	1.051531	1.064966	1.082624
1.3600000	1.042035	1.047718	1.057298	1.070937	1.088873
1.3700000	1.047572	1.053337	1.063055	1.076898	1.095114
1.3799999	1.053100	1.058945	1.068803	1.082850	1.101348
1.3899999	1.058618	1.064545	1.074542	1.088795	1.107574
1.4000000	1.064127	1.070135	1.080272	1.094731	1.113793
1.4100000	1.069628	1.075717	1.085995	1.100659	1.120005
1.4200000	1.075121	1.081292	1.091710	1.106581	1.126211
1.4300000	1.080606	1.086859	1.097417	1.112496	1.132411
1.4400000	1.086084	1.092419	1.103119	1.118405	1.138606
1.4500000	1.091556	1.097972	1.108814	1.124308	1.144796
1.4600000	1.097021	1.103520	1.114503	1.130206	1.150981
1.4700000	1.102482	1.109063	1.120187	1.136099	1.157162
1.4800000	1.107937	1.114600	1.125867	1.141988	1.163339
1.4900000	1.113388	1.120134	1.131542	1.147872	1.169513
1.5000000	1.118834	1.125663	1.137214	1.153753	1.175683
1.5100000	1.124278	1.131189	1.142882	1.159632	1.181851
1.5200000	1.129718	1.136712	1.148547	1.165507	1.188016
1.5300000	1.135156	1.142232	1.154210	1.171380	1.194180
1.5400000	1.140591	1.147751	1.159871	1.177252	1.200341
1.5500000	1.146026	1.153268	1.165531	1.183122	1.206502
1.5600000	1.151459	1.158784	1.171190	1.188991	1.212662
1.5699999	1.156891	1.164299	1.176848	1.194860	1.218822
1.5707963	1.157324	1.164738	1.177299	1.195327	1.219312
1.5707963	1.157323	1.164738	1.177298	1.195327	1.219312

$\alpha = -$ .849999

Θ	K VALUES				
	.318821117	.415016431	.514599755	.613601043	.708073407
.0000000	.000000	.000000	.000000	.000000	.000000
.0100000	.009999	.009999	.009999	.009999	.009999
.0200000	.019998	.019998	.019998	.019998	.019998
.0300000	.029993	.029994	.029994	.029995	.029995
.0400000	.039985	.039986	.039987	.039988	.039989
.0500000	.049971	.049973	.049975	.049977	.049979
.0600000	.059950	.059953	.059957	.059961	.059964
.0700000	.069921	.069926	.069932	.069938	.069943
.0800000	.079882	.079890	.079899	.079907	.079915
.0900000	.089833	.089844	.089856	.089868	.089880
.1000000	.099771	.099787	.099804	.099820	.099836
.1100000	.109696	.109717	.109739	.109761	.109782
.1200000	.119606	.119633	.119662	.119690	.119718
.1300000	.129500	.129535	.129571	.129607	.129642
.1400000	.139377	.139421	.139466	.139511	.139554
.1500000	.149235	.149289	.149345	.149400	.149453
.1600000	.159074	.159139	.159207	.159274	.159338
.1700000	.168892	.168970	.169051	.169132	.169209
.1800000	.178689	.178781	.178877	.178972	.179064
.1900000	.188462	.188570	.188683	.188795	.188903
.2000000	.198211	.198337	.198469	.198600	.198725
.2100000	.207935	.208081	.208233	.208385	.208530
.2200000	.217633	.217801	.217975	.218149	.218316
.2300000	.227304	.227496	.227695	.227893	.228084
.2400000	.236947	.237164	.237390	.237616	.237832
.2500000	.246562	.246807	.247061	.247316	.247561
.2600000	.256146	.256421	.256708	.256994	.257269
.2700000	.265700	.266008	.266328	.266648	.266956
.2800000	.275223	.275565	.275922	.276279	.276622
.2900000	.284714	.285093	.285489	.285885	.286266
.3000000	.294172	.294591	.295028	.295467	.295888
.3100000	.303596	.304058	.304540	.305023	.305488
.3200000	.312987	.313493	.314022	.314553	.315065
.3300000	.322343	.322897	.323476	.324058	.324618
.3400000	.331663	.332268	.332901	.333536	.334149
.3500000	.340948	.341606	.342295	.342988	.343656
.3600000	.350196	.350911	.351660	.352413	.353139
.3700000	.359408	.360182	.360994	.361810	.362599
.3800000	.368583	.369420	.370297	.371181	.372035
.3900000	.377720	.378623	.379569	.380523	.381447

$\alpha = -\ .849999$

θ	K VALUES				
	.318821117	.415016431	.514599755	.613601043	.708073407
.4000000	.386820	.387791	.388810	.389839	.390834
.4100000	.395881	.396924	.398020	.399126	.400198
.4200000	.404904	.406022	.407198	.408386	.409538
.4300000	.413888	.415085	.416345	.417619	.418854
.4400000	.422834	.424113	.425460	.426823	.428147
.4500000	.431740	.433105	.434543	.436000	.437415
.4600000	.440607	.442061	.443595	.445149	.446661
.4700000	.449435	.450982	.452614	.454270	.455883
.4800000	.458224	.459867	.461602	.463364	.465082
.4900000	.466973	.468716	.470559	.472431	.474258
.5000000	.475683	.477529	.479483	.481471	.483412
.5100000	.484353	.486307	.488377	.490484	.492543
.5200000	.492984	.495049	.497239	.499470	.501653
.5300000	.501576	.503756	.506070	.508430	.510741
.5400000	.510128	.512428	.514870	.517364	.519808
.5500000	.518641	.521064	.523639	.526272	.528855
.5600000	.527116	.529665	.532378	.535154	.537881
.5700000	.535551	.538232	.541087	.544012	.546888
.5800000	.543948	.546763	.549766	.552844	.555875
.5900000	.552306	.555261	.558415	.561653	.564844
.6000000	.560626	.563724	.567035	.570437	.573795
.6100000	.568908	.572154	.575626	.579198	.582727
.6200000	.577153	.580550	.584188	.587936	.591643
.6300000	.585360	.588913	.592722	.596651	.600543
.6400000	.593529	.597243	.601229	.605344	.609426
.6500000	.601662	.605540	.609707	.614016	.618295
.6600000	.609758	.613805	.618159	.622667	.627148
.6700000	.617818	.622039	.626585	.631297	.635988
.6800000	.625842	.630241	.634984	.639907	.644815
.6899999	.633831	.638412	.643357	.648497	.653629
.7000000	.641784	.646552	.651706	.657069	.662432
.7100000	.649703	.654662	.660029	.665622	.671224
.7200000	.657587	.662742	.668328	.674158	.680005
.7300000	.665437	.670793	.676604	.682677	.688777
.7400000	.673254	.678815	.684856	.691179	.697540
.7500000	.681037	.686808	.693086	.699665	.706295
.7600000	.688788	.694773	.701293	.708136	.715043
.7700000	.696507	.702711	.709478	.716593	.723785
.7800000	.704193	.710622	.717643	.725035	.732521
.7899999	.711849	.718506	.725786	.733464	.741253

$\alpha = -\ .849999$

θ	K VALUES				
	.318821117	.415016431	.514599755	.613601043	.708073407
.8000000	.719473	.726364	.733910	.741881	.749981
.8100000	.727067	.734196	.742014	.750285	.758705
.8200000	.734631	.742003	.750099	.758679	.767428
.8300000	.742166	.749785	.758166	.767061	.776149
.8400000	.749671	.757543	.766214	.775433	.784870
.8500000	.757148	.765277	.774245	.783796	.793591
.8600000	.764596	.772989	.782260	.792151	.802314
.8700000	.772017	.780677	.790258	.800497	.811039
.8799999	.779411	.788343	.798240	.808836	.819767
.8899999	.786778	.795987	.806207	.817168	.828499
.9000000	.794119	.803610	.814159	.825494	.837235
.9100000	.801434	.811213	.822098	.833815	.845978
.9200000	.808724	.818795	.830022	.842131	.854727
.9300000	.815989	.826357	.837934	.850443	.863484
.9400000	.823230	.833900	.845833	.858751	.872249
.9500000	.830447	.841424	.853720	.867057	.881023
.9600000	.837641	.848929	.861596	.875360	.889807
.9699999	.844812	.856417	.869460	.883662	.898603
.9799999	.851960	.863888	.877315	.891963	.907410
.9899999	.859087	.871341	.885159	.900264	.916230
1.0000000	.866192	.878778	.892994	.908565	.925064
1.0100000	.873277	.886200	.900819	.916867	.933912
1.0200000	.880341	.893605	.908637	.925170	.942775
1.0300000	.887384	.900995	.916446	.933475	.951654
1.0400000	.894409	.908371	.924248	.941783	.960550
1.0500000	.901414	.915733	.932043	.950095	.969464
1.0600000	.908400	.923081	.939831	.958410	.978397
1.0699999	.915369	.930415	.947613	.966729	.987348
1.0799999	.922319	.937737	.955389	.975052	.996319
1.0899999	.929252	.945046	.963160	.983382	1.005311
1.1000000	.936169	.952343	.970926	.991716	1.014325
1.1100000	.943069	.959629	.978687	1.000057	1.023360
1.1200000	.949953	.966903	.986444	1.008405	1.032418
1.1300000	.956821	.974166	.994198	1.016759	1.041500
1.1400000	.963675	.981419	1.001948	1.025121	1.050605
1.1500000	.970513	.988662	1.009694	1.033490	1.059734
1.1600000	.977338	.995894	1.017439	1.041868	1.068889
1.1700000	.984148	1.003118	1.025180	1.050254	1.078068
1.1800000	.990945	1.010333	1.032920	1.058649	1.087274
1.1899999	.997729	1.017538	1.040658	1.067053	1.096506

$\alpha = -.849999$

θ	K VALUES				
	.318821117	.415016431	.514599755	.613601043	.708073407
1.2000000	1.004500	1.024736	1.048395	1.075466	1.105765
1.2100000	1.011259	1.031926	1.056130	1.083889	1.115051
1.2200000	1.018006	1.039107	1.063864	1.092322	1.124364
1.2300000	1.024742	1.046282	1.071597	1.100764	1.133704
1.2400000	1.031466	1.053450	1.079330	1.109217	1.143072
1.2500000	1.038180	1.060610	1.087063	1.117680	1.152468
1.2599999	1.044884	1.067765	1.094795	1.126153	1.161892
1.2699999	1.051577	1.074913	1.102528	1.134637	1.171344
1.2799999	1.058261	1.082055	1.110261	1.143131	1.180823
1.2899999	1.064935	1.089192	1.117994	1.151636	1.190331
1.3000000	1.071601	1.096323	1.125728	1.160151	1.199866
1.3100000	1.078258	1.103450	1.133463	1.168676	1.209429
1.3200000	1.084907	1.110571	1.141198	1.177212	1.219019
1.3300000	1.091548	1.117689	1.148935	1.185759	1.228636
1.3400000	1.098182	1.124801	1.156672	1.194315	1.238279
1.3500000	1.104808	1.131910	1.164411	1.202881	1.247948
1.3600000	1.111428	1.139015	1.172150	1.211457	1.257643
1.3700000	1.118041	1.146116	1.179891	1.220043	1.267363
1.3799999	1.124648	1.153214	1.187633	1.228638	1.277107
1.3899999	1.131249	1.160308	1.195376	1.237243	1.286874
1.4000000	1.137845	1.167400	1.203121	1.245856	1.296664
1.4100000	1.144436	1.174489	1.210867	1.254477	1.306477
1.4200000	1.151021	1.181575	1.218614	1.263107	1.316310
1.4300000	1.157602	1.188658	1.226362	1.271744	1.326163
1.4400000	1.164179	1.195740	1.234111	1.280389	1.336035
1.4500000	1.170752	1.202819	1.241862	1.289041	1.345926
1.4600000	1.177321	1.209897	1.249614	1.297699	1.355833
1.4700000	1.183887	1.216973	1.257367	1.306363	1.365755
1.4800000	1.190450	1.224047	1.265120	1.315033	1.375692
1.4900000	1.197010	1.231120	1.272875	1.323708	1.385642
1.5000000	1.203568	1.238192	1.280630	1.332387	1.395604
1.5100000	1.210124	1.245262	1.288387	1.341071	1.405576
1.5200000	1.216678	1.252332	1.296143	1.349757	1.415557
1.5300000	1.223231	1.259401	1.303901	1.358447	1.425546
1.5400000	1.229782	1.266469	1.311659	1.367139	1.435541
1.5500000	1.236332	1.273537	1.319417	1.375833	1.445540
1.5600000	1.242882	1.280604	1.327175	1.384528	1.455542
1.5699999	1.249431	1.287672	1.334934	1.393224	1.465546
1.5707963	1.249953	1.288235	1.335551	1.393916	1.466343
1.5707963	1.249952	1.288234	1.335551	1.393916	1.466343

$\alpha = -$ .849999

Θ	K VALUES				
	.794250555	.868696860	.928444378	.971111163	.994996249
.0000000	.000000	.000000	.000000	.000000	.000000
.0100000	.009999	.009999	.009999	.009999	.009999
.0200000	.019998	.019998	.019998	.019999	.019999
.0300000	.029995	.029996	.029996	.029996	.029996
.0400000	.039990	.039991	.039991	.039992	.039992
.0500000	.049981	.049982	.049984	.049984	.049985
.0600000	.059967	.059970	.059972	.059973	.059974
.0700000	.069948	.069952	.069956	.069958	.069959
.0800000	.079923	.079929	.079934	.079938	.079940
.0900000	.089890	.089899	.089907	.089912	.089915
.1000000	.099850	.099862	.099872	.099880	.099884
.1100000	.109801	.109818	.109831	.109840	.109846
.1200000	.119742	.119764	.119781	.119793	.119800
.1300000	.129674	.129701	.129723	.129738	.129747
.1400000	.139593	.139628	.139655	.139675	.139685
.1500000	.149502	.149543	.149577	.149601	.149615
.1600000	.159397	.159448	.159489	.159518	.159535
.1700000	.169279	.169340	.169389	.169425	.169444
.1800000	.179148	.179220	.179278	.179320	.179343
.1900000	.189001	.189087	.189155	.189204	.189232
.2000000	.198840	.198939	.199019	.199077	.199109
.2100000	.208663	.208778	.208870	.208937	.208974
.2200000	.218469	.218601	.218708	.218784	.218827
.2300000	.228258	.228410	.228532	.228619	.228668
.2400000	.238031	.238203	.238341	.238441	.238496
.2500000	.247785	.247980	.248136	.248249	.248312
.2600000	.257521	.257740	.257917	.258043	.258114
.2700000	.267239	.267484	.267682	.267823	.267903
.2800000	.276937	.277211	.277432	.277590	.277679
.2900000	.286616	.286920	.287166	.287342	.287441
.3000000	.296276	.296613	.296885	.297080	.297189
.3100000	.305915	.306287	.306588	.306803	.306924
.3200000	.315535	.315944	.316275	.316513	.316646
.3300000	.325134	.325584	.325947	.326208	.326354
.3400000	.334713	.335205	.335603	.335888	.336049
.3500000	.344272	.344809	.345243	.345555	.345730
.3600000	.353810	.354394	.354867	.355207	.355399
.3700000	.363327	.363962	.364477	.364846	.365054
.3800000	.372823	.373512	.374070	.374472	.374697
.3900000	.382299	.383045	.383649	.384084	.384328

$\alpha = -\ .849999$

Θ	K VALUES				
	.794250555	.868696860	.928444378	.971111163	.994996249
.4000000	.391755	.392560	.393213	.393683	.393947
.4100000	.401190	.402058	.402762	.403269	.403554
.4200000	.410605	.411539	.412297	.412843	.413151
.4300000	.419999	.421003	.421818	.422405	.422736
.4400000	.429374	.430451	.431325	.431956	.432312
.4500000	.438729	.439882	.440820	.441497	.441878
.4600000	.448065	.449298	.450302	.451027	.451435
.4700000	.457382	.458699	.459772	.460547	.460984
.4800000	.466679	.468085	.469230	.470058	.470525
.4900000	.475959	.477457	.478678	.479561	.480059
.5000000	.485221	.486814	.488115	.489056	.489588
.5100000	.494465	.496159	.497543	.498545	.499111
.5200000	.503691	.505491	.506962	.508027	.508629
.5300000	.512902	.514811	.516372	.517504	.518144
.5400000	.522096	.524119	.525776	.526977	.527656
.5500000	.531275	.533417	.535172	.536446	.537167
.5600000	.540439	.542705	.544564	.545913	.546678
.5700000	.549588	.551984	.553950	.555379	.556188
.5800000	.558724	.561254	.563332	.564844	.565701
.5900000	.567847	.570516	.572712	.574310	.575216
.6000000	.576958	.579772	.582090	.583778	.584735
.6100000	.586057	.589022	.591467	.593249	.594260
.6200000	.595145	.598268	.600844	.602724	.603791
.6300000	.604222	.607509	.610223	.612204	.613331
.6400000	.613291	.616747	.619604	.621692	.622879
.6500000	.622351	.625983	.628989	.631188	.632439
.6600000	.631403	.635218	.638378	.640693	.642011
.6700000	.640449	.644453	.647775	.650210	.651597
.6800000	.649488	.653689	.657178	.659739	.661198
.6899999	.658523	.662928	.666591	.669282	.670817
.7000000	.667553	.672170	.676014	.678841	.680455
.7100000	.676580	.681416	.685449	.688418	.690114
.7200000	.685605	.690669	.694897	.698014	.699795
.7300000	.694629	.699928	.704360	.707630	.709501
.7400000	.703652	.709196	.713840	.717270	.719234
.7500000	.712677	.718474	.723337	.726934	.728995
.7600000	.721703	.727763	.732854	.736624	.738787
.7700000	.730731	.737064	.742392	.746344	.748612
.7800000	.739764	.746379	.751954	.756094	.758473
.7899999	.748802	.755709	.761540	.765876	.768371

$\alpha = -$ .849999

θ	K VALUES				
	.794250555	.868696860	.928444378	.971111163	.994996249
.8000000	.757846	.765055	.771153	.775694	.778309
.8100000	.766897	.774420	.780795	.785549	.788290
.8200000	.775957	.783805	.790467	.795444	.798316
.8300000	.785026	.793211	.800172	.805381	.808390
.8400000	.794106	.802639	.809911	.815362	.818515
.8500000	.803198	.812092	.819687	.825390	.828694
.8600000	.812303	.821571	.829503	.835469	.838929
.8700000	.821422	.831078	.839359	.845600	.849224
.8799999	.830557	.840615	.849259	.855786	.859583
.8899999	.839708	.850182	.859205	.866031	.870007
.9000000	.848878	.859783	.869199	.876338	.880502
.9100000	.858067	.869418	.879244	.886709	.891071
.9200000	.867277	.879090	.889342	.897149	.901717
.9300000	.876508	.888801	.899496	.907659	.912445
.9400000	.885763	.898551	.909708	.918245	.923258
.9500000	.895042	.908345	.919983	.928910	.934161
.9600000	.904347	.918182	.930321	.939657	.945159
.9699999	.913679	.928066	.940727	.950490	.956256
.9799999	.923039	.937999	.951203	.961414	.967458
.9899999	.932429	.947982	.961752	.972433	.978768
1.0000000	.941850	.958017	.972379	.983551	.990194
1.0100000	.951303	.968107	.983085	.994774	1.001740
1.0200000	.960790	.978254	.993874	1.006105	1.013412
1.0300000	.970312	.988460	1.004751	1.017550	1.025217
1.0400000	.979870	.998727	1.015718	1.029114	1.037161
1.0500000	.989466	1.009058	1.026779	1.040802	1.049251
1.0600000	.999101	1.019455	1.037938	1.052621	1.061495
1.0699999	1.008776	1.029920	1.049198	1.064577	1.073900
1.0799999	1.018492	1.040455	1.060565	1.076675	1.086474
1.0899999	1.028251	1.051063	1.072042	1.088922	1.099226
1.1000000	1.038054	1.061746	1.083634	1.101325	1.112165
1.1100000	1.047902	1.072506	1.095344	1.113891	1.125301
1.1200000	1.057796	1.083347	1.107177	1.126627	1.138643
1.1300000	1.067738	1.094269	1.119138	1.139542	1.152203
1.1400000	1.077729	1.105276	1.131232	1.152644	1.165993
1.1500000	1.087769	1.116370	1.143463	1.165941	1.180023
1.1600000	1.097860	1.127553	1.155836	1.179443	1.194309
1.1700000	1.108003	1.138828	1.168357	1.193158	1.208862
1.1800000	1.118198	1.150197	1.181031	1.207097	1.223700
1.1899999	1.128447	1.161661	1.193862	1.221271	1.238837

$\alpha = -$ .849999

θ	K VALUES				
	.794250555	.868696860	.928444378	.971111163	.994996249
1.2000000	1.138751	1.173225	1.206857	1.235691	1.254291
1.2100000	1.149110	1.184888	1.220021	1.250367	1.270081
1.2200000	1.159524	1.196655	1.233359	1.265312	1.286226
1.2300000	1.169996	1.208525	1.246877	1.280540	1.302748
1.2400000	1.180524	1.220503	1.260580	1.296063	1.319670
1.2500000	1.191111	1.232588	1.274475	1.311895	1.337018
1.2599999	1.201755	1.244784	1.288567	1.328052	1.354818
1.2699999	1.212457	1.257091	1.302861	1.344549	1.373101
1.2799999	1.223218	1.269511	1.317363	1.361403	1.391900
1.2899999	1.234038	1.282045	1.332079	1.378629	1.411249
1.3000000	1.244916	1.294694	1.347014	1.396247	1.431188
1.3100000	1.255852	1.307460	1.362173	1.414275	1.451758
1.3200000	1.266847	1.320341	1.377561	1.432732	1.473008
1.3300000	1.277899	1.333340	1.393182	1.451638	1.494989
1.3400000	1.289007	1.346455	1.409041	1.471014	1.517759
1.3500000	1.300173	1.359687	1.425142	1.490881	1.541380
1.3600000	1.311393	1.373035	1.441487	1.511261	1.565925
1.3700000	1.322668	1.386497	1.458079	1.532176	1.591472
1.3799999	1.333997	1.400074	1.474920	1.553648	1.618109
1.3899999	1.345377	1.413762	1.492011	1.575698	1.645936
1.4000000	1.356807	1.427560	1.509353	1.598348	1.675065
1.4100000	1.368287	1.441465	1.526942	1.621618	1.705621
1.4200000	1.379813	1.455475	1.544778	1.645527	1.737746
1.4300000	1.391384	1.469585	1.562857	1.670089	1.771602
1.4400000	1.402998	1.483792	1.581174	1.695318	1.807369
1.4500000	1.414653	1.498092	1.599722	1.721224	1.845254
1.4600000	1.426346	1.512479	1.618493	1.747809	1.885484
1.4700000	1.438074	1.526949	1.637476	1.775071	1.928317
1.4800000	1.449835	1.541495	1.656662	1.803000	1.974032
1.4900000	1.461626	1.556112	1.676035	1.831577	2.022929
1.5000000	1.473444	1.570792	1.695581	1.860772	2.075313
1.5100000	1.485286	1.585530	1.715282	1.890545	2.131471
1.5200000	1.497149	1.600317	1.735121	1.920846	2.191628
1.5300000	1.509029	1.615145	1.755077	1.951611	2.255885
1.5400000	1.520923	1.630008	1.775130	1.982765	2.324128
1.5500000	1.532828	1.644897	1.795255	2.014224	2.395929
1.5600000	1.544740	1.659804	1.815431	2.045893	2.470475
1.5699999	1.556657	1.674719	1.835633	2.077674	2.546576
1.5707963	1.557605	1.675907	1.837243	2.080207	2.552661
1.5707963	1.557605	1.675906	1.837241	2.080205	2.552660

$\alpha = -\ .799999$

Θ	K VALUES				
	.009966711	.039469502	.087332193	.151646642	.229848846
.0000000	.000000	.000000	.000000	.000000	.000000
.0100000	.009999	.009999	.009999	.009999	.009999
.0200000	.019997	.019997	.019997	.019998	.019998
.0300000	.029992	.029992	.029993	.029993	.029993
.0400000	.039983	.039983	.039983	.039984	.039985
.0500000	.049966	.049967	.049968	.049969	.049971
.0600000	.059942	.059943	.059945	.059948	.059950
.0700000	.069909	.069911	.069913	.069917	.069921
.0800000	.079864	.079867	.079871	.079876	.079883
.0900000	.089807	.089811	.089817	.089825	.089834
.1000000	.099736	.099741	.099749	.099760	.099773
.1100000	.109650	.109656	.109667	.109681	.109698
.1200000	.119546	.119554	.119568	.119586	.119609
.1300000	.129424	.129435	.129452	.129475	.129504
.1400000	.139282	.139295	.139317	.139346	.139381
.1500000	.149119	.149135	.149161	.149197	.149241
.1600000	.158933	.158952	.158985	.159028	.159081
.1700000	.168723	.168746	.168785	.168837	.168900
.1800000	.178487	.178515	.178561	.178622	.178697
.1900000	.188225	.188258	.188312	.188384	.188472
.2000000	.197935	.197974	.198036	.198120	.198222
.2100000	.207616	.207661	.207733	.207829	.207948
.2200000	.217267	.217318	.217401	.217512	.217647
.2300000	.226887	.226944	.227038	.227165	.227320
.2400000	.236474	.236539	.236646	.236789	.236964
.2500000	.246027	.246101	.246221	.246382	.246580
.2600000	.255545	.255628	.255763	.255944	.256166
.2700000	.265028	.265121	.265271	.265474	.265721
.2800000	.274475	.274577	.274744	.274970	.275245
.2900000	.283884	.283997	.284182	.284432	.284737
.3000000	.293254	.293380	.293584	.293859	.294196
.3100000	.302585	.302723	.302948	.303251	.303621
.3200000	.311877	.312028	.312274	.312606	.313012
.3300000	.321127	.321292	.321561	.321924	.322368
.3400000	.330336	.330516	.330809	.331204	.331689
.3500000	.339503	.339698	.340017	.340447	.340973
.3600000	.348627	.348839	.349184	.349650	.350221
.3700000	.357708	.357937	.358310	.358814	.359432
.3800000	.366745	.366992	.367394	.367938	.368605
.3900000	.375737	.376003	.376436	.377022	.377741

$\alpha = -.799999$

Θ	*K* VALUES				
	.009966711	.039469502	.087332193	.151646642	.229848846
.4000000	.384685	.384970	.385435	.386064	.386838
.4100000	.393587	.393892	.394391	.395066	.395896
.4200000	.402443	.402770	.403303	.404027	.404915
.4300000	.411253	.411602	.412172	.412945	.413895
.4400000	.420017	.420389	.420997	.421821	.422836
.4500000	.428734	.429130	.429777	.430655	.431736
.4600000	.437404	.437825	.438513	.439447	.440597
.4700000	.446027	.446474	.447204	.448195	.449417
.4800000	.454603	.455076	.455850	.456901	.458198
.4900000	.463131	.463632	.464451	.465564	.466937
.5000000	.471611	.472140	.473006	.474184	.475637
.5100000	.480044	.480602	.481516	.482760	.484296
.5200000	.488428	.489017	.489981	.491293	.492914
.5300000	.496765	.497386	.498401	.499783	.501492
.5400000	.505055	.505707	.506775	.508230	.510030
.5500000	.513296	.513981	.515104	.516633	.518527
.5600000	.521490	.522209	.523387	.524993	.526983
.5700000	.529636	.530390	.531625	.533311	.535400
.5800000	.537735	.538524	.539818	.541585	.543776
.5900000	.545786	.546612	.547967	.549816	.552113
.6000000	.553790	.554653	.556070	.558005	.560409
.6100000	.561747	.562649	.564129	.566152	.568666
.6200000	.569657	.570598	.572143	.574256	.576884
.6300000	.577521	.578502	.580113	.582318	.585063
.6400000	.585338	.586360	.588040	.590339	.593202
.6500000	.593109	.594173	.595922	.598317	.601303
.6600000	.600834	.601941	.603761	.606255	.609365
.6700000	.608514	.609664	.611557	.614151	.617390
.6800000	.616148	.617344	.619310	.622007	.625376
.6899999	.623738	.624979	.627020	.629823	.633325
.7000000	.631283	.632570	.634689	.637598	.641237
.7100000	.638784	.640118	.642315	.645334	.649112
.7200000	.646241	.647623	.649900	.653030	.656951
.7300000	.653655	.655086	.657444	.660687	.664753
.7400000	.661026	.662506	.664947	.668306	.672520
.7500000	.668354	.669885	.672410	.675886	.680251
.7600000	.675640	.677223	.679833	.683429	.687947
.7700000	.682885	.684519	.687216	.690934	.695609
.7800000	.690088	.691775	.694560	.698402	.703236
.7899999	.697250	.698991	.701866	.705834	.710830

$\alpha = -$ •799999

Θ	K VALUES				
	•009966711	•039469502	•087332193	•151646642	•229848846
•8000000	•704372	•706168	•709134	•713229	•718391
•8100000	•711455	•713305	•716363	•720589	•725918
•8200000	•718497	•720404	•723556	•727913	•733413
•8300000	•725501	•727464	•730711	•735203	•740876
•8400000	•732467	•734487	•737831	•742458	•748308
•8500000	•739394	•741473	•744914	•749679	•755708
•8600000	•746284	•748422	•751962	•756867	•763078
•8700000	•753137	•755335	•758975	•764022	•770417
•8799999	•759954	•762212	•765954	•771144	•777727
•8899999	•766735	•769054	•772898	•778235	•785007
•9000000	•773481	•775861	•779810	•785294	•792259
•9100000	•780191	•782634	•786688	•792321	•799482
•9200000	•786868	•789374	•793534	•799318	•806677
•9300000	•793510	•796080	•800348	•806285	•813845
•9400000	•800120	•802754	•807130	•813223	•820985
•9500000	•806697	•809396	•813882	•820131	•828100
•9600000	•813241	•816006	•820603	•827011	•835188
•9699999	•819754	•822586	•827295	•833862	•842250
•9799999	•826236	•829134	•833957	•840686	•849288
•9899999	•832687	•835653	•840590	•847483	•856301
1•0000000	•839109	•842143	•847195	•854253	•863289
1•0100000	•845500	•848603	•853772	•860997	•870254
1•0200000	•851863	•855036	•860322	•867715	•877196
1•0300000	•858198	•861440	•866845	•874408	•884115
1•0400000	•864505	•867817	•873341	•881076	•891012
1•0500000	•870784	•874168	•879812	•887721	•897887
1•0600000	•877037	•880492	•886258	•894341	•904740
1•0699999	•883263	•886791	•892679	•900938	•911573
1•0799999	•889464	•893064	•899076	•907513	•918385
1•0899999	•895640	•899313	•905449	•914065	•925177
1•1000000	•901791	•905538	•911799	•920596	•931950
1•1100000	•907918	•911739	•918126	•927105	•938704
1•1200000	•914022	•917917	•924431	•933594	•945439
1•1300000	•920102	•924073	•930715	•940063	•952156
1•1400000	•926161	•930206	•936977	•946511	•958855
1•1500000	•932197	•936319	•943219	•952940	•965537
1•1600000	•938212	•942410	•949440	•959351	•972202
1•1700000	•944206	•948481	•955642	•965743	•978851
1•1800000	•950180	•954532	•961825	•972117	•985484
1•1899999	•956135	•960564	•967989	•978474	•992101

$\alpha = -.799999$

Θ	K VALUES				
	.009966711	.039469502	.087332193	.151646642	.229848846
.2000000	.962070	.966577	.974135	.984814	.998703
.2100000	.967986	.972571	.980264	.991138	1.005291
.2200000	.973884	.978548	.986375	.997445	1.011864
.2300000	.979765	.984508	.992470	1.003737	1.018424
.2400000	.985628	.990450	.998549	1.010014	1.024970
.2500000	.991475	.996377	1.004612	1.016276	1.031504
.2599999	.997305	1.002288	1.010660	1.022524	1.038024
.2699999	1.003121	1.008183	1.016693	1.028759	1.044533
.2799999	1.008921	1.014064	1.022712	1.034980	1.051030
.2899999	1.014706	1.019931	1.028718	1.041189	1.057516
.3000000	1.020478	1.025783	1.034710	1.047385	1.063991
.3100000	1.026236	1.031623	1.040690	1.053570	1.070456
.3200000	1.031981	1.037450	1.046657	1.059743	1.076911
.3300000	1.037714	1.043265	1.052612	1.065905	1.083355
.3400000	1.043435	1.049068	1.058557	1.072057	1.089791
.3500000	1.049144	1.054859	1.064490	1.078199	1.096218
.3600000	1.054842	1.060640	1.070414	1.084331	1.102637
.3700000	1.060530	1.066411	1.076327	1.090454	1.109047
.3799999	1.066208	1.072172	1.082231	1.096568	1.115450
.3899999	1.071876	1.077924	1.088127	1.102674	1.121845
.4000000	1.077536	1.083667	1.094013	1.108772	1.128234
.4100000	1.083187	1.089402	1.099892	1.114863	1.134616
.4200000	1.088830	1.095129	1.105764	1.120947	1.140992
.4300000	1.094466	1.100849	1.111628	1.127024	1.147363
.4400000	1.100095	1.106562	1.117486	1.133096	1.153728
.4500000	1.105717	1.112269	1.123338	1.139161	1.160088
.4600000	1.111334	1.117969	1.129184	1.145222	1.166444
.4700000	1.116945	1.123665	1.135025	1.151277	1.172795
.4800000	1.122551	1.129355	1.140862	1.157329	1.179143
.4900000	1.128152	1.135042	1.146694	1.163376	1.185487
.5000000	1.133750	1.140724	1.152523	1.169420	1.191829
.5100000	1.139344	1.146403	1.158348	1.175461	1.198167
.5200000	1.144935	1.152079	1.164171	1.181500	1.204504
.5300000	1.150523	1.157753	1.169991	1.187536	1.210838
.5400000	1.156110	1.163424	1.175809	1.193570	1.217171
.5500000	1.161695	1.169095	1.181626	1.199604	1.223503
1.5600000	1.167279	1.174764	1.187442	1.205636	1.229834
1.5699999	1.172863	1.180432	1.193257	1.211668	1.236164
1.5707963	1.173307	1.180884	1.193720	1.212148	1.236669
1.5707963	1.173307	1.180883	1.193720	1.212147	1.236668

$\alpha = -.799999$

Θ	K VALUES				
	.318821117	.415016431	.514599755	.613601043	.708073407
.0000000	.000000	.000000	.000000	.000000	.000000
.0100000	.009999	.009999	.009999	.009999	.009999
.0200000	.019998	.019998	.019998	.019998	.019998
.0300000	.029994	.029994	.029995	.029995	.029996
.0400000	.039986	.039987	.039988	.039989	.039990
.0500000	.049973	.049975	.049977	.049979	.049981
.0600000	.059954	.059957	.059961	.059964	.059968
.0700000	.069927	.069932	.069938	.069943	.069949
.0800000	.079891	.079899	.079907	.079916	.079924
.0900000	.089845	.089856	.089869	.089881	.089892
.1000000	.099787	.099803	.099820	.099836	.099852
.1100000	.109718	.109739	.109761	.109783	.109804
.1200000	.119634	.119662	.119690	.119719	.119746
.1300000	.129536	.129571	.129607	.129643	.129678
.1400000	.139422	.139465	.139511	.139556	.139599
.1500000	.149290	.149344	.149400	.149455	.149508
.1600000	.159141	.159206	.159273	.159341	.159405
.1700000	.168972	.169050	.169131	.169211	.169288
.1800000	.178782	.178875	.178971	.179067	.179158
.1900000	.188572	.188680	.188793	.188906	.189013
.2000000	.198339	.198465	.198597	.198728	.198853
.2100000	.208082	.208229	.208381	.208532	.208678
.2200000	.217802	.217970	.218144	.218319	.218486
.2300000	.227496	.227688	.227887	.228086	.228277
.2400000	.237164	.237382	.237608	.237834	.238051
.2500000	.246806	.247051	.247306	.247561	.247806
.2600000	.256419	.256695	.256981	.257268	.257544
.2700000	.266004	.266312	.266633	.266954	.267263
.2800000	.275560	.275903	.276260	.276618	.276962
.2900000	.285086	.285466	.285863	.286260	.286642
.3000000	.294582	.295002	.295440	.295880	.296302
.3100000	.304046	.304508	.304992	.305476	.305942
.3200000	.313478	.313986	.314517	.315049	.315562
.3300000	.322878	.323434	.324015	.324598	.325161
.3400000	.332245	.332852	.333486	.334124	.334738
.3500000	.341578	.342239	.342930	.343625	.344295
.3600000	.350878	.351595	.352346	.353102	.353831
.3700000	.360143	.360920	.361734	.362554	.363345
.3800000	.369373	.370213	.371094	.371981	.372838
.3900000	.378568	.379474	.380425	.381383	.382310

$\alpha = -.799999$

Θ	K VALUES				
	.318821117	.415016431	.514599755	.613601043	.708073407
.4000000	.387728	.388703	.389727	.390760	.391760
.4100000	.396852	.397899	.399000	.400112	.401188
.4200000	.405940	.407063	.408245	.409438	.410595
.4300000	.414991	.416194	.417460	.418739	.419981
.4400000	.424006	.425292	.426646	.428015	.429346
.4500000	.432984	.434356	.435802	.437266	.438689
.4600000	.441926	.443387	.444929	.446492	.448012
.4700000	.450830	.452385	.454027	.455692	.457314
.4800000	.459697	.461350	.463096	.464868	.466595
.4900000	.468528	.470281	.472135	.474019	.475856
.5000000	.477321	.479179	.481145	.483145	.485097
.5100000	.486076	.488043	.490126	.492247	.494319
.5200000	.494795	.496874	.499078	.501324	.503521
.5300000	.503477	.505672	.508001	.510378	.512705
.5400000	.512121	.514437	.516896	.519408	.521869
.5500000	.520728	.523168	.525762	.528414	.531016
.5600000	.529299	.531867	.534601	.537398	.540145
.5700000	.537833	.540534	.543411	.546358	.549257
.5800000	.546330	.549168	.552193	.555296	.558351
.5900000	.554791	.557769	.560949	.564213	.567430
.6000000	.563215	.566339	.569677	.573108	.576493
.6100000	.571604	.574877	.578378	.581981	.585541
.6200000	.579957	.583383	.587053	.590834	.594574
.6300000	.588274	.591858	.595702	.599666	.603593
.6400000	.596555	.600303	.604325	.608479	.612598
.6500000	.604802	.608716	.612923	.617272	.621591
.6600000	.613014	.617100	.621495	.626046	.630571
.6700000	.621192	.625453	.630044	.634802	.639540
.6800000	.629335	.633777	.638568	.643540	.648498
.6899999	.637445	.642072	.647068	.652261	.657446
.7000000	.645521	.650338	.655545	.660965	.666385
.7100000	.653564	.658576	.664000	.669653	.675315
.7200000	.661574	.666785	.672432	.678325	.684236
.7300000	.669552	.674967	.680842	.686982	.693151
.7400000	.677498	.683121	.689230	.695625	.702059
.7500000	.685413	.691249	.697598	.704254	.710961
.7600000	.693296	.699350	.705946	.712870	.719859
.7700000	.701148	.707426	.714273	.721473	.728752
.7800000	.708970	.715475	.722581	.730064	.737642
.7899999	.716762	.723500	.730870	.738643	.746529

$\alpha = -.799999$

Θ	K VALUES				
	.318821117	.415016431	.514599755	.613601043	.708073407
.8000000	.724524	.731500	.739141	.747212	.755415
.8100000	.732258	.739476	.747394	.755771	.764300
.8200000	.739962	.747428	.755629	.764320	.773185
.8300000	.747639	.755357	.763847	.772860	.782070
.8400000	.755287	.763263	.772050	.781393	.790957
.8500000	.762908	.771147	.780236	.789917	.799847
.8600000	.770503	.779009	.788407	.798435	.808741
.8700000	.778071	.786849	.796563	.806946	.817638
.8799999	.785612	.794669	.804705	.815452	.826541
.8899999	.793129	.802468	.812834	.823953	.835449
.9000000	.800620	.810247	.820949	.832450	.844365
.9100000	.808086	.818007	.829051	.840942	.853288
.9200000	.815529	.825747	.837142	.849432	.862220
.9300000	.822947	.833469	.845220	.857920	.871162
.9400000	.830343	.841173	.853288	.866405	.880114
.9500000	.837715	.848859	.861345	.874890	.889077
.9600000	.845065	.856528	.869392	.883373	.898052
.9699999	.852393	.864180	.877429	.891857	.907041
.9799999	.859700	.871815	.885457	.900342	.916043
.9899999	.866986	.879435	.893476	.908828	.925060
1.0000000	.874251	.887040	.901487	.917316	.934092
1.0100000	.881496	.894629	.909491	.925806	.943141
1.0200000	.888721	.902204	.917487	.934300	.952207
1.0300000	.895928	.909765	.925476	.942797	.961291
1.0400000	.903115	.917312	.933459	.951298	.970394
1.0500000	.910284	.924846	.941436	.959803	.979516
1.0600000	.917435	.932367	.949408	.968314	.988659
1.0699999	.924569	.939876	.957375	.976831	.997823
1.0799999	.931686	.947372	.965337	.985353	1.007009
1.0899999	.938786	.954857	.973294	.993883	1.016217
1.1000000	.945870	.962331	.981248	1.002419	1.025449
1.1100000	.952938	.969794	.989199	1.010963	1.034704
1.1200000	.959990	.977246	.997146	1.019515	1.043984
1.1300000	.967028	.984689	1.005090	1.028076	1.053289
1.1400000	.974051	.992121	1.013032	1.036645	1.062620
1.1500000	.981060	.999545	1.020973	1.045223	1.071977
1.1600000	.988056	1.006959	1.028911	1.053811	1.081361
1.1700000	.995038	1.014364	1.036848	1.062408	1.090772
1.1800000	1.002007	1.021761	1.044783	1.071015	1.100211
1.1899999	1.008963	1.029151	1.052718	1.079633	1.109678

$\alpha = -.799999$

Θ	K VALUES				
	.318821117	.415016431	.514599755	.613601043	.708073407
.2000000	1.015908	1.036532	1.060652	1.088262	1.119173
.2100000	1.022840	1.043907	1.068586	1.096901	1.128697
.2200000	1.029762	1.051274	1.076520	1.105551	1.138251
.2300000	1.036672	1.058634	1.084454	1.114212	1.147833
.2400000	1.043571	1.065988	1.092388	1.122885	1.157445
.2500000	1.050460	1.073336	1.100323	1.131569	1.167086
.2599999	1.057339	1.080678	1.108258	1.140264	1.176757
.2699999	1.064209	1.088014	1.116194	1.148971	1.186458
.2799999	1.071069	1.095345	1.124131	1.157690	1.196188
.2899999	1.077921	1.102671	1.132070	1.166420	1.205947
1.3000000	1.084764	1.109992	1.140009	1.175161	1.215736
1.3100000	1.091599	1.117309	1.147950	1.183914	1.225554
1.3200000	1.098426	1.124621	1.155893	1.192679	1.235401
1.3300000	1.105245	1.131929	1.163837	1.201454	1.245276
1.3400000	1.112057	1.139233	1.171782	1.210241	1.255178
1.3500000	1.118862	1.146534	1.179730	1.219039	1.265109
1.3600000	1.125661	1.153831	1.187679	1.227847	1.275066
1.3700000	1.132454	1.161125	1.195629	1.236666	1.285049
1.3799999	1.139240	1.168415	1.203582	1.245494	1.295058
1.3899999	1.146021	1.175703	1.211536	1.254333	1.305092
1.4000000	1.152797	1.182988	1.219492	1.263181	1.315149
1.4100000	1.159568	1.190271	1.227450	1.272039	1.325230
1.4200000	1.166334	1.197551	1.235409	1.280905	1.335332
1.4300000	1.173096	1.204830	1.243370	1.289779	1.345456
1.4400000	1.179853	1.212106	1.251332	1.298662	1.355600
1.4500000	1.186607	1.219380	1.259296	1.307551	1.365762
1.4600000	1.193357	1.226653	1.267262	1.316448	1.375943
1.4700000	1.200105	1.233924	1.275229	1.325352	1.386139
1.4800000	1.206849	1.241194	1.283197	1.334261	1.396351
1.4900000	1.213591	1.248462	1.291166	1.343176	1.406576
1.5000000	1.220330	1.255730	1.299136	1.352096	1.416813
1.5100000	1.227068	1.262996	1.307107	1.361020	1.427062
1.5200000	1.233803	1.270262	1.315079	1.369947	1.437320
1.5300000	1.240538	1.277527	1.323052	1.378878	1.447586
1.5400000	1.247271	1.284791	1.331025	1.387811	1.457858
1.5500000	1.254003	1.292055	1.338998	1.396747	1.468135
1.5600000	1.260735	1.299319	1.346972	1.405683	1.478415
1.5699999	1.267466	1.306583	1.354946	1.414620	1.488697
1.5707963	1.268002	1.307161	1.355581	1.415332	1.489516
1.5707963	1.268001	1.307161	1.355581	1.415332	1.489515

$\alpha = -.799999$

Θ	K VALUES				
	.794250555	.868696860	.928444378	.971111163	.994996249
.0000000	.000000	.000000	.000000	.000000	.000000
.0100000	.009999	.009999	.009999	.009999	.009999
.0200000	.019998	.019999	.019999	.019999	.019999
.0300000	.029996	.029996	.029996	.029997	.029997
.0400000	.039991	.039992	.039992	.039993	.039993
.0500000	.049983	.049984	.049986	.049986	.049987
.0600000	.059971	.059973	.059975	.059977	.059978
.0700000	.069954	.069958	.069961	.069964	.069965
.0800000	.079931	.079938	.079943	.079946	.079948
.0900000	.089902	.089912	.089919	.089924	.089927
.1000000	.099867	.099879	.099889	.099896	.099900
.1100000	.109823	.109840	.109853	.109862	.109868
.1200000	.119771	.119792	.119810	.119822	.119829
.1300000	.129710	.129737	.129759	.129774	.129783
.1400000	.139638	.139672	.139700	.139719	.139730
.1500000	.149557	.149599	.149632	.149656	.149670
.1600000	.159464	.159515	.159556	.159585	.159601
.1700000	.169359	.169420	.169469	.169504	.169524
.1800000	.179242	.179315	.179373	.179415	.179438
.1900000	.189112	.189197	.189266	.189315	.189343
.2000000	.198968	.199068	.199148	.199205	.199237
.2100000	.208811	.208926	.209019	.209085	.209123
.2200000	.218639	.218771	.218878	.218955	.218997
.2300000	.228452	.228603	.228725	.228813	.228862
.2400000	.238249	.238422	.238560	.238660	.238716
.2500000	.248031	.248226	.248383	.248495	.248558
.2600000	.257797	.258016	.258193	.258319	.258390
.2700000	.267546	.267791	.267990	.268132	.268211
.2800000	.277278	.277552	.277773	.277932	.278021
.2900000	.286993	.287298	.287544	.287720	.287819
.3000000	.296691	.297029	.297301	.297497	.297607
.3100000	.306371	.306744	.307045	.307261	.307383
.3200000	.316033	.316444	.316776	.317014	.317147
.3300000	.325678	.326129	.326493	.326754	.326901
.3400000	.335305	.335798	.336197	.336483	.336644
.3500000	.344913	.345452	.345888	.346201	.346376
.3600000	.354504	.355090	.355565	.355906	.356098
.3700000	.364076	.364713	.365230	.365601	.365810
.3800000	.373630	.374321	.374882	.375284	.375511
.3900000	.383166	.383914	.384521	.384957	.385203

$\alpha = -.799999$

Θ	*K* VALUES				
	.794250555	.868696860	.928444378	.971111163	.994996249
.4000000	.392684	.393492	.394148	.394620	.394885
.4100000	.402184	.403056	.403763	.404272	.404559
.4200000	.411667	.412605	.413367	.413915	.414224
.4300000	.421132	.422140	.422959	.423549	.423882
.4400000	.430579	.431661	.432541	.433175	.433532
.4500000	.440010	.441169	.442112	.442792	.443175
.4600000	.449424	.450664	.451673	.452402	.452812
.4700000	.458821	.460146	.461225	.462004	.462444
.4800000	.468202	.469616	.470768	.471601	.472070
.4900000	.477568	.479074	.480303	.481192	.481693
.5000000	.486918	.488522	.489831	.490778	.491312
.5100000	.496253	.497958	.499351	.500360	.500929
.5200000	.505574	.507385	.508866	.509938	.510544
.5300000	.514880	.516802	.518375	.519515	.520159
.5400000	.524173	.526211	.527879	.529089	.529774
.5500000	.533454	.535612	.537380	.538663	.539390
.5600000	.542722	.545005	.546878	.548238	.549008
.5700000	.551978	.554392	.556374	.557814	.558630
.5800000	.561223	.563773	.565868	.567392	.568256
.5900000	.570458	.573149	.575363	.576974	.577888
.6000000	.579683	.582521	.584858	.586561	.587526
.6100000	.588898	.591890	.594356	.596153	.597173
.6200000	.598106	.601257	.603856	.605753	.606830
.6300000	.607306	.610622	.613361	.615361	.616497
.6400000	.616499	.619987	.622871	.624979	.626177
.6500000	.625686	.629352	.632387	.634608	.635871
.6600000	.634868	.638719	.641911	.644249	.645580
.6700000	.644045	.648089	.651445	.653904	.655306
.6800000	.653219	.657463	.660988	.663575	.665050
.6899999	.662391	.666842	.670544	.673263	.674815
.7000000	.671561	.676226	.680112	.682970	.684601
.7100000	.680730	.685618	.689696	.692697	.694412
.7200000	.689899	.695019	.699295	.702446	.704248
.7300000	.699069	.704429	.708912	.712219	.714112
.7400000	.708242	.713850	.718548	.722018	.724006
.7500000	.717418	.723284	.728205	.731845	.733931
.7600000	.726598	.732731	.737884	.741701	.743890
.7700000	.735783	.742193	.747588	.751588	.753886
.7800000	.744975	.751672	.757317	.761510	.763920
.7899999	.754174	.761169	.767075	.771467	.773994

$\alpha = -.799999$

Θ	K VALUES				
	.794250555	.868696860	.928444378	.971111163	.994996249
.8000000	.763382	.770685	.776862	.781463	.784113
.8100000	.772599	.780221	.786680	.791499	.794277
.8200000	.781827	.789780	.796532	.801577	.804489
.8300000	.791067	.799363	.806420	.811701	.814753
.8400000	.800320	.808972	.816346	.821873	.825071
.8500000	.809588	.818608	.826311	.832096	.835446
.8600000	.818871	.828272	.836318	.842371	.845882
.8700000	.828171	.837967	.846369	.852703	.856381
.8799999	.837488	.847694	.856468	.863093	.866946
.8899999	.846825	.857456	.866615	.873546	.877582
.9000000	.856183	.867253	.876813	.884063	.888292
.9100000	.865562	.877087	.887066	.894649	.899079
.9200000	.874964	.886962	.897375	.905307	.909948
.9300000	.884390	.896877	.907743	.916039	.920902
.9400000	.893842	.906836	.918174	.926851	.931946
.9500000	.903321	.916840	.928669	.937745	.943084
.9600000	.912828	.926892	.939232	.948725	.954321
.9699999	.922365	.936992	.949866	.959796	.965662
.9799999	.931932	.947144	.960574	.970962	.977111
.9899999	.941531	.957350	.971359	.982227	.988674
1.0000000	.951165	.967611	.982225	.993596	1.000357
1.0100000	.960832	.977931	.993174	1.005072	1.012164
1.0200000	.970536	.988310	1.004210	1.016663	1.024104
1.0300000	.980278	.998751	1.015337	1.028371	1.036181
1.0400000	.990058	1.009257	1.026559	1.040204	1.048402
1.0500000	.999878	1.019829	1.037879	1.052166	1.060776
1.0600000	1.009740	1.030471	1.049301	1.064264	1.073308
1.0699999	1.019645	1.041184	1.060829	1.076503	1.086007
1.0799999	1.029593	1.051971	1.072467	1.088890	1.098882
1.0899999	1.039587	1.062834	1.084220	1.101431	1.111941
1.1000000	1.049627	1.073776	1.096092	1.114135	1.125193
1.1100000	1.059715	1.084798	1.108088	1.127007	1.138649
1.1200000	1.069852	1.095904	1.120211	1.140056	1.152318
1.1300000	1.080039	1.107096	1.132467	1.153289	1.166212
1.1400000	1.090277	1.118376	1.144860	1.166716	1.180343
1.1500000	1.100567	1.129746	1.157396	1.180344	1.194724
1.1600000	1.110911	1.141210	1.170080	1.194184	1.209367
1.1700000	1.121310	1.152769	1.182916	1.208245	1.224288
1.1800000	1.131763	1.164425	1.195911	1.222537	1.239501
1.1899999	1.142273	1.176182	1.209069	1.237072	1.255023

$\alpha = -\ .799999$

Θ	K VALUES				
	.794250555	.868696860	.928444378	.971111163	.994996249
.2000000	1.152840	1.188041	1.222396	1.251860	1.270872
.2100000	1.163465	1.200004	1.235898	1.266913	1.287068
.2200000	1.174149	1.212074	1.249580	1.282244	1.303629
.2300000	1.184891	1.224252	1.263448	1.297866	1.320579
.2400000	1.195694	1.236541	1.277508	1.313793	1.337942
.2500000	1.206556	1.248942	1.291766	1.330039	1.355742
.2599999	1.217480	1.261458	1.306227	1.346620	1.374010
.2699999	1.228464	1.274089	1.320897	1.363551	1.392774
.2799999	1.239509	1.286837	1.335783	1.380849	1.412069
.2899999	1.250616	1.299703	1.350889	1.398533	1.431931
.3000000	1.261783	1.312689	1.366221	1.416619	1.452400
.3100000	1.273011	1.325795	1.381784	1.435128	1.473520
.3200000	1.284300	1.339021	1.397584	1.454079	1.495338
1.3300000	1.295648	1.352368	1.413624	1.473492	1.517909
1.3400000	1.307056	1.365837	1.429910	1.493390	1.541292
1.3500000	1.318523	1.379426	1.446445	1.513793	1.565551
1.3600000	1.330047	1.393134	1.463233	1.534725	1.590759
1.3700000	1.341628	1.406962	1.480275	1.556207	1.616999
1.3799999	1.353264	1.420908	1.497574	1.578262	1.644360
1.3899999	1.364954	1.434969	1.515131	1.600913	1.672945
1.4000000	1.376697	1.449143	1.532945	1.624182	1.702869
1.4100000	1.388490	1.463429	1.551016	1.648088	1.734261
1.4200000	1.400332	1.477822	1.569341	1.672651	1.767267
1.4300000	1.412221	1.492320	1.587916	1.697888	1.802052
1.4400000	1.424154	1.506918	1.606736	1.723811	1.838803
1.4500000	1.436130	1.521611	1.625795	1.750430	1.877730
1.4600000	1.448145	1.536395	1.645083	1.777748	1.919070
1.4700000	1.460197	1.551264	1.664591	1.805763	1.963085
1.4800000	1.472283	1.566212	1.684306	1.834464	2.010064
1.4900000	1.484400	1.581233	1.704215	1.863830	2.060313
1.5000000	1.496546	1.596320	1.724302	1.893834	2.114148
1.5100000	1.508716	1.611466	1.744550	1.924433	2.171862
1.5200000	1.520907	1.626663	1.764939	1.955574	2.233687
1.5300000	1.533117	1.641904	1.785449	1.987192	2.299727
1.5400000	1.545342	1.657179	1.806058	2.019211	2.369864
1.5500000	1.557577	1.672481	1.826742	2.051543	2.443658
1.5600000	1.569820	1.687802	1.847479	2.084092	2.520274
1.5699999	1.582067	1.703132	1.868242	2.116756	2.598490
1.5707963	1.583043	1.704352	1.869896	2.119359	2.604744
1.5707963	1.583042	1.704352	1.869895	2.119358	2.604743

$\alpha = -$ .750000

θ	K VALUES				
	.009966711	.039469502	.087332193	.151646642	.229848846
.0000000	.000000	.000000	.000000	.000000	.000000
.0100000	.009999	.009999	.009999	.009999	.009999
.0200000	.019998	.019998	.019998	.019998	.019998
.0300000	.029993	.029993	.029993	.029993	.029994
.0400000	.039984	.039984	.039984	.039985	.039986
.0500000	.049969	.049969	.049970	.049971	.049973
.0600000	.059946	.059947	.059949	.059951	.059954
.0700000	.069915	.069916	.069919	.069923	.069927
.0800000	.079873	.079875	.079879	.079885	.079892
.0900000	.089819	.089823	.089829	.089837	.089846
.1000000	.099753	.099758	.099766	.099776	.099789
.1100000	.109672	.109678	.109689	.109703	.109720
.1200000	.119574	.119583	.119596	.119615	.119637
.1300000	.129460	.129471	.129488	.129511	.129540
.1400000	.139327	.139340	.139362	.139391	.139426
.1500000	.149173	.149190	.149216	.149252	.149296
.1600000	.158999	.159019	.159051	.159094	.159147
.1700000	.168802	.168826	.168864	.168916	.168979
.1800000	.178581	.178609	.178655	.178716	.178791
.1900000	.188335	.188368	.188422	.188494	.188582
.2000000	.198063	.198101	.198164	.198248	.198350
.2100000	.207764	.207808	.207880	.207977	.208095
.2200000	.217436	.217486	.217569	.217680	.217816
.2300000	.227078	.227136	.227230	.227357	.227512
.2400000	.236690	.236755	.236862	.237006	.237181
.2500000	.246270	.246344	.246464	.246626	.246824
.2600000	.255818	.255900	.256035	.256217	.256439
.2700000	.265331	.265424	.265575	.265778	.266026
.2800000	.274811	.274914	.275081	.275307	.275583
.2900000	.284255	.284369	.284554	.284804	.285110
.3000000	.293663	.293788	.293993	.294269	.294607
.3100000	.303033	.303171	.303396	.303700	.304072
.3200000	.312366	.312518	.312764	.313097	.313505
.3300000	.321660	.321826	.322095	.322460	.322905
.3400000	.330916	.331096	.331390	.331786	.332272
.3500000	.340131	.340327	.340646	.341077	.341606
.3600000	.349305	.349518	.349864	.350332	.350905
.3700000	.358439	.358669	.359043	.359549	.360169
.3800000	.367531	.367778	.368182	.368728	.369399
.3900000	.376581	.376847	.377282	.377870	.378592

$\alpha = -.750000$

Θ	K VALUES				
	.009966711	.039469502	.087332193	.151646642	.229848846
.4000000	.385588	.385874	.386341	.386973	.387750
.4100000	.394552	.394858	.395359	.396038	.396871
.4200000	.403472	.403800	.404336	.405063	.405956
.4300000	.412349	.412699	.413272	.414048	.415003
.4400000	.421181	.421555	.422166	.422994	.424014
.4500000	.429969	.430367	.431018	.431900	.432987
.4600000	.438712	.439136	.439827	.440766	.441922
.4700000	.447411	.447860	.448594	.449591	.450820
.4800000	.456064	.456540	.457318	.458375	.459679
.4900000	.464671	.465175	.465999	.467119	.468501
.5000000	.473233	.473766	.474637	.475822	.477284
.5100000	.481750	.482312	.483232	.484484	.486029
.5200000	.490221	.490814	.491784	.493104	.494736
.5300000	.498646	.499270	.500292	.501684	.503405
.5400000	.507025	.507682	.508758	.510222	.512035
.5500000	.515359	.516049	.517179	.518720	.520627
.5600000	.523647	.524371	.525558	.527176	.529181
.5700000	.531889	.532649	.533894	.535592	.537697
.5800000	.540086	.540881	.542186	.543966	.546175
.5900000	.548237	.549070	.550435	.552300	.554614
.6000000	.556343	.557213	.558642	.560593	.563017
.6100000	.564403	.565313	.566805	.568845	.571381
.6200000	.572419	.573368	.574926	.577058	.579708
.6300000	.580389	.581379	.583005	.585230	.587998
.6400000	.588315	.589347	.591042	.593362	.596251
.6500000	.596197	.597271	.599036	.601454	.604467
.6600000	.604034	.605152	.606989	.609506	.612646
.6700000	.611828	.612990	.614900	.617520	.620790
.6800000	.619578	.620785	.622770	.625494	.628897
.6899999	.627284	.628537	.630600	.633430	.636968
.7000000	.634948	.636248	.638388	.641327	.645004
.7100000	.642568	.643916	.646136	.649187	.653005
.7200000	.650147	.651543	.653845	.657008	.660971
.7300000	.657683	.659129	.661513	.664792	.668902
.7400000	.665178	.666675	.669142	.672539	.676799
.7500000	.672632	.674180	.676733	.680249	.684663
.7600000	.680044	.681644	.684284	.687922	.692493
.7700000	.687416	.689069	.691798	.695560	.700289
.7800000	.694749	.696455	.699274	.703162	.708053
.7899999	.702041	.703803	.706712	.710728	.715785

$\alpha = -\ .750000$

θ	K VALUES				
	.009966711	.039469502	.087332193	.151646642	.229848846
.8000000	.709294	.711111	.714114	.718260	.723485
.8100000	.716509	.718382	.721479	.725757	.731153
.8200000	.723685	.725615	.728807	.733220	.738791
.8300000	.730823	.732812	.736100	.740650	.746397
.8400000	.737924	.739971	.743358	.748046	.753973
.8500000	.744988	.747094	.750581	.755410	.761519
.8600000	.752016	.754182	.757770	.762741	.769036
.8700000	.759008	.761235	.764924	.770040	.776523
.8799999	.765964	.768252	.772046	.777308	.783982
.8899999	.772885	.775236	.779134	.784545	.791413
.9000000	.779771	.782185	.786189	.791751	.798816
.9100000	.786624	.789101	.793213	.798928	.806192
.9200000	.793443	.795985	.800205	.806074	.813541
.9300000	.800229	.802836	.807166	.813191	.820863
.9400000	.806982	.809655	.814097	.820280	.828159
.9500000	.813703	.816443	.820997	.827340	.835430
.9600000	.820393	.823200	.827867	.834373	.842676
.9699999	.827052	.829927	.834709	.841378	.849896
.9799999	.833681	.836624	.841522	.848356	.857093
.9899999	.840279	.843292	.848306	.855308	.864266
1.0000000	.846849	.849931	.855063	.862234	.871416
1.0100000	.853389	.856541	.861793	.869134	.878543
1.0200000	.859901	.863124	.868496	.876010	.885647
1.0300000	.866385	.869680	.875173	.882861	.892729
1.0400000	.872841	.876209	.881824	.889688	.899790
1.0500000	.879271	.882711	.888450	.896491	.906829
1.0600000	.885675	.889188	.895051	.903271	.913848
1.0699999	.892053	.895640	.901628	.910029	.920847
1.0799999	.898405	.902067	.908182	.916765	.927826
1.0899999	.904733	.908470	.914712	.923479	.934786
1.1000000	.911037	.914849	.921219	.930171	.941727
1.1100000	.917317	.921205	.927705	.936843	.948649
1.1200000	.923574	.927538	.934168	.943495	.955553
1.1300000	.929809	.933849	.940610	.950127	.962440
1.1400000	.936021	.940139	.947032	.956739	.969309
1.1500000	.942212	.946408	.953433	.963333	.976162
1.1600000	.948381	.952656	.959815	.969908	.982999
1.1700000	.954530	.958883	.966177	.976466	.989819
1.1800000	.960660	.965092	.972520	.983005	.996624
1.1899999	.966769	.971281	.978846	.989528	1.003414

$\alpha = -.750000$

θ	K VALUES				
	.009966711	.039469502	.087332193	.151646642	.229848846
1.2000000	.972860	.977452	.985153	.996035	1.010190
1.2100000	.978932	.983604	.991443	1.002525	1.016951
1.2200000	.984987	.989739	.997716	1.008999	1.023699
1.2300000	.991024	.995857	1.003973	1.015459	1.030433
1.2400000	.997044	1.001959	1.010214	1.021903	1.037154
1.2500000	1.003047	1.008044	1.016440	1.028333	1.043863
1.2599999	1.009035	1.014114	1.022651	1.034750	1.050559
1.2699999	1.015007	1.020169	1.028847	1.041153	1.057244
1.2799999	1.020965	1.026210	1.035030	1.047543	1.063917
1.2899999	1.026908	1.032236	1.041199	1.053921	1.070580
1.3000000	1.032837	1.038249	1.047355	1.060287	1.077232
1.3100000	1.038753	1.044248	1.053498	1.066641	1.083873
1.3200000	1.044656	1.050236	1.059629	1.072984	1.090505
1.3300000	1.050547	1.056211	1.065749	1.079316	1.097128
1.3400000	1.056426	1.062174	1.071858	1.085638	1.103742
1.3500000	1.062294	1.068127	1.077956	1.091950	1.110347
1.3600000	1.068150	1.074068	1.084044	1.098252	1.116944
1.3700000	1.073997	1.080000	1.090123	1.104546	1.123533
1.3799999	1.079833	1.085922	1.096192	1.110831	1.130115
1.3899999	1.085661	1.091835	1.102252	1.117108	1.136689
1.4000000	1.091479	1.097739	1.108304	1.123377	1.143257
1.4100000	1.097289	1.103635	1.114348	1.129639	1.149819
1.4200000	1.103091	1.109524	1.120385	1.135895	1.156375
1.4300000	1.108886	1.115405	1.126415	1.142144	1.162925
1.4400000	1.114674	1.121279	1.132439	1.148386	1.169470
1.4500000	1.120455	1.127148	1.138456	1.154624	1.176011
1.4600000	1.126231	1.133010	1.144468	1.160856	1.182546
1.4700000	1.132001	1.138867	1.150475	1.167084	1.189078
1.4800000	1.137767	1.144720	1.156478	1.173307	1.195606
1.4900000	1.143528	1.150568	1.162476	1.179527	1.202131
1.5000000	1.149285	1.156412	1.168470	1.185743	1.208653
1.5100000	1.155038	1.162253	1.174462	1.191956	1.215172
1.5200000	1.160789	1.168091	1.180450	1.198167	1.221689
1.5300000	1.166537	1.173926	1.186437	1.204375	1.228205
1.5400000	1.172283	1.179760	1.192421	1.210582	1.234718
1.5500000	1.178027	1.185592	1.198404	1.216787	1.241231
1.5600000	1.183771	1.191423	1.204386	1.222992	1.247743
1.5699999	1.189514	1.197254	1.210367	1.229196	1.254254
1.5707963	1.189971	1.197718	1.210844	1.229690	1.254773
1.5707963	1.189971	1.197717	1.210843	1.229690	1.254772

$\alpha = -$ .750000

Θ	K VALUES				
	.318821117	.415016431	.514599755	.613601043	.708073407
.0000000	.000000	.000000	.000000	.000000	.000000
.0100000	.009999	.009999	.009999	.009999	.009999
.0200000	.019998	.019998	.019998	.019998	.019998
.0300000	.029994	.029995	.029995	.029996	.029996
.0400000	.039987	.039988	.039989	.039990	.039991
.0500000	.049975	.049977	.049979	.049981	.049983
.0600000	.059957	.059961	.059964	.059968	.059971
.0700000	.069932	.069938	.069943	.069949	.069954
.0800000	.079899	.079907	.079916	.079924	.079932
.0900000	.089857	.089868	.089881	.089893	.089904
.1000000	.099804	.099820	.099837	.099853	.099869
.1100000	.109740	.109761	.109783	.109805	.109826
.1200000	.119663	.119690	.119719	.119747	.119774
.1300000	.129572	.129607	.129643	.129680	.129714
.1400000	.139467	.139510	.139556	.139601	.139644
.1500000	.149345	.149399	.149455	.149510	.149563
.1600000	.159207	.159272	.159340	.159407	.159472
.1700000	.169051	.169129	.169210	.169291	.169368
.1800000	.178876	.178969	.179065	.179161	.179253
.1900000	.188682	.188791	.188904	.189016	.189124
.2000000	.198467	.198593	.198725	.198856	.198982
.2100000	.208230	.208376	.208529	.208681	.208826
.2200000	.217971	.218139	.218314	.218488	.218656
.2300000	.227688	.227880	.228080	.228279	.228470
.2400000	.237382	.237599	.237826	.238052	.238269
.2500000	.247050	.247296	.247552	.247807	.248053
.2600000	.256693	.256969	.257256	.257544	.257820
.2700000	.266309	.266618	.266940	.267261	.267570
.2800000	.275899	.276242	.276601	.276959	.277304
.2900000	.285460	.285841	.286239	.286637	.287020
.3000000	.294993	.295415	.295854	.296295	.296718
.3100000	.304497	.304961	.305446	.305932	.306399
.3200000	.313972	.314481	.315014	.315547	.316062
.3300000	.323416	.323974	.324557	.325142	.325706
.3400000	.332830	.333439	.334075	.334715	.335332
.3500000	.342213	.342875	.343569	.344266	.344939
.3600000	.351564	.352283	.353037	.353795	.354527
.3700000	.360883	.361663	.362480	.363302	.364097
.3800000	.370169	.371012	.371896	.372787	.373648
.3900000	.379423	.380333	.381287	.382249	.383180

$\alpha = -.750000$

θ	K VALUES				
	.318821117	.415016431	.514599755	.613601043	.708073407
.4000000	.388644	.389623	.390651	.391688	.392692
.4100000	.397831	.398883	.399989	.401105	.402187
.4200000	.406985	.408113	.409300	.410499	.411662
.4300000	.416104	.417313	.418585	.419871	.421118
.4400000	.425190	.426482	.427843	.429219	.430556
.4500000	.434241	.435620	.437074	.438545	.439976
.4600000	.443258	.444728	.446278	.447849	.449377
.4700000	.452240	.453804	.455455	.457130	.458760
.4800000	.461188	.462850	.464606	.466388	.468126
.4900000	.470100	.471864	.473729	.475625	.477473
.5000000	.478978	.480848	.482826	.484839	.486804
.5100000	.487821	.489800	.491897	.494031	.496117
.5200000	.496629	.498722	.500941	.503202	.505414
.5300000	.505403	.507613	.509958	.512351	.514694
.5400000	.514141	.516473	.518950	.521479	.523959
.5500000	.522845	.525302	.527915	.530587	.533208
.5600000	.531514	.534101	.536855	.539673	.542441
.5700000	.540148	.542870	.545769	.548740	.551661
.5800000	.548748	.551608	.554658	.557786	.560865
.5900000	.557314	.560317	.563522	.566813	.570057
.6000000	.565846	.568995	.572361	.575821	.579235
.6100000	.574344	.577644	.581176	.584810	.588400
.6200000	.582807	.586264	.589966	.593780	.597554
.6300000	.591238	.594855	.598733	.602733	.606695
.6400000	.599635	.603417	.607476	.611668	.615826
.6500000	.607999	.611950	.616196	.620586	.624947
.6600000	.616330	.620455	.624893	.629488	.634058
.6700000	.624629	.628932	.633568	.638374	.643159
.6800000	.632895	.637382	.642221	.647244	.652253
.6899999	.641130	.645804	.650852	.656099	.661338
.7000000	.649332	.654200	.659462	.664939	.670417
.7100000	.657504	.662569	.668051	.673766	.679490
.7200000	.665644	.670912	.676620	.682579	.688556
.7300000	.673754	.679229	.685170	.691380	.697618
.7400000	.681834	.687520	.693699	.700168	.706676
.7500000	.689883	.695787	.702210	.708944	.715731
.7600000	.697903	.704029	.710702	.717709	.724782
.7700000	.705894	.712247	.719177	.726464	.733833
.7800000	.713856	.720441	.727633	.735209	.742882
.7899999	.721790	.728611	.736073	.743944	.751930

$\alpha = -\ .750000$

Θ	K VALUES				
	.318821117	.415016431	.514599755	.613601043	.708073407
.8000000	.729695	.736759	.744496	.752671	.760980
.8100000	.737573	.744884	.752903	.761390	.770031
.8200000	.745424	.752987	.761295	.770101	.779084
.8300000	.753248	.761068	.769671	.778805	.788140
.8400000	.761045	.769128	.778033	.787504	.797201
.8500000	.768816	.777167	.786381	.796196	.806266
.8600000	.776562	.785186	.794715	.804884	.815336
.8700000	.784283	.793184	.803036	.813567	.824414
.8799999	.791979	.801164	.811344	.822247	.833498
.8899999	.799650	.809124	.819640	.830923	.842591
.9000000	.807298	.817066	.827925	.839597	.851693
.9100000	.814922	.824989	.836199	.848270	.860805
.9200000	.822523	.832895	.844462	.856941	.869927
.9300000	.830102	.840783	.852715	.865611	.879062
.9400000	.837658	.848655	.860958	.874282	.888209
.9500000	.845193	.856510	.869192	.882953	.897369
.9600000	.852707	.864349	.877418	.891625	.906544
.9699999	.860199	.872173	.885635	.900299	.915734
.9799999	.867671	.879981	.893845	.908976	.924939
.9899999	.875123	.887775	.902047	.917656	.934162
1.0000000	.882556	.895555	.910243	.926339	.943403
1.0100000	.889969	.903321	.918432	.935026	.952661
1.0200000	.897364	.911073	.926615	.943719	.961940
1.0300000	.904740	.918812	.934793	.952416	.971238
1.0400000	.912098	.926539	.942966	.961119	.980557
1.0500000	.919439	.934253	.951134	.969829	.989898
1.0600000	.926763	.941956	.959299	.978545	.999262
1.0699999	.934070	.949647	.967459	.987268	1.008649
1.0799999	.941361	.957327	.975616	.996000	1.018059
1.0899999	.948636	.964996	.983769	1.004739	1.027494
1.1000000	.955895	.972656	.991921	1.013488	1.036955
1.1100000	.963140	.980305	1.000070	1.022245	1.046442
1.1200000	.970370	.987944	1.008217	1.031012	1.055955
1.1300000	.977585	.995575	1.016362	1.039789	1.065495
1.1400000	.984787	1.003196	1.024506	1.048576	1.075063
1.1500000	.991975	1.010809	1.032649	1.057373	1.084659
1.1600000	.999151	1.018414	1.040791	1.066181	1.094285
1.1700000	1.006313	1.026011	1.048933	1.075001	1.103939
1.1800000	1.013463	1.033600	1.057075	1.083832	1.113623
1.1899999	1.020601	1.041183	1.065217	1.092675	1.123337

$\alpha = -.750000$

θ	K VALUES				
	.318821117	.415016431	.514599755	.613601043	.708073407
1.2000000	1.027728	1.048758	1.073360	1.101530	1.133082
1.2100000	1.034843	1.056327	1.081502	1.110397	1.142857
1.2200000	1.041948	1.063889	1.089646	1.119276	1.152663
1.2300000	1.049042	1.071445	1.097791	1.128168	1.162500
1.2400000	1.056125	1.078995	1.105937	1.137072	1.172369
1.2500000	1.063199	1.086540	1.114085	1.145989	1.182269
1.2599999	1.070264	1.094080	1.122234	1.154918	1.192200
1.2699999	1.077319	1.101615	1.130384	1.163861	1.202163
1.2799999	1.084366	1.109145	1.138537	1.172816	1.212157
1.2899999	1.091404	1.116670	1.146691	1.181783	1.222183
1.3000000	1.098434	1.124191	1.154848	1.190764	1.232239
1.3100000	1.105456	1.131708	1.163007	1.199757	1.242326
1.3200000	1.112470	1.139221	1.171167	1.208762	1.252443
1.3300000	1.119478	1.146731	1.179331	1.217780	1.262590
1.3400000	1.126478	1.154237	1.187496	1.226810	1.272767
1.3500000	1.133472	1.161740	1.195664	1.235851	1.282973
1.3600000	1.140460	1.169240	1.203834	1.244904	1.293207
1.3700000	1.147442	1.176737	1.212006	1.253969	1.303468
1.3799999	1.154418	1.184232	1.220181	1.263044	1.313757
1.3899999	1.161389	1.191724	1.228358	1.272130	1.324071
1.4000000	1.168355	1.199213	1.236537	1.281227	1.334411
1.4100000	1.175316	1.206701	1.244719	1.290334	1.344775
1.4200000	1.182273	1.214186	1.252902	1.299449	1.355163
1.4300000	1.189226	1.221670	1.261088	1.308574	1.365572
1.4400000	1.196174	1.229152	1.269275	1.317708	1.376003
1.4500000	1.203119	1.236632	1.277465	1.326849	1.386453
1.4600000	1.210061	1.244111	1.285656	1.335999	1.396922
1.4700000	1.217000	1.251588	1.293849	1.345155	1.407408
1.4800000	1.223936	1.259065	1.302044	1.354317	1.417909
1.4900000	1.230869	1.266540	1.310239	1.363486	1.428426
1.5000000	1.237801	1.274015	1.318437	1.372659	1.438955
1.5100000	1.244730	1.281488	1.326635	1.381838	1.449495
1.5200000	1.251658	1.288961	1.334834	1.391020	1.460046
1.5300000	1.258584	1.296434	1.343034	1.400206	1.470604
1.5400000	1.265510	1.303905	1.351235	1.409394	1.481170
1.5500000	1.272434	1.311377	1.359436	1.418585	1.491740
1.5600000	1.279358	1.318848	1.367638	1.427776	1.502314
1.5699999	1.286282	1.326320	1.375840	1.436969	1.512890
1.5707963	1.286833	1.326915	1.376493	1.437701	1.513732
1.5707963	1.286833	1.326914	1.376493	1.437700	1.513732

$\alpha = - .750000$

Θ	K VALUES				
	.794250555	.868696860	.928444378	.971111163	.994996249
.0000000	.000000	.000000	.000000	.000000	.000000
.0100000	.009999	.009999	.009999	.009999	.009999
.0200000	.019999	.019999	.019999	.019999	.019999
.0300000	.029996	.029997	.029997	.029997	.029997
.0400000	.039992	.039993	.039993	.039994	.039994
.0500000	.049985	.049986	.049988	.049989	.049989
.0600000	.059974	.059977	.059979	.059981	.059981
.0700000	.069959	.069964	.069967	.069970	.069971
.0800000	.079940	.079946	.079951	.079955	.079957
.0900000	.089915	.089924	.089931	.089936	.089939
.1000000	.099883	.099896	.099905	.099913	.099917
.1100000	.109845	.109861	.109875	.109884	.109890
.1200000	.119799	.119821	.119838	.119850	.119857
.1300000	.129746	.129773	.129795	.129811	.129819
.1400000	.139683	.139717	.139745	.139764	.139775
.1500000	.149612	.149654	.149688	.149712	.149725
.1600000	.159530	.159581	.159622	.159652	.159668
.1700000	.169439	.169500	.169549	.169584	.169604
.1800000	.179336	.179409	.179467	.179509	.179533
.1900000	.189223	.189308	.189377	.189426	.189454
.2000000	.199097	.199197	.199277	.199334	.199367
.2100000	.208959	.209075	.209168	.209234	.209271
.2200000	.218809	.218942	.219049	.219125	.219168
.2300000	.228645	.228797	.228920	.229007	.229056
.2400000	.238468	.238641	.238780	.238880	.238936
.2500000	.248278	.248473	.248630	.248743	.248806
.2600000	.258073	.258293	.258470	.258597	.258668
.2700000	.267854	.268100	.268299	.268441	.268521
.2800000	.277620	.277895	.278117	.278276	.278365
.2900000	.287372	.287677	.287924	.288101	.288200
.3000000	.297108	.297446	.297720	.297916	.298026
.3100000	.306829	.307203	.307505	.307722	.307843
.3200000	.316535	.316946	.317279	.317518	.317652
.3300000	.326225	.326677	.327042	.327305	.327452
.3400000	.335900	.336395	.336795	.337082	.337244
.3500000	.345559	.346099	.346536	.346851	.347027
.3600000	.355202	.355791	.356268	.356610	.356803
.3700000	.364830	.365470	.365988	.366361	.366570
.3800000	.374443	.375137	.375699	.376104	.376331
.3900000	.384039	.384791	.385400	.385838	.386085

$\alpha = -$ .750000

Θ	K VALUES				
	.794250555	.868696860	.928444378	.971111163	.994996249
.4000000	.393621	.394433	.395091	.395565	.395832
.4100000	.403187	.404063	.404773	.405285	.405573
.4200000	.412738	.413681	.414446	.414998	.415308
.4300000	.422275	.423288	.424111	.424704	.425038
.4400000	.431796	.432884	.433768	.434405	.434764
.4500000	.441304	.442469	.443417	.444100	.444486
.4600000	.450797	.452044	.453058	.453791	.454204
.4700000	.460276	.461609	.462694	.463478	.463920
.4800000	.469742	.471164	.472323	.473161	.473633
.4900000	.479195	.480711	.481947	.482841	.483346
.5000000	.488636	.490250	.491567	.492520	.493058
.5100000	.498064	.499780	.501182	.502197	.502771
.5200000	.507480	.509304	.510794	.511874	.512484
.5300000	.516885	.518821	.520404	.521552	.522201
.5400000	.526279	.528331	.530012	.531231	.531920
.5500000	.535663	.537837	.539619	.540912	.541643
.5600000	.545038	.547339	.549226	.550596	.551372
.5700000	.554403	.556836	.558833	.560285	.561107
.5800000	.563760	.566331	.568443	.569979	.570850
.5900000	.573110	.575823	.578055	.579680	.580601
.6000000	.582452	.585315	.587672	.589389	.590363
.6100000	.591788	.594805	.597293	.599106	.600135
.6200000	.601118	.604297	.606920	.608834	.609921
.6300000	.610443	.613790	.616554	.618573	.619720
.6400000	.619764	.623285	.626196	.628324	.629534
.6500000	.629081	.632783	.635848	.638090	.639366
.6600000	.638397	.642287	.645510	.647871	.649215
.6700000	.647710	.651795	.655185	.657670	.659085
.6800000	.657023	.661310	.664873	.667487	.668977
.6899999	.666335	.670833	.674575	.677324	.678892
.7000000	.675649	.680365	.684294	.687183	.688832
.7100000	.684964	.689907	.694030	.697065	.698799
.7200000	.694282	.699460	.703785	.706973	.708795
.7300000	.703605	.709026	.713561	.716908	.718822
.7400000	.712931	.718606	.723359	.726871	.728882
.7500000	.722264	.728201	.733181	.736866	.738977
.7600000	.731603	.737812	.743029	.746893	.749110
.7700000	.740951	.747441	.752903	.756955	.759281
.7800000	.750307	.757089	.762807	.767054	.769495
.7899999	.759673	.766759	.772742	.777192	.779753

$\alpha = - .750000$

Θ	K VALUES				
	.794250555	.868696860	.928444378	.971111163	.994996249
.8000000	.769051	.776450	.782709	.787372	.790057
.8100000	.778440	.786165	.792711	.797595	.800411
.8200000	.787843	.795905	.802750	.807865	.810818
.8300000	.797261	.805672	.812828	.818184	.821279
.8400000	.806694	.815468	.822946	.828553	.831797
.8500000	.816144	.825293	.833108	.838977	.842377
.8600000	.825612	.835151	.843315	.849458	.853021
.8700000	.835100	.845042	.853569	.859998	.863732
.8799999	.844608	.854968	.863874	.870601	.874513
.8899999	.854138	.864930	.874230	.881269	.885369
.9000000	.863691	.874932	.884642	.892006	.896302
.9100000	.873268	.884975	.895111	.902816	.907318
.9200000	.882871	.895060	.905641	.913701	.918418
.9300000	.892501	.905189	.916233	.924665	.929609
.9400000	.902159	.915365	.926890	.935712	.940893
.9500000	.911846	.925589	.937617	.946846	.952277
.9600000	.921564	.935864	.948415	.958070	.963763
.9699999	.931315	.946191	.959287	.969390	.975358
.9799999	.941098	.956573	.970237	.980808	.987066
.9899999	.950917	.967012	.981268	.992330	.998893
1.0000000	.960772	.977509	.992384	1.003960	1.010845
1.0100000	.970664	.988068	1.003587	1.015704	1.022927
1.0200000	.980596	.998690	1.014882	1.027565	1.035146
1.0300000	.990567	1.009378	1.026272	1.039551	1.047508
1.0400000	1.000580	1.020133	1.037760	1.051665	1.060020
1.0500000	1.010635	1.030959	1.049351	1.063913	1.072690
1.0600000	1.020735	1.041858	1.061049	1.076303	1.085524
1.0699999	1.030880	1.052831	1.072857	1.088840	1.098532
1.0799999	1.041072	1.063882	1.084781	1.101530	1.111722
1.0899999	1.051312	1.075013	1.096823	1.114380	1.125103
1.1000000	1.061602	1.086226	1.108990	1.127399	1.138684
1.1100000	1.071942	1.097524	1.121285	1.140592	1.152475
1.1200000	1.082333	1.108909	1.133712	1.153969	1.166488
1.1300000	1.092777	1.120384	1.146278	1.167537	1.180734
1.1400000	1.103276	1.131950	1.158987	1.181305	1.195224
1.1500000	1.113829	1.143611	1.171843	1.195282	1.209972
1.1600000	1.124439	1.155370	1.184853	1.209477	1.224992
1.1700000	1.135106	1.167227	1.198021	1.223902	1.240298
1.1800000	1.145831	1.179187	1.211353	1.238565	1.255907
1.1899999	1.156616	1.191250	1.224855	1.253479	1.271834

$\alpha = - .750000$

Θ	K VALUES				
	.794250555	.868696860	.928444378	.971111163	.994996249
1.2000000	1.167460	1.203420	1.238532	1.268655	1.288099
1.2100000	1.178365	1.215699	1.252389	1.284105	1.304721
1.2200000	1.189331	1.228088	1.266434	1.299842	1.321721
1.2300000	1.200360	1.240590	1.280671	1.315880	1.339122
1.2400000	1.211451	1.253207	1.295106	1.332232	1.356949
1.2500000	1.222605	1.265941	1.309747	1.348914	1.375227
1.2599999	1.233823	1.278794	1.324597	1.365941	1.393986
1.2699999	1.245104	1.291766	1.339664	1.383330	1.413258
1.2799999	1.256449	1.304860	1.354953	1.401098	1.433076
1.2899999	1.267857	1.318077	1.370471	1.419263	1.453479
1.3000000	1.279330	1.331418	1.386222	1.437843	1.474507
1.3100000	1.290866	1.344883	1.402212	1.456860	1.496206
1.3200000	1.302465	1.358473	1.418446	1.476331	1.518624
1.3300000	1.314126	1.372188	1.434929	1.496280	1.541818
1.3400000	1.325850	1.386029	1.451665	1.516728	1.565847
1.3500000	1.337634	1.399995	1.468659	1.537697	1.590779
1.3600000	1.349479	1.414085	1.485913	1.559211	1.616688
1.3700000	1.361382	1.428298	1.503430	1.581292	1.643659
1.3799999	1.373344	1.442633	1.521213	1.603964	1.671785
1.3899999	1.385361	1.457088	1.539261	1.627249	1.701171
1.4000000	1.397434	1.471661	1.557575	1.651171	1.731935
1.4100000	1.409559	1.486348	1.576154	1.675749	1.764209
1.4200000	1.421734	1.501147	1.594996	1.701005	1.798145
1.4300000	1.433959	1.516053	1.614095	1.726954	1.833912
1.4400000	1.446229	1.531064	1.633447	1.753610	1.871702
1.4500000	1.458544	1.546173	1.653045	1.780982	1.911731
1.4600000	1.470900	1.561376	1.672881	1.809075	1.954243
1.4700000	1.483294	1.576667	1.692942	1.837885	1.999508
1.4800000	1.495723	1.592041	1.713218	1.867401	2.047822
1.4900000	1.508185	1.607489	1.733693	1.897604	2.099501
1.5000000	1.520677	1.623006	1.754353	1.928462	2.154868
1.5100000	1.533194	1.638583	1.775177	1.959932	2.214227
1.5200000	1.545733	1.654214	1.796148	1.991962	2.277816
1.5300000	1.558291	1.669889	1.817243	2.024482	2.345740
1.5400000	1.570865	1.685601	1.838440	2.057415	2.417880
1.5500000	1.583450	1.701340	1.859716	2.090671	2.493782
1.5600000	1.596043	1.717098	1.881044	2.124150	2.572587
1.5699999	1.608640	1.732866	1.902401	2.157747	2.653037
1.5707963	1.609643	1.734121	1.904102	2.160424	2.659469
1.5707963	1.609642	1.734121	1.904101	2.160423	2.659468

$\alpha = -\ .699999$

Θ	K VALUES				
	.009966711	.039469502	.087332193	.151646642	.229848846
.0000000	.000000	.000000	.000000	.000000	.000000
.0100000	.009999	.009999	.009999	.009999	.009999
.0200000	.019998	.019998	.019998	.019998	.019998
.0300000	.029993	.029993	.029994	.029994	.029994
.0400000	.039985	.039985	.039986	.039986	.039987
.0500000	.049971	.049971	.049972	.049974	.049975
.0600000	.059950	.059951	.059952	.059955	.059958
.0700000	.069920	.069922	.069925	.069928	.069933
.0800000	.079881	.079884	.079888	.079893	.079900
.0900000	.089832	.089835	.089841	.089849	.089858
.1000000	.099769	.099774	.099782	.099793	.099806
.1100000	.109693	.109700	.109710	.109725	.109742
.1200000	.119603	.119611	.119625	.119643	.119666
.1300000	.129496	.129506	.129524	.129547	.129576
.1400000	.139371	.139385	.139406	.139436	.139471
.1500000	.149228	.149245	.149271	.149307	.149351
.1600000	.159065	.159085	.159117	.159161	.159214
.1700000	.168881	.168905	.168944	.168996	.169059
.1800000	.178675	.178703	.178749	.178810	.178885
.1900000	.188445	.188478	.188532	.188604	.188692
.2000000	.198191	.198229	.198292	.198376	.198478
.2100000	.207911	.207955	.208027	.208124	.208243
.2200000	.217604	.217655	.217738	.217849	.217985
.2300000	.227270	.227328	.227422	.227549	.227704
.2400000	.236907	.236973	.237079	.237223	.237399
.2500000	.246514	.246588	.246709	.246871	.247069
.2600000	.256091	.256174	.256309	.256491	.256713
.2700000	.265636	.265729	.265879	.266083	.266331
.2800000	.275148	.275252	.275419	.275646	.275922
.2900000	.284628	.284742	.284928	.285179	.285485
.3000000	.294073	.294199	.294404	.294681	.295019
.3100000	.303483	.303622	.303848	.304152	.304525
.3200000	.312858	.313010	.313258	.313591	.314000
.3300000	.322197	.322363	.322633	.322998	.323445
.3400000	.331498	.331679	.331974	.332372	.332860
.3500000	.340762	.340959	.341279	.341712	.342242
.3600000	.349988	.350201	.350548	.351018	.351593
.3700000	.359175	.359406	.359781	.360289	.360912
.3800000	.368323	.368571	.368977	.369525	.370198
.3900000	.377431	.377698	.378135	.378725	.379450

$\alpha = -.699999$

Θ	K VALUES				
	.009966711	.039469502	.087332193	.151646642	.229848846
.4000000	.386498	.386786	.387255	.387890	.388669
.4100000	.395525	.395833	.396336	.397017	.397855
.4200000	.404510	.404840	.405379	.406108	.407005
.4300000	.413454	.413807	.414382	.415162	.416122
.4400000	.422357	.422733	.423346	.424179	.425203
.4500000	.431217	.431617	.432271	.433158	.434250
.4600000	.440034	.440460	.441155	.442099	.443261
.4700000	.448809	.449261	.449999	.451002	.452237
.4800000	.457541	.458020	.458803	.459866	.461178
.4900000	.466230	.466737	.467566	.468692	.470083
.5000000	.474876	.475412	.476288	.477480	.478952
.5100000	.483478	.484044	.484970	.486229	.487785
.5200000	.492037	.492633	.493610	.494939	.496582
.5300000	.500552	.501180	.502209	.503610	.505343
.5400000	.509023	.509685	.510768	.512243	.514068
.5500000	.517451	.518146	.519285	.520836	.522757
.5600000	.525835	.526565	.527761	.529391	.531411
.5700000	.534176	.534941	.536196	.537907	.540028
.5800000	.542473	.543275	.544590	.546384	.548610
.5900000	.550727	.551566	.552943	.554822	.557156
.6000000	.558937	.559815	.561255	.563222	.565666
.6100000	.567104	.568021	.569526	.571583	.574141
.6200000	.575227	.576185	.577757	.579906	.582580
.6300000	.583308	.584307	.585947	.588191	.590985
.6400000	.591346	.592387	.594097	.596438	.599354
.6500000	.599341	.600425	.602207	.604647	.607688
.6600000	.607294	.608422	.610277	.612818	.615988
.6700000	.615204	.616378	.618307	.620952	.624254
.6800000	.623073	.624292	.626298	.629049	.632485
.6899999	.630900	.632166	.634249	.637109	.640683
.7000000	.638686	.639999	.642162	.645132	.648847
.7100000	.646430	.647792	.650036	.653119	.656977
.7200000	.654134	.655545	.657871	.661069	.665075
.7300000	.661797	.663259	.665669	.668984	.673140
.7400000	.669420	.670933	.673429	.676863	.681172
.7500000	.677003	.678569	.681151	.684707	.689172
.7600000	.684547	.686165	.688836	.692516	.697140
.7700000	.692051	.693724	.696485	.700291	.705077
.7800000	.699517	.701244	.704097	.708031	.712983
.7899999	.706944	.708727	.711673	.715738	.720858

$\alpha = -\ .699999$

Θ	K VALUES				
	.009966711	.039469502	.087332193	.151646642	.229848846
.8000000	.714334	.716174	.719213	.723411	.728702
.8100000	.721686	.723583	.726719	.731051	.736517
.8200000	.729001	.730956	.734189	.738659	.744301
.8300000	.736279	.738293	.741625	.746234	.752057
.8400000	.743521	.745594	.749026	.753777	.759783
.8500000	.750727	.752861	.756395	.761289	.767481
.8600000	.757897	.760093	.763729	.768769	.775151
.8700000	.765033	.767291	.771032	.776219	.782792
.8799999	.772134	.774455	.778301	.783638	.790407
.8899999	.779201	.781585	.785539	.791028	.797995
.9000000	.786235	.788683	.792745	.798388	.805556
.9100000	.793235	.795749	.799921	.805719	.813090
.9200000	.800203	.802783	.807065	.813021	.820599
.9300000	.807138	.809785	.814180	.820295	.828083
.9400000	.814042	.816756	.821264	.827542	.835542
.9500000	.820915	.823697	.828320	.834761	.842976
.9600000	.827757	.830607	.835347	.841953	.850387
.9699999	.834568	.837488	.842345	.849119	.857773
.9799999	.841350	.844340	.849315	.856259	.865136
.9899999	.848103	.851164	.856259	.863373	.872477
1.0000000	.854827	.857959	.863175	.870462	.879795
1.0100000	.861523	.864727	.870065	.877527	.887091
1.0200000	.868191	.871468	.876928	.884567	.894366
1.0300000	.874832	.878182	.883767	.891584	.901619
1.0400000	.881446	.884870	.890580	.898577	.908852
1.0500000	.888033	.891532	.897368	.905547	.916064
1.0600000	.894595	.898169	.904133	.912495	.923257
1.0699999	.901132	.904781	.910874	.919421	.930430
1.0799999	.907644	.911370	.917592	.926326	.937584
1.0899999	.914132	.917934	.924287	.933210	.944720
1.1000000	.920596	.924476	.930960	.940072	.951837
1.1100000	.927037	.930994	.937611	.946915	.958937
1.1200000	.933455	.937491	.944241	.953738	.966019
1.1300000	.939851	.943966	.950850	.960542	.973084
1.1400000	.946226	.950420	.957439	.967327	.980133
1.1500000	.952579	.956853	.964009	.974094	.987165
1.1600000	.958911	.963265	.970559	.980843	.994182
1.1700000	.965224	.969658	.977090	.987574	1.001184
1.1800000	.971516	.976032	.983602	.994288	1.008170
1.1899999	.977790	.982387	.990097	1.000986	1.015142

$\alpha = -\ .699999$

Θ	K VALUES				
	•009966711	•039469502	•087332193	•151646642	•229848846
1•2000000	•984045	•988724	•996574	1•007667	1•022101
1•2100000	•990281	•995044	1•003035	1•014333	1•029045
1•2200000	•996500	1•001346	1•009479	1•020984	1•035976
1•2300000	1•002702	1•007631	1•015907	1•027620	1•042894
1•2400000	1•008887	1•013900	1•022319	1•034241	1•049800
1•2500000	1•015056	1•020153	1•028716	1•040849	1•056693
1•2599999	1•021210	1•026391	1•035099	1•047443	1•063575
1•2699999	1•027348	1•032614	1•041467	1•054024	1•070446
1•2799999	1•033472	1•038823	1•047822	1•060592	1•077305
1•2899999	1•039581	1•045018	1•054164	1•067148	1•084154
1•3000000	1•045677	1•051200	1•060493	1•073693	1•090993
1•3100000	1•051760	1•057368	1•066809	1•080226	1•097822
1•3200000	1•057830	1•063525	1•073114	1•086748	1•104641
1•3300000	1•063888	1•069669	1•079408	1•093260	1•111452
1•3400000	1•069934	1•075802	1•085690	1•099762	1•118254
1•3500000	1•075969	1•081925	1•091962	1•106254	1•125047
1•3600000	1•081993	1•088036	1•098224	1•112737	1•131833
1•3700000	1•088007	1•094138	1•104477	1•119211	1•138611
1•3799999	1•094011	1•100230	1•110721	1•125677	1•145382
1•3899999	1•100007	1•106314	1•116956	1•132134	1•152146
1•4000000	1•105993	1•112388	1•123182	1•138585	1•158904
1•4100000	1•111971	1•118455	1•129402	1•145028	1•165655
1•4200000	1•117942	1•124514	1•135613	1•151465	1•172401
1•4300000	1•123905	1•130566	1•141819	1•157895	1•179142
1•4400000	1•129861	1•136612	1•148017	1•164320	1•185877
1•4500000	1•135811	1•142651	1•154210	1•170739	1•192608
1•4600000	1•141755	1•148684	1•160398	1•177153	1•199334
1•4700000	1•147694	1•154713	1•166580	1•183563	1•206057
1•4800000	1•153628	1•160736	1•172758	1•189968	1•212776
1•4900000	1•159558	1•166756	1•178932	1•196370	1•219492
1•5000000	1•165483	1•172771	1•185102	1•202768	1•226205
1•5100000	1•171406	1•178783	1•191269	1•209163	1•232916
1•5200000	1•177325	1•184793	1•197434	1•215556	1•239624
1•5300000	1•183242	1•190800	1•203596	1•221947	1•246331
1•5400000	1•189157	1•196805	1•209756	1•228336	1•253036
1•5500000	1•195070	1•202808	1•215915	1•234724	1•259740
1•5600000	1•200983	1•208811	1•222073	1•241111	1•266443
1•5699999	1•206895	1•214813	1•228230	1•247498	1•273146
1•5707963	1•207366	1•215291	1•228721	1•248006	1•273680
1•5707963	1•207365	1•215290	1•228720	1•248006	1•273680

$\alpha = -.699999$

Θ	K VALUES				
	.318821117	.415016431	.514599755	.613601043	.708073407
.0000000	.000000	.000000	.000000	.000000	.000000
.0100000	.009999	.009999	.009999	.009999	.009999
.0200000	.019998	.019998	.019998	.019998	.019999
.0300000	.029995	.029995	.029996	.029996	.029996
.0400000	.039988	.039989	.039990	.039991	.039992
.0500000	.049977	.049979	.049981	.049983	.049985
.0600000	.059961	.059964	.059968	.059971	.059975
.0700000	.069938	.069943	.069949	.069955	.069960
.0800000	.079908	.079916	.079924	.079933	.079941
.0900000	.089869	.089881	.089893	.089905	.089916
.1000000	.099820	.099836	.099853	.099870	.099885
.1100000	.109762	.109783	.109805	.109827	.109848
.1200000	.119691	.119719	.119747	.119776	.119803
.1300000	.129608	.129643	.129679	.129716	.129750
.1400000	.139511	.139555	.139601	.139646	.139689
.1500000	.149400	.149454	.149510	.149565	.149618
.1600000	.159274	.159339	.159407	.159474	.159538
.1700000	.169131	.169209	.169290	.169371	.169448
.1800000	.178971	.179063	.179160	.179255	.179347
.1900000	.188792	.188901	.189014	.189127	.189235
.2000000	.198595	.198722	.198854	.198985	.199111
.2100000	.208378	.208525	.208677	.208829	.208975
.2200000	.218140	.218309	.218484	.218659	.218826
.2300000	.227881	.228073	.228273	.228473	.228664
.2400000	.237600	.237818	.238045	.238272	.238489
.2500000	.247296	.247542	.247798	.248054	.248300
.2600000	.256968	.257244	.257532	.257820	.258097
.2700000	.266616	.266925	.267247	.267570	.267879
.2800000	.276239	.276583	.276942	.277301	.277647
.2900000	.285836	.286218	.286616	.287016	.287399
.3000000	.295407	.295829	.296270	.296712	.297137
.3100000	.304952	.305417	.305902	.306390	.306858
.3200000	.314469	.314980	.315513	.316049	.316564
.3300000	.323958	.324517	.325102	.325689	.326254
.3400000	.333419	.334030	.334668	.335310	.335929
.3500000	.342851	.343516	.344212	.344912	.345587
.3600000	.352254	.352977	.353733	.354494	.355229
.3700000	.361628	.362411	.363231	.364057	.364854
.3800000	.370971	.371818	.372705	.373599	.374463
.3900000	.380285	.381198	.382156	.383122	.384057

$\alpha = -.699999$

Θ	K VALUES				
	.318821117	.415016431	.514599755	.613601043	.708073407
.4000000	.389567	.390551	.391583	.392625	.393633
.4100000	.398819	.399876	.400986	.402108	.403194
.4200000	.408039	.409173	.410366	.411570	.412738
.4300000	.417228	.418443	.419721	.421013	.422267
.4400000	.426386	.427684	.429052	.430435	.431779
.4500000	.435511	.436897	.438358	.439838	.441276
.4600000	.444605	.446082	.447641	.449220	.450757
.4700000	.453666	.455239	.456899	.458583	.460223
.4800000	.462695	.464367	.466133	.467926	.469674
.4900000	.471692	.473466	.475343	.477250	.479110
.5000000	.480656	.482537	.484528	.486554	.488531
.5100000	.489588	.491580	.493690	.495838	.497938
.5200000	.498488	.500594	.502828	.505104	.507331
.5300000	.507355	.509580	.511942	.514351	.516711
.5400000	.516189	.518538	.521032	.523580	.526077
.5500000	.524991	.527467	.530099	.532790	.535430
.5600000	.533761	.536368	.539143	.541982	.544772
.5700000	.542499	.545241	.548163	.551157	.554101
.5800000	.551204	.554087	.557161	.560314	.563418
.5900000	.559877	.562905	.566136	.569454	.572725
.6000000	.568519	.571695	.575089	.578578	.582022
.6100000	.577129	.580458	.584020	.587686	.591308
.6200000	.585707	.589194	.592929	.596777	.600585
.6300000	.594254	.597903	.601817	.605854	.609853
.6400000	.602769	.606586	.610683	.614915	.619112
.6500000	.611254	.615242	.619529	.623962	.628365
.6600000	.619708	.623873	.628354	.632995	.637610
.6700000	.628131	.632478	.637160	.642014	.646848
.6800000	.636524	.641057	.645945	.651020	.656081
.6899999	.644887	.649611	.654711	.660013	.665309
.7000000	.653221	.658140	.663459	.668995	.674532
.7100000	.661525	.666645	.672187	.677965	.683752
.7200000	.669800	.675126	.680898	.686924	.692968
.7300000	.678046	.683583	.689591	.695872	.702183
.7400000	.686264	.692016	.698266	.704810	.711395
.7500000	.694454	.700426	.706925	.713739	.720607
.7600000	.702615	.708814	.715567	.722659	.729819
.7700000	.710750	.717179	.724194	.731571	.739032
.7800000	.718857	.725522	.732805	.740475	.748246
.7899999	.726937	.733844	.741401	.749373	.757462

$\alpha = -.699999$

Θ	K VALUES				
	.318821117	.415016431	.514599755	.613601043	.708073407
.8000000	.734991	.742145	.749982	.758263	.766681
.8100000	.743019	.750425	.758549	.767148	.775905
.8200000	.751021	.758684	.767103	.776028	.785133
.8300000	.758998	.766923	.775643	.784902	.794366
.8400000	.766950	.775143	.784171	.793773	.803607
.8500000	.774878	.783344	.792686	.802641	.812854
.8600000	.782782	.791526	.801190	.811505	.822109
.8700000	.790661	.799690	.809683	.820367	.831373
.8799999	.798518	.807835	.818164	.829228	.840647
.8899999	.806351	.815964	.826636	.838087	.849932
.9000000	.814162	.824075	.835097	.846947	.859228
.9100000	.821951	.832169	.843549	.855806	.868537
.9200000	.829718	.840247	.851993	.864666	.877858
.9300000	.837463	.848310	.860428	.873528	.887194
.9400000	.845188	.856357	.868854	.882391	.896545
.9500000	.852892	.864389	.877274	.891258	.905911
.9600000	.860577	.872406	.885686	.900127	.915294
.9699999	.868241	.880409	.894092	.909000	.924695
.9799999	.875886	.888398	.902492	.917878	.934114
.9899999	.883512	.896374	.910886	.926760	.943552
1.0000000	.891120	.904337	.919275	.935648	.953010
1.0100000	.898709	.912287	.927659	.944542	.962489
1.0200000	.906281	.920226	.936038	.953443	.971990
1.0300000	.913836	.928152	.944414	.962350	.981513
1.0400000	.921373	.936067	.952786	.971266	.991060
1.0500000	.928894	.943970	.961154	.980189	1.000630
1.0600000	.936399	.951864	.969520	.989121	1.010225
1.0699999	.943888	.959746	.977884	.998062	1.019845
1.0799999	.951362	.967619	.986246	1.007012	1.029492
1.0899999	.958821	.975482	.994605	1.015973	1.039166
1.1000000	.966265	.983336	1.002964	1.024943	1.048867
1.1100000	.973695	.991181	1.011322	1.033925	1.058597
1.1200000	.981112	.999018	1.019678	1.042918	1.068355
1.1300000	.988514	1.006846	1.028035	1.051922	1.078143
1.1400000	.995904	1.014667	1.036391	1.060938	1.087960
1.1500000	1.003281	1.022479	1.044748	1.069966	1.097808
1.1600000	1.010645	1.030285	1.053105	1.079007	1.107687
1.1700000	1.017998	1.038083	1.061463	1.088061	1.117598
1.1800000	1.025339	1.045875	1.069822	1.097127	1.127540
1.1899999	1.032668	1.053660	1.078183	1.106207	1.137515

$\alpha = -.699999$

Θ	K VALUES				
	.318821117	.415016431	.514599755	.613601043	.708073407
1.2000000	1.039987	1.061440	1.086544	1.115301	1.147522
1.2100000	1.047295	1.069213	1.094908	1.124408	1.157562
1.2200000	1.054592	1.076981	1.103273	1.133528	1.167635
1.2300000	1.061880	1.084744	1.111641	1.142663	1.177741
1.2400000	1.069158	1.092502	1.120010	1.151812	1.187880
1.2500000	1.076427	1.100255	1.128382	1.160974	1.198053
1.2599999	1.083687	1.108003	1.136757	1.170151	1.208259
1.2699999	1.090939	1.115747	1.145134	1.179342	1.218499
1.2799999	1.098182	1.123487	1.153514	1.188547	1.228772
1.2899999	1.105417	1.131223	1.161896	1.197765	1.239078
1.3000000	1.112644	1.138955	1.170282	1.206998	1.249416
1.3100000	1.119864	1.146684	1.178671	1.216245	1.259788
1.3200000	1.127077	1.154410	1.187062	1.225505	1.270191
1.3300000	1.134283	1.162133	1.195457	1.234778	1.280626
1.3400000	1.141483	1.169852	1.203855	1.244064	1.291092
1.3500000	1.148676	1.177569	1.212255	1.253364	1.301589
1.3600000	1.155864	1.185284	1.220659	1.262676	1.312116
1.3700000	1.163046	1.192996	1.229066	1.272001	1.322672
1.3799999	1.170223	1.200706	1.237475	1.281337	1.333256
1.3899999	1.177395	1.208414	1.245888	1.290685	1.343868
.4000000	1.184562	1.216119	1.254304	1.300044	1.354506
.4100000	1.191724	1.223824	1.262722	1.309414	1.365170
.4200000	1.198883	1.231526	1.271143	1.318794	1.375859
.4300000	1.206037	1.239227	1.279566	1.328184	1.386570
.4400000	1.213188	1.246926	1.287992	1.337584	1.397304
.4500000	1.220336	1.254625	1.296420	1.346991	1.408059
.4600000	1.227480	1.262322	1.304850	1.356408	1.418833
.4700000	1.234621	1.270018	1.313282	1.365831	1.429626
.4800000	1.241760	1.277713	1.321717	1.375262	1.440435
.4900000	1.248897	1.285407	1.330153	1.384699	1.451259
.5000000	1.256031	1.293101	1.338590	1.394141	1.462097
.5100000	1.263164	1.300794	1.347029	1.403589	1.472946
.5200000	1.270295	1.308486	1.355469	1.413041	1.483806
.5300000	1.277425	1.316178	1.363910	1.422496	1.494675
.5400000	1.284554	1.323869	1.372352	1.431955	1.505551
.5500000	1.291682	1.331560	1.380794	1.441415	1.516433
.5600000	1.298810	1.339252	1.389237	1.450878	1.527317
.5699999	1.305937	1.346942	1.397680	1.460340	1.538204
.5707963	1.306505	1.347555	1.398352	1.461094	1.539071
.5707963	1.306504	1.347554	1.398352	1.461093	1.539071

$\alpha = -\ .699999$

Θ	K VALUES				
	.794250555	.868696860	.928444378	.971111163	.994996249
.0000000	.000000	.000000	.000000	.000000	.000000
.0100000	.009999	.009999	.009999	.009999	.009999
.0200000	.019999	.019999	.019999	.019999	.019999
.0300000	.029997	.029997	.029997	.029998	.029998
.0400000	.039993	.039994	.039995	.039995	.039995
.0500000	.049987	.049988	.049990	.049991	.049991
.0600000	.059978	.059980	.059983	.059984	.059985
.0700000	.069965	.069969	.069973	.069975	.069977
.0800000	.079948	.079955	.079960	.079963	.079965
.0900000	.089927	.089936	.089943	.089948	.089951
.1000000	.099900	.099912	.099922	.099929	.099933
.1100000	.109867	.109883	.109897	.109906	.109912
.1200000	.119828	.119849	.119867	.119879	.119886
.1300000	.129782	.129809	.129831	.129847	.129855
.1400000	.139728	.139762	.139790	.139810	.139820
.1500000	.149667	.149709	.149743	.149767	.149780
.1600000	.159597	.159648	.159689	.159719	.159735
.1700000	.169519	.169580	.169629	.169664	.169684
.1800000	.179431	.179504	.179562	.179604	.179627
.1900000	.189334	.189419	.189488	.189537	.189565
.2000000	.199226	.199326	.199406	.199464	.199496
.2100000	.209108	.209224	.209317	.209383	.209421
.2200000	.218980	.219113	.219220	.219296	.219339
.2300000	.228840	.228992	.229114	.229202	.229251
.2400000	.238688	.238861	.239001	.239100	.239156
.2500000	.248525	.248721	.248879	.248992	.249055
.2600000	.258351	.258571	.258748	.258875	.258947
.2700000	.268163	.268410	.268609	.268752	.268832
.2800000	.277964	.278239	.278462	.278621	.278710
.2900000	.287752	.288058	.288305	.288483	.288582
.3000000	.297527	.297867	.298141	.298337	.298447
.3100000	.307289	.307664	.307967	.308184	.308306
.3200000	.317039	.317452	.317785	.318025	.318159
.3300000	.326775	.327229	.327595	.327858	.328006
.3400000	.336498	.336995	.337396	.337685	.337847
.3500000	.346209	.346751	.347190	.347505	.347682
.3600000	.355906	.356497	.356975	.357319	.357512
.3700000	.365590	.366233	.366753	.367127	.367337
.3800000	.375261	.375958	.376523	.376929	.377157
.3900000	.384920	.385675	.386286	.386726	.386974

$\alpha = -.699999$

Θ	K VALUES				
	.794250555	.868696860	.928444378	.971111163	.994996249
.4000000	.394566	.395381	.396042	.396518	.396786
.4100000	.404199	.405078	.405792	.406306	.406595
.4200000	.413820	.414767	.415536	.416090	.416402
.4300000	.423429	.424447	.425274	.425870	.426206
.4400000	.433025	.434118	.435007	.435647	.436008
.4500000	.442611	.443782	.444735	.445422	.445810
.4600000	.452185	.453438	.454459	.455195	.455611
.4700000	.461748	.463088	.464179	.464967	.465412
.4800000	.471300	.472731	.473896	.474739	.475214
.4900000	.480842	.482367	.483611	.484511	.485018
.5000000	.490374	.491999	.493324	.494284	.494825
.5100000	.499897	.501625	.503037	.504058	.504635
.5200000	.509411	.511247	.512748	.513836	.514450
.5300000	.518917	.520866	.522461	.523616	.524270
.5400000	.528414	.530481	.532174	.533402	.534096
.5500000	.537905	.540095	.541890	.543192	.543930
.5600000	.547388	.549707	.551608	.552990	.553772
.5700000	.556865	.559317	.561331	.562794	.563623
.5800000	.566337	.568928	.571058	.572607	.573485
.5900000	.575804	.578540	.580791	.582430	.583359
.6000000	.585266	.588154	.590531	.592263	.593246
.6100000	.594725	.597770	.600279	.602109	.603147
.6200000	.604181	.607389	.610036	.611968	.613065
.6300000	.613635	.617013	.619803	.621841	.622999
.6400000	.623088	.626642	.629582	.631730	.632952
.6500000	.632540	.636278	.639373	.641637	.642925
.6600000	.641992	.645921	.649177	.651562	.652920
.6700000	.651445	.655573	.658997	.661508	.662938
.6800000	.660901	.665234	.668834	.671476	.672982
.6899999	.670359	.674906	.678688	.681467	.683052
.7000000	.679821	.684589	.688561	.691483	.693150
.7100000	.689287	.694286	.698456	.701525	.703279
.7200000	.698760	.703997	.708372	.711597	.713440
.7300000	.708238	.713724	.718312	.721698	.723636
.7400000	.717725	.723467	.728278	.731832	.733868
.7500000	.727220	.733229	.738271	.742000	.744139
.7600000	.736724	.743010	.748292	.752205	.754450
.7700000	.746239	.752812	.758344	.762448	.764804
.7800000	.755766	.762636	.768428	.772731	.775204
.7899999	.765306	.772484	.778547	.783057	.785652

$\alpha = -.699999$

Θ	K VALUES				
	.794250555	.868696860	.928444378	.971111163	.994996249
.8000000	.774859	.782358	.788702	.793428	.796150
.8100000	.784428	.792258	.798894	.803846	.806701
.8200000	.794013	.802186	.809127	.814314	.817308
.8300000	.803614	.812145	.819402	.824835	.827974
.8400000	.813235	.822135	.829721	.835410	.838702
.8500000	.822875	.832158	.840087	.846043	.849494
.8600000	.832536	.842216	.850502	.856737	.860354
.8700000	.842219	.852310	.860968	.867495	.871286
.8799999	.851925	.862443	.871487	.878318	.882292
.8899999	.861656	.872616	.882062	.889212	.893377
.9000000	.871413	.882832	.892696	.900179	.904544
.9100000	.881197	.893091	.903391	.911221	.915797
.9200000	.891009	.903396	.914150	.922344	.927140
.9300000	.900851	.913748	.924976	.933550	.938577
.9400000	.910724	.924151	.935871	.944843	.950113
.9500000	.920630	.934605	.946839	.956227	.961752
.9600000	.930569	.945113	.957882	.967707	.973500
.9699999	.940543	.955678	.969004	.979286	.985360
.9799999	.950553	.966300	.980207	.990968	.997340
.9899999	.960601	.976982	.991496	1.002760	1.009443
1.0000000	.970688	.987727	1.002874	1.014664	1.021676
1.0100000	.980816	.998537	1.014344	1.026687	1.034046
1.0200000	.990985	1.009414	1.025909	1.038833	1.046557
1.0300000	1.001197	1.020360	1.037574	1.051107	1.059218
1.0400000	1.011454	1.031377	1.049342	1.063516	1.072035
1.0500000	1.021757	1.042469	1.061218	1.076066	1.085016
1.0600000	1.032106	1.053637	1.073205	1.088762	1.098168
1.0699999	1.042504	1.064884	1.085308	1.101611	1.111500
1.0799999	1.052952	1.076212	1.097530	1.114620	1.125021
1.0899999	1.063451	1.087625	1.109877	1.127795	1.138740
1.1000000	1.074002	1.099123	1.122353	1.141145	1.152667
1.1100000	1.084606	1.110710	1.134963	1.154676	1.166811
1.1200000	1.095266	1.122388	1.147711	1.168397	1.181185
1.1300000	1.105981	1.134160	1.160602	1.182317	1.195800
1.1400000	1.116753	1.146029	1.173642	1.196444	1.210668
1.1500000	1.127584	1.157996	1.186836	1.210788	1.225803
1.1600000	1.138473	1.170064	1.200189	1.225358	1.241219
1.1700000	1.149424	1.182236	1.213707	1.240165	1.256932
1.1800000	1.160435	1.194515	1.227394	1.255220	1.272956
1.1899999	1.171508	1.206902	1.241258	1.270533	1.289311

$\alpha = -$ .699999

θ	K VALUES				
	.794250555	.868696860	.928444378	.971111163	.994996249
.2000000	1.182645	1.219400	1.255303	1.286118	1.306014
.2100000	1.193845	1.232011	1.269536	1.301987	1.323086
.2200000	1.205110	1.244737	1.283963	1.318152	1.340549
.2300000	1.216439	1.257581	1.298589	1.334627	1.358425
.2400000	1.227835	1.270544	1.313420	1.351429	1.376741
.2500000	1.239296	1.283629	1.328464	1.368570	1.395523
.2599999	1.250824	1.296837	1.343726	1.386069	1.414801
.2699999	1.262419	1.310170	1.359211	1.403941	1.434608
.2799999	1.274080	1.323629	1.374927	1.422204	1.454980
.2899999	1.285808	1.337216	1.390878	1.440877	1.475953
.3000000	1.297603	1.350931	1.407072	1.459980	1.497572
.3100000	1.309464	1.364776	1.423512	1.479532	1.519882
.3200000	1.321391	1.378750	1.440205	1.499554	1.542935
.3300000	1.333383	1.392855	1.457156	1.520069	1.566786
.3400000	1.345440	1.407089	1.474368	1.541098	1.591499
.3500000	1.357561	1.421453	1.491847	1.562666	1.617142
.3600000	1.369744	1.435946	1.509594	1.584795	1.643792
.3700000	1.381989	1.450567	1.527614	1.607509	1.671537
.3799999	1.394294	1.465314	1.545908	1.630832	1.700471
.3899999	1.406658	1.480186	1.564476	1.654789	1.730703
.4000000	1.419079	1.495179	1.583320	1.679401	1.762356
.4100000	1.431555	1.510291	1.602436	1.704691	1.795564
.4200000	1.444084	1.525519	1.621824	1.730678	1.830484
.4300000	1.456663	1.540859	1.641478	1.757381	1.867289
.4400000	1.469291	1.556306	1.661393	1.784813	1.906179
.4500000	1.481964	1.571856	1.681562	1.812983	1.947374
.4600000	1.494680	1.587502	1.701976	1.841895	1.991127
.4700000	1.507437	1.603240	1.722624	1.871547	2.037714
.4800000	1.520230	1.619063	1.743493	1.901926	2.087441
.4900000	1.533057	1.634964	1.764568	1.933013	2.140634
.5000000	1.545914	1.650936	1.785832	1.964776	2.197625
.5100000	1.558798	1.666970	1.807268	1.997170	2.258725
.5200000	1.571706	1.683059	1.828854	2.030140	2.324180
.5300000	1.584633	1.699195	1.850569	2.063616	2.394100
.5400000	1.597576	1.715368	1.872389	2.097517	2.468359
.5500000	1.610531	1.731570	1.894290	2.131750	2.546493
.5600000	1.623494	1.747792	1.916246	2.166213	2.627615
.5699999	1.636462	1.764024	1.938231	2.200798	2.710432
.5707963	1.637494	1.765316	1.939982	2.203554	2.717054
.5707963	1.637493	1.765315	1.939981	2.203553	2.717052

$\alpha = -.649999$

θ	K VALUES				
	.009966711	.039469502	.087332193	.151646642	.229848846
.0000000	.000000	.000000	.000000	.000000	.000000
.0100000	.009999	.009999	.009999	.009999	.009999
.0200000	.019998	.019998	.019998	.019998	.019998
.0300000	.029994	.029994	.029994	.029994	.029995
.0400000	.039986	.039986	.039987	.039987	.039988
.0500000	.049973	.049973	.049974	.049976	.049977
.0600000	.059953	.059954	.059956	.059958	.059961
.0700000	.069926	.069928	.069930	.069934	.069939
.0800000	.079890	.079892	.079896	.079902	.079909
.0900000	.089844	.089847	.089853	.089861	.089870
.1000000	.099786	.099791	.099799	.099809	.099822
.1100000	.109715	.109722	.109732	.109747	.109764
.1200000	.119631	.119640	.119653	.119672	.119694
.1300000	.129532	.129543	.129560	.129583	.129612
.1400000	.139416	.139430	.139451	.139480	.139516
.1500000	.149283	.149300	.149326	.149362	.149406
.1600000	.159132	.159152	.159184	.159227	.159280
.1700000	.168961	.168985	.169023	.169075	.169138
.1800000	.178769	.178797	.178843	.178905	.178980
.1900000	.188556	.188589	.188642	.188715	.188803
.2000000	.198319	.198357	.198420	.198504	.198607
.2100000	.208059	.208103	.208175	.208273	.208391
.2200000	.217774	.217824	.217907	.218019	.218155
.2300000	.227462	.227521	.227615	.227742	.227897
.2400000	.237125	.237190	.237297	.237442	.237618
.2500000	.246759	.246833	.246954	.247117	.247315
.2600000	.256365	.256448	.256584	.256766	.256989
.2700000	.265941	.266034	.266185	.266389	.266638
.2800000	.275487	.275591	.275759	.275986	.276263
.2900000	.285002	.285117	.285303	.285555	.285862
.3000000	.294486	.294612	.294818	.295095	.295434
.3100000	.303936	.304075	.304301	.304607	.304980
.3200000	.313353	.313506	.313754	.314089	.314498
.3300000	.322737	.322903	.323174	.323540	.323989
.3400000	.332085	.332267	.332562	.332961	.333450
.3500000	.341398	.341596	.341917	.342351	.342883
.3600000	.350676	.350890	.351238	.351709	.352287
.3700000	.359917	.360148	.360525	.361035	.361660
.3800000	.369121	.369370	.369777	.370328	.371003
.3900000	.378287	.378556	.378994	.379587	.380316

$\alpha = -\ .649999$

Θ	K VALUES				
	.009966711	.039469502	.087332193	.151646642	.229848846
.4000000	.387416	.387705	.388176	.388814	.389597
.4100000	.396507	.396816	.397321	.398006	.398847
.4200000	.405558	.405890	.406431	.407164	.408065
.4300000	.414571	.414925	.415503	.416287	.417251
.4400000	.423544	.423922	.424539	.425375	.426405
.4500000	.432477	.432880	.433537	.434428	.435526
.4600000	.441370	.441798	.442497	.443446	.444615
.4700000	.450223	.450678	.451420	.452428	.453671
.4800000	.459036	.459517	.460305	.461374	.462694
.4900000	.467807	.468317	.469151	.470285	.471683
.5000000	.476538	.477077	.477959	.479159	.480639
.5100000	.485228	.485797	.486729	.487996	.489562
.5200000	.493876	.494477	.495460	.496798	.498451
.5300000	.502483	.503116	.504152	.505563	.507307
.5400000	.511049	.511715	.512805	.514291	.516129
.5500000	.519573	.520273	.521420	.522983	.524918
.5600000	.528056	.528791	.529996	.531638	.533673
.5700000	.536497	.537268	.538533	.540257	.542395
.5800000	.544897	.545705	.547031	.548839	.551083
.5900000	.553256	.554102	.555490	.557385	.559737
.6000000	.561573	.562458	.563910	.565894	.568359
.6100000	.569849	.570774	.572292	.574367	.576947
.6200000	.578084	.579050	.580636	.582804	.585502
.6300000	.586278	.587285	.588941	.591205	.594024
.6400000	.594431	.595481	.597207	.599570	.602513
.6500000	.602543	.603637	.605436	.607899	.610969
.6600000	.610615	.611754	.613626	.616192	.619393
.6700000	.618646	.619831	.621779	.624450	.627785
.6800000	.626637	.627868	.629894	.632673	.636145
.6899999	.634588	.635867	.637972	.640861	.644472
.7000000	.642500	.643827	.646013	.649014	.652769
.7100000	.650372	.651749	.654017	.657133	.661033
.7200000	.658205	.659632	.661984	.665217	.669267
.7300000	.665999	.667478	.669915	.673267	.677469
.7400000	.673755	.675286	.677809	.681283	.685641
.7500000	.681472	.683056	.685668	.689266	.693783
.7600000	.689152	.690789	.693492	.697216	.701895
.7700000	.696793	.698486	.701280	.705132	.709977
.7800000	.704398	.706146	.709034	.713017	.718029
.7899999	.711965	.713770	.716752	.720869	.726053

$\alpha = - .649999$

Θ	K VALUES				
	.009966711	.039469502	.087332193	.151646642	.229848846
.8000000	.719496	.721359	.724437	.728689	.734047
.8100000	.726991	.728912	.732088	.736477	.742013
.8200000	.734450	.736430	.739706	.744234	.749951
.8300000	.741874	.743914	.747290	.751961	.757862
.8400000	.749262	.751363	.754842	.759657	.765744
.8500000	.756616	.758779	.762361	.767322	.773600
.8600000	.763935	.766161	.769848	.774958	.781429
.8700000	.771221	.773510	.777304	.782565	.789232
.8799999	.778474	.780827	.784729	.790142	.797009
.8899999	.785693	.788112	.792122	.797691	.804760
.9000000	.792880	.795364	.799486	.805211	.812486
.9100000	.800035	.802586	.806819	.812704	.820187
.9200000	.807158	.809776	.814123	.820169	.827863
.9300000	.814250	.816936	.821398	.827607	.835516
.9400000	.821311	.824066	.828644	.835019	.843144
.9500000	.828342	.831167	.835862	.842404	.850750
.9600000	.835343	.838238	.843052	.849764	.858332
.9699999	.842314	.845281	.850215	.857098	.865892
.9799999	.849257	.852295	.857350	.864407	.873430
.9899999	.856171	.859282	.864460	.871691	.880946
1.0000000	.863057	.866241	.871543	.878952	.888441
1.0100000	.869916	.873174	.878600	.886188	.895915
1.0200000	.876748	.880080	.885633	.893401	.903368
1.0300000	.883553	.886960	.892640	.900592	.910801
1.0400000	.890332	.893815	.899624	.907760	.918214
1.0500000	.897086	.900645	.906583	.914905	.925608
1.0600000	.903814	.907450	.913519	.922030	.932983
1.0699999	.910518	.914232	.920432	.929133	.940340
1.0799999	.917198	.920990	.927323	.936215	.947678
1.0899999	.923854	.927724	.934192	.943277	.954999
1.1000000	.930487	.934437	.941039	.950319	.962302
1.1100000	.937097	.941127	.947865	.957342	.969588
1.1200000	.943685	.947795	.954671	.964345	.976857
1.1300000	.950251	.954442	.961456	.971330	.984111
1.1400000	.956796	.961069	.968221	.978297	.991348
1.1500000	.963320	.967675	.974967	.985246	.998570
1.1600000	.969824	.974262	.981695	.992178	1.005777
1.1700000	.976309	.980829	.988404	.999092	1.012969
1.1800000	.982774	.987378	.995095	1.005991	1.020148
1.1899999	.989220	.993908	1.001769	1.012873	1.027312

$\alpha = -\ .649999$

Θ	K VALUES				
	.009966711	.039469502	.087332193	.151646642	.229848846
1.2000000	.995648	1.000420	1.008425	1.019739	1.034463
1.2100000	1.002058	1.006915	1.015066	1.026591	1.041600
1.2200000	1.008451	1.013394	1.021690	1.033427	1.048725
1.2300000	1.014828	1.019855	1.028298	1.040250	1.055838
1.2400000	1.021187	1.026301	1.034891	1.047058	1.062938
1.2500000	1.027531	1.032732	1.041470	1.053853	1.070027
1.2599999	1.033860	1.039147	1.048034	1.060635	1.077105
1.2699999	1.040173	1.045548	1.054585	1.067404	1.084171
1.2799999	1.046473	1.051935	1.061122	1.074160	1.091228
1.2899999	1.052758	1.058308	1.067646	1.080905	1.098274
1.3000000	1.059030	1.064669	1.074158	1.087639	1.105310
1.3100000	1.065289	1.071016	1.080658	1.094362	1.112337
1.3200000	1.071536	1.077352	1.087146	1.101074	1.119355
1.3300000	1.077771	1.083676	1.093623	1.107775	1.126365
1.3400000	1.083994	1.089988	1.100090	1.114467	1.133366
1.3500000	1.090206	1.096290	1.106546	1.121150	1.140359
1.3600000	1.096408	1.102582	1.112993	1.127824	1.147344
1.3700000	1.102599	1.108864	1.119430	1.134489	1.154322
1.3799999	1.108781	1.115137	1.125858	1.141146	1.161294
1.3899999	1.114954	1.121400	1.132278	1.147796	1.168258
1.4000000	1.121119	1.127656	1.138690	1.154438	1.175217
1.4100000	1.127275	1.133903	1.145095	1.161073	1.182170
1.4200000	1.133424	1.140143	1.151492	1.167702	1.189117
1.4300000	1.139565	1.146376	1.157883	1.174325	1.196059
1.4400000	1.145700	1.152603	1.164267	1.180942	1.202996
1.4500000	1.151828	1.158823	1.170646	1.187554	1.209929
1.4600000	1.157951	1.165038	1.177019	1.194161	1.216858
1.4700000	1.164069	1.171248	1.183388	1.200763	1.223783
1.4800000	1.170182	1.177453	1.189752	1.207362	1.230705
1.4900000	1.176290	1.183654	1.196112	1.213956	1.237623
1.5000000	1.182395	1.189851	1.202469	1.220548	1.244539
1.5100000	1.188496	1.196045	1.208822	1.227137	1.251452
1.5200000	1.194595	1.202236	1.215173	1.233723	1.258364
1.5300000	1.200691	1.208425	1.221522	1.240307	1.265273
1.5400000	1.206785	1.214612	1.227868	1.246890	1.272181
1.5500000	1.212877	1.220797	1.234214	1.253471	1.279088
1.5600000	1.218969	1.226982	1.240558	1.260052	1.285995
1.5699999	1.225060	1.233166	1.246902	1.266632	1.292901
1.5707963	1.225545	1.233658	1.247408	1.267156	1.293451
1.5707963	1.225545	1.233657	1.247407	1.267155	1.293450

$\alpha = -.649999$

θ	K VALUES				
	.318821117	.415016431	.514599755	.613601043	.708073407
.0000000	.000000	.000000	.000000	.000000	.000000
.0100000	.009999	.009999	.009999	.009999	.009999
.0200000	.019998	.019998	.019998	.019999	.019999
.0300000	.029995	.029996	.029996	.029996	.029997
.0400000	.039989	.039990	.039991	.039992	.039993
.0500000	.049979	.049981	.049983	.049985	.049987
.0600000	.059964	.059968	.059971	.059975	.059978
.0700000	.069944	.069949	.069955	.069960	.069966
.0800000	.079916	.079924	.079933	.079941	.079949
.0900000	.089881	.089893	.089905	.089917	.089928
.1000000	.099837	.099853	.099870	.099886	.099902
.1100000	.109784	.109805	.109827	.109849	.109870
.1200000	.119719	.119747	.119776	.119804	.119831
.1300000	.129644	.129679	.129715	.129752	.129786
.1400000	.139556	.139600	.139645	.139691	.139734
.1500000	.149455	.149509	.149565	.149621	.149674
.1600000	.159340	.159406	.159473	.159541	.159605
.1700000	.169211	.169289	.169370	.169451	.169528
.1800000	.179065	.179158	.179254	.179350	.179442
.1900000	.188903	.189012	.189125	.189238	.189346
.2000000	.198724	.198851	.198983	.199114	.199240
.2100000	.208526	.208673	.208826	.208978	.209124
.2200000	.218310	.218479	.218654	.218829	.218997
.2300000	.228075	.228267	.228467	.228667	.228859
.2400000	.237819	.238037	.238264	.238492	.238709
.2500000	.247542	.247789	.248045	.248302	.248548
.2600000	.257244	.257521	.257809	.258098	.258375
.2700000	.266923	.267233	.267556	.267879	.268189
.2800000	.276580	.276925	.277285	.277645	.277991
.2900000	.286214	.286596	.286996	.287396	.287781
.3000000	.295823	.296246	.296688	.297131	.297557
.3100000	.305408	.305875	.306362	.306850	.307320
.3200000	.314968	.315481	.316016	.316553	.317070
.3300000	.324503	.325064	.325650	.326239	.326806
.3400000	.334012	.334624	.335265	.335909	.336529
.3500000	.343494	.344161	.344860	.345562	.346239
.3600000	.352950	.353675	.354434	.355198	.355935
.3700000	.362379	.363164	.363988	.364816	.365617
.3800000	.371780	.372630	.373521	.374418	.375286
.3900000	.381153	.382070	.383032	.384002	.384941

$\alpha =$ - .649999

Θ	K VALUES				
	.318821117	.415016431	.514599755	.613601043	.708073407
.4000000	.390498	.391486	.392523	.393569	.394582
.4100000	.399815	.400877	.401993	.403119	.404210
.4200000	.409103	.410243	.411441	.412651	.413825
.4300000	.418363	.419583	.420867	.422166	.423426
.4400000	.427593	.428898	.430273	.431663	.433014
.4500000	.436794	.438188	.439656	.441144	.442589
.4600000	.445966	.447451	.449018	.450607	.452152
.4700000	.455107	.456689	.458359	.460053	.461702
.4800000	.464220	.465901	.467678	.469482	.471240
.4900000	.473302	.475087	.476975	.478894	.480765
.5000000	.482355	.484248	.486251	.488290	.490279
.5100000	.491377	.493382	.495506	.497669	.499782
.5200000	.500370	.502491	.504740	.507032	.509274
.5300000	.509333	.511574	.513952	.516378	.518754
.5400000	.518266	.520631	.523143	.525709	.528225
.5500000	.527168	.529662	.532314	.535025	.537685
.5600000	.536041	.538668	.541464	.544325	.547136
.5700000	.544884	.547649	.550594	.553611	.556578
.5800000	.553698	.556604	.559703	.562882	.566012
.5900000	.562482	.565534	.568792	.572138	.575437
.6000000	.571236	.574439	.577862	.581381	.584854
.6100000	.579961	.583319	.586912	.590610	.594265
.6200000	.588656	.592175	.595943	.599827	.603668
.6300000	.597323	.601006	.604955	.609030	.613066
.6400000	.605960	.609813	.613949	.618221	.622459
.6500000	.614569	.618596	.622924	.627400	.631846
.6600000	.623149	.627355	.631881	.636568	.641229
.6700000	.631701	.636091	.640821	.645725	.650609
.6800000	.640225	.644804	.649743	.654871	.659986
.6899999	.648721	.653494	.658649	.664007	.669360
.7000000	.657189	.662162	.667538	.673134	.678733
.7100000	.665631	.670807	.676410	.682252	.688104
.7200000	.674044	.679430	.685267	.691361	.697476
.7300000	.682432	.688031	.694109	.700463	.706847
.7400000	.690792	.696611	.702935	.709557	.716220
.7500000	.699127	.705171	.711747	.718644	.725595
.7600000	.707435	.713709	.720545	.727724	.734973
.7700000	.715718	.722227	.729329	.736799	.744354
.7800000	.723976	.730725	.738100	.745869	.753739
.7899999	.732209	.739204	.746858	.754933	.763129

$\alpha = -.649999$

θ	K VALUES				
	.318821117	.415016431	.514599755	.613601043	.708073407
.8000000	.740417	.747664	.755604	.763994	.772525
.8100000	.748601	.756104	.764337	.773052	.781928
.8200000	.756761	.764526	.773059	.782106	.791337
.8300000	.764897	.772930	.781770	.791158	.800755
.8400000	.773010	.781317	.790470	.800209	.810183
.8500000	.781100	.789685	.799161	.809258	.819619
.8600000	.789168	.798037	.807841	.818306	.829067
.8700000	.797214	.806373	.816512	.827355	.838526
.8799999	.805237	.814692	.825175	.836404	.847998
.8899999	.813240	.822995	.833829	.845455	.857483
.9000000	.821221	.831284	.842475	.854507	.866981
.9100000	.829181	.839557	.851113	.863562	.876495
.9200000	.837122	.847815	.859745	.872620	.886025
.9300000	.845042	.856059	.868370	.881681	.895571
.9400000	.852943	.864289	.876989	.890747	.905135
.9500000	.860824	.872506	.885602	.899817	.914717
.9600000	.868687	.880710	.894210	.908893	.924318
.9699999	.876531	.888901	.902813	.917974	.933939
.9799999	.884358	.897079	.911412	.927062	.943582
.9899999	.892166	.905246	.920007	.936157	.953246
1.0000000	.899958	.913401	.928598	.945260	.962932
1.0100000	.907732	.921545	.937186	.954370	.972642
1.0200000	.915490	.929678	.945771	.963489	.982376
1.0300000	.923231	.937801	.954354	.972618	.992135
1.0400000	.930957	.945913	.962935	.981755	1.001920
1.0500000	.938667	.954016	.971515	.990903	1.011731
1.0600000	.946363	.962109	.980093	1.000062	1.021569
1.0699999	.954043	.970193	.988670	1.009231	1.031436
1.0799999	.961709	.978269	.997247	1.018412	1.041331
1.0899999	.969362	.986336	1.005824	1.027605	1.051255
1.1000000	.977000	.994395	1.014400	1.036810	1.061210
1.1100000	.984625	1.002446	1.022978	1.046027	1.071195
1.1200000	.992238	1.010490	1.031556	1.055258	1.081211
1.1300000	.999838	1.018527	1.040134	1.064502	1.091259
1.1400000	1.007425	1.026556	1.048715	1.073759	1.101340
1.1500000	1.015001	1.034580	1.057297	1.083031	1.111453
1.1600000	1.022565	1.042597	1.065880	1.092317	1.121600
1.1700000	1.030118	1.050608	1.074466	1.101617	1.131781
1.1800000	1.037660	1.058613	1.083054	1.110932	1.141996
1.1899999	1.045191	1.066613	1.091645	1.120262	1.152245

$\alpha = -.649999$

θ	K VALUES				
	.318821117	.415016431	.514599755	.613601043	.708073407
1.2000000	1.052712	1.074608	1.100238	1.129608	1.162529
1.2100000	1.060224	1.082598	1.108834	1.138968	1.172849
1.2200000	1.067726	1.090583	1.117433	1.148344	1.183203
1.2300000	1.075218	1.098563	1.126036	1.157735	1.193593
1.2400000	1.082702	1.106540	1.134642	1.167142	1.204019
1.2500000	1.090177	1.114513	1.143251	1.176564	1.214480
1.2599999	1.097643	1.122481	1.151864	1.186002	1.224977
1.2699999	1.105102	1.130447	1.160481	1.195455	1.235509
1.2799999	1.112552	1.138409	1.169101	1.204924	1.246076
1.2899999	1.119996	1.146368	1.177725	1.214408	1.256679
1.3000000	1.127432	1.154323	1.186353	1.223908	1.267316
1.3100000	1.134862	1.162277	1.194985	1.233423	1.277988
1.3200000	1.142284	1.170227	1.203621	1.242952	1.288694
1.3300000	1.149701	1.178175	1.212260	1.252496	1.299434
1.3400000	1.157111	1.186121	1.220904	1.262055	1.310207
1.3500000	1.164516	1.194064	1.229551	1.271627	1.321012
1.3600000	1.171915	1.202006	1.238202	1.281213	1.331848
1.3700000	1.179310	1.209946	1.246857	1.290813	1.342716
1.3799999	1.186699	1.217884	1.255516	1.300426	1.353614
1.3899999	1.194083	1.225820	1.264178	1.310051	1.364540
1.4000000	1.201463	1.233755	1.272844	1.319689	1.375495
1.4100000	1.208839	1.241689	1.281513	1.329338	1.386477
1.4200000	1.216212	1.249622	1.290185	1.338998	1.397484
1.4300000	1.223580	1.257553	1.298860	1.348669	1.408516
1.4400000	1.230945	1.265483	1.307539	1.358350	1.419572
1.4500000	1.238307	1.273412	1.316220	1.368040	1.430650
1.4600000	1.245666	1.281341	1.324903	1.377739	1.441748
1.4700000	1.253023	1.289268	1.333589	1.387447	1.452865
1.4800000	1.260377	1.297195	1.342278	1.397161	1.463999
1.4900000	1.267729	1.305122	1.350968	1.406883	1.475150
1.5000000	1.275079	1.313048	1.359660	1.416611	1.486315
1.5100000	1.282427	1.320973	1.368354	1.426344	1.497493
1.5200000	1.289774	1.328898	1.377050	1.436082	1.508681
1.5300000	1.297119	1.336823	1.385746	1.445823	1.519879
1.5400000	1.304464	1.344747	1.394443	1.455568	1.531085
1.5500000	1.311808	1.352671	1.403142	1.465315	1.542295
1.5600000	1.319152	1.360595	1.411840	1.475064	1.553510
1.5699999	1.326495	1.368519	1.420539	1.484814	1.564727
1.5707963	1.327080	1.369150	1.421232	1.485590	1.565620
1.5707963	1.327079	1.369150	1.421231	1.485590	1.565619

$\alpha = -\ .649999$

θ	K VALUES				
	.794250555	.868696860	.928444378	.971111163	.994996249
.0000000	.000000	.000000	.000000	.000000	.000000
.0100000	.009999	.009999	.009999	.009999	.009999
.0200000	.019999	.019999	.019999	.019999	.019999
.0300000	.029997	.029998	.029998	.029998	.029998
.0400000	.039994	.039995	.039996	.039996	.039996
.0500000	.049989	.049991	.049992	.049993	.049993
.0600000	.059981	.059984	.059986	.059988	.059989
.0700000	.069971	.069975	.069978	.069981	.069982
.0800000	.079957	.079963	.079968	.079972	.079974
.0900000	.089939	.089948	.089955	.089960	.089963
.1000000	.099916	.099929	.099939	.099946	.099950
.1100000	.109889	.109905	.109919	.109928	.109934
.1200000	.119856	.119878	.119895	.119907	.119914
.1300000	.129818	.129845	.129867	.129883	.129892
.1400000	.139773	.139808	.139835	.139855	.139866
.1500000	.149722	.149764	.149798	.149822	.149836
.1600000	.159664	.159715	.159756	.159786	.159802
.1700000	.169599	.169660	.169709	.169745	.169764
.1800000	.179526	.179599	.179657	.179699	.179723
.1900000	.189445	.189531	.189599	.189649	.189676
.2000000	.199356	.199455	.199536	.199593	.199626
.2100000	.209258	.209373	.209466	.209533	.209571
.2200000	.219151	.219284	.219391	.219468	.219511
.2300000	.229035	.229187	.229310	.229397	.229447
.2400000	.238909	.239082	.239222	.239322	.239378
.2500000	.248774	.248970	.249128	.249241	.249304
.2600000	.258629	.258850	.259028	.259155	.259226
.2700000	.268474	.268722	.268921	.269064	.269144
.2800000	.278309	.278585	.278808	.278968	.279057
.2900000	.288134	.288441	.288689	.288867	.288966
.3000000	.297948	.298289	.298563	.298760	.298871
.3100000	.307752	.308128	.308432	.308650	.308772
.3200000	.317546	.317960	.318294	.318534	.318669
.3300000	.327329	.327783	.328151	.328415	.328563
.3400000	.337101	.337599	.338002	.338291	.338454
.3500000	.346863	.347407	.347847	.348163	.348341
.3600000	.356614	.357208	.357687	.358032	.358226
.3700000	.366356	.367001	.367523	.367898	.368109
.3800000	.376087	.376786	.377353	.377761	.377990
.3900000	.385808	.386565	.387179	.387621	.387870

$\alpha = -\ .649999$

Θ	K VALUES				
	.794250555	.868696860	.928444378	.971111163	.994996249
.4000000	.395518	.396337	.397001	.397479	.397748
.4100000	.405220	.406103	.406820	.407336	.407627
.4200000	.414911	.415863	.416635	.417192	.417505
.4300000	.424594	.425617	.426448	.427047	.427385
.4400000	.434267	.435365	.436258	.436902	.437265
.4500000	.443931	.445109	.446067	.446758	.447147
.4600000	.453587	.454848	.455874	.456615	.457033
.4700000	.463235	.464583	.465681	.466474	.466921
.4800000	.472876	.474315	.475488	.476335	.476814
.4900000	.482509	.484043	.485295	.486200	.486711
.5000000	.492135	.493770	.495104	.496069	.496614
.5100000	.501754	.503494	.504915	.505943	.506524
.5200000	.511368	.513217	.514728	.515823	.516442
.5300000	.520976	.522939	.524545	.525709	.526368
.5400000	.530579	.532662	.534367	.535604	.536303
.5500000	.540178	.542385	.544194	.545506	.546249
.5600000	.549773	.552110	.554026	.555419	.556207
.5700000	.559365	.561837	.563866	.565342	.566177
.5800000	.568954	.571567	.573714	.575276	.576161
.5900000	.578541	.581301	.583571	.585224	.586161
.6000000	.588127	.591040	.593438	.595186	.596177
.6100000	.597712	.600785	.603317	.605163	.606211
.6200000	.607298	.610536	.613207	.615157	.616264
.6300000	.616884	.620294	.623111	.625168	.626337
.6400000	.626472	.630061	.633029	.635199	.636433
.6500000	.636062	.639838	.642964	.645251	.646552
.6600000	.645656	.649625	.652915	.655325	.656696
.6700000	.655254	.659424	.662885	.665422	.666867
.6800000	.664856	.669236	.672874	.675545	.677067
.6899999	.674465	.679061	.682885	.685694	.687297
.7000000	.684080	.688902	.692918	.695873	.697559
.7100000	.693703	.698758	.702976	.706081	.707855
.7200000	.703334	.708633	.713059	.716321	.718187
.7300000	.712975	.718525	.723169	.726596	.728557
.7400000	.722626	.728438	.733308	.736906	.738967
.7500000	.732289	.738373	.743478	.747254	.749419
.7600000	.741965	.748330	.753679	.757642	.759916
.7700000	.751654	.758311	.763915	.768072	.770460
.7800000	.761357	.768318	.774187	.778546	.781052
.7899999	.771077	.778352	.784496	.789067	.791697

$\alpha = -\ .649999$

Θ	K VALUES				
	.794250555	.868696860	.928444378	.971111163	.994996249
.8000000	.780813	.788414	.794845	.799636	.802396
.8100000	.790568	.798506	.805236	.810257	.813153
.8200000	.800341	.808630	.815670	.820931	.823969
.8300000	.810135	.818788	.826150	.831662	.834848
.8400000	.819950	.828980	.836678	.842452	.845792
.8500000	.829788	.839208	.847257	.853303	.856806
.8600000	.839650	.849475	.857888	.864219	.867892
.8700000	.849536	.859782	.868574	.875203	.879054
.8799999	.859450	.870131	.879317	.886257	.890295
.8899999	.869390	.880524	.890120	.897386	.901618
.9000000	.879360	.890962	.900986	.908591	.913029
.9100000	.889360	.901447	.911917	.919878	.924530
.9200000	.899391	.911982	.922916	.931248	.936126
.9300000	.909455	.922568	.933986	.942707	.947821
.9400000	.919553	.933208	.945129	.954257	.959619
.9500000	.929686	.943902	.956349	.965903	.971526
.9600000	.939856	.954655	.967649	.977650	.983547
.9699999	.950064	.965467	.979032	.989501	.995686
.9799999	.960312	.976341	.990501	1.001460	1.007949
.9899999	.970600	.987279	1.002060	1.013533	1.020342
1.0000000	.980931	.998283	1.013713	1.025725	1.032871
1.0100000	.991305	1.009356	1.025462	1.038041	1.045541
1.0200000	1.001724	1.020500	1.037311	1.050485	1.058360
1.0300000	1.012189	1.031717	1.049265	1.063064	1.071335
1.0400000	1.022702	1.043010	1.061327	1.075783	1.084472
1.0500000	1.033264	1.054381	1.073502	1.088648	1.097779
1.0600000	1.043876	1.065832	1.085793	1.101666	1.111265
1.0699999	1.054540	1.077367	1.098205	1.114843	1.124938
1.0799999	1.065256	1.088987	1.110742	1.128187	1.138807
1.0899999	1.076027	1.100694	1.123409	1.141704	1.152881
1.1000000	1.086854	1.112493	1.136210	1.155402	1.167171
1.1100000	1.097737	1.124384	1.149151	1.169289	1.181688
1.1200000	1.108678	1.136372	1.162237	1.183373	1.196442
1.1300000	1.119679	1.148457	1.175471	1.197663	1.211445
1.1400000	1.130739	1.160643	1.188860	1.212168	1.226712
1.1500000	1.141862	1.172933	1.202410	1.226899	1.242255
1.1600000	1.153046	1.185328	1.216125	1.241864	1.258089
1.1700000	1.164295	1.197832	1.230011	1.257074	1.274229
1.1800000	1.175608	1.210447	1.244073	1.272542	1.290693
1.1899999	1.186986	1.223175	1.258319	1.288277	1.307498

$\alpha = -\ .649999$

Θ	K VALUES				
	.794250555	.868696860	.928444378	.971111163	.994996249
1.2000000	1.198431	1.236019	1.272753	1.304294	1.324664
1.2100000	1.209943	1.248981	1.287382	1.320604	1.342211
1.2200000	1.221523	1.262063	1.302212	1.337221	1.360162
1.2300000	1.233171	1.275268	1.317249	1.354159	1.378541
1.2400000	1.244888	1.288598	1.332499	1.371435	1.397373
1.2500000	1.256674	1.302053	1.347969	1.389062	1.416688
1.2599999	1.268530	1.315637	1.363665	1.407058	1.436515
1.2699999	1.280456	1.329351	1.379593	1.425441	1.456888
1.2799999	1.292452	1.343196	1.395760	1.444229	1.477843
1.2899999	1.304518	1.357174	1.412171	1.463439	1.499421
1.3000000	1.316654	1.371286	1.428832	1.483094	1.521665
1.3100000	1.328859	1.385532	1.445750	1.503213	1.544622
1.3200000	1.341132	1.399913	1.462928	1.523818	1.568345
1.3300000	1.353475	1.414429	1.480374	1.544932	1.592893
1.3400000	1.365885	1.429080	1.498090	1.566577	1.618329
1.3500000	1.378361	1.443866	1.516082	1.588778	1.644725
1.3600000	1.390904	1.458786	1.534352	1.611558	1.672160
1.3700000	1.403510	1.473839	1.552904	1.634943	1.700724
1.3799999	1.416179	1.489022	1.571739	1.658957	1.730515
1.3899999	1.428910	1.504335	1.590858	1.683624	1.761644
1.4000000	1.441700	1.519774	1.610262	1.708968	1.794237
1.4100000	1.454548	1.535337	1.629948	1.735011	1.828435
1.4200000	1.467451	1.551019	1.649914	1.761775	1.864397
1.4300000	1.480406	1.566818	1.670156	1.789276	1.902304
1.4400000	1.493412	1.582728	1.690668	1.817530	1.942358
1.4500000	1.506466	1.598744	1.711443	1.846545	1.984791
1.4600000	1.519565	1.614861	1.732470	1.876326	2.029858
1.4700000	1.532705	1.631073	1.753739	1.906871	2.077847
1.4800000	1.545883	1.647372	1.775237	1.938166	2.129073
1.4900000	1.559097	1.663753	1.796948	1.970191	2.183870
1.5000000	1.572343	1.680207	1.818855	2.002912	2.242582
1.5100000	1.585617	1.696726	1.840938	2.036285	2.305529
1.5200000	1.598914	1.713302	1.863177	2.070252	2.372964
1.5300000	1.612233	1.729926	1.885549	2.104741	2.445000
1.5400000	1.625568	1.746589	1.908030	2.139669	2.521508
1.5500000	1.638915	1.763282	1.930594	2.174939	2.602008
1.5600000	1.652271	1.779995	1.953216	2.210447	2.685589
1.5699999	1.665632	1.796718	1.975866	2.246080	2.770914
1.5707963	1.666695	1.798050	1.977671	2.248919	2.777737
1.5707963	1.666695	1.798049	1.977669	2.248917	2.777735

$\alpha = -.599999$

θ	K VALUES				
	.009966711	.039469502	.087332193	.151646642	.229848846
.0000000	.000000	.000000	.000000	.000000	.000000
.0100000	.009999	.009999	.009999	.009999	.009999
.0200000	.019998	.019998	.019998	.019998	.019998
.0300000	.029994	.029994	.029995	.029995	.029995
.0400000	.039987	.039987	.039988	.039988	.039989
.0500000	.049975	.049975	.049976	.049978	.049979
.0600000	.059957	.059958	.059960	.059962	.059965
.0700000	.069932	.069933	.069936	.069940	.069944
.0800000	.079898	.079901	.079905	.079910	.079917
.0900000	.089856	.089859	.089865	.089873	.089882
.1000000	.099802	.099807	.099815	.099826	.099839
.1100000	.109737	.109744	.109754	.109769	.109786
.1200000	.119660	.119668	.119682	.119700	.119722
.1300000	.129568	.129579	.129596	.129619	.129648
.1400000	.139461	.139475	.139496	.139525	.139561
.1500000	.149338	.149355	.149381	.149417	.149461
.1600000	.159199	.159218	.159251	.159294	.159347
.1700000	.169041	.169064	.169103	.169155	.169218
.1800000	.178863	.178892	.178937	.178999	.179074
.1900000	.188666	.188699	.188753	.188825	.188913
.2000000	.198447	.198486	.198549	.198633	.198735
.2100000	.208207	.208251	.208324	.208421	.208540
.2200000	.217943	.217994	.218077	.218189	.218325
.2300000	.227656	.227714	.227808	.227936	.228091
.2400000	.237343	.237409	.237516	.237661	.237837
.2500000	.247005	.247079	.247200	.247363	.247562
.2600000	.256640	.256724	.256859	.257042	.257265
.2700000	.266248	.266341	.266493	.266697	.266947
.2800000	.275828	.275932	.276100	.276327	.276605
.2900000	.285379	.285494	.285680	.285932	.286240
.3000000	.294900	.295027	.295233	.295511	.295851
.3100000	.304391	.304530	.304757	.305063	.305438
.3200000	.313851	.314004	.314253	.314588	.314999
.3300000	.323279	.323446	.323718	.324086	.324535
.3400000	.332675	.332857	.333154	.333554	.334045
.3500000	.342038	.342236	.342559	.342994	.343528
.3600000	.351368	.351583	.351932	.352405	.352985
.3700000	.360664	.360896	.361274	.361786	.362414
.3800000	.369925	.370176	.370584	.371137	.371815
.3900000	.379151	.379421	.379861	.380457	.381188

$\alpha = -.599999$

Θ	K VALUES				
	.009966711	.039469502	.087332193	.151646642	.229848846
.4000000	.388342	.388632	.389105	.389745	.390532
.4100000	.397497	.397808	.398315	.399003	.399848
.4200000	.406616	.406949	.407492	.408229	.409134
.4300000	.415698	.416054	.416635	.417422	.418391
.4400000	.424743	.425123	.425743	.426584	.427618
.4500000	.433751	.434155	.434816	.435712	.436816
.4600000	.442721	.443151	.443854	.444808	.445983
.4700000	.451653	.452110	.452857	.453871	.455120
.4800000	.460547	.461032	.461824	.462900	.464227
.4900000	.469403	.469916	.470755	.471896	.473303
.5000000	.478221	.478763	.479651	.480858	.482348
.5100000	.487000	.487573	.488511	.489786	.491362
.5200000	.495740	.496344	.497334	.498681	.500346
.5300000	.504441	.505078	.506121	.507541	.509298
.5400000	.513103	.513773	.514872	.516368	.518220
.5500000	.521726	.522431	.523586	.525160	.527110
.5600000	.530309	.531050	.532264	.533919	.535969
.5700000	.538854	.539631	.540905	.542643	.544798
.5800000	.547359	.548174	.549510	.551333	.553595
.5900000	.555826	.556679	.558078	.559989	.562361
.6000000	.564253	.565146	.566610	.568611	.571096
.6100000	.572641	.573574	.575105	.577199	.579801
.6200000	.580990	.581965	.583564	.585752	.588474
.6300000	.589300	.590317	.591987	.594273	.597117
.6400000	.597572	.598632	.600374	.602759	.605730
.6500000	.605804	.606909	.608725	.611212	.614312
.6600000	.613998	.615149	.617040	.619631	.622864
.6700000	.622154	.623351	.625319	.628017	.631385
.6800000	.630272	.631516	.633562	.636370	.639877
.6899999	.638351	.639644	.641770	.644690	.648339
.7000000	.646393	.647735	.649944	.652977	.656772
.7100000	.654398	.655789	.658082	.661232	.665175
.7200000	.662364	.663807	.666185	.669454	.673549
.7300000	.670294	.671789	.674254	.677644	.681895
.7400000	.678187	.679735	.682288	.685802	.690211
.7500000	.686043	.687646	.690289	.693929	.698500
.7600000	.693863	.695521	.698256	.702024	.706760
.7700000	.701647	.703361	.706189	.710088	.714993
.7800000	.709396	.711166	.714089	.718122	.723197
.7899999	.717109	.718937	.721956	.726125	.731375

$\alpha = -.599999$

θ	K VALUES				
	.009966711	.039469502	.087332193	.151646642	.229848846
.8000000	.724787	.726673	.729791	.734097	.739526
.8100000	.732430	.734376	.737594	.742040	.747649
.8200000	.740039	.742045	.745364	.749953	.755747
.8300000	.747613	.749681	.753103	.757837	.763818
.8400000	.755155	.757285	.760811	.765692	.771864
.8500000	.762662	.764856	.768487	.773518	.779884
.8600000	.770137	.772395	.776134	.781316	.787880
.8700000	.777580	.779902	.783750	.789086	.795850
.8799999	.784990	.787378	.791336	.796828	.803796
.8899999	.792368	.794822	.798892	.804543	.811718
.9000000	.799715	.802237	.806420	.812232	.819616
.9100000	.807032	.809621	.813919	.819893	.827491
.9200000	.814317	.816976	.821389	.827529	.835342
.9300000	.821573	.824301	.828832	.835139	.843171
.9400000	.828798	.831597	.836247	.842723	.850978
.9500000	.835995	.838865	.843635	.850282	.858762
.9600000	.843162	.846104	.850996	.857817	.866525
.9699999	.850302	.853316	.858331	.865327	.874267
.9799999	.857413	.860501	.865640	.872814	.881988
.9899999	.864497	.867659	.872923	.880277	.889688
1.0000000	.871553	.874791	.880182	.887716	.897368
1.0100000	.878583	.881896	.887415	.895134	.905029
1.0200000	.885587	.888976	.894625	.902528	.912670
1.0300000	.892565	.896031	.901810	.909901	.920292
1.0400000	.899518	.903062	.908973	.917253	.927895
1.0500000	.906446	.910068	.916112	.924583	.935480
1.0600000	.913349	.917050	.923228	.931893	.943046
1.0699999	.920229	.924010	.930323	.939182	.950596
1.0799999	.927085	.930946	.937396	.946451	.958128
1.0899999	.933918	.937860	.944447	.953701	.965643
1.1000000	.940729	.944752	.951478	.960932	.973142
1.1100000	.947517	.951623	.958488	.968144	.980625
1.1200000	.954284	.958472	.965478	.975338	.988092
1.1300000	.961030	.965301	.972449	.982514	.995543
1.1400000	.967755	.972110	.979401	.989673	1.002980
1.1500000	.974460	.978899	.986334	.996814	1.010402
1.1600000	.981145	.985669	.993249	1.003939	1.017810
1.1700000	.987811	.992421	1.000146	1.011047	1.025204
1.1800000	.994459	.999154	1.007025	1.018140	1.032584
1.1899999	1.001088	1.005869	1.013888	1.025217	1.039951

$\alpha = - .599999$

Θ	K VALUES				
	.009966711	.039469502	.087332193	.151646642	.229848846
1.2000000	1.007699	1.012567	1.020734	1.032279	1.047306
1.2100000	1.014292	1.019248	1.027565	1.039327	1.054648
1.2200000	1.020869	1.025913	1.034379	1.046360	1.061977
1.2300000	1.027430	1.032561	1.041179	1.053379	1.069295
1.2400000	1.033974	1.039194	1.047964	1.060385	1.076602
1.2500000	1.040503	1.045812	1.054734	1.067378	1.083898
1.2599999	1.047017	1.052416	1.061491	1.074359	1.091183
1.2699999	1.053516	1.059005	1.068234	1.081327	1.098458
1.2799999	1.060002	1.065580	1.074964	1.088283	1.105722
1.2899999	1.066474	1.072143	1.081682	1.095228	1.112977
1.3000000	1.072932	1.078692	1.088387	1.102162	1.120223
1.3100000	1.079378	1.085230	1.095081	1.109086	1.127460
1.3200000	1.085812	1.091755	1.101764	1.115999	1.134688
1.3300000	1.092234	1.098269	1.108436	1.122902	1.141908
1.3400000	1.098645	1.104772	1.115097	1.129796	1.149121
1.3500000	1.105045	1.111265	1.121749	1.136681	1.156325
1.3600000	1.111435	1.117747	1.128391	1.143557	1.163523
1.3700000	1.117815	1.124220	1.135024	1.150425	1.170713
1.3799999	1.124186	1.130684	1.141649	1.157285	1.177897
1.3899999	1.130547	1.137140	1.148265	1.164138	1.185075
1.4000000	1.136901	1.143587	1.154873	1.170984	1.192247
1.4100000	1.143246	1.150026	1.161474	1.177823	1.199413
1.4200000	1.149584	1.156458	1.168069	1.184656	1.206574
1.4300000	1.155915	1.162883	1.174656	1.191483	1.213730
1.4400000	1.162239	1.169302	1.181238	1.198304	1.220882
1.4500000	1.168557	1.175715	1.187814	1.205121	1.228029
1.4600000	1.174870	1.182123	1.194385	1.211932	1.235173
1.4700000	1.181177	1.188525	1.200951	1.218740	1.242312
1.4800000	1.187480	1.194923	1.207513	1.225543	1.249449
1.4900000	1.193779	1.201317	1.214071	1.232343	1.256583
1.5000000	1.200073	1.207707	1.220626	1.239140	1.263714
1.5100000	1.206365	1.214094	1.227177	1.245934	1.270843
1.5200000	1.212653	1.220478	1.233726	1.252726	1.277970
1.5300000	1.218940	1.226860	1.240273	1.259515	1.285095
1.5400000	1.225224	1.233240	1.246818	1.266304	1.292219
1.5500000	1.231507	1.239618	1.253361	1.273091	1.299342
1.5600000	1.237789	1.245996	1.259904	1.279877	1.306464
1.5699999	1.244070	1.252373	1.266446	1.286662	1.313586
1.5707963	1.244571	1.252881	1.266967	1.287203	1.314153
1.5707963	1.244570	1.252881	1.266967	1.287202	1.314152

$\alpha = -.599999$

Θ	K VALUES				
	.318821117	.415016431	.514599755	.613601043	.708073407
.0000000	.000000	.000000	.000000	.000000	.000000
.0100000	.009999	.009999	.009999	.009999	.009999
.0200000	.019998	.019998	.019999	.019999	.019999
.0300000	.029996	.029996	.029996	.029997	.029997
.0400000	.039990	.039991	.039992	.039993	.039994
.0500000	.049981	.049983	.049985	.049987	.049989
.0600000	.059968	.059971	.059975	.059978	.059982
.0700000	.069949	.069955	.069960	.069966	.069972
.0800000	.079925	.079933	.079941	.079950	.079958
.0900000	.089893	.089905	.089917	.089929	.089940
.1000000	.099854	.099870	.099886	.099903	.099918
.1100000	.109805	.109827	.109849	.109871	.109892
.1200000	.119748	.119776	.119804	.119833	.119860
.1300000	.129680	.129715	.129752	.129788	.129822
.1400000	.139601	.139645	.139691	.139736	.139779
.1500000	.149511	.149564	.149620	.149676	.149729
.1600000	.159407	.159473	.159540	.159608	.159672
.1700000	.169291	.169369	.169450	.169531	.169608
.1800000	.179160	.179252	.179349	.179445	.179537
.1900000	.189014	.189123	.189236	.189349	.189457
.2000000	.198853	.198980	.199112	.199244	.199370
.2100000	.208675	.208822	.208975	.209127	.209274
.2200000	.218481	.218650	.218825	.219000	.219168
.2300000	.228269	.228461	.228662	.228862	.229054
.2400000	.238038	.238257	.238485	.238712	.238931
.2500000	.247789	.248036	.248293	.248551	.248797
.2600000	.257521	.257798	.258087	.258377	.258654
.2700000	.267232	.267543	.267866	.268190	.268501
.2800000	.276923	.277269	.277630	.277991	.278338
.2900000	.286593	.286977	.287377	.287778	.288164
.3000000	.296241	.296665	.297108	.297552	.297979
.3100000	.305867	.306335	.306823	.307313	.307784
.3200000	.315471	.315984	.316521	.317060	.317578
.3300000	.325051	.325614	.326202	.326793	.327362
.3400000	.334608	.335223	.335866	.336511	.337134
.3500000	.344141	.344811	.345512	.346216	.346895
.3600000	.353650	.354378	.355140	.355906	.356646
.3700000	.363135	.363924	.364750	.365582	.366385
.3800000	.372594	.373447	.374342	.375243	.376114
.3900000	.382029	.382950	.383916	.384890	.385832

$\alpha =$ - .599999

Θ	K VALUES				
	.318821117	.415016431	.514599755	.613601043	.708073407
.4000000	.391437	.392429	.393471	.394522	.395539
.4100000	.400820	.401887	.403008	.404139	.405235
.4200000	.410177	.411322	.412526	.413742	.414921
.4300000	.419508	.420735	.422025	.423330	.424596
.4400000	.428813	.430124	.431506	.432904	.434261
.4500000	.438090	.439491	.440968	.442463	.443917
.4600000	.447341	.448835	.450411	.452008	.453562
.4700000	.456565	.458156	.459835	.461539	.463198
.4800000	.465762	.467454	.469241	.471055	.472824
.4900000	.474932	.476728	.478628	.480558	.482441
.5000000	.484074	.485979	.487996	.490047	.492050
.5100000	.493190	.495208	.497346	.499522	.501650
.5200000	.502277	.504413	.506677	.508984	.511242
.5300000	.511338	.513595	.515990	.518433	.520826
.5400000	.520371	.522754	.525285	.527869	.530403
.5500000	.529377	.531890	.534561	.537293	.539973
.5600000	.538356	.541003	.543820	.546704	.549537
.5700000	.547307	.550093	.553061	.556103	.559094
.5800000	.556231	.559161	.562285	.565490	.568646
.5900000	.565128	.568206	.571492	.574866	.578192
.6000000	.573998	.577228	.580681	.584231	.587734
.6100000	.582841	.586229	.589854	.593585	.597272
.6200000	.591657	.595207	.599010	.602929	.606807
.6300000	.600447	.604164	.608150	.612263	.616338
.6400000	.609210	.613099	.617275	.621588	.625867
.6500000	.617946	.622012	.626383	.630903	.635393
.6600000	.626657	.630905	.635476	.640210	.644919
.6700000	.635341	.639776	.644554	.649509	.654444
.6800000	.644000	.648627	.653618	.658800	.663969
.6899999	.652633	.657457	.662667	.668084	.673495
.7000000	.661241	.666267	.671702	.677361	.683022
.7100000	.669823	.675057	.680724	.686632	.692550
.7200000	.678381	.683828	.689732	.695896	.702082
.7300000	.686914	.692579	.698727	.705156	.711617
.7400000	.695423	.701311	.707710	.714411	.721156
.7500000	.703908	.710024	.716681	.723662	.730699
.7600000	.712368	.718719	.725640	.732909	.740249
.7700000	.720805	.727396	.734587	.742152	.749804
.7800000	.729219	.736055	.743524	.751394	.759367
.7899999	.737610	.744696	.752451	.760633	.768938

$\alpha =$ - .599999

θ	K VALUES				
	.318821117	.415016431	.514599755	.613601043	.708073407
.8000000	.745979	.753321	.761367	.769870	.778517
.8100000	.754325	.761929	.770273	.779107	.788106
.8200000	.762649	.770520	.779171	.788344	.797705
.8300000	.770951	.779095	.788059	.797580	.807315
.8400000	.779231	.787655	.796939	.806818	.816937
.8500000	.787491	.796199	.805811	.816056	.826571
.8600000	.795730	.804728	.814676	.825297	.836219
.8700000	.803948	.813243	.823534	.834540	.845882
.8799999	.812147	.821743	.832384	.843786	.855559
.8899999	.820325	.830229	.841229	.853036	.865253
.9000000	.828485	.838702	.850068	.862291	.874964
.9100000	.836625	.847162	.858901	.871550	.884692
.9200000	.844746	.855609	.867730	.880814	.894439
.9300000	.852849	.864043	.876554	.890084	.904206
.9400000	.860934	.872465	.885374	.899361	.913992
.9500000	.869001	.880875	.894190	.908645	.923800
.9600000	.877051	.889274	.903003	.917937	.933630
.9699999	.885084	.897662	.911813	.927237	.943482
.9799999	.893100	.906039	.920620	.936545	.953359
.9899999	.901100	.914406	.929426	.945863	.963260
1.0000000	.909084	.922763	.938229	.955191	.973186
1.0100000	.917053	.931110	.947032	.964529	.983138
1.0200000	.925006	.939448	.955833	.973877	.993117
1.0300000	.932944	.947777	.964634	.983237	1.003124
1.0400000	.940867	.956097	.973435	.992609	1.013159
1.0500000	.948777	.964409	.982236	1.001993	1.023224
1.0600000	.956672	.972713	.991037	1.011390	1.033318
1.0699999	.964554	.981009	.999839	1.020800	1.043443
1.0799999	.972423	.989298	1.008643	1.030223	1.053600
1.0899999	.980279	.997580	1.017448	1.039661	1.063788
1.1000000	.988122	1.005855	1.026254	1.049112	1.074009
1.1100000	.995953	1.014123	1.035063	1.058579	1.084264
1.1200000	1.003772	1.022386	1.043874	1.068060	1.094552
1.1300000	1.011580	1.030642	1.052687	1.077557	1.104875
1.1400000	1.019376	1.038893	1.061504	1.087069	1.115233
1.1500000	1.027162	1.047138	1.070323	1.096597	1.125627
1.1600000	1.034937	1.055378	1.079146	1.106142	1.136056
1.1700000	1.042701	1.063614	1.087972	1.115703	1.146522
1.1800000	1.050456	1.071845	1.096802	1.125280	1.157025
1.1899999	1.058200	1.080071	1.105636	1.134875	1.167565

$\alpha = -.599999$

Θ	K VALUES				
	.318821117	.415016431	.514599755	.613601043	.708073407
1.2000000	1.065936	1.088294	1.114474	1.144486	1.178142
1.2100000	1.073662	1.096512	1.123317	1.154114	1.188756
1.2200000	1.081380	1.104727	1.132163	1.163760	1.199409
1.2300000	1.089089	1.112939	1.141015	1.173423	1.210099
1.2400000	1.096790	1.121147	1.149870	1.183103	1.220828
1.2500000	1.104483	1.129352	1.158731	1.192800	1.231594
1.2599999	1.112168	1.137554	1.167596	1.202514	1.242398
1.2699999	1.119846	1.145754	1.176466	1.212246	1.253240
1.2799999	1.127517	1.153951	1.185341	1.221994	1.264120
1.2899999	1.135181	1.162146	1.194221	1.231760	1.275037
1.3000000	1.142839	1.170339	1.203105	1.241542	1.285991
1.3100000	1.150490	1.178529	1.211995	1.251341	1.296982
1.3200000	1.158135	1.186718	1.220890	1.261156	1.308008
1.3300000	1.165775	1.194905	1.229789	1.270987	1.319071
1.3400000	1.173409	1.203090	1.238693	1.280833	1.330168
1.3500000	1.181037	1.211274	1.247602	1.290696	1.341300
1.3600000	1.188661	1.219457	1.256516	1.300573	1.352466
1.3700000	1.196280	1.227638	1.265434	1.310465	1.363664
1.3799999	1.203895	1.235818	1.274357	1.320370	1.374894
1.3899999	1.211505	1.243997	1.283284	1.330290	1.386155
1.4000000	1.219111	1.252176	1.292215	1.340223	1.397445
1.4100000	1.226714	1.260353	1.301150	1.350168	1.408764
1.4200000	1.234313	1.268530	1.310089	1.360126	1.420111
1.4300000	1.241909	1.276705	1.319032	1.370095	1.431483
1.4400000	1.249501	1.284881	1.327979	1.380075	1.442880
1.4500000	1.257091	1.293055	1.336928	1.390065	1.454300
1.4600000	1.264678	1.301229	1.345881	1.400065	1.465742
1.4700000	1.272263	1.309403	1.354837	1.410073	1.477204
1.4800000	1.279845	1.317576	1.363795	1.420090	1.488685
1.4900000	1.287426	1.325749	1.372756	1.430114	1.500182
1.5000000	1.295005	1.333922	1.381719	1.440144	1.511695
1.5100000	1.302582	1.342094	1.390684	1.450181	1.523221
1.5200000	1.310158	1.350266	1.399650	1.460222	1.534759
1.5300000	1.317733	1.358438	1.408618	1.470268	1.546306
1.5400000	1.325307	1.366610	1.417587	1.480317	1.557861
1.5500000	1.332881	1.374782	1.426557	1.490369	1.569422
1.5600000	1.340454	1.382954	1.435527	1.500422	1.580987
1.5699999	1.348026	1.391125	1.444498	1.510477	1.592555
1.5707963	1.348629	1.391776	1.445212	1.511277	1.593476
1.5707963	1.348629	1.391775	1.445212	1.511277	1.593475

$\alpha = -.599999$

θ	K VALUES				
	.794250555	.868696860	.928444378	.971111163	.994996249
.0000000	.000000	.000000	.000000	.000000	.000000
.0100000	.009999	.009999	.009999	.009999	.009999
.0200000	.019999	.019999	.019999	.019999	.019999
.0300000	.029998	.029998	.029998	.029998	.029999
.0400000	.039995	.039996	.039997	.039997	.039997
.0500000	.049991	.049993	.049994	.049995	.049995
.0600000	.059985	.059988	.059990	.059991	.059992
.0700000	.069976	.069981	.069984	.069987	.069988
.0800000	.079965	.079972	.079977	.079980	.079982
.0900000	.089951	.089960	.089967	.089972	.089975
.1000000	.099933	.099945	.099955	.099962	.099966
.1100000	.109911	.109927	.109941	.109950	.109956
.1200000	.119885	.119906	.119924	.119936	.119943
.1300000	.129854	.129881	.129903	.129919	.129928
.1400000	.139818	.139853	.139880	.139900	.139911
.1500000	.149778	.149820	.149854	.149878	.149891
.1600000	.159731	.159782	.159823	.159853	.159869
.1700000	.169679	.169741	.169790	.169825	.169845
.1800000	.179621	.179694	.179752	.179794	.179818
.1900000	.189556	.189642	.189711	.189760	.189788
.2000000	.199485	.199585	.199666	.199723	.199756
.2100000	.209407	.209523	.209616	.209683	.209721
.2200000	.219322	.219456	.219563	.219640	.219683
.2300000	.229230	.229383	.229506	.229593	.229643
.2400000	.239131	.239304	.239444	.239544	.239600
.2500000	.249024	.249220	.249378	.249491	.249555
.2600000	.258909	.259130	.259308	.259436	.259507
.2700000	.268786	.269034	.269234	.269377	.269458
.2800000	.278656	.278933	.279156	.279316	.279406
.2900000	.288518	.288826	.289074	.289252	.289352
.3000000	.298372	.298713	.298988	.299186	.299297
.3100000	.308217	.308595	.308899	.309117	.309240
.3200000	.318055	.318471	.318806	.319047	.319182
.3300000	.327885	.328342	.328710	.328975	.329124
.3400000	.337707	.338207	.338611	.338901	.339064
.3500000	.347522	.348068	.348509	.348826	.349005
.3600000	.357328	.357923	.358405	.358751	.358946
.3700000	.367127	.367774	.368298	.368675	.368887
.3800000	.376918	.377621	.378190	.378599	.378829
.3900000	.386702	.387463	.388080	.388524	.388773

$\alpha = -\ .599999$

Θ	K VALUES				
	.794250555	.868696860	.928444378	.971111163	.994996249
.4000000	.396479	.397302	.397969	.398449	.398719
.4100000	.406249	.407137	.407857	.408376	.408668
.4200000	.416013	.416969	.417745	.418304	.418619
.4300000	.425770	.426798	.427633	.428235	.428575
.4400000	.435521	.436625	.437522	.438170	.438534
.4500000	.445266	.446450	.447413	.448108	.448499
.4600000	.455005	.456273	.457305	.458050	.458470
.4700000	.464740	.466096	.467200	.467997	.468447
.4800000	.474470	.475918	.477098	.477950	.478432
.4900000	.484195	.485740	.486999	.487910	.488424
.5000000	.493917	.495562	.496906	.497877	.498426
.5100000	.503635	.505387	.506817	.507853	.508437
.5200000	.513351	.515212	.516734	.517837	.518460
.5300000	.523064	.525041	.526659	.527831	.528494
.5400000	.532775	.534873	.536591	.537837	.538541
.5500000	.542485	.544709	.546531	.547854	.548602
.5600000	.552194	.554549	.556481	.557884	.558679
.5700000	.561903	.564395	.566441	.567929	.568771
.5800000	.571613	.574248	.576413	.577988	.578881
.5900000	.581323	.584107	.586397	.588064	.589009
.6000000	.591036	.593975	.596395	.598157	.599158
.6100000	.600751	.603851	.606407	.608270	.609327
.6200000	.610470	.613738	.616434	.618402	.619520
.6300000	.620192	.623635	.626479	.628556	.629736
.6400000	.629919	.633544	.636541	.638732	.639978
.6500000	.639652	.643466	.646623	.648933	.650248
.6600000	.649391	.653401	.656725	.659160	.660546
.6700000	.659138	.663352	.666850	.669414	.670875
.6800000	.668892	.673319	.676997	.679697	.681236
.6899999	.678656	.683303	.687169	.690010	.691631
.7000000	.688429	.693305	.697368	.700356	.702062
.7100000	.698213	.703327	.707594	.710735	.712530
.7200000	.708009	.713370	.717849	.721151	.723039
.7300000	.717818	.723435	.728135	.731604	.733589
.7400000	.727640	.733524	.738454	.742097	.744184
.7500000	.737477	.743637	.748807	.752631	.754824
.7600000	.747330	.753777	.759195	.763210	.765513
.7700000	.757199	.763944	.769622	.773834	.776253
.7800000	.767086	.774140	.780088	.784506	.787046
.7899999	.776993	.784366	.790595	.795229	.797896

$\alpha = -\ .599999$

Θ	K VALUES				
	.794250555	.868696860	.928444378	.971111163	.994996249
.8000000	.786919	.794625	.801146	.806005	.808804
.8100000	.796867	.804917	.811743	.816836	.819773
.8200000	.806837	.815245	.822387	.827725	.830806
.8300000	.816830	.825609	.833080	.838674	.841907
.8400000	.826848	.836012	.843826	.849686	.853078
.8500000	.836892	.846455	.854626	.860765	.864322
.8600000	.846963	.856940	.865483	.871913	.875644
.8700000	.857062	.867468	.876398	.883133	.887045
.8799999	.867191	.878042	.887375	.894428	.898531
.8899999	.877351	.888663	.898417	.905801	.910104
.9000000	.887542	.899334	.909525	.917257	.921769
.9100000	.897768	.910056	.920702	.928797	.933529
.9200000	.908028	.920831	.931952	.940427	.945389
.9300000	.918324	.931662	.943277	.952150	.957354
.9400000	.928657	.942549	.954680	.963970	.969428
.9500000	.939029	.953496	.966165	.975891	.981616
.9600000	.949441	.964504	.977734	.987917	.993922
.9699999	.959895	.975576	.989390	1.000052	1.006353
.9799999	.970391	.986714	1.001138	1.012302	1.018914
.9899999	.980932	.997921	1.012980	1.024671	1.031611
1.0000000	.991518	1.009197	1.024921	1.037165	1.044449
1.0100000	1.002151	1.020546	1.036963	1.049787	1.057436
1.0200000	1.012832	1.031971	1.049111	1.062545	1.070578
1.0300000	1.023563	1.043473	1.061368	1.075443	1.083882
1.0400000	1.034345	1.055055	1.073739	1.088488	1.097355
1.0500000	1.045180	1.066719	1.086228	1.101685	1.111006
1.0600000	1.056068	1.078468	1.098839	1.115042	1.124843
1.0699999	1.067011	1.090305	1.111576	1.128565	1.138874
1.0799999	1.078011	1.102232	1.124444	1.142261	1.153110
1.0899999	1.089069	1.114252	1.137449	1.156138	1.167558
1.1000000	1.100185	1.126366	1.150593	1.170203	1.182232
1.1100000	1.111362	1.138579	1.163883	1.184465	1.197140
1.1200000	1.122601	1.150892	1.177324	1.198931	1.212295
1.1300000	1.133902	1.163308	1.190921	1.213612	1.227709
1.1400000	1.145267	1.175829	1.204679	1.228517	1.243395
1.1500000	1.156698	1.188459	1.218603	1.243655	1.259369
1.1600000	1.168194	1.201200	1.232700	1.259037	1.275644
1.1700000	1.179758	1.214054	1.246975	1.274674	1.292236
1.1800000	1.191389	1.227024	1.261434	1.290577	1.309164
1.1899999	1.203090	1.240113	1.276083	1.306758	1.326445

$\alpha = -.599999$

Θ	K VALUES				
	.794250555	.868696860	.928444378	.971111163	.994996249
1.2000000	1.214861	1.253323	1.290929	1.323231	1.344100
1.2100000	1.226703	1.266656	1.305976	1.340008	1.362150
1.2200000	1.238615	1.280114	1.321233	1.357103	1.380617
1.2300000	1.250600	1.293701	1.336704	1.374531	1.399527
1.2400000	1.262657	1.307417	1.352398	1.392308	1.418906
1.2500000	1.274788	1.321265	1.368319	1.410450	1.438784
1.2599999	1.286991	1.335247	1.384474	1.428973	1.459192
1.2699999	1.299268	1.349365	1.400871	1.447897	1.480164
1.2799999	1.311618	1.363619	1.417515	1.467239	1.501739
1.2899999	1.324041	1.378011	1.434413	1.487020	1.523956
1.3000000	1.336538	1.392543	1.451570	1.507259	1.546862
1.3100000	1.349108	1.407214	1.468993	1.527979	1.570505
1.3200000	1.361749	1.422026	1.486686	1.549202	1.594939
1.3300000	1.374463	1.436979	1.504656	1.570950	1.620224
1.3400000	1.387247	1.452072	1.522907	1.593248	1.646428
1.3500000	1.400101	1.467305	1.541443	1.616120	1.673622
1.3600000	1.413024	1.482678	1.560267	1.639592	1.701890
1.3700000	1.426014	1.498188	1.579383	1.663688	1.731322
1.3799999	1.439070	1.513835	1.598793	1.688434	1.762022
1.3899999	1.452189	1.529616	1.618497	1.713856	1.794103
1.4000000	1.465372	1.545528	1.638495	1.739977	1.827695
1.4100000	1.478614	1.561569	1.658786	1.766820	1.862943
1.4200000	1.491914	1.577734	1.679366	1.794407	1.900012
1.4300000	1.505269	1.594020	1.700233	1.822756	1.939088
1.4400000	1.518677	1.610421	1.721378	1.851882	1.980380
1.4500000	1.532134	1.626933	1.742796	1.881796	2.024125
1.4600000	1.545639	1.643549	1.764475	1.912500	2.070589
1.4700000	1.559187	1.660264	1.786404	1.943992	2.120067
1.4800000	1.572775	1.677070	1.808569	1.976259	2.172885
1.4900000	1.586400	1.693960	1.830956	2.009280	2.229386
1.5000000	1.600058	1.710926	1.853545	2.043021	2.289926
1.5100000	1.613745	1.727960	1.876316	2.077434	2.354835
1.5200000	1.627458	1.745053	1.899249	2.112460	2.424373
1.5300000	1.641192	1.762196	1.922319	2.148026	2.498657
1.5400000	1.654943	1.779379	1.945502	2.184044	2.577554
1.5500000	1.668707	1.796593	1.968771	2.220416	2.660569
1.5600000	1.682481	1.813829	1.992099	2.257033	2.746761
1.5699999	1.696258	1.831075	2.015458	2.293779	2.834753
1.5707963	1.697356	1.832448	2.017318	2.296708	2.841789
1.5707963	1.697355	1.832447	2.017317	2.296706	2.841787

$\alpha =$ -.549999

θ	K VALUES				
	.009966711	.039469502	.087332193	.151646642	.229848846
.0000000	.000000	.000000	.000000	.000000	.000000
.0100000	.009999	.009999	.009999	.009999	.009999
.0200000	.019998	.019998	.019998	.019998	.019998
.0300000	.029995	.029995	.029995	.029995	.029996
.0400000	.039988	.039988	.039989	.039989	.039990
.0500000	.049977	.049977	.049978	.049980	.049981
.0600000	.059960	.059961	.059963	.059965	.059968
.0700000	.069937	.069939	.069942	.069945	.069950
.0800000	.079907	.079909	.079913	.079919	.079926
.0900000	.089868	.089871	.089877	.089885	.089894
.1000000	.099819	.099824	.099832	.099842	.099855
.1100000	.109759	.109766	.109776	.109790	.109808
.1200000	.119688	.119696	.119710	.119728	.119751
.1300000	.129604	.129615	.129632	.129655	.129684
.1400000	.139506	.139519	.139541	.139570	.139606
.1500000	.149394	.149410	.149437	.149472	.149516
.1600000	.159265	.159285	.159318	.159361	.159414
.1700000	.169120	.169144	.169183	.169235	.169298
.1800000	.178958	.178986	.179032	.179094	.179169
.1900000	.188777	.188810	.188864	.188936	.189024
.2000000	.198576	.198615	.198677	.198762	.198865
.2100000	.208355	.208400	.208472	.208570	.208689
.2200000	.218113	.218164	.218247	.218359	.218496
.2300000	.227849	.227908	.228002	.228130	.228285
.2400000	.237562	.237628	.237736	.237880	.238057
.2500000	.247252	.247326	.247447	.247610	.247810
.2600000	.256917	.257000	.257136	.257319	.257543
.2700000	.266556	.266650	.266801	.267006	.267256
.2800000	.276170	.276274	.276443	.276671	.276949
.2900000	.285757	.285872	.286059	.286312	.286621
.3000000	.295317	.295444	.295650	.295929	.296270
.3100000	.304849	.304988	.305216	.305523	.305898
.3200000	.314352	.314505	.314754	.315091	.315503
.3300000	.323825	.323993	.324266	.324634	.325085
.3400000	.333269	.333452	.333749	.334151	.334644
.3500000	.342683	.342881	.343205	.343642	.344178
.3600000	.352065	.352281	.352632	.353106	.353688
.3700000	.361416	.361649	.362029	.362543	.363173
.3800000	.370736	.370987	.371397	.371952	.372633
.3900000	.380022	.380293	.380735	.381333	.382067

$\alpha =$ -.549999

θ	K VALUES				
	.009966711	.039469502	.087332193	.151646642	.229848846
.4000000	.389276	.389567	.390042	.390685	.391475
.4100000	.398496	.398809	.399318	.400009	.400857
.4200000	.407683	.408018	.408564	.409303	.410213
.4300000	.416836	.417193	.417777	.418569	.419542
.4400000	.425954	.426336	.426959	.427804	.428844
.4500000	.435037	.435444	.436108	.437009	.438119
.4600000	.444086	.444518	.445225	.446185	.447366
.4700000	.453099	.453559	.454310	.455329	.456586
.4800000	.462077	.462564	.463361	.464443	.465778
.4900000	.471019	.471535	.472379	.473526	.474942
.5000000	.479925	.480471	.481364	.482579	.484078
.5100000	.488794	.489371	.490315	.491600	.493186
.5200000	.497628	.498237	.499233	.500589	.502265
.5300000	.506425	.507067	.508117	.509548	.511317
.5400000	.515185	.515861	.516967	.518474	.520340
.5500000	.523909	.524620	.525784	.527370	.529334
.5600000	.532597	.533343	.534566	.536234	.538300
.5700000	.541247	.542030	.543314	.545066	.547238
.5800000	.549861	.550682	.552028	.553866	.556147
.5900000	.558437	.559298	.560709	.562635	.565027
.6000000	.566978	.567878	.569355	.571373	.573880
.6100000	.575481	.576422	.577967	.580078	.582704
.6200000	.583947	.584931	.586545	.588753	.591499
.6300000	.592377	.593403	.595089	.597395	.600267
.6400000	.600771	.601841	.603599	.606007	.609006
.6500000	.609127	.610243	.612076	.614587	.617718
.6600000	.617448	.618609	.620519	.623136	.626401
.6700000	.625732	.626941	.628928	.631654	.635057
.6800000	.633980	.635237	.637304	.640141	.643685
.6899999	.642192	.643498	.645647	.648598	.652286
.7000000	.650368	.651724	.653957	.657024	.660860
.7100000	.658509	.659916	.662234	.665419	.669407
.7200000	.666615	.668074	.670478	.673784	.677926
.7300000	.674685	.676197	.678690	.682119	.686419
.7400000	.682720	.684286	.686869	.690425	.694886
.7500000	.690720	.692342	.695016	.698700	.703326
.7600000	.698686	.700364	.703132	.706947	.711741
.7700000	.706618	.708352	.711216	.715164	.720130
.7800000	.714516	.716308	.719268	.723352	.728493
.7899999	.722380	.724231	.727290	.731512	.736830

$\alpha =$ -.549999

θ	K VALUES				
	.009966711	.039469502	.087332193	.151646642	.229848846
.8000000	.730211	.732122	.735280	.739643	.745143
.8100000	.738008	.739980	.743241	.747747	.753431
.8200000	.745773	.747807	.751170	.755822	.761695
.8300000	.753506	.755602	.759070	.763870	.769934
.8400000	.761206	.763366	.766941	.771890	.778150
.8500000	.768874	.771098	.774782	.779884	.786342
.8600000	.776511	.778801	.782594	.787851	.794510
.8700000	.784117	.786473	.790377	.795791	.802655
.8799999	.791692	.794115	.798132	.803706	.810778
.8899999	.799237	.801728	.805859	.811595	.818879
.9000000	.806751	.809311	.813558	.819458	.826957
.9100000	.814236	.816866	.821230	.827297	.835013
.9200000	.821692	.824392	.828875	.835111	.843048
.9300000	.829119	.831890	.836493	.842900	.851062
.9400000	.836517	.839360	.844085	.850665	.859055
.9500000	.843887	.846803	.851651	.858407	.867027
.9600000	.851229	.854219	.859192	.866125	.874979
.9699999	.858544	.861609	.866708	.873821	.882912
.9799999	.865833	.868973	.874198	.881493	.890825
.9899999	.873094	.876310	.881665	.889144	.898719
1.0000000	.880330	.883623	.889107	.896773	.906594
1.0100000	.887540	.890910	.896526	.904380	.914450
1.0200000	.894725	.898173	.903922	.911965	.922288
1.0300000	.901884	.905412	.911294	.919531	.930109
1.0400000	.909020	.912627	.918645	.927075	.937912
1.0500000	.916131	.919819	.925973	.934600	.945698
1.0600000	.923219	.926988	.933280	.942105	.953467
1.0699999	.930284	.934135	.940565	.949590	.961219
1.0799999	.937326	.941259	.947830	.957057	.968956
1.0899999	.944346	.948362	.955074	.964505	.976676
1.1000000	.951344	.955444	.962299	.971935	.984382
1.1100000	.958321	.962506	.969503	.979347	.992072
1.1200000	.965277	.969546	.976689	.986742	.999748
1.1300000	.972213	.976567	.983856	.994120	1.007409
1.1400000	.979128	.983569	.991004	1.001481	1.015056
1.1500000	.986024	.990552	.998135	1.008825	1.022689
1.1600000	.992901	.997516	1.005248	1.016154	1.030309
1.1700000	.999759	1.004462	1.012343	1.023468	1.037916
1.1800000	1.006599	1.011390	1.019422	1.030766	1.045511
1.1899999	1.013421	1.018301	1.026485	1.038049	1.053093

$\alpha =$ -.549999

θ	K VALUES				
	.009966711	.039469502	.087332193	.151646642	.229848846
.2000000	1.020226	1.025195	1.033532	1.045319	1.060663
.2100000	1.027014	1.032073	1.040564	1.052574	1.068221
.2200000	1.033786	1.038935	1.047580	1.059815	1.075768
.2300000	1.040542	1.045781	1.054582	1.067044	1.083304
.2400000	1.047282	1.052613	1.061570	1.074259	1.090829
.2500000	1.054007	1.059430	1.068544	1.081462	1.098344
.2599999	1.060717	1.066232	1.075504	1.088654	1.105849
.2699999	1.067414	1.073021	1.082452	1.095833	1.113344
.2799999	1.074097	1.079797	1.089387	1.103001	1.120830
.2899999	1.080766	1.086560	1.096310	1.110158	1.128306
.3000000	1.087423	1.093310	1.103221	1.117305	1.135775
.3100000	1.094067	1.100049	1.110121	1.124441	1.143234
.3200000	1.100700	1.106776	1.117010	1.131568	1.150686
.3300000	1.107321	1.113492	1.123889	1.138685	1.158130
.3400000	1.113931	1.120197	1.130758	1.145794	1.165566
.3500000	1.120531	1.126892	1.137617	1.152893	1.172996
.3600000	1.127121	1.133578	1.144467	1.159985	1.180418
.3700000	1.133701	1.140254	1.151308	1.167068	1.187834
.3799999	1.140272	1.146921	1.158141	1.174144	1.195244
.3899999	1.146834	1.153580	1.164966	1.181213	1.202648
1.4000000	1.153389	1.160231	1.171783	1.188275	1.210047
1.4100000	1.159935	1.166874	1.178593	1.195331	1.217440
1.4200000	1.166474	1.173511	1.185397	1.202381	1.224829
1.4300000	1.173006	1.180140	1.192194	1.209425	1.232212
1.4400000	1.179532	1.186764	1.198986	1.216464	1.239592
1.4500000	1.186052	1.193381	1.205772	1.223498	1.246968
1.4600000	1.192567	1.199994	1.212553	1.230527	1.254339
1.4700000	1.199076	1.206601	1.219329	1.237553	1.261708
1.4800000	1.205581	1.213204	1.226102	1.244574	1.269073
1.4900000	1.212082	1.219803	1.232870	1.251593	1.276436
1.5000000	1.218579	1.226399	1.239635	1.258608	1.283797
1.5100000	1.225073	1.232991	1.246398	1.265621	1.291155
1.5200000	1.231564	1.239581	1.253157	1.272631	1.298511
1.5300000	1.238052	1.246168	1.259915	1.279639	1.305866
1.5400000	1.244539	1.252754	1.266671	1.286646	1.313219
1.5500000	1.251025	1.259338	1.273426	1.293652	1.320572
1.5600000	1.257510	1.265922	1.280179	1.300657	1.327924
1.5699999	1.263994	1.272505	1.286933	1.307662	1.335275
1.5707963	1.264510	1.273029	1.287470	1.308220	1.335861
1.5707963	1.264509	1.273028	1.287470	1.308219	1.335860

$\alpha =$ -.549999

Θ	K VALUES				
	.318821117	.415016431	.514599755	.613601043	.708073407
.0000000	.000000	.000000	.000000	.000000	.000000
.0100000	.009999	.009999	.009999	.009999	.009999
.0200000	.019998	.019999	.019999	.019999	.019999
.0300000	.029996	.029996	.029997	.029997	.029998
.0400000	.039991	.039992	.039993	.039994	.039995
.0500000	.049983	.049985	.049987	.049989	.049991
.0600000	.059971	.059975	.059979	.059982	.059985
.0700000	.069955	.069961	.069966	.069972	.069977
.0800000	.079933	.079941	.079950	.079958	.079966
.0900000	.089905	.089917	.089929	.089941	.089952
.1000000	.099870	.099886	.099903	.099919	.099935
.1100000	.109827	.109849	.109871	.109893	.109914
.1200000	.119776	.119804	.119833	.119861	.119888
.1300000	.129716	.129751	.129788	.129824	.129859
.1400000	.139646	.139690	.139736	.139781	.139824
.1500000	.149566	.149620	.149676	.149731	.149784
.1600000	.159474	.159539	.159607	.159675	.159739
.1700000	.169371	.169449	.169530	.169611	.169689
.1800000	.179254	.179347	.179444	.179540	.179632
.1900000	.189125	.189234	.189348	.189461	.189569
.2000000	.198982	.199109	.199241	.199373	.199500
.2100000	.208824	.208971	.209124	.209277	.209423
.2200000	.218652	.218821	.218997	.219172	.219340
.2300000	.228463	.228656	.228857	.229058	.229250
.2400000	.238259	.238478	.238706	.238934	.239152
.2500000	.248037	.248285	.248543	.248800	.249047
.2600000	.257799	.258077	.258367	.258656	.258934
.2700000	.267542	.267853	.268178	.268502	.268814
.2800000	.277268	.277614	.277976	.278337	.278685
.2900000	.286974	.287359	.287760	.288162	.288549
.3000000	.296661	.297087	.297531	.297976	.298404
.3100000	.306329	.306797	.307287	.307778	.308251
.3200000	.315976	.316491	.317029	.317569	.318090
.3300000	.325603	.326167	.326757	.327349	.327920
.3400000	.335208	.335825	.336470	.337118	.337742
.3500000	.344793	.345465	.346168	.346874	.347556
.3600000	.354356	.355086	.355850	.356619	.357362
.3700000	.363897	.364688	.365518	.366353	.367159
.3800000	.373415	.374272	.375170	.376074	.376949
.3900000	.382911	.383836	.384806	.385784	.386730

α = -.549999

θ	K VALUES				
	.318821117	.415016431	.514599755	.613601043	.708073407
.4000000	.392385	.393381	.394427	.395482	.396504
.4100000	.401835	.402906	.404032	.405168	.406269
.4200000	.411261	.412412	.413621	.414843	.416027
.4300000	.420665	.421897	.423194	.424506	.425778
.4400000	.430044	.431363	.432752	.434157	.435521
.4500000	.439400	.440809	.442293	.443796	.445258
.4600000	.448732	.450234	.451819	.453425	.454987
.4700000	.458039	.459639	.461328	.463042	.464710
.4800000	.467322	.469024	.470822	.472648	.474427
.4900000	.476581	.478389	.480300	.482243	.484137
.5000000	.485815	.487733	.489762	.491827	.493842
.5100000	.495025	.497057	.499209	.501400	.503542
.5200000	.504210	.506360	.508640	.510964	.513237
.5300000	.513371	.515644	.518056	.520517	.522927
.5400000	.522507	.524907	.527456	.530060	.532613
.5500000	.531618	.534150	.536842	.539594	.542295
.5600000	.540705	.543372	.546212	.549118	.551973
.5700000	.549767	.552575	.555568	.558634	.561649
.5800000	.558804	.561758	.564909	.568140	.571322
.5900000	.567818	.570921	.574235	.577639	.580994
.6000000	.576806	.580065	.583548	.587129	.590663
.6100000	.585771	.589189	.592847	.596612	.600332
.6200000	.594711	.598294	.602132	.606087	.610001
.6300000	.603627	.607379	.611404	.615556	.619669
.6400000	.612519	.616446	.620662	.625018	.629338
.6500000	.621388	.625494	.629908	.634474	.639009
.6600000	.630232	.634523	.639141	.643924	.648681
.6700000	.639053	.643534	.648362	.653369	.658356
.6800000	.647851	.652527	.657571	.662809	.668034
.6899999	.656626	.661502	.666769	.672245	.677716
.7000000	.665378	.670460	.675955	.681678	.687402
.7100000	.674107	.679400	.685131	.691107	.697094
.7200000	.682813	.688323	.694296	.700532	.706791
.7300000	.691498	.697229	.703450	.709956	.716495
.7400000	.700160	.706118	.712595	.719378	.726206
.7500000	.708800	.714991	.721730	.728798	.735924
.7600000	.717419	.723848	.730856	.738218	.745652
.7700000	.726016	.732690	.739974	.747637	.755389
.7800000	.734592	.741516	.749083	.757056	.765136
.7899999	.743147	.750327	.758184	.766476	.774894

$\alpha =$ -.549999

Θ	K VALUES				
	.318821117	.415016431	.514599755	.613601043	.708073407
.8000000	.751682	.759123	.767278	.775898	.784664
.8100000	.760197	.767905	.776364	.785321	.794447
.8200000	.768692	.776672	.785444	.794747	.804242
.8300000	.777166	.785426	.794518	.804176	.814052
.8400000	.785622	.794166	.803585	.813608	.823877
.8500000	.794058	.802893	.812647	.823045	.833718
.8600000	.802476	.811607	.821704	.832485	.843575
.8700000	.810875	.820309	.830756	.841932	.853450
.8799999	.819255	.828998	.839804	.851384	.863343
.8899999	.827618	.837676	.848848	.860842	.873255
.9000000	.835963	.846342	.857888	.870307	.883187
.9100000	.844291	.854997	.866925	.879780	.893140
.9200000	.852602	.863640	.875960	.889261	.903114
.9300000	.860897	.872274	.884992	.898750	.913111
.9400000	.869174	.880897	.894022	.908248	.923132
.9500000	.877436	.889510	.903051	.917756	.933176
.9600000	.885682	.898114	.912079	.927274	.943246
.9699999	.893913	.906708	.921106	.936803	.953341
.9799999	.902129	.915294	.930133	.946343	.963463
.9899999	.910330	.923871	.939159	.955895	.973612
1.0000000	.918516	.932440	.948186	.965460	.983790
1.0100000	.926689	.941001	.957214	.975037	.993997
1.0200000	.934847	.949554	.966243	.984627	1.004234
1.0300000	.942992	.958100	.975273	.994231	1.014502
1.0400000	.951124	.966639	.984305	1.003849	1.024801
1.0500000	.959243	.975171	.993339	1.013481	1.035132
1.0600000	.967350	.983697	1.002376	1.023129	1.045496
1.0699999	.975444	.992216	1.011415	1.032792	1.055894
1.0799999	.983526	1.000730	1.020457	1.042472	1.066326
1.0899999	.991597	1.009238	1.029503	1.052167	1.076793
1.1000000	.999656	1.017741	1.038552	1.061879	1.087296
1.1100000	1.007704	1.026239	1.047605	1.071608	1.097835
1.1200000	1.015742	1.034732	1.056662	1.081354	1.108411
1.1300000	1.023769	1.043221	1.065724	1.091118	1.119024
1.1400000	1.031786	1.051705	1.074789	1.100899	1.129675
1.1500000	1.039793	1.060185	1.083860	1.110699	1.140364
1.1600000	1.047791	1.068661	1.092936	1.120517	1.151093
1.1700000	1.055779	1.077134	1.102016	1.130354	1.161860
1.1800000	1.063758	1.085604	1.111102	1.140209	1.172667
1.1899999	1.071729	1.094070	1.120194	1.150083	1.183514

$\alpha =$ -.549999

Θ	K VALUES				
	.318821117	.415016431	.514599755	.613601043	.708073407
1.2000000	1.079691	1.102534	1.129291	1.159976	1.194402
1.2100000	1.087645	1.110995	1.138394	1.169888	1.205329
1.2200000	1.095591	1.119453	1.147503	1.179819	1.216297
1.2300000	1.103530	1.127909	1.156617	1.189769	1.227306
1.2400000	1.111461	1.136362	1.165738	1.199739	1.238355
1.2500000	1.119385	1.144814	1.174864	1.209727	1.249444
1.2599999	1.127302	1.153264	1.183997	1.219735	1.260575
1.2699999	1.135213	1.161712	1.193136	1.229761	1.271745
1.2799999	1.143117	1.170158	1.202281	1.239807	1.282956
1.2899999	1.151016	1.178604	1.211432	1.249871	1.294207
1.3000000	1.158908	1.187048	1.220590	1.259953	1.305497
1.3100000	1.166795	1.195490	1.229753	1.270053	1.316826
1.3200000	1.174676	1.203932	1.238922	1.280171	1.328193
1.3300000	1.182553	1.212373	1.248098	1.290307	1.339599
1.3400000	1.190424	1.220813	1.257279	1.300460	1.351042
1.3500000	1.198291	1.229252	1.266466	1.310630	1.362521
1.3600000	1.206153	1.237691	1.275658	1.320816	1.374036
1.3700000	1.214011	1.246129	1.284856	1.331018	1.385585
1.3799999	1.221865	1.254566	1.294059	1.341236	1.397168
1.3899999	1.229716	1.263003	1.303268	1.351468	1.408784
1.4000000	1.237563	1.271440	1.312482	1.361715	1.420432
1.4100000	1.245406	1.279877	1.321700	1.371976	1.432109
1.4200000	1.253246	1.288313	1.330923	1.382250	1.443816
1.4300000	1.261084	1.296749	1.340150	1.392536	1.455550
1.4400000	1.268918	1.305184	1.349382	1.402834	1.467310
1.4500000	1.276750	1.313620	1.358617	1.413143	1.479095
1.4600000	1.284580	1.322056	1.367856	1.423462	1.490903
1.4700000	1.292408	1.330491	1.377099	1.433791	1.502732
1.4800000	1.300233	1.338926	1.386344	1.444129	1.514581
1.4900000	1.308057	1.347362	1.395593	1.454475	1.526448
1.5000000	1.315880	1.355797	1.404844	1.464828	1.538331
1.5100000	1.323701	1.364232	1.414097	1.475187	1.550227
1.5200000	1.331521	1.372667	1.423352	1.485552	1.562136
1.5300000	1.339340	1.381103	1.432609	1.495921	1.574056
1.5400000	1.347158	1.389538	1.441867	1.506294	1.585983
1.5500000	1.354975	1.397973	1.451126	1.516670	1.597917
1.5600000	1.362793	1.406408	1.460386	1.527048	1.609855
1.5699999	1.370610	1.414844	1.469646	1.537427	1.621796
1.5707963	1.371232	1.415515	1.470383	1.538253	1.622746
1.5707963	1.371232	1.415515	1.470383	1.538252	1.622746

$\alpha =$ -.549999

θ	K VALUES				
	.794250555	.868696860	.928444378	.971111163	.994996249
.0000000	.000000	.000000	.000000	.000000	.000000
.0100000	.009999	.009999	.009999	.009999	.009999
.0200000	.019999	.019999	.019999	.019999	.019999
.0300000	.029998	.029998	.029999	.029999	.029999
.0400000	.039996	.039997	.039998	.039998	.039998
.0500000	.049993	.049995	.049996	.049997	.049997
.0600000	.059989	.059991	.059993	.059995	.059996
.0700000	.069982	.069986	.069990	.069992	.069994
.0800000	.079974	.079980	.079985	.079989	.079991
.0900000	.089963	.089972	.089979	.089984	.089987
.1000000	.099949	.099962	.099972	.099979	.099983
.1100000	.109933	.109949	.109963	.109972	.109978
.1200000	.119913	.119935	.119952	.119964	.119971
.1300000	.129890	.129918	.129940	.129955	.129964
.1400000	.139864	.139898	.139925	.139945	.139956
.1500000	.149833	.149875	.149909	.149933	.149947
.1600000	.159799	.159850	.159891	.159920	.159937
.1700000	.169760	.169821	.169870	.169906	.169925
.1800000	.179716	.179789	.179848	.179890	.179913
.1900000	.189668	.189754	.189823	.189872	.189900
.2000000	.199615	.199715	.199796	.199854	.199886
.2100000	.209557	.209673	.209767	.209834	.209871
.2200000	.219494	.219628	.219735	.219812	.219856
.2300000	.229426	.229579	.229702	.229790	.229840
.2400000	.239353	.239527	.239667	.239767	.239823
.2500000	.249274	.249471	.249629	.249742	.249806
.2600000	.259190	.259411	.259590	.259717	.259789
.2700000	.269100	.269348	.269548	.269692	.269772
.2800000	.279004	.279282	.279506	.279666	.279756
.2900000	.288904	.289212	.289461	.289640	.289740
.3000000	.298797	.299139	.299415	.299614	.299725
.3100000	.308685	.309063	.309369	.309588	.309711
.3200000	.318568	.318985	.319321	.319563	.319698
.3300000	.328445	.328903	.329273	.329538	.329687
.3400000	.338318	.338819	.339224	.339515	.339679
.3500000	.348185	.348732	.349176	.349494	.349673
.3600000	.358047	.358644	.359127	.359475	.359670
.3700000	.367904	.368554	.369080	.369458	.369671
.3800000	.377756	.378462	.379033	.379444	.379675
.3900000	.387604	.388369	.388988	.389433	.389684

$\alpha =$ -.549999

Θ	K VALUES				
	.794250555	.868696860	.928444378	.971111163	.994996249
.4000000	.397448	.398274	.398944	.399427	.399698
.4100000	.407288	.408180	.408903	.409424	.409718
.4200000	.417124	.418085	.418865	.419427	.419744
.4300000	.426957	.427991	.428830	.429435	.429776
.4400000	.436787	.437897	.438799	.439450	.439817
.4500000	.446614	.447805	.448773	.449472	.449865
.4600000	.456439	.457714	.458751	.459501	.459923
.4700000	.466261	.467625	.468736	.469538	.469990
.4800000	.476083	.477539	.478727	.479585	.480069
.4900000	.485903	.487457	.488724	.489641	.490158
.5000000	.495722	.497378	.498730	.499708	.500260
.5100000	.505541	.507304	.508744	.509787	.510376
.5200000	.515360	.517235	.518768	.519878	.520505
.5300000	.525181	.527172	.528802	.529983	.530650
.5400000	.535002	.537116	.538846	.540102	.540812
.5500000	.544826	.547067	.548903	.550236	.550991
.5600000	.554652	.557026	.558973	.560387	.561188
.5700000	.564481	.566994	.569057	.570556	.571406
.5800000	.574314	.576971	.579155	.580744	.581644
.5900000	.584152	.586960	.589269	.590951	.591905
.6000000	.593994	.596959	.599401	.601180	.602189
.6100000	.603843	.606972	.609550	.611431	.612498
.6200000	.613698	.616997	.619719	.621706	.622834
.6300000	.623561	.627037	.629908	.632006	.633198
.6400000	.633431	.637092	.640119	.642332	.643591
.6500000	.643311	.647163	.650353	.652687	.654015
.6600000	.653200	.657252	.660611	.663071	.664472
.6700000	.663100	.667359	.670895	.673487	.674963
.6800000	.673011	.677486	.681205	.683935	.685491
.6899999	.682935	.687634	.691544	.694417	.696056
.7000000	.692872	.697804	.701913	.704936	.706662
.7100000	.702823	.707997	.712314	.715493	.717309
.7200000	.712789	.718214	.722748	.726089	.728000
.7300000	.722771	.728458	.733216	.736728	.738737
.7400000	.732770	.738728	.743720	.747410	.749523
.7500000	.742788	.749027	.754263	.758137	.760358
.7600000	.752824	.759356	.764845	.768913	.771247
.7700000	.762881	.769716	.775470	.779739	.782191
.7800000	.772959	.780108	.786137	.790617	.793192
.7899999	.783060	.790535	.796851	.801550	.804254

$\alpha =$ -.549999

θ	K VALUES				
	.794250555	.868696860	.928444378	.971111163	.994996249
.8000000	.793184	.800998	.807612	.812540	.815379
.8100000	.803332	.811498	.818422	.823590	.826570
.8200000	.813506	.822038	.829285	.834702	.837830
.8300000	.823708	.832618	.840201	.845879	.849161
.8400000	.833937	.843240	.851173	.857124	.860568
.8500000	.844196	.853906	.862204	.868440	.872053
.8600000	.854485	.864618	.873296	.879829	.883620
.8700000	.864806	.875378	.884452	.891295	.895272
.8799999	.875160	.886187	.895673	.902842	.907012
.8899999	.885549	.897048	.906963	.914471	.918846
.9000000	.895973	.907962	.918325	.926188	.930777
.9100000	.906434	.918931	.929760	.937995	.942809
.9200000	.916934	.929958	.941272	.949897	.954946
.9300000	.927473	.941044	.952865	.961896	.967193
.9400000	.938053	.952191	.964540	.973998	.979555
.9500000	.948675	.963402	.976302	.986206	.992037
.9600000	.959341	.974679	.988153	.998526	1.004644
.9699999	.970052	.986024	1.000096	1.010960	1.017381
.9799999	.980810	.997439	1.012136	1.023515	1.030255
.9899999	.991615	1.008927	1.024276	1.036195	1.043270
1.0000000	1.002470	1.020489	1.036519	1.049005	1.056434
1.0100000	1.013375	1.032129	1.048870	1.061951	1.069754
1.0200000	1.024332	1.043849	1.061331	1.075038	1.083235
1.0300000	1.035343	1.055650	1.073908	1.088272	1.096885
1.0400000	1.046408	1.067537	1.086604	1.101660	1.110713
1.0500000	1.057530	1.079510	1.099424	1.115207	1.124726
1.0600000	1.068709	1.091573	1.112372	1.128921	1.138932
1.0699999	1.079947	1.103729	1.125452	1.142808	1.153341
1.0799999	1.091245	1.115979	1.138670	1.156875	1.167963
1.0899999	1.102605	1.128327	1.152029	1.171131	1.182807
1.1000000	1.114028	1.140776	1.165536	1.185584	1.197884
1.1100000	1.125515	1.153327	1.179195	1.200241	1.213205
1.1200000	1.137068	1.165984	1.193011	1.215112	1.228784
1.1300000	1.148687	1.178749	1.206990	1.230206	1.244631
1.1400000	1.160373	1.191625	1.221137	1.245532	1.260762
1.1500000	1.172129	1.204614	1.235458	1.261101	1.277190
1.1600000	1.183955	1.217720	1.249959	1.276924	1.293931
1.1700000	1.195852	1.230945	1.264646	1.293012	1.311002
1.1800000	1.207821	1.244291	1.279524	1.309376	1.328421
1.1899999	1.219863	1.257762	1.294600	1.326029	1.346206

$\alpha =$ -.549999

Θ	K VALUES				
	.794250555	.868696860	.928444378	.971111163	.994996249
1.2000000	1.231979	1.271359	1.309881	1.342984	1.364378
1.2100000	1.244169	1.285084	1.325372	1.360256	1.382960
1.2200000	1.256435	1.298942	1.341080	1.377857	1.401974
1.2300000	1.268776	1.312933	1.357012	1.395804	1.421446
1.2400000	1.281194	1.327059	1.373175	1.414113	1.441405
1.2500000	1.293689	1.341323	1.389574	1.432799	1.461880
1.2599999	1.306260	1.355727	1.406218	1.451882	1.482904
1.2699999	1.318909	1.370273	1.423111	1.471379	1.504512
1.2799999	1.331635	1.384961	1.440262	1.491310	1.526743
1.2899999	1.344438	1.399793	1.457676	1.511695	1.549640
1.3000000	1.357319	1.414770	1.475359	1.532555	1.573248
1.3100000	1.370275	1.429893	1.493318	1.553913	1.597619
1.3200000	1.383307	1.445163	1.511558	1.575791	1.622808
1.3300000	1.396415	1.460579	1.530085	1.598214	1.648877
1.3400000	1.409597	1.476141	1.548904	1.621205	1.675895
1.3500000	1.422852	1.491850	1.568018	1.644791	1.703938
1.3600000	1.436179	1.507703	1.587431	1.668997	1.733091
1.3700000	1.449576	1.523700	1.607147	1.693849	1.763447
1.3799999	1.463043	1.539839	1.627167	1.719374	1.795112
1.3899999	1.476577	1.556118	1.647493	1.745597	1.828205
1.4000000	1.490175	1.572533	1.668123	1.772544	1.862859
1.4100000	1.503837	1.589082	1.689057	1.800238	1.899224
1.4200000	1.517559	1.605761	1.710291	1.828701	1.937470
1.4300000	1.531339	1.622564	1.731821	1.857952	1.977789
1.4400000	1.545175	1.639489	1.753641	1.888007	2.020397
1.4500000	1.559062	1.656528	1.775742	1.918875	2.065538
1.4600000	1.572998	1.673675	1.798114	1.950561	2.113488
1.4700000	1.586980	1.690925	1.820746	1.983062	2.164551
1.4800000	1.601004	1.708270	1.843622	2.016364	2.219062
1.4900000	1.615066	1.725703	1.866727	2.050445	2.277378
1.5000000	1.629163	1.743214	1.890042	2.085270	2.339864
1.5100000	1.643291	1.760796	1.913546	2.120790	2.406860
1.5200000	1.657445	1.778439	1.937217	2.156944	2.478637
1.5300000	1.671621	1.796134	1.961031	2.193655	2.555314
1.5400000	1.685816	1.813872	1.984961	2.230834	2.636754
1.5500000	1.700024	1.831641	2.008980	2.268379	2.722446
1.5600000	1.714241	1.849432	2.033060	2.306177	2.811417
1.5699999	1.728464	1.867234	2.057172	2.344109	2.902248
1.5707963	1.729596	1.868652	2.059093	2.347131	2.909511
1.5707963	1.729595	1.868651	2.059092	2.347130	2.909509

$\alpha = -.500000$

Θ	K VALUES				
	.009966711	.039469502	.087332193	.151646642	.229848846
.0000000	.000000	.000000	.000000	.000000	.000000
.0100000	.009999	.009999	.009999	.009999	.009999
.0200000	.019998	.019998	.019998	.019998	.019998
.0300000	.029995	.029995	.029995	.029996	.029996
.0400000	.039989	.039989	.039990	.039990	.039991
.0500000	.049979	.049980	.049981	.049982	.049984
.0600000	.059964	.059965	.059967	.059969	.059972
.0700000	.069943	.069945	.069947	.069951	.069956
.0800000	.079915	.079918	.079922	.079927	.079934
.0900000	.089880	.089883	.089889	.089897	.089906
.1000000	.099835	.099840	.099848	.099859	.099872
.1100000	.109781	.109788	.109798	.109812	.109830
.1200000	.119716	.119725	.119739	.119757	.119779
.1300000	.129640	.129651	.129668	.129692	.129720
.1400000	.139551	.139565	.139586	.139615	.139651
.1500000	.149449	.149465	.149492	.149528	.149571
.1600000	.159332	.159352	.159384	.159428	.159481
.1700000	.169200	.169224	.169263	.169315	.169378
.1800000	.179053	.179081	.179127	.179188	.179264
.1900000	.188888	.188921	.188975	.189047	.189136
.2000000	.198705	.198744	.198807	.198891	.198994
.2100000	.208504	.208549	.208621	.208719	.208838
.2200000	.218284	.218335	.218418	.218530	.218667
.2300000	.228044	.228102	.228197	.228325	.228480
.2400000	.237782	.237848	.237956	.238101	.238278
.2500000	.247499	.247574	.247695	.247859	.248058
.2600000	.257194	.257278	.257414	.257597	.257822
.2700000	.266866	.266959	.267111	.267316	.267567
.2800000	.276514	.276618	.276787	.277015	.277294
.2900000	.286137	.286252	.286440	.286693	.287003
.3000000	.295736	.295863	.296070	.296350	.296692
.3100000	.305308	.305449	.305677	.305984	.306361
.3200000	.314855	.315009	.315259	.315597	.316010
.3300000	.324375	.324543	.324816	.325186	.325638
.3400000	.333867	.334050	.334349	.334752	.335246
.3500000	.343332	.343531	.343855	.344294	.344832
.3600000	.352768	.352984	.353336	.353812	.354396
.3700000	.362175	.362409	.362790	.363305	.363938
.3800000	.371552	.371805	.372216	.372773	.373457
.3900000	.380900	.381172	.381616	.382216	.382953

$\alpha = -\ .500000$

Θ	K VALUES				
	.009966711	.039469502	.087332193	.151646642	.229848846
.4000000	.390218	.390510	.390987	.391633	.392426
.4100000	.399504	.399818	.400330	.401024	.401876
.4200000	.408760	.409096	.409645	.410388	.411302
.4300000	.417985	.418344	.418931	.419726	.420704
.4400000	.427177	.427561	.428187	.429037	.430082
.4500000	.436338	.436747	.437414	.438320	.439436
.4600000	.445466	.445901	.446612	.447576	.448764
.4700000	.454561	.455024	.455779	.456804	.458068
.4800000	.463624	.464114	.464916	.466005	.467347
.4900000	.472654	.473173	.474022	.475177	.476601
.5000000	.481650	.482200	.483098	.484321	.485830
.5100000	.490613	.491193	.492144	.493436	.495033
.5200000	.499542	.500155	.501158	.502523	.504211
.5300000	.508437	.509083	.510141	.511582	.513363
.5400000	.517298	.517979	.519093	.520611	.522490
.5500000	.526125	.526841	.528014	.529612	.531591
.5600000	.534918	.535671	.536903	.538584	.540666
.5700000	.543677	.544467	.545761	.547527	.549716
.5800000	.552402	.553230	.554588	.556441	.558740
.5900000	.561092	.561960	.563383	.565325	.567738
.6000000	.569748	.570656	.572146	.574181	.576710
.6100000	.578370	.579319	.580878	.583008	.585657
.6200000	.586957	.587949	.589579	.591806	.594578
.6300000	.595510	.596546	.598248	.600576	.603474
.6400000	.604029	.605110	.606885	.609316	.612344
.6500000	.612514	.613640	.615492	.618027	.621189
.6600000	.620965	.622138	.624067	.626710	.630008
.6700000	.629381	.630602	.632611	.635364	.638803
.6800000	.637764	.639034	.641123	.643990	.647572
.6899999	.646113	.647433	.649605	.652588	.656316
.7000000	.654429	.655799	.658057	.661157	.665036
.7100000	.662711	.664133	.666477	.669698	.673731
.7200000	.670959	.672435	.674867	.678211	.682401
.7300000	.679175	.680705	.683227	.686697	.691047
.7400000	.687358	.688943	.691556	.695154	.699669
.7500000	.695508	.697149	.699856	.703585	.708268
.7600000	.703625	.705323	.708126	.711988	.716842
.7700000	.711710	.713466	.716366	.720364	.725393
.7800000	.719763	.721579	.724577	.728713	.733920
.7899999	.727784	.729660	.732759	.737036	.742425

$\alpha = -$ •500000

θ	K VALUES				
	•009966711	•039469502	•087332193	•151646642	•229848846
•8000000	•735774	•737711	•740912	•745333	•750907
•8100000	•743733	•745731	•749036	•753603	•759366
•8200000	•751660	•753722	•757132	•761847	•767802
•8300000	•759557	•761682	•765199	•770066	•776217
•8400000	•767423	•769613	•773239	•778260	•784609
•8500000	•775259	•777515	•781252	•786428	•792980
•8600000	•783065	•785388	•789237	•794571	•801329
•8700000	•790842	•793233	•797195	•802690	•809658
•8799999	•798589	•801049	•805126	•810785	•817965
•8899999	•806308	•808837	•813031	•818856	•826252
•9000000	•813998	•816597	•820910	•826903	•834519
•9100000	•821660	•824330	•828763	•834926	•842766
•9200000	•829293	•832036	•836591	•842927	•850993
•9300000	•836900	•839716	•844393	•850905	•859200
•9400000	•844479	•847369	•852171	•858860	•867389
•9500000	•852031	•854996	•859924	•866793	•875558
•9600000	•859557	•862597	•867653	•874704	•883709
•9699999	•867057	•870173	•875359	•882594	•891842
•9799999	•874531	•877725	•883041	•890462	•899957
•9899999	•881980	•885252	•890699	•898310	•908054
1•0000000	•889404	•892754	•898336	•906137	•916134
1•0100000	•896803	•900233	•905949	•913944	•924197
1•0200000	•904178	•907689	•913541	•921731	•932243
1•0300000	•911530	•915121	•921111	•929498	•940272
1•0400000	•918858	•922531	•928660	•937247	•948286
1•0500000	•926163	•929919	•936188	•944976	•956284
1•0600000	•933445	•937285	•943695	•952687	•964266
1•0699999	•940706	•944629	•951182	•960380	•972233
1•0799999	•947944	•951952	•958649	•968055	•980186
1•0899999	•955161	•959255	•966097	•975712	•988123
1•1000000	•962358	•966538	•973526	•983353	•996047
1•1100000	•969534	•973800	•980937	•990976	1•003957
1•1200000	•976690	•981043	•988329	•998583	1•011853
1•1300000	•983826	•988268	•995703	1•006174	1•019735
1•1400000	•990943	•995473	1•003059	1•013750	1•027605
1•1500000	•998041	1•002660	1•010399	1•021310	1•035462
1•1600000	1•005120	1•009830	1•017721	1•028855	1•043307
1•1700000	1•012182	1•016982	1•025028	1•036385	1•051140
1•1800000	1•019226	1•024117	1•032318	1•043902	1•058961
1•1899999	1•026253	1•031236	1•039593	1•051404	1•066771

$\alpha = -.500000$

Θ	K VALUES				
	.009966711	.039469502	.087332193	.151646642	.229848846
1.2000000	1.033264	1.038338	1.046853	1.058893	1.074569
1.2100000	1.040258	1.045425	1.054098	1.066368	1.082357
1.2200000	1.047236	1.052496	1.061329	1.073831	1.090134
1.2300000	1.054199	1.059553	1.068545	1.081281	1.097901
1.2400000	1.061147	1.066595	1.075749	1.088719	1.105659
1.2500000	1.068080	1.073623	1.082938	1.096145	1.113406
1.2599999	1.075000	1.080637	1.090116	1.103560	1.121145
1.2699999	1.081906	1.087638	1.097280	1.110964	1.128874
1.2799999	1.088798	1.094627	1.104433	1.118357	1.136595
1.2899999	1.095678	1.101603	1.111574	1.125740	1.144307
1.3000000	1.102545	1.108567	1.118704	1.133112	1.152012
1.3100000	1.109401	1.115519	1.125823	1.140476	1.159709
1.3200000	1.116245	1.122461	1.132932	1.147830	1.167398
1.3300000	1.123078	1.129392	1.140031	1.155175	1.175080
1.3400000	1.129900	1.136312	1.147120	1.162511	1.182755
1.3500000	1.136713	1.143223	1.154200	1.169839	1.190423
1.3600000	1.143515	1.150124	1.161271	1.177160	1.198086
1.3700000	1.150308	1.157017	1.168334	1.184473	1.205742
1.3799999	1.157093	1.163900	1.175389	1.191779	1.213393
1.3899999	1.163869	1.170776	1.182436	1.199078	1.221038
1.4000000	1.170637	1.177644	1.189476	1.206370	1.228678
1.4100000	1.177398	1.184505	1.196509	1.213657	1.236313
1.4200000	1.184151	1.191359	1.203536	1.220938	1.243944
1.4300000	1.190898	1.198206	1.210557	1.228214	1.251570
1.4400000	1.197639	1.205048	1.217572	1.235484	1.259193
1.4500000	1.204374	1.211884	1.224582	1.242750	1.266812
1.4600000	1.211104	1.218715	1.231587	1.250012	1.274427
1.4700000	1.217828	1.225541	1.238587	1.257270	1.282040
1.4800000	1.224549	1.232363	1.245584	1.264524	1.289649
1.4900000	1.231265	1.239181	1.252577	1.271775	1.297256
1.5000000	1.237978	1.245995	1.259567	1.279023	1.304861
1.5100000	1.244688	1.252807	1.266554	1.286269	1.312463
1.5200000	1.251395	1.259615	1.273538	1.293513	1.320064
1.5300000	1.258099	1.266422	1.280521	1.300754	1.327664
1.5400000	1.264802	1.273227	1.287502	1.307995	1.335262
1.5500000	1.271504	1.280031	1.294482	1.315234	1.342860
1.5600000	1.278205	1.286834	1.301460	1.322472	1.350457
1.5699999	1.284905	1.293636	1.308439	1.329710	1.358054
1.5707963	1.285438	1.294178	1.308994	1.330287	1.358659
1.5707963	1.285438	1.294177	1.308994	1.330286	1.358658

$\alpha = -.500000$

θ	K VALUES				
	.318821117	.415016431	.514599755	.613601043	.708073407
.0000000	.000000	.000000	.000000	.000000	.000000
.0100000	.009999	.009999	.009999	.009999	.009999
.0200000	.019999	.019999	.019999	.019999	.019999
.0300000	.029996	.029997	.029997	.029998	.029998
.0400000	.039992	.039993	.039994	.039995	.039996
.0500000	.049985	.049987	.049989	.049991	.049993
.0600000	.059975	.059979	.059982	.059986	.059989
.0700000	.069961	.069966	.069972	.069978	.069983
.0800000	.079942	.079950	.079958	.079967	.079975
.0900000	.089917	.089929	.089941	.089953	.089964
.1000000	.099887	.099903	.099919	.099936	.099951
.1100000	.109849	.109871	.109893	.109915	.109936
.1200000	.119805	.119833	.119861	.119890	.119917
.1300000	.129752	.129788	.129824	.129860	.129895
.1400000	.139691	.139735	.139781	.139826	.139869
.1500000	.149621	.149675	.149731	.149787	.149840
.1600000	.159541	.159607	.159674	.159742	.159807
.1700000	.169451	.169529	.169611	.169692	.169769
.1800000	.179349	.179442	.179539	.179635	.179727
.1900000	.189236	.189346	.189459	.189573	.189681
.2000000	.199111	.199239	.199371	.199503	.199630
.2100000	.208974	.209121	.209274	.209427	.209574
.2200000	.218823	.218992	.219168	.219344	.219513
.2300000	.228658	.228852	.229053	.229254	.229446
.2400000	.238480	.238699	.238928	.239156	.239375
.2500000	.248286	.248534	.248792	.249050	.249298
.2600000	.258078	.258357	.258647	.258937	.259216
.2700000	.267854	.268166	.268490	.268816	.269128
.2800000	.277614	.277961	.278323	.278686	.279034
.2900000	.287357	.287743	.288145	.288548	.288935
.3000000	.297083	.297510	.297955	.298401	.298830
.3100000	.306792	.307263	.307754	.308246	.308720
.3200000	.316484	.317001	.317540	.318082	.318604
.3300000	.326157	.326724	.327315	.327909	.328482
.3400000	.335812	.336431	.337078	.337728	.338355
.3500000	.345449	.346123	.346828	.347537	.348222
.3600000	.355066	.355799	.356566	.357338	.358083
.3700000	.364664	.365459	.366292	.367130	.367939
.3800000	.374243	.375103	.376004	.376912	.377790
.3900000	.383801	.384730	.385704	.386686	.387636

$\alpha =$ - •500000

Θ	K VALUES				
	•318821117	•415016431	•514599755	•613601043	•708073407
•4000000	•393340	•394340	•395391	•396451	•397477
•4100000	•402858	•403934	•405065	•406207	•407313
•4200000	•412356	•413511	•414726	•415954	•417144
•4300000	•421833	•423071	•424375	•425693	•426971
•4400000	•431289	•432614	•434010	•435422	•436794
•4500000	•440724	•442140	•443632	•445144	•446613
•4600000	•450138	•451648	•453242	•454857	•456428
•4700000	•459530	•461139	•462838	•464562	•466240
•4800000	•468901	•470613	•472422	•474259	•476049
•4900000	•478251	•480069	•481993	•483948	•485855
•5000000	•487579	•489508	•491551	•493629	•495658
•5100000	•496885	•498930	•501097	•503303	•505459
•5200000	•506169	•508334	•510630	•512970	•515259
•5300000	•515432	•517721	•520151	•522629	•525057
•5400000	•524673	•527091	•529659	•532282	•534854
•5500000	•533892	•536443	•539156	•541929	•544651
•5600000	•543090	•545778	•548640	•551570	•554448
•5700000	•552265	•555097	•558113	•561204	•564245
•5800000	•561419	•564398	•567575	•570833	•574042
•5900000	•570552	•573682	•577025	•580457	•583842
•6000000	•579663	•582950	•586464	•590077	•593643
•6100000	•588752	•592201	•595892	•599691	•603446
•6200000	•597820	•601436	•605310	•609302	•613253
•6300000	•606866	•610654	•614717	•618909	•623062
•6400000	•615891	•619856	•624114	•628513	•632876
•6500000	•624895	•629043	•633501	•638113	•642695
•6600000	•633878	•638214	•642879	•647711	•652519
•6700000	•642841	•647369	•652248	•657308	•662348
•6800000	•651782	•656508	•661607	•666902	•672184
•6899999	•660703	•665633	•670958	•676495	•682028
•7000000	•669604	•674743	•680301	•686088	•691879
•7100000	•678485	•683838	•689635	•695681	•701738
•7200000	•687345	•692919	•698962	•705273	•711607
•7300000	•696186	•701985	•708282	•714867	•721486
•7400000	•705007	•711038	•717595	•724462	•731375
•7500000	•713809	•720077	•726901	•734058	•741275
•7600000	•722591	•729103	•736200	•743657	•751188
•7700000	•731355	•738115	•745494	•753258	•761113
•7800000	•740100	•747115	•754782	•762863	•771052
•7899999	•748826	•756102	•764066	•772471	•781005

$\alpha = -.500000$

Θ	K VALUES				
	.318821117	.415016431	.514599755	.613601043	.708073407
.8000000	.757534	.765077	.773344	.782084	.790974
.8100000	.766224	.774039	.782618	.791702	.800958
.8200000	.774897	.782990	.791888	.801325	.810959
.8300000	.783552	.791930	.801154	.810954	.820977
.8400000	.792189	.800859	.810417	.820589	.831014
.8500000	.800810	.809776	.819677	.830232	.841069
.8600000	.809414	.818684	.828934	.839882	.851145
.8700000	.818002	.827581	.838190	.849541	.861241
.8799999	.826573	.836468	.847443	.859208	.871360
.8899999	.835129	.845345	.856695	.868884	.881500
.9000000	.843669	.854213	.865947	.878570	.891664
.9100000	.852193	.863073	.875198	.888266	.901852
.9200000	.860703	.871923	.884448	.897974	.912065
.9300000	.869198	.880765	.893699	.907692	.922303
.9400000	.877678	.889599	.902950	.917423	.932569
.9500000	.886144	.898426	.912202	.927166	.942862
.9600000	.894596	.907244	.921455	.936922	.953183
.9699999	.903035	.916056	.930710	.946692	.963533
.9799999	.911460	.924861	.939967	.956475	.973913
.9899999	.919873	.933659	.949227	.966273	.984324
1.0000000	.928272	.942450	.958489	.976086	.994767
1.0100000	.936659	.951236	.967753	.985915	1.005242
1.0200000	.945034	.960016	.977022	.995759	1.015750
1.0300000	.953397	.968791	.986294	1.005620	1.026293
1.0400000	.961748	.977560	.995569	1.015498	1.036870
1.0500000	.970088	.986324	1.004849	1.025393	1.047482
1.0600000	.978417	.995084	1.014134	1.035306	1.058131
1.0699999	.986736	1.003840	1.023423	1.045236	1.068816
1.0799999	.995043	1.012591	1.032718	1.055185	1.079539
1.0899999	1.003341	1.021338	1.042018	1.065153	1.090301
1.1000000	1.011628	1.030082	1.051323	1.075140	1.101101
1.1100000	1.019906	1.038822	1.060634	1.085147	1.111940
1.1200000	1.028175	1.047559	1.069952	1.095173	1.122820
1.1300000	1.036434	1.056293	1.079275	1.105219	1.133740
1.1400000	1.044684	1.065025	1.088605	1.115286	1.144702
1.1500000	1.052926	1.073753	1.097942	1.125372	1.155705
1.1600000	1.061160	1.082480	1.107285	1.135480	1.166749
1.1700000	1.069385	1.091204	1.116635	1.145609	1.177836
1.1800000	1.077603	1.099927	1.125992	1.155758	1.188966
1.1899999	1.085813	1.108647	1.135357	1.165929	1.200139

$\alpha = - .500000$

Θ	K VALUES				
	.318821117	.415016431	.514599755	.613601043	.708073407
1.2000000	1.094015	1.117366	1.144729	1.176120	1.211355
1.2100000	1.102211	1.126084	1.154108	1.186333	1.222614
1.2200000	1.110400	1.134800	1.163495	1.196568	1.233917
1.2300000	1.118582	1.143516	1.172889	1.206823	1.245263
1.2400000	1.126757	1.152230	1.182291	1.217100	1.256653
1.2500000	1.134927	1.160943	1.191700	1.227398	1.268086
1.2599999	1.143091	1.169656	1.201117	1.237717	1.279563
1.2699999	1.151249	1.178368	1.210542	1.248057	1.291083
1.2799999	1.159401	1.187080	1.219974	1.258417	1.302645
1.2899999	1.167548	1.195792	1.229413	1.268799	1.314251
1.3000000	1.175690	1.204503	1.238860	1.279200	1.325898
1.3100000	1.183828	1.213214	1.248315	1.289621	1.337587
1.3200000	1.191960	1.221924	1.257776	1.300062	1.349317
1.3300000	1.200089	1.230635	1.267245	1.310522	1.361087
1.3400000	1.208213	1.239346	1.276721	1.321001	1.372897
1.3500000	1.216333	1.248057	1.286204	1.331498	1.384746
1.3600000	1.224449	1.256768	1.295693	1.342013	1.396633
1.3700000	1.232562	1.265480	1.305189	1.352546	1.408556
1.3799999	1.240671	1.274191	1.314692	1.363095	1.420516
1.3899999	1.248777	1.282903	1.324200	1.373661	1.432510
1.4000000	1.256880	1.291615	1.333714	1.384243	1.444538
1.4100000	1.264980	1.300328	1.343234	1.394839	1.456597
1.4200000	1.273078	1.309041	1.352760	1.405450	1.468688
1.4300000	1.281172	1.317754	1.362290	1.416074	1.480808
1.4400000	1.289265	1.326467	1.371826	1.426711	1.492955
1.4500000	1.297355	1.335181	1.381366	1.437360	1.505129
1.4600000	1.305444	1.343895	1.390910	1.448020	1.517327
1.4700000	1.313530	1.352610	1.400458	1.458691	1.529547
1.4800000	1.321615	1.361325	1.410010	1.469371	1.541789
1.4900000	1.329699	1.370040	1.419565	1.480060	1.554049
1.5000000	1.337781	1.378755	1.429124	1.490757	1.566326
1.5100000	1.345862	1.387471	1.438684	1.501461	1.578618
1.5200000	1.353942	1.396187	1.448247	1.512170	1.590924
1.5300000	1.362021	1.404903	1.457812	1.522885	1.603240
1.5400000	1.370100	1.413619	1.467379	1.533603	1.615564
1.5500000	1.378178	1.422335	1.476946	1.544325	1.627896
1.5600000	1.386256	1.431051	1.486515	1.555048	1.640232
1.5699999	1.394333	1.439768	1.496083	1.565773	1.652570
1.5707963	1.394976	1.440462	1.496845	1.566627	1.653553
1.5707963	1.394976	1.440461	1.496845	1.566626	1.653552

$\alpha = - .500000$

Θ	K VALUES				
	.794250555	.868696860	.928444378	.971111163	.994996249
.0000000	.000000	.000000	.000000	.000000	.000000
.0100000	.009999	.009999	.009999	.010000	.010000
.0200000	.019999	.019999	.019999	.019999	.020000
.0300000	.029999	.029999	.029999	.029999	.029999
.0400000	.039997	.039998	.039999	.039999	.039999
.0500000	.049995	.049997	.049998	.049999	.049999
.0600000	.059992	.059995	.059997	.059999	.059999
.0700000	.069988	.069992	.069996	.069998	.069999
.0800000	.079982	.079989	.079994	.079997	.079999
.0900000	.089975	.089984	.089991	.089996	.089999
.1000000	.099966	.099978	.099988	.099995	.099999
.1100000	.109955	.109971	.109985	.109994	.110000
.1200000	.119942	.119963	.119981	.119993	.120000
.1300000	.129927	.129954	.129976	.129992	.130000
.1400000	.139909	.139943	.139971	.139990	.140001
.1500000	.149889	.149931	.149965	.149989	.150002
.1600000	.159866	.159917	.159958	.159987	.160004
.1700000	.169840	.169902	.169951	.169986	.170006
.1800000	.179812	.179885	.179943	.179985	.180009
.1900000	.189780	.189866	.189935	.189984	.190012
.2000000	.199745	.199846	.199926	.199984	.200016
.2100000	.209708	.209824	.209918	.209984	.210022
.2200000	.219667	.219801	.219908	.219985	.220029
.2300000	.229623	.229776	.229899	.229987	.230037
.2400000	.239576	.239750	.239890	.239990	.240047
.2500000	.249525	.249722	.249881	.249995	.250058
.2600000	.259471	.259693	.259872	.260000	.260072
.2700000	.269414	.269663	.269864	.270008	.270088
.2800000	.279354	.279632	.279857	.280017	.280107
.2900000	.289291	.289600	.289850	.290029	.290129
.3000000	.299225	.299568	.299845	.300043	.300155
.3100000	.309156	.309535	.309841	.310061	.310184
.3200000	.319084	.319501	.319839	.320081	.320217
.3300000	.329009	.329468	.329839	.330105	.330255
.3400000	.338932	.339435	.339841	.340133	.340297
.3500000	.348852	.349402	.349847	.350166	.350346
.3600000	.358770	.359370	.359855	.360204	.360400
.3700000	.368687	.369339	.369867	.370247	.370460
.3800000	.378601	.379309	.379883	.380295	.380527
.3900000	.388514	.389281	.389903	.390351	.390602

$\alpha = -$ •500000

Θ	K VALUES				
	•794250555	•868696860	•928444378	•971111163	•994996249
•4000000	•398426	•399255	•399928	•400413	•400685
•4100000	•408337	•409232	•409959	•410483	•410777
•4200000	•418247	•419212	•419996	•420560	•420878
•4300000	•428157	•429195	•430039	•430647	•430990
•4400000	•438067	•439182	•440089	•440743	•441112
•4500000	•447977	•449174	•450147	•450850	•451246
•4600000	•457888	•459170	•460214	•460967	•461392
•4700000	•467801	•469172	•470289	•471096	•471552
•4800000	•477715	•479180	•480375	•481238	•481725
•4900000	•487631	•489195	•490471	•491393	•491914
•5000000	•497550	•499217	•500578	•501562	•502118
•5100000	•507472	•509247	•510697	•511747	•512340
•5200000	•517397	•519285	•520829	•521947	•522579
•5300000	•527327	•529333	•530975	•532164	•532837
•5400000	•537262	•539391	•541135	•542400	•543115
•5500000	•547202	•549460	•551311	•552655	•553415
•5600000	•557148	•559540	•561503	•562929	•563737
•5700000	•567100	•569633	•571713	•573226	•574082
•5800000	•577060	•579740	•581942	•583544	•584452
•5900000	•587027	•589860	•592190	•593887	•594849
•6000000	•597004	•599996	•602459	•604254	•605273
•6100000	•606989	•610147	•612750	•614648	•615726
•6200000	•616985	•620316	•623064	•625070	•626209
•6300000	•626992	•630502	•633402	•635520	•636724
•6400000	•637010	•640708	•643766	•646001	•647273
•6500000	•647041	•650933	•654156	•656515	•657857
•6600000	•657085	•661180	•664575	•667061	•668477
•6700000	•667143	•671449	•675023	•677643	•679136
•6800000	•677216	•681741	•685502	•688262	•689836
•6899999	•687305	•692058	•696013	•698919	•700577
•7000000	•697411	•702401	•706559	•709617	•711363
•7100000	•707535	•712771	•717140	•720357	•722195
•7200000	•717677	•723169	•727758	•731141	•733076
•7300000	•727840	•733597	•738415	•741971	•744006
•7400000	•738023	•744056	•749112	•752849	•754989
•7500000	•748227	•754547	•759852	•763777	•766028
•7600000	•758455	•765072	•770636	•774758	•777123
•7700000	•768706	•775633	•781465	•785793	•788279
•7800000	•778982	•786230	•792343	•796885	•799497
•7899999	•789284	•796865	•803270	•808037	•810780

$\alpha = -.500000$

Θ	K VALUES				
	.794250555	.868696860	.928444378	.971111163	.994996249
.8000000	.799614	.807541	.814250	.819250	.822131
.8100000	.809972	.818257	.825283	.830528	.833552
.8200000	.820359	.829017	.836373	.841872	.845048
.8300000	.830777	.839822	.847521	.853287	.856620
.8400000	.841227	.850673	.858730	.864774	.868272
.8500000	.851710	.861572	.870002	.876337	.880008
.8600000	.862227	.872522	.881340	.887979	.891831
.8700000	.872780	.883523	.892746	.899703	.903745
.8799999	.883370	.894579	.904223	.911512	.915753
.8899999	.893998	.905690	.915773	.923409	.927860
.9000000	.904665	.916858	.927400	.935400	.940069
.9100000	.915374	.928087	.939105	.947486	.952385
.9200000	.926124	.939377	.950893	.959672	.964812
.9300000	.936918	.950731	.962765	.971961	.977356
.9400000	.947757	.962151	.974726	.984359	.990020
.9500000	.958642	.973639	.986778	.996869	1.002810
.9600000	.969574	.985198	.998926	1.009496	1.015732
.9699999	.980556	.996829	1.011171	1.022245	1.028791
.9799999	.991588	1.008535	1.023518	1.035120	1.041993
.9899999	1.002672	1.020319	1.035971	1.048127	1.055344
1.0000000	1.013809	1.032183	1.048533	1.061270	1.068851
1.0100000	1.025000	1.044128	1.061207	1.074556	1.082520
1.0200000	1.036248	1.056158	1.074000	1.087990	1.096358
1.0300000	1.047553	1.068276	1.086913	1.101579	1.110374
1.0400000	1.058917	1.080483	1.099952	1.115327	1.124575
1.0500000	1.070342	1.092782	1.113120	1.129243	1.138969
1.0600000	1.081828	1.105177	1.126424	1.143334	1.153566
1.0699999	1.093377	1.117669	1.139866	1.157605	1.168374
1.0799999	1.104990	1.130261	1.153452	1.172065	1.183403
1.0899999	1.116669	1.142956	1.167187	1.186722	1.198664
1.1000000	1.128416	1.155757	1.181077	1.201584	1.214168
1.1100000	1.140230	1.168666	1.195125	1.216659	1.229927
1.1200000	1.152115	1.181687	1.209338	1.231957	1.245953
1.1300000	1.164070	1.194821	1.223721	1.247487	1.262259
1.1400000	1.176097	1.208072	1.238281	1.263260	1.278859
1.1500000	1.188197	1.221442	1.253021	1.279286	1.295769
1.1600000	1.200372	1.234935	1.267950	1.295575	1.313004
1.1700000	1.212622	1.248552	1.283072	1.312140	1.330582
1.1800000	1.224949	1.262297	1.298395	1.328993	1.348520
1.1899999	1.237352	1.276172	1.313924	1.346146	1.366839

$\alpha =$ - .500000

Θ	K VALUES				
	.794250555	.868696860	.928444378	.971111163	.994996249
1.2000000	1.249834	1.290179	1.329666	1.363614	1.385561
1.2100000	1.262394	1.304322	1.345627	1.381409	1.404706
1.2200000	1.275034	1.318602	1.361815	1.399548	1.424301
1.2300000	1.287755	1.333022	1.378236	1.418046	1.444371
1.2400000	1.300555	1.347584	1.394897	1.436919	1.464945
1.2500000	1.313437	1.362291	1.411805	1.456184	1.486054
1.2599999	1.326400	1.377143	1.428966	1.475861	1.507732
1.2699999	1.339444	1.392143	1.446387	1.495967	1.530016
1.2799999	1.352569	1.407292	1.464076	1.516524	1.552945
1.2899999	1.365776	1.422591	1.482039	1.537551	1.576563
1.3000000	1.379064	1.438042	1.500282	1.559072	1.600918
1.3100000	1.392432	1.453646	1.518812	1.581108	1.626063
1.3200000	1.405880	1.469402	1.537633	1.603684	1.652055
1.3300000	1.419406	1.485312	1.556753	1.626824	1.678958
1.3400000	1.433011	1.501374	1.576175	1.650553	1.706844
1.3500000	1.446693	1.517588	1.595905	1.674898	1.735790
1.3600000	1.460451	1.533954	1.615945	1.699886	1.765884
1.3700000	1.474282	1.550469	1.636300	1.725544	1.797223
1.3799999	1.488186	1.567132	1.656970	1.751897	1.829917
1.3899999	1.502161	1.583941	1.677958	1.778974	1.864087
1.4000000	1.516204	1.600892	1.699262	1.806801	1.899873
1.4100000	1.530312	1.617982	1.720880	1.835401	1.937428
1.4200000	1.544484	1.635208	1.742811	1.864797	1.976928
1.4300000	1.558717	1.652564	1.765048	1.895010	2.018572
1.4400000	1.573008	1.670045	1.787587	1.926054	2.062582
1.4500000	1.587353	1.687646	1.810416	1.957940	2.109213
1.4600000	1.601750	1.705360	1.833528	1.990673	2.158747
1.4700000	1.616194	1.723181	1.856908	2.024249	2.211500
1.4800000	1.630683	1.741100	1.880542	2.058655	2.267816
1.4900000	1.645212	1.759111	1.904414	2.093866	2.328067
1.5000000	1.659777	1.777204	1.928503	2.129847	2.392627
1.5100000	1.674374	1.795370	1.952788	2.166548	2.461850
1.5200000	1.688999	1.813600	1.977247	2.203905	2.536015
1.5300000	1.703647	1.831884	2.001853	2.241838	2.615244
1.5400000	1.718314	1.850212	2.026580	2.280255	2.699397
1.5500000	1.732996	1.868574	2.051400	2.319050	2.787943
1.5600000	1.747687	1.886958	2.076282	2.358108	2.879880
1.5699999	1.762384	1.905353	2.101198	2.397305	2.973738
1.5707963	1.763554	1.906818	2.103183	2.400428	2.981243
1.5707963	1.763553	1.906817	2.103181	2.400426	2.981241

$\alpha = -.449999$

Θ	K VALUES				
	.009966711	.039469502	.087332193	.151646642	.229848846
.0000000	.000000	.000000	.000000	.000000	.000000
.0100000	.009999	.009999	.009999	.009999	.009999
.0200000	.019998	.019998	.019998	.019999	.019999
.0300000	.029996	.029996	.029996	.029996	.029997
.0400000	.039990	.039990	.039991	.039992	.039992
.0500000	.049981	.049982	.049983	.049984	.049986
.0600000	.059968	.059969	.059970	.059973	.059975
.0700000	.069949	.069950	.069953	.069957	.069961
.0800000	.079924	.079926	.079930	.079936	.079943
.0900000	.089892	.089895	.089901	.089909	.089918
.1000000	.099852	.099857	.099865	.099875	.099888
.1100000	.109803	.109810	.109820	.109834	.109852
.1200000	.119745	.119753	.119767	.119785	.119808
.1300000	.129676	.129687	.129704	.129728	.129756
.1400000	.139596	.139610	.139631	.139660	.139696
.1500000	.149504	.149521	.149547	.149583	.149627
.1600000	.159399	.159419	.159451	.159495	.159548
.1700000	.169281	.169304	.169343	.169395	.169459
.1800000	.179147	.179176	.179222	.179283	.179359
.1900000	.188999	.189032	.189086	.189159	.189247
.2000000	.198835	.198873	.198936	.199021	.199124
.2100000	.208654	.208698	.208771	.208869	.208988
.2200000	.218455	.218506	.218590	.218702	.218839
.2300000	.228238	.228297	.228392	.228520	.228676
.2400000	.238003	.238069	.238177	.238322	.238499
.2500000	.247748	.247823	.247944	.248108	.248308
.2600000	.257472	.257556	.257693	.257877	.258101
.2700000	.267176	.267270	.267423	.267628	.267879
.2800000	.276859	.276963	.277133	.277361	.277641
.2900000	.286519	.286635	.286823	.287076	.287387
.3000000	.296157	.296284	.296492	.296772	.297115
.3100000	.305771	.305911	.306140	.306449	.306826
.3200000	.315361	.315515	.315766	.316105	.316520
.3300000	.324928	.325096	.325370	.325741	.326195
.3400000	.334469	.334653	.334952	.335356	.335852
.3500000	.343985	.344185	.344510	.344950	.345490
.3600000	.353475	.353692	.354045	.354523	.355109
.3700000	.362939	.363173	.363556	.364073	.364708
.3800000	.372375	.372629	.373042	.373601	.374288
.3900000	.381785	.382058	.382504	.383107	.383847

$\alpha =$ - .449999

θ	K VALUES				
	.009966711	.039469502	.087332193	.151646642	.229848846
.4000000	.391167	.391461	.391940	.392589	.393386
.4100000	.400522	.400837	.401351	.402048	.402904
.4200000	.409847	.410185	.410736	.411483	.412402
.4300000	.419145	.419506	.420096	.420895	.421878
.4400000	.428413	.428799	.429428	.430282	.431333
.4500000	.437652	.438063	.438734	.439645	.440766
.4600000	.446861	.447298	.448013	.448983	.450178
.4700000	.456040	.456505	.457265	.458296	.459568
.4800000	.465190	.465683	.466489	.467585	.468936
.4900000	.474309	.474831	.475686	.476848	.478281
.5000000	.483397	.483950	.484855	.486085	.487604
.5100000	.492455	.493039	.493996	.495297	.496905
.5200000	.501481	.502099	.503109	.504484	.506183
.5300000	.510477	.511128	.512193	.513644	.515439
.5400000	.519441	.520127	.521250	.522779	.524671
.5500000	.528374	.529096	.530277	.531887	.533882
.5600000	.537276	.538034	.539276	.540970	.543069
.5700000	.546146	.546942	.548247	.550026	.552233
.5800000	.554985	.555819	.557188	.559057	.561375
.5900000	.563791	.564666	.566101	.568061	.570494
.6000000	.572567	.573482	.574985	.577039	.579590
.6100000	.581310	.582268	.583841	.585990	.588663
.6200000	.590022	.591023	.592667	.594916	.597713
.6300000	.598702	.599747	.601465	.603815	.606741
.6400000	.607350	.608441	.610233	.612688	.615746
.6500000	.615966	.617104	.618974	.621535	.624728
.6600000	.624551	.625736	.627685	.630356	.633688
.6700000	.633105	.634339	.636368	.639151	.642625
.6800000	.641627	.642910	.645022	.647920	.651540
.6899999	.650117	.651452	.653648	.656663	.660432
.7000000	.658577	.659963	.662245	.665380	.669303
.7100000	.667005	.668444	.670815	.674072	.678151
.7200000	.675402	.676895	.679356	.682739	.686978
.7300000	.683769	.685317	.687869	.691380	.695783
.7400000	.692105	.693709	.696354	.699996	.704566
.7500000	.700410	.702071	.704812	.708587	.713328
.7600000	.708684	.710404	.713242	.717153	.722069
.7700000	.716929	.718708	.721644	.725694	.730788
.7800000	.725144	.726983	.730020	.734211	.739487
.7899999	.733329	.735229	.738369	.742704	.748165

$\alpha = -\ .449999$

Θ	K VALUES				
	.009966711	.039469502	.087332193	.151646642	.229848846
.8000000	.741484	.743447	.746691	.751172	.756822
.8100000	.749610	.751636	.754986	.759616	.765459
.8200000	.757707	.759797	.763255	.768037	.774076
.8300000	.765775	.767931	.771498	.776434	.782673
.8400000	.773814	.776037	.779715	.784808	.791251
.8500000	.781826	.784115	.787906	.793159	.799809
.8600000	.789809	.792166	.796072	.801487	.808347
.8700000	.797764	.800191	.804213	.809793	.816867
.8799999	.805692	.808189	.812329	.818076	.825368
.8899999	.813592	.816161	.820421	.826337	.833850
.9000000	.821466	.824107	.828488	.834576	.842315
.9100000	.829313	.832027	.836531	.842794	.850761
.9200000	.837134	.839921	.844550	.850990	.859189
.9300000	.844929	.847791	.852546	.859166	.867600
.9400000	.852698	.855636	.860519	.867320	.875994
.9500000	.860442	.863456	.868469	.875455	.884370
.9600000	.868161	.871253	.876396	.883569	.892730
.9699999	.875855	.879025	.884301	.891663	.901074
.9799999	.883524	.886774	.892184	.899737	.909401
.9899999	.891170	.894500	.900045	.907792	.917713
1.0000000	.898793	.902203	.907885	.915829	.926008
1.0100000	.906391	.909884	.915704	.923846	.934289
1.0200000	.913967	.917543	.923503	.931845	.942554
1.0300000	.921521	.925180	.931281	.939826	.950804
1.0400000	.929052	.932795	.939039	.947789	.959040
1.0500000	.936562	.940389	.946778	.955735	.967262
1.0600000	.944050	.947963	.954497	.963664	.975469
1.0699999	.951517	.955517	.962197	.971575	.983663
1.0799999	.958963	.963050	.969879	.979470	.991844
1.0899999	.966389	.970564	.977542	.987349	1.000011
1.1000000	.973795	.978059	.985188	.995213	1.008166
1.1100000	.981182	.985535	.992815	1.003060	1.016308
1.1200000	.988549	.992992	1.000426	1.010892	1.024437
1.1300000	.995898	1.000431	1.008020	1.018709	1.032555
1.1400000	1.003229	1.007853	1.015597	1.026512	1.040661
1.1500000	1.010541	1.015257	1.023158	1.034300	1.048755
1.1600000	1.017836	1.022645	1.030703	1.042075	1.056838
1.1700000	1.025113	1.030016	1.038233	1.049836	1.064911
1.1800000	1.032374	1.037370	1.045748	1.057583	1.072973
1.1899999	1.039619	1.044709	1.053248	1.065318	1.081024

$\alpha = -\ .449999$

Θ	K VALUES				
	.009966711	.039469502	.087332193	.151646642	.229848846
1.2000000	1.046848	1.052033	1.060734	1.073040	1.089065
1.2100000	1.054061	1.059341	1.068206	1.080749	1.097097
1.2200000	1.061259	1.066636	1.075665	1.088447	1.105119
1.2300000	1.068442	1.073915	1.083110	1.096133	1.113132
1.2400000	1.075611	1.081181	1.090542	1.103807	1.121136
1.2500000	1.082766	1.088434	1.097962	1.111471	1.129131
1.2599999	1.089908	1.095674	1.105369	1.119124	1.137118
1.2699999	1.097037	1.102901	1.112765	1.126767	1.145097
1.2799999	1.104152	1.110116	1.120150	1.134399	1.153068
1.2899999	1.111256	1.117319	1.127523	1.142022	1.161032
1.3000000	1.118348	1.124510	1.134886	1.149636	1.168988
1.3100000	1.125428	1.131691	1.142239	1.157241	1.176937
1.3200000	1.132498	1.138861	1.149582	1.164837	1.184879
1.3300000	1.139557	1.146021	1.156915	1.172425	1.192815
1.3400000	1.146605	1.153171	1.164240	1.180004	1.200745
1.3500000	1.153644	1.160312	1.171555	1.187576	1.208669
1.3600000	1.160674	1.167443	1.178862	1.195141	1.216587
1.3700000	1.167695	1.174566	1.186161	1.202699	1.224499
1.3799999	1.174707	1.181681	1.193453	1.210250	1.232407
1.3899999	1.181711	1.188789	1.200737	1.217795	1.240309
1.4000000	1.188708	1.195888	1.208015	1.225334	1.248207
1.4100000	1.195697	1.202981	1.215286	1.232867	1.256101
1.4200000	1.202679	1.210068	1.222551	1.240395	1.263990
1.4300000	1.209656	1.217148	1.229810	1.247918	1.271876
1.4400000	1.216626	1.224222	1.237064	1.255436	1.279758
1.4500000	1.223590	1.231291	1.244313	1.262950	1.287637
1.4600000	1.230550	1.238355	1.251558	1.270459	1.295512
1.4700000	1.237505	1.245415	1.258798	1.277966	1.303385
1.4800000	1.244455	1.252471	1.266034	1.285468	1.311255
1.4900000	1.251402	1.259522	1.273267	1.292968	1.319123
1.5000000	1.258346	1.266571	1.280497	1.300465	1.326989
1.5100000	1.265286	1.273617	1.287724	1.307960	1.334853
1.5200000	1.272224	1.280660	1.294949	1.315453	1.342716
1.5300000	1.279159	1.287701	1.302172	1.322944	1.350577
1.5400000	1.286093	1.294740	1.309394	1.330434	1.358437
1.5500000	1.293026	1.301779	1.316614	1.337923	1.366297
1.5600000	1.299958	1.308816	1.323833	1.345411	1.374155
1.5699999	1.306889	1.315853	1.331052	1.352898	1.382014
1.5707963	1.307441	1.316413	1.331627	1.353495	1.382640
1.5707963	1.307440	1.316413	1.331627	1.353494	1.382639

$\alpha = -\ .449999$

Θ	K VALUES				
	.318821117	.415016431	.514599755	.613601043	.708073407
.0000000	.000000	.000000	.000000	.000000	.000000
.0100000	.009999	.009999	.009999	.009999	.009999
.0200000	.019999	.019999	.019999	.019999	.019999
.0300000	.029997	.029997	.029998	.029998	.029999
.0400000	.039993	.039994	.039995	.039996	.039997
.0500000	.049987	.049989	.049992	.049994	.049996
.0600000	.059979	.059982	.059986	.059989	.059993
.0700000	.069966	.069972	.069978	.069983	.069989
.0800000	.079950	.079958	.079967	.079975	.079983
.0900000	.089929	.089941	.089953	.089965	.089977
.1000000	.099903	.099919	.099936	.099952	.099968
.1100000	.109871	.109893	.109915	.109937	.109958
.1200000	.119833	.119861	.119890	.119918	.119946
.1300000	.129789	.129824	.129860	.129897	.129931
.1400000	.139737	.139780	.139826	.139871	.139915
.1500000	.149677	.149731	.149786	.149842	.149896
.1600000	.159608	.159674	.159742	.159809	.159874
.1700000	.169531	.169610	.169691	.169772	.169850
.1800000	.179445	.179538	.179634	.179731	.179823
.1900000	.189348	.189458	.189571	.189684	.189793
.2000000	.199241	.199369	.199501	.199634	.199760
.2100000	.209124	.209271	.209425	.209578	.209724
.2200000	.218995	.219164	.219341	.219517	.219686
.2300000	.228854	.229048	.229249	.229451	.229643
.2400000	.238702	.238921	.239150	.239379	.239598
.2500000	.248536	.248785	.249043	.249302	.249550
.2600000	.258358	.258637	.258928	.259219	.259498
.2700000	.268166	.268479	.268805	.269130	.269443
.2800000	.277961	.278309	.278672	.279036	.279385
.2900000	.287742	.288128	.288532	.288935	.289324
.3000000	.297508	.297935	.298382	.298829	.299259
.3100000	.307259	.307730	.308223	.308716	.309192
.3200000	.316995	.317513	.318055	.318598	.319121
.3300000	.326716	.327283	.327877	.328473	.329047
.3400000	.336420	.337041	.337690	.338342	.338971
.3500000	.346109	.346786	.347493	.348205	.348891
.3600000	.355782	.356517	.357287	.358062	.358810
.3700000	.365437	.366235	.367071	.367912	.368725
.3800000	.375077	.375940	.376845	.377757	.378638
.3900000	.384699	.385631	.386609	.387595	.388549

$\alpha = -.449999$

θ	K VALUES				
	.318821117	.415016431	.514599755	.613601043	.708073407
.4000000	.394303	.395308	.396363	.397428	.398459
.4100000	.403891	.404972	.406108	.407255	.408366
.4200000	.413460	.414621	.415842	.417076	.418272
.4300000	.423012	.424257	.425567	.426891	.428176
.4400000	.432546	.433878	.435281	.436701	.438080
.4500000	.442061	.443485	.444986	.446506	.447983
.4600000	.451559	.453078	.454681	.456305	.457885
.4700000	.461038	.462657	.464366	.466099	.467788
.4800000	.470499	.472221	.474041	.475889	.477690
.4900000	.479941	.481771	.483706	.485674	.487593
.5000000	.489364	.491307	.493363	.495454	.497497
.5100000	.498769	.500828	.503009	.505231	.507402
.5200000	.508155	.510335	.512647	.515003	.517308
.5300000	.517522	.519828	.522275	.524772	.527217
.5400000	.526871	.529306	.531894	.534537	.537128
.5500000	.536201	.538771	.541505	.544299	.547043
.5600000	.545512	.548221	.551106	.554059	.556960
.5700000	.554804	.557658	.560699	.563816	.566882
.5800000	.564077	.567081	.570284	.573571	.576807
.5900000	.573332	.576489	.579861	.583324	.586738
.6000000	.582568	.585885	.589430	.593076	.596674
.6100000	.591786	.595267	.598992	.602826	.606616
.6200000	.600985	.604635	.608545	.612576	.616564
.6300000	.610165	.613990	.618092	.622325	.626519
.6400000	.619328	.623332	.627632	.632075	.636482
.6500000	.628472	.632661	.637165	.641825	.646454
.6600000	.637598	.641978	.646692	.651575	.656433
.6700000	.646706	.651282	.656213	.661327	.666423
.6800000	.655796	.660573	.665728	.671081	.676422
.6899999	.664868	.669853	.675237	.680837	.686433
.7000000	.673923	.679120	.684742	.690596	.696454
.7100000	.682960	.688376	.694241	.700358	.706488
.7200000	.691980	.697620	.703736	.710124	.716534
.7300000	.700983	.706853	.713227	.719893	.726594
.7400000	.709969	.716075	.722714	.729667	.736668
.7500000	.718939	.725286	.732197	.739446	.746757
.7600000	.727891	.734487	.741677	.749231	.756862
.7700000	.736828	.743677	.751154	.759022	.766983
.7800000	.745748	.752857	.760629	.768819	.777121
.7899999	.754652	.762028	.770101	.778624	.787277

$\alpha = -\ .449999$

Θ	K VALUES				
	.318821117	.415016431	.514599755	.613601043	.708073407
.8000000	.763541	.771188	.779572	.788436	.797452
.8100000	.772414	.780340	.789041	.798256	.807647
.8200000	.781272	.789482	.798509	.808085	.817862
.8300000	.790115	.798616	.807976	.817923	.828097
.8400000	.798943	.807741	.817443	.827771	.838355
.8500000	.807756	.816858	.826910	.837629	.848636
.8600000	.816555	.825967	.836377	.847498	.858940
.8700000	.825340	.835069	.845845	.857378	.869268
.8799999	.834111	.844163	.855315	.867270	.879622
.8899999	.842869	.853250	.864785	.877175	.890001
.9000000	.851613	.862330	.874257	.887092	.900408
.9100000	.860343	.871403	.883732	.897023	.910842
.9200000	.869061	.880471	.893209	.906968	.921305
.9300000	.877767	.889532	.902689	.916927	.931798
.9400000	.886460	.898587	.912172	.926902	.942320
.9500000	.895140	.907637	.921659	.936892	.952874
.9600000	.903809	.916682	.931149	.946898	.963460
.9699999	.912466	.925722	.940644	.956921	.974078
.9799999	.921112	.934757	.950143	.966961	.984730
.9899999	.929747	.943788	.959647	.977018	.995417
1.0000000	.938371	.952815	.969157	.987093	1.006139
1.0100000	.946984	.961837	.978672	.997187	1.016896
1.0200000	.955587	.970857	.988192	1.007300	1.027691
1.0300000	.964180	.979872	.997719	1.017431	1.038523
1.0400000	.972763	.988885	1.007252	1.027583	1.049393
1.0500000	.981337	.997895	1.016792	1.037755	1.060303
1.0600000	.989901	1.006902	1.026339	1.047947	1.071252
1.0699999	.998456	1.015906	1.035892	1.058161	1.082241
1.0799999	1.007002	1.024908	1.045454	1.068395	1.093272
1.0899999	1.015539	1.033909	1.055022	1.078651	1.104345
1.1000000	1.024068	1.042907	1.064599	1.088930	1.115460
1.1100000	1.032589	1.051904	1.074184	1.099230	1.126618
1.1200000	1.041102	1.060900	1.083776	1.109553	1.137819
1.1300000	1.049608	1.069894	1.093378	1.119898	1.149065
1.1400000	1.058106	1.078887	1.102988	1.130266	1.160355
1.1500000	1.066596	1.087880	1.112606	1.140658	1.171690
1.1600000	1.075080	1.096871	1.122233	1.151073	1.183071
1.1700000	1.083557	1.105863	1.131870	1.161511	1.194497
1.1800000	1.092028	1.114853	1.141515	1.171973	1.205969
1.1899999	1.100492	1.123844	1.151169	1.182458	1.217488

$\alpha = -$ .449999

Θ	K VALUES				
	.318821117	.415016431	.514599755	.613601043	.708073407
1.2000000	1.108950	1.132835	1.160833	1.192968	1.229053
1.2100000	1.117402	1.141825	1.170506	1.203501	1.240665
1.2200000	1.125849	1.150816	1.180188	1.214057	1.252324
1.2300000	1.134290	1.159807	1.189880	1.224637	1.264029
1.2400000	1.142725	1.168799	1.199581	1.235241	1.275781
1.2500000	1.151156	1.177791	1.209291	1.245868	1.287580
1.2599999	1.159582	1.186783	1.219010	1.256518	1.299425
1.2699999	1.168003	1.195777	1.228739	1.267192	1.311316
1.2799999	1.176420	1.204771	1.238476	1.277888	1.323254
1.2899999	1.184832	1.213766	1.248223	1.288607	1.335237
1.3000000	1.193240	1.222761	1.257979	1.299348	1.347265
1.3100000	1.201645	1.231758	1.267744	1.310111	1.359337
1.3200000	1.210045	1.240756	1.277517	1.320896	1.371453
1.3300000	1.218442	1.249755	1.287299	1.331702	1.383613
1.3400000	1.226835	1.258754	1.297089	1.342528	1.395814
1.3500000	1.235226	1.267755	1.306887	1.353375	1.408057
1.3600000	1.243613	1.276757	1.316693	1.364241	1.420341
1.3700000	1.251997	1.285760	1.326507	1.375126	1.432663
1.3799999	1.260379	1.294764	1.336328	1.386030	1.445024
1.3899999	1.268757	1.303769	1.346157	1.396951	1.457422
1.4000000	1.277134	1.312775	1.355992	1.407890	1.469856
1.4100000	1.285508	1.321783	1.365834	1.418844	1.482324
1.4200000	1.293880	1.330791	1.375683	1.429815	1.494824
1.4300000	1.302250	1.339800	1.385537	1.440800	1.507356
1.4400000	1.310618	1.348810	1.395397	1.451799	1.519917
1.4500000	1.318984	1.357821	1.405263	1.462811	1.532506
1.4600000	1.327349	1.366833	1.415133	1.473836	1.545120
1.4700000	1.335712	1.375846	1.425008	1.484872	1.557759
1.4800000	1.344074	1.384859	1.434887	1.495918	1.570420
1.4900000	1.352435	1.393873	1.444770	1.506974	1.583101
1.5000000	1.360795	1.402888	1.454657	1.518038	1.595800
1.5100000	1.369154	1.411903	1.464546	1.529110	1.608514
1.5200000	1.377512	1.420919	1.474438	1.540188	1.621243
1.5300000	1.385869	1.429935	1.484332	1.551271	1.633983
1.5400000	1.394226	1.438952	1.494228	1.562359	1.646733
1.5500000	1.402582	1.447968	1.504126	1.573450	1.659489
1.5600000	1.410939	1.456985	1.514024	1.584543	1.672250
1.5699999	1.419295	1.466002	1.523922	1.595638	1.685014
1.5707963	1.419960	1.466720	1.524711	1.596521	1.686031
1.5707963	1.419960	1.466719	1.524710	1.596520	1.686030

$\alpha = -.449999$

Θ	K VALUES				
	.794250555	.868696860	.928444378	.971111163	.994996249
.0000000	.000000	.000000	.000000	.000000	.000000
.0100000	.009999	.010000	.010000	.010000	.010000
.0200000	.019999	.019999	.020000	.020000	.020000
.0300000	.029999	.029999	.030000	.030000	.030000
.0400000	.039998	.039999	.040000	.040000	.040001
.0500000	.049997	.049999	.050000	.050001	.050002
.0600000	.059996	.059998	.060001	.060002	.060003
.0700000	.069994	.069998	.070001	.070004	.070005
.0800000	.079991	.079997	.080002	.080006	.080008
.0900000	.089987	.089996	.090003	.090009	.090011
.1000000	.099982	.099995	.100005	.100012	.100016
.1100000	.109977	.109994	.110007	.110016	.110022
.1200000	.119970	.119992	.120009	.120022	.120029
.1300000	.129963	.129990	.130012	.130028	.130037
.1400000	.139954	.139988	.140016	.140036	.140047
.1500000	.149944	.149986	.150020	.150044	.150058
.1600000	.159933	.159984	.160025	.160055	.160071
.1700000	.169921	.169982	.170032	.170067	.170087
.1800000	.179907	.179980	.180039	.180081	.180104
.1900000	.189892	.189978	.190047	.190097	.190125
.2000000	.199876	.199976	.200057	.200115	.200147
.2100000	.209859	.209975	.210069	.210136	.210173
.2200000	.219840	.219974	.220082	.220159	.220202
.2300000	.229820	.229973	.230097	.230185	.230235
.2400000	.239799	.239974	.240114	.240215	.240271
.2500000	.249777	.249975	.250134	.250248	.250311
.2600000	.259754	.259977	.260156	.260284	.260356
.2700000	.269730	.269980	.270181	.270325	.270406
.2800000	.279706	.279984	.280209	.280370	.280461
.2900000	.289681	.289991	.290241	.290420	.290521
.3000000	.299655	.299999	.300276	.300475	.300587
.3100000	.309629	.310009	.310316	.310536	.310660
.3200000	.319602	.320021	.320360	.320603	.320739
.3300000	.329576	.330036	.330408	.330676	.330826
.3400000	.339550	.340054	.340462	.340755	.340920
.3500000	.349524	.350076	.350522	.350843	.351023
.3600000	.359499	.360101	.360588	.360938	.361134
.3700000	.369475	.370130	.370660	.371041	.371255
.3800000	.379452	.380163	.380739	.381154	.381387
.3900000	.389431	.390202	.390826	.391275	.391528

$\alpha = -.449999$

θ	K VALUES				
	.794250555	.868696860	.928444378	.971111163	.994996249
.4000000	.399412	.400245	.400921	.401407	.401681
.4100000	.409394	.410294	.411024	.411550	.411846
.4200000	.419380	.420350	.421137	.421705	.422024
.4300000	.429368	.430412	.431260	.431871	.432215
.4400000	.439359	.440481	.441393	.442050	.442421
.4500000	.449354	.450558	.451537	.452243	.452641
.4600000	.459353	.460643	.461693	.462450	.462878
.4700000	.469357	.470737	.471861	.472673	.473131
.4800000	.479366	.480841	.482043	.482912	.483402
.4900000	.489381	.490955	.492239	.493167	.493691
.5000000	.499401	.501079	.502449	.503440	.504000
.5100000	.509428	.511215	.512675	.513733	.514330
.5200000	.519462	.521364	.522918	.524044	.524681
.5300000	.529504	.531525	.533179	.534377	.535055
.5400000	.539554	.541700	.543457	.544732	.545453
.5500000	.549613	.551890	.553755	.555109	.555876
.5600000	.559682	.562094	.564073	.565511	.566325
.5700000	.569761	.572315	.574413	.575938	.576802
.5800000	.579851	.582554	.584775	.586391	.587307
.5900000	.589952	.592810	.595161	.596872	.597843
.6000000	.600066	.603085	.605571	.607383	.608411
.6100000	.610192	.613380	.616007	.617923	.619011
.6200000	.620333	.623695	.626470	.628496	.629646
.6300000	.630488	.634033	.636962	.639101	.640317
.6400000	.640658	.644393	.647483	.649742	.651026
.6500000	.650845	.654778	.658035	.660418	.661774
.6600000	.661048	.665187	.668619	.671133	.672564
.6700000	.671270	.675623	.679237	.681887	.683396
.6800000	.681511	.686087	.689890	.692682	.694273
.6899999	.691771	.696579	.700580	.703520	.705197
.7000000	.702052	.707101	.711308	.714403	.716170
.7100000	.712354	.717654	.722076	.725332	.727193
.7200000	.722679	.728239	.732885	.736310	.738269
.7300000	.733028	.738858	.743737	.747339	.749401
.7400000	.743401	.749513	.754635	.758421	.760589
.7500000	.753800	.760204	.765579	.769557	.771838
.7600000	.764226	.770933	.776572	.780750	.783148
.7700000	.774679	.781702	.787615	.792003	.794524
.7800000	.785162	.792511	.798711	.803318	.805967
.7899999	.795674	.803364	.809861	.814697	.817480

$\alpha = -\ .449999$

Θ	K VALUES				
	.794250555	.868696860	.928444378	.971111163	.994996249
.8000000	.806218	.814260	.821068	.826143	.829066
.8100000	.816794	.825203	.832334	.837658	.840728
.8200000	.827403	.836193	.843661	.849245	.852469
.8300000	.838047	.847232	.855051	.860907	.864293
.8400000	.848727	.858322	.866507	.872648	.876202
.8500000	.859445	.869465	.878031	.884469	.888200
.8600000	.870200	.880663	.889626	.896375	.900291
.8700000	.880996	.891917	.901294	.908368	.912479
.8799999	.891832	.903230	.913038	.920452	.924766
.8899999	.902711	.914603	.924860	.932630	.937159
.9000000	.913633	.926038	.936765	.944907	.949659
.9100000	.924600	.937538	.948753	.957285	.962273
.9200000	.935614	.949105	.960830	.969769	.975005
.9300000	.946675	.960740	.972996	.982364	.987859
.9400000	.957786	.972447	.985257	.995072	1.000841
.9500000	.968947	.984226	.997615	1.007900	1.013956
.9600000	.980160	.996081	1.010073	1.020850	1.027209
.9699999	.991426	1.008014	1.022636	1.033929	1.040606
.9799999	1.002747	1.020026	1.035306	1.047141	1.054153
.9899999	1.014124	1.032122	1.048088	1.060492	1.067858
1.0000000	1.025558	1.044302	1.060986	1.073987	1.081725
1.0100000	1.037052	1.056570	1.074003	1.087631	1.095763
1.0200000	1.048606	1.068928	1.087143	1.101431	1.109979
1.0300000	1.060222	1.081378	1.100412	1.115393	1.124380
1.0400000	1.071901	1.093924	1.113812	1.129523	1.138974
1.0500000	1.083645	1.106568	1.127349	1.143829	1.153771
1.0600000	1.095455	1.119312	1.141028	1.158317	1.168780
1.0699999	1.107333	1.132160	1.154853	1.172994	1.184009
1.0799999	1.119280	1.145113	1.168829	1.187869	1.199470
1.0899999	1.131297	1.158175	1.182962	1.202950	1.215172
1.1000000	1.143386	1.171350	1.197256	1.218245	1.231129
1.1100000	1.155547	1.184638	1.211717	1.233763	1.247350
1.1200000	1.167783	1.198043	1.226350	1.249513	1.263850
1.1300000	1.180094	1.211569	1.241162	1.265507	1.280641
1.1400000	1.192482	1.225217	1.256158	1.281752	1.297740
1.1500000	1.204948	1.238992	1.271344	1.298262	1.315160
1.1600000	1.217493	1.252894	1.286726	1.315047	1.332919
1.1700000	1.230117	1.266928	1.302311	1.332118	1.351035
1.1800000	1.242823	1.281096	1.318105	1.349490	1.369525
1.1899999	1.255611	1.295400	1.334115	1.367174	1.388412

$\alpha = - .449999$

Θ	*K* VALUES				
	.794250555	.868696860	.928444378	.971111163	.994996249
1.2000000	1.268481	1.309844	1.350347	1.385186	1.407716
1.2100000	1.281435	1.324429	1.366808	1.403538	1.427461
1.2200000	1.294473	1.339159	1.383506	1.422248	1.447672
1.2300000	1.307596	1.354036	1.400447	1.441331	1.468378
1.2400000	1.320804	1.369061	1.417637	1.460805	1.489606
1.2500000	1.334097	1.384237	1.435085	1.480686	1.511390
1.2599999	1.347476	1.399566	1.452798	1.500995	1.533765
1.2699999	1.360941	1.415050	1.470782	1.521750	1.556767
1.2799999	1.374492	1.430690	1.489044	1.542972	1.580439
1.2899999	1.388129	1.446488	1.507591	1.564684	1.604826
1.3000000	1.401851	1.462444	1.526430	1.586908	1.629977
1.3100000	1.415657	1.478559	1.545568	1.609667	1.655947
1.3200000	1.429548	1.494835	1.565009	1.632986	1.682795
1.3300000	1.443522	1.511270	1.584760	1.656891	1.710587
1.3400000	1.457578	1.527864	1.604827	1.681407	1.739398
1.3500000	1.471715	1.544618	1.625213	1.706563	1.769307
1.3600000	1.485931	1.561530	1.645922	1.732384	1.800405
1.3700000	1.500226	1.578598	1.666958	1.758901	1.832793
1.3799999	1.514597	1.595821	1.688323	1.786139	1.866585
1.3899999	1.529042	1.613195	1.710016	1.814128	1.901905
1.4000000	1.543558	1.630719	1.732040	1.842893	1.938899
1.4100000	1.558144	1.648387	1.754390	1.872461	1.977724
1.4200000	1.572797	1.666196	1.777064	1.902854	2.018564
1.4300000	1.587514	1.684142	1.800057	1.934093	2.061622
1.4400000	1.602291	1.702219	1.823362	1.966194	2.107131
1.4500000	1.617125	1.720420	1.846971	1.999168	2.155352
1.4600000	1.632014	1.738739	1.870872	2.033019	2.206579
1.4700000	1.646953	1.757170	1.895052	2.067744	2.261136
1.4800000	1.661938	1.775703	1.919496	2.103328	2.319383
1.4900000	1.676965	1.794332	1.944186	2.139748	2.381700
1.5000000	1.692030	1.813046	1.969103	2.176965	2.448478
1.5100000	1.707129	1.831837	1.994223	2.214927	2.520081
1.5200000	1.722257	1.850694	2.019523	2.253569	2.596797
1.5300000	1.737410	1.869608	2.044977	2.292808	2.678755
1.5400000	1.752582	1.888567	2.070556	2.332549	2.765807
1.5500000	1.767770	1.907562	2.096231	2.372682	2.857405
1.5600000	1.782968	1.926579	2.121971	2.413086	2.952512
1.5699999	1.798171	1.945609	2.147746	2.453634	3.049606
1.5707963	1.799382	1.947125	2.149799	2.456865	3.057370
1.5707963	1.799381	1.947124	2.149798	2.456863	3.057368

$\alpha = -\ .399999$

θ	K VALUES				
	.009966711	.039469502	.087332193	.151646642	.229848846
.0000000	.000000	.000000	.000000	.000000	.000000
.0100000	.009999	.009999	.009999	.009999	.009999
.0200000	.019998	.019998	.019999	.019999	.019999
.0300000	.029996	.029996	.029996	.029997	.029997
.0400000	.039991	.039991	.039992	.039993	.039993
.0500000	.049983	.049984	.049985	.049986	.049988
.0600000	.059971	.059972	.059974	.059976	.059979
.0700000	.069954	.069956	.069959	.069963	.069967
.0800000	.079932	.079935	.079939	.079944	.079951
.0900000	.089904	.089907	.089913	.089921	.089931
.1000000	.099868	.099873	.099881	.099892	.099905
.1100000	.109825	.109832	.109842	.109856	.109874
.1200000	.119773	.119782	.119796	.119814	.119836
.1300000	.129712	.129723	.129741	.129764	.129792
.1400000	.139641	.139655	.139676	.139706	.139741
.1500000	.149559	.149576	.149603	.149639	.149682
.1600000	.159466	.159486	.159518	.159562	.159615
.1700000	.169361	.169385	.169423	.169476	.169539
.1800000	.179242	.179271	.179317	.179379	.179454
.1900000	.189111	.189144	.189198	.189270	.189359
.2000000	.198964	.199003	.199066	.199151	.199254
.2100000	.208803	.208848	.208921	.209018	.209138
.2200000	.218627	.218678	.218761	.218874	.219011
.2300000	.228434	.228492	.228588	.228716	.228872
.2400000	.238224	.238291	.238399	.238544	.238721
.2500000	.247997	.248072	.248194	.248358	.248558
.2600000	.257752	.257836	.257973	.258157	.258382
.2700000	.267488	.267582	.267735	.267941	.268193
.2800000	.277205	.277310	.277480	.277709	.277990
.2900000	.286903	.287018	.287207	.287461	.287772
.3000000	.296580	.296708	.296916	.297197	.297541
.3100000	.306236	.306377	.306606	.306915	.307294
.3200000	.315871	.316025	.316277	.316616	.317032
.3300000	.325484	.325653	.325928	.326300	.326755
.3400000	.335074	.335259	.335559	.335965	.336462
.3500000	.344642	.344843	.345170	.345611	.346153
.3600000	.354187	.354405	.354759	.355239	.355827
.3700000	.363708	.363944	.364328	.364847	.365484
.3800000	.373205	.373460	.373875	.374436	.375125
.3900000	.382678	.382952	.383399	.384005	.384748

$\alpha = -$ .399999

Θ	*K* VALUES				
	.009966711	.039469502	.087332193	.151646642	.229848846
.4000000	.392125	.392421	.392902	.393553	.394354
.4100000	.401548	.401865	.402382	.403082	.403942
.4200000	.410945	.411285	.411838	.412589	.413512
.4300000	.420316	.420679	.421272	.422075	.423063
.4400000	.429661	.430049	.430682	.431540	.432597
.4500000	.438980	.439393	.440068	.440984	.442111
.4600000	.448272	.448712	.449430	.450406	.451608
.4700000	.457537	.458004	.458768	.459806	.461085
.4800000	.466774	.467270	.468082	.469184	.470543
.4900000	.475984	.476510	.477370	.478539	.479982
.5000000	.485167	.485724	.486634	.487872	.489401
.5100000	.494321	.494910	.495873	.497183	.498802
.5200000	.503448	.504069	.505087	.506471	.508182
.5300000	.512546	.513202	.514275	.515736	.517544
.5400000	.521616	.522307	.523438	.524978	.526885
.5500000	.530657	.531384	.532575	.534197	.536207
.5600000	.539670	.540434	.541686	.543393	.545509
.5700000	.548654	.549457	.550772	.552566	.554791
.5800000	.557610	.558452	.559832	.561716	.564054
.5900000	.566536	.567419	.568866	.570842	.573296
.6000000	.575434	.576358	.577874	.579946	.582519
.6100000	.584302	.585269	.586856	.589025	.591722
.6200000	.593142	.594153	.595812	.598082	.600906
.6300000	.601953	.603008	.604742	.607115	.610069
.6400000	.610734	.611836	.613646	.616125	.619213
.6500000	.619487	.620636	.622524	.625111	.628337
.6600000	.628211	.629408	.631377	.634075	.637441
.6700000	.636905	.638152	.640203	.643015	.646526
.6800000	.645571	.646869	.649003	.651932	.655592
.6899999	.654208	.655557	.657778	.660826	.664638
.7000000	.662817	.664219	.666527	.669697	.673665
.7100000	.671397	.672852	.675250	.678546	.682672
.7200000	.679948	.681459	.683948	.687371	.691661
.7300000	.688471	.690037	.692620	.696174	.700630
.7400000	.696965	.698589	.701267	.704954	.709581
.7500000	.705432	.707114	.709889	.713711	.718513
.7600000	.713870	.715611	.718486	.722447	.727426
.7700000	.722281	.724082	.727057	.731160	.736321
.7800000	.730663	.732527	.735604	.739851	.745198
.7899999	.739019	.740945	.744127	.748521	.754056

$\alpha = -.399999$

Θ	K VALUES				
	.009966711	.039469502	.087332193	.151646642	.229848846
.8000000	.747347	.749336	.752625	.757168	.762897
.8100000	.755647	.757702	.761099	.765794	.771720
.8200000	.763921	.766041	.769548	.774399	.780525
.8300000	.772168	.774355	.777974	.782983	.789313
.8400000	.780389	.782644	.786376	.791545	.798084
.8500000	.788583	.790907	.794755	.800087	.806837
.8600000	.796751	.799145	.803110	.808608	.815574
.8700000	.804894	.807358	.811443	.817109	.824294
.8799999	.813011	.815547	.819752	.825589	.832998
.8899999	.821102	.823711	.828039	.834050	.841685
.9000000	.829168	.831851	.836304	.842491	.850356
.9100000	.837210	.839968	.844546	.850913	.859012
.9200000	.845227	.848061	.852767	.859315	.867652
.9300000	.853220	.856130	.860966	.867698	.876277
.9400000	.861189	.864177	.869143	.876062	.884886
.9500000	.869134	.872201	.877300	.884408	.893481
.9600000	.877056	.880202	.885436	.892735	.902060
.9699999	.884955	.888182	.893551	.901045	.910626
.9799999	.892831	.896139	.901646	.909336	.919177
.9899999	.900684	.904075	.909721	.917610	.927714
1.0000000	.908516	.911989	.917776	.925867	.936238
1.0100000	.916325	.919883	.925812	.934107	.944748
1.0200000	.924114	.927756	.933829	.942330	.953244
1.0300000	.931881	.935609	.941827	.950537	.961728
1.0400000	.939627	.943442	.949807	.958727	.970199
1.0500000	.947352	.951255	.957768	.966901	.978657
1.0600000	.955058	.959048	.965711	.975060	.987103
1.0699999	.962744	.966823	.973637	.983204	.995537
1.0799999	.970410	.974579	.981546	.991332	1.003959
1.0899999	.978057	.982317	.989437	.999446	1.012370
1.1000000	.985686	.990036	.997312	1.007545	1.020769
1.1100000	.993296	.997739	1.005171	1.015630	1.029157
1.1200000	1.000888	1.005423	1.013013	1.023701	1.037535
1.1300000	1.008462	1.013091	1.020840	1.031758	1.045902
1.1400000	1.016019	1.020742	1.028652	1.039802	1.054258
1.1500000	1.023559	1.028377	1.036448	1.047833	1.062605
1.1600000	1.031083	1.035996	1.044230	1.055851	1.070941
1.1700000	1.038590	1.043599	1.051998	1.063857	1.079268
1.1800000	1.046082	1.051188	1.059751	1.071850	1.087586
1.1899999	1.053558	1.058761	1.067491	1.079832	1.095895

$\alpha = -.399999$

Θ	K VALUES				
	.009966711	.039469502	.087332193	.151646642	.229848846
1.2000000	1.061019	1.066320	1.075218	1.087802	1.104195
1.2100000	1.068465	1.073865	1.082931	1.095761	1.112486
1.2200000	1.075897	1.081396	1.090632	1.103709	1.120769
1.2300000	1.083315	1.088914	1.098320	1.111646	1.129044
1.2400000	1.090720	1.096419	1.105997	1.119572	1.137311
1.2500000	1.098111	1.103911	1.113661	1.127489	1.145570
1.2599999	1.105490	1.111391	1.121315	1.135396	1.153822
1.2699999	1.112856	1.118859	1.128957	1.143294	1.162067
1.2799999	1.120210	1.126315	1.136589	1.151182	1.170305
1.2899999	1.127553	1.133761	1.144211	1.159061	1.178536
1.3000000	1.134884	1.141195	1.151823	1.166932	1.186761
1.3100000	1.142205	1.148619	1.159425	1.174795	1.194980
1.3200000	1.149515	1.156034	1.167018	1.182650	1.203193
1.3300000	1.156815	1.163438	1.174602	1.190497	1.211400
1.3400000	1.164106	1.170834	1.182177	1.198337	1.219601
1.3500000	1.171387	1.178220	1.189744	1.206169	1.227798
1.3600000	1.178659	1.185598	1.197304	1.213995	1.235989
1.3700000	1.185923	1.192968	1.204856	1.221815	1.244176
1.3799999	1.193179	1.200330	1.212401	1.229628	1.252358
1.3899999	1.200427	1.207685	1.219939	1.237436	1.260536
1.4000000	1.207668	1.215032	1.227471	1.245238	1.268710
1.4100000	1.214902	1.222374	1.234996	1.253035	1.276880
1.4200000	1.222130	1.229709	1.242516	1.260827	1.285046
1.4300000	1.229351	1.237038	1.250031	1.268614	1.293209
1.4400000	1.236567	1.244362	1.257540	1.276397	1.301369
1.4500000	1.243778	1.251680	1.265045	1.284177	1.309526
1.4600000	1.250983	1.258994	1.272546	1.291952	1.317680
1.4700000	1.258185	1.266304	1.280043	1.299724	1.325832
1.4800000	1.265382	1.273610	1.287536	1.307493	1.333981
1.4900000	1.272575	1.280912	1.295026	1.315259	1.342129
1.5000000	1.279766	1.288212	1.302513	1.323023	1.350274
1.5100000	1.286953	1.295508	1.309997	1.330785	1.358418
1.5200000	1.294138	1.302802	1.317480	1.338545	1.366561
1.5300000	1.301321	1.310095	1.324960	1.346303	1.374703
1.5400000	1.308502	1.317385	1.332439	1.354060	1.382843
1.5500000	1.315683	1.324675	1.339917	1.361816	1.390983
1.5600000	1.322862	1.331963	1.347395	1.369571	1.399123
1.5699999	1.330041	1.339251	1.354871	1.377326	1.407262
1.5707963	1.330612	1.339832	1.355467	1.377944	1.407910
1.5707963	1.330612	1.339831	1.355466	1.377943	1.407910

$\alpha = -\ .399999$

Θ	K VALUES				
	.318821117	.415016431	.514599755	.613601043	.708073407
.0000000	.000000	.000000	.000000	.000000	.000000
.0100000	.009999	.009999	.009999	.009999	.009999
.0200000	.019999	.019999	.019999	.019999	.019999
.0300000	.029997	.029998	.029998	.029999	.029999
.0400000	.039994	.039995	.039996	.039998	.039999
.0500000	.049990	.049992	.049994	.049996	.049998
.0600000	.059982	.059986	.059989	.059993	.059996
.0700000	.069972	.069978	.069983	.069989	.069994
.0800000	.079959	.079967	.079975	.079984	.079992
.0900000	.089941	.089953	.089965	.089977	.089989
.1000000	.099920	.099936	.099952	.099969	.099985
.1100000	.109893	.109915	.109937	.109959	.109980
.1200000	.119862	.119890	.119918	.119947	.119974
.1300000	.129825	.129860	.129897	.129933	.129967
.1400000	.139782	.139826	.139871	.139917	.139960
.1500000	.149732	.149786	.149842	.149898	.149951
.1600000	.159675	.159741	.159809	.159877	.159941
.1700000	.169612	.169690	.169772	.169853	.169930
.1800000	.179540	.179633	.179730	.179826	.179918
.1900000	.189460	.189569	.189683	.189797	.189905
.2000000	.199371	.199499	.199632	.199764	.199891
.2100000	.209274	.209422	.209575	.209729	.209875
.2200000	.219167	.219337	.219514	.219690	.219859
.2300000	.229051	.229245	.229446	.229648	.229841
.2400000	.238924	.239144	.239374	.239603	.239822
.2500000	.248787	.249036	.249295	.249554	.249802
.2600000	.258639	.258919	.259211	.259502	.259782
.2700000	.268481	.268794	.269120	.269446	.269760
.2800000	.278310	.278659	.279023	.279387	.279737
.2900000	.288128	.288516	.288920	.289325	.289714
.3000000	.297934	.298363	.298810	.299259	.299690
.3100000	.307728	.308201	.308694	.309189	.309666
.3200000	.317509	.318029	.318572	.319116	.319641
.3300000	.327277	.327847	.328442	.329040	.329616
.3400000	.337032	.337655	.338306	.338960	.339591
.3500000	.346774	.347453	.348163	.348877	.349566
.3600000	.356502	.357240	.358013	.358791	.359541
.3700000	.366217	.367017	.367856	.368701	.369517
.3800000	.375917	.376784	.377693	.378608	.379493
.3900000	.385603	.386540	.387522	.388512	.389470

$\alpha = -.399999$

Θ	K VALUES				
	.318821117	.415016431	.514599755	.613601043	.708073407
.4000000	.395275	.396285	.397344	.398414	.399449
.4100000	.404932	.406019	.407160	.408312	.409429
.4200000	.414575	.415742	.416969	.418208	.419410
.4300000	.424203	.425454	.426771	.428102	.429394
.4400000	.433816	.435155	.436566	.437993	.439379
.4500000	.443414	.444845	.446354	.447882	.449368
.4600000	.452996	.454524	.456136	.457769	.459359
.4700000	.462563	.464192	.465911	.467655	.469353
.4800000	.472115	.473848	.475679	.477539	.479351
.4900000	.481652	.483494	.485442	.487422	.489353
.5000000	.491173	.493128	.495198	.497303	.499359
.5100000	.500678	.502751	.504948	.507184	.509370
.5200000	.510168	.512363	.514692	.517065	.519387
.5300000	.519642	.521965	.524430	.526945	.529408
.5400000	.529101	.531555	.534162	.536825	.539436
.5500000	.538544	.541134	.543889	.546706	.549471
.5600000	.547971	.550703	.553611	.556587	.559512
.5700000	.557383	.560261	.563327	.566470	.569561
.5800000	.566779	.569808	.573039	.576354	.579618
.5900000	.576159	.579345	.582746	.586239	.589684
.6000000	.585525	.588871	.592449	.596127	.599759
.6100000	.594874	.598387	.602147	.606017	.609843
.6200000	.604208	.607893	.611841	.615910	.619937
.6300000	.613527	.617389	.621532	.625806	.630042
.6400000	.622831	.626875	.631219	.635706	.640159
.6500000	.632119	.636352	.640902	.645610	.650288
.6600000	.641392	.645819	.650583	.655518	.660429
.6700000	.650651	.655276	.660261	.665432	.670583
.6800000	.659894	.664725	.669937	.675350	.680752
.6899999	.669123	.674164	.679610	.685275	.690934
.7000000	.678338	.683595	.689282	.695205	.701133
.7100000	.687537	.693017	.698952	.705143	.711347
.7200000	.696723	.702431	.708621	.715087	.721577
.7300000	.705894	.711837	.718290	.725039	.731825
.7400000	.715052	.721234	.727957	.735000	.742091
.7500000	.724195	.730624	.737624	.744969	.752376
.7600000	.733325	.740007	.747292	.754947	.762681
.7700000	.742441	.749382	.756960	.764935	.773005
.7800000	.751544	.758750	.766628	.774933	.783351
.7899999	.760634	.768111	.776298	.784941	.793719

$\alpha = -.399999$

Θ	K VALUES				
	.318821117	.415016431	.514599755	.613601043	.708073407
.8000000	.769711	.777466	.785969	.794961	.804109
.8100000	.778774	.786814	.795642	.804992	.814523
.8200000	.787826	.796157	.805317	.815036	.824961
.8300000	.796865	.805493	.814994	.825092	.835424
.8400000	.805892	.814824	.824674	.835162	.845912
.8500000	.814907	.824149	.834358	.845245	.856428
.8600000	.823910	.833469	.844045	.855343	.866971
.8700000	.832901	.842785	.853735	.865456	.877542
.8799999	.841881	.852096	.863430	.875584	.888143
.8899999	.850850	.861402	.873129	.885727	.898773
.9000000	.859808	.870704	.882834	.895888	.909435
.9100000	.868755	.880003	.892543	.906065	.920128
.9200000	.877692	.889298	.902258	.916259	.930853
.9300000	.886619	.898589	.911979	.926472	.941612
.9400000	.895535	.907877	.921705	.936703	.952405
.9500000	.904442	.917163	.931439	.946953	.963234
.9600000	.913339	.926445	.941179	.957222	.974098
.9699999	.922226	.935726	.950926	.967512	.984999
.9799999	.931104	.945004	.960681	.977821	.995937
.9899999	.939974	.954280	.970444	.988152	1.006914
1.0000000	.948835	.963555	.980214	.998504	1.017930
1.0100000	.957687	.972828	.989993	1.008877	1.028986
1.0200000	.966530	.982099	.999780	1.019273	1.040083
1.0300000	.975366	.991370	1.009576	1.029691	1.051221
1.0400000	.984194	1.000640	1.019381	1.040133	1.062401
1.0500000	.993014	1.009909	1.029195	1.050597	1.073625
1.0600000	1.001827	1.019177	1.039019	1.061086	1.084892
1.0699999	1.010633	1.028446	1.048853	1.071598	1.096204
1.0799999	1.019431	1.037714	1.058697	1.082135	1.107560
1.0899999	1.028223	1.046982	1.068550	1.092697	1.118963
1.1000000	1.037008	1.056251	1.078415	1.103283	1.130411
1.1100000	1.045787	1.065520	1.088289	1.113895	1.141907
1.1200000	1.054559	1.074790	1.098174	1.124533	1.153450
1.1300000	1.063326	1.084060	1.108071	1.135196	1.165041
1.1400000	1.072087	1.093331	1.117977	1.145885	1.176680
1.1500000	1.080842	1.102604	1.127895	1.156600	1.188368
1.1600000	1.089591	1.111877	1.137825	1.167341	1.200105
1.1700000	1.098336	1.121152	1.147765	1.178109	1.211892
1.1800000	1.107075	1.130429	1.157717	1.188903	1.223729
1.1899999	1.115810	1.139707	1.167679	1.199724	1.235615

$\alpha = -.399999$

Θ	K VALUES				
	.318821117	.415016431	.514599755	.613601043	.708073407
1.2000000	1.124540	1.148986	1.177654	1.210571	1.247552
1.2100000	1.133265	1.158267	1.187639	1.221444	1.259540
1.2200000	1.141986	1.167551	1.197636	1.232344	1.271577
1.2300000	1.150703	1.176836	1.207645	1.243270	1.283665
1.2400000	1.159416	1.186122	1.217664	1.254222	1.295803
1.2500000	1.168125	1.195411	1.227695	1.265200	1.307992
1.2599999	1.176831	1.204702	1.237737	1.276204	1.320230
1.2699999	1.185533	1.213996	1.247790	1.287233	1.332518
1.2799999	1.194231	1.223291	1.257854	1.298287	1.344855
1.2899999	1.202927	1.232588	1.267928	1.309367	1.357241
1.3000000	1.211619	1.241888	1.278014	1.320471	1.369675
1.3100000	1.220308	1.251190	1.288110	1.331599	1.382157
1.3200000	1.228995	1.260494	1.298216	1.342751	1.394686
1.3300000	1.237679	1.269800	1.308332	1.353926	1.407261
1.3400000	1.246360	1.279109	1.318458	1.365124	1.419881
1.3500000	1.255039	1.288419	1.328593	1.376344	1.432545
1.3600000	1.263716	1.297732	1.338738	1.387585	1.445253
1.3700000	1.272391	1.307047	1.348891	1.398847	1.458003
1.3799999	1.281063	1.316364	1.359054	1.410130	1.470793
1.3899999	1.289734	1.325682	1.369225	1.421431	1.483623
1.4000000	1.298403	1.335003	1.379404	1.432752	1.496491
1.4100000	1.307070	1.344326	1.389591	1.444090	1.509395
1.4200000	1.315736	1.353650	1.399785	1.455446	1.522334
1.4300000	1.324400	1.362976	1.409986	1.466817	1.535307
1.4400000	1.333063	1.372304	1.420193	1.478204	1.548310
1.4500000	1.341725	1.381633	1.430407	1.489605	1.561344
1.4600000	1.350386	1.390964	1.440626	1.501020	1.574404
1.4700000	1.359045	1.400296	1.450851	1.512447	1.587491
1.4800000	1.367704	1.409629	1.461081	1.523885	1.600601
1.4900000	1.376362	1.418963	1.471315	1.535333	1.613732
1.5000000	1.385019	1.428299	1.481553	1.546791	1.626883
1.5100000	1.393675	1.437635	1.491795	1.558257	1.640050
1.5200000	1.402331	1.446972	1.502039	1.569730	1.653233
1.5300000	1.410987	1.456310	1.512286	1.581208	1.666427
1.5400000	1.419642	1.465648	1.522535	1.592692	1.679631
1.5500000	1.428296	1.474986	1.532786	1.604179	1.692843
1.5600000	1.436951	1.484325	1.543038	1.615668	1.706060
1.5699999	1.445606	1.493664	1.553290	1.627159	1.719280
1.5707963	1.446295	1.494408	1.554106	1.628074	1.720333
1.5707963	1.446294	1.494407	1.554106	1.628073	1.720332

$\alpha = -.399999$

Θ	K VALUES				
	.794250555	.868696860	.928444378	.971111163	.994996249
.0000000	.000000	.000000	.000000	.000000	.000000
.0100000	.010000	.010000	.010000	.010000	.010000
.0200000	.020000	.020000	.020000	.020000	.020000
.0300000	.029999	.030000	.030000	.030000	.030000
.0400000	.039999	.040000	.040001	.040001	.040002
.0500000	.049999	.050001	.050002	.050003	.050004
.0600000	.059999	.060002	.060004	.060006	.060007
.0700000	.069999	.070004	.070007	.070009	.070011
.0800000	.079999	.080006	.080011	.080014	.080016
.0900000	.089999	.090008	.090015	.090021	.090024
.1000000	.099999	.100011	.100021	.100029	.100033
.1100000	.109999	.110016	.110029	.110038	.110044
.1200000	.119999	.120021	.120038	.120050	.120057
.1300000	.129999	.130027	.130049	.130064	.130073
.1400000	.139999	.140034	.140061	.140081	.140092
.1500000	.150000	.150042	.150076	.150100	.150114
.1600000	.160001	.160052	.160093	.160122	.160139
.1700000	.170002	.170063	.170113	.170148	.170168
.1800000	.180003	.180076	.180135	.180177	.180200
.1900000	.190005	.190091	.190160	.190209	.190237
.2000000	.200007	.200107	.200188	.200246	.200279
.2100000	.210010	.210126	.210220	.210287	.210325
.2200000	.220014	.220148	.220256	.220333	.220376
.2300000	.230018	.230172	.230295	.230384	.230433
.2400000	.240024	.240198	.240339	.240440	.240496
.2500000	.250030	.250228	.250387	.250502	.250566
.2600000	.260038	.260261	.260441	.260569	.260642
.2700000	.270048	.270298	.270499	.270644	.270725
.2800000	.280059	.280338	.280563	.280725	.280815
.2900000	.290072	.290383	.290633	.290813	.290914
.3000000	.300087	.300432	.300710	.300909	.301022
.3100000	.310104	.310485	.310793	.311014	.311138
.3200000	.320124	.320544	.320883	.321127	.321264
.3300000	.330146	.330608	.330981	.331249	.331400
.3400000	.340172	.340678	.341088	.341381	.341547
.3500000	.350201	.350754	.351202	.351524	.351705
.3600000	.360233	.360837	.361326	.361677	.361875
.3700000	.370270	.370927	.371459	.371842	.372057
.3800000	.380310	.381024	.381603	.382019	.382253
.3900000	.390356	.391130	.391757	.392208	.392462

$\alpha = -$ .399999

Θ	K VALUES				
	.794250555	.868696860	.928444378	.971111163	.994996249
.4000000	.400406	.401243	.401922	.402411	.402686
.4100000	.410462	.411366	.412100	.412628	.412925
.4200000	.420523	.421498	.422289	.422860	.423181
.4300000	.430591	.431640	.432493	.433107	.433453
.4400000	.440665	.441793	.442710	.443371	.443743
.4500000	.450746	.451957	.452941	.453651	.454052
.4600000	.460835	.462132	.463188	.463950	.464380
.4700000	.470932	.472320	.473451	.474268	.474729
.4800000	.481038	.482522	.483731	.484605	.485098
.4900000	.491152	.492737	.494029	.494963	.495491
.5000000	.501276	.502966	.504345	.505343	.505906
.5100000	.511411	.513211	.514681	.515745	.516347
.5200000	.521556	.523471	.525037	.526171	.526812
.5300000	.531712	.533748	.535414	.536622	.537305
.5400000	.541881	.544043	.545814	.547098	.547825
.5500000	.552062	.554356	.556237	.557602	.558374
.5600000	.562256	.564689	.566684	.568133	.568954
.5700000	.572465	.575041	.577157	.578694	.579566
.5800000	.582688	.585415	.587656	.589286	.590210
.5900000	.592927	.595810	.598182	.599910	.600889
.6000000	.603181	.606229	.608738	.610567	.611604
.6100000	.613453	.616671	.619324	.621258	.622356
.6200000	.623742	.627138	.629940	.631986	.633148
.6300000	.634050	.637631	.640590	.642751	.643979
.6400000	.644378	.648152	.651273	.653555	.654853
.6500000	.654725	.658700	.661992	.664401	.665771
.6600000	.665094	.669278	.672747	.675288	.676735
.6700000	.675484	.679886	.683540	.686220	.687746
.6800000	.685898	.690526	.694373	.697197	.698807
.6899999	.696335	.701199	.705247	.708222	.709920
.7000000	.706797	.711906	.716164	.719297	.721086
.7100000	.717285	.722649	.727126	.730423	.732307
.7200000	.727799	.733429	.738133	.741602	.743586
.7300000	.738341	.744247	.749189	.752837	.754926
.7400000	.748912	.755104	.760294	.764130	.766328
.7500000	.759513	.766003	.771451	.775483	.777794
.7600000	.770145	.776944	.782661	.786897	.789329
.7700000	.780809	.787929	.793926	.798377	.800933
.7800000	.791506	.798960	.805249	.809923	.812610
.7899999	.802237	.810039	.816632	.821539	.824363

$\alpha =$ - •399999

Θ	K VALUES				
	•794250555	•868696860	•928444378	•971111163	•994996249
•8000000	•813004	•821166	•828076	•833227	•836195
•8100000	•823807	•832344	•839584	•844989	•848108
•8200000	•834648	•843574	•851158	•856830	•860105
•8300000	•845529	•854858	•862801	•868751	•872191
•8400000	•856449	•866198	•874515	•880756	•884369
•8500000	•867411	•877595	•886303	•892848	•896641
•8600000	•878417	•889053	•898166	•905029	•909012
•8700000	•889466	•900572	•910109	•917304	•921486
•8799999	•900560	•912154	•922133	•929676	•934067
•8899999	•911702	•923802	•934241	•942149	•946759
•9000000	•922892	•935517	•946436	•954726	•959565
•9100000	•934131	•947302	•958722	•967411	•972492
•9200000	•945421	•959159	•971102	•980209	•985543
•9300000	•956763	•971090	•983578	•993123	•998724
•9400000	•968159	•983098	•996153	1•006159	1•012040
•9500000	•979611	•995183	1•008833	1•019320	1•025495
•9600000	•991118	1•007350	1•021619	1•032611	1•039097
•9699999	1•002684	1•019600	1•034516	1•046038	1•052851
•9799999	1•014309	1•031936	1•047527	1•059605	1•066762
•9899999	1•025996	1•044360	1•060656	1•073319	1•080839
1•0000000	1•037744	1•056875	1•073908	1•087184	1•095087
1•0100000	1•049556	1•069483	1•087286	1•101206	1•109514
1•0200000	1•061434	1•082187	1•100794	1•115393	1•124128
1•0300000	1•073378	1•094989	1•114437	1•129749	1•138936
1•0400000	1•085391	1•107893	1•128220	1•144283	1•153947
1•0500000	1•097473	1•120901	1•142147	1•159000	1•169170
1•0600000	1•109626	1•134015	1•156223	1•173909	1•184614
1•0699999	1•121852	1•147239	1•170453	1•189016	1•200290
1•0799999	1•134152	1•160575	1•184842	1•204330	1•216207
1•0899999	1•146526	1•174026	1•199395	1•219860	1•232378
1•1000000	1•158978	1•187596	1•214119	1•235615	1•248813
1•1100000	1•171508	1•201286	1•229017	1•251602	1•265525
1•1200000	1•184116	1•215100	1•244097	1•267833	1•282528
1•1300000	1•196806	1•229041	1•259363	1•284317	1•299835
1•1400000	1•209577	1•243112	1•274823	1•301065	1•317462
1•1500000	1•222431	1•257315	1•290482	1•318089	1•335425
1•1600000	1•235369	1•271653	1•306346	1•335400	1•353741
1•1700000	1•248392	1•286130	1•322423	1•353010	1•372428
1•1800000	1•261501	1•300748	1•338719	1•370933	1•391505
1•1899999	1•274697	1•315509	1•355240	1•389183	1•410995

$\alpha = -.399999$

Θ	K VALUES				
	.794250555	.868696860	.928444378	.971111163	.994996249
1.2000000	1.287981	1.330417	1.371994	1.407773	1.430920
1.2100000	1.301354	1.345474	1.388987	1.426719	1.451303
1.2200000	1.314816	1.360683	1.406228	1.446037	1.472172
1.2300000	1.328367	1.376045	1.423722	1.465744	1.493554
1.2400000	1.342009	1.391564	1.441477	1.485857	1.515480
1.2500000	1.355742	1.407242	1.459502	1.506395	1.537983
1.2599999	1.369565	1.423080	1.477802	1.527377	1.561100
1.2699999	1.383479	1.439080	1.496385	1.548825	1.584870
1.2799999	1.397483	1.455244	1.515259	1.570758	1.609335
1.2899999	1.411579	1.471572	1.534430	1.593200	1.634542
1.3000000	1.425764	1.488068	1.553906	1.616175	1.660543
1.3100000	1.440039	1.504730	1.573692	1.639706	1.687393
1.3200000	1.454403	1.521559	1.593796	1.663819	1.715155
1.3300000	1.468854	1.538556	1.614222	1.688541	1.743898
1.3400000	1.483392	1.555720	1.634977	1.713898	1.773696
1.3500000	1.498016	1.573050	1.656065	1.739919	1.804634
1.3600000	1.512723	1.590546	1.677489	1.766633	1.836807
1.3700000	1.527513	1.608205	1.699254	1.794067	1.870317
1.3799999	1.542383	1.626026	1.721360	1.822252	1.905282
1.3899999	1.557331	1.644006	1.743810	1.851215	1.941833
1.4000000	1.572355	1.662141	1.766602	1.880986	1.980118
1.4100000	1.587452	1.680428	1.789735	1.911589	2.020303
1.4200000	1.602619	1.698863	1.813205	1.943048	2.062576
1.4300000	1.617853	1.717440	1.837006	1.975386	2.107149
1.4400000	1.633151	1.736153	1.861133	2.008618	2.154262
1.4500000	1.648509	1.754997	1.885575	2.042757	2.204186
1.4600000	1.663924	1.773965	1.910322	2.077805	2.257224
1.4700000	1.679392	1.793048	1.935359	2.113760	2.313715
1.4800000	1.694909	1.812239	1.960670	2.150607	2.374028
1.4900000	1.710470	1.831530	1.986237	2.188320	2.438559
1.5000000	1.726071	1.850910	2.012040	2.226861	2.507712
1.5100000	1.741708	1.870369	2.038055	2.266176	2.581864
1.5200000	1.757375	1.889899	2.064256	2.306194	2.661315
1.5300000	1.773068	1.909487	2.090618	2.346833	2.746195
1.5400000	1.788782	1.929123	2.117109	2.387992	2.836353
1.5500000	1.804512	1.948795	2.143701	2.429557	2.931221
1.5600000	1.820252	1.968492	2.170361	2.471404	3.029724
1.5699999	1.835998	1.988201	2.197056	2.513400	3.130286
1.5707963	1.837252	1.989771	2.199182	2.516747	3.138327
1.5707963	1.837251	1.989770	2.199181	2.516745	3.138325

$\alpha = -.349999$

θ	K VALUES				
	.009966711	.039469502	.087332193	.151646642	.229848846
.0000000	.000000	.000000	.000000	.000000	.000000
.0100000	.009999	.009999	.009999	.009999	.009999
.0200000	.019999	.019999	.019999	.019999	.019999
.0300000	.029996	.029997	.029997	.029997	.029997
.0400000	.039992	.039992	.039993	.039994	.039995
.0500000	.049985	.049986	.049987	.049988	.049990
.0600000	.059975	.059976	.059978	.059980	.059983
.0700000	.069960	.069962	.069965	.069968	.069973
.0800000	.079941	.079943	.079947	.079953	.079960
.0900000	.089916	.089920	.089925	.089933	.089943
.1000000	.099885	.099890	.099898	.099908	.099922
.1100000	.109847	.109854	.109864	.109878	.109896
.1200000	.119802	.119810	.119824	.119843	.119865
.1300000	.129749	.129759	.129777	.129800	.129829
.1400000	.139686	.139700	.139722	.139751	.139786
.1500000	.149615	.149631	.149658	.149694	.149738
.1600000	.159533	.159553	.159586	.159629	.159682
.1700000	.169441	.169465	.169504	.169556	.169620
.1800000	.179338	.179366	.179412	.179474	.179549
.1900000	.189222	.189255	.189310	.189382	.189471
.2000000	.199094	.199133	.199196	.199281	.199384
.2100000	.208953	.208998	.209071	.209169	.209288
.2200000	.218799	.218850	.218934	.219046	.219183
.2300000	.228630	.228689	.228784	.228912	.229069
.2400000	.238446	.238513	.238621	.238767	.238944
.2500000	.248247	.248322	.248444	.248609	.248809
.2600000	.258033	.258117	.258254	.258438	.258664
.2700000	.267802	.267896	.268049	.268255	.268507
.2800000	.277554	.277658	.277829	.278059	.278339
.2900000	.287288	.287404	.287593	.287848	.288160
.3000000	.297005	.297133	.297342	.297624	.297968
.3100000	.306703	.306844	.307074	.307385	.307764
.3200000	.316383	.316538	.316790	.317131	.317548
.3300000	.326043	.326213	.326489	.326862	.327318
.3400000	.335684	.335869	.336170	.336577	.337076
.3500000	.345304	.345506	.345833	.346277	.346820
.3600000	.354904	.355123	.355479	.355960	.356550
.3700000	.364484	.364720	.365106	.365627	.366267
.3800000	.374041	.374297	.374714	.375277	.375969
.3900000	.383578	.383853	.384302	.384910	.385657

$\alpha = -$ .349999

Θ	K VALUES				
	.009966711	.039469502	.087332193	.151646642	.229848846
.4000000	.393092	.393388	.393872	.394526	.395330
.4100000	.402584	.402902	.403421	.404124	.404988
.4200000	.412053	.412394	.412951	.413705	.414632
.4300000	.421500	.421864	.422460	.423267	.424260
.4400000	.430923	.431312	.431949	.432812	.433873
.4500000	.440322	.440738	.441417	.442337	.443471
.4600000	.449698	.450141	.450863	.451844	.453053
.4700000	.459050	.459520	.460289	.461333	.462619
.4800000	.468378	.468877	.469693	.470802	.472169
.4900000	.477681	.478210	.479076	.480252	.481704
.5000000	.486959	.487520	.488436	.489683	.491222
.5100000	.496213	.496806	.497775	.499094	.500724
.5200000	.505441	.506067	.507092	.508486	.510209
.5300000	.514645	.515305	.516386	.517858	.519679
.5400000	.523823	.524519	.525658	.527210	.529131
.5500000	.532975	.533708	.534907	.536543	.538568
.5600000	.542102	.542872	.544134	.545855	.547988
.5700000	.551203	.552012	.553338	.555147	.557391
.5800000	.560279	.561128	.562520	.564420	.566777
.5900000	.569328	.570218	.571678	.573672	.576147
.6000000	.578352	.579284	.580814	.582904	.585501
.6100000	.587349	.588325	.589926	.592116	.594838
.6200000	.596320	.597341	.599016	.601307	.604158
.6300000	.605266	.606332	.608082	.610478	.613461
.6400000	.614185	.615298	.617126	.619629	.622748
.6500000	.623078	.624239	.626146	.628760	.632019
.6600000	.631945	.633155	.635144	.637871	.641273
.6700000	.640786	.642046	.644119	.646961	.650510
.6800000	.649601	.650912	.653070	.656031	.659731
.6899999	.658389	.659753	.661999	.665081	.668936
.7000000	.667152	.668570	.670905	.674112	.678125
.7100000	.675889	.677362	.679788	.683122	.687297
.7200000	.684600	.686129	.688648	.692112	.696454
.7300000	.693285	.694871	.697485	.701083	.705594
.7400000	.701945	.703589	.706300	.710033	.714719
.7500000	.710579	.712282	.715093	.718964	.723828
.7600000	.719187	.720951	.723863	.727876	.732921
.7700000	.727770	.729596	.732611	.736768	.741998
.7800000	.736328	.738217	.741336	.745641	.751060
.7899999	.744861	.746814	.750040	.754494	.760107

$\alpha = -\ .349999$

θ	K VALUES				
	.009966711	.039469502	.087332193	.151646642	.229848846
.8000000	.753369	.755387	.758722	.763329	.769139
.8100000	.761853	.763936	.767382	.772145	.778156
.8200000	.770311	.772462	.776020	.780942	.787158
.8300000	.778746	.780965	.784637	.789720	.796145
.8400000	.787156	.789444	.793233	.798480	.805118
.8500000	.795542	.797901	.801808	.807222	.814076
.8600000	.803904	.806334	.810361	.815945	.823020
.8700000	.812242	.814745	.818894	.824650	.831950
.8799999	.820557	.823134	.827407	.833338	.840867
.8899999	.828849	.831500	.835899	.842008	.849769
.9000000	.837118	.839845	.844371	.850661	.858658
.9100000	.845364	.848168	.852823	.859297	.867534
.9200000	.853587	.856469	.861255	.867915	.876396
.9300000	.861788	.864749	.869668	.876517	.885246
.9400000	.869968	.873008	.878061	.885102	.894082
.9500000	.878125	.881246	.886436	.893670	.902906
.9600000	.886261	.889464	.894791	.902223	.911718
.9699999	.894375	.897661	.903128	.910759	.920517
.9799999	.902469	.905838	.911447	.919280	.929305
.9899999	.910542	.913996	.919747	.927785	.938080
1.0000000	.918595	.922134	.928030	.936275	.946844
1.0100000	.926627	.930252	.936295	.944750	.955597
1.0200000	.934639	.938352	.944543	.953210	.964338
1.0300000	.942632	.946433	.952774	.961655	.973069
1.0400000	.950606	.954496	.960987	.970086	.981788
1.0500000	.958561	.962541	.969185	.978503	.990498
1.0600000	.966497	.970568	.977366	.986906	.999196
1.0699999	.974414	.978577	.985531	.995295	1.007885
1.0799999	.982314	.986569	.993680	1.003671	1.016563
1.0899999	.990196	.994544	1.001814	1.012033	1.025232
1.1000000	.998061	1.002503	1.009933	1.020383	1.033891
1.1100000	1.005908	1.010445	1.018036	1.028720	1.042541
1.1200000	1.013739	1.018372	1.026125	1.037045	1.051182
1.1300000	1.021553	1.026282	1.034200	1.045357	1.059814
1.1400000	1.029351	1.034178	1.042261	1.053658	1.068437
1.1500000	1.037134	1.042058	1.050308	1.061947	1.077052
1.1600000	1.044901	1.049923	1.058342	1.070225	1.085658
1.1700000	1.052653	1.057775	1.066363	1.078491	1.094257
1.1800000	1.060390	1.065612	1.074370	1.086747	1.102847
1.1899999	1.068113	1.073435	1.082366	1.094992	1.111430

$\alpha = -$ .349999

θ	K VALUES				
	.009966711	.039469502	.087332193	.151646642	.229848846
1.2000000	1.075822	1.081245	1.090349	1.103227	1.120006
1.2100000	1.083517	1.089042	1.098320	1.111451	1.128574
1.2200000	1.091199	1.096826	1.106279	1.119666	1.137135
1.2300000	1.098867	1.104598	1.114227	1.127872	1.145690
1.2400000	1.106523	1.112358	1.122165	1.136068	1.154237
1.2500000	1.114167	1.120106	1.130091	1.144255	1.162779
1.2599999	1.121799	1.127842	1.138007	1.152433	1.171314
1.2699999	1.129419	1.135568	1.145913	1.160603	1.179843
1.2799999	1.137028	1.143283	1.153810	1.168765	1.188367
1.2899999	1.144627	1.150987	1.161697	1.176918	1.196884
1.3000000	1.152214	1.158682	1.169575	1.185064	1.205397
1.3100000	1.159792	1.166367	1.177444	1.193203	1.213904
1.3200000	1.167360	1.174042	1.185304	1.201335	1.222407
1.3300000	1.174918	1.181709	1.193157	1.209460	1.230904
1.3400000	1.182468	1.189367	1.201001	1.217578	1.239397
1.3500000	1.190008	1.197017	1.208838	1.225690	1.247886
1.3600000	1.197541	1.204658	1.216668	1.233795	1.256370
1.3700000	1.205065	1.212293	1.224491	1.241896	1.264851
1.3799999	1.212582	1.219920	1.232307	1.249990	1.273327
1.3899999	1.220092	1.227540	1.240118	1.258080	1.281800
1.4000000	1.227595	1.235154	1.247922	1.266164	1.290270
1.4100000	1.235091	1.242761	1.255721	1.274244	1.298736
1.4200000	1.242582	1.250363	1.263514	1.282319	1.307200
1.4300000	1.250067	1.257959	1.271303	1.290391	1.315660
1.4400000	1.257546	1.265551	1.279087	1.298458	1.324118
1.4500000	1.265021	1.273137	1.286866	1.306522	1.332573
1.4600000	1.272491	1.280720	1.294642	1.314583	1.341027
1.4700000	1.279956	1.288298	1.302414	1.322640	1.349478
1.4800000	1.287418	1.295873	1.310183	1.330695	1.357927
1.4900000	1.294877	1.303444	1.317949	1.338747	1.366375
1.5000000	1.302332	1.311012	1.325712	1.346797	1.374821
1.5100000	1.309785	1.318578	1.333473	1.354846	1.383265
1.5200000	1.317236	1.326142	1.341231	1.362892	1.391709
1.5300000	1.324684	1.333704	1.348989	1.370937	1.400152
1.5400000	1.332131	1.341264	1.356744	1.378981	1.408594
1.5500000	1.339577	1.348823	1.364499	1.387024	1.417035
1.5600000	1.347022	1.356382	1.372253	1.395067	1.425476
1.5699999	1.354467	1.363940	1.380007	1.403109	1.433917
1.5707963	1.355060	1.364542	1.380625	1.403750	1.434589
1.5707963	1.355059	1.364541	1.380624	1.403749	1.434588

$\alpha = -\ .349999$

Θ	K VALUES				
	.318821117	.415016431	.514599755	.613601043	.708073407
.0000000	.000000	.000000	.000000	.000000	.000000
.0100000	.009999	.009999	.009999	.009999	.010000
.0200000	.019999	.019999	.019999	.019999	.020000
.0300000	.029998	.029998	.029999	.029999	.030000
.0400000	.039995	.039996	.039998	.039999	.040000
.0500000	.049992	.049994	.049996	.049998	.050000
.0600000	.059986	.059989	.059993	.059996	.060000
.0700000	.069978	.069983	.069989	.069995	.070000
.0800000	.079967	.079975	.079984	.079992	.080000
.0900000	.089953	.089965	.089977	.089989	.090001
.1000000	.099936	.099952	.099969	.099985	.100001
.1100000	.109915	.109937	.109959	.109981	.110002
.1200000	.119891	.119918	.119947	.119975	.120003
.1300000	.129861	.129896	.129933	.129969	.130004
.1400000	.139827	.139871	.139916	.139962	.140005
.1500000	.149788	.149842	.149898	.149953	.150007
.1600000	.159743	.159808	.159876	.159944	.160009
.1700000	.169692	.169771	.169852	.169934	.170011
.1800000	.179635	.179729	.179825	.179922	.180014
.1900000	.189572	.189682	.189796	.189909	.190018
.2000000	.199502	.199630	.199763	.199895	.200022
.2100000	.209425	.209573	.209726	.209880	.210027
.2200000	.219340	.219510	.219687	.219863	.220033
.2300000	.229248	.229442	.229644	.229846	.230039
.2400000	.239147	.239368	.239598	.239827	.240047
.2500000	.249039	.249288	.249548	.249807	.250056
.2600000	.258922	.259202	.259494	.259786	.260066
.2700000	.268796	.269110	.269437	.269764	.270078
.2800000	.278661	.279011	.279375	.279741	.280091
.2900000	.288517	.288905	.289310	.289716	.290106
.3000000	.298363	.298793	.299241	.299691	.300123
.3100000	.308199	.308673	.309168	.309665	.310143
.3200000	.318026	.318547	.319092	.319638	.320164
.3300000	.327842	.328414	.329011	.329610	.330188
.3400000	.337648	.338273	.338926	.339582	.340215
.3500000	.347443	.348124	.348837	.349554	.350245
.3600000	.357228	.357969	.358744	.359525	.360278
.3700000	.367002	.367805	.368648	.369495	.370315
.3800000	.376764	.377634	.378547	.379466	.380355
.3900000	.386516	.387456	.388442	.389437	.390399

$\alpha = -$ .349999

Θ	K VALUES				
	.318821117	.415016431	.514599755	.613601043	.708073407
.4000000	.396255	.397269	.398334	.399408	.400448
.4100000	.405984	.407075	.408222	.409379	.410501
.4200000	.415701	.416873	.418106	.419352	.420559
.4300000	.425406	.426663	.427986	.429324	.430623
.4400000	.435099	.436445	.437863	.439298	.440692
.4500000	.444780	.446220	.447737	.449274	.450767
.4600000	.454450	.455986	.457607	.459250	.460849
.4700000	.464107	.465745	.467474	.469228	.470937
.4800000	.473752	.475495	.477338	.479209	.481032
.4900000	.483385	.485238	.487199	.489191	.491135
.5000000	.493005	.494973	.497057	.499176	.501246
.5100000	.502613	.504701	.506912	.509164	.511366
.5200000	.512209	.514420	.516765	.519155	.521494
.5300000	.521793	.524132	.526616	.529150	.531631
.5400000	.531364	.533837	.536464	.539148	.541779
.5500000	.540923	.543534	.546310	.549150	.551937
.5600000	.550470	.553223	.556155	.559156	.562105
.5700000	.560004	.562906	.565998	.569167	.572285
.5800000	.569526	.572581	.575840	.579184	.582477
.5900000	.579036	.582249	.585681	.589205	.592681
.6000000	.588533	.591910	.595521	.599233	.602898
.6100000	.598019	.601565	.605360	.609267	.613129
.6200000	.607492	.611212	.615199	.619307	.623374
.6300000	.616953	.620853	.625037	.629355	.633634
.6400000	.626403	.630488	.634876	.639410	.643909
.6500000	.635840	.640117	.644715	.649472	.654200
.6600000	.645266	.649739	.654555	.659543	.664507
.6700000	.654680	.659356	.664395	.669623	.674832
.6800000	.664082	.668966	.674237	.679712	.685175
.6899999	.673473	.678572	.684081	.689811	.695537
.7000000	.682852	.688172	.693926	.699920	.705918
.7100000	.692221	.697766	.703773	.710039	.716319
.7200000	.701578	.707356	.713623	.720169	.726741
.7300000	.710924	.716941	.723475	.730311	.737184
.7400000	.720259	.726521	.733331	.740465	.747650
.7500000	.729583	.736097	.743189	.750631	.758138
.7600000	.738897	.745668	.753052	.760811	.768650
.7700000	.748201	.755236	.762918	.771003	.779187
.7800000	.757494	.764800	.772789	.781210	.789749
.7899999	.766777	.774360	.782664	.791432	.800337

$\alpha = -\ .349999$

θ	K VALUES				
	.318821117	.415016431	.514599755	.613601043	.708073407
.8000000	.776050	.783917	.792544	.801668	.810952
.8100000	.785313	.793471	.802429	.811920	.821595
.8200000	.794567	.803022	.812321	.822188	.832266
.8300000	.803811	.812570	.822218	.832473	.842966
.8400000	.813046	.822116	.832121	.842774	.853697
.8500000	.822271	.831660	.842031	.853094	.864458
.8600000	.831488	.841201	.851947	.863431	.875251
.8700000	.840696	.850741	.861871	.873787	.886077
.8799999	.849896	.860279	.871803	.884162	.896937
.8899999	.859087	.869816	.881742	.894557	.907830
.9000000	.868269	.879352	.891690	.904973	.918759
.9100000	.877444	.888886	.901646	.915408	.929724
.9200000	.886611	.898421	.911611	.925865	.940726
.9300000	.895770	.907954	.921586	.936344	.951765
.9400000	.904922	.917488	.931569	.946845	.962843
.9500000	.914066	.927021	.941563	.957369	.973961
.9600000	.923204	.936555	.951566	.967916	.985118
.9699999	.932334	.946088	.961580	.978486	.996317
.9799999	.941458	.955623	.971604	.989081	1.007558
.9899999	.950575	.965158	.981639	.999700	1.018841
1.0000000	.959686	.974694	.991685	1.010344	1.030168
1.0100000	.968790	.984232	1.001743	1.021013	1.041539
1.0200000	.977889	.993771	1.011812	1.031708	1.052956
1.0300000	.986981	1.003311	1.021893	1.042430	1.064418
1.0400000	.996069	1.012853	1.031986	1.053178	1.075927
1.0500000	1.005150	1.022397	1.042091	1.063953	1.087483
1.0600000	1.014227	1.031942	1.052209	1.074755	1.099087
1.0699999	1.023298	1.041490	1.062339	1.085584	1.110740
1.0799999	1.032364	1.051041	1.072483	1.096442	1.122443
1.0899999	1.041426	1.060594	1.082639	1.107328	1.134195
1.1000000	1.050483	1.070149	1.092808	1.118242	1.145998
1.1100000	1.059536	1.079708	1.102991	1.129185	1.157852
1.1200000	1.068584	1.089269	1.113187	1.140157	1.169758
1.1300000	1.077628	1.098833	1.123397	1.151158	1.181716
1.1400000	1.086669	1.108400	1.133620	1.162188	1.193727
1.1500000	1.095705	1.117971	1.143856	1.173248	1.205791
1.1600000	1.104738	1.127544	1.154107	1.184337	1.217908
1.1700000	1.113767	1.137121	1.164371	1.195455	1.230079
1.1800000	1.122793	1.146702	1.174649	1.206603	1.242303
1.1899999	1.131816	1.156286	1.184941	1.217781	1.254582

$\alpha =$ - .349999

θ	K VALUES				
	.318821117	.415016431	.514599755	.613601043	.708073407
1.2000000	1.140836	1.165874	1.195246	1.228988	1.266916
1.2100000	1.149853	1.175465	1.205566	1.240225	1.279303
1.2200000	1.158867	1.185060	1.215898	1.251491	1.291745
1.2300000	1.167879	1.194659	1.226245	1.262786	1.304242
1.2400000	1.176887	1.204261	1.236605	1.274110	1.316792
1.2500000	1.185894	1.213867	1.246978	1.285463	1.329397
1.2599999	1.194898	1.223477	1.257365	1.296844	1.342055
1.2699999	1.203900	1.233091	1.267764	1.308254	1.354767
1.2799999	1.212900	1.242708	1.278177	1.319692	1.367532
1.2899999	1.221898	1.252329	1.288602	1.331157	1.380349
1.3000000	1.230895	1.261954	1.299040	1.342649	1.393218
1.3100000	1.239889	1.271583	1.309491	1.354168	1.406138
1.3200000	1.248882	1.281215	1.319953	1.365713	1.419109
1.3300000	1.257873	1.290850	1.330427	1.377283	1.432128
1.3400000	1.266863	1.300489	1.340912	1.388879	1.445197
1.3500000	1.275851	1.310132	1.351409	1.400499	1.458313
1.3600000	1.284838	1.319778	1.361917	1.412142	1.471475
1.3700000	1.293824	1.329427	1.372435	1.423808	1.484682
1.3799999	1.302809	1.339079	1.382963	1.435497	1.497932
1.3899999	1.311792	1.348734	1.393501	1.447206	1.511225
1.4000000	1.320775	1.358392	1.404048	1.458937	1.524559
1.4100000	1.329757	1.368053	1.414605	1.470687	1.537931
1.4200000	1.338738	1.377716	1.425170	1.482455	1.551341
1.4300000	1.347718	1.387382	1.435742	1.494241	1.564786
1.4400000	1.356697	1.397051	1.446323	1.506044	1.578265
1.4500000	1.365676	1.406722	1.456911	1.517862	1.591775
1.4600000	1.374654	1.416394	1.467505	1.529695	1.605315
1.4700000	1.383632	1.426069	1.478105	1.541542	1.618882
1.4800000	1.392609	1.435746	1.488711	1.553401	1.632475
1.4900000	1.401586	1.445424	1.499322	1.565271	1.646090
1.5000000	1.410562	1.455104	1.509938	1.577151	1.659725
1.5100000	1.419538	1.464785	1.520557	1.589040	1.673379
1.5200000	1.428514	1.474467	1.531181	1.600937	1.687048
1.5300000	1.437490	1.484149	1.541807	1.612840	1.700731
1.5400000	1.446465	1.493833	1.552435	1.624749	1.714424
1.5500000	1.455440	1.503517	1.563065	1.636661	1.728125
1.5600000	1.464415	1.513202	1.573696	1.648576	1.741831
1.5699999	1.473390	1.522887	1.584328	1.660492	1.755540
1.5707963	1.474105	1.523658	1.585175	1.661441	1.756632
1.5707963	1.474104	1.523657	1.585174	1.661440	1.756631

$\alpha = -\ .349999$

θ	K VALUES				
	.794250555	.868696860	.928444378	.971111163	.994996249
.0000000	.000000	.000000	.000000	.000000	.000000
.0100000	.010000	.010000	.010000	.010000	.010000
.0200000	.020000	.020000	.020000	.020000	.020000
.0300000	.030000	.030000	.030001	.030001	.030001
.0400000	.040001	.040001	.040002	.040002	.040003
.0500000	.050002	.050003	.050004	.050005	.050006
.0600000	.060003	.060006	.060008	.060009	.060010
.0700000	.070005	.070009	.070013	.070015	.070016
.0800000	.080008	.080014	.080019	.080023	.080025
.0900000	.090011	.090020	.090028	.090033	.090036
.1000000	.100016	.100028	.100038	.100045	.100049
.1100000	.110021	.110038	.110051	.110060	.110066
.1200000	.120028	.120049	.120067	.120079	.120086
.1300000	.130036	.130063	.130085	.130101	.130110
.1400000	.140045	.140079	.140107	.140126	.140137
.1500000	.150056	.150098	.150132	.150156	.150170
.1600000	.160068	.160119	.160161	.160190	.160207
.1700000	.170082	.170144	.170194	.170229	.170249
.1800000	.180099	.180172	.180231	.180273	.180296
.1900000	.190117	.190203	.190273	.190322	.190350
.2000000	.200138	.200239	.200320	.200378	.200410
.2100000	.210162	.210278	.210372	.210439	.210477
.2200000	.220188	.220322	.220430	.220507	.220551
.2300000	.230217	.230370	.230494	.230583	.230632
.2400000	.240249	.240424	.240565	.240666	.240722
.2500000	.250284	.250482	.250642	.250756	.250821
.2600000	.260323	.260547	.260727	.260856	.260928
.2700000	.270366	.270617	.270819	.270964	.271045
.2800000	.280414	.280693	.280919	.281081	.281172
.2900000	.290465	.290777	.291028	.291208	.291309
.3000000	.300521	.300867	.301146	.301346	.301458
.3100000	.310582	.310964	.311273	.311494	.311619
.3200000	.320648	.321070	.321410	.321655	.321792
.3300000	.330720	.331184	.331558	.331827	.331978
.3400000	.340798	.341306	.341717	.342012	.342177
.3500000	.350882	.351438	.351887	.352210	.352391
.3600000	.360973	.361579	.362069	.362422	.362620
.3700000	.371070	.371730	.372264	.372649	.372865
.3800000	.381175	.381892	.382473	.382891	.383125
.3900000	.391288	.392065	.392695	.393149	.393403

$\alpha = -\ .349999$

Θ	K VALUES				
	.794250555	.868696860	.928444378	.971111163	.994996249
.4000000	.401409	.402250	.402932	.403423	.403699
.4100000	.411539	.412447	.413185	.413715	.414014
.4200000	.421678	.422657	.423453	.424026	.424348
.4300000	.431826	.432881	.433738	.434355	.434703
.4400000	.441985	.443119	.444040	.444705	.445079
.4500000	.452154	.453371	.454361	.455075	.455478
.4600000	.462334	.463639	.464700	.465467	.465899
.4700000	.472526	.473922	.475060	.475882	.476345
.4800000	.482730	.484223	.485440	.486320	.486816
.4900000	.492946	.494541	.495842	.496782	.497313
.5000000	.503176	.504877	.506266	.507271	.507838
.5100000	.513420	.515233	.516713	.517785	.518391
.5200000	.523679	.525608	.527185	.528328	.528974
.5300000	.533953	.536004	.537682	.538899	.539587
.5400000	.544242	.546421	.548206	.549501	.550233
.5500000	.554548	.556861	.558757	.560133	.560912
.5600000	.564872	.567324	.569336	.570798	.571625
.5700000	.575213	.577812	.579945	.581497	.582375
.5800000	.585573	.588324	.590585	.592230	.593162
.5900000	.595953	.598863	.601257	.603000	.603988
.6000000	.606353	.609429	.611962	.613808	.614855
.6100000	.616774	.620023	.622701	.624655	.625763
.6200000	.627217	.630646	.633476	.635542	.636716
.6300000	.637682	.641300	.644288	.646472	.647713
.6400000	.648171	.651985	.655139	.657446	.658757
.6500000	.658685	.662702	.666030	.668465	.669851
.6600000	.669224	.673454	.676961	.679531	.680994
.6700000	.679789	.684240	.687936	.690646	.692191
.6800000	.690381	.695063	.698955	.701812	.703441
.6899999	.701001	.705924	.710020	.713031	.714749
.7000000	.711651	.716823	.721133	.724304	.726115
.7100000	.722331	.727762	.732295	.735634	.737542
.7200000	.733042	.738743	.743508	.747022	.749032
.7300000	.743785	.749767	.754774	.758471	.760587
.7400000	.754561	.760836	.766095	.769983	.772211
.7500000	.765372	.771950	.777473	.781561	.783905
.7600000	.776218	.783112	.788909	.793206	.795672
.7700000	.787101	.794323	.800406	.804921	.807514
.7800000	.798021	.805584	.811965	.816708	.819435
.7899999	.808981	.816898	.823590	.828571	.831438

$\alpha = -.349999$

Θ	*K* VALUES				
	.794250555	.868696860	.928444378	.971111163	.994996249
.8000000	.819980	.828266	.835282	.840512	.843525
.8100000	.831021	.839689	.847043	.852533	.855700
.8200000	.842105	.851170	.858876	.864638	.867966
.8300000	.853232	.862711	.870783	.876830	.880326
.8400000	.864404	.874312	.882767	.889111	.892784
.8500000	.875623	.885976	.894830	.901486	.905344
.8600000	.886889	.897705	.906975	.913956	.918009
.8700000	.898204	.909502	.919205	.926527	.930783
.8799999	.909570	.921367	.931523	.939201	.943671
.8899999	.920987	.933303	.943931	.951983	.956677
.9000000	.932458	.945313	.956432	.964875	.969805
.9100000	.943983	.957397	.969030	.977883	.983060
.9200000	.955563	.969559	.981728	.991010	.996447
.9300000	.967201	.981801	.994530	1.004261	1.009972
.9400000	.978898	.994126	1.007437	1.017641	1.023639
.9500000	.990655	1.006534	1.020455	1.031153	1.037454
.9600000	1.002474	1.019030	1.033587	1.044803	1.051423
.9699999	1.014356	1.031614	1.046836	1.058597	1.065552
.9799999	1.026302	1.044291	1.060207	1.072539	1.079849
.9899999	1.038315	1.057062	1.073703	1.086636	1.094318
1.0000000	1.050395	1.069930	1.087328	1.100892	1.108969
1.0100000	1.062544	1.082898	1.101088	1.115315	1.123807
1.0200000	1.074764	1.095968	1.114985	1.129910	1.138842
1.0300000	1.087056	1.109142	1.129025	1.144684	1.154081
1.0400000	1.099421	1.122425	1.143213	1.159644	1.169533
1.0500000	1.111861	1.135818	1.157553	1.174798	1.185207
1.0600000	1.124378	1.149325	1.172050	1.190153	1.201113
1.0699999	1.136973	1.162948	1.186709	1.205716	1.217262
1.0799999	1.149647	1.176690	1.201536	1.221497	1.233664
1.0899999	1.162401	1.190554	1.216536	1.237503	1.250330
1.1000000	1.175238	1.204544	1.231715	1.253745	1.267274
1.1100000	1.188159	1.218661	1.247079	1.270231	1.284508
1.1200000	1.201164	1.232910	1.262632	1.286972	1.302045
1.1300000	1.214255	1.247292	1.278382	1.303979	1.319901
1.1400000	1.227434	1.261812	1.294335	1.321261	1.338090
1.1500000	1.240701	1.276471	1.310498	1.338832	1.356630
1.1600000	1.254058	1.291274	1.326876	1.356703	1.375539
1.1700000	1.267505	1.306222	1.343476	1.374887	1.394835
1.1800000	1.281044	1.321319	1.360306	1.393398	1.414538
1.1899999	1.294676	1.336568	1.377373	1.412250	1.434671

$\alpha = -.349999$

θ	K VALUES				
	.794250555	.868696860	.928444378	.971111163	.994996249
.2000000	1.308401	1.351971	1.394683	1.431458	1.455258
.2100000	1.322221	1.367531	1.412244	1.451037	1.476322
.2200000	1.336135	1.383251	1.430064	1.471004	1.497892
.2300000	1.350144	1.399132	1.448149	1.491376	1.519996
.2400000	1.364250	1.415179	1.466508	1.512173	1.542667
.2500000	1.378451	1.431391	1.485148	1.533412	1.565939
.2599999	1.392749	1.447773	1.504076	1.555115	1.589849
.2699999	1.407142	1.464325	1.523300	1.577302	1.614439
.2799999	1.421632	1.481049	1.542828	1.599995	1.639751
.2899999	1.436218	1.497946	1.562667	1.623219	1.665836
.3000000	1.450900	1.515018	1.582823	1.646997	1.692746
.3100000	1.465676	1.532265	1.603304	1.671354	1.720539
.3200000	1.480546	1.549688	1.624117	1.696317	1.749280
.3300000	1.495508	1.567286	1.645266	1.721913	1.779039
.3400000	1.510563	1.585060	1.666758	1.748171	1.809896
.3500000	1.525708	1.603008	1.688597	1.775120	1.841937
.3600000	1.540942	1.621129	1.710788	1.802789	1.875260
.3700000	1.556262	1.639422	1.733333	1.831208	1.909973
.3799999	1.571667	1.657884	1.756235	1.860407	1.946196
.3899999	1.587154	1.676513	1.779495	1.890416	1.984067
.4000000	1.602722	1.695305	1.803112	1.921263	2.023737
.4100000	1.618367	1.714255	1.827084	1.952977	2.065381
.4200000	1.634085	1.733360	1.851408	1.985581	2.109191
.4300000	1.649875	1.752614	1.876077	2.019097	2.155389
.4400000	1.665731	1.772012	1.901085	2.053544	2.204223
.4500000	1.681652	1.791545	1.926422	2.088931	2.255974
.4600000	1.697632	1.811208	1.952076	2.125265	2.310957
.4700000	1.713668	1.830993	1.978033	2.162541	2.369523
.4800000	1.729756	1.850890	2.004275	2.200743	2.432055
.4900000	1.745890	1.870890	2.030784	2.239846	2.498963
.5000000	1.762067	1.890985	2.057539	2.279808	2.570666
.5100000	1.778281	1.911163	2.084514	2.320574	2.647556
.5200000	1.794527	1.931414	2.111683	2.362071	2.729942
.5300000	1.810800	1.951727	2.139019	2.404213	2.817961
.5400000	1.827095	1.972089	2.166491	2.446894	2.911455
.5500000	1.843407	1.992490	2.194067	2.489998	3.009835
.5600000	1.859731	2.012916	2.221714	2.533395	3.111985
.5699999	1.876060	2.033356	2.249398	2.576946	3.216272
.5707963	1.877361	2.034984	2.251604	2.580417	3.224610
.5707963	1.877359	2.034982	2.251602	2.580415	3.224608

$\alpha = -$ .299999

Θ	K VALUES				
	.009966711	.039469502	.087332193	.151646642	.229848846
.0000000	.000000	.000000	.000000	.000000	.000000
.0100000	.009999	.009999	.009999	.009999	.009999
.0200000	.019999	.019999	.019999	.019999	.019999
.0300000	.029997	.029997	.029997	.029997	.029998
.0400000	.039993	.039994	.039994	.039995	.039996
.0500000	.049987	.049988	.049989	.049990	.049992
.0600000	.059978	.059979	.059981	.059983	.059986
.0700000	.069966	.069968	.069970	.069974	.069978
.0800000	.079949	.079952	.079956	.079961	.079968
.0900000	.089928	.089932	.089937	.089945	.089955
.1000000	.099902	.099906	.099914	.099925	.099938
.1100000	.109869	.109876	.109886	.109901	.109918
.1200000	.119831	.119839	.119853	.119871	.119894
.1300000	.129785	.129796	.129813	.129836	.129865
.1400000	.139732	.139745	.139767	.139796	.139832
.1500000	.149670	.149687	.149714	.149750	.149793
.1600000	.159601	.159621	.159653	.159697	.159750
.1700000	.169522	.169546	.169584	.169637	.169700
.1800000	.179433	.179461	.179507	.179569	.179645
.1900000	.189334	.189367	.189422	.189494	.189583
.2000000	.199225	.199263	.199326	.199411	.199515
.2100000	.209104	.209149	.209221	.209320	.209439
.2200000	.218971	.219023	.219106	.219219	.219356
.2300000	.228827	.228885	.228981	.229109	.229266
.2400000	.238669	.238736	.238844	.238990	.239168
.2500000	.248499	.248574	.248696	.248861	.249062
.2600000	.258314	.258399	.258536	.258721	.258947
.2700000	.268116	.268210	.268364	.268571	.268823
.2800000	.277903	.278008	.278179	.278409	.278691
.2900000	.287675	.287792	.287981	.288237	.288549
.3000000	.297432	.297561	.297770	.298053	.298398
.3100000	.307173	.307315	.307545	.307856	.308237
.3200000	.316898	.317053	.317306	.317648	.318066
.3300000	.326606	.326776	.327053	.327427	.327885
.3400000	.336297	.336483	.336785	.337193	.337694
.3500000	.345971	.346173	.346502	.346947	.347492
.3600000	.355627	.355846	.356203	.356687	.357279
.3700000	.365265	.365502	.365889	.366413	.367055
.3800000	.374884	.375141	.375559	.376125	.376820
.3900000	.384485	.384762	.385213	.385823	.386573

$\alpha = -$ .299999

Θ	K VALUES				
	.009966711	.039469502	.087332193	.151646642	.229848846
.4000000	.394067	.394365	.394850	.395507	.396315
.4100000	.403629	.403949	.404470	.405177	.406045
.4200000	.413172	.413515	.414074	.414832	.415763
.4300000	.422695	.423061	.423660	.424471	.425470
.4400000	.432197	.432589	.433229	.434096	.435164
.4500000	.441679	.442097	.442780	.443705	.444845
.4600000	.451141	.451586	.452313	.453299	.454515
.4700000	.460581	.461055	.461828	.462878	.464172
.4800000	.470001	.470503	.471324	.472440	.473816
.4900000	.479399	.479932	.480803	.481987	.483447
.5000000	.488775	.489340	.490262	.491517	.493066
.5100000	.498130	.498727	.499703	.501031	.502672
.5200000	.507463	.508093	.509125	.510529	.512265
.5300000	.516774	.517439	.518528	.520011	.521845
.5400000	.526063	.526764	.527912	.529476	.531412
.5500000	.535329	.536067	.537276	.538924	.540965
.5600000	.544573	.545349	.546621	.548356	.550506
.5700000	.553794	.554610	.555947	.557771	.560033
.5800000	.562993	.563849	.565253	.567169	.569547
.5900000	.572168	.573066	.574539	.576550	.579048
.6000000	.581321	.582262	.583806	.585915	.588536
.6100000	.590452	.591436	.593053	.595263	.598010
.6200000	.599559	.600589	.602280	.604593	.607471
.6300000	.608643	.609719	.611487	.613907	.616919
.6400000	.617704	.618828	.620675	.623203	.626354
.6500000	.626742	.627915	.629842	.632483	.635776
.6600000	.635757	.636980	.638990	.641746	.645184
.6700000	.644749	.646023	.648118	.650991	.654580
.6800000	.653718	.655044	.657226	.660220	.663962
.6899999	.662664	.664043	.666314	.669432	.673331
.7000000	.671586	.673021	.675383	.678627	.682688
.7100000	.680486	.681976	.684431	.687805	.692031
.7200000	.689363	.690910	.693460	.696967	.701362
.7300000	.698217	.699822	.702469	.706111	.710680
.7400000	.707048	.708713	.711459	.715240	.719985
.7500000	.715856	.717582	.720429	.724351	.729278
.7600000	.724642	.726429	.729379	.733446	.738558
.7700000	.733405	.735256	.738311	.742524	.747826
.7800000	.742146	.744060	.747223	.751587	.757082
.7899999	.750864	.752844	.756115	.760633	.766325

$\alpha = -.299999$

Θ	K VALUES				
	.009966711	.039469502	.087332193	.151646642	.229848846
.8000000	.759560	.761607	.764989	.769663	.775557
.8100000	.768234	.770348	.773844	.778676	.784776
.8200000	.776886	.779069	.782679	.787674	.793984
.8300000	.785516	.787769	.791497	.796657	.803180
.8400000	.794125	.796448	.800295	.805623	.812364
.8500000	.802711	.805107	.809075	.814574	.821537
.8600000	.811277	.813746	.817837	.823510	.830699
.8700000	.819821	.822364	.826580	.832430	.839849
.8799999	.828344	.830963	.835306	.841335	.848988
.8899999	.836846	.839542	.844013	.850225	.858117
.9000000	.845328	.848101	.852703	.859101	.867235
.9100000	.853789	.856641	.861376	.867961	.876342
.9200000	.862230	.865162	.870031	.876808	.885438
.9300000	.870651	.873663	.878669	.885640	.894525
.9400000	.879052	.882146	.887290	.894457	.903601
.9500000	.887433	.890610	.895894	.903261	.912667
.9600000	.895795	.899056	.904482	.912051	.921723
.9699999	.904137	.907484	.913053	.920827	.930770
.9799999	.912461	.915893	.921608	.929590	.939807
.9899999	.920766	.924285	.930147	.938339	.948835
1.0000000	.929052	.932660	.938670	.947076	.957853
1.0100000	.937320	.941017	.947178	.955800	.966863
1.0200000	.945570	.949357	.955670	.964510	.975864
1.0300000	.953803	.957680	.964148	.973209	.984856
1.0400000	.962018	.965987	.972610	.981895	.993839
1.0500000	.970215	.974277	.981058	.990569	1.002814
1.0600000	.978396	.982551	.989491	.999231	1.011781
1.0699999	.986560	.990810	.997910	1.007881	1.020740
1.0799999	.994708	.999053	1.006315	1.016520	1.029691
1.0899999	1.002839	1.007281	1.014707	1.025147	1.038634
1.1000000	1.010955	1.015494	1.023085	1.033764	1.047570
1.1100000	1.019055	1.023692	1.031449	1.042369	1.056499
1.1200000	1.027140	1.031875	1.039801	1.050964	1.065420
1.1300000	1.035210	1.040045	1.048140	1.059549	1.074334
1.1400000	1.043266	1.048200	1.056467	1.068123	1.083242
1.1500000	1.051306	1.056342	1.064781	1.076687	1.092142
1.1600000	1.059333	1.064471	1.073083	1.085242	1.101037
1.1700000	1.067346	1.072587	1.081374	1.093786	1.109925
1.1800000	1.075346	1.080689	1.089653	1.102322	1.118807
1.1899999	1.083332	1.088780	1.097922	1.110849	1.127682

$\alpha = - .299999$

Θ	K VALUES				
	.009966711	.039469502	.087332193	.151646642	.229848846
1.2000000	1.091306	1.096858	1.106179	1.119366	1.136552
1.2100000	1.099267	1.104925	1.114425	1.127875	1.145417
1.2200000	1.107216	1.112979	1.122662	1.136376	1.154276
1.2300000	1.115153	1.121023	1.130888	1.144868	1.163129
1.2400000	1.123078	1.129056	1.139104	1.153352	1.171978
1.2500000	1.130992	1.137077	1.147311	1.161829	1.180821
1.2599999	1.138895	1.145089	1.155508	1.170298	1.189660
1.2699999	1.146788	1.153091	1.163697	1.178759	1.198494
1.2799999	1.154670	1.161082	1.171877	1.187214	1.207323
1.2899999	1.162542	1.169065	1.180048	1.195662	1.216148
1.3000000	1.170405	1.177038	1.188211	1.204103	1.224969
1.3100000	1.178258	1.185003	1.196367	1.212538	1.233786
1.3200000	1.186102	1.192959	1.204514	1.220967	1.242599
1.3300000	1.193938	1.200907	1.212655	1.229390	1.251408
1.3400000	1.201765	1.208846	1.220788	1.237807	1.260214
1.3500000	1.209585	1.216779	1.228915	1.246218	1.269016
1.3600000	1.217397	1.224704	1.237035	1.254625	1.277815
1.3700000	1.225201	1.232623	1.245149	1.263026	1.286611
1.3799999	1.232999	1.240534	1.253258	1.271423	1.295404
1.3899999	1.240790	1.248440	1.261360	1.279816	1.304194
1.4000000	1.248575	1.256340	1.269458	1.288204	1.312982
1.4100000	1.256353	1.264234	1.277550	1.296588	1.321767
1.4200000	1.264127	1.272122	1.285638	1.304968	1.330550
1.4300000	1.271894	1.280006	1.293721	1.313345	1.339331
1.4400000	1.279658	1.287885	1.301800	1.321718	1.348109
1.4500000	1.287416	1.295760	1.309875	1.330088	1.356886
1.4600000	1.295170	1.303631	1.317947	1.338456	1.365661
1.4700000	1.302921	1.311498	1.326015	1.346820	1.374434
1.4800000	1.310668	1.319362	1.334081	1.355183	1.383206
1.4900000	1.318412	1.327223	1.342143	1.363543	1.391977
1.5000000	1.326153	1.335081	1.350204	1.371902	1.400747
1.5100000	1.333891	1.342937	1.358262	1.380258	1.409515
1.5200000	1.341627	1.350791	1.366319	1.388614	1.418283
1.5300000	1.349362	1.358643	1.374374	1.396968	1.427049
1.5400000	1.357095	1.366494	1.382428	1.405321	1.435816
1.5500000	1.364827	1.374344	1.390481	1.413673	1.444581
1.5600000	1.372559	1.382193	1.398533	1.422025	1.453347
1.5699999	1.380290	1.390042	1.406585	1.430377	1.462112
1.5707963	1.380905	1.390667	1.407226	1.431042	1.462810
1.5707963	1.380905	1.390666	1.407225	1.431041	1.462810

$\alpha = -.299999$

Θ	K VALUES				
	.318821117	.415016431	.514599755	.613601043	.708073407
.0000000	.000000	.000000	.000000	.000000	.000000
.0100000	.009999	.009999	.009999	.010000	.010000
.0200000	.019999	.019999	.019999	.020000	.020000
.0300000	.029998	.029999	.029999	.030000	.030000
.0400000	.039997	.039998	.039999	.040000	.040001
.0500000	.049994	.049996	.049998	.050000	.050002
.0600000	.059989	.059993	.059996	.060000	.060003
.0700000	.069984	.069989	.069995	.070000	.070006
.0800000	.079976	.079984	.079992	.080001	.080009
.0900000	.089966	.089977	.089989	.090001	.090013
.1000000	.099953	.099969	.099986	.100002	.100018
.1100000	.109938	.109959	.109981	.110003	.110024
.1200000	.119919	.119947	.119976	.120004	.120031
.1300000	.129897	.129933	.129969	.130006	.130040
.1400000	.139872	.139916	.139962	.140007	.140051
.1500000	.149843	.149897	.149953	.150009	.150063
.1600000	.159810	.159876	.159944	.160012	.160077
.1700000	.169773	.169852	.169933	.170015	.170092
.1800000	.179731	.179824	.179921	.180018	.180110
.1900000	.189684	.189794	.189908	.190022	.190131
.2000000	.199633	.199761	.199894	.200026	.200153
.2100000	.209576	.209724	.209878	.210032	.210179
.2200000	.219513	.219684	.219861	.220038	.220207
.2300000	.229445	.229640	.229842	.230044	.230238
.2400000	.239371	.239592	.239822	.240052	.240273
.2500000	.249291	.249541	.249801	.250061	.250311
.2600000	.259205	.259486	.259779	.260071	.260352
.2700000	.269113	.269427	.269755	.270083	.270397
.2800000	.279013	.279364	.279729	.280095	.280447
.2900000	.288907	.289296	.289703	.290109	.290501
.3000000	.298794	.299225	.299675	.300125	.300559
.3100000	.308673	.309149	.309645	.310143	.310622
.3200000	.318546	.319069	.319615	.320163	.320690
.3300000	.328411	.328984	.329583	.330184	.330764
.3400000	.338268	.338895	.339550	.340209	.340843
.3500000	.348117	.348801	.349516	.350235	.350929
.3600000	.357959	.358702	.359481	.360264	.361020
.3700000	.367793	.368600	.369445	.370296	.371118
.3800000	.377618	.378492	.379408	.380331	.381223
.3900000	.387435	.388380	.389371	.390369	.391336

$\alpha = -\ .299999$

Θ	K VALUES				
	.318821117	.415016431	.514599755	.613601043	.708073407
.4000000	.397244	.398263	.399332	.400411	.401456
.4100000	.407045	.408141	.409293	.410457	.411583
.4200000	.416837	.418015	.419254	.420506	.421720
.4300000	.426621	.427885	.429215	.430559	.431865
.4400000	.436396	.437749	.439175	.440617	.442019
.4500000	.446162	.447609	.449135	.450680	.452182
.4600000	.455919	.457465	.459095	.460748	.462356
.4700000	.465668	.467316	.469056	.470821	.472540
.4800000	.475408	.477163	.479017	.480899	.482734
.4900000	.485139	.487005	.488978	.490984	.492940
.5000000	.494861	.496843	.498940	.501074	.503158
.5100000	.504575	.506677	.508903	.511171	.513388
.5200000	.514279	.516506	.518868	.521275	.523631
.5300000	.523975	.526332	.528833	.531386	.533887
.5400000	.533661	.536153	.538801	.541505	.544157
.5500000	.543339	.545971	.548769	.551631	.554441
.5600000	.553008	.555784	.558740	.561766	.564740
.5700000	.562668	.565595	.568713	.571910	.575054
.5800000	.572320	.575401	.578689	.582062	.585384
.5900000	.581962	.585204	.588667	.592224	.595731
.6000000	.591596	.595004	.598648	.602395	.606095
.6100000	.601221	.604801	.608632	.612577	.616476
.6200000	.610838	.614595	.618620	.622769	.626876
.6300000	.620446	.624385	.628611	.632973	.637295
.6400000	.630046	.634174	.638607	.643188	.647734
.6500000	.639637	.643959	.648606	.653414	.658193
.6600000	.649220	.653742	.658610	.663654	.668672
.6700000	.658795	.663523	.668619	.673906	.679174
.6800000	.668362	.673302	.678633	.684171	.689698
.6899999	.677920	.683079	.688652	.694450	.700244
.7000000	.687471	.692854	.698677	.704743	.710815
.7100000	.697014	.702627	.708708	.715051	.721410
.7200000	.706549	.712400	.718745	.725374	.732030
.7300000	.716077	.722171	.728789	.735713	.742676
.7400000	.725597	.731941	.738839	.746068	.753349
.7500000	.735110	.741710	.748897	.756440	.764050
.7600000	.744615	.751478	.758963	.766829	.774778
.7700000	.754114	.761247	.769036	.777235	.785536
.7800000	.763605	.771015	.779117	.787660	.796323
.7899999	.773090	.780783	.789207	.798103	.807141

$\alpha = -.299999$

Θ	K VALUES				
	.318821117	.415016431	.514599755	.613601043	.708073407
.8000000	.782568	.790551	.799305	.808566	.817991
.8100000	.792039	.800319	.809413	.819049	.828873
.8200000	.801505	.810089	.819530	.829551	.839788
.8300000	.810963	.819859	.829657	.840075	.850736
.8400000	.820416	.829629	.839794	.850619	.861720
.8500000	.829863	.839402	.849941	.861186	.872739
.8600000	.839303	.849175	.860099	.871775	.883795
.8700000	.848739	.858950	.870268	.882386	.894888
.8799999	.858168	.868727	.880448	.893021	.906019
.8899999	.867593	.878506	.890640	.903680	.917189
.9000000	.877012	.888287	.900844	.914363	.928399
.9100000	.886426	.898071	.911059	.925071	.939650
.9200000	.895835	.907857	.921288	.935805	.950943
.9300000	.905239	.917646	.931529	.946564	.962278
.9400000	.914639	.927438	.941783	.957350	.973656
.9500000	.924034	.937233	.952051	.968162	.985078
.9600000	.933425	.947031	.962332	.979002	.996546
.9699999	.942812	.956832	.972627	.989869	1.008059
.9799999	.952195	.966638	.982936	1.000765	1.019619
.9899999	.961574	.976447	.993259	1.011689	1.031227
1.0000000	.970950	.986260	1.003597	1.022642	1.042883
1.0100000	.980321	.996078	1.013950	1.033625	1.054588
1.0200000	.989690	1.005899	1.024318	1.044637	1.066343
1.0300000	.999055	1.015725	1.034701	1.055680	1.078149
1.0400000	1.008417	1.025556	1.045099	1.066753	1.090006
1.0500000	1.017776	1.035391	1.055513	1.077857	1.101915
1.0600000	1.027133	1.045232	1.065943	1.088992	1.113877
1.0699999	1.036486	1.055077	1.076389	1.100159	1.125893
1.0799999	1.045837	1.064927	1.086851	1.111357	1.137962
1.0899999	1.055186	1.074782	1.097329	1.122588	1.150087
1.1000000	1.064532	1.084643	1.107823	1.133851	1.162267
1.1100000	1.073876	1.094509	1.118333	1.145146	1.174503
1.1200000	1.083218	1.104381	1.128860	1.156474	1.186795
1.1300000	1.092558	1.114258	1.139404	1.167835	1.199144
1.1400000	1.101897	1.124140	1.149964	1.179229	1.211551
1.1500000	1.111233	1.134029	1.160541	1.190656	1.224015
1.1600000	1.120568	1.143923	1.171134	1.202115	1.236538
1.1700000	1.129902	1.153822	1.181744	1.213608	1.249118
1.1800000	1.139234	1.163728	1.192370	1.225134	1.261758
1.1899999	1.148565	1.173639	1.203013	1.236693	1.274456

$\alpha = -\ .299999$

Θ	K VALUES				
	.318821117	.415016431	.514599755	.613601043	.708073407
1.2000000	1.157894	1.183556	1.213673	1.248286	1.287213
1.2100000	1.167223	1.193479	1.224349	1.259911	1.300029
1.2200000	1.176550	1.203407	1.235041	1.271568	1.312903
1.2300000	1.185877	1.213342	1.245749	1.283258	1.325837
1.2400000	1.195203	1.223282	1.256473	1.294981	1.338829
1.2500000	1.204528	1.233228	1.267213	1.306735	1.351879
1.2599999	1.213852	1.243179	1.277969	1.318521	1.364987
1.2699999	1.223176	1.253136	1.288740	1.330338	1.378153
1.2799999	1.232499	1.263099	1.299527	1.342187	1.391376
1.2899999	1.241821	1.273067	1.310328	1.354065	1.404655
1.3000000	1.251143	1.283041	1.321144	1.365974	1.417991
1.3100000	1.260465	1.293019	1.331975	1.377912	1.431381
1.3200000	1.269786	1.303003	1.342819	1.389879	1.444825
1.3300000	1.279108	1.312992	1.353678	1.401874	1.458323
1.3400000	1.288428	1.322986	1.364549	1.413896	1.471872
1.3500000	1.297749	1.332985	1.375434	1.425945	1.485473
1.3600000	1.307069	1.342989	1.386331	1.438021	1.499123
1.3700000	1.316390	1.352997	1.397241	1.450121	1.512822
1.3799999	1.325710	1.363009	1.408162	1.462246	1.526567
1.3899999	1.335030	1.373026	1.419095	1.474394	1.540358
1.4000000	1.344350	1.383047	1.430038	1.486565	1.554192
1.4100000	1.353670	1.393071	1.440992	1.498757	1.568068
1.4200000	1.362990	1.403100	1.451955	1.510970	1.581984
1.4300000	1.372310	1.413131	1.462928	1.523202	1.595938
1.4400000	1.381630	1.423166	1.473910	1.535452	1.609928
1.4500000	1.390950	1.433205	1.484900	1.547719	1.623951
1.4600000	1.400270	1.443246	1.495897	1.560003	1.638006
1.4700000	1.409589	1.453289	1.506902	1.572301	1.652091
1.4800000	1.418909	1.463335	1.517913	1.584613	1.666202
1.4900000	1.428230	1.473384	1.528930	1.596937	1.680338
1.5000000	1.437550	1.483434	1.539952	1.609272	1.694496
1.5100000	1.446870	1.493486	1.550979	1.621617	1.708673
1.5200000	1.456190	1.503539	1.562009	1.633970	1.722867
1.5300000	1.465510	1.513594	1.573043	1.646331	1.737074
1.5400000	1.474830	1.523650	1.584080	1.658696	1.751293
1.5500000	1.484150	1.533707	1.595119	1.671067	1.765521
1.5600000	1.493471	1.543764	1.606159	1.683440	1.779755
1.5699999	1.502791	1.553821	1.617200	1.695814	1.793991
1.5707963	1.503533	1.554622	1.618079	1.696800	1.795125
1.5707963	1.503532	1.554621	1.618078	1.696799	1.795124

$\alpha = -.299999$

Θ	K VALUES				
	.794250555	.868696860	.928444378	.971111163	.994996249
.0000000	.000000	.000000	.000000	.000000	.000000
.0100000	.010000	.010000	.010000	.010000	.010000
.0200000	.020000	.020000	.020000	.020000	.020000
.0300000	.030000	.030001	.030001	.030001	.030001
.0400000	.040002	.040002	.040003	.040003	.040004
.0500000	.050004	.050005	.050006	.050007	.050008
.0600000	.060007	.060009	.060011	.060013	.060014
.0700000	.070011	.070015	.070018	.070021	.070022
.0800000	.080016	.080023	.080028	.080031	.080033
.0900000	.090023	.090032	.090040	.090045	.090048
.1000000	.100032	.100045	.100055	.100062	.100066
.1100000	.110043	.110060	.110073	.110083	.110088
.1200000	.120056	.120078	.120095	.120108	.120114
.1300000	.130072	.130099	.130121	.130137	.130146
.1400000	.140090	.140125	.140152	.140172	.140183
.1500000	.150111	.150154	.150188	.150212	.150225
.1600000	.160136	.160187	.160228	.160258	.160274
.1700000	.170164	.170225	.170275	.170310	.170330
.1800000	.180195	.180268	.180327	.180369	.180393
.1900000	.190230	.190316	.190386	.190435	.190463
.2000000	.200270	.200370	.200451	.200509	.200542
.2100000	.210314	.210430	.210524	.210592	.210629
.2200000	.220362	.220497	.220605	.220682	.220726
.2300000	.230416	.230570	.230694	.230782	.230832
.2400000	.240475	.240650	.240791	.240892	.240949
.2500000	.250539	.250738	.250898	.251012	.251076
.2600000	.260610	.260833	.261014	.261143	.261215
.2700000	.270686	.270937	.271140	.271285	.271366
.2800000	.280770	.281050	.281277	.281439	.281530
.2900000	.290860	.291172	.291424	.291605	.291707
.3000000	.300958	.301304	.301584	.301785	.301897
.3100000	.311063	.311446	.311756	.311978	.312102
.3200000	.321176	.321599	.321940	.322185	.322323
.3300000	.331298	.331762	.332138	.332408	.332559
.3400000	.341428	.341938	.342350	.342646	.342812
.3500000	.351568	.352126	.352576	.352900	.353082
.3600000	.361718	.362326	.362818	.363172	.363371
.3700000	.371877	.372540	.373076	.373462	.373678
.3800000	.382047	.382767	.383350	.383770	.384005
.3900000	.392229	.393009	.393642	.394097	.394353

$\alpha = -$ .299999

Θ	K VALUES				
	.794250555	.868696860	.928444378	.971111163	.994996249
.4000000	.402421	.403266	.403951	.404444	.404722
.4100000	.412626	.413539	.414280	.414813	.415113
.4200000	.422844	.423828	.424627	.425203	.425528
.4300000	.433074	.434134	.434996	.435616	.435966
.4400000	.443318	.444458	.445385	.446053	.446430
.4500000	.453577	.454800	.455796	.456514	.456919
.4600000	.463850	.465162	.466230	.467001	.467436
.4700000	.474138	.475543	.476688	.477515	.477981
.4800000	.484442	.485945	.487170	.488055	.488555
.4900000	.494763	.496368	.497678	.498625	.499159
.5000000	.505102	.506814	.508212	.509224	.509795
.5100000	.515457	.517283	.518774	.519854	.520463
.5200000	.525832	.527775	.529364	.530515	.531166
.5300000	.536226	.538293	.539984	.541210	.541903
.5400000	.546639	.548836	.550634	.551939	.552677
.5500000	.557074	.559405	.561317	.562704	.563489
.5600000	.567530	.570003	.572032	.573506	.574340
.5700000	.578007	.580628	.582781	.584345	.585232
.5800000	.588508	.591284	.593565	.595225	.596165
.5900000	.599033	.601970	.604386	.606145	.607143
.6000000	.609582	.612687	.615244	.617108	.618165
.6100000	.620157	.623437	.626142	.628115	.629235
.6200000	.630758	.634221	.637080	.639167	.640352
.6300000	.641385	.645040	.648060	.650267	.651521
.6400000	.652041	.655895	.659084	.661415	.662741
.6500000	.662726	.666788	.670152	.672614	.674015
.6600000	.673441	.677719	.681266	.683865	.685345
.6700000	.684187	.688690	.692428	.695170	.696732
.6800000	.694964	.699702	.703640	.706531	.708180
.6899999	.705774	.710756	.714903	.717950	.719689
.7000000	.716618	.721854	.726218	.729429	.731263
.7100000	.727497	.732998	.737589	.740970	.742903
.7200000	.738412	.744188	.749015	.752575	.754611
.7300000	.749364	.755426	.760500	.764247	.766391
.7400000	.760354	.766714	.772045	.775987	.778245
.7500000	.771383	.778052	.783653	.787798	.790175
.7600000	.782452	.789444	.795324	.799683	.802184
.7700000	.793563	.800890	.807062	.811643	.814275
.7800000	.804717	.812392	.818868	.823682	.826451
.7899999	.815914	.823951	.830745	.835803	.838714

$\alpha = -\ .299999$

Θ	K VALUES				
	.794250555	.868696860	.928444378	.971111163	.994996249
.8000000	.827157	.835571	.842696	.848007	.851069
.8100000	.838446	.847251	.854721	.860299	.863517
.8200000	.849783	.858994	.866824	.872681	.876063
.8300000	.861168	.870802	.879008	.885155	.888710
.8400000	.872604	.882677	.891274	.897727	.901462
.8500000	.884091	.894621	.903627	.910397	.914323
.8600000	.895632	.906635	.916067	.923171	.927296
.8700000	.907226	.918723	.928599	.936052	.940385
.8799999	.918876	.930885	.941225	.949044	.953596
.8899999	.930583	.943124	.953948	.962150	.966932
.9000000	.942349	.955443	.966771	.975374	.980398
.9100000	.954175	.967843	.979698	.988721	.993999
.9200000	.966061	.980326	.992731	1.002195	1.007740
.9300000	.978011	.992896	1.005875	1.015801	1.021626
.9400000	.990025	1.005554	1.019133	1.029543	1.035663
.9500000	1.002105	1.018303	1.032508	1.043426	1.049858
.9600000	1.014251	1.031146	1.046004	1.057456	1.064215
.9699999	1.026467	1.044084	1.059626	1.071637	1.078741
.9799999	1.038753	1.057121	1.073376	1.085975	1.093443
.9899999	1.051111	1.070259	1.087260	1.100477	1.108329
1.0000000	1.063542	1.083500	1.101281	1.115147	1.123405
1.0100000	1.076047	1.096849	1.115445	1.129993	1.138679
1.0200000	1.088630	1.110306	1.129754	1.145021	1.154159
1.0300000	1.101290	1.123876	1.144215	1.160238	1.169855
1.0400000	1.114029	1.137560	1.158832	1.175651	1.185774
1.0500000	1.126849	1.151363	1.173610	1.191267	1.201927
1.0600000	1.139752	1.165286	1.188554	1.207095	1.218324
1.0699999	1.152739	1.179333	1.203670	1.223143	1.234975
1.0799999	1.165811	1.193506	1.218962	1.239419	1.251892
1.0899999	1.178969	1.207810	1.234437	1.255933	1.269087
1.1000000	1.192216	1.222246	1.250101	1.272693	1.286572
1.1100000	1.205553	1.236818	1.265959	1.289710	1.304360
1.1200000	1.218980	1.251529	1.282018	1.306995	1.322467
1.1300000	1.232500	1.266382	1.298283	1.324558	1.340907
1.1400000	1.246113	1.281380	1.314762	1.342410	1.359696
1.1500000	1.259820	1.296527	1.331461	1.360564	1.378852
1.1600000	1.273624	1.311824	1.348386	1.379033	1.398392
1.1700000	1.287524	1.327276	1.365546	1.397830	1.418338
1.1800000	1.301522	1.342885	1.382947	1.416968	1.438710
1.1899999	1.315619	1.358654	1.400596	1.436463	1.459530

$\alpha =$ - .299999

Θ	K VALUES				
	.794250555	.868696860	.928444378	.971111163	.994996249
1.2000000	1.329816	1.374586	1.418501	1.456331	1.480824
1.2100000	1.344113	1.390684	1.436669	1.476586	1.502616
1.2200000	1.358511	1.406950	1.455108	1.497248	1.524935
1.2300000	1.373010	1.423387	1.473826	1.518333	1.547813
1.2400000	1.387612	1.439998	1.492830	1.539861	1.571281
1.2500000	1.402315	1.456784	1.512129	1.561851	1.595376
1.2599999	1.417121	1.473748	1.531730	1.584325	1.620136
1.2699999	1.432029	1.490891	1.551641	1.607304	1.645604
1.2799999	1.447039	1.508215	1.571870	1.630813	1.671825
1.2899999	1.462151	1.525722	1.592424	1.654874	1.698850
1.3000000	1.477364	1.543412	1.613311	1.679513	1.726735
1.3100000	1.492678	1.561287	1.634537	1.704756	1.755540
1.3200000	1.508091	1.579346	1.656110	1.730632	1.785331
1.3300000	1.523603	1.597590	1.678035	1.757167	1.816182
1.3400000	1.539212	1.616018	1.700318	1.784392	1.848175
1.3500000	1.554917	1.634630	1.722965	1.812337	1.881401
1.3600000	1.570715	1.653423	1.745979	1.841032	1.915959
1.3700000	1.586606	1.672397	1.769363	1.870508	1.951964
1.3799999	1.602586	1.691548	1.793120	1.900798	1.989540
1.3899999	1.618653	1.710874	1.817251	1.931930	2.028828
1.4000000	1.634805	1.730372	1.841755	1.963936	2.069989
1.4100000	1.651039	1.750036	1.866629	1.996843	2.113200
1.4200000	1.667351	1.769862	1.891871	2.030678	2.158664
1.4300000	1.683738	1.789845	1.917474	2.065463	2.206609
1.4400000	1.700196	1.809977	1.943430	2.101215	2.257295
1.4500000	1.716721	1.830253	1.969730	2.137948	2.311013
1.4600000	1.733310	1.850665	1.996360	2.175664	2.368089
1.4700000	1.749957	1.871203	2.023307	2.214361	2.428887
1.4800000	1.766659	1.891860	2.050551	2.254023	2.493807
1.4900000	1.783411	1.912626	2.078074	2.294621	2.563274
1.5000000	1.800207	1.933490	2.105853	2.336113	2.637723
1.5100000	1.817042	1.954442	2.133862	2.378441	2.717560
1.5200000	1.833911	1.975470	2.162074	2.421531	2.803108
1.5300000	1.850810	1.996562	2.190460	2.465291	2.894507
1.5400000	1.867731	2.017707	2.218987	2.509612	2.991593
1.5500000	1.884670	2.038892	2.247623	2.554373	3.093755
1.5600000	1.901621	2.060104	2.276334	2.599439	3.199833
1.5699999	1.918579	2.081329	2.305082	2.644665	3.308130
1.5707963	1.919929	2.083020	2.307372	2.648269	3.316790
1.5707963	1.919928	2.083018	2.307371	2.648267	3.316788

$\alpha = -$ .250000

θ	K VALUES				
	.009966711	.039469502	.087332193	.151646642	.229848846
.0000000	.000000	.000000	.000000	.000000	.000000
.0100000	.009999	.009999	.009999	.009999	.009999
.0200000	.019999	.019999	.019999	.019999	.019999
.0300000	.029997	.029997	.029998	.029998	.029998
.0400000	.039994	.039995	.039995	.039996	.039997
.0500000	.049989	.049990	.049991	.049992	.049994
.0600000	.059982	.059983	.059985	.059987	.059990
.0700000	.069972	.069973	.069976	.069980	.069984
.0800000	.079958	.079960	.079964	.079970	.079977
.0900000	.089940	.089944	.089950	.089957	.089967
.1000000	.099918	.099923	.099931	.099942	.099955
.1100000	.109891	.109898	.109908	.109923	.109940
.1200000	.119859	.119868	.119881	.119900	.119922
.1300000	.129821	.129832	.129849	.129873	.129901
.1400000	.139777	.139790	.139812	.139841	.139877
.1500000	.149726	.149743	.149769	.149805	.149849
.1600000	.159668	.159688	.159720	.159764	.159817
.1700000	.169602	.169626	.169665	.169717	.169781
.1800000	.179529	.179557	.179603	.179665	.179741
.1900000	.189446	.189480	.189534	.189607	.189696
.2000000	.199355	.199394	.199457	.199542	.199646
.2100000	.209255	.209300	.209372	.209471	.209590
.2200000	.219144	.219196	.219280	.219392	.219530
.2300000	.229024	.229083	.229178	.229307	.229464
.2400000	.238893	.238960	.239068	.239214	.239392
.2500000	.248751	.248826	.248948	.249113	.249315
.2600000	.258597	.258682	.258819	.259005	.259231
.2700000	.268432	.268527	.268680	.268888	.269141
.2800000	.278255	.278360	.278531	.278762	.279044
.2900000	.288065	.288181	.288371	.288627	.288941
.3000000	.297862	.297991	.298201	.298484	.298830
.3100000	.307646	.307788	.308019	.308331	.308713
.3200000	.317416	.317572	.317826	.318168	.318588
.3300000	.327172	.327343	.327621	.327996	.328456
.3400000	.336915	.337101	.337404	.337814	.338316
.3500000	.346642	.346845	.347175	.347621	.348168
.3600000	.356355	.356575	.356933	.357418	.358013
.3700000	.366052	.366291	.366679	.367205	.367849
.3800000	.375734	.375992	.376412	.376980	.377677
.3900000	.385400	.385678	.386131	.386744	.387497

$\alpha = -.250000$

Θ	K VALUES				
	.009966711	.039469502	.087332193	.151646642	.229848846
.4000000	.395050	.395349	.395837	.396497	.397308
.4100000	.404684	.405005	.405529	.406239	.407111
.4200000	.414302	.414646	.415208	.415969	.416906
.4300000	.423902	.424270	.424872	.425688	.426691
.4400000	.433485	.433879	.434522	.435394	.436467
.4500000	.443051	.443472	.444158	.445089	.446235
.4600000	.452600	.453048	.453779	.454771	.455993
.4700000	.462131	.462607	.463385	.464441	.465743
.4800000	.471644	.472149	.472976	.474098	.475483
.4900000	.481139	.481675	.482552	.483743	.485214
.5000000	.490616	.491183	.492112	.493375	.494935
.5100000	.500074	.500675	.501658	.502995	.504647
.5200000	.509513	.510148	.511187	.512601	.514350
.5300000	.518934	.519604	.520701	.522195	.524043
.5400000	.528336	.529043	.530199	.531776	.533726
.5500000	.537719	.538463	.539682	.541343	.543400
.5600000	.547083	.547866	.549148	.550897	.553065
.5700000	.556428	.557250	.558598	.560438	.562719
.5800000	.565753	.566617	.568033	.569966	.572365
.5900000	.575059	.575965	.577451	.579480	.582000
.6000000	.584345	.585294	.586852	.588981	.591626
.6100000	.593612	.594606	.596238	.598468	.601242
.6200000	.602859	.603899	.605607	.607942	.610849
.6300000	.612086	.613173	.614959	.617403	.620446
.6400000	.621294	.622429	.624295	.626850	.630033
.6500000	.630482	.631667	.633615	.636283	.639611
.6600000	.639650	.640886	.642918	.645703	.649179
.6700000	.648798	.650086	.652204	.655110	.658738
.6800000	.657926	.659267	.661474	.664503	.668287
.6899999	.667035	.668430	.670728	.673882	.677827
.7000000	.676124	.677575	.679965	.683248	.687357
.7100000	.685193	.686701	.689185	.692601	.696878
.7200000	.694242	.695808	.698389	.701940	.706390
.7300000	.703271	.704897	.707577	.711266	.715892
.7400000	.712281	.713967	.716748	.720578	.725386
.7500000	.721271	.723019	.725903	.729878	.734870
.7600000	.730241	.732052	.735042	.739164	.744345
.7700000	.739192	.741067	.744165	.748437	.753812
.7800000	.748123	.750064	.753271	.757696	.763269
.7899999	.757035	.759043	.762361	.766943	.772718

$\alpha = -$ .250000

θ	K VALUES				
	.009966711	.039469502	.087332193	.151646642	.229848846
.8000000	.765928	.768003	.771435	.776177	.782158
.8100000	.774801	.776946	.780494	.785398	.791590
.8200000	.783655	.785871	.789536	.794607	.801013
.8300000	.792490	.794777	.798563	.803802	.810427
.8400000	.801307	.803666	.807574	.812985	.819833
.8500000	.810104	.812538	.816569	.822156	.829231
.8600000	.818883	.821392	.825549	.831314	.838621
.8700000	.827643	.830229	.834514	.840460	.848003
.8799999	.836385	.839048	.843463	.849594	.857377
.8899999	.845109	.847850	.852398	.858716	.866743
.9000000	.853815	.856636	.861317	.867826	.876102
.9100000	.862503	.865404	.870222	.876924	.885453
.9200000	.871173	.874156	.879112	.886010	.894797
.9300000	.879825	.882892	.887988	.895085	.904133
.9400000	.888460	.891611	.896849	.904148	.913462
.9500000	.897077	.900314	.905696	.913200	.922784
.9600000	.905678	.909001	.914529	.922241	.932099
.9699999	.914262	.917672	.923348	.931271	.941407
.9799999	.922829	.926327	.932153	.940290	.950708
.9899999	.931379	.934968	.940944	.949299	.960003
1.0000000	.939914	.943593	.949723	.958297	.969291
1.0100000	.948432	.952202	.958488	.967284	.978574
1.0200000	.956934	.960797	.967240	.976261	.987849
1.0300000	.965421	.969378	.975979	.985228	.997119
1.0400000	.973892	.977944	.984705	.994185	1.006383
1.0500000	.982348	.986495	.993419	1.003132	1.015641
1.0600000	.990789	.995033	1.002121	1.012070	1.024893
1.0699999	.999215	1.003557	1.010810	1.020998	1.034139
1.0799999	1.007627	1.012067	1.019488	1.029917	1.043381
1.0899999	1.016025	1.020564	1.028154	1.038827	1.052616
1.1000000	1.024408	1.029048	1.036808	1.047727	1.061847
1.1100000	1.032778	1.037518	1.045451	1.056619	1.071073
1.1200000	1.041134	1.045977	1.054083	1.065502	1.080293
1.1300000	1.049477	1.054422	1.062704	1.074377	1.089509
1.1400000	1.057807	1.062856	1.071314	1.083244	1.098720
1.1500000	1.066124	1.071278	1.079914	1.092102	1.107927
1.1600000	1.074429	1.079687	1.088504	1.100953	1.117129
1.1700000	1.082721	1.088086	1.097084	1.109795	1.126326
1.1800000	1.091001	1.096473	1.105654	1.118631	1.135520
1.1899999	1.099270	1.104849	1.114214	1.127458	1.144710

$\alpha =$ - .250000

Θ	K VALUES				
	.009966711	.039469502	.087332193	.151646642	.229848846
.2000000	1.107527	1.113215	1.122765	1.136279	1.153895
.2100000	1.115773	1.121570	1.131307	1.145092	1.163077
.2200000	1.124008	1.129915	1.139840	1.153899	1.172255
.2300000	1.132233	1.138250	1.148364	1.162699	1.181429
.2400000	1.140447	1.146576	1.156880	1.171493	1.190600
.2500000	1.148651	1.154892	1.165387	1.180280	1.199768
.2599999	1.156845	1.163198	1.173887	1.189061	1.208932
.2699999	1.165030	1.171496	1.182379	1.197836	1.218093
.2799999	1.173206	1.179786	1.190863	1.206606	1.227251
.2899999	1.181373	1.188067	1.199340	1.215370	1.236406
.3000000	1.189531	1.196340	1.207810	1.224128	1.245559
.3100000	1.197681	1.204605	1.216274	1.232882	1.254709
.3200000	1.205823	1.212863	1.224730	1.241630	1.263856
.3300000	1.213957	1.221113	1.233181	1.250374	1.273001
.3400000	1.222083	1.229357	1.241625	1.259112	1.282143
.3500000	1.230203	1.237594	1.250064	1.267847	1.291283
.3600000	1.238316	1.245824	1.258497	1.276577	1.300421
.3700000	1.246422	1.254049	1.266925	1.285304	1.309557
.3799999	1.254522	1.262267	1.275347	1.294026	1.318691
.3899999	1.262616	1.270480	1.283765	1.302745	1.327824
.4000000	1.270704	1.278688	1.292178	1.311460	1.336954
.4100000	1.278787	1.286891	1.300587	1.320172	1.346083
.4200000	1.286865	1.295089	1.308992	1.328881	1.355210
.4300000	1.294939	1.303283	1.317393	1.337587	1.364336
.4400000	1.303008	1.311473	1.325791	1.346291	1.373461
.4500000	1.311073	1.319659	1.334185	1.354991	1.382584
.4600000	1.319134	1.327841	1.342576	1.363690	1.391706
.4700000	1.327192	1.336020	1.350964	1.372386	1.400828
.4800000	1.335246	1.344196	1.359350	1.381081	1.409948
.4900000	1.343298	1.352370	1.367733	1.389774	1.419067
.5000000	1.351347	1.360541	1.376115	1.398465	1.428186
.5100000	1.359394	1.368710	1.384494	1.407155	1.437304
.5200000	1.367439	1.376877	1.392872	1.415843	1.446421
.5300000	1.375483	1.385043	1.401249	1.424531	1.455538
.5400000	1.383525	1.393208	1.409625	1.433218	1.464655
.5500000	1.391566	1.401371	1.417999	1.441904	1.473771
.5600000	1.399607	1.409534	1.426374	1.450590	1.482887
.5699999	1.407647	1.417697	1.434748	1.459276	1.492003
.5707963	1.408287	1.418347	1.435415	1.459967	1.492729
.5707963	1.408286	1.418346	1.435414	1.459966	1.492728

$\alpha = - .250000$

Θ	K VALUES				
	.318821117	.415016431	.514599755	.613601043	.708073407
.0000000	.000000	.000000	.000000	.000000	.000000
.0100000	.009999	.009999	.010000	.010000	.010000
.0200000	.019999	.019999	.020000	.020000	.020000
.0300000	.029999	.029999	.030000	.030000	.030000
.0400000	.039998	.039999	.040000	.040001	.040002
.0500000	.049996	.049998	.050000	.050002	.050004
.0600000	.059993	.059996	.060000	.060004	.060007
.0700000	.069989	.069995	.070000	.070006	.070011
.0800000	.079984	.079992	.080001	.080009	.080017
.0900000	.089978	.089989	.090001	.090013	.090025
.1000000	.099969	.099986	.100002	.100019	.100034
.1100000	.109960	.109981	.110003	.110025	.110046
.1200000	.119948	.119975	.120004	.120033	.120060
.1300000	.129934	.129969	.130006	.130042	.130077
.1400000	.139918	.139962	.140007	.140053	.140096
.1500000	.149899	.149953	.150009	.150065	.150118
.1600000	.159878	.159943	.160011	.160079	.160144
.1700000	.169854	.169932	.170014	.170096	.170174
.1800000	.179827	.179920	.180017	.180114	.180207
.1900000	.189797	.189907	.190021	.190135	.190244
.2000000	.199764	.199892	.200025	.200158	.200285
.2100000	.209727	.209876	.210030	.210184	.210331
.2200000	.219687	.219858	.220035	.220212	.220382
.2300000	.229644	.229838	.230041	.230244	.230438
.2400000	.239596	.239818	.240048	.240278	.240499
.2500000	.249545	.249795	.250056	.250316	.250566
.2600000	.259490	.259771	.260064	.260358	.260639
.2700000	.269431	.269746	.270074	.270403	.270718
.2800000	.279367	.279718	.280085	.280452	.280804
.2900000	.289299	.289690	.290097	.290505	.290897
.3000000	.299227	.299659	.300110	.300562	.300997
.3100000	.309150	.309627	.310125	.310624	.311104
.3200000	.319069	.319593	.320141	.320690	.321220
.3300000	.328983	.329558	.330159	.330762	.331343
.3400000	.338892	.339521	.340178	.340839	.341476
.3500000	.348796	.349482	.350200	.350921	.351617
.3600000	.358695	.359442	.360223	.361009	.361768
.3700000	.368590	.369400	.370248	.371103	.371928
.3800000	.378479	.379356	.380276	.381203	.382099
.3900000	.388363	.389312	.390307	.391310	.392280

$\alpha = -\ .250000$

Θ	K VALUES				
	.318821117	.415016431	.514599755	.613601043	.708073407
.4000000	.398242	.399265	.400339	.401423	.402472
.4100000	.408116	.409218	.410375	.411544	.412676
.4200000	.417985	.419169	.420414	.421671	.422891
.4300000	.427848	.429118	.430455	.431807	.433119
.4400000	.437706	.439067	.440500	.441951	.443359
.4500000	.447559	.449014	.450548	.452102	.453613
.4600000	.457406	.458961	.460600	.462263	.463880
.4700000	.467248	.468906	.470656	.472432	.474162
.4800000	.477085	.478850	.480716	.482611	.484458
.4900000	.486916	.488794	.490780	.492799	.494769
.5000000	.496742	.498737	.500849	.502998	.505096
.5100000	.506563	.508680	.510922	.513206	.515439
.5200000	.516379	.518622	.521001	.523426	.525799
.5300000	.526189	.528563	.531084	.533656	.536176
.5400000	.535994	.538505	.541173	.543898	.546571
.5500000	.545793	.548446	.551267	.554152	.556985
.5600000	.555588	.558387	.561367	.564419	.567417
.5700000	.565377	.568328	.571474	.574698	.577869
.5800000	.575161	.578270	.581587	.584990	.588342
.5900000	.584940	.588212	.591706	.595295	.598835
.6000000	.594715	.598155	.601833	.605615	.609350
.6100000	.604484	.608098	.611966	.615949	.619887
.6200000	.614248	.618042	.622107	.626298	.630447
.6300000	.624008	.627987	.632256	.636663	.641030
.6400000	.633763	.637934	.642413	.647043	.651637
.6500000	.643513	.647881	.652578	.657439	.662269
.6600000	.653259	.657831	.662752	.667852	.672927
.6700000	.663000	.667781	.672935	.678282	.683611
.6800000	.672737	.677734	.683127	.688730	.694322
.6899999	.682470	.687689	.693329	.699196	.705061
.7000000	.692198	.697646	.703540	.709681	.715828
.7100000	.701922	.707605	.713762	.720185	.726624
.7200000	.711642	.717567	.723994	.730708	.737451
.7300000	.721359	.727532	.734236	.741252	.748308
.7400000	.731071	.737499	.744490	.751816	.759196
.7500000	.740780	.747470	.754755	.762402	.770117
.7600000	.750486	.757444	.765032	.773009	.781071
.7700000	.760187	.767421	.775321	.783638	.792059
.7800000	.769886	.777402	.785622	.794290	.803082
.7899999	.779581	.787387	.795936	.804966	.814140

$\alpha = -\ .250000$

Θ	K VALUES				
	.318821117	.415016431	.514599755	.613601043	.708073407
.8000000	.789274	.797376	.806263	.815665	.825235
.8100000	.798963	.807369	.816603	.826388	.836367
.8200000	.808649	.817367	.826956	.837137	.847537
.8300000	.818333	.827369	.837324	.847910	.858746
.8400000	.828014	.837376	.847706	.858709	.869995
.8500000	.837692	.847388	.858102	.869535	.881285
.8600000	.847368	.857405	.868513	.880388	.892616
.8700000	.857042	.867427	.878939	.891268	.903990
.8799999	.866714	.877455	.889381	.902176	.915407
.8899999	.876384	.887489	.899838	.913112	.926868
.9000000	.886052	.897528	.910311	.924078	.938374
.9100000	.895718	.907574	.920801	.935073	.949926
.9200000	.905382	.917626	.931307	.946098	.961525
.9300000	.915045	.927684	.941830	.957153	.973172
.9400000	.924707	.937748	.952369	.968239	.984867
.9500000	.934367	.947820	.962927	.979356	.996612
.9600000	.944027	.957898	.973501	.990506	1.008407
.9699999	.953685	.967983	.984094	1.001687	1.020253
.9799999	.963342	.978075	.994705	1.012901	1.032151
.9899999	.972999	.988174	1.005333	1.024149	1.044102
1.0000000	.982655	.998281	1.015981	1.035429	1.056107
1.0100000	.992310	1.008395	1.026647	1.046744	1.068166
1.0200000	1.001965	1.018517	1.037331	1.058093	1.080280
1.0300000	1.011619	1.028647	1.048035	1.069477	1.092451
1.0400000	1.021273	1.038784	1.058758	1.080896	1.104678
1.0500000	1.030927	1.048930	1.069500	1.092349	1.116962
1.0600000	1.040581	1.059083	1.080262	1.103839	1.129305
1.0699999	1.050235	1.069244	1.091043	1.115364	1.141706
1.0799999	1.059889	1.079414	1.101844	1.126926	1.154167
1.0899999	1.069544	1.089591	1.112664	1.138524	1.166688
1.1000000	1.079198	1.099778	1.123505	1.150158	1.179270
1.1100000	1.088853	1.109972	1.134365	1.161830	1.191913
1.1200000	1.098509	1.120175	1.145245	1.173538	1.204618
1.1300000	1.108165	1.130386	1.156145	1.185283	1.217385
1.1400000	1.117822	1.140605	1.167065	1.197065	1.230214
1.1500000	1.127479	1.150833	1.178005	1.208884	1.243107
1.1600000	1.137137	1.161069	1.188965	1.220741	1.256063
1.1700000	1.146796	1.171314	1.199945	1.232634	1.269082
1.1800000	1.156455	1.181567	1.210944	1.244565	1.282165
1.1899999	1.166116	1.191828	1.221963	1.256532	1.295311

$\alpha = -.250000$

θ	K VALUES				
	.318821117	.415016431	.514599755	.613601043	.708073407
1.2000000	1.175777	1.202098	1.233002	1.268537	1.308522
1.2100000	1.185440	1.212376	1.244060	1.280578	1.321797
1.2200000	1.195103	1.222663	1.255137	1.292655	1.335135
1.2300000	1.204768	1.232957	1.266234	1.304769	1.348537
1.2400000	1.214434	1.243259	1.277349	1.316919	1.362003
1.2500000	1.224100	1.253570	1.288483	1.329104	1.375531
1.2599999	1.233768	1.263888	1.299635	1.341324	1.389123
1.2699999	1.243437	1.274214	1.310805	1.353579	1.402776
1.2799999	1.253107	1.284547	1.321993	1.365869	1.416492
1.2899999	1.262779	1.294888	1.333198	1.378192	1.430268
1.3000000	1.272451	1.305237	1.344421	1.390548	1.444104
1.3100000	1.282125	1.315593	1.355661	1.402937	1.458000
1.3200000	1.291800	1.325955	1.366916	1.415358	1.471954
1.3300000	1.301476	1.336325	1.378188	1.427809	1.485966
1.3400000	1.311153	1.346701	1.389476	1.440291	1.500034
1.3500000	1.320831	1.357083	1.400778	1.452803	1.514156
1.3600000	1.330511	1.367472	1.412095	1.465343	1.528332
1.3700000	1.340191	1.377867	1.423426	1.477912	1.542560
1.3799999	1.349873	1.388268	1.434771	1.490507	1.556839
1.3899999	1.359556	1.398674	1.446129	1.503127	1.571166
1.4000000	1.369239	1.409086	1.457499	1.515773	1.585540
1.4100000	1.378924	1.419503	1.468882	1.528442	1.599959
1.4200000	1.388609	1.429924	1.480275	1.541134	1.614420
1.4300000	1.398296	1.440351	1.491680	1.553847	1.628923
1.4400000	1.407983	1.450781	1.503094	1.566580	1.643464
1.4500000	1.417671	1.461216	1.514518	1.579332	1.658042
1.4600000	1.427360	1.471654	1.525951	1.592101	1.672653
1.4700000	1.437049	1.482096	1.537391	1.604887	1.687296
1.4800000	1.446739	1.492541	1.548840	1.617688	1.701968
1.4900000	1.456430	1.502989	1.560295	1.630502	1.716665
1.5000000	1.466121	1.513439	1.571756	1.643329	1.731387
1.5100000	1.475813	1.523892	1.583222	1.656165	1.746129
1.5200000	1.485505	1.534347	1.594693	1.669011	1.760889
1.5300000	1.495197	1.544803	1.606167	1.681865	1.775664
1.5400000	1.504890	1.555260	1.617645	1.694725	1.790451
1.5500000	1.514582	1.565719	1.629125	1.707590	1.805248
1.5600000	1.524275	1.576178	1.640607	1.720458	1.820051
1.5699999	1.533968	1.586638	1.652089	1.733327	1.834856
1.5707963	1.534740	1.587471	1.653004	1.734352	1.836036
1.5707963	1.534740	1.587470	1.653003	1.734351	1.836034

$\alpha =$ - .250000

θ	K VALUES				
	.794250555	.868696860	.928444378	.971111163	.994996249
.0000000	.000000	.000000	.000000	.000000	.000000
.0100000	.010000	.010000	.010000	.010000	.010000
.0200000	.020000	.020000	.020000	.020000	.020000
.0300000	.030001	.030001	.030001	.030002	.030002
.0400000	.040003	.040003	.040004	.040005	.040005
.0500000	.050006	.050007	.050008	.050009	.050010
.0600000	.060010	.060013	.060015	.060017	.060017
.0700000	.070016	.070021	.070024	.070027	.070028
.0800000	.080025	.080031	.080036	.080040	.080042
.0900000	.090035	.090045	.090052	.090057	.090060
.1000000	.100049	.100061	.100071	.100078	.100082
.1100000	.110065	.110082	.110095	.110105	.110110
.1200000	.120085	.120107	.120124	.120136	.120143
.1300000	.130108	.130136	.130158	.130174	.130182
.1400000	.140136	.140170	.140198	.140217	.140228
.1500000	.150167	.150210	.150244	.150268	.150281
.1600000	.160204	.160255	.160296	.160326	.160342
.1700000	.170245	.170306	.170356	.170391	.170411
.1800000	.180291	.180365	.180423	.180466	.180489
.1900000	.190343	.190430	.190499	.190549	.190577
.2000000	.200401	.200502	.200583	.200642	.200674
.2100000	.210466	.210583	.210677	.210744	.210782
.2200000	.220537	.220672	.220780	.220858	.220901
.2300000	.230616	.230770	.230894	.230983	.231033
.2400000	.240701	.240877	.241018	.241120	.241176
.2500000	.250795	.250994	.251154	.251269	.251333
.2600000	.260897	.261121	.261302	.261431	.261504
.2700000	.271008	.271259	.271462	.271607	.271689
.2800000	.281128	.281409	.281636	.281798	.281889
.2900000	.291257	.291570	.291823	.292004	.292106
.3000000	.301396	.301744	.302024	.302225	.302338
.3100000	.311546	.311930	.312241	.312464	.312589
.3200000	.321707	.322131	.322473	.322719	.322857
.3300000	.331879	.332345	.332722	.332992	.333144
.3400000	.342063	.342574	.342987	.343284	.343451
.3500000	.352259	.352818	.353271	.353596	.353779
.3600000	.362468	.363078	.363573	.363928	.364127
.3700000	.372690	.373355	.373894	.374281	.374498
.3800000	.382926	.383649	.384235	.384656	.384892
.3900000	.393177	.393961	.394596	.395053	.395311

$\alpha = -\ .250000$

θ	K VALUES				
	.794250555	.868696860	.928444378	.971111163	.994996249
.4000000	.403443	.404291	.404979	.405475	.405754
.4100000	.413724	.414641	.415385	.415921	.416222
.4200000	.424021	.425010	.425814	.426392	.426718
.4300000	.434335	.435400	.436266	.436890	.437242
.4400000	.444666	.445812	.446744	.447416	.447794
.4500000	.455015	.456246	.457247	.457970	.458377
.4600000	.465383	.466703	.467777	.468553	.468990
.4700000	.475770	.477184	.478335	.479167	.479636
.4800000	.486177	.487689	.488922	.489813	.490315
.4900000	.496604	.498220	.499538	.500491	.501029
.5000000	.507052	.508777	.510185	.511203	.511778
.5100000	.517523	.519361	.520863	.521951	.522565
.5200000	.528016	.529974	.531574	.532734	.533390
.5300000	.538533	.540615	.542320	.543555	.544254
.5400000	.549073	.551287	.553100	.554415	.555159
.5500000	.559639	.561990	.563917	.565316	.566107
.5600000	.570231	.572725	.574771	.576258	.577099
.5700000	.580849	.583493	.585664	.587242	.588136
.5800000	.591494	.594295	.596597	.598271	.599221
.5900000	.602168	.605132	.607571	.609347	.610353
.6000000	.612871	.616006	.618588	.620469	.621537
.6100000	.623604	.626917	.629648	.631641	.632772
.6200000	.634367	.637866	.640755	.642863	.644060
.6300000	.645163	.648856	.651908	.654137	.655404
.6400000	.655991	.659887	.663109	.665466	.666806
.6500000	.666853	.670960	.674361	.676850	.678267
.6600000	.677750	.682076	.685664	.688292	.689789
.6700000	.688682	.693238	.697020	.699794	.701375
.6800000	.699651	.704445	.708431	.711357	.713026
.6899999	.710658	.715701	.719899	.722984	.724745
.7000000	.721704	.727006	.731425	.734677	.736534
.7100000	.732789	.738361	.743011	.746437	.748395
.7200000	.743916	.749768	.754660	.758267	.760331
.7300000	.755085	.761229	.766372	.770170	.772344
.7400000	.766297	.772745	.778151	.782147	.784437
.7500000	.777553	.784317	.789997	.794202	.796613
.7600000	.788855	.795948	.801914	.806336	.808875
.7700000	.800204	.807639	.813903	.818553	.821224
.7800000	.811601	.819392	.825967	.830855	.833666
.7899999	.823047	.831208	.838108	.843244	.846201

$\alpha = -\ .250000$

Θ	K VALUES				
	.794250555	.868696860	.928444378	.971111163	.994996249
.8000000	.834544	.843090	.850328	.855725	.858835
.8100000	.846093	.855039	.862630	.868299	.871570
.8200000	.857694	.867057	.875016	.880970	.884409
.8300000	.869351	.879146	.887490	.893742	.897357
.8400000	.881063	.891307	.900052	.906616	.910417
.8500000	.892832	.903544	.912708	.919598	.923593
.8600000	.904660	.915858	.925458	.932691	.936889
.8700000	.916547	.928251	.938307	.945897	.950310
.8799999	.928497	.940726	.951257	.959222	.963860
.8899999	.940509	.953284	.964311	.972670	.977543
.9000000	.952585	.965928	.977474	.986243	.991365
.9100000	.964728	.978660	.990747	.999948	1.005330
.9200000	.976937	.991482	1.004134	1.013788	1.019444
.9300000	.989215	1.004398	1.017639	1.027768	1.033712
.9400000	1.001564	1.017408	1.031266	1.041892	1.048141
.9500000	1.013984	1.030517	1.045019	1.056167	1.062735
.9600000	1.026478	1.043726	1.058901	1.070597	1.077503
.9699999	1.039047	1.057039	1.072916	1.085189	1.092449
.9799999	1.051692	1.070457	1.087068	1.099946	1.107581
.9899999	1.064415	1.083983	1.101363	1.114877	1.122907
1.0000000	1.077218	1.097621	1.115804	1.129986	1.138434
1.0100000	1.090102	1.111373	1.130395	1.145281	1.154170
1.0200000	1.103069	1.125242	1.145142	1.160769	1.170124
1.0300000	1.116120	1.139231	1.160050	1.176455	1.186304
1.0400000	1.129257	1.153342	1.175123	1.192349	1.202720
1.0500000	1.142481	1.167580	1.190366	1.208458	1.219382
1.0600000	1.155794	1.181946	1.205786	1.224789	1.236301
1.0699999	1.169198	1.196444	1.221387	1.241352	1.253487
1.0799999	1.182694	1.211077	1.237175	1.258156	1.270952
1.0899999	1.196283	1.225848	1.253156	1.275210	1.288709
1.1000000	1.209967	1.240761	1.269337	1.292523	1.306771
1.1100000	1.223747	1.255818	1.285723	1.310107	1.325151
1.1200000	1.237625	1.271022	1.302320	1.327971	1.343865
1.1300000	1.251602	1.286378	1.319135	1.346128	1.362928
1.1400000	1.265679	1.301887	1.336176	1.364589	1.382358
1.1500000	1.279857	1.317553	1.353448	1.383367	1.402172
1.1600000	1.294138	1.333380	1.370960	1.402474	1.422389
1.1700000	1.308523	1.349371	1.388718	1.421926	1.443030
1.1800000	1.323013	1.365527	1.406729	1.441736	1.464117
1.1899999	1.337608	1.381854	1.425002	1.461920	1.485673

$\alpha = -\ .250000$

θ	K VALUES				
	.794250555	.868696860	.928444378	.971111163	.994996249
1.2000000	1.352309	1.398353	1.443543	1.482494	1.507723
1.2100000	1.367118	1.415027	1.462362	1.503475	1.530296
1.2200000	1.382035	1.431879	1.481465	1.524881	1.553419
1.2300000	1.397060	1.448912	1.500861	1.546730	1.577126
1.2400000	1.412193	1.466127	1.520558	1.569042	1.601449
1.2500000	1.427436	1.483529	1.540565	1.591839	1.626427
1.2599999	1.442787	1.501118	1.560888	1.615141	1.652100
1.2699999	1.458247	1.518896	1.581537	1.638972	1.678511
1.2799999	1.473816	1.536865	1.602519	1.663355	1.705709
1.2899999	1.489494	1.555027	1.623842	1.688317	1.733745
1.3000000	1.505279	1.573383	1.645514	1.713882	1.762679
1.3100000	1.521171	1.591932	1.667542	1.740079	1.792571
1.3200000	1.537169	1.610676	1.689933	1.766935	1.823491
1.3300000	1.553271	1.629615	1.712693	1.794481	1.855518
1.3400000	1.569477	1.648747	1.735828	1.822747	1.888734
1.3500000	1.585784	1.668073	1.759344	1.851765	1.923235
1.3600000	1.602191	1.687591	1.783244	1.881565	1.959125
1.3700000	1.618696	1.707298	1.807532	1.912181	1.996521
1.3799999	1.635296	1.727192	1.832211	1.943645	2.035554
1.3899999	1.651988	1.747270	1.857280	1.975988	2.076370
1.4000000	1.668771	1.767528	1.882740	2.009243	2.119137
1.4100000	1.685639	1.787961	1.908588	2.043438	2.164038
1.4200000	1.702591	1.808565	1.934820	2.078600	2.211286
1.4300000	1.719622	1.829334	1.961429	2.114752	2.261117
1.4400000	1.736729	1.850260	1.988408	2.151913	2.313800
1.4500000	1.753907	1.871336	2.015747	2.190097	2.369639
1.4600000	1.771152	1.892556	2.043431	2.229306	2.428974
1.4700000	1.788460	1.913908	2.071445	2.269537	2.492183
1.4800000	1.805825	1.935386	2.099772	2.310773	2.559680
1.4900000	1.823242	1.956977	2.128389	2.352985	2.631910
1.5000000	1.840707	1.978672	2.157274	2.396130	2.709323
1.5100000	1.858213	2.000459	2.186400	2.440145	2.792343
1.5200000	1.875756	2.022326	2.215738	2.484954	2.881304
1.5300000	1.893329	2.044261	2.245257	2.530461	2.976352
1.5400000	1.910927	2.066250	2.274924	2.576554	3.077318
1.5500000	1.928543	2.088282	2.304705	2.623105	3.183564
1.5600000	1.946172	2.110342	2.334563	2.669973	3.293885
1.5699999	1.963807	2.132417	2.364462	2.717008	3.406514
1.5707963	1.965212	2.134175	2.366844	2.720756	3.415520
1.5707963	1.965211	2.134173	2.366842	2.720754	3.415517

$\alpha = -.199999$

Θ	K VALUES				
	.009966711	.039469502	.087332193	.151646642	.229848846
.0000000	.000000	.000000	.000000	.000000	.000000
.0100000	.009999	.009999	.009999	.009999	.009999
.0200000	.019999	.019999	.019999	.019999	.019999
.0300000	.029998	.029998	.029998	.029998	.029999
.0400000	.039995	.039996	.039996	.039997	.039998
.0500000	.049991	.049992	.049993	.049994	.049996
.0600000	.059986	.059987	.059988	.059991	.059993
.0700000	.069977	.069979	.069982	.069985	.069990
.0800000	.079966	.079969	.079973	.079978	.079985
.0900000	.089952	.089956	.089962	.089969	.089979
.1000000	.099935	.099940	.099948	.099958	.099971
.1100000	.109913	.109920	.109930	.109945	.109962
.1200000	.119888	.119896	.119910	.119928	.119951
.1300000	.129857	.129868	.129886	.129909	.129938
.1400000	.139822	.139836	.139857	.139887	.139922
.1500000	.149782	.149798	.149825	.149861	.149905
.1600000	.159735	.159755	.159788	.159832	.159885
.1700000	.169683	.169707	.169746	.169798	.169862
.1800000	.179624	.179653	.179699	.179761	.179837
.1900000	.189559	.189592	.189646	.189719	.189808
.2000000	.199486	.199525	.199588	.199673	.199777
.2100000	.209406	.209451	.209524	.209622	.209742
.2200000	.219318	.219370	.219453	.219566	.219704
.2300000	.229222	.229281	.229376	.229505	.229663
.2400000	.239117	.239184	.239293	.239439	.239618
.2500000	.249004	.249079	.249202	.249367	.249569
.2600000	.258881	.258966	.259104	.259289	.259516
.2700000	.268749	.268844	.268998	.269206	.269460
.2800000	.278608	.278713	.278885	.279116	.279399
.2900000	.288456	.288573	.288763	.289020	.289334
.3000000	.298294	.298423	.298633	.298917	.299265
.3100000	.308121	.308263	.308495	.308808	.309191
.3200000	.317937	.318094	.318348	.318692	.319112
.3300000	.327742	.327913	.328192	.328569	.329030
.3400000	.337536	.337723	.338027	.338438	.338942
.3500000	.347318	.347521	.347853	.348300	.348849
.3600000	.357088	.357309	.357669	.358155	.358752
.3700000	.366846	.367085	.367475	.368002	.368649
.3800000	.376591	.376849	.377271	.377842	.378542
.3900000	.386323	.386602	.387057	.387673	.388429

$\alpha = - .199999$

Θ	K VALUES				
	.009966711	.039469502	.087332193	.151646642	.229848846
.4000000	.396043	.396343	.396833	.397496	.398311
.4100000	.405749	.406072	.406598	.407311	.408188
.4200000	.415442	.415788	.416353	.417118	.418059
.4300000	.425121	.425492	.426097	.426916	.427925
.4400000	.434787	.435183	.435829	.436706	.437785
.4500000	.444439	.444861	.445551	.446487	.447640
.4600000	.454076	.454526	.455261	.456259	.457489
.4700000	.463699	.464178	.464960	.466023	.467333
.4800000	.473307	.473816	.474648	.475777	.477170
.4900000	.482901	.483441	.484323	.485523	.487003
.5000000	.492480	.493052	.493987	.495259	.496829
.5100000	.502044	.502649	.503639	.504986	.506650
.5200000	.511593	.512232	.513279	.514703	.516465
.5300000	.521127	.521802	.522907	.524412	.526274
.5400000	.530645	.531357	.532522	.534111	.536077
.5500000	.540147	.540897	.542126	.543800	.545874
.5600000	.549634	.550423	.551717	.553480	.555666
.5700000	.559106	.559935	.561295	.563150	.565451
.5800000	.568561	.569432	.570861	.572811	.575231
.5900000	.578001	.578915	.580414	.582462	.585005
.6000000	.587424	.588382	.589955	.592103	.594773
.6100000	.596832	.597835	.599483	.601735	.604535
.6200000	.606223	.607273	.608998	.611357	.614292
.6300000	.615598	.616696	.618500	.620969	.624043
.6400000	.624957	.626105	.627990	.630571	.633787
.6500000	.634300	.635498	.637466	.640163	.643527
.6600000	.643626	.644876	.646930	.649746	.653260
.6700000	.652937	.654239	.656381	.659319	.662988
.6800000	.662230	.663587	.665819	.668882	.672710
.6899999	.671508	.672919	.675244	.678435	.682427
.7000000	.680769	.682237	.684656	.687979	.692138
.7100000	.690013	.691540	.694055	.697512	.701843
.7200000	.699241	.700827	.703441	.707036	.711543
.7300000	.708453	.710100	.712815	.716551	.721238
.7400000	.717649	.719357	.722175	.726055	.730927
.7500000	.726828	.728599	.731523	.735550	.740611
.7600000	.735991	.737827	.740857	.745036	.750290
.7700000	.745137	.747039	.750180	.754512	.759963
.7800000	.754268	.756236	.759489	.763978	.769631
.7899999	.763382	.765419	.768786	.773435	.779295

$\alpha = -\ .199999$

Θ	K VALUES				
	.009966711	.039469502	.087332193	.151646642	.229848846
.8000000	.772480	.774587	.778070	.782882	.788953
.8100000	.781562	.783740	.787341	.792321	.798607
.8200000	.790629	.792878	.796600	.801749	.808255
.8300000	.799679	.802002	.805846	.811169	.817899
.8400000	.808714	.811111	.815081	.820579	.827538
.8500000	.817732	.820206	.824302	.829981	.837172
.8600000	.826736	.829286	.833512	.839373	.846802
.8700000	.835723	.838352	.842709	.848756	.856428
.8799999	.844696	.847404	.851895	.858131	.866049
.8899999	.853653	.856441	.861068	.867497	.875665
.9000000	.862595	.865465	.870230	.876854	.885278
.9100000	.871521	.874475	.879379	.886202	.894886
.9200000	.880433	.883471	.888518	.895542	.904491
.9300000	.889330	.892454	.897644	.904873	.914091
.9400000	.898213	.901423	.906759	.914197	.923687
.9500000	.907081	.910378	.915863	.923511	.933280
.9600000	.915934	.919321	.924955	.932818	.942869
.9699999	.924773	.928250	.934037	.942117	.952454
.9799999	.933598	.937166	.943107	.951408	.962035
.9899999	.942410	.946070	.952167	.960691	.971614
1.0000000	.951207	.954961	.961216	.969966	.981189
1.0100000	.959991	.963839	.970254	.979234	.990760
1.0200000	.968761	.972705	.979282	.988494	1.000328
1.0300000	.977518	.981559	.988300	.997747	1.009893
1.0400000	.986262	.990401	.997307	1.006992	1.019455
1.0500000	.994994	.999230	1.006305	1.016230	1.029015
1.0600000	1.003712	1.008049	1.015292	1.025462	1.038571
1.0699999	1.012418	1.016855	1.024270	1.034686	1.048124
1.0799999	1.021112	1.025651	1.033238	1.043904	1.057675
1.0899999	1.029793	1.034435	1.042197	1.053115	1.067223
1.1000000	1.038463	1.043208	1.051147	1.062319	1.076769
1.1100000	1.047120	1.051970	1.060087	1.071517	1.086312
1.1200000	1.055767	1.060722	1.069019	1.080709	1.095852
1.1300000	1.064402	1.069464	1.077942	1.089894	1.105391
1.1400000	1.073025	1.078195	1.086856	1.099073	1.114927
1.1500000	1.081638	1.086916	1.095762	1.108247	1.124461
1.1600000	1.090240	1.095627	1.104660	1.117415	1.133993
1.1700000	1.098832	1.104329	1.113549	1.126577	1.143523
1.1800000	1.107414	1.113021	1.122431	1.135733	1.153051
1.1899999	1.115985	1.121704	1.131304	1.144884	1.162577

$\alpha =$ -.199999

Θ	K VALUES				
	.009966711	.039469502	.087332193	.151646642	.229848846
1.2000000	1.124547	1.130379	1.140171	1.154030	1.172101
1.2100000	1.133099	1.139044	1.149030	1.163171	1.181624
1.2200000	1.141642	1.147701	1.157881	1.172307	1.191145
1.2300000	1.150176	1.156349	1.166726	1.181438	1.200664
1.2400000	1.158701	1.164990	1.175564	1.190564	1.210182
1.2500000	1.167217	1.173622	1.184395	1.199685	1.219698
1.2599999	1.175725	1.182247	1.193220	1.208802	1.229213
1.2699999	1.184225	1.190864	1.202039	1.217915	1.238727
1.2799999	1.192716	1.199474	1.210851	1.227024	1.248239
1.2899999	1.201201	1.208077	1.219658	1.236128	1.257750
1.3000000	1.209678	1.216673	1.228459	1.245229	1.267260
1.3100000	1.218147	1.225262	1.237254	1.254326	1.276769
1.3200000	1.226610	1.233846	1.246044	1.263419	1.286277
1.3300000	1.235066	1.242423	1.254829	1.272509	1.295784
1.3400000	1.243516	1.250994	1.263610	1.281595	1.305289
1.3500000	1.251959	1.259560	1.272385	1.290678	1.314794
1.3600000	1.260397	1.268120	1.281156	1.299759	1.324299
1.3700000	1.268829	1.276675	1.289922	1.308836	1.333802
1.3799999	1.277256	1.285225	1.298685	1.317910	1.343304
1.3899999	1.285678	1.293771	1.307443	1.326982	1.352806
1.4000000	1.294095	1.302312	1.316198	1.336051	1.362307
1.4100000	1.302507	1.310849	1.324950	1.345118	1.371808
1.4200000	1.310915	1.319382	1.333698	1.354182	1.381308
1.4300000	1.319319	1.327911	1.342443	1.363245	1.390807
1.4400000	1.327719	1.336436	1.351185	1.372305	1.400306
1.4500000	1.336115	1.344959	1.359924	1.381364	1.409805
1.4600000	1.344508	1.353478	1.368661	1.390421	1.419303
1.4700000	1.352899	1.361995	1.377395	1.399476	1.428801
1.4800000	1.361286	1.370509	1.386128	1.408530	1.438298
1.4900000	1.369671	1.379021	1.394858	1.417583	1.447795
1.5000000	1.378054	1.387531	1.403587	1.426634	1.457292
1.5100000	1.386436	1.396039	1.412315	1.435685	1.466788
1.5200000	1.394815	1.404546	1.421041	1.444734	1.476285
1.5300000	1.403193	1.413052	1.429766	1.453783	1.485781
1.5400000	1.411570	1.421556	1.438490	1.462832	1.495277
1.5500000	1.419946	1.430060	1.447214	1.471880	1.504773
1.5600000	1.428321	1.438563	1.455937	1.480928	1.514268
1.5699999	1.436697	1.447066	1.464660	1.489975	1.523764
1.5707963	1.437364	1.447743	1.465355	1.490696	1.524520
1.5707963	1.437363	1.447742	1.465354	1.490695	1.524520

$\alpha = -.199999$

Θ	K VALUES				
	.318821117	.415016431	.514599755	.613601043	.708073407
.0000000	.000000	.000000	.000000	.000000	.000000
.0100000	.009999	.010000	.010000	.010000	.010000
.0200000	.019999	.020000	.020000	.020000	.020000
.0300000	.029999	.030000	.030000	.030000	.030001
.0400000	.039999	.040000	.040001	.040002	.040003
.0500000	.049998	.050000	.050002	.050004	.050006
.0600000	.059997	.060000	.060004	.060007	.060011
.0700000	.069995	.070000	.070006	.070012	.070017
.0800000	.079993	.080001	.080009	.080018	.080026
.0900000	.089990	.090001	.090014	.090026	.090037
.1000000	.099986	.100002	.100019	.100035	.100051
.1100000	.109982	.110003	.110025	.110047	.110068
.1200000	.119976	.120004	.120033	.120061	.120089
.1300000	.129970	.130005	.130042	.130078	.130113
.1400000	.139963	.140007	.140053	.140098	.140142
.1500000	.149955	.150009	.150065	.150121	.150174
.1600000	.159945	.160011	.160079	.160147	.160212
.1700000	.169935	.170014	.170095	.170177	.170255
.1800000	.179923	.180016	.180113	.180210	.180303
.1900000	.189910	.190020	.190134	.190248	.190357
.2000000	.199895	.200023	.200157	.200290	.200417
.2100000	.209879	.210028	.210182	.210336	.210484
.2200000	.219861	.220032	.220210	.220387	.220557
.2300000	.229842	.230038	.230241	.230443	.230638
.2400000	.239822	.240044	.240274	.240505	.240726
.2500000	.249800	.250050	.250311	.250572	.250822
.2600000	.259776	.260058	.260351	.260645	.260927
.2700000	.269750	.270066	.270395	.270724	.271040
.2800000	.279722	.280075	.280442	.280810	.281163
.2900000	.289693	.290085	.290493	.290902	.291295
.3000000	.299662	.300096	.300548	.301001	.301437
.3100000	.309629	.310108	.310607	.311107	.311589
.3200000	.319595	.320121	.320670	.321221	.321752
.3300000	.329558	.330135	.330738	.331343	.331926
.3400000	.339520	.340151	.340810	.341473	.342112
.3500000	.349479	.350168	.350888	.351612	.352310
.3600000	.359437	.360186	.360970	.361759	.362521
.3700000	.369393	.370206	.371058	.371916	.372745
.3800000	.379347	.380228	.381152	.382082	.382982
.3900000	.389299	.390251	.391251	.392258	.393233

$\alpha = -\ .199999$

Θ	K VALUES				
	.318821117	.415016431	.514599755	.613601043	.708073407
.4000000	.399249	.400276	.401356	.402444	.403498
.4100000	.409197	.410304	.411467	.412641	.413779
.4200000	.419143	.420333	.421584	.422848	.424074
.4300000	.429088	.430365	.431708	.433067	.434386
.4400000	.439030	.440398	.441840	.443298	.444714
.4500000	.448971	.450435	.451978	.453540	.455059
.4600000	.458910	.460474	.462123	.463795	.465422
.4700000	.468847	.470515	.472276	.474063	.475803
.4800000	.478783	.480559	.482437	.484344	.486202
.4900000	.488716	.490607	.492606	.494638	.496621
.5000000	.498649	.500657	.502783	.504947	.507059
.5100000	.508579	.510711	.512969	.515270	.517518
.5200000	.518508	.520768	.523164	.525607	.527998
.5300000	.528436	.530828	.533368	.535960	.538499
.5400000	.538362	.540892	.543582	.546329	.549023
.5500000	.548286	.550960	.553805	.556714	.559569
.5600000	.558210	.561032	.564038	.567115	.570139
.5700000	.568132	.571108	.574281	.577533	.580733
.5800000	.578052	.581189	.584535	.587969	.591351
.5900000	.587972	.591274	.594800	.598423	.601995
.6000000	.597891	.601363	.605076	.608895	.612666
.6100000	.607809	.611458	.615364	.619386	.623363
.6200000	.617725	.621557	.625663	.629897	.634087
.6300000	.627641	.631662	.635975	.640427	.644840
.6400000	.637557	.641771	.646299	.650978	.655622
.6500000	.647471	.651887	.656635	.661549	.666433
.6600000	.657385	.662008	.666985	.672142	.677275
.6700000	.667299	.672135	.677348	.682757	.688148
.6800000	.677212	.682268	.687724	.693394	.699053
.6899999	.687125	.692407	.698115	.704054	.709991
.7000000	.697038	.702552	.708520	.714738	.720962
.7100000	.706950	.712705	.718939	.725445	.731967
.7200000	.716863	.722864	.729374	.736177	.743008
.7300000	.726776	.733030	.739824	.746933	.754084
.7400000	.736689	.743203	.750289	.757716	.765198
.7500000	.746602	.753383	.760770	.768524	.776348
.7600000	.756515	.763571	.771267	.779359	.787537
.7700000	.766430	.773767	.781781	.790221	.798766
.7800000	.776344	.783970	.792312	.801110	.810034
.7899999	.786260	.794182	.802860	.812028	.821344

$\alpha = -.199999$

Θ	K VALUES				
	.318821117	.415016431	.514599755	.613601043	.708073407
.8000000	.796176	.804402	.813426	.822975	.832695
.8100000	.806093	.814631	.824009	.833950	.844089
.8200000	.816012	.824867	.834611	.844956	.855527
.8300000	.825931	.835113	.845231	.855992	.867009
.8400000	.835852	.845368	.855870	.867058	.878536
.8500000	.845774	.855632	.866527	.878157	.890110
.8600000	.855697	.865905	.877205	.889287	.901731
.8700000	.865622	.876187	.887901	.900449	.913399
.8799999	.875549	.886480	.898618	.911645	.925117
.8899999	.885477	.896782	.909355	.922874	.936885
.9000000	.895408	.907094	.920113	.934137	.948703
.9100000	.905340	.917416	.930891	.945434	.960574
.9200000	.915274	.927748	.941690	.956766	.972496
.9300000	.925210	.938090	.952510	.968134	.984472
.9400000	.935149	.948443	.963352	.979538	.996503
.9500000	.945090	.958807	.974216	.990978	1.008588
.9600000	.955033	.969181	.985101	1.002455	1.020730
.9699999	.964978	.979567	.996009	1.013970	1.032929
.9799999	.974927	.989963	1.006940	1.025522	1.045186
.9899999	.984878	1.000370	1.017892	1.037112	1.057501
1.0000000	.994831	1.010789	1.028868	1.048741	1.069876
1.0100000	1.004788	1.021218	1.039866	1.060408	1.082311
1.0200000	1.014747	1.031659	1.050888	1.072115	1.094807
1.0300000	1.024709	1.042112	1.061933	1.083861	1.107365
1.0400000	1.034674	1.052575	1.073001	1.095648	1.119986
1.0500000	1.044642	1.063051	1.084093	1.107474	1.132670
1.0600000	1.054613	1.073538	1.095208	1.119342	1.145419
1.0699999	1.064588	1.084036	1.106347	1.131249	1.158232
1.0799999	1.074565	1.094547	1.117510	1.143198	1.171110
1.0899999	1.084546	1.105068	1.128696	1.155188	1.184054
1.1000000	1.094530	1.115602	1.139907	1.167220	1.197066
1.1100000	1.104517	1.126147	1.151141	1.179293	1.210144
1.1200000	1.114508	1.136704	1.162398	1.191407	1.223290
1.1300000	1.124502	1.147273	1.173680	1.203563	1.236503
1.1400000	1.134500	1.157853	1.184986	1.215761	1.249786
1.1500000	1.144500	1.168444	1.196315	1.228001	1.263137
1.1600000	1.154504	1.179048	1.207667	1.240282	1.276557
1.1700000	1.164512	1.189662	1.219044	1.252605	1.290046
1.1800000	1.174523	1.200288	1.230443	1.264970	1.303605
1.1899999	1.184537	1.210926	1.241866	1.277376	1.317233

$\alpha = -.199999$

Θ	K VALUES				
	.318821117	.415016431	.514599755	.613601043	.708073407
1.2000000	1.194555	1.221574	1.253312	1.289823	1.330931
1.2100000	1.204577	1.232234	1.264780	1.302311	1.344699
1.2200000	1.214601	1.242904	1.276271	1.314840	1.358535
1.2300000	1.224629	1.253586	1.287785	1.327409	1.372441
1.2400000	1.234660	1.264278	1.299320	1.340018	1.386416
1.2500000	1.244695	1.274981	1.310878	1.352667	1.400460
1.2599999	1.254733	1.285694	1.322457	1.365355	1.414571
1.2699999	1.264774	1.296417	1.334057	1.378082	1.428750
1.2799999	1.274818	1.307150	1.345677	1.390846	1.442996
1.2899999	1.284865	1.317893	1.357318	1.403649	1.457307
1.3000000	1.294916	1.328646	1.368979	1.416488	1.471684
1.3100000	1.304969	1.339408	1.380660	1.429362	1.486125
1.3200000	1.315025	1.350179	1.392359	1.442273	1.500630
1.3300000	1.325084	1.360959	1.404078	1.455217	1.515196
1.3400000	1.335146	1.371747	1.415814	1.468196	1.529823
1.3500000	1.345211	1.382544	1.427567	1.481207	1.544509
1.3600000	1.355278	1.393349	1.439338	1.494250	1.559253
1.3700000	1.365348	1.404162	1.451124	1.507323	1.574053
1.3799999	1.375420	1.414983	1.462927	1.520426	1.588908
1.3899999	1.385494	1.425810	1.474744	1.533558	1.603814
1.4000000	1.395571	1.436645	1.486576	1.546717	1.618772
1.4100000	1.405650	1.447486	1.498422	1.559902	1.633778
1.4200000	1.415731	1.458333	1.510281	1.573112	1.648830
1.4300000	1.425814	1.469186	1.522152	1.586345	1.663927
1.4400000	1.435899	1.480044	1.534035	1.599601	1.679064
1.4500000	1.445985	1.490908	1.545929	1.612877	1.694241
1.4600000	1.456073	1.501776	1.557832	1.626173	1.709455
1.4700000	1.466162	1.512649	1.569745	1.639486	1.724702
1.4800000	1.476253	1.523526	1.581667	1.652816	1.739980
1.4900000	1.486345	1.534406	1.593596	1.666161	1.755287
1.5000000	1.496438	1.545290	1.605533	1.679519	1.770619
1.5100000	1.506532	1.556177	1.617475	1.692889	1.785973
1.5200000	1.516627	1.567066	1.629422	1.706269	1.801346
1.5300000	1.526722	1.577957	1.641374	1.719657	1.816736
1.5400000	1.536818	1.588850	1.653330	1.733053	1.832139
1.5500000	1.546915	1.599744	1.665288	1.746453	1.847551
1.5600000	1.557011	1.610639	1.677248	1.759857	1.862971
1.5699999	1.567108	1.621535	1.689209	1.773262	1.878393
1.5707963	1.567912	1.622402	1.690161	1.774330	1.879622
1.5707963	1.567911	1.622401	1.690160	1.774329	1.879620

$\alpha = -.199999$

Θ	K VALUES				
	.794250555	.868696860	.928444378	.971111163	.994996249
.0000000	.000000	.000000	.000000	.000000	.000000
.0100000	.010000	.010000	.010000	.010000	.010000
.0200000	.020000	.020000	.020000	.020000	.020000
.0300000	.030001	.030002	.030002	.030002	.030002
.0400000	.040004	.040005	.040005	.040006	.040006
.0500000	.050008	.050009	.050011	.050011	.050012
.0600000	.060014	.060016	.060019	.060020	.060021
.0700000	.070022	.070026	.070030	.070032	.070034
.0800000	.080033	.080040	.080045	.080048	.080050
.0900000	.090048	.090057	.090064	.090069	.090072
.1000000	.100065	.100078	.100088	.100095	.100099
.1100000	.110087	.110104	.110117	.110127	.110132
.1200000	.120114	.120135	.120153	.120165	.120172
.1300000	.130145	.130172	.130194	.130210	.130219
.1400000	.140181	.140216	.140243	.140263	.140274
.1500000	.150223	.150266	.150300	.150324	.150337
.1600000	.160271	.160323	.160364	.160394	.160410
.1700000	.170326	.170388	.170437	.170473	.170493
.1800000	.180388	.180461	.180520	.180562	.180586
.1900000	.190457	.190543	.190613	.190662	.190690
.2000000	.200534	.200635	.200716	.200774	.200807
.2100000	.210619	.210736	.210830	.210898	.210935
.2200000	.220713	.220848	.220956	.221034	.221078
.2300000	.230816	.230970	.231095	.231184	.231234
.2400000	.240929	.241105	.241246	.241348	.241405
.2500000	.251052	.251251	.251412	.251526	.251591
.2600000	.261186	.261410	.261591	.261721	.261794
.2700000	.271331	.271583	.271786	.271931	.272013
.2800000	.281487	.281769	.281996	.282159	.282251
.2900000	.291656	.291970	.292223	.292405	.292507
.3000000	.301837	.302186	.302467	.302669	.302782
.3100000	.312032	.312418	.312729	.312952	.313078
.3200000	.322241	.322666	.323009	.323256	.323394
.3300000	.332463	.332931	.333309	.333580	.333733
.3400000	.342701	.343214	.343629	.343927	.344094
.3500000	.352954	.353516	.353970	.354296	.354480
.3600000	.363224	.363837	.364333	.364689	.364889
.3700000	.373509	.374177	.374718	.375106	.375325
.3800000	.383813	.384538	.385126	.385549	.385787
.3900000	.394134	.394921	.395559	.396018	.396276

$\alpha = -.199999$

Θ	K VALUES				
	.794250555	.868696860	.928444378	.971111163	.994996249
.4000000	.404473	.405325	.406017	.406514	.406794
.4100000	.414831	.415753	.416501	.417039	.417342
.4200000	.425210	.426204	.427011	.427593	.427921
.4300000	.435608	.436680	.437550	.438177	.438531
.4400000	.446028	.447181	.448117	.448793	.449174
.4500000	.456470	.457708	.458715	.459441	.459851
.4600000	.466934	.468262	.469343	.470123	.470563
.4700000	.477421	.478844	.480002	.480840	.481312
.4800000	.487932	.489454	.490695	.491592	.492098
.4900000	.498468	.500095	.501422	.502382	.502923
.5000000	.509030	.510766	.512184	.513209	.513789
.5100000	.519617	.521469	.522982	.524077	.524696
.5200000	.530232	.532204	.533817	.534985	.535646
.5300000	.540874	.542973	.544691	.545936	.546640
.5400000	.551545	.553777	.555604	.556930	.557680
.5500000	.562246	.564616	.566559	.567970	.568768
.5600000	.572976	.575492	.577556	.579055	.579904
.5700000	.583738	.586406	.588596	.590189	.591091
.5800000	.594532	.597359	.599682	.601372	.602330
.5900000	.605360	.608352	.610814	.612606	.613623
.6000000	.616221	.619386	.621993	.623893	.624971
.6100000	.627117	.630463	.633222	.635235	.636377
.6200000	.638048	.641583	.644502	.646632	.647842
.6300000	.649017	.652749	.655833	.658087	.659368
.6400000	.660023	.663961	.667219	.669602	.670957
.6500000	.671068	.675221	.678660	.681178	.682611
.6600000	.682153	.686529	.690158	.692818	.694332
.6700000	.693279	.697888	.701716	.704523	.706123
.6800000	.704446	.709299	.713333	.716295	.717985
.6899999	.715657	.720763	.725013	.728138	.729921
.7000000	.726912	.732282	.736758	.740052	.741933
.7100000	.738213	.743857	.748569	.752040	.754024
.7200000	.749559	.755490	.760448	.764104	.766196
.7300000	.760954	.767182	.772397	.776248	.778452
.7400000	.772397	.778936	.784418	.788472	.790795
.7500000	.783891	.790752	.796514	.800781	.803227
.7600000	.795435	.802633	.808687	.813175	.815752
.7700000	.807032	.814579	.820938	.825659	.828372
.7800000	.818683	.826594	.833271	.838235	.841090
.7899999	.830389	.838679	.845688	.850906	.853911

$\alpha = -.199999$

Θ	K VALUES				
	.794250555	.868696860	.928444378	.971111163	.994996249
.8000000	.842152	.850835	.858191	.863675	.866837
.8100000	.853973	.863065	.870782	.876546	.879871
.8200000	.865852	.875371	.883465	.889520	.893018
.8300000	.877792	.887754	.896242	.902602	.906281
.8400000	.889794	.900217	.909116	.915796	.919664
.8500000	.901859	.912762	.922089	.929104	.933172
.8600000	.913990	.925390	.935166	.942531	.946808
.8700000	.926186	.938105	.948348	.956081	.960577
.8799999	.938450	.950908	.961639	.969757	.974484
.8899999	.950783	.963802	.975043	.983564	.988533
.9000000	.963188	.976789	.988562	.997506	1.002730
.9100000	.975664	.989872	1.002201	1.011588	1.017079
.9200000	.988214	1.003052	1.015961	1.025814	1.031587
.9300000	1.000840	1.016333	1.029849	1.040189	1.046259
.9400000	1.013542	1.029716	1.043866	1.054719	1.061101
.9500000	1.026323	1.043206	1.058018	1.069408	1.076119
.9600000	1.039184	1.056803	1.072308	1.084262	1.091321
.9699999	1.052127	1.070512	1.086740	1.099288	1.106712
.9799999	1.065153	1.084334	1.101319	1.114490	1.122300
.9899999	1.078264	1.098273	1.116050	1.129876	1.138093
1.0000000	1.091462	1.112332	1.130936	1.145451	1.154099
1.0100000	1.104748	1.126512	1.145982	1.161223	1.170325
1.0200000	1.118124	1.140819	1.161194	1.177199	1.186782
1.0300000	1.131591	1.155253	1.176577	1.193385	1.203478
1.0400000	1.145151	1.169819	1.192135	1.209791	1.220423
1.0500000	1.158805	1.184520	1.207875	1.226424	1.237627
1.0600000	1.172556	1.199358	1.223801	1.243292	1.255102
1.0699999	1.186404	1.214337	1.239920	1.260405	1.272858
1.0799999	1.200352	1.229460	1.256237	1.277771	1.290908
1.0899999	1.214401	1.244731	1.272759	1.295402	1.309266
1.1000000	1.228552	1.260152	1.289491	1.313306	1.327944
1.1100000	1.242806	1.275728	1.306441	1.331495	1.346957
1.1200000	1.257166	1.291460	1.323614	1.349979	1.366320
1.1300000	1.271632	1.307353	1.341019	1.368771	1.386051
1.1400000	1.286206	1.323409	1.358660	1.387884	1.406166
1.1500000	1.300888	1.339633	1.376547	1.407330	1.426685
1.1600000	1.315681	1.356027	1.394686	1.427122	1.447627
1.1700000	1.330586	1.372595	1.413085	1.447277	1.469013
1.1800000	1.345602	1.389340	1.431752	1.467807	1.490867
1.1899999	1.360732	1.406264	1.450694	1.488731	1.513212

$\alpha = -\ .199999$

Θ	K VALUES				
	.794250555	.868696860	.928444378	.971111163	.994996249
1.2000000	1.375976	1.423371	1.469920	1.510064	1.536076
1.2100000	1.391334	1.440665	1.489437	1.531823	1.559487
1.2200000	1.406808	1.458146	1.509254	1.554029	1.583475
1.2300000	1.422398	1.475820	1.529379	1.576700	1.608072
1.2400000	1.438104	1.493687	1.549821	1.599856	1.633316
1.2500000	1.453926	1.511750	1.570589	1.623520	1.659244
1.2599999	1.469865	1.530012	1.591690	1.647713	1.685899
1.2699999	1.485920	1.548474	1.613133	1.672461	1.713327
1.2799999	1.502091	1.567138	1.634926	1.697788	1.741576
1.2899999	1.518378	1.586006	1.657078	1.723719	1.770702
1.3000000	1.534780	1.605079	1.679597	1.750283	1.800766
1.3100000	1.551295	1.624356	1.702489	1.777508	1.831831
1.3200000	1.567924	1.643839	1.725763	1.805423	1.863971
1.3300000	1.584664	1.663528	1.749424	1.834060	1.897265
1.3400000	1.601514	1.683421	1.773479	1.863449	1.931802
1.3500000	1.618472	1.703518	1.797933	1.893625	1.967679
1.3600000	1.635537	1.723817	1.822791	1.924619	2.005007
1.3700000	1.652705	1.744317	1.848056	1.956466	2.043907
1.3799999	1.669975	1.765013	1.873730	1.989199	2.084514
1.3899999	1.687343	1.785904	1.899814	2.022852	2.126983
1.4000000	1.704806	1.806985	1.926308	2.057457	2.171486
1.4100000	1.722362	1.828250	1.953208	2.093044	2.218216
1.4200000	1.740006	1.849695	1.980510	2.129641	2.267392
1.4300000	1.757734	1.871313	2.008209	2.167273	2.319263
1.4400000	1.775542	1.893098	2.036295	2.205959	2.374108
1.4500000	1.793427	1.915041	2.064758	2.245712	2.432243
1.4600000	1.811383	1.937135	2.093583	2.286537	2.494022
1.4700000	1.829404	1.959369	2.122754	2.328429	2.559840
1.4800000	1.847487	1.981734	2.152251	2.371370	2.630129
1.4900000	1.865626	2.004220	2.182054	2.415331	2.705349
1.5000000	1.883815	2.026815	2.212136	2.460264	2.785973
1.5100000	1.902048	2.049506	2.242471	2.506107	2.872439
1.5200000	1.920320	2.072282	2.273028	2.552778	2.965097
1.5300000	1.938624	2.095129	2.303775	2.600178	3.064099
1.5400000	1.956954	2.118034	2.334677	2.648189	3.169267
1.5500000	1.975304	2.140983	2.365698	2.696678	3.279938
1.5600000	1.993667	2.163962	2.396800	2.745499	3.394854
1.5699999	2.012038	2.186956	2.427945	2.794494	3.512176
1.5707963	2.013501	2.188788	2.430426	2.798398	3.521557
1.5707963	2.013499	2.188786	2.430424	2.798395	3.521554

$\alpha = -$ .149999

θ	K VALUES				
	.009966711	.039469502	.087332193	.151646642	.229848846
.0000000	.000000	.000000	.000000	.000000	.000000
.0100000	.009999	.009999	.009999	.009999	.009999
.0200000	.019999	.019999	.019999	.019999	.019999
.0300000	.029998	.029998	.029999	.029999	.029999
.0400000	.039996	.039997	.039997	.039998	.039999
.0500000	.049993	.049994	.049995	.049996	.049998
.0600000	.059989	.059990	.059992	.059994	.059997
.0700000	.069983	.069985	.069987	.069991	.069996
.0800000	.079975	.079977	.079981	.079987	.079994
.0900000	.089964	.089968	.089974	.089982	.089991
.1000000	.099951	.099956	.099964	.099975	.099988
.1100000	.109935	.109942	.109953	.109967	.109984
.1200000	.119916	.119925	.119939	.119957	.119979
.1300000	.129894	.129905	.129922	.129946	.129974
.1400000	.139868	.139881	.139903	.139932	.139968
.1500000	.149837	.149854	.149881	.149917	.149961
.1600000	.159803	.159823	.159855	.159899	.159952
.1700000	.169764	.169788	.169827	.169879	.169943
.1800000	.179720	.179749	.179795	.179857	.179933
.1900000	.189671	.189705	.189759	.189832	.189921
.2000000	.199617	.199656	.199719	.199805	.199908
.2100000	.209558	.209603	.209676	.209774	.209894
.2200000	.219492	.219544	.219628	.219741	.219879
.2300000	.229420	.229479	.229575	.229704	.229862
.2400000	.239342	.239409	.239518	.239665	.239844
.2500000	.249258	.249333	.249456	.249622	.249824
.2600000	.259166	.259251	.259389	.259575	.259803
.2700000	.269068	.269163	.269317	.269525	.269780
.2800000	.278962	.279068	.279240	.279472	.279755
.2900000	.288849	.288966	.289157	.289414	.289729
.3000000	.298728	.298857	.299068	.299353	.299701
.3100000	.308599	.308741	.308974	.309288	.309672
.3200000	.318461	.318618	.318874	.319218	.319640
.3300000	.328316	.328487	.328767	.329145	.329607
.3400000	.338162	.338349	.338654	.339067	.339572
.3500000	.347998	.348203	.348535	.348984	.349535
.3600000	.357826	.358048	.358409	.358898	.359497
.3700000	.367645	.367885	.368277	.368806	.369456
.3800000	.377454	.377714	.378137	.378710	.379413
.3900000	.387254	.387534	.387991	.388610	.389369

$\alpha =$ - .149999

Θ	K VALUES				
	.009966711	.039469502	.087332193	.151646642	.229848846
.4000000	.397044	.397346	.397838	.398504	.399322
.4100000	.406824	.407148	.407677	.408394	.409274
.4200000	.416594	.416942	.417509	.418278	.419224
.4300000	.426353	.426726	.427334	.428158	.429171
.4400000	.436103	.436501	.437151	.438032	.439117
.4500000	.445841	.446266	.446960	.447901	.449060
.4600000	.455569	.456022	.456761	.457765	.459002
.4700000	.465286	.465768	.466555	.467624	.468942
.4800000	.474992	.475504	.476340	.477477	.478879
.4900000	.484687	.485230	.486118	.487325	.488815
.5000000	.494370	.494946	.495887	.497168	.498749
.5100000	.504042	.504652	.505648	.507005	.508680
.5200000	.513703	.514347	.515401	.516836	.518610
.5300000	.523352	.524032	.525145	.526662	.528538
.5400000	.532989	.533706	.534881	.536482	.538464
.5500000	.542614	.543370	.544609	.546297	.548387
.5600000	.552228	.553023	.554327	.556106	.558309
.5700000	.561829	.562666	.564037	.565909	.568230
.5800000	.571419	.572298	.573739	.575706	.578148
.5900000	.580996	.581918	.583431	.585498	.588064
.6000000	.590561	.591528	.593115	.595284	.597979
.6100000	.600113	.601127	.602790	.605064	.607892
.6200000	.609654	.610714	.612456	.614838	.617803
.6300000	.619182	.620291	.622113	.624607	.627712
.6400000	.628697	.629856	.631761	.634370	.637620
.6500000	.638200	.639410	.641400	.644126	.647526
.6600000	.647690	.648953	.651030	.653877	.657431
.6700000	.657168	.658485	.660651	.663623	.667334
.6800000	.666633	.668005	.670263	.673362	.677235
.6899999	.676085	.677514	.679866	.683096	.687135
.7000000	.685525	.687012	.689460	.692824	.697034
.7100000	.694952	.696498	.699045	.702546	.706931
.7200000	.704367	.705973	.708621	.712262	.716827
.7300000	.713769	.715437	.718187	.721973	.726722
.7400000	.723158	.724889	.727745	.731678	.736615
.7500000	.732534	.734330	.737294	.741377	.746507
.7600000	.741898	.743760	.746833	.751070	.756398
.7700000	.751250	.753178	.756364	.760758	.766288
.7800000	.760588	.762586	.765885	.770440	.776177
.7899999	.769914	.771982	.775398	.780117	.786065

$\alpha = -.149999$

θ	K VALUES				
	.009966711	.039469502	.087332193	.151646642	.229848846
.8000000	.779228	.781366	.784902	.789788	.795952
.8100000	.788529	.790740	.794397	.799454	.805838
.8200000	.797818	.800102	.803883	.809114	.815723
.8300000	.807094	.809454	.813360	.818768	.825608
.8400000	.816358	.818794	.822829	.828418	.835491
.8500000	.825609	.828124	.832288	.838062	.845374
.8600000	.834849	.837442	.841740	.847700	.855257
.8700000	.844076	.846750	.851182	.857334	.865139
.8799999	.853291	.856046	.860616	.866962	.875020
.8899999	.862494	.865332	.870041	.876585	.884901
.9000000	.871686	.874608	.879459	.886203	.894782
.9100000	.880865	.883873	.888867	.895816	.904662
.9200000	.890033	.893127	.898268	.905424	.914542
.9300000	.899189	.902371	.907660	.915027	.924422
.9400000	.908333	.911605	.917044	.924625	.934301
.9500000	.917466	.920828	.926420	.934219	.944180
.9600000	.926588	.930041	.935788	.943807	.954060
.9699999	.935698	.939245	.945148	.953391	.963939
.9799999	.944797	.948438	.954500	.962971	.973818
.9899999	.953886	.957621	.963844	.972545	.983698
1.0000000	.962963	.966795	.973181	.982116	.993577
1.0100000	.972030	.975959	.982511	.991682	1.003457
1.0200000	.981086	.985114	.991832	1.001243	1.013336
1.0300000	.990131	.994259	1.001147	1.010801	1.023216
1.0400000	.999166	1.003395	1.010454	1.020354	1.033097
1.0500000	1.008191	1.012522	1.019754	1.029903	1.042977
1.0600000	1.017205	1.021640	1.029047	1.039448	1.052858
1.0699999	1.026210	1.030749	1.038333	1.048989	1.062740
1.0799999	1.035205	1.039849	1.047612	1.058526	1.072621
1.0899999	1.044190	1.048940	1.056885	1.068059	1.082504
1.1000000	1.053166	1.058023	1.066150	1.077589	1.092386
1.1100000	1.062133	1.067098	1.075410	1.087115	1.102270
1.1200000	1.071090	1.076165	1.084662	1.096637	1.112153
1.1300000	1.080038	1.085223	1.093909	1.106155	1.122038
1.1400000	1.088977	1.094274	1.103149	1.115671	1.131923
1.1500000	1.097908	1.103317	1.112384	1.125183	1.141808
1.1600000	1.106830	1.112352	1.121612	1.134691	1.151695
1.1700000	1.115743	1.121380	1.130834	1.144196	1.161582
1.1800000	1.124649	1.130400	1.140051	1.153699	1.171469
1.1899999	1.133546	1.139413	1.149263	1.163198	1.181357

$\alpha = -$ .149999

Θ	K VALUES				
	.009966711	.039469502	.087332193	.151646642	.229848846
1.2000000	1.142436	1.148420	1.158468	1.172694	1.191247
1.2100000	1.151318	1.157419	1.167669	1.182187	1.201136
1.2200000	1.160192	1.166412	1.176864	1.191677	1.211027
1.2300000	1.169059	1.175398	1.186055	1.201165	1.220918
1.2400000	1.177919	1.184378	1.195240	1.210650	1.230810
1.2500000	1.186772	1.193352	1.204421	1.220132	1.240703
1.2599999	1.195619	1.202320	1.213596	1.229612	1.250596
1.2699999	1.204459	1.211282	1.222768	1.239089	1.260491
1.2799999	1.213292	1.220238	1.231935	1.248564	1.270386
1.2899999	1.222119	1.229189	1.241098	1.258037	1.280281
1.3000000	1.230941	1.238135	1.250256	1.267508	1.290178
1.3100000	1.239757	1.247075	1.259411	1.276976	1.300075
1.3200000	1.248567	1.256011	1.268562	1.286443	1.309973
1.3300000	1.257371	1.264941	1.277709	1.295907	1.319872
1.3400000	1.266171	1.273867	1.286853	1.305370	1.329771
1.3500000	1.274966	1.282789	1.295993	1.314830	1.339671
1.3600000	1.283755	1.291707	1.305130	1.324289	1.349572
1.3700000	1.292541	1.300620	1.314264	1.333747	1.359473
1.3799999	1.301322	1.309530	1.323394	1.343203	1.369375
1.3899999	1.310099	1.318436	1.332522	1.352657	1.379278
1.4000000	1.318872	1.327338	1.341648	1.362110	1.389181
1.4100000	1.327641	1.336237	1.350771	1.371562	1.399085
1.4200000	1.336407	1.345133	1.359891	1.381012	1.408990
1.4300000	1.345169	1.354027	1.369009	1.390461	1.418894
1.4400000	1.353929	1.362917	1.378125	1.399909	1.428800
1.4500000	1.362685	1.371805	1.387239	1.409356	1.438706
1.4600000	1.371439	1.380690	1.396351	1.418802	1.448612
1.4700000	1.380191	1.389574	1.405462	1.428248	1.458518
1.4800000	1.388940	1.398455	1.414571	1.437692	1.468425
1.4900000	1.397688	1.407335	1.423679	1.447136	1.478333
1.5000000	1.406433	1.416213	1.432785	1.456579	1.488240
1.5100000	1.415177	1.425090	1.441891	1.466022	1.498148
1.5200000	1.423920	1.433965	1.450995	1.475464	1.508056
1.5300000	1.432662	1.442840	1.460099	1.484905	1.517964
1.5400000	1.441402	1.451714	1.469202	1.494347	1.527873
1.5500000	1.450142	1.460587	1.478305	1.503788	1.537781
1.5600000	1.458882	1.469460	1.487407	1.513229	1.547690
1.5699999	1.467621	1.478332	1.496509	1.522670	1.557599
1.5707963	1.468317	1.479039	1.497234	1.523422	1.558388
1.5707963	1.468317	1.479038	1.497234	1.523421	1.558387

$\alpha = -.149999$

θ	K VALUES				
	.318821117	.415016431	.514599755	.613601043	.708073407
.0000000	.000000	.000000	.000000	.000000	.000000
.0100000	.010000	.010000	.010000	.010000	.010000
.0200000	.020000	.020000	.020000	.020000	.020000
.0300000	.030000	.030000	.030000	.030001	.030001
.0400000	.040000	.040001	.040002	.040003	.040004
.0500000	.050000	.050002	.050004	.050006	.050008
.0600000	.060000	.060004	.060007	.060011	.060014
.0700000	.070001	.070006	.070012	.070017	.070023
.0800000	.080001	.080009	.080018	.080026	.080034
.0900000	.090002	.090014	.090026	.090038	.090049
.1000000	.100003	.100019	.100035	.100052	.100068
.1100000	.110004	.110025	.110047	.110069	.110090
.1200000	.120005	.120033	.120062	.120090	.120117
.1300000	.130007	.130042	.130078	.130115	.130150
.1400000	.140008	.140053	.140098	.140144	.140187
.1500000	.150011	.150065	.150121	.150177	.150230
.1600000	.160013	.160079	.160147	.160215	.160280
.1700000	.170016	.170095	.170177	.170258	.170336
.1800000	.180019	.180113	.180210	.180307	.180400
.1900000	.190023	.190133	.190247	.190361	.190470
.2000000	.200027	.200155	.200289	.200422	.200549
.2100000	.210031	.210180	.210335	.210489	.210637
.2200000	.220036	.220207	.220385	.220563	.220733
.2300000	.230042	.230237	.230441	.230644	.230838
.2400000	.240048	.240270	.240501	.240732	.240954
.2500000	.250055	.250306	.250567	.250829	.251080
.2600000	.260062	.260345	.260639	.260934	.261216
.2700000	.270071	.270387	.270717	.271047	.271364
.2800000	.280080	.280433	.280801	.281169	.281523
.2900000	.290089	.290482	.290891	.291301	.291695
.3000000	.300100	.300534	.300988	.301442	.301879
.3100000	.310111	.310591	.311091	.311593	.312076
.3200000	.320124	.320651	.321202	.321755	.322288
.3300000	.330137	.330716	.331321	.331928	.332513
.3400000	.340152	.340785	.341447	.342112	.342753
.3500000	.350168	.350858	.351581	.352308	.353009
.3600000	.360184	.360936	.361723	.362515	.363280
.3700000	.370202	.371019	.371874	.372735	.373567
.3800000	.380222	.381106	.382034	.382968	.383872
.3900000	.390242	.391199	.392203	.393215	.394194

$\alpha = -\ .149999$

Θ	K VALUES				
	.318821117	.415016431	.514599755	.613601043	.708073407
.4000000	.400265	.401297	.402381	.403474	.404533
.4100000	.410288	.411400	.412569	.413749	.414892
.4200000	.420313	.421509	.422767	.424037	.425269
.4300000	.430340	.431624	.432975	.434341	.435666
.4400000	.440369	.441744	.443193	.444660	.446084
.4500000	.450399	.451871	.453423	.454995	.456522
.4600000	.460431	.462004	.463664	.465346	.466982
.4700000	.470466	.472144	.473916	.475714	.477464
.4800000	.480502	.482290	.484180	.486099	.487969
.4900000	.490540	.492443	.494456	.496501	.498498
.5000000	.500581	.502603	.504744	.506922	.509050
.5100000	.510624	.512770	.515045	.517362	.519627
.5200000	.520669	.522945	.525359	.527821	.530229
.5300000	.530716	.533127	.535687	.538299	.540858
.5400000	.540767	.543317	.546028	.548797	.551513
.5500000	.550819	.553515	.556383	.559316	.562195
.5600000	.560875	.563722	.566753	.569856	.572906
.5700000	.570933	.573936	.577137	.580418	.583646
.5800000	.580995	.584159	.587536	.591001	.594415
.5900000	.591059	.594391	.597951	.601607	.605214
.6000000	.601127	.604632	.608381	.612237	.616044
.6100000	.611197	.614882	.618827	.622890	.626906
.6200000	.621271	.625142	.629290	.633567	.637801
.6300000	.631349	.635411	.639769	.644269	.648729
.6400000	.641430	.645690	.650266	.654996	.659691
.6500000	.651514	.655978	.660779	.665748	.670687
.6600000	.661602	.666277	.671311	.676527	.681720
.6700000	.671694	.676586	.681861	.687333	.692788
.6800000	.681790	.686906	.692429	.698167	.703895
.6899999	.691891	.697237	.703015	.709028	.715039
.7000000	.701995	.707579	.713621	.719918	.726222
.7100000	.712103	.717931	.724247	.730837	.737445
.7200000	.722216	.728295	.734892	.741785	.748708
.7300000	.732333	.738671	.745557	.752764	.760013
.7400000	.742455	.749059	.756243	.763773	.771360
.7500000	.752581	.759458	.766949	.774814	.782751
.7600000	.762712	.769869	.777677	.785886	.794186
.7700000	.772848	.780293	.788426	.796991	.805665
.7800000	.782989	.790729	.799197	.808129	.817191
.7899999	.793135	.801178	.809990	.819301	.828763

α = - .149999

Θ	K VALUES				
	.318821117	.415016431	.514599755	.613601043	.708073407
.8000000	.803286	.811640	.820806	.830506	.840383
.8100000	.813443	.822115	.831645	.841746	.852052
.8200000	.823604	.832603	.842506	.853022	.863770
.8300000	.833771	.843105	.853391	.864333	.875538
.8400000	.843944	.853620	.864300	.875681	.887358
.8500000	.854122	.864148	.875233	.887066	.899231
.8600000	.864305	.874691	.886190	.898488	.911156
.8700000	.874495	.885248	.897172	.909947	.923136
.8799999	.884690	.895818	.908179	.921446	.935171
.8899999	.894891	.906403	.919210	.932983	.947262
.9000000	.905098	.917003	.930268	.944561	.959410
.9100000	.915312	.927617	.941351	.956178	.971616
.9200000	.925531	.938246	.952460	.967835	.983881
.9300000	.935757	.948889	.963596	.979534	.996206
.9400000	.945988	.959548	.974757	.991274	1.008591
.9500000	.956226	.970221	.985946	1.003057	1.021038
.9600000	.966471	.980910	.997161	1.014881	1.033548
.9699999	.976722	.991614	1.008404	1.026749	1.046121
.9799999	.986979	1.002333	1.019674	1.038660	1.058758
.9899999	.997243	1.013067	1.030971	1.050614	1.071461
1.0000000	1.007513	1.023817	1.042296	1.062613	1.084229
1.0100000	1.017790	1.034583	1.053648	1.074656	1.097065
1.0200000	1.028073	1.045364	1.065029	1.086744	1.109968
1.0300000	1.038363	1.056160	1.076437	1.098877	1.122939
1.0400000	1.048660	1.066972	1.087874	1.111056	1.135980
1.0500000	1.058963	1.077800	1.099338	1.123280	1.149091
1.0600000	1.069273	1.088643	1.110831	1.135551	1.162272
1.0699999	1.079590	1.099502	1.122352	1.147867	1.175525
1.0799999	1.089913	1.110377	1.133902	1.160230	1.188850
1.0899999	1.100243	1.121267	1.145480	1.172640	1.202247
1.1000000	1.110580	1.132172	1.157086	1.185096	1.215718
1.1100000	1.120924	1.143094	1.168721	1.197600	1.229262
1.1200000	1.131274	1.154030	1.180384	1.210150	1.242881
1.1300000	1.141630	1.164982	1.192074	1.222747	1.256574
1.1400000	1.151993	1.175949	1.203793	1.235391	1.270342
1.1500000	1.162363	1.186931	1.215540	1.248082	1.284186
1.1600000	1.172739	1.197929	1.227315	1.260820	1.298105
1.1700000	1.183121	1.208941	1.239117	1.273605	1.312099
1.1800000	1.193510	1.219968	1.250947	1.286436	1.326170
1.1899999	1.203906	1.231010	1.262804	1.299314	1.340316

$\alpha = -.149999$

θ	K VALUES				
	.318821117	.415016431	.514599755	.613601043	.708073407
1.2000000	1.214307	1.242066	1.274689	1.312238	1.354539
1.2100000	1.224715	1.253137	1.286599	1.325207	1.368837
1.2200000	1.235128	1.264222	1.298537	1.338222	1.383211
1.2300000	1.245548	1.275320	1.310500	1.351283	1.397660
1.2400000	1.255974	1.286433	1.322489	1.364388	1.412185
1.2500000	1.266405	1.297559	1.334503	1.377537	1.426783
1.2599999	1.276842	1.308698	1.346543	1.390729	1.441456
1.2699999	1.287285	1.319850	1.358607	1.403965	1.456202
1.2799999	1.297733	1.331015	1.370695	1.417243	1.471021
1.2899999	1.308187	1.342193	1.382807	1.430563	1.485912
1.3000000	1.318646	1.353383	1.394942	1.443924	1.500873
1.3100000	1.329110	1.364584	1.407100	1.457325	1.515904
1.3200000	1.339579	1.375797	1.419279	1.470765	1.531004
1.3300000	1.350052	1.387022	1.431480	1.484243	1.546170
1.3400000	1.360531	1.398257	1.443702	1.497759	1.561403
1.3500000	1.371014	1.409503	1.455945	1.511311	1.576700
1.3600000	1.381501	1.420759	1.468206	1.524898	1.592059
1.3700000	1.391993	1.432025	1.480487	1.538519	1.607479
1.3799999	1.402488	1.443300	1.492785	1.552173	1.622958
1.3899999	1.412988	1.454584	1.505101	1.565859	1.638494
1.4000000	1.423491	1.465877	1.517434	1.579574	1.654084
1.4100000	1.433998	1.477178	1.529783	1.593319	1.669727
1.4200000	1.444508	1.488487	1.542146	1.607091	1.685420
1.4300000	1.455021	1.499803	1.554524	1.620889	1.701160
1.4400000	1.465537	1.511126	1.566915	1.634712	1.716946
1.4500000	1.476056	1.522456	1.579319	1.648558	1.732774
1.4600000	1.486577	1.533791	1.591734	1.662425	1.748641
1.4700000	1.497101	1.545132	1.604160	1.676311	1.764544
1.4800000	1.507627	1.556478	1.616596	1.690216	1.780482
1.4900000	1.518155	1.567829	1.629041	1.704138	1.796450
1.5000000	1.528685	1.579183	1.641493	1.718074	1.812445
1.5100000	1.539216	1.590542	1.653953	1.732023	1.828464
1.5200000	1.549749	1.601903	1.666418	1.745983	1.844504
1.5300000	1.560282	1.613267	1.678889	1.759952	1.860562
1.5400000	1.570817	1.624633	1.691364	1.773929	1.876633
1.5500000	1.581352	1.636000	1.703841	1.787912	1.892716
1.5600000	1.591887	1.647369	1.716321	1.801898	1.908805
1.5699999	1.602423	1.658738	1.728802	1.815887	1.924898
1.5707963	1.603262	1.659643	1.729796	1.817001	1.926180
1.5707963	1.603261	1.659642	1.729795	1.817000	1.926179

$\alpha =$ - .149999

Θ	K VALUES				
	.794250555	.868696860	.928444378	.971111163	.994996249
.0000000	.000000	.000000	.000000	.000000	.000000
.0100000	.010000	.010000	.010000	.010000	.010000
.0200000	.020000	.020000	.020000	.020000	.020000
.0300000	.030002	.030002	.030002	.030003	.030003
.0400000	.040005	.040006	.040006	.040007	.040007
.0500000	.050010	.050011	.050013	.050014	.050014
.0600000	.060017	.060020	.060022	.060024	.060025
.0700000	.070028	.070032	.070036	.070038	.070039
.0800000	.080042	.080048	.080053	.080057	.080059
.0900000	.090060	.090069	.090076	.090081	.090084
.1000000	.100082	.100095	.100105	.100112	.100116
.1100000	.110110	.110126	.110139	.110149	.110154
.1200000	.120142	.120164	.120181	.120194	.120201
.1300000	.130181	.130209	.130231	.130247	.130256
.1400000	.140227	.140261	.140289	.140309	.140320
.1500000	.150279	.150322	.150356	.150380	.150394
.1600000	.160339	.160391	.160432	.160462	.160478
.1700000	.170408	.170469	.170519	.170555	.170574
.1800000	.180484	.180558	.180617	.180659	.180683
.1900000	.190570	.190657	.190726	.190776	.190804
.2000000	.200666	.200767	.200848	.200907	.200939
.2100000	.210772	.210889	.210984	.211051	.211089
.2200000	.220889	.221024	.221133	.221210	.221254
.2300000	.231017	.231172	.231296	.231385	.231435
.2400000	.241157	.241333	.241475	.241577	.241634
.2500000	.251310	.251509	.251670	.251785	.251850
.2600000	.261475	.261700	.261882	.262012	.262084
.2700000	.271655	.271907	.272111	.272257	.272339
.2800000	.281848	.282131	.282359	.282522	.282614
.2900000	.292057	.292371	.292625	.292807	.292910
.3000000	.302281	.302630	.302912	.303114	.303228
.3100000	.312521	.312907	.313220	.313443	.313569
.3200000	.322778	.323204	.323549	.323796	.323935
.3300000	.333052	.333521	.333900	.334172	.334325
.3400000	.343344	.343859	.344275	.344574	.344742
.3500000	.353655	.354218	.354674	.355001	.355185
.3600000	.363985	.364600	.365098	.365456	.365657
.3700000	.374335	.375005	.375548	.375938	.376158
.3800000	.384706	.385435	.386025	.386450	.386689
.3900000	.395098	.395889	.396530	.396991	.397250

$\alpha =$ - .149999

Θ	K VALUES				
	.794250555	.868696860	.928444378	.971111163	.994996249
.4000000	.405512	.406369	.407063	.407563	.407845
.4100000	.415950	.416875	.417627	.418168	.418472
.4200000	.426410	.427410	.428221	.428806	.429135
.4300000	.436895	.437972	.438847	.439478	.439833
.4400000	.447405	.448564	.449506	.450185	.450568
.4500000	.457941	.459186	.460199	.460929	.461341
.4600000	.468503	.469839	.470926	.471711	.472154
.4700000	.479093	.480524	.481690	.482533	.483008
.4800000	.489711	.491243	.492491	.493394	.493903
.4900000	.500357	.501995	.503331	.504297	.504842
.5000000	.511034	.512783	.514210	.515243	.515827
.5100000	.521741	.523606	.525130	.526234	.526857
.5200000	.532480	.534467	.536092	.537270	.537935
.5300000	.543251	.545367	.547098	.548353	.549062
.5400000	.554056	.556305	.558148	.559485	.560241
.5500000	.564894	.567285	.569244	.570666	.571472
.5600000	.575768	.578306	.580387	.581900	.582756
.5700000	.586678	.589369	.591580	.593187	.594097
.5800000	.597625	.600477	.602822	.604528	.605495
.5900000	.608610	.611631	.614116	.615926	.616953
.6000000	.619634	.622830	.625464	.627382	.628471
.6100000	.630698	.634078	.636866	.638899	.640053
.6200000	.641803	.645375	.648324	.650477	.651699
.6300000	.652950	.656723	.659840	.662118	.663413
.6400000	.664140	.668122	.671416	.673825	.675196
.6500000	.675374	.679574	.683053	.685600	.687050
.6600000	.686654	.691082	.694754	.697444	.698977
.6700000	.697980	.702645	.706519	.709360	.710980
.6800000	.709354	.714267	.718351	.721350	.723061
.6899999	.720777	.725947	.730252	.733416	.735222
.7000000	.732249	.737689	.742223	.745560	.747466
.7100000	.743773	.749492	.754267	.757785	.759796
.7200000	.755349	.761360	.766386	.770093	.772214
.7300000	.766978	.773294	.778582	.782487	.784723
.7400000	.778662	.785295	.790856	.794969	.797326
.7500000	.790403	.797365	.803212	.807542	.810025
.7600000	.802201	.809506	.815652	.820209	.822825
.7700000	.814057	.821720	.828178	.832972	.835727
.7800000	.825974	.834009	.840792	.845835	.848736
.7899999	.837952	.846375	.853497	.858800	.861854

$\alpha =$ - .149999

θ	K VALUES				
	.794250555	.868696860	.928444378	.971111163	.994996249
.8000000	.849993	.858819	.866296	.871872	.875086
.8100000	.862099	.871344	.879191	.885052	.888434
.8200000	.874270	.883951	.892185	.898345	.901904
.8300000	.886508	.896643	.905280	.911754	.915498
.8400000	.898814	.909423	.918481	.925282	.929221
.8500000	.911191	.922291	.931789	.938934	.943077
.8600000	.923639	.935251	.945209	.952713	.957071
.8700000	.936161	.948304	.958742	.966624	.971207
.8799999	.948757	.961454	.972393	.980670	.985490
.8899999	.961429	.974702	.986165	.994856	.999925
.9000000	.974179	.988052	1.000062	1.009187	1.014518
.9100000	.987009	1.001504	1.014086	1.023667	1.029273
.9200000	.999919	1.015063	1.028242	1.038302	1.044198
.9300000	1.012912	1.028730	1.042533	1.053095	1.059297
.9400000	1.025989	1.042509	1.056964	1.068054	1.074576
.9500000	1.039152	1.056401	1.071539	1.083182	1.090044
.9600000	1.052403	1.070411	1.086262	1.098486	1.105705
.9699999	1.065743	1.084540	1.101137	1.113973	1.121569
.9799999	1.079174	1.098792	1.116169	1.129647	1.137641
.9899999	1.092697	1.113169	1.131362	1.145517	1.153931
1.0000000	1.106315	1.127675	1.146722	1.161588	1.170446
1.0100000	1.120028	1.142312	1.162253	1.177868	1.187195
1.0200000	1.133839	1.157084	1.177960	1.194363	1.204187
1.0300000	1.147750	1.171993	1.193849	1.211083	1.221433
1.0400000	1.161761	1.187044	1.209925	1.228034	1.238942
1.0500000	1.175875	1.202239	1.226194	1.245227	1.256725
1.0600000	1.190093	1.217582	1.242662	1.262668	1.274793
1.0699999	1.204416	1.233075	1.259334	1.280368	1.293159
1.0799999	1.218848	1.248722	1.276217	1.298337	1.311835
1.0899999	1.233388	1.264527	1.293316	1.316584	1.330834
1.1000000	1.248038	1.280493	1.310640	1.335120	1.350172
1.1100000	1.262801	1.296624	1.328194	1.353957	1.369863
1.1200000	1.277677	1.312922	1.345985	1.373107	1.389923
1.1300000	1.292668	1.329391	1.364020	1.392581	1.410369
1.1400000	1.307775	1.346035	1.382308	1.412392	1.431220
1.1500000	1.322999	1.362858	1.400854	1.432555	1.452496
1.1600000	1.338342	1.379861	1.419668	1.453084	1.474216
1.1700000	1.353805	1.397050	1.438756	1.473993	1.496404
1.1800000	1.369388	1.414426	1.458127	1.495299	1.519082
1.1899999	1.385093	1.431994	1.477789	1.517018	1.542278

$\alpha = -.149999$

Θ	K VALUES				
	.794250555	.868696860	.928444378	.971111163	.994996249
1.2000000	1.400921	1.449757	1.497751	1.539168	1.566017
1.2100000	1.416872	1.467717	1.518021	1.561767	1.590330
1.2200000	1.432946	1.485877	1.538607	1.584834	1.615249
1.2300000	1.449145	1.504241	1.559519	1.608390	1.640808
1.2400000	1.465468	1.522810	1.580765	1.632457	1.667044
1.2500000	1.481917	1.541588	1.602354	1.657057	1.693998
1.2599999	1.498490	1.560576	1.624294	1.682213	1.721713
1.2699999	1.515187	1.579777	1.646595	1.707951	1.750238
1.2799999	1.532009	1.599192	1.669266	1.734296	1.779624
1.2899999	1.548954	1.618823	1.692313	1.761277	1.809928
1.3000000	1.566023	1.638671	1.715747	1.788921	1.841214
1.3100000	1.583213	1.658736	1.739575	1.817257	1.873548
1.3200000	1.600524	1.679018	1.763803	1.846318	1.907006
1.3300000	1.617954	1.699518	1.788440	1.876135	1.941673
1.3400000	1.635501	1.720235	1.813491	1.906742	1.977640
1.3500000	1.653164	1.741168	1.838961	1.938171	2.015009
1.3600000	1.670941	1.762314	1.864857	1.970459	2.053894
1.3700000	1.688829	1.783673	1.891180	2.003640	2.094424
1.3799999	1.706824	1.805239	1.917933	2.037749	2.136738
1.3899999	1.724925	1.827011	1.945118	2.072821	2.180999
1.4000000	1.743127	1.848984	1.972732	2.108891	2.227385
1.4100000	1.761428	1.871152	2.000774	2.145988	2.276098
1.4200000	1.779823	1.893510	2.029239	2.184143	2.327368
1.4300000	1.798308	1.916051	2.058120	2.223382	2.381452
1.4400000	1.816878	1.938767	2.087408	2.263723	2.438644
1.4500000	1.835530	1.961652	2.117091	2.305181	2.499272
1.4600000	1.854257	1.984694	2.147154	2.347760	2.563706
1.4700000	1.873055	2.007886	2.177581	2.391455	2.632358
1.4800000	1.891918	2.031216	2.208351	2.436249	2.705678
1.4900000	1.910840	2.054673	2.239441	2.482108	2.784148
1.5000000	1.929816	2.078245	2.270825	2.528986	2.868259
1.5100000	1.948839	2.101919	2.302474	2.576814	2.958471
1.5200000	1.967903	2.125683	2.334356	2.625509	3.055146
1.5300000	1.987001	2.149521	2.366437	2.674966	3.158445
1.5400000	2.006127	2.173421	2.398681	2.725062	3.268180
1.5500000	2.025274	2.197367	2.431050	2.775658	3.383660
1.5600000	2.044436	2.221345	2.463504	2.826601	3.503572
1.5699999	2.063605	2.245339	2.496003	2.877726	3.625994
1.5707963	2.065132	2.247250	2.498592	2.881800	3.635783
1.5707963	2.065130	2.247249	2.498590	2.881797	3.635780

$\alpha = -\ .099999$

Θ	K VALUES				
	.009966711	.039469502	.087332193	.151646642	.229848846
.0000000	.000000	.000000	.000000	.000000	.000000
.0100000	.009999	.009999	.009999	.009999	.010000
.0200000	.019999	.019999	.019999	.019999	.020000
.0300000	.029999	.029999	.029999	.029999	.030000
.0400000	.039997	.039998	.039998	.039999	.040000
.0500000	.049996	.049996	.049997	.049999	.050000
.0600000	.059993	.059994	.059995	.059998	.060001
.0700000	.069989	.069990	.069993	.069997	.070001
.0800000	.079983	.079986	.079990	.079995	.080002
.0900000	.089977	.089980	.089986	.089994	.090003
.1000000	.099968	.099973	.099981	.099991	.100005
.1100000	.109957	.109964	.109975	.109989	.110006
.1200000	.119945	.119953	.119967	.119986	.120008
.1300000	.129930	.129941	.129958	.129982	.130011
.1400000	.139913	.139926	.139948	.139978	.140013
.1500000	.149893	.149910	.149937	.149973	.150017
.1600000	.159871	.159891	.159923	.159967	.160020
.1700000	.169845	.169869	.169908	.169960	.170024
.1800000	.179816	.179845	.179891	.179953	.180029
.1900000	.189784	.189818	.189872	.189945	.190034
.2000000	.199749	.199788	.199851	.199936	.200040
.2100000	.209710	.209755	.209828	.209926	.210047
.2200000	.219666	.219718	.219802	.219916	.220054
.2300000	.229619	.229678	.229775	.229904	.230062
.2400000	.239568	.239635	.239744	.239891	.240070
.2500000	.249513	.249588	.249711	.249877	.250080
.2600000	.259453	.259538	.259676	.259862	.260090
.2700000	.269388	.269483	.269638	.269846	.270101
.2800000	.279318	.279424	.279597	.279829	.280113
.2900000	.289244	.289361	.289553	.289811	.290126
.3000000	.299164	.299294	.299505	.299791	.300140
.3100000	.309079	.309222	.309455	.309770	.310155
.3200000	.318989	.319146	.319402	.319748	.320171
.3300000	.328893	.329065	.329346	.329724	.330188
.3400000	.338791	.338979	.339286	.339700	.340206
.3500000	.348684	.348889	.349222	.349673	.350226
.3600000	.358570	.358793	.359155	.359646	.360247
.3700000	.368451	.368692	.369085	.369617	.370269
.3800000	.378325	.378586	.379011	.379586	.380292
.3900000	.388193	.388474	.388933	.389554	.390317

$\alpha = - .099999$

Θ	K VALUES				
	.009966711	.039469502	.087332193	.151646642	.229848846
.4000000	.398054	.398357	.398852	.399521	.400343
.4100000	.407909	.408235	.408766	.409486	.410371
.4200000	.417757	.418106	.418677	.419450	.420400
.4300000	.427598	.427972	.428583	.429412	.430431
.4400000	.437432	.437833	.438486	.439372	.440463
.4500000	.447260	.447687	.448385	.449331	.450497
.4600000	.457080	.457535	.458279	.459289	.460533
.4700000	.466892	.467377	.468169	.469245	.470571
.4800000	.476698	.477213	.478055	.479199	.480610
.4900000	.486495	.487042	.487936	.489152	.490651
.5000000	.496286	.496865	.497813	.499103	.500695
.5100000	.506069	.506682	.507686	.509052	.510740
.5200000	.515844	.516492	.517554	.519000	.520787
.5300000	.525611	.526296	.527418	.528946	.530836
.5400000	.535370	.536093	.537277	.538891	.540888
.5500000	.545121	.545883	.547132	.548834	.550942
.5600000	.554865	.555667	.556982	.558775	.560998
.5700000	.564600	.565444	.566827	.568715	.571056
.5800000	.574327	.575214	.576668	.578653	.581117
.5900000	.584046	.584977	.586504	.588590	.591180
.6000000	.593757	.594733	.596335	.598525	.601246
.6100000	.603459	.604482	.606162	.608458	.611314
.6200000	.613153	.614224	.615983	.618390	.621385
.6300000	.622838	.623959	.625800	.628320	.631458
.6400000	.632515	.633687	.635612	.638249	.641534
.6500000	.642184	.643408	.645419	.648176	.651613
.6600000	.651844	.653121	.655222	.658101	.661695
.6700000	.661496	.662828	.665019	.668025	.671780
.6800000	.671139	.672527	.674812	.677948	.681867
.6899999	.680773	.682219	.684600	.687869	.691958
.7000000	.690399	.691904	.694382	.697788	.702051
.7100000	.700016	.701581	.704160	.707706	.712148
.7200000	.709624	.711252	.713933	.717623	.722248
.7300000	.719224	.720915	.723702	.727538	.732351
.7400000	.728815	.730570	.733465	.737451	.742457
.7500000	.738398	.740219	.743223	.747364	.752566
.7600000	.747972	.749860	.752977	.757275	.762679
.7700000	.757537	.759494	.762726	.767184	.772795
.7800000	.767094	.769121	.772469	.777092	.782915
.7899999	.776642	.778740	.782208	.786999	.793038

$\alpha = -.099999$

Θ	K VALUES				
	.009966711	.039469502	.087332193	.151646642	.229848846
.8000000	.786181	.788353	.791943	.796905	.803165
.8100000	.795712	.797958	.801672	.806809	.813295
.8200000	.805234	.807556	.811397	.816712	.823429
.8300000	.814748	.817146	.821117	.826614	.833566
.8400000	.824253	.826730	.830832	.836514	.843708
.8500000	.833750	.836306	.840542	.846414	.853852
.8600000	.843238	.845876	.850248	.856312	.864001
.8700000	.852718	.855438	.859949	.866209	.874154
.8799999	.862189	.864994	.869645	.876105	.884310
.8899999	.871652	.874542	.879337	.886000	.894470
.9000000	.881107	.884084	.889024	.895894	.904634
.9100000	.890554	.893618	.898707	.905787	.914802
.9200000	.899993	.903146	.908385	.915679	.924974
.9300000	.909423	.912667	.918059	.925570	.935150
.9400000	.918846	.922182	.927728	.935460	.945330
.9500000	.928260	.931689	.937393	.945349	.955514
.9600000	.937667	.941190	.947054	.955237	.965701
.9699999	.947065	.950685	.956710	.965125	.975893
.9799999	.956456	.960173	.966362	.975011	.986089
.9899999	.965840	.969654	.976010	.984897	.996289
1.0000000	.975215	.979130	.985653	.994782	1.006493
1.0100000	.984584	.988598	.995293	1.004666	1.016702
1.0200000	.993944	.998061	1.004929	1.014549	1.026914
1.0300000	1.003297	1.007518	1.014560	1.024432	1.037130
1.0400000	1.012644	1.016968	1.024188	1.034314	1.047351
1.0500000	1.021982	1.026413	1.033811	1.044195	1.057575
1.0600000	1.031314	1.035851	1.043431	1.054076	1.067804
1.0699999	1.040639	1.045284	1.053047	1.063956	1.078036
1.0799999	1.049957	1.054711	1.062659	1.073836	1.088273
1.0899999	1.059268	1.064132	1.072268	1.083715	1.098513
1.1000000	1.068572	1.073548	1.081873	1.093593	1.108758
1.1100000	1.077870	1.082958	1.091475	1.103471	1.119006
1.1200000	1.087161	1.092363	1.101073	1.113348	1.129259
1.1300000	1.096446	1.101762	1.110667	1.123225	1.139515
1.1400000	1.105725	1.111156	1.120258	1.133102	1.149776
1.1500000	1.114998	1.120545	1.129846	1.142978	1.160040
1.1600000	1.124264	1.129929	1.139431	1.152854	1.170308
1.1700000	1.133525	1.139309	1.149012	1.162729	1.180580
1.1800000	1.142780	1.148683	1.158591	1.172604	1.190855
1.1899999	1.152029	1.158052	1.168166	1.182478	1.201134

$\alpha = -.099999$

Θ	K VALUES				
	.009966711	.039469502	.087332193	.151646642	.229848846
1.2000000	1.161272	1.167417	1.177739	1.192353	1.211417
1.2100000	1.170510	1.176778	1.187308	1.202227	1.221704
1.2200000	1.179743	1.186134	1.196875	1.212100	1.231993
1.2300000	1.188971	1.195485	1.206439	1.221973	1.242287
1.2400000	1.198193	1.204833	1.216000	1.231847	1.252584
1.2500000	1.207411	1.214176	1.225559	1.241719	1.262884
1.2599999	1.216624	1.223516	1.235115	1.251592	1.273187
1.2699999	1.225832	1.232851	1.244668	1.261464	1.283494
1.2799999	1.235036	1.242183	1.254220	1.271337	1.293804
1.2899999	1.244235	1.251511	1.263769	1.281209	1.304116
1.3000000	1.253431	1.260836	1.273315	1.291080	1.314432
1.3100000	1.262622	1.270157	1.282860	1.300952	1.324751
1.3200000	1.271809	1.279475	1.292402	1.310824	1.335073
1.3300000	1.280992	1.288789	1.301943	1.320695	1.345397
1.3400000	1.290172	1.298101	1.311481	1.330566	1.355724
1.3500000	1.299348	1.307410	1.321018	1.340437	1.366053
1.3600000	1.308520	1.316716	1.330553	1.350308	1.376385
1.3700000	1.317690	1.326019	1.340086	1.360179	1.386720
1.3799999	1.326856	1.335319	1.349618	1.370050	1.397056
1.3899999	1.336020	1.344618	1.359148	1.379921	1.407395
1.4000000	1.345180	1.353913	1.368676	1.389791	1.417736
1.4100000	1.354338	1.363207	1.378203	1.399662	1.428079
1.4200000	1.363494	1.372499	1.387729	1.409532	1.438423
1.4300000	1.372647	1.381788	1.397254	1.419403	1.448770
1.4400000	1.381798	1.391076	1.406777	1.429273	1.459118
1.4500000	1.390947	1.400362	1.416300	1.439143	1.469467
1.4600000	1.400094	1.409647	1.425821	1.449014	1.479818
1.4700000	1.409239	1.418930	1.435341	1.458884	1.490171
1.4800000	1.418383	1.428212	1.444861	1.468754	1.500524
1.4900000	1.427525	1.437492	1.454380	1.478624	1.510879
1.5000000	1.436666	1.446772	1.463898	1.488494	1.521234
1.5100000	1.445806	1.456050	1.473416	1.498365	1.531591
1.5200000	1.454945	1.465328	1.482933	1.508235	1.541948
1.5300000	1.464084	1.474605	1.492450	1.518105	1.552306
1.5400000	1.473221	1.483882	1.501967	1.527975	1.562664
1.5500000	1.482358	1.493158	1.511483	1.537845	1.573023
1.5600000	1.491495	1.502434	1.520999	1.547715	1.583382
1.5699999	1.500632	1.511710	1.530515	1.557585	1.593741
1.5707963	1.501359	1.512449	1.531273	1.558371	1.594565
1.5707963	1.501358	1.512448	1.531272	1.558370	1.594565

$\alpha = -\ .099999$

Θ	K VALUES				
	.318821117	.415016431	.514599755	.613601043	.708073407
.0000000	.000000	.000000	.000000	.000000	.000000
.0100000	.010000	.010000	.010000	.010000	.010000
.0200000	.020000	.020000	.020000	.020000	.020000
.0300000	.030000	.030000	.030001	.030001	.030002
.0400000	.040001	.040002	.040003	.040004	.040005
.0500000	.050002	.050004	.050006	.050008	.050010
.0600000	.060004	.060007	.060011	.060014	.060018
.0700000	.070006	.070012	.070018	.070023	.070029
.0800000	.080010	.080018	.080026	.080035	.080043
.0900000	.090014	.090026	.090038	.090050	.090061
.1000000	.100019	.100035	.100052	.100069	.100084
.1100000	.110026	.110047	.110069	.110091	.110112
.1200000	.120034	.120062	.120090	.120119	.120146
.1300000	.130043	.130078	.130115	.130151	.130186
.1400000	.140054	.140098	.140144	.140189	.140233
.1500000	.150067	.150121	.150177	.150233	.150286
.1600000	.160081	.160147	.160215	.160283	.160348
.1700000	.170097	.170176	.170258	.170340	.170418
.1800000	.180115	.180209	.180306	.180403	.180496
.1900000	.190136	.190246	.190361	.190475	.190584
.2000000	.200159	.200287	.200421	.200554	.200682
.2100000	.210184	.210333	.210488	.210642	.210790
.2200000	.220212	.220383	.220561	.220739	.220909
.2300000	.230242	.230438	.230641	.230845	.231040
.2400000	.240275	.240498	.240729	.240961	.241183
.2500000	.250311	.250563	.250825	.251087	.251338
.2600000	.260350	.260633	.260928	.261223	.261506
.2700000	.270393	.270710	.271040	.271371	.271689
.2800000	.280438	.280792	.281161	.281530	.281885
.2900000	.290487	.290881	.291291	.291702	.292097
.3000000	.300540	.300975	.301430	.301885	.302324
.3100000	.310596	.311077	.311579	.312082	.312567
.3200000	.320656	.321185	.321738	.322292	.322826
.3300000	.330720	.331301	.331907	.332516	.333103
.3400000	.340788	.341423	.342088	.342755	.343398
.3500000	.350860	.351554	.352279	.353008	.353712
.3600000	.360937	.361692	.362482	.363277	.364044
.3700000	.371018	.371838	.372697	.373561	.374396
.3800000	.381104	.381992	.382924	.383862	.384769
.3900000	.391194	.392155	.393163	.394179	.395163

$\alpha = -.099999$

Θ	K VALUES				
	.318821117	.415016431	.514599755	.613601043	.708073407
.4000000	.401289	.402327	.403416	.404514	.405578
.4100000	.411390	.412507	.413681	.414867	.416015
.4200000	.421495	.422697	.423961	.425238	.426476
.4300000	.431606	.432896	.434254	.435627	.436960
.4400000	.441722	.443105	.444562	.446036	.447468
.4500000	.451844	.453324	.454884	.456465	.458002
.4600000	.461971	.463553	.465222	.466914	.468561
.4700000	.472104	.473792	.475575	.477384	.479146
.4800000	.482243	.484043	.485944	.487876	.489759
.4900000	.492388	.494304	.496330	.498389	.500399
.5000000	.502539	.504576	.506732	.508925	.511068
.5100000	.512697	.514859	.517151	.519484	.521766
.5200000	.522861	.525154	.527587	.530067	.532494
.5300000	.533032	.535461	.538041	.540673	.543252
.5400000	.543209	.545781	.548513	.551305	.554043
.5500000	.553394	.556112	.559004	.561961	.564865
.5600000	.563585	.566456	.569513	.572644	.575720
.5700000	.573784	.576813	.580042	.583352	.586609
.5800000	.583990	.587183	.590591	.594088	.597533
.5900000	.594203	.597566	.601160	.604851	.608492
.6000000	.604424	.607963	.611749	.615642	.619487
.6100000	.614652	.618374	.622359	.626462	.630520
.6200000	.624888	.628799	.632990	.637311	.641590
.6300000	.635133	.639238	.643643	.648190	.652698
.6400000	.645385	.649691	.654317	.659100	.663847
.6500000	.655645	.660159	.665015	.670040	.675035
.6600000	.665914	.670643	.675735	.681012	.686265
.6700000	.676191	.681141	.686478	.692016	.697537
.6800000	.686477	.691655	.697244	.703053	.708851
.6899999	.696771	.702184	.708035	.714123	.720210
.7000000	.707075	.712729	.718849	.725227	.731614
.7100000	.717387	.723291	.729689	.736366	.743063
.7200000	.727708	.733869	.740553	.747540	.754558
.7300000	.738038	.744463	.751443	.758750	.766101
.7400000	.748378	.755074	.762359	.769996	.777693
.7500000	.758727	.765701	.773301	.781280	.789333
.7600000	.769085	.776346	.784269	.792600	.801024
.7700000	.779453	.787009	.795264	.803959	.812767
.7800000	.789830	.797689	.806287	.815357	.824561
.7899999	.800218	.808386	.817337	.826795	.836409

$\alpha = -.099999$

Θ	K VALUES				
	.318821117	.415016431	.514599755	.613601043	.708073407
.8000000	.810615	.819102	.828415	.838272	.848310
.8100000	.821022	.829835	.839521	.849790	.860267
.8200000	.831439	.840587	.850655	.861349	.872280
.8300000	.841866	.851357	.861819	.872950	.884350
.8400000	.852304	.862146	.873012	.884593	.896478
.8500000	.862751	.872954	.884234	.896279	.908665
.8600000	.873209	.883780	.895487	.908009	.920911
.8700000	.883678	.894626	.906769	.919782	.933219
.8799999	.894157	.905491	.918082	.931601	.945589
.8899999	.904646	.916375	.929426	.943464	.958022
.9000000	.915146	.927279	.940801	.955374	.970518
.9100000	.925657	.938202	.952206	.967329	.983080
.9200000	.936178	.949145	.963644	.979331	.995707
.9300000	.946710	.960107	.975113	.991381	1.008401
.9400000	.957253	.971090	.986614	1.003478	1.021163
.9500000	.967807	.982092	.998147	1.015623	1.033994
.9600000	.978371	.993115	1.009713	1.027817	1.046894
.9699999	.988946	1.004157	1.021311	1.040060	1.059865
.9799999	.999532	1.015220	1.032942	1.052353	1.072908
.9899999	1.010129	1.026303	1.044606	1.064696	1.086022
1.0000000	1.020737	1.037406	1.056303	1.077089	1.099211
1.0100000	1.031356	1.048530	1.068034	1.089533	1.112473
1.0200000	1.041985	1.059674	1.079797	1.102027	1.125810
1.0300000	1.052626	1.070838	1.091594	1.114573	1.139223
1.0400000	1.063277	1.082022	1.103424	1.127171	1.152713
1.0500000	1.073939	1.093226	1.115288	1.139821	1.166280
1.0600000	1.084611	1.104451	1.127185	1.152523	1.179925
1.0699999	1.095295	1.115696	1.139116	1.165277	1.193649
1.0799999	1.105989	1.126961	1.151080	1.178084	1.207452
1.0899999	1.116694	1.138246	1.163078	1.190944	1.221336
1.1000000	1.127409	1.149551	1.175109	1.203857	1.235300
1.1100000	1.138134	1.160876	1.187174	1.216822	1.249345
1.1200000	1.148871	1.172220	1.199271	1.229840	1.263471
1.1300000	1.159617	1.183584	1.211402	1.242912	1.277680
1.1400000	1.170373	1.194968	1.223566	1.256036	1.291971
1.1500000	1.181140	1.206371	1.235763	1.269213	1.306344
1.1600000	1.191917	1.217793	1.247992	1.282443	1.320801
1.1700000	1.202704	1.229233	1.260254	1.295725	1.335340
1.1800000	1.213500	1.240693	1.272548	1.309059	1.349963
1.1899999	1.224306	1.252171	1.284874	1.322446	1.364668

$\alpha = -\ .099999$

Θ	K VALUES				
	.318821117	.415016431	.514599755	.613601043	.708073407
1.2000000	1.235122	1.263668	1.297231	1.335885	1.379457
1.2100000	1.245947	1.275183	1.309620	1.349374	1.394329
1.2200000	1.256781	1.286715	1.322039	1.362915	1.409283
1.2300000	1.267624	1.298265	1.334489	1.376506	1.424320
1.2400000	1.278477	1.309832	1.346968	1.390148	1.439439
1.2500000	1.289338	1.321416	1.359478	1.403838	1.454639
1.2599999	1.300207	1.333017	1.372016	1.417578	1.469919
1.2699999	1.311085	1.344634	1.384583	1.431365	1.485280
1.2799999	1.321971	1.356267	1.397178	1.445200	1.500720
1.2899999	1.332866	1.367916	1.409800	1.459081	1.516238
1.3000000	1.343768	1.379580	1.422449	1.473008	1.531833
1.3100000	1.354677	1.391258	1.435125	1.486979	1.547505
1.3200000	1.365594	1.402951	1.447825	1.500995	1.563250
1.3300000	1.376518	1.414658	1.460551	1.515053	1.579069
1.3400000	1.387449	1.426379	1.473301	1.529152	1.594959
1.3500000	1.398387	1.438112	1.486074	1.543292	1.610920
1.3600000	1.409331	1.449858	1.498870	1.557470	1.626948
1.3700000	1.420281	1.461617	1.511687	1.571687	1.643042
1.3799999	1.431237	1.473387	1.524525	1.585940	1.659200
1.3899999	1.442199	1.485168	1.537384	1.600228	1.675420
1.4000000	1.453167	1.496960	1.550262	1.614550	1.691700
1.4100000	1.464139	1.508762	1.563158	1.628904	1.708036
1.4200000	1.475116	1.520574	1.576071	1.643289	1.724426
1.4300000	1.486098	1.532394	1.589000	1.657702	1.740869
1.4400000	1.497084	1.544223	1.601945	1.672142	1.757360
1.4500000	1.508075	1.556060	1.614905	1.686608	1.773896
1.4600000	1.519068	1.567905	1.627877	1.701098	1.790476
1.4700000	1.530066	1.579756	1.640863	1.715610	1.807095
1.4800000	1.541066	1.591614	1.653859	1.730141	1.823751
1.4900000	1.552069	1.603477	1.666865	1.744691	1.840440
1.5000000	1.563075	1.615345	1.679881	1.759257	1.857158
1.5100000	1.574083	1.627217	1.692905	1.773838	1.873903
1.5200000	1.585093	1.639093	1.705935	1.788431	1.890670
1.5300000	1.596105	1.650973	1.718972	1.803034	1.907456
1.5400000	1.607117	1.662855	1.732013	1.817646	1.924257
1.5500000	1.618131	1.674739	1.745057	1.832263	1.941070
1.5600000	1.629146	1.686624	1.758104	1.846886	1.957891
1.5699999	1.640160	1.698510	1.771152	1.861510	1.974716
1.5707963	1.641037	1.699456	1.772191	1.862674	1.976056
1.5707963	1.641036	1.699455	1.772191	1.862673	1.976054

$\alpha = -.099999$

Θ	K VALUES				
	.794250555	.868696860	.928444378	.971111163	.994996249
.0000000	.000000	.000000	.000000	.000000	.000000
.0100000	.010000	.010000	.010000	.010000	.010000
.0200000	.020000	.020000	.020000	.020001	.020001
.0300000	.030002	.030003	.030003	.030003	.030003
.0400000	.040006	.040007	.040007	.040008	.040008
.0500000	.050012	.050013	.050015	.050016	.050016
.0600000	.060021	.060024	.060026	.060027	.060028
.0700000	.070034	.070038	.070041	.070044	.070045
.0800000	.080050	.080057	.080062	.080065	.080068
.0900000	.090072	.090081	.090088	.090093	.090096
.1000000	.100099	.100111	.100121	.100128	.100132
.1100000	.110132	.110148	.110162	.110171	.110177
.1200000	.120171	.120193	.120210	.120223	.120229
.1300000	.130218	.130245	.130267	.130283	.130292
.1400000	.140272	.140307	.140334	.140354	.140365
.1500000	.150335	.150378	.150412	.150436	.150450
.1600000	.160407	.160459	.160500	.160530	.160546
.1700000	.170489	.170551	.170601	.170636	.170656
.1800000	.180581	.180655	.180714	.180756	.180780
.1900000	.190684	.190771	.190841	.190890	.190918
.2000000	.200799	.200900	.200981	.201040	.201072
.2100000	.210926	.211043	.211137	.211205	.211243
.2200000	.221065	.221201	.221309	.221387	.221431
.2300000	.231218	.231373	.231498	.231588	.231638
.2400000	.241386	.241562	.241705	.241806	.241863
.2500000	.251568	.251768	.251929	.252045	.252109
.2600000	.261766	.261992	.262173	.262303	.262376
.2700000	.271980	.272233	.272437	.272584	.272666
.2800000	.282211	.282494	.282723	.282886	.282978
.2900000	.292460	.292775	.293030	.293212	.293315
.3000000	.302726	.303077	.303359	.303562	.303676
.3100000	.313012	.313400	.313713	.313938	.314064
.3200000	.323318	.323746	.324091	.324339	.324478
.3300000	.333644	.334115	.334495	.334768	.334921
.3400000	.343991	.344508	.344925	.345225	.345394
.3500000	.354360	.354926	.355383	.355712	.355896
.3600000	.364752	.365370	.365869	.366229	.366430
.3700000	.375167	.375840	.376385	.376777	.376997
.3800000	.385607	.386339	.386931	.387358	.387598
.3900000	.396071	.396866	.397509	.397972	.398233

$\alpha = -.099999$

Θ	K VALUES				
	.794250555	.868696860	.928444378	.971111163	.994996249
.4000000	.406562	.407422	.408120	.408622	.408905
.4100000	.417078	.418009	.418764	.419308	.419614
.4200000	.427623	.428627	.429443	.430030	.430361
.4300000	.438195	.439278	.440158	.440792	.441149
.4400000	.448797	.449962	.450909	.451593	.451977
.4500000	.459428	.460681	.461699	.462434	.462849
.4600000	.470091	.471435	.472529	.473319	.473764
.4700000	.480785	.482225	.483399	.484246	.484725
.4800000	.491511	.493053	.494311	.495219	.495732
.4900000	.502271	.503920	.505265	.506238	.506787
.5000000	.513066	.514827	.516265	.517305	.517893
.5100000	.523896	.525774	.527310	.528421	.529049
.5200000	.534762	.536764	.538402	.539588	.540258
.5300000	.545665	.547797	.549542	.550807	.551522
.5400000	.556606	.558874	.560732	.562080	.562842
.5500000	.567587	.569997	.571973	.573408	.574220
.5600000	.578607	.581167	.583267	.584793	.585657
.5700000	.589669	.592385	.594615	.596237	.597156
.5800000	.600773	.603652	.606019	.607742	.608718
.5900000	.611921	.614971	.617481	.619308	.620345
.6000000	.623113	.626341	.629001	.630939	.632039
.6100000	.634350	.637765	.640581	.642636	.643802
.6200000	.645634	.649244	.652224	.654400	.655636
.6300000	.656965	.660779	.663931	.666234	.667543
.6400000	.668346	.672372	.675704	.678141	.679526
.6500000	.679776	.684025	.687544	.690121	.691587
.6600000	.691258	.695738	.699454	.702177	.703728
.6700000	.702792	.707514	.711435	.714311	.715951
.6800000	.714379	.719353	.723489	.726526	.728258
.6899999	.726021	.731259	.735619	.738824	.740654
.7000000	.737720	.743231	.747826	.751208	.753139
.7100000	.749476	.755273	.760113	.763679	.765718
.7200000	.761290	.767385	.772482	.776241	.778391
.7300000	.773164	.779570	.784934	.788896	.791164
.7400000	.785100	.791829	.797473	.801646	.804038
.7500000	.797099	.804165	.810100	.814495	.817016
.7600000	.809161	.816578	.822819	.827446	.830103
.7700000	.821289	.829072	.835631	.840502	.843300
.7800000	.833484	.841647	.848540	.853665	.856613
.7899999	.845747	.854307	.861547	.866938	.870043

$\alpha = - .099999$

Θ	K VALUES				
	.794250555	.868696860	.928444378	.971111163	.994996249
.8000000	.858080	.867053	.874656	.880327	.883596
.8100000	.870484	.879887	.887869	.893833	.897274
.8200000	.882961	.892812	.901190	.907460	.911082
.8300000	.895513	.905829	.914621	.921212	.925024
.8400000	.908140	.918941	.928166	.935093	.939105
.8500000	.920844	.932150	.941827	.949106	.953328
.8600000	.933628	.945459	.955608	.963256	.967698
.8700000	.946492	.958870	.969512	.977548	.982221
.8799999	.959439	.972386	.983542	.991985	.996902
.8899999	.972469	.986008	.997703	1.006572	1.011745
.9000000	.985585	.999740	1.011998	1.021314	1.026756
.9100000	.998788	1.013585	1.026431	1.036216	1.041942
.9200000	1.012080	1.027544	1.041005	1.051283	1.057307
.9300000	1.025462	1.041621	1.055725	1.066520	1.072859
.9400000	1.038937	1.055818	1.070595	1.081933	1.088603
.9500000	1.052506	1.070139	1.085619	1.097528	1.104547
.9600000	1.066171	1.084586	1.100802	1.113310	1.120698
.9699999	1.079933	1.099163	1.116148	1.129287	1.137063
.9799999	1.093794	1.113871	1.131661	1.145464	1.153651
.9899999	1.107756	1.128715	1.147348	1.161848	1.170469
1.0000000	1.121822	1.143698	1.163213	1.178447	1.187527
1.0100000	1.135991	1.158822	1.179260	1.195269	1.204833
1.0200000	1.150267	1.174091	1.195496	1.212319	1.222398
1.0300000	1.164651	1.189508	1.211926	1.229608	1.240230
1.0400000	1.179144	1.205077	1.228555	1.247143	1.258342
1.0500000	1.193749	1.220801	1.245390	1.264934	1.276743
1.0600000	1.208467	1.236683	1.262437	1.282989	1.295447
1.0699999	1.223300	1.252727	1.279702	1.301318	1.314466
1.0799999	1.238250	1.268936	1.297191	1.319932	1.333812
1.0899999	1.253317	1.285314	1.314911	1.338840	1.353501
1.1000000	1.268504	1.301865	1.332869	1.358056	1.373547
1.1100000	1.283813	1.318592	1.351071	1.377589	1.393966
1.1200000	1.299244	1.335498	1.369526	1.397453	1.414774
1.1300000	1.314799	1.352587	1.388240	1.417660	1.435990
1.1400000	1.330479	1.369863	1.407222	1.438224	1.457633
1.1500000	1.346287	1.387329	1.426479	1.459159	1.479723
1.1600000	1.362222	1.404990	1.446019	1.480480	1.502282
1.1700000	1.378286	1.422847	1.465850	1.502203	1.525333
1.1800000	1.394481	1.440905	1.485981	1.524345	1.548901
1.1899999	1.410807	1.459168	1.506420	1.546922	1.573014

$\alpha = -.099999$

Θ	K VALUES				
	.794250555	.868696860	.928444378	.971111163	.994996249
1.2000000	1.427265	1.477637	1.527177	1.569954	1.597698
1.2100000	1.443855	1.496318	1.548260	1.593459	1.622987
1.2200000	1.460579	1.515211	1.569678	1.617458	1.648912
1.2300000	1.477436	1.534322	1.591439	1.641972	1.675510
1.2400000	1.494428	1.553651	1.613555	1.667024	1.702820
1.2500000	1.511553	1.573202	1.636033	1.692637	1.730884
1.2599999	1.528813	1.592978	1.658882	1.718835	1.759747
1.2699999	1.546206	1.612979	1.682113	1.745646	1.789461
1.2799999	1.563733	1.633208	1.705733	1.773096	1.820079
1.2899999	1.581393	1.653666	1.729752	1.801213	1.851660
1.3000000	1.599184	1.674354	1.754179	1.830028	1.884271
1.3100000	1.617107	1.695274	1.779021	1.859572	1.917982
1.3200000	1.635158	1.716424	1.804287	1.889876	1.952872
1.3300000	1.653338	1.737806	1.829982	1.920975	1.989030
1.3400000	1.671643	1.759417	1.856115	1.952903	2.026550
1.3500000	1.690072	1.781258	1.882691	1.985696	2.065540
1.3600000	1.708623	1.803325	1.909714	2.019390	2.106119
1.3700000	1.727293	1.825617	1.937188	2.054022	2.148420
1.3799999	1.746078	1.848130	1.965115	2.089628	2.192592
1.3899999	1.764976	1.870861	1.993497	2.126245	2.238801
1.4000000	1.783983	1.893805	2.022332	2.163908	2.287237
1.4100000	1.803095	1.916955	2.051617	2.202650	2.338110
1.4200000	1.822307	1.940307	2.081347	2.242501	2.391659
1.4300000	1.841616	1.963853	2.111516	2.283489	2.448154
1.4400000	1.861017	1.987585	2.142112	2.325633	2.507902
1.4500000	1.880504	2.011495	2.173125	2.368948	2.571246
1.4600000	1.900072	2.035572	2.204539	2.413440	2.638574
1.4700000	1.919716	2.059807	2.236334	2.459101	2.710314
1.4800000	1.939429	2.084189	2.268491	2.505913	2.786940
1.4900000	1.959205	2.108705	2.300985	2.553843	2.868953
1.5000000	1.979039	2.133343	2.333788	2.602841	2.956867
1.5100000	1.998924	2.158089	2.366870	2.652835	3.051163
1.5200000	2.018852	2.182929	2.400197	2.703737	3.152221
1.5300000	2.038816	2.207849	2.433734	2.755437	3.260206
1.5400000	2.058811	2.232834	2.467442	2.807808	3.374923
1.5500000	2.078828	2.257868	2.501281	2.860702	3.495649
1.5600000	2.098860	2.282936	2.535210	2.913960	3.621010
1.5699999	2.118901	2.308020	2.569186	2.967409	3.748997
1.5707963	2.120497	2.310018	2.571892	2.971668	3.759231
1.5707963	2.120495	2.310017	2.571890	2.971665	3.759228

$\alpha =$ -.079999

Θ	K VALUES				
	.009966711	.039469502	.087332193	.151646642	.229848846
.0000000	.000000	.000000	.000000	.000000	.000000
.0100000	.009999	.009999	.009999	.010000	.010000
.0200000	.019999	.019999	.019999	.019999	.020000
.0300000	.029999	.029999	.029999	.029999	.030000
.0400000	.039998	.039998	.039999	.039999	.040000
.0500000	.049996	.049997	.049998	.049999	.050001
.0600000	.059994	.059995	.059997	.059999	.060002
.0700000	.069991	.069993	.069995	.069999	.070004
.0800000	.079987	.079989	.079993	.079999	.080006
.0900000	.089981	.089985	.089991	.089999	.090008
.1000000	.099975	.099979	.099987	.099998	.100011
.1100000	.109966	.109973	.109983	.109998	.110015
.1200000	.119956	.119965	.119979	.119997	.120020
.1300000	.129945	.129956	.129973	.129997	.130025
.1400000	.139931	.139945	.139966	.139996	.140032
.1500000	.149916	.149932	.149959	.149995	.150039
.1600000	.159898	.159918	.159950	.159994	.160047
.1700000	.169878	.169902	.169941	.169993	.170057
.1800000	.179855	.179883	.179930	.179992	.180068
.1900000	.189830	.189863	.189917	.189990	.190080
.2000000	.199801	.199840	.199904	.199989	.200093
.2100000	.209770	.209816	.209889	.209987	.210108
.2200000	.219736	.219788	.219872	.219986	.220124
.2300000	.229699	.229758	.229854	.229984	.230142
.2400000	.239659	.239726	.239835	.239982	.240161
.2500000	.249615	.249691	.249814	.249980	.250182
.2600000	.259567	.259652	.259791	.259977	.260205
.2700000	.269516	.269611	.269766	.269975	.270230
.2800000	.279461	.279567	.279740	.279972	.280257
.2900000	.289402	.289520	.289711	.289970	.290285
.3000000	.299339	.299469	.299681	.299967	.300316
.3100000	.309272	.309415	.309649	.309964	.310349
.3200000	.319201	.319358	.319614	.319961	.320384
.3300000	.329125	.329297	.329578	.329957	.330422
.3400000	.339044	.339233	.339539	.339954	.340461
.3500000	.348959	.349164	.349499	.349950	.350504
.3600000	.358870	.359092	.359455	.359946	.360548
.3700000	.368775	.369016	.369410	.369943	.370596
.3800000	.378675	.378937	.379362	.379939	.380646
.3900000	.388571	.388853	.389312	.389935	.390698

$\alpha =$ −.079999

Θ	K VALUES				
	.009966711	.039469502	.087332193	.151646642	.229848846
.4000000	.398461	.398765	.399260	.399930	.400754
.4100000	.408346	.408672	.409205	.409926	.410812
.4200000	.418226	.418576	.419147	.419922	.420874
.4300000	.428100	.428475	.429087	.429917	.430938
.4400000	.437968	.438369	.439024	.439912	.441006
.4500000	.447831	.448260	.448959	.449908	.451076
.4600000	.457689	.458145	.458891	.459903	.461150
.4700000	.467540	.468026	.468820	.469898	.471228
.4800000	.477386	.477902	.478747	.479894	.481308
.4900000	.487226	.487774	.488670	.489889	.491393
.5000000	.497060	.497641	.498591	.499884	.501480
.5100000	.506887	.507503	.508509	.509879	.511572
.5200000	.516709	.517359	.518425	.519874	.521667
.5300000	.526524	.527211	.528337	.529870	.531766
.5400000	.536333	.537058	.538246	.539865	.541869
.5500000	.546136	.546900	.548153	.549860	.551975
.5600000	.555932	.556737	.558056	.559856	.562086
.5700000	.565722	.566569	.567957	.569851	.572201
.5800000	.575505	.576395	.577854	.579847	.582319
.5900000	.585282	.586216	.587749	.589842	.592443
.6000000	.595052	.596032	.597640	.599838	.602570
.6100000	.604815	.605843	.607529	.609834	.612702
.6200000	.614572	.615648	.617414	.619831	.622838
.6300000	.624322	.625448	.627296	.629827	.632978
.6400000	.634066	.635242	.637176	.639824	.643123
.6500000	.643802	.645031	.647052	.649820	.653273
.6600000	.653532	.654815	.656925	.659817	.663427
.6700000	.663255	.664593	.666795	.669815	.673587
.6800000	.672971	.674366	.676661	.679812	.683751
.6899999	.682680	.684133	.686525	.689810	.693919
.7000000	.692382	.693895	.696386	.699809	.704093
.7100000	.702077	.703651	.706243	.709807	.714272
.7200000	.711766	.713401	.716097	.719806	.724456
.7300000	.721447	.723146	.725949	.729805	.734644
.7400000	.731122	.732886	.735797	.739805	.744838
.7500000	.740789	.742620	.745642	.749805	.755037
.7600000	.750450	.752349	.755483	.759806	.765242
.7700000	.760103	.762072	.765322	.769807	.775451
.7800000	.769750	.771789	.775158	.779808	.785666
.7899999	.779390	.781501	.784990	.789810	.795887

$\alpha =$ -.079999

θ	K VALUES				
	.009966711	.039469502	.087332193	.151646642	.229848846
.8000000	.789022	.791207	.794820	.799813	.806113
.8100000	.798648	.800908	.804646	.809816	.816344
.8200000	.808267	.810604	.814470	.819820	.826581
.8300000	.817879	.820294	.824290	.829824	.836823
.8400000	.827485	.829978	.834108	.839829	.847071
.8500000	.837083	.839657	.843922	.849834	.857325
.8600000	.846675	.849331	.853733	.859840	.867584
.8700000	.856259	.858999	.863542	.869847	.877849
.8799999	.865837	.868662	.873347	.879855	.888119
.8899999	.875409	.878320	.883150	.889863	.898396
.9000000	.884974	.887972	.892950	.899871	.908678
.9100000	.894532	.897619	.902746	.909881	.918965
.9200000	.904083	.907261	.912540	.919891	.929259
.9300000	.913628	.916897	.922332	.929902	.939558
.9400000	.923167	.926529	.932120	.939914	.949864
.9500000	.932698	.936155	.941905	.949926	.960175
.9600000	.942224	.945776	.951688	.959940	.970491
.9699999	.951743	.955393	.961468	.969954	.980814
.9799999	.961256	.965004	.971246	.979969	.991142
.9899999	.970763	.974610	.981020	.989984	1.001477
1.0000000	.980264	.984212	.990793	1.000001	1.011817
1.0100000	.989758	.993808	1.000562	1.010018	1.022162
1.0200000	.999246	1.003400	1.010329	1.020037	1.032514
1.0300000	1.008729	1.012987	1.020094	1.030056	1.042871
1.0400000	1.018205	1.022570	1.029856	1.040076	1.053234
1.0500000	1.027676	1.032147	1.039615	1.050097	1.063603
1.0600000	1.037141	1.041721	1.049372	1.060118	1.073978
1.0699999	1.046600	1.051289	1.059127	1.070141	1.084358
1.0799999	1.056054	1.060854	1.068879	1.080164	1.094744
1.0899999	1.065502	1.070414	1.078629	1.090189	1.105135
1.1000000	1.074945	1.079969	1.088377	1.100214	1.115532
1.1100000	1.084382	1.089521	1.098123	1.110240	1.125934
1.1200000	1.093814	1.099068	1.107866	1.120267	1.136342
1.1300000	1.103241	1.108611	1.117607	1.130295	1.146755
1.1400000	1.112663	1.118150	1.127346	1.140324	1.157174
1.1500000	1.122080	1.127685	1.137084	1.150354	1.167598
1.1600000	1.131491	1.137217	1.146819	1.160384	1.178027
1.1700000	1.140899	1.146744	1.156552	1.170416	1.188461
1.1800000	1.150301	1.156268	1.166283	1.180448	1.198900
1.1899999	1.159699	1.165788	1.176012	1.190481	1.209344

$\alpha =$ -.079999

Θ	K VALUES				
	.009966711	.039469502	.087332193	.151646642	.229848846
1.2000000	1.169092	1.175304	1.185739	1.200515	1.219794
1.2100000	1.178481	1.184817	1.195465	1.210550	1.230248
1.2200000	1.187865	1.194327	1.205189	1.220586	1.240707
1.2300000	1.197245	1.203833	1.214911	1.230623	1.251170
1.2400000	1.206621	1.213336	1.224631	1.240660	1.261638
1.2500000	1.215993	1.222836	1.234350	1.250698	1.272111
1.2599999	1.225361	1.232333	1.244067	1.260737	1.282588
1.2699999	1.234726	1.241827	1.253782	1.270777	1.293069
1.2799999	1.244087	1.251317	1.263497	1.280817	1.303555
1.2899999	1.253444	1.260805	1.273209	1.290859	1.314045
1.3000000	1.262797	1.270291	1.282921	1.300901	1.324539
1.3100000	1.272148	1.279774	1.292631	1.310944	1.335036
1.3200000	1.281495	1.289254	1.302339	1.320987	1.345537
1.3300000	1.290839	1.298731	1.312047	1.331031	1.356042
1.3400000	1.300180	1.308207	1.321753	1.341076	1.366551
1.3500000	1.309518	1.317680	1.331458	1.351121	1.377063
1.3600000	1.318853	1.327151	1.341162	1.361167	1.387578
1.3700000	1.328186	1.336619	1.350865	1.371214	1.398096
1.3799999	1.337516	1.346086	1.360566	1.381261	1.408617
1.3899999	1.346844	1.355551	1.370267	1.391309	1.419141
1.4000000	1.356169	1.365014	1.379967	1.401357	1.429668
1.4100000	1.365493	1.374476	1.389666	1.411406	1.440198
1.4200000	1.374814	1.383935	1.399365	1.421455	1.450730
1.4300000	1.384133	1.393394	1.409062	1.431504	1.461264
1.4400000	1.393451	1.402851	1.418759	1.441554	1.471800
1.4500000	1.402767	1.412306	1.428455	1.451605	1.482339
1.4600000	1.412081	1.421760	1.438151	1.461656	1.492879
1.4700000	1.421394	1.431214	1.447846	1.471707	1.503421
1.4800000	1.430705	1.440666	1.457540	1.481758	1.513965
1.4900000	1.440016	1.450117	1.467234	1.491810	1.524510
1.5000000	1.449325	1.459568	1.476928	1.501862	1.535056
1.5100000	1.458634	1.469018	1.486621	1.511914	1.545604
1.5200000	1.467942	1.478467	1.496314	1.521966	1.556152
1.5300000	1.477249	1.487915	1.506007	1.532019	1.566701
1.5400000	1.486555	1.497364	1.515699	1.542071	1.577251
1.5500000	1.495862	1.506811	1.525392	1.552124	1.587802
1.5600000	1.505167	1.516259	1.535084	1.562177	1.598352
1.5699999	1.514473	1.525707	1.544776	1.572230	1.608903
1.5707963	1.515214	1.526459	1.545548	1.573030	1.609743
1.5707963	1.515213	1.526458	1.545547	1.573029	1.609742

$\alpha =$ -.079999

θ	K VALUES				
	.318821117	.415016431	.514599755	.613601043	.708073407
.0000000	.000000	.000000	.000000	.000000	.000000
.0100000	.010000	.010000	.010000	.010000	.010000
.0200000	.020000	.020000	.020000	.020000	.020000
.0300000	.030000	.030001	.030001	.030002	.030002
.0400000	.040001	.040002	.040003	.040004	.040005
.0500000	.050003	.050005	.050007	.050009	.050011
.0600000	.060005	.060009	.060012	.060016	.060019
.0700000	.070009	.070014	.070020	.070025	.070031
.0800000	.080013	.080021	.080030	.080038	.080046
.0900000	.090019	.090031	.090043	.090055	.090066
.1000000	.100026	.100042	.100059	.100075	.100091
.1100000	.110035	.110056	.110078	.110100	.110121
.1200000	.120045	.120073	.120102	.120130	.120158
.1300000	.130058	.130093	.130130	.130166	.130201
.1400000	.140072	.140116	.140162	.140207	.140251
.1500000	.150089	.150143	.150199	.150255	.150309
.1600000	.160108	.160174	.160242	.160310	.160375
.1700000	.170130	.170209	.170291	.170372	.170450
.1800000	.180154	.180248	.180345	.180442	.180535
.1900000	.190181	.190292	.190406	.190520	.190630
.2000000	.200212	.200340	.200474	.200607	.200735
.2100000	.210245	.210394	.210549	.210703	.210852
.2200000	.220282	.220453	.220631	.220809	.220980
.2300000	.230322	.230518	.230722	.230925	.231121
.2400000	.240366	.240589	.240821	.241052	.241274
.2500000	.250414	.250666	.250928	.251190	.251441
.2600000	.260466	.260749	.261044	.261339	.261623
.2700000	.270522	.270839	.271170	.271501	.271819
.2800000	.280582	.280936	.281306	.281675	.282030
.2900000	.290647	.291041	.291451	.291863	.292258
.3000000	.300716	.301152	.301607	.302063	.302502
.3100000	.310791	.311272	.311775	.312278	.312764
.3200000	.320870	.321400	.321953	.322508	.323043
.3300000	.330954	.331535	.332143	.332753	.333341
.3400000	.341044	.341680	.342345	.343013	.343658
.3500000	.351139	.351833	.352560	.353290	.353994
.3600000	.361240	.361995	.362787	.363583	.364352
.3700000	.371346	.372167	.373027	.373893	.374730
.3800000	.381459	.382348	.383281	.384221	.385130
.3900000	.391577	.392540	.393550	.394568	.395553

$\alpha =$ -.079999

Θ	K VALUES				
	.318821117	.415016431	.514599755	.613601043	.708073407
.4000000	.401702	.402741	.403832	.404933	.405998
.4100000	.411833	.412953	.414129	.415317	.416468
.4200000	.421971	.423175	.424442	.425721	.426962
.4300000	.432116	.433409	.434770	.436146	.437481
.4400000	.442267	.443653	.445113	.446591	.448026
.4500000	.452426	.453910	.455474	.457058	.458598
.4600000	.462592	.464178	.465851	.467547	.469198
.4700000	.472765	.474458	.476245	.478059	.479825
.4800000	.482946	.484750	.486657	.488593	.490481
.4900000	.493134	.495055	.497086	.499152	.501167
.5000000	.503330	.505372	.507534	.509734	.511883
.5100000	.513535	.515703	.518001	.520342	.522630
.5200000	.523747	.526047	.528487	.530975	.533409
.5300000	.533968	.536405	.538993	.541634	.544221
.5400000	.544197	.546777	.549518	.552319	.555066
.5500000	.554435	.557163	.560064	.563032	.565945
.5600000	.564682	.567563	.570631	.573772	.576859
.5700000	.574938	.577978	.581219	.584541	.587809
.5800000	.585203	.588408	.591828	.595338	.598796
.5900000	.595477	.598853	.602460	.606166	.609821
.6000000	.605760	.609314	.613114	.617023	.620883
.6100000	.616053	.619790	.623791	.627911	.631985
.6200000	.626356	.630282	.634491	.638831	.643127
.6300000	.636668	.640791	.645215	.649782	.654310
.6400000	.646991	.651316	.655963	.660766	.665534
.6500000	.657323	.661858	.666735	.671783	.676801
.6600000	.667666	.672416	.677532	.682834	.688112
.6700000	.678019	.682992	.688354	.693919	.699467
.6800000	.688383	.693586	.699203	.705040	.710868
.6899999	.698757	.704197	.710077	.716196	.722314
.7000000	.709142	.714826	.720978	.727389	.733808
.7100000	.719538	.725473	.731905	.738618	.745350
.7200000	.729945	.736139	.742860	.749885	.756941
.7300000	.740363	.746823	.753842	.761190	.768583
.7400000	.750792	.757526	.764853	.772534	.780275
.7500000	.761233	.768248	.775891	.783917	.792019
.7600000	.771685	.778989	.786959	.795340	.803815
.7700000	.782149	.789750	.798056	.806804	.815666
.7800000	.792624	.800531	.809182	.818310	.827572
.7899999	.803111	.811331	.820338	.829857	.839533

$\alpha =$ −.079999

θ	K VALUES				
	.318821117	.415016431	.514599755	.613601043	.708073407
.8000000	.813610	.822151	.831525	.841447	.851552
.8100000	.824121	.832992	.842742	.853079	.863628
.8200000	.834644	.843853	.853989	.864756	.875763
.8300000	.845179	.854735	.865269	.876477	.887957
.8400000	.855726	.865637	.876579	.888243	.900213
.8500000	.866286	.876561	.887922	.900054	.912530
.8600000	.876858	.887505	.899297	.911911	.924910
.8700000	.887442	.898471	.910704	.923815	.937354
.8799999	.898039	.909458	.922144	.935767	.949863
.8899999	.908648	.920466	.933618	.947766	.962438
.9000000	.919270	.931497	.945125	.959813	.975080
.9100000	.929905	.942549	.956665	.971910	.987789
.9200000	.940552	.953622	.968239	.984055	1.000568
.9300000	.951212	.964718	.979848	.996251	1.013416
.9400000	.961885	.975836	.991490	1.008497	1.026335
.9500000	.972570	.986976	1.003168	1.020794	1.039326
.9600000	.983268	.998138	1.014880	1.033142	1.052389
.9699999	.993979	1.009322	1.026627	1.045543	1.065527
.9799999	1.004702	1.020528	1.038409	1.057995	1.078738
.9899999	1.015439	1.031757	1.050226	1.070500	1.092026
1.0000000	1.026188	1.043008	1.062079	1.083058	1.105390
1.0100000	1.036950	1.054282	1.073967	1.095670	1.118831
1.0200000	1.047724	1.065577	1.085891	1.108335	1.132350
1.0300000	1.058512	1.076895	1.097851	1.121054	1.145948
1.0400000	1.069311	1.088236	1.109846	1.133828	1.159626
1.0500000	1.080124	1.099599	1.121877	1.146656	1.173385
1.0600000	1.090949	1.110983	1.133944	1.159540	1.187225
1.0699999	1.101786	1.122390	1.146047	1.172478	1.201147
1.0799999	1.112636	1.133820	1.158186	1.185471	1.215151
1.0899999	1.123498	1.145271	1.170360	1.198520	1.229239
1.1000000	1.134373	1.156744	1.182570	1.211625	1.243410
1.1100000	1.145260	1.168238	1.194816	1.224785	1.257666
1.1200000	1.156158	1.179755	1.207097	1.238000	1.272007
1.1300000	1.167069	1.191293	1.219413	1.251272	1.286432
1.1400000	1.177991	1.202852	1.231765	1.264598	1.300944
1.1500000	1.188925	1.214432	1.244151	1.277980	1.315541
1.1600000	1.199871	1.226033	1.256573	1.291418	1.330224
1.1700000	1.210829	1.237655	1.269028	1.304910	1.344993
1.1800000	1.221797	1.249297	1.281518	1.318457	1.359849
1.1899999	1.232777	1.260960	1.294042	1.332059	1.374791

$\alpha =$ -.079999

θ	K VALUES				
	.318821117	.415016431	.514599755	.613601043	.708073407
1.2000000	1.243767	1.272643	1.306599	1.345715	1.389819
1.2100000	1.254769	1.284345	1.319190	1.359425	1.404933
1.2200000	1.265781	1.296067	1.331813	1.373188	1.420133
1.2300000	1.276804	1.307808	1.344468	1.387004	1.435419
1.2400000	1.287837	1.319567	1.357156	1.400872	1.450789
1.2500000	1.298879	1.331346	1.369875	1.414792	1.466243
1.2599999	1.309932	1.343142	1.382624	1.428763	1.481782
1.2699999	1.320995	1.354956	1.395404	1.442784	1.497403
1.2799999	1.332066	1.366787	1.408214	1.456854	1.513106
1.2899999	1.343147	1.378636	1.421053	1.470974	1.528890
1.3000000	1.354237	1.390501	1.433920	1.485141	1.544754
1.3100000	1.365336	1.402381	1.446815	1.499354	1.560697
1.3200000	1.376443	1.414278	1.459737	1.513614	1.576717
1.3300000	1.387558	1.426190	1.472685	1.527917	1.592813
1.3400000	1.398682	1.438116	1.485659	1.542265	1.608982
1.3500000	1.409812	1.450057	1.498658	1.556654	1.625224
1.3600000	1.420950	1.462012	1.511680	1.571084	1.641537
1.3700000	1.432096	1.473979	1.524726	1.585554	1.657917
1.3799999	1.443248	1.485960	1.537794	1.600062	1.674364
1.3899999	1.454406	1.497952	1.550883	1.614606	1.690875
1.4000000	1.465571	1.509956	1.563992	1.629186	1.707447
1.4100000	1.476741	1.521971	1.577121	1.643799	1.724079
1.4200000	1.487917	1.533997	1.590268	1.658444	1.740766
1.4300000	1.499098	1.546032	1.603432	1.673118	1.757507
1.4400000	1.510285	1.558076	1.616613	1.687822	1.774298
1.4500000	1.521475	1.570130	1.629809	1.702552	1.791136
1.4600000	1.532670	1.582191	1.643019	1.717307	1.808019
1.4700000	1.543869	1.594259	1.656242	1.732084	1.824943
1.4800000	1.555072	1.606334	1.669477	1.746883	1.841905
1.4900000	1.566277	1.618415	1.682722	1.761700	1.858900
1.5000000	1.577486	1.630502	1.695978	1.776535	1.875927
1.5100000	1.588697	1.642594	1.709242	1.791384	1.892980
1.5200000	1.599910	1.654689	1.722513	1.806246	1.910057
1.5300000	1.611125	1.666788	1.735790	1.821119	1.927153
1.5400000	1.622341	1.678890	1.749073	1.836001	1.944265
1.5500000	1.633559	1.690994	1.762359	1.850890	1.961389
1.5600000	1.644777	1.703099	1.775647	1.865783	1.978521
1.5699999	1.655996	1.715205	1.788937	1.880678	1.995658
1.5707963	1.656889	1.716169	1.789995	1.881864	1.997022
1.5707963	1.656888	1.716168	1.789994	1.881863	1.997021

$\alpha =$ -.079999

θ	K VALUES				
	.794250555	.868696860	.928444378	.971111163	.994996249
.0000000	.000000	.000000	.000000	.000000	.000000
.0100000	.010000	.010000	.010000	.010000	.010000
.0200000	.020000	.020000	.020001	.020001	.020001
.0300000	.030002	.030003	.030003	.030003	.030003
.0400000	.040006	.040007	.040008	.040008	.040008
.0500000	.050013	.050014	.050016	.050016	.050017
.0600000	.060022	.060025	.060027	.060029	.060030
.0700000	.070036	.070040	.070044	.070046	.070047
.0800000	.080054	.080060	.080065	.080069	.080071
.0900000	.090077	.090086	.090093	.090098	.090101
.1000000	.100105	.100118	.100128	.100135	.100139
.1100000	.110141	.110157	.110171	.110180	.110185
.1200000	.120183	.120204	.120222	.120234	.120241
.1300000	.130233	.130260	.130282	.130298	.130307
.1400000	.140291	.140325	.140353	.140372	.140384
.1500000	.150358	.150400	.150434	.150459	.150472
.1600000	.160435	.160486	.160528	.160557	.160574
.1700000	.170522	.170584	.170633	.170669	.170689
.1800000	.180620	.180694	.180753	.180795	.180819
.1900000	.190730	.190817	.190886	.190936	.190964
.2000000	.200852	.200953	.201035	.201093	.201126
.2100000	.210987	.211105	.211199	.211267	.211305
.2200000	.221136	.221271	.221380	.221458	.221502
.2300000	.231299	.231454	.231579	.231669	.231719
.2400000	.241478	.241654	.241797	.241898	.241955
.2500000	.251672	.251872	.252033	.252149	.252213
.2600000	.261883	.262108	.262290	.262420	.262494
.2700000	.272111	.272364	.272568	.272715	.272797
.2800000	.282357	.282640	.282869	.283032	.283124
.2900000	.292621	.292937	.293192	.293375	.293477
.3000000	.302905	.303256	.303539	.303742	.303856
.3100000	.313210	.313598	.313911	.314136	.314262
.3200000	.323535	.323963	.324309	.324557	.324697
.3300000	.333882	.334353	.334734	.335007	.335161
.3400000	.344251	.344768	.345187	.345487	.345656
.3500000	.354644	.355210	.355668	.355997	.356182
.3600000	.365060	.365679	.366179	.366539	.366741
.3700000	.375502	.376176	.376722	.377114	.377335
.3800000	.385969	.386702	.387296	.387723	.387963
.3900000	.396463	.397259	.397903	.398367	.398629

$\alpha =$ -.079999

θ	K VALUES				
	.794250555	.868696860	.928444378	.971111163	.994996249
.4000000	.406984	.407846	.408545	.409048	.409331
.4100000	.417533	.418465	.419222	.419766	.420073
.4200000	.428111	.429118	.429935	.430524	.430855
.4300000	.438719	.439804	.440686	.441321	.441679
.4400000	.449358	.450526	.451475	.452160	.452546
.4500000	.460028	.461283	.462305	.463041	.463457
.4600000	.470731	.472078	.473175	.473967	.474413
.4700000	.481468	.482912	.484088	.484938	.485417
.4800000	.492238	.493784	.495045	.495956	.496470
.4900000	.503044	.504698	.506046	.507022	.507573
.5000000	.513887	.515653	.517095	.518138	.518727
.5100000	.524766	.526651	.528190	.529305	.529935
.5200000	.535684	.537692	.539335	.540525	.541198
.5300000	.546641	.548780	.550530	.551799	.552517
.5400000	.557638	.559913	.561777	.563129	.563894
.5500000	.568676	.571095	.573078	.574517	.575332
.5600000	.579757	.582325	.584433	.585964	.586831
.5700000	.590881	.593606	.595845	.597472	.598395
.5800000	.602049	.604939	.607315	.609043	.610023
.5900000	.613263	.616324	.618844	.620679	.621719
.6000000	.624523	.627765	.630435	.632381	.633485
.6100000	.635831	.639261	.642088	.644151	.645322
.6200000	.647188	.650814	.653807	.655992	.657233
.6300000	.658595	.662426	.665592	.667905	.669220
.6400000	.670054	.674098	.677445	.679893	.681285
.6500000	.681564	.685833	.689368	.691957	.693430
.6600000	.693129	.697630	.701364	.704100	.705659
.6700000	.704748	.709493	.713434	.716324	.717972
.6800000	.716423	.721422	.725579	.728632	.730373
.6899999	.728156	.733420	.737803	.741025	.742864
.7000000	.739947	.745488	.750107	.753507	.755449
.7100000	.751798	.757627	.762494	.766080	.768130
.7200000	.763711	.769840	.774965	.778746	.780909
.7300000	.775686	.782129	.787524	.791508	.793790
.7400000	.787726	.794494	.800171	.804370	.806775
.7500000	.799830	.806939	.812911	.817333	.819869
.7600000	.812002	.819465	.825744	.830401	.833074
.7700000	.824242	.832074	.838675	.843577	.846393
.7800000	.836552	.844768	.851705	.856864	.859831
.7899999	.848933	.857549	.864837	.870265	.873391

$\alpha =$ -.079999

θ	K VALUES				
	.794250555	.868696860	.928444378	.971111163	.994996249
.8000000	.861387	.870420	.878075	.883785	.887076
.8100000	.873914	.883382	.891420	.897425	.900891
.8200000	.886518	.896438	.904876	.911191	.914839
.8300000	.899199	.909590	.918446	.925085	.928925
.8400000	.911960	.922840	.932133	.939112	.943154
.8500000	.924800	.936191	.945941	.953276	.957530
.8600000	.937723	.949645	.959872	.967580	.972057
.8700000	.950730	.963204	.973930	.982030	.986741
.8799999	.963822	.976872	.988118	.996629	1.001586
.8899999	.977001	.990650	1.002441	1.011383	1.016599
.9000000	.990269	1.004542	1.016902	1.026296	1.031785
.9100000	1.003628	1.018549	1.031505	1.041374	1.047149
.9200000	1.017079	1.032675	1.046253	1.056621	1.062698
.9300000	1.030624	1.046923	1.061152	1.072043	1.078438
.9400000	1.044264	1.061296	1.076205	1.087646	1.094377
.9500000	1.058003	1.075795	1.091416	1.103435	1.110520
.9600000	1.071840	1.090425	1.106791	1.119417	1.126875
.9699999	1.085779	1.105188	1.122334	1.135599	1.143450
.9799999	1.099820	1.120088	1.138049	1.151986	1.160253
.9899999	1.113966	1.135127	1.153942	1.168586	1.177293
1.0000000	1.128219	1.150309	1.170018	1.185406	1.194578
1.0100000	1.142579	1.165637	1.186282	1.202454	1.212118
1.0200000	1.157050	1.181115	1.202739	1.219738	1.229922
1.0300000	1.171632	1.196745	1.219396	1.237265	1.248000
1.0400000	1.186328	1.212531	1.236258	1.255045	1.266365
1.0500000	1.201139	1.228477	1.253330	1.273087	1.285026
1.0600000	1.216068	1.244585	1.270620	1.291399	1.303997
1.0699999	1.231114	1.260861	1.288134	1.309993	1.323290
1.0799999	1.246282	1.277306	1.305878	1.328878	1.342918
1.0899999	1.261571	1.293925	1.323858	1.348065	1.362897
1.1000000	1.276984	1.310722	1.342083	1.367566	1.383241
1.1100000	1.292522	1.327700	1.360559	1.387392	1.403966
1.1200000	1.308187	1.344862	1.379294	1.407557	1.425089
1.1300000	1.323979	1.362213	1.398294	1.428073	1.446630
1.1400000	1.339902	1.379755	1.417568	1.448954	1.468606
1.1500000	1.355955	1.397493	1.437125	1.470215	1.491040
1.1600000	1.372140	1.415430	1.456971	1.491870	1.513953
1.1700000	1.388459	1.433570	1.477116	1.513937	1.537368
1.1800000	1.404912	1.451916	1.497568	1.536431	1.561312
1.1899999	1.421500	1.470472	1.518336	1.559372	1.585812

$\alpha =$ -.079999

θ	K VALUES				
	.794250555	.868696860	.928444378	.971111163	.994996249
1.2000000	1.438224	1.489241	1.539428	1.582776	1.610896
1.2100000	1.455085	1.508225	1.560855	1.606665	1.636597
1.2200000	1.472083	1.527429	1.582624	1.631058	1.662948
1.2300000	1.489219	1.546856	1.604746	1.655977	1.689986
1.2400000	1.506494	1.566507	1.627229	1.681446	1.717750
1.2500000	1.523906	1.586385	1.650084	1.707487	1.746284
1.2599999	1.541456	1.606494	1.673318	1.734128	1.775634
1.2699999	1.559145	1.626834	1.696943	1.761393	1.805851
1.2799999	1.576970	1.647408	1.720966	1.789310	1.836991
1.2899999	1.594933	1.668217	1.745397	1.817910	1.869114
1.3000000	1.613031	1.689262	1.770245	1.847222	1.902287
1.3100000	1.631264	1.710544	1.795517	1.877277	1.936582
1.3200000	1.649630	1.732063	1.821223	1.908110	1.972081
1.3300000	1.668128	1.753819	1.847368	1.939753	2.008870
1.3400000	1.686755	1.775810	1.873960	1.972242	2.047050
1.3500000	1.705509	1.798036	1.901005	2.005614	2.086728
1.3600000	1.724389	1.820495	1.928507	2.039906	2.128027
1.3700000	1.743391	1.843184	1.956471	2.075154	2.171081
1.3799999	1.762512	1.866099	1.984897	2.111396	2.216042
1.3899999	1.781749	1.889237	2.013787	2.148669	2.263080
1.4000000	1.801098	1.912594	2.043141	2.187010	2.312388
1.4100000	1.820554	1.936162	2.072955	2.226451	2.364178
1.4200000	1.840115	1.959937	2.103223	2.267024	2.418697
1.4300000	1.859775	1.983910	2.133939	2.308756	2.476218
1.4400000	1.879528	2.008074	2.165093	2.351668	2.537054
1.4500000	1.899371	2.032420	2.196672	2.395773	2.601554
1.4600000	1.919297	2.056938	2.228660	2.441078	2.670113
1.4700000	1.939300	2.081617	2.261038	2.487576	2.743168
1.4800000	1.959376	2.106446	2.293786	2.535248	2.821200
1.4900000	1.979516	2.131413	2.326877	2.584060	2.904722
1.5000000	1.999715	2.156505	2.360285	2.633960	2.994256
1.5100000	2.019966	2.181708	2.393976	2.684876	3.090291
1.5200000	2.040262	2.207007	2.427919	2.736718	3.193215
1.5300000	2.060596	2.232388	2.462076	2.789374	3.303196
1.5400000	2.080960	2.257835	2.496407	2.842713	3.420035
1.5500000	2.101348	2.283332	2.530873	2.896587	3.542995
1.5600000	2.121751	2.308863	2.565430	2.950830	3.670677
1.5699999	2.142162	2.334413	2.600035	3.005269	3.801034
1.5707963	2.143788	2.336448	2.602791	3.009607	3.811457
1.5707963	2.143786	2.336446	2.602789	3.009604	3.811454

$\alpha = -.059999$

θ	K VALUES				
	.009966711	.039469502	.087332193	.151646642	.229848846
.0000000	.000000	.000000	.000000	.000000	.000000
.0100000	.009999	.009999	.010000	.010000	.010000
.0200000	.019999	.019999	.019999	.020000	.020000
.0300000	.029999	.029999	.029999	.030000	.030000
.0400000	.039998	.039999	.039999	.040000	.040001
.0500000	.049997	.049998	.049999	.050000	.050002
.0600000	.059996	.059997	.059998	.060001	.060003
.0700000	.069993	.069995	.069998	.070001	.070006
.0800000	.079990	.079993	.079997	.080002	.080009
.0900000	.089986	.089990	.089996	.090003	.090013
.1000000	.099981	.099986	.099994	.100005	.100018
.1100000	.109975	.109982	.109992	.110007	.110024
.1200000	.119968	.119976	.119990	.120009	.120031
.1300000	.129959	.129970	.129988	.130011	.130040
.1400000	.139949	.139963	.139985	.140014	.140050
.1500000	.149938	.149954	.149981	.150017	.150061
.1600000	.159925	.159945	.159977	.160021	.160074
.1700000	.169910	.169934	.169973	.170026	.170089
.1800000	.179893	.179922	.179968	.180030	.180106
.1900000	.189875	.189908	.189963	.190036	.190125
.2000000	.199854	.199893	.199957	.200042	.200146
.2100000	.209831	.209877	.209950	.210049	.210169
.2200000	.219806	.219858	.219942	.220056	.220194
.2300000	.229779	.229838	.229934	.230064	.230222
.2400000	.239749	.239817	.239926	.240073	.240252
.2500000	.249717	.249793	.249916	.250082	.250285
.2600000	.259682	.259767	.259906	.260093	.260321
.2700000	.269645	.269740	.269895	.270104	.270359
.2800000	.279604	.279710	.279883	.280116	.280401
.2900000	.289561	.289679	.289870	.290129	.290445
.3000000	.299515	.299645	.299857	.300143	.300493
.3100000	.309465	.309609	.309842	.310158	.310544
.3200000	.319413	.319571	.319827	.320174	.320598
.3300000	.329357	.329530	.329811	.330191	.330656
.3400000	.339298	.339487	.339794	.340209	.340717
.3500000	.349236	.349441	.349776	.350228	.350782
.3600000	.359170	.359393	.359756	.360248	.360851
.3700000	.369100	.369342	.369736	.370270	.370924
.3800000	.379027	.379288	.379715	.380292	.381000
.3900000	.388950	.389232	.389693	.390316	.391081

$\alpha = -.059999$

θ	K VALUES				
	.009966711	.039469502	.087332193	.151646642	.229848846
.4000000	.398869	.399173	.399669	.400341	.401166
.4100000	.408784	.409111	.409645	.410368	.411256
.4200000	.418696	.419047	.419619	.420395	.421349
.4300000	.428603	.428979	.429593	.430424	.431448
.4400000	.438507	.438909	.439565	.440455	.441551
.4500000	.448406	.448835	.449536	.450487	.451658
.4600000	.458301	.458758	.459506	.460521	.461771
.4700000	.468192	.468679	.469475	.470555	.471888
.4800000	.478078	.478596	.479442	.480592	.482010
.4900000	.487960	.488510	.489408	.490630	.492138
.5000000	.497837	.498420	.499373	.500670	.502271
.5100000	.507710	.508328	.509337	.510711	.512409
.5200000	.517579	.518232	.519300	.520754	.522552
.5300000	.527443	.528132	.529261	.530799	.532701
.5400000	.537302	.538030	.539222	.540845	.542855
.5500000	.547157	.547924	.549180	.550893	.553015
.5600000	.557006	.557814	.559138	.560943	.563181
.5700000	.566851	.567701	.569094	.570995	.573353
.5800000	.576691	.577585	.579049	.581049	.583531
.5900000	.586527	.587465	.589003	.591105	.593714
.6000000	.596357	.597341	.598956	.601162	.603904
.6100000	.606183	.607214	.608907	.611222	.614100
.6200000	.616003	.617083	.618857	.621283	.624303
.6300000	.625819	.626949	.628805	.631346	.634511
.6400000	.635629	.636811	.638753	.641412	.644726
.6500000	.645435	.646669	.648699	.651479	.654948
.6600000	.655235	.656524	.658643	.661549	.665176
.6700000	.665030	.666375	.668587	.671621	.675411
.6800000	.674820	.676222	.678529	.681695	.685652
.6899999	.684605	.686065	.688469	.691771	.695900
.7000000	.694385	.695905	.698409	.701849	.706156
.7100000	.704160	.705741	.708347	.711930	.716418
.7200000	.713929	.715574	.718284	.722012	.726687
.7300000	.723694	.725402	.728220	.732097	.736963
.7400000	.733453	.735227	.738154	.742185	.747246
.7500000	.743207	.745048	.748087	.752274	.757536
.7600000	.752956	.754866	.758019	.762366	.767834
.7700000	.762699	.764679	.767949	.772461	.778139
.7800000	.772438	.774489	.777878	.782557	.788451
.7899999	.782171	.784295	.787806	.792656	.798771

$\alpha = -.059999$

θ	K VALUES				
	.009966711	.039469502	.087332193	.151646642	.229848846
.8000000	.791899	.794098	.797733	.802758	.809098
.8100000	.801622	.803896	.807659	.812862	.819432
.8200000	.811340	.813691	.817583	.822968	.829774
.8300000	.821052	.823483	.827506	.833077	.840123
.8400000	.830760	.833270	.837428	.843188	.850480
.8500000	.840462	.843054	.847348	.853302	.860845
.8600000	.850159	.852834	.857268	.863418	.871217
.8700000	.859851	.862611	.867186	.873537	.881597
.8799999	.869538	.872384	.877103	.883658	.891984
.8899999	.879221	.882153	.887019	.893782	.902379
.9000000	.888898	.891919	.896934	.903908	.912782
.9100000	.898570	.901681	.906848	.914037	.923193
.9200000	.908237	.911439	.916760	.924169	.933611
.9300000	.917899	.921194	.926672	.934303	.944037
.9400000	.927556	.930946	.936582	.944439	.954470
.9500000	.937209	.940694	.946491	.954578	.964912
.9600000	.946856	.950438	.956399	.964720	.975361
.9699999	.956499	.960179	.966306	.974864	.985817
.9799999	.966137	.969917	.976212	.985011	.996282
.9899999	.975771	.979652	.986118	.995160	1.006754
1.0000000	.985400	.989383	.996022	1.005312	1.017233
1.0100000	.995024	.999110	1.005925	1.015466	1.027721
1.0200000	1.004644	1.008835	1.015827	1.025623	1.038215
1.0300000	1.014259	1.018556	1.025728	1.035782	1.048718
1.0400000	1.023869	1.028274	1.035628	1.045944	1.059227
1.0500000	1.033476	1.037989	1.045527	1.056109	1.069745
1.0600000	1.043078	1.047701	1.055426	1.066275	1.080269
1.0699999	1.052675	1.057410	1.065323	1.076445	1.090801
1.0799999	1.062269	1.067115	1.075220	1.086616	1.101341
1.0899999	1.071858	1.076818	1.085115	1.096790	1.111887
1.1000000	1.081443	1.086518	1.095010	1.106967	1.122441
1.1100000	1.091024	1.096215	1.104905	1.117146	1.133002
1.1200000	1.100602	1.105909	1.114798	1.127327	1.143570
1.1300000	1.110175	1.115600	1.124690	1.137511	1.154145
1.1400000	1.119744	1.125289	1.134582	1.147697	1.164726
1.1500000	1.129310	1.134975	1.144473	1.157885	1.175315
1.1600000	1.138872	1.144658	1.154363	1.168075	1.185910
1.1700000	1.148430	1.154338	1.164252	1.178268	1.196512
1.1800000	1.157984	1.164016	1.174141	1.188463	1.207121
1.1899999	1.167536	1.173692	1.184029	1.198660	1.217735

$\alpha =$ - .059999

Θ	K VALUES				
	.009966711	.039469502	.087332193	.151646642	.229848846
1.2000000	1.177083	1.183365	1.193917	1.208859	1.228357
1.2100000	1.186628	1.193036	1.203803	1.219060	1.238984
1.2200000	1.196169	1.202704	1.213689	1.229263	1.249617
1.2300000	1.205707	1.212370	1.223575	1.239469	1.260257
1.2400000	1.215241	1.222034	1.233460	1.249676	1.270902
1.2500000	1.224773	1.231696	1.243344	1.259885	1.281553
1.2599999	1.234302	1.241355	1.253228	1.270096	1.292210
1.2699999	1.243828	1.251013	1.263111	1.280309	1.302872
1.2799999	1.253351	1.260668	1.272993	1.290524	1.313539
1.2899999	1.262871	1.270322	1.282876	1.300740	1.324212
1.3000000	1.272389	1.279974	1.292757	1.310959	1.334890
1.3100000	1.281904	1.289623	1.302639	1.321178	1.345573
1.3200000	1.291417	1.299272	1.312519	1.331400	1.356260
1.3300000	1.300927	1.308918	1.322399	1.341623	1.366952
1.3400000	1.310436	1.318563	1.332279	1.351847	1.377649
1.3500000	1.319941	1.328206	1.342159	1.362073	1.388349
1.3600000	1.329445	1.337848	1.352038	1.372301	1.399054
1.3700000	1.338947	1.347488	1.361917	1.382529	1.409763
1.3799999	1.348447	1.357127	1.371795	1.392759	1.420476
1.3899999	1.357945	1.366765	1.381673	1.402990	1.431192
1.4000000	1.367441	1.376402	1.391551	1.413223	1.441912
1.4100000	1.376936	1.386037	1.401428	1.423456	1.452635
1.4200000	1.386429	1.395671	1.411305	1.433691	1.463361
1.4300000	1.395921	1.405304	1.421182	1.443926	1.474090
1.4400000	1.405411	1.414937	1.431059	1.454162	1.484822
1.4500000	1.414900	1.424568	1.440935	1.464400	1.495556
1.4600000	1.424388	1.434198	1.450811	1.474638	1.506293
1.4700000	1.433875	1.443828	1.460687	1.484876	1.517032
1.4800000	1.443361	1.453457	1.470563	1.495116	1.527773
1.4900000	1.452846	1.463086	1.480439	1.505356	1.538515
1.5000000	1.462330	1.472713	1.490314	1.515597	1.549260
1.5100000	1.471813	1.482341	1.500190	1.525838	1.560005
1.5200000	1.481296	1.491968	1.510065	1.536079	1.570752
1.5300000	1.490778	1.501594	1.519940	1.546321	1.581500
1.5400000	1.500260	1.511221	1.529815	1.556563	1.592249
1.5500000	1.509742	1.520847	1.539690	1.566805	1.602998
1.5600000	1.519223	1.530473	1.549565	1.577048	1.613748
1.5699999	1.528705	1.540098	1.559440	1.587290	1.624498
1.5707963	1.529460	1.540865	1.560227	1.588106	1.625354
1.5707963	1.529459	1.540864	1.560226	1.588105	1.625353

α = - .059999

θ	K VALUES				
	.318821117	.415016431	.514599755	.613601043	.708073407
.0000000	.000000	.000000	.000000	.000000	.000000
.0100000	.010000	.010000	.010000	.010000	.010000
.0200000	.020000	.020000	.020000	.020000	.020000
.0300000	.030000	.030001	.030001	.030002	.030002
.0400000	.040002	.040003	.040004	.040005	.040006
.0500000	.050004	.050006	.050008	.050010	.050012
.0600000	.060007	.060010	.060014	.060017	.060021
.0700000	.070011	.070016	.070022	.070028	.070033
.0800000	.080017	.080025	.080033	.080042	.080050
.0900000	.090024	.090035	.090048	.090060	.090071
.1000000	.100033	.100049	.100065	.100082	.100098
.1100000	.110044	.110065	.110087	.110109	.110130
.1200000	.120057	.120085	.120113	.120142	.120169
.1300000	.130072	.130108	.130144	.130181	.130215
.1400000	.140090	.140135	.140180	.140226	.140269
.1500000	.150111	.150166	.150222	.150278	.150331
.1600000	.160135	.160201	.160269	.160337	.160403
.1700000	.170162	.170241	.170323	.170405	.170483
.1800000	.180193	.180287	.180384	.180481	.180574
.1900000	.190227	.190337	.190452	.190566	.190675
.2000000	.200265	.200393	.200527	.200660	.200788
.2100000	.210306	.210455	.210610	.210765	.210913
.2200000	.220352	.220524	.220702	.220880	.221051
.2300000	.230403	.230599	.230802	.231006	.231201
.2400000	.240457	.240680	.240912	.241144	.241366
.2500000	.250517	.250769	.251031	.251293	.251545
.2600000	.260582	.260865	.261160	.261456	.261739
.2700000	.270651	.270969	.271300	.271631	.271949
.2800000	.280726	.281081	.281450	.281820	.282176
.2900000	.290807	.291201	.291612	.292024	.292420
.3000000	.300893	.301330	.301785	.302242	.302681
.3100000	.310986	.311468	.311971	.312475	.312961
.3200000	.321084	.321615	.322168	.322724	.323260
.3300000	.331189	.331771	.332379	.332990	.333578
.3400000	.341300	.341937	.342603	.343272	.343918
.3500000	.351418	.352113	.352841	.353572	.354278
.3600000	.361543	.362300	.363093	.363890	.364660
.3700000	.371675	.372498	.373359	.374227	.375064
.3800000	.381815	.382706	.383641	.384582	.385492
.3900000	.391962	.392926	.393937	.394957	.395944

$\alpha = -\ .059999$

Θ	K VALUES				
	.318821117	.415016431	.514599755	.613601043	.708073407
.4000000	.402116	.403157	.404250	.405353	.406420
.4100000	.412279	.413400	.414579	.415769	.416922
.4200000	.422449	.423656	.424925	.426207	.427450
.4300000	.432628	.433924	.435287	.436666	.438005
.4400000	.442815	.444204	.445668	.447148	.448587
.4500000	.453011	.454498	.456066	.457654	.459198
.4600000	.463215	.464805	.466482	.468183	.469837
.4700000	.473429	.475126	.476918	.478736	.480507
.4800000	.483652	.485461	.487373	.489314	.491207
.4900000	.493884	.495810	.497847	.499918	.501939
.5000000	.504126	.506174	.508342	.510548	.512702
.5100000	.514377	.516552	.518857	.521204	.523499
.5200000	.524638	.526946	.529393	.531888	.534330
.5300000	.534910	.537355	.539950	.542600	.545195
.5400000	.545192	.547780	.550530	.553340	.556095
.5500000	.555484	.558220	.561132	.564109	.567032
.5600000	.565786	.568677	.571756	.574908	.578006
.5700000	.576100	.579151	.582404	.585737	.589018
.5800000	.586424	.589642	.593075	.596598	.600069
.5900000	.596760	.600149	.603770	.607490	.611159
.6000000	.607107	.610675	.614490	.618414	.622290
.6100000	.617465	.621217	.625234	.629372	.633462
.6200000	.627835	.631778	.636004	.640362	.644677
.6300000	.638217	.642357	.646800	.651387	.655935
.6400000	.648610	.652955	.657622	.662447	.667236
.6500000	.659016	.663571	.668471	.673542	.678583
.6600000	.669434	.674206	.679346	.684673	.689976
.6700000	.679864	.684861	.690249	.695841	.701416
.6800000	.690307	.695535	.701180	.707046	.712903
.6899999	.700762	.706229	.712139	.718290	.724439
.7000000	.711230	.716944	.723127	.729572	.736026
.7100000	.721712	.727678	.734144	.740893	.747662
.7200000	.732206	.738433	.745191	.752255	.759350
.7300000	.742713	.749209	.756267	.763657	.771091
.7400000	.753234	.760005	.767374	.775100	.782886
.7500000	.763768	.770823	.778512	.786585	.794735
.7600000	.774315	.781663	.789680	.798113	.806639
.7700000	.784876	.792524	.800881	.809683	.818601
.7800000	.795451	.803407	.812113	.821298	.830619
.7899999	.806040	.814312	.823377	.832957	.842697

$\alpha =$ -.059999

Θ	K VALUES				
	.318821117	.415016431	.514599755	.613601043	.708073407
.8000000	.816643	.825240	.834674	.844662	.854834
.8100000	.827260	.836190	.846004	.856412	.867032
.8200000	.837891	.847162	.857368	.868208	.879291
.8300000	.848536	.858158	.868765	.880052	.891614
.8400000	.859196	.869176	.880196	.891942	.903999
.8500000	.869870	.880218	.891661	.903882	.916450
.8600000	.880558	.891283	.903161	.915870	.928967
.8700000	.891261	.902371	.914696	.927907	.941550
.8799999	.901978	.913483	.926267	.939994	.954201
.8899999	.912710	.924619	.937873	.952132	.966922
.9000000	.923457	.935779	.949515	.964321	.979712
.9100000	.934218	.946963	.961193	.976562	.992573
.9200000	.944994	.958170	.972907	.988855	1.005506
.9300000	.955785	.969402	.984658	1.001200	1.018512
.9400000	.966591	.980659	.996446	1.013599	1.031592
.9500000	.977411	.991939	1.008271	1.026051	1.044747
.9600000	.988246	1.003244	1.020133	1.038558	1.057978
.9699999	.999096	1.014574	1.032032	1.051119	1.071286
.9799999	1.009961	1.025928	1.043970	1.063735	1.084672
.9899999	1.020841	1.037306	1.055945	1.076407	1.098136
1.0000000	1.031735	1.048709	1.067957	1.089135	1.111681
1.0100000	1.042644	1.060137	1.080008	1.101919	1.125305
1.0200000	1.053567	1.071589	1.092097	1.114759	1.139012
1.0300000	1.064506	1.083065	1.104224	1.127656	1.152800
1.0400000	1.075458	1.094566	1.116389	1.140611	1.166672
1.0500000	1.086426	1.106092	1.128593	1.153623	1.180628
1.0600000	1.097407	1.117641	1.140834	1.166693	1.194668
1.0699999	1.108403	1.129215	1.153114	1.179820	1.208793
1.0799999	1.119414	1.140813	1.165432	1.193006	1.223005
1.0899999	1.130438	1.152436	1.177789	1.206250	1.237303
1.1000000	1.141477	1.164082	1.190183	1.219552	1.251688
1.1100000	1.152529	1.175752	1.202615	1.232913	1.266161
1.1200000	1.163596	1.187445	1.215085	1.246332	1.280722
1.1300000	1.174676	1.199162	1.227593	1.259809	1.295372
1.1400000	1.185769	1.210902	1.240138	1.273344	1.310111
1.1500000	1.196876	1.222665	1.252720	1.286938	1.324938
1.1600000	1.207996	1.234451	1.265339	1.300589	1.339855
1.1700000	1.219130	1.246260	1.277995	1.314298	1.354862
1.1800000	1.230276	1.258091	1.290687	1.328065	1.369959
1.1899999	1.241435	1.269944	1.303415	1.341889	1.385144

$\alpha = -.059999$

Θ	K VALUES				
	.318821117	.415016431	.514599755	.613601043	.708073407
1.2000000	1.252606	1.281819	1.316179	1.355769	1.400420
1.2100000	1.263790	1.293715	1.328979	1.369706	1.415785
1.2200000	1.274986	1.305633	1.341812	1.383699	1.431238
1.2300000	1.286194	1.317571	1.354681	1.397747	1.446781
1.2400000	1.297414	1.329530	1.367583	1.411850	1.462411
1.2500000	1.308645	1.341509	1.380518	1.426007	1.478129
1.2599999	1.319887	1.353507	1.393486	1.440218	1.493933
1.2699999	1.331140	1.365525	1.406487	1.454481	1.509824
1.2799999	1.342404	1.377561	1.419519	1.468795	1.525800
1.2899999	1.353678	1.389616	1.432581	1.483161	1.541859
1.3000000	1.364963	1.401690	1.445674	1.497576	1.558002
1.3100000	1.376257	1.413780	1.458797	1.512041	1.574225
1.3200000	1.387561	1.425887	1.471948	1.526553	1.590529
1.3300000	1.398874	1.438011	1.485127	1.541111	1.606912
1.3400000	1.410196	1.450151	1.498333	1.555715	1.623371
1.3500000	1.421527	1.462307	1.511565	1.570363	1.639904
1.3600000	1.432866	1.474477	1.524823	1.585054	1.656511
1.3700000	1.444214	1.486662	1.538105	1.599786	1.673189
1.3799999	1.455568	1.498860	1.551410	1.614558	1.689935
1.3899999	1.466931	1.511071	1.564738	1.629368	1.706747
1.4000000	1.478300	1.523295	1.578088	1.644214	1.723623
1.4100000	1.489676	1.535531	1.591458	1.659096	1.740560
1.4200000	1.501058	1.547778	1.604847	1.674011	1.757555
1.4300000	1.512446	1.560036	1.618255	1.688957	1.774605
1.4400000	1.523839	1.572304	1.631680	1.703933	1.791708
1.4500000	1.535238	1.584581	1.645121	1.718937	1.808860
1.4600000	1.546642	1.596867	1.658577	1.733966	1.826057
1.4700000	1.558049	1.609161	1.672047	1.749020	1.843297
1.4800000	1.569461	1.621462	1.685530	1.764095	1.860576
1.4900000	1.580877	1.633769	1.699024	1.779190	1.877890
1.5000000	1.592296	1.646083	1.712528	1.794303	1.895236
1.5100000	1.603718	1.658401	1.726041	1.809432	1.912609
1.5200000	1.615142	1.670725	1.739562	1.824574	1.930007
1.5300000	1.626568	1.683051	1.753089	1.839727	1.947426
1.5400000	1.637996	1.695381	1.766622	1.854889	1.964860
1.5500000	1.649425	1.707713	1.780158	1.870058	1.982307
1.5600000	1.660855	1.720047	1.793697	1.885232	1.999762
1.5699999	1.672285	1.732381	1.807238	1.900408	2.017222
1.5707963	1.673195	1.733363	1.808316	1.901617	2.018613
1.5707963	1.673194	1.733362	1.808315	1.901615	2.018611

$\alpha = -\ .059999$

Θ	K VALUES				
	.794250555	.868696860	.928444378	.971111163	.994996249
.0000000	.000000	.000000	.000000	.000000	.000000
.0100000	.010000	.010000	.010000	.010000	.010000
.0200000	.020000	.020001	.020001	.020001	.020001
.0300000	.030003	.030003	.030003	.030003	.030003
.0400000	.040007	.040008	.040008	.040009	.040009
.0500000	.050014	.050015	.050016	.050017	.050018
.0600000	.060024	.060027	.060029	.060030	.060031
.0700000	.070038	.070042	.070046	.070048	.070050
.0800000	.080057	.080064	.080069	.080072	.080074
.0900000	.090082	.090091	.090098	.090103	.090106
.1000000	.100112	.100125	.100135	.100142	.100146
.1100000	.110149	.110166	.110179	.110189	.110194
.1200000	.120194	.120216	.120233	.120246	.120253
.1300000	.130247	.130275	.130297	.130313	.130321
.1400000	.140309	.140343	.140371	.140391	.140402
.1500000	.150380	.150423	.150457	.150481	.150495
.1600000	.160462	.160513	.160555	.160584	.160601
.1700000	.170555	.170616	.170666	.170702	.170722
.1800000	.180659	.180732	.180792	.180834	.180858
.1900000	.190775	.190862	.190932	.190982	.191010
.2000000	.200905	.201007	.201088	.201146	.201179
.2100000	.211049	.211166	.211261	.211329	.211367
.2200000	.221207	.221342	.221451	.221529	.221573
.2300000	.231380	.231535	.231660	.231750	.231800
.2400000	.241570	.241746	.241889	.241991	.242048
.2500000	.251776	.251976	.252137	.252253	.252318
.2600000	.261999	.262225	.262407	.262538	.262611
.2700000	.272241	.272495	.272700	.272846	.272928
.2800000	.282502	.282786	.283015	.283179	.283271
.2900000	.292783	.293099	.293354	.293537	.293640
.3000000	.303085	.303436	.303719	.303922	.304036
.3100000	.313407	.313796	.314110	.314335	.314461
.3200000	.323752	.324181	.324527	.324776	.324916
.3300000	.334120	.334592	.334973	.335247	.335401
.3400000	.344512	.345030	.345449	.345749	.345918
.3500000	.354928	.355495	.355954	.356283	.356469
.3600000	.365370	.365989	.366490	.366851	.367053
.3700000	.375838	.376513	.377059	.377452	.377673
.3800000	.386333	.387067	.387662	.388090	.388330
.3900000	.396856	.397653	.398299	.398764	.399025

$\alpha = -$ .059999

θ	K VALUES				
	.794250555	.868696860	.928444378	.971111163	.994996249
.4000000	.407408	.408271	.408972	.409476	.409760
.4100000	.417989	.418923	.419681	.420227	.420534
.4200000	.428602	.429610	.430429	.431019	.431351
.4300000	.439245	.440333	.441216	.441853	.442211
.4400000	.449921	.451092	.452043	.452730	.453116
.4500000	.460631	.461889	.462912	.463651	.464067
.4600000	.471375	.472725	.473825	.474618	.475066
.4700000	.482154	.483601	.484781	.485633	.486113
.4800000	.492969	.494519	.495783	.496696	.497212
.4900000	.503821	.505479	.506832	.507810	.508362
.5000000	.514712	.516483	.517929	.518975	.519566
.5100000	.525642	.527532	.529076	.530194	.530826
.5200000	.536611	.538626	.540274	.541468	.542142
.5300000	.547623	.549768	.551524	.552798	.553518
.5400000	.558676	.560959	.562829	.564186	.564953
.5500000	.569773	.572200	.574189	.575634	.576452
.5600000	.580914	.583492	.585607	.587144	.588014
.5700000	.592100	.594836	.597083	.598717	.599642
.5800000	.603334	.606234	.608619	.610355	.611338
.5900000	.614615	.617688	.620218	.622060	.623105
.6000000	.625945	.629199	.631880	.633834	.634943
.6100000	.637324	.640768	.643608	.645679	.646855
.6200000	.648756	.652397	.655403	.657597	.658844
.6300000	.660239	.664087	.667267	.669590	.670911
.6400000	.671776	.675840	.679202	.681661	.683059
.6500000	.683369	.687657	.691209	.693810	.695291
.6600000	.695017	.699540	.703292	.706042	.707607
.6700000	.706722	.711491	.715451	.718357	.720012
.6800000	.718487	.723511	.727690	.730758	.732508
.6899999	.730311	.735603	.740009	.743249	.745097
.7000000	.742197	.747767	.752412	.755830	.757783
.7100000	.754145	.760006	.764900	.768506	.770567
.7200000	.766158	.772322	.777476	.781278	.783453
.7300000	.778236	.784715	.790142	.794150	.796445
.7400000	.790380	.797189	.802900	.807124	.809544
.7500000	.802593	.809745	.815754	.820203	.822755
.7600000	.814876	.822386	.828705	.833390	.836080
.7700000	.827230	.835112	.841756	.846689	.849524
.7800000	.839657	.847927	.854910	.860102	.863090
.7899999	.852158	.860833	.868170	.873634	.876781

$\alpha = -.059999$

Θ	K VALUES				
	.794250555	.868696860	.928444378	.971111163	.994996249
.8000000	.864735	.873831	.881538	.887287	.890601
.8100000	.877390	.886923	.895018	.901065	.904555
.8200000	.890123	.900113	.908612	.914972	.918647
.8300000	.902936	.913403	.922324	.929011	.932880
.8400000	.915832	.926794	.936156	.943188	.947260
.8500000	.928812	.940289	.950113	.957505	.961792
.8600000	.941877	.953891	.964198	.971967	.976479
.8700000	.955029	.967602	.978413	.986578	.991327
.8799999	.968271	.981425	.992763	1.001344	1.006342
.8899999	.981602	.995363	1.007252	1.016268	1.021528
.9000000	.995026	1.009418	1.021882	1.031357	1.036892
.9100000	1.008544	1.023592	1.036659	1.046614	1.052440
.9200000	1.022158	1.037890	1.051586	1.062045	1.068177
.9300000	1.035869	1.052312	1.066668	1.077657	1.084111
.9400000	1.049680	1.066864	1.081909	1.093454	1.100247
.9500000	1.063592	1.081547	1.097312	1.109443	1.116595
.9600000	1.077607	1.096364	1.112884	1.125630	1.133160
.9699999	1.091726	1.111319	1.128629	1.142022	1.149950
.9799999	1.105952	1.126415	1.144551	1.158625	1.166974
.9899999	1.120287	1.141654	1.160656	1.175446	1.184241
1.0000000	1.134732	1.157042	1.176949	1.192494	1.201760
1.0100000	1.149289	1.172579	1.193435	1.209774	1.219539
1.0200000	1.163960	1.188271	1.210120	1.227297	1.237589
1.0300000	1.178746	1.204119	1.227010	1.245070	1.255921
1.0400000	1.193650	1.220129	1.244110	1.263102	1.274545
1.0500000	1.208674	1.236303	1.261427	1.281401	1.293474
1.0600000	1.223818	1.252645	1.278968	1.299979	1.312719
1.0699999	1.239085	1.269159	1.296738	1.318845	1.332295
1.0799999	1.254476	1.285847	1.314744	1.338009	1.352213
1.0899999	1.269994	1.302715	1.332993	1.357483	1.372490
1.1000000	1.285639	1.319765	1.351493	1.377278	1.393141
1.1100000	1.301414	1.337001	1.370250	1.397407	1.414182
1.1200000	1.317320	1.354428	1.389273	1.417881	1.435630
1.1300000	1.333358	1.372047	1.408568	1.438716	1.457505
1.1400000	1.349530	1.389865	1.428144	1.459924	1.479826
1.1500000	1.365836	1.407883	1.448010	1.481520	1.502614
1.1600000	1.382280	1.426106	1.468172	1.503521	1.525892
1.1700000	1.398861	1.444537	1.488641	1.525943	1.549684
1.1800000	1.415580	1.463181	1.509424	1.548801	1.574016
1.1899999	1.432439	1.482039	1.530531	1.572116	1.598916

$\alpha = -\ .059999$

θ	K VALUES				
	.794250555	.868696860	.928444378	.971111163	.994996249
1.2000000	1.449438	1.501117	1.551971	1.595906	1.624413
1.2100000	1.466579	1.520416	1.573752	1.620190	1.650539
1.2200000	1.483861	1.539941	1.595885	1.644990	1.677330
1.2300000	1.501285	1.559694	1.618379	1.670329	1.704822
1.2400000	1.518851	1.579677	1.641243	1.696228	1.733056
1.2500000	1.536560	1.599895	1.664486	1.722714	1.762076
1.2599999	1.554412	1.620348	1.688119	1.749810	1.791930
1.2699999	1.572405	1.641039	1.712151	1.777546	1.822668
1.2799999	1.590540	1.661970	1.736591	1.805948	1.854348
1.2899999	1.608816	1.683142	1.761448	1.835046	1.887032
1.3000000	1.627232	1.704556	1.786732	1.864872	1.920787
1.3100000	1.645786	1.726213	1.812450	1.895458	1.955687
1.3200000	1.664477	1.748113	1.838611	1.926837	1.991814
1.3300000	1.683305	1.770257	1.865222	1.959044	2.029259
1.3400000	1.702265	1.792642	1.892290	1.992114	2.068122
1.3500000	1.721357	1.815267	1.919821	2.026086	2.108513
1.3600000	1.740577	1.838131	1.947820	2.060996	2.150557
1.3700000	1.759924	1.861231	1.976290	2.096883	2.194392
1.3799999	1.779392	1.884564	2.005233	2.133785	2.240171
1.3899999	1.798980	1.908124	2.034651	2.171739	2.288068
1.4000000	1.818684	1.931909	2.064543	2.210782	2.338279
1.4100000	1.838498	1.955910	2.094904	2.250948	2.391021
1.4200000	1.858419	1.980123	2.125731	2.292270	2.446545
1.4300000	1.878443	2.004540	2.157015	2.334773	2.505130
1.4400000	1.898562	2.029152	2.188747	2.378480	2.567094
1.4500000	1.918774	2.053950	2.220913	2.423406	2.632793
1.4600000	1.939071	2.078925	2.253496	2.469554	2.702629
1.4700000	1.959448	2.104065	2.286479	2.516921	2.777048
1.4800000	1.979899	2.129359	2.319839	2.565484	2.856540
1.4900000	2.000417	2.154794	2.353551	2.615211	2.941626
1.5000000	2.020995	2.180356	2.387585	2.666047	3.032840
1.5100000	2.041626	2.206032	2.421910	2.717920	3.130680
1.5200000	2.062304	2.231807	2.456491	2.770737	3.235540
1.5300000	2.083021	2.257666	2.491291	2.824385	3.347592
1.5400000	2.103769	2.283592	2.526269	2.878729	3.466633
1.5500000	2.124541	2.309571	2.561385	2.933618	3.591912
1.5600000	2.145329	2.335584	2.596594	2.988885	3.722002
1.5699999	2.166125	2.361615	2.631852	3.044351	3.854818
1.5707963	2.167782	2.363688	2.634660	3.048771	3.865439
1.5707963	2.167780	2.363687	2.634658	3.048768	3.865435

$\alpha = -\ .039999$

θ	K VALUES				
	.009966711	.039469502	.087332193	.151646642	.229848846
.0000000	.000000	.000000	.000000	.000000	.000000
.0100000	.009999	.009999	.010000	.010000	.010000
.0200000	.019999	.019999	.020000	.020000	.020000
.0300000	.029999	.029999	.030000	.030000	.030000
.0400000	.039999	.039999	.040000	.040000	.040001
.0500000	.049998	.049999	.050000	.050001	.050003
.0600000	.059997	.059998	.060000	.060002	.060005
.0700000	.069996	.069997	.070000	.070004	.070008
.0800000	.079994	.079996	.080000	.080006	.080012
.0900000	.089991	.089995	.090000	.090008	.090018
.1000000	.099988	.099993	.100001	.100011	.100024
.1100000	.109984	.109991	.110001	.110015	.110033
.1200000	.119979	.119988	.120002	.120020	.120043
.1300000	.129974	.129985	.130002	.130026	.130054
.1400000	.139968	.139981	.140003	.140032	.140068
.1500000	.149960	.149977	.150004	.150040	.150084
.1600000	.159952	.159972	.160005	.160048	.160102
.1700000	.169943	.169967	.170006	.170058	.170122
.1800000	.179932	.179960	.180007	.180069	.180145
.1900000	.189920	.189954	.190008	.190081	.190170
.2000000	.199907	.199946	.200009	.200095	.200199
.2100000	.209892	.209938	.210011	.210110	.210230
.2200000	.219877	.219928	.220013	.220126	.220265
.2300000	.229859	.229918	.230015	.230144	.230302
.2400000	.239840	.239907	.240017	.240164	.240343
.2500000	.249820	.249896	.250019	.250185	.250388
.2600000	.259797	.259883	.260021	.260208	.260436
.2700000	.269774	.269869	.270024	.270233	.270489
.2800000	.279748	.279854	.280027	.280260	.280545
.2900000	.289720	.289838	.290030	.290289	.290605
.3000000	.299691	.299821	.300033	.300320	.300670
.3100000	.309659	.309803	.310037	.310352	.310739
.3200000	.319626	.319784	.320040	.320387	.320812
.3300000	.329590	.329763	.330044	.330425	.330890
.3400000	.339552	.339741	.340049	.340464	.340973
.3500000	.349513	.349718	.350053	.350506	.351061
.3600000	.359471	.359694	.360058	.360551	.361154
.3700000	.369426	.369668	.370063	.370597	.371253
.3800000	.379379	.379641	.380069	.380647	.381356
.3900000	.389330	.389613	.390074	.390699	.391465

$\alpha = -.039999$

Θ	K VALUES				
	.009966711	.039469502	.087332193	.151646642	.229848846
.4000000	.399279	.399583	.400080	.400753	.401580
.4100000	.409225	.409552	.410087	.410811	.411701
.4200000	.419168	.419520	.420093	.420871	.421827
.4300000	.429109	.429486	.430100	.430934	.431959
.4400000	.439047	.439450	.440108	.441000	.442098
.4500000	.448983	.449413	.450116	.451069	.452243
.4600000	.458916	.459374	.460124	.461141	.462394
.4700000	.468846	.469334	.470132	.471216	.472552
.4800000	.478773	.479292	.480141	.481294	.482716
.4900000	.488698	.489249	.490150	.491375	.492887
.5000000	.498620	.499204	.500160	.501460	.503065
.5100000	.508538	.509157	.510170	.511548	.513250
.5200000	.518454	.519109	.520181	.521639	.523442
.5300000	.528367	.529059	.530192	.531734	.533642
.5400000	.538277	.539007	.540203	.541832	.543848
.5500000	.548184	.548954	.550215	.551934	.554063
.5600000	.558088	.558899	.560227	.562039	.564284
.5700000	.567989	.568842	.570240	.572148	.574514
.5800000	.577886	.578783	.580253	.582260	.584751
.5900000	.587781	.588722	.590267	.592376	.594996
.6000000	.597673	.598660	.600281	.602496	.605249
.6100000	.607561	.608596	.610296	.612620	.615510
.6200000	.617446	.618530	.620311	.622747	.625779
.6300000	.627328	.628462	.630327	.632879	.636057
.6400000	.637206	.638393	.640343	.643014	.646343
.6500000	.647081	.648321	.650360	.653153	.656637
.6600000	.656953	.658248	.660377	.663297	.666940
.6700000	.666822	.668173	.670395	.673444	.677252
.6800000	.676688	.678096	.680414	.683595	.687572
.6899999	.686550	.688017	.690433	.693751	.697901
.7000000	.696409	.697936	.700453	.703910	.708239
.7100000	.706264	.707854	.710473	.714074	.718586
.7200000	.716116	.717769	.720494	.724242	.728942
.7300000	.725965	.727683	.730515	.734414	.739307
.7400000	.735810	.737594	.740537	.744591	.749681
.7500000	.745652	.747504	.750560	.754771	.760064
.7600000	.755491	.757412	.760583	.764956	.770456
.7700000	.765326	.767318	.770607	.775146	.780858
.7800000	.775158	.777222	.780632	.785339	.791269
.7899999	.784987	.787124	.790657	.795537	.801690

$\alpha = -\ .039999$

θ	K VALUES				
	.009966711	.039469502	.087332193	.151646642	.229848846
.8000000	.794812	.797025	.800683	.805740	.812120
.8100000	.804634	.806923	.810710	.815947	.822560
.8200000	.814452	.816820	.820737	.826158	.833009
.8300000	.824268	.826714	.830765	.836373	.843468
.8400000	.834079	.836607	.840793	.846593	.853936
.8500000	.843888	.846498	.850822	.856818	.864414
.8600000	.853693	.856387	.860852	.867047	.874902
.8700000	.863495	.866274	.870883	.877280	.885399
.8799999	.873294	.876160	.880914	.887518	.895906
.8899999	.883089	.886043	.890946	.897760	.906423
.9000000	.892881	.895925	.900979	.908007	.916949
.9100000	.902670	.905805	.911012	.918258	.927485
.9200000	.912455	.915683	.921046	.928514	.938031
.9300000	.922238	.925559	.931081	.938774	.948587
.9400000	.932017	.935434	.941116	.949038	.959152
.9500000	.941793	.945307	.951152	.959307	.969727
.9600000	.951566	.955178	.961189	.969580	.980312
.9699999	.961336	.965047	.971226	.979858	.990906
.9799999	.971102	.974915	.981265	.990140	1.001510
.9899999	.980866	.984781	.991304	1.000426	1.012123
1.0000000	.990627	.994645	1.001343	1.010717	1.022747
1.0100000	1.000384	1.004507	1.011384	1.021012	1.033379
1.0200000	1.010139	1.014368	1.021425	1.031311	1.044021
1.0300000	1.019890	1.024228	1.031466	1.041615	1.054672
1.0400000	1.029639	1.034085	1.041509	1.051923	1.065333
1.0500000	1.039385	1.043941	1.051552	1.062235	1.076003
1.0600000	1.049128	1.053796	1.061595	1.072551	1.086683
1.0699999	1.058868	1.063649	1.071640	1.082871	1.097371
1.0799999	1.068606	1.073500	1.081685	1.093195	1.108068
1.0899999	1.078340	1.083350	1.091731	1.103524	1.118775
1.1000000	1.088072	1.093198	1.101777	1.113856	1.129490
1.1100000	1.097802	1.103045	1.111824	1.124193	1.140215
1.1200000	1.107528	1.112891	1.121872	1.134533	1.150948
1.1300000	1.117253	1.122735	1.131921	1.144877	1.161689
1.1400000	1.126974	1.132578	1.141970	1.155225	1.172439
1.1500000	1.136693	1.142419	1.152019	1.165577	1.183198
1.1600000	1.146410	1.152259	1.162070	1.175932	1.193965
1.1700000	1.156124	1.162098	1.172121	1.186292	1.204740
1.1800000	1.165836	1.171935	1.182172	1.196654	1.215523
1.1899999	1.175546	1.181771	1.192224	1.207021	1.226314

$\alpha = -\ .039999$

θ	K VALUES				
	.009966711	.039469502	.087332193	.151646642	.229848846
1.2000000	1.185254	1.191606	1.202277	1.217390	1.237113
1.2100000	1.194959	1.201440	1.212331	1.227763	1.247919
1.2200000	1.204662	1.211272	1.222384	1.238140	1.258733
1.2300000	1.214363	1.221103	1.232439	1.248520	1.269555
1.2400000	1.224062	1.230934	1.242494	1.258903	1.280383
1.2500000	1.233759	1.240763	1.252549	1.269289	1.291219
1.2599999	1.243453	1.250591	1.262606	1.279678	1.302061
1.2699999	1.253147	1.260418	1.272662	1.290070	1.312910
1.2799999	1.262838	1.270244	1.282719	1.300465	1.323766
1.2899999	1.272527	1.280069	1.292777	1.310863	1.334628
1.3000000	1.282215	1.289893	1.302835	1.321264	1.345497
1.3100000	1.291901	1.299716	1.312894	1.331667	1.356371
1.3200000	1.301585	1.309538	1.322953	1.342073	1.367252
1.3300000	1.311268	1.319360	1.333012	1.352481	1.378138
1.3400000	1.320950	1.329180	1.343072	1.362892	1.389029
1.3500000	1.330629	1.339000	1.353132	1.373305	1.399926
1.3600000	1.340308	1.348819	1.363193	1.383720	1.410827
1.3700000	1.349985	1.358637	1.373254	1.394138	1.421734
1.3799999	1.359661	1.368455	1.383315	1.404557	1.432645
1.3899999	1.369336	1.378272	1.393377	1.414979	1.443561
1.4000000	1.379009	1.388088	1.403439	1.425402	1.454481
1.4100000	1.388682	1.397904	1.413502	1.435827	1.465404
1.4200000	1.398353	1.407719	1.423564	1.446254	1.476332
1.4300000	1.408024	1.417534	1.433627	1.456682	1.487263
1.4400000	1.417693	1.427348	1.443690	1.467112	1.498198
1.4500000	1.427362	1.437162	1.453754	1.477543	1.509135
1.4600000	1.437030	1.446975	1.463817	1.487975	1.520076
1.4700000	1.446697	1.456788	1.473881	1.498409	1.531019
1.4800000	1.456364	1.466601	1.483945	1.508844	1.541965
1.4900000	1.466030	1.476413	1.494010	1.519279	1.552912
1.5000000	1.475696	1.486225	1.504074	1.529716	1.563862
1.5100000	1.485361	1.496037	1.514139	1.540153	1.574814
1.5200000	1.495025	1.505848	1.524203	1.550591	1.585767
1.5300000	1.504690	1.515659	1.534268	1.561029	1.596721
1.5400000	1.514354	1.525471	1.544333	1.571468	1.607676
1.5500000	1.524018	1.535282	1.554398	1.581907	1.618632
1.5600000	1.533681	1.545093	1.564462	1.592346	1.629588
1.5699999	1.543345	1.554904	1.574527	1.602786	1.640545
1.5707963	1.544115	1.555685	1.575329	1.603617	1.641417
1.5707963	1.544114	1.555684	1.575328	1.603616	1.641416

$\alpha = -.039999$

θ	K VALUES				
	.318821117	.415016431	.514599755	.613601043	.708073407
.0000000	.000000	.000000	.000000	.000000	.000000
.0100000	.010000	.010000	.010000	.010000	.010000
.0200000	.020000	.020000	.020000	.020000	.020000
.0300000	.030001	.030001	.030001	.030002	.030002
.0400000	.040002	.040003	.040004	.040005	.040006
.0500000	.050005	.050007	.050009	.050011	.050013
.0600000	.060008	.060012	.060015	.060019	.060022
.0700000	.070013	.070019	.070024	.070030	.070035
.0800000	.080020	.080028	.080037	.080045	.080053
.0900000	.090029	.090040	.090052	.090064	.090076
.1000000	.100039	.100055	.100072	.100089	.100104
.1100000	.110052	.110074	.110096	.110118	.110139
.1200000	.120068	.120096	.120125	.120153	.120181
.1300000	.130087	.130122	.130159	.130195	.130230
.1400000	.140109	.140153	.140198	.140244	.140288
.1500000	.150134	.150188	.150244	.150300	.150354
.1600000	.160162	.160228	.160297	.160365	.160430
.1700000	.170195	.170274	.170356	.170438	.170516
.1800000	.180231	.180325	.180423	.180520	.180613
.1900000	.190272	.190383	.190497	.190612	.190721
.2000000	.200317	.200446	.200580	.200714	.200841
.2100000	.210368	.210517	.210672	.210826	.210975
.2200000	.220423	.220594	.220773	.220951	.221121
.2300000	.230483	.230679	.230883	.231087	.231282
.2400000	.240549	.240772	.241004	.241235	.241458
.2500000	.250620	.250872	.251135	.251397	.251649
.2600000	.260697	.260981	.261277	.261572	.261856
.2700000	.270781	.271099	.271430	.271762	.272080
.2800000	.280871	.281226	.281596	.281966	.282322
.2900000	.290967	.291362	.291773	.292185	.292582
.3000000	.301071	.301508	.301964	.302421	.302860
.3100000	.311181	.311664	.312167	.312672	.313159
.3200000	.321299	.321830	.322385	.322941	.323477
.3300000	.331424	.332007	.332616	.333228	.333817
.3400000	.341557	.342195	.342862	.343532	.344178
.3500000	.351699	.352395	.353123	.353855	.354562
.3600000	.361848	.362606	.363400	.364198	.364969
.3700000	.372006	.372829	.373692	.374561	.375400
.3800000	.382172	.383065	.384001	.384944	.385856
.3900000	.392347	.393313	.394327	.395348	.396337

$\alpha = -\ .039999$

θ	K VALUES				
	.318821117	.415016431	.514599755	.613601043	.708073407
.4000000	.402532	.403575	.404670	.405774	.406844
.4100000	.412726	.413849	.415030	.416223	.417378
.4200000	.422929	.424138	.425409	.426694	.427940
.4300000	.433142	.434440	.435807	.437189	.438530
.4400000	.443365	.444757	.446224	.447708	.449150
.4500000	.453598	.455089	.456660	.458252	.459800
.4600000	.463842	.465436	.467117	.468822	.470480
.4700000	.474096	.475798	.477594	.479417	.481192
.4800000	.484362	.486175	.488092	.490039	.491937
.4900000	.494638	.496569	.498612	.500688	.502715
.5000000	.504926	.506979	.509153	.511366	.513526
.5100000	.515225	.517406	.519717	.522072	.524373
.5200000	.525535	.527849	.530304	.532807	.535256
.5300000	.535858	.538310	.540914	.543572	.546175
.5400000	.546192	.548789	.551548	.554367	.557132
.5500000	.556539	.559285	.562206	.565194	.568127
.5600000	.566898	.569799	.572889	.576052	.579161
.5700000	.577270	.580333	.583597	.586943	.590235
.5800000	.587655	.590884	.594330	.597867	.601351
.5900000	.598053	.601455	.605090	.608824	.612508
.6000000	.608464	.612046	.615876	.619816	.623708
.6100000	.618889	.622656	.626690	.630844	.634951
.6200000	.629327	.633286	.637530	.641907	.646240
.6300000	.639779	.643937	.648399	.653006	.657573
.6400000	.650244	.654608	.659296	.664142	.668954
.6500000	.660724	.665300	.670222	.675317	.680381
.6600000	.671218	.676013	.681177	.686529	.691858
.6700000	.681727	.686748	.692162	.697781	.703383
.6800000	.692250	.697504	.703177	.709072	.714959
.6899999	.702787	.708282	.714222	.720404	.726586
.7000000	.713340	.719083	.725299	.731778	.738265
.7100000	.723908	.729906	.736407	.743192	.749998
.7200000	.734491	.740752	.747547	.754650	.761785
.7300000	.745089	.751621	.758719	.766150	.773628
.7400000	.755702	.762513	.769924	.777695	.785526
.7500000	.766331	.773428	.781162	.789283	.797482
.7600000	.776976	.784368	.792434	.800917	.809497
.7700000	.787637	.795331	.803739	.812597	.821570
.7800000	.798313	.806319	.815079	.824323	.833705
.7899999	.809006	.817331	.826454	.836097	.845901

$\alpha = -.039999$

θ	K VALUES				
	.318821117	.415016431	.514599755	.613601043	.708073407
.8000000	.819715	.828367	.837864	.847918	.858159
.8100000	.830440	.839429	.849309	.859788	.870481
.8200000	.841181	.850515	.860791	.871706	.882868
.8300000	.851939	.861627	.872308	.883675	.895320
.8400000	.862713	.872764	.883862	.895694	.907839
.8500000	.873503	.883926	.895453	.907764	.920426
.8600000	.884311	.895114	.907081	.919885	.933082
.8700000	.895135	.906328	.918747	.932059	.945808
.8799999	.905975	.917568	.930450	.944285	.958605
.8899999	.916833	.928834	.942192	.956565	.971474
.9000000	.927708	.940127	.953972	.968899	.984416
.9100000	.938599	.951446	.965791	.981287	.997432
.9200000	.949507	.962791	.977649	.993731	1.010524
.9300000	.960432	.974162	.989546	1.006230	1.023692
.9400000	.971374	.985561	1.001483	1.018785	1.036937
.9500000	.982333	.996986	1.013459	1.031397	1.050260
.9600000	.993309	1.008438	1.025475	1.044066	1.063663
.9699999	1.004301	1.019916	1.037532	1.056792	1.077146
.9799999	1.015311	1.031422	1.049628	1.069577	1.090710
.9899999	1.026338	1.042954	1.061765	1.082420	1.104357
1.0000000	1.037381	1.054513	1.073942	1.095322	1.118086
1.0100000	1.048441	1.066099	1.086160	1.108283	1.131900
1.0200000	1.059518	1.077711	1.098418	1.121303	1.145799
1.0300000	1.070611	1.089351	1.110717	1.134384	1.159783
1.0400000	1.081721	1.101017	1.123057	1.147524	1.173854
1.0500000	1.092848	1.112710	1.135438	1.160725	1.188012
1.0600000	1.103991	1.124429	1.147860	1.173987	1.202259
1.0699999	1.115150	1.136175	1.160322	1.187310	1.216594
1.0799999	1.126326	1.147947	1.172825	1.200693	1.231019
1.0899999	1.137518	1.159746	1.185368	1.214138	1.245534
1.1000000	1.148725	1.171570	1.197953	1.227644	1.260139
1.1100000	1.159949	1.183421	1.210577	1.241211	1.274836
1.1200000	1.171188	1.195297	1.223242	1.254840	1.289625
1.1300000	1.182443	1.207198	1.235947	1.268529	1.304505
1.1400000	1.193713	1.219125	1.248692	1.282280	1.319479
1.1500000	1.204998	1.231077	1.261476	1.296092	1.334544
1.1600000	1.216298	1.243054	1.274299	1.309964	1.349703
1.1700000	1.227614	1.255056	1.287162	1.323897	1.364955
1.1800000	1.238943	1.267082	1.300063	1.337891	1.380300
1.1899999	1.250287	1.279131	1.313002	1.351944	1.395738

$\alpha = -.039999$

Θ	K VALUES				
	.318821117	.415016431	.514599755	.613601043	.708073407
1.2000000	1.261646	1.291205	1.325980	1.366057	1.411269
1.2100000	1.273018	1.303302	1.338995	1.380229	1.426893
1.2200000	1.284404	1.315422	1.352047	1.394459	1.442609
1.2300000	1.295804	1.327564	1.365135	1.408747	1.458416
1.2400000	1.307216	1.339729	1.378259	1.423093	1.474316
1.2500000	1.318642	1.351915	1.391419	1.437495	1.490306
1.2599999	1.330080	1.364123	1.404613	1.451954	1.506386
1.2699999	1.341531	1.376351	1.417841	1.466467	1.522556
1.2799999	1.352994	1.388600	1.431103	1.481034	1.538813
1.2899999	1.364468	1.400869	1.444398	1.495655	1.555158
1.3000000	1.375954	1.413158	1.457725	1.510328	1.571589
1.3100000	1.387451	1.425466	1.471083	1.525052	1.588104
1.3200000	1.398959	1.437792	1.484471	1.539826	1.604702
1.3300000	1.410478	1.450135	1.497889	1.554648	1.621381
1.3400000	1.422006	1.462497	1.511336	1.569518	1.638140
1.3500000	1.433544	1.474874	1.524810	1.584434	1.654977
1.3600000	1.445092	1.487268	1.538312	1.599395	1.671889
1.3700000	1.456649	1.499678	1.551839	1.614399	1.688874
1.3799999	1.468214	1.512102	1.565391	1.629444	1.705931
1.3899999	1.479787	1.524541	1.578967	1.644530	1.723056
1.4000000	1.491369	1.536993	1.592565	1.659654	1.740247
1.4100000	1.502958	1.549458	1.606186	1.674814	1.757501
1.4200000	1.514554	1.561935	1.619827	1.690009	1.774815
1.4300000	1.526156	1.574424	1.633487	1.705237	1.792186
1.4400000	1.537765	1.586923	1.647166	1.720496	1.809612
1.4500000	1.549379	1.599433	1.660861	1.735784	1.827088
1.4600000	1.560999	1.611952	1.674573	1.751099	1.844612
1.4700000	1.572624	1.624480	1.688299	1.766439	1.862180
1.4800000	1.584254	1.637015	1.702039	1.781801	1.879788
1.4900000	1.595887	1.649558	1.715790	1.797185	1.897433
1.5000000	1.607525	1.662107	1.729553	1.812587	1.915111
1.5100000	1.619165	1.674661	1.743325	1.828005	1.932817
1.5200000	1.630808	1.687221	1.757105	1.843437	1.950549
1.5300000	1.642454	1.699784	1.770892	1.858881	1.968301
1.5400000	1.654101	1.712351	1.784684	1.874334	1.986071
1.5500000	1.665750	1.724920	1.798481	1.889795	2.003853
1.5600000	1.677400	1.737490	1.812280	1.905261	2.021644
1.5699999	1.689050	1.750062	1.826081	1.920729	2.039439
1.5707963	1.689978	1.751063	1.827180	1.921960	2.040856
1.5707963	1.689976	1.751062	1.827179	1.921959	2.040855

$\alpha = -$ .039999

θ	K VALUES				
	.794250555	.868696860	.928444378	.971111163	.994996249
.0000000	.000000	.000000	.000000	.000000	.000000
.0100000	.010000	.010000	.010000	.010000	.010000
.0200000	.020000	.020001	.020001	.020001	.020001
.0300000	.030003	.030003	.030003	.030004	.030004
.0400000	.040007	.040008	.040009	.040009	.040009
.0500000	.050014	.050016	.050017	.050018	.050019
.0600000	.060025	.060028	.060030	.060032	.060033
.0700000	.070040	.070045	.070048	.070051	.070052
.0800000	.080061	.080067	.080072	.080076	.080078
.0900000	.090086	.090096	.090103	.090108	.090111
.1000000	.100119	.100131	.100141	.100148	.100152
.1100000	.110158	.110175	.110188	.110198	.110203
.1200000	.120206	.120227	.120245	.120257	.120264
.1300000	.130262	.130289	.130311	.130327	.130336
.1400000	.140327	.140362	.140389	.140409	.140420
.1500000	.150403	.150445	.150479	.150504	.150517
.1600000	.160489	.160541	.160582	.160612	.160628
.1700000	.170587	.170649	.170699	.170735	.170755
.1800000	.180698	.180771	.180831	.180873	.180897
.1900000	.190821	.190908	.190978	.191028	.191056
.2000000	.200958	.201060	.201141	.201200	.201232
.2100000	.211110	.211228	.211323	.211390	.211428
.2200000	.221278	.221413	.221522	.221600	.221644
.2300000	.231461	.231616	.231741	.231831	.231881
.2400000	.241662	.241839	.241981	.242083	.242140
.2500000	.251880	.252080	.252242	.252357	.252422
.2600000	.262117	.262343	.262525	.262655	.262728
.2700000	.272372	.272626	.272831	.272978	.273060
.2800000	.282649	.282932	.283161	.283326	.283418
.2900000	.292946	.293262	.293517	.293700	.293803
.3000000	.303264	.303616	.303899	.304103	.304217
.3100000	.313606	.313995	.314309	.314534	.314661
.3200000	.323970	.324400	.324746	.324995	.325135
.3300000	.334359	.334832	.335214	.335488	.335642
.3400000	.344773	.345292	.345711	.346012	.346182
.3500000	.355213	.355781	.356241	.356571	.356756
.3600000	.365680	.366300	.366802	.367163	.367366
.3700000	.376175	.376851	.377398	.377792	.378013
.3800000	.386698	.387433	.388029	.388458	.388699
.3900000	.397250	.398049	.398696	.399162	.399424

$\alpha = -$ .039999

θ	K VALUES				
	.794250555	.868696860	.928444378	.971111163	.994996249
.4000000	.407833	.408698	.409400	.409905	.410189
.4100000	.418447	.419383	.420143	.420690	.420997
.4200000	.429094	.430104	.430925	.431516	.431849
.4300000	.439774	.440863	.441748	.442387	.442746
.4400000	.450487	.451660	.452614	.453302	.453689
.4500000	.461236	.462497	.463523	.464263	.464681
.4600000	.472021	.473375	.474477	.475273	.475721
.4700000	.482843	.484295	.485477	.486331	.486813
.4800000	.493703	.495258	.496525	.497441	.497957
.4900000	.504602	.506265	.507621	.508602	.509156
.5000000	.515542	.517318	.518768	.519818	.520410
.5100000	.526522	.528418	.529967	.531088	.531722
.5200000	.537545	.539566	.541219	.542416	.543093
.5300000	.548611	.550763	.552525	.553802	.554525
.5400000	.559721	.562012	.563888	.565249	.566019
.5500000	.570877	.573312	.575309	.576758	.577579
.5600000	.582079	.584666	.586789	.588331	.589204
.5700000	.593329	.596075	.598330	.599970	.600899
.5800000	.604628	.607540	.609934	.611676	.612663
.5900000	.615977	.619063	.621602	.623452	.624500
.6000000	.627377	.630645	.633337	.635299	.636412
.6100000	.638830	.642288	.645139	.647220	.648401
.6200000	.650336	.653993	.657012	.659216	.660468
.6300000	.661897	.665762	.668956	.671290	.672617
.6400000	.673514	.677596	.680974	.683444	.684849
.6500000	.685189	.689498	.693067	.695680	.697168
.6600000	.696922	.701468	.705238	.708001	.709575
.6700000	.708716	.713508	.717489	.720409	.722073
.6800000	.720571	.725621	.729821	.732905	.734664
.6899999	.732488	.737808	.742238	.745494	.747353
.7000000	.744470	.750071	.754740	.758177	.760141
.7100000	.756517	.762411	.767332	.770958	.773031
.7200000	.768631	.774830	.780014	.783838	.786026
.7300000	.780813	.787331	.792789	.796821	.799129
.7400000	.793065	.799915	.805660	.809909	.812344
.7500000	.805389	.812584	.818630	.823106	.825674
.7600000	.817785	.825341	.831700	.836415	.839123
.7700000	.830255	.838188	.844874	.849839	.852693
.7800000	.842801	.851126	.858154	.863382	.866389
.7899999	.855425	.864157	.871544	.877046	.880214

$\alpha = -.039999$

θ	K VALUES				
	.794250555	.868696860	.928444378	.971111163	.994996249
.8000000	.868128	.877285	.885046	.890835	.894173
.8100000	.880911	.890511	.898663	.904754	.908269
.8200000	.893776	.903838	.912398	.918805	.922507
.8300000	.906725	.917268	.926255	.932992	.936890
.8400000	.919759	.930803	.940236	.947321	.951425
.8500000	.932881	.944446	.954346	.961795	.966115
.8600000	.946092	.958199	.968587	.976418	.980966
.8700000	.959393	.972066	.982963	.991195	.995982
.8799999	.972786	.986048	.997479	1.006130	1.011170
.8899999	.986274	1.000149	1.012137	1.021229	1.026534
.9000000	.999858	1.014371	1.026941	1.036497	1.042080
.9100000	1.013539	1.028716	1.041897	1.051939	1.057816
.9200000	1.027319	1.043189	1.057007	1.067559	1.073746
.9300000	1.041201	1.057791	1.072276	1.083365	1.089878
.9400000	1.055186	1.072526	1.087709	1.099362	1.106218
.9500000	1.069276	1.087397	1.103310	1.115555	1.122775
.9600000	1.083473	1.102407	1.119084	1.131952	1.139555
.9699999	1.097778	1.117558	1.135036	1.148560	1.156566
.9799999	1.112194	1.132855	1.151170	1.165384	1.173818
.9899999	1.126723	1.148301	1.167492	1.182433	1.191318
1.0000000	1.141365	1.163899	1.184008	1.199713	1.209076
1.0100000	1.156124	1.179652	1.200723	1.217234	1.227101
1.0200000	1.171001	1.195563	1.217642	1.235002	1.245405
1.0300000	1.185997	1.211637	1.234772	1.253027	1.263997
1.0400000	1.201115	1.227877	1.252118	1.271318	1.282889
1.0500000	1.216357	1.244286	1.269687	1.289884	1.302092
1.0600000	1.231723	1.260868	1.287485	1.308734	1.321621
1.0699999	1.247217	1.277626	1.305518	1.327880	1.341486
1.0799999	1.262839	1.294566	1.323795	1.347332	1.361704
1.0899999	1.278592	1.311689	1.342321	1.367101	1.382289
1.1000000	1.294478	1.329000	1.361104	1.387200	1.403256
1.1100000	1.310496	1.346503	1.380152	1.407640	1.424622
1.1200000	1.326651	1.364202	1.399471	1.428434	1.446406
1.1300000	1.342941	1.382099	1.419071	1.449597	1.468625
1.1400000	1.359371	1.400200	1.438959	1.471143	1.491301
1.1500000	1.375939	1.418508	1.459143	1.493086	1.514455
1.1600000	1.392649	1.437026	1.479632	1.515443	1.538110
1.1700000	1.409500	1.455758	1.500435	1.538231	1.562291
1.1800000	1.426495	1.474709	1.521561	1.561466	1.587024
1.1899999	1.443634	1.493880	1.543018	1.585168	1.612336

$\alpha = -\ .039999$

θ	K VALUES				
	.794250555	.868696860	.928444378	.971111163	.994996249
1.2000000	1.460918	1.513277	1.564816	1.609355	1.638260
1.2100000	1.478347	1.532902	1.586965	1.634049	1.664827
1.2200000	1.495922	1.552758	1.609473	1.659270	1.692072
1.2300000	1.513644	1.572848	1.632351	1.685042	1.720035
1.2400000	1.531513	1.593176	1.655609	1.711387	1.748755
1.2500000	1.549529	1.613743	1.679255	1.738331	1.778278
1.2599999	1.567692	1.634553	1.703300	1.765901	1.808652
1.2699999	1.586001	1.655607	1.727754	1.794123	1.839929
1.2799999	1.604456	1.676908	1.752625	1.823026	1.872169
1.2899999	1.623056	1.698456	1.777924	1.852642	1.905433
1.3000000	1.641801	1.720253	1.803659	1.883000	1.939790
1.3100000	1.660688	1.742298	1.829839	1.914135	1.975317
1.3200000	1.679717	1.764594	1.856472	1.946080	2.012096
1.3300000	1.698886	1.787138	1.883566	1.978871	2.050220
1.3400000	1.718192	1.809931	1.911127	2.012544	2.089791
1.3500000	1.737633	1.832971	1.939162	2.047137	2.130922
1.3600000	1.757207	1.856255	1.967675	2.082689	2.173739
1.3700000	1.776910	1.879782	1.996671	2.119239	2.218382
1.3799999	1.796740	1.903546	2.026150	2.156824	2.265010
1.3899999	1.816692	1.927545	2.056116	2.195484	2.313798
1.4000000	1.836763	1.951774	2.086565	2.235256	2.364945
1.4100000	1.856949	1.976225	2.117495	2.276174	2.418676
1.4200000	1.877244	2.000893	2.148901	2.318272	2.475243
1.4300000	1.897644	2.025769	2.180775	2.361576	2.534932
1.4400000	1.918144	2.050846	2.213105	2.406109	2.598066
1.4500000	1.938738	2.076114	2.245880	2.451885	2.665009
1.4600000	1.959421	2.101563	2.279083	2.498910	2.736171
1.4700000	1.980186	2.127181	2.312693	2.547177	2.812006
1.4800000	2.001026	2.152957	2.346689	2.596667	2.893013
1.4900000	2.021936	2.178878	2.381044	2.647343	2.979724
1.5000000	2.042908	2.204929	2.415729	2.699151	3.072683
1.5100000	2.063934	2.231097	2.450712	2.752017	3.172396
1.5200000	2.085008	2.257366	2.485956	2.805847	3.279267
1.5300000	2.106123	2.283721	2.521423	2.860524	3.393469
1.5400000	2.127269	2.310146	2.557074	2.915913	3.514797
1.5500000	2.148440	2.336623	2.592864	2.971857	3.642483
1.5600000	2.169628	2.363136	2.628750	3.028186	3.775074
1.5699999	2.190825	2.389668	2.664686	3.084718	3.910445
1.5707963	2.192513	2.391781	2.667548	3.089223	3.921269
1.5707963	2.192511	2.391779	2.667546	3.089220	3.921266

$\alpha = -$ .019999

Θ	K VALUES				
	.009966711	.039469502	.087332193	.151646642	.229848846
.0000000	.000000	.000000	.000000	.000000	.000000
.0100000	.010000	.010000	.010000	.010000	.010000
.0200000	.019999	.020000	.020000	.020000	.020000
.0300000	.029999	.030000	.030000	.030000	.030000
.0400000	.039999	.040000	.040000	.040001	.040002
.0500000	.049999	.050000	.050001	.050002	.050003
.0600000	.059998	.060000	.060001	.060004	.060006
.0700000	.069998	.070000	.070002	.070006	.070010
.0800000	.079997	.079999	.080004	.080009	.080016
.0900000	.089996	.089999	.090005	.090013	.090023
.1000000	.099995	.099999	.100007	.100018	.100031
.1100000	.109993	.109999	.110010	.110024	.110042
.1200000	.119991	.119999	.120013	.120032	.120054
.1300000	.129989	.129999	.130017	.130040	.130069
.1400000	.139986	.139999	.140021	.140050	.140086
.1500000	.149983	.149999	.150026	.150062	.150106
.1600000	.159979	.159999	.160032	.160076	.160129
.1700000	.169975	.169999	.170038	.170091	.170155
.1800000	.179971	.179999	.180045	.180108	.180184
.1900000	.189965	.189999	.190053	.190127	.190216
.2000000	.199960	.199999	.200062	.200148	.200252
.2100000	.209954	.209999	.210072	.210171	.210291
.2200000	.219947	.219999	.220083	.220196	.220335
.2300000	.229939	.229999	.230095	.230224	.230383
.2400000	.239931	.239998	.240108	.240255	.240435
.2500000	.249922	.249998	.250122	.250288	.250491
.2600000	.259913	.259998	.260137	.260324	.260552
.2700000	.269903	.269998	.270153	.270363	.270618
.2800000	.279891	.279998	.280171	.280404	.280689
.2900000	.289880	.289998	.290190	.290449	.290765
.3000000	.299867	.299997	.300210	.300496	.300847
.3100000	.309853	.309997	.310231	.310547	.310934
.3200000	.319839	.319997	.320254	.320602	.321027
.3300000	.329824	.329997	.330279	.330659	.331126
.3400000	.339808	.339997	.340305	.340721	.341230
.3500000	.349790	.349996	.350332	.350786	.351341
.3600000	.359772	.359996	.360361	.360854	.361459
.3700000	.369753	.369996	.370391	.370926	.371583
.3800000	.379733	.379996	.380424	.381003	.381713
.3900000	.389712	.389995	.390457	.391083	.391851

$\alpha =$ - .019999

Θ	K VALUES				
	.009966711	.039469502	.087332193	.151646642	.229848846
.4000000	.399690	.399995	.400493	.401167	.401995
.4100000	.409667	.409995	.410530	.411256	.412147
.4200000	.419642	.419995	.420569	.421349	.422306
.4300000	.429617	.429994	.430610	.431446	.432473
.4400000	.439590	.439994	.440653	.441547	.442648
.4500000	.449563	.449994	.450698	.451653	.452830
.4600000	.459534	.459993	.460744	.461764	.463020
.4700000	.469504	.469993	.470793	.471879	.473219
.4800000	.479472	.479993	.480844	.482000	.483425
.4900000	.489440	.489993	.490896	.492125	.493640
.5000000	.499406	.499992	.500951	.502254	.503864
.5100000	.509371	.509992	.511008	.512389	.514097
.5200000	.519335	.519992	.521066	.522529	.524338
.5300000	.529298	.529991	.531127	.532674	.534588
.5400000	.539259	.539991	.541191	.542825	.544848
.5500000	.549219	.549991	.551256	.552980	.555117
.5600000	.559177	.559991	.561324	.563141	.565395
.5700000	.569134	.569990	.571393	.573308	.575683
.5800000	.579090	.579990	.581466	.583480	.585980
.5900000	.589045	.589990	.591540	.593657	.596287
.6000000	.598998	.599990	.601617	.603841	.606604
.6100000	.608950	.609989	.611696	.614029	.616931
.6200000	.618900	.619989	.621777	.624224	.627268
.6300000	.628849	.629989	.631861	.634424	.637616
.6400000	.638797	.639989	.641948	.644630	.647974
.6500000	.648743	.649989	.652036	.654842	.658342
.6600000	.658688	.659988	.662128	.665060	.668721
.6700000	.668631	.669988	.672221	.675284	.679110
.6800000	.678573	.679988	.682317	.685514	.689510
.6899999	.688513	.689988	.692416	.695750	.699922
.7000000	.698452	.699988	.702517	.705993	.710344
.7100000	.708390	.709988	.712621	.716241	.720777
.7200000	.718326	.719988	.722727	.726496	.731221
.7300000	.728261	.729988	.732836	.736757	.741676
.7400000	.738194	.739988	.742947	.747024	.752143
.7500000	.748125	.749988	.753061	.757297	.762620
.7600000	.758056	.759988	.763178	.767577	.773110
.7700000	.767984	.769988	.773297	.777863	.783610
.7800000	.777912	.779988	.783419	.788156	.794122
.7899999	.787838	.789988	.793543	.798454	.804646

α = - •019999

Θ	K VALUES				
	•009966711	•039469502	•087332193	•151646642	•229848846
•8000000	•797762	•799989	•803671	•808760	•815182
•8100000	•807685	•809989	•813800	•819072	•825729
•8200000	•817606	•819989	•823932	•829390	•836287
•8300000	•827526	•829989	•834067	•839714	•846858
•8400000	•837445	•839990	•844205	•850046	•857440
•8500000	•847362	•849990	•854345	•860383	•868034
•8600000	•857277	•859991	•864488	•870727	•878639
•8700000	•867191	•869991	•874633	•881078	•889257
•8799999	•877104	•879992	•884781	•891435	•899886
•8899999	•887015	•889992	•894932	•901798	•910528
•9000000	•896925	•899993	•905085	•912168	•921181
•9100000	•906834	•909993	•915241	•922545	•931846
•9200000	•916741	•919994	•925400	•932927	•942522
•9300000	•926646	•929995	•935561	•943317	•953211
•9400000	•936550	•939996	•945725	•953712	•963911
•9500000	•946453	•949996	•955891	•964114	•974623
•9600000	•956355	•959997	•966060	•974523	•985347
•9699999	•966255	•969998	•976231	•984937	•996083
•9799999	•976153	•979999	•986405	•995358	1•006830
•9899999	•986051	•990000	•996581	1•005786	1•017589
1•0000000	•995947	1•000001	1•006760	1•016219	1•028359
1•0100000	1•005842	1•010002	1•016942	1•026659	1•039141
1•0200000	1•015735	1•020004	1•027125	1•037105	1•049935
1•0300000	1•025627	1•030005	1•037312	1•047557	1•060739
1•0400000	1•035518	1•040006	1•047500	1•058015	1•071555
1•0500000	1•045407	1•050008	1•057692	1•068479	1•082383
1•0600000	1•055296	1•060009	1•067885	1•078949	1•093221
1•0699999	1•065183	1•070010	1•078081	1•089425	1•104071
1•0799999	1•075068	1•080012	1•088279	1•099906	1•114931
1•0899999	1•084953	1•090013	1•098480	1•110394	1•125803
1•1000000	1•094837	1•100015	1•108682	1•120887	1•136685
1•1100000	1•104719	1•110017	1•118887	1•131386	1•147578
1•1200000	1•114600	1•120019	1•129095	1•141890	1•158481
1•1300000	1•124480	1•130020	1•139304	1•152400	1•169395
1•1400000	1•134359	1•140022	1•149516	1•162915	1•180319
1•1500000	1•144236	1•150024	1•159729	1•173436	1•191253
1•1600000	1•154113	1•160026	1•169945	1•183962	1•202197
1•1700000	1•163989	1•170028	1•180163	1•194493	1•213151
1•1800000	1•173863	1•180030	1•190383	1•205029	1•224114
1•1899999	1•183737	1•190032	1•200604	1•215571	1•235087

$\alpha = -.019999$

θ	K VALUES				
	.009966711	.039469502	.087332193	.151646642	.229848846
1.2000000	1.193609	1.200035	1.210828	1.226117	1.246070
1.2100000	1.203481	1.210037	1.221054	1.236668	1.257062
1.2200000	1.213352	1.220039	1.231281	1.247223	1.268062
1.2300000	1.223221	1.230041	1.241511	1.257784	1.279072
1.2400000	1.233090	1.240044	1.251742	1.268348	1.290090
1.2500000	1.242958	1.250046	1.261975	1.278918	1.301117
1.2599999	1.252825	1.260049	1.272210	1.289491	1.312152
1.2699999	1.262691	1.270051	1.282446	1.300069	1.323195
1.2799999	1.272556	1.280054	1.292684	1.310651	1.334246
1.2899999	1.282421	1.290056	1.302923	1.321237	1.345304
1.3000000	1.292285	1.300059	1.313164	1.331827	1.356370
1.3100000	1.302148	1.310062	1.323406	1.342420	1.367444
1.3200000	1.312010	1.320065	1.333650	1.353017	1.378524
1.3300000	1.321872	1.330067	1.343896	1.363618	1.389611
1.3400000	1.331733	1.340070	1.354142	1.374222	1.400704
1.3500000	1.341593	1.350073	1.364390	1.384829	1.411804
1.3600000	1.351453	1.360076	1.374639	1.395439	1.422910
1.3700000	1.361312	1.370079	1.384889	1.406053	1.434022
1.3799999	1.371171	1.380082	1.395141	1.416669	1.445139
1.3899999	1.381029	1.390085	1.405393	1.427288	1.456261
1.4000000	1.390887	1.400088	1.415646	1.437909	1.467389
1.4100000	1.400744	1.410091	1.425901	1.448533	1.478521
1.4200000	1.410600	1.420094	1.436156	1.459160	1.489658
1.4300000	1.420456	1.430097	1.446412	1.469788	1.500799
1.4400000	1.430312	1.440100	1.456669	1.480419	1.511944
1.4500000	1.440168	1.450104	1.466927	1.491051	1.523093
1.4600000	1.450023	1.460107	1.477185	1.501686	1.534245
1.4700000	1.459877	1.470110	1.487444	1.512321	1.545401
1.4800000	1.469732	1.480113	1.497704	1.522959	1.556559
1.4900000	1.479586	1.490116	1.507964	1.533597	1.567720
1.5000000	1.489440	1.500120	1.518225	1.544237	1.578883
1.5100000	1.499294	1.510123	1.528486	1.554878	1.590048
1.5200000	1.509147	1.520126	1.538747	1.565520	1.601215
1.5300000	1.519001	1.530130	1.549009	1.576163	1.612384
1.5400000	1.528854	1.540133	1.559271	1.586806	1.623553
1.5500000	1.538707	1.550136	1.569533	1.597450	1.634724
1.5600000	1.548561	1.560140	1.579795	1.608094	1.645895
1.5699999	1.558414	1.570143	1.590057	1.618738	1.657066
1.5707963	1.559198	1.570940	1.590875	1.619585	1.657956
1.5707963	1.559198	1.570939	1.590874	1.619584	1.657955

$\alpha = -.019999$

θ	K VALUES				
	.318821117	.415016431	.514599755	.613601043	.708073407
.0000000	.000000	.000000	.000000	.000000	.000000
.0100000	.010000	.010000	.010000	.010000	.010000
.0200000	.020000	.020000	.020000	.020000	.020000
.0300000	.030001	.030001	.030002	.030002	.030003
.0400000	.040002	.040004	.040005	.040006	.040007
.0500000	.050005	.050007	.050009	.050011	.050013
.0600000	.060010	.060013	.060017	.060020	.060024
.0700000	.070015	.070021	.070027	.070032	.070038
.0800000	.080023	.080032	.080040	.080049	.080057
.0900000	.090033	.090045	.090057	.090069	.090081
.1000000	.100046	.100062	.100079	.100095	.100111
.1100000	.110061	.110083	.110105	.110127	.110148
.1200000	.120080	.120108	.120136	.120165	.120192
.1300000	.130102	.130137	.130173	.130210	.130245
.1400000	.140127	.140171	.140217	.140262	.140306
.1500000	.150156	.150210	.150267	.150323	.150376
.1600000	.160190	.160255	.160324	.160392	.160457
.1700000	.170228	.170307	.170389	.170470	.170549
.1800000	.180270	.180364	.180461	.180559	.180652
.1900000	.190318	.190428	.190543	.190657	.190767
.2000000	.200371	.200499	.200633	.200767	.200895
.2100000	.210429	.210578	.210733	.210888	.211036
.2200000	.220493	.220665	.220843	.221022	.221192
.2300000	.230563	.230760	.230964	.231168	.231363
.2400000	.240640	.240863	.241095	.241327	.241550
.2500000	.250723	.250976	.251238	.251501	.251753
.2600000	.260814	.261098	.261393	.261689	.261973
.2700000	.270911	.271229	.271561	.271893	.272211
.2800000	.281016	.281371	.281741	.282112	.282468
.2900000	.291128	.291523	.291935	.292347	.292744
.3000000	.301249	.301686	.302142	.302600	.303040
.3100000	.311377	.311860	.312364	.312870	.313357
.3200000	.321514	.322046	.322601	.323158	.323695
.3300000	.331660	.332244	.332853	.333466	.334056
.3400000	.341815	.342454	.343122	.343793	.344439
.3500000	.351979	.352677	.353406	.354139	.354847
.3600000	.362153	.362912	.363707	.364507	.365279
.3700000	.372337	.373162	.374026	.374896	.375737
.3800000	.382530	.383425	.384362	.385307	.386220
.3900000	.392734	.393702	.394717	.395741	.396731

$\alpha = -.019999$

Θ	K VALUES				
	.318821117	.415016431	.514599755	.613601043	.708073407
.4000000	.402949	.403994	.405091	.406197	.407269
.4100000	.413174	.414300	.415483	.416678	.417836
.4200000	.423411	.424622	.425896	.427184	.428432
.4300000	.433658	.434960	.436329	.437714	.439058
.4400000	.443918	.445313	.446783	.448270	.449715
.4500000	.454189	.455683	.457258	.458853	.460404
.4600000	.464472	.466069	.467755	.469463	.471126
.4700000	.474767	.476473	.478274	.480101	.481881
.4800000	.485075	.486894	.488816	.490767	.492670
.4900000	.495396	.497332	.499381	.501463	.503495
.5000000	.505730	.507789	.509970	.512188	.514355
.5100000	.516077	.518264	.520583	.522944	.525253
.5200000	.526437	.528758	.531221	.533731	.536188
.5300000	.536811	.539272	.541884	.544550	.547162
.5400000	.547199	.549804	.552572	.555401	.558175
.5500000	.557602	.560357	.563288	.566285	.569229
.5600000	.568018	.570929	.574029	.577204	.580324
.5700000	.578449	.581522	.584798	.588157	.591461
.5800000	.588895	.592136	.595595	.599145	.602642
.5900000	.599356	.602771	.606420	.610169	.613867
.6000000	.609832	.613428	.617274	.621230	.625137
.6100000	.620324	.624106	.628156	.632328	.636453
.6200000	.630831	.634807	.639069	.643464	.647815
.6300000	.641354	.645530	.650011	.654639	.659226
.6400000	.651892	.656275	.660985	.665853	.670686
.6500000	.662447	.667044	.671989	.677107	.682196
.6600000	.673019	.677836	.683025	.688402	.693757
.6700000	.683607	.688652	.694092	.699739	.705369
.6800000	.694211	.699492	.705193	.711118	.717035
.6899999	.704833	.710355	.716326	.722540	.728754
.7000000	.715471	.721244	.727493	.734006	.740529
.7100000	.726127	.732157	.738693	.745516	.752359
.7200000	.736800	.743096	.749928	.757071	.764247
.7300000	.747490	.754059	.761198	.768672	.776192
.7400000	.758199	.765048	.772503	.780319	.788197
.7500000	.768925	.776063	.783843	.792013	.800262
.7600000	.779668	.787105	.795220	.803755	.812388
.7700000	.790430	.798172	.806633	.815546	.824577
.7800000	.801210	.809266	.818083	.827386	.836828
.7899999	.812009	.820387	.829570	.839276	.849145

$\alpha = -$ •019999

Θ	K VALUES				
	•318821117	•415016431	•514599755	•613601043	•708073407
•8000000	•822826	•831535	•841095	•851217	•861527
•8100000	•833661	•842710	•852658	•863208	•873976
•8200000	•844515	•853913	•864260	•875252	•886492
•8300000	•855387	•865143	•875900	•887348	•899077
•8400000	•866278	•876401	•887580	•899498	•911733
•8500000	•877189	•887687	•899299	•911701	•924459
•8600000	•888118	•899001	•911058	•923959	•937257
•8700000	•899066	•910344	•922857	•936272	•950129
•8799999	•910033	•921715	•934697	•948641	•963075
•8899999	•921019	•933114	•946578	•961066	•976096
•9000000	•932024	•944542	•958500	•973546	•989194
•9100000	•943048	•955999	•970463	•986088	1•002369
•9200000	•954092	•967485	•982468	•998686	1•015623
•9300000	•965154	•979000	•994515	1•011342	1•028957
•9400000	•976236	•990544	1•006604	1•024058	1•042372
•9500000	•987337	1•002117	1•018736	1•036833	1•055868
•9600000	•998457	1•013720	1•030910	1•049669	1•069447
•9699999	1•009597	1•025351	1•043127	1•062565	1•083110
•9799999	1•020755	1•037012	1•055387	1•075523	1•096857
•9899999	1•031933	1•048703	1•067690	1•088541	1•110691
1•0000000	1•043129	1•060422	1•080036	1•101622	1•124611
1•0100000	1•054345	1•072171	1•092426	1•114766	1•138619
1•0200000	1•065579	1•083949	1•104858	1•127971	1•152715
1•0300000	1•076832	1•095756	1•117335	1•141240	1•166901
1•0400000	1•088104	1•107592	1•129855	1•154572	1•181176
1•0500000	1•099395	1•119457	1•142418	1•167968	1•195543
1•0600000	1•110704	1•131351	1•155024	1•181427	1•210002
1•0699999	1•122032	1•143274	1•167675	1•194951	1•224554
1•0799999	1•133378	1•155226	1•180368	1•208538	1•239198
1•0899999	1•144742	1•167206	1•193105	1•222190	1•253937
1•1000000	1•156124	1•179214	1•205885	1•235906	1•268770
1•1100000	1•167524	1•191251	1•218708	1•249687	1•283698
1•1200000	1•178941	1•203315	1•231574	1•263531	1•298721
1•1300000	1•190376	1•215408	1•244482	1•277440	1•313840
1•1400000	1•201828	1•227528	1•257433	1•291413	1•329055
1•1500000	1•213298	1•239675	1•270426	1•305451	1•344367
1•1600000	1•224784	1•251849	1•283460	1•319551	1•359775
1•1700000	1•236287	1•264050	1•296536	1•333716	1•375280
1•1800000	1•247807	1•276277	1•309653	1•347943	1•390882
1•1899999	1•259342	1•288530	1•322811	1•362234	1•406581

$\alpha = -.019999$

θ	K VALUES				
	.318821117	.415016431	.514599755	.613601043	.708073407
1.2000000	1.270894	1.300809	1.336010	1.376587	1.422376
1.2100000	1.282461	1.313113	1.349247	1.391002	1.438267
1.2200000	1.294044	1.325442	1.362525	1.405478	1.454255
1.2300000	1.305642	1.337796	1.375841	1.420015	1.470338
1.2400000	1.317254	1.350173	1.389195	1.434612	1.486515
1.2500000	1.328881	1.362574	1.402586	1.449268	1.502788
1.2599999	1.340523	1.374999	1.416015	1.463983	1.519153
1.2699999	1.352178	1.387446	1.429480	1.478755	1.535612
1.2799999	1.363847	1.399915	1.442980	1.493585	1.552161
1.2899999	1.375529	1.412406	1.456515	1.508469	1.568802
1.3000000	1.387224	1.424918	1.470084	1.523409	1.585531
1.3100000	1.398931	1.437451	1.483686	1.538402	1.602348
1.3200000	1.410650	1.450003	1.497321	1.553448	1.619251
1.3300000	1.422381	1.462575	1.510986	1.568544	1.636238
1.3400000	1.434124	1.475165	1.524682	1.583690	1.653308
1.3500000	1.445877	1.487774	1.538408	1.598884	1.670459
1.3600000	1.457641	1.500400	1.552162	1.614125	1.687687
1.3700000	1.469415	1.513043	1.565944	1.629411	1.704992
1.3799999	1.481198	1.525702	1.579752	1.644740	1.722371
1.3899999	1.492991	1.538376	1.593585	1.660112	1.739820
1.4000000	1.504793	1.551065	1.607442	1.675523	1.757338
1.4100000	1.516603	1.563768	1.621323	1.690973	1.774921
1.4200000	1.528421	1.576484	1.635225	1.706459	1.792567
1.4300000	1.540246	1.589213	1.649147	1.721979	1.810272
1.4400000	1.552078	1.601953	1.663089	1.737532	1.828033
1.4500000	1.563917	1.614704	1.677050	1.753115	1.845847
1.4600000	1.575762	1.627465	1.691026	1.768726	1.863710
1.4700000	1.587612	1.640236	1.705019	1.784363	1.881619
1.4800000	1.599468	1.653015	1.719025	1.800025	1.899569
1.4900000	1.611328	1.665802	1.733045	1.815707	1.917557
1.5000000	1.623192	1.678595	1.747075	1.831410	1.935580
1.5100000	1.635060	1.691395	1.761116	1.847129	1.953632
1.5200000	1.646931	1.704200	1.775166	1.862863	1.971710
1.5300000	1.658804	1.717009	1.789222	1.878609	1.989810
1.5400000	1.670679	1.729822	1.803285	1.894365	2.007927
1.5500000	1.682556	1.742637	1.817352	1.910129	2.026058
1.5600000	1.694434	1.755454	1.831422	1.925897	2.044198
1.5699999	1.706313	1.768272	1.845493	1.941669	2.062342
1.5707963	1.707259	1.769293	1.846614	1.942925	2.063787
1.5707963	1.707258	1.769292	1.846613	1.942923	2.063785

$\alpha = - .019999$

Θ	K VALUES				
	.794250555	.868696860	.928444378	.971111163	.994996249
.0000000	.000000	.000000	.000000	.000000	.000000
.0100000	.010000	.010000	.010000	.010000	.010000
.0200000	.020001	.020001	.020001	.020001	.020001
.0300000	.030003	.030003	.030004	.030004	.030004
.0400000	.040008	.040008	.040009	.040009	.040010
.0500000	.050015	.050017	.050018	.050019	.050019
.0600000	.060027	.060029	.060032	.060033	.060034
.0700000	.070043	.070047	.070050	.070053	.070054
.0800000	.080064	.080070	.080075	.080079	.080081
.0900000	.090091	.090100	.090108	.090113	.090116
.1000000	.100125	.100138	.100148	.100155	.100159
.1100000	.110167	.110184	.110197	.110207	.110212
.1200000	.120217	.120239	.120256	.120269	.120276
.1300000	.130276	.130304	.130326	.130342	.130351
.1400000	.140346	.140380	.140408	.140427	.140438
.1500000	.150425	.150468	.150502	.150526	.150540
.1600000	.160517	.160568	.160610	.160639	.160656
.1700000	.170620	.170682	.170732	.170767	.170787
.1800000	.180737	.180810	.180869	.180912	.180936
.1900000	.190867	.190954	.191023	.191073	.191101
.2000000	.201012	.201113	.201195	.201253	.201286
.2100000	.211172	.211290	.211385	.211452	.211490
.2200000	.221349	.221484	.221594	.221672	.221715
.2300000	.231542	.231698	.231823	.231912	.231963
.2400000	.241754	.241931	.242073	.242175	.242233
.2500000	.251984	.252185	.252346	.252462	.252527
.2600000	.262234	.262460	.262642	.262773	.262846
.2700000	.272504	.272758	.272963	.273109	.273192
.2800000	.282795	.283079	.283308	.283473	.283565
.2900000	.293108	.293425	.293680	.293864	.293967
.3000000	.303444	.303796	.304080	.304284	.304398
.3100000	.313804	.314194	.314508	.314734	.314860
.3200000	.324189	.324619	.324966	.325215	.325355
.3300000	.334599	.335072	.335454	.335729	.335883
.3400000	.345035	.345555	.345975	.346276	.346446
.3500000	.355499	.356068	.356528	.356858	.357044
.3600000	.365991	.366613	.367115	.367477	.367680
.3700000	.376512	.377190	.377738	.378132	.378354
.3800000	.387064	.387800	.388397	.388827	.389068
.3900000	.397646	.398446	.399094	.399561	.399823

$\alpha = -.019999$

Θ	K VALUES				
	.794250555	.868696860	.928444378	.971111163	.994996249
.4000000	.408260	.409127	.409830	.410336	.410621
.4100000	.418907	.419845	.420606	.421154	.421462
.4200000	.429588	.430601	.431423	.432016	.432349
.4300000	.440304	.441396	.442283	.442923	.443283
.4400000	.451056	.452231	.453187	.453877	.454265
.4500000	.461844	.463108	.464137	.464879	.465297
.4600000	.472671	.474028	.475133	.475930	.476380
.4700000	.483536	.484991	.486177	.487033	.487516
.4800000	.494441	.496000	.497271	.498189	.498707
.4900000	.505388	.507055	.508415	.509399	.509954
.5000000	.516376	.518158	.519612	.520664	.521259
.5100000	.527408	.529309	.530863	.531988	.532623
.5200000	.538484	.540511	.542169	.543370	.544049
.5300000	.549605	.551765	.553532	.554814	.555538
.5400000	.560773	.563071	.564954	.566320	.567092
.5500000	.571988	.574432	.576435	.577890	.578713
.5600000	.583252	.585848	.587979	.589527	.590403
.5700000	.594566	.597322	.599586	.601232	.602164
.5800000	.605932	.608855	.611258	.613007	.613998
.5900000	.617349	.620447	.622997	.624854	.625907
.6000000	.628821	.632102	.634805	.636775	.637893
.6100000	.640347	.643820	.646683	.648772	.649959
.6200000	.651929	.655602	.658634	.660848	.662106
.6300000	.663569	.667451	.670660	.673004	.674337
.6400000	.675268	.679368	.682761	.685243	.686655
.6500000	.687026	.691355	.694942	.697567	.699062
.6600000	.698846	.703414	.707202	.709979	.711560
.6700000	.710729	.715545	.719545	.722480	.724153
.6800000	.722675	.727752	.731974	.735074	.736842
.6899999	.734687	.740035	.744489	.747763	.749631
.7000000	.746767	.752398	.757093	.760549	.762523
.7100000	.758914	.764840	.769789	.773436	.775520
.7200000	.771131	.777366	.782579	.786426	.788626
.7300000	.783420	.789976	.795466	.799522	.801844
.7400000	.795781	.802672	.808452	.812727	.815177
.7500000	.808217	.815457	.821540	.826044	.828629
.7600000	.820728	.828332	.834732	.839477	.842202
.7700000	.833317	.841301	.848031	.853029	.855901
.7800000	.845985	.854364	.861440	.866702	.869730
.7899999	.858733	.867525	.874962	.880502	.883692

$\alpha = -\ .019999$

θ	K VALUES				
	.794250555	.868696860	.928444378	.971111163	.994996249
.8000000	.871564	.880785	.888600	.894430	.897791
.8100000	.884479	.894147	.902357	.908492	.912032
.8200000	.897479	.907614	.916236	.922690	.926419
.8300000	.910566	.921187	.930241	.937029	.940957
.8400000	.923742	.934869	.944374	.951514	.955650
.8500000	.937009	.948663	.958640	.966148	.970502
.8600000	.950368	.962571	.973042	.980935	.985520
.8700000	.963822	.976597	.987583	.995881	1.000708
.8799999	.977371	.990742	1.002267	1.010991	1.016073
.8899999	.991019	1.005009	1.017098	1.026269	1.031619
.9000000	1.004766	1.019402	1.032081	1.041720	1.047352
.9100000	1.018614	1.033923	1.047219	1.057350	1.063280
.9200000	1.032566	1.048575	1.062517	1.073165	1.079408
.9300000	1.046622	1.063361	1.077978	1.089170	1.095743
.9400000	1.060786	1.078285	1.093609	1.105371	1.112292
.9500000	1.075059	1.093348	1.109412	1.121774	1.129063
.9600000	1.089442	1.108555	1.125393	1.138387	1.146064
.9699999	1.103938	1.123909	1.141558	1.155216	1.163302
.9799999	1.118549	1.139413	1.157910	1.172268	1.180787
.9899999	1.133277	1.155070	1.174456	1.189550	1.198527
1.0000000	1.148122	1.170884	1.191201	1.207070	1.216531
1.0100000	1.163088	1.186859	1.208151	1.224837	1.234810
1.0200000	1.178177	1.202997	1.225311	1.242858	1.253374
1.0300000	1.193389	1.219302	1.242687	1.261143	1.272234
1.0400000	1.208727	1.235778	1.260286	1.279700	1.291401
1.0500000	1.224193	1.252429	1.278114	1.298539	1.310888
1.0600000	1.239789	1.269258	1.296177	1.317671	1.330707
1.0699999	1.255517	1.286270	1.314482	1.337106	1.350872
1.0799999	1.271377	1.303467	1.333037	1.356854	1.371398
1.0899999	1.287373	1.320854	1.351849	1.376927	1.392299
1.1000000	1.303505	1.338435	1.370924	1.397339	1.413593
1.1100000	1.319776	1.356213	1.390271	1.418100	1.435295
1.1200000	1.336186	1.374192	1.409897	1.439224	1.457424
1.1300000	1.352738	1.392376	1.429811	1.460726	1.480000
1.1400000	1.369433	1.410770	1.450020	1.482620	1.503043
1.1500000	1.386272	1.429376	1.470534	1.504922	1.526574
1.1600000	1.403256	1.448199	1.491360	1.527647	1.550619
1.1700000	1.420388	1.467243	1.512509	1.550813	1.575201
1.1800000	1.437667	1.486510	1.533988	1.574437	1.600347
1.1899999	1.455095	1.506005	1.555807	1.598539	1.626088

$\alpha = -\ .019999$

Θ	K VALUES				
	.794250555	.868696860	.928444378	.971111163	.994996249
1.2000000	1.472673	1.525732	1.577977	1.623138	1.652452
1.2100000	1.490401	1.545693	1.600505	1.648255	1.679475
1.2200000	1.508280	1.565892	1.623402	1.673912	1.707191
1.2300000	1.526310	1.586332	1.646678	1.700131	1.735639
1.2400000	1.544492	1.607016	1.670343	1.726938	1.764863
1.2500000	1.562826	1.627946	1.694406	1.754358	1.794906
1.2599999	1.581311	1.649125	1.718878	1.782416	1.825819
1.2699999	1.599947	1.670556	1.743769	1.811143	1.857656
1.2799999	1.618734	1.692239	1.769087	1.840566	1.890474
1.2899999	1.637670	1.714176	1.794843	1.870716	1.924340
1.3000000	1.656756	1.736369	1.821046	1.901627	1.959322
1.3100000	1.675988	1.758818	1.847705	1.933330	1.995498
1.3200000	1.695367	1.781523	1.874827	1.965862	2.032953
1.3300000	1.714889	1.804484	1.902421	1.999259	2.071781
1.3400000	1.734553	1.827700	1.930494	2.033557	2.112086
1.3500000	1.754357	1.851169	1.959051	2.068795	2.153984
1.3600000	1.774297	1.874890	1.988099	2.105013	2.197603
1.3700000	1.794371	1.898858	2.017639	2.142250	2.243085
1.3799999	1.814575	1.923072	2.047676	2.180545	2.290593
1.3899999	1.834906	1.947526	2.078209	2.219937	2.340306
1.4000000	1.855359	1.972215	2.109237	2.260466	2.392426
1.4100000	1.875929	1.997133	2.140758	2.302165	2.447182
1.4200000	1.896613	2.022273	2.172765	2.345068	2.504832
1.4300000	1.917405	2.047627	2.205250	2.389204	2.565667
1.4400000	1.938300	2.073187	2.238204	2.434594	2.630017
1.4500000	1.959292	2.098943	2.271611	2.481254	2.698252
1.4600000	1.980375	2.124884	2.305456	2.529189	2.770791
1.4700000	2.001542	2.150999	2.339719	2.578393	2.848097
1.4800000	2.022787	2.177276	2.374375	2.628844	2.930679
1.4900000	2.044104	2.203701	2.409399	2.680506	3.019078
1.5000000	2.065485	2.230260	2.444760	2.733325	3.113849
1.5100000	2.086922	2.256939	2.480426	2.787223	3.215509
1.5200000	2.108408	2.283721	2.516359	2.842105	3.324469
1.5300000	2.129935	2.310592	2.552520	2.897852	3.440906
1.5400000	2.151496	2.337534	2.588869	2.954325	3.564609
1.5500000	2.173082	2.364530	2.625361	3.011366	3.694797
1.5600000	2.194685	2.391563	2.661950	3.068799	3.829988
1.5699999	2.216297	2.418615	2.698590	3.126440	3.968013
1.5707963	2.218018	2.420770	2.701509	3.131033	3.979049
1.5707963	2.218017	2.420768	2.701507	3.131030	3.979046

$\alpha =$ .049999

Θ	K VALUES				
	.009966711	.039469502	.087332193	.151646642	.229848846
.0000000	.000000	.000000	.000000	.000000	.000000
.0100000	.010000	.010000	.010000	.010000	.010000
.0200000	.020000	.020000	.020000	.020000	.020000
.0300000	.030000	.030000	.030000	.030001	.030001
.0400000	.040001	.040001	.040002	.040002	.040003
.0500000	.050002	.050002	.050003	.050005	.050006
.0600000	.060003	.060005	.060006	.060009	.060011
.0700000	.070006	.070008	.070010	.070014	.070018
.0800000	.080009	.080011	.080016	.080021	.080028
.0900000	.090013	.090016	.090022	.090030	.090040
.1000000	.100018	.100023	.100031	.100041	.100054
.1100000	.110024	.110030	.110041	.110055	.110073
.1200000	.120031	.120040	.120053	.120072	.120094
.1300000	.130040	.130050	.130068	.130091	.130120
.1400000	.140050	.140063	.140085	.140114	.140150
.1500000	.150061	.150078	.150105	.150141	.150185
.1600000	.160074	.160094	.160127	.160171	.160224
.1700000	.170089	.170113	.170152	.170205	.170269
.1800000	.180106	.180134	.180181	.180243	.180319
.1900000	.190124	.190158	.190213	.190286	.190375
.2000000	.200145	.200184	.200248	.200333	.200438
.2100000	.210168	.210213	.210287	.210386	.210506
.2200000	.220193	.220245	.220330	.220443	.220582
.2300000	.230221	.230280	.230376	.230506	.230665
.2400000	.240250	.240318	.240427	.240575	.240755
.2500000	.250283	.250359	.250483	.250650	.250853
.2600000	.260318	.260404	.260543	.260730	.260959
.2700000	.270356	.270452	.270607	.270817	.271074
.2800000	.280397	.280503	.280677	.280911	.281197
.2900000	.290440	.290559	.290751	.291011	.291329
.3000000	.300487	.300618	.300831	.301119	.301471
.3100000	.310537	.310681	.310916	.311233	.311622
.3200000	.320590	.320748	.321007	.321356	.321783
.3300000	.330646	.330820	.331103	.331485	.331954
.3400000	.340706	.340896	.341205	.341623	.342135
.3500000	.350769	.350976	.351313	.351769	.352328
.3600000	.360836	.361061	.361428	.361923	.362531
.3700000	.370906	.371150	.371548	.372086	.372746
.3800000	.380981	.381245	.381675	.382258	.382972
.3900000	.391059	.391344	.391809	.392438	.393211

$\alpha =$ .049999

Θ	K VALUES				
	.009966711	.039469502	.087332193	.151646642	.229848846
.4000000	.401141	.401448	.401949	.402628	.403461
.4100000	.411227	.411557	.412096	.412827	.413724
.4200000	.421317	.421672	.422251	.423035	.424000
.4300000	.431411	.431791	.432412	.433254	.434289
.4400000	.441510	.441917	.442581	.443482	.444591
.4500000	.451613	.452047	.452757	.453720	.454907
.4600000	.461720	.462183	.462941	.463969	.465236
.4700000	.471832	.472325	.473132	.474228	.475579
.4800000	.481948	.482473	.483332	.484498	.485937
.4900000	.492069	.492627	.493539	.494779	.496309
.5000000	.502194	.502786	.503754	.505071	.506696
.5100000	.512324	.512952	.513978	.515374	.517099
.5200000	.522460	.523123	.524209	.525688	.527516
.5300000	.532599	.533301	.534450	.536014	.537949
.5400000	.542744	.543485	.544698	.546351	.548398
.5500000	.552894	.553675	.554955	.556700	.558862
.5600000	.563049	.563872	.565222	.567062	.569343
.5700000	.573209	.574076	.575496	.577435	.579840
.5800000	.583374	.584285	.585780	.587821	.590354
.5900000	.593544	.594502	.596073	.598219	.600884
.6000000	.603720	.604725	.606375	.608630	.611432
.6100000	.613901	.614955	.616686	.619053	.621997
.6200000	.624087	.625192	.627006	.629489	.632579
.6300000	.634278	.635435	.637336	.639938	.643179
.6400000	.644475	.645686	.647675	.650400	.653796
.6500000	.654678	.655943	.658024	.660875	.664432
.6600000	.664886	.666208	.668382	.671364	.675085
.6700000	.675099	.676479	.678750	.681865	.685757
.6800000	.685318	.686758	.689128	.692381	.696447
.6899999	.695543	.697044	.699515	.702909	.707156
.7000000	.705773	.707337	.709913	.713452	.717883
.7100000	.716009	.717637	.720320	.724008	.728629
.7200000	.726251	.727945	.730737	.734578	.739395
.7300000	.736498	.738259	.741164	.745162	.750179
.7400000	.746751	.748581	.751601	.755760	.760983
.7500000	.757010	.758911	.762048	.766371	.771806
.7600000	.767274	.769247	.772505	.776997	.782648
.7700000	.777545	.779592	.782972	.787637	.793510
.7800000	.787821	.789943	.793450	.798291	.804391
.7899999	.798103	.800302	.803937	.808959	.815292

$\alpha =$ •049999

Θ	K VALUES				
	•009966711	•039469502	•087332193	•151646642	•229848846
•8000000	•808390	•810668	•814435	•819642	•826214
•8100000	•818684	•821042	•824943	•830339	•837154
•8200000	•828983	•831423	•835461	•841050	•848115
•8300000	•839288	•841811	•845989	•851775	•859096
•8400000	•849599	•852207	•856528	•862515	•870096
•8500000	•859915	•862611	•867077	•873269	•881117
•8600000	•870238	•873021	•877635	•884038	•892158
•8700000	•880566	•883439	•888204	•894820	•903219
•8799999	•890900	•893865	•898784	•905618	•914300
•8899999	•901239	•904297	•909373	•916429	•925401
•9000000	•911585	•914738	•919973	•927255	•936522
•9100000	•921936	•925185	•930582	•938095	•947664
•9200000	•932293	•935640	•941202	•948949	•958825
•9300000	•942655	•946102	•951832	•959817	•970007
•9400000	•953023	•956571	•962471	•970700	•981208
•9500000	•963397	•967047	•973121	•981596	•992429
•9600000	•973776	•977531	•983780	•992507	1•003671
•9699999	•984161	•988021	•994450	1•003431	1•014932
•9799999	•994551	•998519	1•005129	1•014370	1•026213
•9899999	1•004946	1•009023	1•015818	1•025322	1•037513
1•0000000	1•015348	1•019535	1•026516	1•036288	1•048834
1•0100000	1•025754	1•030053	1•037224	1•047268	1•060173
1•0200000	1•036166	1•040579	1•047942	1•058261	1•071532
1•0300000	1•046583	1•051111	1•058669	1•069268	1•082911
1•0400000	1•057005	1•061649	1•069405	1•080288	1•094308
1•0500000	1•067433	1•072195	1•080150	1•091321	1•105724
1•0600000	1•077866	1•082747	1•090905	1•102368	1•117159
1•0699999	1•088303	1•093305	1•101669	1•113427	1•128613
1•0799999	1•098746	1•103870	1•112442	1•124499	1•140086
1•0899999	1•109194	1•114442	1•123223	1•135584	1•151576
1•1000000	1•119646	1•125019	1•134013	1•146682	1•163085
1•1100000	1•130104	1•135603	1•144812	1•157791	1•174612
1•1200000	1•140566	1•146193	1•155620	1•168914	1•186156
1•1300000	1•151033	1•156789	1•166436	1•180048	1•197718
1•1400000	1•161504	1•167391	1•177260	1•191194	1•209298
1•1500000	1•171980	1•177999	1•188092	1•202352	1•220894
1•1600000	1•182461	1•188612	1•198933	1•213521	1•232507
1•1700000	1•192946	1•199231	1•209781	1•224702	1•244137
1•1800000	1•203435	1•209856	1•220637	1•235894	1•255783
1•1899999	1•213928	1•220486	1•231500	1•247097	1•267445

$\alpha =$ .049999

Θ	K VALUES				
	.009966711	.039469502	.087332193	.151646642	.229848846
1.2000000	1.224426	1.231121	1.242371	1.258311	1.279123
1.2100000	1.234928	1.241762	1.253250	1.269535	1.290816
1.2200000	1.245433	1.252408	1.264135	1.280770	1.302525
1.2300000	1.255943	1.263058	1.275028	1.292015	1.314248
1.2400000	1.266456	1.273714	1.285927	1.303270	1.325986
1.2500000	1.276973	1.284375	1.296833	1.314534	1.337738
1.2599999	1.287494	1.295040	1.307746	1.325808	1.349504
1.2699999	1.298018	1.305709	1.318665	1.337091	1.361283
1.2799999	1.308545	1.316383	1.329590	1.348384	1.373076
1.2899999	1.319076	1.327061	1.340521	1.359684	1.384881
1.3000000	1.329611	1.337744	1.351458	1.370994	1.396699
1.3100000	1.340148	1.348430	1.362400	1.382311	1.408530
1.3200000	1.350688	1.359120	1.373348	1.393637	1.420371
1.3300000	1.361231	1.369815	1.384301	1.404970	1.432224
1.3400000	1.371777	1.380512	1.395260	1.416311	1.444089
1.3500000	1.382326	1.391213	1.406223	1.427658	1.455963
1.3600000	1.392877	1.401918	1.417191	1.439013	1.467848
1.3700000	1.403431	1.412625	1.428163	1.450374	1.479742
1.3799999	1.413987	1.423336	1.439140	1.461741	1.491646
1.3899999	1.424545	1.434050	1.450120	1.473114	1.503559
1.4000000	1.435106	1.444766	1.461105	1.484494	1.515480
1.4100000	1.445668	1.455485	1.472093	1.495878	1.527409
1.4200000	1.456233	1.466207	1.483085	1.507267	1.539346
1.4300000	1.466799	1.476931	1.494080	1.518662	1.551289
1.4400000	1.477367	1.487657	1.505079	1.530061	1.563240
1.4500000	1.487937	1.498385	1.516080	1.541464	1.575197
1.4600000	1.498508	1.509115	1.527083	1.552870	1.587159
1.4700000	1.509080	1.519846	1.538089	1.564281	1.599127
1.4800000	1.519654	1.530579	1.549098	1.575694	1.611099
1.4900000	1.530228	1.541314	1.560108	1.587111	1.623076
1.5000000	1.540804	1.552050	1.571120	1.598530	1.635057
1.5100000	1.551381	1.562787	1.582134	1.609952	1.647041
1.5200000	1.561958	1.573525	1.593149	1.621375	1.659028
1.5300000	1.572536	1.584264	1.604165	1.632800	1.671018
1.5400000	1.583114	1.595003	1.615182	1.644226	1.683010
1.5500000	1.593693	1.605743	1.626200	1.655654	1.695003
1.5600000	1.604272	1.616483	1.637218	1.667082	1.706997
1.5699999	1.614851	1.627224	1.648236	1.678510	1.718991
1.5707963	1.615694	1.628079	1.649114	1.679420	1.719946
1.5707963	1.615693	1.628078	1.649112	1.679419	1.719945

$\alpha =$ .049999

Θ	K VALUES				
	.318821117	.415016431	.514599755	.613601043	.708073407
.0000000	.000000	.000000	.000000	.000000	.000000
.0100000	.010000	.010000	.010000	.010000	.010000
.0200000	.020000	.020000	.020000	.020000	.020001
.0300000	.030001	.030002	.030002	.030003	.030003
.0400000	.040004	.040005	.040006	.040007	.040008
.0500000	.050008	.050010	.050012	.050014	.050016
.0600000	.060015	.060018	.060022	.060025	.060029
.0700000	.070023	.070029	.070035	.070040	.070046
.0800000	.080035	.080043	.080052	.080060	.080069
.0900000	.090050	.090062	.090074	.090086	.090098
.1000000	.100069	.100085	.100102	.100119	.100134
.1100000	.110092	.110114	.110136	.110158	.110179
.1200000	.120120	.120148	.120177	.120205	.120233
.1300000	.130153	.130188	.130225	.130261	.130296
.1400000	.140191	.140235	.140281	.140326	.140370
.1500000	.150235	.150289	.150345	.150402	.150455
.1600000	.160285	.160351	.160419	.160488	.160553
.1700000	.170342	.170421	.170503	.170585	.170663
.1800000	.180406	.180500	.180597	.180695	.180788
.1900000	.190477	.190588	.190703	.190817	.190927
.2000000	.200557	.200686	.200820	.200954	.201082
.2100000	.210644	.210794	.210949	.211104	.211253
.2200000	.220741	.220913	.221091	.221270	.221441
.2300000	.230846	.231043	.231247	.231452	.231648
.2400000	.240961	.241185	.241417	.241650	.241873
.2500000	.251086	.251339	.251602	.251866	.252118
.2600000	.261221	.261506	.261803	.262099	.262384
.2700000	.271367	.271686	.272019	.272352	.272672
.2800000	.281524	.281881	.282252	.282624	.282981
.2900000	.291693	.292089	.292502	.292916	.293314
.3000000	.301874	.302313	.302771	.303230	.303672
.3100000	.312066	.312551	.313058	.313565	.314054
.3200000	.322272	.322806	.323364	.323923	.324462
.3300000	.332491	.333077	.333689	.334304	.334897
.3400000	.342723	.343365	.344036	.344710	.345360
.3500000	.352969	.353670	.354403	.355140	.355851
.3600000	.363229	.363993	.364792	.365596	.366372
.3700000	.373504	.374334	.375203	.376078	.376923
.3800000	.383794	.384694	.385637	.386587	.387506
.3900000	.394100	.395073	.396095	.397125	.398121

$\alpha =$ .049999

Θ	K VALUES				
	.318821117	.415016431	.514599755	.613601043	.708073407
.4000000	.404421	.405472	.406577	.407691	.408769
.4100000	.414758	.415892	.417083	.418286	.419452
.4200000	.425112	.426332	.427616	.428912	.430170
.4300000	.435483	.436794	.438174	.439569	.440923
.4400000	.445871	.447277	.448759	.450258	.451714
.4500000	.456276	.457783	.459371	.460979	.462543
.4600000	.466700	.468311	.470011	.471734	.473411
.4700000	.477142	.478862	.480679	.482523	.484319
.4800000	.487602	.489438	.491377	.493347	.495268
.4900000	.498082	.500037	.502105	.504207	.506259
.5000000	.508581	.510661	.512863	.515104	.517293
.5100000	.519099	.521310	.523652	.526038	.528371
.5200000	.529638	.531984	.534473	.537011	.539494
.5300000	.540197	.542684	.545326	.548022	.550663
.5400000	.550776	.553411	.556212	.559073	.561880
.5500000	.561377	.564165	.567131	.570165	.573144
.5600000	.571999	.574946	.578085	.581299	.584458
.5700000	.582642	.585755	.589073	.592475	.595822
.5800000	.593307	.596592	.600096	.603694	.607238
.5900000	.603995	.607457	.611156	.614957	.618706
.6000000	.614705	.618352	.622252	.626265	.630228
.6100000	.625438	.629276	.633385	.637618	.641804
.6200000	.636194	.640230	.644556	.649018	.653436
.6300000	.646974	.651214	.655766	.660465	.665126
.6400000	.657777	.662230	.667014	.671961	.676873
.6500000	.668604	.673276	.678302	.683505	.688679
.6600000	.679455	.684353	.689630	.695099	.700546
.6700000	.690330	.695463	.700998	.706744	.712474
.6800000	.701231	.706605	.712408	.718440	.724464
.6899999	.712156	.717779	.723860	.730189	.736519
.7000000	.723106	.728987	.735354	.741991	.748639
.7100000	.734082	.740228	.746891	.753846	.760824
.7200000	.745083	.751503	.758471	.765757	.773077
.7300000	.756110	.762811	.770095	.777722	.785399
.7400000	.767163	.774154	.781764	.789745	.797790
.7500000	.778242	.785532	.793478	.801824	.810252
.7600000	.789348	.796945	.805238	.813962	.822787
.7700000	.800480	.808393	.817043	.826158	.835395
.7800000	.811639	.819877	.828895	.838414	.848077
.7899999	.822824	.831397	.840795	.850730	.860835

$\alpha =$ .049999

Θ	K VALUES				
	.318821117	.415016431	.514599755	.613601043	.708073407
.8000000	.834037	.842953	.852742	.863108	.873671
.8100000	.845277	.854546	.864737	.875548	.886584
.8200000	.856544	.866175	.876780	.888050	.899577
.8300000	.867839	.877841	.888872	.900616	.912651
.8400000	.879161	.889544	.901014	.913246	.925807
.8500000	.890510	.901285	.913205	.925941	.939046
.8600000	.901888	.913063	.925446	.938702	.952369
.8700000	.913293	.924879	.937739	.951529	.965778
.8799999	.924726	.936733	.950082	.964423	.979274
.8899999	.936187	.948625	.962476	.977385	.992858
.9000000	.947676	.960556	.974922	.990416	1.006532
.9100000	.959192	.972525	.987420	1.003516	1.020296
.9200000	.970737	.984532	.999970	1.016686	1.034152
.9300000	.982310	.996578	1.012572	1.029926	1.048100
.9400000	.993911	1.008663	1.025227	1.043237	1.062143
.9500000	1.005540	1.020786	1.037936	1.056620	1.076281
.9600000	1.017197	1.032948	1.050697	1.070075	1.090515
.9699999	1.028881	1.045150	1.063512	1.083602	1.104847
.9799999	1.040594	1.057389	1.076381	1.097203	1.119277
.9899999	1.052334	1.069668	1.089304	1.110878	1.133807
1.0000000	1.064102	1.081986	1.102280	1.124626	1.148438
1.0100000	1.075898	1.094342	1.115310	1.138449	1.163170
1.0200000	1.087721	1.106737	1.128395	1.152347	1.178005
1.0300000	1.099571	1.119171	1.141533	1.166320	1.192944
1.0400000	1.111449	1.131643	1.154726	1.180369	1.207987
1.0500000	1.123354	1.144154	1.167972	1.194493	1.223135
1.0600000	1.135286	1.156703	1.181273	1.208694	1.238390
1.0699999	1.147244	1.169290	1.194628	1.222970	1.253752
1.0799999	1.159229	1.181915	1.208037	1.237323	1.269222
1.0899999	1.171241	1.194577	1.221499	1.251753	1.284800
1.1000000	1.183278	1.207277	1.235015	1.266259	1.300487
1.1100000	1.195342	1.220015	1.248584	1.280841	1.316284
1.1200000	1.207431	1.232789	1.262207	1.295500	1.332190
1.1300000	1.219545	1.245599	1.275882	1.310235	1.348208
1.1400000	1.231684	1.258446	1.289609	1.325047	1.364336
1.1500000	1.243848	1.271329	1.303389	1.339934	1.380575
1.1600000	1.256037	1.284248	1.317221	1.354897	1.396925
1.1700000	1.268250	1.297201	1.331103	1.369935	1.413387
1.1800000	1.280486	1.310189	1.345037	1.385048	1.429960
1.1899999	1.292746	1.323212	1.359021	1.400236	1.446644

$\alpha =$ .049999

Θ	K VALUES				
	.318821117	.415016431	.514599755	.613601043	.708073407
1.2000000	1.305029	1.336268	1.373055	1.415498	1.463439
1.2100000	1.317335	1.349358	1.387138	1.430833	1.480345
1.2200000	1.329662	1.362480	1.401269	1.446240	1.497361
1.2300000	1.342012	1.375634	1.415448	1.461719	1.514486
1.2400000	1.354383	1.388820	1.429675	1.477270	1.531721
1.2500000	1.366775	1.402037	1.443947	1.492890	1.549063
1.2599999	1.379187	1.415285	1.458265	1.508580	1.566513
1.2699999	1.391620	1.428562	1.472628	1.524337	1.584069
1.2799999	1.404072	1.441868	1.487034	1.540162	1.601730
1.2899999	1.416543	1.455203	1.501484	1.556052	1.619494
1.3000000	1.429033	1.468565	1.515975	1.572007	1.637360
1.3100000	1.441540	1.481954	1.530507	1.588025	1.655327
1.3200000	1.454065	1.495369	1.545078	1.604104	1.673391
1.3300000	1.466607	1.508810	1.559688	1.620244	1.691553
1.3400000	1.479165	1.522275	1.574336	1.636442	1.709808
1.3500000	1.491738	1.535764	1.589020	1.652697	1.728156
1.3600000	1.504327	1.549275	1.603738	1.669007	1.746593
1.3700000	1.516931	1.562809	1.618491	1.685370	1.765117
1.3799999	1.529548	1.576363	1.633276	1.701784	1.783725
1.3899999	1.542179	1.589938	1.648092	1.718247	1.802414
1.4000000	1.554822	1.603532	1.662937	1.734758	1.821181
1.4100000	1.567477	1.617144	1.677811	1.751313	1.840023
1.4200000	1.580144	1.630773	1.692712	1.767911	1.858936
1.4300000	1.592821	1.644419	1.707637	1.784550	1.877917
1.4400000	1.605509	1.658080	1.722587	1.801226	1.896962
1.4500000	1.618205	1.671755	1.737559	1.817939	1.916066
1.4600000	1.630911	1.685443	1.752551	1.834684	1.935227
1.4700000	1.643624	1.699144	1.767562	1.851460	1.954439
1.4800000	1.656345	1.712856	1.782591	1.868264	1.973700
1.4900000	1.669072	1.726577	1.797635	1.885093	1.993003
1.5000000	1.681805	1.740308	1.812694	1.901946	2.012345
1.5100000	1.694543	1.754046	1.827764	1.918818	2.031722
1.5200000	1.707286	1.767792	1.842846	1.935707	2.051127
1.5300000	1.720032	1.781543	1.857936	1.952611	2.070558
1.5400000	1.732781	1.795298	1.873033	1.969527	2.090009
1.5500000	1.745533	1.809057	1.888136	1.986451	2.109474
1.5600000	1.758286	1.822818	1.903242	2.003381	2.128950
1.5699999	1.771040	1.836581	1.918351	2.020315	2.148431
1.5707963	1.772055	1.837677	1.919554	2.021663	2.149983
1.5707963	1.772054	1.837675	1.919552	2.021661	2.149981

$\alpha =$ .049999

Θ	K VALUES				
	.794250555	.868696860	.928444378	.971111163	.994996249
.0000000	.000000	.000000	.000000	.000000	.000000
.0100000	.010000	.010000	.010000	.010000	.010000
.0200000	.020001	.020001	.020001	.020001	.020001
.0300000	.030004	.030004	.030004	.030004	.030004
.0400000	.040009	.040010	.040010	.040011	.040011
.0500000	.050018	.050020	.050021	.050022	.050022
.0600000	.060032	.060034	.060037	.060038	.060039
.0700000	.070051	.070055	.070058	.070061	.070062
.0800000	.080076	.080082	.080087	.080091	.080093
.0900000	.090108	.090117	.090125	.090130	.090133
.1000000	.100149	.100161	.100171	.100178	.100182
.1100000	.110198	.110215	.110228	.110238	.110243
.1200000	.120258	.120279	.120297	.120309	.120316
.1300000	.130328	.130355	.130377	.130393	.130402
.1400000	.140410	.140444	.140472	.140492	.140503
.1500000	.150504	.150547	.150581	.150605	.150619
.1600000	.160612	.160664	.160705	.160735	.160752
.1700000	.170735	.170797	.170847	.170882	.170902
.1800000	.180873	.180947	.181006	.181048	.181072
.1900000	.191027	.191114	.191184	.191234	.191262
.2000000	.201199	.201300	.201382	.201441	.201473
.2100000	.211389	.211507	.211602	.211669	.211707
.2200000	.221598	.221734	.221843	.221921	.221965
.2300000	.231827	.231983	.232108	.232198	.232248
.2400000	.242077	.242255	.242398	.242500	.242557
.2500000	.252350	.252551	.252713	.252829	.252894
.2600000	.262645	.262872	.263055	.263186	.263259
.2700000	.272965	.273220	.273425	.273572	.273655
.2800000	.283309	.283595	.283825	.283989	.284082
.2900000	.293680	.293998	.294254	.294438	.294541
.3000000	.304078	.304431	.304716	.304920	.305035
.3100000	.314503	.314894	.315210	.315436	.315564
.3200000	.324958	.325390	.325738	.325988	.326129
.3300000	.335443	.335918	.336302	.336578	.336733
.3400000	.345959	.346480	.346902	.347205	.347376
.3500000	.356507	.357078	.357541	.357873	.358059
.3600000	.367088	.367713	.368218	.368581	.368786
.3700000	.377704	.378385	.378936	.379333	.379556
.3800000	.388355	.389096	.389696	.390128	.390371
.3900000	.399042	.399847	.400499	.400969	.401233

$\alpha =$ .049999

Θ	K VALUES				
	.794250555	.868696860	.928444378	.971111163	.994996249
.4000000	.409767	.410640	.411347	.411857	.412143
.4100000	.420531	.421475	.422241	.422793	.423104
.4200000	.431334	.432354	.433183	.433779	.434115
.4300000	.442179	.443279	.444173	.444817	.445180
.4400000	.453065	.454250	.455214	.455909	.456300
.4500000	.463995	.465270	.466307	.467055	.467477
.4600000	.474969	.476338	.477453	.478257	.478711
.4700000	.485989	.487458	.488654	.489518	.490006
.4800000	.497056	.498629	.499912	.500839	.501362
.4900000	.508171	.509854	.511228	.512221	.512782
.5000000	.519335	.521134	.522604	.523667	.524267
.5100000	.530549	.532471	.534041	.535178	.535820
.5200000	.541815	.543865	.545541	.546756	.547442
.5300000	.553135	.555319	.557107	.558403	.559136
.5400000	.564508	.566834	.568739	.570121	.570903
.5500000	.575937	.578411	.580440	.581912	.582746
.5600000	.587424	.590053	.592211	.593778	.594666
.5700000	.598968	.601760	.604054	.605722	.606666
.5800000	.610572	.613535	.615971	.617744	.618749
.5900000	.622238	.625379	.627965	.629848	.630916
.6000000	.633965	.637294	.640037	.642036	.643170
.6100000	.645757	.649282	.652189	.654309	.655513
.6200000	.657614	.661343	.664423	.666671	.667948
.6300000	.669537	.673481	.676741	.679124	.680478
.6400000	.681529	.685697	.689146	.691669	.693105
.6500000	.693591	.697993	.701640	.704311	.705831
.6600000	.705723	.710370	.714226	.717051	.718660
.6700000	.717929	.722832	.726904	.729892	.731595
.6800000	.730208	.735379	.739679	.742837	.744638
.6899999	.742564	.748013	.752552	.755888	.757793
.7000000	.754997	.760738	.765526	.769050	.771063
.7100000	.767509	.773554	.778603	.782323	.784450
.7200000	.780102	.786465	.791786	.795713	.797959
.7300000	.792778	.799472	.805079	.809221	.811593
.7400000	.805537	.812577	.818483	.822851	.825355
.7500000	.818382	.825783	.832001	.836607	.839250
.7600000	.831315	.839092	.845637	.850492	.853280
.7700000	.844337	.852506	.859394	.864510	.867451
.7800000	.857450	.866029	.873274	.878664	.881765
.7899999	.870655	.879661	.887281	.892958	.896228

$\alpha =$ .049999

θ	K VALUES				
	.794250555	.868696860	.928444378	.971111163	.994996249
.8000000	.883956	.893407	.901419	.907397	.910844
.8100000	.897352	.907268	.915690	.921983	.925616
.8200000	.910848	.921247	.930097	.936722	.940551
.8300000	.924443	.935347	.944646	.951618	.955653
.8400000	.938140	.949571	.959338	.966676	.970927
.8500000	.951942	.963920	.974178	.981899	.986378
.8600000	.965849	.978399	.989171	.997293	1.002012
.8700000	.979864	.993010	1.004319	1.012864	1.017834
.8799999	.993990	1.007756	1.019627	1.028615	1.033852
.8899999	1.008227	1.022641	1.035100	1.044553	1.050069
.9000000	1.022578	1.037666	1.050741	1.060684	1.066495
.9100000	1.037045	1.052836	1.066555	1.077012	1.083134
.9200000	1.051630	1.068153	1.082547	1.093545	1.099994
.9300000	1.066335	1.083621	1.098722	1.110287	1.117082
.9400000	1.081162	1.099243	1.115084	1.127247	1.134406
.9500000	1.096113	1.115023	1.131639	1.144431	1.151975
.9600000	1.111191	1.130964	1.148391	1.161845	1.169796
.9699999	1.126397	1.147070	1.165347	1.179498	1.187878
.9799999	1.141733	1.163343	1.182512	1.197396	1.206231
.9899999	1.157202	1.179789	1.199891	1.215549	1.224864
1.0000000	1.172805	1.196410	1.217491	1.233964	1.243788
1.0100000	1.188546	1.213211	1.235317	1.252649	1.263012
1.0200000	1.204424	1.230194	1.253376	1.271615	1.282549
1.0300000	1.220444	1.247365	1.271675	1.290870	1.302410
1.0400000	1.236607	1.264727	1.290219	1.310424	1.322607
1.0500000	1.252914	1.282284	1.309017	1.330289	1.343154
1.0600000	1.269369	1.300039	1.328075	1.350474	1.364064
1.0699999	1.285972	1.317998	1.347400	1.370991	1.385353
1.0799999	1.302726	1.336164	1.367000	1.391852	1.407035
1.0899999	1.319633	1.354542	1.386883	1.413069	1.429127
1.1000000	1.336694	1.373135	1.407057	1.434655	1.451647
1.1100000	1.353912	1.391948	1.427530	1.456625	1.474612
1.1200000	1.371288	1.410984	1.448310	1.478992	1.498043
1.1300000	1.388823	1.430249	1.469407	1.501771	1.521959
1.1400000	1.406519	1.449746	1.490829	1.524978	1.546384
1.1500000	1.424378	1.469479	1.512585	1.548631	1.571342
1.1600000	1.442401	1.489453	1.534685	1.572745	1.596856
1.1700000	1.460589	1.509671	1.557138	1.597340	1.622955
1.1800000	1.478944	1.530138	1.579954	1.622435	1.649667
1.1899999	1.497466	1.550857	1.603143	1.648050	1.677023

$\alpha =$ .049999

Θ	K VALUES				
	.794250555	.868696860	.928444378	.971111163	.994996249
1.2000000	1.516157	1.571833	1.626716	1.674206	1.705057
1.2100000	1.535016	1.593068	1.650682	1.700927	1.733804
1.2200000	1.554046	1.614567	1.675052	1.728234	1.763303
1.2300000	1.573245	1.636332	1.699837	1.756153	1.793596
1.2400000	1.592614	1.658366	1.725048	1.784711	1.824727
1.2500000	1.612154	1.680673	1.750694	1.813934	1.856747
1.2599999	1.631863	1.703255	1.776787	1.843852	1.889708
1.2699999	1.651742	1.726115	1.803337	1.874494	1.923668
1.2799999	1.671790	1.749253	1.830355	1.905891	1.958689
1.2899999	1.692006	1.772673	1.857851	1.938079	1.994842
1.3000000	1.712388	1.796374	1.885835	1.971090	2.032202
1.3100000	1.732935	1.820357	1.914315	2.004960	2.070850
1.3200000	1.753646	1.844623	1.943302	2.039728	2.110880
1.3300000	1.774517	1.869171	1.972803	2.075433	2.152391
1.3400000	1.795547	1.893999	2.002826	2.112114	2.195496
1.3500000	1.816733	1.919107	2.033377	2.149812	2.240319
1.3600000	1.838072	1.944491	2.064461	2.188570	2.286997
1.3700000	1.859560	1.970148	2.096083	2.228430	2.335684
1.3799999	1.881194	1.996075	2.128245	2.269434	2.386553
1.3899999	1.902969	2.022266	2.160947	2.311625	2.439797
1.4000000	1.924880	2.048715	2.194188	2.355044	2.495635
1.4100000	1.946923	2.075417	2.227965	2.399728	2.554310
1.4200000	1.969093	2.102362	2.262270	2.445713	2.616100
1.4300000	1.991383	2.129543	2.297096	2.493028	2.681318
1.4400000	2.013787	2.156950	2.332431	2.541699	2.750318
1.4500000	2.036300	2.184572	2.368260	2.591740	2.823499
1.4600000	2.058915	2.212398	2.404563	2.643157	2.901307
1.4700000	2.081624	2.240415	2.441321	2.695944	2.984243
1.4800000	2.104419	2.268609	2.478506	2.750077	3.072850
1.4900000	2.127294	2.296966	2.516091	2.805516	3.167713
1.5000000	2.150241	2.325471	2.554042	2.862203	3.269425
1.5100000	2.173251	2.354106	2.592323	2.920055	3.378542
1.5200000	2.196315	2.382856	2.630895	2.978967	3.495504
1.5300000	2.219425	2.411702	2.669716	3.038813	3.620502
1.5400000	2.242572	2.440627	2.708739	3.099442	3.753308
1.5500000	2.265748	2.469611	2.747918	3.160682	3.893082
1.5600000	2.288942	2.498635	2.787202	3.222346	4.038231
1.5699999	2.312146	2.527681	2.826543	3.284234	4.186426
1.5707963	2.313994	2.529994	2.829676	3.289166	4.198275
1.5707963	2.313992	2.529991	2.829673	3.289162	4.198269

$\alpha =$ .099999

Θ	K VALUES				
	.009966711	.039469502	.087332193	.151646642	.229848846
.0000000	.000000	.000000	.000000	.000000	.000000
.0100000	.010000	.010000	.010000	.010000	.010000
.0200000	.020000	.020000	.020000	.020000	.020000
.0300000	.030000	.030001	.030001	.030001	.030001
.0400000	.040002	.040002	.040003	.040003	.040004
.0500000	.050004	.050005	.050006	.050007	.050008
.0600000	.060007	.060008	.060010	.060012	.060015
.0700000	.070012	.070013	.070016	.070020	.070024
.0800000	.080017	.080020	.080024	.080030	.080036
.0900000	.090025	.090029	.090034	.090042	.090052
.1000000	.100034	.100039	.100047	.100058	.100071
.1100000	.110046	.110053	.110063	.110077	.110095
.1200000	.120060	.120068	.120082	.120101	.120123
.1300000	.130076	.130087	.130104	.130128	.130157
.1400000	.140095	.140109	.140131	.140160	.140196
.1500000	.150117	.150134	.150161	.150197	.150241
.1600000	.160142	.160162	.160195	.160239	.160292
.1700000	.170171	.170195	.170234	.170287	.170351
.1800000	.180203	.180231	.180278	.180340	.180416
.1900000	.190238	.190272	.190326	.190400	.190489
.2000000	.200278	.200317	.200381	.200466	.200571
.2100000	.210322	.210367	.210440	.210540	.210660
.2200000	.220370	.220422	.220506	.220620	.220759
.2300000	.230422	.230482	.230578	.230708	.230867
.2400000	.240479	.240547	.240657	.240805	.240985
.2500000	.250542	.250618	.250742	.250909	.251113
.2600000	.260609	.260694	.260834	.261022	.261251
.2700000	.270681	.270777	.270933	.271144	.271401
.2800000	.280759	.280866	.281040	.281275	.281562
.2900000	.290843	.290962	.291155	.291415	.291734
.3000000	.300932	.301064	.301277	.301566	.301919
.3100000	.311028	.311173	.311408	.311727	.312116
.3200000	.321130	.321289	.321548	.321898	.322326
.3300000	.331238	.331412	.331696	.332080	.332550
.3400000	.341353	.341543	.341854	.342273	.342787
.3500000	.351474	.351682	.352020	.352478	.353038
.3600000	.361602	.361828	.362196	.362694	.363304
.3700000	.371738	.371983	.372382	.372922	.373585
.3800000	.381881	.382146	.382578	.383163	.383881
.3900000	.392031	.392317	.392784	.393416	.394193

$\alpha =$ .099999

Θ	K VALUES				
	.009966711	.039469502	.087332193	.151646642	.229848846
.4000000	.402189	.402497	.403001	.403683	.404520
.4100000	.412354	.412686	.413228	.413962	.414864
.4200000	.422528	.422884	.423466	.424255	.425225
.4300000	.432709	.433092	.433716	.434562	.435602
.4400000	.442899	.443308	.443976	.444882	.445998
.4500000	.453097	.453535	.454249	.455217	.456411
.4600000	.463304	.463771	.464533	.465567	.466842
.4700000	.473520	.474017	.474829	.475932	.477291
.4800000	.483744	.484273	.485137	.486311	.487760
.4900000	.493977	.494539	.495457	.496706	.498247
.5000000	.504220	.504816	.505791	.507117	.508754
.5100000	.514471	.515103	.516137	.517543	.519281
.5200000	.524732	.525401	.526496	.527986	.529828
.5300000	.535003	.535710	.536868	.538444	.540395
.5400000	.545283	.546030	.547253	.548920	.550983
.5500000	.555573	.556361	.557652	.559412	.561592
.5600000	.565873	.566704	.568065	.569921	.572223
.5700000	.576183	.577057	.578491	.580448	.582875
.5800000	.586503	.587423	.588932	.590992	.593549
.5900000	.596833	.597800	.599386	.601553	.604245
.6000000	.607174	.608189	.609855	.612133	.614964
.6100000	.617525	.618590	.620339	.622730	.625705
.6200000	.627886	.629003	.630837	.633346	.636469
.6300000	.638259	.639428	.641350	.643980	.647257
.6400000	.648641	.649866	.651878	.654633	.658068
.6500000	.659035	.660315	.662420	.665305	.668903
.6600000	.669440	.670778	.672978	.675995	.679762
.6700000	.679855	.681253	.683551	.686705	.690645
.6800000	.690282	.691740	.694140	.697434	.701552
.6899999	.700720	.702240	.704744	.708182	.712484
.7000000	.711169	.712753	.715363	.718950	.723441
.7100000	.721629	.723279	.725999	.729738	.734423
.7200000	.732101	.733818	.736650	.740545	.745430
.7300000	.742584	.744370	.747316	.751372	.756462
.7400000	.753078	.754935	.757999	.762219	.767520
.7500000	.763584	.765514	.768698	.773087	.778604
.7600000	.774102	.776105	.779413	.783974	.789713
.7700000	.784631	.786710	.790144	.794882	.800849
.7800000	.795171	.797327	.800891	.805811	.812010
.7899999	.805723	.807959	.811654	.816759	.823198

$\alpha =$ .099999

θ	K VALUES				
	.009966711	.039469502	.087332193	.151646642	.229848846
.8000000	.816287	.818603	.822434	.827729	.834412
.8100000	.826863	.829261	.833229	.838719	.845653
.8200000	.837450	.839933	.844042	.849729	.856920
.8300000	.848049	.850617	.854870	.860761	.868214
.8400000	.858659	.861315	.865715	.871813	.879535
.8500000	.869282	.872027	.876576	.882885	.890882
.8600000	.879916	.882752	.887454	.893979	.902256
.8700000	.890561	.893490	.898348	.905093	.913657
.8799999	.901219	.904242	.909258	.916228	.925085
.8899999	.911888	.915007	.920185	.927384	.936540
.9000000	.922568	.925786	.931128	.938561	.948021
.9100000	.933261	.936577	.942088	.949758	.959530
.9200000	.943964	.947382	.953063	.960976	.971065
.9300000	.954680	.958201	.964055	.972214	.982628
.9400000	.965407	.969032	.975063	.983474	.994217
.9500000	.976145	.979877	.986087	.994753	1.005833
.9600000	.986895	.990734	.997127	1.006053	1.017475
.9699999	.997656	1.001605	1.008183	1.017374	1.029144
.9799999	1.008428	1.012489	1.019254	1.028714	1.040840
.9899999	1.019211	1.023385	1.030342	1.040075	1.052562
1.0000000	1.030006	1.034295	1.041445	1.051456	1.064311
1.0100000	1.040812	1.045217	1.052564	1.062857	1.076086
1.0200000	1.051629	1.056151	1.063698	1.074278	1.087886
1.0300000	1.062456	1.067098	1.074848	1.085718	1.099713
1.0400000	1.073295	1.078058	1.086013	1.097178	1.111565
1.0500000	1.084144	1.089029	1.097193	1.108658	1.123443
1.0600000	1.095003	1.100013	1.108388	1.120156	1.135346
1.0699999	1.105874	1.111009	1.119598	1.131674	1.147275
1.0799999	1.116754	1.122017	1.130822	1.143210	1.159228
1.0899999	1.127645	1.133037	1.142061	1.154765	1.171206
1.1000000	1.138546	1.144069	1.153314	1.166339	1.183209
1.1100000	1.149457	1.155111	1.164581	1.177931	1.195236
1.1200000	1.160378	1.166166	1.175863	1.189540	1.207286
1.1300000	1.171309	1.177231	1.187158	1.201168	1.219361
1.1400000	1.182249	1.188308	1.198467	1.212813	1.231458
1.1500000	1.193199	1.199395	1.209789	1.224476	1.243579
1.1600000	1.204158	1.210493	1.221124	1.236155	1.255723
1.1700000	1.215126	1.221602	1.232473	1.247851	1.267889
1.1800000	1.226103	1.232721	1.243834	1.259564	1.280076
1.1899999	1.237089	1.243850	1.255207	1.271293	1.292286

$\alpha =$ .099999

Θ	K VALUES				
	.009966711	.039469502	.087332193	.151646642	.229848846
1.2000000	1.248084	1.254989	1.266593	1.283038	1.304517
1.2100000	1.259088	1.266138	1.277991	1.294799	1.316769
1.2200000	1.270099	1.277297	1.289401	1.306575	1.329041
1.2300000	1.281119	1.288464	1.300822	1.318365	1.341334
1.2400000	1.292147	1.299641	1.312255	1.330171	1.353646
1.2500000	1.303182	1.310827	1.323699	1.341991	1.365977
1.2599999	1.314225	1.322022	1.335153	1.353825	1.378328
1.2699999	1.325276	1.333225	1.346618	1.365672	1.390696
1.2799999	1.336334	1.344437	1.358093	1.377533	1.403083
1.2899999	1.347398	1.355656	1.369579	1.389407	1.415487
1.3000000	1.358470	1.366884	1.381074	1.401293	1.427908
1.3100000	1.369548	1.378119	1.392578	1.413192	1.440345
1.3200000	1.380632	1.389361	1.404091	1.425102	1.452798
1.3300000	1.391723	1.400610	1.415613	1.437023	1.465267
1.3400000	1.402820	1.411866	1.427143	1.448956	1.477750
1.3500000	1.413922	1.423129	1.438682	1.460899	1.490248
1.3600000	1.425029	1.434398	1.450228	1.472853	1.502760
1.3700000	1.436142	1.445673	1.461782	1.484816	1.515284
1.3799999	1.447260	1.456954	1.473343	1.496788	1.527822
1.3899999	1.458383	1.468240	1.484911	1.508769	1.540371
1.4000000	1.469511	1.479532	1.496485	1.520759	1.552932
1.4100000	1.480642	1.490829	1.508065	1.532757	1.565504
1.4200000	1.491778	1.502130	1.519651	1.544762	1.578086
1.4300000	1.502918	1.513436	1.531243	1.556775	1.590678
1.4400000	1.514061	1.524745	1.542840	1.568794	1.603279
1.4500000	1.525207	1.536059	1.554441	1.580819	1.615888
1.4600000	1.536357	1.547376	1.566047	1.592851	1.628505
1.4700000	1.547509	1.558697	1.577657	1.604887	1.641130
1.4800000	1.558664	1.570020	1.589271	1.616928	1.653761
1.4900000	1.569822	1.581346	1.600888	1.628974	1.666397
1.5000000	1.580981	1.592675	1.612508	1.641024	1.679040
1.5100000	1.592143	1.604005	1.624131	1.653076	1.691686
1.5200000	1.603306	1.615338	1.635755	1.665132	1.704337
1.5300000	1.614470	1.626672	1.647382	1.677191	1.716991
1.5400000	1.625635	1.638007	1.659010	1.689251	1.729648
1.5500000	1.636801	1.649343	1.670640	1.701313	1.742307
1.5600000	1.647967	1.660680	1.682270	1.713375	1.754967
1.5699999	1.659134	1.672017	1.693900	1.725439	1.767628
1.5707963	1.660024	1.672920	1.694826	1.726399	1.768636
1.5707963	1.660023	1.672919	1.694825	1.726399	1.768636

$\alpha =$ .099999

Θ	K VALUES				
	.318821117	.415016431	.514599755	.613601043	.708073407
.0000000	.000000	.000000	.000000	.000000	.000000
.0100000	.010000	.010000	.010000	.010000	.010000
.0200000	.020000	.020000	.020000	.020001	.020001
.0300000	.030002	.030002	.030003	.030003	.030004
.0400000	.040005	.040006	.040007	.040008	.040009
.0500000	.050010	.050012	.050014	.050016	.050018
.0600000	.060018	.060022	.060025	.060029	.060032
.0700000	.070029	.070035	.070040	.070046	.070051
.0800000	.080044	.080052	.080061	.080069	.080077
.0900000	.090063	.090074	.090086	.090098	.090110
.1000000	.100086	.100102	.100119	.100135	.100151
.1100000	.110115	.110136	.110158	.110180	.110201
.1200000	.120149	.120177	.120205	.120234	.120261
.1300000	.130189	.130225	.130261	.130298	.130333
.1400000	.140237	.140281	.140326	.140372	.140416
.1500000	.150291	.150345	.150402	.150458	.150512
.1600000	.160353	.160419	.160488	.160556	.160621
.1700000	.170424	.170503	.170585	.170667	.170745
.1800000	.180503	.180597	.180695	.180792	.180885
.1900000	.190592	.190702	.190817	.190932	.191042
.2000000	.200690	.200819	.200953	.201087	.201216
.2100000	.210798	.210948	.211104	.211259	.211408
.2200000	.220918	.221090	.221269	.221448	.221619
.2300000	.231049	.231246	.231451	.231655	.231851
.2400000	.241191	.241415	.241648	.241881	.242105
.2500000	.251346	.251600	.251863	.252127	.252380
.2600000	.261514	.261799	.262096	.262394	.262679
.2700000	.271695	.272015	.272348	.272682	.273002
.2800000	.281890	.282247	.282619	.282992	.283350
.2900000	.292099	.292496	.292910	.293325	.293724
.3000000	.302323	.302763	.303222	.303683	.304126
.3100000	.312562	.313048	.313556	.314065	.314555
.3200000	.322817	.323353	.323912	.324473	.325014
.3300000	.333089	.333676	.334291	.334908	.335503
.3400000	.343377	.344020	.344694	.345370	.346022
.3500000	.353682	.354385	.355121	.355861	.356574
.3600000	.364005	.364771	.365573	.366381	.367160
.3700000	.374346	.375179	.376052	.376930	.377779
.3800000	.384706	.385610	.386557	.387511	.388434
.3900000	.395086	.396063	.397089	.398124	.399125

$\alpha =$ .099999

Θ	K VALUES				
	.318821117	.415016431	.514599755	.613601043	.708073407
.4000000	.405484	.406541	.407650	.408769	.409853
.4100000	.415903	.417042	.418240	.419449	.420620
.4200000	.426342	.427569	.428859	.430162	.431426
.4300000	.436803	.438121	.439508	.440911	.442273
.4400000	.447285	.448699	.450189	.451697	.453161
.4500000	.457789	.459304	.460901	.462519	.464092
.4600000	.468315	.469936	.471646	.473380	.475067
.4700000	.478864	.480595	.482424	.484280	.486087
.4800000	.489436	.491284	.493236	.495220	.497153
.4900000	.500032	.502000	.504083	.506200	.508266
.5000000	.510652	.512747	.514965	.517223	.519428
.5100000	.521296	.523523	.525884	.528288	.530639
.5200000	.531966	.534331	.536839	.539397	.541900
.5300000	.542661	.545169	.547832	.550550	.553213
.5400000	.553382	.556039	.558863	.561749	.564579
.5500000	.564129	.566941	.569933	.572994	.575999
.5600000	.574902	.577876	.581043	.584286	.587475
.5700000	.585703	.588844	.592193	.595627	.599007
.5800000	.596531	.599846	.603385	.607017	.610596
.5900000	.607386	.610883	.614619	.618457	.622245
.6000000	.618270	.621954	.625895	.629949	.633953
.6100000	.629183	.633061	.637214	.641492	.645723
.6200000	.640124	.644204	.648577	.653088	.657556
.6300000	.651094	.655383	.659985	.664738	.669452
.6400000	.662094	.666599	.671439	.676443	.681413
.6500000	.673124	.677852	.682938	.688204	.693441
.6600000	.684185	.689143	.694484	.700022	.705536
.6700000	.695275	.700473	.706078	.711897	.717700
.6800000	.706397	.711841	.717719	.723831	.729935
.6899999	.717550	.723248	.729410	.735825	.742241
.7000000	.728734	.734696	.741150	.747879	.754619
.7100000	.739951	.746183	.752939	.759994	.767072
.7200000	.751199	.757711	.764780	.772172	.779600
.7300000	.762480	.769280	.776671	.784413	.792205
.7400000	.773793	.780890	.788615	.796718	.804888
.7500000	.785139	.792542	.800611	.809089	.817651
.7600000	.796518	.804236	.812661	.821525	.830494
.7700000	.807931	.815972	.824764	.834029	.843419
.7800000	.819377	.827752	.836921	.846600	.856428
.7899999	.830856	.839574	.849133	.859240	.869522

$\alpha =$ .099999

θ	K VALUES				
	.318821117	.415016431	.514599755	.613601043	.708073407
.8000000	.842370	.851441	.861401	.871950	.882702
.8100000	.853918	.863351	.873724	.884731	.895969
.8200000	.865500	.875305	.886104	.897583	.909326
.8300000	.877117	.887304	.898541	.910507	.922772
.8400000	.888768	.899348	.911036	.923504	.936310
.8500000	.900454	.911436	.923588	.936575	.949942
.8600000	.912175	.923570	.936200	.949721	.963667
.8700000	.923931	.935749	.948869	.962943	.977489
.8799999	.935722	.947974	.961599	.976241	.991407
.8899999	.947548	.960245	.974388	.989616	1.005424
.9000000	.959409	.972563	.987237	1.003069	1.019541
.9100000	.971305	.984926	1.000147	1.016601	1.033758
.9200000	.983237	.997336	1.013118	1.030212	1.048078
.9300000	.995204	1.009792	1.026149	1.043903	1.062502
.9400000	1.007206	1.022295	1.039243	1.057675	1.077031
.9500000	1.019244	1.034845	1.052398	1.071528	1.091666
.9600000	1.031317	1.047441	1.065615	1.085463	1.106408
.9699999	1.043425	1.060084	1.078894	1.099481	1.121259
.9799999	1.055568	1.072774	1.092236	1.113582	1.136220
.9899999	1.067746	1.085511	1.105641	1.127767	1.151292
1.0000000	1.079960	1.098295	1.119108	1.142036	1.166476
1.0100000	1.092208	1.111125	1.132639	1.156389	1.181774
1.0200000	1.104491	1.124002	1.146232	1.170827	1.197186
1.0300000	1.116808	1.136926	1.159888	1.185351	1.212713
1.0400000	1.129160	1.149896	1.173607	1.199960	1.228357
1.0500000	1.141546	1.162913	1.187389	1.214656	1.244118
1.0600000	1.153967	1.175975	1.201235	1.229438	1.259997
1.0699999	1.166421	1.189084	1.215143	1.244306	1.275996
1.0799999	1.178908	1.202238	1.229114	1.259260	1.292114
1.0899999	1.191429	1.215438	1.243147	1.274302	1.308353
1.1000000	1.203983	1.228683	1.257243	1.289430	1.324713
1.1100000	1.216570	1.241972	1.271401	1.304645	1.341195
1.1200000	1.229189	1.255306	1.285620	1.319947	1.357799
1.1300000	1.241840	1.268685	1.299901	1.335335	1.374526
1.1400000	1.254523	1.282107	1.314244	1.350810	1.391376
1.1500000	1.267237	1.295572	1.328647	1.366370	1.408349
1.1600000	1.279982	1.309081	1.343110	1.382016	1.425446
1.1700000	1.292758	1.322631	1.357632	1.397748	1.442667
1.1800000	1.305563	1.336224	1.372214	1.413564	1.460011
1.1899999	1.318399	1.349858	1.386855	1.429465	1.477478

$\alpha =$ .099999

Θ	K VALUES				
	.318821117	.415016431	.514599755	.613601043	.708073407
1.2000000	1.331264	1.363532	1.401553	1.445449	1.495069
1.2100000	1.344157	1.377247	1.416309	1.461517	1.512782
1.2200000	1.357079	1.391001	1.431121	1.477666	1.530618
1.2300000	1.370028	1.404794	1.445989	1.493897	1.548575
1.2400000	1.383004	1.418626	1.460911	1.510208	1.566653
1.2500000	1.396007	1.432494	1.475887	1.526599	1.584850
1.2599999	1.409036	1.446400	1.490916	1.543068	1.603167
1.2699999	1.422090	1.460341	1.505997	1.559613	1.621601
1.2799999	1.435169	1.474317	1.521129	1.576235	1.640151
1.2899999	1.448273	1.488328	1.536311	1.592931	1.658815
1.3000000	1.461399	1.502372	1.551542	1.609700	1.677593
1.3100000	1.474549	1.516448	1.566819	1.626540	1.696482
1.3200000	1.487720	1.530556	1.582143	1.643449	1.715479
1.3300000	1.500913	1.544694	1.597512	1.660427	1.734584
1.3400000	1.514127	1.558862	1.612924	1.677471	1.753792
1.3500000	1.527361	1.573059	1.628379	1.694579	1.773103
1.3600000	1.540613	1.587283	1.643874	1.711749	1.792512
1.3700000	1.553885	1.601534	1.659408	1.728979	1.812018
1.3799999	1.567174	1.615810	1.674980	1.746266	1.831616
1.3899999	1.580479	1.630110	1.690588	1.763610	1.851304
1.4000000	1.593801	1.644434	1.706230	1.781007	1.871079
1.4100000	1.607139	1.658779	1.721905	1.798454	1.890936
1.4200000	1.620490	1.673146	1.737611	1.815949	1.910872
1.4300000	1.633855	1.687532	1.753347	1.833491	1.930882
1.4400000	1.647233	1.701936	1.769110	1.851075	1.950963
1.4500000	1.660623	1.716358	1.784899	1.868699	1.971111
1.4600000	1.674024	1.730795	1.800712	1.886361	1.991320
1.4700000	1.687435	1.745247	1.816547	1.904058	2.011587
1.4800000	1.700855	1.759713	1.832402	1.921786	2.031906
1.4900000	1.714283	1.774191	1.848275	1.939543	2.052273
1.5000000	1.727719	1.788680	1.864165	1.957325	2.072683
1.5100000	1.741162	1.803178	1.880069	1.975130	2.093131
1.5200000	1.754610	1.817684	1.895985	1.992955	2.113611
1.5300000	1.768062	1.832197	1.911912	2.010796	2.134119
1.5400000	1.781519	1.846716	1.927847	2.028650	2.154648
1.5500000	1.794978	1.861238	1.943788	2.046513	2.175195
1.5600000	1.808440	1.875764	1.959733	2.064384	2.195752
1.5699999	1.821902	1.890291	1.975681	2.082258	2.216316
1.5707963	1.822974	1.891448	1.976951	2.083681	2.217953
1.5707963	1.822974	1.891447	1.976950	2.083681	2.217953

$\alpha =$ .099999

Θ	K VALUES				
	.794250555	.868696860	.928444378	.971111163	.994996249
.0000000	.000000	.000000	.000000	.000000	.000000
.0100000	.010000	.010000	.010000	.010000	.010000
.0200000	.020001	.020001	.020001	.020001	.020001
.0300000	.030004	.030004	.030005	.030005	.030005
.0400000	.040010	.040011	.040012	.040012	.040012
.0500000	.050020	.050022	.050023	.050024	.050024
.0600000	.060035	.060038	.060040	.060042	.060043
.0700000	.070056	.070061	.070064	.070067	.070068
.0800000	.080084	.080091	.080096	.080100	.080102
.0900000	.090120	.090130	.090137	.090142	.090145
.1000000	.100165	.100178	.100188	.100195	.100199
.1100000	.110220	.110237	.110250	.110260	.110265
.1200000	.120286	.120308	.120325	.120338	.120345
.1300000	.130364	.130392	.130414	.130430	.130439
.1400000	.140456	.140490	.140518	.140537	.140549
.1500000	.150561	.150603	.150637	.150662	.150675
.1600000	.160681	.160732	.160774	.160804	.160820
.1700000	.170817	.170879	.170929	.170965	.170985
.1800000	.180971	.181044	.181104	.181146	.181170
.1900000	.191142	.191229	.191299	.191349	.191377
.2000000	.201333	.201435	.201516	.201575	.201608
.2100000	.211544	.211662	.211757	.211825	.211863
.2200000	.221776	.221913	.222022	.222100	.222144
.2300000	.232031	.232187	.232313	.232403	.232453
.2400000	.242310	.242487	.242630	.242733	.242790
.2500000	.252612	.252814	.252976	.253092	.253158
.2600000	.262941	.263168	.263351	.263483	.263556
.2700000	.273296	.273551	.273757	.273905	.273988
.2800000	.283679	.283965	.284195	.284360	.284453
.2900000	.294091	.294409	.294667	.294851	.294954
.3000000	.304533	.304887	.305173	.305377	.305493
.3100000	.315006	.315398	.315715	.315942	.316069
.3200000	.325511	.325944	.326294	.326545	.326686
.3300000	.336050	.336527	.336912	.337189	.337344
.3400000	.346623	.347147	.347570	.347874	.348045
.3500000	.357232	.357806	.358270	.358604	.358791
.3600000	.367878	.368505	.369013	.369378	.369583
.3700000	.378563	.379246	.379800	.380198	.380422
.3800000	.389286	.390030	.390633	.391067	.391311
.3900000	.400050	.400858	.401514	.401985	.402251

$\alpha =$ .099999

Θ	K VALUES				
	.794250555	.868696860	.928444378	.971111163	.994996249
.4000000	.410855	.411732	.412443	.412955	.413243
.4100000	.421704	.422653	.423423	.423978	.424290
.4200000	.432597	.433622	.434455	.435055	.435393
.4300000	.443535	.444642	.445540	.446188	.446553
.4400000	.454520	.455712	.456681	.457380	.457774
.4500000	.465553	.466835	.467878	.468631	.469056
.4600000	.476635	.478013	.479134	.479944	.480401
.4700000	.487768	.489246	.490451	.491320	.491811
.4800000	.498953	.500537	.501829	.502762	.503289
.4900000	.510191	.511887	.513270	.514271	.514835
.5000000	.521484	.523297	.524777	.525849	.526454
.5100000	.532833	.534770	.536352	.537498	.538145
.5200000	.544240	.546306	.547995	.549220	.549912
.5300000	.555705	.557907	.559710	.561017	.561756
.5400000	.567230	.569576	.571497	.572891	.573680
.5500000	.578817	.581313	.583359	.584845	.585686
.5600000	.590467	.593121	.595298	.596881	.597777
.5700000	.602182	.605001	.607317	.609000	.609954
.5800000	.613963	.616955	.619416	.621206	.622221
.5900000	.625812	.628986	.631598	.633500	.634579
.6000000	.637730	.641094	.643865	.645886	.647032
.6100000	.649719	.653282	.656220	.658364	.659582
.6200000	.661779	.665551	.668665	.670939	.672231
.6300000	.673914	.677904	.681202	.683612	.684982
.6400000	.686125	.690343	.693833	.696387	.697839
.6500000	.698412	.702869	.706562	.709265	.710804
.6600000	.710779	.715485	.719389	.722251	.723881
.6700000	.723226	.728193	.732319	.735346	.737071
.6800000	.735755	.740995	.745353	.748554	.750380
.6899999	.748368	.753893	.758494	.761878	.763809
.7000000	.761067	.766890	.771746	.775320	.777362
.7100000	.773854	.779987	.785109	.788885	.791043
.7200000	.786730	.793187	.798589	.802575	.804856
.7300000	.799696	.806493	.812187	.816394	.818803
.7400000	.812756	.819907	.825907	.830345	.832889
.7500000	.825911	.833431	.839751	.844433	.847118
.7600000	.839162	.847068	.853723	.858660	.861495
.7700000	.852512	.860820	.867826	.873030	.876022
.7800000	.865962	.874691	.882064	.887549	.890705
.7899999	.879515	.888682	.896439	.902219	.905548

$\alpha =$ .099999

Θ	K VALUES				
	.794250555	.868696860	.928444378	.971111163	.994996249
.8000000	.893173	.902797	.910956	.917045	.920556
.8100000	.906937	.917038	.925618	.932031	.935734
.8200000	.920809	.931408	.940428	.947182	.951086
.8300000	.934792	.945910	.955392	.962503	.966618
.8400000	.948888	.960547	.970511	.977998	.982336
.8500000	.963098	.975322	.985791	.993673	.998245
.8600000	.977425	.990238	1.001236	1.009532	1.014351
.8700000	.991872	1.005298	1.016850	1.025581	1.030660
.8799999	1.006439	1.020506	1.032638	1.041825	1.047179
.8899999	1.021130	1.035864	1.048603	1.058271	1.063913
.9000000	1.035946	1.051376	1.064751	1.074924	1.080871
.9100000	1.050890	1.067046	1.081087	1.091791	1.098058
.9200000	1.065963	1.082877	1.097615	1.108878	1.115483
.9300000	1.081169	1.098871	1.114341	1.126191	1.133154
.9400000	1.096510	1.115034	1.131269	1.143738	1.151078
.9500000	1.111986	1.131369	1.148406	1.161525	1.169264
.9600000	1.127602	1.147879	1.165756	1.179561	1.187721
.9699999	1.143359	1.164568	1.183326	1.197854	1.206459
.9799999	1.159259	1.181440	1.201122	1.216410	1.225486
.9899999	1.175305	1.198499	1.219150	1.235240	1.244815
1.0000000	1.191499	1.215750	1.237415	1.254352	1.264454
1.0100000	1.207843	1.233195	1.255926	1.273754	1.284416
1.0200000	1.224340	1.250839	1.274687	1.293457	1.304713
1.0300000	1.240991	1.268686	1.293707	1.313471	1.325356
1.0400000	1.257799	1.286741	1.312992	1.333806	1.346360
1.0500000	1.274766	1.305008	1.332549	1.354474	1.367737
1.0600000	1.291894	1.323490	1.352387	1.375485	1.389504
1.0699999	1.309185	1.342193	1.372513	1.396852	1.411674
1.0799999	1.326641	1.361121	1.392935	1.418587	1.434265
1.0899999	1.344265	1.380278	1.413661	1.440704	1.457295
1.1000000	1.362059	1.399669	1.434701	1.463217	1.480780
1.1100000	1.380023	1.419298	1.456062	1.486140	1.504742
1.1200000	1.398160	1.439169	1.477753	1.509487	1.529200
1.1300000	1.416473	1.459287	1.499785	1.533276	1.554176
1.1400000	1.434961	1.479657	1.522166	1.557522	1.579695
1.1500000	1.453628	1.500283	1.544906	1.582244	1.605781
1.1600000	1.472474	1.521169	1.568015	1.607460	1.632460
1.1700000	1.491500	1.542319	1.591503	1.633189	1.659762
1.1800000	1.510709	1.563738	1.615381	1.659451	1.687717
1.1899999	1.530101	1.585430	1.639659	1.686269	1.716357

$\alpha =$ .099999

θ	K VALUES				
	.794250555	.868696860	.928444378	.971111163	.994996249
1.2000000	1.549677	1.607399	1.664348	1.713664	1.745719
1.2100000	1.569437	1.629649	1.689459	1.741661	1.775839
1.2200000	1.589383	1.652183	1.715003	1.770283	1.806759
1.2300000	1.609515	1.675004	1.740991	1.799558	1.838523
1.2400000	1.629832	1.698117	1.767435	1.829514	1.871178
1.2500000	1.650335	1.721524	1.794346	1.860177	1.904777
1.2599999	1.671023	1.745228	1.821735	1.891581	1.939375
1.2699999	1.691896	1.769230	1.849613	1.923755	1.975033
1.2799999	1.712954	1.793534	1.877992	1.956734	2.011818
1.2899999	1.734194	1.818141	1.906881	1.990553	2.049803
1.3000000	1.755616	1.843051	1.936293	2.025248	2.089069
1.3100000	1.777218	1.868265	1.966235	2.060858	2.129701
1.3200000	1.798998	1.893784	1.996718	2.097421	2.171798
1.3300000	1.820953	1.919606	2.027751	2.134979	2.215465
1.3400000	1.843081	1.945731	2.059341	2.173575	2.260820
1.3500000	1.865379	1.972156	2.091496	2.213251	2.307995
1.3600000	1.887843	1.998879	2.124219	2.254053	2.357134
1.3700000	1.910470	2.025896	2.157517	2.296026	2.408402
1.3799999	1.933255	2.053203	2.191390	2.339213	2.461979
1.3899999	1.956194	2.080794	2.225841	2.383659	2.518069
1.4000000	1.979281	2.108663	2.260866	2.429409	2.576904
1.4100000	2.002512	2.136803	2.296462	2.476500	2.638740
1.4200000	2.025880	2.165206	2.332623	2.524971	2.703872
1.4300000	2.049380	2.193861	2.369339	2.574854	2.772628
1.4400000	2.073004	2.222760	2.406597	2.626173	2.845384
1.4500000	2.096746	2.251890	2.444381	2.678946	2.922559
1.4600000	2.120598	2.281239	2.482672	2.733178	3.004626
1.4700000	2.144553	2.310793	2.521446	2.788860	3.092112
1.4800000	2.168602	2.340537	2.560676	2.845970	3.185592
1.4900000	2.192737	2.370457	2.600332	2.904464	3.285682
1.5000000	2.216951	2.400535	2.640378	2.964280	3.393008
1.5100000	2.241232	2.430754	2.680776	3.025331	3.508159
1.5200000	2.265574	2.461095	2.721483	3.087505	3.631596
1.5300000	2.289965	2.491540	2.762455	3.150668	3.763522
1.5400000	2.314396	2.522069	2.803643	3.214660	3.903696
1.5500000	2.338858	2.552662	2.844997	3.279300	4.051229
1.5600000	2.363341	2.583299	2.886464	3.344389	4.204440
1.5699999	2.387834	2.613958	2.927989	3.409715	4.360867
1.5707963	2.389785	2.616400	2.931297	3.414920	4.373375
1.5707963	2.389784	2.616399	2.931296	3.414919	4.373373

$\alpha =$ .149999

θ	K VALUES				
	.009966711	.039469502	.087332193	.151646642	.229848846
.0000000	.000000	.000000	.000000	.000000	.000000
.0100000	.010000	.010000	.010000	.010000	.010000
.0200000	.020000	.020000	.020000	.020000	.020000
.0300000	.030001	.030001	.030001	.030002	.030002
.0400000	.040003	.040003	.040004	.040004	.040005
.0500000	.050006	.050007	.050008	.050009	.050011
.0600000	.060011	.060012	.060013	.060016	.060019
.0700000	.070017	.070019	.070022	.070025	.070030
.0800000	.080026	.080028	.080033	.080038	.080045
.0900000	.090037	.090041	.090047	.090054	.090064
.1000000	.100051	.100056	.100064	.100075	.100088
.1100000	.110068	.110075	.110085	.110100	.110117
.1200000	.120089	.120097	.120111	.120129	.120152
.1300000	.130113	.130124	.130141	.130165	.130193
.1400000	.140141	.140154	.140176	.140206	.140242
.1500000	.150173	.150190	.150217	.150253	.150297
.1600000	.160211	.160231	.160263	.160307	.160361
.1700000	.170253	.170277	.170316	.170368	.170433
.1800000	.180300	.180328	.180375	.180437	.180513
.1900000	.190352	.190386	.190441	.190514	.190604
.2000000	.200411	.200450	.200514	.200600	.200704
.2100000	.210476	.210521	.210595	.210694	.210815
.2200000	.220547	.220599	.220683	.220798	.220937
.2300000	.230624	.230684	.230781	.230911	.231070
.2400000	.240709	.240777	.240887	.241035	.241216
.2500000	.250801	.250878	.251002	.251169	.251374
.2600000	.260901	.260987	.261126	.261315	.261545
.2700000	.271008	.271104	.271261	.271472	.271729
.2800000	.281124	.281231	.281405	.281640	.281928
.2900000	.291248	.291367	.291560	.291822	.292141
.3000000	.301380	.301512	.301726	.302016	.302369
.3100000	.311522	.311667	.311904	.312223	.312613
.3200000	.321673	.321833	.322093	.322444	.322873
.3300000	.331834	.332008	.332293	.332678	.333150
.3400000	.342004	.342195	.342507	.342927	.343443
.3500000	.352184	.352393	.352732	.353191	.353754
.3600000	.362375	.362602	.362971	.363471	.364083
.3700000	.372576	.372822	.373223	.373765	.374431
.3800000	.382788	.383055	.383489	.384076	.384797
.3900000	.393012	.393299	.393769	.394403	.395183

$\alpha =$ •149999

Θ	K VALUES				
	•009966711	•039469502	•087332193	•151646642	•229848846
•4000000	•403246	•403557	•404062	•404747	•405589
•4100000	•413493	•413827	•414371	•415109	•416015
•4200000	•423751	•424110	•424694	•425487	•426462
•4300000	•434022	•434406	•435033	•435884	•436930
•4400000	•444304	•444716	•445387	•446299	•447420
•4500000	•454600	•455039	•455758	•456732	•457932
•4600000	•464908	•465377	•466144	•467185	•468467
•4700000	•475229	•475729	•476547	•477657	•479025
•4800000	•485564	•486096	•486966	•488148	•489607
•4900000	•495912	•496478	•497403	•498660	•500212
•5000000	•506274	•506875	•507857	•509192	•510842
•5100000	•516650	•517287	•518328	•519745	•521496
•5200000	•527041	•527714	•528818	•530319	•532176
•5300000	•537445	•538158	•539325	•540914	•542881
•5400000	•547864	•548617	•549851	•551532	•553612
•5500000	•558298	•559093	•560395	•562171	•564370
•5600000	•568748	•569586	•570959	•572832	•575154
•5700000	•579212	•580095	•581542	•583516	•585966
•5800000	•589692	•590620	•592144	•594223	•596805
•5900000	•600187	•601163	•602765	•604954	•607672
•6000000	•610698	•611724	•613407	•615708	•618568
•6100000	•621225	•622301	•624069	•626485	•629492
•6200000	•631768	•632897	•634751	•637287	•640444
•6300000	•642327	•643510	•645453	•648113	•651427
•6400000	•652903	•654141	•656176	•658964	•662439
•6500000	•663495	•664791	•666921	•669839	•673480
•6600000	•674105	•675459	•677686	•680740	•684553
•6700000	•684730	•686145	•688473	•691666	•695655
•6800000	•695373	•696850	•699281	•702617	•706789
•6899999	•706033	•707574	•710110	•713594	•717954
•7000000	•716711	•718317	•720962	•724598	•729150
•7100000	•727406	•729079	•731836	•735627	•740378
•7200000	•738118	•739860	•742731	•746683	•751638
•7300000	•748847	•750660	•753649	•757765	•762930
•7400000	•759595	•761480	•764589	•768873	•774254
•7500000	•770360	•772319	•775552	•780009	•785612
•7600000	•781143	•783178	•786538	•791172	•797002
•7700000	•791944	•794057	•797546	•802361	•808425
•7800000	•802763	•804955	•808577	•813579	•819881
•7899999	•813600	•815873	•819631	•824823	•831371

$\alpha =$ .149999

θ	K VALUES				
	.009966711	.039469502	.087332193	.151646642	.229848846
.8000000	.824456	.826812	.830708	.836095	.842895
.8100000	.835329	.837770	.841808	.847395	.854452
.8200000	.846221	.848748	.852931	.858722	.866044
.8300000	.857131	.859747	.864078	.870077	.877669
.8400000	.868059	.870765	.875247	.881460	.889329
.8500000	.879006	.881804	.886440	.892871	.901022
.8600000	.889971	.892862	.897656	.904310	.912751
.8700000	.900954	.903941	.908896	.915776	.924513
.8799999	.911956	.915041	.920159	.927271	.936310
.8899999	.922976	.926160	.931445	.938794	.948142
.9000000	.934014	.937299	.942755	.950345	.960008
.9100000	.945071	.948459	.954088	.961924	.971909
.9200000	.956146	.959639	.965444	.973531	.983845
.9300000	.967239	.970839	.976823	.985166	.995815
.9400000	.978351	.982058	.988226	.996829	1.007819
.9500000	.989480	.993298	.999651	1.008519	1.019858
.9600000	1.000628	1.004558	1.011100	1.020238	1.031932
.9699999	1.011794	1.015837	1.022572	1.031984	1.044040
.9799999	1.022977	1.027136	1.034066	1.043757	1.056182
.9899999	1.034179	1.038455	1.045583	1.055559	1.068359
1.0000000	1.045398	1.049793	1.057123	1.067387	1.080569
1.0100000	1.056635	1.061151	1.068686	1.079243	1.092814
1.0200000	1.067889	1.072528	1.080271	1.091126	1.105092
1.0300000	1.079161	1.083924	1.091878	1.103035	1.117403
1.0400000	1.090450	1.095339	1.103507	1.114972	1.129749
1.0500000	1.101756	1.106773	1.115158	1.126935	1.142127
1.0600000	1.113079	1.118226	1.126830	1.138924	1.154538
1.0699999	1.124419	1.129697	1.138525	1.150940	1.166982
1.0799999	1.135776	1.141187	1.150240	1.162981	1.179459
1.0899999	1.147149	1.152695	1.161977	1.175048	1.191967
1.1000000	1.158539	1.164221	1.173735	1.187140	1.204508
1.1100000	1.169945	1.175765	1.185513	1.199258	1.217080
1.1200000	1.181366	1.187326	1.197312	1.211400	1.229683
1.1300000	1.192804	1.198904	1.209130	1.223566	1.242318
1.1400000	1.204257	1.210500	1.220969	1.235757	1.254982
1.1500000	1.215725	1.222112	1.232828	1.247972	1.267677
1.1600000	1.227209	1.233741	1.244705	1.260210	1.280402
1.1700000	1.238707	1.245387	1.256602	1.272472	1.293155
1.1800000	1.250220	1.257049	1.268518	1.284756	1.305938
1.1899999	1.261747	1.268726	1.280452	1.297063	1.318749

$\alpha =$ .149999

Θ	K VALUES				
	.009966711	.039469502	.087332193	.151646642	.229848846
1.2000000	1.273289	1.280419	1.292404	1.309392	1.331588
1.2100000	1.284844	1.292127	1.304373	1.321743	1.344455
1.2200000	1.296413	1.303850	1.316360	1.334114	1.357348
1.2300000	1.307995	1.315588	1.328365	1.346507	1.370268
1.2400000	1.319590	1.327340	1.340386	1.358920	1.383214
1.2500000	1.331198	1.339106	1.352423	1.371353	1.396185
1.2599999	1.342818	1.350886	1.364476	1.383805	1.409180
1.2699999	1.354450	1.362679	1.376544	1.396276	1.422200
1.2799999	1.366095	1.374485	1.388628	1.408766	1.435243
1.2899999	1.377750	1.386304	1.400727	1.421274	1.448310
1.3000000	1.389417	1.398135	1.412840	1.433799	1.461398
1.3100000	1.401094	1.409978	1.424966	1.446341	1.474509
1.3200000	1.412782	1.421832	1.437106	1.458900	1.487640
1.3300000	1.424480	1.433697	1.449259	1.471475	1.500791
1.3400000	1.436188	1.445573	1.461425	1.484064	1.513962
1.3500000	1.447905	1.457460	1.473602	1.496669	1.527152
1.3600000	1.459631	1.469356	1.485791	1.509288	1.540360
1.3700000	1.471366	1.481262	1.497992	1.521920	1.553586
1.3799999	1.483109	1.493177	1.510203	1.534566	1.566828
1.3899999	1.494860	1.505101	1.522424	1.547224	1.580086
1.4000000	1.506619	1.517033	1.534654	1.559894	1.593360
1.4100000	1.518384	1.528973	1.546894	1.572575	1.606648
1.4200000	1.530157	1.540920	1.559143	1.585266	1.619949
1.4300000	1.541935	1.552875	1.571399	1.597968	1.633263
1.4400000	1.553720	1.564835	1.583664	1.610679	1.646589
1.4500000	1.565510	1.576802	1.595935	1.623399	1.659927
1.4600000	1.577305	1.588775	1.608213	1.636127	1.673274
1.4700000	1.589105	1.600752	1.620497	1.648862	1.686632
1.4800000	1.600909	1.612735	1.632786	1.661604	1.699998
1.4900000	1.612717	1.624721	1.645081	1.674352	1.713371
1.5000000	1.624529	1.636712	1.657380	1.687105	1.726752
1.5100000	1.636343	1.648706	1.669683	1.699864	1.740139
1.5200000	1.648160	1.660702	1.681989	1.712626	1.753531
1.5300000	1.659979	1.672701	1.694298	1.725392	1.766928
1.5400000	1.671800	1.684702	1.706609	1.738161	1.780328
1.5500000	1.683623	1.696704	1.718922	1.750931	1.793731
1.5600000	1.695446	1.708708	1.731236	1.763703	1.807136
1.5699999	1.707270	1.720712	1.743550	1.776476	1.820541
1.5707963	1.708211	1.721668	1.744531	1.777493	1.821609
1.5707963	1.708210	1.721667	1.744530	1.777492	1.821608

$\alpha =$ .149999

Θ	K VALUES				
	.318821117	.415016431	.514599755	.613601043	.708073407
.0000000	.000000	.000000	.000000	.000000	.000000
.0100000	.010000	.010000	.010000	.010000	.010000
.0200000	.020000	.020000	.020001	.020001	.020001
.0300000	.030002	.030003	.030003	.030004	.030004
.0400000	.040006	.040007	.040008	.040009	.040010
.0500000	.050012	.050014	.050016	.050019	.050021
.0600000	.060022	.060025	.060029	.060032	.060036
.0700000	.070035	.070040	.070046	.070052	.070057
.0800000	.080052	.080061	.080069	.080078	.080086
.0900000	.090075	.090086	.090099	.090111	.090122
.1000000	.100103	.100119	.100135	.100152	.100168
.1100000	.110137	.110158	.110180	.110202	.110223
.1200000	.120178	.120205	.120234	.120263	.120290
.1300000	.130226	.130261	.130298	.130334	.130369
.1400000	.140282	.140327	.140372	.140418	.140462
.1500000	.150347	.150402	.150458	.150514	.150568
.1600000	.160422	.160488	.160556	.160624	.160690
.1700000	.170506	.170585	.170667	.170749	.170828
.1800000	.180600	.180694	.180792	.180890	.180983
.1900000	.190706	.190817	.190932	.191047	.191157
.2000000	.200823	.200953	.201087	.201221	.201350
.2100000	.210953	.211103	.211259	.211414	.211563
.2200000	.221096	.221268	.221448	.221627	.221798
.2300000	.231252	.231449	.231654	.231859	.232056
.2400000	.241422	.241647	.241880	.242113	.242337
.2500000	.251607	.251861	.252125	.252390	.252643
.2600000	.261808	.262094	.262391	.262689	.262975
.2700000	.272024	.272345	.272679	.273013	.273334
.2800000	.282257	.282615	.282988	.283362	.283721
.2900000	.292507	.292905	.293320	.293736	.294136
.3000000	.302775	.303216	.303676	.304138	.304582
.3100000	.313061	.313548	.314057	.314568	.315059
.3200000	.323366	.323903	.324464	.325027	.325569
.3300000	.333690	.334280	.334896	.335515	.336112
.3400000	.344035	.344681	.345356	.346035	.346690
.3500000	.354400	.355106	.355844	.356587	.357303
.3600000	.364787	.365556	.366361	.367171	.367953
.3700000	.375195	.376031	.376908	.377790	.378642
.3800000	.385626	.386533	.387485	.388443	.389370
.3900000	.396080	.397062	.398093	.399132	.400138

$\alpha =$ .149999

Θ	K VALUES				
	.318821117	.415016431	.514599755	.613601043	.708073407
.4000000	.406557	.407619	.408734	.409858	.410947
.4100000	.417059	.418204	.419407	.420622	.421799
.4200000	.427585	.428818	.430115	.431425	.432696
.4300000	.438137	.439462	.440857	.442268	.443637
.4400000	.448715	.450137	.451635	.453152	.454625
.4500000	.459319	.460843	.462450	.464078	.465660
.4600000	.469949	.471580	.473301	.475046	.476744
.4700000	.480608	.482351	.484191	.486059	.487878
.4800000	.491294	.493154	.495120	.497117	.499064
.4900000	.502009	.503992	.506089	.508221	.510302
.5000000	.512753	.514864	.517098	.519372	.521593
.5100000	.523527	.525771	.528149	.530572	.532940
.5200000	.534331	.536714	.539242	.541820	.544343
.5300000	.545165	.547694	.550378	.553119	.555804
.5400000	.556031	.558711	.561559	.564469	.567324
.5500000	.566928	.569765	.572784	.575872	.578904
.5600000	.577858	.580859	.584055	.587328	.590546
.5700000	.588820	.591991	.595372	.598839	.602250
.5800000	.599816	.603164	.606737	.610405	.614019
.5900000	.610845	.614377	.618150	.622028	.625854
.6000000	.621908	.625630	.629612	.633709	.637755
.6100000	.633006	.636926	.641124	.645448	.649725
.6200000	.644139	.648264	.652686	.657248	.661765
.6300000	.655308	.659645	.664300	.669108	.673876
.6400000	.666512	.671069	.675966	.681030	.686060
.6500000	.677753	.682537	.687685	.693016	.698317
.6600000	.689030	.694050	.699458	.705066	.710650
.6700000	.700345	.705608	.711286	.717181	.723060
.6800000	.711697	.717213	.723169	.729362	.735548
.6899999	.723088	.728863	.735108	.741611	.748116
.7000000	.734517	.740560	.747105	.753929	.760765
.7100000	.745984	.752305	.759159	.766315	.773497
.7200000	.757491	.764098	.771271	.778773	.786313
.7300000	.769037	.775939	.783443	.791302	.799215
.7400000	.780623	.787829	.795674	.803904	.812203
.7500000	.792249	.799768	.807967	.816580	.825281
.7600000	.803916	.811758	.820320	.829331	.838449
.7700000	.815623	.823798	.832736	.842157	.851708
.7800000	.827371	.835889	.845214	.855061	.865061
.7899999	.839161	.848030	.857756	.868043	.878508

$\alpha =$ .149999

Θ	K VALUES				
	.318821117	.415016431	.514599755	.613601043	.708073407
.8000000	.850993	.860224	.870362	.881103	.892051
.8100000	.862866	.872470	.883033	.894244	.905693
.8200000	.874781	.884768	.895769	.907465	.919433
.8300000	.886739	.897119	.908572	.920769	.933275
.8400000	.898739	.909523	.921440	.934155	.947218
.8500000	.910782	.921981	.934376	.947626	.961266
.8600000	.922868	.934493	.947380	.961181	.975419
.8700000	.934996	.947058	.960452	.974822	.989678
.8799999	.947168	.959678	.973592	.988549	1.004047
.8899999	.959383	.972353	.986802	1.002365	1.018525
.9000000	.971642	.985083	1.000082	1.016268	1.033114
.9100000	.983944	.997868	1.013432	1.030261	1.047816
.9200000	.996289	1.010708	1.026852	1.044344	1.062633
.9300000	1.008678	1.023603	1.040343	1.058518	1.077565
.9400000	1.021111	1.036554	1.053906	1.072784	1.092615
.9500000	1.033587	1.049561	1.067541	1.087142	1.107783
.9600000	1.046107	1.062624	1.081247	1.101593	1.123071
.9699999	1.058670	1.075743	1.095026	1.116138	1.138481
.9799999	1.071277	1.088917	1.108877	1.130777	1.154013
.9899999	1.083927	1.102148	1.122801	1.145511	1.169669
1.0000000	1.096621	1.115434	1.136798	1.160341	1.185450
1.0100000	1.109358	1.128776	1.150868	1.175267	1.201358
1.0200000	1.122138	1.142174	1.165011	1.190290	1.217394
1.0300000	1.134960	1.155628	1.179228	1.205409	1.233558
1.0400000	1.147826	1.169138	1.193517	1.220626	1.249852
1.0500000	1.160734	1.182703	1.207880	1.235941	1.266277
1.0600000	1.173684	1.196323	1.222316	1.251353	1.282834
1.0699999	1.186676	1.209998	1.236826	1.266864	1.299524
1.0799999	1.199710	1.223728	1.251408	1.282474	1.316348
1.0899999	1.212786	1.237512	1.266063	1.298181	1.333306
1.1000000	1.225903	1.251351	1.280790	1.313988	1.350399
1.1100000	1.239060	1.265243	1.295590	1.329893	1.367628
1.1200000	1.252258	1.279189	1.310462	1.345896	1.384994
1.1300000	1.265495	1.293187	1.325405	1.361998	1.402497
1.1400000	1.278773	1.307238	1.340420	1.378197	1.420136
1.1500000	1.292089	1.321341	1.355505	1.394495	1.437914
1.1600000	1.305444	1.335496	1.370660	1.410890	1.455829
1.1700000	1.318837	1.349702	1.385885	1.427382	1.473882
1.1800000	1.332268	1.363957	1.401178	1.443970	1.492072
1.1899999	1.345736	1.378263	1.416540	1.460654	1.510400

$\alpha =$ .149999

Θ	K VALUES				
	.318821117	.415016431	.514599755	.613601043	.708073407
1.2000000	1.359240	1.392618	1.431969	1.477433	1.528865
1.2100000	1.372780	1.407020	1.447465	1.494306	1.547467
1.2200000	1.386356	1.421471	1.463026	1.511273	1.566205
1.2300000	1.399966	1.435967	1.478653	1.528332	1.585079
1.2400000	1.413610	1.450510	1.494343	1.545483	1.604086
1.2500000	1.427287	1.465098	1.510096	1.562723	1.623228
1.2599999	1.440997	1.479730	1.525910	1.580053	1.642501
1.2699999	1.454738	1.494406	1.541785	1.597470	1.661906
1.2799999	1.468511	1.509123	1.557720	1.614973	1.681440
1.2899999	1.482314	1.523882	1.573712	1.632560	1.701101
1.3000000	1.496146	1.538681	1.589762	1.650230	1.720888
1.3100000	1.510007	1.553519	1.605866	1.667981	1.740799
1.3200000	1.523896	1.568395	1.622024	1.685812	1.760831
1.3300000	1.537811	1.583307	1.638234	1.703719	1.780981
1.3400000	1.551753	1.598256	1.654496	1.721702	1.801248
1.3500000	1.565719	1.613239	1.670806	1.739757	1.821628
1.3600000	1.579710	1.628255	1.687164	1.757883	1.842118
1.3700000	1.593724	1.643303	1.703567	1.776077	1.862715
1.3799999	1.607760	1.658381	1.720014	1.794337	1.883415
1.3899999	1.621817	1.673489	1.736504	1.812660	1.904215
1.4000000	1.635895	1.688625	1.753034	1.831043	1.925112
1.4100000	1.649991	1.703788	1.769601	1.849484	1.946099
1.4200000	1.664106	1.718975	1.786205	1.867980	1.967175
1.4300000	1.678238	1.734187	1.802844	1.886527	1.988333
1.4400000	1.692386	1.749420	1.819514	1.905124	2.009570
1.4500000	1.706549	1.764675	1.836215	1.923766	2.030881
1.4600000	1.720726	1.779948	1.852943	1.942450	2.052260
1.4700000	1.734915	1.795239	1.869697	1.961174	2.073704
1.4800000	1.749116	1.810547	1.886475	1.979934	2.095205
1.4900000	1.763328	1.825869	1.903274	1.998726	2.116760
1.5000000	1.777549	1.841204	1.920092	2.017548	2.138363
1.5100000	1.791778	1.856551	1.936927	2.036395	2.160007
1.5200000	1.806014	1.871907	1.953776	2.055264	2.181688
1.5300000	1.820256	1.887272	1.970637	2.074152	2.203398
1.5400000	1.834503	1.902643	1.987508	2.093054	2.225134
1.5500000	1.848754	1.918019	2.004386	2.111968	2.246888
1.5600000	1.863006	1.933399	2.021269	2.130889	2.268654
1.5699999	1.877261	1.948781	2.038155	2.149815	2.290427
1.5707963	1.878396	1.950006	2.039499	2.151322	2.292161
1.5707963	1.878395	1.950004	2.039498	2.151321	2.292160

$\alpha =$ .149999

Θ	K VALUES				
	.794250555	.868696860	.928444378	.971111163	.994996249
.0000000	.000000	.000000	.000000	.000000	.000000
.0100000	.010000	.010000	.010000	.010000	.010000
.0200000	.020001	.020001	.020001	.020001	.020001
.0300000	.030004	.030005	.030005	.030005	.030005
.0400000	.040011	.040012	.040013	.040013	.040013
.0500000	.050022	.050024	.050025	.050026	.050027
.0600000	.060039	.060042	.060044	.060045	.060046
.0700000	.070062	.070066	.070070	.070072	.070074
.0800000	.080093	.080099	.080105	.080108	.080110
.0900000	.090133	.090142	.090149	.090154	.090157
.1000000	.100182	.100195	.100205	.100212	.100216
.1100000	.110243	.110259	.110273	.110282	.110288
.1200000	.120315	.120337	.120354	.120367	.120374
.1300000	.130401	.130429	.130451	.130467	.130476
.1400000	.140501	.140536	.140564	.140583	.140594
.1500000	.150617	.150660	.150694	.150718	.150732
.1600000	.160749	.160801	.160843	.160872	.160889
.1700000	.170899	.170962	.171011	.171047	.171067
.1800000	.181068	.181142	.181202	.181244	.181268
.1900000	.191257	.191344	.191414	.191464	.191493
.2000000	.201467	.201569	.201651	.201710	.201742
.2100000	.211700	.211818	.211913	.211981	.212019
.2200000	.221956	.222092	.222202	.222280	.222324
.2300000	.232236	.232392	.232518	.232608	.232659
.2400000	.242542	.242720	.242864	.242966	.243024
.2500000	.252876	.253078	.253240	.253357	.253422
.2600000	.263238	.263465	.263649	.263780	.263854
.2700000	.273629	.273884	.274091	.274239	.274322
.2800000	.284050	.284337	.284568	.284733	.284826
.2900000	.294504	.294823	.295081	.295266	.295369
.3000000	.304990	.305345	.305632	.305837	.305953
.3100000	.315511	.315905	.316222	.316450	.316578
.3200000	.326068	.326502	.326853	.327105	.327246
.3300000	.336661	.337139	.337526	.337804	.337960
.3400000	.347293	.347818	.348243	.348548	.348719
.3500000	.357963	.358539	.359005	.359340	.359528
.3600000	.368675	.369304	.369814	.370180	.370386
.3700000	.379428	.380115	.380671	.381071	.381296
.3800000	.390225	.390973	.391578	.392014	.392259
.3900000	.401067	.401879	.402537	.403011	.403278

$\alpha =$ .149999

Θ	K VALUES				
	.794250555	.868696860	.928444378	.971111163	.994996249
.4000000	.411954	.412835	.413550	.414064	.414353
.4100000	.422889	.423843	.424617	.425174	.425488
.4200000	.433873	.434903	.435740	.436344	.436683
.4300000	.444906	.446019	.446923	.447574	.447941
.4400000	.455992	.457190	.458165	.458868	.459264
.4500000	.467130	.468420	.469469	.470226	.470653
.4600000	.478322	.479708	.480837	.481652	.482111
.4700000	.489571	.491058	.492270	.493146	.493640
.4800000	.500876	.502471	.503771	.504711	.505241
.4900000	.512241	.513948	.515341	.516349	.516918
.5000000	.523665	.525492	.526983	.528062	.528672
.5100000	.535152	.537103	.538698	.539852	.540505
.5200000	.546702	.548785	.550488	.551722	.552420
.5300000	.558317	.560537	.562355	.563673	.564419
.5400000	.569998	.572364	.574302	.575708	.576504
.5500000	.581747	.584265	.586330	.587830	.588678
.5600000	.593566	.596244	.598442	.600040	.600944
.5700000	.605456	.608303	.610641	.612341	.613304
.5800000	.617420	.620442	.622927	.624735	.625760
.5900000	.629458	.632664	.635304	.637226	.638316
.6000000	.641572	.644972	.647773	.649815	.650974
.6100000	.653765	.657367	.660338	.662506	.663737
.6200000	.666037	.669851	.673001	.675301	.676608
.6300000	.678391	.682427	.685764	.688203	.689590
.6400000	.690828	.695097	.698630	.701215	.702685
.6500000	.703350	.707863	.711602	.714340	.715898
.6600000	.715960	.720727	.724681	.727580	.729232
.6700000	.728658	.733691	.737872	.740940	.742689
.6800000	.741447	.746759	.751176	.754422	.756273
.6899999	.754329	.759931	.764598	.768029	.769988
.7000000	.767306	.773212	.778139	.781765	.783837
.7100000	.780379	.786603	.791802	.795634	.797825
.7200000	.793550	.800106	.805591	.809639	.811955
.7300000	.806822	.813726	.819509	.823783	.826230
.7400000	.820197	.827463	.833560	.838071	.840656
.7500000	.833676	.841321	.847746	.852506	.855237
.7600000	.847262	.855302	.862071	.867092	.869976
.7700000	.860957	.869410	.876538	.881834	.884879
.7800000	.874763	.883647	.891152	.896736	.899950
.7899999	.888682	.898016	.905916	.911802	.915194

$\alpha =$ .149999

Θ	K VALUES				
	.794250555	.868696860	.928444378	.971111163	.994996249
.8000000	.902716	.912520	.920833	.927038	.930616
.8100000	.916868	.927162	.935908	.942446	.946221
.8200000	.931139	.941945	.951145	.958033	.962015
.8300000	.945533	.956873	.966547	.973804	.978003
.8400000	.960050	.971948	.982119	.989763	.994192
.8500000	.974695	.987175	.997866	1.005916	1.010587
.8600000	.989468	1.002555	1.013792	1.022268	1.027194
.8700000	1.004372	1.018093	1.029901	1.038827	1.044020
.8799999	1.019411	1.033792	1.046199	1.055596	1.061072
.8899999	1.034585	1.049655	1.062689	1.072583	1.078358
.9000000	1.049897	1.065687	1.079378	1.089794	1.095883
.9100000	1.065350	1.081891	1.096271	1.107236	1.113656
.9200000	1.080947	1.098271	1.113372	1.124915	1.131686
.9300000	1.096689	1.114830	1.130687	1.142838	1.149979
.9400000	1.112579	1.131572	1.148223	1.161014	1.168546
.9500000	1.128620	1.148502	1.165984	1.179450	1.187395
.9600000	1.144814	1.165623	1.183977	1.198154	1.206535
.9699999	1.161163	1.182940	1.202208	1.217134	1.225977
.9799999	1.177670	1.200456	1.220683	1.236399	1.245732
.9899999	1.194338	1.218176	1.239409	1.255958	1.265809
1.0000000	1.211169	1.236105	1.258393	1.275822	1.286221
1.0100000	1.228165	1.254246	1.277642	1.295998	1.306979
1.0200000	1.245329	1.272604	1.297162	1.316498	1.328097
1.0300000	1.262663	1.291183	1.316962	1.337333	1.349587
1.0400000	1.280170	1.309989	1.337049	1.358514	1.371464
1.0500000	1.297851	1.329025	1.357430	1.380052	1.393742
1.0600000	1.315711	1.348297	1.378115	1.401960	1.416437
1.0699999	1.333749	1.367808	1.399111	1.424251	1.439566
1.0799999	1.351970	1.387564	1.420427	1.446938	1.463146
1.0899999	1.370374	1.407570	1.442071	1.470034	1.487196
1.1000000	1.388965	1.427830	1.464054	1.493556	1.511734
1.1100000	1.407744	1.448349	1.486383	1.517518	1.536782
1.1200000	1.426713	1.469131	1.509069	1.541936	1.562362
1.1300000	1.445874	1.490182	1.532122	1.566828	1.588496
1.1400000	1.465229	1.511507	1.555552	1.592211	1.615211
1.1500000	1.484780	1.533109	1.579369	1.618104	1.642532
1.1600000	1.504528	1.554995	1.603584	1.644526	1.670488
1.1700000	1.524474	1.577167	1.628207	1.671498	1.699110
1.1800000	1.544620	1.599632	1.653250	1.699042	1.728429
1.1899999	1.564967	1.622392	1.678724	1.727181	1.758480

$\alpha =$ •149999

Θ	K VALUES				
	•794250555	•868696860	•928444378	•971111163	•994996249
•2000000	1•585517	1•645453	1•704641	1•755938	1•789301
•2100000	1•606268	1•668819	1•731012	1•785339	1•820933
•2200000	1•627223	1•692493	1•757848	1•815410	1•853417
•2300000	1•648382	1•716480	1•785163	1•846179	1•886802
•2400000	1•669745	1•740782	1•812968	1•877676	1•921137
•2500000	1•691311	1•765402	1•841274	1•909930	1•956478
•2599999	1•713080	1•790345	1•870094	1•942974	1•992884
•2699999	1•735053	1•815611	1•899440	1•976843	2•030420
•2799999	1•757227	1•841204	1•929324	2•011571	2•069156
•2899999	1•779601	1•867124	1•959756	2•047195	2•109170
•3000000	1•802175	1•893374	1•990748	2•083756	2•150546
•3100000	1•824946	1•919953	2•022311	2•121292	2•193377
•3200000	1•847911	1•946860	2•054454	2•159846	2•237765
•3300000	1•871069	1•974097	2•087186	2•199461	2•283824
•3400000	1•894416	2•001661	2•120516	2•240183	2•331678
•3500000	1•917949	2•029549	2•154451	2•282057	2•381465
•3600000	1•941664	2•057760	2•188997	2•325130	2•433341
•3700000	1•965557	2•086289	2•224158	2•369451	2•487477
•3799999	1•989623	2•115130	2•259936	2•415066	2•544066
•3899999	2•013857	2•144280	2•296332	2•462023	2•603324
•4000000	2•038254	2•173730	2•333344	2•510367	2•665496
•4100000	2•062807	2•203472	2•370967	2•560140	2•730854
•4200000	2•087511	2•233499	2•409195	2•611382	2•799708
•4300000	2•112359	2•263798	2•448017	2•664127	2•872409
•4400000	2•137343	2•294360	2•487420	2•718400	2•949352
•4500000	2•162455	2•325172	2•527385	2•774220	3•030983
•4600000	2•187689	2•356220	2•567893	2•831592	3•117803
•4700000	2•213034	2•387490	2•608918	2•890507	3•210367
•4800000	2•238483	2•418965	2•650431	2•950940	3•309288
•4900000	2•264026	2•450630	2•692399	3•012845	3•415214
•5000000	2•289654	2•482465	2•734785	3•076156	3•528811
•5100000	2•315357	2•514452	2•777547	3•140779	3•650701
•5200000	2•341124	2•546572	2•820641	3•206598	3•781372
•5300000	2•366947	2•578804	2•864017	3•273467	3•921040
•5400000	2•392813	2•611126	2•907624	3•341217	4•069446
•5500000	2•418713	2•643517	2•951409	3•409657	4•225651
•5600000	2•444635	2•675955	2•995314	3•478573	4•387872
•5699999	2•470569	2•708417	3•039282	3•547742	4•553500
•5707963	2•472635	2•711003	3•042784	3•553254	4•566744
•5707963	2•472633	2•711001	3•042781	3•553250	4•566739

$\alpha =$ .199999

Θ	K VALUES				
	.009966711	.039469502	.087332193	.151646642	.229848846
.0000000	.000000	.000000	.000000	.000000	.000000
.0100000	.010000	.010000	.010000	.010000	.010000
.0200000	.020000	.020000	.020000	.020000	.020000
.0300000	.030001	.030001	.030002	.030002	.030002
.0400000	.040004	.040004	.040005	.040005	.040006
.0500000	.050008	.050009	.050010	.050011	.050013
.0600000	.060014	.060015	.060017	.060019	.060022
.0700000	.070023	.070025	.070027	.070031	.070036
.0800000	.080035	.080037	.080041	.080047	.080053
.0900000	.090049	.090053	.090059	.090067	.090076
.1000000	.100068	.100073	.100081	.100091	.100104
.1100000	.110090	.110097	.110108	.110122	.110139
.1200000	.120117	.120126	.120140	.120158	.120181
.1300000	.130149	.130160	.130178	.130201	.130230
.1400000	.140187	.140200	.140222	.140251	.140287
.1500000	.150230	.150246	.150273	.150309	.150353
.1600000	.160279	.160299	.160332	.160376	.160429
.1700000	.170334	.170359	.170398	.170450	.170515
.1800000	.180397	.180426	.180472	.180535	.180611
.1900000	.190467	.190500	.190555	.190629	.190718
.2000000	.200544	.200584	.200647	.200733	.200838
.2100000	.210630	.210675	.210749	.210849	.210970
.2200000	.220724	.220776	.220861	.220976	.221115
.2300000	.230827	.230887	.230984	.231114	.231274
.2400000	.240940	.241007	.241118	.241266	.241447
.2500000	.251062	.251138	.251263	.251430	.251635
.2600000	.261194	.261280	.261420	.261609	.261839
.2700000	.271336	.271433	.271590	.271801	.272059
.2800000	.281490	.281597	.281772	.282008	.282296
.2900000	.291655	.291774	.291968	.292230	.292550
.3000000	.301831	.301963	.302178	.302468	.302822
.3100000	.312019	.312165	.312402	.312722	.313113
.3200000	.322220	.322380	.322640	.322993	.323423
.3300000	.332433	.332609	.332894	.333281	.333753
.3400000	.342660	.342851	.343164	.343586	.344104
.3500000	.352899	.353109	.353450	.353910	.354475
.3600000	.363153	.363381	.363752	.364253	.364868
.3700000	.373421	.373668	.374071	.374615	.375283
.3800000	.383704	.383971	.384407	.384997	.385721
.3900000	.394001	.394290	.394762	.395399	.396182

$\alpha =$ .199999

Θ	K VALUES				
	.009966711	.039469502	.087332193	.151646642	.229848846
.4000000	.404314	.404626	.405134	.405822	.406668
.4100000	.414643	.414978	.415525	.416266	.417177
.4200000	.424987	.425347	.425935	.426732	.427712
.4300000	.435348	.435734	.436365	.437220	.438272
.4400000	.445725	.446139	.446815	.447731	.448859
.4500000	.456120	.456562	.457285	.458265	.459472
.4600000	.466532	.467004	.467775	.468823	.470113
.4700000	.476961	.477464	.478287	.479404	.480781
.4800000	.487409	.487944	.488820	.490010	.491478
.4900000	.497874	.498444	.499375	.500642	.502204
.5000000	.508359	.508964	.509953	.511298	.512960
.5100000	.518862	.519504	.520553	.521981	.523745
.5200000	.529385	.530064	.531176	.532689	.534561
.5300000	.539927	.540646	.541822	.543425	.545407
.5400000	.550489	.551249	.552493	.554188	.556286
.5500000	.561072	.561873	.563187	.564978	.567196
.5600000	.571674	.572520	.573906	.575796	.578139
.5700000	.582298	.583189	.584649	.586643	.589115
.5800000	.592942	.593880	.595418	.597518	.600125
.5900000	.603608	.604594	.606212	.608423	.611168
.6000000	.614295	.615331	.617032	.619357	.622246
.6100000	.625004	.626092	.627878	.630321	.633359
.6200000	.635735	.636876	.638751	.641315	.644507
.6300000	.646489	.647685	.649650	.652340	.655692
.6400000	.657264	.658517	.660576	.663396	.666912
.6500000	.668063	.669374	.671530	.674484	.678169
.6600000	.678885	.680256	.682511	.685603	.689463
.6700000	.689730	.691162	.693519	.696754	.700794
.6800000	.700598	.702094	.704556	.707937	.712164
.6899999	.711490	.713051	.715622	.719153	.723571
.7000000	.722406	.724034	.726716	.730402	.735018
.7100000	.733346	.735043	.737839	.741684	.746503
.7200000	.744310	.746077	.748991	.753000	.758028
.7300000	.755298	.757138	.760172	.764349	.769592
.7400000	.766311	.768225	.771382	.775732	.781196
.7500000	.777349	.779339	.782623	.787150	.792841
.7600000	.788411	.790479	.793893	.798601	.804526
.7700000	.799499	.801646	.805193	.810088	.816253
.7800000	.810612	.812840	.816523	.821610	.828020
.7899999	.821750	.824062	.827884	.833166	.839829

$\alpha =$ .199999

θ	K VALUES				
	.009966711	.039469502	.087332193	.151646642	.229848846
.8000000	.832913	.835310	.839275	.844758	.851679
.8100000	.844102	.846586	.850697	.856385	.863572
.8200000	.855316	.857890	.862150	.868048	.875506
.8300000	.866556	.869221	.873633	.879746	.887483
.8400000	.877821	.880579	.885148	.891481	.899503
.8500000	.889113	.891965	.896693	.903251	.911565
.8600000	.900430	.903380	.908270	.915057	.923670
.8700000	.911773	.914821	.919878	.926900	.935818
.8799999	.923142	.926291	.931517	.938778	.948009
.8899999	.934537	.937789	.943187	.950693	.960243
.9000000	.945958	.949314	.954888	.962645	.972521
.9100000	.957405	.960868	.966621	.974632	.984841
.9200000	.968878	.972449	.978385	.986656	.997206
.9300000	.980377	.984058	.990181	.998716	1.009613
.9400000	.991901	.995695	1.002007	1.010813	1.022064
.9500000	1.003452	1.007360	1.013865	1.022945	1.034558
.9600000	1.015028	1.019052	1.025754	1.035114	1.047096
.9699999	1.026630	1.030773	1.037673	1.047319	1.059677
.9799999	1.038257	1.042520	1.049624	1.059560	1.072301
.9899999	1.049910	1.054295	1.061606	1.071837	1.084969
1.0000000	1.061589	1.066098	1.073618	1.084150	1.097679
1.0100000	1.073292	1.077927	1.085661	1.096498	1.110432
1.0200000	1.085021	1.089784	1.097734	1.108882	1.123228
1.0300000	1.096775	1.101668	1.109838	1.121301	1.136067
1.0400000	1.108554	1.113578	1.121971	1.133756	1.148947
1.0500000	1.120358	1.125515	1.134135	1.146245	1.161870
1.0600000	1.132186	1.137479	1.146328	1.158769	1.174835
1.0699999	1.144038	1.149468	1.158550	1.171327	1.187841
1.0799999	1.155914	1.161484	1.170802	1.183919	1.200889
1.0899999	1.167815	1.173525	1.183083	1.196545	1.213977
1.1000000	1.179739	1.185592	1.195392	1.209205	1.227106
1.1100000	1.191687	1.197683	1.207730	1.221898	1.240275
1.1200000	1.203657	1.209800	1.220096	1.234624	1.253484
1.1300000	1.215651	1.221942	1.232489	1.247382	1.266733
1.1400000	1.227667	1.234108	1.244910	1.260173	1.280020
1.1500000	1.239705	1.246297	1.257358	1.272995	1.293346
1.1600000	1.251766	1.258511	1.269833	1.285848	1.306710
1.1700000	1.263848	1.270748	1.282334	1.298732	1.320112
1.1800000	1.275952	1.283008	1.294860	1.311647	1.333550
1.1899999	1.288076	1.295290	1.307413	1.324591	1.347025

$\alpha =$ .199999

Θ	K VALUES				
	.009966711	.039469502	.087332193	.151646642	.229848846
1.2000000	1.300222	1.307595	1.319990	1.337565	1.360536
1.2100000	1.312387	1.319921	1.332592	1.350568	1.374082
1.2200000	1.324573	1.332269	1.345218	1.363599	1.387662
1.2300000	1.336778	1.344638	1.357868	1.376658	1.401277
1.2400000	1.349002	1.357028	1.370541	1.389744	1.414925
1.2500000	1.361244	1.369438	1.383236	1.402857	1.428605
1.2599999	1.373505	1.381867	1.395954	1.415996	1.442317
1.2699999	1.385784	1.394315	1.408693	1.429161	1.456061
1.2799999	1.398080	1.406782	1.421454	1.442350	1.469835
1.2899999	1.410393	1.419268	1.434235	1.455563	1.483638
1.3000000	1.422723	1.431771	1.447036	1.468800	1.497470
1.3100000	1.435068	1.444291	1.459856	1.482060	1.511330
1.3200000	1.447429	1.456828	1.472695	1.495341	1.525218
1.3300000	1.459805	1.469381	1.485552	1.508644	1.539131
1.3400000	1.472195	1.481949	1.498427	1.521968	1.553070
1.3500000	1.484599	1.494533	1.511318	1.535312	1.567033
1.3600000	1.497017	1.507131	1.524226	1.548675	1.581020
1.3700000	1.509447	1.519742	1.537150	1.562056	1.595030
1.3799999	1.521890	1.532367	1.550088	1.575455	1.609061
1.3899999	1.534344	1.545005	1.563040	1.588870	1.623113
1.4000000	1.546810	1.557654	1.576007	1.602302	1.637184
1.4100000	1.559286	1.570315	1.588986	1.615749	1.651274
1.4200000	1.571772	1.582987	1.601977	1.629210	1.665382
1.4300000	1.584267	1.595668	1.614979	1.642685	1.679507
1.4400000	1.596772	1.608360	1.627993	1.656172	1.693647
1.4500000	1.609284	1.621060	1.641016	1.669671	1.707801
1.4600000	1.621804	1.633768	1.654048	1.683181	1.721969
1.4700000	1.634331	1.646484	1.667089	1.696701	1.736150
1.4800000	1.646865	1.659207	1.680138	1.710230	1.750341
1.4900000	1.659404	1.671936	1.693194	1.723768	1.764543
1.5000000	1.671949	1.684670	1.706256	1.737313	1.778755
1.5100000	1.684498	1.697409	1.719324	1.750864	1.792974
1.5200000	1.697050	1.710153	1.732396	1.764421	1.807200
1.5300000	1.709606	1.722900	1.745472	1.777983	1.821431
1.5400000	1.722165	1.735650	1.758552	1.791548	1.835668
1.5500000	1.734726	1.748402	1.771633	1.805116	1.849908
1.5600000	1.747288	1.761155	1.784717	1.818687	1.864150
1.5699999	1.759850	1.773909	1.797801	1.832258	1.878393
1.5707963	1.760851	1.774925	1.798843	1.833338	1.879527
1.5707963	1.760850	1.774924	1.798842	1.833337	1.879526

$\alpha =$ •199999

θ	K VALUES				
	•318821117	•415016431	•514599755	•613601043	•708073407
•0000000	•000000	•000000	•000000	•000000	•000000
•0100000	•010000	•010000	•010000	•010000	•010000
•0200000	•020000	•020001	•020001	•020001	•020001
•0300000	•030003	•030003	•030004	•030004	•030005
•0400000	•040007	•040008	•040009	•040010	•040011
•0500000	•050014	•050017	•050019	•050021	•050023
•0600000	•060025	•060029	•060032	•060036	•060039
•0700000	•070041	•070046	•070052	•070058	•070063
•0800000	•080061	•080069	•080078	•080086	•080094
•0900000	•090087	•090099	•090111	•090123	•090134
•1000000	•100119	•100135	•100152	•100169	•100184
•1100000	•110159	•110180	•110203	•110225	•110246
•1200000	•120206	•120234	•120263	•120292	•120319
•1300000	•130263	•130298	•130335	•130371	•130406
•1400000	•140328	•140372	•140418	•140464	•140508
•1500000	•150404	•150458	•150515	•150571	•150625
•1600000	•160490	•160556	•160625	•160693	•160758
•1700000	•170588	•170667	•170750	•170832	•170910
•1800000	•180698	•180792	•180890	•180988	•181081
•1900000	•190821	•190932	•191047	•191162	•191272
•2000000	•200957	•201087	•201221	•201356	•201484
•2100000	•211108	•211258	•211414	•211570	•211719
•2200000	•221274	•221447	•221626	•221806	•221978
•2300000	•231456	•231653	•231859	•232064	•232261
•2400000	•241654	•241879	•242113	•242346	•242571
•2500000	•251869	•252124	•252389	•252653	•252907
•2600000	•262103	•262389	•262687	•262986	•263273
•2700000	•272354	•272676	•273010	•273345	•273667
•2800000	•282626	•282984	•283358	•283733	•284093
•2900000	•292917	•293316	•293732	•294149	•294550
•3000000	•303229	•303671	•304133	•304596	•305041
•3100000	•313562	•314051	•314562	•315074	•315566
•3200000	•323917	•324456	•325019	•325584	•326127
•3300000	•334296	•334887	•335506	•336127	•336725
•3400000	•344697	•345346	•346024	•346705	•347361
•3500000	•355123	•355832	•356573	•357318	•358037
•3600000	•365574	•366346	•367155	•367968	•368753
•3700000	•376051	•376890	•377770	•378656	•379512
•3800000	•386554	•387465	•388420	•389383	•390313
•3900000	•397083	•398070	•399106	•400149	•401159

$\alpha =$ .199999

Θ	K VALUES				
	.318821117	.415016431	.514599755	.613601043	.708073407
.4000000	.407641	.408707	.409827	.410957	.412051
.4100000	.418227	.419377	.420587	.421808	.422991
.4200000	.428841	.430081	.431384	.432701	.433979
.4300000	.439486	.440818	.442221	.443640	.445016
.4400000	.450161	.451591	.453098	.454624	.456105
.4500000	.460867	.462400	.464017	.465654	.467247
.4600000	.471604	.473246	.474977	.476733	.478442
.4700000	.482374	.484129	.485981	.487862	.489693
.4800000	.493177	.495050	.497030	.499040	.501000
.4900000	.504014	.506011	.508123	.510270	.512366
.5000000	.514885	.517011	.519262	.521553	.523791
.5100000	.525791	.528052	.530449	.532890	.535277
.5200000	.536733	.539135	.541683	.544282	.546826
.5300000	.547711	.550260	.552967	.555730	.558438
.5400000	.558725	.561428	.564301	.567236	.570116
.5500000	.569777	.572640	.575685	.578801	.581860
.5600000	.580868	.583896	.587122	.590425	.593673
.5700000	.591997	.595198	.598611	.602111	.605556
.5800000	.603165	.606546	.610155	.613859	.617510
.5900000	.614373	.617941	.621753	.625671	.629536
.6000000	.625622	.629383	.633407	.637547	.641638
.6100000	.636912	.640874	.645118	.649490	.653815
.6200000	.648243	.652414	.656887	.661500	.666069
.6300000	.659617	.664004	.668714	.673578	.678402
.6400000	.671033	.675645	.680601	.685726	.690816
.6500000	.682493	.687336	.692548	.697945	.703313
.6600000	.693997	.699080	.704557	.710236	.715893
.6700000	.705545	.710877	.716629	.722601	.728558
.6800000	.717137	.722726	.728763	.735041	.741311
.6899999	.728775	.734630	.740962	.747556	.754152
.7000000	.740460	.746589	.753227	.760148	.767084
.7100000	.752190	.758603	.765557	.772819	.780108
.7200000	.763967	.770673	.777954	.785570	.793225
.7300000	.775792	.782799	.790419	.798401	.806438
.7400000	.787664	.794983	.802953	.811314	.819748
.7500000	.799584	.807225	.815556	.824311	.833156
.7600000	.811553	.819525	.828230	.837392	.846665
.7700000	.823571	.831884	.840975	.850559	.860276
.7800000	.835639	.844303	.853792	.863813	.873991
.7899999	.847756	.856782	.866682	.877155	.887811

$\alpha =$ .199999

Θ	K VALUES				
	.318821117	.415016431	.514599755	.613601043	.708073407
.8000000	.859923	.869322	.879646	.890586	.901739
.8100000	.872140	.881923	.892684	.904107	.915776
.8200000	.884409	.894585	.905798	.917721	.929924
.8300000	.896728	.907310	.918987	.931426	.944184
.8400000	.909098	.920097	.932253	.945226	.958558
.8500000	.921520	.932947	.945596	.959121	.973048
.8600000	.933994	.945860	.959018	.973111	.987655
.8700000	.946520	.958838	.972518	.987199	1.002382
.8799999	.959099	.971879	.986097	1.001385	1.017230
.8899999	.971729	.984985	.999756	1.015671	1.032201
.9000000	.984413	.998156	1.013496	1.030056	1.047296
.9100000	.997149	1.011392	1.027317	1.044543	1.062517
.9200000	1.009938	1.024693	1.041220	1.059132	1.077866
.9300000	1.022780	1.038060	1.055204	1.073824	1.093344
.9400000	1.035675	1.051493	1.069271	1.088620	1.108953
.9500000	1.048622	1.064991	1.083421	1.103521	1.124695
.9600000	1.061624	1.078556	1.097654	1.118527	1.140571
.9699999	1.074678	1.092187	1.111972	1.133641	1.156582
.9799999	1.087785	1.105885	1.126373	1.148861	1.172731
.9899999	1.100945	1.119649	1.140858	1.164189	1.189018
1.0000000	1.114159	1.133479	1.155428	1.179626	1.205445
1.0100000	1.127425	1.147376	1.170083	1.195172	1.222014
1.0200000	1.140743	1.161339	1.184822	1.210828	1.238726
1.0300000	1.154115	1.175368	1.199647	1.226595	1.255582
1.0400000	1.167538	1.189464	1.214556	1.242472	1.272583
1.0500000	1.181014	1.203625	1.229551	1.258460	1.289730
1.0600000	1.194542	1.217853	1.244631	1.274560	1.307025
1.0699999	1.208121	1.232146	1.259796	1.290771	1.324469
1.0799999	1.221752	1.246504	1.275045	1.307095	1.342063
1.0899999	1.235433	1.260927	1.290379	1.323531	1.359807
1.1000000	1.249165	1.275415	1.305798	1.340079	1.377703
1.1100000	1.262947	1.289967	1.321301	1.356739	1.395750
1.1200000	1.276780	1.304583	1.336887	1.373512	1.413951
1.1300000	1.290661	1.319262	1.352557	1.390396	1.432304
1.1400000	1.304591	1.334004	1.368310	1.407393	1.450811
1.1500000	1.318569	1.348809	1.384145	1.424500	1.469472
1.1600000	1.332595	1.363675	1.400062	1.441719	1.488288
1.1700000	1.346669	1.378602	1.416060	1.459048	1.507257
1.1800000	1.360788	1.393589	1.432138	1.476488	1.526381
1.1899999	1.374954	1.408636	1.448295	1.494036	1.545659

$\alpha =$ •199999

Θ	K VALUES				
	•318821117	•415016431	•514599755	•613601043	•708073407
1•2000000	1•389165	1•423741	1•464532	1•511693	1•565090
1•2100000	1•403420	1•438905	1•480846	1•529458	1•584674
1•2200000	1•417719	1•454125	1•497237	1•547329	1•604411
1•2300000	1•432061	1•469402	1•513704	1•565305	1•624299
1•2400000	1•446445	1•484733	1•530245	1•583386	1•644338
1•2500000	1•460871	1•500119	1•546859	1•601569	1•664527
1•2599999	1•475336	1•515558	1•563546	1•619854	1•684863
1•2699999	1•489842	1•531049	1•580303	1•638239	1•705346
1•2799999	1•504386	1•546590	1•597130	1•656722	1•725973
1•2899999	1•518967	1•562182	1•614025	1•675302	1•746744
1•3000000	1•533585	1•577821	1•630986	1•693976	1•767655
1•3100000	1•548239	1•593508	1•648011	1•712743	1•788705
1•3200000	1•562927	1•609240	1•665100	1•731600	1•809890
1•3300000	1•577649	1•625017	1•682249	1•750545	1•831208
1•3400000	1•592403	1•640837	1•699459	1•769576	1•852656
1•3500000	1•607189	1•656699	1•716725	1•788689	1•874231
1•3600000	1•622004	1•672600	1•734047	1•807884	1•895929
1•3700000	1•636849	1•688540	1•751423	1•827157	1•917747
1•3799999	1•651721	1•704517	1•768850	1•846504	1•939681
1•3899999	1•666620	1•720529	1•786326	1•865924	1•961726
1•4000000	1•681544	1•736575	1•803850	1•885412	1•983878
1•4100000	1•696492	1•752653	1•821418	1•904967	2•006133
1•4200000	1•711462	1•768762	1•839029	1•924584	2•028486
1•4300000	1•726454	1•784899	1•856680	1•944260	2•050933
1•4400000	1•741466	1•801063	1•874369	1•963993	2•073467
1•4500000	1•756497	1•817251	1•892092	1•983777	2•096083
1•4600000	1•771545	1•833464	1•909849	2•003610	2•118777
1•4700000	1•786609	1•849697	1•927636	2•023488	2•141542
1•4800000	1•801687	1•865951	1•945450	2•043406	2•164372
1•4900000	1•816779	1•882221	1•963289	2•063363	2•187261
1•5000000	1•831882	1•898508	1•981151	2•083352	2•210204
1•5100000	1•846996	1•914809	1•999032	2•103371	2•233194
1•5200000	1•862118	1•931121	2•016930	2•123414	2•256224
1•5300000	1•877248	1•947444	2•034842	2•143479	2•279289
1•5400000	1•892384	1•963774	2•052766	2•163561	2•302380
1•5500000	1•907525	1•980111	2•070698	2•183656	2•325493
1•5600000	1•922668	1•996451	2•088636	2•203760	2•348619
1•5699999	1•937813	2•012794	2•106577	2•223868	2•371753
1•5707963	1•939019	2•014096	2•108006	2•225470	2•373595
1•5707963	1•939018	2•014094	2•108004	2•225468	2•373593

$\alpha =$ •199999

Θ	K VALUES				
	•794250555	•868696860	•928444378	•971111163	•994996249
•0000000	•000000	•000000	•000000	•000000	•000000
•0100000	•010000	•010000	•010000	•010000	•010000
•0200000	•020001	•020001	•020001	•020001	•020001
•0300000	•030005	•030005	•030005	•030006	•030006
•0400000	•040012	•040013	•040014	•040014	•040014
•0500000	•050024	•050026	•050027	•050028	•050029
•0600000	•060043	•060045	•060047	•060049	•060050
•0700000	•070068	•070072	•070076	•070078	•070079
•0800000	•080102	•080108	•080113	•080117	•080119
•0900000	•090145	•090154	•090161	•090166	•090169
•1000000	•100199	•100211	•100221	•100229	•100233
•1100000	•110265	•110282	•110295	•110305	•110310
•1200000	•120344	•120366	•120383	•120396	•120403
•1300000	•130438	•130466	•130488	•130504	•130512
•1400000	•140547	•140582	•140610	•140629	•140641
•1500000	•150674	•150716	•150750	•150775	•150788
•1600000	•160818	•160870	•160911	•160941	•160958
•1700000	•170982	•171044	•171094	•171130	•171150
•1800000	•181166	•181240	•181300	•181342	•181366
•1900000	•191373	•191460	•191530	•191580	•191608
•2000000	•201602	•201704	•201786	•201845	•201877
•2100000	•211856	•211974	•212069	•212137	•212176
•2200000	•222135	•222272	•222381	•222460	•222504
•2300000	•232442	•232598	•232724	•232814	•232865
•2400000	•242776	•242954	•243098	•243201	•243259
•2500000	•253140	•253343	•253505	•253622	•253688
•2600000	•263535	•263764	•263948	•264079	•264153
•2700000	•273963	•274219	•274426	•274574	•274657
•2800000	•284423	•284710	•284942	•285108	•285201
•2900000	•294919	•295239	•295497	•295683	•295787
•3000000	•305450	•305806	•306094	•306300	•306415
•3100000	•316020	•316414	•316733	•316961	•317089
•3200000	•326628	•327063	•327415	•327668	•327810
•3300000	•337276	•337756	•338144	•338423	•338579
•3400000	•347966	•348494	•348920	•349226	•349398
•3500000	•358700	•359278	•359745	•360081	•360270
•3600000	•369478	•370110	•370621	•370989	•371195
•3700000	•380301	•380991	•381549	•381951	•382176
•3800000	•391173	•391924	•392532	•392969	•393215
•3900000	•402093	•402909	•403570	•404046	•404314

$\alpha =$ .199999

Θ	K VALUES				
	.794250555	.868696860	.928444378	.971111163	.994996249
.4000000	.413063	.413949	.414666	.415183	.415474
.4100000	.424086	.425044	.425822	.426382	.426698
.4200000	.435162	.436198	.437039	.437646	.437987
.4300000	.446292	.447411	.448320	.448975	.449344
.4400000	.457480	.458685	.459666	.460373	.460771
.4500000	.468725	.470023	.471079	.471841	.472270
.4600000	.480030	.481425	.482561	.483381	.483843
.4700000	.491396	.492894	.494114	.494995	.495493
.4800000	.502825	.504431	.505740	.506687	.507221
.4900000	.514319	.516039	.517442	.518457	.519030
.5000000	.525879	.527719	.529221	.530309	.530923
.5100000	.537506	.539473	.541080	.542244	.542901
.5200000	.549203	.551303	.553020	.554265	.554968
.5300000	.560972	.563211	.565045	.566374	.567125
.5400000	.572813	.575200	.577155	.578574	.579377
.5500000	.584729	.587270	.589354	.590867	.591724
.5600000	.596722	.599426	.601644	.603257	.604170
.5700000	.608793	.611667	.614028	.615745	.616718
.5800000	.620944	.623997	.626507	.628334	.629370
.5900000	.633178	.636418	.639085	.641028	.642129
.6000000	.645495	.648932	.651764	.653828	.655000
.6100000	.657899	.661541	.664546	.666739	.667983
.6200000	.670390	.674248	.677435	.679762	.681084
.6300000	.682971	.687055	.690432	.692901	.694304
.6400000	.695643	.699965	.703542	.706159	.707648
.6500000	.708410	.712979	.716766	.719539	.721118
.6600000	.721272	.726101	.730108	.733045	.734718
.6700000	.734232	.739333	.743570	.746680	.748453
.6800000	.747292	.752677	.757157	.760447	.762325
.6899999	.760454	.766136	.770870	.774351	.776338
.7000000	.773720	.779714	.784713	.788394	.790497
.7100000	.787093	.793411	.798690	.802581	.804805
.7200000	.800574	.807233	.812803	.816914	.819267
.7300000	.814166	.821180	.827057	.831400	.833887
.7400000	.827871	.835256	.841454	.846040	.848669
.7500000	.841692	.849465	.856000	.860841	.863619
.7600000	.855630	.863809	.870696	.875805	.878740
.7700000	.869688	.878291	.885547	.890938	.894038
.7800000	.883868	.892914	.900557	.906245	.909518
.7899999	.898174	.907682	.915731	.921729	.925185

$\alpha =$ .199999

θ	K VALUES				
	.794250555	.868696860	.928444378	.971111163	.994996249
.8000000	.912606	.922598	.931072	.937397	.941045
.8100000	.927168	.937664	.946584	.953252	.957102
.8200000	.941862	.952886	.962271	.969301	.973364
.8300000	.956691	.968265	.978140	.985548	.989836
.8400000	.971657	.983805	.994193	1.002000	1.006524
.8500000	.986763	.999511	1.010435	1.018662	1.023436
.8600000	1.002010	1.015386	1.026873	1.035540	1.040576
.8700000	1.017403	1.031432	1.043510	1.052640	1.057954
.8799999	1.032943	1.047656	1.060351	1.069970	1.075576
.8899999	1.048634	1.064059	1.077403	1.087534	1.093449
.9000000	1.064477	1.080647	1.094671	1.105342	1.111582
.9100000	1.080475	1.097422	1.112159	1.123399	1.129982
.9200000	1.096632	1.114390	1.129875	1.141713	1.148659
.9300000	1.112950	1.131554	1.147823	1.160292	1.167621
.9400000	1.129431	1.148919	1.166010	1.179144	1.186878
.9500000	1.146078	1.166489	1.184443	1.198277	1.206440
.9600000	1.162894	1.184269	1.203128	1.217699	1.226316
.9699999	1.179882	1.202262	1.222071	1.237421	1.246518
.9799999	1.197045	1.220473	1.241279	1.257451	1.267056
.9899999	1.214385	1.238908	1.260760	1.277799	1.287943
1.0000000	1.231905	1.257571	1.280522	1.298475	1.309190
1.0100000	1.249607	1.276465	1.300570	1.319490	1.330811
1.0200000	1.267495	1.295598	1.320914	1.340855	1.352819
1.0300000	1.285570	1.314972	1.341560	1.362581	1.375229
1.0400000	1.303836	1.334593	1.362519	1.384681	1.398055
1.0500000	1.322296	1.354467	1.383797	1.407166	1.421313
1.0600000	1.340951	1.374597	1.405404	1.430051	1.445021
1.0699999	1.359805	1.394990	1.427348	1.453349	1.469194
1.0799999	1.378859	1.415651	1.449639	1.477074	1.493853
1.0899999	1.398117	1.436583	1.472287	1.501241	1.519017
1.1000000	1.417580	1.457794	1.495301	1.525867	1.544707
1.1100000	1.437251	1.479288	1.518691	1.550967	1.570945
1.1200000	1.457132	1.501069	1.542468	1.576558	1.597754
1.1300000	1.477225	1.523144	1.566642	1.602660	1.625159
1.1400000	1.497531	1.545517	1.591224	1.629291	1.653188
1.1500000	1.518054	1.568193	1.616225	1.656471	1.681867
1.1600000	1.538794	1.591178	1.641656	1.684221	1.711228
1.1700000	1.559753	1.614477	1.667530	1.712564	1.741303
1.1800000	1.580933	1.638094	1.693858	1.741521	1.772126
1.1899999	1.602335	1.662034	1.720652	1.771118	1.803735

$\alpha =$ .199999

Θ	K VALUES				
	.794250555	.868696860	.928444378	.971111163	.994996249
1.2000000	1.623959	1.686302	1.747925	1.801380	1.836169
1.2100000	1.645807	1.710901	1.775688	1.832333	1.869471
1.2200000	1.667879	1.735837	1.803955	1.864007	1.903687
1.2300000	1.690175	1.761114	1.832739	1.896431	1.938867
1.2400000	1.712696	1.786734	1.862051	1.929635	1.975065
1.2500000	1.735442	1.812701	1.891906	1.963654	2.012339
1.2599999	1.758412	1.839019	1.922315	1.998521	2.050752
1.2699999	1.781605	1.865690	1.953292	2.034271	2.090374
1.2799999	1.805021	1.892716	1.984849	2.070944	2.131279
1.2899999	1.828658	1.920098	2.016998	2.108578	2.173550
1.3000000	1.852514	1.947839	2.049751	2.147216	2.217277
1.3100000	1.876587	1.975938	2.083119	2.186899	2.262558
1.3200000	1.900875	2.004395	2.117113	2.227672	2.309502
1.3300000	1.925375	2.033210	2.151742	2.269583	2.358229
1.3400000	1.950083	2.062380	2.187015	2.312679	2.408873
1.3500000	1.974995	2.091904	2.222940	2.357008	2.461579
1.3600000	2.000108	2.121778	2.259522	2.402621	2.516514
1.3700000	2.025417	2.151998	2.296767	2.449569	2.573858
1.3799999	2.050917	2.182558	2.334676	2.497902	2.633818
1.3899999	2.076602	2.213452	2.373251	2.547669	2.696624
1.4000000	2.102466	2.244672	2.412488	2.598920	2.762534
1.4100000	2.128502	2.276211	2.452384	2.651699	2.831839
1.4200000	2.154704	2.308058	2.492929	2.706047	2.904868
1.4300000	2.181064	2.340201	2.534114	2.762002	2.981993
1.4400000	2.207573	2.372630	2.575923	2.819590	3.063636
1.4500000	2.234225	2.405330	2.618337	2.878830	3.150269
1.4600000	2.261009	2.438286	2.661335	2.939728	3.242424
1.4700000	2.287916	2.471483	2.704888	3.002274	3.340694
1.4800000	2.314937	2.504903	2.748966	3.066441	3.445726
1.4900000	2.342062	2.538528	2.793533	3.132180	3.558212
1.5000000	2.369281	2.572339	2.838550	3.199419	3.678858
1.5100000	2.396581	2.606315	2.883970	3.268060	3.808325
1.5200000	2.423953	2.640434	2.929746	3.337976	3.947132
1.5300000	2.451385	2.674675	2.975826	3.409013	4.095505
1.5400000	2.478865	2.709014	3.022154	3.480991	4.253172
1.5500000	2.506382	2.743428	3.068673	3.553705	4.419132
1.5600000	2.533924	2.777893	3.115321	3.626927	4.591488
1.5699999	2.561480	2.812384	3.162037	3.700418	4.767468
1.5707963	2.563674	2.815131	3.165758	3.706275	4.781539
1.5707963	2.563671	2.815128	3.165755	3.706270	4.781530

$\alpha =$ .250000

Θ	K VALUES				
	.009966711	.039469502	.087332193	.151646642	.229848846
.0000000	.000000	.000000	.000000	.000000	.000000
.0100000	.010000	.010000	.010000	.010000	.010000
.0200000	.020000	.020000	.020000	.020000	.020000
.0300000	.030002	.030002	.030002	.030002	.030003
.0400000	.040005	.040005	.040006	.040006	.040007
.0500000	.050010	.050011	.050012	.050013	.050015
.0600000	.060018	.060019	.060021	.060023	.060026
.0700000	.070029	.070030	.070033	.070037	.070041
.0800000	.080043	.080046	.080050	.080055	.080062
.0900000	.090061	.090065	.090071	.090079	.090088
.1000000	.100084	.100089	.100097	.100108	.100121
.1100000	.110113	.110119	.110130	.110144	.110161
.1200000	.120146	.120155	.120169	.120187	.120210
.1300000	.130186	.130197	.130214	.130238	.130267
.1400000	.140233	.140246	.140268	.140297	.140333
.1500000	.150286	.150303	.150330	.150366	.150410
.1600000	.160347	.160367	.160400	.160444	.160498
.1700000	.170416	.170441	.170480	.170533	.170597
.1800000	.180494	.180523	.180570	.180632	.180709
.1900000	.190581	.190615	.190670	.190744	.190833
.2000000	.200678	.200717	.200781	.200867	.200972
.2100000	.210785	.210830	.210904	.211004	.211125
.2200000	.220902	.220955	.221040	.221154	.221294
.2300000	.231031	.231091	.231188	.231318	.231478
.2400000	.241171	.241239	.241349	.241498	.241679
.2500000	.251323	.251400	.251525	.251693	.251898
.2600000	.261488	.261574	.261715	.261904	.262135
.2700000	.271666	.271763	.271920	.272132	.272390
.2800000	.281858	.281965	.282141	.282377	.282666
.2900000	.292063	.292183	.292378	.292640	.292961
.3000000	.302284	.302416	.302631	.302922	.303278
.3100000	.312519	.312665	.312903	.313224	.313616
.3200000	.322770	.322930	.323192	.323545	.323977
.3300000	.333036	.333213	.333499	.333887	.334361
.3400000	.343320	.343512	.343826	.344250	.344769
.3500000	.353620	.353830	.354172	.354635	.355201
.3600000	.363938	.364166	.364538	.365042	.365659
.3700000	.374273	.374521	.374925	.375472	.376143
.3800000	.384627	.384896	.385334	.385926	.386653
.3900000	.395000	.395290	.395764	.396404	.397191

$\alpha =$ .250000

Θ	K VALUES				
	.009966711	.039469502	.087332193	.151646642	.229848846
.4000000	.405392	.405705	.406216	.406907	.407757
.4100000	.415804	.416141	.416691	.417436	.418351
.4200000	.426236	.426598	.427189	.427990	.428975
.4300000	.436689	.437077	.437712	.438572	.439629
.4400000	.447163	.447579	.448258	.449180	.450314
.4500000	.457658	.458103	.458830	.459816	.461031
.4600000	.468176	.468651	.469427	.470481	.471779
.4700000	.478716	.479222	.480050	.481175	.482561
.4800000	.489278	.489818	.490700	.491898	.493376
.4900000	.499864	.500438	.501376	.502651	.504225
.5000000	.510474	.511083	.512080	.513435	.515109
.5100000	.521108	.521754	.522812	.524250	.526028
.5200000	.531767	.532451	.533572	.535097	.536984
.5300000	.542450	.543175	.544361	.545977	.547976
.5400000	.553159	.553925	.555180	.556889	.559006
.5500000	.563894	.564703	.566028	.567835	.570073
.5600000	.574655	.575508	.576907	.578814	.581179
.5700000	.585442	.586342	.587816	.589828	.592325
.5800000	.596257	.597204	.598757	.600878	.603510
.5900000	.607098	.608095	.609729	.611962	.614736
.6000000	.617968	.619015	.620734	.623083	.626003
.6100000	.628865	.629965	.631771	.634240	.637311
.6200000	.639791	.640945	.642840	.645434	.648662
.6300000	.650746	.651956	.653944	.656665	.660055
.6400000	.661730	.662997	.665081	.667934	.671492
.6500000	.672743	.674070	.676252	.679242	.682973
.6600000	.683786	.685174	.687457	.690588	.694498
.6700000	.694859	.696310	.698698	.701974	.706068
.6800000	.705963	.707478	.709974	.713399	.717683
.6899999	.717097	.718679	.721285	.724865	.729344
.7000000	.728262	.729913	.732633	.736371	.741052
.7100000	.739459	.741180	.744016	.747918	.752807
.7200000	.750687	.752480	.755437	.759506	.764609
.7300000	.761946	.763814	.766894	.771135	.776459
.7400000	.773238	.775182	.778389	.782807	.788358
.7500000	.784563	.786584	.789921	.794521	.800305
.7600000	.795920	.798021	.801491	.806277	.812301
.7700000	.807309	.809492	.813099	.818077	.824346
.7800000	.818732	.820999	.824745	.829920	.836442
.7899999	.830188	.832540	.836430	.841806	.848588

$\alpha =$ .250000

Θ	K VALUES				
	.009966711	.039469502	.087332193	.151646642	.229848846
.8000000	.841677	.844118	.848154	.853737	.860785
.8100000	.853200	.855730	.859917	.865711	.873032
.8200000	.864756	.867379	.871719	.877730	.885331
.8300000	.876347	.879063	.883561	.889793	.897681
.8400000	.887971	.890783	.895442	.901901	.910084
.8500000	.899630	.902540	.907363	.914054	.922538
.8600000	.911323	.914333	.919324	.926252	.935045
.8700000	.923050	.926162	.931325	.938496	.947604
.8799999	.934812	.938028	.943366	.950785	.960216
.8899999	.946608	.949931	.955447	.963119	.972882
.9000000	.958439	.961870	.967569	.975500	.985600
.9100000	.970305	.973846	.979731	.987926	.998371
.9200000	.982205	.985859	.991933	1.000398	1.011196
.9300000	.994140	.997909	1.004176	1.012915	1.024075
.9400000	1.006110	1.009995	1.016459	1.025479	1.037006
.9500000	1.018114	1.022118	1.028783	1.038088	1.049992
.9600000	1.030153	1.034278	1.041147	1.050744	1.063031
.9699999	1.042227	1.046475	1.053552	1.063445	1.076123
.9799999	1.054335	1.058708	1.065996	1.076192	1.089269
.9899999	1.066477	1.070978	1.078481	1.088985	1.102469
1.0000000	1.078654	1.083284	1.091006	1.101823	1.115722
1.0100000	1.090865	1.095626	1.103571	1.114707	1.129028
1.0200000	1.103111	1.108005	1.116176	1.127636	1.142387
1.0300000	1.115390	1.120420	1.128820	1.140610	1.155799
1.0400000	1.127703	1.132870	1.141504	1.153629	1.169264
1.0500000	1.140049	1.145357	1.154227	1.166693	1.182781
1.0600000	1.152429	1.157878	1.166989	1.179801	1.196351
1.0699999	1.164842	1.170435	1.179790	1.192954	1.209973
1.0799999	1.177289	1.183027	1.192630	1.206150	1.223646
1.0899999	1.189767	1.195653	1.205507	1.219390	1.237370
1.1000000	1.202279	1.208314	1.218423	1.232673	1.251146
1.1100000	1.214822	1.221009	1.231376	1.245999	1.264972
1.1200000	1.227397	1.233738	1.244366	1.259367	1.278848
1.1300000	1.240003	1.246500	1.257393	1.272777	1.292773
1.1400000	1.252641	1.259295	1.270456	1.286229	1.306748
1.1500000	1.265309	1.272122	1.283555	1.299722	1.320771
1.1600000	1.278008	1.284982	1.296690	1.313255	1.334842
1.1700000	1.290737	1.297873	1.309859	1.326829	1.348961
1.1800000	1.303495	1.310796	1.323064	1.340442	1.363126
1.1899999	1.316282	1.323750	1.336302	1.354094	1.377337

$\alpha =$ •250000

θ	K VALUES				
	•009966711	•039469502	•087332193	•151646642	•229848846
1•2000000	1•329098	1•336734	1•349574	1•367784	1•391594
1•2100000	1•341942	1•349748	1•362878	1•381512	1•405895
1•2200000	1•354813	1•362791	1•376215	1•395277	1•420240
1•2300000	1•367712	1•375863	1•389584	1•409078	1•434628
1•2400000	1•380637	1•388963	1•402984	1•422915	1•449059
1•2500000	1•393588	1•402091	1•416414	1•436786	1•463531
1•2599999	1•406564	1•415245	1•429874	1•450692	1•478044
1•2699999	1•419566	1•428426	1•443363	1•464631	1•492596
1•2799999	1•432591	1•441633	1•456880	1•478603	1•507187
1•2899999	1•445641	1•454865	1•470425	1•492606	1•521815
1•3000000	1•458713	1•468121	1•483997	1•506640	1•536481
1•3100000	1•471807	1•481401	1•497595	1•520704	1•551182
1•3200000	1•484923	1•494704	1•511219	1•534797	1•565917
1•3300000	1•498060	1•508029	1•524866	1•548919	1•580687
1•3400000	1•511217	1•521375	1•538538	1•563067	1•595488
1•3500000	1•524394	1•534742	1•552233	1•577242	1•610321
1•3600000	1•537590	1•548129	1•565949	1•591442	1•625184
1•3700000	1•550803	1•561536	1•579687	1•605666	1•640077
1•3799999	1•564034	1•574960	1•593445	1•619914	1•654996
1•3899999	1•577281	1•588402	1•607222	1•634184	1•669943
1•4000000	1•590544	1•601861	1•621018	1•648475	1•684915
1•4100000	1•603822	1•615336	1•634831	1•662786	1•699910
1•4200000	1•617114	1•628825	1•648660	1•677115	1•714929
1•4300000	1•630419	1•642329	1•662505	1•691463	1•729968
1•4400000	1•643737	1•655845	1•676365	1•705828	1•745028
1•4500000	1•657066	1•669375	1•690238	1•720208	1•760107
1•4600000	1•670406	1•682915	1•704124	1•734603	1•775203
1•4700000	1•683756	1•696466	1•718022	1•749011	1•790314
1•4800000	1•697115	1•710027	1•731930	1•763431	1•805441
1•4900000	1•710482	1•723596	1•745848	1•777862	1•820580
1•5000000	1•723856	1•737173	1•759774	1•792303	1•835732
1•5100000	1•737237	1•750757	1•773708	1•806753	1•850893
1•5200000	1•750623	1•764346	1•787648	1•821210	1•866064
1•5300000	1•764014	1•777940	1•801593	1•835673	1•881241
1•5400000	1•777408	1•791539	1•815543	1•850141	1•896425
1•5500000	1•790806	1•805140	1•829496	1•864613	1•911614
1•5600000	1•804205	1•818743	1•843452	1•879088	1•926805
1•5699999	1•817605	1•832348	1•857408	1•893564	1•941998
1•5707963	1•818672	1•833431	1•858519	1•894716	1•943208
1•5707963	1•818671	1•833430	1•858518	1•894715	1•943207

$\alpha =$ .250000

Θ	K VALUES				
	.318821117	.415016431	.514599755	.613601043	.708073407
.0000000	.000000	.000000	.000000	.000000	.000000
.0100000	.010000	.010000	.010000	.010000	.010000
.0200000	.020001	.020001	.020001	.020001	.020001
.0300000	.030003	.030004	.030004	.030005	.030005
.0400000	.040008	.040009	.040010	.040011	.040012
.0500000	.050017	.050019	.050021	.050023	.050025
.0600000	.060029	.060032	.060036	.060040	.060043
.0700000	.070046	.070052	.070058	.070063	.070069
.0800000	.080069	.080078	.080086	.080095	.080103
.0900000	.090099	.090111	.090123	.090135	.090146
.1000000	.100136	.100152	.100169	.100185	.100201
.1100000	.110181	.110203	.110225	.110247	.110268
.1200000	.120235	.120263	.120292	.120321	.120348
.1300000	.130299	.130335	.130371	.130408	.130443
.1400000	.140374	.140418	.140464	.140510	.140553
.1500000	.150460	.150515	.150571	.150627	.150681
.1600000	.160559	.160625	.160693	.160762	.160827
.1700000	.170670	.170750	.170832	.170914	.170993
.1800000	.180796	.180890	.180988	.181086	.181179
.1900000	.190936	.191047	.191162	.191277	.191387
.2000000	.201091	.201221	.201356	.201490	.201619
.2100000	.211264	.211414	.211570	.211726	.211875
.2200000	.221453	.221626	.221806	.221985	.222158
.2300000	.231660	.231858	.232064	.232270	.232467
.2400000	.241887	.242112	.242346	.242580	.242805
.2500000	.252132	.252387	.252653	.252918	.253172
.2600000	.262399	.262686	.262985	.263284	.263571
.2700000	.272686	.273008	.273344	.273680	.274002
.2800000	.282996	.283356	.283731	.284106	.284467
.2900000	.293329	.293729	.294146	.294565	.294967
.3000000	.303685	.304129	.304592	.305056	.305503
.3100000	.314066	.314557	.315069	.315582	.316076
.3200000	.324473	.325013	.325577	.326144	.326689
.3300000	.334905	.335499	.336119	.336742	.337343
.3400000	.345365	.346015	.346695	.347379	.348038
.3500000	.355852	.356563	.357307	.358055	.358776
.3600000	.366368	.367143	.367955	.368771	.369559
.3700000	.376914	.377757	.378640	.379529	.380389
.3800000	.387489	.388404	.389364	.390330	.391265
.3900000	.398096	.399087	.400127	.401176	.402191

$\alpha =$ .250000

Θ	K VALUES				
	.318821117	.415016431	.514599755	.613601043	.708073407
.4000000	.408735	.409806	.410932	.412067	.413166
.4100000	.419406	.420562	.421778	.423005	.424194
.4200000	.430111	.431356	.432667	.433991	.435275
.4300000	.440850	.442189	.443600	.445026	.446411
.4400000	.451624	.453062	.454578	.456112	.457603
.4500000	.462434	.463976	.465603	.467250	.468852
.4600000	.473280	.474932	.476675	.478442	.480161
.4700000	.484164	.485930	.487795	.489688	.491531
.4800000	.495086	.496972	.498965	.500990	.502963
.4900000	.506048	.508059	.510186	.512349	.514460
.5000000	.517049	.519191	.521458	.523767	.526021
.5100000	.528090	.530369	.532784	.535244	.537650
.5200000	.539173	.541595	.544164	.546784	.549348
.5300000	.550298	.552869	.555599	.558385	.561116
.5400000	.561466	.564192	.567090	.570051	.572956
.5500000	.572677	.575565	.578638	.581782	.584870
.5600000	.583933	.586990	.590246	.593580	.596859
.5700000	.595234	.598466	.601913	.605446	.608925
.5800000	.606581	.609995	.613640	.617382	.621070
.5900000	.617974	.621578	.625430	.629389	.633295
.6000000	.629414	.633216	.637283	.641468	.645602
.6100000	.640903	.644909	.649200	.653620	.657994
.6200000	.652440	.656659	.661182	.665848	.670471
.6300000	.664027	.668465	.673231	.678153	.683035
.6400000	.675663	.680330	.685347	.690535	.695688
.6500000	.687351	.692254	.697532	.702997	.708433
.6600000	.699089	.704238	.709786	.715540	.721270
.6700000	.710880	.716283	.722112	.728165	.734202
.6800000	.722724	.728389	.734509	.740873	.747231
.6899999	.734621	.740558	.746979	.753667	.760358
.7000000	.746572	.752790	.759524	.766547	.773585
.7100000	.758578	.765085	.772143	.779515	.786914
.7200000	.770639	.777446	.784839	.792573	.800348
.7300000	.782755	.789872	.797612	.805721	.813887
.7400000	.794928	.802365	.810463	.818961	.827534
.7500000	.807158	.814924	.823394	.832296	.841290
.7600000	.819445	.827552	.836405	.845725	.855159
.7700000	.831791	.840248	.849497	.859250	.869141
.7800000	.844195	.853013	.862672	.872874	.883238
.7899999	.856658	.865848	.875930	.886597	.897453

$\alpha =$ •250000

Θ	K VALUES				
	•318821117	•415016431	•514599755	•613601043	•708073407
•8000000	•869180	•878754	•889272	•900420	•911788
•8100000	•881762	•891731	•902700	•914345	•926244
•8200000	•894405	•904780	•916213	•928374	•940823
•8300000	•907108	•917901	•929814	•942507	•955527
•8400000	•919873	•931096	•943502	•956746	•970359
•8500000	•932699	•944364	•957280	•971093	•985321
•8600000	•945587	•957706	•971147	•985548	1•000413
•8700000	•958537	•971123	•985104	1•000113	1•015639
•8799999	•971550	•984615	•999152	1•014789	1•031000
•8899999	•984626	•998182	1•013293	1•029577	1•046498
•9000000	•997764	1•011826	1•027526	1•044479	1•062135
•9100000	1•010966	1•025546	1•041852	1•059496	1•077913
•9200000	1•024232	1•039343	1•056273	1•074629	1•093833
•9300000	1•037561	1•053217	1•070788	1•089878	1•109899
•9400000	1•050954	1•067168	1•085398	1•105246	1•126111
•9500000	1•064411	1•081198	1•100104	1•120732	1•142471
•9600000	1•077931	1•095305	1•114907	1•136339	1•158981
•9699999	1•091516	1•109490	1•129806	1•152066	1•175644
•9799999	1•105165	1•123754	1•144802	1•167916	1•192460
•9899999	1•118879	1•138096	1•159896	1•183888	1•209432
1•0000000	1•132656	1•152517	1•175088	1•199984	1•226560
1•0100000	1•146497	1•167016	1•190378	1•216204	1•243847
1•0200000	1•160402	1•181594	1•205766	1•232549	1•261295
1•0300000	1•174371	1•196250	1•221253	1•249020	1•278904
1•0400000	1•188403	1•210985	1•236839	1•265617	1•296676
1•0500000	1•202499	1•225798	1•252524	1•282341	1•314612
1•0600000	1•216658	1•240689	1•268307	1•299192	1•332715
1•0699999	1•230880	1•255658	1•284190	1•316171	1•350984
1•0799999	1•245164	1•270705	1•300170	1•333277	1•369421
1•0899999	1•259510	1•285829	1•316250	1•350512	1•388028
1•1000000	1•273919	1•301031	1•332428	1•367875	1•406804
1•1100000	1•288388	1•316308	1•348704	1•385366	1•425752
1•1200000	1•302919	1•331662	1•365077	1•402985	1•444871
1•1300000	1•317509	1•347092	1•381548	1•420732	1•464163
1•1400000	1•332160	1•362596	1•398115	1•438608	1•483627
1•1500000	1•346870	1•378175	1•414779	1•456611	1•503264
1•1600000	1•361638	1•393827	1•431538	1•474740	1•523075
1•1700000	1•376464	1•409553	1•448391	1•492997	1•543060
1•1800000	1•391347	1•425351	1•465339	1•511379	1•563217
1•1899999	1•406287	1•441220	1•482380	1•529887	1•583549

$\alpha =$ .250000

Θ	K VALUES				
	.318821117	.415016431	.514599755	.613601043	.708073407
1.2000000	1.421283	1.457159	1.499513	1.548519	1.604053
1.2100000	1.436333	1.473168	1.516736	1.567274	1.624729
1.2200000	1.451437	1.489245	1.534050	1.586151	1.645577
1.2300000	1.466594	1.505390	1.551453	1.605149	1.666596
1.2400000	1.481803	1.521601	1.568942	1.624266	1.687784
1.2500000	1.497063	1.537877	1.586518	1.643502	1.709140
1.2599999	1.512373	1.554217	1.604179	1.662854	1.730663
1.2699999	1.527732	1.570619	1.621922	1.682321	1.752352
1.2799999	1.543138	1.587083	1.639747	1.701901	1.774203
1.2899999	1.558592	1.603606	1.657652	1.721591	1.796215
1.3000000	1.574090	1.620188	1.675634	1.741390	1.818386
1.3100000	1.589633	1.636827	1.693693	1.761295	1.840713
1.3200000	1.605219	1.653520	1.711825	1.781304	1.863192
1.3300000	1.620846	1.670267	1.730030	1.801414	1.885822
1.3400000	1.636514	1.687066	1.748304	1.821623	1.908597
1.3500000	1.652220	1.703916	1.766646	1.841928	1.931516
1.3600000	1.667964	1.720813	1.785054	1.862325	1.954574
1.3700000	1.683744	1.737758	1.803524	1.882811	1.977766
1.3799999	1.699558	1.754747	1.822055	1.903385	2.001089
1.3899999	1.715405	1.771778	1.840644	1.924041	2.024537
1.4000000	1.731284	1.788851	1.859289	1.944776	2.048107
1.4100000	1.747192	1.805962	1.877986	1.965587	2.071793
1.4200000	1.763129	1.823110	1.896734	1.986471	2.095589
1.4300000	1.779093	1.840293	1.915528	2.007422	2.119489
1.4400000	1.795081	1.857508	1.934367	2.028438	2.143489
1.4500000	1.811093	1.874754	1.953248	2.049513	2.167582
1.4600000	1.827126	1.892028	1.972168	2.070645	2.191762
1.4700000	1.843180	1.909328	1.991123	2.091828	2.216021
1.4800000	1.859251	1.926651	2.010110	2.113059	2.240355
1.4900000	1.875339	1.943996	2.029127	2.134332	2.264756
1.5000000	1.891442	1.961361	2.048170	2.155644	2.289217
1.5100000	1.907557	1.978742	2.067237	2.176990	2.313730
1.5200000	1.923684	1.996137	2.086323	2.198364	2.338289
1.5300000	1.939819	2.013545	2.105426	2.219763	2.362887
1.5400000	1.955963	2.030962	2.124542	2.241182	2.387515
1.5500000	1.972111	2.048387	2.143669	2.262615	2.412167
1.5600000	1.988264	2.065816	2.162802	2.284059	2.436835
1.5699999	2.004419	2.083249	2.181939	2.305507	2.461511
1.5707963	2.005705	2.084637	2.183463	2.307215	2.463476
1.5707963	2.005704	2.084635	2.183461	2.307213	2.463474

$\alpha =$ .250000

Θ	K VALUES				
	.794250555	.868696860	.928444378	.971111163	.994996249
.0000000	.000000	.000000	.000000	.000000	.000000
.0100000	.010000	.010000	.010000	.010000	.010000
.0200000	.020001	.020001	.020001	.020001	.020002
.0300000	.030005	.030006	.030006	.030006	.030006
.0400000	.040013	.040014	.040015	.040015	.040015
.0500000	.050026	.050028	.050029	.050030	.050031
.0600000	.060046	.060049	.060051	.060053	.060053
.0700000	.070074	.070078	.070081	.070084	.070085
.0800000	.080110	.080116	.080122	.080125	.080127
.0900000	.090157	.090166	.090173	.090179	.090182
.1000000	.100216	.100228	.100238	.100245	.100249
.1100000	.110287	.110304	.110317	.110327	.110332
.1200000	.120373	.120395	.120412	.120425	.120432
.1300000	.130475	.130502	.130525	.130540	.130549
.1400000	.140593	.140628	.140656	.140675	.140687
.1500000	.150730	.150773	.150807	.150831	.150845
.1600000	.160887	.160939	.160980	.161010	.161027
.1700000	.171064	.171127	.171177	.171212	.171233
.1800000	.181264	.181338	.181398	.181441	.181464
.1900000	.191488	.191575	.191646	.191696	.191724
.2000000	.201737	.201839	.201921	.201980	.202013
.2100000	.212012	.212131	.212226	.212294	.212333
.2200000	.222315	.222452	.222562	.222641	.222685
.2300000	.232648	.232804	.232930	.233021	.233071
.2400000	.243011	.243189	.243333	.243436	.243494
.2500000	.253406	.253608	.253772	.253888	.253954
.2600000	.263834	.264063	.264247	.264379	.264454
.2700000	.274298	.274555	.274762	.274911	.274994
.2800000	.284798	.285086	.285318	.285484	.285578
.2900000	.295336	.295657	.295916	.296102	.296206
.3000000	.305913	.306270	.306558	.306765	.306881
.3100000	.316531	.316927	.317246	.317475	.317604
.3200000	.327191	.327628	.327981	.328235	.328377
.3300000	.337896	.338377	.338766	.339045	.339202
.3400000	.348645	.349174	.349602	.349909	.350082
.3500000	.359442	.360022	.360491	.360828	.361017
.3600000	.370287	.370921	.371434	.371803	.372011
.3700000	.381182	.381874	.382435	.382838	.383064
.3800000	.392128	.392882	.393493	.393933	.394180
.3900000	.403128	.403948	.404612	.405091	.405360

$\alpha =$ .250000

Θ	K VALUES				
	.794250555	.868696860	.928444378	.971111163	.994996249
.4000000	.414183	.415073	.415794	.416313	.416606
.4100000	.425295	.426258	.427040	.427603	.427920
.4200000	.436464	.437506	.438352	.438962	.439305
.4300000	.447694	.448819	.449733	.450392	.450763
.4400000	.458985	.460198	.461184	.461895	.462296
.4500000	.470340	.471646	.472708	.473475	.473907
.4600000	.481759	.483163	.484306	.485132	.485597
.4700000	.493246	.494754	.495982	.496869	.497370
.4800000	.504801	.506418	.507737	.508690	.509228
.4900000	.516427	.518159	.519573	.520595	.521172
.5000000	.528125	.529979	.531493	.532589	.533207
.5100000	.539897	.541879	.543499	.544672	.545335
.5200000	.551745	.553862	.555593	.556848	.557557
.5300000	.563671	.565930	.567779	.569120	.569878
.5400000	.575677	.578085	.580058	.581489	.582299
.5500000	.587765	.590330	.592433	.593960	.594824
.5600000	.599937	.602666	.604906	.606534	.607456
.5700000	.612194	.615097	.617481	.619215	.620198
.5800000	.624540	.627624	.630160	.632005	.633052
.5900000	.636975	.640250	.642945	.644908	.646022
.6000000	.649503	.652977	.655840	.657927	.659112
.6100000	.662124	.665808	.668847	.671065	.672324
.6200000	.674842	.678746	.681970	.684324	.685662
.6300000	.687658	.691793	.695211	.697709	.699130
.6400000	.700575	.704951	.708573	.711223	.712731
.6500000	.713595	.718224	.722060	.724869	.726469
.6600000	.726721	.731614	.735675	.738652	.740347
.6700000	.739953	.745124	.749421	.752573	.754371
.6800000	.753296	.758757	.763301	.766639	.768543
.6899999	.766751	.772516	.777319	.780851	.782868
.7000000	.780320	.786403	.791478	.795215	.797350
.7100000	.794007	.800423	.805783	.809735	.811994
.7200000	.807812	.814577	.820236	.824414	.826804
.7300000	.821740	.828868	.834842	.839257	.841785
.7400000	.835792	.843302	.849604	.854268	.856942
.7500000	.849972	.857879	.864527	.869453	.872280
.7600000	.864281	.872605	.879614	.884816	.887803
.7700000	.878722	.887481	.894870	.900361	.903518
.7800000	.893298	.902512	.910300	.916095	.919430
.7899999	.908011	.917702	.925906	.932021	.935544

$\alpha =$ .250000

Θ	K VALUES				
	.794250555	.868696860	.928444378	.971111163	.994996249
.8000000	.922865	.933053	.941695	.948146	.951867
.8100000	.937862	.948570	.957670	.964475	.968404
.8200000	.953005	.964255	.973837	.981013	.985162
.8300000	.968296	.980114	.990200	.997767	1.002148
.8400000	.983739	.996150	1.006764	1.014743	1.019368
.8500000	.999336	1.012366	1.023535	1.031947	1.036829
.8600000	1.015090	1.028768	1.040518	1.049385	1.054539
.8700000	1.031004	1.045358	1.057718	1.067065	1.072505
.8799999	1.047081	1.062142	1.075142	1.084993	1.090735
.8899999	1.063324	1.079123	1.092794	1.103176	1.109238
.9000000	1.079736	1.096306	1.110682	1.121623	1.128022
.9100000	1.096319	1.113695	1.128810	1.140341	1.147095
.9200000	1.113078	1.131295	1.147185	1.159337	1.166468
.9300000	1.130015	1.149111	1.165815	1.178621	1.186150
.9400000	1.147132	1.167146	1.184704	1.198201	1.206151
.9500000	1.164434	1.185407	1.203862	1.218086	1.226481
.9600000	1.181922	1.203897	1.223293	1.238285	1.247152
.9699999	1.199601	1.222622	1.243006	1.258808	1.268175
.9799999	1.217473	1.241586	1.263009	1.279666	1.289562
.9899999	1.235541	1.260795	1.283308	1.300869	1.311326
1.0000000	1.253809	1.280254	1.303913	1.322428	1.333481
1.0100000	1.272279	1.299968	1.324831	1.344354	1.356039
1.0200000	1.290954	1.319943	1.346070	1.366659	1.379016
1.0300000	1.309837	1.340183	1.367639	1.389356	1.402427
1.0400000	1.328932	1.360694	1.389548	1.412458	1.426288
1.0500000	1.348241	1.381482	1.411805	1.435978	1.450617
1.0600000	1.367766	1.402552	1.434420	1.459931	1.475430
1.0699999	1.387512	1.423910	1.457403	1.484331	1.500748
1.0799999	1.407480	1.445561	1.480764	1.509194	1.526590
1.0899999	1.427674	1.467511	1.504512	1.534536	1.552977
1.1000000	1.448095	1.489766	1.528659	1.560374	1.579931
1.1100000	1.468747	1.512331	1.553216	1.586725	1.607478
1.1200000	1.489632	1.535213	1.578193	1.613609	1.635640
1.1300000	1.510752	1.558415	1.603602	1.641045	1.664446
1.1400000	1.532109	1.581946	1.629455	1.669054	1.693924
1.1500000	1.553705	1.605809	1.655764	1.697656	1.724104
1.1600000	1.575542	1.630010	1.682542	1.726874	1.755019
1.1700000	1.597623	1.654555	1.709800	1.756732	1.786702
1.1800000	1.619948	1.679449	1.737551	1.787256	1.819192
1.1899999	1.642519	1.704697	1.765809	1.818470	1.852528

$\alpha =$ •250000

θ	K VALUES				
	•794250555	•868696860	•928444378	•971111163	•994996249
1•2000000	1•665337	1•730305	1•794588	1•850402	1•886753
1•2100000	1•688403	1•756276	1•823899	1•883082	1•921912
1•2200000	1•711718	1•782616	1•853758	1•916539	1•958054
1•2300000	1•735281	1•809329	1•884177	1•950806	1•995234
1•2400000	1•759094	1•836418	1•915171	1•985915	2•033507
1•2500000	1•783156	1•863888	1•946753	2•021902	2•072938
1•2599999	1•807467	1•891742	1•978937	2•058803	2•113593
1•2699999	1•832025	1•919982	2•011737	2•096658	2•155547
1•2799999	1•856830	1•948611	2•045166	2•135506	2•198879
1•2899999	1•881880	1•977631	2•079237	2•175390	2•243677
1•3000000	1•907173	2•007043	2•113963	2•216355	2•290038
1•3100000	1•932706	2•036846	2•149356	2•258446	2•338066
1•3200000	1•958478	2•067042	2•185426	2•301710	2•387878
1•3300000	1•984484	2•097629	2•222185	2•346199	2•439603
1•3400000	2•010722	2•128605	2•259642	2•391962	2•493381
1•3500000	2•037186	2•159968	2•297804	2•439052	2•549370
1•3600000	2•063873	2•191713	2•336678	2•487523	2•607746
1•3700000	2•090776	2•223837	2•376270	2•537429	2•668704
1•3799999	2•117891	2•256333	2•416580	2•588823	2•732462
1•3899999	2•145211	2•289194	2•457610	2•641759	2•799266
1•4000000	2•172730	2•322412	2•499358	2•696289	2•869393
1•4100000	2•200439	2•355977	2•541818	2•752460	2•943152
1•4200000	2•228332	2•389880	2•584980	2•810316	3•020895
1•4300000	2•256400	2•424106	2•628834	2•869897	3•103018
1•4400000	2•284634	2•458644	2•673362	2•931231	3•189971
1•4500000	2•313025	2•493478	2•718546	2•994338	3•282259
1•4600000	2•341563	2•528593	2•764359	3•059223	3•380450
1•4700000	2•370238	2•563970	2•810773	3•125877	3•485174
1•4800000	2•399039	2•599591	2•857754	3•194270	3•597123
1•4900000	2•427954	2•635436	2•905263	3•264349	3•717035
1•5000000	2•456973	2•671484	2•953257	3•336037	3•845663
1•5100000	2•486083	2•707712	3•001688	3•409227	3•983711
1•5200000	2•515272	2•744096	3•050503	3•483785	4•131733
1•5300000	2•544528	2•780613	3•099646	3•559545	4•289970
1•5400000	2•573837	2•817238	3•149058	3•636313	4•458130
1•5500000	2•603187	2•853944	3•198675	3•713869	4•635144
1•5600000	2•632565	2•890705	3•248432	3•791972	4•818987
1•5699999	2•661957	2•927496	3•298262	3•870362	5•006698
1•5707963	2•664298	2•930426	3•302232	3•876609	5•021707
1•5707963	2•664295	2•930423	3•302228	3•876604	5•021699

$\alpha =$ .299999

Θ	K VALUES				
	.009966711	.039469502	.087332193	.151646642	.229848846
.0000000	.000000	.000000	.000000	.000000	.000000
.0100000	.010000	.010000	.010000	.010000	.010000
.0200000	.020000	.020000	.020000	.020001	.020001
.0300000	.030002	.030002	.030003	.030003	.030003
.0400000	.040006	.040006	.040007	.040008	.040008
.0500000	.050012	.050013	.050014	.050015	.050017
.0600000	.060021	.060023	.060024	.060027	.060029
.0700000	.070034	.070036	.070039	.070043	.070047
.0800000	.080052	.080054	.080058	.080064	.080070
.0900000	.090074	.090077	.090083	.090091	.090100
.1000000	.100101	.100106	.100114	.100125	.100138
.1100000	.110135	.110141	.110152	.110166	.110184
.1200000	.120175	.120184	.120197	.120216	.120239
.1300000	.130223	.130234	.130251	.130275	.130303
.1400000	.140278	.140292	.140314	.140343	.140379
.1500000	.150342	.150359	.150386	.150422	.150466
.1600000	.160416	.160436	.160469	.160513	.160566
.1700000	.170499	.170523	.170562	.170615	.170679
.1800000	.180592	.180621	.180667	.180730	.180806
.1900000	.190696	.190730	.190785	.190859	.190948
.2000000	.200812	.200851	.200915	.201001	.201106
.2100000	.210940	.210986	.211060	.211159	.211281
.2200000	.221081	.221133	.221218	.221333	.221473
.2300000	.231235	.231295	.231392	.231523	.231683
.2400000	.241403	.241471	.241582	.241731	.241912
.2500000	.251586	.251663	.251788	.251956	.252161
.2600000	.261784	.261870	.262011	.262200	.262431
.2700000	.271997	.272094	.272251	.272464	.272723
.2800000	.282227	.282335	.282511	.282748	.283037
.2900000	.292474	.292594	.292789	.293053	.293374
.3000000	.302739	.302872	.303088	.303379	.303736
.3100000	.313021	.313168	.313406	.313728	.314122
.3200000	.323323	.323484	.323746	.324101	.324534
.3300000	.333644	.333820	.334108	.334497	.334973
.3400000	.343984	.344178	.344492	.344918	.345439
.3500000	.354346	.354557	.354900	.355364	.355933
.3600000	.364728	.364957	.365331	.365837	.366456
.3700000	.375132	.375381	.375787	.376336	.377009
.3800000	.385559	.385828	.386268	.386863	.387593
.3900000	.396008	.396299	.396775	.397418	.398208

$\alpha =$ .299999

Θ	K VALUES				
	.009966711	.039469502	.087332193	.151646642	.229848846
.4000000	.406480	.406795	.407308	.408003	.408856
.4100000	.416977	.417316	.417868	.418617	.419537
.4200000	.427498	.427862	.428456	.429262	.430252
.4300000	.438045	.438435	.439073	.439938	.441001
.4400000	.448617	.449035	.449719	.450646	.451787
.4500000	.459215	.459663	.460394	.461386	.462608
.4600000	.469840	.470319	.471100	.472160	.473467
.4700000	.480493	.481003	.481836	.482968	.484364
.4800000	.491174	.491717	.492605	.493811	.495299
.4900000	.501883	.502461	.503405	.504689	.506275
.5000000	.512621	.513235	.514239	.515604	.517290
.5100000	.523389	.524040	.525106	.526555	.528347
.5200000	.534187	.534877	.536007	.537544	.539446
.5300000	.545016	.545746	.546942	.548572	.550587
.5400000	.555876	.556648	.557913	.559638	.561773
.5500000	.566767	.567583	.568920	.570743	.573002
.5600000	.577691	.578552	.579964	.581889	.584276
.5700000	.588648	.589556	.591044	.593076	.595597
.5800000	.599637	.600594	.602163	.604304	.606963
.5900000	.610661	.611668	.613319	.615575	.618378
.6000000	.621719	.622777	.624514	.626889	.629840
.6100000	.632812	.633924	.635749	.638245	.641351
.6200000	.643940	.645107	.647024	.649646	.652911
.6300000	.655103	.656327	.658339	.661092	.664522
.6400000	.666303	.667586	.669695	.672583	.676184
.6500000	.677540	.678883	.681092	.684120	.687897
.6600000	.688813	.690219	.692532	.695703	.699663
.6700000	.700124	.701595	.704014	.707334	.711482
.6800000	.711473	.713010	.715539	.719012	.723354
.6899999	.722861	.724465	.727108	.730738	.735280
.7000000	.734287	.735962	.738721	.742513	.747262
.7100000	.745753	.747499	.750378	.754337	.759299
.7200000	.757258	.759078	.762080	.766211	.771393
.7300000	.768803	.770699	.773828	.778135	.783543
.7400000	.780388	.782363	.785621	.790110	.795750
.7500000	.792015	.794069	.797460	.802136	.808016
.7600000	.803682	.805818	.809347	.814214	.820340
.7700000	.815391	.817611	.821280	.826344	.832723
.7800000	.827141	.829448	.833261	.838527	.845166
.7899999	.838933	.841329	.845289	.850763	.857669

$\alpha =$ .299999

θ	K VALUES				
	.009966711	.039469502	.087332193	.151646642	.229848846
.8000000	.850768	.853254	.857366	.863052	.870232
.8100000	.862646	.865224	.869491	.875395	.882857
.8200000	.874566	.877239	.881664	.887792	.895543
.8300000	.886530	.889300	.893887	.900243	.908291
.8400000	.898537	.901406	.906159	.912750	.921101
.8500000	.910587	.913557	.918481	.925311	.933974
.8600000	.922682	.925755	.930852	.937929	.946910
.8700000	.934820	.937999	.943274	.950601	.959910
.8799999	.947003	.950290	.955746	.963330	.972973
.8899999	.959230	.962627	.968268	.976115	.986101
.9000000	.971501	.975011	.980841	.988956	.999293
.9100000	.983817	.987442	.993465	1.001854	1.012549
.9200000	.996178	.999919	1.006139	1.014808	1.025870
.9300000	1.008584	1.012444	1.018865	1.027820	1.039256
.9400000	1.021034	1.025016	1.031642	1.040888	1.052708
.9500000	1.033529	1.037635	1.044470	1.054013	1.066224
.9600000	1.046070	1.050301	1.057349	1.067196	1.079806
.9699999	1.058655	1.063015	1.070279	1.080435	1.093454
.9799999	1.071285	1.075776	1.083260	1.093732	1.107166
.9899999	1.083960	1.088583	1.096292	1.107086	1.120945
1.0000000	1.096680	1.101438	1.109376	1.120496	1.134789
1.0100000	1.109445	1.114340	1.122510	1.133964	1.148698
1.0200000	1.122254	1.127289	1.135695	1.147488	1.162672
1.0300000	1.135107	1.140284	1.148931	1.161069	1.176712
1.0400000	1.148005	1.153326	1.162218	1.174707	1.190816
1.0500000	1.160947	1.166415	1.175555	1.188401	1.204986
1.0600000	1.173933	1.179549	1.188941	1.202151	1.219219
1.0699999	1.186963	1.192730	1.202378	1.215956	1.233517
1.0799999	1.200036	1.205956	1.215864	1.229817	1.247880
1.0899999	1.213152	1.219227	1.229400	1.243734	1.262305
1.1000000	1.226311	1.232544	1.242984	1.257705	1.276794
1.1100000	1.239513	1.245905	1.256617	1.271730	1.291346
1.1200000	1.252757	1.259310	1.270297	1.285809	1.305959
1.1300000	1.266042	1.272760	1.284026	1.299942	1.320635
1.1400000	1.279369	1.286252	1.297802	1.314127	1.335372
1.1500000	1.292737	1.299788	1.311624	1.328365	1.350169
1.1600000	1.306145	1.313366	1.325492	1.342654	1.365026
1.1700000	1.319593	1.326987	1.339406	1.356995	1.379943
1.1800000	1.333080	1.340648	1.353366	1.371386	1.394918
1.1899999	1.346607	1.354351	1.367369	1.385827	1.409950

$\alpha =$ .299999

Θ	K VALUES				
	.009966711	.039469502	.087332193	.151646642	.229848846
1.2000000	1.360171	1.368093	1.381416	1.400317	1.425040
1.2100000	1.373774	1.381876	1.395507	1.414856	1.440186
1.2200000	1.387413	1.395697	1.409639	1.429442	1.455387
1.2300000	1.401089	1.409557	1.423813	1.444075	1.470642
1.2400000	1.414800	1.423454	1.438028	1.458753	1.485951
1.2500000	1.428547	1.437388	1.452283	1.473477	1.501311
1.2599999	1.442328	1.451358	1.466577	1.488244	1.516723
1.2699999	1.456142	1.465363	1.480910	1.503055	1.532185
1.2799999	1.469989	1.479402	1.495280	1.517908	1.547696
1.2899999	1.483868	1.493475	1.509686	1.532801	1.563255
1.3000000	1.497778	1.507581	1.524128	1.547735	1.578861
1.3100000	1.511718	1.521719	1.538604	1.562708	1.594511
1.3200000	1.525688	1.535887	1.553114	1.577718	1.610206
1.3300000	1.539686	1.550086	1.567656	1.592765	1.625943
1.3400000	1.553711	1.564313	1.582230	1.607847	1.641721
1.3500000	1.567763	1.578568	1.596834	1.622963	1.657539
1.3600000	1.581840	1.592850	1.611468	1.638112	1.673396
1.3700000	1.595942	1.607157	1.626129	1.653293	1.689290
1.3799999	1.610068	1.621490	1.640817	1.668504	1.705218
1.3899999	1.624216	1.635846	1.655531	1.683744	1.721181
1.4000000	1.638386	1.650224	1.670270	1.699012	1.737176
1.4100000	1.652575	1.664624	1.685032	1.714306	1.753202
1.4200000	1.666784	1.679045	1.699815	1.729624	1.769256
1.4300000	1.681012	1.693484	1.714620	1.744966	1.785338
1.4400000	1.695256	1.707941	1.729444	1.760330	1.801446
1.4500000	1.709516	1.722415	1.744286	1.775715	1.817577
1.4600000	1.723791	1.736904	1.759145	1.791118	1.833731
1.4700000	1.738079	1.751408	1.774020	1.806539	1.849905
1.4800000	1.752380	1.765924	1.788908	1.821976	1.866098
1.4900000	1.766691	1.780453	1.803810	1.837427	1.882307
1.5000000	1.781013	1.794992	1.818723	1.852891	1.898532
1.5100000	1.795344	1.809540	1.833645	1.868366	1.914770
1.5200000	1.809682	1.824095	1.848577	1.883852	1.931019
1.5300000	1.824026	1.838658	1.863515	1.899345	1.947278
1.5400000	1.838376	1.853226	1.878460	1.914844	1.963544
1.5500000	1.852729	1.867798	1.893409	1.930349	1.979816
1.5600000	1.867085	1.882372	1.908360	1.945857	1.996093
1.5699999	1.881442	1.896948	1.923314	1.961367	2.012371
1.5707963	1.882585	1.898109	1.924504	1.962602	2.013667
1.5707963	1.882584	1.898108	1.924503	1.962601	2.013666

$\alpha =$ .299999

Θ	K VALUES				
	.318821117	.415016431	.514599755	.613601043	.708073407
.0000000	.000000	.000000	.000000	.000000	.000000
.0100000	.010000	.010000	.010000	.010000	.010000
.0200000	.020001	.020001	.020001	.020001	.020001
.0300000	.030004	.030004	.030005	.030005	.030005
.0400000	.040009	.040010	.040011	.040012	.040013
.0500000	.050019	.050021	.050023	.050025	.050027
.0600000	.060033	.060036	.060040	.060043	.060047
.0700000	.070052	.070058	.070063	.070069	.070074
.0800000	.080078	.080086	.080095	.080103	.080111
.0900000	.090111	.090123	.090135	.090147	.090159
.1000000	.100153	.100169	.100185	.100202	.100218
.1100000	.110203	.110225	.110247	.110269	.110290
.1200000	.120264	.120292	.120321	.120350	.120377
.1300000	.130336	.130372	.130408	.130445	.130480
.1400000	.140420	.140464	.140510	.140556	.140600
.1500000	.150517	.150571	.150628	.150684	.150738
.1600000	.160627	.160693	.160762	.160831	.160896
.1700000	.170753	.170832	.170914	.170997	.171075
.1800000	.180893	.180988	.181086	.181184	.181277
.1900000	.191051	.191162	.191278	.191393	.191503
.2000000	.201226	.201356	.201491	.201625	.201754
.2100000	.211419	.211570	.211726	.211883	.212032
.2200000	.221632	.221806	.221986	.222166	.222338
.2300000	.231865	.232064	.232270	.232476	.232673
.2400000	.242120	.242345	.242580	.242815	.243040
.2500000	.252396	.252652	.252918	.253183	.253438
.2600000	.262696	.262984	.263283	.263583	.263871
.2700000	.273020	.273342	.273679	.274015	.274338
.2800000	.283368	.283729	.284105	.284481	.284843
.2900000	.293743	.294144	.294563	.294982	.295385
.3000000	.304144	.304589	.305053	.305519	.305967
.3100000	.314573	.315065	.315579	.316094	.316589
.3200000	.325031	.325573	.326139	.326708	.327255
.3300000	.335519	.336114	.336737	.337362	.337964
.3400000	.346037	.346689	.347372	.348058	.348719
.3500000	.356586	.357299	.358046	.358797	.359521
.3600000	.367168	.367946	.368761	.369580	.370372
.3700000	.377783	.378630	.379517	.380410	.381273
.3800000	.388433	.389352	.390316	.391287	.392225
.3900000	.399118	.400113	.401158	.402212	.403231

$\alpha =$ .299999

Θ	K VALUES				
	.318821117	.415016431	.514599755	.613601043	.708073407
.4000000	.409839	.410916	.412046	.413187	.414292
.4100000	.420597	.421759	.422981	.424214	.425409
.4200000	.431393	.432646	.433963	.435294	.436585
.4300000	.442228	.443576	.444994	.446428	.447820
.4400000	.453104	.454551	.456075	.457618	.459117
.4500000	.464020	.465572	.467208	.468866	.470477
.4600000	.474977	.476639	.478393	.480172	.481902
.4700000	.485978	.487755	.489633	.491538	.493394
.4800000	.497022	.498921	.500927	.502966	.504954
.4900000	.508111	.510136	.512279	.514457	.516584
.5000000	.519245	.521403	.523688	.526013	.528285
.5100000	.530425	.532722	.535156	.537636	.540061
.5200000	.541653	.544094	.546684	.549326	.551911
.5300000	.552929	.555522	.558275	.561085	.563839
.5400000	.564254	.567004	.569928	.572915	.575846
.5500000	.575630	.578544	.581645	.584818	.587934
.5600000	.587056	.590141	.593428	.596795	.600105
.5700000	.598534	.601798	.605278	.608847	.612360
.5800000	.610065	.613514	.617196	.620976	.624702
.5900000	.621649	.625291	.629184	.633184	.637132
.6000000	.633288	.637131	.641242	.645473	.649653
.6100000	.644982	.649033	.653373	.657843	.662266
.6200000	.656733	.661000	.665576	.670297	.674974
.6300000	.668541	.673032	.677855	.682837	.687778
.6400000	.680406	.685131	.690209	.695462	.700681
.6500000	.692330	.697296	.702641	.708177	.713683
.6600000	.704314	.709531	.715152	.720981	.726789
.6700000	.716359	.721834	.727742	.733878	.739999
.6800000	.728464	.734208	.740413	.746867	.753316
.6899999	.740632	.746653	.753167	.759952	.766741
.7000000	.752862	.759171	.766005	.773133	.780278
.7100000	.765156	.771763	.778928	.786413	.793927
.7200000	.777515	.784428	.791937	.799793	.807692
.7300000	.789938	.797169	.805033	.813274	.821574
.7400000	.802428	.809986	.818219	.826859	.835575
.7500000	.814984	.822881	.831494	.840548	.849699
.7600000	.827607	.835853	.844861	.854345	.863946
.7700000	.840298	.848905	.858320	.868249	.878320
.7800000	.853058	.862036	.871872	.882263	.892822
.7899999	.865887	.875249	.885520	.896389	.907454

$\alpha =$ •299999

Θ	K VALUES				
	•318821117	•415016431	•514599755	•613601043	•708073407
•8000000	•878786	•888543	•899264	•910629	•922220
•8100000	•891756	•901919	•913104	•924982	•937121
•8200000	•904796	•915379	•927043	•939453	•952159
•8300000	•917909	•928923	•941082	•954041	•967337
•8400000	•931093	•942551	•955221	•968748	•982657
•8500000	•944351	•956265	•969461	•983577	•998121
•8600000	•957681	•970065	•983804	•998529	1•013732
•8700000	•971085	•983952	•998251	1•013604	1•029491
•8799999	•984564	•997927	1•012802	1•028806	1•045402
•8899999	•998117	1•011990	1•027458	1•044134	1•061466
•9000000	1•011745	1•026142	1•042222	1•059591	1•077685
•9100000	1•025448	1•040383	1•057092	1•075178	1•094062
•9200000	1•039227	1•054714	1•072071	1•090896	1•110599
•9300000	1•053081	1•069135	1•087158	1•106747	1•127298
•9400000	1•067012	1•083647	1•102355	1•122731	1•144161
•9500000	1•081019	1•098250	1•117663	1•138851	1•161191
•9600000	1•095103	1•112945	1•133082	1•155108	1•178389
•9699999	1•109264	1•127731	1•148612	1•171502	1•195757
•9799999	1•123502	1•142610	1•164255	1•188035	1•213298
•9899999	1•137816	1•157581	1•180011	1•204707	1•231014
1•0000000	1•152208	1•172644	1•195880	1•221521	1•248907
1•0100000	1•166676	1•187801	1•211863	1•238476	1•266977
1•0200000	1•181222	1•203050	1•227960	1•255574	1•285228
1•0300000	1•195844	1•218392	1•244172	1•272816	1•303661
1•0400000	1•210543	1•233826	1•260498	1•290201	1•322277
1•0500000	1•225318	1•249354	1•276939	1•307732	1•341079
1•0600000	1•240170	1•264974	1•293495	1•325407	1•360067
1•0699999	1•255098	1•280687	1•310166	1•343229	1•379244
1•0799999	1•270102	1•296492	1•326952	1•361198	1•398610
1•0899999	1•285182	1•312388	1•343853	1•379313	1•418167
1•1000000	1•300336	1•328377	1•360869	1•397575	1•437916
1•1100000	1•315565	1•344457	1•377999	1•415984	1•457858
1•1200000	1•330868	1•360627	1•395243	1•434540	1•477994
1•1300000	1•346245	1•376887	1•412601	1•453243	1•498324
1•1400000	1•361694	1•393237	1•430072	1•472093	1•518850
1•1500000	1•377216	1•409676	1•447655	1•491090	1•539571
1•1600000	1•392809	1•426203	1•465350	1•510233	1•560489
1•1700000	1•408473	1•442818	1•483157	1•529521	1•581603
1•1800000	1•424208	1•459518	1•501073	1•548954	1•602913
1•1899999	1•440011	1•476305	1•519099	1•568532	1•624420

$\alpha =$ .299999

Θ	K VALUES				
	.318821117	.415016431	.514599755	.613601043	.708073407
.2000000	1.455883	1.493176	1.537233	1.588252	1.646122
.2100000	1.471822	1.510130	1.555474	1.608115	1.668019
.2200000	1.487827	1.527166	1.573820	1.628118	1.690111
.2300000	1.503897	1.544284	1.592271	1.648261	1.712396
.2400000	1.520031	1.561481	1.610825	1.668542	1.734873
.2500000	1.536228	1.578757	1.629481	1.688959	1.757541
.2599999	1.552487	1.596109	1.648236	1.709510	1.780399
.2699999	1.568807	1.613537	1.667089	1.730194	1.803443
.2799999	1.585185	1.631039	1.686037	1.751008	1.826672
.2899999	1.601621	1.648613	1.705081	1.771951	1.850084
.3000000	1.618113	1.666258	1.724216	1.793019	1.873676
.3100000	1.634659	1.683971	1.743441	1.814210	1.897445
.3200000	1.651259	1.701751	1.762753	1.835521	1.921387
.3300000	1.667911	1.719595	1.782151	1.856949	1.945499
1.3400000	1.684612	1.737503	1.801631	1.878491	1.969778
1.3500000	1.701362	1.755471	1.821191	1.900144	1.994219
1.3600000	1.718158	1.773499	1.840829	1.921905	2.018818
1.3700000	1.734998	1.791582	1.860541	1.943769	2.043570
1.3799999	1.751882	1.809720	1.880326	1.965733	2.068470
1.3899999	1.768807	1.827910	1.900179	1.987794	2.093513
1.4000000	1.785771	1.846149	1.920098	2.009947	2.118693
1.4100000	1.802772	1.864436	1.940079	2.032187	2.144006
1.4200000	1.819809	1.882767	1.960120	2.054511	2.169443
1.4300000	1.836878	1.901141	1.980217	2.076915	2.195000
1.4400000	1.853979	1.919554	2.000367	2.099392	2.220670
1.4500000	1.871109	1.938004	2.020566	2.121940	2.246445
1.4600000	1.888266	1.956488	2.040811	2.144552	2.272319
1.4700000	1.905448	1.975004	2.061099	2.167225	2.298284
1.4800000	1.922652	1.993549	2.081425	2.189952	2.324333
1.4900000	1.939877	2.012120	2.101786	2.212729	2.350459
1.5000000	1.957121	2.030714	2.122178	2.235551	2.376652
1.5100000	1.974380	2.049329	2.142598	2.258412	2.402906
1.5200000	1.991653	2.067961	2.163041	2.281306	2.429212
1.5300000	2.008938	2.086609	2.183505	2.304229	2.455561
1.5400000	2.026232	2.105268	2.203984	2.327175	2.481945
1.5500000	2.043534	2.123936	2.224476	2.350137	2.508357
1.5600000	2.060840	2.142610	2.244975	2.373112	2.534786
1.5699999	2.078148	2.161287	2.265479	2.396093	2.561224
1.5707963	2.079527	2.162775	2.267112	2.397923	2.563329
1.5707963	2.079525	2.162773	2.267110	2.397921	2.563327

$\alpha =$ .299999

Θ	K VALUES				
	.794250555	.868696860	.928444378	.971111163	.994996249
.0000000	.000000	.000000	.000000	.000000	.000000
.0100000	.010000	.010000	.010000	.010000	.010000
.0200000	.020001	.020001	.020002	.020002	.020002
.0300000	.030006	.030006	.030006	.030007	.030007
.0400000	.040014	.040015	.040016	.040016	.040017
.0500000	.050029	.050030	.050031	.050032	.050033
.0600000	.060050	.060052	.060055	.060056	.060057
.0700000	.070079	.070084	.070087	.070089	.070091
.0800000	.080119	.080125	.080130	.080134	.080136
.0900000	.090169	.090178	.090186	.090191	.090194
.1000000	.100232	.100245	.100255	.100262	.100266
.1100000	.110309	.110326	.110340	.110349	.110354
.1200000	.120402	.120424	.120441	.120454	.120461
.1300000	.130512	.130539	.130561	.130577	.130586
.1400000	.140639	.140674	.140702	.140722	.140733
.1500000	.150787	.150830	.150864	.150888	.150902
.1600000	.160956	.161008	.161049	.161079	.161096
.1700000	.171147	.171210	.171260	.171295	.171315
.1800000	.181363	.181437	.181497	.181539	.181563
.1900000	.191604	.191691	.191762	.191812	.191840
.2000000	.201872	.201974	.202057	.202115	.202148
.2100000	.212169	.212288	.212383	.212452	.212490
.2200000	.222496	.222633	.222743	.222822	.222866
.2300000	.232854	.233011	.233138	.233228	.233279
.2400000	.243246	.243425	.243569	.243672	.243730
.2500000	.253672	.253875	.254039	.254156	.254222
.2600000	.264135	.264364	.264549	.264681	.264755
.2700000	.274635	.274893	.275100	.275249	.275333
.2800000	.285175	.285463	.285696	.285862	.285956
.2900000	.295755	.296077	.296337	.296523	.296627
.3000000	.306378	.306736	.307025	.307232	.307348
.3100000	.317045	.317442	.317762	.317992	.318121
.3200000	.327758	.328197	.328551	.328805	.328948
.3300000	.338519	.339002	.339392	.339673	.339830
.3400000	.349328	.349859	.350289	.350597	.350770
.3500000	.360189	.360771	.361242	.361580	.361771
.3600000	.371102	.371739	.372254	.372625	.372833
.3700000	.382069	.382764	.383327	.383732	.383960
.3800000	.393092	.393850	.394463	.394905	.395153
.3900000	.404173	.404997	.405664	.406145	.406415

$\alpha =$ .299999

Θ	*K* VALUES				
	.794250555	.868696860	.928444378	.971111163	.994996249
.4000000	.415314	.416208	.416932	.417454	.417748
.4100000	.426516	.427484	.428270	.428836	.429154
.4200000	.437781	.438828	.439679	.440292	.440637
.4300000	.449111	.450242	.451161	.451824	.452197
.4400000	.460508	.461728	.462720	.463436	.463839
.4500000	.471974	.473288	.474357	.475128	.475563
.4600000	.483511	.484924	.486074	.486905	.487374
.4700000	.495120	.496638	.497875	.498768	.499272
.4800000	.506804	.508433	.509761	.510721	.511262
.4900000	.518565	.520311	.521735	.522765	.523346
.5000000	.530405	.532273	.533799	.534903	.535527
.5100000	.542325	.544323	.545956	.547138	.547807
.5200000	.554328	.556463	.558209	.559474	.560189
.5300000	.566416	.568695	.570560	.571912	.572677
.5400000	.578592	.581021	.583012	.584456	.585273
.5500000	.590856	.593445	.595568	.597109	.597982
.5600000	.603212	.605968	.608230	.609874	.610805
.5700000	.615662	.618594	.621002	.622754	.623746
.5800000	.628208	.631324	.633886	.635752	.636809
.5900000	.640852	.644162	.646886	.648871	.649997
.6000000	.653597	.657110	.660005	.662116	.663313
.6100000	.666444	.670171	.673245	.675488	.676762
.6200000	.679397	.683348	.686610	.688993	.690347
.6300000	.692458	.696643	.700104	.702634	.704072
.6400000	.705629	.710061	.713729	.716413	.717940
.6500000	.718913	.723603	.727489	.730336	.731957
.6600000	.732313	.737272	.741388	.744406	.746125
.6700000	.745830	.751073	.755430	.758627	.760450
.6800000	.759467	.765007	.769617	.773003	.774935
.6899999	.773228	.779079	.783954	.787539	.789586
.7000000	.787115	.793291	.798444	.802239	.804407
.7100000	.801130	.807647	.813093	.817107	.819403
.7200000	.815277	.822150	.827903	.832149	.834579
.7300000	.829557	.836804	.842878	.847368	.849939
.7400000	.843975	.851613	.858024	.862770	.865490
.7500000	.858532	.866579	.873345	.878359	.881237
.7600000	.873232	.881707	.888845	.894142	.897184
.7700000	.888078	.897000	.904528	.910123	.913339
.7800000	.903072	.912463	.920400	.926307	.929708
.7899999	.918218	.928098	.936465	.942702	.946296

$\alpha =$ •299999

Θ	K VALUES				
	•794250555	•868696860	•928444378	•971111163	•994996249
•8000000	•933519	•943911	•952728	•959312	•963109
•8100000	•948977	•959905	•969195	•976143	•980156
•8200000	•964596	•976085	•985871	•993202	•997441
•8300000	•980380	•992454	1•002761	1•010495	1•014974
•8400000	•996331	1•009018	1•019870	1•028030	1•032760
•8500000	1•012452	1•025779	1•037205	1•045812	1•050808
•8600000	1•028747	1•042744	1•054771	1•063849	1•069126
•8700000	1•045219	1•059916	1•072574	1•082148	1•087722
•8799999	1•061871	1•077300	1•090621	1•100718	1•106604
•8899999	1•078707	1•094901	1•108918	1•119565	1•125783
•9000000	1•095730	1•112724	1•127472	1•138699	1•145266
•9100000	1•112943	1•130773	1•146288	1•158127	1•165064
•9200000	1•130350	1•149055	1•165375	1•177859	1•185186
•9300000	1•147955	1•167573	1•184739	1•197903	1•205644
•9400000	1•165760	1•186333	1•204387	1•218270	1•226449
•9500000	1•183770	1•205340	1•224328	1•238968	1•247611
•9600000	1•201986	1•224600	1•244569	1•260008	1•269142
•9699999	1•220414	1•244119	1•265118	1•281402	1•291056
•9799999	1•239057	1•263901	1•285983	1•303159	1•313366
•9899999	1•257918	1•283952	1•307172	1•325291	1•336084
1•0000000	1•277000	1•304279	1•328696	1•347811	1•359226
1•0100000	1•296307	1•324886	1•350561	1•370731	1•382807
1•0200000	1•315842	1•345781	1•372779	1•394064	1•406842
1•0300000	1•335608	1•366967	1•395357	1•417822	1•431348
1•0400000	1•355610	1•388453	1•418307	1•442022	1•456343
1•0500000	1•375850	1•410244	1•441637	1•466676	1•481845
1•0600000	1•396332	1•432345	1•465359	1•491801	1•507873
1•0699999	1•417058	1•454764	1•489483	1•517413	1•534448
1•0799999	1•438032	1•477506	1•514021	1•543529	1•561592
1•0899999	1•459257	1•500577	1•538982	1•570165	1•589327
1•1000000	1•480737	1•523985	1•564380	1•597341	1•617677
1•1100000	1•502472	1•547734	1•590225	1•625076	1•646669
1•1200000	1•524467	1•571832	1•616531	1•653390	1•676329
1•1300000	1•546724	1•596284	1•643309	1•682303	1•706687
1•1400000	1•569246	1•621098	1•670572	1•711839	1•737772
1•1500000	1•592035	1•646278	1•698333	1•742020	1•769618
1•1600000	1•615092	1•671831	1•726606	1•772871	1•802260
1•1700000	1•638421	1•697764	1•755405	1•804417	1•835735
1•1800000	1•662022	1•724081	1•784743	1•836685	1•870082
1•1899999	1•685898	1•750789	1•814635	1•869704	1•905345

$\alpha =$ •299999

Θ	K VALUES				
	•794250555	•868696860	•928444378	•971111163	•994996249
1•2000000	1•710050	1•777893	1•845095	1•903502	1•941570
1•2100000	1•734478	1•805398	1•876137	1•938112	1•978805
1•2200000	1•759183	1•833309	1•907777	1•973565	2•017104
1•2300000	1•784167	1•861631	1•940030	2•009896	2•056523
1•2400000	1•809428	1•890369	1•972909	2•047141	2•097126
1•2500000	1•834968	1•919526	2•006431	2•085338	2•138978
1•2599999	1•860785	1•949106	2•040610	2•124527	2•182153
1•2699999	1•886879	1•979112	2•075460	2•164748	2•226730
1•2799999	1•913248	2•009547	2•110997	2•206046	2•272794
1•2899999	1•939891	2•040412	2•147235	2•248467	2•320441
1•3000000	1•966805	2•071708	2•184187	2•292057	2•369774
1•3100000	1•993988	2•103437	2•221865	2•336867	2•420904
1•3200000	2•021437	2•135598	2•260283	2•382947	2•473958
1•3300000	2•049147	2•168189	2•299451	2•430351	2•529072
1•3400000	2•077116	2•201209	2•339379	2•479134	2•586399
1•3500000	2•105338	2•234655	2•380076	2•529352	2•646107
1•3600000	2•133808	2•268523	2•421549	2•581063	2•708385
1•3700000	2•162521	2•302806	2•463802	2•634324	2•773442
1•3799999	2•191470	2•337500	2•506839	2•689194	2•841512
1•3899999	2•220647	2•372595	2•550659	2•745730	2•912859
1•4000000	2•250047	2•408084	2•595261	2•803986	2•987778
1•4100000	2•279660	2•443954	2•640636	2•864015	3•066603
1•4200000	2•309477	2•480196	2•686777	2•925863	3•149710
1•4300000	2•339490	2•516794	2•733669	2•989572	3•237524
1•4400000	2•369688	2•553735	2•781295	3•055174	3•330527
1•4500000	2•400062	2•591002	2•829634	3•122687	3•429260
1•4600000	2•430600	2•628577	2•878657	3•192120	3•534331
1•4700000	2•461290	2•666441	2•928334	3•263460	3•646416
1•4800000	2•492121	2•704573	2•978627	3•336674	3•766258
1•4900000	2•523080	2•742952	3•029494	3•411706	3•894645
1•5000000	2•554155	2•781553	3•080888	3•488472	4•032386
1•5100000	2•585332	2•820353	3•132757	3•566858	4•180234
1•5200000	2•616596	2•859325	3•185044	3•646718	4•338782
1•5300000	2•647935	2•898442	3•237687	3•727873	4•508288
1•5400000	2•679334	2•937678	3•290621	3•810115	4•688438
1•5500000	2•710779	2•977003	3•343779	3•893205	4•878084
1•5600000	2•742254	3•016390	3•397089	3•976884	5•075053
1•5699999	2•773745	3•055808	3•450478	4•060874	5•276171
1•5707963	2•776253	3•058947	3•454731	4•067567	5•292253
1•5707963	2•776251	3•058945	3•454728	4•067563	5•292244

$\alpha =$ .349999

Θ	K VALUES				
	.009966711	.039469502	.087332193	.151646642	.229848846
.0000000	.000000	.000000	.000000	.000000	.000000
.0100000	.010000	.010000	.010000	.010000	.010000
.0200000	.020000	.020000	.020001	.020001	.020001
.0300000	.030003	.030003	.030003	.030003	.030004
.0400000	.040007	.040007	.040008	.040009	.040009
.0500000	.050014	.050015	.050016	.050017	.050019
.0600000	.060025	.060026	.060028	.060030	.060033
.0700000	.070040	.070042	.070045	.070048	.070053
.0800000	.080060	.080063	.080067	.080072	.080079
.0900000	.090086	.090089	090095	.090103	.090113
.1000000	.100118	.100123	.100131	.100141	.100155
.1100000	.110157	.110164	.110174	.110188	.110206
.1200000	.120204	.120213	.120226	.120245	.120267
.1300000	.130260	.130270	.130288	.130311	.130340
.1400000	.140324	.140338	.140360	.140389	.140425
.1500000	.150399	.150416	.150443	.150479	.150523
.1600000	.160484	.160504	.160537	.160581	.160635
.1700000	.170581	.170605	.170644	.170697	.170762
.1800000	.180690	.180719	.180765	.180828	.180904
.1900000	.190811	.190845	.190900	.190974	.191064
.2000000	.200946	.200986	.201050	.201136	.201241
.2100000	.211096	.211141	.211215	.211315	.211437
.2200000	.221260	.221312	.221398	.221512	.221652
.2300000	.231440	.231500	.231597	.231728	.231888
.2400000	.241636	.241704	.241815	.241964	.242146
.2500000	.251849	.251926	.252051	.252220	.252426
.2600000	.262080	.262167	.262308	.262498	.262730
.2700000	.272330	.272427	.272585	.272797	.273057
.2800000	.282599	.282707	.282883	.283120	.283410
.2900000	.292887	.293007	.293203	.293467	.293790
.3000000	.303196	.303330	.303546	.303839	.304196
.3100000	.313527	.313674	.313913	.314236	.314631
.3200000	.323880	.324041	.324304	.324660	.325095
.3300000	.334255	.334432	.334721	.335111	.335588
.3400000	.344654	.344848	.345164	.345590	.346113
.3500000	.355077	.355288	.355633	.356099	.356670
.3600000	.365525	.365755	.366130	.366638	.367260
.3700000	.375998	.376248	.376656	.377207	.377883
.3800000	.386498	.386769	.387210	.387808	.388541
.3900000	.397025	.397318	.397795	.398442	.399235

$\alpha =$ .349999

Θ	K VALUES				
	.009966711	.039469502	.087332193	.151646642	.229848846
.4000000	.407579	.407895	.408411	.409109	.409966
.4100000	.418162	.418502	.419058	.419810	.420735
.4200000	.428774	.429140	.429737	.430547	.431542
.4300000	.439415	.439808	.440450	.441319	.442389
.4400000	.450088	.450509	.451196	.452128	.453276
.4500000	.460791	.461241	.461977	.462975	.464205
.4600000	.471526	.472008	.472794	.473861	.475176
.4700000	.482294	.482808	.483647	.484786	.486191
.4800000	.493096	.493642	.494536	.495751	.497250
.4900000	.503931	.504512	.505464	.506757	.508354
.5000000	.514800	.515419	.516430	.517806	.519505
.5100000	.525706	.526362	.527436	.528897	.530702
.5200000	.536647	.537342	.538481	.540031	.541948
.5300000	.547624	.548361	.549567	.551210	.553243
.5400000	.558640	.559419	.560695	.562435	.564588
.5500000	.569693	.570516	.571866	.573705	.575984
.5600000	.580785	.581654	.583079	.585022	.587432
.5700000	.591916	.592833	.594336	.596388	.598933
.5800000	.603087	.604053	.605638	.607801	.610487
.5900000	.614299	.615316	.616984	.619264	.622096
.6000000	.625552	.626622	.628377	.630777	.633761
.6100000	.636847	.637971	.639817	.642341	.645482
.6200000	.648185	.649365	.651304	.653957	.657260
.6300000	.659565	.660804	.662839	.665625	.669097
.6400000	.670990	.672288	.674423	.677347	.680992
.6500000	.682459	.683819	.686056	.689122	.692948
.6600000	.693973	.695397	.697740	.700953	.704965
.6700000	.705532	.707022	.709474	.712838	.717043
.6800000	.717138	.718696	.721260	.724781	.729184
.6899999	.728791	.730418	.733098	.736780	.741388
.7000000	.740491	.742190	.744989	.748837	.753656
.7100000	.752238	.754011	.756933	.760952	.765990
.7200000	.764034	.765883	.768931	.773126	.778389
.7300000	.775880	.777806	.780984	.785360	.790855
.7400000	.787774	.789781	.793092	.797655	.803388
.7500000	.799719	.801808	.805256	.810010	.815990
.7600000	.811714	.813887	.817476	.822428	.828660
.7700000	.823760	.826020	.829753	.834907	.841400
.7800000	.835858	.838206	.842088	.847450	.854210
.7899999	.848007	.850446	.854480	.860056	.867092

$\alpha =$ .349999

θ	K VALUES				
	.009966711	.039469502	.087332193	.151646642	.229848846
.8000000	.860209	.862742	.866932	.872727	.880045
.8100000	.872464	.875092	.879441	.885461	.893070
.8200000	.884771	.887497	.892011	.898261	.906169
.8300000	.897133	.899959	.904640	.911127	.919341
.8400000	.909548	.912477	.917330	.924059	.932587
.8500000	.922018	.925051	.930080	.937058	.945908
.8600000	.934542	.937683	.942891	.950123	.959304
.8700000	.947122	.950372	.955764	.963256	.972776
.8799999	.959756	.963118	.968699	.976457	.986324
.8899999	.972447	.975923	.981696	.989727	.999949
.9000000	.985193	.988786	.994755	1.003065	1.013651
.9100000	.997995	1.001707	1.007877	1.016471	1.027430
.9200000	1.010853	1.014687	1.021062	1.029947	1.041288
.9300000	1.023768	1.027726	1.034310	1.043493	1.055224
.9400000	1.036740	1.040824	1.047621	1.057108	1.069238
.9500000	1.049768	1.053982	1.060996	1.070793	1.083331
.9600000	1.062853	1.067198	1.074435	1.084549	1.097503
.9699999	1.075996	1.080474	1.087937	1.098374	1.111754
.9799999	1.089195	1.093810	1.101503	1.112270	1.126085
.9899999	1.102451	1.107205	1.115134	1.126236	1.140495
1.0000000	1.115765	1.120660	1.128828	1.140272	1.154985
1.0100000	1.129135	1.134175	1.142586	1.154379	1.169555
1.0200000	1.142563	1.147748	1.156407	1.168557	1.184204
1.0300000	1.156047	1.161382	1.170293	1.182804	1.198932
1.0400000	1.169588	1.175074	1.184242	1.197122	1.213740
1.0500000	1.183186	1.188826	1.198254	1.211510	1.228628
1.0600000	1.196840	1.202636	1.212330	1.225967	1.243594
1.0699999	1.210551	1.216505	1.226469	1.240494	1.258639
1.0799999	1.224318	1.230433	1.240671	1.255091	1.273763
1.0899999	1.238140	1.244419	1.254935	1.269756	1.288966
1.1000000	1.252018	1.258463	1.269261	1.284490	1.304246
1.1100000	1.265951	1.272564	1.283649	1.299292	1.319603
1.1200000	1.279938	1.286722	1.298098	1.314162	1.335038
1.1300000	1.293980	1.300937	1.312608	1.329099	1.350549
1.1400000	1.308075	1.315208	1.327178	1.344103	1.366135
1.1500000	1.322224	1.329535	1.341808	1.359172	1.381797
1.1600000	1.336426	1.343917	1.356497	1.374308	1.397534
1.1700000	1.350679	1.358353	1.371245	1.389507	1.413344
1.1800000	1.364985	1.372843	1.386050	1.404771	1.429227
1.1899999	1.379341	1.387386	1.400913	1.420098	1.445182

$\alpha =$ .349999

Θ	K VALUES				
	.009966711	.039469502	.087332193	.151646642	.229848846
1.2000000	1.393747	1.401982	1.415832	1.435488	1.461208
1.2100000	1.408203	1.416629	1.430807	1.450939	1.477304
1.2200000	1.422708	1.431327	1.445836	1.466450	1.493470
1.2300000	1.437261	1.446075	1.460919	1.482021	1.509703
1.2400000	1.451861	1.460873	1.476055	1.497650	1.526003
1.2500000	1.466507	1.475718	1.491242	1.513337	1.542369
1.2599999	1.481198	1.490611	1.506481	1.529081	1.558800
1.2699999	1.495933	1.505551	1.521769	1.544879	1.575293
1.2799999	1.510712	1.520535	1.537106	1.560731	1.591848
1.2899999	1.525534	1.535564	1.552491	1.576636	1.608463
1.3000000	1.540397	1.550636	1.567922	1.592593	1.625137
1.3100000	1.555299	1.565750	1.583398	1.608599	1.641869
1.3200000	1.570241	1.580904	1.598917	1.624654	1.658655
1.3300000	1.585221	1.596098	1.614480	1.640756	1.675496
1.3400000	1.600237	1.611330	1.630083	1.656904	1.692389
1.3500000	1.615289	1.626599	1.645726	1.673096	1.709333
1.3600000	1.630374	1.641904	1.661408	1.689330	1.726325
1.3700000	1.645493	1.657243	1.677126	1.705605	1.743365
1.3799999	1.660643	1.672615	1.692880	1.721919	1.760449
1.3899999	1.675823	1.688019	1.708667	1.738271	1.777576
1.4000000	1.691032	1.703452	1.724487	1.754659	1.794745
1.4100000	1.706269	1.718914	1.740337	1.771081	1.811952
1.4200000	1.721531	1.734403	1.756217	1.787535	1.829196
1.4300000	1.736817	1.749918	1.772124	1.804019	1.846476
1.4400000	1.752126	1.765456	1.788056	1.820532	1.863788
1.4500000	1.767457	1.781016	1.804012	1.837071	1.881130
1.4600000	1.782807	1.796597	1.819991	1.853635	1.898501
1.4700000	1.798176	1.812198	1.835990	1.870222	1.915898
1.4800000	1.813561	1.827815	1.852008	1.886830	1.933319
1.4900000	1.828962	1.843448	1.868043	1.903456	1.950761
1.5000000	1.844376	1.859096	1.884093	1.920099	1.968223
1.5100000	1.859801	1.874755	1.900156	1.936757	1.985702
1.5200000	1.875237	1.890426	1.916230	1.953428	2.003195
1.5300000	1.890681	1.906105	1.932314	1.970109	2.020700
1.5400000	1.906132	1.921791	1.948406	1.986799	2.038215
1.5500000	1.921588	1.937483	1.964504	2.003495	2.055738
1.5600000	1.937048	1.953178	1.980605	2.020195	2.073266
1.5699999	1.952509	1.968875	1.996708	2.036898	2.090796
1.5707963	1.953741	1.970125	1.997991	2.038228	2.092192
1.5707963	1.953739	1.970124	1.997990	2.038227	2.092190

$\alpha =$ .349999

Θ	K VALUES				
	.318821117	.415016431	.514599755	.613601043	.708073407
.0000000	.000000	.000000	.000000	.000000	.000000
.0100000	.010000	.010000	.010000	.010000	.010000
.0200000	.020001	.020001	.020001	.020001	.020001
.0300000	.030004	.030005	.030005	.030005	.030006
.0400000	.040010	.040011	.040012	.040014	.040015
.0500000	.050021	.050023	.050025	.050027	.050029
.0600000	.060036	.060040	.060043	.060047	.060050
.0700000	.070058	.070063	.070069	.070075	.070080
.0800000	.080087	.080095	.080103	.080112	.080120
.0900000	.090123	.090135	.090147	.090159	.090171
.1000000	.100169	.100185	.100202	.100219	.100235
.1100000	.110226	.110247	.110269	.110291	.110313
.1200000	.120293	.120321	.120350	.120379	.120406
.1300000	.130373	.130408	.130445	.130482	.130517
.1400000	.140466	.140510	.140556	.140602	.140646
.1500000	.150573	.150628	.150684	.150741	.150795
.1600000	.160696	.160762	.160831	.160899	.160965
.1700000	.170835	.170915	.170997	.171079	.171158
.1800000	.180992	.181086	.181184	.181282	.181376
.1900000	.191166	.191278	.191393	.191509	.191619
.2000000	.201361	.201491	.201626	.201761	.201890
.2100000	.211576	.211726	.211883	.212039	.212189
.2200000	.221812	.221986	.222166	.222346	.222519
.2300000	.232071	.232270	.232476	.232683	.232881
.2400000	.242354	.242580	.242815	.243050	.243276
.2500000	.252661	.252917	.253184	.253450	.253705
.2600000	.262995	.263283	.263583	.263883	.264172
.2700000	.273355	.273678	.274015	.274352	.274676
.2800000	.283742	.284104	.284480	.284858	.285220
.2900000	.294159	.294561	.294981	.295401	.295805
.3000000	.304606	.305052	.305517	.305984	.306433
.3100000	.315083	.315577	.316092	.316608	.317105
.3200000	.325593	.326137	.326705	.327275	.327824
.3300000	.336136	.336733	.337358	.337985	.338590
.3400000	.346713	.347368	.348053	.348741	.349405
.3500000	.357325	.358041	.358791	.359544	.360271
.3600000	.367974	.368755	.369573	.370396	.371191
.3700000	.378660	.379510	.380401	.381298	.382164
.3800000	.389385	.390308	.391276	.392251	.393194
.3900000	.400149	.401149	.402199	.403257	.404281

$\alpha =$ .349999

Θ	K VALUES				
	.318821117	.415016431	.514599755	.613601043	.708073407
.4000000	.410954	.412036	.413172	.414318	.415429
.4100000	.421800	.422968	.424196	.425436	.426637
.4200000	.432689	.433949	.435273	.436611	.437909
.4300000	.443623	.444977	.446404	.447846	.449246
.4400000	.454601	.456056	.457590	.459142	.460650
.4500000	.465625	.467186	.468833	.470501	.472123
.4600000	.476696	.478369	.480134	.481924	.483666
.4700000	.487816	.489605	.491495	.493413	.495282
.4800000	.498984	.500896	.502917	.504970	.506972
.4900000	.510203	.512244	.514402	.516597	.518739
.5000000	.521474	.523648	.525951	.528294	.530584
.5100000	.532797	.535112	.537565	.540065	.542509
.5200000	.544174	.546635	.549246	.551910	.554517
.5300000	.555605	.558220	.560996	.563831	.566609
.5400000	.567092	.569867	.572816	.575831	.578788
.5500000	.578636	.581577	.584707	.587910	.591055
.5600000	.590238	.593353	.596672	.600071	.603413
.5700000	.601899	.605195	.608710	.612315	.615863
.5800000	.613620	.617105	.620825	.624644	.628409
.5900000	.625402	.629083	.633017	.637061	.641051
.6000000	.637247	.641132	.645288	.649566	.653793
.6100000	.649154	.653251	.657640	.662162	.666637
.6200000	.661126	.665444	.670074	.674851	.679584
.6300000	.673163	.677710	.682591	.687634	.692637
.6400000	.685267	.690051	.695193	.700513	.705798
.6500000	.697438	.702468	.707883	.713491	.719070
.6600000	.709677	.714963	.720660	.726568	.732455
.6700000	.721986	.727537	.733527	.739748	.745955
.6800000	.734366	.740191	.746485	.753031	.759573
.6899999	.746817	.752926	.759535	.766420	.773311
.7000000	.759340	.765744	.772681	.779917	.787171
.7100000	.771937	.778645	.785921	.793524	.801157
.7200000	.784608	.791631	.799260	.807242	.815270
.7300000	.797354	.804703	.812696	.821074	.829513
.7400000	.810177	.817862	.826234	.835021	.843888
.7500000	.823077	.831110	.839873	.849086	.858398
.7600000	.836055	.844447	.853615	.863270	.873046
.7700000	.849111	.857874	.867462	.877575	.887834
.7800000	.862248	.871394	.881415	.892003	.902764
.7899999	.875466	.885006	.895476	.906557	.917840

$\alpha =$ .349999

Θ	K VALUES				
	.318821117	.415016431	.514599755	.613601043	.708073407
.8000000	.888765	.898712	.909645	.921237	.933063
.8100000	.902146	.912514	.923926	.936047	.948437
.8200000	.915611	.926411	.938318	.950988	.963964
.8300000	.929159	.940405	.952823	.966061	.979647
.8400000	.942792	.954497	.967443	.981269	.995488
.8500000	.956511	.968688	.982179	.996614	1.011490
.8600000	.970315	.982979	.997032	1.012097	1.027656
.8700000	.984206	.997371	1.012003	1.027720	1.043988
.8799999	.998185	1.011864	1.027094	1.043485	1.060489
.8899999	1.012251	1.026460	1.042306	1.059394	1.077161
.9000000	1.026406	1.041159	1.057640	1.075449	1.094008
.9100000	1.040650	1.055962	1.073098	1.091651	1.111031
.9200000	1.054984	1.070870	1.088679	1.108002	1.128234
.9300000	1.069407	1.085883	1.104386	1.124504	1.145619
.9400000	1.083921	1.101002	1.120219	1.141158	1.163187
.9500000	1.098526	1.116228	1.136180	1.157965	1.180943
.9600000	1.113222	1.131561	1.152269	1.174928	1.198889
.9699999	1.128009	1.147002	1.168487	1.192048	1.217026
.9799999	1.142888	1.162551	1.184834	1.209325	1.235358
.9899999	1.157859	1.178209	1.201313	1.226763	1.253886
1.0000000	1.172923	1.193976	1.217923	1.244361	1.272613
1.0100000	1.188078	1.209851	1.234664	1.262121	1.291542
1.0200000	1.203326	1.225837	1.251538	1.280044	1.310674
1.0300000	1.218665	1.241931	1.268545	1.298132	1.330011
1.0400000	1.234098	1.258136	1.285686	1.316384	1.349556
1.0500000	1.249622	1.274450	1.302960	1.334803	1.369310
1.0600000	1.265238	1.290874	1.320368	1.353389	1.389276
1.0699999	1.280946	1.307408	1.337911	1.372142	1.409454
1.0799999	1.296746	1.324051	1.355587	1.391064	1.429848
1.0899999	1.312637	1.340804	1.373398	1.410154	1.450458
1.1000000	1.328619	1.357666	1.391343	1.429413	1.471286
1.1100000	1.344692	1.374636	1.409422	1.448842	1.492332
1.1200000	1.360854	1.391715	1.427634	1.468440	1.513599
1.1300000	1.377106	1.408901	1.445980	1.488208	1.535087
1.1400000	1.393447	1.426194	1.464459	1.508146	1.556796
1.1500000	1.409876	1.443593	1.483069	1.528252	1.578729
1.1600000	1.426392	1.461098	1.501812	1.548528	1.600884
1.1700000	1.442994	1.478708	1.520685	1.568972	1.623263
1.1800000	1.459683	1.496421	1.539688	1.589583	1.645865
1.1899999	1.476455	1.514237	1.558819	1.610362	1.668691

$\alpha =$ .349999

Θ	K VALUES				
	.318821117	.415016431	.514599755	.613601043	.708073407
1.2000000	1.493312	1.532155	1.578079	1.631306	1.691740
1.2100000	1.510251	1.550174	1.597465	1.652415	1.715012
1.2200000	1.527272	1.568291	1.616975	1.673688	1.738505
1.2300000	1.544373	1.586506	1.636609	1.695122	1.762219
1.2400000	1.561552	1.604818	1.656365	1.716717	1.786153
1.2500000	1.578809	1.623224	1.676241	1.738470	1.810304
1.2599999	1.596142	1.641723	1.696235	1.760379	1.834671
1.2699999	1.613550	1.660313	1.716346	1.782443	1.859253
1.2799999	1.631030	1.678993	1.736570	1.804658	1.884045
1.2899999	1.648582	1.697760	1.756906	1.827022	1.909047
1.3000000	1.666204	1.716613	1.777352	1.849533	1.934255
1.3100000	1.683893	1.735549	1.797904	1.872187	1.959665
1.3200000	1.701648	1.754567	1.818561	1.894981	1.985273
1.3300000	1.719468	1.773663	1.839319	1.917912	2.011077
1.3400000	1.737349	1.792836	1.860175	1.940977	2.037071
1.3500000	1.755290	1.812082	1.881127	1.964170	2.063250
1.3600000	1.773289	1.831401	1.902171	1.987489	2.089611
1.3700000	1.791344	1.850788	1.923305	2.010930	2.116147
1.3799999	1.809452	1.870241	1.944524	2.034487	2.142853
1.3899999	1.827612	1.889758	1.965826	2.058157	2.169724
1.4000000	1.845821	1.909336	1.987206	2.081935	2.196752
1.4100000	1.864075	1.928971	2.008661	2.105816	2.223930
1.4200000	1.882374	1.948661	2.030187	2.129795	2.251253
1.4300000	1.900715	1.968402	2.051780	2.153866	2.278713
1.4400000	1.919094	1.988192	2.073437	2.178024	2.306302
1.4500000	1.937510	2.008027	2.095153	2.202265	2.334012
1.4600000	1.955960	2.027904	2.116923	2.226581	2.361836
1.4700000	1.974441	2.047820	2.138745	2.250968	2.389764
1.4800000	1.992950	2.067771	2.160612	2.275419	2.417789
1.4900000	2.011485	2.087755	2.182522	2.299928	2.445902
1.5000000	2.030044	2.107767	2.204469	2.324490	2.474093
1.5100000	2.048622	2.127804	2.226449	2.349097	2.502352
1.5200000	2.067217	2.147863	2.248458	2.373745	2.530672
1.5300000	2.085828	2.167940	2.270490	2.398425	2.559041
1.5400000	2.104450	2.188032	2.292542	2.423132	2.587451
1.5500000	2.123080	2.208134	2.314608	2.447860	2.615892
1.5600000	2.141717	2.228245	2.336684	2.472601	2.644353
1.5699999	2.160357	2.248359	2.358764	2.497349	2.672825
1.5707963	2.161841	2.249960	2.360523	2.499320	2.675093
1.5707963	2.161841	2.249958	2.360521	2.499318	2.675090

$\alpha =$ .349999

Θ	K VALUES				
	.794250555	.868696860	.928444378	.971111163	.994996249
.0000000	.000000	.000000	.000000	.000000	.000000
.0100000	.010000	.010000	.010000	.010000	.010000
.0200000	.020002	.020002	.020002	.020002	.020002
.0300000	.030006	.030007	.030007	.030007	.030007
.0400000	.040015	.040016	.040017	.040017	.040018
.0500000	.050031	.050032	.050033	.050034	.050035
.0600000	.060053	.060056	.060058	.060060	.060061
.0700000	.070085	.070089	.070093	.070095	.070097
.0800000	.080127	.080134	.080139	.080142	.080144
.0900000	.090181	.090190	.090198	.090203	.090206
.1000000	.100249	.100262	.100272	.100279	.100283
.1100000	.110332	.110348	.110362	.110371	.110377
.1200000	.120431	.120453	.120470	.120483	.120490
.1300000	.130549	.130576	.130598	.130614	.130623
.1400000	.140686	.140720	.140748	.140768	.140779
.1500000	.150844	.150886	.150921	.150945	.150959
.1600000	.161025	.161077	.161118	.161148	.161165
.1700000	.171230	.171292	.171343	.171378	.171398
.1800000	.181461	.181536	.181595	.181638	.181662
.1900000	.191720	.191808	.191878	.191928	.191956
.2000000	.202008	.202110	.202192	.202251	.202284
.2100000	.212326	.212445	.212541	.212609	.212648
.2200000	.222677	.222814	.222925	.223003	.223048
.2300000	.233062	.233219	.233346	.233436	.233487
.2400000	.243482	.243661	.243806	.243909	.243967
.2500000	.253940	.254143	.254307	.254424	.254490
.2600000	.264436	.264666	.264851	.264983	.265058
.2700000	.274973	.275232	.275440	.275589	.275673
.2800000	.285553	.285842	.286075	.286242	.286336
.2900000	.296176	.296499	.296759	.296946	.297051
.3000000	.306846	.307204	.307494	.307702	.307819
.3100000	.317563	.317960	.318282	.318512	.318642
.3200000	.328329	.328768	.329124	.329379	.329522
.3300000	.339146	.339631	.340023	.340304	.340462
.3400000	.350016	.350549	.350980	.351290	.351463
.3500000	.360942	.361526	.361999	.362338	.362529
.3600000	.371923	.372563	.373080	.373452	.373661
.3700000	.382964	.383662	.384227	.384634	.384862
.3800000	.394065	.394825	.395442	.395885	.396134
.3900000	.405228	.406055	.406726	.407208	.407480

$\alpha =$ .349999

Θ	K VALUES				
	.794250555	.868696860	.928444378	.971111163	.994996249
.4000000	.416455	.417353	.418082	.418606	.418901
.4100000	.427749	.428723	.429512	.430081	.430402
.4200000	.439111	.440165	.441020	.441636	.441983
.4300000	.450544	.451682	.452606	.453273	.453648
.4400000	.462049	.463276	.464274	.464994	.465400
.4500000	.473629	.474951	.476026	.476803	.477240
.4600000	.485285	.486707	.487865	.488701	.489173
.4700000	.497020	.498548	.499793	.500693	.501200
.4800000	.508836	.510476	.511813	.512780	.513326
.4900000	.520735	.522493	.523928	.524966	.525552
.5000000	.532720	.534602	.536140	.537253	.537881
.5100000	.544792	.546806	.548452	.549644	.550318
.5200000	.556954	.559107	.560867	.562143	.562864
.5300000	.569209	.571507	.573388	.574753	.575524
.5400000	.581558	.584010	.586019	.587476	.588301
.5500000	.594005	.596618	.598761	.600317	.601198
.5600000	.606551	.609334	.611618	.613278	.614218
.5700000	.619199	.622160	.624593	.626363	.627365
.5800000	.631952	.635100	.637690	.639575	.640644
.5900000	.644811	.648157	.650912	.652919	.654057
.6000000	.657781	.661334	.664262	.666397	.667609
.6100000	.670863	.674633	.677744	.680014	.681303
.6200000	.684060	.688059	.691361	.693773	.695143
.6300000	.697375	.701613	.705117	.707679	.709135
.6400000	.710811	.715299	.719016	.721735	.723282
.6500000	.724369	.729121	.733061	.735946	.737588
.6600000	.738054	.743083	.747256	.750316	.752059
.6700000	.751868	.757186	.761605	.764849	.766698
.6800000	.765814	.771436	.776114	.779551	.781511
.6899999	.779896	.785835	.790784	.794425	.796503
.7000000	.794115	.800388	.805622	.809477	.811679
.7100000	.808475	.815097	.820631	.824711	.827044
.7200000	.822979	.829967	.835815	.840133	.842604
.7300000	.837631	.845002	.851180	.855747	.858363
.7400000	.852433	.860205	.866730	.871560	.874329
.7500000	.867389	.875581	.882471	.887576	.890507
.7600000	.882502	.891134	.898406	.903803	.906903
.7700000	.897776	.906868	.914541	.920244	.923523
.7800000	.913213	.922788	.930882	.936907	.940375
.7899999	.928818	.938897	.947433	.953798	.957465

$\alpha =$ •349999

θ	K VALUES				
	•794250555	•868696860	•928444378	•971111163	•994996249
•8000000	•944593	•955200	•964201	•970923	•974801
•8100000	•960542	•971702	•981191	•988289	•992388
•8200000	•976669	•988408	•998409	1•005902	1•010236
•8300000	•992978	1•005321	1•015860	1•023771	1•028351
•8400000	1•009471	1•022448	1•033552	1•041901	1•046743
•8500000	1•026153	1•039793	1•051489	1•060302	1•065418
•8600000	1•043027	1•057361	1•069680	1•078981	1•084388
•8700000	1•060098	1•075156	1•088130	1•097945	1•103659
•8799999	1•077368	1•093186	1•106847	1•117203	1•123242
•8899999	1•094842	1•111454	1•125837	1•136765	1•143147
•9000000	1•112523	1•129966	1•145108	1•156639	1•163384
•9100000	1•130416	1•148728	1•164667	1•176834	1•183964
•9200000	1•148524	1•167745	1•184522	1•197360	1•204896
•9300000	1•166851	1•187023	1•204681	1•218227	1•226194
•9400000	1•185402	1•206569	1•225152	1•239446	1•247869
•9500000	1•204179	1•226387	1•245943	1•261027	1•269934
•9600000	1•223188	1•246484	1•267064	1•282982	1•292401
•9699999	1•242431	1•266866	1•288522	1•305322	1•315285
•9799999	1•261914	1•287540	1•310327	1•328059	1•338599
•9899999	1•281639	1•308511	1•332489	1•351207	1•362360
1•0000000	1•301612	1•329786	1•355016	1•374778	1•386582
1•0100000	1•321835	1•351372	1•377920	1•398786	1•411282
1•0200000	1•342313	1•373274	1•401210	1•423244	1•436478
1•0300000	1•363050	1•395501	1•424897	1•448169	1•462186
1•0400000	1•384050	1•418058	1•448991	1•473576	1•488428
1•0500000	1•405315	1•440953	1•473504	1•499479	1•515222
1•0600000	1•426851	1•464192	1•498447	1•525898	1•542590
1•0699999	1•448660	1•487782	1•523831	1•552848	1•570554
1•0799999	1•470747	1•511731	1•549670	1•580349	1•599137
1•0899999	1•493115	1•536044	1•575976	1•608419	1•628365
1•1000000	1•515767	1•560730	1•602761	1•637080	1•658264
1•1100000	1•538707	1•585795	1•630038	1•666351	1•688862
1•1200000	1•561937	1•611246	1•657820	1•696254	1•720188
1•1300000	1•585461	1•637091	1•686122	1•726814	1•752273
1•1400000	1•609282	1•663335	1•714958	1•758053	1•785152
1•1500000	1•633402	1•689987	1•744342	1•789998	1•818859
1•1600000	1•657824	1•717052	1•774288	1•822674	1•853432
1•1700000	1•682551	1•744538	1•804812	1•856110	1•888913
1•1800000	1•707583	1•772451	1•835929	1•890335	1•925343
1•1899999	1•732924	1•800798	1•867655	1•925380	1•962769

$\alpha =$ .349999

Θ	K VALUES				
	.794250555	.868696860	.928444378	.971111163	.994996249
1.2000000	1.758574	1.829584	1.900005	1.961276	2.001242
1.2100000	1.784535	1.858815	1.932996	1.998057	2.040814
1.2200000	1.810808	1.888497	1.966643	2.035760	2.081542
1.2300000	1.837394	1.918636	2.000963	2.074421	2.123490
1.2400000	1.864292	1.949235	2.035973	2.114079	2.166723
1.2500000	1.891503	1.980300	2.071688	2.154775	2.211314
1.2599999	1.919025	2.011834	2.108125	2.196553	2.257341
1.2699999	1.946860	2.043842	2.145300	2.239457	2.304891
1.2799999	1.975003	2.076324	2.183229	2.283535	2.354056
1.2899999	2.003455	2.109285	2.221927	2.328836	2.404938
1.3000000	2.032213	2.142725	2.261410	2.375411	2.457649
1.3100000	2.061273	2.176645	2.301690	2.423315	2.512310
1.3200000	2.090632	2.211044	2.342781	2.472602	2.569056
1.3300000	2.120286	2.245921	2.384696	2.523331	2.628036
1.3400000	2.150231	2.281274	2.427446	2.575560	2.689413
1.3500000	2.180461	2.317100	2.471038	2.629351	2.753370
1.3600000	2.210970	2.353393	2.515482	2.684766	2.820108
1.3700000	2.241753	2.390148	2.560781	2.741867	2.889855
1.3799999	2.272801	2.427358	2.606939	2.800717	2.962863
1.3899999	2.304107	2.465014	2.653957	2.861377	3.039415
1.4000000	2.335664	2.503106	2.701830	2.923908	3.119831
1.4100000	2.367460	2.541622	2.750552	2.988363	3.204469
1.4200000	2.399487	2.580549	2.800112	3.054796	3.293735
1.4300000	2.431735	2.619872	2.850495	3.123248	3.388087
1.4400000	2.464191	2.659575	2.901683	3.193755	3.488044
1.4500000	2.496845	2.699640	2.953651	3.266337	3.594189
1.4600000	2.529684	2.740046	3.006368	3.341002	3.707178
1.4700000	2.562695	2.780773	3.059801	3.417735	3.827739
1.4800000	2.595864	2.821798	3.113908	3.496502	3.956670
1.4900000	2.629178	2.863095	3.168644	3.577241	4.094822
1.5000000	2.662622	2.904640	3.223957	3.659861	4.243065
1.5100000	2.696181	2.946404	3.279789	3.744236	4.402210
1.5200000	2.729839	2.988360	3.336079	3.830209	4.572896
1.5300000	2.763581	3.030476	3.392758	3.917587	4.755399
1.5400000	2.797391	3.072724	3.449757	4.006142	4.949379
1.5500000	2.831251	3.115071	3.506999	4.095618	5.153598
1.5600000	2.865147	3.157486	3.564408	4.185732	5.365712
1.5699999	2.899060	3.199937	3.621904	4.276181	5.582300
1.5707963	2.901761	3.203318	3.626484	4.283389	5.599619
1.5707963	2.901758	3.203314	3.626479	4.283383	5.599608

$\alpha =$ .399999

Θ	K VALUES				
	.009966711	.039469502	.087332193	.151646642	.229848846
.0000000	.000000	.000000	.000000	.000000	.000000
.0100000	.010000	.010000	.010000	.010000	.010000
.0200000	.020001	.020001	.020001	.020001	.020001
.0300000	.030003	.030003	.030004	.030004	.030004
.0400000	.040008	.040008	.040009	.040010	.040011
.0500000	.050016	.050017	.050018	.050019	.050021
.0600000	.060029	.060030	.060031	.060034	.060037
.0700000	.070046	.070048	.070050	.070054	.070058
.0800000	.080069	.080071	.080075	.080081	.080087
.0900000	.090098	.090102	.090107	.090115	.090125
.1000000	.100135	.100139	.100147	.100158	.100171
.1100000	.110179	.110186	.110196	.110211	.110228
.1200000	.120233	.120241	.120255	.120274	.120296
.1300000	.130296	.130307	.130325	.130348	.130377
.1400000	.140370	.140384	.140406	.140435	.140471
.1500000	.150456	.150472	.150499	.150535	.150580
.1600000	.160553	.160573	.160606	.160650	.160704
.1700000	.170664	.170688	.170727	.170780	.170844
.1800000	.180788	.180817	.180863	.180926	.181003
.1900000	.190927	.190961	.191015	.191089	.191179
.2000000	.201081	.201121	.201185	.201271	.201376
.2100000	.211252	.211297	.211372	.211472	.211593
.2200000	.221440	.221492	.221577	.221692	.221833
.2300000	.231645	.231705	.231803	.231934	.232095
.2400000	.241870	.241938	.242049	.242198	.242381
.2500000	.252114	.252191	.252316	.252485	.252692
.2600000	.262378	.262465	.262606	.262796	.263029
.2700000	.272664	.272761	.272919	.273133	.273393
.2800000	.282972	.283080	.283257	.283495	.283785
.2900000	.293302	.293423	.293619	.293884	.294207
.3000000	.303657	.303790	.304007	.304301	.304659
.3100000	.314036	.314183	.314423	.314746	.315143
.3200000	.324440	.324602	.324866	.325222	.325658
.3300000	.334870	.335048	.335338	.335729	.336208
.3400000	.345328	.345523	.345839	.346268	.346792
.3500000	.355813	.356026	.356372	.356839	.357412
.3600000	.366328	.366559	.366935	.367445	.368069
.3700000	.376871	.377122	.377532	.378085	.378764
.3800000	.387446	.387718	.388161	.388761	.389498
.3900000	.398051	.398345	.398825	.399475	.400272

$\alpha =$ .399999

Θ	K VALUES				
	.009966711	.039469502	.087332193	.151646642	.229848846
.4000000	.408688	.409006	.409524	.410225	.411087
.4100000	.419359	.419701	.420259	.421015	.421945
.4200000	.430063	.430431	.431031	.431845	.432846
.4300000	.440802	.441197	.441842	.442716	.443792
.4400000	.451576	.451999	.452691	.453629	.454783
.4500000	.462387	.462840	.463580	.464584	.465821
.4600000	.473234	.473718	.474510	.475584	.476907
.4700000	.484120	.484637	.485481	.486628	.488042
.4800000	.495044	.495595	.496495	.497719	.499228
.4900000	.506008	.506594	.507553	.508856	.510464
.5000000	.517013	.517636	.518655	.520041	.521753
.5100000	.528059	.528720	.529803	.531275	.533095
.5200000	.539147	.539848	.540997	.542560	.544492
.5300000	.550278	.551021	.552238	.553895	.555945
.5400000	.561453	.562239	.563527	.565282	.567455
.5500000	.572673	.573504	.574865	.576722	.579022
.5600000	.583938	.584815	.586254	.588216	.590649
.5700000	.595249	.596175	.597693	.599765	.602336
.5800000	.606608	.607584	.609184	.611370	.614084
.5900000	.618014	.619042	.620728	.623032	.625894
.6000000	.629470	.630551	.632326	.634752	.637769
.6100000	.640974	.642111	.643978	.646531	.649707
.6200000	.652530	.653724	.655685	.658370	.661712
.6300000	.664136	.665390	.667449	.670269	.673783
.6400000	.675795	.677109	.679270	.682231	.685922
.6500000	.687506	.688884	.691150	.694255	.698131
.6600000	.699271	.700714	.703088	.706343	.710409
.6700000	.711090	.712600	.715086	.718496	.722759
.6800000	.722964	.724544	.727144	.730715	.735180
.6899999	.734894	.736545	.739264	.743000	.747675
.7000000	.746881	.748606	.751447	.755352	.760245
.7100000	.758926	.760726	.763692	.767773	.772890
.7200000	.771028	.772906	.776002	.780264	.785611
.7300000	.783189	.785147	.788376	.792824	.798409
.7400000	.795410	.797450	.800816	.805456	.811286
.7500000	.807691	.809815	.813323	.818159	.824242
.7600000	.820033	.822244	.825896	.830936	.837279
.7700000	.832436	.834737	.838538	.843786	.850397
.7800000	.844902	.847294	.851248	.856710	.863597
.7899999	.857431	.859917	.864027	.869710	.876881

$\alpha =$ .399999

θ	K VALUES				
	.009966711	.039469502	.087332193	.151646642	.229848846
.8000000	.870023	.872605	.876877	.882786	.890249
.8100000	.882680	.885360	.889797	.895938	.903701
.8200000	.895401	.898183	.902789	.909168	.917240
.8300000	.908188	.911073	.915853	.922477	.930865
.8400000	.921040	.924032	.928989	.935864	.944577
.8500000	.933959	.937060	.942199	.949331	.958378
.8600000	.946946	.950157	.955483	.962878	.972268
.8700000	.959999	.963324	.968841	.976506	.986248
.8799999	.973121	.976562	.982274	.990216	1.000318
.8899999	.986311	.989871	.995783	1.004008	1.014480
.9000000	.999570	1.003251	1.009367	1.017883	1.028733
.9100000	1.012898	1.016703	1.023028	1.031840	1.043079
.9200000	1.026296	1.030228	1.036766	1.045882	1.057518
.9300000	1.039764	1.043825	1.050582	1.060007	1.072050
.9400000	1.053302	1.057495	1.064474	1.074217	1.086677
.9500000	1.066911	1.071239	1.078445	1.088512	1.101397
.9600000	1.080590	1.085056	1.092494	1.102892	1.116213
.9699999	1.094341	1.098947	1.106622	1.117358	1.131125
.9799999	1.108163	1.112912	1.120828	1.131909	1.146132
.9899999	1.122057	1.126951	1.135114	1.146546	1.161234
1.0000000	1.136022	1.141064	1.149478	1.161270	1.176434
1.0100000	1.150059	1.155252	1.163922	1.176080	1.191729
1.0200000	1.164167	1.169514	1.178444	1.190977	1.207121
1.0300000	1.178348	1.183851	1.193046	1.205959	1.222610
1.0400000	1.192600	1.198262	1.207728	1.221029	1.238195
1.0500000	1.206923	1.212748	1.222488	1.236184	1.253877
1.0600000	1.221318	1.227308	1.237328	1.251426	1.269656
1.0699999	1.235785	1.241942	1.252246	1.266755	1.285531
1.0799999	1.250323	1.256650	1.267243	1.282169	1.301502
1.0899999	1.264932	1.271432	1.282319	1.297668	1.317569
1.1000000	1.279611	1.286287	1.297473	1.313254	1.333732
1.1100000	1.294361	1.301215	1.312704	1.328924	1.349990
1.1200000	1.309181	1.316215	1.328013	1.344678	1.366343
1.1300000	1.324070	1.331288	1.343399	1.360517	1.382790
1.1400000	1.339028	1.346433	1.358861	1.376439	1.399331
1.1500000	1.354055	1.361649	1.374399	1.392444	1.415965
1.1600000	1.369150	1.376935	1.390012	1.408531	1.432691
1.1700000	1.384312	1.392291	1.405700	1.424699	1.449508
1.1800000	1.399541	1.407716	1.421461	1.440949	1.466417
1.1899999	1.414835	1.423210	1.437295	1.457277	1.483415

$\alpha =$ .399999

Θ	K VALUES				
	.009966711	.039469502	.087332193	.151646642	.229848846
1.2000000	1.430195	1.438772	1.453201	1.473685	1.500501
1.2100000	1.445619	1.454400	1.469178	1.490171	1.517675
1.2200000	1.461106	1.470093	1.485226	1.506733	1.534936
1.2300000	1.476656	1.485852	1.501342	1.523371	1.552281
1.2400000	1.492267	1.501675	1.517526	1.540083	1.569711
1.2500000	1.507938	1.517560	1.533777	1.556868	1.587223
1.2599999	1.523669	1.533506	1.550094	1.573725	1.604815
1.2699999	1.539458	1.549513	1.566475	1.590652	1.622487
1.2799999	1.555303	1.565579	1.582919	1.607649	1.640237
1.2899999	1.571204	1.581702	1.599424	1.624712	1.658063
1.3000000	1.587160	1.597883	1.615989	1.641842	1.675963
1.3100000	1.603168	1.614117	1.632613	1.659036	1.693935
1.3200000	1.619227	1.630405	1.649294	1.676291	1.711977
1.3300000	1.635337	1.646745	1.666030	1.693608	1.730088
1.3400000	1.651495	1.663135	1.682819	1.710983	1.748266
1.3500000	1.667699	1.679574	1.699661	1.728415	1.766507
1.3600000	1.683949	1.696060	1.716552	1.745902	1.784810
1.3700000	1.700242	1.712591	1.733491	1.763441	1.803173
1.3799999	1.716577	1.729165	1.750477	1.781032	1.821594
1.3899999	1.732952	1.745781	1.767507	1.798670	1.840069
1.4000000	1.749365	1.762436	1.784579	1.816356	1.858597
1.4100000	1.765814	1.779129	1.801692	1.834085	1.877174
1.4200000	1.782298	1.795858	1.818842	1.851856	1.895799
1.4300000	1.798814	1.812620	1.836029	1.869666	1.914468
1.4400000	1.815361	1.829414	1.853249	1.887513	1.933179
1.4500000	1.831936	1.846237	1.870500	1.905395	1.951929
1.4600000	1.848537	1.863088	1.887781	1.923309	1.970716
1.4700000	1.865163	1.879965	1.905089	1.941253	1.989536
1.4800000	1.881811	1.896864	1.922421	1.959223	2.008386
1.4900000	1.898479	1.913784	1.939776	1.977218	2.027265
1.5000000	1.915165	1.930723	1.957151	1.995235	2.046168
1.5100000	1.931867	1.947678	1.974543	2.013271	2.065092
1.5200000	1.948582	1.964647	1.991950	2.031324	2.084036
1.5300000	1.965309	1.981628	2.009369	2.049390	2.102995
1.5400000	1.982044	1.998619	2.026799	2.067468	2.121966
1.5500000	1.998787	2.015617	2.044237	2.085554	2.140947
1.5600000	2.015535	2.032619	2.061679	2.103645	2.159935
1.5699999	2.032285	2.049625	2.079125	2.121740	2.178926
1.5707963	2.033618	2.050979	2.080514	2.123180	2.180438
1.5707963	2.033617	2.050977	2.080512	2.123179	2.180437

$\alpha =$ .399999

Θ	K VALUES				
	.318821117	.415016431	.514599755	.613601043	.708073407
.0000000	.000000	.000000	.000000	.000000	.000000
.0100000	.010000	.010000	.010000	.010000	.010000
.0200000	.020001	.020001	.020001	.020001	.020002
.0300000	.030005	.030005	.030005	.030006	.030006
.0400000	.040011	.040012	.040014	.040015	.040016
.0500000	.050023	.050025	.050027	.050029	.050031
.0600000	.060040	.060043	.060047	.060050	.060054
.0700000	.070064	.070069	.070075	.070080	.070086
.0800000	.080095	.080103	.080112	.080120	.080128
.0900000	.090136	.090147	.090159	.090172	.090183
.1000000	.100186	.100202	.100219	.100235	.100251
.1100000	.110248	.110269	.110292	.110314	.110335
.1200000	.120322	.120350	.120379	.120408	.120435
.1300000	.130410	.130445	.130482	.130519	.130553
.1400000	.140512	.140556	.140602	.140648	.140692
.1500000	.150630	.150685	.150741	.150798	.150851
.1600000	.160765	.160831	.160900	.160968	.161034
.1700000	.170918	.170997	.171080	.171162	.171241
.1800000	.181090	.181184	.181283	.181381	.181474
.1900000	.191282	.191394	.191509	.191625	.191735
.2000000	.201496	.201626	.201761	.201896	.202026
.2100000	.211732	.211883	.212040	.212197	.212347
.2200000	.221993	.222166	.222347	.222528	.222700
.2300000	.232278	.232477	.232684	.232890	.233088
.2400000	.242589	.242815	.243051	.243286	.243512
.2500000	.252928	.253184	.253451	.253717	.253973
.2600000	.263294	.263583	.263884	.264185	.264474
.2700000	.273691	.274015	.274353	.274691	.275015
.2800000	.284118	.284480	.284858	.285236	.285599
.2900000	.294577	.294981	.295401	.295823	.296228
.3000000	.305070	.305517	.305984	.306452	.306902
.3100000	.315596	.316091	.316608	.317126	.317624
.3200000	.326159	.326704	.327274	.327845	.328396
.3300000	.336757	.337357	.337984	.338613	.339219
.3400000	.347394	.348052	.348739	.349430	.350096
.3500000	.358070	.358789	.359541	.360298	.361027
.3600000	.368787	.369571	.370392	.371218	.372016
.3700000	.379544	.380398	.381292	.382193	.383063
.3800000	.390345	.391272	.392244	.393224	.394171
.3900000	.401190	.402195	.403249	.404312	.405341

$\alpha =$ .399999

Θ	K VALUES				
	.318821117	.415016431	.514599755	.613601043	.708073407
.4000000	.412079	.413167	.414308	.415461	.416576
.4100000	.423016	.424190	.425424	.426670	.427878
.4200000	.434000	.435266	.436597	.437943	.439248
.4300000	.445032	.446395	.447829	.449280	.450688
.4400000	.456116	.457580	.459122	.460684	.462201
.4500000	.467250	.468821	.470478	.472156	.473788
.4600000	.478437	.480121	.481898	.483699	.485452
.4700000	.489678	.491480	.493383	.495314	.497195
.4800000	.500974	.502900	.504935	.507003	.509019
.4900000	.512327	.514382	.516557	.518768	.520926
.5000000	.523737	.525928	.528249	.530610	.532918
.5100000	.535207	.537540	.540013	.542533	.544997
.5200000	.546736	.549218	.551851	.554537	.557166
.5300000	.558327	.560964	.563765	.566625	.569427
.5400000	.569981	.572780	.575756	.578798	.581783
.5500000	.581699	.584667	.587827	.591059	.594234
.5600000	.593482	.596627	.599978	.603410	.606785
.5700000	.605332	.608661	.612211	.615853	.619437
.5800000	.617249	.620770	.624529	.628389	.632193
.5900000	.629236	.632957	.636933	.641021	.645055
.6000000	.641293	.645222	.649425	.653751	.658026
.6100000	.653422	.657566	.662006	.666581	.671108
.6200000	.665624	.669993	.674679	.679513	.684304
.6300000	.677900	.682502	.687444	.692550	.697616
.6400000	.690251	.695096	.700305	.705693	.711046
.6500000	.702679	.707776	.713262	.718945	.724599
.6600000	.715186	.720543	.726317	.732307	.738275
.6700000	.727771	.733399	.739473	.745783	.752079
.6800000	.740437	.746346	.752731	.759374	.766012
.6899999	.753184	.759384	.766093	.773082	.780077
.7000000	.766015	.772516	.779560	.786910	.794278
.7100000	.778929	.785743	.793135	.800860	.808616
.7200000	.791929	.799066	.806820	.814934	.823095
.7300000	.805016	.812487	.820615	.829135	.837718
.7400000	.818190	.826007	.834523	.843464	.852488
.7500000	.831453	.839628	.848546	.857925	.867406
.7600000	.844806	.853350	.862686	.872519	.882478
.7700000	.858251	.867176	.876944	.887249	.897704
.7800000	.871787	.881108	.891322	.902116	.913089
.7899999	.885418	.895145	.905821	.917124	.928636

$\alpha =$ .399999

Θ	K VALUES				
	.318821117	.415016431	.514599755	.613601043	.708073407
.8000000	.899142	.909290	.920445	.932275	.944346
.8100000	.912963	.923544	.935193	.947570	.960225
.8200000	.926879	.937908	.950069	.963013	.976273
.8300000	.940894	.952383	.965073	.978605	.992496
.8400000	.955007	.966972	.980208	.994348	1.008895
.8500000	.969220	.981674	.995475	1.010246	1.025473
.8600000	.983533	.996492	1.010875	1.026300	1.042235
.8700000	.997948	1.011426	1.026411	1.042512	1.059183
.8799999	1.012465	1.026478	1.042084	1.058885	1.076320
.8899999	1.027086	1.041649	1.057895	1.075421	1.093649
.9000000	1.041810	1.056939	1.073846	1.092121	1.111173
.9100000	1.056640	1.072350	1.089939	1.108989	1.128896
.9200000	1.071575	1.087884	1.106174	1.126026	1.146820
.9300000	1.086616	1.103540	1.122553	1.143234	1.164949
.9400000	1.101763	1.119319	1.139078	1.160615	1.183285
.9500000	1.117019	1.135224	1.155750	1.178172	1.201832
.9600000	1.132382	1.151253	1.172569	1.195905	1.220593
.9699999	1.147854	1.167409	1.189538	1.213817	1.239570
.9799999	1.163436	1.183692	1.206657	1.231910	1.258767
.9899999	1.179126	1.200102	1.223928	1.250186	1.278186
1.0000000	1.194927	1.216641	1.241351	1.268646	1.297830
1.0100000	1.210837	1.233308	1.258927	1.287291	1.317701
1.0200000	1.226858	1.250104	1.276657	1.306123	1.337804
1.0300000	1.242990	1.267029	1.294542	1.325144	1.358139
1.0400000	1.259232	1.284084	1.312582	1.344355	1.378710
1.0500000	1.275585	1.301269	1.330778	1.363757	1.399518
1.0600000	1.292049	1.318585	1.349131	1.383351	1.420568
1.0699999	1.308623	1.336030	1.367640	1.403138	1.441859
1.0799999	1.325308	1.353606	1.386307	1.423120	1.463395
1.0899999	1.342103	1.371312	1.405131	1.443296	1.485177
1.1000000	1.359009	1.389147	1.424113	1.463668	1.507208
1.1100000	1.376024	1.407113	1.443252	1.484236	1.529489
1.1200000	1.393148	1.425207	1.462548	1.505001	1.552021
1.1300000	1.410381	1.443431	1.482001	1.525962	1.574806
1.1400000	1.427721	1.461782	1.501611	1.547120	1.597845
1.1500000	1.445170	1.480262	1.521377	1.568474	1.621138
1.1600000	1.462725	1.498868	1.541298	1.590025	1.644687
1.1700000	1.480385	1.517600	1.561374	1.611772	1.668492
1.1800000	1.498151	1.536456	1.581603	1.633714	1.692554
1.1899999	1.516020	1.555437	1.601985	1.655850	1.716871

$\alpha =$ •399999

Θ	K VALUES				
	•318821117	•415016431	•514599755	•613601043	•708073407
•2000000	1•533992	1•574541	1•622519	1•678181	1•741446
•2100000	1•552065	1•593765	1•643203	1•700703	1•766275
•2200000	1•570239	1•613110	1•664035	1•723417	1•791360
•2300000	1•588511	1•632573	1•685015	1•746320	1•816699
•2400000	1•606881	1•652153	1•706139	1•769410	1•842290
•2500000	1•625346	1•671848	1•727407	1•792686	1•868132
•2599999	1•643906	1•691655	1•748815	1•816145	1•894224
•2699999	1•662557	1•711574	1•770363	1•839786	1•920562
•2799999	1•681299	1•731602	1•792046	1•863604	1•947144
•2899999	1•700130	1•751737	1•813864	1•887598	1•973966
•3000000	1•719047	1•771976	1•835813	1•911764	2•001027
•3100000	1•738048	1•792316	1•857890	1•936098	2•028322
•3200000	1•757131	1•812756	1•880091	1•960597	2•055846
•3300000	1•776295	1•833293	1•902415	1•985258	2•083596
•3400000	1•795535	1•853923	1•924857	2•010075	2•111566
•3500000	1•814851	1•874644	1•947414	2•035045	2•139751
•3600000	1•834239	1•895453	1•970082	2•060164	2•168145
•3700000	1•853696	1•916346	1•992857	2•085425	2•196743
•3799999	1•873221	1•937321	2•015736	2•110825	2•225538
•3899999	1•892809	1•958374	2•038714	2•136358	2•254523
1•4000000	1•912459	1•979502	2•061786	2•162018	2•283690
1•4100000	1•932168	2•000700	2•084950	2•187800	2•313033
1•4200000	1•951931	2•021966	2•108199	2•213698	2•342543
1•4300000	1•971747	2•043295	2•131529	2•239706	2•372212
1•4400000	1•991612	2•064684	2•154936	2•265817	2•402030
1•4500000	2•011523	2•086129	2•178414	2•292024	2•431990
1•4600000	2•031476	2•107626	2•201959	2•318322	2•462081
1•4700000	2•051469	2•129171	2•225565	2•344704	2•492294
1•4800000	2•071497	2•150760	2•249228	2•371162	2•522619
1•4900000	2•091558	2•172388	2•272941	2•397689	2•553045
1•5000000	2•111648	2•194052	2•296700	2•424278	2•583563
1•5100000	2•131763	2•215747	2•320498	2•450921	2•614161
1•5200000	2•151900	2•237469	2•344331	2•477612	2•644828
1•5300000	2•172056	2•259213	2•368193	2•504341	2•675553
1•5400000	2•192226	2•280976	2•392078	2•531103	2•706326
1•5500000	2•212408	2•302752	2•415981	2•557889	2•737134
1•5600000	2•232597	2•324537	2•439896	2•584691	2•767966
1•5699999	2•252790	2•346327	2•463817	2•611501	2•798810
1•5707963	2•254398	2•348062	2•465722	2•613636	2•801267
1•5707963	2•254397	2•348060	2•465720	2•613634	2•801264

$\alpha =$ .399999

Θ	K VALUES				
	.794250555	.868696860	.928444378	.971111163	.994996249
.0000000	.000000	.000000	.000000	.000000	.000000
.0100000	.010000	.010000	.010000	.010000	.010000
.0200000	.020002	.020002	.020002	.020002	.020002
.0300000	.030007	.030007	.030007	.030007	.030008
.0400000	.040017	.040017	.040018	.040018	.040019
.0500000	.050033	.050034	.050036	.050036	.050037
.0600000	.060057	.060060	.060062	.060063	.060064
.0700000	.070091	.070095	.070098	.070101	.070102
.0800000	.080136	.080142	.080147	.080151	.080153
.0900000	.090194	.090203	.090210	.090215	.090218
.1000000	.100266	.100278	.100288	.100296	.100300
.1100000	.110354	.110371	.110384	.110394	.110399
.1200000	.120460	.120482	.120499	.120512	.120519
.1300000	.130585	.130613	.130635	.130651	.130660
.1400000	.140732	.140766	.140794	.140814	.140825
.1500000	.150901	.150943	.150978	.151002	.151016
.1600000	.161094	.161146	.161188	.161217	.161234
.1700000	.171313	.171376	.171426	.171462	.171482
.1800000	.181560	.181634	.181694	.181737	.181761
.1900000	.191836	.191924	.191994	.192045	.192073
.2000000	.202144	.202246	.202329	.202388	.202421
.2100000	.212484	.212603	.212699	.212767	.212806
.2200000	.222859	.222996	.223107	.223186	.223230
.2300000	.233270	.233427	.233554	.233645	.233696
.2400000	.243719	.243899	.244043	.244147	.244205
.2500000	.254208	.254412	.254576	.254694	.254760
.2600000	.264739	.264969	.265154	.265287	.265362
.2700000	.275313	.275572	.275781	.275930	.276014
.2800000	.285933	.286223	.286457	.286624	.286718
.2900000	.296600	.296923	.297184	.297372	.297477
.3000000	.307316	.307676	.307966	.308174	.308291
.3100000	.318083	.318482	.318804	.319035	.319165
.3200000	.328903	.329344	.329700	.329956	.330100
.3300000	.339778	.340264	.340657	.340939	.341098
.3400000	.350709	.351244	.351676	.351987	.352162
.3500000	.361700	.362287	.362761	.363102	.363294
.3600000	.372752	.373394	.373913	.374287	.374496
.3700000	.383866	.384567	.385135	.385543	.385773
.3800000	.395046	.395810	.396429	.396874	.397125
.3900000	.406292	.407123	.407797	.408282	.408555

$\alpha =$ .399999

Θ	K VALUES				
	.794250555	.868696860	.928444378	.971111163	.994996249
.4000000	.417608	.418511	.419243	.419770	.420066
.4100000	.428995	.429974	.430768	.431340	.431662
.4200000	.440456	.441515	.442375	.442995	.443344
.4300000	.451993	.453138	.454067	.454738	.455115
.4400000	.463608	.464843	.465847	.466571	.466979
.4500000	.475304	.476634	.477717	.478498	.478938
.4600000	.487082	.488514	.489679	.490521	.490996
.4700000	.498945	.500484	.501738	.502644	.503155
.4800000	.510896	.512548	.513895	.514869	.515418
.4900000	.522937	.524708	.526154	.527200	.527790
.5000000	.535070	.536968	.538517	.539639	.540272
.5100000	.547298	.549329	.550989	.552191	.552870
.5200000	.559624	.561795	.563571	.564857	.565585
.5300000	.572050	.574368	.576267	.577643	.578421
.5400000	.584578	.587053	.589080	.590551	.591383
.5500000	.597212	.599850	.602014	.603585	.604474
.5600000	.609954	.612765	.615072	.616748	.617698
.5700000	.622807	.625799	.628257	.630045	.631058
.5800000	.635774	.638956	.641574	.643479	.644559
.5900000	.648857	.652240	.655025	.657054	.658205
.6000000	.662060	.665653	.668615	.670775	.672001
.6100000	.675385	.679200	.682348	.684645	.685949
.6200000	.688835	.692883	.696226	.698668	.700056
.6300000	.702414	.706706	.710255	.712850	.714325
.6400000	.716125	.720673	.724438	.727194	.728761
.6500000	.729970	.734787	.738780	.741705	.743370
.6600000	.743953	.749052	.753284	.756388	.758156
.6700000	.758077	.763473	.767956	.771248	.773124
.6800000	.772346	.778052	.782800	.786289	.788280
.6899999	.786763	.792794	.797820	.801518	.803629
.7000000	.801331	.807704	.813022	.816939	.819177
.7100000	.816053	.822784	.828410	.832558	.834930
.7200000	.830934	.838040	.843988	.848380	.850893
.7300000	.845977	.853476	.859763	.864411	.867073
.7400000	.861185	.869097	.875740	.880657	.883477
.7500000	.876562	.884906	.891923	.897125	.900110
.7600000	.892112	.900908	.908319	.913820	.916980
.7700000	.907839	.917109	.924933	.930749	.934094
.7800000	.923746	.933513	.941771	.947920	.951459
.7899999	.939838	.950125	.958840	.965338	.969083

$\alpha =$ .399999

θ	K VALUES				
	.794250555	.868696860	.928444378	.971111163	.994996249
.8000000	.956118	.966950	.976144	.983011	.986973
.8100000	.972590	.983994	.993691	1.000946	1.005137
.8200000	.989259	1.001261	1.011487	1.019151	1.023584
.8300000	1.006129	1.018756	1.029539	1.037635	1.042323
.8400000	1.023203	1.036486	1.047854	1.056404	1.061362
.8500000	1.040486	1.054456	1.066438	1.075468	1.080711
.8600000	1.057982	1.072671	1.085299	1.094835	1.100380
.8700000	1.075696	1.091138	1.104445	1.114514	1.120378
.8799999	1.093632	1.109862	1.123883	1.134515	1.140716
.8899999	1.111794	1.128849	1.143621	1.154847	1.161404
.9000000	1.130187	1.148107	1.163667	1.175520	1.182456
.9100000	1.148815	1.167639	1.184030	1.196545	1.203880
.9200000	1.167683	1.187454	1.204718	1.217932	1.225691
.9300000	1.186795	1.207558	1.225740	1.239693	1.247901
.9400000	1.206155	1.227957	1.247105	1.261838	1.270523
.9500000	1.225769	1.248658	1.268823	1.284381	1.293570
.9600000	1.245641	1.269668	1.290903	1.307333	1.317058
.9699999	1.265776	1.290994	1.313355	1.330708	1.341002
.9799999	1.286178	1.312643	1.336189	1.354518	1.365417
.9899999	1.306852	1.334622	1.359415	1.378778	1.390319
1.0000000	1.327802	1.356939	1.383046	1.403503	1.415727
1.0100000	1.349033	1.379600	1.407091	1.428708	1.441658
1.0200000	1.370550	1.402614	1.431562	1.454407	1.468132
1.0300000	1.392357	1.425988	1.456471	1.480618	1.495167
1.0400000	1.414459	1.449729	1.481830	1.507358	1.522786
1.0500000	1.436859	1.473846	1.507652	1.534645	1.551010
1.0600000	1.459564	1.498346	1.533948	1.562497	1.579863
1.0699999	1.482576	1.523237	1.560733	1.590933	1.609369
1.0799999	1.505900	1.548527	1.588019	1.619975	1.639554
1.0899999	1.529540	1.574224	1.615821	1.649642	1.670445
1.1000000	1.553501	1.600336	1.644154	1.679958	1.702072
1.1100000	1.577786	1.626871	1.673030	1.710946	1.734463
1.1200000	1.602399	1.653836	1.702466	1.742629	1.767653
1.1300000	1.627343	1.681241	1.732476	1.775033	1.801675
1.1400000	1.652622	1.709092	1.763077	1.808184	1.836567
1.1500000	1.678239	1.737398	1.794284	1.842111	1.872365
1.1600000	1.704197	1.766165	1.826114	1.876843	1.909113
1.1700000	1.730499	1.795403	1.858583	1.912410	1.946855
1.1800000	1.757147	1.825118	1.891709	1.948844	1.985637
1.1899999	1.784144	1.855317	1.925509	1.986179	2.025510

$\alpha =$ .399999

Θ	K VALUES				
	.794250555	.868696860	.928444378	.971111163	.994996249
1.2000000	1.811492	1.886008	1.959999	2.024451	2.066528
1.2100000	1.839191	1.917196	1.995199	2.063695	2.108750
1.2200000	1.867244	1.948889	2.031126	2.103952	2.152237
1.2300000	1.895651	1.981092	2.067797	2.145261	2.197058
1.2400000	1.924412	2.013812	2.105232	2.187666	2.243286
1.2500000	1.953528	2.047051	2.143448	2.231212	2.290999
1.2599999	1.982998	2.080817	2.182463	2.275946	2.340283
1.2699999	2.012821	2.115111	2.222295	2.321916	2.391231
1.2799999	2.042996	2.149938	2.262961	2.369175	2.443944
1.2899999	2.073521	2.185300	2.304478	2.417776	2.498533
1.3000000	2.104393	2.221199	2.346863	2.467776	2.555120
1.3100000	2.135608	2.257634	2.390131	2.519232	2.613835
1.3200000	2.167163	2.294607	2.434296	2.572206	2.674826
1.3300000	2.199054	2.332114	2.479372	2.626761	2.738254
1.3400000	2.231275	2.370155	2.525371	2.682961	2.804297
1.3500000	2.263820	2.408725	2.572303	2.740872	2.873153
1.3600000	2.296684	2.447818	2.620175	2.800563	2.945041
1.3700000	2.329858	2.487429	2.668994	2.862100	3.020206
1.3799999	2.363334	2.527548	2.718763	2.925552	3.098923
1.3899999	2.397105	2.568168	2.769480	2.990987	3.181500
1.4000000	2.431159	2.609276	2.821143	3.058468	3.268283
1.4100000	2.465487	2.650858	2.873744	3.128055	3.359659
1.4200000	2.500078	2.692901	2.927271	3.199804	3.456071
1.4300000	2.534919	2.735388	2.981708	3.273763	3.558013
1.4400000	2.569999	2.778299	3.037032	3.349968	3.666049
1.4500000	2.605303	2.821616	3.093218	3.428442	3.780810
1.4600000	2.640818	2.865316	3.150232	3.509191	3.903006
1.4700000	2.676529	2.909374	3.208035	3.592202	4.033428
1.4800000	2.712421	2.953765	3.266583	3.677433	4.172941
1.4900000	2.748477	2.998462	3.325825	3.764818	4.322466
1.5000000	2.784682	3.043436	3.385703	3.854257	4.482945
1.5100000	2.821017	3.088655	3.446154	3.945613	4.655256
1.5200000	2.857465	3.134089	3.507110	4.038714	4.840093
1.5300000	2.894009	3.179703	3.568497	4.133347	5.037751
1.5400000	2.930630	3.225464	3.630235	4.229267	5.247862
1.5500000	2.967309	3.271336	3.692242	4.326190	5.469080
1.5600000	3.004028	3.317284	3.754433	4.423810	5.698863
1.5699999	3.040768	3.363272	3.816720	4.521796	5.933498
1.5707963	3.043694	3.366934	3.821681	4.529605	5.952260
1.5707963	3.043691	3.366931	3.821677	4.529600	5.952253

$\alpha =$ .449999

Θ	K VALUES				
	.009966711	.039469502	.087332193	.151646642	.229848846
.0000000	.000000	.000000	.000000	.000000	.000000
.0100000	.010000	.010000	.010000	.010000	.010000
.0200000	.020001	.020001	.020001	.020001	.020001
.0300000	.030004	.030004	.030004	.030004	.030005
.0400000	.040009	.040010	.040010	.040011	.040012
.0500000	.050018	.050019	.050020	.050021	.050023
.0600000	.060032	.060033	.060035	.060037	.060040
.0700000	.070052	.070053	.070056	.070060	.070064
.0800000	.080077	.080080	.080084	.080089	.080096
.0900000	.090110	.090114	.090120	.090127	.090137
.1000000	.100151	.100156	.100164	.100175	.100188
.1100000	.110202	.110208	.110219	.110233	.110250
.1200000	.120262	.120270	.120284	.120303	.120325
.1300000	.130333	.130344	.130361	.130385	.130414
.1400000	.140416	.140430	.140452	.140481	.140517
.1500000	.150512	.150529	.150556	.150592	.150636
.1600000	.160622	.160642	.160675	.160719	.160773
.1700000	.170746	.170770	.170810	.170863	.170927
.1800000	.180886	.180915	.180961	.181024	.181101
.1900000	.191042	.191076	.191131	.191205	.191295
.2000000	.201216	.201256	.201320	.201406	.201511
.2100000	.211408	.211454	.211528	.211628	.211750
.2200000	.221620	.221672	.221758	.221873	.222013
.2300000	.231851	.231912	.232009	.232141	.232302
.2400000	.242104	.242173	.242284	.242433	.242616
.2500000	.252379	.252457	.252582	.252752	.252958
.2600000	.262677	.262764	.262906	.263096	.263329
.2700000	.273000	.273097	.273255	.273469	.273730
.2800000	.283347	.283455	.283632	.283871	.284162
.2900000	.293720	.293840	.294037	.294302	.294627
.3000000	.304119	.304253	.304471	.304765	.305124
.3100000	.314547	.314695	.314935	.315260	.315657
.3200000	.325004	.325166	.325431	.325788	.326226
.3300000	.335490	.335668	.335959	.336351	.336832
.3400000	.346007	.346202	.346520	.346950	.347476
.3500000	.356555	.356769	.357116	.357585	.358160
.3600000	.367137	.367369	.367747	.368258	.368885
.3700000	.377752	.378004	.378415	.378971	.379652
.3800000	.388401	.388675	.389120	.389723	.390463
.3900000	.399087	.399382	.399864	.400517	.401318

$\alpha =$ .449999

Θ	K VALUES				
	.009966711	.039469502	.087332193	.151646642	.229848846
.4000000	.409809	.410128	.410648	.411353	.412219
.4100000	.420568	.420912	.421473	.422233	.423167
.4200000	.431366	.431736	.432340	.433158	.434164
.4300000	.442204	.442601	.443249	.444129	.445211
.4400000	.453082	.453508	.454203	.455147	.456308
.4500000	.464002	.464458	.465202	.466213	.467458
.4600000	.474964	.475452	.476248	.477329	.478661
.4700000	.485970	.486490	.487341	.488495	.489919
.4800000	.497021	.497575	.498482	.499714	.501234
.4900000	.508117	.508707	.509673	.510985	.512606
.5000000	.519260	.519887	.520914	.522311	.524036
.5100000	.530450	.531117	.532208	.533692	.535527
.5200000	.541689	.542396	.543554	.545130	.547079
.5300000	.552978	.553727	.554954	.556626	.558694
.5400000	.564317	.565111	.566410	.568181	.570373
.5500000	.575709	.576547	.577922	.579796	.582117
.5600000	.587152	.588038	.589491	.591472	.593929
.5700000	.598650	.599585	.601118	.603211	.605808
.5800000	.610202	.611188	.612806	.615014	.617756
.5900000	.621810	.622849	.624553	.626882	.629776
.6000000	.633475	.634569	.636363	.638817	.641867
.6100000	.645198	.646348	.648236	.650819	.654032
.6200000	.656979	.658188	.660173	.662889	.666271
.6300000	.668821	.670090	.672175	.675030	.678587
.6400000	.680723	.682054	.684243	.687241	.690980
.6500000	.692687	.694083	.696378	.699525	.703452
.6600000	.704714	.706176	.708582	.711882	.716003
.6700000	.716805	.718336	.720856	.724314	.728637
.6800000	.728960	.730562	.733200	.736822	.741353
.6899999	.741182	.742857	.745616	.749407	.754153
.7000000	.753470	.755220	.758105	.762070	.767038
.7100000	.765826	.767654	.770668	.774813	.780010
.7200000	.778251	.780159	.783305	.787636	.793070
.7300000	.790745	.792736	.796019	.800541	.806220
.7400000	.803310	.805385	.808810	.813529	.819460
.7500000	.815947	.818109	.821678	.826600	.832791
.7600000	.828657	.830908	.834626	.839757	.846216
.7700000	.841439	.843783	.847654	.853000	.859736
.7800000	.854297	.856734	.860763	.866330	.873350
.7899999	.867229	.869764	.873955	.879749	.887062

$\alpha =$ .449999

Θ	K VALUES				
	.009966711	.039469502	.087332193	.151646642	.229848846
.8000000	.880238	.882872	.887229	.893257	.900872
.8100000	.893324	.896059	.900588	.906856	.914780
.8200000	.906487	.909328	.914031	.920546	.928789
.8300000	.919730	.922677	.927560	.934328	.942900
.8400000	.933051	.936109	.941176	.948204	.957113
.8500000	.946454	.949624	.954880	.962175	.971430
.8600000	.959937	.963222	.968672	.976240	.985852
.8700000	.973502	.976905	.982553	.990403	1.000379
.8799999	.987149	.990674	.996525	1.004662	1.015013
.8899999	1.000880	1.004528	1.010587	1.019019	1.029755
.9000000	1.014695	1.018470	1.024742	1.033475	1.044606
.9100000	1.028594	1.032498	1.038988	1.048031	1.059567
.9200000	1.042579	1.046615	1.053328	1.062687	1.074638
.9300000	1.056649	1.060820	1.067761	1.077444	1.089820
.9400000	1.070805	1.075115	1.082288	1.092303	1.105115
.9500000	1.085049	1.089499	1.096910	1.107265	1.120522
.9600000	1.099379	1.103974	1.111628	1.122329	1.136043
.9699999	1.113798	1.118539	1.126442	1.137497	1.151678
.9799999	1.128304	1.133196	1.141352	1.152769	1.167428
.9899999	1.142899	1.147944	1.156358	1.168146	1.183294
1.0000000	1.157583	1.162784	1.171462	1.183627	1.199275
1.0100000	1.172356	1.177716	1.186663	1.199214	1.215373
1.0200000	1.187219	1.192740	1.201962	1.214906	1.231588
1.0300000	1.202171	1.207857	1.217358	1.230705	1.247919
1.0400000	1.217212	1.223067	1.232853	1.246609	1.264368
1.0500000	1.232344	1.238369	1.248446	1.262619	1.280934
1.0600000	1.247565	1.253764	1.264137	1.278736	1.297618
1.0699999	1.262876	1.269252	1.279926	1.294958	1.314419
1.0799999	1.278276	1.284833	1.295813	1.311287	1.331338
1.0899999	1.293766	1.300507	1.311798	1.327722	1.348375
1.1000000	1.309346	1.316273	1.327881	1.344263	1.365529
1.1100000	1.325015	1.332130	1.344062	1.360909	1.382800
1.1200000	1.340772	1.348080	1.360339	1.377660	1.400187
1.1300000	1.356618	1.364121	1.376713	1.394516	1.417691
1.1400000	1.372551	1.380253	1.393183	1.411477	1.435310
1.1500000	1.388572	1.396476	1.409749	1.428540	1.453044
1.1600000	1.404680	1.412788	1.426410	1.445707	1.470893
1.1700000	1.420874	1.429189	1.443166	1.462976	1.488856
1.1800000	1.437154	1.445679	1.460014	1.480347	1.506931
1.1899999	1.453518	1.462256	1.476956	1.497817	1.525117

$\alpha =$ .449999

Θ	K VALUES				
	.009966711	.039469502	.087332193	.151646642	.229848846
1.2000000	1.469966	1.478920	1.493989	1.515388	1.543415
1.2100000	1.486497	1.495670	1.511113	1.533056	1.561821
1.2200000	1.503110	1.512504	1.528326	1.550822	1.580336
1.2300000	1.519803	1.529422	1.545628	1.568683	1.598957
1.2400000	1.536576	1.546422	1.563017	1.586639	1.617684
1.2500000	1.553427	1.563503	1.580491	1.604688	1.636514
1.2599999	1.570355	1.580664	1.598050	1.622829	1.655446
1.2699999	1.587359	1.597902	1.615692	1.641059	1.674478
1.2799999	1.604437	1.615218	1.633414	1.659377	1.693608
1.2899999	1.621588	1.632608	1.651217	1.677781	1.712834
1.3000000	1.638809	1.650072	1.669097	1.696270	1.732155
1.3100000	1.656100	1.667608	1.687052	1.714841	1.751567
1.3200000	1.673458	1.685213	1.705082	1.733492	1.771068
1.3300000	1.690881	1.702886	1.723183	1.752221	1.790657
1.3400000	1.708368	1.720624	1.741354	1.771026	1.810329
1.3500000	1.725917	1.738427	1.759592	1.789904	1.830084
1.3600000	1.743525	1.756290	1.777895	1.808853	1.849918
1.3700000	1.761191	1.774214	1.796262	1.827870	1.869827
1.3799999	1.778912	1.792194	1.814689	1.846952	1.889810
1.3899999	1.796685	1.810229	1.833173	1.866098	1.909864
1.4000000	1.814510	1.828316	1.851713	1.885304	1.929985
1.4100000	1.832382	1.846453	1.870306	1.904567	1.950169
1.4200000	1.850300	1.864638	1.888949	1.923884	1.970414
1.4300000	1.868261	1.882866	1.907638	1.943252	1.990716
1.4400000	1.886262	1.901137	1.926373	1.962668	2.011073
1.4500000	1.904301	1.919446	1.945148	1.982130	2.031479
1.4600000	1.922376	1.937792	1.963962	2.001634	2.051933
1.4700000	1.940482	1.956172	1.982812	2.021176	2.072429
1.4800000	1.958619	1.974582	2.001694	2.040753	2.092965
1.4900000	1.976782	1.993020	2.020605	2.060362	2.113537
1.5000000	1.994969	2.011483	2.039543	2.080000	2.134140
1.5100000	2.013177	2.029967	2.058504	2.099663	2.154772
1.5200000	2.031404	2.048471	2.077484	2.119347	2.175428
1.5300000	2.049645	2.066990	2.096482	2.139049	2.196104
1.5400000	2.067899	2.085521	2.115492	2.158766	2.216796
1.5500000	2.086162	2.104062	2.134513	2.178494	2.237501
1.5600000	2.104431	2.122610	2.153541	2.198230	2.258213
1.5699999	2.122704	2.141161	2.172572	2.217969	2.278931
1.5707963	2.124159	2.142638	2.174087	2.219541	2.280581
1.5707963	2.124157	2.142637	2.174086	2.219540	2.280579

$\alpha =$ .449999

Θ	K VALUES				
	.318821117	.415016431	.514599755	.613601043	.708073407
.0000000	.000000	.000000	.000000	.000000	.000000
.0100000	.010000	.010000	.010000	.010000	.010000
.0200000	.020001	.020001	.020001	.020002	.020002
.0300000	.030005	.030005	.030006	.030006	.030007
.0400000	.040013	.040014	.040015	.040016	.040017
.0500000	.050025	.050027	.050029	.050031	.050033
.0600000	.060043	.060047	.060050	.060054	.060057
.0700000	.070069	.070075	.070080	.070086	.070092
.0800000	.080104	.080112	.080120	.080129	.080137
.0900000	.090148	.090159	.090172	.090184	.090195
.1000000	.100203	.100219	.100236	.100252	.100268
.1100000	.110270	.110292	.110314	.110336	.110357
.1200000	.120351	.120379	.120408	.120437	.120464
.1300000	.130447	.130482	.130519	.130555	.130590
.1400000	.140558	.140602	.140648	.140694	.140738
.1500000	.150687	.150741	.150798	.150854	.150908
.1600000	.160834	.160900	.160969	.161038	.161103
.1700000	.171001	.171080	.171163	.171245	.171324
.1800000	.181188	.181283	.181381	.181479	.181573
.1900000	.191398	.191510	.191626	.191741	.191852
.2000000	.201632	.201762	.201897	.202032	.202162
.2100000	.211890	.212041	.212198	.212354	.212505
.2200000	.222174	.222348	.222529	.222709	.222882
.2300000	.232485	.232684	.232891	.233098	.233297
.2400000	.242825	.243052	.243288	.243523	.243750
.2500000	.253195	.253451	.253719	.253986	.254242
.2600000	.263595	.263885	.264186	.264488	.264777
.2700000	.274029	.274354	.274692	.275031	.275356
.2800000	.284496	.284859	.285237	.285616	.285980
.2900000	.294998	.295402	.295824	.296246	.296652
.3000000	.305536	.305985	.306453	.306922	.307374
.3100000	.316112	.316609	.317127	.317646	.318146
.3200000	.326728	.327275	.327846	.328420	.328972
.3300000	.337383	.337985	.338613	.339245	.339853
.3400000	.348080	.348740	.349430	.350123	.350791
.3500000	.358821	.359542	.360297	.361056	.361789
.3600000	.369606	.370393	.371217	.372047	.372848
.3700000	.380436	.381293	.382191	.383096	.383969
.3800000	.391314	.392245	.393221	.394205	.395157
.3900000	.402240	.403250	.404309	.405377	.406411

$\alpha =$ .449999

Θ	K VALUES				
	.318821117	.415016431	.514599755	.613601043	.708073407
.4000000	.413216	.414309	.415456	.416614	.417735
.4100000	.424244	.425424	.426664	.427917	.429131
.4200000	.435324	.436597	.437936	.439288	.440601
.4300000	.446458	.447829	.449271	.450730	.452146
.4400000	.457648	.459121	.460673	.462244	.463770
.4500000	.468895	.470477	.472144	.473833	.475475
.4600000	.480201	.481896	.483684	.485497	.487262
.4700000	.491566	.493380	.495296	.497241	.499135
.4800000	.502993	.504932	.506982	.509065	.511095
.4900000	.514482	.516553	.518743	.520971	.523145
.5000000	.526036	.528244	.530582	.532963	.535288
.5100000	.537655	.540007	.542501	.545041	.547526
.5200000	.549342	.551844	.554500	.557209	.559860
.5300000	.561097	.563757	.566583	.569468	.572295
.5400000	.572922	.575747	.578750	.581820	.584832
.5500000	.584819	.587816	.591005	.594269	.597474
.5600000	.596789	.599965	.603349	.606816	.610224
.5700000	.608834	.612197	.615784	.619463	.623085
.5800000	.620955	.624513	.628312	.632213	.636058
.5900000	.633154	.636915	.640935	.645068	.649148
.6000000	.645431	.649404	.653655	.658031	.662356
.6100000	.657790	.661983	.666475	.671104	.675685
.6200000	.670230	.674652	.679395	.684290	.689139
.6300000	.682755	.687415	.692419	.697590	.702721
.6400000	.695364	.700272	.705548	.711008	.716432
.6500000	.708061	.713225	.718785	.724545	.730277
.6600000	.720845	.726277	.732132	.738206	.744258
.6700000	.733720	.739429	.745590	.751991	.758379
.6800000	.746686	.752682	.759162	.765903	.772642
.6899999	.759745	.766039	.772850	.779946	.787050
.7000000	.772898	.779501	.786656	.794122	.801608
.7100000	.786147	.793070	.800582	.808433	.816318
.7200000	.799493	.806748	.814631	.822883	.831183
.7300000	.812938	.820537	.828805	.837473	.846206
.7400000	.826484	.834438	.843105	.852206	.861392
.7500000	.840131	.848453	.857535	.867086	.876743
.7600000	.853882	.862585	.872095	.882114	.892263
.7700000	.867738	.876834	.886789	.897294	.907956
.7800000	.881699	.891202	.901618	.912629	.923824
.7899999	.895769	.905692	.916585	.928120	.939871

$\alpha =$ .449999

θ	K VALUES				
	.318821117	.415016431	.514599755	.613601043	.708073407
.8000000	.909947	.920304	.931692	.943772	.956101
.8100000	.924236	.935042	.946941	.959586	.972518
.8200000	.938637	.949905	.962334	.975565	.989125
.8300000	.953151	.964896	.977873	.991713	1.005925
.8400000	.967779	.980017	.993560	1.008031	1.022923
.8500000	.982523	.995269	1.009397	1.024523	1.040121
.8600000	.997385	1.010654	1.025387	1.041192	1.057524
.8700000	1.012364	1.026174	1.041532	1.058039	1.075136
.8799999	1.027463	1.041829	1.057833	1.075068	1.092960
.8899999	1.042683	1.057621	1.074292	1.092282	1.110999
.9000000	1.058025	1.073553	1.090912	1.109683	1.129258
.9100000	1.073490	1.089625	1.107694	1.127273	1.147740
.9200000	1.089078	1.105838	1.124640	1.145056	1.166449
.9300000	1.104792	1.122194	1.141752	1.163033	1.185389
.9400000	1.120632	1.138695	1.159032	1.181209	1.204563
.9500000	1.136599	1.155340	1.176481	1.199584	1.223975
.9600000	1.152693	1.172133	1.194101	1.218161	1.243628
.9699999	1.168917	1.189073	1.211894	1.236943	1.263527
.9799999	1.185269	1.206162	1.229860	1.255932	1.283674
.9899999	1.201752	1.223401	1.248003	1.275131	1.304074
1.0000000	1.218366	1.240791	1.266323	1.294540	1.324729
1.0100000	1.235111	1.258332	1.284821	1.314164	1.345643
1.0200000	1.251988	1.276026	1.303498	1.334002	1.366819
1.0300000	1.268998	1.293872	1.322356	1.354058	1.388261
1.0400000	1.286140	1.311872	1.341396	1.374333	1.409972
1.0500000	1.303415	1.330026	1.360618	1.394829	1.431954
1.0600000	1.320823	1.348335	1.380024	1.415548	1.454210
1.0699999	1.338365	1.366799	1.399613	1.436490	1.476744
1.0799999	1.356040	1.385417	1.419388	1.457657	1.499559
1.0899999	1.373848	1.404191	1.439348	1.479051	1.522655
1.1000000	1.391790	1.423121	1.459493	1.500672	1.546037
1.1100000	1.409865	1.442205	1.479824	1.522521	1.569705
1.1200000	1.428072	1.461445	1.500341	1.544599	1.593663
1.1300000	1.446412	1.480839	1.521044	1.566907	1.617911
1.1400000	1.464884	1.500387	1.541932	1.589444	1.642452
1.1500000	1.483486	1.520089	1.563006	1.612211	1.667287
1.1600000	1.502220	1.539943	1.584264	1.635209	1.692417
1.1700000	1.521082	1.559950	1.605707	1.658436	1.717842
1.1800000	1.540074	1.580108	1.627332	1.681892	1.743564
1.1899999	1.559193	1.600417	1.649140	1.705577	1.769582

$\alpha =$ .449999

Θ	K VALUES				
	.318821117	.415016431	.514599755	.613601043	.708073407
1.2000000	1.578438	1.620874	1.671128	1.729489	1.795898
1.2100000	1.597809	1.641478	1.693296	1.753628	1.822509
1.2200000	1.617303	1.662228	1.715643	1.777992	1.849417
1.2300000	1.636919	1.683123	1.738165	1.802579	1.876619
1.2400000	1.656656	1.704160	1.760861	1.827388	1.904115
1.2500000	1.676511	1.725338	1.783730	1.852417	1.931903
1.2599999	1.696483	1.746653	1.806769	1.877662	1.959981
1.2699999	1.716571	1.768105	1.829975	1.903122	1.988346
1.2799999	1.736770	1.789691	1.853345	1.928793	2.016995
1.2899999	1.757080	1.811407	1.876877	1.954671	2.045926
1.3000000	1.777499	1.833252	1.900567	1.980755	2.075134
1.3100000	1.798022	1.855223	1.924413	2.007039	2.104615
1.3200000	1.818649	1.877315	1.948410	2.033519	2.134365
1.3300000	1.839375	1.899527	1.972554	2.060191	2.164378
1.3400000	1.860198	1.921854	1.996842	2.087050	2.194649
1.3500000	1.881116	1.944294	2.021270	2.114092	2.225172
1.3600000	1.902125	1.966843	2.045833	2.141310	2.255941
1.3700000	1.923221	1.989496	2.070527	2.168700	2.286947
1.3799999	1.944402	2.012250	2.095347	2.196254	2.318185
1.3899999	1.965664	2.035102	2.120288	2.223968	2.349646
1.4000000	1.987004	2.058046	2.145344	2.251835	2.381321
1.4100000	2.008417	2.081078	2.170511	2.279847	2.413202
1.4200000	2.029900	2.104194	2.195783	2.307998	2.445280
1.4300000	2.051450	2.127389	2.221154	2.336281	2.477544
1.4400000	2.073061	2.150659	2.246619	2.364688	2.509984
1.4500000	2.094731	2.173998	2.272171	2.393211	2.542590
1.4600000	2.116454	2.197403	2.297805	2.421842	2.575351
1.4700000	2.138228	2.220867	2.323514	2.450573	2.608256
1.4800000	2.160047	2.244386	2.349292	2.479397	2.641292
1.4900000	2.181907	2.267954	2.375133	2.508303	2.674447
1.5000000	2.203805	2.291567	2.401029	2.537284	2.707711
1.5100000	2.225734	2.315219	2.426974	2.566331	2.741068
1.5200000	2.247692	2.338904	2.452961	2.595434	2.774508
1.5300000	2.269673	2.362618	2.478984	2.624585	2.808016
1.5400000	2.291672	2.386354	2.505036	2.653774	2.841579
1.5500000	2.313686	2.410107	2.531109	2.682991	2.875184
1.5600000	2.335710	2.433872	2.557197	2.712229	2.908818
1.5699999	2.357739	2.457643	2.583292	2.741476	2.942466
1.5707963	2.359493	2.459536	2.585370	2.743806	2.945146
1.5707963	2.359492	2.459536	2.585368	2.743803	2.945143

$\alpha =$ .449999

θ	K VALUES				
	.794250555	.868696860	.928444378	.971111163	.994996249
.0000000	.000000	.000000	.000000	.000000	.000000
.0100000	.010000	.010000	.010000	.010000	.010000
.0200000	.020002	.020002	.020002	.020002	.020002
.0300000	.030007	.030007	.030008	.030008	.030008
.0400000	.040018	.040018	.040019	.040019	.040020
.0500000	.050035	.050036	.050038	.050039	.050039
.0600000	.060061	.060063	.060065	.060067	.060068
.0700000	.070097	.070101	.070104	.070107	.070108
.0800000	.080144	.080151	.080156	.080160	.080162
.0900000	.090206	.090215	.090222	.090227	.090230
.1000000	.100283	.100295	.100305	.100312	.100316
.1100000	.110376	.110393	.110407	.110416	.110421
.1200000	.120489	.120511	.120528	.120541	.120548
.1300000	.130622	.130650	.130672	.130688	.130697
.1400000	.140778	.140813	.140840	.140860	.140871
.1500000	.150958	.151000	.151035	.151059	.151073
.1600000	.161163	.161215	.161257	.161287	.161303
.1700000	.171396	.171459	.171509	.171545	.171565
.1800000	.181659	.181733	.181793	.181836	.181860
.1900000	.191953	.192041	.192111	.192162	.192190
.2000000	.202280	.202383	.202465	.202524	.202557
.2100000	.212642	.212761	.212857	.212926	.212964
.2200000	.223041	.223178	.223289	.223368	.223413
.2300000	.233479	.233636	.233763	.233854	.233905
.2400000	.243957	.244137	.244282	.244385	.244443
.2500000	.254478	.254682	.254846	.254964	.255030
.2600000	.265043	.265273	.265459	.265592	.265667
.2700000	.275655	.275914	.276123	.276273	.276357
.2800000	.286315	.286605	.286840	.287008	.287102
.2900000	.297025	.297350	.297612	.297799	.297904
.3000000	.307788	.308149	.308441	.308650	.308767
.3100000	.318606	.319006	.319329	.319561	.319691
.3200000	.329480	.329923	.330280	.330537	.330681
.3300000	.340413	.340901	.341296	.341579	.341738
.3400000	.351407	.351944	.352378	.352689	.352864
.3500000	.362464	.363053	.363529	.363871	.364064
.3600000	.373586	.374231	.374752	.375127	.375338
.3700000	.384776	.385480	.386050	.386460	.386690
.3800000	.396035	.396803	.397425	.397872	.398123
.3900000	.407367	.408202	.408879	.409366	.409640

$\alpha =$ .449999

θ	K VALUES				
	.794250555	.868696860	.928444378	.971111163	.994996249
.4000000	.418772	.419679	.420415	.420945	.421243
.4100000	.430255	.431238	.432036	.432611	.432935
.4200000	.441816	.442881	.443745	.444368	.444719
.4300000	.453459	.454610	.455545	.456219	.456599
.4400000	.465186	.466429	.467438	.468167	.468577
.4500000	.477000	.478339	.479428	.480214	.480658
.4600000	.488903	.490344	.491517	.492365	.492843
.4700000	.500897	.502447	.503709	.504621	.505136
.4800000	.512986	.514650	.516007	.516988	.517541
.4900000	.525172	.526957	.528413	.529467	.530062
.5000000	.537457	.539370	.540932	.542063	.542701
.5100000	.549846	.551893	.553566	.554778	.555463
.5200000	.562339	.564529	.566320	.567618	.568351
.5300000	.574941	.577280	.579196	.580584	.581370
.5400000	.587654	.590151	.592197	.593682	.594523
.5500000	.600481	.603144	.605329	.606916	.607814
.5600000	.613425	.616264	.618594	.620288	.621247
.5700000	.626489	.629513	.631997	.633804	.634827
.5800000	.639677	.642894	.645541	.647467	.648559
.5900000	.652992	.656413	.659230	.661282	.662446
.6000000	.666436	.670072	.673068	.675253	.676493
.6100000	.680013	.683875	.687061	.689386	.690706
.6200000	.693727	.697825	.701211	.703684	.705089
.6300000	.707581	.711928	.715523	.718152	.719647
.6400000	.721578	.726187	.730003	.732796	.734385
.6500000	.735722	.740606	.744654	.747620	.749309
.6600000	.750017	.755189	.759482	.762630	.764424
.6700000	.764465	.769940	.774491	.777832	.779736
.6800000	.779072	.784865	.789687	.793230	.795251
.6899999	.793841	.799967	.805073	.808830	.810975
.7000000	.808775	.815252	.820657	.824639	.826914
.7100000	.823879	.830723	.836443	.840662	.843075
.7200000	.839156	.846385	.852437	.856906	.859463
.7300000	.854611	.862245	.868645	.873376	.876087
.7400000	.870248	.878305	.885071	.890081	.892953
.7500000	.886071	.894572	.901724	.907025	.910068
.7600000	.902084	.911052	.918608	.924218	.927441
.7700000	.918292	.927748	.935730	.941665	.945078
.7800000	.934698	.944667	.953097	.959374	.962988
.7899999	.951309	.961814	.970715	.977353	.981179

$\alpha =$ •449999

Θ	K VALUES				
	•794250555	•868696860	•928444378	•971111163	•994996249
•8000000	•968127	•979196	•988592	•995611	•999661
•8100000	•985158	•996817	1•006734	1•014154	1•018441
•8200000	1•002406	1•014684	1•025149	1•032993	1•037530
•8300000	1•019877	1•032803	1•043844	1•052135	1•056936
•8400000	1•037574	1•051180	1•062827	1•071589	1•076670
•8500000	1•055504	1•069822	1•082106	1•091366	1•096743
•8600000	1•073670	1•088734	1•101689	1•111474	1•117164
•8700000	1•092077	1•107924	1•121585	1•131924	1•137946
•8799999	1•110732	1•127399	1•141802	1•152727	1•159099
•8899999	1•129639	1•147165	1•162349	1•173892	1•180636
•9000000	1•148803	1•167229	1•183236	1•195432	1•202570
•9100000	1•168229	1•187599	1•204472	1•217358	1•224912
•9200000	1•187923	1•208282	1•226065	1•239681	1•247678
•9300000	1•207889	1•229285	1•248028	1•262415	1•270881
•9400000	1•228134	1•250615	1•270369	1•285572	1•294536
•9500000	1•248663	1•272282	1•293099	1•309166	1•318659
•9600000	1•269481	1•294292	1•316230	1•333211	1•343265
•9699999	1•290593	1•316653	1•339772	1•357720	1•368371
•9799999	1•312005	1•339374	1•363736	1•382710	1•393995
•9899999	1•333723	1•362463	1•388136	1•408195	1•420155
1•0000000	1•355752	1•385929	1•412983	1•434193	1•446870
1•0100000	1•378097	1•409779	1•438289	1•460719	1•474162
1•0200000	1•400763	1•434022	1•464068	1•487792	1•502050
1•0300000	1•423757	1•458668	1•490332	1•515429	1•530556
1•0400000	1•447083	1•483725	1•517096	1•543650	1•559705
1•0500000	1•470747	1•509201	1•544374	1•572476	1•589521
1•0600000	1•494754	1•535107	1•572179	1•601926	1•620029
1•0699999	1•519109	1•561451	1•600527	1•632022	1•651257
1•0799999	1•543817	1•588241	1•629433	1•662787	1•683234
1•0899999	1•568884	1•615489	1•658912	1•694244	1•715988
1•1000000	1•594314	1•643202	1•688982	1•726419	1•749554
1•1100000	1•620111	1•671389	1•719657	1•759337	1•783964
1•1200000	1•646281	1•700061	1•750955	1•793024	1•819253
1•1300000	1•672828	1•729226	1•782893	1•827510	1•855461
1•1400000	1•699755	1•758893	1•815489	1•862823	1•892627
1•1500000	1•727067	1•789071	1•848761	1•898995	1•930795
1•1600000	1•754767	1•819770	1•882727	1•936058	1•970009
1•1700000	1•782859	1•850998	1•917407	1•974046	2•010320
1•1800000	1•811347	1•882763	1•952818	2•012994	2•051778
1•1899999	1•840232	1•915074	1•988982	2•052940	2•094439

$\alpha =$ •449999

Θ	K VALUES				
	•794250555	•868696860	•928444378	•971111163	•994996249
1•2000000	1•869517	1•947940	2•025916	2•093923	2•138364
1•2100000	1•899204	1•981367	2•063642	2•135984	2•183616
1•2200000	1•929295	2•015362	2•102180	2•179166	2•230263
1•2300000	1•959792	2•049934	2•141548	2•223514	2•278381
1•2400000	1•990694	2•085088	2•181769	2•269075	2•328050
1•2500000	2•022002	2•120831	2•222862	2•315899	2•379355
1•2599999	2•053715	2•157167	2•264847	2•364039	2•432391
1•2699999	2•085834	2•194101	2•307745	2•413547	2•487260
1•2799999	2•118356	2•231637	2•351574	2•464481	2•544073
1•2899999	2•151279	2•269777	2•396353	2•516901	2•602952
1•3000000	2•184600	2•308524	2•442102	2•570869	2•664028
1•3100000	2•218316	2•347879	2•488836	2•626448	2•727448
1•3200000	2•252423	2•387841	2•536572	2•683705	2•793370
1•3300000	2•286915	2•428408	2•585326	2•742710	2•861973
1•3400000	2•321787	2•469578	2•635109	2•803534	2•933449
1•3500000	2•357032	2•511347	2•685934	2•866249	3•008016
1•3600000	2•392643	2•553709	2•737809	2•930930	3•085915
1•3700000	2•428611	2•596656	2•790740	2•997651	3•167412
1•3799999	2•464928	2•640180	2•844730	3•066487	3•252808
1•3899999	2•501583	2•684269	2•899780	3•137510	3•342438
1•4000000	2•538565	2•728911	2•955885	3•210793	3•436683
1•4100000	2•575863	2•774091	3•013036	3•286400	3•535964
1•4200000	2•613463	2•819791	3•071221	3•364393	3•640763
1•4300000	2•651353	2•865995	3•130419	3•444821	3•751624
1•4400000	2•689516	2•912679	3•190608	3•527726	3•869159
1•4500000	2•727940	2•959823	3•251757	3•613133	3•994058
1•4600000	2•766606	3•007399	3•313830	3•701047	4•127097
1•4700000	2•805498	3•055382	3•376782	3•791452	4•269137
1•4800000	2•844599	3•103743	3•440565	3•884303	4•421123
1•4900000	2•883889	3•152449	3•505120	3•979527	4•584061
1•5000000	2•923351	3•201469	3•570386	4•077013	4•758977
1•5100000	2•962963	3•250767	3•636290	4•176608	4•946831
1•5200000	3•002707	3•300307	3•702756	4•278125	5•148376
1•5300000	3•042560	3•350053	3•769701	4•381329	5•363935
1•5400000	3•082502	3•399964	3•837038	4•485948	5•593102
1•5500000	3•122512	3•450001	3•904676	4•591672	5•834406
1•5600000	3•162567	3•500124	3•972518	4•698162	6•085068
1•5699999	3•202646	3•550292	4•040467	4•805055	6•341033
1•5707963	3•205838	3•554288	4•045880	4•813574	6•361501
1•5707963	3•205835	3•554284	4•045875	4•813569	6•361491

$\alpha =$ .500000

θ	K VALUES				
	.009966711	.039469502	.087332193	.151646642	.229848846
.0000000	.000000	.000000	.000000	.000000	.000000
.0100000	.010000	.010000	.010000	.010000	.010000
.0200000	.020001	.020001	.020001	.020001	.020001
.0300000	.030004	.030004	.030004	.030005	.030005
.0400000	.040010	.040011	.040011	.040012	.040013
.0500000	.050021	.050021	.050022	.050024	.050025
.0600000	.060036	.060037	.060039	.060041	.060044
.0700000	.070057	.070059	.070062	.070065	.070070
.0800000	.080086	.080088	.080092	.080098	.080105
.0900000	.090122	.090126	.090132	.090140	.090149
.1000000	.100168	.100173	.100181	.100192	.100205
.1100000	.110224	.110230	.110241	.110255	.110273
.1200000	.120291	.120299	.120313	.120332	.120354
.1300000	.130370	.130381	.130398	.130422	.130451
.1400000	.140462	.140476	.140498	.140527	.140563
.1500000	.150569	.150586	.150613	.150649	.150693
.1600000	.160691	.160711	.160744	.160788	.160842
.1700000	.170829	.170853	.170893	.170945	.171010
.1800000	.180984	.181013	.181060	.181123	.181200
.1900000	.191158	.191192	.191247	.191321	.191411
.2000000	.201351	.201391	.201455	.201542	.201647
.2100000	.211565	.211611	.211685	.211786	.211908
.2200000	.221800	.221853	.221939	.222054	.222195
.2300000	.232058	.232118	.232216	.232348	.232509
.2400000	.242340	.242408	.242519	.242669	.242852
.2500000	.252646	.252723	.252849	.253019	.253226
.2600000	.262978	.263065	.263207	.263398	.263631
.2700000	.273337	.273434	.273593	.273807	.274069
.2800000	.283723	.283832	.284009	.284249	.284541
.2900000	.294139	.294260	.294457	.294723	.295048
.3000000	.304585	.304719	.304937	.305232	.305592
.3100000	.315062	.315210	.315451	.315777	.316175
.3200000	.325571	.325734	.325999	.326358	.326797
.3300000	.336113	.336292	.336584	.336978	.337460
.3400000	.346690	.346886	.347205	.347637	.348165
.3500000	.357303	.357517	.357865	.358337	.358914
.3600000	.367952	.368185	.368565	.369078	.369708
.3700000	.378640	.378893	.379305	.379864	.380548
.3800000	.389366	.389640	.390088	.390693	.391437
.3900000	.400132	.400429	.400914	.401569	.402374

$\alpha =$ .500000

Θ	K VALUES				
	.009966711	.039469502	.087332193	.151646642	.229848846
.4000000	.410940	.411261	.411784	.412492	.413362
.4100000	.421790	.422136	.422700	.423464	.424403
.4200000	.432683	.433055	.433662	.434485	.435497
.4300000	.443622	.444021	.444674	.445558	.446646
.4400000	.454606	.455035	.455734	.456683	.457851
.4500000	.465637	.466096	.466846	.467863	.469115
.4600000	.476717	.477207	.478009	.479097	.480438
.4700000	.487846	.488370	.489226	.490389	.491822
.4800000	.499026	.499584	.500497	.501738	.503269
.4900000	.510257	.510852	.511824	.513147	.514779
.5000000	.521542	.522174	.523209	.524617	.526355
.5100000	.532880	.533552	.534652	.536149	.537998
.5200000	.544275	.544988	.546155	.547744	.549710
.5300000	.555726	.556481	.557719	.559405	.561492
.5400000	.567234	.568035	.569346	.571133	.573345
.5500000	.578802	.579649	.581036	.582928	.585272
.5600000	.590431	.591325	.592792	.594793	.597273
.5700000	.602121	.603065	.604614	.606728	.609351
.5800000	.613873	.614870	.616504	.618736	.621507
.5900000	.625690	.626740	.628463	.630818	.633743
.6000000	.637573	.638678	.640493	.642975	.646060
.6100000	.649522	.650685	.652595	.655208	.658459
.6200000	.661538	.662761	.664770	.667520	.670943
.6300000	.673624	.674909	.677020	.679911	.683513
.6400000	.685780	.687129	.689346	.692383	.696171
.6500000	.698008	.699423	.701749	.704938	.708917
.6600000	.710309	.711792	.714231	.717577	.721755
.6700000	.722684	.724237	.726793	.730301	.734685
.6800000	.735135	.736760	.739437	.743112	.747710
.6899999	.747662	.749363	.752163	.756012	.760830
.7000000	.760267	.762045	.764975	.769002	.774048
.7100000	.772952	.774809	.777871	.782083	.787365
.7200000	.785717	.787656	.790855	.795258	.800783
.7300000	.798563	.800587	.803927	.808526	.814303
.7400000	.811493	.813604	.817088	.821891	.827927
.7500000	.824507	.826708	.830341	.835352	.841656
.7600000	.837606	.839899	.843686	.848913	.855493
.7700000	.850792	.853180	.857125	.862574	.869439
.7800000	.864067	.866551	.870660	.876336	.883495
.7899999	.877430	.880015	.884290	.890201	.897663

$\alpha =$ .500000

θ	K VALUES				
	.009966711	.039469502	.087332193	.151646642	.229848846
.8000000	.890883	.893571	.898018	.904171	.911945
.8100000	.904428	.907222	.911846	.918247	.926342
.8200000	.918066	.920968	.925773	.932430	.940855
.8300000	.931798	.934811	.939802	.946722	.955487
.8400000	.945624	.948751	.953934	.961124	.970239
.8500000	.959547	.962791	.968170	.975637	.985112
.8600000	.973566	.976931	.982511	.990263	1.000108
.8700000	.987685	.991172	.996959	1.005002	1.015227
.8799999	1.001902	1.005515	1.011514	1.019857	1.030473
.8899999	1.016220	1.019962	1.026177	1.034828	1.045845
.9000000	1.030639	1.034513	1.040951	1.049917	1.061346
.9100000	1.045161	1.049170	1.055835	1.065124	1.076976
.9200000	1.059785	1.063933	1.070831	1.080451	1.092737
.9300000	1.074514	1.078803	1.085940	1.095899	1.108630
.9400000	1.089348	1.093782	1.101163	1.111470	1.124657
.9500000	1.104288	1.108870	1.116500	1.127163	1.140818
.9600000	1.119335	1.124068	1.131953	1.142980	1.157114
.9699999	1.134489	1.139376	1.147523	1.158922	1.173547
.9799999	1.149752	1.154797	1.163210	1.174990	1.190118
.9899999	1.165123	1.170329	1.179014	1.191184	1.206827
1.0000000	1.180604	1.185974	1.194938	1.207506	1.223676
1.0100000	1.196195	1.201733	1.210980	1.223955	1.240665
1.0200000	1.211896	1.217605	1.227142	1.240533	1.257795
1.0300000	1.227708	1.233592	1.243425	1.257241	1.275066
1.0400000	1.243632	1.249694	1.259829	1.274078	1.292480
1.0500000	1.259668	1.265911	1.276353	1.291045	1.310036
1.0600000	1.275815	1.282243	1.292999	1.308142	1.327735
1.0699999	1.292075	1.298691	1.309767	1.325370	1.345578
1.0799999	1.308447	1.315255	1.326656	1.342729	1.363564
1.0899999	1.324932	1.331934	1.343668	1.360219	1.381695
1.1000000	1.341529	1.348730	1.360801	1.377840	1.399969
1.1100000	1.358239	1.365641	1.378056	1.395592	1.418387
1.1200000	1.375060	1.382668	1.395433	1.413475	1.436949
1.1300000	1.391994	1.399811	1.412931	1.431488	1.455654
1.1400000	1.409039	1.417068	1.430550	1.449631	1.474502
1.1500000	1.426195	1.434440	1.448290	1.467904	1.493493
1.1600000	1.443462	1.451926	1.466150	1.486306	1.512626
1.1700000	1.460839	1.469525	1.484129	1.504836	1.531900
1.1800000	1.478325	1.487237	1.502226	1.523494	1.551315
1.1899999	1.495919	1.505061	1.520442	1.542279	1.570869

$\alpha =$ .500000

Θ	K VALUES				
	.009966711	.039469502	.087332193	.151646642	.229848846
1.2000000	1.513622	1.522995	1.538774	1.561189	1.590562
1.2100000	1.531431	1.541040	1.557222	1.580224	1.610392
1.2200000	1.549345	1.559193	1.575784	1.599381	1.630357
1.2300000	1.567364	1.577454	1.594459	1.618661	1.650457
1.2400000	1.585485	1.595821	1.613246	1.638061	1.670689
1.2500000	1.603709	1.614293	1.632143	1.657579	1.691052
1.2599999	1.622032	1.632868	1.651149	1.677214	1.711544
1.2699999	1.640453	1.651544	1.670262	1.696964	1.732163
1.2799999	1.658972	1.670319	1.689479	1.716828	1.752907
1.2899999	1.677584	1.689193	1.708799	1.736801	1.773773
1.3000000	1.696290	1.708162	1.728220	1.756884	1.794758
1.3100000	1.715087	1.727225	1.747740	1.777072	1.815861
1.3200000	1.733972	1.746378	1.767355	1.797364	1.837078
1.3300000	1.752943	1.765621	1.787064	1.817757	1.858406
1.3400000	1.771998	1.784950	1.806864	1.838247	1.879843
1.3500000	1.791134	1.804362	1.826752	1.858833	1.901384
1.3600000	1.810348	1.823856	1.846725	1.879510	1.923027
1.3700000	1.829639	1.843428	1.866781	1.900276	1.944768
1.3799999	1.849002	1.863075	1.886916	1.921128	1.966604
1.3899999	1.868436	1.882795	1.907127	1.942062	1.988530
1.4000000	1.887937	1.902583	1.927411	1.963074	2.010543
1.4100000	1.907502	1.922438	1.947764	1.984161	2.032639
1.4200000	1.927127	1.942355	1.968184	2.005319	2.054814
1.4300000	1.946810	1.962331	1.988665	2.026544	2.077062
1.4400000	1.966546	1.982363	2.009205	2.047832	2.099381
1.4500000	1.986334	2.002447	2.029800	2.069179	2.121765
1.4600000	2.006168	2.022579	2.050446	2.090582	2.144210
1.4700000	2.026045	2.042756	2.071139	2.112035	2.166711
1.4800000	2.045962	2.062974	2.091875	2.133534	2.189263
1.4900000	2.065915	2.083228	2.112650	2.155076	2.211862
1.5000000	2.085901	2.103516	2.133460	2.176655	2.234502
1.5100000	2.105914	2.123833	2.154300	2.198267	2.257179
1.5200000	2.125951	2.144175	2.175167	2.219908	2.279888
1.5300000	2.146009	2.164538	2.196056	2.241572	2.302622
1.5400000	2.166084	2.184918	2.216963	2.263256	2.325379
1.5500000	2.186171	2.205311	2.237883	2.284954	2.348151
1.5600000	2.206266	2.225713	2.258812	2.306662	2.370934
1.5699999	2.226365	2.246118	2.279747	2.328375	2.393723
1.5707963	2.227966	2.247744	2.281414	2.330104	2.395538
1.5707963	2.227964	2.247742	2.281412	2.330103	2.395536

$\alpha =$ .500000

Θ	K VALUES				
	.318821117	.415016431	.514599755	.613601043	.708073407
.0000000	.000000	.000000	.000000	.000000	.000000
.0100000	.010000	.010000	.010000	.010000	.010000
.0200000	.020001	.020001	.020002	.020002	.020002
.0300000	.030005	.030006	.030006	.030007	.030007
.0400000	.040014	.040015	.040016	.040017	.040018
.0500000	.050027	.050029	.050031	.050033	.050035
.0600000	.060047	.060050	.060054	.060058	.060061
.0700000	.070075	.070080	.070086	.070092	.070097
.0800000	.080112	.080120	.080129	.080137	.080146
.0900000	.090160	.090172	.090184	.090196	.090207
.1000000	.100220	.100236	.100252	.100269	.100285
.1100000	.110293	.110314	.110336	.110358	.110379
.1200000	.120380	.120408	.120437	.120466	.120493
.1300000	.130484	.130519	.130556	.130592	.130627
.1400000	.140604	.140649	.140695	.140740	.140784
.1500000	.150744	.150798	.150855	.150911	.150965
.1600000	.160903	.160969	.161038	.161107	.161173
.1700000	.171084	.171163	.171246	.171329	.171408
.1800000	.181287	.181382	.181480	.181578	.181672
.1900000	.191514	.191626	.191742	.191858	.191969
.2000000	.201767	.201898	.202033	.202169	.202298
.2100000	.212047	.212198	.212356	.212513	.212663
.2200000	.222355	.222529	.222711	.222892	.223065
.2300000	.232693	.232892	.233100	.233307	.233506
.2400000	.243061	.243289	.243525	.243761	.243988
.2500000	.253463	.253720	.253988	.254256	.254513
.2600000	.263898	.264188	.264490	.264792	.265082
.2700000	.274368	.274694	.275033	.275372	.275698
.2800000	.284875	.285239	.285618	.285998	.286363
.2900000	.295420	.295826	.296249	.296672	.297079
.3000000	.306005	.306455	.306925	.307395	.307848
.3100000	.316631	.317129	.317649	.318170	.318671
.3200000	.327300	.327849	.328422	.328998	.329552
.3300000	.338013	.338616	.339247	.339881	.340491
.3400000	.348771	.349433	.350126	.350821	.351492
.3500000	.359577	.360301	.361059	.361821	.362556
.3600000	.370431	.371221	.372049	.372882	.373686
.3700000	.381335	.382196	.383098	.384006	.384883
.3800000	.392291	.393226	.394207	.395196	.396151
.3900000	.403300	.404315	.405379	.406453	.407491

$\alpha =$ .500000

Θ	K VALUES				
	.318821117	.415016431	.514599755	.613601043	.708073407
.4000000	.414364	.415462	.416615	.417779	.418906
.4100000	.425485	.426671	.427918	.429177	.430397
.4200000	.436663	.437943	.439289	.440649	.441969
.4300000	.447901	.449279	.450730	.452197	.453621
.4400000	.459200	.460682	.462243	.463823	.465359
.4500000	.470562	.472153	.473830	.475530	.477183
.4600000	.481988	.483694	.485494	.487320	.489096
.4700000	.493480	.495307	.497236	.499194	.501102
.4800000	.505040	.506994	.509058	.511156	.513202
.4900000	.516670	.518756	.520963	.523208	.525399
.5000000	.528371	.530596	.532953	.535352	.537696
.5100000	.540144	.542515	.545029	.547590	.550095
.5200000	.551992	.554516	.557194	.559926	.562601
.5300000	.563916	.566600	.569450	.572361	.575214
.5400000	.575918	.578769	.581800	.584898	.587938
.5500000	.587999	.591025	.594245	.597540	.600777
.5600000	.600163	.603370	.606788	.610289	.613732
.5700000	.612409	.615807	.619431	.623148	.626808
.5800000	.624740	.628336	.632176	.636119	.640006
.5900000	.637158	.640961	.645026	.649206	.653331
.6000000	.649665	.653683	.657984	.662411	.666786
.6100000	.662262	.666505	.671050	.675736	.680372
.6200000	.674951	.679427	.684229	.689185	.694095
.6300000	.687734	.692453	.697522	.702760	.707957
.6400000	.700613	.705585	.710931	.716464	.721961
.6500000	.713589	.718824	.724460	.730300	.736111
.6600000	.726665	.732173	.738111	.744271	.750411
.6700000	.739842	.745634	.751885	.758381	.764864
.6800000	.753123	.759209	.765786	.772631	.779473
.6899999	.766508	.772900	.779817	.787025	.794242
.7000000	.780001	.786709	.793979	.801567	.809175
.7100000	.793602	.800639	.808276	.816258	.824276
.7200000	.807313	.814692	.822710	.831103	.839548
.7300000	.821138	.828869	.837283	.846104	.854995
.7400000	.835076	.843173	.851998	.861265	.870621
.7500000	.849131	.857607	.866858	.876589	.886430
.7600000	.863304	.872172	.881865	.892079	.902427
.7700000	.877596	.886870	.897022	.907738	.918614
.7800000	.892010	.901705	.912333	.923569	.934996
.7899999	.906548	.916677	.927798	.939577	.951578

$\alpha =$ .500000

Θ	K VALUES				
	.318821117	.415016431	.514599755	.613601043	.708073407
.8000000	.921212	.931789	.943421	.955763	.968363
.8100000	.936002	.947043	.959205	.972133	.985356
.8200000	.950922	.962442	.975152	.988687	1.002561
.8300000	.965972	.977987	.991266	1.005431	1.019982
.8400000	.981154	.993681	1.007547	1.022368	1.037624
.8500000	.996471	1.009526	1.024000	1.039501	1.055490
.8600000	1.011924	1.025523	1.040626	1.056832	1.073586
.8700000	1.027514	1.041675	1.057429	1.074367	1.091916
.8799999	1.043244	1.057984	1.074410	1.092107	1.110484
.8899999	1.059114	1.074452	1.091573	1.110056	1.129295
.9000000	1.075127	1.091080	1.108920	1.128219	1.148353
.9100000	1.091284	1.107871	1.126454	1.146596	1.167662
.9200000	1.107587	1.124827	1.144176	1.165194	1.187228
.9300000	1.124036	1.141949	1.162089	1.184013	1.207054
.9400000	1.140634	1.159239	1.180196	1.203058	1.227146
.9500000	1.157382	1.176699	1.198498	1.222332	1.247507
.9600000	1.174281	1.194331	1.216999	1.241838	1.268143
.9699999	1.191332	1.212136	1.235699	1.261578	1.289057
.9799999	1.208537	1.230115	1.254602	1.281557	1.310254
.9899999	1.225896	1.248271	1.273710	1.301776	1.331738
1.0000000	1.243412	1.266604	1.293024	1.322239	1.353514
1.0100000	1.261084	1.285117	1.312545	1.342948	1.375586
1.0200000	1.278913	1.303809	1.332277	1.363907	1.397958
1.0300000	1.296902	1.322682	1.352220	1.385117	1.420633
1.0400000	1.315049	1.341738	1.372377	1.406581	1.443617
1.0500000	1.333356	1.360977	1.392748	1.428302	1.466913
1.0600000	1.351824	1.380400	1.413335	1.450281	1.490524
1.0699999	1.370453	1.400008	1.434138	1.472522	1.514455
1.0799999	1.389243	1.419801	1.455161	1.495024	1.538708
1.0899999	1.408195	1.439781	1.476402	1.517792	1.563288
1.1000000	1.427309	1.459947	1.497863	1.540825	1.588197
1.1100000	1.446585	1.480299	1.519545	1.564126	1.613438
1.1200000	1.466022	1.500838	1.541448	1.587695	1.639013
1.1300000	1.485621	1.521563	1.563572	1.611534	1.664926
1.1400000	1.505381	1.542475	1.585917	1.635643	1.691179
1.1500000	1.525301	1.563572	1.608484	1.660024	1.717773
1.1600000	1.545382	1.584856	1.631271	1.684675	1.744711
1.1700000	1.565623	1.606324	1.654280	1.709599	1.771993
1.1800000	1.586022	1.627976	1.677508	1.734793	1.799621
1.1899999	1.606578	1.649811	1.700955	1.760259	1.827596

$\alpha =$ .500000

θ	K VALUES				
	.318821117	.415016431	.514599755	.613601043	.708073407
1.2000000	1.627291	1.671828	1.724621	1.785995	1.855919
1.2100000	1.648159	1.694026	1.748503	1.812000	1.884588
1.2200000	1.669181	1.716402	1.772600	1.838273	1.913604
1.2300000	1.690355	1.738956	1.796910	1.864813	1.942966
1.2400000	1.711678	1.761684	1.821432	1.891617	1.972673
1.2500000	1.733150	1.784586	1.846163	1.918683	2.002723
1.2599999	1.754768	1.807658	1.871100	1.946009	2.033114
1.2699999	1.776530	1.830899	1.896240	1.973591	2.063844
1.2799999	1.798434	1.854305	1.921582	2.001427	2.094910
1.2899999	1.820476	1.877873	1.947120	2.029513	2.126308
1.3000000	1.842654	1.901601	1.972853	2.057844	2.158033
1.3100000	1.864965	1.925485	1.998775	2.086417	2.190082
1.3200000	1.887406	1.949521	2.024883	2.115227	2.222449
1.3300000	1.909973	1.973705	2.051172	2.144268	2.255128
1.3400000	1.932663	1.998034	2.077637	2.173535	2.288113
1.3500000	1.955473	2.022504	2.104275	2.203023	2.321397
1.3600000	1.978398	2.047110	2.131079	2.232724	2.354972
1.3700000	2.001435	2.071847	2.158044	2.262633	2.388831
1.3799999	2.024580	2.096710	2.185165	2.292742	2.422964
1.3899999	2.047828	2.121696	2.212435	2.323044	2.457364
1.4000000	2.071175	2.146798	2.239848	2.353532	2.492019
1.4100000	2.094615	2.172011	2.267398	2.384197	2.526919
1.4200000	2.118146	2.197330	2.295079	2.415031	2.562053
1.4300000	2.141761	2.222749	2.322882	2.446025	2.597410
1.4400000	2.165456	2.248262	2.350802	2.477170	2.632977
1.4500000	2.189225	2.273863	2.378830	2.508457	2.668743
1.4600000	2.213064	2.299546	2.406960	2.539876	2.704694
1.4700000	2.236967	2.325305	2.435183	2.571417	2.740816
1.4800000	2.260928	2.351133	2.463492	2.603070	2.777096
1.4900000	2.284943	2.377024	2.491879	2.634825	2.813519
1.5000000	2.309005	2.402971	2.520335	2.666671	2.850070
1.5100000	2.333108	2.428968	2.548852	2.698598	2.886735
1.5200000	2.357248	2.455007	2.577422	2.730593	2.923498
1.5300000	2.381418	2.481082	2.606037	2.762647	2.960342
1.5400000	2.405612	2.507185	2.634687	2.794747	2.997253
1.5500000	2.429824	2.533311	2.663363	2.826882	3.034214
1.5600000	2.454049	2.559451	2.692059	2.859042	3.071210
1.5699999	2.478280	2.585598	2.720763	2.891214	3.108223
1.5707963	2.480210	2.587681	2.723049	2.893776	3.111170
1.5707963	2.480209	2.587680	2.723047	2.893774	3.111168

$\alpha =$ .500000

θ	K VALUES				
	.794250555	.868696860	.928444378	.971111163	.994996249
.0000000	.000000	.000000	.000000	.000000	.000000
.0100000	.010000	.010000	.010000	.010000	.010000
.0200000	.020002	.020002	.020002	.020002	.020002
.0300000	.030008	.030008	.030008	.030008	.030008
.0400000	.040019	.040019	.040020	.040021	.040021
.0500000	.050037	.050038	.050040	.050041	.050041
.0600000	.060064	.060067	.060069	.060071	.060071
.0700000	.070102	.070107	.070110	.070112	.070114
.0800000	.080153	.080159	.080164	.080168	.080170
.0900000	.090218	.090227	.090234	.090240	.090243
.1000000	.100299	.100312	.100322	.100329	.100333
.1100000	.110399	.110415	.110429	.110438	.110444
.1200000	.120518	.120540	.120557	.120570	.120577
.1300000	.130659	.130687	.130709	.130725	.130734
.1400000	.140824	.140859	.140887	.140907	.140918
.1500000	.151015	.151057	.151092	.151116	.151130
.1600000	.161233	.161284	.161326	.161356	.161373
.1700000	.171480	.171542	.171592	.171628	.171648
.1800000	.181758	.181833	.181892	.181935	.181959
.1900000	.192070	.192158	.192228	.192279	.192307
.2000000	.202417	.202519	.202602	.202661	.202694
.2100000	.212801	.212920	.213016	.213085	.213123
.2200000	.223224	.223361	.223472	.223552	.223596
.2300000	.233688	.233846	.233973	.234064	.234115
.2400000	.244195	.244376	.244521	.244625	.244683
.2500000	.254748	.254953	.255117	.255235	.255302
.2600000	.265348	.265579	.265765	.265899	.265974
.2700000	.275998	.276258	.276467	.276617	.276702
.2800000	.286699	.286990	.287225	.287393	.287488
.2900000	.297453	.297778	.298041	.298229	.298335
.3000000	.308264	.308626	.308918	.309127	.309245
.3100000	.319133	.319534	.319858	.320091	.320221
.3200000	.330062	.330505	.330864	.331121	.331266
.3300000	.341053	.341543	.341939	.342223	.342382
.3400000	.352110	.352649	.353084	.353397	.353573
.3500000	.363234	.363825	.364303	.364647	.364840
.3600000	.374428	.375075	.375599	.375975	.376187
.3700000	.385693	.386400	.386973	.387385	.387616
.3800000	.397034	.397805	.398429	.398879	.399131
.3900000	.408451	.409290	.409970	.410460	.410735

$\alpha =$ .500000

Θ	K VALUES				
	.794250555	.868696860	.928444378	.971111163	.994996249
.4000000	.419948	.420859	.421599	.422131	.422431
.4100000	.431527	.432516	.433318	.433896	.434221
.4200000	.443191	.444261	.445131	.445757	.446110
.4300000	.454942	.456100	.457040	.457718	.458100
.4400000	.466783	.468033	.469049	.469782	.470195
.4500000	.478718	.480065	.481162	.481953	.482399
.4600000	.490748	.492199	.493380	.494233	.494714
.4700000	.502876	.504437	.505708	.506627	.507145
.4800000	.515106	.516783	.518149	.519137	.519695
.4900000	.527441	.529239	.530707	.531769	.532368
.5000000	.539883	.541811	.543385	.544525	.545168
.5100000	.552435	.554499	.556187	.557409	.558099
.5200000	.565101	.567310	.569116	.570426	.571166
.5300000	.577884	.580244	.582177	.583579	.584371
.5400000	.590786	.593307	.595373	.596872	.597720
.5500000	.603813	.606503	.608709	.610311	.611218
.5600000	.616965	.619833	.622188	.623899	.624868
.5700000	.630249	.633304	.635814	.637641	.638675
.5800000	.643665	.646918	.649593	.651541	.652645
.5900000	.657219	.660679	.663529	.665604	.666782
.6000000	.670914	.674593	.677625	.679836	.681091
.6100000	.684753	.688662	.691888	.694241	.695578
.6200000	.698741	.702892	.706320	.708825	.710248
.6300000	.712881	.717286	.720929	.723592	.725107
.6400000	.727177	.731849	.735717	.738549	.740160
.6500000	.741633	.746586	.750692	.753700	.755413
.6600000	.756253	.761501	.765857	.769052	.770872
.6700000	.771042	.776600	.781219	.784611	.786544
.6800000	.786003	.791886	.796783	.800382	.802436
.6899999	.801141	.807366	.812555	.816373	.818553
.7000000	.816461	.823045	.828541	.832590	.834903
.7100000	.831966	.838927	.844747	.849039	.851494
.7200000	.847662	.855019	.861178	.865727	.868331
.7300000	.863552	.871325	.877843	.882662	.885423
.7400000	.879643	.887851	.894746	.899851	.902778
.7500000	.895937	.904604	.911895	.917301	.920405
.7600000	.912442	.921589	.929298	.935021	.938310
.7700000	.929161	.938812	.946960	.953019	.956504
.7800000	.946099	.956279	.964890	.971302	.974994
.7899999	.963263	.973998	.983095	.989880	.993792

$\alpha =$ .500000

Θ	K VALUES				
	.794250555	.868696860	.928444378	.971111163	.994996249
.8000000	.980656	.991974	1.001583	1.008762	1.012905
.8100000	.998285	1.010213	1.020362	1.027956	1.032345
.8200000	1.016155	1.028724	1.039440	1.047473	1.052121
.8300000	1.034271	1.047512	1.058825	1.067322	1.072244
.8400000	1.052639	1.066586	1.078528	1.087514	1.092726
.8500000	1.071264	1.085951	1.098556	1.108058	1.113578
.8600000	1.090153	1.105617	1.118918	1.128967	1.134812
.8700000	1.109312	1.125589	1.139625	1.150251	1.156441
.8799999	1.128745	1.145877	1.160687	1.171922	1.178477
.8899999	1.148460	1.166488	1.182112	1.193993	1.200935
.9000000	1.168463	1.187430	1.203913	1.216475	1.223829
.9100000	1.188759	1.208712	1.226099	1.239382	1.247172
.9200000	1.209354	1.230342	1.248682	1.262728	1.270980
.9300000	1.230256	1.252328	1.271672	1.286527	1.295269
.9400000	1.251470	1.274680	1.295083	1.310792	1.320057
.9500000	1.273003	1.297406	1.318925	1.335540	1.345359
.9600000	1.294861	1.320516	1.343211	1.360786	1.371194
.9699999	1.317050	1.344018	1.367954	1.386546	1.397581
.9799999	1.339578	1.367923	1.393168	1.412838	1.424541
.9899999	1.362451	1.392240	1.418865	1.439679	1.452092
1.0000000	1.385675	1.416979	1.445060	1.467087	1.480257
1.0100000	1.409257	1.442149	1.471767	1.495081	1.509059
1.0200000	1.433203	1.467761	1.499001	1.523682	1.538521
1.0300000	1.457519	1.493825	1.526777	1.552910	1.568669
1.0400000	1.482214	1.520351	1.555111	1.582787	1.599528
1.0500000	1.507292	1.547350	1.584018	1.613335	1.631125
1.0600000	1.532760	1.574833	1.613516	1.644577	1.663490
1.0699999	1.558625	1.602809	1.643621	1.676539	1.696654
1.0799999	1.584892	1.631290	1.674351	1.709245	1.730647
1.0899999	1.611568	1.660287	1.705723	1.742722	1.765505
1.1000000	1.638659	1.689810	1.737756	1.776998	1.801263
1.1100000	1.666170	1.719870	1.770469	1.812103	1.837959
1.1200000	1.694107	1.750478	1.803881	1.848065	1.875632
1.1300000	1.722476	1.781645	1.838012	1.884918	1.914325
1.1400000	1.751281	1.813382	1.872881	1.922695	1.954084
1.1500000	1.780529	1.845699	1.908511	1.961430	1.994956
1.1600000	1.810222	1.878606	1.944921	2.001159	2.036992
1.1700000	1.840366	1.912115	1.982133	2.041922	2.080246
1.1800000	1.870965	1.946234	2.020170	2.083757	2.124777
1.1899999	1.902022	1.980975	2.059052	2.126706	2.170646

$\alpha =$ .500000

Θ	K VALUES				
	.794250555	.868696860	.928444378	.971111163	.994996249
1.2000000	1.933540	2.016347	2.098804	2.170815	2.217921
1.2100000	1.965523	2.052358	2.139446	2.216128	2.266671
1.2200000	1.997972	2.089018	2.181003	2.262694	2.316975
1.2300000	2.030889	2.126334	2.223498	2.310562	2.368913
1.2400000	2.064276	2.164315	2.266953	2.359787	2.422575
1.2500000	2.098133	2.202968	2.311391	2.410424	2.478057
1.2599999	2.132460	2.242298	2.356837	2.462530	2.535464
1.2699999	2.167257	2.282312	2.403311	2.516166	2.594908
1.2799999	2.202521	2.323013	2.450836	2.571397	2.656513
1.2899999	2.238252	2.364406	2.499434	2.628287	2.720412
1.3000000	2.274445	2.406493	2.549126	2.686906	2.786754
1.3100000	2.311098	2.449275	2.599930	2.747325	2.855696
1.3200000	2.348205	2.492752	2.651866	2.809620	2.927418
1.3300000	2.385760	2.536922	2.704949	2.873866	3.002114
1.3400000	2.423759	2.581784	2.759196	2.940142	3.079998
1.3500000	2.462192	2.627331	2.814618	3.008531	3.161311
1.3600000	2.501052	2.673557	2.871225	3.079112	3.246316
1.3700000	2.540329	2.720455	2.929025	3.151971	3.335310
1.3799999	2.580012	2.768013	2.988021	3.227188	3.428622
1.3899999	2.620090	2.816220	3.048213	3.304845	3.526625
1.4000000	2.660552	2.865062	3.109595	3.385021	3.629734
1.4100000	2.701381	2.914520	3.172158	3.467788	3.738417
1.4200000	2.742564	2.964576	3.235887	3.553213	3.853204
1.4300000	2.784086	3.015208	3.300761	3.641352	3.974692
1.4400000	2.825929	3.066393	3.366752	3.732249	4.103557
1.4500000	2.868075	3.118105	3.433827	3.825931	4.240559
1.4600000	2.910506	3.170314	3.501943	3.922405	4.386552
1.4700000	2.953202	3.222989	3.571052	4.021651	4.542483
1.4800000	2.996142	3.276098	3.641097	4.123619	4.709392
1.4900000	3.039304	3.329603	3.712014	4.228227	4.888386
1.5000000	3.082667	3.383469	3.783731	4.335349	5.080595
1.5100000	3.126206	3.437655	3.856169	4.444819	5.287073
1.5200000	3.169899	3.492118	3.929240	4.556424	5.508647
1.5300000	3.213721	3.546817	4.002852	4.669905	5.745671
1.5400000	3.257647	3.601707	4.076906	4.784959	5.997696
1.5500000	3.301652	3.656741	4.151298	4.901241	6.263098
1.5600000	3.345711	3.711874	4.225920	5.018375	6.538814
1.5699999	3.389798	3.767058	4.300664	5.135957	6.820373
1.5707963	3.393309	3.771453	4.306618	5.145327	6.842887
1.5707963	3.393306	3.771450	4.306613	5.145322	6.842877

$\alpha =$ .519999

Θ	K VALUES				
	.009966711	.039469502	.087332193	.151646642	.229848846
.0000000	.000000	.000000	.000000	.000000	.000000
.0100000	.010000	.010000	.010000	.010000	.010000
.0200000	.020001	.020001	.020001	.020001	.020001
.0300000	.030004	.030004	.030005	.030005	.030005
.0400000	.040011	.040011	.040012	.040012	.040013
.0500000	.050021	.050022	.050023	.050024	.050026
.0600000	.060037	.060038	.060040	.060042	.060045
.0700000	.070060	.070061	.070064	.070068	.070072
.0800000	.080089	.080092	.080096	.080101	.080108
.0900000	.090127	.090131	.090137	.090144	.090154
.1000000	.100175	.100180	.100188	.100198	.100211
.1100000	.110233	.110239	.110250	.110264	.110282
.1200000	.120302	.120311	.120325	.120343	.120366
.1300000	.130385	.130396	.130413	.130437	.130466
.1400000	.140481	.140494	.140516	.140546	.140582
.1500000	.150592	.150608	.150635	.150672	.150716
.1600000	.160718	.160739	.160771	.160816	.160869
.1700000	.170862	.170886	.170926	.170979	.171043
.1800000	.181024	.181053	.181099	.181162	.181239
.1900000	.191205	.191239	.191294	.191368	.191458
.2000000	.201406	.201445	.201509	.201596	.201701
.2100000	.211628	.211674	.211748	.211849	.211971
.2200000	.221873	.221926	.222011	.222127	.222267
.2300000	.232141	.232201	.232299	.232431	.232592
.2400000	.242434	.242503	.242614	.242764	.242947
.2500000	.252753	.252830	.252956	.253126	.253333
.2600000	.263098	.263186	.263327	.263518	.263752
.2700000	.273472	.273570	.273728	.273943	.274205
.2800000	.283874	.283983	.284161	.284400	.284693
.2900000	.294307	.294429	.294626	.294892	.295217
.3000000	.304771	.304906	.305124	.305420	.305780
.3100000	.315268	.315417	.315658	.315984	.316383
.3200000	.325799	.325962	.326228	.326587	.327026
.3300000	.336364	.336543	.336835	.337229	.337712
.3400000	.346965	.347161	.347481	.347913	.348442
.3500000	.357604	.357818	.358167	.358639	.359217
.3600000	.368281	.368514	.368894	.369408	.370039
.3700000	.378997	.379251	.379664	.380223	.380909
.3800000	.389754	.390029	.390477	.391084	.391828
.3900000	.400553	.400851	.401336	.401993	.402799

$\alpha =$ .519999

Θ	K VALUES				
	.009966711	.039469502	.087332193	.151646642	.229848846
.4000000	.411396	.411717	.412241	.412951	.413823
.4100000	.422282	.422629	.423194	.423959	.424900
.4200000	.433214	.433587	.434196	.435020	.436034
.4300000	.444194	.444594	.445248	.446134	.447224
.4400000	.455221	.455650	.456352	.457303	.458474
.4500000	.466297	.466757	.467509	.468528	.469784
.4600000	.477425	.477916	.478720	.479811	.481155
.4700000	.488604	.489129	.489987	.491153	.492591
.4800000	.499836	.500396	.501311	.502556	.504091
.4900000	.511122	.511719	.512694	.514021	.515658
.5000000	.522464	.523099	.524137	.525549	.527293
.5100000	.533864	.534538	.535641	.537143	.538998
.5200000	.545321	.546037	.547208	.548803	.550775
.5300000	.556838	.557597	.558839	.560531	.562625
.5400000	.568416	.569220	.570535	.572329	.574549
.5500000	.580056	.580906	.582299	.584198	.586551
.5600000	.591760	.592659	.594131	.596140	.598630
.5700000	.603529	.604477	.606033	.608156	.610789
.5800000	.615364	.616365	.618006	.620247	.623030
.5900000	.627266	.628321	.630052	.632416	.635355
.6000000	.639238	.640349	.642172	.644665	.647764
.6100000	.651280	.652449	.654368	.656993	.660260
.6200000	.663393	.664622	.666641	.669404	.672844
.6300000	.675580	.676871	.678993	.681898	.685519
.6400000	.687841	.689197	.691425	.694478	.698285
.6500000	.700178	.701600	.703939	.707145	.711146
.6600000	.712592	.714083	.716535	.719900	.724102
.6700000	.725084	.726646	.729217	.732745	.737155
.6800000	.737657	.739292	.741984	.745682	.750307
.6899999	.750311	.752022	.754840	.758712	.763560
.7000000	.763047	.764836	.767784	.771838	.776916
.7100000	.775868	.777738	.780819	.785059	.790376
.7200000	.788774	.790727	.793947	.798379	.803942
.7300000	.801768	.803806	.807168	.811799	.817616
.7400000	.814849	.816975	.820484	.825321	.831400
.7500000	.828020	.830237	.833897	.838945	.845295
.7600000	.841282	.843592	.847408	.852674	.859304
.7700000	.854637	.857043	.861019	.866509	.873428
.7800000	.868085	.870590	.874731	.880452	.887669
.7899999	.881629	.884235	.888545	.894505	.902028

$\alpha =$ .519999

Θ	K VALUES				
	.009966711	.039469502	.087332193	.151646642	.229848846
.8000000	.895269	.897979	.902464	.908669	.916508
.8100000	.909007	.911824	.916488	.922945	.931110
.8200000	.922844	.925771	.930619	.937335	.945836
.8300000	.936782	.939822	.944859	.951842	.960687
.8400000	.950821	.953977	.959208	.966465	.975666
.8500000	.964963	.968238	.973669	.981207	.990773
.8600000	.979210	.982607	.988242	.996069	1.006012
.8700000	.993562	.997084	1.002929	1.011053	1.021382
.8799999	1.008021	1.011671	1.017731	1.026160	1.036886
.8899999	1.022588	1.026369	1.032650	1.041392	1.052526
.9000000	1.037264	1.041179	1.047686	1.056749	1.068303
.9100000	1.052050	1.056103	1.062842	1.072234	1.084218
.9200000	1.066948	1.071142	1.078118	1.087847	1.100273
.9300000	1.081958	1.086296	1.093515	1.103590	1.116470
.9400000	1.097082	1.101567	1.109035	1.119464	1.132809
.9500000	1.112320	1.116956	1.124679	1.135471	1.149293
.9600000	1.127673	1.132464	1.140447	1.151610	1.165922
.9699999	1.143143	1.148092	1.156341	1.167885	1.182697
.9799999	1.158731	1.163840	1.172361	1.184294	1.199621
.9899999	1.174436	1.179710	1.188510	1.200840	1.216693
1.0000000	1.190260	1.195702	1.204786	1.217524	1.233916
1.0100000	1.206204	1.211818	1.221192	1.234346	1.251289
1.0200000	1.222268	1.228057	1.237728	1.251307	1.268815
1.0300000	1.238453	1.244420	1.254394	1.268408	1.286493
1.0400000	1.254759	1.260909	1.271192	1.285650	1.304325
1.0500000	1.271188	1.277523	1.288121	1.303032	1.322311
1.0600000	1.287738	1.294263	1.305182	1.320557	1.340452
1.0699999	1.304411	1.311129	1.322376	1.338223	1.358748
1.0799999	1.321207	1.328122	1.339703	1.356031	1.377200
1.0899999	1.338127	1.345241	1.357163	1.373982	1.395808
1.1000000	1.355169	1.362487	1.374756	1.392076	1.414573
1.1100000	1.372335	1.379860	1.392482	1.410313	1.433494
1.1200000	1.389623	1.397360	1.410341	1.428692	1.452571
1.1300000	1.407035	1.414986	1.428333	1.447213	1.471804
1.1400000	1.424569	1.432739	1.446458	1.465877	1.491194
1.1500000	1.442226	1.450617	1.464715	1.484683	1.510738
1.1600000	1.460004	1.468621	1.483104	1.503630	1.530438
1.1700000	1.477904	1.486750	1.501624	1.522718	1.550293
1.1800000	1.495924	1.505003	1.520275	1.541946	1.570301
1.1899999	1.514064	1.523380	1.539055	1.561313	1.590461

$\alpha =$ .519999

Θ	K VALUES				
	.009966711	.039469502	.087332193	.151646642	.229848846
.2000000	1.532324	1.541879	1.557964	1.580818	1.610773
.2100000	1.550701	1.560499	1.577000	1.600460	1.631236
.2200000	1.569195	1.579240	1.596163	1.620238	1.651847
.2300000	1.587805	1.598100	1.615451	1.640150	1.672606
.2400000	1.606529	1.617077	1.634862	1.660194	1.693511
.2500000	1.625365	1.636171	1.654396	1.680370	1.714560
.2599999	1.644313	1.655378	1.674049	1.700674	1.735750
.2699999	1.663370	1.674699	1.693821	1.721106	1.757081
.2799999	1.682535	1.694130	1.713710	1.741663	1.778548
.2899999	1.701805	1.713670	1.733712	1.762342	1.800151
.3000000	1.721179	1.733317	1.753827	1.783141	1.821886
.3100000	1.740654	1.753067	1.774051	1.804058	1.843750
.3200000	1.760228	1.772919	1.794381	1.825090	1.865741
.3300000	1.779897	1.792871	1.814816	1.846234	1.887855
.3400000	1.799661	1.812919	1.835353	1.867487	1.910089
.3500000	1.819515	1.833060	1.855987	1.888845	1.932439
.3600000	1.839458	1.853292	1.876717	1.910305	1.954901
.3700000	1.859485	1.873611	1.897539	1.931865	1.977473
.3799999	1.879595	1.894015	1.918449	1.953520	2.000150
.3899999	1.899782	1.914500	1.939445	1.975266	2.022927
.4000000	1.920046	1.935062	1.960522	1.997099	2.045801
.4100000	1.940381	1.955699	1.981676	2.019017	2.068767
.4200000	1.960784	1.976405	2.002905	2.041013	2.091820
.4300000	1.981251	1.997178	2.024203	2.063084	2.114955
.4400000	2.001780	2.018013	2.045567	2.085226	2.138169
.4500000	2.022365	2.038906	2.066992	2.107435	2.161456
.4600000	2.043002	2.059855	2.088475	2.129704	2.184810
.4700000	2.063689	2.080853	2.110010	2.152031	2.208227
.4800000	2.084420	2.101897	2.131594	2.174409	2.231701
.4900000	2.105192	2.122983	2.153221	2.196834	2.255227
.5000000	2.126000	2.144106	2.174888	2.219302	2.278800
.5100000	2.146840	2.165262	2.196589	2.241807	2.302413
.5200000	2.167707	2.186446	2.218320	2.264343	2.326062
.5300000	2.188597	2.207654	2.240075	2.286906	2.349740
.5400000	2.209506	2.228881	2.261851	2.309491	2.373442
.5500000	2.230428	2.250122	2.283641	2.332092	2.397161
.5600000	2.251360	2.271373	2.305442	2.354704	2.420893
.5699999	2.272297	2.292629	2.327249	2.377322	2.444632
.5707963	2.273965	2.294322	2.328985	2.379123	2.446522
.5707963	2.273963	2.294321	2.328983	2.379121	2.446520

$\alpha =$ .519999

Θ	K VALUES				
	.318821117	.415016431	.514599755	.613601043	.708073407
.0000000	.000000	.000000	.000000	.000000	.000000
.0100000	.010000	.010000	.010000	.010000	.010000
.0200000	.020001	.020001	.020002	.020002	.020002
.0300000	.030006	.030006	.030007	.030007	.030007
.0400000	.040014	.040015	.040016	.040017	.040018
.0500000	.050028	.050030	.050032	.050034	.050036
.0600000	.060048	.060052	.060056	.060059	.060063
.0700000	.070077	.070083	.070088	.070094	.070100
.0800000	.080116	.080124	.080132	.080141	.080149
.0900000	.090165	.090177	.090189	.090201	.090212
.1000000	.100226	.100242	.100259	.100276	.100292
.1100000	.110301	.110323	.110345	.110367	.110388
.1200000	.120392	.120420	.120448	.120477	.120505
.1300000	.130498	.130534	.130571	.130607	.130642
.1400000	.140623	.140667	.140713	.140759	.140803
.1500000	.150766	.150821	.150878	.150934	.150988
.1600000	.160931	.160997	.161066	.161135	.161200
.1700000	.171117	.171197	.171279	.171362	.171441
.1800000	.181327	.181421	.181520	.181618	.181712
.1900000	.191561	.191673	.191789	.191905	.192015
.2000000	.201822	.201952	.202088	.202223	.202353
.2100000	.212110	.212262	.212419	.212576	.212726
.2200000	.222428	.222602	.222784	.222965	.223138
.2300000	.232776	.232976	.233183	.233391	.233590
.2400000	.243156	.243384	.243620	.243857	.244083
.2500000	.253570	.253828	.254096	.254364	.254621
.2600000	.264019	.264309	.264612	.264914	.265204
.2700000	.274504	.274830	.275170	.275509	.275836
.2800000	.285027	.285392	.285771	.286152	.286517
.2900000	.295590	.295996	.296419	.296843	.297251
.3000000	.306194	.306644	.307114	.307585	.308038
.3100000	.316840	.317338	.317858	.318380	.318882
.3200000	.327530	.328080	.328654	.329230	.329785
.3300000	.338266	.338870	.339502	.340136	.340748
.3400000	.349049	.349712	.350405	.351102	.351774
.3500000	.359881	.360606	.361365	.362128	.362865
.3600000	.370763	.371555	.372384	.373218	.374023
.3700000	.381697	.382559	.383463	.384372	.385251
.3800000	.392685	.393621	.394604	.395594	.396551
.3900000	.403727	.404743	.405810	.406885	.407926

$\alpha =$ .519999

Θ	K VALUES				
	.318821117	.415016431	.514599755	.613601043	.708073407
.4000000	.414827	.415927	.417082	.418248	.419377
.4100000	.425985	.427173	.428423	.429685	.430908
.4200000	.437203	.438485	.439834	.441198	.442520
.4300000	.448482	.449864	.451318	.452789	.454216
.4400000	.459826	.461311	.462876	.464460	.466000
.4500000	.471234	.472829	.474511	.476215	.477872
.4600000	.482709	.484420	.486225	.488055	.489837
.4700000	.494253	.496085	.498020	.499983	.501896
.4800000	.505868	.507827	.509897	.512001	.514053
.4900000	.517554	.519647	.521861	.524112	.526310
.5000000	.529315	.531547	.533911	.536318	.538670
.5100000	.541151	.543530	.546052	.548622	.551135
.5200000	.553064	.555597	.558285	.561026	.563710
.5300000	.565057	.567751	.570612	.573533	.576396
.5400000	.577132	.579993	.583036	.586146	.589197
.5500000	.589289	.592326	.595558	.598866	.602116
.5600000	.601531	.604751	.608183	.611698	.615155
.5700000	.613860	.617272	.620911	.624644	.628319
.5800000	.626277	.629889	.633745	.637706	.641610
.5900000	.638785	.642605	.646689	.650887	.655031
.6000000	.651386	.655423	.659743	.664191	.668587
.6100000	.664081	.668344	.672912	.677620	.682279
.6200000	.676872	.681370	.686196	.691177	.696112
.6300000	.689761	.694505	.699600	.704865	.710090
.6400000	.702751	.707750	.713125	.718687	.724214
.6500000	.715843	.721107	.726774	.732647	.738491
.6600000	.729039	.734579	.740550	.746747	.752922
.6700000	.742342	.748167	.754456	.760990	.767512
.6800000	.755752	.761875	.768493	.775380	.782264
.6899999	.769273	.775705	.782665	.789920	.797183
.7000000	.782906	.789658	.796975	.804613	.812271
.7100000	.796653	.803738	.811426	.819462	.827534
.7200000	.810517	.817946	.826019	.834471	.842975
.7300000	.824499	.832285	.840758	.849644	.858599
.7400000	.838601	.846757	.855646	.864982	.874408
.7500000	.852825	.861365	.870686	.880491	.890409
.7600000	.867174	.876111	.885880	.896173	.906604
.7700000	.881649	.890997	.901231	.912033	.922998
.7800000	.896253	.906026	.916742	.928072	.939595
.7899999	.910987	.921201	.932416	.944296	.956401

$\alpha =$ •519999

Θ	K VALUES				
	•318821117	•415016431	•514599755	•613601043	•708073407
•8000000	•925854	•936522	•948256	•960707	•973419
•8100000	•940855	•951994	•964265	•977309	•990654
•8200000	•955993	•967618	•980445	•994106	1•008110
•8300000	•971268	•983396	•996800	1•011101	1•025793
•8400000	•986685	•999332	1•013332	1•028298	1•043706
•8500000	1•002243	1•015426	1•030044	1•045701	1•061854
•8600000	1•017946	1•031682	1•046940	1•063313	1•080243
•8700000	1•033795	1•048102	1•064021	1•081138	1•098876
•8799999	1•049791	1•064688	1•081291	1•099180	1•117760
•8899999	1•065938	1•081442	1•098753	1•117442	1•136898
•9000000	1•082236	1•098367	1•116409	1•135928	1•156295
•9100000	1•098688	1•115464	1•134261	1•154641	1•175957
•9200000	1•115295	1•132736	1•152314	1•173585	1•195888
•9300000	1•132058	1•150185	1•170569	1•192763	1•216093
•9400000	1•148980	1•167813	1•189029	1•212180	1•236576
•9500000	1•166062	1•185622	1•207697	1•231839	1•257344
•9600000	1•183305	1•203613	1•226575	1•251742	1•278400
•9699999	1•200712	1•221789	1•245665	1•271894	1•299750
•9799999	1•218283	1•240151	1•264971	1•292298	1•321398
•9899999	1•236020	1•258701	1•284493	1•312956	1•343350
1•0000000	1•253924	1•277441	1•304236	1•333874	1•365609
1•0100000	1•271996	1•296372	1•324200	1•355052	1•388180
1•0200000	1•290237	1•315496	1•344387	1•376494	1•411069
1•0300000	1•308649	1•334815	1•364800	1•398204	1•434279
1•0400000	1•327233	1•354328	1•385441	1•420184	1•457815
1•0500000	1•345989	1•374038	1•406311	1•442437	1•481681
1•0600000	1•364917	1•393946	1•427411	1•464965	1•505882
1•0699999	1•384020	1•414053	1•448744	1•487770	1•530421
1•0799999	1•403296	1•434358	1•470311	1•510856	1•555302
1•0899999	1•422748	1•454864	1•492112	1•534223	1•580530
1•1000000	1•442374	1•475571	1•514149	1•557874	1•606107
1•1100000	1•462176	1•496479	1•536422	1•581811	1•632037
1•1200000	1•482153	1•517588	1•558933	1•606035	1•658322
1•1300000	1•502305	1•538898	1•581682	1•630547	1•684967
1•1400000	1•522632	1•560410	1•604668	1•655348	1•711973
1•1500000	1•543134	1•582123	1•627893	1•680440	1•739343
1•1600000	1•563810	1•604037	1•651356	1•705822	1•767079
1•1700000	1•584659	1•626152	1•675057	1•731495	1•795182
1•1800000	1•605682	1•648465	1•698995	1•757460	1•823655
1•1899999	1•626876	1•670978	1•723170	1•783715	1•852497

$\alpha =$ .519999

Θ	K VALUES				
	.318821117	.415016431	.514599755	.613601043	.708073407
1.2000000	1.648241	1.693688	1.747580	1.810261	1.881710
1.2100000	1.669775	1.716593	1.772224	1.837096	1.911294
1.2200000	1.691476	1.739694	1.797101	1.864219	1.941249
1.2300000	1.713344	1.762987	1.822208	1.891629	1.971574
1.2400000	1.735377	1.786471	1.847545	1.919324	2.002268
1.2500000	1.757572	1.810143	1.873108	1.947301	2.033330
1.2599999	1.779927	1.834002	1.898895	1.975558	2.064758
1.2699999	1.802439	1.858045	1.924903	2.004092	2.096548
1.2799999	1.825107	1.882268	1.951129	2.032900	2.128698
1.2899999	1.847928	1.906668	1.977570	2.061977	2.161204
1.3000000	1.870898	1.931244	2.004221	2.091321	2.194063
1.3100000	1.894014	1.955989	2.031079	2.120925	2.227269
1.3200000	1.917273	1.980902	2.058139	2.150785	2.260816
1.3300000	1.940672	2.005977	2.085396	2.180896	2.294698
1.3400000	1.964206	2.031211	2.112846	2.211252	2.328910
1.3500000	1.987872	2.056600	2.140484	2.241846	2.363444
1.3600000	2.011666	2.082137	2.168303	2.272673	2.398291
1.3700000	2.035583	2.107819	2.196298	2.303724	2.433443
1.3799999	2.059619	2.133640	2.224463	2.334993	2.468891
1.3899999	2.083769	2.159595	2.252791	2.366471	2.504625
1.4000000	2.108028	2.185679	2.281277	2.398151	2.540635
1.4100000	2.132392	2.211885	2.309912	2.430023	2.576909
1.4200000	2.156855	2.238207	2.338689	2.462079	2.613436
1.4300000	2.181412	2.264639	2.367601	2.494309	2.650202
1.4400000	2.206057	2.291176	2.396640	2.526703	2.687196
1.4500000	2.230785	2.317809	2.425799	2.559251	2.724404
1.4600000	2.255590	2.344533	2.455068	2.591943	2.761812
1.4700000	2.280466	2.371340	2.484441	2.624769	2.799405
1.4800000	2.305406	2.398224	2.513907	2.657716	2.837168
1.4900000	2.330406	2.425178	2.543458	2.690774	2.875085
1.5000000	2.355459	2.452193	2.573086	2.723931	2.913142
1.5100000	2.380558	2.479263	2.602781	2.757176	2.951320
1.5200000	2.405697	2.506380	2.632534	2.790496	2.989605
1.5300000	2.430869	2.533537	2.662335	2.823879	3.027978
1.5400000	2.456069	2.560725	2.692176	2.857313	3.066423
1.5500000	2.481289	2.587938	2.722046	2.890786	3.104922
1.5600000	2.506522	2.615166	2.751936	2.924285	3.143458
1.5699999	2.531763	2.642403	2.781836	2.957797	3.182013
1.5707963	2.533773	2.644572	2.784218	2.960466	3.185083
1.5707963	2.533772	2.644571	2.784220	2.960463	3.185079

$\alpha =$ .519999

Θ	K VALUES				
	.794250555	.868696860	.928444378	.971111163	.994996249
.0000000	.000000	.000000	.000000	.000000	.000000
.0100000	.010000	.010000	.010000	.010000	.010000
.0200000	.020002	.020002	.020002	.020002	.020002
.0300000	.030008	.030008	.030008	.030009	.030009
.0400000	.040019	.040020	.040021	.040021	.040021
.0500000	.050038	.050039	.050041	.050041	.050042
.0600000	.060066	.060068	.060070	.060072	.060073
.0700000	.070105	.070109	.070112	.070115	.070116
.0800000	.080156	.080163	.080168	.080172	.080174
.0900000	.090223	.090232	.090239	.090245	.090247
.1000000	.100306	.100319	.100329	.100336	.100340
.1100000	.110408	.110424	.110438	.110447	.110453
.1200000	.120530	.120552	.120569	.120581	.120588
.1300000	.130674	.130702	.130724	.130740	.130749
.1400000	.140843	.140877	.140905	.140925	.140936
.1500000	.151038	.151080	.151115	.151139	.151153
.1600000	.161260	.161312	.161354	.161384	.161401
.1700000	.171513	.171576	.171626	.171662	.171682
.1800000	.181798	.181872	.181932	.181975	.181999
.1900000	.192117	.192205	.192275	.192326	.192354
.2000000	.202471	.202574	.202657	.202716	.202749
.2100000	.212864	.212984	.213080	.213148	.213187
.2200000	.223297	.223435	.223546	.223625	.223670
.2300000	.233772	.233930	.234057	.234148	.234199
.2400000	.244291	.244471	.244617	.244721	.244779
.2500000	.254857	.255061	.255226	.255344	.255411
.2600000	.265471	.265702	.265888	.266022	.266097
.2700000	.276135	.276395	.276605	.276755	.276840
.2800000	.286853	.287144	.287379	.287548	.287642
.2900000	.297625	.297951	.298213	.298402	.298507
.3000000	.308455	.308817	.309109	.309319	.309437
.3100000	.319344	.319746	.320070	.320303	.320434
.3200000	.330295	.330740	.331099	.331356	.331501
.3300000	.341311	.341801	.342197	.342481	.342641
.3400000	.352393	.352932	.353368	.353681	.353857
.3500000	.363544	.364135	.364614	.364958	.365152
.3600000	.374766	.375414	.375939	.376316	.376528
.3700000	.386063	.386771	.387344	.387757	.387989
.3800000	.397436	.398208	.398834	.399284	.399537
.3900000	.408888	.409728	.410410	.410900	.411176

$\alpha =$ .519999

Θ	K VALUES				
	.794250555	.868696860	.928444378	.971111163	.994996249
.4000000	.420421	.421335	.422076	.422609	.422909
.4100000	.432040	.433030	.433834	.434414	.434740
.4200000	.443745	.444818	.445689	.446317	.446671
.4300000	.455540	.456700	.457643	.458323	.458706
.4400000	.467428	.468681	.469699	.470434	.470848
.4500000	.479411	.480762	.481861	.482654	.483102
.4600000	.491493	.492947	.494132	.494987	.495470
.4700000	.503676	.505240	.506515	.507437	.507956
.4800000	.515963	.517644	.519015	.520006	.520565
.4900000	.528358	.530162	.531634	.532699	.533301
.5000000	.540863	.542798	.544377	.545521	.546166
.5100000	.553483	.555554	.557247	.558473	.559166
.5200000	.566219	.568435	.570248	.571562	.572305
.5300000	.579076	.581445	.583385	.584791	.585587
.5400000	.592056	.594587	.596660	.598165	.599016
.5500000	.605164	.607864	.610079	.611688	.612598
.5600000	.618402	.621281	.623645	.625364	.626337
.5700000	.631774	.634843	.637364	.639198	.640237
.5800000	.645285	.648552	.651239	.653196	.654305
.5900000	.658937	.662413	.665276	.667361	.668544
.6000000	.672735	.676431	.679478	.681700	.682961
.6100000	.686682	.690610	.693851	.696217	.697560
.6200000	.700782	.704954	.708400	.710918	.712348
.6300000	.715040	.719468	.723130	.725808	.727331
.6400000	.729459	.734156	.738046	.740893	.742513
.6500000	.744043	.749024	.753154	.756180	.757902
.6600000	.758798	.764077	.768459	.771673	.773504
.6700000	.773727	.779319	.783967	.787379	.789325
.6800000	.788835	.794756	.799684	.803306	.805372
.6899999	.804126	.810392	.815615	.819458	.821652
.7000000	.819606	.826234	.831768	.835844	.838173
.7100000	.835277	.842287	.848147	.852469	.854942
.7200000	.851147	.858557	.864761	.869343	.871965
.7300000	.867219	.875049	.881615	.886471	.889253
.7400000	.883498	.891769	.898717	.903861	.906811
.7500000	.899990	.908724	.916073	.921522	.924651
.7600000	.916699	.925920	.933692	.939463	.942779
.7700000	.933632	.943363	.951580	.957690	.961205
.7800000	.950793	.961060	.969745	.976214	.979938
.7899999	.968188	.979018	.988196	.995043	.998989

$\alpha =$ •519999

Θ	K VALUES				
	•794250555	•868696860	•928444378	•971111163	•994996249
•8000000	•985823	•997243	1•006941	1•014186	1•018368
•8100000	1•003703	1•015743	1•025987	1•033654	1•038084
•8200000	1•021833	1•034524	1•045344	1•053456	1•058149
•8300000	1•040221	1•053594	1•065020	1•073603	1•078575
•8400000	1•058872	1•072961	1•085026	1•094105	1•099372
•8500000	1•077791	1•092632	1•105370	1•114974	1•120553
•8600000	1•096986	1•112615	1•126062	1•136221	1•142130
•8700000	1•116462	1•132919	1•147112	1•157858	1•164118
•8799999	1•136226	1•153552	1•168531	1•179897	1•186529
•8899999	1•156284	1•174521	1•190330	1•202351	1•209377
•9000000	1•176642	1•195837	1•212519	1•225235	1•232678
•9100000	1•197308	1•217506	1•235109	1•248559	1•256447
•9200000	1•218288	1•239540	1•258113	1•272341	1•280700
•9300000	1•239589	1•261946	1•281543	1•296593	1•305453
•9400000	1•261217	1•284734	1•305410	1•321333	1•330724
•9500000	1•283179	1•307913	1•329728	1•346574	1•356531
•9600000	1•305483	1•331494	1•354509	1•372335	1•382893
•9699999	1•328135	1•355487	1•379768	1•398632	1•409830
•9799999	1•351143	1•379900	1•405519	1•425483	1•437363
•9899999	1•374512	1•404746	1•431774	1•452908	1•465513
1•0000000	1•398252	1•430033	1•458551	1•480924	1•494304
1•0100000	1•422367	1•455774	1•485863	1•509552	1•523758
1•0200000	1•446867	1•481977	1•513726	1•538814	1•553901
1•0300000	1•471756	1•508655	1•542156	1•568731	1•584758
1•0400000	1•497044	1•535819	1•571171	1•599325	1•616358
1•0500000	1•522736	1•563479	1•600786	1•630621	1•648730
1•0600000	1•548840	1•591647	1•631020	1•662643	1•681903
1•0699999	1•575362	1•620335	1•661890	1•695417	1•715909
1•0799999	1•602309	1•649554	1•693415	1•728970	1•750783
1•0899999	1•629688	1•679315	1•725614	1•763329	1•786560
1•1000000	1•657506	1•709630	1•758507	1•798526	1•823277
1•1100000	1•685768	1•740510	1•792113	1•834588	1•860974
1•1200000	1•714481	1•771968	1•826452	1•871549	1•899693
1•1300000	1•743651	1•804015	1•861547	1•909443	1•939479
1•1400000	1•773283	1•836663	1•897417	1•948304	1•980379
1•1500000	1•803383	1•869922	1•934086	1•988168	2•022443
1•1600000	1•833957	1•903805	1•971575	2•029075	2•065725
1•1700000	1•865008	1•938321	2•009907	2•071064	2•110281
1•1800000	1•896541	1•973484	2•049106	2•114177	2•156172
1•1899999	1•928561	2•009302	2•089194	2•158459	2•203464

$\alpha =$ .519999

Θ	K VALUES				
	.794250555	.868696860	.928444378	.971111163	.994996249
1.2000000	1.961072	2.045786	2.130196	2.203956	2.252226
1.2100000	1.994075	2.082947	2.172136	2.250715	2.302532
1.2200000	2.027574	2.120793	2.215038	2.298787	2.354463
1.2300000	2.061571	2.159333	2.258926	2.348226	2.408105
1.2400000	2.096067	2.198576	2.303825	2.399087	2.463550
1.2500000	2.131064	2.238530	2.349760	2.451428	2.520901
1.2599999	2.166561	2.279201	2.396754	2.505310	2.580264
1.2699999	2.202558	2.320595	2.444831	2.560797	2.641759
1.2799999	2.239054	2.362718	2.494016	2.617955	2.705515
1.2899999	2.276046	2.405572	2.544330	2.676855	2.771671
1.3000000	2.313532	2.449162	2.595797	2.737567	2.840381
1.3100000	2.351508	2.493488	2.648435	2.800168	2.911812
1.3200000	2.389968	2.538551	2.702264	2.864734	2.986150
1.3300000	2.428907	2.584348	2.757304	2.931346	3.063597
1.3400000	2.468319	2.630878	2.813568	3.000088	3.144378
1.3500000	2.508195	2.678135	2.871070	3.071044	3.228743
1.3600000	2.548526	2.726112	2.929822	3.144299	3.316968
1.3700000	2.589303	2.774802	2.989829	3.219940	3.409361
1.3799999	2.630515	2.824192	3.051097	3.298054	3.506268
1.3899999	2.672149	2.874269	3.113625	3.378725	3.608073
1.4000000	2.714192	2.925020	3.177407	3.462036	3.715214
1.4100000	2.756629	2.976425	3.242434	3.548061	3.828176
1.4200000	2.799444	3.028465	3.308688	3.636871	3.947512
1.4300000	2.842622	3.081117	3.376149	3.728525	4.073845
1.4400000	2.886143	3.134355	3.444786	3.823068	4.207878
1.4500000	2.929988	3.188151	3.514565	3.920528	4.350405
1.4600000	2.974139	3.242476	3.585442	4.020911	4.502313
1.4700000	3.018573	3.297296	3.657364	4.124197	4.664593
1.4800000	3.063268	3.352575	3.730273	4.230334	4.838325
1.4900000	3.108201	3.408277	3.804100	4.339234	5.024664
1.5000000	3.153349	3.464360	3.878770	4.450767	5.224787
1.5100000	3.198687	3.520783	3.954198	4.564757	5.439790
1.5200000	3.244188	3.577501	4.030294	4.680982	5.670537
1.5300000	3.289828	3.634469	4.106960	4.799170	5.917395
1.5400000	3.335580	3.691640	4.184091	4.919005	6.179892
1.5500000	3.381416	3.748964	4.261579	5.040126	6.456337
1.5600000	3.427309	3.806393	4.339309	5.162137	6.743535
1.5699999	3.473233	3.863876	4.417166	5.284618	7.036824
1.5707963	3.476890	3.868455	4.423368	5.294379	7.060277
1.5707963	3.476886	3.868450	4.423362	5.294372	7.060264

$\alpha =$ .539999

Θ	K VALUES				
	.009966711	.039469502	.087332193	.151646642	.229848846
.0000000	.000000	.000000	.000000	.000000	.000000
.0100000	.010000	.010000	.010000	.010000	.010000
.0200000	.020001	.020001	.020001	.020001	.020001
.0300000	.030004	.030005	.030005	.030005	.030005
.0400000	.040011	.040011	.040012	.040013	.040013
.0500000	.050022	.050023	.050024	.050025	.050027
.0600000	.060039	.060040	.060042	.060044	.060047
.0700000	.070062	.070064	.070066	.070070	.070074
.0800000	.080093	.080095	.080099	.080105	.080111
.0900000	.090132	.090136	.090142	.090149	.090159
.1000000	.100181	.100186	.100194	.100205	.100218
.1100000	.110242	.110248	.110259	.110273	.110291
.1200000	.120314	.120322	.120336	.120355	.120378
.1300000	.130399	.130410	.130428	.130452	.130480
.1400000	.140499	.140513	.140535	.140564	.140600
.1500000	.150614	.150631	.150658	.150694	.150739
.1600000	.160746	.160766	.160799	.160843	.160897
.1700000	.170895	.170919	.170959	.171012	.171076
.1800000	.181063	.181092	.181139	.181202	.181279
.1900000	.191251	.191285	.191340	.191414	.191505
.2000000	.201460	.201500	.201564	.201650	.201756
.2100000	.211691	.211737	.211811	.211912	.212034
.2200000	.221945	.221998	.222084	.222199	.222340
.2300000	.232224	.232285	.232382	.232514	.232676
.2400000	.242529	.242597	.242709	.242859	.243042
.2500000	.252860	.252937	.253063	.253233	.253441
.2600000	.263219	.263306	.263448	.263640	.263873
.2700000	.273607	.273705	.273864	.274079	.274341
.2800000	.284026	.284135	.284313	.284552	.284845
.2900000	.294476	.294597	.294795	.295061	.295387
.3000000	.304959	.305093	.305312	.305607	.305969
.3100000	.315475	.315624	.315866	.316192	.316591
.3200000	.326027	.326191	.326457	.326816	.327256
.3300000	.336615	.336795	.337087	.337482	.337965
.3400000	.347241	.347437	.347757	.348190	.348720
.3500000	.357905	.358120	.358469	.358942	.359521
.3600000	.368610	.368843	.369224	.369739	.370371
.3700000	.379355	.379609	.380023	.380583	.381270
.3800000	.390144	.390419	.390868	.391476	.392222
.3900000	.400976	.401274	.401760	.402418	.403226

$\alpha =$ .539999

Θ	K VALUES				
	.009966711	.039469502	.087332193	.151646642	.229848846
.4000000	.411853	.412175	.412700	.413411	.414285
.4100000	.422777	.423124	.423690	.424457	.425400
.4200000	.433748	.434121	.434731	.435557	.436573
.4300000	.444768	.445169	.445825	.446713	.447806
.4400000	.455839	.456269	.456972	.457926	.459100
.4500000	.466961	.467422	.468175	.469197	.470456
.4600000	.478136	.478629	.479435	.480529	.481877
.4700000	.489365	.489892	.490753	.491922	.493363
.4800000	.500650	.501212	.502130	.503378	.504918
.4900000	.511993	.512591	.513569	.514900	.516542
.5000000	.523393	.524030	.525071	.526487	.528237
.5100000	.534853	.535530	.536637	.538143	.540005
.5200000	.546375	.547093	.548268	.549868	.551847
.5300000	.557959	.558720	.559967	.561665	.563766
.5400000	.569607	.570413	.571734	.573534	.575763
.5500000	.581320	.582174	.583571	.585478	.587839
.5600000	.593101	.594002	.595481	.597497	.599998
.5700000	.604949	.605902	.607463	.609595	.612240
.5800000	.616867	.617872	.619521	.621772	.624567
.5900000	.628857	.629916	.631655	.634030	.636981
.6000000	.640919	.642035	.643867	.646371	.649484
.6100000	.653055	.654230	.656158	.658796	.662078
.6200000	.665267	.666502	.668531	.671307	.674765
.6300000	.677556	.678854	.680986	.683907	.687546
.6400000	.689924	.691286	.693526	.696596	.700423
.6500000	.702371	.703801	.706152	.709376	.713399
.6600000	.714900	.716400	.718866	.722249	.726475
.6700000	.727513	.729084	.731669	.735218	.739653
.6800000	.740210	.741855	.744563	.748283	.752936
.6899999	.752993	.754714	.757550	.761446	.766324
.7000000	.765864	.767664	.770631	.774710	.779821
.7100000	.778824	.780706	.783807	.788075	.793427
.7200000	.791874	.793840	.797082	.801544	.807145
.7300000	.805017	.807070	.810455	.815119	.820977
.7400000	.818254	.820396	.823930	.828801	.834924
.7500000	.831587	.833820	.837507	.842592	.848990
.7600000	.845016	.847343	.851188	.856494	.863175
.7700000	.858543	.860968	.864975	.870508	.877481
.7800000	.872171	.874695	.878869	.884637	.891912
.7899999	.885899	.888527	.892873	.898882	.906468

$\alpha =$ •539999

θ	K VALUES				
	•009966711	•039469502	•087332193	•151646642	•229848846
•8000000	•899731	•902465	•906987	•913245	•921151
•8100000	•913668	•916510	•921214	•927727	•935964
•8200000	•927710	•930664	•935555	•942331	•950908
•8300000	•941860	•944928	•950011	•957058	•965986
•8400000	•956118	•959304	•964585	•971910	•981199
•8500000	•970488	•973794	•979277	•986888	•996548
•8600000	•984968	•988399	•994090	1•001995	1•012037
•8700000	•999563	1•003120	1•009024	1•017232	1•027667
•8799999	1•014271	1•017959	1•024082	1•032600	1•043439
•8899999	1•029096	1•032917	1•039265	1•048101	1•059356
•9000000	1•044038	1•047997	1•054575	1•063737	1•075419
•9100000	1•059099	1•063198	1•070012	1•079509	1•091629
•9200000	1•074280	1•078522	1•085578	1•095419	1•107990
•9300000	1•089582	1•093971	1•101275	1•111469	1•124502
•9400000	1•105007	1•109546	1•117104	1•127659	1•141166
•9500000	1•120556	1•125249	1•133066	1•143991	1•157985
•9600000	1•136229	1•141079	1•149162	1•160467	1•174960
•9699999	1•152028	1•157040	1•165394	1•177087	1•192093
•9799999	1•167954	1•173130	1•181763	1•193854	1•209385
•9899999	1•184009	1•189353	1•198270	1•210768	1•226836
1•0000000	1•200192	1•205708	1•214916	1•227830	1•244450
1•0100000	1•216505	1•222197	1•231702	1•245042	1•262226
1•0200000	1•232949	1•238820	1•248629	1•262404	1•280166
1•0300000	1•249525	1•255578	1•265698	1•279918	1•298270
1•0400000	1•266232	1•272473	1•282909	1•297584	1•316541
1•0500000	1•283073	1•289504	1•300263	1•315402	1•334979
1•0600000	1•300047	1•306672	1•317761	1•333375	1•353584
1•0699999	1•317155	1•323978	1•335403	1•351502	1•372358
1•0799999	1•334398	1•341422	1•353190	1•369784	1•391300
1•0899999	1•351775	1•359005	1•371123	1•388221	1•410412
1•1000000	1•369287	1•376727	1•389201	1•406813	1•429694
1•1100000	1•386934	1•394588	1•407425	1•425562	1•449146
1•1200000	1•404717	1•412587	1•425794	1•444466	1•468768
1•1300000	1•422634	1•430725	1•444309	1•463526	1•488560
1•1400000	1•440686	1•449003	1•462969	1•482741	1•508522
1•1500000	1•458873	1•467418	1•481775	1•502112	1•528654
1•1600000	1•477195	1•485972	1•500725	1•521638	1•548956
1•1700000	1•495650	1•504663	1•519820	1•541318	1•569426
1•1800000	1•514238	1•523492	1•539058	1•561152	1•590064
1•1899999	1•532959	1•542456	1•558439	1•581139	1•610870

$\alpha =$ .539999

θ	K VALUES .009966711	.039469502	.087332193	.151646642	.229848846
1.2000000	1.551812	1.561556	1.577963	1.601277	1.631842
1.2100000	1.570795	1.580791	1.597627	1.621567	1.652979
1.2200000	1.589907	1.600158	1.617430	1.642006	1.674280
1.2300000	1.609148	1.619657	1.637372	1.662593	1.695743
1.2400000	1.628515	1.639287	1.657451	1.683326	1.717366
1.2500000	1.648008	1.659046	1.677665	1.704205	1.739148
1.2599999	1.667625	1.678931	1.698012	1.725226	1.761086
1.2699999	1.687363	1.698942	1.718490	1.746388	1.783179
1.2799999	1.707221	1.719076	1.739098	1.767688	1.805423
1.2899999	1.727196	1.739332	1.759833	1.789124	1.827817
1.3000000	1.747288	1.759706	1.780692	1.810694	1.850357
1.3100000	1.767492	1.780196	1.801673	1.832394	1.873040
1.3200000	1.787806	1.800799	1.822774	1.854222	1.895863
1.3300000	1.808228	1.821514	1.843990	1.876174	1.918822
1.3400000	1.828755	1.842336	1.865320	1.898248	1.941915
1.3500000	1.849384	1.863263	1.886759	1.920439	1.965137
1.3600000	1.870112	1.884292	1.908305	1.942745	1.988484
1.3700000	1.890935	1.905418	1.929954	1.965160	2.011952
1.3799999	1.911849	1.926639	1.951702	1.987682	2.035537
1.3899999	1.932852	1.947951	1.973545	2.010306	2.059234
1.4000000	1.953940	1.969350	1.995480	2.033029	2.083038
1.4100000	1.975108	1.990832	2.017501	2.055844	2.106945
1.4200000	1.996353	2.012393	2.039606	2.078748	2.130950
1.4300000	2.017671	2.034028	2.061788	2.101736	2.155046
1.4400000	2.039057	2.055734	2.084045	2.124803	2.179230
1.4500000	2.060507	2.077505	2.106370	2.147945	2.203495
1.4600000	2.082016	2.099338	2.128760	2.171155	2.227836
1.4700000	2.103581	2.121228	2.151209	2.194429	2.252246
1.4800000	2.125196	2.143169	2.173713	2.217761	2.276721
1.4900000	2.146857	2.165157	2.196266	2.241146	2.301254
1.5000000	2.168558	2.187187	2.218863	2.264578	2.325839
1.5100000	2.190295	2.209254	2.241499	2.288052	2.350469
1.5200000	2.212064	2.231353	2.264168	2.311562	2.375139
1.5300000	2.233858	2.253479	2.286865	2.335101	2.399842
1.5400000	2.255673	2.275626	2.309585	2.358665	2.424571
1.5500000	2.277504	2.297790	2.332321	2.382247	2.449321
1.5600000	2.299345	2.319964	2.355070	2.405842	2.474084
1.5699999	2.321193	2.342144	2.377824	2.429443	2.498854
1.5707963	2.322932	2.343911	2.379636	2.431323	2.500827
1.5707963	2.322931	2.343909	2.379634	2.431321	2.500825

$\alpha =$ .539999

θ	K VALUES				
	.318821117	.415016431	.514599755	.613601043	.708073407
.0000000	.000000	.000000	.000000	.000000	.000000
.0100000	.010000	.010000	.010000	.010000	.010000
.0200000	.020001	.020002	.020002	.020002	.020002
.0300000	.030006	.030006	.030007	.030007	.030008
.0400000	.040014	.040015	.040017	.040018	.040019
.0500000	.050029	.050031	.050033	.050035	.050037
.0600000	.060050	.060053	.060057	.060061	.060064
.0700000	.070080	.070085	.070091	.070096	.070102
.0800000	.080119	.080127	.080136	.080144	.080152
.0900000	.090170	.090181	.090194	.090206	.090217
.1000000	.100233	.100249	.100266	.100282	.100298
.1100000	.110310	.110332	.110354	.110376	.110397
.1200000	.120403	.120431	.120460	.120489	.120516
.1300000	.130513	.130549	.130585	.130622	.130657
.1400000	.140641	.140686	.140732	.140777	.140821
.1500000	.150789	.150844	.150900	.150957	.151011
.1600000	.160958	.161025	.161094	.161162	.161228
.1700000	.171150	.171230	.171313	.171395	.171474
.1800000	.181366	.181461	.181559	.181658	.181752
.1900000	.191608	.191719	.191836	.191951	.192062
.2000000	.201876	.202007	.202143	.202278	.202408
.2100000	.212173	.212325	.212482	.212639	.212790
.2200000	.222501	.222675	.222857	.223038	.223211
.2300000	.232860	.233059	.233267	.233475	.233674
.2400000	.243251	.243479	.243716	.243952	.244179
.2500000	.253678	.253936	.254204	.254472	.254729
.2600000	.264140	.264431	.264733	.265036	.265327
.2700000	.274641	.274967	.275307	.275647	.275973
.2800000	.285180	.285545	.285925	.286305	.286671
.2900000	.295760	.296166	.296590	.297014	.297422
.3000000	.306383	.306833	.307304	.307775	.308229
.3100000	.317049	.317548	.318068	.318591	.319094
.3200000	.327761	.328311	.328886	.329463	.330018
.3300000	.338520	.339125	.339758	.340393	.341005
.3400000	.349328	.349991	.350686	.351383	.352056
.3500000	.360186	.360912	.361672	.362437	.363174
.3600000	.371096	.371889	.372719	.373555	.374362
.3700000	.382060	.382924	.383829	.384740	.385620
.3800000	.393079	.394018	.395002	.395994	.396953
.3900000	.404156	.405174	.406243	.407320	.408362

$\alpha =$ .539999

Θ	K VALUES				
	.318821117	.415016431	.514599755	.613601043	.708073407
.4000000	.415291	.416393	.417551	.418719	.419851
.4100000	.426487	.427678	.428930	.430195	.431420
.4200000	.437745	.439030	.440382	.441748	.443074
.4300000	.449067	.450451	.451909	.453383	.454814
.4400000	.460455	.461944	.463512	.465101	.466643
.4500000	.471910	.473509	.475195	.476904	.478565
.4600000	.483435	.485150	.486960	.488795	.490581
.4700000	.495031	.496868	.498808	.500777	.502695
.4800000	.506700	.508665	.510741	.512851	.514909
.4900000	.518444	.520543	.522764	.525022	.527226
.5000000	.530265	.532504	.534876	.537291	.539650
.5100000	.542164	.544551	.547082	.549660	.552182
.5200000	.554145	.556686	.559383	.562134	.564827
.5300000	.566207	.568910	.571782	.574713	.577587
.5400000	.578354	.581227	.584280	.587402	.590465
.5500000	.590588	.593637	.596882	.600203	.603465
.5600000	.602910	.606144	.609589	.613119	.616590
.5700000	.615323	.618749	.622403	.626152	.629843
.5800000	.627827	.631455	.635328	.639306	.643227
.5900000	.640427	.644264	.648366	.652584	.656747
.6000000	.653123	.657179	.661520	.665988	.670405
.6100000	.665917	.670201	.674791	.679522	.684205
.6200000	.678812	.683333	.688184	.693189	.698150
.6300000	.691810	.696578	.701700	.706992	.712245
.6400000	.704913	.709938	.715342	.720935	.726492
.6500000	.718122	.723415	.729114	.735020	.740897
.6600000	.731441	.737012	.743018	.749250	.755462
.6700000	.744871	.750731	.757057	.763630	.770192
.6800000	.758414	.764574	.771233	.778163	.785090
.6899999	.772073	.778545	.785550	.792851	.800161
.7000000	.785850	.792646	.800011	.807699	.815409
.7100000	.799746	.806878	.814618	.822710	.830837
.7200000	.813765	.821245	.829375	.837887	.846451
.7300000	.827908	.835750	.844284	.853234	.862255
.7400000	.842178	.850394	.859349	.868755	.878252
.7500000	.856576	.865180	.874572	.884454	.894448
.7600000	.871106	.880112	.889957	.900333	.910847
.7700000	.885768	.895191	.905507	.916398	.927453
.7800000	.900566	.910420	.921225	.932651	.944272
.7899999	.915502	.925802	.937114	.949096	.961308

$\alpha =$ .539999

θ	K VALUES				
	.318821117	.415016431	.514599755	.613601043	.708073407
.8000000	.930578	.941339	.953176	.965738	.978565
.8100000	.945796	.957034	.969416	.982580	.996049
.8200000	.961158	.972890	.985837	.999626	1.013764
.8300000	.976666	.988909	1.002440	1.016880	1.031716
.8400000	.992323	1.005093	1.019231	1.034346	1.049909
.8500000	1.008131	1.021446	1.036211	1.052028	1.068348
.8600000	1.024092	1.037969	1.053384	1.069930	1.087039
.8700000	1.040208	1.054666	1.070754	1.088055	1.105987
.8799999	1.056481	1.071538	1.088322	1.106409	1.125197
.8899999	1.072914	1.088589	1.106093	1.124994	1.144673
.9000000	1.089508	1.105821	1.124069	1.143815	1.164423
.9100000	1.106265	1.123236	1.142254	1.162875	1.184450
.9200000	1.123187	1.140836	1.160650	1.182180	1.204759
.9300000	1.140277	1.158625	1.179260	1.201732	1.225357
.9400000	1.157536	1.176603	1.198087	1.221535	1.246249
.9500000	1.174966	1.194774	1.217135	1.241594	1.267440
.9600000	1.192568	1.213140	1.236406	1.261911	1.288934
.9699999	1.210345	1.231703	1.255903	1.282492	1.310738
.9799999	1.228298	1.250464	1.275628	1.303340	1.332857
.9899999	1.246429	1.269427	1.295585	1.324457	1.355296
1.0000000	1.264739	1.288592	1.315775	1.345849	1.378061
1.0100000	1.283230	1.307962	1.336201	1.367518	1.401155
1.0200000	1.301903	1.327538	1.356866	1.389468	1.424585
1.0300000	1.320759	1.347323	1.377772	1.411702	1.448355
1.0400000	1.339800	1.367316	1.398921	1.434223	1.472470
1.0500000	1.359027	1.387521	1.420314	1.457034	1.496936
1.0600000	1.378440	1.407939	1.441955	1.480138	1.521756
1.0699999	1.398041	1.428570	1.463844	1.503539	1.546935
1.0799999	1.417830	1.449415	1.485984	1.527238	1.572477
1.0899999	1.437808	1.470476	1.508375	1.551237	1.598388
1.1000000	1.457975	1.491754	1.531020	1.575541	1.624670
1.1100000	1.478333	1.513248	1.553918	1.600149	1.651328
1.1200000	1.498880	1.534960	1.577072	1.625065	1.678364
1.1300000	1.519618	1.556890	1.600482	1.650289	1.705783
1.1400000	1.540545	1.579037	1.624147	1.675823	1.733587
1.1500000	1.561663	1.601403	1.648070	1.701668	1.761779
1.1600000	1.582971	1.623986	1.672250	1.727826	1.790362
1.1700000	1.604467	1.646786	1.696686	1.754296	1.819337
1.1800000	1.626152	1.669803	1.721378	1.781079	1.848707
1.1899999	1.648024	1.693036	1.746326	1.808174	1.878473

$\alpha =$ .539999

Θ	K VALUES				
	.318821117	.415016431	.514599755	.613601043	.708073407
1.2000000	1.670083	1.716484	1.771529	1.835582	1.908635
1.2100000	1.692327	1.740145	1.796986	1.863302	1.939194
1.2200000	1.714754	1.764017	1.822695	1.891332	1.970151
1.2300000	1.737364	1.788100	1.848654	1.919672	2.001504
1.2400000	1.760154	1.812392	1.874861	1.948318	2.033253
1.2500000	1.783122	1.836889	1.901315	1.977270	2.065397
1.2599999	1.806266	1.861590	1.928012	2.006525	2.097934
1.2699999	1.829583	1.886491	1.954950	2.036078	2.130860
1.2799999	1.853071	1.911591	1.982124	2.065928	2.164173
1.2899999	1.876727	1.936884	2.009533	2.096070	2.197869
1.3000000	1.900547	1.962370	2.037171	2.126500	2.231945
1.3100000	1.924529	1.988042	2.065034	2.157213	2.266394
1.3200000	1.948669	2.013897	2.093118	2.188203	2.301211
1.3300000	1.972962	2.039932	2.121418	2.219466	2.336389
1.3400000	1.997406	2.066141	2.149929	2.250994	2.371923
1.3500000	2.021995	2.092519	2.178644	2.282782	2.407803
1.3600000	2.046725	2.119062	2.207559	2.314822	2.444022
1.3700000	2.071592	2.145764	2.236666	2.347106	2.480570
1.3799999	2.096590	2.172620	2.265959	2.379627	2.517438
1.3899999	2.121716	2.199623	2.295431	2.412377	2.554615
1.4000000	2.146962	2.226768	2.325075	2.445345	2.592090
1.4100000	2.172325	2.254047	2.354883	2.478524	2.629851
1.4200000	2.197797	2.281456	2.384848	2.511902	2.667884
1.4300000	2.223374	2.308986	2.414961	2.545471	2.706178
1.4400000	2.249048	2.336631	2.445214	2.579218	2.744718
1.4500000	2.274815	2.364383	2.475597	2.613134	2.783489
1.4600000	2.300668	2.392236	2.506103	2.647207	2.822477
1.4700000	2.326599	2.420181	2.536722	2.681426	2.861665
1.4800000	2.352603	2.448211	2.567444	2.715777	2.901037
1.4900000	2.378673	2.476318	2.598260	2.750250	2.940577
1.5000000	2.404801	2.504493	2.629160	2.784831	2.980268
1.5100000	2.430981	2.532729	2.660134	2.819507	3.020091
1.5200000	2.457206	2.561017	2.691171	2.854266	3.060029
1.5300000	2.483468	2.589349	2.722263	2.889094	3.100063
1.5400000	2.509760	2.617716	2.753397	2.923978	3.140174
1.5500000	2.536074	2.646110	2.784564	2.958904	3.180345
1.5600000	2.562405	2.674522	2.815753	2.993858	3.220555
1.5699999	2.588743	2.702943	2.846953	3.028828	3.260786
1.5707963	2.590840	2.705206	2.849438	3.031613	3.263990
1.5707963	2.590839	2.705205	2.849438	3.031611	3.263989

$\alpha =$ .539999

Θ	K VALUES				
	.794250555	.868696860	.928444378	.971111163	.994996249
.0000000	.000000	.000000	.000000	.000000	.000000
.0100000	.010000	.010000	.010000	.010000	.010000
.0200000	.020002	.020002	.020002	.020002	.020002
.0300000	.030008	.030008	.030009	.030009	.030009
.0400000	.040020	.040020	.040021	.040021	.040022
.0500000	.050039	.050040	.050041	.050042	.050043
.0600000	.060067	.060070	.060072	.060073	.060074
.0700000	.070107	.070111	.070115	.070117	.070118
.0800000	.080160	.080166	.080171	.080175	.080177
.0900000	.090228	.090237	.090244	.090249	.090252
.1000000	.100313	.100325	.100335	.100342	.100347
.1100000	.110417	.110433	.110447	.110456	.110462
.1200000	.120541	.120563	.120581	.120593	.120600
.1300000	.130689	.130717	.130739	.130755	.130764
.1400000	.140861	.140896	.140924	.140944	.140955
.1500000	.151060	.151103	.151137	.151162	.151176
.1600000	.161288	.161340	.161382	.161412	.161428
.1700000	.171547	.171609	.171659	.171695	.171715
.1800000	.181838	.181912	.181972	.182015	.182039
.1900000	.192164	.192251	.192322	.192373	.192401
.2000000	.202526	.202629	.202712	.202771	.202804
.2100000	.212928	.213047	.213143	.213212	.213251
.2200000	.223370	.223508	.223619	.223699	.223743
.2300000	.233856	.234014	.234142	.234233	.234284
.2400000	.244387	.244567	.244713	.244817	.244875
.2500000	.254965	.255170	.255335	.255453	.255520
.2600000	.265593	.265825	.266011	.266145	.266220
.2700000	.276273	.276533	.276743	.276894	.276978
.2800000	.287007	.287299	.287534	.287703	.287797
.2900000	.297797	.298123	.298386	.298574	.298680
.3000000	.308646	.309009	.309301	.309511	.309629
.3100000	.319556	.319958	.320283	.320516	.320647
.3200000	.330529	.330974	.331334	.331592	.331737
.3300000	.341568	.342059	.342456	.342741	.342901
.3400000	.352676	.353216	.353653	.353966	.354143
.3500000	.363854	.364447	.364926	.365271	.365465
.3600000	.375106	.375755	.376280	.376658	.376870
.3700000	.386433	.387142	.387717	.388130	.388362
.3800000	.397839	.398613	.399240	.399691	.399944
.3900000	.409326	.410168	.410851	.411342	.411619

$\alpha =$ .539999

Θ	K VALUES				
	.794250555	.868696860	.928444378	.971111163	.994996249
.4000000	.420897	.421812	.422555	.423089	.423390
.4100000	.432554	.433547	.434353	.434934	.435260
.4200000	.444301	.445377	.446250	.446879	.447234
.4300000	.456141	.457304	.458249	.458930	.459314
.4400000	.468075	.469331	.470352	.471089	.471504
.4500000	.480108	.481462	.482564	.483359	.483808
.4600000	.492241	.493700	.494888	.495746	.496229
.4700000	.504479	.506049	.507327	.508251	.508772
.4800000	.516825	.518511	.519886	.520880	.521441
.4900000	.529281	.531091	.532567	.533636	.534239
.5000000	.541850	.543791	.545376	.546523	.547171
.5100000	.554537	.556616	.558315	.559545	.560240
.5200000	.567345	.569569	.571388	.572707	.573452
.5300000	.580276	.582654	.584601	.586013	.586811
.5400000	.593335	.595875	.597957	.599467	.600322
.5500000	.606525	.609236	.611460	.613075	.613989
.5600000	.619850	.622741	.625115	.626841	.627818
.5700000	.633313	.636395	.638927	.640769	.641813
.5800000	.646919	.650200	.652900	.654865	.655979
.5900000	.660670	.664163	.667039	.669134	.670322
.6000000	.674573	.678287	.681349	.683581	.684848
.6100000	.688629	.692577	.695834	.698212	.699562
.6200000	.702844	.707037	.710502	.713032	.714470
.6300000	.717221	.721673	.725355	.728048	.729578
.6400000	.731765	.736489	.740401	.743264	.744893
.6500000	.746481	.751491	.755644	.758687	.760420
.6600000	.761373	.766683	.771091	.774325	.776167
.6700000	.776445	.782071	.786748	.790182	.792139
.6800000	.791702	.797661	.802620	.806265	.808345
.6899999	.807150	.813457	.818714	.822583	.824792
.7000000	.822792	.829466	.835037	.839141	.841487
.7100000	.838634	.845693	.851595	.855947	.858437
.7200000	.854681	.862145	.868394	.873009	.875652
.7300000	.870939	.878827	.885443	.890335	.893138
.7400000	.887411	.895746	.902748	.907932	.910906
.7500000	.904105	.912909	.920317	.925810	.928963
.7600000	.921025	.930321	.938157	.943975	.947319
.7700000	.938176	.947990	.956277	.962439	.965984
.7800000	.955566	.965923	.974684	.981209	.984967
.7899999	.973199	.984126	.993387	1.000296	1.004278

$\alpha =$ .539999

θ	K VALUES				
	.794250555	.868696860	.928444378	.971111163	.994996249
.8000000	.991082	1.002607	1.012395	1.019708	1.023929
.8100000	1.009220	1.021374	1.031716	1.039457	1.043931
.8200000	1.027620	1.040434	1.051360	1.059553	1.064293
.8300000	1.046287	1.059794	1.071337	1.080007	1.085030
.8400000	1.065229	1.079464	1.091655	1.100830	1.106152
.8500000	1.084452	1.099450	1.112325	1.122033	1.127672
.8600000	1.103963	1.119762	1.133357	1.143629	1.149605
.8700000	1.123767	1.140409	1.154762	1.165631	1.171963
.8799999	1.143872	1.161398	1.176552	1.188051	1.194761
.8899999	1.164285	1.182738	1.198736	1.210903	1.218014
.9000000	1.185013	1.204440	1.221327	1.234201	1.241738
.9100000	1.206063	1.226513	1.244338	1.257959	1.265948
.9200000	1.227442	1.248965	1.267779	1.282193	1.290662
.9300000	1.249157	1.271807	1.291664	1.306917	1.315897
.9400000	1.271215	1.295048	1.316007	1.332149	1.341671
.9500000	1.293625	1.318700	1.340820	1.357905	1.368003
.9600000	1.316393	1.342772	1.366117	1.384202	1.394914
.9699999	1.339527	1.367275	1.391914	1.411059	1.422425
.9799999	1.363035	1.392219	1.418224	1.438494	1.450557
.9899999	1.386924	1.417617	1.445063	1.466527	1.479332
1.0000000	1.411202	1.443478	1.472447	1.495179	1.508776
1.0100000	1.435877	1.469815	1.500392	1.524471	1.538912
1.0200000	1.460955	1.496638	1.528914	1.554425	1.569768
1.0300000	1.486446	1.523960	1.558030	1.585063	1.601370
1.0400000	1.512356	1.551793	1.587759	1.616411	1.633748
1.0500000	1.538693	1.580147	1.618118	1.648492	1.666932
1.0600000	1.565464	1.609036	1.649125	1.681334	1.700954
1.0699999	1.592678	1.638472	1.680801	1.714963	1.735848
1.0799999	1.620342	1.668467	1.713164	1.749407	1.771648
1.0899999	1.648462	1.699034	1.746234	1.784697	1.808394
1.1000000	1.677047	1.730185	1.780034	1.820864	1.846123
1.1100000	1.706102	1.761932	1.814583	1.857938	1.884878
1.1200000	1.735635	1.794289	1.849903	1.895955	1.924703
1.1300000	1.765652	1.827267	1.886017	1.934950	1.965645
1.1400000	1.796160	1.860879	1.922948	1.974959	2.007754
1.1500000	1.827165	1.895137	1.960718	2.016021	2.051081
1.1600000	1.858672	1.930054	1.999352	2.058177	2.095685
1.1700000	1.890686	1.965642	2.038874	2.101469	2.141623
1.1800000	1.923214	2.001913	2.079308	2.145941	2.188961
1.1899999	1.956258	2.038877	2.120679	2.191640	2.237767

$\alpha =$ .539999

Θ	K VALUES				
	.794250555	.868696860	.928444378	.971111163	.994996249
1.2000000	1.989825	2.076547	2.163013	2.238614	2.288113
1.2100000	2.023916	2.114932	2.206335	2.286915	2.340077
1.2200000	2.058535	2.154044	2.250672	2.336595	2.393745
1.2300000	2.093685	2.193891	2.296048	2.387710	2.449205
1.2400000	2.129367	2.234484	2.342491	2.440319	2.506557
1.2500000	2.165583	2.275829	2.390026	2.494484	2.565905
1.2599999	2.202333	2.317935	2.438678	2.550268	2.627364
1.2699999	2.239617	2.360809	2.488474	2.607737	2.691056
1.2799999	2.277433	2.404455	2.539438	2.666964	2.757118
1.2899999	2.315779	2.448878	2.591594	2.728019	2.825696
1.3000000	2.354653	2.494082	2.644966	2.790980	2.896951
1.3100000	2.394050	2.540068	2.699575	2.855924	2.971057
1.3200000	2.433966	2.586837	2.755442	2.922934	3.048208
1.3300000	2.474395	2.634386	2.812587	2.992095	3.128617
1.3400000	2.515329	2.682713	2.871024	3.063492	3.212519
1.3500000	2.556760	2.731813	2.930770	3.137215	3.300175
1.3600000	2.598680	2.781679	2.991834	3.213354	3.391873
1.3700000	2.641076	2.832302	3.054225	3.291999	3.487936
1.3799999	2.683938	2.883670	3.117947	3.373242	3.588724
1.3899999	2.727253	2.935770	3.182999	3.457171	3.694640
1.4000000	2.771007	2.988586	3.249377	3.543871	3.806140
1.4100000	2.815183	3.042098	3.317068	3.633422	3.923731
1.4200000	2.859765	3.096285	3.386056	3.725897	4.047992
1.4300000	2.904736	3.151123	3.456319	3.821357	4.179572
1.4400000	2.950075	3.206585	3.527824	3.919850	4.319206
1.4500000	2.995763	3.262642	3.600535	4.021405	4.467721
1.4600000	3.041778	3.319261	3.674405	4.126028	4.626046
1.4700000	3.088098	3.376408	3.749379	4.233697	4.795212
1.4800000	3.134698	3.434043	3.825396	4.344358	4.976349
1.4900000	3.181554	3.492128	3.902382	4.457917	5.170662
1.5000000	3.228641	3.550620	3.980258	4.574240	5.379378
1.5100000	3.275931	3.609473	4.058935	4.693139	5.603642
1.5200000	3.323398	3.668641	4.138318	4.814383	5.844353
1.5300000	3.371013	3.728074	4.218301	4.937687	6.101895
1.5400000	3.418748	3.787723	4.298777	5.062718	6.375773
1.5500000	3.466574	3.847536	4.379628	5.189097	6.664220
1.5600000	3.514462	3.907461	4.460736	5.316410	6.963898
1.5699999	3.562382	3.967443	4.541978	5.444216	7.269938
1.5707963	3.566198	3.972220	4.548450	5.454401	7.294411
1.5707963	3.566197	3.972218	4.548448	5.454398	7.294403

$\alpha =$ .559999

Θ	K VALUES				
	.009966711	.039469502	.087332193	.151646642	.229848846
.0000000	.000000	.000000	.000000	.000000	.000000
.0100000	.010000	.010000	.010000	.010000	.010000
.0200000	.020001	.020001	.020001	.020001	.020001
.0300000	.030005	.030005	.030005	.030005	.030006
.0400000	.040012	.040012	.040012	.040013	.040014
.0500000	.050023	.050024	.050025	.050026	.050028
.0600000	.060040	.060041	.060043	.060045	.060048
.0700000	.070064	.070066	.070069	.070072	.070077
.0800000	.080096	.080099	.080103	.080108	.080115
.0900000	.090137	.090141	.090146	.090154	.090164
.1000000	.100188	.100193	.100201	.100212	.100225
.1100000	.110251	.110257	.110268	.110282	.110300
.1200000	.120326	.120334	.120348	.120367	.120389
.1300000	.130414	.130425	.130443	.130466	.130495
.1400000	.140518	.140531	.140553	.140583	.140619
.1500000	.150637	.150654	.150681	.150717	.150761
.1600000	.160774	.160794	.160827	.160871	.160925
.1700000	.170928	.170953	.170992	.171045	.171110
.1800000	.181103	.181132	.181178	.181241	.181318
.1900000	.191298	.191332	.191387	.191461	.191551
.2000000	.201514	.201554	.201618	.201705	.201810
.2100000	.211754	.211800	.211874	.211975	.212097
.2200000	.222018	.222071	.222156	.222272	.222413
.2300000	.232307	.232368	.232466	.232598	.232759
.2400000	.242623	.242692	.242803	.242954	.243137
.2500000	.252967	.253045	.253171	.253341	.253548
.2600000	.263340	.263427	.263569	.263761	.263995
.2700000	.273743	.273841	.274000	.274215	.274477
.2800000	.284178	.284287	.284465	.284704	.284997
.2900000	.294645	.294766	.294964	.295231	.295557
.3000000	.305146	.305281	.305500	.305796	.306157
.3100000	.315683	.315832	.316074	.316400	.316800
.3200000	.326256	.326420	.326686	.327046	.327487
.3300000	.336867	.337047	.337339	.337735	.338219
.3400000	.347517	.347714	.348034	.348468	.348998
.3500000	.358208	.358423	.358773	.359246	.359826
.3600000	.368940	.369174	.369555	.370071	.370704
.3700000	.379715	.379970	.380384	.380945	.381633
.3800000	.390535	.390811	.391260	.391869	.392616
.3900000	.401400	.401699	.402186	.402845	.403654

$\alpha =$ .559999

Θ	K VALUES				
	.009966711	.039469502	.087332193	.151646642	.229848846
.4000000	.412312	.412635	.413161	.413874	.414749
.4100000	.423273	.423621	.424188	.424957	.425902
.4200000	.434284	.434658	.435269	.436097	.437115
.4300000	.445345	.445747	.446404	.447295	.448390
.4400000	.456459	.456891	.457596	.458552	.459728
.4500000	.467628	.468090	.468845	.469870	.471131
.4600000	.478851	.479345	.480153	.481250	.482602
.4700000	.490131	.490660	.491523	.492695	.494141
.4800000	.501470	.502033	.502954	.504206	.505750
.4900000	.512868	.513468	.514450	.515784	.517431
.5000000	.524328	.524966	.526011	.527432	.529187
.5100000	.535850	.536528	.537639	.539150	.541018
.5200000	.547436	.548156	.549336	.550941	.552927
.5300000	.559088	.559852	.561103	.562807	.564915
.5400000	.570807	.571616	.572941	.574748	.576985
.5500000	.582594	.583450	.584854	.586767	.589138
.5600000	.594452	.595357	.596841	.598866	.601377
.5700000	.606381	.607338	.608906	.611046	.613702
.5800000	.618384	.619393	.621049	.623309	.626117
.5900000	.630462	.631526	.633272	.635658	.638622
.6000000	.642616	.643737	.645577	.648093	.651221
.6100000	.654848	.656028	.657966	.660616	.663914
.6200000	.667160	.668401	.670440	.673230	.676704
.6300000	.679553	.680857	.683001	.685936	.689594
.6400000	.692029	.693399	.695650	.698736	.702584
.6500000	.704589	.706027	.708391	.711632	.715678
.6600000	.717236	.718743	.721224	.724626	.728876
.6700000	.729970	.731550	.734151	.737720	.742182
.6800000	.742794	.744449	.747174	.750916	.755597
.6899999	.755709	.757441	.760294	.764215	.769124
.7000000	.768717	.770529	.773514	.777620	.782764
.7100000	.781819	.783713	.786836	.791132	.796519
.7200000	.795018	.796997	.800261	.804754	.810393
.7300000	.808314	.810381	.813790	.818487	.824386
.7400000	.821710	.823867	.827427	.832333	.838501
.7500000	.835207	.837457	.841172	.846295	.852741
.7600000	.848808	.851153	.855027	.860374	.867107
.7700000	.862513	.864956	.868995	.874572	.881601
.7800000	.876324	.878869	.883077	.888891	.896226
.7899999	.890243	.892893	.897275	.903334	.910984

$\alpha =$ .559999

Θ	K VALUES				
	.009966711	.039469502	.087332193	.151646642	.229848846
.8000000	.904273	.907029	.911590	.917902	.925877
.8100000	.918413	.921280	.926026	.932597	.940907
.8200000	.932667	.935647	.940582	.947420	.956076
.8300000	.947035	.950132	.955262	.962375	.971387
.8400000	.961520	.964736	.970067	.977463	.986841
.8500000	.976124	.979462	.984999	.992685	1.002441
.8600000	.990847	.994311	1.000059	1.008044	1.018189
.8700000	1.005691	1.009285	1.015250	1.023542	1.034086
.8799999	1.020658	1.024385	1.030573	1.039181	1.050136
.8899999	1.035751	1.039613	1.046029	1.054961	1.066340
.9000000	1.050969	1.054971	1.061622	1.070886	1.082699
.9100000	1.066315	1.070459	1.077351	1.086957	1.099217
.9200000	1.081790	1.086081	1.093219	1.103175	1.115894
.9300000	1.097396	1.101837	1.109227	1.119543	1.132734
.9400000	1.113134	1.117728	1.125377	1.136062	1.149737
.9500000	1.129005	1.133757	1.141671	1.152734	1.166905
.9600000	1.145012	1.149924	1.158110	1.169560	1.184241
.9699999	1.161155	1.166231	1.174695	1.186542	1.201747
.9799999	1.177435	1.182680	1.191428	1.203681	1.219422
.9899999	1.193854	1.199271	1.208310	1.220979	1.237271
1.0000000	1.210413	1.216006	1.225343	1.238438	1.255293
1.0100000	1.227113	1.232886	1.242527	1.256058	1.273491
1.0200000	1.243955	1.249911	1.259863	1.273841	1.291865
1.0300000	1.260941	1.267084	1.277354	1.291787	1.310418
1.0400000	1.278070	1.284405	1.294999	1.309899	1.329149
1.0500000	1.295344	1.301874	1.312800	1.328177	1.348062
1.0600000	1.312764	1.319494	1.330758	1.346621	1.367156
1.0699999	1.330331	1.337263	1.348873	1.365234	1.386432
1.0799999	1.348044	1.355184	1.367146	1.384015	1.405892
1.0899999	1.365904	1.373256	1.385577	1.402965	1.425536
1.1000000	1.383913	1.391480	1.404168	1.422084	1.445364
1.1100000	1.402070	1.409856	1.422918	1.441374	1.465378
1.1200000	1.420375	1.428385	1.441827	1.460834	1.485576
1.1300000	1.438829	1.447066	1.460896	1.480464	1.505961
1.1400000	1.457431	1.465900	1.480124	1.500265	1.526531
1.1500000	1.476181	1.484886	1.499513	1.520235	1.547286
1.1600000	1.495080	1.504024	1.519060	1.540376	1.568227
1.1700000	1.514126	1.523314	1.538766	1.560687	1.589353
1.1800000	1.533319	1.542755	1.558630	1.581166	1.610663
1.1899999	1.552659	1.562347	1.578652	1.601813	1.632157

$\alpha =$ .559999

Θ	K VALUES				
	.009966711	.039469502	.087332193	.151646642	.229848846
.2000000	1.572144	1.582088	1.598831	1.622629	1.653833
.2100000	1.591774	1.601978	1.619165	1.643610	1.675691
.2200000	1.611548	1.622015	1.639654	1.664756	1.697728
.2300000	1.631464	1.642199	1.660296	1.686065	1.719945
.2400000	1.651521	1.662527	1.681089	1.707537	1.742338
.2500000	1.671717	1.682999	1.702033	1.729169	1.764906
.2599999	1.692051	1.703612	1.723124	1.750959	1.787647
.2699999	1.712521	1.724365	1.744362	1.772905	1.810558
.2799999	1.733124	1.745255	1.765743	1.795005	1.833637
.2899999	1.753859	1.766280	1.787266	1.817255	1.856882
.3000000	1.774723	1.787437	1.808927	1.839655	1.880288
.3100000	1.795713	1.808724	1.830724	1.862199	1.903854
.3200000	1.816827	1.830138	1.852655	1.884886	1.927574
.3300000	1.838061	1.851677	1.874715	1.907711	1.951447
.3400000	1.859413	1.873336	1.896902	1.930671	1.975468
.3500000	1.880879	1.895112	1.919211	1.953763	1.999632
.3600000	1.902456	1.917002	1.941640	1.976983	2.023936
.3700000	1.924140	1.939002	1.964184	2.000326	2.048374
.3799999	1.945927	1.961109	1.986839	2.023787	2.072943
.3899999	1.967814	1.983317	2.009602	2.047363	2.097637
.4000000	1.989796	2.005624	2.032467	2.071049	2.122451
.4100000	2.011869	2.028024	2.055429	2.094840	2.147380
.4200000	2.034028	2.050513	2.078485	2.118729	2.172418
.4300000	2.056270	2.073085	2.101629	2.142714	2.197558
.4400000	2.078588	2.095738	2.124856	2.166787	2.222796
.4500000	2.100979	2.118464	2.148161	2.190943	2.248126
.4600000	2.123437	2.141260	2.171538	2.215177	2.273540
.4700000	2.145957	2.164119	2.194982	2.239482	2.299032
.4800000	2.168534	2.187037	2.218488	2.263853	2.324597
.4900000	2.191163	2.210008	2.242049	2.288283	2.350226
.5000000	2.213838	2.233027	2.265659	2.312767	2.375914
.5100000	2.236554	2.256088	2.289314	2.337297	2.401653
.5200000	2.259305	2.279184	2.313006	2.361868	2.427436
.5300000	2.282085	2.302310	2.336730	2.386472	2.453256
.5400000	2.304889	2.325461	2.360479	2.411104	2.479107
.5500000	2.327710	2.348631	2.384248	2.435757	2.504979
.5600000	2.350544	2.371813	2.408030	2.460423	2.530868
.5699999	2.373385	2.395001	2.431818	2.485097	2.556764
.5707963	2.375203	2.396847	2.433713	2.487062	2.558826
.5707963	2.375202	2.396846	2.433711	2.487060	2.558824

$\alpha =$ .559999

Θ	K VALUES				
	.318821117	.415016431	.514599755	.613601043	.708073407
.0000000	.000000	.000000	.000000	.000000	.000000
.0100000	.010000	.010000	.010000	.010000	.010000
.0200000	.020001	.020002	.020002	.020002	.020002
.0300000	.030006	.030006	.030007	.030007	.030008
.0400000	.040015	.040016	.040017	.040018	.040019
.0500000	.050030	.050032	.050034	.050036	.050038
.0600000	.060051	.060055	.060058	.060062	.060065
.0700000	.070082	.070087	.070093	.070099	.070104
.0800000	.080122	.080131	.080139	.080148	.080156
.0900000	.090175	.090186	.090198	.090211	.090222
.1000000	.100240	.100256	.100273	.100289	.100305
.1100000	.110319	.110341	.110363	.110385	.110406
.1200000	.120415	.120443	.120472	.120500	.120528
.1300000	.130528	.130563	.130600	.130637	.130672
.1400000	.140660	.140704	.140750	.140796	.140840
.1500000	.150812	.150867	.150923	.150980	.151034
.1600000	.160986	.161052	.161121	.161190	.161256
.1700000	.171183	.171263	.171346	.171429	.171508
.1800000	.181406	.181501	.181599	.181697	.181791
.1900000	.191654	.191766	.191882	.191998	.192109
.2000000	.201931	.202061	.202197	.202333	.202462
.2100000	.212237	.212388	.212546	.212703	.212854
.2200000	.222574	.222748	.222930	.223111	.223285
.2300000	.232943	.233143	.233351	.233559	.233758
.2400000	.243347	.243574	.243811	.244048	.244275
.2500000	.253786	.254044	.254312	.254580	.254838
.2600000	.264262	.264553	.264856	.265159	.265449
.2700000	.274777	.275104	.275444	.275784	.276111
.2800000	.285333	.285698	.286078	.286459	.286825
.2900000	.295930	.296337	.296761	.297186	.297594
.3000000	.306572	.307023	.307494	.307966	.308420
.3100000	.317258	.317758	.318279	.318802	.319305
.3200000	.327992	.328543	.329118	.329696	.330252
.3300000	.338774	.339380	.340014	.340650	.341263
.3400000	.349607	.350272	.350967	.351666	.352339
.3500000	.360492	.361219	.361981	.362746	.363485
.3600000	.371430	.372224	.373056	.373893	.374701
.3700000	.382424	.383289	.384196	.385109	.385991
.3800000	.393476	.394416	.395402	.396396	.397356
.3900000	.404586	.405606	.406677	.407756	.408801

$\alpha =$ .559999

Θ	K VALUES				
	.318821117	.415016431	.514599755	.613601043	.708073407
.4000000	.415757	.416862	.418022	.419192	.420326
.4100000	.426991	.428185	.429440	.430707	.431935
.4200000	.438289	.439577	.440932	.442302	.443630
.4300000	.449654	.451041	.452502	.453980	.455414
.4400000	.461086	.462579	.464152	.465744	.467291
.4500000	.472589	.474193	.475883	.477596	.479261
.4600000	.484164	.485884	.487698	.489539	.491330
.4700000	.495813	.497654	.499600	.501575	.503498
.4800000	.507537	.509507	.511590	.513707	.515770
.4900000	.519339	.521444	.523672	.525937	.528148
.5000000	.531221	.533468	.535847	.538269	.540636
.5100000	.543185	.545580	.548119	.550706	.553236
.5200000	.555232	.557782	.560489	.563249	.565952
.5300000	.567366	.570078	.572960	.575902	.578786
.5400000	.579587	.582469	.585535	.588668	.591743
.5500000	.591898	.594958	.598216	.601550	.604825
.5600000	.604301	.607547	.611007	.614551	.618036
.5700000	.616798	.620239	.623909	.627673	.631380
.5800000	.629391	.633035	.636925	.640920	.644859
.5900000	.642083	.645938	.650059	.654296	.658478
.6000000	.654876	.658951	.663313	.667802	.672240
.6100000	.667772	.672076	.676689	.681444	.686149
.6200000	.680772	.685316	.690191	.695222	.700209
.6300000	.693880	.698673	.703822	.709142	.714423
.6400000	.707098	.712150	.717584	.723207	.728795
.6500000	.720427	.725749	.731481	.737420	.743330
.6600000	.733870	.739474	.745515	.751784	.758032
.6700000	.747430	.753325	.759689	.766303	.772904
.6800000	.761109	.767307	.774007	.780980	.787951
.6899999	.774909	.781422	.788472	.795820	.803178
.7000000	.788832	.795673	.803087	.810826	.818588
.7100000	.802881	.810061	.817855	.826002	.834186
.7200000	.817059	.824591	.832778	.841351	.849977
.7300000	.831367	.839265	.847862	.856877	.865965
.7400000	.845808	.854085	.863108	.872585	.882154
.7500000	.860385	.869055	.878519	.888478	.898551
.7600000	.875099	.884177	.894101	.904559	.915159
.7700000	.889954	.899453	.909854	.920835	.931983
.7800000	.904952	.914888	.925784	.937307	.949028
.7899999	.920095	.930483	.941893	.953981	.966300

$\alpha =$ .559999

Θ	K VALUES				
	.318821117	.415016431	.514599755	.613601043	.708073407
.8000000	.935386	.946242	.958185	.970860	.983804
.8100000	.950827	.962168	.974663	.987949	1.001544
.8200000	.966420	.978262	.991331	1.005252	1.019526
.8300000	.982168	.994528	1.008191	1.022772	1.037755
.8400000	.998074	1.010970	1.025248	1.040516	1.056237
.8500000	1.014140	1.027589	1.042505	1.058486	1.074977
.8600000	1.030367	1.044388	1.059965	1.076687	1.093981
.8700000	1.046760	1.061371	1.077633	1.095123	1.113253
.8799999	1.063319	1.078541	1.095510	1.113799	1.132801
.8899999	1.080048	1.095899	1.113601	1.132719	1.152629
.9000000	1.096948	1.113449	1.131909	1.151888	1.172743
.9100000	1.114023	1.131193	1.150438	1.171309	1.193149
.9200000	1.131273	1.149135	1.169190	1.190988	1.213852
.9300000	1.148702	1.167276	1.188170	1.210928	1.234859
.9400000	1.166311	1.185620	1.207380	1.231133	1.256175
.9500000	1.184103	1.204169	1.226824	1.251609	1.277806
.9600000	1.202080	1.222925	1.246504	1.272359	1.299757
.9699999	1.220243	1.241891	1.266425	1.293387	1.322036
.9799999	1.238596	1.261070	1.286589	1.314698	1.344646
.9899999	1.257138	1.280463	1.306999	1.336295	1.367595
1.0000000	1.275874	1.300074	1.327658	1.358184	1.390888
1.0100000	1.294803	1.319903	1.348569	1.380367	1.414530
1.0200000	1.313928	1.339953	1.369734	1.402848	1.438527
1.0300000	1.333251	1.360227	1.391157	1.425632	1.462885
1.0400000	1.352772	1.380725	1.412839	1.448721	1.487609
1.0500000	1.372494	1.401450	1.434784	1.472120	1.512705
1.0600000	1.392417	1.422404	1.456993	1.495831	1.538176
1.0699999	1.412543	1.443587	1.479468	1.519858	1.564030
1.0799999	1.432872	1.465002	1.502212	1.544204	1.590270
1.0899999	1.453406	1.486649	1.525227	1.568872	1.616901
1.1000000	1.474145	1.508530	1.548513	1.593864	1.643929
1.1100000	1.495090	1.530645	1.572073	1.619183	1.671356
1.1200000	1.516242	1.552995	1.595907	1.644831	1.699187
1.1300000	1.537600	1.575581	1.620017	1.670810	1.727426
1.1400000	1.559165	1.598403	1.644404	1.697122	1.756077
1.1500000	1.580937	1.621461	1.669068	1.723768	1.785143
1.1600000	1.602915	1.644756	1.694009	1.750749	1.814626
1.1700000	1.625100	1.668286	1.719227	1.778066	1.844529
1.1800000	1.647491	1.692052	1.744723	1.805721	1.874854
1.1899999	1.670086	1.716053	1.770496	1.833712	1.905604

$\alpha =$ .559999

Θ	K VALUES				
	.318821117	.415016431	.514599755	.613601043	.708073407
1.2000000	1.692885	1.740288	1.796546	1.862041	1.936779
1.2100000	1.715888	1.764755	1.822870	1.890705	1.968380
1.2200000	1.739091	1.789454	1.849468	1.919705	2.000408
1.2300000	1.762494	1.814383	1.876338	1.949039	2.032862
1.2400000	1.786095	1.839539	1.903479	1.978706	2.065741
1.2500000	1.809892	1.864920	1.930887	2.008703	2.099045
1.2599999	1.833883	1.890524	1.958561	2.039027	2.132772
1.2699999	1.858064	1.916349	1.986497	2.069676	2.166918
1.2799999	1.882434	1.942390	2.014691	2.100646	2.201482
1.2899999	1.906988	1.968645	2.043141	2.131933	2.236459
1.3000000	1.931725	1.995110	2.071842	2.163534	2.271844
1.3100000	1.956640	2.021781	2.100789	2.195441	2.307633
.3200000	1.981729	2.048654	2.129978	2.227651	2.343820
.3300000	2.006989	2.075724	2.159404	2.260156	2.380397
.3400000	2.032414	2.102986	2.189060	2.292952	2.417359
.3500000	2.058001	2.130435	2.218941	2.326030	2.454695
.3600000	2.083745	2.158065	2.249040	2.359382	2.492398
.3700000	2.109640	2.185872	2.279351	2.393002	2.530458
.3799999	2.135682	2.213848	2.309866	2.426880	2.568864
.3899999	2.161864	2.241987	2.340578	2.461007	2.607605
.4000000	2.188182	2.270283	2.371480	2.495375	2.646670
.4100000	2.214628	2.298729	2.402562	2.529971	2.686044
.4200000	2.241196	2.327317	2.433817	2.564786	2.725715
.4300000	2.267881	2.356040	2.465234	2.599809	2.765668
.4400000	2.294676	2.384890	2.496806	2.635028	2.805888
.4500000	2.321573	2.413860	2.528522	2.670432	2.846360
.4600000	2.348565	2.442941	2.560373	2.706007	2.887067
.4700000	2.375646	2.472124	2.592349	2.741742	2.927992
.4800000	2.402808	2.501402	2.624439	2.777623	2.969117
.4900000	2.430043	2.530765	2.656632	2.813636	3.010425
.5000000	2.457343	2.560205	2.688919	2.849769	3.051896
.5100000	2.484702	2.589712	2.721287	2.886006	3.093511
.5200000	2.512110	2.619276	2.753725	2.922334	3.135252
.5300000	2.539560	2.648890	2.786223	2.958737	3.177097
.5400000	2.567043	2.678543	2.818768	2.995202	3.219026
.5500000	2.594552	2.708225	2.851350	3.031713	3.261020
.5600000	2.622079	2.737928	2.883955	3.068255	3.303057
.5699999	2.649614	2.767641	2.916574	3.104814	3.345117
.5707963	2.651807	2.770007	2.919172	3.107726	3.348466
.5707963	2.651805	2.770005	2.919171	3.107724	3.348464

$\alpha =$ .559999

Θ	K VALUES				
	.794250555	.868696860	.928444378	.971111163	.994996249
.0000000	.000000	.000000	.000000	.000000	.000000
.0100000	.010000	.010000	.010000	.010000	.010000
.0200000	.020002	.020002	.020002	.020002	.020002
.0300000	.030008	.030008	.030009	.030009	.030009
.0400000	.040020	.040021	.040021	.040022	.040022
.0500000	.050039	.050041	.050042	.050043	.050044
.0600000	.060069	.060071	.060073	.060075	.060076
.0700000	.070109	.070113	.070117	.070119	.070121
.0800000	.080163	.080170	.080175	.080178	.080180
.0900000	.090233	.090242	.090249	.090254	.090257
.1000000	.100319	.100332	.100342	.100349	.100353
.1100000	.110426	.110442	.110456	.110465	.110471
.1200000	.120553	.120575	.120592	.120605	.120612
.1300000	.130704	.130731	.130754	.130770	.130779
.1400000	.140880	.140915	.140942	.140962	.140973
.1500000	.151083	.151126	.151160	.151185	.151199
.1600000	.161316	.161368	.161410	.161440	.161456
.1700000	.171580	.171642	.171693	.171729	.171749
.1800000	.181877	.181952	.182012	.182055	.182079
.1900000	.192210	.192298	.192369	.192420	.192448
.2000000	.202581	.202684	.202767	.202826	.202859
.2100000	.212991	.213111	.213207	.213276	.213315
.2200000	.223444	.223582	.223693	.223772	.223817
.2300000	.233940	.234098	.234226	.234317	.234368
.2400000	.244483	.244663	.244809	.244913	.244971
.2500000	.255074	.255279	.255444	.255563	.255629
.2600000	.265716	.265948	.266134	.266268	.266343
.2700000	.276411	.276672	.276882	.277032	.277117
.2800000	.287161	.287454	.287689	.287858	.287953
.2900000	.297970	.298296	.298559	.298748	.298854
.3000000	.308838	.309201	.309494	.309704	.309822
.3100000	.319768	.320171	.320496	.320730	.320861
.3200000	.330764	.331210	.331569	.331828	.331973
.3300000	.341827	.342319	.342716	.343001	.343161
.3400000	.352960	.353501	.353938	.354252	.354429
.3500000	.364166	.364759	.365240	.365585	.365779
.3600000	.375446	.376097	.376623	.377001	.377214
.3700000	.386805	.387515	.388091	.388505	.388737
.3800000	.398244	.399019	.399647	.400099	.400353
.3900000	.409766	.410610	.411294	.411786	.412063

$\alpha =$ .559999

Θ	K VALUES				
	.794250555	.868696860	.928444378	.971111163	.994996249
.4000000	.421374	.422291	.423035	.423571	.423872
.4100000	.433071	.434066	.434874	.435456	.435783
.4200000	.444860	.445938	.446813	.447444	.447799
.4300000	.456744	.457910	.458857	.459540	.459925
.4400000	.468726	.469985	.471008	.471747	.472163
.4500000	.480808	.482166	.483271	.484068	.484518
.4600000	.492994	.494457	.495648	.496508	.496993
.4700000	.505288	.506862	.508144	.509070	.509593
.4800000	.517692	.519383	.520762	.521759	.522322
.4900000	.530209	.532025	.533506	.534578	.535183
.5000000	.542844	.544791	.546381	.547531	.548181
.5100000	.555599	.557685	.559389	.560624	.561322
.5200000	.568479	.570711	.572537	.573860	.574608
.5300000	.581486	.583872	.585826	.587244	.588045
.5400000	.594624	.597174	.599263	.600780	.601638
.5500000	.607897	.610619	.612852	.614474	.615392
.5600000	.621310	.624213	.626597	.628330	.629311
.5700000	.634865	.637960	.640503	.642353	.643401
.5800000	.648567	.651863	.654575	.656549	.657668
.5900000	.662420	.665929	.668818	.670923	.672117
.6000000	.676428	.680160	.683237	.685480	.686754
.6100000	.690595	.694563	.697837	.700227	.701584
.6200000	.704927	.709142	.712624	.715168	.716614
.6300000	.719426	.723902	.727604	.730311	.731850
.6400000	.734098	.738848	.742782	.745661	.747299
.6500000	.748947	.753985	.758163	.761224	.762967
.6600000	.763978	.769320	.773755	.777008	.778861
.6700000	.779196	.784857	.789563	.793018	.794988
.6800000	.794606	.800602	.805594	.809263	.811356
.6899999	.810213	.816561	.821854	.825748	.827972
.7000000	.826022	.832741	.838351	.842483	.844845
.7100000	.842038	.849146	.855090	.859474	.861982
.7200000	.858266	.865784	.872080	.876729	.879391
.7300000	.874713	.882661	.889327	.894257	.897082
.7400000	.891384	.899784	.906840	.912066	.915063
.7500000	.908284	.917159	.924627	.930164	.933343
.7600000	.925420	.934793	.942694	.948562	.951934
.7700000	.942796	.952694	.961052	.967267	.970843
.7800000	.960421	.970868	.979707	.986291	.990082
.7899999	.978298	.989324	.998670	1.005642	1.009662

$\alpha =$ .559999

Θ	K VALUES				
	.794250555	.868696860	.928444378	.971111163	.994996249
.8000000	.996436	1.008069	1.017949	1.025332	1.029593
.8100000	1.014840	1.027111	1.037553	1.045370	1.049887
.8200000	1.033517	1.046458	1.057493	1.065769	1.070557
.8300000	1.052473	1.066118	1.077778	1.086539	1.091614
.8400000	1.071716	1.086099	1.098419	1.107692	1.113071
.8500000	1.091252	1.106412	1.119426	1.129241	1.134943
.8600000	1.111089	1.127063	1.140810	1.151198	1.157242
.8700000	1.131233	1.148064	1.162583	1.173577	1.179983
.8799999	1.151692	1.169422	1.184755	1.196392	1.203182
.8899999	1.172473	1.191147	1.207339	1.219655	1.226855
.9000000	1.193583	1.213250	1.230348	1.243384	1.251017
.9100000	1.215032	1.235740	1.253793	1.267592	1.275685
.9200000	1.236825	1.258627	1.277689	1.292295	1.300878
.9300000	1.258971	1.281922	1.302048	1.317510	1.326613
.9400000	1.281477	1.305636	1.326885	1.343254	1.352911
.9500000	1.304353	1.329779	1.352214	1.369545	1.379791
.9600000	1.327605	1.354363	1.378050	1.396401	1.407274
.9699999	1.351242	1.379399	1.404407	1.423842	1.435383
.9799999	1.375273	1.404898	1.431302	1.451887	1.464140
.9899999	1.399704	1.430873	1.458751	1.480558	1.493569
1.0000000	1.424546	1.457335	1.486771	1.509875	1.523696
1.0100000	1.449806	1.484296	1.515378	1.539862	1.554548
1.0200000	1.475492	1.511769	1.544591	1.570541	1.586151
1.0300000	1.501612	1.539766	1.574428	1.601937	1.618534
1.0400000	1.528176	1.568301	1.604906	1.634076	1.651730
1.0500000	1.555192	1.597386	1.636047	1.666983	1.685768
1.0600000	1.582666	1.627034	1.667869	1.700687	1.720684
1.0699999	1.610609	1.657258	1.700393	1.735217	1.756512
1.0799999	1.639028	1.688072	1.733639	1.770602	1.793290
1.0899999	1.667931	1.719489	1.767630	1.806874	1.831058
1.1000000	1.697326	1.751523	1.802388	1.844065	1.869857
1.1100000	1.727220	1.784187	1.837935	1.882211	1.909731
1.1200000	1.757621	1.817495	1.874293	1.921345	1.950727
1.1300000	1.788537	1.851460	1.911488	1.961507	1.992894
1.1400000	1.819974	1.886095	1.949543	2.002734	2.036284
1.1500000	1.851939	1.921415	1.988484	2.045068	2.080954
1.1600000	1.884438	1.957432	2.028334	2.088552	2.126962
1.1700000	1.917478	1.994160	2.069121	2.133230	2.174372
1.1800000	1.951064	2.031610	2.110871	2.179150	2.223251
1.1899999	1.985201	2.069797	2.153610	2.226359	2.273669

$\alpha =$ .559999

Θ	K VALUES				
	.794250555	.868696860	.928444378	.971111163	.994996249
.2000000	2.019894	2.108731	2.197366	2.274911	2.325706
.2100000	2.055147	2.148425	2.242165	2.324858	2.379442
.2200000	2.090964	2.188890	2.288035	2.376257	2.434966
.2300000	2.127348	2.230136	2.335004	2.429166	2.492374
.2400000	2.164301	2.272173	2.383100	2.483648	2.551767
.2500000	2.201824	2.315011	2.432351	2.539768	2.613257
.2599999	2.239918	2.358658	2.482783	2.597592	2.676964
.2699999	2.278583	2.403120	2.534424	2.657192	2.743017
.2799999	2.317818	2.448404	2.587301	2.718641	2.811559
.2899999	2.357622	2.494516	2.641439	2.782016	2.882742
.3000000	2.397991	2.541458	2.696864	2.847399	2.956737
.3100000	2.438921	2.589233	2.753597	2.914870	3.033726
.3200000	2.480407	2.637841	2.811662	2.984516	3.113913
.3300000	2.522443	2.687281	2.871079	3.056426	3.197520
.3400000	2.565022	2.737550	2.931865	3.130693	3.284793
.3500000	2.608135	2.788643	2.994035	3.207408	3.376006
.3600000	2.651772	2.840553	3.057602	3.286667	3.471462
.3700000	2.695922	2.893269	3.122573	3.368565	3.571498
.3799999	2.740573	2.946781	3.188954	3.453198	3.676491
.3899999	2.785710	3.001073	3.256743	3.540658	3.786865
.4000000	2.831320	3.056129	3.325936	3.631035	3.903094
.4100000	2.877384	3.111927	3.396520	3.724413	4.025710
.4200000	2.923885	3.168447	3.468478	3.820869	4.155319
.4300000	2.970804	3.225661	3.541785	3.920465	4.292601
.4400000	3.018120	3.283542	3.616408	4.023253	4.438323
.4500000	3.065812	3.342057	3.692308	4.129262	4.593352
.4600000	3.113856	3.401173	3.769435	4.238499	4.758659
.4700000	3.162229	3.460852	3.847733	4.350940	4.935323
.4800000	3.210903	3.521054	3.927133	4.466527	5.124525
.4900000	3.259854	3.581735	4.007560	4.585163	5.327523
1.5000000	3.309053	3.642851	4.088931	4.706704	5.545604
1.5100000	3.358472	3.704353	4.171149	4.830955	5.779962
1.5200000	3.408081	3.766191	4.254115	4.957672	6.031538
1.5300000	3.457850	3.828313	4.337717	5.086554	6.300730
1.5400000	3.507748	3.890666	4.421839	5.217251	6.587022
1.5500000	3.557745	3.953194	4.506360	5.349366	6.888560
1.5600000	3.607809	4.015840	4.591153	5.482462	7.201852
1.5699999	3.657907	4.078549	4.676087	5.616077	7.521801
1.5707963	3.661897	4.083543	4.682853	5.626725	7.547386
1.5707963	3.661894	4.083541	4.682850	5.626721	7.547377

$\alpha =$ •579999

Θ	K VALUES				
	•009966711	•039469502	•087332193	•151646642	•229848846
•0000000	•000000	•000000	•000000	•000000	•000000
•0100000	•010000	•010000	•010000	•010000	•010000
•0200000	•020001	•020001	•020001	•020001	•020001
•0300000	•030005	•030005	•030005	•030005	•030006
•0400000	•040012	•040012	•040013	•040014	•040014
•0500000	•050024	•050025	•050026	•050027	•050028
•0600000	•060042	•060043	•060044	•060047	•060050
•0700000	•070066	•070068	•070071	•070075	•070079
•0800000	•080099	•080102	•080106	•080112	•080118
•0900000	•090142	•090145	•090151	•090159	•090169
•1000000	•100195	•100200	•100208	•100218	•100232
•1100000	•110260	•110266	•110277	•110291	•110308
•1200000	•120337	•120346	•120360	•120378	•120401
•1300000	•130429	•130440	•130457	•130481	•130510
•1400000	•140536	•140550	•140572	•140601	•140637
•1500000	•150660	•150676	•150704	•150740	•150784
•1600000	•160801	•160821	•160854	•160899	•160952
•1700000	•170962	•170986	•171025	•171078	•171143
•1800000	•181142	•181171	•181218	•181281	•181358
•1900000	•191344	•191378	•191433	•191507	•191598
•2000000	•201569	•201608	•201673	•201759	•201865
•2100000	•211817	•211863	•211938	•212038	•212160
•2200000	•222091	•222143	•222229	•222345	•222486
•2300000	•232391	•232451	•232549	•232681	•232842
•2400000	•242718	•242787	•242898	•243049	•243232
•2500000	•253074	•253152	•253278	•253449	•253656
•2600000	•263461	•263548	•263691	•263882	•264116
•2700000	•273879	•273977	•274136	•274351	•274614
•2800000	•284330	•284439	•284617	•284857	•285150
•2900000	•294814	•294936	•295134	•295401	•295727
•3000000	•305334	•305469	•305688	•305985	•306347
•3100000	•315891	•316040	•316282	•316609	•317010
•3200000	•326486	•326650	•326917	•327277	•327718
•3300000	•337120	•337300	•337593	•337989	•338473
•3400000	•347794	•347991	•348312	•348746	•349277
•3500000	•358511	•358726	•359077	•359551	•360132
•3600000	•369271	•369506	•369888	•370404	•371038
•3700000	•380076	•380331	•380746	•381308	•381997
•3800000	•390927	•391204	•391654	•392264	•393012
•3900000	•401826	•402125	•402613	•403273	•404084

$\alpha =$ .579999

Θ	K VALUES				
	.009966711	.039469502	.087332193	.151646642	.229848846
.4000000	.412773	.413097	.413624	.414338	.415215
.4100000	.423772	.424120	.424689	.425459	.426406
.4200000	.434822	.435197	.435809	.436639	.437659
.4300000	.445925	.446328	.446986	.447879	.448977
.4400000	.457083	.457516	.458222	.459180	.460360
.4500000	.468298	.468761	.469518	.470545	.471811
.4600000	.479570	.480066	.480876	.481976	.483331
.4700000	.490902	.491431	.492297	.493472	.494922
.4800000	.502294	.502859	.503783	.505038	.506587
.4900000	.513749	.514351	.515336	.516674	.518326
.5000000	.525268	.525909	.526957	.528382	.530143
.5100000	.536853	.537534	.538648	.540164	.542038
.5200000	.548504	.549227	.550410	.552022	.554014
.5300000	.560225	.560991	.562247	.563957	.566073
.5400000	.572015	.572827	.574158	.575971	.578217
.5500000	.583878	.584738	.586146	.588067	.590447
.5600000	.595814	.596723	.598213	.600246	.602767
.5700000	.607826	.608786	.610361	.612510	.615177
.5800000	.619914	.620928	.622590	.624861	.627680
.5900000	.632081	.633150	.634904	.637300	.640278
.6000000	.644329	.645455	.647304	.649831	.652973
.6100000	.656658	.657844	.659791	.662454	.665768
.6200000	.669072	.670319	.672368	.675172	.678664
.6300000	.681571	.682882	.685036	.687987	.691663
.6400000	.694157	.695534	.697798	.700900	.704769
.6500000	.706832	.708278	.710655	.713914	.717982
.6600000	.719598	.721115	.723609	.727031	.731305
.6700000	.732457	.734046	.736662	.740253	.744741
.6800000	.745410	.747075	.749817	.753582	.758292
.6899999	.758460	.760203	.763074	.767020	.771959
.7000000	.771608	.773432	.776437	.780569	.785746
.7100000	.784856	.786763	.789906	.794231	.799655
.7200000	.798206	.800198	.803484	.808009	.813687
.7300000	.811659	.813740	.817174	.821904	.827845
.7400000	.825218	.827390	.830976	.835919	.842132
.7500000	.838884	.841151	.844893	.850055	.856550
.7600000	.852660	.855024	.858928	.864316	.871102
.7700000	.866547	.869010	.873081	.878703	.885789
.7800000	.880547	.883113	.887356	.893218	.900614
.7899999	.894663	.897334	.901753	.907864	.915579

$\alpha =$ •579999

Θ	K VALUES				
	•009966711	•039469502	•087332193	•151646642	•229848846
•8000000	•908895	•911675	•916276	•922643	•930688
•8100000	•923246	•926138	•930926	•937556	•945941
•8200000	•937717	•940725	•945705	•952606	•961342
•8300000	•952312	•955437	•960616	•967796	•976894
•8400000	•967030	•970277	•975660	•983127	•992597
•8500000	•981876	•985247	•990839	•998602	1•008455
•8600000	•996849	1•000349	1•006155	1•014222	1•024471
•8700000	1•011952	1•015584	1•021611	1•029990	1•040646
•8799999	1•027188	1•030954	1•037208	1•045909	1•056983
•8899999	1•042557	1•046461	1•052948	1•061979	1•073484
•9000000	1•058061	1•062108	1•068834	1•078203	1•090151
•9100000	1•073703	1•077896	1•084867	1•094584	1•106988
•9200000	1•089484	1•093826	1•101048	1•111123	1•123995
•9300000	1•105406	1•109901	1•117381	1•127822	1•141175
•9400000	1•121470	1•126121	1•133866	1•144684	1•158531
•9500000	1•137679	1•142490	1•150505	1•161709	1•176064
•9600000	1•154033	1•159009	1•167301	1•178901	1•193776
•9699999	1•170535	1•175679	1•184255	1•196260	1•211670
•9799999	1•187185	1•192501	1•201368	1•213789	1•229748
•9899999	1•203986	1•209478	1•218643	1•231490	1•248012
1•0000000	1•220939	1•226611	1•236080	1•249363	1•266462
1•0100000	1•238044	1•243900	1•253682	1•267411	1•285102
1•0200000	1•255305	1•261349	1•271449	1•285635	1•303932
1•0300000	1•272721	1•278957	1•289383	1•304037	1•322955
1•0400000	1•290293	1•296726	1•307485	1•322618	1•342172
1•0500000	1•308024	1•314657	1•325756	1•341378	1•361584
1•0600000	1•325914	1•332752	1•344198	1•360321	1•381193
1•0699999	1•343964	1•351011	1•362812	1•379445	1•401000
1•0799999	1•362174	1•369434	1•381598	1•398753	1•421006
1•0899999	1•380546	1•388023	1•400557	1•418246	1•441212
1•1000000	1•399080	1•406779	1•419690	1•437923	1•461619
1•1100000	1•417777	1•425702	1•438997	1•457786	1•482228
1•1200000	1•436636	1•444792	1•458479	1•477836	1•503038
1•1300000	1•455659	1•464049	1•478136	1•498071	1•524051
1•1400000	1•474846	1•483474	1•497969	1•518494	1•545267
1•1500000	1•494195	1•503067	1•517977	1•539103	1•566687
1•1600000	1•513708	1•522828	1•538160	1•559899	1•588309
1•1700000	1•533385	1•542756	1•558518	1•580881	1•610133
1•1800000	1•553223	1•562851	1•579050	1•602049	1•632160
1•1899999	1•573224	1•583112	1•599757	1•623403	1•654388

$\alpha =$ .579999

θ	K VALUES				
	.009966711	.039469502	.087332193	.151646642	.229848846
.2000000	1.593387	1.603540	1.620636	1.644941	1.676818
.2100000	1.613710	1.624131	1.641688	1.666663	1.699447
.2200000	1.634192	1.644887	1.662911	1.688566	1.722274
.2300000	1.654833	1.665805	1.684304	1.710651	1.745299
.2400000	1.675630	1.686884	1.705865	1.732916	1.768518
.2500000	1.696583	1.708122	1.727593	1.755357	1.791931
.2599999	1.717689	1.729518	1.749485	1.777975	1.815536
.2699999	1.738946	1.751069	1.771540	1.800765	1.839329
.2799999	1.760353	1.772773	1.793755	1.823727	1.863308
.2899999	1.781907	1.794629	1.816128	1.846856	1.887471
.3000000	1.803605	1.816632	1.838655	1.870151	1.911813
.3100000	1.825445	1.838781	1.861335	1.893608	1.936333
.3200000	1.847423	1.861072	1.884163	1.917224	1.961025
.3300000	1.869536	1.883503	1.907137	1.940995	1.985886
.3400000	1.891782	1.906068	1.930253	1.964916	2.010912
.3500000	1.914156	1.928766	1.953506	1.988985	2.036099
.3600000	1.936655	1.951591	1.976893	2.013197	2.061441
.3700000	1.959275	1.974541	2.000410	2.037547	2.086934
.3799999	1.982011	1.997610	2.024052	2.062030	2.112573
.3899999	2.004859	2.020794	2.047814	2.086641	2.138351
.4000000	2.027814	2.044088	2.071691	2.111376	2.164265
.4100000	2.050873	2.067488	2.095679	2.136229	2.190306
.4200000	2.074029	2.090988	2.119772	2.161193	2.216470
.4300000	2.097277	2.114584	2.143964	2.186264	2.242749
.4400000	2.120613	2.138269	2.168250	2.211434	2.269138
.4500000	2.144031	2.162038	2.192624	2.236698	2.295629
.4600000	2.167525	2.185885	2.217079	2.262050	2.322216
.4700000	2.191090	2.209804	2.241611	2.287483	2.348890
.4800000	2.214719	2.233790	2.266211	2.312989	2.375646
.4900000	2.238407	2.257836	2.290875	2.338563	2.402474
.5000000	2.262147	2.281936	2.315595	2.364196	2.429369
.5100000	2.285934	2.306084	2.340364	2.389883	2.456321
.5200000	2.309760	2.330272	2.365176	2.415615	2.483323
.5300000	2.333619	2.354494	2.390024	2.441385	2.510367
.5400000	2.357505	2.378744	2.414901	2.467186	2.537444
.5500000	2.381412	2.403015	2.439800	2.493011	2.564547
.5600000	2.405333	2.427300	2.464713	2.518851	2.591667
1.5699999	2.429260	2.451592	2.489635	2.544700	2.618796
1.5707963	2.431166	2.453527	2.491619	2.546758	2.620957
1.5707963	2.431164	2.453525	2.491617	2.546757	2.620955

$\alpha =$ .579999

θ	K VALUES				
	.318821117	.415016431	.514599755	.613601043	.708073407
.0000000	.000000	.000000	.000000	.000000	.000000
.0100000	.010000	.010000	.010000	.010000	.010000
.0200000	.020001	.020002	.020002	.020002	.020002
.0300000	.030006	.030007	.030007	.030007	.030008
.0400000	.040015	.040016	.040017	.040018	.040019
.0500000	.050030	.050032	.050034	.050036	.050038
.0600000	.060053	.060056	.060060	.060063	.060067
.0700000	.070084	.070090	.070095	.070101	.070106
.0800000	.080126	.080134	.080143	.080151	.080159
.0900000	.090179	.090191	.090203	.090215	.090227
.1000000	.100246	.100263	.100279	.100296	.100312
.1100000	.110328	.110350	.110372	.110394	.110415
.1200000	.120427	.120454	.120483	.120512	.120540
.1300000	.130543	.130578	.130615	.130652	.130687
.1400000	.140678	.140723	.140769	.140815	.140858
.1500000	.150835	.150889	.150946	.151003	.151057
.1600000	.161014	.161080	.161149	.161218	.161284
.1700000	.171217	.171297	.171379	.171462	.171541
.1800000	.181445	.181540	.181639	.181737	.181831
.1900000	.191701	.191813	.191929	.192045	.192156
.2000000	.201985	.202116	.202252	.202387	.202517
.2100000	.212300	.212452	.212609	.212767	.212917
.2200000	.222647	.222821	.223003	.223184	.223358
.2300000	.233027	.233227	.233435	.233643	.233842
.2400000	.243442	.243670	.243907	.244144	.244371
.2500000	.253894	.254152	.254420	.254689	.254947
.2600000	.264384	.264675	.264978	.265281	.265572
.2700000	.274914	.275241	.275581	.275922	.276249
.2800000	.285486	.285851	.286232	.286613	.286980
.2900000	.296101	.296508	.296933	.297358	.297767
.3000000	.306761	.307213	.307685	.308157	.308612
.3100000	.317468	.317968	.318490	.319014	.319518
.3200000	.328224	.328775	.329352	.329930	.330487
.3300000	.339030	.339636	.340271	.340907	.341521
.3400000	.349887	.350553	.351249	.351949	.352623
.3500000	.360799	.361527	.362290	.363056	.363796
.3600000	.371765	.372561	.373394	.374232	.375041
.3700000	.382790	.383656	.384564	.385479	.386362
.3800000	.393873	.394815	.395803	.396799	.397761
.3900000	.405018	.406040	.407112	.408194	.409240

$\alpha =$ .579999

Θ	K VALUES				
	.318821117	.415016431	.514599755	.613601043	.708073407
.4000000	.416225	.417332	.418494	.419667	.420803
.4100000	.427497	.428694	.429951	.431221	.432451
.4200000	.438836	.440127	.441485	.442858	.444189
.4300000	.450243	.451634	.453099	.454580	.456018
.4400000	.461721	.463218	.464794	.466390	.467941
.4500000	.473272	.474879	.476574	.478291	.479961
.4600000	.484897	.486621	.488441	.490286	.492082
.4700000	.496599	.498446	.500397	.502377	.504306
.4800000	.508379	.510355	.512444	.514567	.516636
.4900000	.520240	.522352	.524586	.526858	.529076
.5000000	.532184	.534437	.536824	.539254	.541629
.5100000	.544212	.546615	.549162	.551758	.554297
.5200000	.556328	.558887	.561602	.564372	.567085
.5300000	.568532	.571255	.574147	.577100	.579995
.5400000	.580828	.583722	.586799	.589944	.593031
.5500000	.593217	.596290	.599561	.602908	.606196
.5600000	.605703	.608962	.612436	.615995	.619495
.5700000	.618286	.621741	.625427	.629207	.632930
.5800000	.630969	.634628	.638536	.642549	.646506
.5900000	.643755	.647627	.651767	.656024	.660225
.6000000	.656646	.660741	.665123	.669634	.674093
.6100000	.669645	.673970	.678606	.683384	.688113
.6200000	.682752	.687319	.692219	.697276	.702288
.6300000	.695972	.700791	.705966	.711315	.716624
.6400000	.709307	.714387	.719850	.725504	.731124
.6500000	.722758	.728110	.733874	.739847	.745791
.6600000	.736328	.741964	.748041	.754347	.760632
.6700000	.750021	.755951	.762354	.769008	.775650
.6800000	.763838	.770074	.776817	.783833	.790849
.6899999	.777781	.784336	.791432	.798828	.806234
.7000000	.791855	.798740	.806204	.813996	.821810
.7100000	.806060	.813289	.821136	.829340	.837581
.7200000	.820400	.827985	.836231	.844864	.853553
.7300000	.834877	.842832	.851492	.860574	.869730
.7400000	.849494	.857833	.866923	.876473	.886117
.7500000	.864253	.872990	.882528	.892565	.902718
.7600000	.879158	.888307	.898311	.908854	.919541
.7700000	.894210	.903787	.914274	.925346	.936588
.7800000	.909413	.919433	.930421	.942043	.953867
.7899999	.924769	.935247	.946757	.958952	.971382

$\alpha =$ •579999

θ	K VALUES				
	•318821117	•415016431	•514599755	•613601043	•708073407
•8000000	•940281	•951234	•963285	•976075	•989139
•8100000	•955951	•967396	•980008	•993418	1•007143
•8200000	•971783	•983737	•996930	1•010986	1•025400
•8300000	•987779	1•000259	1•014056	1•028782	1•043915
•8400000	1•003941	1•016965	1•031388	1•046811	1•062695
•8500000	1•020273	1•033860	1•048931	1•065079	1•081746
•8600000	1•036776	1•050945	1•066688	1•083589	1•101072
•8700000	1•053455	1•068224	1•084663	1•102348	1•120681
•8799999	1•070311	1•085701	1•102861	1•121358	1•140579
•8899999	1•087346	1•103378	1•121284	1•140625	1•160770
•9000000	1•104565	1•121258	1•139937	1•160155	1•181263
•9100000	1•121968	1•139345	1•158823	1•179951	1•202062
•9200000	1•139560	1•157641	1•177946	1•200018	1•223175
•9300000	1•157341	1•176149	1•197310	1•220361	1•244607
•9400000	1•175316	1•194873	1•216918	1•240986	1•266365
•9500000	1•193486	1•213816	1•236774	1•261896	1•288455
•9600000	1•211853	1•232980	1•256882	1•283097	1•310884
•9699999	1•230420	1•252368	1•277246	1•304593	1•333657
•9799999	1•249190	1•271982	1•297868	1•326388	1•356782
•9899999	1•268164	1•291826	1•318753	1•348488	1•380264
1•0000000	1•287344	1•311903	1•339903	1•370896	1•404111
1•0100000	1•306733	1•332214	1•361321	1•393618	1•428327
1•0200000	1•326333	1•352762	1•383012	1•416658	1•452920
1•0300000	1•346146	1•373549	1•404978	1•440019	1•477896
1•0400000	1•366173	1•394579	1•427222	1•463706	1•503260
1•0500000	1•386415	1•415852	1•449746	1•487723	1•529018
1•0600000	1•406876	1•437370	1•472554	1•512074	1•555177
1•0699999	1•427556	1•459137	1•495649	1•536762	1•581742
1•0799999	1•448455	1•481153	1•519031	1•561792	1•608719
1•0899999	1•469577	1•503419	1•542704	1•587165	1•636113
1•1000000	1•490922	1•525938	1•566670	1•612887	1•663928
1•1100000	1•512489	1•548711	1•590930	1•638958	1•692171
1•1200000	1•534281	1•571738	1•615487	1•665383	1•720845
1•1300000	1•556298	1•595021	1•640340	1•692164	1•749956
1•1400000	1•578541	1•618560	1•665493	1•719302	1•779506
1•1500000	1•601009	1•642355	1•690945	1•746799	1•809501
1•1600000	1•623702	1•666407	1•716697	1•774658	1•839943
1•1700000	1•646620	1•690716	1•742750	1•802880	1•870835
1•1800000	1•669764	1•715281	1•769104	1•831464	1•902181
1•1899999	1•693132	1•740103	1•795758	1•860413	1•933982

$\alpha =$ .579999

Θ	K VALUES				
	.318821117	.415016431	.514599755	.613601043	.708073407
1.2000000	1.716724	1.765179	1.822712	1.889725	1.966240
1.2100000	1.740537	1.790510	1.849965	1.919401	1.998956
1.2200000	1.764572	1.816094	1.877517	1.949441	2.032131
1.2300000	1.788827	1.841929	1.905364	1.979842	2.065766
1.2400000	1.813299	1.868014	1.933507	2.010603	2.099859
1.2500000	1.837987	1.894346	1.961942	2.041723	2.134410
1.2599999	1.862889	1.920922	1.990666	2.073199	2.169417
1.2699999	1.888001	1.947740	2.019677	2.105028	2.204878
1.2799999	1.913321	1.974797	2.048971	2.137206	2.240790
1.2899999	1.938845	2.002090	2.078545	2.169729	2.277148
1.3000000	1.964571	2.029613	2.108393	2.202593	2.313949
1.3100000	1.990494	2.057364	2.138512	2.235792	2.351186
1.3200000	2.016611	2.085337	2.168897	2.269320	2.388855
1.3300000	2.042917	2.113528	2.199541	2.303172	2.426947
1.3400000	2.069407	2.141931	2.230438	2.337340	2.465456
1.3500000	2.096076	2.170541	2.261583	2.371818	2.504372
1.3600000	2.122920	2.199352	2.292969	2.406596	2.543686
1.3700000	2.149932	2.228358	2.324587	2.441666	2.583388
1.3799999	2.177108	2.257552	2.356431	2.477019	2.623466
1.3899999	2.204440	2.286928	2.388492	2.512645	2.663909
1.4000000	2.231923	2.316477	2.420763	2.548534	2.704704
1.4100000	2.259550	2.346193	2.453232	2.584675	2.745836
1.4200000	2.287314	2.376066	2.485892	2.621056	2.787291
1.4300000	2.315207	2.406090	2.518733	2.657665	2.829054
1.4400000	2.343223	2.436256	2.551744	2.694490	2.871108
1.4500000	2.371354	2.466555	2.584916	2.731518	2.913436
1.4600000	2.399592	2.496977	2.618236	2.768735	2.956021
1.4700000	2.427928	2.527514	2.651694	2.806126	2.998843
1.4800000	2.456355	2.558156	2.685279	2.843679	3.041885
1.4900000	2.484865	2.588893	2.718979	2.881378	3.085125
1.5000000	2.513448	2.619716	2.752782	2.919208	3.128544
1.5100000	2.542096	2.650613	2.786676	2.957153	3.172121
1.5200000	2.570799	2.681575	2.820648	2.995197	3.215834
1.5300000	2.599550	2.712592	2.854685	3.033326	3.259662
1.5400000	2.628338	2.743652	2.888775	3.071522	3.303582
1.5500000	2.657155	2.774746	2.922906	3.109769	3.347572
1.5600000	2.685992	2.805862	2.957063	3.148050	3.391610
1.5699999	2.714838	2.836990	2.991235	3.186350	3.435672
1.5707963	2.717135	2.839469	2.993956	3.189400	3.439181
1.5707963	2.717133	2.839467	2.993955	3.189396	3.439177

$\alpha =$ .579999

Θ	K VALUES				
	.794250555	.868696860	.928444378	.971111163	.994996249
.0000000	.000000	.000000	.000000	.000000	.000000
.0100000	.010000	.010000	.010000	.010000	.010000
.0200000	.020002	.020002	.020002	.020002	.020002
.0300000	.030008	.030009	.030009	.030009	.030009
.0400000	.040020	.040021	.040022	.040022	.040023
.0500000	.050040	.050042	.050043	.050044	.050044
.0600000	.060070	.060073	.060075	.060076	.060077
.0700000	.070111	.070116	.070119	.070122	.070123
.0800000	.080167	.080173	.080178	.080182	.080184
.0900000	.090238	.090247	.090254	.090259	.090262
.1000000	.100326	.100339	.100349	.100356	.100360
.1100000	.110435	.110451	.110465	.110474	.110480
.1200000	.120565	.120586	.120604	.120616	.120623
.1300000	.130719	.130746	.130769	.130784	.130793
.1400000	.140898	.140933	.140961	.140981	.140992
.1500000	.151106	.151149	.151183	.151208	.151221
.1600000	.161344	.161396	.161438	.161467	.161484
.1700000	.171613	.171676	.171726	.171762	.171782
.1800000	.181917	.181992	.182052	.182094	.182119
.1900000	.192257	.192345	.192416	.192467	.192495
.2000000	.202636	.202739	.202822	.202881	.202914
.2100000	.213055	.213175	.213271	.213340	.213378
.2200000	.223517	.223655	.223766	.223846	.223891
.2300000	.234025	.234183	.234310	.234402	.234453
.2400000	.244579	.244760	.244905	.245009	.245068
.2500000	.255183	.255388	.255554	.255672	.255738
.2600000	.265839	.266071	.266258	.266392	.266467
.2700000	.276549	.276810	.277021	.277171	.277256
.2800000	.287316	.287609	.287845	.288014	.288109
.2900000	.298142	.298469	.298732	.298921	.299027
.3000000	.309030	.309393	.309687	.309897	.310015
.3100000	.319981	.320385	.320710	.320944	.321075
.3200000	.330999	.331445	.331806	.332064	.332210
.3300000	.342086	.342578	.342976	.343262	.343422
.3400000	.353245	.353787	.354225	.354539	.354716
.3500000	.364478	.365073	.365554	.365899	.366094
.3600000	.375788	.376439	.376966	.377345	.377558
.3700000	.387178	.387890	.388466	.388881	.389114
.3800000	.398650	.399427	.400056	.400508	.400763
.3900000	.410208	.411053	.411739	.412232	.412509

$\alpha =$ .579999

Θ	K VALUES				
	.794250555	.868696860	.928444378	.971111163	.994996249
.4000000	.421853	.422773	.423518	.424055	.424357
.4100000	.433591	.434588	.435397	.435980	.436308
.4200000	.445422	.446502	.447379	.448012	.448368
.4300000	.457351	.458519	.459468	.460153	.460539
.4400000	.469379	.470642	.471668	.472408	.472825
.4500000	.481512	.482874	.483981	.484781	.485231
.4600000	.493751	.495218	.496412	.497275	.497761
.4700000	.506101	.507679	.508965	.509894	.510418
.4800000	.518564	.520260	.521643	.522643	.523207
.4900000	.531144	.532965	.534451	.535526	.536133
.5000000	.543844	.545797	.547392	.548547	.549199
.5100000	.556668	.558761	.560471	.561710	.562410
.5200000	.569620	.571860	.573693	.575021	.575771
.5300000	.582704	.585099	.587061	.588483	.589288
.5400000	.595923	.598482	.600580	.602102	.602964
.5500000	.609281	.612014	.614255	.615883	.616805
.5600000	.622782	.625697	.628091	.629831	.630816
.5700000	.636430	.639538	.642093	.643951	.645004
.5800000	.650230	.653541	.656265	.658248	.659372
.5900000	.664186	.667711	.670614	.672729	.673928
.6000000	.678301	.682052	.685143	.687398	.688678
.6100000	.692582	.696569	.699860	.702262	.703626
.6200000	.707031	.711268	.714769	.717327	.718780
.6300000	.721654	.726154	.729877	.732599	.734146
.6400000	.736456	.741233	.745189	.748084	.749732
.6500000	.751441	.756509	.760711	.763790	.765543
.6600000	.766614	.771988	.776450	.779723	.781587
.6700000	.781981	.787677	.792413	.795890	.797872
.6800000	.797546	.803581	.808605	.812298	.814406
.6899999	.813316	.819707	.825035	.828956	.831195
.7000000	.829295	.836061	.841709	.845871	.848249
.7100000	.845489	.852648	.858635	.863050	.865576
.7200000	.861903	.869477	.875819	.880503	.883185
.7300000	.878544	.886553	.893270	.898238	.901084
.7400000	.895418	.903884	.910996	.916263	.919284
.7500000	.912530	.921477	.929005	.934589	.937794
.7600000	.929887	.939338	.947306	.953224	.956624
.7700000	.947494	.957477	.965908	.972178	.975785
.7800000	.965360	.975900	.984818	.991461	.995287
.7899999	.983489	.994616	1.004048	1.011085	1.015142

$\alpha =$ .579999

θ	K VALUES				
	.794250555	.868696860	.928444378	.971111163	.994996249
.8000000	1.001889	1.013632	1.023606	1.031060	1.035362
.8100000	1.020567	1.032957	1.043502	1.051396	1.055958
.8200000	1.039529	1.052599	1.063747	1.072106	1.076944
.8300000	1.058783	1.072568	1.084350	1.093203	1.098331
.8400000	1.078336	1.092872	1.105324	1.114697	1.120135
.8500000	1.098196	1.113521	1.126679	1.136603	1.142369
.8600000	1.118370	1.134524	1.148427	1.158934	1.165047
.8700000	1.138865	1.155891	1.170579	1.181703	1.188185
.8799999	1.159690	1.177631	1.193148	1.204926	1.211800
.8899999	1.180853	1.199755	1.216147	1.228617	1.235906
.9000000	1.202361	1.222274	1.239589	1.252792	1.260523
.9100000	1.224223	1.245198	1.263487	1.277467	1.285667
.9200000	1.246447	1.268537	1.287855	1.302658	1.311358
.9300000	1.269041	1.292304	1.312707	1.328384	1.337614
.9400000	1.292014	1.316510	1.338059	1.354662	1.364457
.9500000	1.315375	1.341165	1.363925	1.381511	1.391908
.9600000	1.339133	1.366283	1.390322	1.408950	1.419988
.9699999	1.363295	1.391875	1.417265	1.437001	1.448721
.9799999	1.387872	1.417954	1.444772	1.465684	1.478132
.9899999	1.412872	1.444533	1.472859	1.495021	1.508246
1.0000000	1.438304	1.471624	1.501545	1.525035	1.539090
1.0100000	1.464177	1.499240	1.530847	1.555750	1.570690
1.0200000	1.490501	1.527395	1.560785	1.587191	1.603078
1.0300000	1.517284	1.556102	1.591378	1.619383	1.636283
1.0400000	1.544536	1.585376	1.622646	1.652354	1.670337
1.0500000	1.572265	1.615229	1.654610	1.686131	1.705275
1.0600000	1.600481	1.645677	1.687290	1.720744	1.741133
1.0699999	1.629193	1.676733	1.720709	1.756224	1.777947
1.0799999	1.658409	1.708412	1.754889	1.792603	1.815757
1.0899999	1.688140	1.740728	1.789853	1.829913	1.854606
1.1000000	1.718392	1.773697	1.825625	1.868189	1.894537
1.1100000	1.749175	1.807332	1.862228	1.907469	1.935597
1.1200000	1.780497	1.841649	1.899688	1.947789	1.977835
1.1300000	1.812366	1.876661	1.938030	1.989189	2.021302
1.1400000	1.844790	1.912385	1.977281	2.031711	2.066056
1.1500000	1.877777	1.948833	2.017466	2.075398	2.112154
1.1600000	1.911333	1.986022	2.058612	2.120297	2.159658
1.1700000	1.945466	2.023964	2.100749	2.166453	2.208636
1.1800000	1.980182	2.062675	2.143903	2.213917	2.259159
1.1899999	2.015486	2.102167	2.188103	2.262741	2.311302

$\alpha =$ •579999

Θ	K VALUES				
	•794250555	•868696860	•928444378	•971111163	•994996249
1•2000000	2•051385	2•142454	2•233379	2•312979	2•365146
1•2100000	2•087882	2•183549	2•279759	2•364689	2•420779
1•2200000	2•124983	2•225464	2•327273	2•417930	2•478293
1•2300000	2•162690	2•268210	2•375951	2•472764	2•537788
1•2400000	2•201007	2•311799	2•425823	2•529257	2•599374
1•2500000	2•239935	2•356241	2•476917	2•587478	2•663167
1•2599999	2•279475	2•401545	2•529264	2•647498	2•729293
1•2699999	2•319629	2•447718	2•582893	2•709392	2•797888
1•2799999	2•360394	2•494769	2•637832	2•773237	2•869103
1•2899999	2•401770	2•542701	2•694108	2•839116	2•943098
1•3000000	2•443753	2•591521	2•751750	2•907113	3•020052
1•3100000	2•486340	2•641230	2•810779	2•977315	3•100158
1•3200000	2•529525	2•691829	2•871222	3•049813	3•183628
1•3300000	2•573302	2•743316	2•933100	3•124702	3•270697
1•3400000	2•617663	2•795690	2•996430	3•202077	3•361625
1•3500000	2•662600	2•848944	3•061230	3•282038	3•456697
1•3600000	2•708102	2•903072	3•127513	3•364684	3•556231
1•3700000	2•754157	2•958063	3•195288	3•450116	3•660583
1•3799999	2•800751	3•013904	3•264559	3•538433	3•770148
1•3899999	2•847871	3•070581	3•335326	3•629735	3•885369
1•4000000	2•895501	3•128075	3•407583	3•724115	4•006747
1•4100000	2•943621	3•186365	3•481318	3•821662	4•134838
1•4200000	2•992214	3•245426	3•556513	3•922455	4•270276
1•4300000	3•041258	3•305232	3•633140	4•026563	4•413776
1•4400000	3•090732	3•365752	3•711166	4•134037	4•566142
1•4500000	3•140611	3•426951	3•790547	4•244909	4•728283
1•4600000	3•190872	3•488794	3•871233	4•359185	4•901216
1•4700000	3•241487	3•551241	3•953161	4•476840	5•086072
1•4800000	3•292430	3•614247	4•036261	4•597814	5•284089
1•4900000	3•343671	3•677768	4•120452	4•722001	5•496588
1•5000000	3•395182	3•741755	4•205644	4•849251	5•724912
1•5100000	3•446929	3•806156	4•291738	4•979359	5•970316
1•5200000	3•498883	3•870917	4•378625	5•112065	6•233783
1•5300000	3•551011	3•935983	4•466188	5•247053	6•515731
1•5400000	3•603278	4•001295	4•554304	5•383955	6•815613
1•5500000	3•655652	4•066796	4•642843	5•522351	7•131487
1•5600000	3•708098	4•132423	4•731671	5•661782	7•459689
1•5699999	3•760581	4•198118	4•820650	5•801758	7•794872
1•5707963	3•764761	4•203350	4•827738	5•812914	7•821675
1•5707963	3•764756	4•203345	4•827731	5•812905	7•821660

$\alpha =$ .599999

θ	K VALUES				
	.009966711	.039469502	.087332193	.151646642	.229848846
.0000000	.000000	.000000	.000000	.000000	.000000
.0100000	.010000	.010000	.010000	.010000	.010000
.0200000	.020001	.020001	.020001	.020001	.020001
.0300000	.030005	.030005	.030005	.030006	.030006
.0400000	.040012	.040013	.040013	.040014	.040015
.0500000	.050025	.050025	.050026	.050028	.050029
.0600000	.060043	.060044	.060046	.060048	.060051
.0700000	.070069	.070070	.070073	.070077	.070081
.0800000	.080103	.080105	.080110	.080115	.080122
.0900000	.090147	.090150	.090156	.090164	.090174
.1000000	.100201	.100206	.100214	.100225	.100238
.1100000	.110268	.110275	.110286	.110300	.110317
.1200000	.120349	.120357	.120371	.120390	.120412
.1300000	.130444	.130455	.130472	.130496	.130525
.1400000	.140555	.140568	.140590	.140620	.140656
.1500000	.150683	.150699	.150726	.150763	.150807
.1600000	.160829	.160849	.160882	.160926	.160980
.1700000	.170995	.171019	.171059	.171112	.171176
.1800000	.181182	.181211	.181257	.181320	.181397
.1900000	.191391	.191425	.191480	.191554	.191645
.2000000	.201623	.201663	.201727	.201814	.201919
.2100000	.211880	.211926	.212001	.212101	.212224
.2200000	.222163	.222216	.222302	.222418	.222559
.2300000	.232474	.232534	.232632	.232765	.232926
.2400000	.242813	.242882	.242993	.243144	.243327
.2500000	.253182	.253260	.253386	.253556	.253764
.2600000	.263582	.263670	.263812	.264004	.264238
.2700000	.274015	.274113	.274273	.274488	.274751
.2800000	.284482	.284591	.284770	.285010	.285303
.2900000	.294984	.295106	.295304	.295571	.295898
.3000000	.305523	.305658	.305877	.306174	.306536
.3100000	.316100	.316249	.316491	.316819	.317220
.3200000	.326716	.326880	.327147	.327508	.327950
.3300000	.337373	.337553	.337847	.338243	.338729
.3400000	.348072	.348270	.348591	.349025	.349557
.3500000	.358815	.359031	.359382	.359857	.360438
.3600000	.369603	.369838	.370221	.370738	.371373
.3700000	.380438	.380693	.381110	.381672	.382363
.3800000	.391321	.391598	.392049	.392660	.393410
.3900000	.402253	.402553	.403042	.403704	.404516

$\alpha =$ .599999

Θ	K VALUES				
	.009966711	.039469502	.087332193	.151646642	.229848846
.4000000	.413236	.413560	.414089	.414804	.415683
.4100000	.424272	.424621	.425191	.425963	.426912
.4200000	.435362	.435738	.436352	.437183	.438206
.4300000	.446507	.446912	.447571	.448466	.449566
.4400000	.457710	.458144	.458852	.459812	.460995
.4500000	.468971	.469436	.470195	.471225	.472493
.4600000	.480293	.480790	.481602	.482705	.484064
.4700000	.491676	.492207	.493075	.494254	.495708
.4800000	.503124	.503690	.504616	.505875	.507428
.4900000	.514636	.515239	.516227	.517569	.519227
.5000000	.526215	.526857	.527909	.529339	.531105
.5100000	.537862	.538545	.539663	.541185	.543065
.5200000	.549580	.550305	.551493	.553110	.555109
.5300000	.561370	.562139	.563399	.565115	.567239
.5400000	.573233	.574048	.575384	.577204	.579458
.5500000	.585172	.586035	.587449	.589377	.591767
.5600000	.597187	.598100	.599596	.601637	.604168
.5700000	.609282	.610246	.611828	.613986	.616664
.5800000	.621458	.622476	.624145	.626426	.629257
.5900000	.633715	.634789	.636551	.638958	.641950
.6000000	.646058	.647189	.649047	.651586	.654743
.6100000	.658486	.659678	.661634	.664310	.667640
.6200000	.671003	.672257	.674316	.677134	.680644
.6300000	.683610	.684928	.687093	.690059	.693755
.6400000	.696308	.697693	.699969	.703088	.706977
.6500000	.709100	.710554	.712945	.716222	.720313
.6600000	.721989	.723513	.726022	.729464	.733763
.6700000	.734974	.736573	.739205	.742817	.747332
.6800000	.748060	.749735	.752493	.756281	.761020
.6899999	.761247	.763001	.765890	.769861	.774832
.7000000	.774538	.776373	.779398	.783557	.788769
.7100000	.787935	.789854	.793019	.797373	.802833
.7200000	.801439	.803445	.806754	.811310	.817028
.7300000	.815053	.817149	.820607	.825371	.831356
.7400000	.828779	.830967	.834580	.839559	.845819
.7500000	.842619	.844903	.848674	.853875	.860420
.7600000	.856575	.858957	.862891	.868322	.875162
.7700000	.870649	.873132	.877235	.882903	.890046
.7800000	.884843	.887430	.891708	.897619	.905077
.7899999	.899160	.901854	.906311	.912474	.920256

$\alpha =$ .599999

Θ	K VALUES				
	.009966711	.039469502	.087332193	.151646642	.229848846
.8000000	.913601	.916406	.921047	.927470	.935586
.8100000	.928169	.931087	.935918	.942608	.951070
.8200000	.942865	.945900	.950927	.957892	.966710
.8300000	.957692	.960847	.966075	.973324	.982510
.8400000	.972652	.975931	.981366	.988907	.998471
.8500000	.987747	.991153	.996801	1.004642	1.014596
.8600000	1.002980	1.006516	1.012382	1.020533	1.030889
.8700000	1.018351	1.022021	1.028112	1.036581	1.047351
.8799999	1.033864	1.037671	1.043993	1.052789	1.063986
.8899999	1.049521	1.053469	1.060028	1.069160	1.080795
.9000000	1.065323	1.069416	1.076218	1.085696	1.097782
.9100000	1.081272	1.085514	1.092566	1.102399	1.114950
.9200000	1.097372	1.101765	1.109074	1.119271	1.132300
.9300000	1.113622	1.118172	1.125744	1.136315	1.149835
.9400000	1.130027	1.134736	1.142578	1.153534	1.167558
.9500000	1.146587	1.151460	1.159579	1.170929	1.185471
.9600000	1.163304	1.168346	1.176748	1.188502	1.203577
.9699999	1.180181	1.185394	1.194087	1.206256	1.221878
.9799999	1.197219	1.202608	1.211598	1.224193	1.240377
.9899999	1.214419	1.219989	1.229284	1.242315	1.259075
1.0000000	1.231785	1.237539	1.247146	1.260623	1.277975
1.0100000	1.249317	1.255259	1.265186	1.279121	1.297079
1.0200000	1.267016	1.273152	1.283405	1.297809	1.316388
1.0300000	1.284885	1.291218	1.301806	1.316689	1.335906
1.0400000	1.302925	1.309459	1.320389	1.335763	1.355634
1.0500000	1.321137	1.327877	1.339156	1.355034	1.375573
1.0600000	1.339523	1.346474	1.358110	1.374501	1.395725
1.0699999	1.358083	1.365249	1.377250	1.394167	1.416093
1.0799999	1.376820	1.384205	1.396578	1.414032	1.436677
1.0899999	1.395733	1.403342	1.416096	1.434099	1.457478
1.1000000	1.414824	1.422661	1.435804	1.454368	1.478498
1.1100000	1.434094	1.442163	1.455703	1.474840	1.499738
1.1200000	1.453542	1.461850	1.475793	1.495515	1.521199
1.1300000	1.473171	1.481720	1.496076	1.516395	1.542881
1.1400000	1.492979	1.501775	1.516552	1.537480	1.564785
1.1500000	1.512968	1.522015	1.537220	1.558770	1.586911
1.1600000	1.533137	1.542440	1.558082	1.580264	1.609260
1.1700000	1.553486	1.563050	1.579136	1.601965	1.631831
1.1800000	1.574015	1.583844	1.600383	1.623870	1.654625
1.1899999	1.594724	1.604823	1.621823	1.645979	1.677640

$\alpha =$ .599999

Θ	K VALUES				
	.009966711	.039469502	.087332193	.151646642	.229848846
1.2000000	1.615613	1.625985	1.643454	1.668292	1.700877
1.2100000	1.636679	1.647330	1.665276	1.690809	1.724334
1.2200000	1.657923	1.668857	1.687288	1.713527	1.748009
1.2300000	1.679342	1.690565	1.709488	1.736445	1.771903
1.2400000	1.700937	1.712452	1.731876	1.759563	1.796013
1.2500000	1.722705	1.734516	1.754449	1.782877	1.820337
1.2599999	1.744644	1.756756	1.777205	1.806387	1.844873
1.2699999	1.766752	1.779170	1.800143	1.830090	1.869618
1.2799999	1.789027	1.801755	1.823259	1.853984	1.894570
1.2899999	1.811467	1.824510	1.846552	1.878064	1.919726
1.3000000	1.834070	1.847430	1.870018	1.902330	1.945083
1.3100000	1.856831	1.870513	1.893655	1.926776	1.970637
1.3200000	1.879747	1.893756	1.917458	1.951400	1.996383
1.3300000	1.902816	1.917155	1.941424	1.976198	2.022319
1.3400000	1.926034	1.940707	1.965549	2.001165	2.048438
1.3500000	1.949397	1.964407	1.989830	2.026297	2.074737
1.3600000	1.972900	1.988251	2.014261	2.051589	2.101211
1.3700000	1.996539	2.012235	2.038838	2.077037	2.127853
1.3799999	2.020310	2.036355	2.063556	2.102635	2.154659
1.3899999	2.044208	2.060604	2.088410	2.128377	2.181622
1.4000000	2.068227	2.084978	2.113394	2.154258	2.208736
1.4100000	2.092363	2.109471	2.138503	2.180272	2.235995
1.4200000	2.116610	2.134078	2.163730	2.206412	2.263390
1.4300000	2.140961	2.158793	2.189070	2.232672	2.290917
1.4400000	2.165412	2.183609	2.214516	2.259045	2.318566
1.4500000	2.189956	2.208521	2.240062	2.285524	2.346331
1.4600000	2.214586	2.233521	2.265700	2.312102	2.374203
1.4700000	2.239297	2.258604	2.291424	2.338771	2.402175
1.4800000	2.264081	2.283762	2.317227	2.365524	2.430238
1.4900000	2.288931	2.308989	2.343102	2.392353	2.458384
1.5000000	2.313842	2.334277	2.369040	2.419250	2.486604
1.5100000	2.338804	2.359618	2.395034	2.446207	2.514889
1.5200000	2.363813	2.385006	2.421078	2.473216	2.543231
1.5300000	2.388859	2.410433	2.447161	2.500268	2.571619
1.5400000	2.413936	2.435892	2.473278	2.527355	2.600046
1.5500000	2.439036	2.461374	2.499420	2.554468	2.628502
1.5600000	2.464152	2.486873	2.525578	2.581600	2.656977
1.5699999	2.489275	2.512380	2.551745	2.608741	2.685463
1.5707963	2.491276	2.514411	2.553829	2.610902	2.687731
1.5707963	2.491274	2.514409	2.553827	2.610900	2.687729

$\alpha =$ .599999

Θ	K VALUES				
	.318821117	.415016431	.514599755	.613601043	.708073407
.0000000	.000000	.000000	.000000	.000000	.000000
.0100000	.010000	.010000	.010000	.010000	.010000
.0200000	.020002	.020002	.020002	.020002	.020002
.0300000	.030006	.030007	.030007	.030008	.030008
.0400000	.040016	.040017	.040018	.040019	.040020
.0500000	.050031	.050033	.050035	.050037	.050039
.0600000	.060054	.060058	.060061	.060065	.060068
.0700000	.070086	.070092	.070098	.070103	.070109
.0800000	.080129	.080138	.080146	.080155	.080163
.0900000	.090184	.090196	.090208	.090220	.090232
.1000000	.100253	.100269	.100286	.100303	.100318
.1100000	.110337	.110359	.110381	.110403	.110424
.1200000	.120438	.120466	.120495	.120524	.120551
.1300000	.130557	.130593	.130630	.130666	.130701
.1400000	.140697	.140741	.140787	.140833	.140877
.1500000	.150858	.150912	.150969	.151026	.151080
.1600000	.161041	.161108	.161177	.161246	.161311
.1700000	.171250	.171330	.171413	.171495	.171575
.1800000	.181485	.181580	.181679	.181777	.181871
.1900000	.191748	.191860	.191976	.192092	.192203
.2000000	.202040	.202171	.202307	.202442	.202572
.2100000	.212363	.212515	.212673	.212830	.212981
.2200000	.222720	.222895	.223076	.223258	.223432
.2300000	.233110	.233311	.233519	.233727	.233926
.2400000	.243537	.243765	.244002	.244239	.244467
.2500000	.254002	.254260	.254529	.254798	.255056
.2600000	.264506	.264797	.265101	.265404	.265695
.2700000	.275051	.275378	.275719	.276060	.276387
.2800000	.285639	.286005	.286386	.286768	.287135
.2900000	.296272	.296680	.297105	.297530	.297940
.3000000	.306951	.307404	.307876	.308349	.308804
.3100000	.317679	.318179	.318702	.319226	.319731
.3200000	.328456	.329008	.329585	.330164	.330722
.3300000	.339285	.339893	.340528	.341166	.341780
.3400000	.350168	.350835	.351532	.352233	.352908
.3500000	.361106	.361836	.362600	.363367	.364108
.3600000	.372102	.372899	.373733	.374572	.375383
.3700000	.383156	.384025	.384934	.385850	.386735
.3800000	.394272	.395216	.396206	.397203	.398167
.3900000	.405451	.406475	.407550	.408633	.409682

$\alpha =$ .599999

Θ	K VALUES				
	.318821117	.415016431	.514599755	.613601043	.708073407
.4000000	.416695	.417804	.418969	.420144	.421282
.4100000	.428006	.429205	.430465	.431737	.432970
.4200000	.439385	.440679	.442040	.443416	.444750
.4300000	.450836	.452230	.453698	.455183	.456624
.4400000	.462360	.463860	.465440	.467040	.468594
.4500000	.473958	.475570	.477269	.478991	.480665
.4600000	.485634	.487363	.489188	.491038	.492839
.4700000	.497389	.499242	.501198	.503184	.505119
.4800000	.509226	.511208	.513303	.515432	.517508
.4900000	.521146	.523264	.525506	.527785	.530010
.5000000	.533152	.535413	.537808	.540246	.542628
.5100000	.545246	.547657	.550213	.552818	.555365
.5200000	.557430	.559998	.562724	.565504	.568225
.5300000	.569707	.572440	.575342	.578306	.581212
.5400000	.582079	.584984	.588072	.591230	.594328
.5500000	.594548	.597633	.600916	.604277	.607578
.5600000	.607116	.610389	.613877	.617451	.620965
.5700000	.619786	.623256	.626958	.630755	.634494
.5800000	.632561	.636236	.640161	.644192	.648167
.5900000	.645443	.649332	.653491	.657767	.661989
.6000000	.658433	.662547	.666950	.671483	.675964
.6100000	.671536	.675883	.680542	.685344	.690096
.6200000	.684753	.689343	.694268	.699352	.704390
.6300000	.698087	.702931	.708134	.713512	.718849
.6400000	.711540	.716648	.722142	.727827	.733478
.6500000	.725115	.730498	.736295	.742302	.748281
.6600000	.738815	.744484	.750597	.756940	.763263
.6700000	.752643	.758610	.765051	.771746	.778429
.6800000	.766601	.772877	.779661	.786723	.793784
.6899999	.780691	.787289	.794431	.801876	.809331
.7000000	.794918	.801850	.809364	.817208	.825076
.7100000	.809283	.816562	.824463	.832725	.841025
.7200000	.823789	.831428	.839733	.848429	.857181
.7300000	.838439	.846452	.855176	.864327	.873551
.7400000	.853236	.861638	.870798	.880421	.890140
.7500000	.868182	.876987	.886601	.896718	.906953
.7600000	.883282	.892505	.902590	.913220	.923995
.7700000	.898537	.908193	.918768	.929934	.941272
.7800000	.913951	.924056	.935139	.946863	.958791
.7899999	.929526	.940096	.951708	.964012	.976555

$\alpha =$ .599999

θ	K VALUES				
	.318821117	.415016431	.514599755	.613601043	.708073407
.8000000	.945265	.956318	.968478	.981387	.994573
.8100000	.961173	.972724	.985454	.998992	1.012849
.8200000	.977250	.989318	1.002639	1.016832	1.031389
.8300000	.993501	1.006104	1.020038	1.034912	1.050200
.8400000	1.009928	1.023084	1.037654	1.053238	1.069288
.8500000	1.026535	1.040263	1.055493	1.071813	1.088659
.8600000	1.043324	1.057644	1.073557	1.090644	1.108320
.8700000	1.060299	1.075230	1.091852	1.109735	1.128277
.8799999	1.077462	1.093025	1.110381	1.129092	1.148537
.8899999	1.094816	1.111032	1.129148	1.148719	1.169107
.9000000	1.112365	1.129256	1.148159	1.168623	1.189993
.9100000	1.130111	1.147698	1.167416	1.188809	1.211201
.9200000	1.148057	1.166363	1.186925	1.209280	1.232739
.9300000	1.166206	1.185254	1.206689	1.230044	1.254614
.9400000	1.184561	1.204375	1.226712	1.251106	1.276833
.9500000	1.203125	1.223728	1.246999	1.272469	1.299402
.9600000	1.221900	1.243317	1.267554	1.294141	1.322329
.9699999	1.240889	1.263146	1.288380	1.316125	1.345620
.9799999	1.260095	1.283217	1.309482	1.338428	1.369283
.9899999	1.279521	1.303534	1.330864	1.361053	1.393324
1.0000000	1.299169	1.324099	1.352529	1.384008	1.417751
1.0100000	1.319040	1.344916	1.374481	1.407295	1.442571
1.0200000	1.339139	1.365987	1.396724	1.430921	1.467790
1.0300000	1.359467	1.387315	1.419261	1.454890	1.493415
1.0400000	1.380026	1.408903	1.442096	1.479207	1.519453
1.0500000	1.400819	1.430754	1.465232	1.503876	1.545911
1.0600000	1.421846	1.452869	1.488673	1.528902	1.572795
1.0699999	1.443111	1.475251	1.512420	1.554289	1.600112
1.0799999	1.464615	1.497903	1.536478	1.580041	1.627867
1.0899999	1.486359	1.520826	1.560849	1.606162	1.656068
1.1000000	1.508344	1.544022	1.585535	1.632657	1.684720
1.1100000	1.530573	1.567492	1.610539	1.659527	1.713828
1.1200000	1.553046	1.591238	1.635862	1.686777	1.743398
1.1300000	1.575764	1.615262	1.661507	1.714410	1.773435
1.1400000	1.598727	1.639564	1.687475	1.742428	1.803944
1.1500000	1.621937	1.664145	1.713767	1.770834	1.834929
1.1600000	1.645393	1.689006	1.740385	1.799629	1.866394
1.1700000	1.669096	1.714146	1.767329	1.828816	1.898343
1.1800000	1.693045	1.739567	1.794600	1.858396	1.930780
1.1899999	1.717240	1.765267	1.822198	1.888369	1.963707

$\alpha =$ .599999

Θ	K VALUES				
	.318821117	.415016431	.514599755	.613601043	.708073407
1.2000000	1.741681	1.791246	1.850122	1.918737	1.997126
1.2100000	1.766366	1.817504	1.878373	1.949498	2.031039
1.2200000	1.791294	1.844039	1.906948	1.980654	2.065447
1.2300000	1.816464	1.870849	1.935847	2.012203	2.100352
1.2400000	1.841875	1.897933	1.965068	2.044144	2.135752
1.2500000	1.867523	1.925290	1.994609	2.076474	2.171647
1.2599999	1.893407	1.952915	2.024467	2.109192	2.208035
1.2699999	1.919525	1.980807	2.054639	2.142295	2.244916
1.2799999	1.945872	2.008962	2.085122	2.175779	2.282284
1.2899999	1.972446	2.037376	2.115912	2.209639	2.320138
1.3000000	1.999244	2.066046	2.147004	2.243872	2.358472
1.3100000	2.026261	2.094967	2.178394	2.278472	2.397280
1.3200000	2.053492	2.124135	2.210075	2.313432	2.436557
1.3300000	2.080934	2.153544	2.242043	2.348746	2.476295
1.3400000	2.108582	2.183188	2.274291	2.384407	2.516486
1.3500000	2.136429	2.213062	2.306812	2.420407	2.557121
1.3600000	2.164471	2.243159	2.339598	2.456738	2.598190
1.3700000	2.192702	2.273473	2.372642	2.493389	2.639682
1.3799999	2.221114	2.303996	2.405936	2.530352	2.681585
1.3899999	2.249702	2.334721	2.439470	2.567615	2.723886
1.4000000	2.278459	2.365640	2.473236	2.605167	2.766571
1.4100000	2.307377	2.396744	2.507223	2.642997	2.809625
1.4200000	2.336448	2.428025	2.541421	2.681091	2.853033
1.4300000	2.365665	2.459473	2.575819	2.719437	2.896777
1.4400000	2.395019	2.491080	2.610408	2.758021	2.940840
1.4500000	2.424502	2.522835	2.645174	2.796829	2.985203
1.4600000	2.454106	2.554729	2.680105	2.835845	3.029847
1.4700000	2.483820	2.586750	2.715191	2.875056	3.074752
1.4800000	2.513637	2.618890	2.750417	2.914444	3.119897
1.4900000	2.543546	2.651136	2.785772	2.953993	3.165260
1.5000000	2.573538	2.683478	2.821241	2.993687	3.210820
1.5100000	2.603602	2.715903	2.856811	3.033509	3.256552
1.5200000	2.633730	2.748402	2.892468	3.073441	3.302434
1.5300000	2.663911	2.780961	2.928198	3.113466	3.348441
1.5400000	2.694134	2.813570	2.963988	3.153566	3.394550
1.5500000	2.724389	2.846215	2.999822	3.193722	3.440736
1.5600000	2.754666	2.878886	3.035686	3.233916	3.486974
1.5699999	2.784955	2.911570	3.071566	3.274130	3.533240
1.5707963	2.787367	2.914173	3.074424	3.277333	3.536924
1.5707963	2.787365	2.914171	3.074422	3.277330	3.536921

$\alpha =$ .599999

Θ	K VALUES				
	.794250555	.868696860	.928444378	.971111163	.994996249
.0000000	.000000	.000000	.000000	.000000	.000000
.0100000	.010000	.010000	.010000	.010000	.010000
.0200000	.020002	.020002	.020002	.020002	.020002
.0300000	.030008	.030009	.030009	.030009	.030009
.0400000	.040021	.040022	.040022	.040023	.040023
.0500000	.050041	.050043	.050044	.050045	.050045
.0600000	.060071	.060074	.060076	.060078	.060079
.0700000	.070114	.070118	.070121	.070124	.070125
.0800000	.080170	.080176	.080182	.080185	.080187
.0900000	.090242	.090252	.090259	.090264	.090267
.1000000	.100333	.100345	.100355	.100363	.100367
.1100000	.110444	.110460	.110474	.110483	.110489
.1200000	.120576	.120598	.120616	.120628	.120635
.1300000	.130733	.130761	.130783	.130799	.130808
.1400000	.140917	.140952	.140979	.140999	.141011
.1500000	.151129	.151172	.151206	.151231	.151244
.1600000	.161372	.161424	.161465	.161495	.161512
.1700000	.171647	.171709	.171760	.171796	.171816
.1800000	.181957	.182032	.182092	.182134	.182158
.1900000	.192304	.192392	.192463	.192514	.192542
.2000000	.202691	.202794	.202877	.202936	.202969
.2100000	.213119	.213239	.213335	.213404	.213442
.2200000	.223591	.223729	.223840	.223920	.223964
.2300000	.234109	.234267	.234395	.234486	.234537
.2400000	.244675	.244856	.245002	.245106	.245164
.2500000	.255292	.255498	.255663	.255781	.255848
.2600000	.265962	.266194	.266381	.266515	.266591
.2700000	.276688	.276949	.277160	.277310	.277395
.2800000	.287472	.287764	.288000	.288170	.288264
.2900000	.298316	.298642	.298906	.299095	.299201
.3000000	.309222	.309586	.309880	.310091	.310209
.3100000	.320195	.320598	.320925	.321158	.321290
.3200000	.331235	.331682	.332043	.332302	.332447
.3300000	.342346	.342839	.343237	.343523	.343684
.3400000	.353531	.354073	.354512	.354827	.355004
.3500000	.364791	.365387	.365869	.366215	.366409
.3600000	.376131	.376783	.377311	.377691	.377904
.3700000	.387552	.388265	.388843	.389258	.389491
.3800000	.399058	.399836	.400466	.400920	.401175
.3900000	.410651	.411498	.412185	.412679	.412957

$\alpha =$ .599999

Θ	K VALUES				
	.794250555	.868696860	.928444378	.971111163	.994996249
.4000000	.422335	.423256	.424003	.424540	.424843
.4100000	.434112	.435111	.435922	.436506	.436835
.4200000	.445986	.447069	.447948	.448581	.448938
.4300000	.457960	.459131	.460083	.460769	.461155
.4400000	.470037	.471302	.472331	.473073	.473491
.4500000	.482220	.483585	.484695	.485497	.485949
.4600000	.494512	.495983	.497181	.498046	.498533
.4700000	.506918	.508501	.509791	.510723	.511248
.4800000	.519441	.521142	.522530	.523533	.524099
.4900000	.532084	.533911	.535401	.536480	.537088
.5000000	.544850	.546810	.548410	.549569	.550223
.5100000	.557744	.559844	.561561	.562804	.563506
.5200000	.570770	.573018	.574857	.576190	.576943
.5300000	.583931	.586336	.588304	.589732	.590539
.5400000	.597231	.599801	.601907	.603435	.604300
.5500000	.610675	.613419	.615670	.617304	.618230
.5600000	.624266	.627194	.629598	.631345	.632335
.5700000	.638009	.641131	.643696	.645563	.646620
.5800000	.651908	.655234	.657971	.659963	.661092
.5900000	.665968	.669510	.672426	.674551	.675757
.6000000	.680193	.683962	.687069	.689334	.690620
.6100000	.694588	.698596	.701903	.704318	.705689
.6200000	.709157	.713417	.716937	.719508	.720969
.6300000	.723906	.728431	.732174	.734911	.736467
.6400000	.738840	.743644	.747623	.750535	.752192
.6500000	.753963	.759061	.763288	.766385	.768149
.6600000	.769282	.774688	.779178	.782470	.784347
.6700000	.784800	.790532	.795298	.798797	.800792
.6800000	.800524	.806599	.811656	.815373	.817494
.6899999	.816460	.822894	.828259	.832206	.834461
.7000000	.832613	.839426	.845114	.849305	.851700
.7100000	.848989	.856200	.862229	.866677	.869222
.7200000	.865593	.873223	.879613	.884332	.887034
.7300000	.882433	.890503	.897273	.902279	.905148
.7400000	.899515	.908048	.915217	.920527	.923572
.7500000	.916844	.925864	.933455	.939085	.942317
.7600000	.934428	.943959	.951995	.957963	.961393
.7700000	.952272	.962342	.970847	.977173	.980812
.7800000	.970385	.981021	.990020	.996724	1.000585
.7899999	.988773	1.000003	1.009524	1.016627	1.020723

$\alpha =$ .599999

θ	K VALUES				
	.794250555	.868696860	.928444378	.971111163	.994996249
.8000000	1.007444	1.019299	1.029369	1.036895	1.041240
.8100000	1.026403	1.038916	1.049566	1.057539	1.062147
.8200000	1.045660	1.058863	1.070125	1.078571	1.083458
.8300000	1.065222	1.079150	1.091057	1.100003	1.105187
.8400000	1.085095	1.099788	1.112375	1.121850	1.127348
.8500000	1.105290	1.120784	1.134089	1.144125	1.149956
.8600000	1.125812	1.142150	1.156213	1.166842	1.173027
.8700000	1.146672	1.163896	1.178759	1.190016	1.196576
.8799999	1.167876	1.186033	1.201739	1.213662	1.220621
.8899999	1.189435	1.208571	1.225168	1.237796	1.245178
.9000000	1.211355	1.231522	1.249060	1.262435	1.270267
.9100000	1.233647	1.254896	1.273428	1.287595	1.295906
.9200000	1.256319	1.278706	1.298287	1.313294	1.322115
.9300000	1.279380	1.302964	1.323653	1.339552	1.348914
.9400000	1.302840	1.327682	1.349541	1.366386	1.376325
.9500000	1.326708	1.352873	1.375969	1.393817	1.404371
.9600000	1.350993	1.378548	1.402952	1.421866	1.433075
.9699999	1.375704	1.404722	1.430508	1.450555	1.462461
.9799999	1.400853	1.431408	1.458654	1.479905	1.492557
.9899999	1.426448	1.458619	1.487410	1.509940	1.523387
1.0000000	1.452499	1.486370	1.516794	1.540685	1.554982
1.0100000	1.479017	1.514674	1.546826	1.572165	1.587369
1.0200000	1.506010	1.543545	1.577526	1.604406	1.620581
1.0300000	1.533490	1.572999	1.608915	1.637435	1.654650
1.0400000	1.561466	1.603051	1.641014	1.671283	1.689609
1.0500000	1.589948	1.633715	1.673845	1.705977	1.725496
1.0600000	1.618946	1.665007	1.707432	1.741550	1.762347
1.0699999	1.648471	1.696942	1.741796	1.778034	1.800203
1.0799999	1.678531	1.729535	1.776963	1.815463	1.839106
1.0899999	1.709137	1.762804	1.812958	1.853872	1.879099
1.1000000	1.740299	1.796764	1.849804	1.893299	1.920231
1.1100000	1.772025	1.831429	1.887529	1.933782	1.962548
1.1200000	1.804326	1.866818	1.926160	1.975361	2.006105
1.1300000	1.837209	1.902945	1.965722	2.018079	2.050957
1.1400000	1.870685	1.939826	2.006245	2.061980	2.097161
1.1500000	1.904761	1.977479	2.047757	2.107111	2.144781
1.1600000	1.939445	2.015917	2.090287	2.153518	2.193883
1.1700000	1.974746	2.055158	2.133865	2.201253	2.244537
1.1800000	2.010669	2.095216	2.178521	2.250369	2.296818
1.1899999	2.047224	2.136106	2.224286	2.300922	2.350807

$\alpha =$ .599999

Θ	K VALUES				
	.794250555	.868696860	.928444378	.971111163	.994996249
1.2000000	2.084415	2.177843	2.271192	2.352969	2.406589
1.2100000	2.122247	2.220442	2.319269	2.406570	2.464257
1.2200000	2.160727	2.263914	2.368549	2.461790	2.523909
1.2300000	2.199857	2.308275	2.419065	2.518694	2.585651
1.2400000	2.239643	2.353534	2.470847	2.577353	2.649597
1.2500000	2.280085	2.399705	2.523930	2.637839	2.715872
1.2599999	2.321186	2.446797	2.578343	2.700227	2.784607
1.2699999	2.362947	2.494818	2.634118	2.764599	2.855948
1.2799999	2.405366	2.543778	2.691287	2.831035	2.930053
1.2899999	2.448443	2.593682	2.749877	2.899623	3.007091
1.3000000	2.492176	2.644536	2.809920	2.970453	3.087251
1.3100000	2.536559	2.696341	2.871440	3.043616	3.170736
1.3200000	2.581588	2.749100	2.934464	3.119210	3.257770
1.3300000	2.627257	2.802812	2.999014	3.197334	3.348602
1.3400000	2.673556	2.857474	3.065112	3.278091	3.443502
1.3500000	2.720478	2.913081	3.132775	3.361583	3.542774
1.3600000	2.768011	2.969625	3.202016	3.447918	3.646752
1.3700000	2.816142	3.027095	3.272847	3.537202	3.755809
1.3799999	2.864858	3.085478	3.345271	3.629540	3.870361
1.3899999	2.914143	3.144759	3.419289	3.725036	3.990876
1.4000000	2.963980	3.204918	3.494895	3.823791	4.117879
1.4100000	3.014349	3.265931	3.572076	3.925896	4.251955
1.4200000	3.065230	3.327774	3.650811	4.031436	4.393772
1.4300000	3.116601	3.390417	3.731074	4.140483	4.544080
1.4400000	3.168438	3.453828	3.812827	4.253091	4.703725
1.4500000	3.220715	3.517970	3.896025	4.369294	4.873661
1.4600000	3.273407	3.582804	3.980613	4.489096	5.054958
1.4700000	3.326483	3.648287	4.066525	4.612473	5.248804
1.4800000	3.379916	3.714373	4.153686	4.739359	5.456499
1.4900000	3.433672	3.781012	4.242010	4.869642	5.679429
1.5000000	3.487722	3.848153	4.331402	5.003165	5.919008
1.5100000	3.542029	3.915739	4.421754	5.139708	6.176550
1.5200000	3.596560	3.983713	4.512951	5.278997	6.453089
1.5300000	3.651280	4.052015	4.604870	5.420700	6.749060
1.5400000	3.706153	4.120582	4.697377	5.564425	7.063888
1.5500000	3.761141	4.189352	4.790336	5.709729	7.395529
1.5600000	3.816207	4.258260	4.883603	5.856127	7.740130
1.5699999	3.871314	4.327238	4.977030	6.003101	8.092071
1.5707963	3.875703	4.332732	4.984472	6.014814	8.120215
1.5707963	3.875700	4.332728	4.984467	6.014807	8.120202

$\alpha =$ .619999

Θ	K VALUES				
	.009966711	.039469502	.087332193	.151646642	.229848846
.0000000	.000000	.000000	.000000	.000000	.000000
.0100000	.010000	.010000	.010000	.010000	.010000
.0200000	.020001	.020001	.020001	.020001	.020001
.0300000	.030005	.030005	.030005	.030006	.030006
.0400000	.040013	.040013	.040014	.040014	.040015
.0500000	.050026	.050026	.050027	.050029	.050030
.0600000	.060045	.060046	.060047	.060050	.060052
.0700000	.070071	.070073	.070075	.070079	.070084
.0800000	.080106	.080109	.080113	.080118	.080125
.0900000	.090152	.090155	.090161	.090169	.090178
.1000000	.100208	.100213	.100221	.100232	.100245
.1100000	.110277	.110284	.110295	.110309	.110326
.1200000	.120360	.120369	.120383	.120401	.120424
.1300000	.130459	.130469	.130487	.130511	.130539
.1400000	.140573	.140587	.140609	.140638	.140674
.1500000	.150705	.150722	.150749	.150785	.150830
.1600000	.160857	.160877	.160910	.160954	.161008
.1700000	.171028	.171052	.171092	.171145	.171210
.1800000	.181221	.181250	.181297	.181360	.181437
.1900000	.191437	.191471	.191526	.191601	.191691
.2000000	.201678	.201717	.201782	.201868	.201974
.2100000	.211943	.211989	.212064	.212165	.212287
.2200000	.222236	.222289	.222375	.222491	.222632
.2300000	.232557	.232618	.232716	.232848	.233010
.2400000	.242908	.242977	.243089	.243239	.243423
.2500000	.253290	.253367	.253494	.253664	.253872
.2600000	.263704	.263791	.263934	.264126	.264360
.2700000	.274152	.274250	.274409	.274625	.274888
.2800000	.284635	.284744	.284922	.285163	.285457
.2900000	.295154	.295276	.295474	.295742	.296069
.3000000	.305712	.305847	.306067	.306363	.306726
.3100000	.316309	.316458	.316701	.317029	.317430
.3200000	.326947	.327111	.327379	.327740	.328182
.3300000	.337627	.337807	.338101	.338498	.338984
.3400000	.348351	.348549	.348871	.349306	.349838
.3500000	.359121	.359336	.359688	.360163	.360746
.3600000	.369937	.370172	.370555	.371074	.371709
.3700000	.380802	.381057	.381474	.382038	.382730
.3800000	.391716	.391994	.392446	.393058	.393809
.3900000	.402682	.402983	.403472	.404135	.404949

$\alpha =$ .619999

Θ	K VALUES				
	.009966711	.039469502	.087332193	.151646642	.229848846
.4000000	.413701	.414026	.414555	.415272	.416153
.4100000	.424775	.425125	.425696	.426470	.427421
.4200000	.435905	.436282	.436897	.437730	.438755
.4300000	.447093	.447498	.448159	.449056	.450159
.4400000	.458340	.458775	.459484	.460447	.461633
.4500000	.469648	.470114	.470875	.471908	.473179
.4600000	.481020	.481518	.482332	.483438	.484800
.4700000	.492456	.492988	.493858	.495041	.496498
.4800000	.503958	.504526	.505455	.506717	.508275
.4900000	.515528	.516133	.517124	.518470	.520133
.5000000	.527168	.527812	.528867	.530301	.532073
.5100000	.538879	.539564	.540686	.542212	.544099
.5200000	.550664	.551391	.552583	.554205	.556212
.5300000	.562523	.563296	.564560	.566283	.568414
.5400000	.574460	.575278	.576619	.578446	.580708
.5500000	.586476	.587342	.588762	.590698	.593097
.5600000	.598572	.599489	.600991	.603040	.605581
.5700000	.610751	.611720	.613308	.615475	.618165
.5800000	.623015	.624037	.625714	.628005	.630849
.5900000	.635365	.636443	.638213	.640632	.643636
.6000000	.647804	.648940	.650806	.653358	.656530
.6100000	.660333	.661530	.663496	.666185	.669532
.6200000	.672954	.674214	.676284	.679116	.682644
.6300000	.685671	.686995	.689172	.692154	.695869
.6400000	.698483	.699875	.702164	.705300	.709211
.6500000	.711395	.712857	.715260	.718556	.722670
.6600000	.724407	.725941	.728464	.731926	.736250
.6700000	.737522	.739131	.741778	.745412	.749954
.6800000	.750743	.752428	.755203	.759015	.763784
.6899999	.764070	.765836	.768743	.772739	.777742
.7000000	.777508	.779355	.782400	.786586	.791833
.7100000	.791056	.792989	.796175	.800559	.806057
.7200000	.804719	.806739	.810072	.814660	.820418
.7300000	.818498	.820609	.824092	.828891	.834919
.7400000	.832395	.834600	.838239	.843255	.849562
.7500000	.846413	.848714	.852514	.857756	.864351
.7600000	.860554	.862954	.866920	.872394	.879288
.7700000	.874820	.877323	.881460	.887174	.894376
.7800000	.889214	.891822	.896136	.902097	.909618
.7899999	.903738	.906455	.910950	.917167	.925017

$\alpha =$ •619999

Θ	K VALUES				
	•009966711	•039469502	•087332193	•151646642	•229848846
•8000000	•918394	•921223	•925906	•932386	•940576
•8100000	•933185	•936130	•941005	•947757	•956297
•8200000	•948113	•951176	•956251	•963282	•972184
•8300000	•963181	•966366	•971645	•978964	•988239
•8400000	•978390	•981701	•987190	•994806	1•004467
•8500000	•993744	•997184	1•002889	1•010811	1•020868
•8600000	1•009244	1•012817	1•018745	1•026981	1•037448
•8700000	1•024894	1•028603	1•034759	1•043320	1•054207
•8799999	1•040695	1•044544	1•050936	1•059829	1•071151
•8899999	1•056649	1•060642	1•067276	1•076512	1•088281
•9000000	1•072761	1•076901	1•083783	1•093371	1•105600
•9100000	1•089030	1•093322	1•100459	1•110409	1•123112
•9200000	1•105461	1•109908	1•117306	1•127629	1•140819
•9300000	1•122054	1•126661	1•134328	1•145032	1•158724
•9400000	1•138814	1•143583	1•151526	1•162623	1•176831
•9500000	1•155741	1•160678	1•168904	1•180404	1•195141
•9600000	1•172838	1•177947	1•186462	1•198376	1•213658
•9699999	1•190107	1•195392	1•204205	1•216543	1•232385
•9799999	1•207551	1•213016	1•222133	1•234907	1•251324
•9899999	1•225171	1•230821	1•240250	1•253471	1•270478
1•0000000	1•242970	1•248809	1•258558	1•272236	1•289849
1•0100000	1•260949	1•266981	1•277058	1•291206	1•309441
1•0200000	1•279111	1•285341	1•295754	1•310382	1•329255
1•0300000	1•297457	1•303890	1•314646	1•329767	1•349294
1•0400000	1•315990	1•322629	1•333736	1•349362	1•369560
1•0500000	1•334710	1•341561	1•353028	1•369170	1•390056
1•0600000	1•353620	1•360688	1•372521	1•389192	1•410783
1•0699999	1•372721	1•380010	1•392219	1•409431	1•431744
1•0799999	1•392014	1•399529	1•412122	1•429887	1•452940
1•0899999	1•411502	1•419247	1•432232	1•450563	1•474372
1•1000000	1•431185	1•439165	1•452551	1•471460	1•496044
1•1100000	1•451063	1•459284	1•473079	1•492579	1•517955
1•1200000	1•471139	1•479605	1•493817	1•513921	1•540108
1•1300000	1•491412	1•500129	1•514767	1•535488	1•562503
1•1400000	1•511885	1•520856	1•535928	1•557279	1•585141
1•1500000	1•532556	1•541787	1•557303	1•579295	1•608023
1•1600000	1•553427	1•562922	1•578890	1•601538	1•631149
1•1700000	1•574497	1•584262	1•600690	1•624007	1•654520
1•1800000	1•595766	1•605806	1•622704	1•646702	1•678135
1•1899999	1•617236	1•627555	1•644930	1•669623	1•701995

$\alpha =$ •619999

Θ	K VALUES				
	•009966711	•039469502	•087332193	•151646642	•229848846
1•2000000	1•638904	1•649508	1•667369	1•692769	1•726100
1•2100000	1•660770	1•671663	1•690020	1•716140	1•750447
1•2200000	1•682834	1•694021	1•712881	1•739735	1•775037
1•2300000	1•705094	1•716581	1•735952	1•763553	1•799868
1•2400000	1•727549	1•739340	1•759232	1•787592	1•824939
1•2500000	1•750198	1•762297	1•782719	1•811850	1•850247
1•2599999	1•773038	1•785451	1•806410	1•836326	1•875791
1•2699999	1•796068	1•808800	1•830304	1•861018	1•901568
1•2799999	1•819286	1•832340	1•854398	1•885921	1•927576
1•2899999	1•842688	1•856070	1•878690	1•911035	1•953811
1•3000000	1•866273	1•879987	1•903176	1•936355	1•980270
1•3100000	1•890036	1•904086	1•927854	1•961878	2•006949
1•3200000	1•913975	1•928366	1•952718	1•987601	2•033844
1•3300000	1•938086	1•952822	1•977767	2•013518	2•060950
1•3400000	1•962364	1•977450	2•002995	2•039626	2•088263
1•3500000	1•986807	2•002245	2•028397	2•065919	2•115778
1•3600000	2•011408	2•027203	2•053970	2•092393	2•143488
1•3700000	2•036163	2•052320	2•079707	2•119043	2•171389
1•3799999	2•061068	2•077589	2•105604	2•145861	2•199473
1•3899999	2•086116	2•103006	2•131655	2•172843	2•227734
1•4000000	2•111303	2•128565	2•157853	2•199982	2•256166
1•4100000	2•136622	2•154259	2•184193	2•227271	2•284760
1•4200000	2•162067	2•180082	2•210667	2•254703	2•313510
1•4300000	2•187632	2•206027	2•237269	2•282271	2•342407
1•4400000	2•213309	2•232089	2•263991	2•309967	2•371444
1•4500000	2•239092	2•258259	2•290827	2•337783	2•400611
1•4600000	2•264974	2•284530	2•317768	2•365711	2•429900
1•4700000	2•290948	2•310895	2•344808	2•393744	2•459301
1•4800000	2•317005	2•337346	2•371936	2•421871	2•488806
1•4900000	2•343139	2•363874	2•399146	2•450085	2•518405
1•5000000	2•369341	2•390473	2•426429	2•478377	2•548088
1•5100000	2•395602	2•417133	2•453777	2•506737	2•577845
1•5200000	2•421916	2•443847	2•481179	2•535155	2•607666
1•5300000	2•448273	2•470605	2•508628	2•563623	2•637541
1•5400000	2•474665	2•497399	2•536115	2•592131	2•667459
1•5500000	2•501084	2•524220	2•563630	2•620669	2•697410
1•5600000	2•527521	2•551060	2•591164	2•649228	2•727383
1•5699999	2•553967	2•577909	2•618708	2•677797	2•757367
1•5707963	2•556073	2•580047	2•620902	2•680072	2•759755
1•5707963	2•556071	2•580045	2•620900	2•680070	2•759753

$\alpha =$ •619999

Θ	K VALUES				
	•318821117	•415016431	•514599755	•613601043	•708073407
•0000000	•000000	•000000	•000000	•000000	•000000
•0100000	•010000	•010000	•010000	•010000	•010000
•0200000	•020002	•020002	•020002	•020002	•020002
•0300000	•030007	•030007	•030007	•030008	•030008
•0400000	•040016	•040017	•040018	•040019	•040020
•0500000	•050032	•050034	•050036	•050038	•050040
•0600000	•060056	•060059	•060063	•060066	•060070
•0700000	•070089	•070094	•070100	•070106	•070111
•0800000	•080133	•080141	•080149	•080158	•080166
•0900000	•090189	•090201	•090213	•090225	•090237
•1000000	•100260	•100276	•100293	•100309	•100325
•1100000	•110346	•110368	•110390	•110412	•110433
•1200000	•120450	•120478	•120507	•120535	•120563
•1300000	•130572	•130608	•130645	•130681	•130716
•1400000	•140715	•140760	•140806	•140852	•140895
•1500000	•150880	•150935	•150992	•151048	•151102
•1600000	•161069	•161136	•161205	•161273	•161339
•1700000	•171283	•171363	•171446	•171529	•171608
•1800000	•181525	•181620	•181718	•181817	•181911
•1900000	•191795	•191906	•192023	•192139	•192250
•2000000	•202095	•202226	•202362	•202497	•202627
•2100000	•212427	•212579	•212737	•212894	•213045
•2200000	•222793	•222968	•223150	•223331	•223505
•2300000	•233194	•233395	•233603	•233811	•234011
•2400000	•243633	•243861	•244098	•244336	•244563
•2500000	•254110	•254369	•254638	•254907	•255165
•2600000	•264628	•264920	•265223	•265527	•265818
•2700000	•275189	•275516	•275857	•276198	•276526
•2800000	•285793	•286159	•286541	•286923	•287290
•2900000	•296444	•296851	•297277	•297703	•298113
•3000000	•307142	•307595	•308067	•308541	•308997
•3100000	•317890	•318391	•318914	•319439	•319944
•3200000	•328689	•329242	•329820	•330400	•330958
•3300000	•339542	•340150	•340786	•341425	•342040
•3400000	•350450	•351117	•351816	•352517	•353194
•3500000	•361415	•362146	•362911	•363680	•364422
•3600000	•372439	•373237	•374073	•374914	•375726
•3700000	•383525	•384394	•385305	•386223	•387109
•3800000	•394673	•395618	•396610	•397609	•398575
•3900000	•405886	•406912	•407989	•409075	•410125

$\alpha =$ .619999

Θ	K VALUES				
	.318821117	.415016431	.514599755	.613601043	.708073407
.4000000	.417167	.418278	.419445	.420623	.421763
.4100000	.428516	.429718	.430981	.432256	.433492
.4200000	.439937	.441234	.442598	.443977	.445314
.4300000	.451431	.452829	.454300	.455788	.457233
.4400000	.463001	.464505	.466089	.467693	.469251
.4500000	.474648	.476264	.477967	.479694	.481372
.4600000	.486375	.488109	.489938	.491794	.493599
.4700000	.498185	.500042	.502004	.503995	.505936
.4800000	.510078	.512066	.514167	.516302	.518385
.4900000	.522058	.524183	.526431	.528718	.530949
.5000000	.534127	.536395	.538798	.541244	.543634
.5100000	.546287	.548706	.551271	.553884	.556441
.5200000	.558541	.561118	.563853	.566643	.569374
.5300000	.570891	.573634	.576547	.579522	.582438
.5400000	.583339	.586255	.589356	.592525	.595636
.5500000	.595889	.598986	.602282	.605656	.608971
.5600000	.608541	.611828	.615330	.618919	.622448
.5700000	.621300	.624785	.628502	.632315	.636071
.5800000	.634167	.637859	.641801	.645851	.649843
.5900000	.647146	.651053	.655231	.659528	.663769
.6000000	.660238	.664371	.668796	.673351	.677853
.6100000	.673446	.677815	.682497	.687323	.692100
.6200000	.686774	.691388	.696339	.701449	.706513
.6300000	.700224	.705094	.710325	.715732	.721098
.6400000	.713798	.718934	.724459	.730176	.735859
.6500000	.727500	.732914	.738744	.744786	.750800
.6600000	.741332	.747035	.753184	.759565	.765927
.6700000	.755298	.761301	.767782	.774518	.781244
.6800000	.769399	.775715	.782543	.789650	.796756
.6899999	.783640	.790281	.797470	.804964	.812469
.7000000	.798023	.805002	.812567	.820465	.828388
.7100000	.812551	.819881	.827838	.836158	.844517
.7200000	.827227	.834921	.843286	.852046	.860863
.7300000	.842054	.850127	.858917	.868136	.877431
.7400000	.857035	.865502	.874733	.884431	.894227
.7500000	.872174	.881049	.890739	.900937	.911255
.7600000	.887474	.896772	.906940	.917658	.928524
.7700000	.902937	.912674	.923339	.934600	.946037
.7800000	.918568	.928760	.939940	.951767	.963801
.7899999	.934368	.945033	.956749	.969165	.981823

$\alpha =$ .619999

Θ	K VALUES				
	.318821117	.415016431	.514599755	.613601043	.708073407
.8000000	.950343	.961496	.973769	.986799	1.000109
.8100000	.966494	.978154	.991005	1.004674	1.018665
.8200000	.982825	.995010	1.008461	1.022795	1.037498
.8300000	.999339	1.012067	1.026142	1.041168	1.056614
.8400000	1.016040	1.029331	1.044052	1.059799	1.076020
.8500000	1.032931	1.046804	1.062196	1.078693	1.095723
.8600000	1.050016	1.064491	1.080578	1.097855	1.115731
.8700000	1.067298	1.082395	1.099204	1.117291	1.136049
.8799999	1.084779	1.100520	1.118077	1.137007	1.156685
.8899999	1.102464	1.118871	1.137202	1.157009	1.177646
.9000000	1.120356	1.137451	1.156584	1.177302	1.198940
.9100000	1.138458	1.156263	1.176228	1.197892	1.220574
.9200000	1.156773	1.175312	1.196138	1.218786	1.242556
.9300000	1.175305	1.194602	1.216319	1.239988	1.264892
.9400000	1.194057	1.214136	1.236776	1.261504	1.287591
.9500000	1.213033	1.233918	1.257513	1.283342	1.310661
.9600000	1.232234	1.253952	1.278534	1.305505	1.334108
.9699999	1.251665	1.274242	1.299845	1.328001	1.357941
.9799999	1.271329	1.294791	1.321450	1.350835	1.382167
.9899999	1.291228	1.315603	1.343353	1.374012	1.406795
1.0000000	1.311366	1.336682	1.365558	1.397540	1.431832
1.0100000	1.331746	1.358030	1.388071	1.421422	1.457285
1.0200000	1.352369	1.379652	1.410895	1.445665	1.483163
1.0300000	1.373240	1.401550	1.434034	1.470274	1.509472
1.0400000	1.394361	1.423727	1.457492	1.495254	1.536221
1.0500000	1.415733	1.446187	1.481274	1.520612	1.563418
1.0600000	1.437360	1.468933	1.505383	1.546351	1.591068
1.0699999	1.459244	1.491967	1.529822	1.572478	1.619181
1.0799999	1.481388	1.515293	1.554595	1.598996	1.647762
1.0899999	1.503792	1.538911	1.579706	1.625910	1.676819
1.1000000	1.526459	1.562826	1.605157	1.653226	1.706358
1.1100000	1.549390	1.587038	1.630951	1.680946	1.736386
1.1200000	1.572587	1.611550	1.657091	1.709074	1.766910
1.1300000	1.596052	1.636364	1.683579	1.737616	1.797934
1.1400000	1.619785	1.661480	1.710417	1.766572	1.829465
1.1500000	1.643787	1.686901	1.737607	1.795948	1.861508
1.1600000	1.668059	1.712626	1.765151	1.825745	1.894068
1.1700000	1.692602	1.738657	1.793050	1.855966	1.927149
1.1800000	1.717415	1.764994	1.821304	1.886612	1.960756
1.1899999	1.742498	1.791638	1.849915	1.917685	1.994891

$\alpha =$ .619999

Θ	K VALUES				
	.318821117	.415016431	.514599755	.613601043	.708073407
1.2000000	1.767851	1.818587	1.878882	1.949187	2.029558
1.2100000	1.793473	1.845842	1.908205	1.981117	2.064759
1.2200000	1.819364	1.873401	1.937883	2.013475	2.100495
1.2300000	1.845522	1.901263	1.967916	2.046262	2.136769
1.2400000	1.871945	1.929427	1.998302	2.079476	2.173580
1.2500000	1.898631	1.957890	2.029038	2.113115	2.210928
1.2599999	1.925579	1.986651	2.060123	2.147177	2.248812
1.2699999	1.952785	2.015705	2.091553	2.181660	2.287230
1.2799999	1.980247	2.045051	2.123326	2.216560	2.326179
1.2899999	2.007961	2.074684	2.155436	2.251873	2.365656
1.3000000	2.035924	2.104601	2.187880	2.287594	2.405656
1.3100000	2.064130	2.134796	2.220652	2.323717	2.446174
1.3200000	2.092576	2.165264	2.253746	2.360237	2.487203
1.3300000	2.121258	2.196001	2.287158	2.397146	2.528735
1.3400000	2.150168	2.227000	2.320879	2.434436	2.570762
1.3500000	2.179303	2.258254	2.354902	2.472100	2.613275
1.3600000	2.208655	2.289758	2.389221	2.510128	2.656263
1.3700000	2.238218	2.321503	2.423825	2.548510	2.699714
1.3799999	2.267986	2.353482	2.458706	2.587235	2.743616
1.3899999	2.297951	2.385686	2.493855	2.626292	2.787954
1.4000000	2.328105	2.418107	2.529262	2.665670	2.832713
1.4100000	2.358440	2.450736	2.564915	2.705354	2.877878
1.4200000	2.388948	2.483563	2.600803	2.745331	2.923430
1.4300000	2.419620	2.516577	2.636915	2.785587	2.969353
1.4400000	2.450447	2.549770	2.673239	2.826106	3.015626
1.4500000	2.481419	2.583129	2.709761	2.866874	3.062230
1.4600000	2.512527	2.616643	2.746468	2.907873	3.109143
1.4700000	2.543760	2.650302	2.783347	2.949088	3.156344
1.4800000	2.575109	2.684093	2.820383	2.990500	3.203808
1.4900000	2.606562	2.718003	2.857562	3.032091	3.251513
1.5000000	2.638109	2.752022	2.894870	3.073843	3.299435
1.5100000	2.669738	2.786135	2.932291	3.115737	3.347547
1.5200000	2.701438	2.820330	2.969810	3.157754	3.395824
1.5300000	2.733199	2.854593	3.007410	3.199874	3.444239
1.5400000	2.765007	2.888912	3.045077	3.242076	3.492767
1.5500000	2.796852	2.923273	3.082794	3.284342	3.541380
1.5600000	2.828722	2.957662	3.120544	3.326651	3.590050
1.5699999	2.860604	2.992066	3.158313	3.368981	3.638749
1.5707963	2.863143	2.994806	3.161321	3.372353	3.642628
1.5707963	2.863141	2.994804	3.161319	3.372359	3.642624

$\alpha =$ .619999

Θ	K VALUES				
	.794250555	.868696860	.928444378	.971111163	.994996249
.0000000	.000000	.000000	.000000	.000000	.000000
.0100000	.010000	.010000	.010000	.010000	.010000
.0200000	.020002	.020002	.020002	.020002	.020002
.0300000	.030009	.030009	.030009	.030009	.030010
.0400000	.040021	.040022	.040023	.040023	.040023
.0500000	.050042	.050043	.050045	.050046	.050046
.0600000	.060073	.060076	.060078	.060079	.060080
.0700000	.070116	.070120	.070124	.070126	.070128
.0800000	.080173	.080180	.080185	.080189	.080191
.0900000	.090247	.090256	.090264	.090269	.090272
.1000000	.100340	.100352	.100362	.100369	.100373
.1100000	.110452	.110469	.110483	.110492	.110498
.1200000	.120588	.120610	.120627	.120640	.120647
.1300000	.130748	.130776	.130798	.130814	.130823
.1400000	.140936	.140970	.140998	.141018	.141029
.1500000	.151152	.151195	.151229	.151254	.151267
.1600000	.161399	.161451	.161493	.161523	.161540
.1700000	.171680	.171743	.171793	.171829	.171849
.1800000	.181997	.182071	.182131	.182174	.182198
.1900000	.192351	.192439	.192510	.192561	.192589
.2000000	.202746	.202849	.202932	.202991	.203024
.2100000	.213183	.213303	.213399	.213468	.213507
.2200000	.223665	.223803	.223914	.223994	.224038
.2300000	.234193	.234352	.234480	.234571	.234622
.2400000	.244772	.244953	.245098	.245203	.245261
.2500000	.255402	.255607	.255773	.255891	.255958
.2600000	.266086	.266318	.266505	.266639	.266715
.2700000	.276827	.277088	.277299	.277450	.277535
.2800000	.287627	.287920	.288156	.288326	.288421
.2900000	.298489	.298816	.299080	.299270	.299376
.3000000	.309415	.309780	.310074	.310285	.310403
.3100000	.320409	.320813	.321139	.321374	.321505
.3200000	.331472	.331919	.332280	.332540	.332685
.3300000	.342607	.343100	.343499	.343786	.343947
.3400000	.353817	.354361	.354800	.355115	.355293
.3500000	.365106	.365702	.366185	.366531	.366726
.3600000	.376475	.377128	.377657	.378037	.378251
.3700000	.387928	.388642	.389220	.389636	.389870
.3800000	.399467	.400246	.400878	.401332	.401588
.3900000	.411096	.411945	.412633	.413128	.413407

$\alpha =$ .619999

Θ	K VALUES				
	.794250555	.868696860	.928444378	.971111163	.994996249
.4000000	.422818	.423741	.424489	.425028	.425331
.4100000	.434636	.435637	.436450	.437035	.437365
.4200000	.446553	.447638	.448519	.449154	.449512
.4300000	.458572	.459746	.460700	.461388	.461775
.4400000	.470697	.471965	.472997	.473741	.474160
.4500000	.482931	.484300	.485413	.486217	.486670
.4600000	.495278	.496753	.497953	.498821	.499310
.4700000	.507741	.509328	.510621	.511556	.512083
.4800000	.520323	.522030	.523421	.524427	.524995
.4900000	.533030	.534862	.536358	.537440	.538050
.5000000	.545863	.547829	.549435	.550597	.551253
.5100000	.558828	.560935	.562657	.563905	.564610
.5200000	.571928	.574184	.576030	.577367	.578123
.5300000	.585167	.587581	.589557	.590990	.591801
.5400000	.598550	.601130	.603244	.604778	.605646
.5500000	.612080	.614835	.617095	.618737	.619666
.5600000	.625763	.628703	.631117	.632872	.633865
.5700000	.639601	.642737	.645314	.647188	.648251
.5800000	.653601	.656943	.659692	.661693	.662828
.5900000	.667767	.671325	.674256	.676391	.677602
.6000000	.682103	.685890	.689013	.691289	.692582
.6100000	.696614	.700643	.703967	.706394	.707772
.6200000	.711306	.715588	.719127	.721712	.723181
.6300000	.726183	.730733	.734497	.737249	.738814
.6400000	.741251	.746083	.750084	.753013	.754680
.6500000	.756515	.761643	.765896	.769012	.770786
.6600000	.771981	.777421	.781938	.785252	.787139
.6700000	.787655	.793423	.798219	.801741	.803749
.6800000	.803541	.809655	.814746	.818488	.820623
.6899999	.819646	.826124	.831525	.835500	.837770
.7000000	.835977	.842838	.848566	.852787	.855199
.7100000	.852538	.859802	.865876	.870357	.872920
.7200000	.869338	.877025	.883463	.888219	.890941
.7300000	.886381	.894514	.901337	.906382	.909274
.7400000	.903676	.912278	.919505	.924857	.927928
.7500000	.921228	.930323	.937977	.943654	.946914
.7600000	.939045	.948658	.956763	.962783	.966243
.7700000	.957133	.967292	.975872	.982255	.985927
.7800000	.975501	.986233	.995315	1.002081	1.005977
.7899999	.994155	1.005490	1.015101	1.022272	1.026407

$\alpha =$ •619999

Θ	K VALUES				
	•794250555	•868696860	•928444378	•971111163	•994996249
•8000000	1•013103	1•025073	1•035242	1•042842	1•047230
•8100000	1•032354	1•044991	1•055748	1•063802	1•068457
•8200000	1•051914	1•065253	1•076631	1•085166	1•090105
•8300000	1•071793	1•085869	1•097903	1•106946	1•112186
•8400000	1•091998	1•106850	1•119576	1•129157	1•134717
•8500000	1•112538	1•128207	1•141663	1•151814	1•157712
•8600000	1•133422	1•149949	1•164176	1•174931	1•181189
•8700000	1•154659	1•172088	1•187129	1•198524	1•205164
•8799999	1•176257	1•194636	1•210537	1•222609	1•229655
•8899999	1•198226	1•217603	1•234412	1•247202	1•254680
•9000000	1•220575	1•241003	1•258771	1•272323	1•280260
•9100000	1•243314	1•264846	1•283627	1•297988	1•306413
•9200000	1•266453	1•289146	1•308998	1•324216	1•333161
•9300000	1•290001	1•313916	1•334899	1•351027	1•360525
•9400000	1•313968	1•339169	1•361348	1•378442	1•388530
•9500000	1•338365	1•364918	1•388361	1•406481	1•417197
•9600000	1•363201	1•391176	1•415957	1•435167	1•446553
•9699999	1•388488	1•417959	1•444154	1•464523	1•476623
•9799999	1•414235	1•445281	1•472971	1•494572	1•507435
•9899999	1•440454	1•473155	1•502428	1•525340	1•539018
1•0000000	1•467156	1•501598	1•532546	1•556853	1•571401
1•0100000	1•494351	1•530625	1•563344	1•589136	1•604615
1•0200000	1•522049	1•560251	1•594846	1•622219	1•638695
1•0300000	1•550263	1•590491	1•627073	1•656131	1•673673
1•0400000	1•579003	1•621364	1•660049	1•690902	1•709587
1•0500000	1•608280	1•652883	1•693796	1•726565	1•746475
1•0600000	1•638105	1•685067	1•728340	1•763152	1•784378
1•0699999	1•668489	1•717932	1•763706	1•800699	1•823336
1•0799999	1•699443	1•751495	1•799919	1•839241	1•863396
1•0899999	1•730979	1•785774	1•837006	1•878816	1•904603
1•1000000	1•763106	1•820786	1•874994	1•919465	1•947009
1•1100000	1•795835	1•856547	1•913912	1•961227	1•990665
1•1200000	1•829177	1•893077	1•953787	2•004148	2•035626
1•1300000	1•863142	1•930392	1•994651	2•048270	2•081952
1•1400000	1•897739	1•968509	2•036532	2•093642	2•129705
1•1500000	1•932978	2•007447	2•079461	2•140313	2•178951
1•1600000	1•968869	2•047223	2•123471	2•188335	2•229761
1•1700000	2•005420	2•087854	2•168592	2•237762	2•282209
1•1800000	2•042640	2•129356	2•214859	2•288649	2•336376
1•1899999	2•080536	2•171747	2•262304	2•341057	2•392346

$\alpha =$ .619999

Θ	K VALUES				
	.794250555	.868696860	.928444378	.971111163	.994996249
.2000000	2.119115	2.215043	2.310961	2.395047	2.450211
.2100000	2.158384	2.259259	2.360863	2.450684	2.510069
.2200000	2.198349	2.304410	2.412046	2.508035	2.572023
.2300000	2.239015	2.350510	2.464543	2.567172	2.636188
.2400000	2.280386	2.397574	2.518390	2.628169	2.702683
.2500000	2.322465	2.445613	2.573621	2.691103	2.771640
.2599999	2.365255	2.494640	2.630270	2.756055	2.843200
.2699999	2.408757	2.544664	2.688371	2.823110	2.917516
.2799999	2.452971	2.595694	2.747957	2.892357	2.994754
.2899999	2.497895	2.647739	2.809061	2.963886	3.075097
.3000000	2.543529	2.700803	2.871713	3.037795	3.158742
.3100000	2.589867	2.754890	2.935943	3.114181	3.245903
.3200000	2.636904	2.810002	3.001778	3.193147	3.336820
.3300000	2.684635	2.866140	3.069243	3.274798	3.431752
.3400000	2.733050	2.923299	3.138361	3.359245	3.530989
.3500000	2.782140	2.981476	3.209150	3.446596	3.634849
.3600000	2.831894	3.040662	3.281627	3.536965	3.743685
.3700000	2.882298	3.100845	3.355802	3.630464	3.857891
.3799999	2.933337	3.162013	3.431680	3.727206	3.977908
.3899999	2.984995	3.224149	3.509263	3.827301	4.104226
.4000000	3.037254	3.287231	3.588543	3.930855	4.237400
.4100000	3.090092	3.351235	3.669507	4.037965	4.378050
.4200000	3.143488	3.416135	3.752134	4.148722	4.526876
.4300000	3.197417	3.481898	3.836394	4.263200	4.684670
.4400000	3.251855	3.548489	3.922249	4.381457	4.852324
.4500000	3.306773	3.615871	4.009649	4.503528	5.030843
.4600000	3.362142	3.684000	4.098535	4.629420	5.221354
.4700000	3.417932	3.752830	4.188839	4.759103	5.425108
.4800000	3.474109	3.822312	4.280478	4.892508	5.643475
.4900000	3.530641	3.892391	4.373362	5.029518	5.877915
.5000000	3.587493	3.963013	4.467388	5.169963	6.129914
.5100000	3.644626	4.034116	4.562442	5.313610	6.400858
.5200000	3.702004	4.105638	4.658400	5.460171	6.691833
.5300000	3.759588	4.177515	4.755129	5.609291	7.003296
.5400000	3.817339	4.249679	4.852490	5.760555	7.334638
.5500000	3.875216	4.322062	4.950332	5.913493	7.683704
.5600000	3.933178	4.394594	5.048504	6.067591	8.046429
.5699999	3.991186	4.467202	5.146848	6.222300	8.416891
.5707963	3.995806	4.472986	5.154682	6.234629	8.446516
.5707963	3.995801	4.472980	5.154676	6.234621	8.446501

$\alpha =$ •639999

Θ	K VALUES				
	•009966711	•039469502	•087332193	•151646642	•229848846
•0000000	•000000	•000000	•000000	•000000	•000000
•0100000	•010000	•010000	•010000	•010000	•010000
•0200000	•020001	•020001	•020001	•020001	•020002
•0300000	•030005	•030005	•030006	•030006	•030006
•0400000	•040013	•040014	•040014	•040015	•040016
•0500000	•050026	•050027	•050028	•050029	•050031
•0600000	•060046	•060047	•060049	•060051	•060054
•0700000	•070073	•070075	•070078	•070081	•070086
•0800000	•080110	•080112	•080116	•080122	•080129
•0900000	•090157	•090160	•090166	•090174	•090183
•1000000	•100215	•100220	•100228	•100239	•100252
•1100000	•110286	•110293	•110304	•110318	•110335
•1200000	•120372	•120381	•120394	•120413	•120436
•1300000	•130473	•130484	•130502	•130525	•130554
•1400000	•140592	•140605	•140627	•140657	•140693
•1500000	•150728	•150745	•150772	•150808	•150853
•1600000	•160884	•160905	•160937	•160982	•161036
•1700000	•171061	•171086	•171125	•171178	•171243
•1800000	•181261	•181290	•181337	•181400	•181477
•1900000	•191484	•191518	•191573	•191647	•191738
•2000000	•201732	•201772	•201836	•201923	•202029
•2100000	•212007	•212053	•212127	•212228	•212351
•2200000	•222309	•222362	•222448	•222564	•222705
•2300000	•232641	•232701	•232800	•232932	•233094
•2400000	•243003	•243072	•243184	•243334	•243518
•2500000	•253398	•253475	•253602	•253772	•253981
•2600000	•263825	•263913	•264056	•264248	•264482
•2700000	•274288	•274387	•274546	•274762	•275025
•2800000	•284788	•284897	•285076	•285316	•285611
•2900000	•295325	•295447	•295645	•295913	•296240
•3000000	•305901	•306036	•306256	•306553	•306917
•3100000	•316518	•316668	•316911	•317239	•317641
•3200000	•327178	•327343	•327610	•327972	•328415
•3300000	•337882	•338062	•338357	•338754	•339241
•3400000	•348631	•348829	•349151	•349586	•350120
•3500000	•359427	•359643	•359995	•360471	•361055
•3600000	•370271	•370507	•370891	•371410	•372046
•3700000	•381166	•381422	•381840	•382405	•383097
•3800000	•392113	•392391	•392844	•393457	•394209
•3900000	•403113	•403414	•403904	•404569	•405384

$\alpha =$ •639999

Θ	K VALUES				
	•009966711	•039469502	•087332193	•151646642	•229848846
•4000000	•414168	•414493	•415023	•415742	•416624
•4100000	•425280	•425631	•426203	•426978	•427931
•4200000	•436450	•436828	•437444	•438280	•439307
•4300000	•447681	•448087	•448749	•449648	•450754
•4400000	•458973	•459409	•460120	•461086	•462274
•4500000	•470329	•470796	•471559	•472594	•473869
•4600000	•481750	•482250	•483067	•484175	•485541
•4700000	•493239	•493773	•494646	•495831	•497293
•4800000	•504797	•505367	•506298	•507565	•509127
•4900000	•516425	•517033	•518026	•519377	•521044
•5000000	•528126	•528773	•529831	•531270	•533048
•5100000	•539902	•540590	•541715	•543247	•545140
•5200000	•551755	•552485	•553681	•555309	•557322
•5300000	•563685	•564460	•565729	•567458	•569598
•5400000	•575697	•576518	•577864	•579698	•581969
•5500000	•587790	•588660	•590085	•592029	•594437
•5600000	•599968	•600889	•602397	•604455	•607006
•5700000	•612233	•613205	•614800	•616977	•619678
•5800000	•624586	•625613	•627297	•629598	•632455
•5900000	•637030	•638113	•639891	•642320	•645339
•6000000	•649566	•650708	•652583	•655147	•658334
•6100000	•662198	•663401	•665376	•668079	•671442
•6200000	•674926	•676192	•678272	•681119	•684665
•6300000	•687754	•689085	•691274	•694271	•698007
•6400000	•700683	•702083	•704384	•707536	•711469
•6500000	•713716	•715186	•717603	•720918	•725055
•6600000	•726855	•728398	•730936	•734418	•738767
•6700000	•740102	•741720	•744383	•748039	•752609
•6800000	•753460	•755156	•757949	•761784	•766583
•6899999	•766931	•768708	•771634	•775656	•780692
•7000000	•780518	•782378	•785442	•789657	•794939
•7100000	•794222	•796168	•799376	•803790	•809326
•7200000	•808047	•810082	•813437	•818058	•823858
•7300000	•821994	•824121	•827629	•832464	•838536
•7400000	•836067	•838288	•841955	•847009	•853365
•7500000	•850267	•852586	•856416	•861698	•868346
•7600000	•864598	•867018	•871016	•876534	•883484
•7700000	•879062	•881586	•885757	•891518	•898780
•7800000	•893661	•896292	•900642	•906654	•914240
•7899999	•908398	•911139	•915674	•921945	•929865

$\alpha =$ •639999

Θ	K VALUES				
	•009966711	•039469502	•087332193	•151646642	•229848846
•8000000	•923276	•926131	•930856	•937395	•945659
•8100000	•938298	•941270	•946190	•953004	•961625
•8200000	•953465	•956557	•961680	•968778	•977766
•8300000	•968781	•971997	•977328	•984719	•994086
•8400000	•984248	•987592	•993137	1•000830	1•010589
•8500000	•999869	1•003345	1•009109	1•017114	1•027276
•8600000	1•015648	1•019258	1•025249	1•033574	1•044153
•8700000	1•031585	1•035335	1•041559	1•050213	1•061221
•8799999	1•047685	1•051577	1•058041	1•067034	1•078485
•8899999	1•063950	1•067988	1•074698	1•084041	1•095948
•9000000	1•080382	1•084571	1•091534	1•101237	1•113612
•9100000	1•096985	1•101328	1•108552	1•118623	1•131483
•9200000	1•113761	1•118263	1•125753	1•136205	1•149562
•9300000	1•130712	1•135377	1•143142	1•153984	1•167853
•9400000	1•147842	1•152674	1•160720	1•171964	1•186360
•9500000	1•165152	1•170156	1•178492	1•190147	1•205085
•9600000	1•182647	1•187826	1•196458	1•208537	1•224033
•9699999	1•200327	1•205687	1•214624	1•227137	1•243205
•9799999	1•218197	1•223740	1•232990	1•245949	1•262607
•9899999	1•236257	1•241990	1•251559	1•264977	1•282239
1•0000000	1•254512	1•260439	1•270336	1•284223	1•302107
1•0100000	1•272962	1•279088	1•289321	1•303689	1•322212
1•0200000	1•291611	1•297940	1•308517	1•323380	1•342557
1•0300000	1•310461	1•316997	1•327928	1•343296	1•363146
1•0400000	1•329513	1•336263	1•347554	1•363442	1•383981
1•0500000	1•348771	1•355739	1•367399	1•383818	1•405065
1•0600000	1•368236	1•375426	1•387465	1•404428	1•426401
1•0699999	1•387910	1•395328	1•407754	1•425274	1•447990
1•0799999	1•407795	1•415445	1•428267	1•446357	1•469835
1•0899999	1•427893	1•435781	1•449007	1•467681	1•491939
1•1000000	1•448205	1•456336	1•469975	1•489246	1•514304
1•1100000	1•468732	1•477111	1•491173	1•511054	1•536930
1•1200000	1•489477	1•498109	1•512602	1•533107	1•559821
1•1300000	1•510440	1•519331	1•534264	1•555406	1•582977
1•1400000	1•531622	1•540776	1•556159	1•577953	1•606400
1•1500000	1•553024	1•562447	1•578289	1•600748	1•630091
1•1600000	1•574646	1•584344	1•600655	1•623793	1•654051
1•1700000	1•596490	1•606468	1•623256	1•647087	1•678280
1•1800000	1•618556	1•628818	1•646093	1•670631	1•702779
1•1899999	1•640843	1•651396	1•669166	1•694425	1•727548

$\alpha =$ •639999

Θ	K VALUES				
	•009966711	•039469502	•087332193	•151646642	•229848846
1•2000000	1•663351	1•674200	1•692475	1•718469	1•752587
1•2100000	1•686081	1•697230	1•716020	1•742763	1•777896
1•2200000	1•709030	1•720486	1•739799	1•767305	1•803473
1•2300000	1•732199	1•743966	1•763813	1•792095	1•829318
1•2400000	1•755587	1•767670	1•788059	1•817132	1•855429
1•2500000	1•779191	1•791596	1•812536	1•842414	1•881805
1•2599999	1•803010	1•815742	1•837242	1•867939	1•908444
1•2699999	1•827042	1•840106	1•862176	1•893704	1•935343
1•2799999	1•851285	1•864686	1•887334	1•919708	1•962499
1•2899999	1•875736	1•889480	1•912714	1•945947	1•989909
1•3000000	1•900393	1•914483	1•938314	1•972418	2•017571
1•3100000	1•925251	1•939693	1•964128	1•999117	2•045479
1•3200000	1•950307	1•965106	1•990153	2•026040	2•073630
1•3300000	1•975558	1•990719	2•016386	2•053182	2•102018
1•3400000	2•000999	2•016525	2•042822	2•080540	2•130638
1•3500000	2•026626	2•042522	2•069456	2•108108	2•159486
1•3600000	2•052433	2•068704	2•096282	2•135879	2•188555
1•3700000	2•078415	2•095065	2•123294	2•163849	2•217838
1•3799999	2•104567	2•121600	2•150488	2•192011	2•247328
1•3899999	2•130883	2•148303	2•177857	2•220358	2•277019
1•4000000	2•157356	2•175167	2•205393	2•248883	2•306904
1•4100000	2•183980	2•202185	2•233090	2•277579	2•336972
1•4200000	2•210748	2•229351	2•260941	2•306437	2•367217
1•4300000	2•237652	2•256657	2•288937	2•335449	2•397628
1•4400000	2•264686	2•284094	2•317071	2•364608	2•428198
1•4500000	2•291840	2•311656	2•345334	2•393904	2•458917
1•4600000	2•319108	2•339334	2•373718	2•423328	2•489774
1•4700000	2•346481	2•367119	2•402214	2•452870	2•520759
1•4800000	2•373950	2•395003	2•430812	2•482521	2•551862
1•4900000	2•401506	2•422976	2•459503	2•512271	2•583072
1•5000000	2•429140	2•451029	2•488278	2•542110	2•614379
1•5100000	2•456844	2•479152	2•517127	2•572026	2•645769
1•5200000	2•484607	2•507337	2•546038	2•602010	2•677233
1•5300000	2•512420	2•535573	2•575004	2•632051	2•708757
1•5400000	2•540273	2•563850	2•604012	2•662137	2•740331
1•5500000	2•568157	2•592159	2•633053	2•692257	2•771943
1•5600000	2•596061	2•620488	2•662115	2•722401	2•803580
1•5699999	2•623976	2•648829	2•691189	2•752557	2•835230
1•5707963	2•626199	2•651086	2•693505	2•754959	2•837751
1•5707963	2•626197	2•651084	2•693503	2•754957	2•837748

$\alpha =$ .639999

Θ	K VALUES				
	.318821117	.415016431	.514599755	.613601043	.708073407
.0000000	.000000	.000000	.000000	.000000	.000000
.0100000	.010000	.010000	.010000	.010000	.010000
.0200000	.020002	.020002	.020002	.020002	.020002
.0300000	.030007	.030007	.030008	.030008	.030008
.0400000	.040017	.040018	.040019	.040020	.040021
.0500000	.050033	.050035	.050037	.050039	.050041
.0600000	.060057	.060061	.060064	.060068	.060071
.0700000	.070091	.070097	.070102	.070108	.070113
.0800000	.080136	.080144	.080153	.080161	.080170
.0900000	.090194	.090206	.090218	.090230	.090242
.1000000	.100267	.100283	.100299	.100316	.100332
.1100000	.110355	.110377	.110399	.110421	.110442
.1200000	.120461	.120489	.120518	.120547	.120575
.1300000	.130587	.130623	.130659	.130696	.130731
.1400000	.140734	.140778	.140824	.140870	.140914
.1500000	.150903	.150958	.151015	.151071	.151125
.1600000	.161097	.161163	.161233	.161301	.161367
.1700000	.171317	.171397	.171480	.171562	.171642
.1800000	.181564	.181659	.181758	.181857	.181951
.1900000	.191841	.191953	.192070	.192186	.192297
.2000000	.202149	.202280	.202416	.202552	.202682
.2100000	.212490	.212642	.212800	.212958	.213109
.2200000	.222866	.223041	.223223	.223405	.223579
.2300000	.233278	.233479	.233687	.233895	.234095
.2400000	.243729	.243957	.244194	.244432	.244659
.2500000	.254219	.254477	.254747	.255016	.255274
.2600000	.264751	.265042	.265346	.265650	.265942
.2700000	.275326	.275654	.275995	.276337	.276665
.2800000	.285947	.286314	.286695	.287078	.287445
.2900000	.296615	.297024	.297449	.297876	.298286
.3000000	.307333	.307786	.308259	.308733	.309190
.3100000	.318101	.318603	.319127	.319652	.320158
.3200000	.328923	.329476	.330055	.330635	.331194
.3300000	.339799	.340408	.341045	.341685	.342301
.3400000	.350732	.351401	.352100	.352803	.353481
.3500000	.361725	.362456	.363223	.363993	.364736
.3600000	.372778	.373577	.374414	.375256	.376070
.3700000	.383894	.384765	.385678	.386597	.387485
.3800000	.395075	.396022	.397015	.398016	.398984
.3900000	.406323	.407351	.408430	.409517	.410570

$\alpha =$ .639999

Θ	K VALUES				
	.318821117	.415016431	.514599755	.613601043	.708073407
.4000000	.417640	.418754	.419923	.421103	.422246
.4100000	.429029	.430233	.431499	.432777	.434015
.4200000	.440491	.441791	.443158	.444540	.445880
.4300000	.452029	.453430	.454905	.456396	.457844
.4400000	.463645	.465153	.466741	.468349	.469911
.4500000	.475342	.476961	.478670	.480400	.482083
.4600000	.487120	.488859	.490693	.492553	.494364
.4700000	.498984	.500847	.502814	.504812	.506757
.4800000	.510935	.512929	.515037	.517178	.519266
.4900000	.522976	.525107	.527362	.529656	.531895
.5000000	.535108	.537384	.539794	.542248	.544646
.5100000	.547336	.549763	.552336	.554959	.557523
.5200000	.559660	.562246	.564990	.567790	.570531
.5300000	.572084	.574836	.577760	.580746	.583673
.5400000	.584610	.587536	.590649	.593831	.596953
.5500000	.597240	.600350	.603660	.607047	.610375
.5600000	.609978	.613279	.616795	.620399	.623943
.5700000	.622827	.626326	.630060	.633890	.637662
.5800000	.635788	.639496	.643456	.647524	.651534
.5900000	.648864	.652791	.656988	.661305	.665566
.6000000	.662060	.666213	.670659	.675236	.679761
.6100000	.675376	.679767	.684472	.689323	.694124
.6200000	.688817	.693455	.698431	.703568	.708659
.6300000	.702384	.707280	.712540	.717976	.723372
.6400000	.716082	.721247	.726802	.732552	.738266
.6500000	.729913	.735357	.741221	.747299	.753348
.6600000	.743879	.749616	.755802	.762222	.768622
.6700000	.757986	.764026	.770547	.777326	.784094
.6800000	.772234	.778590	.785462	.792615	.799767
.6899999	.786628	.793312	.800549	.808094	.815649
.7000000	.801171	.808197	.815814	.823767	.831745
.7100000	.815865	.823247	.831260	.839640	.848060
.7200000	.830715	.838466	.846892	.855717	.864600
.7300000	.845724	.853858	.862714	.872004	.881371
.7400000	.860895	.869427	.878730	.888505	.898378
.7500000	.876231	.885177	.894945	.905226	.915629
.7600000	.891736	.901111	.911363	.922171	.933129
.7700000	.907413	.917233	.927989	.939348	.950884
.7800000	.923267	.933548	.944827	.956760	.968902
.7899999	.939299	.950060	.961883	.974413	.987189

$\alpha =$ .639999

θ	K VALUES				
	.318821117	.415016431	.514599755	.613601043	.708073407
.8000000	.955515	.966772	.979161	.992314	1.005752
.8100000	.971918	.983689	.996665	1.010467	1.024597
.8200000	.988510	1.000815	1.014401	1.028879	1.043731
.8300000	1.005297	1.018154	1.032373	1.047555	1.063162
.8400000	1.022282	1.035710	1.050587	1.066501	1.082897
.8500000	1.039467	1.053488	1.069047	1.085724	1.102944
.8600000	1.056858	1.071492	1.087758	1.105230	1.123310
.8700000	1.074458	1.089726	1.106727	1.125024	1.144002
.8799999	1.092270	1.108194	1.125957	1.145113	1.165028
.8899999	1.110298	1.126901	1.145453	1.165503	1.186397
.9000000	1.128547	1.145851	1.165222	1.186201	1.208115
.9100000	1.147020	1.165049	1.185268	1.207213	1.230192
.9200000	1.165720	1.184498	1.205597	1.228545	1.252636
.9300000	1.184651	1.204204	1.226213	1.250204	1.275454
.9400000	1.203818	1.224169	1.247122	1.272197	1.298655
.9500000	1.223223	1.244400	1.268328	1.294529	1.322247
.9600000	1.242871	1.264900	1.289839	1.317207	1.346239
.9699999	1.262765	1.285673	1.311657	1.340239	1.370640
.9799999	1.282908	1.306724	1.333789	1.363630	1.395458
.9899999	1.303305	1.328056	1.356239	1.387387	1.420701
1.0000000	1.323959	1.349674	1.379013	1.411516	1.446378
1.0100000	1.344872	1.371581	1.402116	1.436024	1.472499
1.0200000	1.366049	1.393783	1.425552	1.460917	1.499070
1.0300000	1.387492	1.416281	1.449326	1.486202	1.526102
1.0400000	1.409206	1.439082	1.473443	1.511883	1.553602
1.0500000	1.431192	1.462187	1.497907	1.537969	1.581579
1.0600000	1.453454	1.485600	1.522723	1.564464	1.610041
1.0699999	1.475994	1.509325	1.547896	1.591374	1.638996
1.0799999	1.498816	1.533365	1.573428	1.618705	1.668454
1.0899999	1.521921	1.557724	1.599325	1.646462	1.698420
1.1000000	1.545313	1.582403	1.625590	1.674651	1.728904
1.1100000	1.568993	1.607406	1.652226	1.703276	1.759913
1.1200000	1.592964	1.632734	1.679237	1.732341	1.791453
1.1300000	1.617226	1.658391	1.706625	1.761853	1.823532
1.1400000	1.641782	1.684378	1.734394	1.791814	1.856157
1.1500000	1.666633	1.710698	1.762545	1.822228	1.889333
1.1600000	1.691779	1.737350	1.791082	1.853099	1.923066
1.1700000	1.717223	1.764337	1.820005	1.884430	1.957362
1.1800000	1.742964	1.791660	1.849317	1.916222	1.992226
1.1899999	1.769003	1.819318	1.879017	1.948479	2.027661

$\alpha =$ .639999

Θ	K VALUES				
	.318821117	.415016431	.514599755	.613601043	.708073407
1.2000000	1.795340	1.847313	1.909108	1.981203	2.063673
1.2100000	1.821973	1.875643	1.939588	2.014393	2.100263
1.2200000	1.848904	1.904309	1.970459	2.048051	2.137435
1.2300000	1.876129	1.933309	2.001718	2.082176	2.175190
1.2400000	1.903649	1.962642	2.033365	2.116769	2.213529
1.2500000	1.931462	1.992306	2.065398	2.151827	2.252452
1.2599999	1.959564	2.022299	2.097815	2.187349	2.291959
1.2699999	1.987954	2.052618	2.130612	2.223332	2.332049
1.2799999	2.016628	2.083259	2.163788	2.259773	2.372718
1.2899999	2.045584	2.114220	2.197337	2.296668	2.413964
1.3000000	2.074817	2.145496	2.231255	2.334013	2.455782
1.3100000	2.104324	2.177082	2.265537	2.371800	2.498166
1.3200000	2.134098	2.208973	2.300177	2.410025	2.541111
1.3300000	2.164135	2.241163	2.335168	2.448679	2.584607
1.3400000	2.194430	2.273646	2.370503	2.487755	2.628647
1.3500000	2.224976	2.306415	2.406176	2.527244	2.673220
1.3600000	2.255767	2.339463	2.442176	2.567135	2.718314
1.3700000	2.286796	2.372781	2.478495	2.607419	2.763919
1.3799999	2.318054	2.406361	2.515124	2.648084	2.810019
1.3899999	2.349535	2.440195	2.552051	2.689118	2.856600
1.4000000	2.381229	2.474272	2.589266	2.730506	2.903646
1.4100000	2.413128	2.508583	2.626757	2.772236	2.951138
1.4200000	2.445222	2.543116	2.664511	2.814291	2.999059
1.4300000	2.477502	2.577862	2.702516	2.856657	3.047389
1.4400000	2.509957	2.612807	2.740757	2.899317	3.096106
1.4500000	2.542577	2.647940	2.779222	2.942253	3.145189
1.4600000	2.575350	2.683250	2.817894	2.985448	3.194614
1.4700000	2.608266	2.718721	2.856760	3.028882	3.244357
1.4800000	2.641312	2.754342	2.895802	3.072537	3.294392
1.4900000	2.674478	2.790099	2.935006	3.116392	3.344694
1.5000000	2.707749	2.825978	2.974354	3.160428	3.395236
1.5100000	2.741115	2.861963	3.013829	3.204621	3.445989
1.5200000	2.774561	2.898041	3.053414	3.248952	3.496925
1.5300000	2.808076	2.934197	3.093091	3.293398	3.548014
1.5400000	2.841645	2.970416	3.132843	3.337937	3.599228
1.5500000	2.875256	3.006682	3.172651	3.382547	3.650537
1.5600000	2.908895	3.042981	3.212497	3.427204	3.701909
1.5699999	2.942548	3.079296	3.252364	3.471886	3.753314
1.5707963	2.945228	3.082188	3.255539	3.475445	3.757408
1.5707963	2.945226	3.082186	3.255537	3.475445	3.757404

$\alpha =$ •639999

Θ	K VALUES				
	•794250555	•868696860	•928444378	•971111163	•994996249
•0000000	•000000	•000000	•000000	•000000	•000000
•0100000	•010000	•010000	•010000	•010000	•010000
•0200000	•020002	•020002	•020002	•020003	•020003
•0300000	•030009	•030009	•030009	•030010	•030010
•0400000	•040022	•040022	•040023	•040024	•040024
•0500000	•050043	•050044	•050046	•050046	•050047
•0600000	•060074	•060077	•060079	•060081	•060082
•0700000	•070118	•070123	•070126	•070128	•070130
•0800000	•080177	•080183	•080188	•080192	•080194
•0900000	•090252	•090261	•090269	•090274	•090277
•1000000	•100346	•100359	•100369	•100376	•100380
•1100000	•110461	•110478	•110492	•110501	•110507
•1200000	•120600	•120621	•120639	•120651	•120658
•1300000	•130763	•130791	•130813	•130829	•130838
•1400000	•140954	•140989	•141017	•141037	•141048
•1500000	•151175	•151218	•151252	•151276	•151290
•1600000	•161427	•161479	•161521	•161551	•161568
•1700000	•171714	•171776	•171827	•171863	•171883
•1800000	•182037	•182111	•182171	•182214	•182238
•1900000	•192398	•192486	•192557	•192608	•192636
•2000000	•202801	•202904	•202987	•203046	•203080
•2100000	•213247	•213367	•213463	•213532	•213571
•2200000	•223738	•223877	•223988	•224068	•224112
•2300000	•234278	•234437	•234564	•234656	•234707
•2400000	•244868	•245049	•245195	•245299	•245358
•2500000	•255511	•255717	•255882	•256001	•256068
•2600000	•266210	•266442	•266629	•266763	•266839
•2700000	•276966	•277228	•277438	•277590	•277674
•2800000	•287783	•288076	•288313	•288482	•288577
•2900000	•298663	•298991	•299255	•299444	•299551
•3000000	•309609	•309973	•310268	•310479	•310597
•3100000	•320623	•321028	•321355	•321589	•321721
•3200000	•331709	•332157	•332518	•332778	•332924
•3300000	•342868	•343363	•343762	•344049	•344210
•3400000	•354105	•354649	•355089	•355405	•355582
•3500000	•365421	•366018	•366502	•366849	•367044
•3600000	•376820	•377474	•378004	•378385	•378599
•3700000	•388304	•389020	•389600	•390016	•390251
•3800000	•399878	•400659	•401291	•401746	•402002
•3900000	•411543	•412393	•413083	•413579	•413858

$\alpha =$ .639999

Θ	K VALUES				
	.794250555	.868696860	.928444378	.971111163	.994996249
.4000000	.423303	.424228	.424978	.425518	.425821
.4100000	.435162	.436165	.436980	.437566	.437897
.4200000	.447122	.448209	.449092	.449729	.450087
.4300000	.459187	.460364	.461320	.462009	.462398
.4400000	.471360	.472632	.473666	.474412	.474832
.4500000	.483646	.485018	.486135	.486941	.487395
.4600000	.496047	.497526	.498730	.499600	.500090
.4700000	.508568	.510160	.511457	.512394	.512923
.4800000	.521211	.522923	.524319	.525328	.525897
.4900000	.533982	.535820	.537320	.538405	.539018
.5000000	.546883	.548855	.550466	.551632	.552291
.5100000	.559919	.562033	.563762	.565013	.565721
.5200000	.573094	.575359	.577211	.578553	.579312
.5300000	.586413	.588835	.590819	.592258	.593071
.5400000	.599879	.602469	.604591	.606132	.607003
.5500000	.613497	.616264	.618533	.620181	.621114
.5600000	.627272	.630225	.632649	.634411	.635409
.5700000	.641208	.644357	.646946	.648829	.649896
.5800000	.655310	.658667	.661428	.663439	.664579
.5900000	.669583	.673158	.676103	.678248	.679466
.6000000	.684031	.687838	.690976	.693264	.694563
.6100000	.698661	.702711	.706052	.708492	.709877
.6200000	.713477	.717783	.721340	.723939	.725416
.6300000	.728485	.733060	.736845	.739613	.741186
.6400000	.743690	.748549	.752574	.755520	.757196
.6500000	.759098	.764256	.768534	.771669	.773454
.6600000	.774714	.780188	.784733	.788067	.789967
.6700000	.790545	.796351	.801178	.804722	.806744
.6800000	.806597	.812752	.817876	.821643	.823793
.6899999	.822876	.829398	.834837	.838839	.841125
.7000000	.839388	.846297	.852067	.856318	.858748
.7100000	.856140	.863457	.869576	.874090	.876672
.7200000	.873138	.880884	.887371	.892163	.894907
.7300000	.890391	.898587	.905464	.910549	.913464
.7400000	.907903	.916575	.923861	.929258	.932354
.7500000	.925684	.934855	.942574	.948299	.951587
.7600000	.943740	.953436	.961612	.967685	.971175
.7700000	.962079	.972328	.980986	.987426	.991132
.7800000	.980708	.991539	1.000706	1.007535	1.011468
.7899999	.999637	1.011080	1.020783	1.028023	1.032198

$\alpha =$ .639999

Θ	K VALUES				
	.794250555	.868696860	.928444378	.971111163	.994996249
.8000000	1.018872	1.030959	1.041228	1.048904	1.053336
.8100000	1.038422	1.051187	1.062054	1.070191	1.074894
.8200000	1.058296	1.071773	1.083272	1.091897	1.096888
.8300000	1.078502	1.092730	1.104894	1.114036	1.119334
.8400000	1.099050	1.114067	1.126935	1.136624	1.142246
.8500000	1.119948	1.135795	1.149406	1.159675	1.165642
.8600000	1.141206	1.157927	1.172323	1.183206	1.189540
.8700000	1.162834	1.180474	1.195699	1.207234	1.213956
.8799999	1.184840	1.203448	1.219549	1.231774	1.238911
.8899999	1.207236	1.226861	1.243888	1.256846	1.264422
.9000000	1.230031	1.250728	1.268732	1.282467	1.290512
.9100000	1.253236	1.275059	1.294098	1.308658	1.317201
.9200000	1.276861	1.299870	1.320002	1.335437	1.344510
.9300000	1.300916	1.325174	1.346461	1.362826	1.372465
.9400000	1.325413	1.350985	1.373495	1.390847	1.401088
.9500000	1.350363	1.377317	1.401120	1.419522	1.430405
.9600000	1.375776	1.404186	1.429357	1.448875	1.460443
.9699999	1.401665	1.431607	1.458226	1.478930	1.491230
.9799999	1.428041	1.459595	1.487746	1.509712	1.522794
.9899999	1.454916	1.488166	1.517939	1.541249	1.555166
1.0000000	1.482301	1.517337	1.548828	1.573568	1.588378
1.0100000	1.510208	1.547125	1.580434	1.606697	1.622463
1.0200000	1.538649	1.577545	1.612780	1.640668	1.657456
1.0300000	1.567637	1.608616	1.645892	1.675510	1.693394
1.0400000	1.597184	1.640354	1.679793	1.711257	1.730317
1.0500000	1.627301	1.672779	1.714509	1.747944	1.768264
1.0600000	1.658002	1.705907	1.750067	1.785605	1.807278
1.0699999	1.689297	1.739758	1.786493	1.824278	1.847405
1.0799999	1.721200	1.774350	1.823816	1.864001	1.888693
1.0899999	1.753723	1.809702	1.862064	1.904816	1.931191
1.1000000	1.786878	1.845833	1.901268	1.946764	1.974952
1.1100000	1.820675	1.882762	1.941456	1.989890	2.020033
1.1200000	1.855128	1.920509	1.982660	2.034240	2.066492
1.1300000	1.890247	1.959092	2.024912	2.079862	2.114393
1.1400000	1.926044	1.998531	2.068245	2.126808	2.163802
1.1500000	1.962529	2.038846	2.112693	2.175129	2.214789
1.1600000	1.999714	2.080055	2.158288	2.224882	2.267430
1.1700000	2.037607	2.122178	2.205067	2.276123	2.321805
1.1800000	2.076219	2.165233	2.253065	2.328915	2.377998
1.1899999	2.115559	2.209239	2.302317	2.383319	2.436100

$\alpha =$ .639999

Θ	K VALUES				
	.794250555	.868696860	.928444378	.971111163	.994996249
1.2000000	2.155635	2.254214	2.352861	2.439403	2.496210
1.2100000	2.196454	2.300175	2.404734	2.497236	2.558431
1.2200000	2.238024	2.347139	2.457971	2.556891	2.622873
1.2300000	2.280350	2.395122	2.512613	2.618442	2.689657
1.2400000	2.323438	2.444140	2.568695	2.681971	2.758913
1.2500000	2.367293	2.494206	2.626255	2.747560	2.830779
1.2599999	2.411916	2.545333	2.685332	2.815295	2.905405
1.2699999	2.457311	2.597534	2.745961	2.885268	2.982955
1.2799999	2.503477	2.650818	2.808179	2.957573	3.063605
1.2899999	2.550415	2.705194	2.872020	3.032308	3.147547
1.3000000	2.598122	2.760670	2.937520	3.109575	3.234993
1.3100000	2.646595	2.817249	3.004709	3.189480	3.326171
1.3200000	2.695828	2.874934	3.073617	3.272133	3.421332
1.3300000	2.745816	2.933726	3.144273	3.357646	3.520754
1.3400000	2.796549	2.993623	3.216700	3.446135	3.624742
1.3500000	2.848018	3.054618	3.290920	3.537719	3.733634
1.3600000	2.900210	3.116705	3.366949	3.632518	3.847805
1.3700000	2.953112	3.179871	3.444800	3.730651	3.967671
1.3799999	3.006707	3.244102	3.524478	3.832238	4.093699
1.3899999	3.060979	3.309381	3.605986	3.937397	4.226408
1.4000000	3.115907	3.375686	3.689316	4.046240	4.366385
1.4100000	3.171468	3.442989	3.774453	4.158871	4.514284
1.4200000	3.227640	3.511263	3.861376	4.275386	4.670848
1.4300000	3.284397	3.580473	3.950053	4.395865	4.836913
1.4400000	3.341709	3.650581	4.040441	4.520368	5.013422
1.4500000	3.399548	3.721547	4.132490	4.648933	5.201438
1.4600000	3.457882	3.793324	4.226136	4.781565	5.402149
1.4700000	3.516677	3.865862	4.321304	4.918234	5.616879
1.4800000	3.575898	3.939107	4.417907	5.058865	5.847075
1.4900000	3.635507	4.013001	4.515848	5.203333	6.094277
1.5000000	3.695467	4.087484	4.615015	5.351457	6.360055
1.5100000	3.755736	4.162490	4.715286	5.502990	6.645872
1.5200000	3.816275	4.237952	4.816529	5.657623	6.952874
1.5300000	3.877039	4.313798	4.918601	5.814979	7.281539
1.5400000	3.937987	4.389958	5.021351	5.974616	7.631224
1.5500000	3.999073	4.466354	5.124619	6.136035	7.999646
1.5600000	4.060254	4.542912	5.228241	6.298688	8.382508
1.5699999	4.121483	4.619554	5.332048	6.461991	8.773549
1.5707963	4.126360	4.625659	5.340317	6.475006	8.804820
1.5707963	4.126356	4.625655	5.340312	6.474999	8.804810

$\alpha =$ .659999

Θ	K VALUES				
	.009966711	.039469502	.087332193	.151646642	.229848846
.0000000	.000000	.000000	.000000	.000000	.000000
.0100000	.010000	.010000	.010000	.010000	.010000
.0200000	.020001	.020001	.020001	.020001	.020002
.0300000	.030006	.030006	.030006	.030006	.030006
.0400000	.040014	.040014	.040015	.040015	.040016
.0500000	.050027	.050028	.050029	.050030	.050032
.0600000	.060047	.060049	.060050	.060053	.060055
.0700000	.070076	.070077	.070080	.070084	.070088
.0800000	.080113	.080116	.080120	.080125	.080132
.0900000	.090161	.090165	.090171	.090179	.090188
.1000000	.100222	.100227	.100235	.100245	.100258
.1100000	.110295	.110302	.110312	.110327	.110344
.1200000	.120384	.120392	.120406	.120425	.120447
.1300000	.130488	.130499	.130517	.130540	.130569
.1400000	.140610	.140624	.140646	.140675	.140711
.1500000	.150751	.150768	.150795	.150831	.150875
.1600000	.160912	.160932	.160965	.161009	.161063
.1700000	.171095	.171119	.171159	.171212	.171276
.1800000	.181300	.181329	.181376	.181439	.181516
.1900000	.191531	.191565	.191620	.191694	.191785
.2000000	.201787	.201826	.201891	.201978	.202083
.2100000	.212070	.212116	.212191	.212291	.212414
.2200000	.222382	.222435	.222521	.222637	.222778
.2300000	.232725	.232785	.232883	.233016	.233178
.2400000	.243099	.243167	.243279	.243430	.243614
.2500000	.253506	.253584	.253710	.253881	.254089
.2600000	.263947	.264035	.264178	.264370	.264605
.2700000	.274425	.274524	.274683	.274899	.275163
.2800000	.284941	.285051	.285229	.285470	.285765
.2900000	.295495	.295618	.295816	.296084	.296412
.3000000	.306091	.306226	.306446	.306744	.307108
.3100000	.316728	.316878	.317121	.317450	.317852
.3200000	.327410	.327575	.327843	.328205	.328649
.3300000	.338137	.338318	.338613	.339011	.339498
.3400000	.348911	.349109	.349432	.349868	.350403
.3500000	.359734	.359950	.360303	.360780	.361364
.3600000	.370607	.370843	.371227	.371747	.372385
.3700000	.381532	.381789	.382207	.382773	.383467
.3800000	.392511	.392789	.393243	.393857	.394611
.3900000	.403545	.403847	.404338	.405004	.405821

$\alpha =$ .659999

Θ	K VALUES				
	.009966711	.039469502	.087332193	.151646642	.229848846
.4000000	.414637	.414962	.415494	.416214	.417098
.4100000	.425787	.426138	.426712	.427489	.428444
.4200000	.436998	.437376	.437994	.438831	.439861
.4300000	.448271	.448678	.449343	.450244	.451352
.4400000	.459609	.460046	.460759	.461727	.462918
.4500000	.471013	.471481	.472246	.473284	.474562
.4600000	.482485	.482986	.483805	.484916	.486286
.4700000	.494027	.494563	.495438	.496627	.498093
.4800000	.505641	.506212	.507147	.508417	.509984
.4900000	.517328	.517938	.518934	.520289	.521962
.5000000	.529092	.529740	.530802	.532245	.534029
.5100000	.540933	.541623	.542752	.544288	.546188
.5200000	.552853	.553586	.554786	.556420	.558440
.5300000	.564856	.565634	.566908	.568643	.570790
.5400000	.576943	.577767	.579118	.580959	.583239
.5500000	.589115	.589989	.591420	.593371	.595789
.5600000	.601376	.602300	.603815	.605881	.608443
.5700000	.613728	.614704	.616306	.618492	.621204
.5800000	.626171	.627203	.628895	.631206	.634075
.5900000	.638710	.639799	.641585	.644025	.647058
.6000000	.651346	.652494	.654377	.656953	.660156
.6100000	.664081	.665290	.667276	.669992	.673371
.6200000	.676918	.678191	.680282	.683144	.686708
.6300000	.689860	.691198	.693399	.696412	.700167
.6400000	.702907	.704315	.706628	.709799	.713753
.6500000	.716064	.717542	.719973	.723307	.727468
.6600000	.729332	.730884	.733437	.736940	.741315
.6700000	.742714	.744342	.747021	.750699	.755298
.6800000	.756213	.757919	.760729	.764589	.769418
.6899999	.769830	.771618	.774564	.778612	.783681
.7000000	.783570	.785442	.788527	.792771	.798088
.7100000	.797433	.799393	.802623	.807068	.812643
.7200000	.811424	.813473	.816853	.821507	.827349
.7300000	.825544	.827686	.831221	.836091	.842209
.7400000	.839797	.842035	.845729	.850823	.857227
.7500000	.854185	.856522	.860381	.865706	.872406
.7600000	.868711	.871150	.875180	.880743	.887750
.7700000	.883377	.885922	.890128	.895937	.903261
.7800000	.898188	.900841	.905228	.911293	.918944
.7899999	.913144	.915910	.920485	.926812	.934802

$\alpha =$ .659999

θ	K VALUES				
	.009966711	.039469502	.087332193	.151646642	.229848846
.8000000	.928251	.931132	.935900	.942498	.950839
.8100000	.943510	.946510	.951476	.958355	.967057
.8200000	.958924	.962046	.967218	.974386	.983462
.8300000	.974497	.977745	.983128	.990594	1.000055
.8400000	.990231	.993609	.999210	1.006982	1.016842
.8500000	1.006129	1.009641	1.015466	1.023555	1.033826
.8600000	1.022195	1.025845	1.031900	1.040315	1.051010
.8700000	1.038432	1.042223	1.048516	1.057267	1.068399
.8799999	1.054842	1.058778	1.065316	1.074412	1.085995
.8899999	1.071429	1.075515	1.082303	1.091756	1.103804
.9000000	1.088196	1.092435	1.099482	1.109302	1.121828
.9100000	1.105146	1.109542	1.116855	1.127052	1.140072
.9200000	1.122281	1.126840	1.134426	1.145011	1.158539
.9300000	1.139606	1.144331	1.152197	1.163181	1.177233
.9400000	1.157123	1.162019	1.170173	1.181567	1.196158
.9500000	1.174835	1.179907	1.188357	1.200173	1.215318
.9600000	1.192746	1.197997	1.206751	1.219000	1.234717
.9699999	1.210858	1.216294	1.225359	1.238054	1.254357
.9799999	1.229174	1.234799	1.244185	1.257337	1.274243
.9899999	1.247698	1.253517	1.263231	1.276852	1.294379
1.0000000	1.266432	1.272450	1.282500	1.296603	1.314769
1.0100000	1.285379	1.291601	1.301996	1.316594	1.335415
1.0200000	1.304541	1.310972	1.321722	1.336827	1.356321
1.0300000	1.323923	1.330568	1.341680	1.357305	1.377491
1.0400000	1.343526	1.350390	1.361873	1.378033	1.398928
1.0500000	1.363353	1.370441	1.382305	1.399011	1.420635
1.0600000	1.383406	1.390724	1.402977	1.420244	1.442615
1.0699999	1.403689	1.411241	1.423893	1.441735	1.464872
1.0799999	1.424202	1.431995	1.445055	1.463485	1.487408
1.0899999	1.444950	1.452987	1.466465	1.485497	1.510227
1.1000000	1.465933	1.474221	1.488126	1.507775	1.533330
1.1100000	1.487153	1.495698	1.510039	1.530319	1.556720
1.1200000	1.508612	1.517419	1.532207	1.553132	1.580400
1.1300000	1.530313	1.539387	1.554631	1.576216	1.604371
1.1400000	1.552256	1.561604	1.577313	1.599573	1.628635
1.1500000	1.574442	1.584069	1.600254	1.623203	1.653194
1.1600000	1.596873	1.606785	1.623455	1.647109	1.678050
1.1700000	1.619550	1.629752	1.646918	1.671291	1.703202
1.1800000	1.642473	1.652971	1.670643	1.695750	1.728654
1.1899999	1.665643	1.676442	1.694630	1.720487	1.754404

$\alpha =$ .659999

θ	K VALUES				
	.009966711	.039469502	.087332193	.151646642	.229848846
1.2000000	1.689060	1.700166	1.718879	1.745501	1.780453
1.2100000	1.712723	1.724143	1.743392	1.770793	1.806802
1.2200000	1.736633	1.748372	1.768166	1.796362	1.833449
1.2300000	1.760788	1.772852	1.793202	1.822208	1.860394
1.2400000	1.785188	1.797582	1.818498	1.848329	1.887636
1.2500000	1.809832	1.822562	1.844053	1.874724	1.915174
1.2599999	1.834717	1.847789	1.869865	1.901392	1.943005
1.2699999	1.859843	1.873261	1.895933	1.928329	1.971128
1.2799999	1.885206	1.898977	1.922254	1.955535	1.999539
1.2899999	1.910804	1.924934	1.948825	1.983004	2.028235
1.3000000	1.936634	1.951127	1.975643	2.010735	2.057213
1.3100000	1.962693	1.977555	2.002704	2.038724	2.086469
1.3200000	1.988977	2.004213	2.030004	2.066965	2.115999
1.3300000	2.015481	2.031096	2.057539	2.095456	2.145796
1.3400000	2.042201	2.058201	2.085304	2.124189	2.175856
1.3500000	2.069132	2.085521	2.113293	2.153160	2.206172
1.3600000	2.096269	2.113053	2.141502	2.182363	2.236739
1.3700000	2.123606	2.140788	2.169923	2.211791	2.267549
1.3799999	2.151137	2.168722	2.198551	2.241438	2.298594
1.3899999	2.178855	2.196848	2.227378	2.271295	2.329868
1.4000000	2.206754	2.225158	2.256397	2.301356	2.361360
1.4100000	2.234824	2.253645	2.285599	2.331611	2.393063
1.4200000	2.263060	2.282300	2.314977	2.362052	2.424966
1.4300000	2.291453	2.311116	2.344522	2.392669	2.457060
1.4400000	2.319994	2.340084	2.374225	2.423454	2.489335
1.4500000	2.348674	2.369194	2.404076	2.454396	2.521779
1.4600000	2.377485	2.398438	2.434065	2.485484	2.554382
1.4700000	2.406416	2.427805	2.464183	2.516709	2.587131
1.4800000	2.435458	2.457285	2.494419	2.548058	2.620015
1.4900000	2.464600	2.486868	2.524762	2.579520	2.653022
1.5000000	2.493833	2.516544	2.555202	2.611085	2.686139
1.5100000	2.523146	2.546301	2.585725	2.642739	2.719353
1.5200000	2.552527	2.576129	2.616322	2.674470	2.752650
1.5300000	2.581966	2.606015	2.646981	2.706267	2.786018
1.5400000	2.611451	2.635950	2.677689	2.738116	2.819442
1.5500000	2.640972	2.665920	2.708435	2.770005	2.852910
1.5600000	2.670516	2.695915	2.739206	2.801921	2.886406
1.5699999	2.700073	2.725922	2.769990	2.833851	2.919918
1.5707963	2.702427	2.728312	2.772442	2.836393	2.922587
1.5707963	2.702425	2.728310	2.772439	2.836391	2.922585

$\alpha =$ .659999

Θ	K VALUES				
	.318821117	.415016431	.514599755	.613601043	.708073407
.0000000	.000000	.000000	.000000	.000000	.000000
.0100000	.010000	.010000	.010000	.010000	.010000
.0200000	.020002	.020002	.020002	.020002	.020002
.0300000	.030007	.030007	.030008	.030008	.030009
.0400000	.040017	.040018	.040019	.040020	.040021
.0500000	.050034	.050036	.050038	.050040	.050042
.0600000	.060059	.060062	.060066	.060069	.060073
.0700000	.070093	.070099	.070105	.070110	.070116
.0800000	.080140	.080148	.080156	.080165	.080173
.0900000	.090199	.090211	.090223	.090235	.090247
.1000000	.100273	.100289	.100306	.100323	.100339
.1100000	.110364	.110386	.110408	.110430	.110451
.1200000	.120473	.120501	.120530	.120559	.120586
.1300000	.130602	.130637	.130674	.130711	.130746
.1400000	.140752	.140797	.140843	.140889	.140933
.1500000	.150926	.150981	.151038	.151094	.151148
.1600000	.161125	.161191	.161260	.161329	.161395
.1700000	.171350	.171430	.171513	.171596	.171675
.1800000	.181604	.181699	.181798	.181896	.181991
.1900000	.191888	.192000	.192117	.192233	.192344
.2000000	.202204	.202335	.202471	.202607	.202737
.2100000	.212554	.212706	.212864	.213022	.213173
.2200000	.222940	.223115	.223297	.223478	.223653
.2300000	.233362	.233563	.233772	.233980	.234180
.2400000	.243824	.244053	.244290	.244528	.244756
.2500000	.254327	.254586	.254856	.255125	.255384
.2600000	.264873	.265165	.265469	.265774	.266066
.2700000	.275464	.275792	.276134	.276475	.276804
.2800000	.286101	.286468	.286851	.287233	.287601
.2900000	.296788	.297196	.297622	.298049	.298460
.3000000	.307524	.307978	.308451	.308926	.309383
.3100000	.318313	.318816	.319340	.319866	.320372
.3200000	.329157	.329711	.330290	.330872	.331431
.3300000	.340057	.340667	.341305	.341945	.342562
.3400000	.351016	.351685	.352386	.353089	.353768
.3500000	.362035	.362768	.363535	.364307	.365051
.3600000	.373117	.373918	.374756	.375600	.376415
.3700000	.384264	.385137	.386051	.386972	.387861
.3800000	.395478	.396427	.397422	.398425	.399394
.3900000	.406761	.407791	.408872	.409962	.411017

$\alpha =$ .659999

Θ	K VALUES				
	.318821117	.415016431	.514599755	.613601043	.708073407
.4000000	.418116	.419232	.420403	.421586	.422731
.4100000	.429544	.430751	.432019	.433300	.434541
.4200000	.441048	.442351	.443721	.445106	.446449
.4300000	.452630	.454034	.455513	.457008	.458459
.4400000	.464293	.465804	.467396	.469008	.470574
.4500000	.476039	.477663	.479375	.481110	.482798
.4600000	.487870	.489613	.491452	.493317	.495133
.4700000	.499788	.501656	.503630	.505633	.507584
.4800000	.511797	.513797	.515911	.518059	.520154
.4900000	.523899	.526037	.528299	.530600	.532846
.5000000	.536096	.538379	.540797	.543259	.545665
.5100000	.548391	.550826	.553409	.556040	.558614
.5200000	.560786	.563382	.566136	.568946	.571697
.5300000	.573285	.576048	.578983	.581980	.584918
.5400000	.585890	.588828	.591952	.595147	.598281
.5500000	.598603	.601725	.605048	.608449	.611791
.5600000	.611428	.614742	.618273	.621892	.625451
.5700000	.624367	.627882	.631631	.635478	.639266
.5800000	.637423	.641148	.645126	.649212	.653241
.5900000	.650600	.654544	.658761	.663098	.667380
.6000000	.663899	.668073	.672541	.677140	.681688
.6100000	.677325	.681738	.686467	.691343	.696169
.6200000	.690881	.695543	.700545	.705709	.710828
.6300000	.704568	.709491	.714779	.720245	.725671
.6400000	.718391	.723585	.729172	.734954	.740702
.6500000	.732353	.737830	.743728	.749841	.755927
.6600000	.746458	.752229	.758452	.764911	.771351
.6700000	.760707	.766785	.773347	.780169	.786980
.6800000	.775106	.781502	.788419	.795619	.802818
.6899999	.789656	.796385	.803671	.811266	.818873
.7000000	.804362	.811437	.819107	.827116	.835150
.7100000	.819228	.826662	.834733	.843173	.851654
.7200000	.834256	.842064	.850552	.859443	.868393
.7300000	.849451	.857646	.866570	.875932	.885371
.7400000	.864816	.873414	.882791	.892644	.902596
.7500000	.880354	.889372	.899220	.909585	.920075
.7600000	.896070	.905523	.915861	.926762	.937813
.7700000	.911968	.921872	.932721	.944179	.955818
.7800000	.928050	.938423	.949803	.961843	.974096
.7899999	.944322	.955181	.967112	.979759	.992656

$\alpha =$ •659999

Θ	K VALUES				
	•318821117	•415016431	•514599755	•613601043	•708073407
•8000000	•960787	•972150	•984655	•997935	1•011503
•8100000	•977449	•989334	1•002437	1•016375	1•030646
•8200000	•994312	1•006739	1•020461	1•035087	1•050092
•8300000	1•011380	1•024369	1•038735	1•054076	1•069849
•8400000	1•028657	1•042228	1•057263	1•073349	1•089925
•8500000	1•046148	1•060321	1•076050	1•092913	1•110327
•8600000	1•063856	1•078653	1•095103	1•112774	1•131064
•8700000	1•081786	1•097229	1•114427	1•132940	1•152144
•8799999	1•099941	1•116053	1•134028	1•153416	1•173576
•8899999	1•118327	1•135131	1•153911	1•174210	1•195368
•9000000	1•136947	1•154467	1•174082	1•195330	1•217529
•9100000	1•155806	1•174065	1•194547	1•216781	1•240067
•9200000	1•174907	1•193932	1•215312	1•238571	1•262992
•9300000	1•194256	1•214072	1•236382	1•260707	1•286313
•9400000	1•213856	1•234489	1•257764	1•283196	1•310038
•9500000	1•233711	1•255189	1•279462	1•306047	1•334178
•9600000	1•253826	1•276177	1•301484	1•329265	1•358741
•9699999	1•274205	1•297456	1•323835	1•352858	1•383737
•9799999	1•294853	1•319033	1•346520	1•376834	1•409175
•9899999	1•315772	1•340912	1•369546	1•401200	1•435066
1•0000000	1•336968	1•363098	1•392919	1•425963	1•461418
1•0100000	1•358444	1•385595	1•416643	1•451131	1•488241
1•0200000	1•380205	1•408409	1•440725	1•476710	1•515545
1•0300000	1•402253	1•431542	1•465169	1•502708	1•543339
1•0400000	1•424594	1•455001	1•489983	1•529131	1•571633
1•0500000	1•447230	1•478789	1•515170	1•555988	1•600437
1•0600000	1•470165	1•502910	1•540737	1•583284	1•629760
1•0699999	1•493402	1•527369	1•566688	1•611026	1•659611
1•0799999	1•516946	1•552169	1•593028	1•639221	1•690000
1•0899999	1•540798	1•577315	1•619761	1•667875	1•720935
1•1000000	1•564963	1•602809	1•646894	1•696995	1•752426
1•1100000	1•589442	1•628656	1•674429	1•726586	1•784481
1•1200000	1•614238	1•654857	1•702370	1•756654	1•817108
1•1300000	1•639354	1•681417	1•730722	1•787204	1•850316
1•1400000	1•664792	1•708338	1•759489	1•818241	1•884112
1•1500000	1•690554	1•735622	1•788672	1•849770	1•918504
1•1600000	1•716641	1•763271	1•818275	1•881795	1•953499
1•1700000	1•743054	1•791287	1•848301	1•914320	1•989102
1•1800000	1•769796	1•819671	1•878752	1•947348	2•025321
1•1899999	1•796866	1•848425	1•909629	1•980883	2•062160

$\alpha =$ •659999

θ	K VALUES				
	•318821117	•415016431	•514599755	•613601043	•708073407
1•2000000	1•824266	1•877549	1•940934	2•014927	2•099625
1•2100000	1•851994	1•907044	1•972667	2•049481	2•137719
1•2200000	1•880050	1•936909	2•004828	2•084547	2•176445
1•2300000	1•908435	1•967143	2•037418	2•120125	2•215807
1•2400000	1•937147	1•997747	2•070436	2•156216	2•255807
1•2500000	1•966184	2•028717	2•103880	2•192818	2•296444
1•2599999	1•995545	2•060053	2•137748	2•229930	2•337720
1•2699999	2•025226	2•091751	2•172037	2•267550	2•379633
1•2799999	2•055225	2•123808	2•206746	2•305675	2•422182
1•2899999	2•085540	2•156221	2•241869	2•344301	2•465363
1•3000000	2•116165	2•188986	2•277402	2•383423	2•509172
1•3100000	2•147096	2•222098	2•313339	2•423036	2•553603
1•3200000	2•178328	2•255551	2•349675	2•463132	2•598650
1•3300000	2•209857	2•289339	2•386403	2•503705	2•644306
1•3400000	2•241675	2•323455	2•423516	2•544746	2•690560
1•3500000	2•273776	2•357893	2•461004	2•586246	2•737403
1•3600000	2•306154	2•392643	2•498860	2•628193	2•784822
1•3700000	2•338800	2•427699	2•537073	2•670578	2•832804
1•3799999	2•371707	2•463050	2•575633	2•713387	2•881334
1•3899999	2•404865	2•498686	2•614528	2•756606	2•930397
1•4000000	2•438266	2•534598	2•653746	2•800223	2•979976
1•4100000	2•471898	2•570773	2•693274	2•844220	3•030049
1•4200000	2•505752	2•607200	2•733099	2•888582	3•080598
1•4300000	2•539817	2•643867	2•773206	2•933291	3•131601
1•4400000	2•574082	2•680761	2•813580	2•978330	3•183035
1•4500000	2•608534	2•717869	2•854206	3•023678	3•234876
1•4600000	2•643162	2•755175	2•895066	3•069317	3•287097
1•4700000	2•677952	2•792667	2•936144	3•115224	3•339671
1•4800000	2•712891	2•830328	2•977422	3•161379	3•392572
1•4900000	2•747965	2•868143	3•018883	3•207759	3•445770
1•5000000	2•783162	2•906097	3•060507	3•254341	3•499235
1•5100000	2•818465	2•944172	3•102274	3•301102	3•552936
1•5200000	2•853861	2•982353	3•144166	3•348016	3•606841
1•5300000	2•889334	3•020623	3•186163	3•395061	3•660917
1•5400000	2•924871	3•058964	3•228245	3•442210	3•715133
1•5500000	2•960455	3•097360	3•270390	3•489438	3•769453
1•5600000	2•996071	3•135791	3•312578	3•536721	3•823844
1•5699999	3•031704	3•174242	3•354790	3•584031	3•878273
1•5707963	3•034542	3•177305	3•358151	3•587799	3•882608
1•5707963	3•034540	3•177303	3•358150	3•587799	3•882605

$\alpha =$ .659999

Θ	K VALUES				
	.794250555	.868696860	.928444378	.971111163	.994996249
.0000000	.000000	.000000	.000000	.000000	.000000
.0100000	.010000	.010000	.010000	.010000	.010000
.0200000	.020002	.020002	.020003	.020003	.020003
.0300000	.030009	.030009	.030010	.030010	.030010
.0400000	.040022	.040023	.040024	.040024	.040024
.0500000	.050044	.050045	.050046	.050047	.050048
.0600000	.060076	.060078	.060081	.060082	.060083
.0700000	.070121	.070125	.070128	.070131	.070132
.0800000	.080180	.080187	.080192	.080196	.080198
.0900000	.090257	.090266	.090274	.090279	.090282
.1000000	.100353	.100366	.100376	.100383	.100387
.1100000	.110470	.110487	.110501	.110510	.110515
.1200000	.120611	.120633	.120651	.120663	.120670
.1300000	.130778	.130806	.130828	.130844	.130853
.1400000	.140973	.141007	.141035	.141055	.141066
.1500000	.151198	.151240	.151275	.151299	.151313
.1600000	.161455	.161507	.161549	.161579	.161596
.1700000	.171747	.171810	.171860	.171896	.171917
.1800000	.182077	.182151	.182211	.182254	.182278
.1900000	.192446	.192534	.192604	.192655	.192684
.2000000	.202856	.202959	.203042	.203102	.203135
.2100000	.213311	.213431	.213527	.213596	.213635
.2200000	.223812	.223951	.224062	.224142	.224186
.2300000	.234363	.234521	.234649	.234741	.234792
.2400000	.244965	.245146	.245292	.245396	.245455
.2500000	.255621	.255827	.255992	.256111	.256178
.2600000	.266333	.266566	.266753	.266888	.266963
.2700000	.277105	.277367	.277578	.277729	.277814
.2800000	.287939	.288233	.288469	.288639	.288734
.2900000	.298837	.299165	.299430	.299619	.299726
.3000000	.309803	.310168	.310462	.310674	.310792
.3100000	.320838	.321243	.321571	.321805	.321937
.3200000	.331946	.332395	.332757	.333017	.333163
.3300000	.343130	.343625	.344025	.344312	.344474
.3400000	.354393	.354938	.355378	.355695	.355873
.3500000	.365737	.366336	.366820	.367167	.367363
.3600000	.377166	.377822	.378352	.378734	.378948
.3700000	.388683	.389399	.389980	.390397	.390632
.3800000	.400290	.401072	.401706	.402162	.402418
.3900000	.411991	.412844	.413534	.414031	.414311

$\alpha =$ .659999

Θ	K VALUES				
	.794250555	.868696860	.928444378	.971111163	.994996249
.4000000	.423790	.424717	.425468	.426009	.426314
.4100000	.435690	.436695	.437512	.438100	.438431
.4200000	.447693	.448783	.449669	.450307	.450666
.4300000	.459805	.460984	.461943	.462634	.463023
.4400000	.472027	.473302	.474339	.475087	.475508
.4500000	.484365	.485741	.486860	.487668	.488124
.4600000	.496821	.498304	.499511	.500383	.500875
.4700000	.509399	.510996	.512297	.513237	.513767
.4800000	.522104	.523821	.525221	.526233	.526804
.4900000	.534939	.536784	.538289	.539378	.539992
.5000000	.547909	.549888	.551505	.552675	.553335
.5100000	.561018	.563139	.564873	.566130	.566839
.5200000	.574269	.576541	.578400	.579748	.580509
.5300000	.587668	.590099	.592091	.593535	.594351
.5400000	.601218	.603818	.605949	.607496	.608371
.5500000	.614925	.617703	.619982	.621637	.622574
.5600000	.628794	.631759	.634194	.635964	.636966
.5700000	.642828	.645992	.648592	.650483	.651555
.5800000	.657034	.660406	.663181	.665201	.666346
.5900000	.671416	.675009	.677968	.680124	.681347
.6000000	.685979	.689805	.692958	.695258	.696564
.6100000	.700729	.704800	.708159	.710611	.712004
.6200000	.715672	.720000	.723577	.726190	.727675
.6300000	.730812	.735413	.739219	.742002	.743585
.6400000	.746157	.751044	.755092	.758056	.759742
.6500000	.761711	.766900	.771204	.774358	.776154
.6600000	.777481	.782989	.787562	.790917	.792829
.6700000	.793473	.799316	.804174	.807742	.809776
.6800000	.809693	.815889	.821049	.824841	.827006
.6899999	.826149	.832717	.838193	.842224	.844526
.7000000	.842847	.849806	.855618	.859899	.862347
.7100000	.859794	.867165	.873330	.877878	.880479
.7200000	.876996	.884801	.891339	.896168	.898933
.7300000	.894462	.902724	.909655	.914782	.917720
.7400000	.912199	.920942	.928288	.933730	.936851
.7500000	.930214	.939463	.947248	.953023	.956338
.7600000	.948516	.958297	.966545	.972672	.976194
.7700000	.967112	.977454	.986191	.992690	.996430
.7800000	.986011	.996944	1.006196	1.013090	1.017061
.7899999	1.005222	1.016775	1.026572	1.033884	1.038100

$\alpha =$ .659999

θ	K VALUES				
	.794250555	.868696860	.928444378	.971111163	.994996249
.8000000	1.024752	1.036960	1.047332	1.055086	1.059562
.8100000	1.044612	1.057507	1.068487	1.076709	1.081461
.8200000	1.064809	1.078429	1.090050	1.098768	1.103814
.8300000	1.085354	1.099737	1.112035	1.121279	1.126635
.8400000	1.106256	1.121442	1.134456	1.144256	1.149943
.8500000	1.127525	1.143556	1.157326	1.167716	1.173754
.8600000	1.149171	1.166091	1.180661	1.191677	1.198088
.8700000	1.171205	1.189061	1.204475	1.216155	1.222962
.8799999	1.193636	1.212478	1.228785	1.241168	1.248398
.8899999	1.216475	1.236355	1.253606	1.266736	1.274415
.9000000	1.239734	1.260707	1.278956	1.292879	1.301035
.9100000	1.263424	1.285548	1.304852	1.319617	1.328282
.9200000	1.287555	1.310891	1.331312	1.346971	1.356178
.9300000	1.312141	1.336752	1.358355	1.374964	1.384748
.9400000	1.337192	1.363146	1.385999	1.403618	1.414018
.9500000	1.362720	1.390090	1.414265	1.432958	1.444016
.9600000	1.388738	1.417598	1.443174	1.463009	1.474768
.9699999	1.415259	1.445688	1.472747	1.493798	1.506306
.9799999	1.442294	1.474376	1.503006	1.525350	1.538660
.9899999	1.469858	1.503680	1.533973	1.557695	1.571861
1.0000000	1.497962	1.533617	1.565673	1.590863	1.605946
1.0100000	1.526620	1.564206	1.598129	1.624884	1.640948
1.0200000	1.555846	1.595464	1.631367	1.659791	1.676905
1.0300000	1.585651	1.627412	1.665413	1.695616	1.713858
1.0400000	1.616051	1.660067	1.700293	1.732396	1.751846
1.0500000	1.647059	1.693450	1.736035	1.770167	1.790915
1.0600000	1.678688	1.727580	1.772668	1.808966	1.831109
1.0699999	1.710951	1.762478	1.810221	1.848835	1.872478
1.0799999	1.743863	1.798164	1.848724	1.889815	1.915071
1.0899999	1.777437	1.834658	1.888209	1.931949	1.958942
1.1000000	1.811687	1.871983	1.928707	1.975283	2.004149
1.1100000	1.846625	1.910158	1.970251	2.019864	2.050751
1.1200000	1.882265	1.949206	2.012876	2.065743	2.098812
1.1300000	1.918620	1.989147	2.056615	2.112970	2.148398
1.1400000	1.955702	2.030002	2.101504	2.161602	2.199582
1.1500000	1.993525	2.071795	2.147581	2.211694	2.252438
1.1600000	2.032100	2.114545	2.194881	2.263307	2.307047
1.1700000	2.071438	2.158274	2.243444	2.316502	2.363494
1.1800000	2.111550	2.203002	2.293307	2.371346	2.421872
1.1899999	2.152448	2.248751	2.344510	2.427905	2.482276

$\alpha =$ .659999

Θ	*K* VALUES				
	.794250555	.868696860	.928444378	.971111163	.994996249
.2000000	2.194141	2.295541	2.397094	2.486253	2.544811
.2100000	2.236638	2.343391	2.451097	2.546462	2.609588
1.2200000	2.279946	2.392319	2.506562	2.608612	2.676727
1.2300000	2.324075	2.442345	2.563530	2.672784	2.746354
1.2400000	2.369029	2.493485	2.622041	2.739064	2.818609
1.2500000	2.414815	2.545756	2.682136	2.807542	2.893640
1.2599999	2.461436	2.599173	2.743858	2.878310	2.971608
1.2699999	2.508896	2.653748	2.807245	2.951466	3.052685
1.2799999	2.557195	2.709494	2.872337	3.027111	3.137062
1.2899999	2.606335	2.766421	2.939174	3.105352	3.224942
1.3000000	2.656314	2.824538	3.007792	3.186298	3.316552
1.3100000	2.707127	2.883850	3.078226	3.270062	3.412133
1.3200000	2.758772	2.944360	3.150509	3.356763	3.511954
1.3300000	2.811241	3.006070	3.224672	3.446520	3.616312
1.3400000	2.864525	3.068979	3.300741	3.539460	3.725529
1.3500000	2.918615	3.133080	3.378740	3.635707	3.839966
1.3600000	2.973497	3.198366	3.458688	3.735392	3.960021
1.3700000	3.029157	3.264826	3.540598	3.838641	4.086138
1.3799999	3.085578	3.332444	3.624477	3.945585	4.218810
1.3899999	3.142742	3.401201	3.710328	4.056347	4.358591
1.4000000	3.200626	3.471075	3.798144	4.171049	4.506103
1.4100000	3.259207	3.542036	3.887908	4.289802	4.662040
1.4200000	3.318460	3.614054	3.979598	4.412707	4.827191
1.4300000	3.378356	3.687093	4.073180	4.539850	5.002442
1.4400000	3.438864	3.761111	4.168609	4.671296	5.188794
1.4500000	3.499953	3.836063	4.265829	4.807083	5.387373
1.4600000	3.561586	3.911901	4.364773	4.947219	5.599439
1.4700000	3.623729	3.988568	4.465359	5.091669	5.826395
1.4800000	3.686341	4.066008	4.567494	5.240353	6.069774
1.4900000	3.749382	4.144156	4.671073	5.393139	6.331207
1.5000000	3.812810	4.222947	4.775976	5.549830	6.612359
1.5100000	3.876580	4.302310	4.882071	5.710165	6.914777
1.5200000	3.940647	4.382170	4.989215	5.873811	7.239673
1.5300000	4.004964	4.462451	5.097255	6.040366	7.587553
1.5400000	4.069483	4.543073	5.206026	6.209358	7.957730
1.5500000	4.134155	4.623954	5.315357	6.380254	8.347780
1.5600000	4.198932	4.705013	5.425069	6.552467	8.753147
1.5699999	4.263763	4.786162	5.534982	6.725375	9.167188
1.5707963	4.268926	4.792626	5.543737	6.739155	9.200298
1.5707963	4.268924	4.792623	5.543734	6.739150	9.200292

$\alpha =$ .679999

Θ	K VALUES				
	.009966711	.039469502	.087332193	.151646642	.229848846
.0000000	.000000	.000000	.000000	.000000	.000000
.0100000	.010000	.010000	.010000	.010000	.010000
.0200000	.020001	.020001	.020001	.020002	.020002
.0300000	.030006	.030006	.030006	.030006	.030007
.0400000	.040014	.040014	.040015	.040016	.040016
.0500000	.050028	.050029	.050030	.050031	.050033
.0600000	.060049	.060050	.060052	.060054	.060057
.0700000	.070078	.070080	.070082	.070086	.070091
.0800000	.080117	.080119	.080123	.080129	.080135
.0900000	.090166	.090170	.090176	.090184	.090193
.1000000	.100228	.100233	.100241	.100252	.100265
.1100000	.110304	.110311	.110321	.110336	.110353
.1200000	.120395	.120404	.120418	.120436	.120459
.1300000	.130503	.130514	.130531	.130555	.130584
.1400000	.140629	.140642	.140664	.140694	.140730
.1500000	.150774	.150790	.150818	.150854	.150898
.1600000	.160940	.160960	.160993	.161037	.161091
.1700000	.171128	.171152	.171192	.171245	.171310
.1800000	.181340	.181369	.181416	.181479	.181556
.1900000	.191577	.191611	.191667	.191741	.191832
.2000000	.201841	.201881	.201946	.202032	.202138
.2100000	.212134	.212180	.212254	.212355	.212478
.2200000	.222455	.222508	.222594	.222710	.222852
.2300000	.232808	.232869	.232967	.233100	.233262
.2400000	.243194	.243263	.243375	.243526	.243710
.2500000	.253614	.253692	.253819	.253989	.254198
.2600000	.264069	.264157	.264300	.264492	.264727
.2700000	.274562	.274661	.274821	.275037	.275300
.2800000	.285094	.285204	.285383	.285624	.285919
.2900000	.295667	.295789	.295988	.296256	.296584
.3000000	.306281	.306416	.306637	.306935	.307299
.3100000	.316939	.317089	.317333	.317662	.318064
.3200000	.327642	.327807	.328076	.328439	.328883
.3300000	.338393	.338574	.338869	.339268	.339756
.3400000	.349192	.349391	.349714	.350151	.350686
.3500000	.360042	.360259	.360612	.361089	.361675
.3600000	.370944	.371180	.371565	.372086	.372724
.3700000	.381899	.382156	.382575	.383142	.383837
.3800000	.392910	.393189	.393644	.394259	.395015
.3900000	.403979	.404281	.404774	.405441	.406259

$\alpha =$ .679999

Θ	K VALUES				
	.009966711	.039469502	.087332193	.151646642	.229848846
.4000000	.415107	.415434	.415966	.416687	.417573
.4100000	.426296	.426648	.427223	.428002	.428959
.4200000	.437548	.437927	.438547	.439386	.440418
.4300000	.448865	.449273	.449939	.450842	.451953
.4400000	.460249	.460686	.461402	.462372	.463566
.4500000	.471701	.472170	.472937	.473978	.475259
.4600000	.483224	.483726	.484547	.485662	.487035
.4700000	.494820	.495357	.496234	.497427	.498897
.4800000	.506490	.507063	.508000	.509274	.510846
.4900000	.518237	.518848	.519848	.521207	.522885
.5000000	.530063	.530714	.531779	.533227	.535016
.5100000	.541970	.542662	.543795	.545337	.547243
.5200000	.553960	.554696	.555900	.557539	.559567
.5300000	.566036	.566816	.568095	.569836	.571991
.5400000	.578198	.579026	.580382	.582230	.584518
.5500000	.590451	.591328	.592765	.594723	.597151
.5600000	.602796	.603724	.605245	.607319	.609892
.5700000	.615235	.616216	.617824	.620020	.622744
.5800000	.627771	.628607	.630507	.632828	.635710
.5900000	.640407	.641500	.643294	.645746	.648793
.6000000	.653144	.654297	.656189	.658777	.661996
.6100000	.665984	.667199	.669195	.671924	.675321
.6200000	.678932	.680211	.682313	.685189	.688772
.6300000	.691989	.693334	.695546	.698576	.702351
.6400000	.705157	.706572	.708898	.712086	.716063
.6500000	.718440	.719926	.722372	.725724	.729909
.6600000	.731840	.733400	.735969	.739492	.743894
.6700000	.745359	.746997	.749693	.753393	.758020
.6800000	.759001	.760719	.763547	.767431	.772291
.6899999	.772769	.774568	.777533	.781608	.786710
.7000000	.786664	.788549	.791656	.795928	.801281
.7100000	.800691	.802664	.805917	.810393	.816007
.7200000	.814851	.816915	.820320	.825008	.830892
.7300000	.829149	.831307	.834868	.839774	.845939
.7400000	.843586	.845841	.849564	.854697	.861151
.7500000	.858166	.860522	.864412	.869779	.876533
.7600000	.872893	.875352	.879415	.885024	.892089
.7700000	.887768	.890334	.894576	.900435	.907821
.7800000	.902796	.905472	.909898	.916015	.923734
.7899999	.917979	.920769	.925385	.931769	.939832

$\alpha =$ •679999

Θ	K VALUES				
	•009966711	•039469502	•087332193	•151646642	•229848846
•8000000	•933321	•936229	•941041	•947700	•956119
•8100000	•948826	•951854	•956868	•963812	•972598
•8200000	•964495	•967648	•972870	•980108	•989274
•8300000	•980333	•983614	•989051	•996592	1•006151
•8400000	•996343	•999756	1•005415	1•013269	1•023232
•8500000	1•012529	1•016078	1•021965	1•030141	1•040522
•8600000	1•028893	1•032583	1•038705	1•047212	1•058026
•8700000	1•045440	1•049274	1•055638	1•064488	1•075747
•8799999	1•062173	1•066155	1•072768	1•081971	1•093690
•8899999	1•079095	1•083229	1•090099	1•099665	1•111858
•9000000	1•096211	1•100501	1•107634	1•117575	1•130257
•9100000	1•113522	1•117974	1•125378	1•135704	1•148890
•9200000	1•131034	1•135651	1•143334	1•154057	1•167762
•9300000	1•148749	1•153536	1•161506	1•172637	1•186877
•9400000	1•166671	1•171633	1•179898	1•191448	1•206240
•9500000	1•184804	1•189946	1•198513	1•210495	1•225855
•9600000	1•203151	1•208477	1•217356	1•229782	1•245726
•9699999	1•221716	1•227231	1•236429	1•249311	1•265858
•9799999	1•240502	1•246211	1•255738	1•269089	1•286254
•9899999	1•259513	1•265421	1•275285	1•289118	1•306920
1•0000000	1•278752	1•284865	1•295074	1•309402	1•327859
1•0100000	1•298223	1•304545	1•315109	1•329945	1•349076
1•0200000	1•317929	1•324466	1•335394	1•350752	1•370575
1•0300000	1•337873	1•344630	1•355931	1•371825	1•392359
1•0400000	1•358059	1•365042	1•376725	1•393168	1•414434
1•0500000	1•378490	1•385704	1•397779	1•414786	1•436802
1•0600000	1•399168	1•406619	1•419096	1•436681	1•459468
1•0699999	1•420098	1•427791	1•440679	1•458857	1•482435
1•0799999	1•441282	1•449222	1•462532	1•481318	1•505707
1•0899999	1•462722	1•470916	1•484658	1•504065	1•529288
1•1000000	1•484421	1•492875	1•507058	1•527104	1•553180
1•1100000	1•506383	1•515102	1•529737	1•550435	1•577387
1•1200000	1•528608	1•537599	1•552696	1•574063	1•601912
1•1300000	1•551100	1•560368	1•575938	1•597989	1•626757
1•1400000	1•573860	1•583412	1•599465	1•622216	1•651926
1•1500000	1•596891	1•606732	1•623279	1•646745	1•677419
1•1600000	1•620193	1•630330	1•647381	1•671580	1•703240
1•1700000	1•643769	1•654207	1•671774	1•696720	1•729390
1•1800000	1•667619	1•678365	1•696458	1•722168	1•755870
1•1899999	1•691744	1•702805	1•721434	1•747925	1•782682

$\alpha =$ .679999

Θ	K VALUES				
	.009966711	.039469502	.087332193	.151646642	.229848846
1.2000000	1.716146	1.727527	1.746704	1.773991	1.809827
1.2100000	1.740823	1.752530	1.772266	1.800367	1.837305
1.2200000	1.765777	1.777817	1.798122	1.827052	1.865115
1.2300000	1.791006	1.803385	1.824271	1.854047	1.893259
1.2400000	1.816511	1.829235	1.850712	1.881351	1.921734
1.2500000	1.842290	1.855366	1.877445	1.908962	1.950540
1.2599999	1.868342	1.881775	1.904467	1.936879	1.979676
1.2699999	1.894665	1.908462	1.931777	1.965101	2.009138
1.2799999	1.921256	1.935423	1.959373	1.993624	2.038926
1.2899999	1.948114	1.962657	1.987251	2.022445	2.069035
1.3000000	1.975236	1.990161	2.015410	2.051563	2.099462
1.3100000	2.002617	2.017929	2.043844	2.080972	2.130202
1.3200000	2.030254	2.045960	2.072550	2.110668	2.161252
1.3300000	2.058142	2.074247	2.101523	2.140646	2.192606
1.3400000	2.086277	2.102787	2.130758	2.170900	2.224257
1.3500000	2.114654	2.131573	2.160250	2.201426	2.256200
1.3600000	2.143265	2.160600	2.189991	2.232216	2.288428
1.3700000	2.172106	2.189862	2.219976	2.263263	2.320933
1.3799999	2.201169	2.219351	2.250197	2.294560	2.353706
1.3899999	2.230447	2.249059	2.280646	2.326097	2.386739
1.4000000	2.259933	2.278980	2.311316	2.357868	2.420024
1.4100000	2.289617	2.309104	2.342197	2.389862	2.453548
1.4200000	2.319491	2.339422	2.373279	2.422069	2.487303
1.4300000	2.349546	2.369925	2.404554	2.454479	2.521276
1.4400000	2.379773	2.400604	2.436011	2.487082	2.555456
1.4500000	2.410160	2.431447	2.467639	2.519866	2.589832
1.4600000	2.440698	2.462444	2.499427	2.552818	2.624389
1.4700000	2.471376	2.493584	2.531363	2.585928	2.659116
1.4800000	2.502182	2.524855	2.563436	2.619181	2.693998
1.4900000	2.533105	2.556245	2.595632	2.652566	2.729021
1.5000000	2.564132	2.587743	2.627940	2.686068	2.764171
1.5100000	2.595252	2.619335	2.660346	2.719674	2.799433
1.5200000	2.626452	2.651009	2.692837	2.753369	2.834791
1.5300000	2.657719	2.682751	2.725399	2.787140	2.870231
1.5400000	2.689039	2.714549	2.758019	2.820972	2.905736
1.5500000	2.720401	2.746388	2.790682	2.854850	2.941291
1.5600000	2.751791	2.778256	2.823375	2.888759	2.976879
1.5699999	2.783195	2.810139	2.856083	2.922684	3.012485
1.5707963	2.785696	2.812678	2.858687	2.925385	3.015320
1.5707963	2.785694	2.812676	2.858685	2.925383	3.015318

$\alpha =$ .679999

Θ	K VALUES				
	.318821117	.415016431	.514599755	.613601043	.708073407
.0000000	.000000	.000000	.000000	.000000	.000000
.0100000	.010000	.010000	.010000	.010000	.010000
.0200000	.020002	.020002	.020002	.020002	.020002
.0300000	.030007	.030008	.030008	.030008	.030009
.0400000	.040017	.040018	.040020	.040021	.040022
.0500000	.050035	.050037	.050039	.050041	.050043
.0600000	.060060	.060063	.060067	.060071	.060074
.0700000	.070096	.070101	.070107	.070113	.070118
.0800000	.080143	.080151	.080160	.080168	.080176
.0900000	.090204	.090216	.090228	.090240	.090251
.1000000	.100280	.100296	.100313	.100329	.100345
.1100000	.110373	.110394	.110417	.110439	.110460
.1200000	.120485	.120513	.120542	.120570	.120598
.1300000	.130617	.130652	.130689	.130726	.130761
.1400000	.140771	.140815	.140861	.140907	.140951
.1500000	.150949	.151004	.151060	.151117	.151171
.1600000	.161153	.161219	.161288	.161357	.161423
.1700000	.171384	.171464	.171547	.171629	.171709
.1800000	.181644	.181739	.181838	.181936	.182031
.1900000	.191935	.192047	.192164	.192280	.192391
.2000000	.202259	.202390	.202526	.202662	.202792
.2100000	.212618	.212770	.212928	.213086	.213237
.2200000	.223013	.223188	.223370	.223552	.223727
.2300000	.233447	.233647	.233856	.234064	.234264
.2400000	.243920	.244149	.244387	.244624	.244852
.2500000	.254436	.254695	.254965	.255235	.255493
.2600000	.264996	.265288	.265593	.265897	.266189
.2700000	.275602	.275930	.276272	.276615	.276943
.2800000	.286256	.286623	.287006	.287389	.287757
.2900000	.296960	.297369	.297796	.298223	.298634
.3000000	.307716	.308170	.308644	.309120	.309577
.3100000	.318526	.319029	.319554	.320080	.320587
.3200000	.329392	.329947	.330527	.331109	.331669
.3300000	.340316	.340927	.341565	.342206	.342824
.3400000	.351300	.351971	.352672	.353377	.354056
.3500000	.362347	.363081	.363849	.364622	.365367
.3600000	.373458	.374260	.375100	.375945	.376761
.3700000	.384636	.385510	.386426	.387348	.388239
.3800000	.395883	.396834	.397831	.398835	.399807
.3900000	.407202	.408233	.409316	.410408	.411465

$\alpha =$ .679999

Θ	K VALUES				
	.318821117	.415016431	.514599755	.613601043	.708073407
.4000000	.418593	.419711	.420886	.422071	.423218
.4100000	.430061	.431270	.432541	.433825	.435069
.4200000	.441607	.442913	.444286	.445674	.447021
.4300000	.453234	.454642	.456123	.457622	.459077
.4400000	.464944	.466459	.468055	.469671	.471241
.4500000	.476739	.478368	.480085	.481824	.483516
.4600000	.488623	.490371	.492215	.494086	.495906
.4700000	.500597	.502471	.504450	.506458	.508415
.4800000	.512665	.514670	.516791	.518945	.521046
.4900000	.524828	.526973	.529242	.531550	.533803
.5000000	.537090	.539381	.541807	.544277	.546690
.5100000	.549454	.551897	.554488	.557129	.559712
.5200000	.561921	.564526	.567290	.570109	.572871
.5300000	.574495	.577268	.580214	.583223	.586172
.5400000	.587180	.590129	.593266	.596473	.599619
.5500000	.599977	.603111	.606448	.609863	.613218
.5600000	.612889	.616217	.619763	.623397	.626972
.5700000	.625920	.629451	.633217	.637080	.640886
.5800000	.639073	.642815	.646812	.650916	.654964
.5900000	.652351	.656314	.660552	.664909	.669211
.6000000	.665757	.669951	.674441	.679063	.683633
.6100000	.679295	.683730	.688483	.693383	.698234
.6200000	.692967	.697653	.702682	.707874	.713020
.6300000	.706776	.711726	.717043	.722539	.727995
.6400000	.720727	.725951	.731569	.737384	.743165
.6500000	.734823	.740332	.746265	.752414	.758536
.6600000	.749067	.754873	.761135	.767634	.774113
.6700000	.763463	.769579	.776183	.783048	.789903
.6800000	.778015	.784453	.791415	.798662	.805910
.6899999	.792726	.799500	.806835	.814482	.822142
.7000000	.807599	.814723	.822447	.830512	.838603
.7100000	.822639	.830127	.838256	.846758	.855302
.7200000	.837850	.845716	.854268	.863226	.872244
.7300000	.853236	.861494	.870486	.879921	.889435
.7400000	.868799	.877466	.886918	.896850	.906883
.7500000	.884546	.893637	.903566	.914018	.924595
.7600000	.900479	.910011	.920437	.931431	.942578
.7700000	.916602	.926593	.937537	.949096	.960840
.7800000	.932921	.943387	.954869	.967020	.979387
.7899999	.949439	.960398	.972441	.985207	.998227

$\alpha =$ •679999

Θ	K VALUES				
	•318821117	•415016431	•514599755	•613601043	•708073407
•8000000	•966161	•977632	•990258	1•003666	1•017368
•8100000	•983091	•995093	1•008325	1•022403	1•036819
•8200000	1•000233	1•012785	1•026648	1•041424	1•056587
•8300000	1•017592	1•030716	1•045233	1•060737	1•076681
•8400000	1•035172	1•048888	1•064086	1•080349	1•097108
•8500000	1•052979	1•067308	1•083213	1•100266	1•117879
•8600000	1•071016	1•085981	1•102620	1•120496	1•139002
•8700000	1•089288	1•104912	1•122313	1•141047	1•160485
•8799999	1•107801	1•124106	1•142299	1•161926	1•182338
•8899999	1•126558	1•143569	1•162584	1•183141	1•204570
•9000000	1•145565	1•163307	1•183174	1•204699	1•227191
•9100000	1•164826	1•183324	1•204076	1•226608	1•250211
•9200000	1•184347	1•203626	1•225296	1•248875	1•273639
•9300000	1•204131	1•224220	1•246841	1•271510	1•297485
•9400000	1•224184	1•245109	1•268717	1•294520	1•321759
•9500000	1•244511	1•266301	1•290931	1•317913	1•346472
•9600000	1•265117	1•287800	1•313490	1•341697	1•371634
•9699999	1•286005	1•309612	1•336399	1•365880	1•397255
•9799999	1•307182	1•331742	1•359667	1•390472	1•423346
•9899999	1•328652	1•354197	1•383299	1•415479	1•449917
1•0000000	1•350420	1•376981	1•407301	1•440910	1•476980
1•0100000	1•372490	1•400101	1•431682	1•466773	1•504545
1•0200000	1•394867	1•423560	1•456446	1•493077	1•532622
1•0300000	1•417556	1•447365	1•481600	1•519830	1•561224
1•0400000	1•440561	1•471522	1•507152	1•547039	1•590359
1•0500000	1•463886	1•496034	1•533106	1•574713	1•620040
1•0600000	1•487536	1•520907	1•559470	1•602860	1•650277
1•0699999	1•511515	1•546147	1•586249	1•631488	1•681081
1•0799999	1•535828	1•571757	1•613449	1•660604	1•712462
1•0899999	1•560477	1•597742	1•641076	1•690215	1•744431
1•1000000	1•585467	1•624108	1•669135	1•720330	1•776997
1•1100000	1•610801	1•650857	1•697632	1•750954	1•810172
1•1200000	1•636482	1•677994	1•726571	1•782095	1•843964
1•1300000	1•662514	1•705522	1•755957	1•813759	1•878383
1•1400000	1•688900	1•733446	1•785795	1•845953	1•913438
1•1500000	1•715641	1•761768	1•816088	1•878681	1•949139
1•1600000	1•742742	1•790491	1•846842	1•911950	1•985492
1•1700000	1•770202	1•819617	1•878058	1•945764	2•022507
1•1800000	1•798025	1•849149	1•909740	1•980128	2•060190
1•1899999	1•826212	1•879089	1•941890	2•015046	2•098549

$\alpha =$ .679999

Θ	K VALUES				
	.318821117	.415016431	.514599755	.613601043	.708073407
1.2000000	1.854763	1.909438	1.974511	2.050521	2.137589
1.2100000	1.883680	1.940197	2.007604	2.086556	2.177315
1.2200000	1.912962	1.971365	2.041170	2.123153	2.217733
1.2300000	1.942608	2.002944	2.075209	2.160313	2.258845
1.2400000	1.972620	2.034933	2.109721	2.198038	2.300655
1.2500000	2.002995	2.067330	2.144706	2.236326	2.343165
1.2599999	2.033731	2.100134	2.180161	2.275177	2.386375
1.2699999	2.064827	2.133343	2.216085	2.314590	2.430286
1.2799999	2.096280	2.166953	2.252474	2.354562	2.474895
1.2899999	2.128086	2.200962	2.289326	2.395089	2.520202
1.3000000	2.160242	2.235365	2.326635	2.436167	2.566201
1.3100000	2.192743	2.270157	2.364397	2.477790	2.612887
1.3200000	2.225584	2.305332	2.402604	2.519951	2.660254
1.3300000	2.258759	2.340885	2.441250	2.562643	2.708294
1.3400000	2.292262	2.376808	2.480328	2.605857	2.756997
1.3500000	2.326086	2.413093	2.519828	2.649583	2.806353
1.3600000	2.360223	2.449732	2.559740	2.693810	2.856348
1.3700000	2.394665	2.486716	2.600055	2.738526	2.906970
1.3799999	2.429403	2.524034	2.640761	2.783718	2.958202
1.3899999	2.464427	2.561676	2.681845	2.829370	3.010026
1.4000000	2.499728	2.599631	2.723295	2.875468	3.062425
1.4100000	2.535293	2.637885	2.765095	2.921994	3.115376
1.4200000	2.571112	2.676426	2.807230	2.968930	3.168859
1.4300000	2.607172	2.715241	2.849686	3.016257	3.222848
1.4400000	2.643460	2.754313	2.892444	3.063955	3.277319
1.4500000	2.679963	2.793629	2.935488	3.112003	3.332245
1.4600000	2.716667	2.833173	2.978798	3.160378	3.387598
1.4700000	2.753557	2.872928	3.022356	3.209057	3.443347
1.4800000	2.790618	2.912876	3.066142	3.258016	3.499461
1.4900000	2.827835	2.953002	3.110135	3.307229	3.555909
1.5000000	2.865192	2.993285	3.154314	3.356671	3.612656
1.5100000	2.902673	3.033709	3.198658	3.406315	3.669668
1.5200000	2.940259	3.074253	3.243143	3.456133	3.726909
1.5300000	2.977936	3.114899	3.287747	3.506099	3.784344
1.5400000	3.015684	3.155627	3.332448	3.556183	3.841934
1.5500000	3.053488	3.196417	3.377222	3.606357	3.899642
1.5600000	3.091328	3.237249	3.422045	3.656592	3.957430
1.5699999	3.129188	3.278103	3.466894	3.706858	4.015260
1.5707963	3.132203	3.281357	3.470466	3.710862	4.019866
1.5707963	3.132200	3.281354	3.470464	3.710861	4.019862

$\alpha =$ .679999

Θ	K VALUES				
	.794250555	.868696860	.928444378	.971111163	.994996249
.0000000	.000000	.000000	.000000	.000000	.000000
.0100000	.010000	.010000	.010000	.010000	.010000
.0200000	.020002	.020002	.020003	.020003	.020003
.0300000	.030009	.030010	.030010	.030010	.030010
.0400000	.040023	.040023	.040024	.040024	.040025
.0500000	.050044	.050046	.050047	.050048	.050049
.0600000	.060077	.060080	.060082	.060084	.060084
.0700000	.070123	.070127	.070131	.070133	.070134
.0800000	.080184	.080190	.080195	.080199	.080201
.0900000	.090262	.090271	.090278	.090284	.090287
.1000000	.100360	.100372	.100382	.100390	.100394
.1100000	.110479	.110496	.110509	.110519	.110524
.1200000	.120623	.120645	.120662	.120675	.120682
.1300000	.130793	.130821	.130843	.130859	.130868
.1400000	.140991	.141026	.141054	.141074	.141085
.1500000	.151221	.151263	.151298	.151322	.151336
.1600000	.161483	.161535	.161577	.161607	.161624
.1700000	.171781	.171844	.171894	.171930	.171950
.1800000	.182117	.182191	.182251	.182294	.182318
.1900000	.192493	.192581	.192652	.192702	.192731
.2000000	.202911	.203014	.203097	.203157	.203190
.2100000	.213375	.213495	.213591	.213660	.213699
.2200000	.223886	.224025	.224136	.224216	.224261
.2300000	.234448	.234606	.234734	.234826	.234877
.2400000	.245061	.245243	.245389	.245493	.245552
.2500000	.255731	.255937	.256102	.256221	.256288
.2600000	.266458	.266690	.266878	.267012	.267088
.2700000	.277245	.277507	.277718	.277870	.277955
.2800000	.288095	.288389	.288626	.288796	.288891
.2900000	.299012	.299340	.299605	.299795	.299901
.3000000	.309997	.310362	.310657	.310869	.310988
.3100000	.321054	.321459	.321787	.322022	.322154
.3200000	.332185	.332634	.332996	.333257	.333403
.3300000	.343393	.343889	.344289	.344577	.344738
.3400000	.354682	.355228	.355669	.355986	.356164
.3500000	.366054	.366654	.367138	.367487	.367683
.3600000	.377513	.378170	.378702	.379084	.379298
.3700000	.389062	.389780	.390362	.390780	.391015
.3800000	.400704	.401487	.402122	.402579	.402836
.3900000	.412442	.413295	.413988	.414486	.414766

$\alpha =$ .679999

Θ	K VALUES				
	.794250555	.868696860	.928444378	.971111163	.994996249
.4000000	.424279	.425208	.425961	.426503	.426808
.4100000	.436220	.437228	.438046	.438635	.438967
.4200000	.448268	.449360	.450248	.450887	.451247
.4300000	.460426	.461608	.462569	.463262	.463652
.4400000	.472698	.473976	.475015	.475765	.476187
.4500000	.485087	.486467	.487589	.488399	.488856
.4600000	.497599	.499086	.500297	.501171	.501664
.4700000	.510236	.511837	.513142	.514085	.514616
.4800000	.523003	.524725	.526129	.527144	.527717
.4900000	.535903	.537754	.539264	.540356	.540972
.5000000	.548942	.550928	.552550	.553724	.554387
.5100000	.562124	.564253	.565993	.567254	.567966
.5200000	.575452	.577733	.579599	.580951	.581715
.5300000	.588932	.591373	.593372	.594821	.595641
.5400000	.602568	.605179	.607318	.608871	.609749
.5500000	.616366	.619155	.621443	.623105	.624046
.5600000	.630329	.633307	.635752	.637530	.638537
.5700000	.644463	.647641	.650253	.652153	.653229
.5800000	.658774	.662162	.664950	.666979	.668130
.5900000	.673267	.676877	.679850	.682017	.683246
.6000000	.687946	.691791	.694961	.697272	.698584
.6100000	.702819	.706911	.710288	.712753	.714153
.6200000	.717890	.722242	.725838	.728466	.729959
.6300000	.733166	.737792	.741620	.744419	.746011
.6400000	.748652	.753568	.757640	.760621	.762317
.6500000	.764355	.769576	.773906	.777079	.778886
.6600000	.780282	.785824	.790427	.793803	.795727
.6700000	.796438	.802319	.807210	.810801	.812849
.6800000	.812831	.819069	.824263	.828082	.830261
.6899999	.829468	.836082	.841597	.845656	.847974
.7000000	.846356	.853365	.859219	.863532	.865998
.7100000	.863502	.870928	.877139	.881722	.884343
.7200000	.880913	.888779	.895367	.900235	.903022
.7300000	.898598	.906926	.913914	.919082	.922044
.7400000	.916565	.925380	.932788	.938275	.941423
.7500000	.934821	.944149	.952001	.957826	.961171
.7600000	.953375	.963243	.971565	.977747	.981300
.7700000	.972236	.982673	.991490	.998050	1.001825
.7800000	.991413	1.002448	1.011789	1.018749	1.022758
.7899999	1.010914	1.022580	1.032474	1.039858	1.044116

$\alpha =$ •679999

Θ	K VALUES				
	•794250555	•868696860	•928444378	•971111163	•994996249
•8000000	1•030749	1•043079	1•053557	1•061390	1•065913
•8100000	1•050928	1•063957	1•075052	1•083361	1•088164
•8200000	1•071460	1•085226	1•096972	1•105785	1•110886
•8300000	1•092355	1•106896	1•119332	1•128679	1•134097
•8400000	1•113624	1•128982	1•142146	1•152060	1•157813
•8500000	1•135277	1•151495	1•165429	1•175944	1•182055
•8600000	1•157325	1•174450	1•189198	1•200350	1•206841
•8700000	1•179780	1•197859	1•213467	1•225296	1•232190
•8799999	1•202651	1•221736	1•238255	1•250801	1•258126
•8899999	1•225953	1•246096	1•263578	1•276886	1•284669
•9000000	1•249695	1•270954	1•289455	1•303572	1•311843
•9100000	1•273890	1•296324	1•315903	1•330881	1•339671
•9200000	1•298551	1•322224	1•342944	1•358835	1•368178
•9300000	1•323690	1•348667	1•370595	1•387458	1•397392
•9400000	1•349321	1•375672	1•398879	1•416775	1•427340
•9500000	1•375455	1•403255	1•427817	1•446812	1•458049
•9600000	1•402108	1•431434	1•457430	1•477595	1•489552
•9699999	1•429291	1•460226	1•487742	1•509153	1•521878
•9799999	1•457021	1•489650	1•518777	1•541515	1•555061
•9899999	1•485309	1•519725	1•550560	1•574712	1•589137
1•0000000	1•514172	1•550470	1•583115	1•608774	1•624140
1•0100000	1•543622	1•581905	1•616468	1•643736	1•660110
1•0200000	1•573676	1•614049	1•650648	1•679632	1•697087
1•0300000	1•604347	1•646924	1•685683	1•716498	1•735113
1•0400000	1•635651	1•680550	1•721600	1•754371	1•774231
1•0500000	1•667603	1•714950	1•758431	1•793292	1•814490
1•0600000	1•700218	1•750144	1•796206	1•833302	1•855937
1•0699999	1•733511	1•786156	1•834958	1•874443	1•898625
1•0799999	1•767497	1•823007	1•874718	1•916761	1•942609
1•0899999	1•802193	1•860721	1•915521	1•960302	1•987946
1•1000000	1•837612	1•899320	1•957403	2•005116	2•034698
1•1100000	1•873771	1•938829	2•000398	2•051255	2•082927
1•1200000	1•910683	1•979270	2•044544	2•098771	2•132703
1•1300000	1•948364	2•020668	2•089879	2•147721	2•184098
1•1400000	1•986828	2•063046	2•136441	2•198165	2•237189
1•1500000	2•026090	2•106428	2•184270	2•250163	2•292056
1•1600000	2•066163	2•150839	2•233407	2•303780	2•348786
1•1700000	2•107060	2•196301	2•283895	2•359084	2•407471
1•1800000	2•148795	2•242838	2•335774	2•416145	2•468209
1•1899999	2•191379	2•290474	2•389089	2•475037	2•531105

$\alpha =$ .679999

Θ	K VALUES				
	.794250555	.868696860	.928444378	.971111163	.994996249
1.2000000	2.234825	2.339231	2.443884	2.535838	2.596270
1.2100000	2.279143	2.389131	2.500202	2.598628	2.663823
1.2200000	2.324343	2.440196	2.558089	2.663491	2.733892
1.2300000	2.370433	2.492446	2.617589	2.730517	2.806616
1.2400000	2.417423	2.545902	2.678749	2.799798	2.882142
1.2500000	2.465318	2.600581	2.741613	2.871430	2.960630
1.2599999	2.514124	2.656501	2.806227	2.945515	3.042251
1.2699999	2.563845	2.713677	2.872635	3.022157	3.127193
1.2799999	2.614485	2.772123	2.940881	3.101467	3.215657
1.2899999	2.666043	2.831853	3.011007	3.183559	3.307863
1.3000000	2.718520	2.892875	3.083056	3.268552	3.404052
1.3100000	2.771912	2.955196	3.157064	3.356567	3.504484
1.3200000	2.826216	3.018823	3.233069	3.447732	3.609446
1.3300000	2.881426	3.083756	3.311105	3.542178	3.719254
1.3400000	2.937531	3.149995	3.391203	3.640038	3.834254
1.3500000	2.994523	3.217536	3.473387	3.741450	3.954832
1.3600000	3.052387	3.286370	3.557679	3.846551	4.081411
1.3700000	3.111109	3.356486	3.644094	3.955481	4.214465
1.3799999	3.170671	3.427867	3.732643	4.068376	4.354522
1.3899999	3.231052	3.500494	3.823325	4.185373	4.502170
1.4000000	3.292229	3.574343	3.916137	4.306601	4.658074
1.4100000	3.354177	3.649382	4.011060	4.432179	4.822974
1.4200000	3.416868	3.725579	4.108071	4.562215	4.997709
1.4300000	3.480271	3.802894	4.207132	4.696803	5.183222
1.4400000	3.544353	3.881284	4.308197	4.836011	5.380579
1.4500000	3.609077	3.960698	4.411204	4.979882	5.590978
1.4600000	3.674407	4.041082	4.516080	5.128420	5.815761
1.4700000	3.740301	4.122379	4.622739	5.281591	6.056419
1.4800000	3.806717	4.204522	4.731079	5.439308	6.314582
1.4900000	3.873609	4.287444	4.840985	5.601426	6.591987
1.5000000	3.940931	4.371073	4.952328	5.767738	6.890399
1.5100000	4.008633	4.455329	5.064965	5.937959	7.211465
1.5200000	4.076665	4.540132	5.178741	6.111734	7.556471
1.5300000	4.144975	4.625397	5.293489	6.288630	7.925952
1.5400000	4.213511	4.711038	5.409031	6.468142	8.319172
1.5500000	4.282217	4.796964	5.525181	6.649696	8.733550
1.5600000	4.351039	4.883085	5.641745	6.832664	9.164232
1.5699999	4.419921	4.969306	5.758526	7.016377	9.604146
1.5707963	4.425407	4.976173	5.767829	7.031019	9.639325
1.5707963	4.425403	4.976168	5.767822	7.031010	9.639310

$\alpha =$ .699999

θ	K VALUES				
	.009966711	.039469502	.087332193	.151646642	.229848846
.0000000	.000000	.000000	.000000	.000000	.000000
.0100000	.010000	.010000	.010000	.010000	.010000
.0200000	.020001	.020001	.020001	.020002	.020002
.0300000	.030006	.030006	.030006	.030006	.030007
.0400000	.040015	.040015	.040015	.040016	.040017
.0500000	.050029	.050030	.050031	.050032	.050034
.0600000	.060050	.060051	.060053	.060055	.060058
.0700000	.070080	.070082	.070085	.070088	.070093
.0800000	.080120	.080123	.080127	.080132	.080139
.0900000	.090171	.090175	.090181	.090188	.090198
.1000000	.100235	.100240	.100248	.100259	.100272
.1100000	.110313	.110320	.110330	.110345	.110362
.1200000	.120407	.120415	.120429	.120448	.120470
.1300000	.130518	.130529	.130546	.130570	.130599
.1400000	.140647	.140661	.140683	.140712	.140748
.1500000	.150797	.150813	.150840	.150877	.150921
.1600000	.160968	.160988	.161021	.161065	.161119
.1700000	.171161	.171186	.171225	.171278	.171343
.1800000	.181380	.181409	.181456	.181519	.181596
.1900000	.191624	.191658	.191714	.191788	.191879
.2000000	.201896	.201936	.202000	.202087	.202193
.2100000	.212197	.212243	.212318	.212419	.212541
.2200000	.222529	.222582	.222668	.222784	.222925
.2300000	.232892	.232953	.233051	.233184	.233346
.2400000	.243290	.243358	.243471	.243622	.243806
.2500000	.253722	.253800	.253927	.254098	.254307
.2600000	.264192	.264280	.264422	.264615	.264850
.2700000	.274700	.274798	.274959	.275175	.275439
.2800000	.285248	.285358	.285537	.285778	.286073
.2900000	.295838	.295960	.296160	.296428	.296757
.3000000	.306471	.306607	.306828	.307126	.307490
.3100000	.317150	.317300	.317544	.317874	.318277
.3200000	.327876	.328041	.328310	.328673	.329117
.3300000	.338650	.338831	.339127	.339526	.340014
.3400000	.349474	.349673	.349997	.350434	.350970
.3500000	.360351	.360568	.360922	.361400	.361986
.3600000	.371281	.371518	.371904	.372425	.373065
.3700000	.382268	.382525	.382945	.383512	.384209
.3800000	.393311	.393591	.394046	.394663	.395420
.3900000	.404415	.404717	.405211	.405879	.406699

$\alpha =$ .699999

Θ	K VALUES				
	.009966711	.039469502	.087332193	.151646642	.229848846
.4000000	.415580	.415907	.416440	.417163	.418051
.4100000	.426808	.427161	.427736	.428517	.429476
.4200000	.438101	.438481	.439102	.439943	.440977
.4300000	.449461	.449870	.450538	.451443	.452556
.4400000	.460891	.461330	.462047	.463019	.464216
.4500000	.472392	.472863	.473632	.474675	.475960
.4600000	.483967	.484470	.485294	.486411	.487788
.4700000	.495617	.496155	.497035	.498231	.499705
.4800000	.507344	.507919	.508859	.510137	.511713
.4900000	.519152	.519765	.520767	.522131	.523814
.5000000	.531041	.531694	.532762	.534215	.536010
.5100000	.543015	.543709	.544846	.546393	.548305
.5200000	.555075	.555813	.557021	.558666	.560701
.5300000	.567224	.568007	.569290	.571038	.573201
.5400000	.579464	.580295	.581656	.583511	.585808
.5500000	.591798	.592678	.594120	.596087	.598525
.5600000	.604228	.605159	.606686	.608770	.611354
.5700000	.616756	.617741	.619357	.621562	.624298
.5800000	.629386	.630427	.632134	.634465	.637361
.5900000	.642119	.643218	.645020	.647484	.650545
.6000000	.654959	.656117	.658019	.660620	.663854
.6100000	.667907	.669128	.671133	.673876	.677290
.6200000	.680967	.682253	.684365	.687257	.690858
.6300000	.694141	.695494	.697718	.700764	.704560
.6400000	.707432	.708855	.711195	.714401	.718399
.6500000	.720844	.722339	.724798	.728170	.732380
.6600000	.734378	.735948	.738532	.742077	.746505
.6700000	.748038	.749686	.752398	.756122	.760778
.6800000	.761827	.763555	.766401	.770310	.775202
.6899999	.775747	.777559	.780543	.784645	.789782
.7000000	.789803	.791700	.794828	.799130	.804520
.7100000	.803996	.805983	.809259	.813767	.819421
.7200000	.818331	.820410	.823839	.828561	.834489
.7300000	.832810	.834984	.838572	.843516	.849727
.7400000	.847437	.849710	.853461	.858634	.865139
.7500000	.862215	.864589	.868511	.873921	.880730
.7600000	.877147	.879627	.883723	.889379	.896503
.7700000	.892237	.894825	.899103	.905012	.912462
.7800000	.907489	.910189	.914653	.920825	.928613
.7899999	.922906	.925721	.930378	.936821	.944958

$\alpha =$ .699999

Θ	K VALUES				
	.009966711	.039469502	.087332193	.151646642	.229848846
.8000000	.938491	.941425	.946282	.953005	.961503
.8100000	.954248	.957305	.962368	.969379	.978251
.8200000	.970181	.973365	.978640	.985950	.995208
.8300000	.986294	.989608	.995101	1.002720	1.012377
.8400000	1.002590	1.006039	1.011757	1.019694	1.029764
.8500000	1.019074	1.022661	1.028612	1.036876	1.047372
.8600000	1.035748	1.039478	1.045668	1.054271	1.065207
.8700000	1.052617	1.056494	1.062931	1.071883	1.083273
.8799999	1.069686	1.073714	1.080405	1.089717	1.101576
.8899999	1.086957	1.091141	1.098093	1.107776	1.120119
.9000000	1.104435	1.108779	1.116001	1.126066	1.138908
.9100000	1.122124	1.126633	1.134132	1.144591	1.157948
.9200000	1.140029	1.144706	1.152491	1.163355	1.177243
.9300000	1.158152	1.163004	1.171081	1.182363	1.196799
.9400000	1.176498	1.181529	1.189909	1.201620	1.216620
.9500000	1.195072	1.200287	1.208977	1.221130	1.236712
.9600000	1.213878	1.219281	1.228290	1.240898	1.257080
.9699999	1.232919	1.238516	1.247853	1.260929	1.277727
.9799999	1.252199	1.257996	1.267669	1.281227	1.298661
.9899999	1.271724	1.277725	1.287745	1.301797	1.319885
1.0000000	1.291497	1.297708	1.308083	1.322644	1.341405
1.0100000	1.311521	1.317948	1.328687	1.343772	1.363225
1.0200000	1.331802	1.338450	1.349563	1.365185	1.385351
1.0300000	1.352343	1.359217	1.370715	1.386888	1.407787
1.0400000	1.373147	1.380254	1.392146	1.408886	1.430538
1.0500000	1.394220	1.401565	1.413862	1.431182	1.453609
1.0600000	1.415564	1.423153	1.435865	1.453782	1.477004
1.0699999	1.437184	1.445023	1.458160	1.476689	1.500728
1.0799999	1.459082	1.467178	1.480750	1.499908	1.524786
1.0899999	1.481263	1.489622	1.503640	1.523442	1.549181
1.1000000	1.503730	1.512358	1.526833	1.547295	1.573919
1.1100000	1.526486	1.535389	1.550332	1.571471	1.599002
1.1200000	1.549535	1.558718	1.574141	1.595973	1.624435
1.1300000	1.572878	1.582349	1.598263	1.620805	1.650220
1.1400000	1.596519	1.606285	1.622700	1.645969	1.676362
1.1500000	1.620461	1.630527	1.647456	1.671469	1.702864
1.1600000	1.644705	1.655079	1.672532	1.697306	1.729728
1.1700000	1.669253	1.679942	1.697932	1.723485	1.756958
1.1800000	1.694108	1.705118	1.723656	1.750005	1.784554
1.1899999	1.719271	1.730609	1.749707	1.776870	1.812520

$\alpha =$ .699999

Θ	K VALUES				
	.009966711	.039469502	.087332193	.151646642	.229848846
1.2000000	1.744744	1.756415	1.776085	1.804080	1.840856
1.2100000	1.770526	1.782539	1.802792	1.831637	1.869564
1.2200000	1.796619	1.808980	1.829829	1.859541	1.898644
1.2300000	1.823022	1.835738	1.857194	1.887792	1.928097
1.2400000	1.849736	1.862814	1.884889	1.916390	1.957922
1.2500000	1.876760	1.890206	1.912913	1.945335	1.988120
1.2599999	1.904093	1.917914	1.941264	1.974625	2.018688
1.2699999	1.931733	1.945936	1.969941	2.004258	2.049625
1.2799999	1.959679	1.974270	1.998941	2.034233	2.080929
1.2899999	1.987927	2.002914	2.028263	2.064547	2.112596
1.3000000	2.016476	2.031864	2.057903	2.095197	2.144624
1.3100000	2.045321	2.061118	2.087858	2.126177	2.177008
1.3200000	2.074458	2.090670	2.118122	2.157486	2.209744
1.3300000	2.103883	2.120516	2.148692	2.189116	2.242825
1.3400000	2.133591	2.150651	2.179561	2.221062	2.276246
1.3500000	2.163576	2.181070	2.210725	2.253318	2.310000
1.3600000	2.193832	2.211765	2.242175	2.285877	2.344080
1.3700000	2.224352	2.242730	2.273905	2.318732	2.378477
1.3799999	2.255128	2.273957	2.305907	2.351873	2.413182
1.3899999	2.286152	2.305437	2.338173	2.385292	2.448185
1.4000000	2.317416	2.337163	2.370692	2.418979	2.483477
1.4100000	2.348910	2.369123	2.403456	2.452923	2.519046
1.4200000	2.380625	2.401309	2.436453	2.487115	2.554880
1.4300000	2.412549	2.433710	2.469673	2.521541	2.590966
1.4400000	2.444673	2.466313	2.503104	2.556189	2.627292
1.4500000	2.476983	2.499108	2.536734	2.591048	2.663843
1.4600000	2.509469	2.532083	2.570550	2.626102	2.700605
1.4700000	2.542118	2.565223	2.604538	2.661339	2.737562
1.4800000	2.574917	2.598517	2.638685	2.696743	2.774700
1.4900000	2.607851	2.631950	2.672976	2.732300	2.812002
1.5000000	2.640908	2.665508	2.707397	2.767993	2.849451
1.5100000	2.674073	2.699176	2.741933	2.803808	2.887030
1.5200000	2.707331	2.732939	2.776567	2.839726	2.924721
1.5300000	2.740668	2.766783	2.811285	2.875733	2.962507
1.5400000	2.774068	2.800691	2.846070	2.911810	3.000369
1.5500000	2.807516	2.834649	2.880906	2.947942	3.038289
1.5600000	2.840997	2.868639	2.915776	2.984109	3.076248
1.5699999	2.874494	2.902647	2.950665	3.020296	3.114227
1.5707963	2.877162	2.905356	2.953443	3.023178	3.117251
1.5707963	2.877159	2.905353	2.953441	3.023175	3.117249

$\alpha =$ •699999

Θ	K VALUES				
	•318821117	•415016431	•514599755	•613601043	•708073407
•0000000	•000000	•000000	•000000	•000000	•000000
•0100000	•010000	•010000	•010000	•010000	•010000
•0200000	•020002	•020002	•020002	•020002	•020002
•0300000	•030007	•030008	•030008	•030009	•030009
•0400000	•040018	•040019	•040020	•040021	•040022
•0500000	•050035	•050037	•050039	•050042	•050043
•0600000	•060061	•060065	•060069	•060072	•060076
•0700000	•070098	•070103	•070109	•070115	•070120
•0800000	•080146	•080155	•080163	•080172	•080180
•0900000	•090209	•090221	•090233	•090245	•090256
•1000000	•100287	•100303	•100320	•100336	•100352
•1100000	•110382	•110403	•110426	•110448	•110469
•1200000	•120496	•120524	•120553	•120582	•120610
•1300000	•130632	•130667	•130704	•130741	•130776
•1400000	•140789	•140834	•140880	•140926	•140970
•1500000	•150972	•151027	•151083	•151140	•151194
•1600000	•161180	•161247	•161316	•161385	•161451
•1700000	•171417	•171497	•171580	•171663	•171742
•1800000	•181684	•181779	•181878	•181976	•182070
•1900000	•191982	•192094	•192211	•192327	•192438
•2000000	•202314	•202445	•202581	•202717	•202847
•2100000	•212682	•212834	•212992	•213150	•213301
•2200000	•223086	•223262	•223444	•223626	•223801
•2300000	•233531	•233732	•233941	•234149	•234349
•2400000	•244016	•244245	•244483	•244721	•244949
•2500000	•254545	•254804	•255074	•255344	•255603
•2600000	•265119	•265412	•265716	•266021	•266313
•2700000	•275741	•276069	•276411	•276754	•277083
•2800000	•286411	•286778	•287162	•287545	•287914
•2900000	•297133	•297542	•297970	•298397	•298809
•3000000	•307908	•308363	•308837	•309313	•309771
•3100000	•318739	•319242	•319768	•320295	•320803
•3200000	•329627	•330183	•330763	•331346	•331907
•3300000	•340575	•341187	•341826	•342468	•343087
•3400000	•351585	•352257	•352959	•353665	•354345
•3500000	•362659	•363395	•364164	•364938	•365684
•3600000	•373800	•374603	•375444	•376291	•377108
•3700000	•385009	•385885	•386802	•387726	•388619
•3800000	•396290	•397242	•398241	•399247	•400220
•3900000	•407643	•408677	•409762	•410856	•411915

$\alpha =$ .699999

Θ	K VALUES				
	.318821117	.415016431	.514599755	.613601043	.708073407
.4000000	.419073	.420193	.421370	.422557	.423707
.4100000	.430581	.431792	.433066	.434352	.435599
.4200000	.442169	.443478	.444854	.446245	.447595
.4300000	.453841	.455252	.456737	.458239	.459697
.4400000	.465598	.467117	.468717	.470337	.471911
.4500000	.477444	.479076	.480798	.482542	.484238
.4600000	.489381	.491133	.492983	.494858	.496684
.4700000	.501411	.503290	.505274	.507289	.509251
.4800000	.513538	.515549	.517676	.519837	.521944
.4900000	.525763	.527915	.530191	.532507	.534767
.5000000	.538091	.540389	.542823	.545302	.547723
.5100000	.550524	.552976	.555576	.558225	.560817
.5200000	.563064	.565678	.568452	.571282	.574053
.5300000	.575715	.578498	.581455	.584475	.587435
.5400000	.588480	.591441	.594590	.597809	.600968
.5500000	.601361	.604509	.607859	.611288	.614657
.5600000	.614363	.617705	.621266	.624916	.628506
.5700000	.627488	.631033	.634816	.638697	.642519
.5800000	.640739	.644498	.648512	.652636	.656702
.5900000	.654120	.658102	.662359	.666737	.671060
.6000000	.667634	.671848	.676360	.681006	.685599
.6100000	.681284	.685742	.690520	.695446	.700322
.6200000	.695075	.699787	.704842	.710062	.715236
.6300000	.709009	.713986	.719332	.724859	.730346
.6400000	.723090	.728343	.733994	.739843	.745658
.6500000	.737323	.742864	.748832	.755018	.761177
.6600000	.751710	.757551	.763851	.770391	.776911
.6700000	.766255	.772410	.779056	.785965	.792864
.6800000	.780963	.787444	.794451	.801747	.809043
.6899999	.795837	.802657	.810042	.817742	.825455
.7000000	.810882	.818056	.825834	.833957	.842107
.7100000	.826101	.833643	.841832	.850396	.859004
.7200000	.841499	.849423	.858040	.867066	.876154
.7300000	.857080	.865402	.874465	.883974	.893564
.7400000	.872848	.881584	.891112	.901125	.911241
.7500000	.888808	.897974	.907986	.918525	.929193
.7600000	.904964	.914577	.925093	.936183	.947428
.7700000	.921320	.931398	.942439	.954103	.965953
.7800000	.937882	.948443	.960030	.972293	.984776
.7899999	.954654	.965715	.977872	.990760	1.003906

$\alpha =$ .699999

θ	K VALUES				
	.318821117	.415016431	.514599755	.613601043	.708073407
.8000000	.971641	.983222	.995971	1.009512	1.023351
.8100000	.988847	1.000968	1.014333	1.028555	1.043119
.8200000	1.006278	1.018959	1.032965	1.047896	1.063220
.8300000	1.023938	1.037200	1.051872	1.067544	1.083662
.8400000	1.041832	1.055697	1.071062	1.087506	1.104454
.8500000	1.059966	1.074456	1.090540	1.107789	1.125607
.8600000	1.078345	1.093482	1.110315	1.128403	1.147130
.8700000	1.096973	1.112782	1.130392	1.149354	1.169031
.8799999	1.115857	1.132361	1.150779	1.170652	1.191323
.8899999	1.135001	1.152226	1.171482	1.192304	1.214014
.9000000	1.154412	1.172382	1.192509	1.214319	1.237115
.9100000	1.174093	1.192836	1.213867	1.236706	1.260637
.9200000	1.194051	1.213594	1.235563	1.259473	1.284590
.9300000	1.214291	1.234661	1.257605	1.282630	1.308985
.9400000	1.234819	1.256046	1.279999	1.306184	1.333834
.9500000	1.255641	1.277753	1.302753	1.330146	1.359148
.9600000	1.276761	1.299789	1.325875	1.354524	1.384939
.9699999	1.298185	1.322160	1.349372	1.379328	1.411217
.9799999	1.319920	1.344873	1.373252	1.404567	1.437995
.9899999	1.341970	1.367935	1.397522	1.430249	1.465284
1.0000000	1.364341	1.391351	1.422191	1.456386	1.493097
1.0100000	1.387039	1.415127	1.447264	1.482985	1.521446
1.0200000	1.410069	1.439271	1.472751	1.510056	1.550342
1.0300000	1.433436	1.463788	1.498658	1.537608	1.579799
1.0400000	1.457146	1.488685	1.524992	1.565652	1.609828
1.0500000	1.481204	1.513967	1.551762	1.594195	1.640441
1.0600000	1.505615	1.539641	1.578974	1.623248	1.671651
1.0699999	1.530385	1.565713	1.606636	1.652819	1.703470
1.0799999	1.555518	1.592187	1.634754	1.682918	1.735911
1.0899999	1.581018	1.619071	1.663335	1.713553	1.768984
1.1000000	1.606892	1.646369	1.692387	1.744732	1.802703
1.1100000	1.633143	1.674086	1.721915	1.776465	1.837077
1.1200000	1.659775	1.702227	1.751925	1.808759	1.872120
1.1300000	1.686793	1.730798	1.782424	1.841621	1.907842
1.1400000	1.714199	1.759802	1.813416	1.875061	1.944254
1.1500000	1.741999	1.789244	1.844908	1.909084	1.981367
1.1600000	1.770194	1.819127	1.876904	1.943697	2.019189
1.1700000	1.798788	1.849456	1.909409	1.978907	2.057732
1.1800000	1.827784	1.880233	1.942426	2.014719	2.097003
1.1899999	1.857183	1.911460	1.975959	2.051139	2.137012

$\alpha =$ .699999

Θ	K VALUES				
	.318821117	.415016431	.514599755	.613601043	.708073407
1.2000000	1.886987	1.943142	2.010012	2.088171	2.177765
1.2100000	1.917198	1.975277	2.044586	2.125819	2.219270
1.2200000	1.947817	2.007869	2.079685	2.164087	2.261533
1.2300000	1.978843	2.040917	2.115308	2.202976	2.304558
1.2400000	2.010278	2.074423	2.151456	2.242489	2.348351
1.2500000	2.042120	2.108385	2.188130	2.282627	2.392914
1.2599999	2.074367	2.142802	2.225329	2.323389	2.438249
1.2699999	2.107019	2.177672	2.263051	2.364774	2.484357
1.2799999	2.140073	2.212994	2.301293	2.406781	2.531238
1.2899999	2.173526	2.248763	2.340052	2.449406	2.578889
1.3000000	2.207374	2.284976	2.379325	2.492645	2.627309
1.3100000	2.241612	2.321628	2.419105	2.536493	2.676490
1.3200000	2.276236	2.358713	2.459386	2.580943	2.726429
1.3300000	2.311239	2.396225	2.500162	2.625988	2.777116
1.3400000	2.346615	2.434156	2.541424	2.671618	2.828542
1.3500000	2.382357	2.472498	2.583164	2.717823	2.880696
1.3600000	2.418456	2.511243	2.625370	2.764592	2.933565
1.3700000	2.454903	2.550379	2.668032	2.811911	2.987133
1.3799999	2.491688	2.589897	2.711137	2.859766	3.041385
1.3899999	2.528801	2.629785	2.754671	2.908141	3.096300
1.4000000	2.566231	2.670029	2.798621	2.957019	3.151860
1.4100000	2.603965	2.710616	2.842970	3.006382	3.208040
1.4200000	2.641990	2.751531	2.887701	3.056210	3.264817
1.4300000	2.680293	2.792759	2.932797	3.106480	3.322164
1.4400000	2.718859	2.834284	2.978239	3.157172	3.380054
1.4500000	2.757672	2.876088	3.024007	3.208261	3.438456
1.4600000	2.796717	2.918154	3.070080	3.259721	3.497339
1.4700000	2.835977	2.960463	3.116436	3.311528	3.556670
1.4800000	2.875436	3.002996	3.163054	3.363653	3.616414
1.4900000	2.915074	3.045731	3.209909	3.416068	3.676534
1.5000000	2.954875	3.088650	3.256978	3.468744	3.736993
1.5100000	2.994818	3.131730	3.304235	3.521650	3.797751
1.5200000	3.034885	3.174950	3.351656	3.574755	3.858769
1.5300000	3.075055	3.218286	3.399213	3.628029	3.920006
1.5400000	3.115309	3.261718	3.446881	3.681438	3.981419
1.5500000	3.155627	3.305221	3.494633	3.734949	4.042966
1.5600000	3.195988	3.348773	3.542442	3.788530	4.104603
1.5699999	3.236371	3.392350	3.590280	3.842147	4.166288
1.5707963	3.239588	3.395820	3.594090	3.846417	4.171201
1.5707963	3.239585	3.395818	3.594088	3.846416	4.171198

$\alpha =$ .699999

θ	K VALUES				
	.794250555	.868696860	.928444378	.971111163	.994996249
.0000000	.000000	.000000	.000000	.000000	.000000
.0100000	.010000	.010000	.010000	.010000	.010000
.0200000	.020002	.020003	.020003	.020003	.020003
.0300000	.030009	.030010	.030010	.030010	.030010
.0400000	.040023	.040024	.040024	.040025	.040025
.0500000	.050045	.050047	.050048	.050049	.050049
.0600000	.060079	.060081	.060083	.060085	.060086
.0700000	.070125	.070129	.070133	.070135	.070137
.0800000	.080187	.080194	.080199	.080202	.080204
.0900000	.090267	.090276	.090283	.090289	.090291
.1000000	.100366	.100379	.100389	.100396	.100400
.1100000	.110488	.110505	.110518	.110528	.110533
.1200000	.120635	.120656	.120674	.120686	.120693
.1300000	.130808	.130835	.130858	.130874	.130883
.1400000	.141010	.141045	.141073	.141092	.141104
.1500000	.151244	.151286	.151321	.151345	.151359
.1600000	.161511	.161563	.161605	.161635	.161652
.1700000	.171815	.171877	.171928	.171964	.171984
.1800000	.182157	.182231	.182291	.182334	.182358
.1900000	.192540	.192628	.192699	.192750	.192778
.2000000	.202966	.203070	.203153	.203212	.203245
.2100000	.213439	.213559	.213656	.213725	.213763
.2200000	.223960	.224099	.224210	.224290	.224335
.2300000	.234532	.234691	.234819	.234911	.234962
.2400000	.245158	.245340	.245486	.245591	.245649
.2500000	.255841	.256047	.256213	.256332	.256398
.2600000	.266582	.266815	.267003	.267137	.267213
.2700000	.277385	.277647	.277858	.278010	.278095
.2800000	.288252	.288546	.288783	.288953	.289049
.2900000	.299187	.299515	.299781	.299971	.300077
.3000000	.310192	.310558	.310853	.311065	.311184
.3100000	.321270	.321676	.322004	.322239	.322371
.3200000	.332424	.332873	.333236	.333497	.333644
.3300000	.343657	.344153	.344554	.344842	.345004
.3400000	.354972	.355518	.355960	.356278	.356456
.3500000	.366373	.366973	.367458	.367807	.368003
.3600000	.377862	.378520	.379052	.379435	.379650
.3700000	.389443	.390162	.390745	.391164	.391399
.3800000	.401119	.401904	.402540	.402998	.403255
.3900000	.412894	.413749	.414443	.414942	.415222

$\alpha =$ .699999

Θ	K VALUES				
	.794250555	.868696860	.928444378	.971111163	.994996249
.4000000	.424770	.425701	.426455	.426999	.427304
.4100000	.436753	.437763	.438583	.439173	.439506
.4200000	.448845	.449940	.450829	.451470	.451831
.4300000	.461050	.462235	.463198	.463893	.464284
.4400000	.473371	.474653	.475694	.476446	.476869
.4500000	.485814	.487197	.488322	.489135	.489593
.4600000	.498381	.499872	.501087	.501964	.502458
.4700000	.511077	.512683	.513992	.514937	.515471
.4800000	.523907	.525634	.527043	.528061	.528636
.4900000	.536874	.538730	.540244	.541340	.541959
.5000000	.549982	.551975	.553602	.554780	.555445
.5100000	.563238	.565374	.567121	.568386	.569100
.5200000	.576644	.578933	.580806	.582163	.582930
.5300000	.590206	.592656	.594663	.596118	.596941
.5400000	.603929	.606550	.608697	.610256	.611139
.5500000	.617818	.620618	.622916	.624585	.625530
.5600000	.631877	.634868	.637324	.639109	.640121
.5700000	.646113	.649305	.651929	.653837	.654919
.5800000	.660531	.663935	.666735	.668774	.669930
.5900000	.675135	.678763	.681751	.683928	.685164
.6000000	.689934	.693798	.696983	.699307	.700626
.6100000	.704930	.709044	.712439	.714917	.716324
.6200000	.720132	.724508	.728124	.730766	.732268
.6300000	.735545	.740199	.744048	.746863	.748464
.6400000	.751176	.756122	.760218	.763216	.764923
.6500000	.767031	.772285	.776641	.779834	.781652
.6600000	.783118	.788695	.793327	.796725	.798662
.6700000	.799442	.805362	.810284	.813899	.815961
.6800000	.816011	.822292	.827521	.831366	.833561
.6899999	.832833	.839494	.845048	.849136	.851471
.7000000	.849915	.856976	.862873	.867218	.869702
.7100000	.867265	.874748	.881006	.885624	.888266
.7200000	.884891	.892818	.899459	.904364	.907174
.7300000	.902800	.911196	.918240	.923451	.926438
.7400000	.921003	.929892	.937363	.942896	.946071
.7500000	.939507	.948915	.956836	.962712	.966087
.7600000	.958321	.968277	.976674	.982912	.986498
.7700000	.977454	.987987	.996887	1.003508	1.007319
.7800000	.996916	1.008057	1.017488	1.024516	1.028564
.7899999	1.016717	1.028498	1.038490	1.045949	1.050250

$\alpha =$ .699999

θ	K VALUES				
	.794250555	.868696860	.928444378	.971111163	.994996249
.8000000	1.036866	1.049322	1.059908	1.067822	1.072392
.8100000	1.057375	1.070541	1.081754	1.090152	1.095007
.8200000	1.078252	1.092167	1.104043	1.112954	1.118111
.8300000	1.099510	1.114214	1.126791	1.136245	1.141724
.8400000	1.121158	1.136694	1.150012	1.160043	1.165865
.8500000	1.143210	1.159622	1.173724	1.184366	1.190552
.8600000	1.165676	1.183011	1.197942	1.209234	1.215807
.8700000	1.188568	1.206876	1.222685	1.234666	1.241651
.8799999	1.211898	1.231232	1.247969	1.260683	1.268107
.8899999	1.235680	1.256094	1.273815	1.287306	1.295197
.9000000	1.259926	1.281480	1.300241	1.314558	1.322947
.9100000	1.284649	1.307404	1.327266	1.342463	1.351382
.9200000	1.309863	1.333884	1.354913	1.371044	1.380529
.9300000	1.335581	1.360937	1.383202	1.400326	1.410417
.9400000	1.361819	1.388581	1.412155	1.430338	1.441073
.9500000	1.388589	1.416835	1.441797	1.461105	1.472530
.9600000	1.415907	1.445718	1.472150	1.492658	1.504819
.9699999	1.443788	1.475248	1.503240	1.525025	1.537974
.9799999	1.472247	1.505447	1.535092	1.558239	1.572032
.9899999	1.501300	1.536335	1.567733	1.592333	1.607028
1.0000000	1.530963	1.567932	1.601190	1.627340	1.643002
1.0100000	1.561251	1.600261	1.635493	1.663296	1.679995
1.0200000	1.592181	1.633343	1.670670	1.700238	1.718050
1.0300000	1.623770	1.667201	1.706752	1.738207	1.757212
1.0400000	1.656033	1.701858	1.743770	1.777241	1.797530
1.0500000	1.688989	1.737338	1.781758	1.817385	1.839053
1.0600000	1.722653	1.773665	1.820749	1.858682	1.881835
1.0699999	1.757044	1.810864	1.860778	1.901179	1.925930
1.0799999	1.792178	1.848959	1.901880	1.944925	1.971399
1.0899999	1.828072	1.887975	1.944093	1.989971	2.018303
1.1000000	1.864744	1.927940	1.987456	2.036371	2.066708
1.1100000	1.902211	1.968879	2.032008	2.084179	2.116683
1.1200000	1.940490	2.010817	2.077788	2.133454	2.168301
1.1300000	1.979597	2.053782	2.124838	2.184257	2.221642
1.1400000	2.019550	2.097800	2.173202	2.236653	2.276787
1.1500000	2.060364	2.142898	2.222923	2.290708	2.333824
1.1600000	2.102057	2.189103	2.274046	2.346492	2.392847
1.1700000	2.144642	2.236441	2.326617	2.404078	2.453954
1.1800000	2.188136	2.284940	2.380683	2.463544	2.517252
1.1899999	2.232552	2.334625	2.436292	2.524970	2.582853

$\alpha =$ .699999

Θ	K VALUES				
	.794250555	.868696860	.928444378	.971111163	.994996249
1.2000000	2.277905	2.385522	2.493492	2.588439	2.650878
1.2100000	2.324207	2.437657	2.552331	2.654040	2.721456
1.2200000	2.371470	2.491053	2.612861	2.721865	2.794724
1.2300000	2.419705	2.545735	2.675130	2.792010	2.870833
1.2400000	2.468923	2.601725	2.739190	2.864576	2.949940
1.2500000	2.519131	2.659044	2.805090	2.939667	3.032218
1.2599999	2.570337	2.717714	2.872881	3.017395	3.117853
1.2699999	2.622547	2.777751	2.942613	3.097873	3.207046
1.2799999	2.675764	2.839173	3.014333	3.181221	3.300014
1.2899999	2.729991	2.901995	3.088090	3.267562	3.396993
1.3000000	2.785230	2.966228	3.163929	3.357028	3.498244
1.3100000	2.841477	3.031881	3.241894	3.449748	3.604045
1.3200000	2.898729	3.098962	3.322026	3.545863	3.714706
1.3300000	2.956980	3.167473	3.404362	3.645513	3.830565
1.3400000	3.016223	3.237416	3.488937	3.748845	3.951995
1.3500000	3.076445	3.308786	3.575781	3.856006	4.079409
1.3600000	3.137635	3.381575	3.664917	3.967147	4.213262
1.3700000	3.199775	3.455772	3.756363	4.082418	4.354061
1.3799999	3.262847	3.531361	3.850130	4.201967	4.502373
1.3899999	3.326829	3.608320	3.946221	4.325942	4.658828
1.4000000	3.391697	3.686623	4.044631	4.454483	4.824137
1.4100000	3.457423	3.766238	4.145343	4.587718	4.999092
1.4200000	3.523975	3.847129	4.248329	4.725765	5.184591
1.4300000	3.591321	3.929253	4.353552	4.868724	5.381643
1.4400000	3.659425	4.012562	4.460959	5.016669	5.591386
1.4500000	3.728246	4.097002	4.570486	5.169645	5.815102
1.4600000	3.797743	4.182514	4.682052	5.327659	6.054224
1.4700000	3.867871	4.269034	4.795564	5.490671	6.310345
1.4800000	3.938582	4.356490	4.910911	5.658588	6.585206
1.4900000	4.009826	4.444807	5.027967	5.831254	6.880659
1.5000000	4.081551	4.533906	5.146593	6.008444	7.198591
1.5100000	4.153702	4.623699	5.266632	6.189851	7.540756
1.5200000	4.226223	4.714097	5.387915	6.375092	7.908525
1.5300000	4.299056	4.805007	5.510259	6.563699	8.302466
1.5400000	4.372140	4.896333	5.633471	6.755127	8.721789
1.5500000	4.445417	4.987975	5.757347	6.948758	9.163730
1.5600000	4.518823	5.079831	5.881675	7.143913	9.623100
1.5699999	4.592296	5.171800	6.006240	7.339872	10.092338
1.5707963	4.598148	5.179125	6.016163	7.355489	10.129862
1.5707963	4.598146	5.179122	6.016160	7.355484	10.129851

$\alpha =$ .719999

θ	K VALUES				
	.009966711	.039469502	.087332193	.151646642	.229848846
.0000000	.000000	.000000	.000000	.000000	.000000
.0100000	.010000	.010000	.010000	.010000	.010000
.0200000	.020001	.020001	.020002	.020002	.020002
.0300000	.030006	.030006	.030006	.030007	.030007
.0400000	.040015	.040015	.040016	.040017	.040017
.0500000	.050030	.050030	.050031	.050033	.050034
.0600000	.060052	.060053	.060055	.060057	.060060
.0700000	.070083	.070084	.070087	.070091	.070095
.0800000	.080123	.080126	.080130	.080136	.080142
.0900000	.090176	.090180	.090185	.090193	.090203
.1000000	.100242	.100247	.100255	.100265	.100278
.1100000	.110322	.110329	.110339	.110354	.110371
.1200000	.120418	.120427	.120441	.120459	.120482
.1300000	.130533	.130543	.130561	.130585	.130614
.1400000	.140666	.140679	.140701	.140731	.140767
.1500000	.150819	.150836	.150863	.150900	.150944
.1600000	.160995	.161016	.161048	.161093	.161147
.1700000	.171195	.171219	.171259	.171312	.171377
.1800000	.181420	.181448	.181495	.181559	.181636
.1900000	.191671	.191705	.191760	.191835	.191926
.2000000	.201951	.201991	.202055	.202142	.202248
.2100000	.212261	.212307	.212381	.212482	.212605
.2200000	.222602	.222655	.222741	.222857	.222999
.2300000	.232976	.233037	.233135	.233268	.233430
.2400000	.243385	.243454	.243566	.243717	.243902
.2500000	.253831	.253909	.254036	.254207	.254416
.2600000	.264314	.264402	.264545	.264738	.264973
.2700000	.274837	.274936	.275096	.275313	.275577
.2800000	.285402	.285512	.285691	.285933	.286228
.2900000	.296010	.296132	.296332	.296601	.296930
.3000000	.306662	.306798	.307019	.307318	.307683
.3100000	.317362	.317512	.317756	.318086	.318490
.3200000	.328109	.328275	.328544	.328908	.329353
.3300000	.338907	.339089	.339385	.339784	.340274
.3400000	.349757	.349956	.350280	.350718	.351255
.3500000	.360661	.360878	.361233	.361712	.362299
.3600000	.371620	.371857	.372244	.372766	.373407
.3700000	.382637	.382895	.383316	.383884	.384582
.3800000	.393714	.393994	.394450	.395068	.395826
.3900000	.404852	.405155	.405650	.406319	.407141

$\alpha =$ .719999

Θ	K VALUES				
	.009966711	.039469502	.087332193	.151646642	.229848846
.4000000	.416054	.416382	.416916	.417641	.418530
.4100000	.427321	.427675	.428252	.429034	.429995
.4200000	.438656	.439037	.439659	.440502	.441539
.4300000	.450061	.450470	.451139	.452047	.453163
.4400000	.461537	.461977	.462696	.463670	.464870
.4500000	.473087	.473559	.474330	.475376	.476664
.4600000	.484714	.485219	.486044	.487165	.488546
.4700000	.496418	.496958	.497841	.499040	.500519
.4800000	.508204	.508780	.509723	.511005	.512585
.4900000	.520072	.520687	.521693	.523060	.524749
.5000000	.532025	.532680	.533752	.535210	.537011
.5100000	.544066	.544763	.545904	.547456	.549375
.5200000	.556197	.556938	.558151	.559802	.561844
.5300000	.568421	.569207	.570495	.572250	.574421
.5400000	.580740	.581574	.582940	.584802	.587108
.5500000	.593156	.594039	.595487	.597462	.599909
.5600000	.605672	.606607	.608141	.610233	.612827
.5700000	.618291	.619280	.620902	.623117	.625865
.5800000	.631015	.632061	.633776	.636118	.639026
.5900000	.643848	.644952	.646763	.649238	.652313
.6000000	.656792	.657956	.659867	.662481	.665730
.6100000	.669849	.671077	.673092	.675849	.679280
.6200000	.683024	.684316	.686440	.689347	.692967
.6300000	.696318	.697678	.699914	.702976	.706793
.6400000	.709734	.711165	.713518	.716742	.720763
.6500000	.723277	.724781	.727254	.730646	.734880
.6600000	.736948	.738528	.741127	.744693	.749148
.6700000	.750751	.752409	.755139	.758886	.763571
.6800000	.764690	.766429	.769294	.773228	.778152
.6899999	.778767	.780590	.783595	.787724	.792896
.7000000	.792986	.794897	.798046	.802377	.807806
.7100000	.807350	.809351	.812651	.817191	.822886
.7200000	.821863	.823958	.827412	.832169	.838142
.7300000	.836529	.838720	.842335	.847316	.853576
.7400000	.851350	.853641	.857422	.862636	.869193
.7500000	.866331	.868725	.872678	.878133	.884998
.7600000	.881475	.883976	.888107	.893810	.900994
.7700000	.896787	.899397	.903712	.909673	.917188
.7800000	.912269	.914993	.919498	.925724	.933582
.7899999	.927926	.930768	.935468	.941970	.950183

$\alpha =$ .719999

θ	K VALUES				
	.009966711	.039469502	.087332193	.151646642	.229848846
.8000000	.943763	.946725	.951628	.958414	.966994
.8100000	.959781	.962869	.967980	.975061	.984020
.8200000	.975987	.979203	.984531	.991915	1.001267
.8300000	.992385	.995733	1.001283	1.008981	1.018740
.8400000	1.008977	1.012463	1.018242	1.026264	1.036442
.8500000	1.025769	1.029396	1.035412	1.043768	1.054381
.8600000	1.042766	1.046538	1.052798	1.061499	1.072560
.8700000	1.059970	1.063892	1.070404	1.079461	1.090985
.8799999	1.077388	1.081464	1.088235	1.097659	1.109662
.8899999	1.095023	1.099258	1.106296	1.116099	1.128596
.9000000	1.112880	1.117279	1.124592	1.134785	1.147792
.9100000	1.130964	1.135531	1.143127	1.153723	1.167257
.9200000	1.149278	1.154019	1.161907	1.172917	1.186995
.9300000	1.167829	1.172748	1.180936	1.192374	1.207012
.9400000	1.186621	1.191722	1.200220	1.212098	1.227314
.9500000	1.205658	1.210948	1.219764	1.232095	1.247907
.9600000	1.224945	1.230429	1.239572	1.252369	1.268796
.9699999	1.244487	1.250170	1.259649	1.272928	1.289987
.9799999	1.264289	1.270177	1.280002	1.293775	1.311487
.9899999	1.284356	1.290454	1.300635	1.314916	1.333300
1.0000000	1.304693	1.311006	1.321553	1.336357	1.355434
1.0100000	1.325303	1.331839	1.342761	1.358103	1.377893
1.0200000	1.346193	1.352956	1.364264	1.380159	1.400683
1.0300000	1.367367	1.374364	1.386067	1.402532	1.423811
1.0400000	1.388830	1.396066	1.408176	1.425225	1.447281
1.0500000	1.410585	1.418068	1.430596	1.448245	1.471100
1.0600000	1.432639	1.440374	1.453331	1.471596	1.495274
1.0699999	1.454996	1.462990	1.476385	1.495284	1.519807
1.0799999	1.477660	1.485918	1.499765	1.519314	1.544705
1.0899999	1.500635	1.509165	1.523474	1.543690	1.569973
1.1000000	1.523925	1.532735	1.547518	1.568418	1.595618
1.1100000	1.547536	1.556631	1.571899	1.593501	1.621642
1.1200000	1.571470	1.580857	1.596623	1.618945	1.648053
1.1300000	1.595732	1.605418	1.621694	1.644754	1.674853
1.1400000	1.620325	1.630317	1.647115	1.670931	1.702047
1.1500000	1.645252	1.655558	1.672890	1.697481	1.729641
1.1600000	1.670517	1.681143	1.699023	1.724407	1.757636
1.1700000	1.696122	1.707076	1.725516	1.751712	1.786038
1.1800000	1.722071	1.733360	1.752372	1.779399	1.814848
1.1899999	1.748365	1.759996	1.779593	1.807472	1.844071

$\alpha =$ .719999

Θ	K VALUES				
	.009966711	.039469502	.087332193	.151646642	.229848846
1.2000000	1.775007	1.786988	1.807183	1.835931	1.873708
1.2100000	1.801998	1.814336	1.835142	1.864779	1.903761
1.2200000	1.829339	1.842042	1.863471	1.894018	1.934232
1.2300000	1.857031	1.870106	1.892173	1.923648	1.965123
1.2400000	1.885074	1.898529	1.921246	1.953670	1.996433
1.2500000	1.913470	1.927312	1.950692	1.984083	2.028163
1.2599999	1.942216	1.956453	1.980509	2.014888	2.060312
1.2699999	1.971312	1.985951	2.010696	2.046082	2.092878
1.2799999	2.000757	2.015805	2.041253	2.077665	2.125861
1.2899999	2.030547	2.046012	2.072175	2.109634	2.159258
1.3000000	2.060681	2.076571	2.103462	2.141986	2.193065
1.3100000	2.091156	2.107476	2.135108	2.174717	2.227278
1.3200000	2.121966	2.138725	2.167110	2.207822	2.261892
1.3300000	2.153107	2.170312	2.199462	2.241297	2.296903
1.3400000	2.184574	2.202232	2.232160	2.275135	2.332303
1.3500000	2.216361	2.234478	2.265196	2.309330	2.368086
1.3600000	2.248462	2.267045	2.298564	2.343874	2.404243
1.3700000	2.280868	2.299923	2.332255	2.378759	2.440766
1.3799999	2.313571	2.333106	2.366262	2.413976	2.477645
1.3899999	2.346563	2.366583	2.400573	2.449514	2.514868
1.4000000	2.379834	2.400345	2.435181	2.485364	2.552426
1.4100000	2.413374	2.434381	2.470072	2.521513	2.590304
1.4200000	2.447170	2.468680	2.505235	2.557948	2.628490
1.4300000	2.481212	2.503229	2.540658	2.594657	2.666970
1.4400000	2.515486	2.538016	2.576328	2.631626	2.705728
1.4500000	2.549980	2.573027	2.612230	2.668840	2.744749
1.4600000	2.584679	2.608248	2.648350	2.706283	2.784015
1.4700000	2.619570	2.643664	2.684672	2.743939	2.823511
1.4800000	2.654636	2.679260	2.721180	2.781791	2.863217
1.4900000	2.689863	2.715019	2.757857	2.819822	2.903114
1.5000000	2.725233	2.750926	2.794687	2.858014	2.943184
1.5100000	2.760731	2.786962	2.831652	2.896347	2.983406
1.5200000	2.796338	2.823110	2.868733	2.934803	3.023760
1.5300000	2.832038	2.859353	2.905912	2.973362	3.064225
1.5400000	2.867813	2.895673	2.943170	3.012005	3.104778
1.5500000	2.903645	2.932050	2.980489	3.050711	3.145400
1.5600000	2.939514	2.968466	3.017847	3.089459	3.186068
1.5699999	2.975404	3.004903	3.055227	3.128230	3.226759
1.5707963	2.978262	3.007805	3.058204	3.131318	3.230000
1.5707963	2.978260	3.007802	3.058202	3.131316	3.229998

$\alpha =$ .719999

θ	K VALUES				
	.318821117	.415016431	.514599755	.613601043	.708073407
.0000000	.000000	.000000	.000000	.000000	.000000
.0100000	.010000	.010000	.010000	.010000	.010000
.0200000	.020002	.020002	.020002	.020002	.020002
.0300000	.030007	.030008	.030008	.030009	.030009
.0400000	.040018	.040019	.040020	.040021	.040022
.0500000	.050036	.050038	.050040	.050042	.050044
.0600000	.060063	.060066	.060070	.060074	.060077
.0700000	.070100	.070106	.070111	.070117	.070123
.0800000	.080150	.080158	.080167	.080175	.080183
.0900000	.090214	.090225	.090238	.090250	.090261
.1000000	.100293	.100310	.100326	.100343	.100359
.1100000	.110391	.110412	.110435	.110457	.110478
.1200000	.120508	.120536	.120565	.120594	.120621
.1300000	.130646	.130682	.130719	.130755	.130791
.1400000	.140808	.140852	.140899	.140945	.140988
.1500000	.150995	.151049	.151106	.151163	.151217
.1600000	.161208	.161275	.161344	.161413	.161479
.1700000	.171450	.171531	.171614	.171696	.171776
.1800000	.181723	.181819	.181918	.182016	.182110
.1900000	.192029	.192141	.192258	.192374	.192485
.2000000	.202369	.202500	.202636	.202772	.202903
.2100000	.212745	.212898	.213056	.213214	.213365
.2200000	.223160	.223336	.223518	.223700	.223875
.2300000	.233615	.233816	.234025	.234234	.234434
.2400000	.244113	.244342	.244580	.244818	.245046
.2500000	.254654	.254914	.255184	.255454	.255713
.2600000	.265243	.265535	.265840	.266145	.266438
.2700000	.275879	.276208	.276550	.276893	.277223
.2800000	.286566	.286934	.287317	.287701	.288070
.2900000	.297306	.297716	.298144	.298572	.298984
.3000000	.308101	.308556	.309031	.309507	.309966
.3100000	.318952	.319456	.319983	.320511	.321019
.3200000	.329863	.330419	.331001	.331584	.332146
.3300000	.340835	.341448	.342088	.342731	.343351
.3400000	.351871	.352543	.353247	.353953	.354635
.3500000	.362973	.363709	.364480	.365255	.366003
.3600000	.374143	.374947	.375790	.376638	.377456
.3700000	.385384	.386261	.387180	.388105	.389000
.3800000	.396698	.397652	.398652	.399660	.400635
.3900000	.408087	.409123	.410210	.411306	.412367

$\alpha =$ .719999

Θ	K VALUES				
	.318821117	.415016431	.514599755	.613601043	.708073407
.4000000	.419554	.420677	.421856	.423046	.424198
.4100000	.431102	.432317	.433593	.434882	.436131
.4200000	.442734	.444045	.445425	.446819	.448171
.4300000	.454450	.455865	.457353	.458859	.460321
.4400000	.466256	.467778	.469382	.471006	.472584
.4500000	.478152	.479789	.481515	.483264	.484965
.4600000	.490142	.491900	.493754	.495635	.497466
.4700000	.502229	.504113	.506104	.508124	.510092
.4800000	.514416	.516433	.518566	.520734	.522848
.4900000	.526704	.528862	.531146	.533469	.535736
.5000000	.539099	.541404	.543846	.546333	.548762
.5100000	.551601	.554062	.556671	.559329	.561930
.5200000	.564215	.566838	.569622	.572463	.575244
.5300000	.576944	.579738	.582706	.585737	.588708
.5400000	.589790	.592763	.595924	.599156	.602328
.5500000	.602758	.605918	.609282	.612725	.616108
.5600000	.615850	.619206	.622782	.626447	.630053
.5700000	.629069	.632631	.636430	.640328	.644167
.5800000	.642420	.646196	.650229	.654372	.658457
.5900000	.655905	.659906	.664184	.668584	.672927
.6000000	.669529	.673765	.678299	.682968	.687584
.6100000	.683295	.687776	.692578	.697529	.702431
.6200000	.697206	.701943	.707026	.712273	.717476
.6300000	.711267	.716271	.721647	.727205	.732723
.6400000	.725481	.730764	.736447	.742331	.748179
.6500000	.739852	.745426	.751430	.757654	.763851
.6600000	.754385	.760263	.766602	.773182	.779743
.6700000	.769083	.775277	.781966	.788920	.795864
.6800000	.783951	.790474	.797529	.804873	.812219
.6899999	.798992	.805859	.813295	.821048	.828816
.7000000	.814212	.821437	.829271	.837452	.845661
.7100000	.829615	.837211	.845461	.854089	.862761
.7200000	.845204	.853188	.861871	.870967	.880125
.7300000	.860986	.869373	.878507	.888092	.897759
.7400000	.876963	.885770	.895375	.905471	.915671
.7500000	.893142	.902385	.912481	.923111	.933870
.7600000	.909528	.919224	.929831	.941018	.952364
.7700000	.926124	.936292	.947432	.959201	.971160
.7800000	.942936	.953594	.965289	.977667	.990268
.7899999	.959970	.971136	.983409	.996422	1.009696

$\alpha =$ .719999

θ	K VALUES				
	.318821117	.415016431	.514599755	.613601043	.708073407
.8000000	.977230	.988925	1.001800	1.015476	1.029454
.8100000	.994722	1.006965	1.020466	1.034834	1.049551
.8200000	1.012451	1.025264	1.039417	1.054507	1.069996
.8300000	1.030423	1.043827	1.058658	1.074502	1.090798
.8400000	1.048642	1.062660	1.078197	1.094826	1.111969
.8500000	1.067116	1.081771	1.098040	1.115490	1.133518
.8600000	1.085850	1.101164	1.118197	1.136501	1.155456
.8700000	1.104848	1.120848	1.138673	1.157869	1.177793
.8799999	1.124119	1.140827	1.159477	1.179603	1.200541
.8899999	1.143666	1.161110	1.180616	1.201711	1.223710
.9000000	1.163497	1.181704	1.202099	1.224203	1.247312
.9100000	1.183617	1.202614	1.223933	1.247089	1.271358
.9200000	1.204033	1.223848	1.246127	1.270379	1.295860
.9300000	1.224751	1.245412	1.268688	1.294082	1.320831
.9400000	1.245777	1.267315	1.291625	1.318207	1.346283
.9500000	1.267117	1.289563	1.314947	1.342767	1.372228
.9600000	1.288779	1.312164	1.338661	1.367770	1.398679
.9699999	1.310767	1.335124	1.362777	1.393226	1.425649
.9799999	1.333089	1.358452	1.387303	1.419147	1.453151
.9899999	1.355752	1.382154	1.412247	1.445543	1.481198
1.0000000	1.378761	1.406237	1.437619	1.472425	1.509805
1.0100000	1.402123	1.430710	1.463426	1.499802	1.538983
1.0200000	1.425845	1.455579	1.489678	1.527687	1.568748
1.0300000	1.449932	1.480852	1.516384	1.556088	1.599112
1.0400000	1.474392	1.506536	1.543551	1.585019	1.630091
1.0500000	1.499230	1.532638	1.571189	1.614488	1.661697
1.0600000	1.524453	1.559166	1.599306	1.644507	1.693945
1.0699999	1.550067	1.586126	1.627911	1.675086	1.726849
1.0799999	1.576078	1.613525	1.657011	1.706236	1.760422
1.0899999	1.602491	1.641371	1.686616	1.737967	1.794679
1.1000000	1.629314	1.669670	1.716733	1.770290	1.829634
1.1100000	1.656550	1.698428	1.747369	1.803214	1.865300
1.1200000	1.684206	1.727651	1.778533	1.836749	1.901690
1.1300000	1.712287	1.757345	1.810231	1.870905	1.938817
1.1400000	1.740797	1.787517	1.842471	1.905691	1.976695
1.1500000	1.769741	1.818171	1.875260	1.941114	2.015335
1.1600000	1.799123	1.849313	1.908603	1.977185	2.054751
1.1700000	1.828948	1.880948	1.942507	2.013911	2.094953
1.1800000	1.859220	1.913079	1.976977	2.051299	2.135952
1.1899999	1.889940	1.945710	2.012018	2.089356	2.177759

$\alpha =$ .719999

θ	K VALUES				
	.318821117	.415016431	.514599755	.613601043	.708073407
1.2000000	1.921113	1.978845	2.047634	2.128088	2.220383
1.2100000	1.952740	2.012487	2.083829	2.167501	2.263834
1.2200000	1.984823	2.046638	2.120606	2.207599	2.308118
1.2300000	2.017364	2.081300	2.157968	2.248387	2.353243
1.2400000	2.050363	2.116473	2.195916	2.289867	2.399216
1.2500000	2.083821	2.152158	2.234451	2.332041	2.446040
1.2599999	2.117736	2.188355	2.273573	2.374911	2.493720
1.2699999	2.152108	2.225062	2.313282	2.418476	2.542257
1.2799999	2.186935	2.262278	2.353575	2.462736	2.591652
1.2899999	2.222214	2.300000	2.394451	2.507688	2.641905
1.3000000	2.257942	2.338225	2.435905	2.553329	2.693014
1.3100000	2.294114	2.376947	2.477931	2.599654	2.744974
1.3200000	2.330726	2.416161	2.520525	2.646656	2.797779
1.3300000	2.367770	2.455860	2.563679	2.694327	2.851422
1.3400000	2.405241	2.496038	2.607385	2.742659	2.905894
1.3500000	2.443131	2.536685	2.651633	2.791642	2.961182
1.3600000	2.481431	2.577791	2.696412	2.841261	3.017274
1.3700000	2.520130	2.619347	2.741711	2.891505	3.074154
1.3799999	2.559220	2.661340	2.787516	2.942357	3.131803
1.3899999	2.598687	2.703757	2.833811	2.993800	3.190201
1.4000000	2.638520	2.746584	2.880582	3.045817	3.249327
1.4100000	2.678704	2.789807	2.927811	3.098385	3.309155
1.4200000	2.719225	2.833408	2.975478	3.151483	3.369659
1.4300000	2.760068	2.877370	3.023565	3.205088	3.430810
1.4400000	2.801216	2.921676	3.072050	3.259174	3.492576
1.4500000	2.842652	2.966305	3.120910	3.313715	3.554925
1.4600000	2.884357	3.011237	3.170123	3.368682	3.617820
1.4700000	2.926313	3.056451	3.219662	3.424045	3.681224
1.4800000	2.968500	3.101924	3.269503	3.479775	3.745099
1.4900000	3.010897	3.147634	3.319619	3.535837	3.809403
1.5000000	3.053483	3.193556	3.369982	3.592200	3.874093
1.5100000	3.096235	3.239666	3.420563	3.648827	3.939125
1.5200000	3.139132	3.285939	3.471333	3.705684	4.004453
1.5300000	3.182151	3.332348	3.522262	3.762734	4.070031
1.5400000	3.225267	3.378867	3.573319	3.819940	4.135811
1.5500000	3.268458	3.425470	3.624474	3.877265	4.201743
1.5600000	3.311699	3.472130	3.675695	3.934669	4.267779
1.5699999	3.354967	3.518819	3.726950	3.992116	4.333869
1.5707963	3.358412	3.522538	3.731032	3.996691	4.339133
1.5707963	3.358410	3.522535	3.731030	3.996690	4.339143

$\alpha =$ .719999

Θ	K VALUES				
	.794250555	.868696860	.928444378	.971111163	.994996249
.0000000	.000000	.000000	.000000	.000000	.000000
.0100000	.010000	.010000	.010000	.010000	.010000
.0200000	.020002	.020003	.020003	.020003	.020003
.0300000	.030010	.030010	.030010	.030010	.030010
.0400000	.040023	.040024	.040025	.040025	.040026
.0500000	.050046	.050048	.050049	.050050	.050050
.0600000	.060080	.060083	.060085	.060086	.060087
.0700000	.070127	.070132	.070135	.070138	.070139
.0800000	.080191	.080197	.080202	.080206	.080208
.0900000	.090272	.090281	.090288	.090293	.090296
.1000000	.100373	.100386	.100396	.100403	.100407
.1100000	.110497	.110514	.110527	.110537	.110542
.1200000	.120646	.120668	.120686	.120698	.120705
.1300000	.130823	.130850	.130873	.130889	.130897
.1400000	.141029	.141063	.141091	.141111	.141122
.1500000	.151267	.151309	.151344	.151368	.151382
.1600000	.161539	.161591	.161633	.161663	.161680
.1700000	.171848	.171911	.171961	.171997	.172018
.1800000	.182197	.182271	.182332	.182374	.182399
.1900000	.192587	.192675	.192746	.192797	.192825
.2000000	.203022	.203125	.203208	.203268	.203301
.2100000	.213503	.213623	.213720	.213789	.213828
.2200000	.224034	.224173	.224285	.224364	.224409
.2300000	.234618	.234777	.234905	.234996	.235048
.2400000	.245255	.245437	.245583	.245688	.245747
.2500000	.255951	.256157	.256323	.256442	.256509
.2600000	.266706	.266939	.267127	.267262	.267338
.2700000	.277525	.277787	.277999	.278151	.278236
.2800000	.288409	.288704	.288941	.289111	.289207
.2900000	.299362	.299691	.299957	.300147	.300254
.3000000	.310387	.310753	.311049	.311261	.311380
.3100000	.321486	.321893	.322221	.322457	.322589
.3200000	.332663	.333113	.333477	.333738	.333885
.3300000	.343921	.344418	.344820	.345108	.345270
.3400000	.355263	.355810	.356253	.356570	.356749
.3500000	.366692	.367293	.367779	.368129	.368325
.3600000	.378211	.378870	.379404	.379787	.380002
.3700000	.389825	.390546	.391129	.391549	.391785
.3800000	.401536	.402322	.402960	.403418	.403676
.3900000	.413347	.414205	.414899	.415399	.415681

$\alpha =$ •719999

Θ	K VALUES				
	•794250555	•868696860	•928444378	•971111163	•994996249
•4000000	•425264	•426196	•426952	•427496	•427803
•4100000	•437288	•438300	•439122	•439714	•440047
•4200000	•449424	•450522	•451413	•452055	•452417
•4300000	•461676	•462865	•463830	•464526	•464918
•4400000	•474048	•475333	•476377	•477131	•477555
•4500000	•486544	•487931	•489059	•489874	•490333
•4600000	•499168	•500663	•501881	•502760	•503256
•4700000	•511924	•513534	•514847	•515795	•516330
•4800000	•524816	•526549	•527962	•528984	•529560
•4900000	•537850	•539712	•541232	•542331	•542952
•5000000	•551029	•553029	•554661	•555843	•556511
•5100000	•564359	•566503	•568256	•569525	•570243
•5200000	•577844	•580142	•582021	•583384	•584154
•5300000	•591490	•593949	•595963	•597424	•598250
•5400000	•605300	•607932	•610088	•611653	•612539
•5500000	•619282	•622094	•624401	•626077	•627026
•5600000	•633439	•636443	•638910	•640703	•641718
•5700000	•647777	•650984	•653619	•655537	•656623
•5800000	•662303	•665724	•668537	•670586	•671748
•5900000	•677022	•680668	•683671	•685859	•687100
•6000000	•691941	•695824	•699027	•701362	•702688
•6100000	•707064	•711199	•714612	•717104	•718519
•6200000	•722399	•726799	•730435	•733092	•734602
•6300000	•737952	•742632	•746504	•749335	•750945
•6400000	•753730	•758705	•762826	•765842	•767559
•6500000	•769741	•775026	•779410	•782622	•784452
•6600000	•785990	•791603	•796265	•799685	•801634
•6700000	•802485	•808444	•813400	•817039	•819115
•6800000	•819234	•825558	•830824	•834696	•836905
•6899999	•836245	•842954	•848548	•852665	•855017
•7000000	•853526	•860640	•866580	•870958	•873460
•7100000	•871085	•878625	•884932	•889585	•892248
•7200000	•888930	•896920	•903614	•908559	•911391
•7300000	•907071	•915535	•922638	•927892	•930903
•7400000	•925515	•934480	•942014	•947596	•950798
•7500000	•944273	•953764	•961756	•967684	•971088
•7600000	•963354	•973401	•981874	•988170	•991789
•7700000	•982768	•993400	1•002384	1•009068	1•012915
•7800000	1•002524	1•013773	1•023296	1•030393	1•034482
•7899999	1•022634	1•034533	1•044627	1•052161	1•056506

$\alpha =$ .719999

θ	K VALUES				
	.794250555	.868696860	.928444378	.971111163	.994996249
.8000000	1.043108	1.055693	1.066389	1.074386	1.079004
.8100000	1.063957	1.077264	1.088598	1.097087	1.101995
.8200000	1.085192	1.099261	1.111269	1.120279	1.125495
.8300000	1.106824	1.121696	1.134418	1.143981	1.149525
.8400000	1.128867	1.144585	1.158061	1.168212	1.174104
.8500000	1.151332	1.167942	1.182217	1.192992	1.199254
.8600000	1.174231	1.191783	1.206903	1.218339	1.224997
.8700000	1.197578	1.216122	1.232137	1.244277	1.251354
.8799999	1.221386	1.240977	1.257940	1.270826	1.278351
.8899999	1.245669	1.266363	1.284329	1.298010	1.306012
.9000000	1.270440	1.292298	1.311328	1.325853	1.334364
.9100000	1.295715	1.318801	1.338956	1.354379	1.363433
.9200000	1.321507	1.345888	1.367237	1.383616	1.393249
.9300000	1.347832	1.373579	1.396193	1.413589	1.423841
.9400000	1.374706	1.401894	1.425849	1.444329	1.455241
.9500000	1.402143	1.430852	1.456229	1.475863	1.487482
.9600000	1.430161	1.460475	1.487360	1.508224	1.520599
.9699999	1.458776	1.490783	1.519268	1.541444	1.554627
.9799999	1.488005	1.521798	1.551982	1.575556	1.589605
.9899999	1.517865	1.553544	1.585529	1.610596	1.625573
1.0000000	1.548374	1.586042	1.619941	1.646601	1.662573
1.0100000	1.579548	1.619317	1.655247	1.683610	1.700649
1.0200000	1.611407	1.653393	1.691481	1.721662	1.739847
1.0300000	1.643970	1.688295	1.728675	1.760801	1.780217
1.0400000	1.677253	1.724048	1.766864	1.801070	1.821809
1.0500000	1.711278	1.760678	1.806084	1.842516	1.864679
1.0600000	1.746062	1.798213	1.846372	1.885186	1.908883
1.0699999	1.781625	1.836680	1.887765	1.929132	1.954482
1.0799999	1.817986	1.876106	1.930303	1.974406	2.001539
1.0899999	1.855165	1.916519	1.974028	2.021065	2.050122
1.1000000	1.893182	1.957950	2.018981	2.069165	2.100302
1.1100000	1.932055	2.000425	2.065205	2.118768	2.152153
1.1200000	1.971806	2.043975	2.112744	2.169938	2.205756
1.1300000	2.012452	2.088631	2.161646	2.222740	2.261195
1.1400000	2.054013	2.134421	2.211957	2.277245	2.318560
1.1500000	2.096508	2.181376	2.263726	2.333526	2.377946
1.1600000	2.139956	2.229527	2.317002	2.391659	2.439454
1.1700000	2.184374	2.278903	2.371836	2.451725	2.503192
1.1800000	2.229782	2.329536	2.428281	2.513807	2.569275
1.1899999	2.276194	2.381454	2.486389	2.577993	2.637825

$\alpha =$ .719999

Θ	K VALUES				
	.794250555	.868696860	.928444378	.971111163	.994996249
1.2000000	2.323629	2.434688	2.546215	2.644377	2.708973
1.2100000	2.372102	2.489266	2.607812	2.713053	2.782859
1.2200000	2.421626	2.545216	2.671237	2.784122	2.859633
1.2300000	2.472215	2.602567	2.736546	2.857691	2.939456
1.2400000	2.523883	2.661344	2.803794	2.933869	3.022501
1.2500000	2.576639	2.721573	2.873039	3.012771	3.108955
1.2599999	2.630493	2.783276	2.944336	3.094518	3.199018
1.2699999	2.685453	2.846476	3.017741	3.179236	3.292910
1.2799999	2.741525	2.911193	3.093308	3.267055	3.390864
1.2899999	2.798712	2.977444	3.171091	3.358110	3.493139
1.3000000	2.857019	3.045245	3.251143	3.452545	3.600014
1.3100000	2.916443	3.114606	3.333512	3.550502	3.711790
1.3200000	2.976982	3.185538	3.418243	3.652135	3.828804
1.3300000	3.038630	3.258045	3.505382	3.757597	3.951420
1.3400000	3.101381	3.332130	3.594966	3.867048	4.080042
1.3500000	3.165223	3.407789	3.687029	3.980650	4.215114
1.3600000	3.230143	3.485016	3.781599	4.098567	4.357128
1.3700000	3.296124	3.563800	3.878697	4.220963	4.506630
1.3799999	3.363147	3.644122	3.978337	4.348000	4.664231
1.3899999	3.431187	3.725962	4.080523	4.479838	4.830610
1.4000000	3.500219	3.809292	4.185251	4.616630	5.006531
1.4100000	3.570212	3.894077	4.292502	4.758517	5.192847
1.4200000	3.641133	3.980278	4.402249	4.905627	5.390523
1.4300000	3.712946	4.067848	4.514450	5.058067	5.600644
1.4400000	3.785610	4.156735	4.629050	5.215919	5.824433
1.4500000	3.859081	4.246881	4.745977	5.379231	6.063266
1.4600000	3.933313	4.338220	4.865145	5.548011	6.318681
1.4700000	4.008256	4.430680	4.986451	5.722216	6.592389
1.4800000	4.083856	4.524184	5.109773	5.901745	6.886255
1.4900000	4.160058	4.618647	5.234975	6.086426	7.202269
1.5000000	4.236803	4.713981	5.361904	6.276017	7.542452
1.5100000	4.314029	4.810089	5.490386	6.470183	7.908685
1.5200000	4.391673	4.906873	5.620236	6.668509	8.302433
1.5300000	4.469669	5.004229	5.751254	6.870488	8.724303
1.5400000	4.547950	5.102048	5.883226	7.075527	9.173441
1.5500000	4.626448	5.200220	6.015929	7.282955	9.646874
1.5600000	4.705093	5.298631	6.149130	7.492037	10.139025
1.5699999	4.783814	5.397168	6.282591	7.701991	10.641775
1.5707963	4.790084	5.405017	6.293223	7.718724	10.681980
1.5707963	4.790080	5.405012	6.293217	7.718717	10.681967

$\alpha =$ •739999

Θ	K VALUES				
	•009966711	•039469502	•087332193	•151646642	•229848846
•0000000	•000000	•000000	•000000	•000000	•000000
•0100000	•010000	•010000	•010000	•010000	•010000
•0200000	•020001	•020002	•020002	•020002	•020002
•0300000	•030006	•030006	•030007	•030007	•030007
•0400000	•040015	•040016	•040016	•040017	•040018
•0500000	•050031	•050031	•050032	•050034	•050035
•0600000	•060053	•060054	•060056	•060058	•060061
•0700000	•070085	•070087	•070089	•070093	•070097
•0800000	•080127	•080129	•080133	•080139	•080146
•0900000	•090181	•090185	•090190	•090198	•090208
•1000000	•100248	•100253	•100261	•100272	•100285
•1100000	•110331	•110338	•110348	•110363	•110380
•1200000	•120430	•120439	•120453	•120471	•120494
•1300000	•130547	•130558	•130576	•130600	•130628
•1400000	•140684	•140698	•140720	•140749	•140785
•1500000	•150842	•150859	•150886	•150923	•150967
•1600000	•161023	•161043	•161076	•161121	•161175
•1700000	•171228	•171253	•171292	•171345	•171410
•1800000	•181459	•181488	•181535	•181598	•181675
•1900000	•191718	•191752	•191807	•191882	•191972
•2000000	•202006	•202045	•202110	•202197	•202303
•2100000	•212324	•212370	•212445	•212546	•212669
•2200000	•222675	•222728	•222814	•222931	•223072
•2300000	•233060	•233121	•233220	•233352	•233515
•2400000	•243481	•243550	•243662	•243814	•243998
•2500000	•253939	•254018	•254145	•254316	•254525
•2600000	•264437	•264525	•264668	•264861	•265097
•2700000	•274975	•275074	•275235	•275451	•275715
•2800000	•285557	•285667	•285846	•286088	•286384
•2900000	•296182	•296305	•296504	•296774	•297103
•3000000	•306854	•306990	•307211	•307510	•307875
•3100000	•317574	•317724	•317969	•318299	•318703
•3200000	•328344	•328509	•328779	•329143	•329589
•3300000	•339165	•339347	•339643	•340044	•340534
•3400000	•350041	•350240	•350565	•351003	•351541
•3500000	•360972	•361189	•361544	•362024	•362612
•3600000	•371960	•372198	•372585	•373108	•373750
•3700000	•383008	•383267	•383688	•384257	•384956
•3800000	•394118	•394398	•394856	•395474	•396234
•3900000	•405291	•405595	•406090	•406761	•407585

$\alpha =$ .739999

Θ	K VALUES				
	.009966711	.039469502	.087332193	.151646642	.229848846
.4000000	.416530	.416859	.417394	.418120	.419011
.4100000	.427837	.428192	.428770	.429554	.430517
.4200000	.439214	.439596	.440219	.441064	.442103
.4300000	.450663	.451073	.451744	.452653	.453772
.4400000	.462186	.462627	.463347	.464325	.465528
.4500000	.473786	.474259	.475032	.476080	.477372
.4600000	.485465	.485971	.486799	.487923	.489307
.4700000	.497225	.497766	.498652	.499854	.501337
.4800000	.509068	.509647	.510592	.511878	.513463
.4900000	.520998	.521615	.522624	.523996	.525689
.5000000	.533016	.533674	.534749	.536211	.538018
.5100000	.545126	.545825	.546969	.548527	.550452
.5200000	.557328	.558072	.559289	.560946	.562995
.5300000	.569627	.570417	.571709	.573470	.575649
.5400000	.582025	.582862	.584234	.586103	.588419
.5500000	.594525	.595412	.596866	.598849	.601306
.5600000	.607128	.608068	.609608	.611708	.614314
.5700000	.619839	.620833	.622462	.624686	.627447
.5800000	.632660	.633710	.635433	.637785	.640707
.5900000	.645594	.646703	.648522	.651009	.654099
.6000000	.658643	.659813	.661734	.664360	.667626
.6100000	.671812	.673046	.675071	.677842	.681291
.6200000	.685103	.686402	.688537	.691459	.695099
.6300000	.698519	.699886	.702135	.705214	.709052
.6400000	.712063	.713502	.715868	.719110	.723155
.6500000	.725739	.727252	.729740	.733152	.737411
.6600000	.739550	.741139	.743754	.747342	.751825
.6700000	.753500	.755168	.757915	.761686	.766401
.6800000	.767591	.769342	.772225	.776186	.781142
.6899999	.781829	.783665	.786689	.790847	.796053
.7000000	.796215	.798139	.801311	.805672	.811139
.7100000	.810755	.812770	.816093	.820666	.826403
.7200000	.825451	.827561	.831041	.835834	.841851
.7300000	.840307	.842515	.846158	.851178	.857486
.7400000	.855328	.857637	.861449	.866705	.873314
.7500000	.870518	.872932	.876917	.882417	.889339
.7600000	.885880	.888402	.892568	.898320	.905566
.7700000	.901420	.904053	.908405	.914418	.922000
.7800000	.917140	.919888	.924433	.930717	.938647
.7899999	.933045	.935913	.940657	.947220	.955510

$\alpha =$ .739999

Θ	K VALUES				
	.009966711	.039469502	.087332193	.151646642	.229848846
.8000000	.949140	.952131	.957081	.963933	.972596
.8100000	.965430	.968547	.973710	.980861	.989910
.8200000	.981918	.985167	.990548	.998009	1.007458
.8300000	.998610	1.001994	1.007602	1.015381	1.025244
.8400000	1.015510	1.019033	1.024875	1.032984	1.043274
.8500000	1.032622	1.036290	1.042373	1.050823	1.061555
.8600000	1.049953	1.053769	1.060101	1.068902	1.080092
.8700000	1.067507	1.071475	1.078064	1.087229	1.098891
.8799999	1.085288	1.089414	1.096267	1.105807	1.117958
.8899999	1.103303	1.107591	1.114717	1.124644	1.137300
.9000000	1.121555	1.126011	1.133418	1.143744	1.156921
.9100000	1.140052	1.144679	1.152376	1.163114	1.176830
.9200000	1.158796	1.163601	1.171597	1.182759	1.197031
.9300000	1.177795	1.182782	1.191086	1.202685	1.217532
.9400000	1.197054	1.202229	1.210849	1.222900	1.238338
.9500000	1.216578	1.221946	1.230892	1.243408	1.259458
.9600000	1.236372	1.241939	1.251221	1.264215	1.280896
.9699999	1.256442	1.262214	1.271842	1.285329	1.302660
.9799999	1.276795	1.282777	1.292760	1.306756	1.324758
.9899999	1.297435	1.303633	1.313982	1.328501	1.347194
1.0000000	1.318368	1.324789	1.335514	1.350571	1.369977
1.0100000	1.339601	1.346249	1.357361	1.372973	1.393114
1.0200000	1.361137	1.368021	1.379531	1.395713	1.416610
1.0300000	1.382985	1.390109	1.402028	1.418796	1.440473
1.0400000	1.405148	1.412520	1.424859	1.442231	1.464710
1.0500000	1.427633	1.435260	1.448030	1.466022	1.489327
1.0600000	1.450446	1.458333	1.471546	1.490177	1.514332
1.0699999	1.473591	1.481747	1.495415	1.514700	1.539731
1.0799999	1.497075	1.505506	1.519641	1.539600	1.565530
1.0899999	1.520903	1.529615	1.544230	1.564881	1.591737
1.1000000	1.545081	1.554082	1.569189	1.590550	1.618357
1.1100000	1.569612	1.578910	1.594521	1.616612	1.645397
1.1200000	1.594503	1.604105	1.620234	1.643073	1.672863
1.1300000	1.619758	1.629671	1.646331	1.669939	1.700761
1.1400000	1.645383	1.655615	1.672819	1.697214	1.729096
1.1500000	1.671381	1.681940	1.699701	1.724904	1.757874
1.1600000	1.697756	1.708650	1.726982	1.753014	1.787101
1.1700000	1.724514	1.735750	1.754667	1.781547	1.816780
1.1800000	1.751656	1.763243	1.782759	1.810509	1.846916
1.1899999	1.779188	1.791133	1.811261	1.839902	1.877514

$\alpha =$ .739999

Θ	K VALUES				
	.009966711	.039469502	.087332193	.151646642	.229848846
1.2000000	1.807112	1.819424	1.840179	1.869731	1.908577
1.2100000	1.835430	1.848116	1.869512	1.899998	1.940108
1.2200000	1.864144	1.877214	1.899265	1.930706	1.972111
1.2300000	1.893257	1.906718	1.929439	1.961856	2.004586
1.2400000	1.922770	1.936631	1.960036	1.993450	2.037536
1.2500000	1.952683	1.966952	1.991055	2.025490	2.070962
1.2599999	1.982997	1.997682	2.022498	2.057974	2.104865
1.2699999	2.013711	2.028820	2.054365	2.090903	2.139242
1.2799999	2.044825	2.060366	2.086653	2.124276	2.174095
1.2899999	2.076336	2.092318	2.119361	2.158091	2.209419
1.3000000	2.108242	2.124674	2.152487	2.192346	2.245215
1.3100000	2.140540	2.157429	2.186028	2.227036	2.281476
1.3200000	2.173227	2.190581	2.219979	2.262157	2.318198
1.3300000	2.206297	2.224124	2.254335	2.297705	2.355377
1.3400000	2.239745	2.258053	2.289091	2.333673	2.393006
1.3500000	2.273565	2.292362	2.324240	2.370055	2.431077
1.3600000	2.307749	2.327043	2.359774	2.406842	2.469582
1.3700000	2.342290	2.362087	2.395685	2.444025	2.508511
1.3799999	2.377179	2.397487	2.431963	2.481595	2.547853
1.3899999	2.412405	2.433231	2.468599	2.519540	2.587598
1.4000000	2.447958	2.469309	2.505580	2.557849	2.627732
1.4100000	2.483827	2.505709	2.542894	2.596508	2.668240
1.4200000	2.519997	2.542417	2.580528	2.635503	2.709109
1.4300000	2.556457	2.579420	2.618467	2.674820	2.750322
1.4400000	2.593191	2.616704	2.656697	2.714442	2.791862
1.4500000	2.630185	2.654252	2.695200	2.754352	2.833710
1.4600000	2.667421	2.692048	2.733961	2.794533	2.875848
1.4700000	2.704884	2.730076	2.772961	2.834965	2.918255
1.4800000	2.742555	2.768315	2.812181	2.875629	2.960910
1.4900000	2.780416	2.806749	2.851601	2.916505	3.003792
1.5000000	2.818449	2.845358	2.891203	2.957570	3.046877
1.5100000	2.856632	2.884120	2.930964	2.998804	3.090142
1.5200000	2.894946	2.923016	2.970864	3.040183	3.133563
1.5300000	2.933370	2.962025	3.010880	3.081684	3.177115
1.5400000	2.971883	3.001124	3.050990	3.123285	3.220774
1.5500000	3.010464	3.040292	3.091171	3.164960	3.264512
1.5600000	3.049090	3.079507	3.131401	3.206687	3.308305
1.5699999	3.087740	3.118746	3.171656	3.248439	3.352126
1.5707963	3.090818	3.121871	3.174862	3.251765	3.355616
1.5707963	3.090815	3.121869	3.174859	3.251762	3.355613

$\alpha =$ .739999

Θ	K VALUES				
	.318821117	.415016431	.514599755	.613601043	.708073407
.0000000	.000000	.000000	.000000	.000000	.000000
.0100000	.010000	.010000	.010000	.010000	.010000
.0200000	.020002	.020002	.020002	.020002	.020002
.0300000	.030008	.030008	.030008	.030009	.030009
.0400000	.040019	.040020	.040021	.040022	.040023
.0500000	.050037	.050039	.050041	.050043	.050045
.0600000	.060064	.060068	.060071	.060075	.060078
.0700000	.070103	.070108	.070114	.070119	.070125
.0800000	.080153	.080162	.080170	.080179	.080187
.0900000	.090219	.090230	.090242	.090255	.090266
.1000000	.100300	.100316	.100333	.100350	.100365
.1100000	.110400	.110421	.110444	.110466	.110487
.1200000	.120520	.120548	.120576	.120605	.120633
.1300000	.130661	.130697	.130734	.130770	.130805
.1400000	.140827	.140871	.140917	.140963	.141007
.1500000	.151018	.151072	.151129	.151186	.151240
.1600000	.161236	.161303	.161372	.161441	.161507
.1700000	.171484	.171564	.171647	.171730	.171809
.1800000	.181763	.181859	.181957	.182056	.182150
.1900000	.192076	.192188	.192305	.192421	.192533
.2000000	.202424	.202555	.202692	.202828	.202958
.2100000	.212809	.212962	.213120	.213278	.213429
.2200000	.223234	.223409	.223592	.223774	.223949
.2300000	.233700	.233901	.234110	.234319	.234519
.2400000	.244209	.244438	.244676	.244915	.245143
.2500000	.254764	.255023	.255294	.255564	.255823
.2600000	.265366	.265659	.265964	.266269	.266562
.2700000	.276018	.276347	.276690	.277033	.277363
.2800000	.286722	.287090	.287474	.287858	.288227
.2900000	.297480	.297890	.298318	.298747	.299159
.3000000	.308294	.308749	.309225	.309702	.310161
.3100000	.319166	.319671	.320198	.320727	.321235
.3200000	.330099	.330657	.331239	.331823	.332386
.3300000	.341096	.341709	.342350	.342994	.343615
.3400000	.352158	.352831	.353535	.354243	.354926
.3500000	.363287	.364025	.364797	.365573	.366322
.3600000	.374487	.375293	.376137	.376986	.377806
.3700000	.385759	.386638	.387559	.388486	.389382
.3800000	.397107	.398063	.399065	.400075	.401052
.3900000	.408532	.409570	.410659	.411758	.412821

$\alpha =$ •739999

Θ	K VALUES				
	•318821117	•415016431	•514599755	•613601043	•708073407
•4000000	•420038	•421163	•422344	•423536	•424691
•4100000	•431626	•432843	•434123	•435414	•436666
•4200000	•443301	•444615	•445998	•447395	•448751
•4300000	•455063	•456480	•457973	•459482	•460948
•4400000	•466916	•468443	•470051	•471679	•473261
•4500000	•478864	•480505	•482236	•483989	•485694
•4600000	•490908	•492670	•494530	•496416	•498252
•4700000	•503052	•504942	•506938	•508964	•510938
•4800000	•515299	•517323	•519462	•521637	•523757
•4900000	•527651	•529816	•532107	•534438	•536712
•5000000	•540113	•542426	•544876	•547371	•549809
•5100000	•552686	•555155	•557773	•560441	•563051
•5200000	•565375	•568007	•570802	•573652	•576444
•5300000	•578182	•580986	•583966	•587008	•589991
•5400000	•591111	•594095	•597269	•600514	•603699
•5500000	•604166	•607338	•610716	•614174	•617571
•5600000	•617349	•620719	•624311	•627992	•631613
•5700000	•630665	•634242	•638058	•641974	•645831
•5800000	•644117	•647910	•651962	•656124	•660229
•5900000	•657708	•661728	•666027	•670448	•674813
•6000000	•671444	•675700	•680257	•684950	•689589
•6100000	•685326	•689830	•694658	•699635	•704563
•6200000	•699361	•704123	•709233	•714509	•719740
•6300000	•713550	•718582	•723989	•729578	•735127
•6400000	•727900	•733213	•738930	•744847	•750731
•6500000	•742413	•748020	•754061	•760322	•766557
•6600000	•757094	•763008	•769387	•776009	•782612
•6700000	•771948	•778182	•784914	•791914	•798904
•6800000	•786979	•793546	•800648	•808042	•815438
•6899999	•802192	•809106	•816594	•824401	•832224
•7000000	•817591	•824867	•832757	•840998	•849267
•7100000	•833181	•840834	•849145	•857838	•866576
•7200000	•848967	•857012	•865762	•874929	•884159
•7300000	•864954	•873408	•882615	•892277	•902023
•7400000	•881147	•890026	•899711	•909890	•920177
•7500000	•897552	•906873	•917055	•927776	•938629
•7600000	•914173	•923954	•934655	•945941	•957389
•7700000	•931016	•941275	•952517	•964395	•976464
•7800000	•948087	•958843	•970648	•983144	•995866
•7899999	•965390	•976664	•989056	1•002196	1•015602

$\alpha =$ •739999

Θ	K VALUES				
	•318821117	•415016431	•514599755	•613601043	•708073407
•8000000	•982933	•994743	1•007747	1•021562	1•035683
•8100000	1•000720	1•013089	1•026729	1•041247	1•056119
•8200000	1•018758	1•031706	1•046010	1•061263	1•076920
•8300000	1•037052	1•050602	1•065596	1•081616	1•098097
•8400000	1•055610	1•069785	1•085497	1•102318	1•119660
•8500000	1•074436	1•089260	1•105720	1•123376	1•141621
•8600000	1•093538	1•109035	1•126273	1•144801	1•163990
•8700000	1•112923	1•129118	1•147164	1•166602	1•186780
•8799999	1•132595	1•149515	1•168403	1•188789	1•210003
•8899999	1•152563	1•170234	1•189997	1•211373	1•233670
•9000000	1•172834	1•191284	1•211956	1•234364	1•257795
•9100000	1•193413	1•212671	1•234288	1•257772	1•282390
•9200000	1•214308	1•234403	1•257003	1•281608	1•307468
•9300000	1•235526	1•256489	1•280109	1•305884	1•333042
•9400000	1•257075	1•278936	1•303616	1•330609	1•359126
•9500000	1•278961	1•301753	1•327534	1•355796	1•385735
•9600000	1•301192	1•324948	1•351872	1•381457	1•412881
•9699999	1•323775	1•348529	1•376640	1•407602	1•440580
•9799999	1•346717	1•372505	1•401847	1•434243	1•468847
•9899999	1•370027	1•396884	1•427504	1•461393	1•497695
1•0000000	1•393712	1•421674	1•453620	1•489063	1•527141
1•0100000	1•417778	1•446885	1•480206	1•517267	1•557199
1•0200000	1•442235	1•472524	1•507271	1•546015	1•587886
1•0300000	1•467088	1•498601	1•534826	1•575320	1•619216
1•0400000	1•492347	1•525124	1•562881	1•605195	1•651206
1•0500000	1•518017	1•552101	1•591445	1•635652	1•683872
1•0600000	1•544108	1•579541	1•620529	1•666703	1•717229
1•0699999	1•570626	1•607453	1•650143	1•698362	1•751294
1•0799999	1•597578	1•635844	1•680297	1•730639	1•786083
1•0899999	1•624972	1•664723	1•711001	1•763549	1•821612
1•1000000	1•652816	1•694099	1•742264	1•797102	1•857897
1•1100000	1•681115	1•723979	1•774095	1•831310	1•894954
1•1200000	1•709876	1•754370	1•806505	1•866186	1•932798
1•1300000	1•739106	1•785281	1•839501	1•901740	1•971446
1•1400000	1•768812	1•816718	1•873094	1•937985	2•010913
1•1500000	1•798999	1•848689	1•907291	1•974930	2•051213
1•1600000	1•829674	1•881200	1•942100	2•012587	2•092361
1•1700000	1•860841	1•914257	1•977529	2•050965	2•134372
1•1800000	1•892505	1•947867	2•013585	2•090073	2•177258
1•1899999	1•924671	1•982034	2•050275	2•129921	2•221032

$\alpha =$ .739999

Θ	K VALUES				
	.318821117	.415016431	.514599755	.613601043	.708073407
1.2000000	1.957344	2.016764	2.087605	2.170517	2.265708
1.2100000	1.990526	2.052060	2.125580	2.211868	2.311295
1.2200000	2.024222	2.087927	2.164205	2.253981	2.357804
1.2300000	2.058432	2.124367	2.203484	2.296861	2.405245
1.2400000	2.093160	2.161382	2.243419	2.340514	2.453626
1.2500000	2.128406	2.198975	2.284014	2.384943	2.502953
1.2599999	2.164171	2.237146	2.325270	2.430151	2.553233
1.2699999	2.200455	2.275895	2.367187	2.476139	2.604469
1.2799999	2.237255	2.315220	2.409765	2.522907	2.656664
1.2899999	2.274572	2.355121	2.453000	2.570455	2.709819
1.3000000	2.312401	2.395593	2.496892	2.618780	2.763933
1.3100000	2.350738	2.436633	2.541434	2.667878	2.819003
1.3200000	2.389579	2.478235	2.586622	2.717742	2.875025
1.3300000	2.428918	2.520393	2.632449	2.768366	2.931990
1.3400000	2.468748	2.563100	2.678906	2.819741	2.989891
1.3500000	2.509060	2.606346	2.725984	2.871855	3.048715
1.3600000	2.549846	2.650121	2.773670	2.924697	3.108448
1.3700000	2.591096	2.694415	2.821953	2.978250	3.169075
1.3799999	2.632797	2.739213	2.870818	3.032500	3.230576
1.3899999	2.674936	2.784503	2.920249	3.087427	3.292929
1.4000000	2.717502	2.830268	2.970228	3.143012	3.356111
1.4100000	2.760476	2.876492	3.020736	3.199230	3.420094
1.4200000	2.803845	2.923156	3.071753	3.256059	3.484849
1.4300000	2.847589	2.970242	3.123255	3.313471	3.550343
1.4400000	2.891690	3.017727	3.175220	3.371439	3.616542
1.4500000	2.936128	3.065590	3.227621	3.429932	3.683408
1.4600000	2.980883	3.113807	3.280431	3.488918	3.750902
1.4700000	3.025932	3.162354	3.333623	3.548363	3.818981
1.4800000	3.071253	3.211206	3.387167	3.608232	3.887601
1.4900000	3.116821	3.260334	3.441031	3.668488	3.956714
1.5000000	3.162611	3.309713	3.495184	3.729092	4.026273
1.5100000	3.208598	3.359311	3.549592	3.790003	4.096225
1.5200000	3.254756	3.409101	3.604221	3.851182	4.166518
1.5300000	3.301057	3.459051	3.659036	3.912585	4.237100
1.5400000	3.347474	3.509131	3.714001	3.974170	4.307914
1.5500000	3.393978	3.559310	3.769081	4.035893	4.378905
1.5600000	3.440542	3.609555	3.824237	4.097709	4.450016
1.5699999	3.487137	3.659835	3.879434	4.159574	4.521189
1.5707963	3.490848	3.663840	3.883830	4.164501	4.526858
1.5707963	3.490846	3.663837	3.883828	4.164500	4.526864

$\alpha =$ .739999

Θ	K VALUES				
	.794250555	.868696860	.928444378	.971111163	.994996249
.0000000	.000000	.000000	.000000	.000000	.000000
.0100000	.010000	.010000	.010000	.010000	.010000
.0200000	.020003	.020003	.020003	.020003	.020003
.0300000	.030010	.030010	.030010	.030011	.030011
.0400000	.040024	.040025	.040025	.040026	.040026
.0500000	.050047	.050049	.050050	.050051	.050051
.0600000	.060082	.060084	.060086	.060088	.060089
.0700000	.070130	.070134	.070137	.070140	.070141
.0800000	.080194	.080200	.080206	.080209	.080211
.0900000	.090277	.090286	.090293	.090298	.090301
.1000000	.100380	.100392	.100403	.100410	.100414
.1100000	.110506	.110523	.110536	.110546	.110551
.1200000	.120658	.120680	.120697	.120710	.120717
.1300000	.130837	.130865	.130887	.130903	.130912
.1400000	.141047	.141082	.141110	.141130	.141141
.1500000	.151289	.151332	.151367	.151391	.151405
.1600000	.161567	.161619	.161661	.161691	.161708
.1700000	.171882	.171945	.171995	.172031	.172051
.1800000	.182237	.182312	.182372	.182415	.182439
.1900000	.192634	.192723	.192794	.192844	.192873
.2000000	.203077	.203180	.203264	.203323	.203356
.2100000	.213568	.213688	.213784	.213854	.213892
.2200000	.224109	.224247	.224359	.224439	.224484
.2300000	.234703	.234862	.234990	.235082	.235133
.2400000	.245353	.245534	.245681	.245785	.245844
.2500000	.256061	.256267	.256434	.256553	.256620
.2600000	.266831	.267064	.267252	.267387	.267463
.2700000	.277665	.277928	.278140	.278292	.278377
.2800000	.288566	.288861	.289099	.289269	.289365
.2900000	.299538	.299867	.300133	.300323	.300430
.3000000	.310582	.310949	.311245	.311457	.311577
.3100000	.321703	.322110	.322439	.322675	.322808
.3200000	.332903	.333354	.333718	.333980	.334126
.3300000	.344186	.344684	.345086	.345375	.345537
.3400000	.355555	.356103	.356546	.356864	.357043
.3500000	.367012	.367614	.368101	.368451	.368648
.3600000	.378562	.379222	.379756	.380140	.380356
.3700000	.390208	.390930	.391515	.391935	.392172
.3800000	.401954	.402742	.403381	.403840	.404098
.3900000	.413803	.414662	.415358	.415859	.416141

$\alpha =$ .739999

Θ	K VALUES				
	.794250555	.868696860	.928444378	.971111163	.994996249
.4000000	.425759	.426693	.427451	.427996	.428303
.4100000	.437825	.438840	.439663	.440256	.440590
.4200000	.450006	.451107	.452000	.452644	.453006
.4300000	.462306	.463497	.464465	.465163	.465556
.4400000	.474729	.476017	.477064	.477819	.478245
.4500000	.487278	.488669	.489800	.490617	.491077
.4600000	.499959	.501458	.502680	.503561	.504059
.4700000	.512775	.514390	.515707	.516658	.517194
.4800000	.525731	.527470	.528887	.529912	.530490
.4900000	.538833	.540701	.542225	.543328	.543951
.5000000	.552084	.554089	.555728	.556913	.557583
.5100000	.565489	.567641	.569399	.570673	.571393
.5200000	.579054	.581360	.583246	.584614	.585387
.5300000	.592783	.595252	.597274	.598741	.599570
.5400000	.606683	.609325	.611490	.613061	.613951
.5500000	.620758	.623582	.625899	.627582	.628535
.5600000	.635014	.638031	.640509	.642310	.643330
.5700000	.649457	.652678	.655326	.657252	.658343
.5800000	.664093	.667529	.670357	.672415	.673582
.5900000	.678928	.682592	.685609	.687808	.689056
.6000000	.693968	.697872	.701091	.703438	.704771
.6100000	.709220	.713377	.716809	.719314	.720736
.6200000	.724691	.729115	.732772	.735443	.736962
.6300000	.740387	.745093	.748988	.751836	.753455
.6400000	.756315	.761319	.765465	.768500	.770227
.6500000	.772483	.777802	.782213	.785445	.787286
.6600000	.788898	.794548	.799240	.802682	.804644
.6700000	.805569	.811568	.816557	.820221	.822311
.6800000	.822502	.828870	.834173	.838071	.840297
.6899999	.839707	.846463	.852098	.856245	.858614
.7000000	.857191	.864357	.870342	.874753	.877275
.7100000	.874964	.882562	.888918	.893608	.896291
.7200000	.893034	.901088	.907836	.912821	.915676
.7300000	.911411	.919945	.927107	.932406	.935443
.7400000	.930104	.939145	.946745	.952375	.955605
.7500000	.949123	.958699	.966761	.972743	.976178
.7600000	.968479	.978618	.987170	.993524	.997177
.7700000	.988181	.998914	1.007984	1.014733	1.018617
.7800000	1.008241	1.019601	1.029218	1.036386	1.040515
.7899999	1.028670	1.040690	1.050886	1.058498	1.062889

$\alpha =$ •739999

Θ	K VALUES				
	•794250555	•868696860	•928444378	•971111163	•994996249
•8000000	1•049479	1•062196	1•073005	1•081088	1•085755
•8100000	1•070680	1•084131	1•095589	1•104171	1•109134
•8200000	1•092284	1•106511	1•118654	1•127768	1•133043
•8300000	1•114306	1•129349	1•142219	1•151896	1•157505
•8400000	1•136757	1•152662	1•166301	1•176576	1•182540
•8500000	1•159650	1•176466	1•190918	1•201828	1•208170
•8600000	1•183000	1•200775	1•216090	1•227675	1•234419
•8700000	1•206821	1•225608	1•241836	1•254138	1•261311
•8799999	1•231126	1•250982	1•268177	1•281242	1•288872
•8899999	1•255931	1•276914	1•295135	1•309011	1•317128
•9000000	1•281252	1•303425	1•322731	1•337471	1•346108
•9100000	1•307103	1•330531	1•350990	1•366648	1•375840
•9200000	1•333500	1•358254	1•379935	1•396571	1•406356
•9300000	1•360461	1•386615	1•409590	1•427268	1•437687
•9400000	1•388003	1•415633	1•439983	1•458772	1•469868
•9500000	1•416142	1•445332	1•471141	1•491113	1•502933
•9600000	1•444897	1•475734	1•503090	1•524324	1•536920
•9699999	1•474286	1•506861	1•535861	1•558442	1•571869
•9799999	1•504327	1•538738	1•569483	1•593502	1•607819
•9899999	1•535040	1•571391	1•603989	1•629543	1•644814
1•0000000	1•566444	1•604843	1•639411	1•666605	1•682900
1•0100000	1•598558	1•639121	1•675782	1•704730	1•722124
1•0200000	1•631404	1•674252	1•713138	1•743961	1•762537
1•0300000	1•665002	1•710264	1•751515	1•784345	1•804191
1•0400000	1•699373	1•747185	1•790951	1•825929	1•847141
1•0500000	1•734538	1•785043	1•831486	1•868763	1•891448
1•0600000	1•770518	1•823870	1•873159	1•912902	1•937173
1•0699999	1•807336	1•863694	1•916013	1•958398	1•984381
1•0799999	1•845014	1•904547	1•960091	2•005312	2•033141
1•0899999	1•883573	1•946460	2•005439	2•053702	2•083527
1•1000000	1•923037	1•989468	2•052103	2•103634	2•135617
1•1100000	1•963427	2•033600	2•100130	2•155172	2•189491
1•1200000	2•004766	2•078891	2•149570	2•208387	2•245237
1•1300000	2•047077	2•125375	2•200475	2•263352	2•302947
1•1400000	2•090381	2•173086	2•252896	2•320143	2•362718
1•1500000	2•134701	2•222058	2•306888	2•378841	2•424655
1•1600000	2•180059	2•272326	2•362506	2•439530	2•488867
1•1700000	2•226476	2•323924	2•419808	2•502298	2•555473
1•1800000	2•273973	2•376886	2•478850	2•567237	2•624597
1•1899999	2•322571	2•431248	2•539693	2•634445	2•696373

$\alpha =$ .739999

Θ	*K* VALUES				
	.794250555	.868696860	.928444378	.971111163	.994996249
1.2000000	2.372288	2.487044	2.602398	2.704023	2.770945
1.2100000	2.423144	2.544306	2.667024	2.776076	2.848464
1.2200000	2.475156	2.603067	2.733636	2.850716	2.929096
1.2300000	2.528342	2.663361	2.802296	2.928059	3.013014
1.2400000	2.582715	2.725217	2.873067	3.008228	3.100410
1.2500000	2.638292	2.788665	2.946013	3.091348	3.191485
1.2599999	2.695083	2.853733	3.021199	3.177554	3.286461
1.2699999	2.753099	2.920448	3.098685	3.266983	3.385574
1.2799999	2.812349	2.988833	3.178536	3.359779	3.489081
1.2899999	2.872839	3.058910	3.260811	3.456093	3.597262
1.3000000	2.934575	3.130698	3.345571	3.556081	3.710421
1.3100000	2.997556	3.204212	3.432870	3.659903	3.828890
1.3200000	3.061782	3.279463	3.522762	3.767725	3.953030
1.3300000	3.127248	3.356461	3.615298	3.879719	4.083241
1.3400000	3.193949	3.435209	3.710521	3.996060	4.219959
1.3500000	3.261874	3.515706	3.808471	4.116927	4.363668
1.3600000	3.331009	3.597947	3.909181	4.242500	4.514903
1.3700000	3.401337	3.681921	4.012676	4.372959	4.674256
1.3799999	3.472837	3.767611	4.118974	4.508484	4.842387
1.3899999	3.545485	3.854993	4.228080	4.649251	5.020033
1.4000000	3.619253	3.944039	4.339992	4.795427	5.208023
1.4100000	3.694106	4.034712	4.454691	4.947167	5.407278
1.4200000	3.770010	4.126969	4.572148	5.104612	5.618842
1.4300000	3.846924	4.220759	4.692319	5.267881	5.843889
1.4400000	3.924803	4.316026	4.815143	5.437062	6.083740
1.4500000	4.003598	4.412704	4.940544	5.612209	6.339880
1.4600000	4.083258	4.510721	5.068425	5.793330	6.613972
1.4700000	4.163726	4.609998	5.198674	5.980378	6.907859
1.4800000	4.244942	4.710447	5.331157	6.173242	7.223556
1.4900000	4.326843	4.811976	5.465724	6.371737	7.563206
1.5000000	4.409363	4.914484	5.602204	6.575595	7.928989
1.5100000	4.492432	5.017863	5.740407	6.784452	8.322931
1.5200000	4.575977	5.122004	5.880127	6.997852	8.746609
1.5300000	4.659925	5.226788	6.021142	7.215243	9.200670
1.5400000	4.744198	5.332094	6.163215	7.435976	9.684186
1.5500000	4.828718	5.437798	6.306100	7.659319	10.193943
1.5600000	4.913407	5.543773	6.449537	7.884468	10.723915
1.5699999	4.998182	5.649888	6.593263	8.110570	11.265332
1.5707963	5.004934	5.658340	6.604712	8.128590	11.308629
1.5707963	5.004930	5.658335	6.604706	8.128582	11.308614

$\alpha =$ .759999

Θ	K VALUES				
	.009966711	.039469502	.087332193	.151646642	.229848846
.0000000	.000000	.000000	.000000	.000000	.000000
.0100000	.010000	.010000	.010000	.010000	.010000
.0200000	.020002	.020002	.020002	.020002	.020002
.0300000	.030006	.030007	.030007	.030007	.030007
.0400000	.040016	.040016	.040017	.040017	.040018
.0500000	.050031	.050032	.050033	.050034	.050036
.0600000	.060055	.060056	.060057	.060060	.060063
.0700000	.070087	.070089	.070092	.070095	.070100
.0800000	.080130	.080133	.080137	.080142	.080149
.0900000	.090186	.090189	.090195	.090203	.090213
.1000000	.100255	.100260	.100268	.100279	.100292
.1100000	.110340	.110347	.110357	.110372	.110389
.1200000	.120442	.120450	.120464	.120483	.120505
.1300000	.130562	.130573	.130591	.130614	.130643
.1400000	.140703	.140716	.140738	.140768	.140804
.1500000	.150865	.150882	.150909	.150945	.150990
.1600000	.161051	.161071	.161104	.161148	.161202
.1700000	.171262	.171286	.171326	.171379	.171444
.1800000	.181499	.181528	.181575	.181638	.181715
.1900000	.191765	.191799	.191854	.191929	.192020
.2000000	.202061	.202100	.202165	.202252	.202358
.2100000	.212388	.212434	.212509	.212610	.212733
.2200000	.222749	.222802	.222888	.223004	.223146
.2300000	.233144	.233205	.233304	.233437	.233599
.2400000	.243577	.243646	.243758	.243910	.244094
.2500000	.254048	.254127	.254254	.254425	.254634
.2600000	.264560	.264648	.264791	.264984	.265220
.2700000	.275114	.275212	.275373	.275590	.275854
.2800000	.285711	.285822	.286001	.286243	.286539
.2900000	.296355	.296477	.296677	.296947	.297276
.3000000	.307046	.307182	.307403	.307702	.308068
.3100000	.317786	.317937	.318182	.318513	.318917
.3200000	.328579	.328744	.329014	.329379	.329825
.3300000	.339424	.339606	.339903	.340304	.340794
.3400000	.350325	.350525	.350850	.351289	.351827
.3500000	.361283	.361502	.361857	.362338	.362926
.3600000	.372301	.372539	.372927	.373451	.374094
.3700000	.383381	.383639	.384061	.384632	.385332
.3800000	.394523	.394804	.395262	.395882	.396643
.3900000	.405732	.406036	.406533	.407205	.408030

$\alpha =$ .759999

Θ	K VALUES				
	.009966711	.039469502	.087332193	.151646642	.229848846
.4000000	.417008	.417338	.417874	.418602	.419495
.4100000	.428355	.428710	.429290	.430075	.431041
.4200000	.439774	.440157	.440782	.441628	.442670
.4300000	.451268	.451679	.452352	.453263	.454385
.4400000	.462838	.463281	.464003	.464982	.466188
.4500000	.474488	.474963	.475737	.476789	.478084
.4600000	.486220	.486728	.487558	.488685	.490073
.4700000	.498036	.498579	.499467	.500673	.502160
.4800000	.509938	.510518	.511467	.512756	.514347
.4900000	.521930	.522549	.523561	.524937	.526636
.5000000	.534014	.534673	.535752	.537219	.539032
.5100000	.546192	.546894	.548042	.549605	.551537
.5200000	.558467	.559214	.560435	.562098	.564155
.5300000	.570843	.571635	.572933	.574700	.576888
.5400000	.583321	.584162	.585538	.587415	.589739
.5500000	.595905	.596796	.598256	.600246	.602714
.5600000	.608597	.609541	.611087	.613197	.615813
.5700000	.621401	.622399	.624036	.626270	.629042
.5800000	.634320	.635375	.637105	.639469	.642404
.5900000	.647356	.648471	.650299	.652797	.655902
.6000000	.660514	.661690	.663620	.666259	.669541
.6100000	.673795	.675035	.677071	.679857	.683323
.6200000	.687205	.688511	.690657	.693595	.697254
.6300000	.700745	.702120	.704381	.707477	.711336
.6400000	.714419	.715866	.718246	.721507	.725574
.6500000	.728231	.729753	.732256	.735688	.739973
.6600000	.742185	.743784	.746415	.750026	.754536
.6700000	.756284	.757964	.760728	.764523	.769268
.6800000	.770533	.772295	.775197	.779184	.784173
.6899999	.784934	.786782	.789827	.794013	.799256
.7000000	.799492	.801429	.804623	.809016	.814521
.7100000	.814210	.816241	.819588	.824195	.829974
.7200000	.829094	.831220	.834727	.839556	.845619
.7300000	.844147	.846372	.850043	.855103	.861460
.7400000	.859374	.861701	.865543	.870841	.877505
.7500000	.874778	.877211	.881230	.886776	.893756
.7600000	.890364	.892908	.897109	.902911	.910220
.7700000	.906138	.908795	.913186	.919252	.926902
.7800000	.922103	.924877	.929464	.935805	.943808
.7899999	.938265	.941160	.945949	.952574	.960943

$\alpha =$ .759999

Θ	K VALUES				
	.009966711	.039469502	.087332193	.151646642	.229848846
.8000000	.954628	.957648	.962646	.969565	.978314
.8100000	.971197	.974346	.979560	.986784	.995925
.8200000	.987978	.991260	.996698	1.004235	1.013784
.8300000	1.004975	1.008395	1.014063	1.021926	1.031895
.8400000	1.022194	1.025756	1.031662	1.039861	1.050266
.8500000	1.039640	1.043348	1.049501	1.058047	1.068903
.8600000	1.057318	1.061178	1.067584	1.076490	1.087812
.8700000	1.075235	1.079251	1.085919	1.095195	1.107000
.8799999	1.093396	1.097573	1.104511	1.114170	1.126474
.8899999	1.111807	1.116149	1.123367	1.133421	1.146241
.9000000	1.130473	1.134986	1.142492	1.152954	1.166307
.9100000	1.149401	1.154090	1.161892	1.172775	1.186680
.9200000	1.168596	1.173467	1.181575	1.192893	1.207367
.9300000	1.188066	1.193124	1.201546	1.213313	1.228375
.9400000	1.207815	1.213066	1.221813	1.234042	1.249712
.9500000	1.227851	1.233300	1.242382	1.255088	1.271385
.9600000	1.248180	1.253833	1.263260	1.276458	1.293403
.9699999	1.268808	1.274672	1.284454	1.298159	1.315772
.9799999	1.289742	1.295822	1.305970	1.320198	1.338501
.9899999	1.310989	1.317292	1.327816	1.342582	1.361597
1.0000000	1.332556	1.339087	1.349999	1.365320	1.385069
1.0100000	1.354448	1.361215	1.372526	1.388418	1.408925
1.0200000	1.376673	1.383683	1.395403	1.411885	1.433172
1.0300000	1.399238	1.406497	1.418640	1.435727	1.457819
1.0400000	1.422150	1.429664	1.442241	1.459952	1.482874
1.0500000	1.445415	1.453192	1.466216	1.484569	1.508345
1.0600000	1.469040	1.477088	1.490570	1.509584	1.534241
1.0699999	1.493032	1.501357	1.515312	1.535005	1.560569
1.0799999	1.517398	1.526009	1.540448	1.560839	1.587337
1.0899999	1.542145	1.551048	1.565985	1.587095	1.614554
1.1000000	1.567279	1.576483	1.591931	1.613780	1.642228
1.1100000	1.592806	1.602318	1.618292	1.640900	1.670365
1.1200000	1.618733	1.628562	1.645075	1.668463	1.698975
1.1300000	1.645067	1.655221	1.672287	1.696476	1.728064
1.1400000	1.671813	1.682300	1.699934	1.724945	1.757640
1.1500000	1.698978	1.709806	1.728023	1.753878	1.787710
1.1600000	1.726567	1.737745	1.756558	1.783280	1.818280
1.1700000	1.754584	1.766121	1.785547	1.813157	1.849357
1.1800000	1.783037	1.794941	1.814994	1.843516	1.880947
1.1899999	1.811928	1.824208	1.844905	1.874361	1.913056

$\alpha =$ .759999

Θ	K VALUES				
	.009966711	.039469502	.087332193	.151646642	.229848846
1.2000000	1.841263	1.853929	1.875284	1.905698	1.945690
1.2100000	1.871046	1.884106	1.906135	1.937530	1.978852
1.2200000	1.901279	1.914742	1.937462	1.969862	2.012547
1.2300000	1.931967	1.945843	1.969268	2.002697	2.046779
1.2400000	1.963111	1.977408	2.001555	2.036038	2.081551
1.2500000	1.994714	2.009442	2.034327	2.069887	2.116864
1.2599999	2.026776	2.041944	2.067584	2.104245	2.152722
1.2699999	2.059299	2.074916	2.101326	2.139113	2.189124
1.2799999	2.092282	2.108358	2.135554	2.174492	2.226070
1.2899999	2.125724	2.142268	2.170267	2.210379	2.263560
1.3000000	2.159624	2.176645	2.205463	2.246774	2.301592
1.3100000	2.193979	2.211486	2.241139	2.283673	2.340162
1.3200000	2.228785	2.246788	2.277292	2.321072	2.379266
1.3300000	2.264038	2.282546	2.313916	2.358967	2.418900
1.3400000	2.299733	2.318754	2.351007	2.397351	2.459056
1.3500000	2.335863	2.355407	2.388557	2.436218	2.499728
1.3600000	2.372421	2.392495	2.426558	2.475559	2.540906
1.3700000	2.409398	2.430012	2.465002	2.515365	2.582581
1.3799999	2.446785	2.467946	2.503878	2.555624	2.624740
1.3899999	2.484570	2.506286	2.543175	2.596326	2.667371
1.4000000	2.522742	2.545022	2.582880	2.637456	2.710461
1.4100000	2.561287	2.584138	2.622978	2.679000	2.753993
1.4200000	2.600191	2.623620	2.663456	2.720942	2.797950
1.4300000	2.639438	2.663453	2.704296	2.763265	2.842314
1.4400000	2.679013	2.703619	2.745482	2.805951	2.887065
1.4500000	2.718896	2.744100	2.786993	2.848979	2.932183
1.4600000	2.759070	2.784878	2.828812	2.892330	2.977645
1.4700000	2.799515	2.825932	2.870915	2.935980	3.023427
1.4800000	2.840209	2.867240	2.913282	2.979907	3.069506
1.4900000	2.881131	2.908781	2.955890	3.024087	3.115854
1.5000000	2.922258	2.950531	2.998714	3.068494	3.162445
1.5100000	2.963566	2.992467	3.041730	3.113102	3.209252
1.5200000	3.005032	3.034562	3.084912	3.157885	3.256244
1.5300000	3.046630	3.076793	3.128233	3.202815	3.303394
1.5400000	3.088336	3.119134	3.171668	3.247864	3.350671
1.5500000	3.130122	3.161557	3.215189	3.293002	3.398044
1.5600000	3.171964	3.204036	3.258767	3.338202	3.445483
1.5699999	3.213834	3.246544	3.302376	3.383434	3.492955
1.5707963	3.217169	3.249930	3.305849	3.387036	3.496736
1.5707963	3.217166	3.249927	3.305846	3.387033	3.496733

$\alpha =$ .759999

Θ	K VALUES				
	.318821117	.415016431	.514599755	.613601043	.708073407
.0000000	.000000	.000000	.000000	.000000	.000000
.0100000	.010000	.010000	.010000	.010000	.010000
.0200000	.020002	.020002	.020002	.020002	.020002
.0300000	.030008	.030008	.030009	.030009	.030010
.0400000	.040019	.040020	.040021	.040022	.040023
.0500000	.050038	.050040	.050042	.050044	.050046
.0600000	.060066	.060069	.060073	.060076	.060080
.0700000	.070105	.070110	.070116	.070122	.070127
.0800000	.080157	.080165	.080174	.080182	.080190
.0900000	.090223	.090235	.090247	.090259	.090271
.1000000	.100307	.100323	.100340	.100356	.100372
.1100000	.110409	.110430	.110453	.110475	.110496
.1200000	.120531	.120559	.120588	.120617	.120645
.1300000	.130676	.130712	.130748	.130785	.130820
.1400000	.140845	.140890	.140936	.140982	.141026
.1500000	.151040	.151095	.151152	.151209	.151263
.1600000	.161264	.161331	.161400	.161469	.161535
.1700000	.171518	.171598	.171681	.171764	.171843
.1800000	.181803	.181899	.181997	.182096	.182191
.1900000	.192123	.192235	.192352	.192468	.192580
.2000000	.202479	.202610	.202747	.202883	.203013
.2100000	.212873	.213026	.213184	.213342	.213493
.2200000	.223308	.223483	.223666	.223848	.224023
.2300000	.233784	.233986	.234195	.234404	.234604
.2400000	.244305	.244535	.244773	.245012	.245240
.2500000	.254873	.255133	.255404	.255674	.255934
.2600000	.265490	.265783	.266088	.266394	.266687
.2700000	.276157	.276486	.276830	.277173	.277503
.2800000	.286878	.287246	.287630	.288015	.288385
.2900000	.297654	.298064	.298493	.298922	.299335
.3000000	.308487	.308943	.309420	.309897	.310356
.3100000	.319381	.319886	.320414	.320943	.321452
.3200000	.330337	.330895	.331477	.332062	.332626
.3300000	.341357	.341972	.342614	.343258	.343880
.3400000	.352445	.353120	.353825	.354534	.355217
.3500000	.363603	.364341	.365114	.365892	.366642
.3600000	.374832	.375639	.376485	.377335	.378157
.3700000	.386136	.387017	.387939	.388868	.389765
.3800000	.397518	.398476	.399480	.400492	.401470
.3900000	.408979	.410019	.411111	.412211	.413276

$\alpha =$ •759999

Θ	K VALUES				
	•318821117	•415016431	•514599755	•613601043	•708073407
•4000000	•420523	•421650	•422834	•424029	•425186
•4100000	•432153	•433372	•434654	•435949	•437204
•4200000	•443870	•445188	•446573	•447974	•449333
•4300000	•455678	•457099	•458595	•460108	•461577
•4400000	•467581	•469111	•470723	•472355	•473941
•4500000	•479580	•481225	•482960	•484718	•486428
•4600000	•491678	•493445	•495310	•497202	•499043
•4700000	•503880	•505775	•507777	•509809	•511789
•4800000	•516188	•518218	•520364	•522545	•524672
•4900000	•528604	•530776	•533075	•535412	•537694
•5000000	•541134	•543455	•545913	•548416	•550862
•5100000	•553779	•556256	•558884	•561561	•564180
•5200000	•566543	•569185	•571989	•574851	•577652
•5300000	•579430	•582245	•585235	•588290	•591284
•5400000	•592442	•595439	•598625	•601883	•605080
•5500000	•605585	•608771	•612163	•615635	•619046
•5600000	•618861	•622246	•625854	•629550	•633187
•5700000	•632275	•635868	•639702	•643635	•647509
•5800000	•645829	•649640	•653711	•657893	•662017
•5900000	•659529	•663568	•667888	•672330	•676717
•6000000	•673378	•677656	•682236	•686952	•691615
•6100000	•687379	•691907	•696760	•701763	•706717
•6200000	•701539	•706327	•711465	•716770	•722030
•6300000	•715860	•720920	•726357	•731979	•737559
•6400000	•730347	•735692	•741442	•747394	•753313
•6500000	•745005	•750646	•756723	•763023	•769296
•6600000	•759838	•765789	•772208	•778872	•785518
•6700000	•774851	•781125	•787902	•794947	•801984
•6800000	•790049	•796660	•803810	•811255	•818702
•6899999	•805437	•812399	•819939	•827803	•835681
•7000000	•821019	•828348	•836296	•844597	•852927
•7100000	•836802	•844512	•852885	•861645	•870450
•7200000	•852789	•860897	•869715	•878954	•888257
•7300000	•868988	•877509	•886790	•896531	•906357
•7400000	•885402	•894354	•904120	•914385	•924759
•7500000	•902039	•911439	•921709	•932523	•943472
•7600000	•918902	•928770	•939566	•950954	•962506
•7700000	•936000	•946352	•957698	•969686	•981869
•7800000	•953336	•964194	•976112	•988727	1•001573
•7899999	•970919	•982302	•994816	1•008087	1•021628

$\alpha =$ .759999

Θ	K VALUES				
	.318821117	.415016431	.514599755	.613601043	.708073407
.8000000	.988753	1.000682	1.013818	1.027775	1.042043
.8100000	1.006846	1.019343	1.033126	1.047798	1.062830
.8200000	1.025204	1.038290	1.052749	1.068168	1.084000
.8300000	1.043833	1.057532	1.072693	1.088895	1.105564
.8400000	1.062740	1.077077	1.092970	1.109987	1.127534
.8500000	1.081933	1.096931	1.113586	1.131455	1.149922
.8600000	1.101419	1.117103	1.134552	1.153310	1.172740
.8700000	1.121204	1.137601	1.155876	1.175562	1.196002
.8799999	1.141297	1.158434	1.177567	1.198223	1.219720
.8899999	1.161704	1.179609	1.199636	1.221303	1.243908
.9000000	1.182434	1.201135	1.222093	1.244815	1.268580
.9100000	1.203493	1.223021	1.244946	1.268770	1.293748
.9200000	1.224891	1.245276	1.268207	1.293179	1.319429
.9300000	1.246634	1.267909	1.291885	1.318055	1.345637
.9400000	1.268732	1.290928	1.315992	1.343411	1.372386
.9500000	1.291192	1.314344	1.340537	1.369259	1.399692
.9600000	1.314024	1.338165	1.365532	1.395612	1.427572
.9699999	1.337234	1.362401	1.390988	1.422484	1.456041
.9799999	1.360833	1.387063	1.416916	1.449887	1.485115
.9899999	1.384828	1.412158	1.443328	1.477835	1.514812
1.0000000	1.409228	1.437699	1.470234	1.506342	1.545148
1.0100000	1.434043	1.463693	1.497646	1.535422	1.576141
1.0200000	1.459281	1.490152	1.525576	1.565089	1.607809
1.0300000	1.484951	1.517085	1.554036	1.595357	1.640168
1.0400000	1.511062	1.544503	1.583038	1.626240	1.673238
1.0500000	1.537623	1.572416	1.612593	1.657754	1.707036
1.0600000	1.564643	1.600834	1.642713	1.689911	1.741582
1.0699999	1.592131	1.629766	1.673411	1.722728	1.776893
1.0799999	1.620096	1.659224	1.704697	1.756218	1.812989
1.0899999	1.648546	1.689217	1.736584	1.790396	1.849887
1.1000000	1.677491	1.719755	1.769084	1.825277	1.887608
1.1100000	1.706939	1.750847	1.802208	1.860874	1.926169
1.1200000	1.736898	1.782504	1.835967	1.897202	1.965590
1.1300000	1.767377	1.814735	1.870373	1.934274	2.005888
1.1400000	1.798383	1.847549	1.905436	1.972106	2.047083
1.1500000	1.829925	1.880954	1.941168	2.010709	2.089191
1.1600000	1.862010	1.914960	1.977577	2.050097	2.132232
1.1700000	1.894645	1.949575	2.014675	2.090283	2.176221
1.1800000	1.927837	1.984806	2.052471	2.131278	2.221176
1.1899999	1.961592	2.020660	2.090973	2.173094	2.267113

$\alpha =$ .759999

Θ	K VALUES				
	.318821117	.415016431	.514599755	.613601043	.708073407
1.2000000	1.995916	2.057146	2.130190	2.215743	2.314047
1.2100000	2.030815	2.094268	2.170129	2.259232	2.361991
1.2200000	2.066292	2.132032	2.210797	2.303573	2.410961
1.2300000	2.102353	2.170442	2.252200	2.348772	2.460968
1.2400000	2.139001	2.209504	2.294344	2.394838	2.512023
1.2500000	2.176237	2.249220	2.337231	2.441776	2.564136
1.2599999	2.214065	2.289593	2.380867	2.489592	2.617316
1.2699999	2.252485	2.330623	2.425252	2.538288	2.671569
1.2799999	2.291497	2.372312	2.470388	2.587866	2.726900
1.2899999	2.331101	2.414657	2.516273	2.638328	2.783313
1.3000000	2.371293	2.457659	2.562907	2.689673	2.840809
1.3100000	2.412072	2.501312	2.610286	2.741897	2.899385
1.3200000	2.453432	2.545612	2.658404	2.794995	2.959040
1.3300000	2.495368	2.590553	2.707257	2.848961	3.019766
1.3400000	2.537873	2.636128	2.756834	2.903787	3.081556
1.3500000	2.580939	2.682329	2.807128	2.959461	3.144399
1.3600000	2.624557	2.729144	2.858126	3.015972	3.208280
1.3700000	2.668716	2.776561	2.909814	3.073302	3.273182
1.3799999	2.713403	2.824567	2.962177	3.131436	3.339086
1.3899999	2.758604	2.873146	3.015199	3.190353	3.405969
1.4000000	2.804304	2.922283	3.068859	3.250032	3.473804
1.4100000	2.850485	2.971956	3.123137	3.310446	3.542562
1.4200000	2.897131	3.022146	3.178008	3.371569	3.612210
1.4300000	2.944219	3.072832	3.233449	3.433371	3.682712
1.4400000	2.991730	3.123988	3.289431	3.495821	3.754029
1.4500000	3.039641	3.175591	3.345926	3.558883	3.826120
1.4600000	3.087926	3.227612	3.402902	3.622522	3.898938
1.4700000	3.136561	3.280023	3.460328	3.686699	3.972436
1.4800000	3.185518	3.332794	3.518168	3.751372	4.046561
1.4900000	3.234769	3.385894	3.576386	3.816499	4.121262
1.5000000	3.284286	3.439291	3.634946	3.882034	4.196481
1.5100000	3.334037	3.492949	3.693807	3.947932	4.272158
1.5200000	3.383992	3.546834	3.752930	4.014143	4.348234
1.5300000	3.434118	3.600911	3.812273	4.080618	4.424647
1.5400000	3.484382	3.655142	3.871794	4.147308	4.501331
1.5500000	3.534751	3.709491	3.931451	4.214160	4.578221
1.5600000	3.585191	3.763919	3.991199	4.281122	4.655251
1.5699999	3.635669	3.818388	4.050995	4.348141	4.732355
1.5707963	3.639689	3.822726	4.055757	4.353479	4.738496
1.5707963	3.639686	3.822724	4.055755	4.353478	4.738500

$\alpha =$ .759999

Θ	K VALUES				
	.794250555	.868696860	.928444378	.971111163	.994996249
.0000000	.000000	.000000	.000000	.000000	.000000
.0100000	.010000	.010000	.010000	.010000	.010000
.0200000	.020003	.020003	.020003	.020003	.020003
.0300000	.030010	.030010	.030011	.030011	.030011
.0400000	.040024	.040025	.040026	.040026	.040026
.0500000	.050048	.050049	.050051	.050051	.050052
.0600000	.060083	.060086	.060088	.060089	.060090
.0700000	.070132	.070136	.070140	.070142	.070144
.0800000	.080198	.080204	.080209	.080213	.080215
.0900000	.090282	.090291	.090298	.090303	.090306
.1000000	.100387	.100399	.100409	.100416	.100420
.1100000	.110515	.110532	.110545	.110555	.110560
.1200000	.120670	.120691	.120709	.120721	.120728
.1300000	.130852	.130880	.130902	.130918	.130927
.1400000	.141066	.141101	.141128	.141148	.141160
.1500000	.151312	.151355	.151390	.151414	.151428
.1600000	.161595	.161647	.161689	.161719	.161736
.1700000	.171915	.171978	.172029	.172065	.172085
.1800000	.182277	.182352	.182412	.182455	.182479
.1900000	.192682	.192770	.192841	.192892	.192920
.2000000	.203132	.203236	.203319	.203378	.203412
.2100000	.213632	.213752	.213849	.213918	.213957
.2200000	.224183	.224322	.224433	.224513	.224558
.2300000	.234788	.234947	.235075	.235167	.235219
.2400000	.245450	.245632	.245778	.245883	.245942
.2500000	.256172	.256378	.256545	.256664	.256731
.2600000	.266956	.267189	.267378	.267513	.267588
.2700000	.277806	.278069	.278281	.278433	.278518
.2800000	.288724	.289019	.289257	.289427	.289523
.2900000	.299714	.300044	.300310	.300500	.300607
.3000000	.310778	.311146	.311442	.311655	.311774
.3100000	.321921	.322328	.322658	.322894	.323026
.3200000	.333144	.333595	.333960	.334222	.334369
.3300000	.344452	.344950	.345353	.345642	.345804
.3400000	.355847	.356396	.356840	.357158	.357337
.3500000	.367333	.367936	.368424	.368775	.368972
.3600000	.378914	.379575	.380110	.380495	.380711
.3700000	.390593	.391316	.391902	.392323	.392560
.3800000	.402374	.403164	.403803	.404264	.404522
.3900000	.414260	.415121	.415818	.416320	.416603

$\alpha =$ •759999

Θ	K VALUES				
	•794250555	•868696860	•928444378	•971111163	•994996249
•4000000	•426256	•427192	•427952	•428498	•428806
•4100000	•438365	•439382	•440207	•440801	•441136
•4200000	•450591	•451694	•452590	•453235	•453598
•4300000	•462939	•464133	•465103	•465803	•466197
•4400000	•475413	•476704	•477754	•478511	•478938
•4500000	•488016	•489411	•490545	•491364	•491826
•4600000	•500754	•502258	•503483	•504367	•504866
•4700000	•513631	•515252	•516572	•517526	•518064
•4800000	•526652	•528396	•529817	•530845	•531425
•4900000	•539822	•541696	•543225	•544332	•544957
•5000000	•553145	•555157	•556801	•557991	•558663
•5100000	•566626	•568786	•570551	•571829	•572552
•5200000	•580272	•582587	•584480	•585853	•586628
•5300000	•594087	•596566	•598595	•600068	•600900
•5400000	•608076	•610729	•612903	•614481	•615374
•5500000	•622246	•625083	•627410	•629100	•630057
•5600000	•636603	•639634	•642122	•643931	•644956
•5700000	•651152	•654388	•657048	•658983	•660079
•5800000	•665900	•669352	•672193	•674262	•675435
•5900000	•680852	•684534	•687567	•689777	•691031
•6000000	•696017	•699941	•703176	•705536	•706876
•6100000	•711400	•715579	•719029	•721548	•722978
•6200000	•727008	•731457	•735134	•737821	•739348
•6300000	•742849	•747583	•751500	•754365	•755994
•6400000	•758931	•763965	•768136	•771189	•772927
•6500000	•775260	•780612	•785051	•788304	•790157
•6600000	•791845	•797531	•802254	•805719	•807694
•6700000	•808694	•814734	•819757	•823446	•825549
•6800000	•825815	•832228	•837568	•841494	•843735
•6899999	•843218	•850023	•855699	•859877	•862264
•7000000	•860911	•868131	•874161	•878606	•881147
•7100000	•878903	•886560	•892966	•897693	•900398
•7200000	•897203	•905323	•912125	•917151	•920030
•7300000	•915823	•924429	•931651	•936995	•940058
•7400000	•934772	•943891	•951557	•957237	•960496
•7500000	•954060	•963721	•971857	•977893	•981359
•7600000	•973698	•983931	•992563	•998977	1•002665
•7700000	•993698	1•004534	1•013692	1•020507	1•024429
•7800000	1•014071	1•025543	1•035257	1•042497	1•046668
•7899999	1•034828	1•046972	1•057274	1•064966	1•069402

$\alpha =$ .759999

Θ	K VALUES				
	.794250555	.868696860	.928444378	.971111163	.994996249
.8000000	1.055984	1.068835	1.079761	1.087931	1.092649
.8100000	1.077548	1.091148	1.102732	1.111411	1.116429
.8200000	1.099536	1.113924	1.126207	1.135426	1.140763
.8300000	1.121960	1.137181	1.150203	1.159995	1.165672
.8400000	1.144835	1.160934	1.174739	1.185141	1.191179
.8500000	1.168174	1.185200	1.199836	1.210885	1.217308
.8600000	1.191993	1.209998	1.225513	1.237250	1.244084
.8700000	1.216307	1.235345	1.251792	1.264262	1.271533
.8799999	1.241131	1.261260	1.278695	1.291944	1.299682
.8899999	1.266481	1.287763	1.306245	1.320323	1.328559
.9000000	1.292375	1.314873	1.334467	1.349428	1.358196
.9100000	1.318830	1.342613	1.363385	1.379286	1.388622
.9200000	1.345862	1.371002	1.393026	1.409928	1.419872
.9300000	1.373491	1.400065	1.423416	1.441386	1.451979
.9400000	1.401734	1.429823	1.454584	1.473692	1.484979
.9500000	1.430612	1.460301	1.486558	1.506882	1.518912
.9600000	1.460143	1.491524	1.519371	1.540991	1.553817
.9699999	1.490348	1.523516	1.553052	1.576056	1.589737
.9799999	1.521248	1.556305	1.587636	1.612119	1.626715
.9899999	1.552864	1.589917	1.623156	1.649220	1.664798
1.0000000	1.585218	1.624381	1.659649	1.687403	1.704036
1.0100000	1.618331	1.659725	1.697151	1.726713	1.744479
1.0200000	1.652227	1.695979	1.735701	1.767198	1.786184
1.0300000	1.686929	1.733174	1.775339	1.808908	1.829206
1.0400000	1.722459	1.771341	1.816107	1.851895	1.873607
1.0500000	1.758844	1.810513	1.858047	1.896216	1.919450
1.0600000	1.796106	1.850722	1.901205	1.941926	1.966803
1.0699999	1.834271	1.892003	1.945626	1.989088	2.015738
1.0799999	1.873363	1.934390	1.991360	2.037763	2.066330
1.0899999	1.913409	1.977920	2.038456	2.088019	2.118659
1.1000000	1.954435	2.022629	2.086966	2.139926	2.172810
1.1100000	1.996464	2.068553	2.136943	2.193557	2.228871
1.1200000	2.039525	2.115730	2.188442	2.248988	2.286939
1.1300000	2.083643	2.164199	2.241521	2.306300	2.347113
1.1400000	2.128843	2.213999	2.296237	2.365578	2.409501
1.1500000	2.175152	2.265168	2.352652	2.426910	2.474217
1.1600000	2.222596	2.317748	2.410828	2.490389	2.541382
1.1700000	2.271199	2.371776	2.470829	2.556114	2.611126
1.1800000	2.320988	2.427294	2.532719	2.624187	2.683584
1.1899999	2.371985	2.484341	2.596567	2.694714	2.758906

$\alpha =$ .759999

Θ	K VALUES				
	.794250555	.868696860	.928444378	.971111163	.994996249
1.2000000	2.424216	2.542957	2.662442	2.767809	2.837248
1.2100000	2.477702	2.603180	2.730411	2.843589	2.918777
1.2200000	2.532466	2.665050	2.800547	2.922177	3.003673
1.2300000	2.588528	2.728605	2.872920	3.003704	3.092131
1.2400000	2.645907	2.793880	2.947603	3.088304	3.184358
1.2500000	2.704623	2.860912	3.024670	3.176120	3.280577
1.2599999	2.764689	2.929733	3.104192	3.267298	3.381031
1.2699999	2.826122	3.000377	3.186241	3.361993	3.485980
1.2799999	2.888932	3.072871	3.270890	3.460365	3.595707
1.2899999	2.953130	3.147243	3.358208	3.562582	3.710518
1.3000000	3.018722	3.223516	3.448264	3.668818	3.830749
1.3100000	3.085713	3.301711	3.541121	3.779250	3.956761
1.3200000	3.154105	3.381842	3.636844	3.894065	4.088952
1.3300000	3.223894	3.463924	3.735488	4.013453	4.227760
1.3400000	3.295075	3.547962	3.837108	4.137610	4.373663
1.3500000	3.367640	3.633958	3.941750	4.266734	4.527190
1.3600000	3.441575	3.721910	4.049453	4.401026	4.688926
1.3700000	3.516863	3.811806	4.160247	4.540686	4.859518
1.3799999	3.593483	3.903631	4.274155	4.685915	5.039687
1.3899999	3.671408	3.997361	4.391187	4.836907	5.230239
1.4000000	3.750609	4.092965	4.511341	4.993850	5.432075
1.4100000	3.831048	4.190404	4.634600	5.156914	5.646200
1.4200000	3.912688	4.289633	4.760933	5.326257	5.873752
1.4300000	3.995483	4.390595	4.890293	5.502009	6.116008
1.4400000	4.079383	4.493227	5.022614	5.684271	6.374404
1.4500000	4.164334	4.597459	5.157811	5.873102	6.650556
1.4600000	4.250278	4.703208	5.295781	6.068511	6.946270
1.4700000	4.337150	4.810386	5.436396	6.270447	7.263549
1.4800000	4.424884	4.918896	5.579511	6.478788	7.604581
1.4900000	4.513406	5.028632	5.724956	6.693329	7.971689
1.5000000	4.602641	5.139482	5.872542	6.913776	8.367239
1.5100000	4.692509	5.251323	6.022057	7.139728	8.793426
1.5200000	4.782927	5.364030	6.173270	7.370683	9.251957
1.5300000	4.873809	5.477470	6.325934	7.606032	9.743528
1.5400000	4.965068	5.591505	6.479784	7.845062	10.267122
1.5500000	5.056612	5.705993	6.634542	8.086964	10.819240
1.5600000	5.148350	5.820789	6.789919	8.330856	11.393329
1.5699999	5.240189	5.935746	6.945620	8.575797	11.979856
1.5707963	5.247503	5.944903	6.958024	8.595318	12.026762
1.5707963	5.247500	5.944898	6.958019	8.595311	12.026748

$\alpha =$ .779999

Θ	K VALUES				
	.009966711	.039469502	.087332193	.151646642	.229848846
.0000000	.000000	.000000	.000000	.000000	.000000
.0100000	.010000	.010000	.010000	.010000	.010000
.0200000	.020002	.020002	.020002	.020002	.020002
.0300000	.030007	.030007	.030007	.030007	.030008
.0400000	.040016	.040017	.040017	.040018	.040019
.0500000	.050032	.050033	.050034	.050035	.050037
.0600000	.060056	.060057	.060059	.060061	.060064
.0700000	.070089	.070091	.070094	.070098	.070102
.0800000	.080134	.080136	.080140	.080146	.080153
.0900000	.090191	.090194	.090200	.090208	.090218
.1000000	.100262	.100267	.100275	.100286	.100299
.1100000.	.110349	.110355	.110366	.110380	.110398
.1200000	.120453	.120462	.120476	.120494	.120517
.1300000	.130577	.130588	.130605	.130629	.130658
.1400000	.140721	.140735	.140757	.140787	.140823
.1500000	.150888	.150905	.150932	.150968	.151013
.1600000	.161079	.161099	.161132	.161176	.161230
.1700000	.171295	.171319	.171359	.171412	.171477
.1800000	.181539	.181568	.181615	.181678	.181755
.1900000	.191812	.191846	.191901	.191976	.192067
.2000000	.202115	.202155	.202220	.202307	.202413
.2100000	.212452	.212498	.212573	.212674	.212797
.2200000	.222822	.222875	.222962	.223078	.223220
.2300000	.233229	.233290	.233388	.233521	.233684
.2400000	.243673	.243742	.243855	.244006	.244191
.2500000	.254157	.254236	.254363	.254534	.254744
.2600000	.264683	.264771	.264914	.265108	.265344
.2700000	.275252	.275351	.275512	.275728	.275993
.2800000	.285866	.285977	.286156	.286399	.286695
.2900000	.296528	.296651	.296850	.297120	.297450
.3000000	.307238	.307374	.307596	.307896	.308262
.3100000	.318000	.318150	.318395	.318727	.319132
.3200000	.328814	.328980	.329250	.329615	.330062
.3300000	.339684	.339866	.340163	.340564	.341056
.3400000	.350610	.350810	.351136	.351576	.352115
.3500000	.361596	.361815	.362171	.362652	.363242
.3600000	.372643	.372882	.373270	.373795	.374439
.3700000	.383754	.384013	.384436	.385008	.385709
.3800000	.394930	.395212	.395671	.396292	.397054
.3900000	.406175	.406479	.406977	.407650	.408477

$\alpha =$ .779999

Θ	K VALUES				
	.009966711	.039469502	.087332193	.151646642	.229848846
.4000000	.417489	.417819	.418356	.419085	.419980
.4100000	.428875	.429231	.429812	.430599	.431567
.4200000	.440337	.440721	.441347	.442195	.443239
.4300000	.451876	.452288	.452962	.453876	.455000
.4400000	.463494	.463937	.464661	.465643	.466852
.4500000	.475194	.475670	.476447	.477501	.478799
.4600000	.486979	.487489	.488321	.489451	.490843
.4700000	.498852	.499396	.500287	.501496	.502988
.4800000	.510814	.511396	.512347	.513640	.515235
.4900000	.522868	.523489	.524504	.525885	.527589
.5000000	.535018	.535680	.536762	.538234	.540053
.5100000	.547266	.547970	.549123	.550691	.552630
.5200000	.559615	.560364	.561589	.563258	.565323
.5300000	.572068	.572863	.574165	.575939	.578135
.5400000	.584627	.585471	.586853	.588737	.591071
.5500000	.597297	.598191	.599657	.601656	.604133
.5600000	.610079	.611026	.612579	.614698	.617326
.5700000	.622978	.623980	.625624	.627868	.630653
.5800000	.635996	.637055	.638794	.641168	.644117
.5900000	.649136	.650256	.652093	.654603	.657723
.6000000	.662403	.663585	.665525	.668177	.671475
.6100000	.675800	.677046	.679093	.681892	.685377
.6200000	.689330	.690643	.692801	.695754	.699433
.6300000	.702996	.704379	.706652	.709766	.713647
.6400000	.716803	.718259	.720652	.723932	.728023
.6500000	.730755	.732285	.734803	.738256	.742567
.6600000	.744854	.746463	.749111	.752743	.757282
.6700000	.759106	.760796	.763578	.767397	.772173
.6800000	.773514	.775288	.778210	.782223	.787246
.6899999	.788083	.789944	.793010	.797225	.802504
.7000000	.802817	.804768	.807984	.812408	.817954
.7100000	.817719	.819764	.823136	.827777	.833599
.7200000	.832795	.834937	.838471	.843337	.849446
.7300000	.848050	.850292	.853993	.859092	.865500
.7400000	.863487	.865834	.869707	.875049	.881767
.7500000	.879112	.881566	.885619	.891211	.898251
.7600000	.894930	.897495	.901734	.907586	.914959
.7700000	.910945	.913626	.918056	.924178	.931897
.7800000	.927164	.929963	.934592	.940993	.949071
.7899999	.943590	.946512	.951347	.958036	.966487

$\alpha =$ .779999

Θ	K VALUES				
	.009966711	.039469502	.087332193	.151646642	.229848846
.8000000	.960230	.963279	.968327	.975315	.984151
.8100000	.977089	.980269	.985537	.992834	1.002070
.8200000	.994172	.997488	1.002983	1.010601	1.020251
.8300000	1.011486	1.014942	1.020672	1.028621	1.038700
.8400000	1.029036	1.032637	1.038610	1.046901	1.057424
.8500000	1.046828	1.050579	1.056803	1.065448	1.076431
.8600000	1.064869	1.068774	1.075257	1.084269	1.095727
.8700000	1.083165	1.087229	1.093979	1.103370	1.115321
.8799999	1.101721	1.105950	1.112977	1.122758	1.135220
.8899999	1.120546	1.124945	1.132256	1.142441	1.155431
.9000000	1.139645	1.144219	1.151824	1.162427	1.175962
.9100000	1.159025	1.163779	1.171688	1.182723	1.196822
.9200000	1.178693	1.183633	1.191856	1.203336	1.218018
.9300000	1.198657	1.203789	1.212335	1.224274	1.239560
.9400000	1.218923	1.224252	1.233132	1.245546	1.261455
.9500000	1.239499	1.245032	1.254255	1.267159	1.283712
.9600000	1.260392	1.266135	1.275712	1.289122	1.306341
.9699999	1.281610	1.287569	1.297511	1.311443	1.329349
.9799999	1.303160	1.309342	1.319661	1.334130	1.352747
.9899999	1.325051	1.331462	1.342169	1.357193	1.376543
1.0000000	1.347289	1.353937	1.365043	1.380640	1.400747
1.0100000	1.369884	1.376775	1.388293	1.404479	1.425368
1.0200000	1.392843	1.399984	1.411926	1.428720	1.450416
1.0300000	1.416175	1.423573	1.435951	1.453372	1.475900
1.0400000	1.439887	1.447550	1.460378	1.478444	1.501831
1.0500000	1.463988	1.471923	1.485213	1.503945	1.528217
1.0600000	1.488485	1.496701	1.510467	1.529884	1.555069
1.0699999	1.513389	1.521893	1.536148	1.556270	1.582396
1.0799999	1.538706	1.547506	1.562265	1.583113	1.610209
1.0899999	1.564444	1.573549	1.588827	1.610422	1.638518
1.1000000	1.590614	1.600032	1.615842	1.638206	1.667332
1.1100000	1.617221	1.626961	1.643318	1.666473	1.696660
1.1200000	1.644275	1.654345	1.671265	1.695234	1.726513
1.1300000	1.671784	1.682193	1.699691	1.724496	1.756899
1.1400000	1.699755	1.710512	1.728604	1.754269	1.787830
1.1500000	1.728195	1.739310	1.758012	1.784561	1.819312
1.1600000	1.757114	1.768595	1.787923	1.815381	1.851356
1.1700000	1.786517	1.798375	1.818345	1.846735	1.883969
1.1800000	1.816411	1.828655	1.849285	1.878633	1.917161
1.1899999	1.846804	1.859443	1.880749	1.911080	1.950938

$\alpha =$ .779999

Θ	K VALUES				
	.009966711	.039469502	.087332193	.151646642	.229848846
1.2000000	1.877701	1.890746	1.912745	1.944086	1.985309
1.2100000	1.909108	1.922569	1.945279	1.977654	2.020279
1.2200000	1.941030	1.954917	1.978356	2.011792	2.055857
1.2300000	1.973472	1.987795	2.011980	2.046504	2.092046
1.2400000	2.006439	2.021208	2.046157	2.081796	2.128852
1.2500000	2.039933	2.055159	2.080890	2.117671	2.166280
1.2599999	2.073958	2.089651	2.116183	2.154132	2.204332
1.2699999	2.108515	2.124686	2.152036	2.191182	2.243012
1.2799999	2.143607	2.160265	2.188453	2.228822	2.282320
1.2899999	2.179232	2.196389	2.225432	2.267052	2.322257
1.3000000	2.215392	2.233058	2.262974	2.305873	2.362824
1.3100000	2.252082	2.270268	2.301076	2.345281	2.404017
1.3200000	2.289303	2.308018	2.339736	2.385274	2.445833
1.3300000	2.327048	2.346303	2.378949	2.425847	2.488268
1.3400000	2.365313	2.385119	2.418711	2.466996	2.531316
1.3500000	2.404093	2.424459	2.459014	2.508712	2.574970
1.3600000	2.443378	2.464315	2.499851	2.550989	2.619221
1.3700000	2.483161	2.504678	2.541212	2.593815	2.664057
1.3799999	2.523431	2.545538	2.583086	2.637179	2.709468
1.3899999	2.564176	2.586881	2.625460	2.681069	2.755439
1.4000000	2.605382	2.628697	2.668322	2.725469	2.801955
1.4100000	2.647036	2.670967	2.711654	2.770364	2.848997
1.4200000	2.689120	2.713676	2.755441	2.815734	2.896547
1.4300000	2.731617	2.756807	2.799662	2.861561	2.944584
1.4400000	2.774507	2.800339	2.844299	2.907824	2.993085
1.4500000	2.817771	2.844251	2.889329	2.954499	3.042027
1.4600000	2.861385	2.888521	2.934728	3.001562	3.091382
1.4700000	2.905327	2.933125	2.980473	3.048986	3.141123
1.4800000	2.949572	2.978037	3.026536	3.096746	3.191222
1.4900000	2.994093	3.023232	3.072891	3.144811	3.241646
1.5000000	3.038863	3.068680	3.119509	3.193152	3.292365
1.5100000	3.083854	3.114354	3.166359	3.241737	3.343344
1.5200000	3.129036	3.160223	3.213412	3.290535	3.394549
1.5300000	3.174381	3.206257	3.260634	3.339510	3.445945
1.5400000	3.219855	3.252424	3.307995	3.388630	3.497494
1.5500000	3.265429	3.298691	3.355459	3.437860	3.549161
1.5600000	3.311070	3.345028	3.402995	3.487164	3.600907
1.5699999	3.356746	3.391400	3.450567	3.536507	3.652694
1.5707963	3.360384	3.395093	3.454356	3.540436	3.656818
1.5707963	3.360381	3.395090	3.454353	3.540433	3.656815

$\alpha =$ .779999

Θ	K VALUES				
	.318821117	.415016431	.514599755	.613601043	.708073407
.0000000	.000000	.000000	.000000	.000000	.000000
.0100000	.010000	.010000	.010000	.010000	.010000
.0200000	.020002	.020002	.020002	.020002	.020003
.0300000	.030008	.030008	.030009	.030009	.030010
.0400000	.040020	.040021	.040022	.040023	.040024
.0500000	.050039	.050041	.050043	.050045	.050047
.0600000	.060067	.060071	.060074	.060078	.060081
.0700000	.070107	.070113	.070118	.070124	.070129
.0800000	.080160	.080168	.080177	.080185	.080194
.0900000	.090228	.090240	.090252	.090264	.090276
.1000000	.100314	.100330	.100346	.100363	.100379
.1100000	.110418	.110439	.110462	.110484	.110505
.1200000	.120543	.120571	.120600	.120629	.120656
.1300000	.130691	.130726	.130763	.130800	.130835
.1400000	.140864	.140908	.140954	.141000	.141044
.1500000	.151063	.151118	.151175	.151232	.151286
.1600000	.161292	.161358	.161428	.161497	.161563
.1700000	.171551	.171631	.171714	.171797	.171877
.1800000	.181843	.181939	.182037	.182136	.182231
.1900000	.192170	.192283	.192399	.192516	.192627
.2000000	.202534	.202666	.202802	.202938	.203069
.2100000	.212937	.213090	.213248	.213406	.213558
.2200000	.223381	.223557	.223740	.223922	.224097
.2300000	.233869	.234070	.234280	.234489	.234690
.2400000	.244402	.244632	.244870	.245109	.245338
.2500000	.254983	.255243	.255514	.255784	.256044
.2600000	.265614	.265907	.266213	.266518	.266812
.2700000	.276296	.276626	.276970	.277313	.277644
.2800000	.287034	.287403	.287787	.288172	.288542
.2900000	.297828	.298239	.298668	.299098	.299511
.3000000	.308681	.309138	.309615	.310093	.310552
.3100000	.319596	.320102	.320630	.321160	.321670
.3200000	.330574	.331133	.331717	.332302	.332866
.3300000	.341620	.342235	.342878	.343523	.344145
.3400000	.352734	.353409	.354115	.354825	.355510
.3500000	.363919	.364659	.365433	.366212	.366963
.3600000	.375179	.375987	.376834	.377686	.378508
.3700000	.386515	.387396	.388320	.389251	.390150
.3800000	.397930	.398890	.399896	.400910	.401890
.3900000	.409428	.410470	.411564	.412666	.413733

$\alpha =$ .779999

Θ	K VALUES				
	.318821117	.415016431	.514599755	.613601043	.708073407
.4000000	.421011	.422140	.423327	.424524	.425683
.4100000	.432681	.433903	.435188	.436486	.437743
.4200000	.444442	.445763	.447152	.448556	.449917
.4300000	.456297	.457721	.459221	.460738	.462210
.4400000	.468248	.469782	.471399	.473035	.474625
.4500000	.480299	.481949	.483689	.485452	.487166
.4600000	.492453	.494225	.496095	.497992	.499838
.4700000	.504713	.506613	.508621	.510659	.512645
.4800000	.517082	.519118	.521271	.523459	.525592
.4900000	.529564	.531743	.534048	.536394	.538683
.5000000	.542162	.544490	.546957	.549469	.551923
.5100000	.554879	.557365	.560002	.562689	.565317
.5200000	.567720	.570371	.573186	.576058	.578870
.5300000	.580687	.583513	.586515	.589581	.592587
.5400000	.593785	.596793	.599992	.603263	.606473
.5500000	.607017	.610216	.613622	.617108	.620534
.5600000	.620387	.623786	.627410	.631122	.634775
.5700000	.633899	.637509	.641360	.645311	.649203
.5800000	.647558	.651387	.655477	.659679	.663822
.5900000	.661367	.665426	.669767	.674231	.678640
.6000000	.675331	.679631	.684234	.688975	.693662
.6100000	.689454	.694006	.698884	.703914	.708895
.6200000	.703741	.708555	.713722	.719056	.724345
.6300000	.718196	.723285	.728753	.734407	.740020
.6400000	.732824	.738200	.743984	.749972	.755926
.6500000	.747629	.753305	.759419	.765758	.772071
.6600000	.762617	.768606	.775066	.781773	.788461
.6700000	.777793	.784108	.790930	.798022	.805106
.6800000	.793162	.799818	.807017	.814513	.822012
.6899999	.808728	.815740	.823334	.831253	.839188
.7000000	.824499	.831881	.839887	.848250	.856643
.7100000	.840478	.848247	.856684	.865511	.874384
.7200000	.856673	.864844	.873731	.883043	.892421
.7300000	.873088	.881678	.891035	.900856	.910764
.7400000	.889730	.898757	.908605	.918958	.929421
.7500000	.906605	.916087	.926446	.937356	.948402
.7600000	.923718	.933674	.944568	.956060	.967718
.7700000	.941078	.951526	.962977	.975079	.987378
.7800000	.958689	.969651	.981683	.994422	1.007394
.7899999	.976560	.988055	1.000694	1.014099	1.027777

$\alpha =$ .779999

Θ	K VALUES				
	.318821117	.415016431	.514599755	.613601043	.708073407
.8000000	.994696	1.006746	1.020017	1.034119	1.048538
.8100000	1.013105	1.025733	1.039663	1.054493	1.069688
.8200000	1.031793	1.045022	1.059639	1.075230	1.091240
.8300000	1.050770	1.064623	1.079956	1.096343	1.113206
.8400000	1.070041	1.084543	1.100622	1.117841	1.135598
.8500000	1.089615	1.104792	1.121648	1.139735	1.158431
.8600000	1.109500	1.125377	1.143043	1.162038	1.181717
.8700000	1.129704	1.146308	1.164818	1.184760	1.205470
.8799999	1.150234	1.167595	1.186982	1.207915	1.229706
.8899999	1.171100	1.189246	1.209547	1.231515	1.254437
.9000000	1.192310	1.211272	1.232524	1.255571	1.279681
.9100000	1.213873	1.233681	1.255924	1.280098	1.305451
.9200000	1.235798	1.256484	1.279758	1.305109	1.331764
.9300000	1.258093	1.279691	1.304037	1.330617	1.358637
.9400000	1.280769	1.303313	1.328774	1.356636	1.386086
.9500000	1.303835	1.327359	1.353981	1.383180	1.414128
.9600000	1.327299	1.351842	1.379670	1.410265	1.442782
.9699999	1.351173	1.376771	1.405853	1.437904	1.472064
.9799999	1.375466	1.402158	1.432544	1.466114	1.501994
.9899999	1.400188	1.428014	1.459756	1.494909	1.532591
1.0000000	1.425350	1.454350	1.487501	1.524305	1.563873
1.0100000	1.450961	1.481179	1.515793	1.554318	1.595861
1.0200000	1.477032	1.508511	1.544645	1.584965	1.628574
1.0300000	1.503574	1.536360	1.574072	1.616261	1.662032
1.0400000	1.530598	1.564735	1.604087	1.648223	1.696257
1.0500000	1.558113	1.593651	1.634704	1.680868	1.731270
1.0600000	1.586131	1.623118	1.665936	1.714214	1.767092
1.0699999	1.614663	1.653149	1.697799	1.748277	1.803744
1.0799999	1.643719	1.683757	1.730307	1.783074	1.841248
1.0899999	1.673310	1.714952	1.763473	1.818622	1.879626
1.1000000	1.703447	1.746748	1.797312	1.854940	1.918901
1.1100000	1.734141	1.779156	1.831837	1.892043	1.959094
1.1200000	1.765402	1.812189	1.867063	1.929949	2.000227
1.1300000	1.797240	1.845857	1.903004	1.968676	2.042323
1.1400000	1.829666	1.880174	1.939672	2.008240	2.085404
1.1500000	1.862690	1.915149	1.977082	2.048657	2.129491
1.1600000	1.896321	1.950794	2.015247	2.089943	2.174606
1.1700000	1.930569	1.987120	2.054179	2.132116	2.220770
1.1800000	1.965444	2.024136	2.093891	2.175189	2.268004
1.1899999	2.000953	2.061854	2.134393	2.219178	2.316327

$\alpha =$ .779999

Θ	K VALUES				
	.318821117	.415016431	.514599755	.613601043	.708073407
1.2000000	2.037104	2.100282	2.175698	2.264097	2.365760
1.2100000	2.073906	2.139428	2.217815	2.309958	2.416319
1.2200000	2.111365	2.179301	2.260755	2.356775	2.468024
1.2300000	2.149488	2.219908	2.304525	2.404559	2.520890
1.2400000	2.188280	2.261256	2.349135	2.453320	2.574933
1.2500000	2.227746	2.303349	2.394590	2.503068	2.630165
1.2599999	2.267889	2.346193	2.440896	2.553810	2.686600
1.2699999	2.308713	2.389791	2.488058	2.605553	2.744248
1.2799999	2.350219	2.434144	2.536079	2.658301	2.803116
1.2899999	2.392408	2.479254	2.584961	2.712058	2.863212
1.3000000	2.435279	2.525122	2.634703	2.766825	2.924540
1.3100000	2.478831	2.571743	2.685303	2.822600	2.987100
1.3200000	2.523059	2.619115	2.736759	2.879380	3.050891
1.3300000	2.567959	2.667234	2.789064	2.937161	3.115911
1.3400000	2.613526	2.716091	2.842213	2.995935	3.182150
1.3500000	2.659750	2.765679	2.896194	3.055692	3.249601
1.3600000	2.706622	2.815987	2.950996	3.116419	3.318248
1.3700000	2.754132	2.867002	3.006607	3.178100	3.388075
1.3799999	2.802264	2.918710	3.063008	3.240717	3.459062
1.3899999	2.851006	2.971095	3.120183	3.304249	3.531183
1.4000000	2.900340	3.024138	3.178110	3.368672	3.604412
1.4100000	2.950246	3.077817	3.236764	3.433958	3.678715
1.4200000	3.000704	3.132110	3.296121	3.500077	3.754056
1.4300000	3.051691	3.186992	3.356152	3.566996	3.830395
1.4400000	3.103183	3.242435	3.416825	3.634679	3.907689
1.4500000	3.155154	3.298411	3.478108	3.703086	3.985889
1.4600000	3.207574	3.354887	3.539964	3.772175	4.064943
1.4700000	3.260415	3.411830	3.602355	3.841902	4.144796
1.4800000	3.313643	3.469206	3.665241	3.912217	4.225389
1.4900000	3.367226	3.526976	3.728580	3.983071	4.306659
1.5000000	3.421129	3.585102	3.792327	4.054412	4.388541
1.5100000	3.475316	3.643544	3.856435	4.126184	4.470965
1.5200000	3.529748	3.702259	3.920858	4.198330	4.553861
1.5300000	3.584387	3.761205	3.985545	4.270792	4.637153
1.5400000	3.639194	3.820338	4.050445	4.343509	4.720768
1.5500000	3.694128	3.879612	4.115509	4.416419	4.804627
1.5600000	3.749149	3.938982	4.180682	4.489461	4.888652
1.5699999	3.804214	3.998402	4.245913	4.562572	4.972763
1.5707963	3.808600	4.003135	4.251109	4.568395	4.979463
1.5707963	3.808597	4.003132	4.251106	4.568394	4.979464

$\alpha =$ .779999

Θ	K VALUES				
	.794250555	.868696860	.928444378	.971111163	.994996249
.0000000	.000000	.000000	.000000	.000000	.000000
.0100000	.010000	.010000	.010000	.010000	.010000
.0200000	.020003	.020003	.020003	.020003	.020003
.0300000	.030010	.030010	.030011	.030011	.030011
.0400000	.040025	.040025	.040026	.040027	.040027
.0500000	.050049	.050050	.050051	.050052	.050053
.0600000	.060084	.060087	.060089	.060091	.060092
.0700000	.070134	.070139	.070142	.070145	.070146
.0800000	.080201	.080207	.080212	.080216	.080218
.0900000	.090286	.090296	.090303	.090308	.090311
.1000000	.100393	.100406	.100416	.100423	.100427
.1100000	.110524	.110541	.110554	.110564	.110569
.1200000	.120681	.120703	.120721	.120733	.120740
.1300000	.130867	.130895	.130917	.130933	.130942
.1400000	.141084	.141119	.141147	.141167	.141178
.1500000	.151335	.151378	.151413	.151437	.151451
.1600000	.161623	.161675	.161717	.161747	.161764
.1700000	.171949	.172012	.172062	.172098	.172119
.1800000	.182317	.182392	.182452	.182495	.182519
.1900000	.192729	.192817	.192888	.192939	.192968
.2000000	.203188	.203291	.203375	.203434	.203467
.2100000	.213696	.213817	.213913	.213983	.214021
.2200000	.224257	.224396	.224508	.224588	.224633
.2300000	.234873	.235033	.235161	.235253	.235304
.2400000	.245547	.245729	.245876	.245981	.246040
.2500000	.256282	.256489	.256656	.256775	.256842
.2600000	.267081	.267315	.267503	.267638	.267714
.2700000	.277947	.278210	.278422	.278574	.278659
.2800000	.288882	.289177	.289415	.289586	.289682
.2900000	.299890	.300220	.300487	.300678	.300785
.3000000	.310975	.311343	.311639	.311852	.311971
.3100000	.322139	.322547	.322877	.323113	.323246
.3200000	.333386	.333837	.334203	.334465	.334612
.3300000	.344718	.345217	.345621	.345910	.346073
.3400000	.356140	.356690	.357134	.357454	.357633
.3500000	.367656	.368259	.368748	.369099	.369296
.3600000	.379267	.379929	.380465	.380851	.381067
.3700000	.390979	.391704	.392290	.392712	.392949
.3800000	.402795	.403587	.404227	.404689	.404948
.3900000	.414720	.415582	.416281	.416784	.417067

$\alpha =$ .779999

Θ	K VALUES				
	.794250555	.868696860	.928444378	.971111163	.994996249
.4000000	.426755	.427693	.428454	.429002	.429311
.4100000	.438907	.439926	.440753	.441349	.441684
.4200000	.451179	.452284	.453182	.453829	.454193
.4300000	.463575	.464772	.465745	.466446	.466841
.4400000	.476100	.477395	.478447	.479207	.479634
.4500000	.488758	.490156	.491294	.492115	.492578
.4600000	.501554	.503062	.504291	.505177	.505677
.4700000	.514493	.516118	.517442	.518399	.518938
.4800000	.527579	.529328	.530754	.531785	.532367
.4900000	.540817	.542698	.544232	.545342	.545969
.5000000	.554213	.556233	.557882	.559076	.559751
.5100000	.567772	.569939	.571710	.572994	.573719
.5200000	.581499	.583822	.585723	.587101	.587880
.5300000	.595400	.597889	.599927	.601405	.602240
.5400000	.609481	.612145	.614328	.615912	.616809
.5500000	.623748	.626596	.628933	.630630	.631591
.5600000	.638206	.641250	.643750	.645567	.646596
.5700000	.652862	.656113	.658785	.660729	.661831
.5800000	.667723	.671193	.674048	.676126	.677305
.5900000	.682796	.686496	.689544	.691765	.693025
.6000000	.698087	.702031	.705283	.707656	.709002
.6100000	.713603	.717805	.721274	.723806	.725244
.6200000	.729351	.733826	.737524	.740225	.741761
.6300000	.745340	.750102	.754042	.756924	.758563
.6400000	.761578	.766643	.770839	.773912	.775660
.6500000	.778071	.783457	.787925	.791199	.793063
.6600000	.794830	.800554	.805308	.808796	.810783
.6700000	.811861	.817942	.823000	.826714	.828833
.6800000	.829175	.835633	.841011	.844966	.847223
.6899999	.846780	.853636	.859353	.863562	.865967
.7000000	.864686	.871961	.878038	.882517	.885078
.7100000	.882903	.890621	.897078	.901843	.904569
.7200000	.901441	.909626	.916485	.921553	.924455
.7300000	.920310	.928989	.936272	.941662	.944751
.7400000	.939521	.948720	.956454	.962184	.965472
.7500000	.959085	.968834	.977045	.983136	.986635
.7600000	.979015	.989344	.998058	1.004533	1.008256
.7700000	.999321	1.010263	1.019510	1.026393	1.030354
.7800000	1.020017	1.031604	1.041417	1.048731	1.052946
.7899999	1.041114	1.053384	1.063795	1.071568	1.076052

$\alpha =$ .779999

Θ	K VALUES				
	.794250555	.868696860	.928444378	.971111163	.994996249
.8000000	1.062627	1.075617	1.086662	1.094922	1.099692
.8100000	1.084569	1.098320	1.110035	1.118812	1.123887
.8200000	1.106953	1.121507	1.133933	1.143260	1.148660
.8300000	1.129795	1.145197	1.158376	1.168287	1.174033
.8400000	1.153110	1.169407	1.183385	1.193917	1.200031
.8500000	1.176913	1.194155	1.208979	1.220172	1.226679
.8600000	1.201220	1.219461	1.235182	1.247078	1.254004
.8700000	1.226047	1.245344	1.262017	1.274660	1.282033
.8799999	1.251412	1.271824	1.289507	1.302945	1.310795
.8899999	1.277333	1.298922	1.317676	1.331963	1.340322
.9000000	1.303827	1.326662	1.346553	1.361742	1.370646
.9100000	1.330914	1.355064	1.376162	1.392314	1.401799
.9200000	1.358612	1.384153	1.406533	1.423711	1.433818
.9300000	1.386942	1.413953	1.437694	1.455968	1.466740
.9400000	1.415924	1.444490	1.469677	1.489119	1.500605
.9500000	1.445580	1.475789	1.502513	1.523203	1.535452
.9600000	1.475931	1.507878	1.536236	1.558258	1.571326
.9699999	1.507000	1.540785	1.570880	1.594326	1.608272
.9799999	1.538809	1.574539	1.606482	1.631450	1.646338
.9899999	1.571383	1.609169	1.643078	1.669675	1.685575
1.0000000	1.604745	1.644708	1.680709	1.709049	1.726036
1.0100000	1.638921	1.681186	1.719415	1.749620	1.767778
1.0200000	1.673936	1.718637	1.759238	1.791442	1.810859
1.0300000	1.709816	1.757096	1.800222	1.834569	1.855343
1.0400000	1.746589	1.796596	1.842414	1.879058	1.901295
1.0500000	1.784280	1.837175	1.885861	1.924971	1.948785
1.0600000	1.822919	1.878869	1.930613	1.972370	1.997888
1.0699999	1.862533	1.921718	1.976721	2.021322	2.048681
1.0799999	1.903151	1.965760	2.024240	2.071897	2.101247
1.0899999	1.944803	2.011035	2.073225	2.124169	2.155674
1.1000000	1.987518	2.057586	2.123733	2.178214	2.212056
1.1100000	2.031326	2.105453	2.175825	2.234114	2.270490
1.1200000	2.076258	2.154680	2.229562	2.291953	2.331080
1.1300000	2.122344	2.205311	2.285008	2.351822	2.393939
1.1400000	2.169614	2.257391	2.342230	2.413814	2.459184
1.1500000	2.218098	2.310965	2.401295	2.478028	2.526941
1.1600000	2.267829	2.366079	2.462275	2.544568	2.597343
1.1700000	2.318835	2.422778	2.525242	2.613542	2.670534
1.1800000	2.371147	2.481110	2.590270	2.685064	2.746666
1.1899999	2.424794	2.541121	2.657436	2.759256	2.825901

$\alpha =$ .779999

Θ	K VALUES				
	.794250555	.868696860	.928444378	.971111163	.994996249
.2000000	2.479806	2.602858	2.726817	2.836243	2.908414
.2100000	2.536209	2.666366	2.798494	2.916156	2.994390
.2200000	2.594032	2.731692	2.872546	2.999134	3.084028
.2300000	2.653299	2.798880	2.949058	3.085323	3.177544
.2400000	2.714037	2.867975	3.028112	3.174874	3.275168
.2500000	2.776266	2.939019	3.109791	3.267946	3.377148
.2599999	2.840010	3.012054	3.194181	3.364705	3.483750
.2699999	2.905286	3.087117	3.281364	3.465325	3.595266
.2799999	2.972112	3.164245	3.371425	3.569986	3.712008
.2899999	3.040501	3.243473	3.464443	3.678877	3.834315
.3000000	3.110465	3.324830	3.560501	3.792193	3.962560
.3100000	3.182012	3.408342	3.659674	3.910136	4.097141
1.3200000	3.255146	3.494031	3.762035	4.032913	4.238501
1.3300000	3.329868	3.581915	3.867653	4.160742	4.387121
1.3400000	3.406176	3.672005	3.976591	4.293840	4.543532
1.3500000	3.484062	3.764307	4.088905	4.432432	4.708317
1.3600000	3.563513	3.858821	4.204644	4.576743	4.882120
1.3700000	3.644514	3.955538	4.323846	4.727002	5.065657
1.3799999	3.727043	4.054445	4.446539	4.883431	5.259722
1.3899999	3.811072	4.155516	4.572738	5.046251	5.465200
1.4000000	3.896569	4.258722	4.702445	5.215672	5.683084
1.4100000	3.983496	4.364019	4.835644	5.391886	5.914479
1.4200000	4.071809	4.471359	4.972304	5.575072	6.160632
1.4300000	4.161458	4.580680	5.112374	5.765376	6.422946
1.4400000	4.252389	4.691913	5.255783	5.962911	6.702996
1.4500000	4.344540	4.804977	5.402438	6.167745	7.002553
1.4600000	4.437844	4.919783	5.552223	6.379889	7.323593
1.4700000	4.532229	5.036229	5.704999	6.599288	7.668310
1.4800000	4.627616	5.154206	5.860599	6.825806	8.039096
1.4900000	4.723924	5.273593	6.018836	7.059216	8.438492
1.5000000	4.821064	5.394262	6.179496	7.299191	8.869083
1.5100000	4.918943	5.516074	6.342340	7.545286	9.333264
1.5200000	5.017466	5.638884	6.507107	7.796943	9.832897
1.5300000	5.116532	5.762539	6.673518	8.053485	10.368733
1.5400000	5.216038	5.886880	6.841273	8.314117	10.939650
1.5500000	5.315879	6.011744	7.010057	8.577944	11.541808
1.5600000	5.415947	6.136964	7.179543	8.843981	12.168025
1.5699999	5.516133	6.262369	7.349395	9.111185	12.807863
1.5707963	5.524113	6.272359	7.362927	9.132481	12.859033
1.5707963	5.524106	6.272350	7.362917	9.132469	12.859011

$\alpha =$ .799999

Θ	K VALUES				
	.009966711	.039469502	.087332193	.151646642	.229848846
.0000000	.000000	.000000	.000000	.000000	.000000
.0100000	.010000	.010000	.010000	.010000	.010000
.0200000	.020002	.020002	.020002	.020002	.020002
.0300000	.030007	.030007	.030007	.030007	.030008
.0400000	.040017	.040017	.040018	.040018	.040019
.0500000	.050033	.050034	.050035	.050036	.050038
.0600000	.060058	.060059	.060060	.060063	.060065
.0700000	.070092	.070093	.070096	.070100	.070104
.0800000	.080137	.080140	.080144	.080149	.080156
.0900000	.090196	.090199	.090205	.090213	.090222
.1000000	.100269	.100274	.100282	.100292	.100305
.1100000	.110358	.110364	.110375	.110389	.110407
.1200000	.120465	.120474	.120487	.120506	.120529
.1300000	.130592	.130603	.130620	.130644	.130673
.1400000	.140740	.140753	.140775	.140805	.140841
.1500000	.150911	.150928	.150955	.150991	.151036
.1600000	.161107	.161127	.161160	.161204	.161258
.1700000	.171329	.171353	.171393	.171446	.171511
.1800000	.181579	.181608	.181655	.181718	.181795
.1900000	.191859	.191893	.191948	.192023	.192114
.2000000	.202170	.202210	.202275	.202362	.202468
.2100000	.212515	.212562	.212637	.212738	.212861
.2200000	.222896	.222949	.223035	.223152	.223293
.2300000	.233313	.233374	.233473	.233606	.233768
.2400000	.243770	.243839	.243951	.244103	.244288
.2500000	.254267	.254345	.254472	.254644	.254853
.2600000	.264806	.264895	.265038	.265231	.265468
.2700000	.275391	.275490	.275651	.275868	.276133
.2800000	.286022	.286132	.286312	.286554	.286851
.2900000	.296701	.296824	.297024	.297294	.297624
.3000000	.307431	.307567	.307789	.308089	.308456
.3100000	.318213	.318364	.318610	.318941	.319347
.3200000	.329050	.329216	.329487	.329853	.330300
.3300000	.339944	.340127	.340424	.340826	.341318
.3400000	.350897	.351097	.351423	.351863	.352403
.3500000	.361910	.362129	.362485	.362967	.363558
.3600000	.372987	.373225	.373614	.374140	.374785
.3700000	.384129	.384389	.384812	.385385	.386087
.3800000	.395339	.395621	.396081	.396703	.397466
.3900000	.406619	.406924	.407423	.408097	.408926

$\alpha =$ .799999

Θ	K VALUES				
	.009966711	.039469502	.087332193	.151646642	.229848846
.4000000	.417971	.418301	.418841	.419571	.420467
.4100000	.429398	.429755	.430337	.431126	.432095
.4200000	.440902	.441287	.441914	.442765	.443811
.4300000	.452487	.452900	.453576	.454492	.455618
.4400000	.464153	.464597	.465323	.466308	.467520
.4500000	.475904	.476381	.477160	.478217	.479519
.4600000	.487743	.488254	.489088	.490221	.491618
.4700000	.499672	.500219	.501111	.502324	.503820
.4800000	.511694	.512278	.513232	.514529	.516129
.4900000	.523812	.524435	.525454	.526839	.528549
.5000000	.536029	.536693	.537779	.539256	.541081
.5100000	.548348	.549054	.550211	.551785	.553730
.5200000	.560771	.561522	.562753	.564428	.566499
.5300000	.573302	.574100	.575407	.577188	.579392
.5400000	.585944	.586791	.588179	.590070	.592413
.5500000	.598700	.599598	.601070	.603077	.605565
.5600000	.611574	.612525	.614085	.616213	.618852
.5700000	.624568	.625575	.627226	.629480	.632278
.5800000	.637687	.638752	.640498	.642884	.645846
.5900000	.650934	.652059	.653905	.656427	.659562
.6000000	.664312	.665500	.667449	.670115	.673430
.6100000	.677826	.679078	.681136	.683950	.687453
.6200000	.691478	.692799	.694968	.697937	.701636
.6300000	.705274	.706665	.708950	.712081	.715984
.6400000	.719216	.720680	.723087	.726386	.730501
.6500000	.733309	.734849	.737382	.740856	.745193
.6600000	.747558	.749177	.751841	.755496	.760063
.6700000	.761966	.763667	.766467	.770311	.775118
.6800000	.776538	.778323	.781265	.785305	.790361
.6899999	.791278	.793152	.796239	.800484	.805800
.7000000	.806191	.808157	.811396	.815852	.821438
.7100000	.821282	.823343	.826740	.831415	.837281
.7200000	.836556	.838715	.842275	.847179	.853336
.7300000	.852018	.854278	.858008	.863148	.869608
.7400000	.867672	.870037	.873943	.879329	.886103
.7500000	.883524	.885999	.890086	.895726	.902827
.7600000	.899580	.902167	.906443	.912347	.919786
.7700000	.915845	.918549	.923020	.929197	.936988
.7800000	.932324	.935149	.939822	.946283	.954438
.7899999	.949024	.951974	.956856	.963610	.972144

$\alpha =$ .799999

θ	K VALUES				
	.009966711	.039469502	.087332193	.151646642	.229848846
.8000000	.965950	.969030	.974128	.981186	.990112
.8100000	.983108	.986322	.991644	.999017	1.008350
.8200000	1.000506	1.003858	1.009411	1.017110	1.026865
.8300000	1.018148	1.021643	1.027436	1.035473	1.045664
.8400000	1.036042	1.039685	1.045725	1.054111	1.064756
.8500000	1.054195	1.057990	1.064287	1.073034	1.084147
.8600000	1.072613	1.076566	1.083127	1.092248	1.103848
.8700000	1.091304	1.095419	1.102253	1.111762	1.123864
.8799999	1.110274	1.114558	1.121674	1.131582	1.144206
.8899999	1.129532	1.133989	1.141397	1.151718	1.164882
.9000000	1.149084	1.153720	1.161430	1.172179	1.185901
.9100000	1.168939	1.173760	1.181780	1.192971	1.207271
.9200000	1.189104	1.194115	1.202457	1.214105	1.229003
.9300000	1.209587	1.214796	1.223469	1.235588	1.251106
.9400000	1.230398	1.235809	1.244825	1.257431	1.273589
.9500000	1.251543	1.257164	1.266533	1.279643	1.296463
.9600000	1.273033	1.278869	1.288603	1.302233	1.319737
.9699999	1.294875	1.300934	1.311043	1.325210	1.343423
.9799999	1.317079	1.323367	1.333864	1.348586	1.367530
.9899999	1.339653	1.346178	1.357075	1.372369	1.392069
1.0000000	1.362608	1.369377	1.380686	1.396570	1.417053
1.0100000	1.385952	1.392972	1.404707	1.421200	1.442490
1.0200000	1.409695	1.416973	1.429147	1.446269	1.468393
1.0300000	1.433847	1.441392	1.454017	1.471788	1.494773
1.0400000	1.458417	1.466237	1.479327	1.497767	1.521642
1.0500000	1.483416	1.491518	1.505089	1.524218	1.549012
1.0600000	1.508853	1.517247	1.531311	1.551152	1.576894
1.0699999	1.534740	1.543432	1.558006	1.578580	1.605300
1.0799999	1.561085	1.570086	1.585183	1.606513	1.634242
1.0899999	1.587899	1.597217	1.612854	1.634962	1.663733
1.1000000	1.615192	1.624837	1.641030	1.663940	1.693785
1.1100000	1.642975	1.652956	1.669721	1.693457	1.724409
1.1200000	1.671258	1.681584	1.698937	1.723524	1.755618
1.1300000	1.700051	1.710732	1.728690	1.754152	1.787424
1.1400000	1.729364	1.740410	1.758990	1.785354	1.819838
1.1500000	1.759207	1.770628	1.789848	1.817139	1.852872
1.1600000	1.789590	1.801397	1.821274	1.849519	1.886539
1.1700000	1.820522	1.832724	1.853278	1.882505	1.920848
1.1800000	1.852013	1.864622	1.885870	1.916105	1.955812
1.1899999	1.884071	1.897097	1.919059	1.950331	1.991440

$\alpha =$ .799999

Θ	K VALUES				
	.009966711	.039469502	.087332193	.151646642	.229848846
.2000000	1.916705	1.930160	1.952854	1.985193	2.027744
.2100000	1.949924	1.963819	1.987265	2.020697	2.064732
.2200000	1.983735	1.998080	2.022298	2.056855	2.102414
.2300000	2.018144	2.032953	2.057962	2.093672	2.140798
.2400000	2.053160	2.068442	2.094263	2.131158	2.179892
.2500000	2.088787	2.104555	2.131208	2.169317	2.219702
.2599999	2.125030	2.141296	2.168801	2.208155	2.260236
.2699999	2.161894	2.178669	2.207048	2.247678	2.301497
.2799999	2.199382	2.216678	2.245951	2.287888	2.343490
.2899999	2.237496	2.255325	2.285513	2.328789	2.386217
.3000000	2.276237	2.294612	2.325736	2.370382	2.429680
.3100000	2.315605	2.334538	2.366618	2.412665	2.473878
.3200000	2.355599	2.375101	2.408159	2.455638	2.518811
.3300000	2.396215	2.416298	2.450355	2.499298	2.564474
1.3400000	2.437450	2.458126	2.493202	2.543640	2.610862
1.3500000	2.479298	2.500579	2.536694	2.588657	2.657970
1.3600000	2.521751	2.543649	2.580824	2.634342	2.705789
1.3700000	2.564801	2.587326	2.625581	2.680685	2.754307
1.3799999	2.608436	2.631600	2.670954	2.727673	2.803513
1.3899999	2.652643	2.676457	2.716930	2.775292	2.853390
1.4000000	2.697409	2.721884	2.763494	2.823528	2.903924
1.4100000	2.742716	2.767862	2.810627	2.872360	2.955092
1.4200000	2.788546	2.814374	2.858311	2.921770	3.006875
1.4300000	2.834879	2.861397	2.906525	2.971733	3.059249
1.4400000	2.881693	2.908911	2.955244	3.022227	3.112186
1.4500000	2.928962	2.956889	3.004443	3.073224	3.165659
1.4600000	2.976662	3.005306	3.054094	3.124695	3.219637
1.4700000	3.024763	3.054132	3.104169	3.176609	3.274087
1.4800000	3.073237	3.103337	3.154636	3.228933	3.328974
1.4900000	3.122051	3.152889	3.205460	3.281633	3.384261
1.5000000	3.171173	3.202755	3.256609	3.334673	3.439909
1.5100000	3.220567	3.252899	3.308045	3.388013	3.495877
1.5200000	3.270198	3.303284	3.359730	3.441615	3.552124
1.5300000	3.320029	3.353873	3.411626	3.495437	3.608606
1.5400000	3.370022	3.404627	3.463692	3.549438	3.665277
1.5500000	3.420138	3.455507	3.515887	3.603574	3.722093
1.5600000	3.470337	3.506471	3.568170	3.657802	3.779007
1.5699999	3.520580	3.557479	3.620499	3.712078	3.835972
1.5707963	3.524582	3.561542	3.624667	3.716401	3.840509
1.5707963	3.524579	3.561538	3.624663	3.716397	3.840506

$\alpha =$ .799999

Θ	K VALUES				
	.318821117	.415016431	.514599755	.613601043	.708073407
.0000000	.000000	.000000	.000000	.000000	.000000
.0100000	.010000	.010000	.010000	.010000	.010000
.0200000	.020002	.020002	.020002	.020002	.020003
.0300000	.030008	.030009	.030009	.030009	.030010
.0400000	.040020	.040021	.040022	.040023	.040024
.0500000	.050040	.050042	.050044	.050046	.050048
.0600000	.060069	.060072	.060076	.060079	.060083
.0700000	.070109	.070115	.070121	.070126	.070132
.0800000	.080164	.080172	.080180	.080189	.080197
.0900000	.090233	.090245	.090257	.090269	.090281
.1000000	.100320	.100336	.100353	.100370	.100386
.1100000	.110427	.110448	.110471	.110493	.110514
.1200000	.120555	.120583	.120611	.120640	.120668
.1300000	.130706	.130741	.130778	.130815	.130850
.1400000	.140882	.140927	.140973	.141019	.141063
.1500000	.151086	.151141	.151198	.151255	.151309
.1600000	.161320	.161386	.161456	.161525	.161591
.1700000	.171585	.171665	.171748	.171831	.171910
.1800000	.181883	.181979	.182078	.182176	.182271
.1900000	.192217	.192330	.192447	.192563	.192674
.2000000	.202589	.202721	.202857	.202994	.203124
.2100000	.213001	.213154	.213312	.213471	.213622
.2200000	.223455	.223631	.223814	.223997	.224172
.2300000	.233954	.234155	.234365	.234574	.234775
.2400000	.244499	.244728	.244967	.245206	.245435
.2500000	.255093	.255353	.255624	.255895	.256155
.2600000	.265738	.266031	.266337	.266643	.266937
.2700000	.276436	.276766	.277110	.277454	.277784
.2800000	.287190	.287559	.287944	.288330	.288700
.2900000	.298003	.298414	.298844	.299274	.299687
.3000000	.308875	.309333	.309810	.310289	.310749
.3100000	.319811	.320318	.320847	.321377	.321888
.3200000	.330813	.331372	.331957	.332543	.333108
.3300000	.341882	.342498	.343142	.343789	.344412
.3400000	.353023	.353699	.354407	.355118	.355803
.3500000	.364236	.364977	.365753	.366533	.367285
.3600000	.375526	.376336	.377184	.378037	.378861
.3700000	.386894	.387778	.388703	.389635	.390536
.3800000	.398344	.399306	.400314	.401329	.402311
.3900000	.409879	.410923	.412018	.413123	.414192

$\alpha =$ .799999

Θ	K VALUES				
	.318821117	.415016431	.514599755	.613601043	.708073407
.4000000	.421500	.422632	.423821	.425020	.426182
.4100000	.433212	.434437	.435725	.437025	.438285
.4200000	.445017	.446341	.447733	.449140	.450505
.4300000	.456918	.458346	.459849	.461370	.462846
.4400000	.468919	.470457	.472077	.473718	.475312
.4500000	.481023	.482677	.484421	.486189	.487908
.4600000	.493232	.495009	.496884	.498786	.500638
.4700000	.505551	.507457	.509470	.511515	.513506
.4800000	.517982	.520024	.522184	.524378	.526518
.4900000	.530529	.532715	.535028	.537381	.539678
.5000000	.543197	.545533	.548008	.550528	.552991
.5100000	.555987	.558482	.561128	.563824	.566462
.5200000	.568905	.571567	.574392	.577274	.580097
.5300000	.581954	.584790	.587804	.590882	.593900
.5400000	.595138	.598158	.601370	.604654	.607877
.5500000	.608460	.611673	.615093	.618594	.622034
.5600000	.621926	.625340	.628979	.632708	.636377
.5700000	.635539	.639165	.643033	.647002	.650912
.5800000	.649304	.653151	.657260	.661482	.665645
.5900000	.663224	.667303	.671665	.676152	.680582
.6000000	.677305	.681627	.686254	.691019	.695730
.6100000	.691552	.696127	.701031	.706089	.711096
.6200000	.705968	.710809	.716004	.721368	.726687
.6300000	.720559	.725677	.731177	.736863	.742509
.6400000	.735330	.740738	.746557	.752581	.758571
.6500000	.750286	.755997	.762149	.768528	.774880
.6600000	.765432	.771460	.777961	.784712	.791444
.6700000	.780774	.787132	.793999	.801139	.808271
.6800000	.796318	.803019	.810268	.817817	.825369
.6899999	.812068	.819129	.826777	.834754	.842747
.7000000	.828031	.835467	.843533	.851958	.860415
.7100000	.844213	.852040	.860542	.869438	.878381
.7200000	.860619	.868855	.877813	.887200	.896654
.7300000	.877257	.885918	.895352	.905255	.915245
.7400000	.894133	.903236	.913168	.923610	.934165
.7500000	.911253	.920818	.931269	.942276	.953422
.7600000	.928624	.938670	.949663	.961262	.973028
.7700000	.946254	.956800	.968359	.980576	.992995
.7800000	.964149	.975216	.987366	1.000231	1.013333
.7899999	.982316	.993927	1.006693	1.020235	1.034055

$\alpha =$ •799999

θ	K VALUES				
	•318821117	•415016431	•514599755	•613601043	•708073407
•8000000	1•000765	1•012940	1•026349	1•040600	1•055173
•8100000	1•019501	1•032264	1•046344	1•061336	1•076699
•8200000	1•038533	1•051908	1•066688	1•082455	1•098647
•8300000	1•057870	1•071881	1•087390	1•103968	1•121030
•8400000	1•077519	1•092192	1•108462	1•125888	1•143862
•8500000	1•097490	1•112850	1•129914	1•148226	1•167157
•8600000	1•117791	1•133866	1•151756	1•170995	1•190930
•8700000	1•138430	1•155250	1•174001	1•194208	1•215197
•8799999	1•159418	1•177011	1•196659	1•217879	1•239972
•8899999	1•180764	1•199160	1•219744	1•242021	1•265273
•9000000	1•202478	1•221708	1•243266	1•266649	1•291115
•9100000	1•224569	1•244666	1•267239	1•291777	1•317516
•9200000	1•247047	1•268045	1•291674	1•317419	1•344494
•9300000	1•269923	1•291857	1•316586	1•343591	1•372067
•9400000	1•293208	1•316113	1•341988	1•370309	1•400253
•9500000	1•316912	1•340825	1•367892	1•397588	1•429072
•9600000	1•341047	1•366006	1•394315	1•425446	1•458543
•9699999	1•365623	1•391669	1•421269	1•453899	1•488688
•9799999	1•390653	1•417825	1•448769	1•482964	1•519525
•9899999	1•416147	1•444489	1•476830	1•512658	1•551077
1•0000000	1•442119	1•471674	1•505469	1•543001	1•583367
1•0100000	1•468579	1•499392	1•534699	1•574009	1•616415
1•0200000	1•495541	1•527658	1•564536	1•605702	1•650245
1•0300000	1•523016	1•556485	1•594998	1•638098	1•684880
1•0400000	1•551017	1•585888	1•626099	1•671218	1•720344
1•0500000	1•579558	1•615881	1•657857	1•705080	1•756661
1•0600000	1•608651	1•646479	1•690287	1•739704	1•793857
1•0699999	1•638308	1•677695	1•723408	1•775111	1•831956
1•0799999	1•668544	1•709545	1•757235	1•811321	1•870983
1•0899999	1•699372	1•742044	1•791787	1•848355	1•910964
1•1000000	1•730804	1•775206	1•827080	1•886233	1•951927
1•1100000	1•762854	1•809046	1•863130	1•924976	1•993895
1•1200000	1•795535	1•843579	1•899957	1•964604	2•036897
1•1300000	1•828860	1•878820	1•937575	2•005139	2•080959
1•1400000	1•862842	1•914783	1•976004	2•046601	2•126107
1•1500000	1•897493	1•951482	2•015258	2•089010	2•172367
1•1600000	1•932828	1•988932	2•055356	2•132388	2•219767
1•1700000	1•968857	2•027147	2•096312	2•176753	2•268332
1•1800000	2•005594	2•066140	2•138144	2•222126	2•318087
1•1899999	2•043049	2•105925	2•180866	2•268526	2•369059

$\alpha =$ .799999

Θ	K VALUES				
	.318821117	.415016431	.514599755	.613601043	.708073407
.2000000	2.081233	2.146514	2.224494	2.315971	2.421272
.2100000	2.120158	2.187918	2.269041	2.364478	2.474748
.2200000	2.159833	2.230150	2.314520	2.414065	2.529512
.2300000	2.200268	2.273220	2.360946	2.464747	2.585584
.2400000	2.241471	2.317138	2.408327	2.516539	2.642985
.2500000	2.283450	2.361911	2.456677	2.569454	2.701735
.2599999	2.326210	2.407548	2.506002	2.623504	2.761849
.2699999	2.369759	2.454056	2.556312	2.678701	2.823345
.2799999	2.414099	2.501438	2.607613	2.735051	2.886233
.2899999	2.459235	2.549699	2.659908	2.792563	2.950527
.3000000	2.505168	2.598842	2.713203	2.851240	3.016234
.3100000	2.551897	2.648865	2.767495	2.911085	3.083358
.3200000	2.599421	2.699768	2.822785	2.972097	3.151904
.3300000	2.647737	2.751546	2.879069	3.034273	3.221869
.3400000	2.696839	2.804195	2.936342	3.097608	3.293249
.3500000	2.746721	2.857706	2.994594	3.162093	3.366036
.3600000	2.797373	2.912071	3.053816	3.227716	3.440219
.3700000	2.848783	2.967275	3.113992	3.294462	3.515780
.3799999	2.900938	3.023304	3.175107	3.362311	3.592698
.3899999	2.953822	3.080140	3.237141	3.431243	3.670949
.4000000	3.007417	3.137765	3.300071	3.501230	3.750503
.4100000	3.061700	3.196153	3.363870	3.572243	3.831323
.4200000	3.116650	3.255279	3.428511	3.644248	3.913371
.4300000	3.172240	3.315115	3.493960	3.717208	3.996601
.4400000	3.228442	3.375629	3.560183	3.791081	4.080964
.4500000	3.285224	3.436787	3.627140	3.865822	4.166405
.4600000	3.342555	3.498553	3.694789	3.941382	4.252863
.4700000	3.400397	3.560887	3.763087	4.017709	4.340276
.4800000	3.458713	3.623746	3.831984	4.094745	4.428572
.4900000	3.517463	3.687087	3.901430	4.172432	4.517679
1.5000000	3.576606	3.750863	3.971373	4.250707	4.607519
1.5100000	3.636095	3.815025	4.041756	4.329503	4.698010
1.5200000	3.695887	3.879521	4.112522	4.408753	4.789068
1.5300000	3.755933	3.944300	4.183610	4.488385	4.880603
1.5400000	3.816186	4.009308	4.254959	4.568327	4.972525
1.5500000	3.876595	4.074490	4.326507	4.648504	5.064742
1.5600000	3.937110	4.139789	4.398189	4.728841	5.157159
1.5699999	3.997681	4.205151	4.469942	4.809261	5.249679
1.5707963	4.002505	4.210356	4.475657	4.815667	5.257049
1.5707963	4.002502	4.210353	4.475654	4.815665	5.257050

$\alpha =$ .799999

Θ	K VALUES				
	.794250555	.868696860	.928444378	.971111163	.994996249
.0000000	.000000	.000000	.000000	.000000	.000000
.0100000	.010000	.010000	.010000	.010000	.010000
.0200000	.020003	.020003	.020003	.020003	.020003
.0300000	.030010	.030011	.030011	.030011	.030011
.0400000	.040025	.040026	.040027	.040027	.040027
.0500000	.050049	.050051	.050052	.050053	.050054
.0600000	.060086	.060089	.060091	.060092	.060093
.0700000	.070137	.070141	.070144	.070147	.070148
.0800000	.080204	.080211	.080216	.080220	.080222
.0900000	.090291	.090301	.090308	.090313	.090316
.1000000	.100400	.100413	.100423	.100430	.100434
.1100000	.110533	.110550	.110563	.110573	.110578
.1200000	.120693	.120715	.120732	.120745	.120752
.1300000	.130882	.130910	.130932	.130948	.130957
.1400000	.141103	.141138	.141166	.141186	.141197
.1500000	.151358	.151401	.151436	.151460	.151474
.1600000	.161651	.161703	.161745	.161775	.161792
.1700000	.171983	.172046	.172096	.172132	.172152
.1800000	.182357	.182432	.182492	.182535	.182559
.1900000	.192776	.192865	.192936	.192987	.193015
.2000000	.203243	.203347	.203430	.203490	.203523
.2100000	.213761	.213881	.213978	.214047	.214086
.2200000	.224332	.224471	.224583	.224663	.224707
.2300000	.234959	.235118	.235247	.235339	.235390
.2400000	.245645	.245827	.245974	.246079	.246138
.2500000	.256393	.256600	.256767	.256886	.256953
.2600000	.267206	.267440	.267629	.267764	.267840
.2700000	.278088	.278351	.278564	.278716	.278801
.2800000	.289040	.289336	.289574	.289745	.289841
.2900000	.300067	.300398	.300664	.300855	.300963
.3000000	.311172	.311540	.311837	.312050	.312170
.3100000	.322358	.322766	.323096	.323333	.323466
.3200000	.333628	.334080	.334446	.334708	.334855
.3300000	.344985	.345485	.345889	.346179	.346342
.3400000	.356435	.356985	.357430	.357750	.357929
.3500000	.367979	.368584	.369073	.369425	.369622
.3600000	.379622	.380285	.380822	.381207	.381424
.3700000	.391367	.392093	.392680	.393103	.393341
.3800000	.403219	.404011	.404653	.405115	.405375
.3900000	.415180	.416044	.416745	.417249	.417532

$\alpha =$ .799999

Θ	*K* VALUES				
	.794250555	.868696860	.928444378	.971111163	.994996249
.4000000	.427257	.428197	.428959	.429508	.429817
.4100000	.439452	.440473	.441302	.441899	.442235
.4200000	.451769	.452877	.453777	.454425	.454790
.4300000	.464214	.465414	.466389	.467092	.467488
.4400000	.476791	.478089	.479144	.479906	.480335
.4500000	.489504	.490906	.492047	.492870	.493334
.4600000	.502359	.503871	.505103	.505992	.506494
.4700000	.515359	.516989	.518317	.519277	.519818
.4800000	.528511	.530266	.531696	.532730	.533314
.4900000	.541819	.543706	.545245	.546359	.546988
.5000000	.555289	.557315	.558971	.560169	.560845
.5100000	.568926	.571101	.572879	.574166	.574894
.5200000	.582736	.585068	.586976	.588358	.589140
.5300000	.596724	.599223	.601268	.602752	.603591
.5400000	.610898	.613572	.615764	.617355	.618255
.5500000	.625262	.628122	.630469	.632174	.633139
.5600000	.639823	.642881	.645392	.647217	.648251
.5700000	.654589	.657855	.660539	.662492	.663599
.5800000	.669565	.673051	.675920	.678008	.679193
.5900000	.684759	.688478	.691541	.693774	.695040
.6000000	.700178	.704143	.707413	.709797	.711151
.6100000	.715829	.720055	.723543	.726089	.727535
.6200000	.731721	.736221	.739940	.742657	.744202
.6300000	.747861	.752651	.756615	.759513	.761162
.6400000	.764257	.769354	.773576	.776667	.778427
.6500000	.780919	.786339	.790835	.794130	.796007
.6600000	.797854	.803616	.808402	.811913	.813914
.6700000	.815072	.821195	.826287	.830028	.832161
.6800000	.832582	.839086	.844503	.848486	.850760
.6899999	.850395	.857301	.863062	.867302	.869725
.7000000	.868520	.875851	.881975	.886488	.889069
.7100000	.886967	.894747	.901255	.906058	.908807
.7200000	.905747	.914001	.920916	.926027	.928953
.7300000	.924872	.933626	.940972	.946409	.949525
.7400000	.944353	.953635	.961438	.967220	.970537
.7500000	.964202	.974041	.982328	.988476	.992008
.7600000	.984432	.994859	1.003657	1.010195	1.013954
.7700000	1.005054	1.016104	1.025443	1.032395	1.036396
.7800000	1.026083	1.037789	1.047703	1.055093	1.059351
.7899999	1.047532	1.059931	1.070453	1.078310	1.082842

$\alpha =$ .799999

Θ	K VALUES				
	.794250555	.868696860	.928444378	.971111163	.994996249
.8000000	1.069415	1.082547	1.093713	1.102065	1.106889
.8100000	1.091747	1.105653	1.117502	1.126381	1.131515
.8200000	1.114543	1.129267	1.141840	1.151278	1.156743
.8300000	1.137819	1.153407	1.166747	1.176781	1.182598
.8400000	1.161590	1.178091	1.192246	1.202913	1.209106
.8500000	1.185875	1.203341	1.218359	1.229700	1.236294
.8600000	1.210690	1.229176	1.245110	1.257168	1.264190
.8700000	1.236054	1.255618	1.272524	1.285346	1.292824
.8799999	1.261984	1.282688	1.300627	1.314262	1.322227
.8899999	1.288501	1.310410	1.329444	1.343947	1.352434
.9000000	1.315624	1.338808	1.359006	1.374433	1.383477
.9100000	1.343374	1.367905	1.389340	1.405754	1.415393
.9200000	1.371772	1.397729	1.420478	1.437944	1.448221
.9300000	1.400840	1.428305	1.452451	1.471040	1.482000
.9400000	1.430601	1.459662	1.485293	1.505082	1.516774
.9500000	1.461078	1.491828	1.519039	1.540110	1.552586
.9600000	1.492295	1.524833	1.553724	1.576166	1.589484
.9699999	1.524278	1.558709	1.589388	1.613295	1.627517
.9799999	1.557052	1.593486	1.626069	1.651544	1.666738
.9899999	1.590643	1.629198	1.663809	1.690964	1.707201
1.0000000	1.625079	1.665881	1.702651	1.731604	1.748965
1.0100000	1.660388	1.703568	1.742640	1.773521	1.792090
1.0200000	1.696599	1.742298	1.783822	1.816771	1.836642
1.0300000	1.733741	1.782109	1.826248	1.861414	1.882690
1.0400000	1.771844	1.823039	1.869967	1.907514	1.930306
1.0500000	1.810940	1.865130	1.915033	1.955138	1.979566
1.0600000	1.851061	1.908424	1.961501	2.004355	2.030552
1.0699999	1.892238	1.952964	2.009430	2.055239	2.083350
1.0799999	1.934506	1.998794	2.058878	2.107868	2.138051
1.0899999	1.977898	2.045961	2.109909	2.162324	2.194752
1.1000000	2.022449	2.094511	2.162588	2.218692	2.253556
1.1100000	2.068193	2.144494	2.216981	2.277061	2.314572
1.1200000	2.115165	2.195957	2.273159	2.337528	2.377915
1.1300000	2.163403	2.248952	2.331194	2.400192	2.443709
1.1400000	2.212941	2.303531	2.391162	2.465159	2.512084
1.1500000	2.263816	2.359746	2.453140	2.532539	2.583182
1.1600000	2.316065	2.417651	2.517208	2.602448	2.657150
1.1700000	2.369724	2.477299	2.583449	2.675009	2.734147
1.1800000	2.424829	2.538746	2.651950	2.750351	2.814344
1.1899999	2.481417	2.602045	2.722796	2.828609	2.897922

$\alpha =$ .799999

Θ	K VALUES				
	.794250555	.868696860	.928444378	.971111163	.994996249
1.2000000	2.539522	2.667254	2.796080	2.909925	2.985075
1.2100000	2.599179	2.734426	2.871891	2.994449	3.076011
1.2200000	2.660422	2.803617	2.950325	3.082336	3.170953
1.2300000	2.723284	2.874880	3.031477	3.173752	3.270140
1.2400000	2.787797	2.948269	3.115444	3.268869	3.373832
1.2500000	2.853989	3.023837	3.202324	3.367867	3.482305
1.2599999	2.921888	3.101633	3.292216	3.470935	3.595859
1.2699999	2.991521	3.181707	3.385219	3.578271	3.714818
1.2799999	3.062911	3.264103	3.481430	3.690080	3.839532
1.2899999	3.136077	3.348864	3.580946	3.806577	3.970383
1.3000000	3.211037	3.436031	3.683863	3.927986	4.107786
1.3100000	3.287804	3.525636	3.790272	4.054534	4.252187
1.3200000	3.366388	3.617711	3.900261	4.186461	4.404082
1.3300000	3.446794	3.712280	4.013913	4.324013	4.564007
1.3400000	3.529024	3.809361	4.131305	4.467441	4.732557
1.3500000	3.613072	3.908967	4.252507	4.616999	4.910381
1.3600000	3.698930	4.011101	4.377578	4.772947	5.098199
1.3700000	3.786582	4.115760	4.506568	4.935544	5.296808
1.3799999	3.876007	4.222932	4.639513	5.105045	5.507090
1.3899999	3.967177	4.332593	4.776438	5.281703	5.730033
1.4000000	4.060060	4.444713	4.917349	5.465758	5.966737
1.4100000	4.154612	4.559247	5.062232	5.657430	6.218430
1.4200000	4.250786	4.676142	5.211057	5.856923	6.486497
1.4300000	4.348528	4.795331	5.363771	6.064406	6.772491
1.4400000	4.447775	4.916737	5.520297	6.280009	7.078156
1.4500000	4.548459	5.040271	5.680531	6.503809	7.405451
1.4600000	4.650502	5.165830	5.844346	6.735824	7.756563
1.4700000	4.753821	5.293299	6.011583	6.975991	8.133912
1.4800000	4.858326	5.422553	6.182057	7.224161	8.540141
1.4900000	4.963921	5.553452	6.355552	7.480079	8.978053
1.5000000	5.070502	5.685850	6.531828	7.743379	9.450497
1.5100000	5.177961	5.819584	6.710609	8.013560	9.960110
1.5200000	5.286184	5.954485	6.891600	8.289996	10.508938
1.5300000	5.395053	6.090377	7.074478	8.571924	11.097800
1.5400000	5.504446	6.227072	7.258901	8.858452	11.725443
1.5500000	5.614238	6.364381	7.444506	9.148573	12.387616
1.5600000	5.724300	6.502107	7.630919	9.441180	13.076375
1.5699999	5.834503	6.640050	7.817754	9.735099	13.780183
1.5707963	5.843281	6.651038	7.832639	9.758525	13.836470
1.5707963	5.843322	6.651032	7.832631	9.758515	13.836451

$\alpha =$ .809999

Θ	K VALUES				
	.009966711	.039469502	.087332193	.151646642	.229848846
.0000000	.000000	.000000	.000000	.000000	.000000
.0100000	.010000	.010000	.010000	.010000	.010000
.0200000	.020002	.020002	.020002	.020002	.020002
.0300000	.030007	.030007	.030007	.030007	.030008
.0400000	.040017	.040017	.040018	.040018	.040019
.0500000	.050034	.050034	.050035	.050036	.050038
.0600000	.060058	.060059	.060061	.060063	.060066
.0700000	.070093	.070095	.070097	.070101	.070105
.0800000	.080139	.080141	.080146	.080151	.080158
.0900000	.090198	.090202	.090207	.090215	.090225
.1000000	.100272	.100277	.100285	.100296	.100309
.1100000	.110362	.110369	.110380	.110394	.110411
.1200000	.120471	.120479	.120493	.120512	.120535
.1300000	.130599	.130610	.130628	.130651	.130680
.1400000	.140749	.140763	.140785	.140814	.140850
.1500000	.150922	.150939	.150966	.151003	.151047
.1600000	.161120	.161141	.161174	.161218	.161272
.1700000	.171345	.171370	.171409	.171463	.171527
.1800000	.181599	.181628	.181675	.181738	.181815
.1900000	.191882	.191916	.191972	.192046	.192137
.2000000	.202198	.202238	.202302	.202390	.202496
.2100000	.212547	.212594	.212669	.212770	.212893
.2200000	.222933	.222986	.223072	.223189	.223330
.2300000	.233355	.233416	.233515	.233648	.233811
.2400000	.243818	.243887	.243999	.244151	.244336
.2500000	.254321	.254400	.254527	.254699	.254908
.2600000	.264868	.264956	.265100	.265293	.265530
.2700000	.275460	.275559	.275720	.275937	.276203
.2800000	.286099	.286210	.286390	.286633	.286929
.2900000	.296788	.296911	.297111	.297381	.297712
.3000000	.307527	.307664	.307886	.308186	.308553
.3100000	.318320	.318471	.318717	.319048	.319454
.3200000	.329169	.329335	.329606	.329971	.330419
.3300000	.340074	.340257	.340555	.340957	.341449
.3400000	.351040	.351240	.351567	.352008	.352548
.3500000	.362067	.362286	.362643	.363126	.363717
.3600000	.373159	.373398	.373787	.374313	.374959
.3700000	.384317	.384577	.385000	.385574	.386277
.3800000	.395544	.395826	.396286	.396909	.397673
.3900000	.406842	.407147	.407646	.408321	.409151

$\alpha =$ .809999

Θ	K VALUES				
	.009966711	.039469502	.087332193	.151646642	.229848846
.4000000	.418213	.418544	.419083	.419814	.420712
.4100000	.429660	.430017	.430600	.431390	.432360
.4200000	.441186	.441571	.442199	.443051	.444098
.4300000	.452793	.453207	.453884	.454800	.455929
.4400000	.464484	.464929	.465655	.466641	.467855
.4500000	.476261	.476738	.477518	.478576	.479880
.4600000	.488127	.488638	.489474	.490608	.492007
.4700000	.500084	.500631	.501526	.502740	.504238
.4800000	.512137	.512721	.513677	.514976	.516579
.4900000	.524287	.524911	.525931	.527318	.529030
.5000000	.536537	.537202	.538290	.539770	.541597
.5100000	.548891	.549599	.550758	.552334	.554283
.5200000	.561352	.562105	.563337	.565015	.567091
.5300000	.573923	.574723	.576032	.577816	.580025
.5400000	.586606	.587455	.588846	.590741	.593088
.5500000	.599406	.600306	.601781	.603793	.606285
.5600000	.612326	.613280	.614842	.616975	.619620
.5700000	.625369	.626378	.628033	.630292	.633096
.5800000	.638539	.639606	.641357	.643748	.646717
.5900000	.651840	.652967	.654817	.657346	.660489
.6000000	.665274	.666465	.668419	.671091	.674415
.6100000	.678847	.680103	.682165	.684987	.688499
.6200000	.692562	.693886	.696061	.699038	.702747
.6300000	.706422	.707817	.710109	.713249	.717163
.6400000	.720433	.721902	.724316	.727624	.731752
.6500000	.734599	.736143	.738684	.742168	.746518
.6600000	.748923	.750547	.753219	.756886	.761468
.6700000	.763410	.765116	.767925	.771782	.776605
.6800000	.778065	.779857	.782808	.786862	.791936
.6899999	.792893	.794773	.797872	.802131	.807465
.7000000	.807898	.809870	.813122	.817594	.823200
.7100000	.823085	.825153	.828563	.833256	.839144
.7200000	.838459	.840626	.844201	.849123	.855305
.7300000	.854027	.856296	.860041	.865202	.871688
.7400000	.869791	.872167	.876089	.881497	.888299
.7500000	.885760	.888245	.892350	.898015	.905146
.7600000	.901937	.904536	.908831	.914761	.922234
.7700000	.918329	.921046	.925538	.931744	.939570
.7800000	.934942	.937781	.942476	.948968	.957162
.7899999	.951782	.954747	.959653	.966441	.975016

$\alpha =$ .809999

Θ	K VALUES				
	.009966711	.039469502	.087332193	.151646642	.229848846
.8000000	.968855	.971951	.977075	.984169	.993141
.8100000	.986168	.989398	.994748	1.002160	1.011542
.8200000	1.003727	1.007097	1.012680	1.020421	1.030229
.8300000	1.021538	1.025052	1.030878	1.038959	1.049208
.8400000	1.039610	1.043273	1.049348	1.057783	1.068489
.8500000	1.057948	1.061766	1.068099	1.076899	1.088079
.8600000	1.076561	1.080538	1.087139	1.096316	1.107987
.8700000	1.095456	1.099597	1.106474	1.116042	1.128223
.8799999	1.114640	1.118951	1.126114	1.136086	1.148794
.8899999	1.134121	1.138608	1.146066	1.156457	1.169710
.9000000	1.153909	1.158576	1.166339	1.177163	1.190981
.9100000	1.174009	1.178864	1.186942	1.198213	1.212617
.9200000	1.194432	1.199480	1.207883	1.219617	1.234626
.9300000	1.215186	1.220433	1.229173	1.241384	1.257021
.9400000	1.236280	1.241733	1.250819	1.263524	1.279810
.9500000	1.257722	1.263388	1.272832	1.286048	1.303005
.9600000	1.279523	1.285407	1.295221	1.308965	1.326616
.9699999	1.301691	1.307801	1.317997	1.332285	1.350656
.9799999	1.324237	1.330580	1.341169	1.356021	1.375134
.9899999	1.347169	1.353753	1.364749	1.380181	1.400063
1.0000000	1.370500	1.377331	1.388746	1.404779	1.425454
1.0100000	1.394237	1.401324	1.413171	1.429824	1.451320
1.0200000	1.418392	1.425742	1.438036	1.455328	1.477673
1.0300000	1.442976	1.450598	1.463351	1.481303	1.504526
1.0400000	1.468000	1.475900	1.489128	1.507762	1.531890
1.0500000	1.493473	1.501662	1.515378	1.534715	1.559779
1.0600000	1.519408	1.527893	1.542114	1.562175	1.588206
1.0699999	1.545815	1.554606	1.569346	1.590155	1.617184
1.0799999	1.572706	1.581812	1.597086	1.618667	1.646727
1.0899999	1.600092	1.609522	1.625348	1.647724	1.676847
1.1000000	1.627985	1.637749	1.654142	1.677337	1.707558
1.1100000	1.656396	1.666503	1.683481	1.707521	1.738874
1.1200000	1.685336	1.695797	1.713376	1.738287	1.770809
1.1300000	1.714818	1.725641	1.743840	1.769647	1.803374
1.1400000	1.744851	1.756049	1.774885	1.801616	1.836585
1.1500000	1.775448	1.787031	1.806523	1.834205	1.870455
1.1600000	1.806620	1.818598	1.838765	1.867426	1.904996
1.1700000	1.838378	1.850762	1.871624	1.901292	1.940221
1.1800000	1.870732	1.883534	1.905109	1.935814	1.976144
1.1899999	1.903694	1.916925	1.939234	1.971005	2.012776

$\alpha =$ .809999

Θ	K VALUES				
	.009966711	.039469502	.087332193	.151646642	.229848846
1.2000000	1.937273	1.950945	1.974007	2.006874	2.050130
1.2100000	1.971478	1.985603	2.009439	2.043434	2.088217
1.2200000	2.006319	2.020909	2.045540	2.080693	2.127047
1.2300000	2.041805	2.056871	2.082319	2.118662	2.166631
1.2400000	2.077943	2.093499	2.119785	2.157349	2.206979
1.2500000	2.114742	2.130799	2.157944	2.196763	2.248099
1.2599999	2.152207	2.168778	2.196805	2.236911	2.289998
1.2699999	2.190343	2.207442	2.236372	2.277798	2.332684
1.2799999	2.229156	2.246795	2.276650	2.319430	2.376161
1.2899999	2.268650	2.286841	2.317644	2.361811	2.420435
1.3000000	2.308825	2.327582	2.359356	2.404943	2.465507
1.3100000	2.349684	2.369019	2.401786	2.448827	2.511379
1.3200000	2.391225	2.411152	2.444935	2.493464	2.558050
1.3300000	2.433448	2.453978	2.488799	2.538850	2.605518
1.3400000	2.476347	2.497495	2.533376	2.584981	2.653780
1.3500000	2.519919	2.541696	2.578660	2.631853	2.702828
1.3600000	2.564155	2.586575	2.624643	2.679458	2.752656
1.3700000	2.609048	2.632122	2.671316	2.727784	2.803251
1.3799999	2.654585	2.678327	2.718668	2.776821	2.854602
1.3899999	2.700755	2.725175	2.766684	2.826554	2.906693
1.4000000	2.747541	2.772652	2.815350	2.876967	2.959508
1.4100000	2.794927	2.820740	2.864645	2.928039	3.013024
1.4200000	2.842892	2.869418	2.914550	2.979750	3.067219
1.4300000	2.891415	2.918664	2.965043	3.032075	3.122068
1.4400000	2.940472	2.968454	3.016096	3.084989	3.177542
1.4500000	2.990036	3.018762	3.067684	3.138461	3.233611
1.4600000	3.040079	3.069557	3.119775	3.192461	3.290241
1.4700000	3.090570	3.120809	3.172338	3.246954	3.347396
1.4800000	3.141476	3.172484	3.225337	3.301905	3.405037
1.4900000	3.192763	3.224546	3.278737	3.357275	3.463125
1.5000000	3.244394	3.276960	3.332498	3.413024	3.521616
1.5100000	3.296330	3.329683	3.386580	3.469109	3.580464
1.5200000	3.348531	3.382678	3.440942	3.525486	3.639623
1.5300000	3.400956	3.435900	3.495539	3.582109	3.699045
1.5400000	3.453563	3.489307	3.550327	3.638933	3.758679
1.5500000	3.506307	3.542855	3.605259	3.695908	3.818474
1.5600000	3.559145	3.596498	3.660290	3.752986	3.878380
1.5699999	3.612031	3.650190	3.715372	3.810118	3.938342
1.5707963	3.616243	3.654466	3.719760	3.814669	3.943118
1.5707963	3.616240	3.654463	3.719756	3.814666	3.943114

$\alpha =$ .809999

Θ	K VALUES				
	.318821117	.415016431	.514599755	.613601043	.708073407
.0000000	.000000	.000000	.000000	.000000	.000000
.0100000	.010000	.010000	.010000	.010000	.010000
.0200000	.020002	.020002	.020002	.020002	.020003
.0300000	.030008	.030009	.030009	.030010	.030010
.0400000	.040020	.040021	.040022	.040023	.040024
.0500000	.050040	.050042	.050044	.050046	.050048
.0600000	.060069	.060073	.060076	.060080	.060083
.0700000	.070111	.070116	.070122	.070127	.070133
.0800000	.080165	.080174	.080182	.080191	.080199
.0900000	.090236	.090247	.090260	.090272	.090283
.1000000	.100324	.100340	.100356	.100373	.100389
.1100000	.110431	.110453	.110475	.110497	.110518
.1200000	.120560	.120588	.120617	.120646	.120674
.1300000	.130713	.130749	.130786	.130822	.130858
.1400000	.140892	.140936	.140982	.141028	.141072
.1500000	.151098	.151153	.151210	.151266	.151320
.1600000	.161334	.161400	.161470	.161539	.161605
.1700000	.171601	.171682	.171765	.171848	.171927
.1800000	.181903	.181999	.182098	.182196	.182291
.1900000	.192241	.192353	.192470	.192587	.192698
.2000000	.202617	.202748	.202885	.203021	.203152
.2100000	.213033	.213186	.213345	.213503	.213654
.2200000	.223492	.223668	.223851	.224034	.224209
.2300000	.233996	.234198	.234408	.234617	.234818
.2400000	.244547	.244777	.245016	.245255	.245484
.2500000	.255148	.255408	.255679	.255950	.256210
.2600000	.265800	.266094	.266400	.266706	.267000
.2700000	.276506	.276836	.277180	.277524	.277855
.2800000	.287269	.287638	.288023	.288409	.288779
.2900000	.298090	.298502	.298931	.299362	.299776
.3000000	.308973	.309430	.309908	.310387	.310847
.3100000	.319919	.320426	.320955	.321486	.321997
.3200000	.330932	.331492	.332077	.332664	.333229
.3300000	.342014	.342630	.343275	.343922	.344545
.3400000	.353168	.353845	.354553	.355264	.355950
.3500000	.364395	.365137	.365913	.366694	.367447
.3600000	.375700	.376511	.377360	.378214	.379038
.3700000	.387085	.387969	.388895	.389828	.390729
.3800000	.398552	.399514	.400523	.401540	.402523
.3900000	.410105	.411150	.412246	.413352	.414422

$\alpha =$ •809999

Θ	K VALUES				
	•318821117	•415016431	•514599755	•613601043	•708073407
•4000000	•421746	•422879	•424069	•425270	•426432
•4100000	•433478	•434705	•435994	•437295	•438557
•4200000	•445305	•446630	•448024	•449433	•450800
•4300000	•457230	•458660	•460165	•461687	•463165
•4400000	•469256	•470796	•472418	•474061	•475657
•4500000	•481386	•483042	•484789	•486559	•488280
•4600000	•493623	•495402	•497280	•499185	•501039
•4700000	•505971	•507880	•509897	•511944	•513939
•4800000	•518434	•520479	•522642	•524840	•526983
•4900000	•531014	•533204	•535521	•537877	•540178
•5000000	•543717	•546057	•548537	•551061	•553528
•5100000	•556544	•559044	•561694	•564395	•567038
•5200000	•569501	•572168	•574998	•577885	•580713
•5300000	•582591	•585433	•588453	•591536	•594560
•5400000	•595818	•598844	•602063	•605353	•608583
•5500000	•609187	•612406	•615833	•619342	•622789
•5600000	•622701	•626122	•629769	•633507	•637184
•5700000	•636364	•639998	•643876	•647854	•651773
•5800000	•650183	•654039	•658158	•662389	•666563
•5900000	•664160	•668249	•672621	•677119	•681560
•6000000	•678300	•682633	•687271	•692049	•696773
•6100000	•692609	•697196	•702114	•707185	•712206
•6200000	•707091	•711945	•717155	•722534	•727867
•6300000	•721751	•726884	•732400	•738103	•743765
•6400000	•736595	•742019	•747855	•753898	•759906
•6500000	•751627	•757356	•763527	•769926	•776298
•6600000	•766854	•772900	•779423	•786195	•792950
•6700000	•782280	•788659	•795549	•802713	•809869
•6800000	•797912	•804637	•811911	•819487	•827065
•6899999	•813756	•820843	•828518	•836524	•844546
•7000000	•829817	•837281	•845377	•853834	•862323
•7100000	•846102	•853959	•862494	•871424	•880403
•7200000	•862617	•870885	•879879	•889304	•898797
•7300000	•879368	•888064	•897538	•907482	•917515
•7400000	•896363	•905505	•915480	•925967	•936568
•7500000	•913609	•923216	•933713	•944770	•955966
•7600000	•931112	•941203	•952247	•963899	•975721
•7700000	•948879	•959475	•971090	•983366	•995845
•7800000	•966919	•978041	•990251	1•003180	1•016348
•7899999	•985240	•996909	1•009740	1•023352	1•037244

$\alpha =$ .809999

Θ	K VALUES				
	.318821117	.415016431	.514599755	.613601043	.708073407
.8000000	1.003848	1.016087	1.029567	1.043893	1.058545
.8100000	1.022753	1.035584	1.049741	1.064816	1.080264
.8200000	1.041961	1.055410	1.070273	1.086130	1.102416
.8300000	1.061483	1.075575	1.091174	1.107850	1.125013
.8400000	1.081327	1.096087	1.112455	1.129986	1.148071
.8500000	1.101502	1.116957	1.134126	1.152553	1.171605
.8600000	1.122018	1.138195	1.156199	1.175563	1.195629
.8700000	1.142883	1.159812	1.178687	1.199029	1.220161
.8799999	1.164107	1.181818	1.201601	1.222967	1.245215
.8899999	1.185701	1.204225	1.224953	1.247390	1.270810
.9000000	1.207676	1.227044	1.248758	1.272314	1.296963
.9100000	1.230040	1.250286	1.273028	1.297753	1.323691
.9200000	1.252806	1.273964	1.297776	1.323723	1.351014
.9300000	1.275984	1.298090	1.323017	1.350240	1.378951
.9400000	1.299586	1.322676	1.348764	1.377322	1.407521
.9500000	1.323623	1.347736	1.375032	1.404984	1.436744
.9600000	1.348107	1.373281	1.401837	1.433246	1.466642
.9699999	1.373051	1.399327	1.429194	1.462123	1.497236
.9799999	1.398465	1.425886	1.457117	1.491635	1.528549
.9899999	1.424365	1.452973	1.485624	1.521801	1.560602
1.0000000	1.450761	1.480602	1.514731	1.552640	1.593419
1.0100000	1.477667	1.508788	1.544453	1.584171	1.627024
1.0200000	1.505097	1.537544	1.574809	1.616414	1.661442
1.0300000	1.533064	1.566888	1.605816	1.649390	1.696697
1.0400000	1.561581	1.596833	1.637490	1.683120	1.732815
1.0500000	1.590664	1.627395	1.669851	1.717625	1.769822
1.0600000	1.620325	1.658591	1.702916	1.752927	1.807744
1.0699999	1.650580	1.690436	1.736703	1.789047	1.846610
1.0799999	1.681443	1.722946	1.771232	1.826007	1.886446
1.0899999	1.712928	1.756138	1.806521	1.863831	1.927281
1.1000000	1.745050	1.790029	1.842588	1.902540	1.969142
1.1100000	1.777824	1.824633	1.879453	1.942158	2.012059
1.1200000	1.811264	1.859969	1.917135	1.982708	2.056060
1.1300000	1.845386	1.896052	1.955653	2.024211	2.101175
1.1400000	1.880203	1.932898	1.995026	2.066692	2.147433
1.1500000	1.915731	1.970525	2.035273	2.110174	2.194863
1.1600000	1.951983	2.008948	2.076412	2.154678	2.243494
1.1700000	1.988975	2.048184	2.118462	2.200228	2.293355
1.1800000	2.026719	2.088246	2.161441	2.246846	2.344476
1.1899999	2.065229	2.129152	2.205367	2.294553	2.396883

$\alpha =$ .809999

Θ	K VALUES				
	.318821117	.415016431	.514599755	.613601043	.708073407
1.2000000	2.104518	2.170915	2.250257	2.343370	2.450607
1.2100000	2.144599	2.213550	2.296127	2.393318	2.505671
1.2200000	2.185484	2.257069	2.342993	2.444416	2.562104
1.2300000	2.227183	2.301485	2.390870	2.496683	2.619930
1.2400000	2.269707	2.346811	2.439771	2.550136	2.679172
1.2500000	2.313066	2.393057	2.489711	2.604791	2.739853
1.2599999	2.357268	2.440232	2.540698	2.660664	2.801994
1.2699999	2.402320	2.488345	2.592745	2.717766	2.865612
1.2799999	2.448228	2.537403	2.645860	2.776108	2.930724
1.2899999	2.494997	2.587411	2.700048	2.835701	2.997345
1.3000000	2.542631	2.638373	2.755315	2.896551	3.065484
1.3100000	2.591129	2.690290	2.811663	2.958662	3.135151
1.3200000	2.640493	2.743162	2.869093	3.022035	3.206349
1.3300000	2.690719	2.796988	2.927603	3.086669	3.279080
1.3400000	2.741803	2.851762	2.987187	3.152561	3.353342
1.3500000	2.793740	2.907478	3.047839	3.219702	3.429127
1.3600000	2.846519	2.964126	3.109548	3.288082	3.506426
1.3700000	2.900130	3.021693	3.172301	3.357685	3.585222
1.3799999	2.954560	3.080166	3.236081	3.428493	3.665494
1.3899999	3.009790	3.139525	3.300867	3.500484	3.747218
1.4000000	3.065804	3.199750	3.366638	3.573630	3.830362
1.4100000	3.122578	3.260816	3.433364	3.647901	3.914890
1.4200000	3.180087	3.322696	3.501016	3.723260	4.000760
1.4300000	3.238305	3.385361	3.569559	3.799668	4.087924
1.4400000	3.297200	3.448775	3.638955	3.877082	4.176330
1.4500000	3.356739	3.512902	3.709162	3.955451	4.265918
1.4600000	3.416886	3.577703	3.780136	4.034724	4.356625
1.4700000	3.477602	3.643133	3.851826	4.114842	4.448380
1.4800000	3.538845	3.709148	3.924181	4.195745	4.541108
1.4900000	3.600571	3.775697	3.997146	4.277367	4.634729
1.5000000	3.662735	3.842731	4.070661	4.359641	4.729158
1.5100000	3.725285	3.910194	4.144666	4.442491	4.824305
1.5200000	3.788173	3.978030	4.219095	4.525844	4.920077
1.5300000	3.851345	4.046181	4.293884	4.609622	5.016377
1.5400000	3.914747	4.114587	4.368963	4.693743	5.113105
1.5500000	3.978325	4.183187	4.444263	4.778125	5.210159
1.5600000	4.042021	4.251919	4.519713	4.862684	5.307433
1.5699999	4.105778	4.320719	4.595241	4.947336	5.404822
1.5707963	4.110857	4.326199	4.601257	4.954079	5.412579
1.5707963	4.110853	4.326196	4.601254	4.954077	5.412580

$\alpha =$ .809999

Θ	K VALUES				
	.794250555	.868696860	.928444378	.971111163	.994996249
.0000000	.000000	.000000	.000000	.000000	.000000
.0100000	.010000	.010000	.010000	.010000	.010000
.0200000	.020003	.020003	.020003	.020003	.020003
.0300000	.030010	.030011	.030011	.030011	.030011
.0400000	.040025	.040026	.040027	.040027	.040027
.0500000	.050050	.050051	.050053	.050054	.050054
.0600000	.060087	.060089	.060091	.060093	.060094
.0700000	.070138	.070142	.070146	.070148	.070149
.0800000	.080206	.080212	.080218	.080221	.080223
.0900000	.090294	.090303	.090310	.090316	.090318
.1000000	.100404	.100416	.100426	.100433	.100437
.1100000	.110538	.110554	.110568	.110577	.110583
.1200000	.120699	.120721	.120738	.120751	.120758
.1300000	.130890	.130917	.130940	.130956	.130964
.1400000	.141112	.141147	.141175	.141195	.141206
.1500000	.151370	.151413	.151447	.151472	.151486
.1600000	.161665	.161717	.161759	.161789	.161806
.1700000	.172000	.172063	.172113	.172149	.172169
.1800000	.182377	.182452	.182512	.182555	.182579
.1900000	.192800	.192888	.192960	.193010	.193039
.2000000	.203271	.203375	.203458	.203517	.203551
.2100000	.213793	.213914	.214010	.214080	.214118
.2200000	.224369	.224508	.224620	.224700	.224745
.2300000	.235002	.235161	.235290	.235382	.235433
.2400000	.245694	.245876	.246023	.246128	.246187
.2500000	.256449	.256656	.256822	.256942	.257009
.2600000	.267269	.267503	.267692	.267827	.267903
.2700000	.278158	.278422	.278634	.278787	.278872
.2800000	.289120	.289415	.289654	.289825	.289921
.2900000	.300156	.300486	.300753	.300944	.301052
.3000000	.311271	.311639	.311936	.312149	.312269
.3100000	.322467	.322876	.323206	.323443	.323576
.3200000	.333749	.334202	.334567	.334830	.334977
.3300000	.345119	.345619	.346023	.346314	.346477
.3400000	.356582	.357133	.357578	.357898	.358078
.3500000	.368141	.368746	.369236	.369588	.369785
.3600000	.379799	.380463	.381000	.381386	.381604
.3700000	.391561	.392288	.392876	.393299	.393537
.3800000	.403431	.404224	.404867	.405329	.405589
.3900000	.415412	.416276	.416977	.417482	.417766

$\alpha =$ •809999

Θ	K VALUES				
	•794250555	•868696860	•928444378	•971111163	•994996249
•4000000	•427508	•428449	•429213	•429762	•430071
•4100000	•439725	•440747	•441577	•442175	•442511
•4200000	•452066	•453175	•454075	•454724	•455090
•4300000	•464535	•465736	•466713	•467417	•467813
•4400000	•477138	•478438	•479494	•480256	•480686
•4500000	•489879	•491283	•492425	•493249	•493714
•4600000	•502763	•504277	•505511	•506401	•506904
•4700000	•515795	•517427	•518757	•519718	•520260
•4800000	•528979	•530737	•532170	•533205	•533790
•4900000	•542323	•544212	•545754	•546870	•547500
•5000000	•555830	•557860	•559518	•560718	•561396
•5100000	•569506	•571685	•573466	•574756	•575485
•5200000	•583358	•585694	•587605	•588991	•589774
•5300000	•597390	•599893	•601943	•603430	•604271
•5400000	•611610	•614290	•616486	•618081	•618983
•5500000	•626024	•628890	•631242	•632951	•633918
•5600000	•640637	•643702	•646218	•648048	•649084
•5700000	•655458	•658732	•661422	•663380	•664489
•5800000	•670492	•673987	•676863	•678956	•680144
•5900000	•685748	•689476	•692548	•694786	•696055
•6000000	•701232	•705208	•708486	•710877	•712234
•6100000	•716952	•721189	•724686	•727240	•728690
•6200000	•732916	•737429	•741159	•743884	•745433
•6300000	•749133	•753937	•757912	•760820	•762473
•6400000	•765610	•770722	•774957	•778058	•779823
•6500000	•782356	•787794	•792304	•795610	•797493
•6600000	•799381	•805162	•809964	•813487	•815495
•6700000	•816694	•822838	•827948	•831702	•833842
•6800000	•834304	•840832	•846268	•850266	•852548
•6899999	•852222	•859154	•864937	•869193	•871625
•7000000	•870459	•877818	•883966	•888497	•891088
•7100000	•889023	•896834	•903369	•908192	•910951
•7200000	•907927	•916215	•923160	•928292	•931231
•7300000	•927183	•935974	•943353	•948813	•951943
•7400000	•946802	•956125	•963963	•969771	•973104
•7500000	•966796	•976681	•985006	•991183	•994731
•7600000	•987179	•997657	1•006497	1•013067	1•016844
•7700000	1•007963	1•019067	1•028454	1•035440	1•039462
•7800000	1•029162	1•040929	1•050894	1•058323	1•062604
•7899999	1•050791	1•063257	1•073836	1•081735	1•086291

$\alpha =$ .809999

Θ	K VALUES				
	.794250555	.868696860	.928444378	.971111163	.994996249
.8000000	1.072864	1.086069	1.097298	1.105696	1.110547
.8100000	1.095397	1.109382	1.121300	1.130230	1.135394
.8200000	1.118404	1.133215	1.145863	1.155358	1.160856
.8300000	1.141903	1.157586	1.171009	1.181105	1.186959
.8400000	1.165910	1.182516	1.196761	1.207496	1.213729
.8500000	1.190444	1.208024	1.223141	1.234557	1.241195
.8600000	1.215521	1.234132	1.250175	1.262316	1.269386
.8700000	1.241161	1.260862	1.277888	1.290801	1.298333
.8799999	1.267384	1.288237	1.306307	1.320043	1.328068
.8899999	1.294209	1.316282	1.335460	1.350074	1.358625
.9000000	1.321658	1.345020	1.365377	1.380926	1.390042
.9100000	1.349752	1.374479	1.396087	1.412635	1.422353
.9200000	1.378513	1.404684	1.427623	1.445236	1.455601
.9300000	1.407965	1.435664	1.460018	1.478770	1.489826
.9400000	1.438131	1.467447	1.493307	1.513275	1.525073
.9500000	1.469035	1.500065	1.527526	1.548794	1.561389
.9600000	1.500705	1.533548	1.562714	1.585372	1.598821
.9699999	1.533165	1.567929	1.598910	1.623056	1.637422
.9799999	1.566443	1.603242	1.636156	1.661894	1.677246
.9899999	1.600568	1.639521	1.674495	1.701939	1.718351
1.0000000	1.635568	1.676803	1.713972	1.743245	1.760798
1.0100000	1.671472	1.715126	1.754635	1.785868	1.804650
1.0200000	1.708311	1.754529	1.796533	1.829869	1.849976
1.0300000	1.746118	1.795052	1.839718	1.875311	1.896848
1.0400000	1.784924	1.836737	1.884243	1.922261	1.945341
1.0500000	1.824762	1.879627	1.930165	1.970789	1.995537
1.0600000	1.865667	1.923767	1.977542	2.020969	2.047520
1.0699999	1.907674	1.969204	2.026435	2.072877	2.101381
1.0799999	1.950818	2.015984	2.076909	2.126597	2.157216
1.0899999	1.995135	2.064157	2.129028	2.182214	2.215127
1.1000000	2.040664	2.113774	2.182864	2.239820	2.275222
1.1100000	2.087441	2.164885	2.238486	2.299508	2.337616
1.1200000	2.135506	2.217544	2.295969	2.361380	2.402431
1.1300000	2.184896	2.271807	2.355392	2.425542	2.469798
1.1400000	2.235652	2.327727	2.416833	2.492106	2.539854
1.1500000	2.287813	2.385363	2.480378	2.561189	2.612749
1.1600000	2.341419	2.444772	2.546110	2.632914	2.688638
1.1700000	2.396511	2.506013	2.614120	2.707413	2.767692
1.1800000	2.453128	2.569145	2.684500	2.784821	2.850089
1.1899999	2.511309	2.634228	2.757342	2.865284	2.936021

$\alpha =$ .809999

Θ	K VALUES				
	.794250555	.868696860	.928444378	.971111163	.994996249
1.2000000	2.571096	2.701323	2.832746	2.948953	3.025696
1.2100000	2.632525	2.770490	2.910809	3.035987	3.119332
1.2200000	2.695635	2.841790	2.991634	3.126553	3.217168
1.2300000	2.760462	2.915281	3.075323	3.220828	3.319458
1.2400000	2.827044	2.991025	3.161984	3.318995	3.426475
1.2500000	2.895412	3.069077	3.251721	3.421249	3.538515
1.2599999	2.965600	3.149495	3.344642	3.527791	3.655896
1.2699999	3.037637	3.232333	3.440856	3.638833	3.778962
1.2799999	3.111550	3.317642	3.540468	3.754595	3.908086
1.2899999	3.187364	3.405471	3.643586	3.875308	4.043673
1.3000000	3.265100	3.495866	3.750314	4.001212	4.186163
1.3100000	3.344774	3.588864	3.860752	4.132552	4.336032
1.3200000	3.426399	3.684502	3.974997	4.269585	4.493805
1.3300000	3.509985	3.782810	4.093143	4.412576	4.660055
1.3400000	3.595534	3.883810	4.215274	4.561793	4.835409
1.3500000	3.683044	3.987519	4.341468	4.717512	5.020558
1.3600000	3.772509	4.093944	4.471794	4.880012	5.216267
1.3700000	3.863913	4.203084	4.606306	5.049570	5.423379
1.3799999	3.957238	4.314928	4.745049	5.226463	5.642831
1.3899999	4.052454	4.429456	4.888050	5.410961	5.875668
1.4000000	4.149529	4.546637	5.035321	5.603323	6.123057
1.4100000	4.248418	4.666425	5.186851	5.803789	6.386297
1.4200000	4.349072	4.788765	5.342609	6.012575	6.666852
1.4300000	4.451434	4.913588	5.502541	6.229865	6.966364
1.4400000	4.555438	5.040812	5.666568	6.455800	7.286679
1.4500000	4.661009	5.170343	5.834581	6.690465	7.629863
1.4600000	4.768065	5.302071	6.006444	6.933879	7.998226
1.4700000	4.876518	5.435873	6.181990	7.185979	8.394324
1.4800000	4.986268	5.571614	6.361020	7.446604	8.820943
1.4900000	5.097212	5.709145	6.543305	7.715487	9.281040
1.5000000	5.209238	5.848305	6.728584	7.992236	9.777617
1.5100000	5.322226	5.988920	6.916564	8.276319	10.313452
1.5200000	5.436053	6.130807	7.106927	8.567069	10.890700
1.5300000	5.550589	6.273772	7.299325	8.863673	11.510215
1.5400000	5.665701	6.417614	7.493388	9.165180	12.170670
1.5500000	5.781250	6.562124	7.688728	9.470516	12.867570
1.5600000	5.897097	6.707088	7.884939	9.778503	13.592531
1.5699999	6.013099	6.852290	8.081605	10.087888	14.333374
1.5707963	6.022339	6.863856	8.097273	10.112547	14.392623
1.5707963	6.022361	6.863849	8.097263	10.112535	14.392601

$\alpha =$ .819999

Θ	K VALUES				
	.009966711	.039469502	.087332193	.151646642	.229848846
.0000000	.000000	.000000	.000000	.000000	.000000
.0100000	.010000	.010000	.010000	.010000	.010000
.0200000	.020002	.020002	.020002	.020002	.020002
.0300000	.030007	.030007	.030007	.030008	.030008
.0400000	.040017	.040017	.040018	.040019	.040019
.0500000	.050034	.050035	.050036	.050037	.050039
.0600000	.060059	.060060	.060062	.060064	.060067
.0700000	.070094	.070096	.070098	.070102	.070107
.0800000	.080141	.080143	.080147	.080153	.080159
.0900000	.090200	.090204	.090210	.090218	.090227
.1000000	.100275	.100280	.100288	.100299	.100312
.1100000	.110367	.110373	.110384	.110398	.110416
.1200000	.120477	.120485	.120499	.120518	.120540
.1300000	.130607	.130618	.130635	.130659	.130688
.1400000	.140758	.140772	.140794	.140824	.140860
.1500000	.150934	.150950	.150978	.151014	.151059
.1600000	.161134	.161155	.161188	.161232	.161286
.1700000	.171362	.171386	.171426	.171479	.171544
.1800000	.181619	.181648	.181695	.181758	.181835
.1900000	.191906	.191940	.191995	.192070	.192161
.2000000	.202225	.202265	.202330	.202417	.202523
.2100000	.212579	.212626	.212701	.212802	.212925
.2200000	.222970	.223023	.223109	.223225	.223367
.2300000	.233398	.233459	.233557	.233691	.233853
.2400000	.243866	.243935	.244048	.244199	.244384
.2500000	.254376	.254454	.254582	.254753	.254963
.2600000	.264930	.265018	.265162	.265355	.265592
.2700000	.275530	.275629	.275790	.276007	.276272
.2800000	.286177	.286288	.286468	.286711	.287007
.2900000	.296875	.296998	.297198	.297469	.297799
.3000000	.307624	.307761	.307983	.308283	.308650
.3100000	.318427	.318578	.318824	.319156	.319562
.3200000	.329287	.329453	.329724	.330090	.330538
.3300000	.340205	.340388	.340686	.341088	.341581
.3400000	.351184	.351384	.351711	.352152	.352692
.3500000	.362225	.362444	.362801	.363284	.363875
.3600000	.373331	.373570	.373960	.374487	.375133
.3700000	.384505	.384765	.385189	.385763	.386467
.3800000	.395749	.396031	.396492	.397115	.397880
.3900000	.407065	.407371	.407870	.408546	.409376

$\alpha =$ •819999

Θ	K VALUES				
	•009966711	•039469502	•087332193	•151646642	•229848846
•4000000	•418455	•418786	•419327	•420058	•420957
•4100000	•429923	•430281	•430864	•431654	•432626
•4200000	•441471	•441856	•442485	•443337	•444386
•4300000	•453100	•453515	•454192	•455110	•456240
•4400000	•464815	•465261	•465988	•466976	•468191
•4500000	•476618	•477096	•477877	•478937	•480242
•4600000	•488511	•489023	•489860	•490996	•492397
•4700000	•500498	•501046	•501941	•503158	•504658
•4800000	•512581	•513166	•514123	•515424	•517029
•4900000	•524763	•525388	•526409	•527799	•529514
•5000000	•537047	•537713	•538803	•540285	•542116
•5100000	•549437	•550146	•551307	•552886	•554838
•5200000	•561936	•562690	•563924	•565605	•567685
•5300000	•574546	•575347	•576659	•578447	•580660
•5400000	•587271	•588122	•589515	•591414	•593766
•5500000	•600116	•601017	•602495	•604511	•607009
•5600000	•613082	•614037	•615604	•617741	•620391
•5700000	•626174	•627185	•628844	•631108	•633918
•5800000	•639395	•640465	•642219	•644616	•647592
•5900000	•652750	•653880	•655735	•658270	•661420
•6000000	•666241	•667435	•669394	•672073	•675405
•6100000	•679874	•681133	•683201	•686030	•689551
•6200000	•693651	•694979	•697160	•700145	•703865
•6300000	•707578	•708977	•711275	•714424	•718349
•6400000	•721658	•723131	•725552	•728870	•733010
•6500000	•735896	•737446	•739994	•743489	•747852
•6600000	•750297	•751926	•754607	•758285	•762881
•6700000	•764864	•766576	•769394	•773264	•778102
•6800000	•779603	•781401	•784362	•788430	•793521
•6899999	•794519	•796407	•799516	•803790	•809143
•7000000	•809617	•811597	•814860	•819348	•824975
•7100000	•824902	•826977	•830400	•835111	•841021
•7200000	•840378	•842553	•846142	•851084	•857289
•7300000	•856052	•858331	•862091	•867273	•873785
•7400000	•871930	•874315	•878253	•883684	•890515
•7500000	•888016	•890512	•894634	•900323	•907486
•7600000	•904317	•906927	•911241	•917198	•924704
•7700000	•920839	•923568	•928080	•934315	•942178
•7800000	•937587	•940440	•945157	•951680	•959914
•7899999	•954570	•957549	•962479	•969301	•977919

$\alpha =$ .819999

Θ	K VALUES				
	.009966711	.039469502	.087332193	.151646642	.229848846
.8000000	.971792	.974904	.980054	.987184	.996202
.8100000	.989262	.992509	.997887	1.005338	1.014770
.8200000	1.006985	1.010373	1.015987	1.023770	1.033631
.8300000	1.024969	1.028503	1.034360	1.042488	1.052795
.8400000	1.043221	1.046905	1.053016	1.061499	1.072268
.8500000	1.061749	1.065589	1.071961	1.080813	1.092061
.8600000	1.080561	1.084562	1.091203	1.100438	1.112182
.8700000	1.099664	1.103831	1.110752	1.120382	1.132640
.8799999	1.119067	1.123406	1.130616	1.140654	1.153446
.8899999	1.138778	1.143294	1.150803	1.161264	1.174609
.9000000	1.158805	1.163505	1.171322	1.182222	1.196138
.9100000	1.179158	1.184048	1.192184	1.203536	1.218045
.9200000	1.199846	1.204931	1.213396	1.225217	1.240340
.9300000	1.220877	1.226164	1.234970	1.247276	1.263034
.9400000	1.242262	1.247758	1.256915	1.269722	1.286138
.9500000	1.264010	1.269721	1.279242	1.292566	1.309663
.9600000	1.286131	1.292064	1.301960	1.315819	1.333621
.9699999	1.308635	1.314798	1.325081	1.339494	1.358025
.9799999	1.331533	1.337932	1.348616	1.363600	1.382886
.9899999	1.354835	1.361479	1.372575	1.388150	1.408217
1.0000000	1.378553	1.385449	1.396971	1.413156	1.434031
1.0100000	1.402698	1.409853	1.421815	1.438631	1.460340
1.0200000	1.427280	1.434703	1.447120	1.464586	1.487159
1.0300000	1.452312	1.460011	1.472896	1.491035	1.514500
1.0400000	1.477805	1.485790	1.499157	1.517990	1.542379
1.0500000	1.503772	1.512050	1.525916	1.545465	1.570808
1.0600000	1.530224	1.538804	1.553184	1.573473	1.599802
1.0699999	1.557174	1.566066	1.580976	1.602028	1.629375
1.0799999	1.584634	1.593848	1.609304	1.631143	1.659543
1.0899999	1.612617	1.622162	1.638181	1.660833	1.690319
1.1000000	1.641136	1.651022	1.667621	1.691112	1.721720
1.1100000	1.670204	1.680441	1.697638	1.721992	1.753760
1.1200000	1.699832	1.710431	1.728245	1.753490	1.786454
1.1300000	1.730035	1.741007	1.759455	1.785619	1.819817
1.1400000	1.760826	1.772181	1.791283	1.818393	1.853865
1.1500000	1.792216	1.803966	1.823741	1.851827	1.888613
1.1600000	1.824220	1.836375	1.856843	1.885934	1.924075
1.1700000	1.856849	1.869422	1.890603	1.920729	1.960267
1.1800000	1.890116	1.903118	1.925033	1.956225	1.997203
1.1899999	1.924033	1.937477	1.960146	1.992436	2.034897

$\alpha =$ •819999

Θ	K VALUES				
	•009966711	•039469502	•087332193	•151646642	•229848846
1•2000000	1•958612	1•972510	1•995955	2•029374	2•073364
1•2100000	1•993864	2•008229	2•032472	2•067053	2•112616
1•2200000	2•029801	2•044645	2•069708	2•105483	2•152667
1•2300000	2•066432	2•081768	2•107675	2•144678	2•193530
1•2400000	2•103768	2•119610	2•146382	2•184647	2•235214
1•2500000	2•141817	2•158178	2•185839	2•225401	2•277732
1•2599999	2•180589	2•197482	2•226054	2•266949	2•321093
1•2699999	2•220089	2•237528	2•267036	2•309298	2•365305
1•2799999	2•260325	2•278323	2•308791	2•352456	2•410376
1•2899999	2•301301	2•319872	2•351324	2•396428	2•456311
1•3000000	2•343021	2•362180	2•394640	2•441219	2•503117
1•3100000	2•385488	2•405248	2•438740	2•486830	2•550794
1•3200000	2•428702	2•449077	2•483625	2•533263	2•599344
1•3300000	2•472662	2•493667	2•529295	2•580518	2•648766
1•3400000	2•517366	2•539014	2•575747	2•628590	2•699058
1•3500000	2•562810	2•585114	2•622977	2•677476	2•750214
1•3600000	2•608986	2•631961	2•670976	2•727167	2•802226
1•3700000	2•655887	2•679545	2•719737	2•777656	2•855084
1•3799999	2•703500	2•727856	2•769247	2•828928	2•908776
1•3899999	2•751814	2•776880	2•819494	2•880971	2•963287
1•4000000	2•800812	2•826602	2•870460	2•933766	3•018598
1•4100000	2•850475	2•877001	2•922125	2•987294	3•074686
1•4200000	2•900784	2•928057	2•974469	3•041532	3•131529
1•4300000	2•951714	2•979747	3•027466	3•096453	3•189099
1•4400000	3•003240	3•032043	3•081089	3•152030	3•247366
1•4500000	3•055333	3•084917	3•135309	3•208230	3•306295
1•4600000	3•107962	3•138337	3•190092	3•265020	3•365851
1•4700000	3•161093	3•192268	3•245402	3•322362	3•425995
1•4800000	3•214689	3•246674	3•301202	3•380217	3•486682
1•4900000	3•268713	3•301515	3•357451	3•438541	3•547869
1•5000000	3•323123	3•356749	3•414107	3•497291	3•609509
1•5100000	3•377876	3•412333	3•471123	3•556418	3•671549
1•5200000	3•432928	3•468221	3•528453	3•615874	3•733939
1•5300000	3•488232	3•524366	3•586048	3•675607	3•796623
1•5400000	3•543740	3•580719	3•643857	3•735565	3•859547
1•5500000	3•599404	3•637231	3•701831	3•795694	3•922652
1•5600000	3•655173	3•693849	3•759914	3•855938	3•985881
1•5699999	3•710996	3•750524	3•818056	3•916244	4•049173
1•5707963	3•715443	3•755038	3•822687	3•921047	4•054215
1•5707963	3•715439	3•755035	3•822684	3•921043	4•054211

$\alpha =$ •819999

Θ	K VALUES				
	•318821117	•415016431	•514599755	•613601043	•708073407
•0000000	•000000	•000000	•000000	•000000	•000000
•0100000	•010000	•010000	•010000	•010000	•010000
•0200000	•020002	•020002	•020002	•020003	•020003
•0300000	•030008	•030009	•030009	•030010	•030010
•0400000	•040020	•040021	•040023	•040024	•040025
•0500000	•050040	•050042	•050044	•050047	•050048
•0600000	•060070	•060074	•060077	•060081	•060084
•0700000	•070112	•070117	•070123	•070129	•070134
•0800000	•080167	•080175	•080184	•080192	•080200
•0900000	•090238	•090250	•090262	•090274	•090286
•1000000	•100327	•100343	•100360	•100376	•100392
•1100000	•110436	•110457	•110479	•110502	•110523
•1200000	•120566	•120594	•120623	•120652	•120680
•1300000	•130721	•130756	•130793	•130830	•130865
•1400000	•140901	•140945	•140992	•141038	•141082
•1500000	•151109	•151164	•151221	•151278	•151332
•1600000	•161348	•161414	•161484	•161553	•161619
•1700000	•171618	•171698	•171782	•171865	•171944
•1800000	•181923	•182019	•182118	•182216	•182311
•1900000	•192265	•192377	•192494	•192610	•192722
•2000000	•202645	•202776	•202913	•203049	•203179
•2100000	•213065	•213218	•213377	•213535	•213687
•2200000	•223529	•223705	•223888	•224071	•224246
•2300000	•234039	•234240	•234450	•234660	•234860
•2400000	•244596	•244826	•245065	•245304	•245533
•2500000	•255203	•255463	•255734	•256005	•256266
•2600000	•265862	•266156	•266462	•266768	•267062
•2700000	•276576	•276906	•277250	•277595	•277925
•2800000	•287347	•287717	•288102	•288488	•288858
•2900000	•298178	•298590	•299019	•299450	•299864
•3000000	•309070	•309528	•310006	•310485	•310946
•3100000	•320027	•320535	•321064	•321595	•322107
•3200000	•331052	•331612	•332197	•332784	•333350
•3300000	•342146	•342763	•343408	•344055	•344679
•3400000	•353313	•353990	•354699	•355411	•356097
•3500000	•364555	•365297	•366074	•366855	•367608
•3600000	•375875	•376686	•377535	•378390	•379216
•3700000	•387276	•388160	•389087	•390021	•390923
•3800000	•398760	•399723	•400733	•401750	•402734
•3900000	•410331	•411377	•412475	•413582	•414653

$\alpha =$ •819999

Θ	K VALUES				
	•318821117	•415016431	•514599755	•613601043	•708073407
•4000000	•421992	•423126	•424317	•425519	•426683
•4100000	•433745	•434973	•436263	•437566	•438829
•4200000	•445595	•446921	•448317	•449727	•451095
•4300000	•457543	•458974	•460481	•462005	•463485
•4400000	•469594	•471135	•472760	•474405	•476003
•4500000	•481750	•483409	•485158	•486930	•488654
•4600000	•494015	•495797	•497678	•499585	•501442
•4700000	•506393	•508305	•510325	•512375	•514373
•4800000	•518887	•520936	•523102	•525303	•527450
•4900000	•531501	•533694	•536015	•538375	•540680
•5000000	•544239	•546583	•549067	•551595	•554066
•5100000	•557103	•559607	•562262	•564968	•567615
•5200000	•570099	•572771	•575606	•578499	•581332
•5300000	•583231	•586078	•589104	•592194	•595223
•5400000	•596502	•599534	•602759	•606056	•609293
•5500000	•609916	•613142	•616577	•620093	•623547
•5600000	•623479	•626908	•630563	•634309	•637994
•5700000	•637194	•640836	•644722	•648710	•652637
•5800000	•651066	•654931	•659060	•663302	•667485
•5900000	•665100	•669199	•673582	•678091	•682544
•6000000	•679300	•683644	•688295	•693084	•697820
•6100000	•693672	•698272	•703202	•708287	•713322
•6200000	•708220	•713088	•718312	•723706	•729055
•6300000	•722950	•728098	•733629	•739349	•745028
•6400000	•737867	•743308	•749161	•755222	•761249
•6500000	•752977	•758723	•764914	•771333	•777725
•6600000	•768285	•774351	•780894	•787689	•794466
•6700000	•783797	•790196	•797110	•804298	•811479
•6800000	•799518	•806267	•813566	•821168	•828774
•6899999	•815456	•822568	•830272	•838307	•846359
•7000000	•831617	•839109	•847235	•855724	•864245
•7100000	•848006	•855894	•864462	•873427	•882441
•7200000	•864630	•872931	•881962	•891425	•900957
•7300000	•881497	•890229	•899742	•909728	•919804
•7400000	•898613	•907794	•917812	•928345	•938993
•7500000	•915986	•925635	•936180	•947287	•958534
•7600000	•933622	•943760	•954855	•966562	•978440
•7700000	•951531	•962177	•973847	•986183	•998723
•7800000	•969718	•980895	•993165	1•006159	1•019394
•7899999	•988194	•999922	1•012819	1•026501	1•040466

$\alpha =$ •819999

Θ	K VALUES				
	•318821117	•415016431	•514599755	•613601043	•708073407
•8000000	1•006965	1•019268	1•032820	1•047223	1•061954
•8100000	1•026041	1•038942	1•053176	1•068335	1•083870
•8200000	1•045429	1•058954	1•073901	1•089849	1•106229
•8300000	1•065140	1•079313	1•095004	1•111778	1•129045
•8400000	1•085183	1•100030	1•116497	1•134136	1•152334
•8500000	1•105566	1•121116	1•138392	1•156936	1•176111
•8600000	1•126301	1•142581	1•160702	1•180192	1•200392
•8700000	1•147396	1•164436	1•183437	1•203917	1•225194
•8799999	1•168862	1•186694	1•206612	1•228128	1•250534
•8899999	1•190711	1•209364	1•230240	1•252838	1•276430
•9000000	1•212952	1•232460	1•254334	1•278065	1•302901
•9100000	1•235597	1•255995	1•278909	1•303823	1•329965
•9200000	1•258658	1•279979	1•303977	1•330130	1•357641
•9300000	1•282146	1•304428	1•329555	1•357002	1•385952
•9400000	1•306074	1•329353	1•355658	1•384457	1•414916
•9500000	1•330453	1•354769	1•382301	1•412514	1•444555
•9600000	1•355297	1•380691	1•409499	1•441190	1•474893
•9699999	1•380618	1•407131	1•437270	1•470505	1•505951
•9799999	1•406431	1•434106	1•465630	1•500479	1•537752
•9899999	1•432747	1•461629	1•494597	1•531131	1•570322
1•0000000	1•459583	1•489718	1•524188	1•562483	1•603685
1•0100000	1•486950	1•518386	1•554420	1•594554	1•637867
1•0200000	1•514865	1•547651	1•585312	1•627367	1•672893
1•0300000	1•543341	1•577529	1•616884	1•660945	1•708790
1•0400000	1•572394	1•608037	1•649153	1•695308	1•745586
1•0500000	1•602040	1•639191	1•682140	1•730481	1•783309
1•0600000	1•632293	1•671009	1•715865	1•766486	1•821989
1•0699999	1•663169	1•703508	1•750346	1•803348	1•861653
1•0799999	1•694685	1•736706	1•785606	1•841091	1•902332
1•0899999	1•726856	1•770622	1•821663	1•879739	1•944057
1•1000000	1•759700	1•805273	1•858541	1•919318	1•986858
1•1100000	1•793231	1•840677	1•896258	1•959851	2•030767
1•1200000	1•827467	1•876854	1•934837	2•001366	2•075815
1•1300000	1•862424	1•913820	1•974298	2•043886	2•122035
1•1400000	1•898119	1•951596	2•014663	2•087437	2•169458
1•1500000	1•934568	1•990198	2•055953	2•132046	2•218118
1•1600000	1•971787	2•029646	2•098189	2•177738	2•268046
1•1700000	2•009793	2•069957	2•141393	2•224537	2•319275
1•1800000	2•048602	2•111150	2•185584	2•272470	2•371837
1•1899999	2•088228	2•153241	2•230784	2•321560	2•425764

$\alpha =$ •819999

Θ	K VALUES				
	•318821117	•415016431	•514599755	•613601043	•708073407
1•2000000	2•128688	2•196249	2•277011	2•371832	2•481088
1•2100000	2•169996	2•240188	2•324285	2•423308	2•537838
1•2200000	2•212166	2•285076	2•372624	2•476013	2•596045
1•2300000	2•255212	2•330926	2•422047	2•529967	2•655738
1•2400000	2•299145	2•377754	2•472569	2•585191	2•716943
1•2500000	2•343978	2•425572	2•524206	2•641705	2•779688
1•2599999	2•389721	2•474393	2•576972	2•699525	2•843995
1•2699999	2•436384	2•524226	2•630880	2•758669	2•909888
1•2799999	2•483975	2•575082	2•685941	2•819150	2•977387
1•2899999	2•532500	2•626967	2•742163	2•880981	3•046509
1•3000000	2•581965	2•679889	2•799556	2•944170	3•117268
1•3100000	2•632372	2•733849	2•858121	3•008725	3•189676
1•3200000	2•683723	2•788850	2•917863	3•074650	3•263741
1•3300000	2•736016	2•844891	2•978781	3•141945	3•339466
1•3400000	2•789250	2•901970	3•040872	3•210608	3•416852
1•3500000	2•843418	2•960079	3•104130	3•280634	3•495893
1•3600000	2•898511	3•019211	3•168545	3•352012	3•576581
1•3700000	2•954521	3•079353	3•234105	3•424729	3•658902
1•3799999	3•011431	3•140492	3•300792	3•498765	3•742834
1•3899999	3•069227	3•202607	3•368588	3•574099	3•828353
1•4000000	3•127889	3•265679	3•437467	3•650703	3•915428
1•4100000	3•187392	3•329681	3•507402	3•728544	4•004019
1•4200000	3•247711	3•394585	3•578359	3•807585	4•094084
1•4300000	3•308817	3•460358	3•650302	3•887785	4•185573
1•4400000	3•370676	3•526964	3•723191	3•969094	4•278429
1•4500000	3•433253	3•594363	3•796981	4•051462	4•372588
1•4600000	3•496508	3•662512	3•871621	4•134831	4•467981
1•4700000	3•560398	3•731363	3•947060	4•219138	4•564533
1•4800000	3•624878	3•800866	4•023238	4•304316	4•662161
1•4900000	3•689898	3•870967	4•100096	4•390294	4•760778
1•5000000	3•755407	3•941609	4•177569	4•476996	4•860290
1•5100000	3•821351	4•012731	4•255588	4•564340	4•960599
1•5200000	3•887673	4•084272	4•334082	4•652245	5•061601
1•5300000	3•954313	4•156165	4•412977	4•740623	5•163189
1•5400000	4•021213	4•228345	4•492198	4•829384	5•265252
1•5500000	4•088309	4•300742	4•571666	4•918437	5•367677
1•5600000	4•155539	4•373287	4•651301	5•007687	5•470348
1•5699999	4•222838	4•445908	4•731025	5•097041	5•573146
1•5707963	4•228198	4•451693	4•737374	5•104158	5•581334
1•5707963	4•228195	4•451690	4•737372	5•104157	5•581336

$\alpha =$ .819999

Θ	K VALUES				
	.794250555	.868696860	.928444378	.971111163	.994996249
.0000000	.000000	.000000	.000000	.000000	.000000
.0100000	.010000	.010000	.010000	.010000	.010000
.0200000	.020003	.020003	.020003	.020003	.020003
.0300000	.030010	.030011	.030011	.030011	.030011
.0400000	.040026	.040026	.040027	.040027	.040028
.0500000	.050050	.050052	.050053	.050054	.050054
.0600000	.060087	.060090	.060092	.060094	.060095
.0700000	.070139	.070143	.070147	.070149	.070151
.0800000	.080208	.080214	.080219	.080223	.080225
.0900000	.090296	.090305	.090313	.090318	.090321
.1000000	.100407	.100419	.100429	.100437	.100441
.1100000	.110542	.110559	.110572	.110582	.110587
.1200000	.120705	.120726	.120744	.120756	.120763
.1300000	.130897	.130925	.130947	.130963	.130972
.1400000	.141122	.141157	.141184	.141204	.141216
.1500000	.151381	.151424	.151459	.151483	.151497
.1600000	.161679	.161731	.161773	.161803	.161820
.1700000	.172017	.172079	.172130	.172166	.172186
.1800000	.182397	.182472	.182532	.182575	.182600
.1900000	.192824	.192912	.192983	.193034	.193063
.2000000	.203299	.203402	.203486	.203545	.203579
.2100000	.213826	.213946	.214043	.214112	.214151
.2200000	.224406	.224545	.224657	.224737	.224782
.2300000	.235044	.235204	.235333	.235425	.235476
.2400000	.245743	.245925	.246072	.246177	.246236
.2500000	.256504	.256711	.256878	.256997	.257064
.2600000	.267332	.267566	.267755	.267890	.267966
.2700000	.278229	.278493	.278705	.278858	.278943
.2800000	.289199	.289495	.289733	.289904	.290000
.2900000	.300244	.300575	.300842	.301033	.301141
.3000000	.311369	.311738	.312035	.312248	.312368
.3100000	.322577	.322986	.323316	.323553	.323686
.3200000	.333870	.334323	.334689	.334952	.335100
.3300000	.345253	.345754	.346158	.346449	.346612
.3400000	.356730	.357281	.357727	.358047	.358227
.3500000	.368303	.368909	.369399	.369751	.369949
.3600000	.379977	.380641	.381179	.381566	.381783
.3700000	.391756	.392483	.393072	.393495	.393733
.3800000	.403643	.404437	.405081	.405543	.405804
.3900000	.415643	.416509	.417211	.417716	.418000

$\alpha =$ .819999

Θ	K VALUES				
	.794250555	.868696860	.928444378	.971111163	.994996249
.4000000	.427760	.428702	.429466	.430017	.430326
.4100000	.439999	.441022	.441853	.442451	.442788
.4200000	.452363	.453473	.454375	.455024	.455390
.4300000	.464857	.466059	.467037	.467742	.468139
.4400000	.477486	.478787	.479845	.480608	.481038
.4500000	.490255	.491660	.492804	.493630	.494095
.4600000	.503168	.504685	.505920	.506812	.507315
.4700000	.516231	.517866	.519198	.520160	.520703
.4800000	.529449	.531209	.532644	.533682	.534268
.4900000	.542828	.544720	.546265	.547382	.548013
.5000000	.556372	.558406	.560066	.561269	.561948
.5100000	.570088	.572271	.574055	.575347	.576078
.5200000	.583982	.586322	.588237	.589625	.590410
.5300000	.598059	.600567	.602621	.604110	.604953
.5400000	.612326	.615011	.617212	.618809	.619713
.5500000	.626789	.629662	.632019	.633731	.634700
.5600000	.641455	.644526	.647049	.648882	.649920
.5700000	.656331	.659613	.662310	.664272	.665384
.5800000	.671424	.674928	.677810	.679909	.681099
.5900000	.686742	.690480	.693559	.695803	.697076
.6000000	.702292	.706278	.709565	.711962	.713323
.6100000	.718081	.722329	.725836	.728397	.729851
.6200000	.734118	.738644	.742384	.745117	.746671
.6300000	.750412	.755230	.759217	.762134	.763792
.6400000	.766970	.772098	.776347	.779457	.781228
.6500000	.783803	.789258	.793783	.797099	.798988
.6600000	.800919	.806719	.811537	.815072	.817087
.6700000	.818327	.824493	.829621	.833387	.835536
.6800000	.836039	.842590	.848046	.852058	.854348
.6899999	.854064	.861022	.866825	.871098	.873539
.7000000	.872412	.879800	.885972	.890521	.893122
.7100000	.891096	.898938	.905500	.910342	.913113
.7200000	.910126	.918448	.925422	.930576	.933527
.7300000	.929514	.938343	.945754	.951238	.954382
.7400000	.949272	.958637	.966511	.972345	.975693
.7500000	.969414	.979345	.987709	.993916	.997481
.7600000	.989953	1.000481	1.009364	1.015966	1.019762
.7700000	1.010901	1.022061	1.031495	1.038517	1.042559
.7800000	1.032274	1.044101	1.054119	1.061587	1.065890
.7899999	1.054086	1.066619	1.077254	1.085196	1.089778

$\alpha =$ .819999

Θ	K VALUES				
	.794250555	.868696860	.928444378	.971111163	.994996249
.8000000	1.076352	1.089630	1.100922	1.109368	1.114247
.8100000	1.099088	1.113155	1.125141	1.134124	1.139318
.8200000	1.122311	1.137210	1.149935	1.159487	1.165019
.8300000	1.146038	1.161818	1.175324	1.185483	1.191374
.8400000	1.170285	1.186996	1.201333	1.212138	1.218412
.8500000	1.195072	1.212768	1.227986	1.239479	1.246162
.8600000	1.220417	1.239155	1.255309	1.267534	1.274654
.8700000	1.246341	1.266180	1.283328	1.296334	1.303920
.8799999	1.272862	1.293867	1.312071	1.325909	1.333994
.8899999	1.300003	1.322242	1.341567	1.356293	1.364912
.9000000	1.327786	1.351330	1.371847	1.387520	1.396709
.9100000	1.356232	1.381158	1.402943	1.419627	1.429427
.9200000	1.385366	1.411754	1.434887	1.452651	1.463105
.9300000	1.415211	1.443149	1.467716	1.486633	1.497788
.9400000	1.445793	1.475371	1.501464	1.521614	1.533522
.9500000	1.477138	1.508453	1.536171	1.557639	1.570354
.9600000	1.509273	1.542428	1.571876	1.594755	1.608336
.9699999	1.542225	1.577330	1.608620	1.633010	1.647522
.9799999	1.576024	1.613195	1.646448	1.672456	1.687969
.9899999	1.610699	1.650059	1.685405	1.713146	1.729737
1.0000000	1.646280	1.687961	1.725539	1.755138	1.772890
1.0100000	1.682800	1.726941	1.766899	1.798492	1.817494
1.0200000	1.720291	1.767041	1.809538	1.843271	1.863621
1.0300000	1.758786	1.808302	1.853509	1.889542	1.911347
1.0400000	1.798321	1.850770	1.898871	1.937373	1.960751
1.0500000	1.838930	1.894490	1.945681	1.986841	2.011918
1.0600000	1.880651	1.939511	1.994003	2.038021	2.064938
1.0699999	1.923521	1.985881	2.043901	2.090996	2.119906
1.0799999	1.967578	2.033651	2.095443	2.145853	2.176922
1.0899999	2.012861	2.082874	2.148699	2.202682	2.236096
1.1000000	2.059412	2.133604	2.203743	2.261581	2.297540
1.1100000	2.107271	2.185897	2.260650	2.322649	2.361376
1.1200000	2.156479	2.239810	2.319502	2.385993	2.427733
1.1300000	2.207079	2.295401	2.380379	2.451727	2.496750
1.1400000	2.259114	2.352731	2.443370	2.519968	2.568572
1.1500000	2.312627	2.411861	2.508561	2.590842	2.643357
1.1600000	2.367664	2.472854	2.576047	2.664481	2.721271
1.1700000	2.424266	2.535775	2.645923	2.741023	2.802492
1.1800000	2.482480	2.600688	2.718287	2.820615	2.887213
1.1899999	2.542348	2.667658	2.793242	2.903410	2.975637

$\alpha =$ .819999

Θ	K VALUES				
	.794250555	.868696860	.928444378	.971111163	.994996249
1.2000000	2.603916	2.736752	2.870892	2.989572	3.067984
1.2100000	2.667225	2.808036	2.951344	3.079270	3.164487
1.2200000	2.732319	2.881577	3.034710	3.172684	3.265399
1.2300000	2.799240	2.957442	3.121102	3.270002	3.370990
1.2400000	2.868027	3.035695	3.210634	3.371422	3.481554
1.2500000	2.938720	3.116401	3.303422	3.477153	3.597403
1.2599999	3.011356	3.199624	3.399584	3.587410	3.718878
1.2699999	3.085969	3.285424	3.499238	3.702423	3.846345
1.2799999	3.162591	3.373860	3.602501	3.822428	3.980202
1.2899999	3.241252	3.464986	3.709491	3.947674	4.120880
1.3000000	3.321977	3.558856	3.820323	4.078419	4.268849
1.3100000	3.404786	3.655514	3.935107	4.214928	4.424617
1.3200000	3.489698	3.755003	4.053952	4.357479	4.588742
1.3300000	3.576724	3.857358	4.176961	4.506355	4.761835
1.3400000	3.665872	3.962607	4.304230	4.661850	4.944566
1.3500000	3.757142	4.070771	4.435846	4.824260	5.137671
1.3600000	3.850529	4.181863	4.571886	4.993885	5.341962
1.3700000	3.946022	4.295885	4.712416	5.171027	5.558338
1.3799999	4.043601	4.412828	4.857484	5.355986	5.787796
1.3899999	4.143240	4.532675	5.007126	5.549052	6.031447
1.4000000	4.244903	4.655396	5.161359	5.750508	6.290531
1.4100000	4.348547	4.780942	5.320174	5.960611	6.566427
1.4200000	4.454119	4.909260	5.483542	6.179599	6.860690
1.4300000	4.561559	5.040275	5.651409	6.407670	7.175063
1.4400000	4.670798	5.173904	5.823692	6.644977	7.511501
1.4500000	4.781755	5.310043	6.000278	6.891616	7.872197
1.4600000	4.894344	5.448577	6.181021	7.147607	8.259594
1.4700000	5.008466	5.589375	6.365744	7.412886	8.676401
1.4800000	5.124016	5.732289	6.554235	7.687285	9.125565
1.4900000	5.240879	5.877158	6.746247	7.970516	9.610215
1.5000000	5.358935	6.023809	6.941500	8.262162	10.133523
1.5100000	5.478052	6.172052	7.139677	8.561655	10.698426
1.5200000	5.598095	6.321687	7.340434	8.868282	11.307196
1.5300000	5.718921	6.472502	7.543397	9.181173	11.960731
1.5400000	5.840382	6.624278	7.748166	9.499312	12.657618
1.5500000	5.962327	6.776787	7.954317	9.821548	13.393091
1.5600000	6.084601	6.929794	8.161413	10.146621	14.158270
1.5699999	6.207045	7.083060	8.369002	10.473189	14.940261
1.5707963	6.216799	7.095269	8.385541	10.499218	15.002802
1.5707963	6.216818	7.095260	8.385529	10.499203	15.002775

$\alpha =$ •829999

Θ	K VALUES				
	•009966711	•039469502	•087332193	•151646642	•229848846
•0000000	•000000	•000000	•000000	•000000	•000000
•0100000	•010000	•010000	•010000	•010000	•010000
•0200000	•020002	•020002	•020002	•020002	•020002
•0300000	•030007	•030007	•030007	•030008	•030008
•0400000	•040017	•040018	•040018	•040019	•040020
•0500000	•050034	•050035	•050036	•050037	•050039
•0600000	•060060	•060061	•060063	•060065	•060068
•0700000	•070095	•070097	•070100	•070103	•070108
•0800000	•080142	•080145	•080149	•080154	•080161
•0900000	•090203	•090207	•090212	•090220	•090230
•1000000	•100279	•100284	•100292	•100302	•100315
•1100000	•110371	•110378	•110389	•110403	•110420
•1200000	•120483	•120491	•120505	•120524	•120546
•1300000	•130614	•130625	•130643	•130666	•130695
•1400000	•140768	•140781	•140803	•140833	•140869
•1500000	•150945	•150962	•150989	•151026	•151070
•1600000	•161148	•161169	•161202	•161246	•161300
•1700000	•171379	•171403	•171443	•171496	•171561
•1800000	•181639	•181668	•181715	•181778	•181855
•1900000	•191929	•191963	•192019	•192093	•192184
•2000000	•202253	•202293	•202358	•202445	•202551
•2100000	•212611	•212658	•212733	•212834	•212957
•2200000	•223006	•223060	•223146	•223262	•223404
•2300000	•233440	•233501	•233600	•233733	•233896
•2400000	•243914	•243983	•244096	•244248	•244433
•2500000	•254431	•254509	•254637	•254808	•255018
•2600000	•264992	•265080	•265224	•265417	•265654
•2700000	•275599	•275698	•275859	•276077	•276342
•2800000	•286255	•286366	•286546	•286789	•287086
•2900000	•296962	•297085	•297285	•297556	•297887
•3000000	•307721	•307857	•308080	•308380	•308747
•3100000	•318535	•318686	•318932	•319264	•319670
•3200000	•329406	•329572	•329843	•330209	•330658
•3300000	•340336	•340519	•340817	•341220	•341713
•3400000	•351327	•351528	•351855	•352296	•352837
•3500000	•362383	•362602	•362959	•363442	•364035
•3600000	•373504	•373743	•374133	•374660	•375307
•3700000	•384694	•384954	•385379	•385953	•386657
•3800000	•395954	•396237	•396698	•397322	•398088
•3900000	•407288	•407595	•408095	•408771	•409602

$\alpha =$ .829999

Θ	K VALUES				
	.009966711	.039469502	.087332193	.151646642	.229848846
.4000000	.418698	.419030	.419570	.420303	.421202
.4100000	.430186	.430544	.431128	.431920	.432892
.4200000	.441756	.442141	.442771	.443625	.444674
.4300000	.453408	.453824	.454501	.455421	.456552
.4400000	.465148	.465594	.466322	.467311	.468527
.4500000	.476976	.477455	.478237	.479298	.480605
.4600000	.488897	.489410	.490248	.491385	.492788
.4700000	.500912	.501461	.502358	.503576	.505078
.4800000	.513026	.513612	.514571	.515874	.517481
.4900000	.525240	.525866	.526889	.528281	.529999
.5000000	.537559	.538226	.539317	.540802	.542636
.5100000	.549985	.550695	.551857	.553440	.555395
.5200000	.562521	.563277	.564514	.566198	.568281
.5300000	.575171	.575974	.577289	.579080	.581297
.5400000	.587939	.588791	.590187	.592090	.594447
.5500000	.600828	.601731	.603212	.605232	.607735
.5600000	.613841	.614798	.616368	.618510	.621166
.5700000	.626982	.627996	.629658	.631927	.634743
.5800000	.640255	.641327	.643086	.645488	.648472
.5900000	.653664	.654797	.656656	.659198	.662356
.6000000	.667213	.668410	.670374	.673060	.676400
.6100000	.680906	.682168	.684242	.687078	.690609
.6200000	.694747	.696078	.698265	.701259	.704988
.6300000	.708740	.710143	.712448	.715606	.719542
.6400000	.722890	.724367	.726796	.730124	.734276
.6500000	.737202	.738756	.741312	.744818	.749195
.6600000	.751680	.753314	.756003	.759693	.764304
.6700000	.766328	.768046	.770873	.774755	.779610
.6800000	.781153	.782957	.785928	.790010	.795118
.6899999	.796158	.798052	.801172	.805461	.810834
.7000000	.811350	.813337	.816612	.821117	.826764
.7100000	.826733	.828816	.832252	.836981	.842914
.7200000	.842313	.844496	.848099	.853060	.859290
.7300000	.858095	.860383	.864158	.869361	.875900
.7400000	.874087	.876482	.880436	.885890	.892750
.7500000	.890292	.892799	.896940	.902653	.909847
.7600000	.906719	.909341	.913674	.919658	.927198
.7700000	.923372	.926114	.930647	.936911	.944811
.7800000	.940259	.943125	.947865	.954419	.962693
.7899999	.957387	.960381	.965335	.972190	.980852

$\alpha =$ .829999

Θ	K VALUES				
	.009966711	.039469502	.087332193	.151646642	.229848846
.8000000	.974761	.977888	.983065	.990232	.999297
.8100000	.992390	.995655	1.001061	1.008552	1.018034
.8200000	1.010281	1.013687	1.019332	1.027158	1.037074
.8300000	1.028441	1.031994	1.037885	1.046059	1.056425
.8400000	1.046877	1.050583	1.056729	1.065262	1.076095
.8500000	1.065599	1.069462	1.075872	1.084778	1.096094
.8600000	1.084614	1.088639	1.095322	1.104614	1.116433
.8700000	1.103930	1.108124	1.115089	1.124781	1.137119
.8799999	1.123556	1.127924	1.135182	1.145287	1.158165
.8899999	1.143502	1.148049	1.155609	1.166143	1.179579
.9000000	1.163776	1.168509	1.176381	1.187358	1.201374
.9100000	1.184388	1.189313	1.197508	1.208943	1.223559
.9200000	1.205347	1.210470	1.218999	1.230909	1.246147
.9300000	1.226663	1.231991	1.240865	1.253266	1.269148
.9400000	1.248347	1.253887	1.263117	1.276026	1.292575
.9500000	1.270409	1.276167	1.285766	1.299201	1.316440
.9600000	1.292860	1.298843	1.308823	1.322801	1.340756
.9699999	1.315710	1.321927	1.332300	1.346839	1.365535
.9799999	1.338972	1.345429	1.356209	1.371329	1.390791
.9899999	1.362657	1.369361	1.380561	1.396281	1.416537
1.0000000	1.386776	1.393737	1.405369	1.421710	1.442787
1.0100000	1.411341	1.418567	1.430647	1.447629	1.469556
1.0200000	1.436366	1.443864	1.456406	1.474051	1.496857
1.0300000	1.461863	1.469642	1.482661	1.500991	1.524706
1.0400000	1.487844	1.495913	1.509425	1.528462	1.553118
1.0500000	1.514323	1.522692	1.536712	1.556479	1.582108
1.0600000	1.541313	1.549991	1.564535	1.585057	1.611692
1.0699999	1.568828	1.577824	1.592910	1.614211	1.641886
1.0799999	1.596882	1.606207	1.621850	1.643956	1.672706
1.0899999	1.625489	1.635152	1.651371	1.674307	1.704168
1.1000000	1.654663	1.664675	1.681487	1.705281	1.736291
1.1100000	1.684418	1.694790	1.712214	1.736893	1.769088
1.1200000	1.714769	1.725511	1.743567	1.769158	1.802579
1.1300000	1.745730	1.756854	1.775561	1.802094	1.836780
1.1400000	1.777317	1.788834	1.808211	1.835715	1.871708
1.1500000	1.809543	1.821465	1.841533	1.870039	1.907381
1.1600000	1.842423	1.854763	1.875543	1.905081	1.943815
1.1700000	1.875972	1.888741	1.910254	1.940857	1.981027
1.1800000	1.910205	1.923416	1.945684	1.977383	2.019035
1.1899999	1.945134	1.958800	1.981845	2.014675	2.057855

$\alpha =$ .829999

Θ	K VALUES				
	.009966711	.039469502	.087332193	.151646642	.229848846
1.2000000	1.980775	1.994909	2.018754	2.052748	2.097503
1.2100000	2.017141	2.031756	2.056424	2.091616	2.137995
1.2200000	2.054244	2.069354	2.094869	2.131294	2.179346
1.2300000	2.092097	2.107716	2.134102	2.171796	2.221571
1.2400000	2.130713	2.146854	2.174135	2.213135	2.264684
1.2500000	2.170101	2.186780	2.214981	2.255324	2.308699
1.2599999	2.210274	2.227504	2.256650	2.298372	2.353626
1.2699999	2.251239	2.269035	2.299152	2.342292	2.399478
1.2799999	2.293005	2.311382	2.342495	2.387092	2.446263
1.2899999	2.335580	2.354552	2.386687	2.432780	2.493991
1.3000000	2.378969	2.398552	2.431735	2.479362	2.542668
1.3100000	2.423175	2.443384	2.477642	2.526841	2.592298
1.3200000	2.468202	2.489052	2.524410	2.575222	2.642885
1.3300000	2.514049	2.535555	2.572041	2.624505	2.694429
1.3400000	2.560717	2.582894	2.620533	2.674689	2.746929
1.3500000	2.608200	2.631064	2.669882	2.725769	2.800381
1.3600000	2.656494	2.680059	2.720083	2.777739	2.854779
1.3700000	2.705590	2.729872	2.771127	2.830592	2.910112
1.3799999	2.755479	2.780490	2.823002	2.884314	2.966370
1.3899999	2.806145	2.831902	2.875696	2.938891	3.023535
1.4000000	2.857574	2.884090	2.929190	2.994306	3.081590
1.4100000	2.909746	2.937035	2.983465	3.050537	3.140511
1.4200000	2.962639	2.990714	3.038498	3.107561	3.200274
1.4300000	3.016228	3.045102	3.094261	3.165349	3.260849
1.4400000	3.070485	3.100170	3.150727	3.223871	3.322204
1.4500000	3.125379	3.155887	3.207862	3.283093	3.384302
1.4600000	3.180875	3.212217	3.265629	3.342978	3.447103
1.4700000	3.236937	3.269124	3.323991	3.403483	3.510564
1.4800000	3.293523	3.326564	3.382904	3.464565	3.574637
1.4900000	3.350592	3.384496	3.442324	3.526177	3.639273
1.5000000	3.408098	3.442873	3.502202	3.588270	3.704419
1.5100000	3.465991	3.501645	3.562489	3.650788	3.770018
1.5200000	3.524223	3.560762	3.623130	3.713678	3.836012
1.5300000	3.582740	3.620169	3.684071	3.776882	3.902338
1.5400000	3.641489	3.679812	3.745256	3.840340	3.968935
1.5500000	3.700414	3.739634	3.806626	3.903992	4.035738
1.5600000	3.759458	3.799578	3.868122	3.967775	4.102680
1.5699999	3.818565	3.859586	3.929682	4.031627	4.169695
1.5707963	3.823273	3.864365	3.934586	4.036712	4.175033
1.5707963	3.823269	3.864362	3.934582	4.036709	4.175029

$\alpha =$ .829999

Θ	K VALUES				
	.318821117	.415016431	.514599755	.613601043	.708073407
.0000000	.000000	.000000	.000000	.000000	.000000
.0100000	.010000	.010000	.010000	.010000	.010000
.0200000	.020002	.020002	.020002	.020003	.020003
.0300000	.030008	.030009	.030009	.030010	.030010
.0400000	.040021	.040022	.040023	.040024	.040025
.0500000	.050041	.050043	.050045	.050047	.050049
.0600000	.060071	.060074	.060078	.060081	.060085
.0700000	.070113	.070118	.070124	.070130	.070135
.0800000	.080169	.080177	.080186	.080194	.080202
.0900000	.090241	.090252	.090265	.090277	.090288
.1000000	.100330	.100346	.100363	.100380	.100396
.1100000	.110440	.110462	.110484	.110506	.110527
.1200000	.120572	.120600	.120629	.120658	.120685
.1300000	.130728	.130764	.130801	.130837	.130872
.1400000	.140910	.140955	.141001	.141047	.141091
.1500000	.151121	.151176	.151233	.151289	.151343
.1600000	.161362	.161428	.161498	.161567	.161633
.1700000	.171635	.171715	.171798	.171881	.171961
.1800000	.181943	.182039	.182138	.182236	.182331
.1900000	.192288	.192401	.192517	.192634	.192746
.2000000	.202672	.202804	.202940	.203077	.203207
.2100000	.213098	.213250	.213409	.213567	.213719
.2200000	.223567	.223743	.223926	.224108	.224283
.2300000	.234081	.234283	.234493	.234702	.234903
.2400000	.244644	.244874	.245113	.245352	.245582
.2500000	.255258	.255518	.255790	.256061	.256321
.2600000	.265924	.266218	.266525	.266831	.267125
.2700000	.276646	.276976	.277321	.277665	.277996
.2800000	.287425	.287795	.288181	.288567	.288938
.2900000	.298265	.298678	.299108	.299538	.299953
.3000000	.309168	.309626	.310104	.310583	.311044
.3100000	.320136	.320643	.321173	.321704	.322216
.3200000	.331172	.331732	.332318	.332905	.333471
.3300000	.342278	.342895	.343541	.344188	.344813
.3400000	.353458	.354136	.354845	.355558	.356245
.3500000	.364714	.365457	.366234	.367016	.367770
.3600000	.376050	.376861	.377712	.378567	.379393
.3700000	.387467	.388352	.389280	.390214	.391117
.3800000	.398968	.399932	.400943	.401961	.402946
.3900000	.410558	.411605	.412704	.413812	.414884

$\alpha =$ .829999

Θ	K VALUES				
	.318821117	.415016431	.514599755	.613601043	.708073407
.4000000	.422238	.423374	.424566	.425769	.426935
.4100000	.434013	.435242	.436533	.437838	.439102
.4200000	.445884	.447212	.448609	.450021	.451391
.4300000	.457856	.459289	.460798	.462324	.463805
.4400000	.469932	.471476	.473102	.474749	.476350
.4500000	.482115	.483776	.485527	.487302	.489028
.4600000	.494409	.496193	.498076	.499987	.501846
.4700000	.506816	.508731	.510754	.512807	.514808
.4800000	.519342	.521394	.523564	.525768	.527918
.4900000	.531989	.534186	.536510	.538875	.541183
.5000000	.544762	.547111	.549598	.552131	.554607
.5100000	.557664	.560173	.562832	.565543	.568195
.5200000	.570700	.573376	.576217	.579115	.581954
.5300000	.583873	.586726	.589757	.592853	.595888
.5400000	.597188	.600226	.603458	.606762	.610005
.5500000	.610649	.613881	.617323	.620847	.624309
.5600000	.624260	.627697	.631360	.635114	.638807
.5700000	.638027	.641677	.645573	.649569	.653506
.5800000	.651953	.655828	.659967	.664219	.668412
.5900000	.666044	.670154	.674548	.679068	.683532
.6000000	.680305	.684660	.689323	.694125	.698874
.6100000	.694741	.699353	.704297	.709395	.714443
.6200000	.709356	.714237	.719476	.724885	.730249
.6300000	.724156	.729319	.734867	.740603	.746299
.6400000	.739148	.744604	.750476	.756555	.762600
.6500000	.754335	.760099	.766310	.772749	.779162
.6600000	.769725	.775811	.782376	.789193	.795992
.6700000	.785323	.791745	.798681	.805894	.813100
.6800000	.801136	.807908	.815233	.822862	.830494
.6899999	.817169	.824307	.832039	.840104	.848185
.7000000	.833430	.840950	.849107	.857629	.866183
.7100000	.849925	.857844	.866445	.875446	.884496
.7200000	.866661	.874995	.884062	.893564	.903136
.7300000	.883644	.892413	.901966	.911994	.922113
.7400000	.900883	.910104	.920165	.930745	.941440
.7500000	.918385	.928078	.938670	.949827	.961126
.7600000	.936157	.946342	.957489	.969251	.981185
.7700000	.954208	.964905	.976632	.989027	1.001629
.7800000	.972546	.983777	.996109	1.009168	1.022471
.7899999	.991179	1.002967	1.015931	1.029685	1.043723

$\alpha =$ •829999

Θ	K VALUES				
	•318821117	•415016431	•514599755	•613601043	•708073407
•8000000	1•010116	1•022484	1•036108	1•050589	1•065401
•8100000	1•029366	1•042338	1•056651	1•071894	1•087517
•8200000	1•048938	1•062538	1•077571	1•093611	1•110088
•8300000	1•068841	1•083097	1•098881	1•115755	1•133127
•8400000	1•089086	1•104024	1•120591	1•138339	1•156651
•8500000	1•109683	1•125330	1•142715	1•161377	1•180676
•8600000	1•130641	1•147026	1•165265	1•184884	1•205219
•8700000	1•151972	1•169126	1•188254	1•208874	1•230298
•8799999	1•173686	1•191639	1•211697	1•233364	1•255930
•8899999	1•195794	1•214580	1•235606	1•258369	1•282134
•9000000	1•218309	1•237960	1•259996	1•283906	1•308931
•9100000	1•241242	1•261794	1•284883	1•309991	1•336339
•9200000	1•264606	1•286093	1•310281	1•336643	1•364379
•9300000	1•288412	1•310873	1•336206	1•363879	1•393073
•9400000	1•312675	1•336147	1•362673	1•391719	1•422442
•9500000	1•337406	1•361931	1•389701	1•420181	1•452510
•9600000	1•362621	1•388238	1•417305	1•449285	1•483300
•9699999	1•388332	1•415086	1•445504	1•479051	1•514836
•9799999	1•414554	1•442489	1•474314	1•509501	1•547143
•9899999	1•441302	1•470464	1•503755	1•540655	1•580246
1•0000000	1•468591	1•499027	1•533846	1•572537	1•614174
1•0100000	1•496436	1•528196	1•564606	1•605168	1•648951
1•0200000	1•524853	1•557987	1•596055	1•638572	1•684607
1•0300000	1•553858	1•588420	1•628212	1•672772	1•721171
1•0400000	1•583467	1•619511	1•661099	1•707793	1•758672
1•0500000	1•613697	1•651280	1•694737	1•743660	1•797139
1•0600000	1•644566	1•683745	1•729148	1•780398	1•836605
1•0699999	1•676090	1•716926	1•764353	1•818034	1•877102
1•0799999	1•708288	1•750843	1•800374	1•856592	1•918660
1•0899999	1•741176	1•785514	1•837236	1•896102	1•961315
1•1000000	1•774773	1•820961	1•874960	1•936589	2•005099
1•1100000	1•809098	1•857203	1•913569	1•978082	2•050047
1•1200000	1•844168	1•894261	1•953088	2•020608	2•096193
1•1300000	1•880003	1•932155	1•993540	2•064195	2•143573
1•1400000	1•916621	1•970907	2•034949	2•108873	2•192223
1•1500000	1•954040	2•010537	2•077338	2•154670	2•242177
1•1600000	1•992279	2•051066	2•120732	2•201613	2•293474
1•1700000	2•031357	2•092515	2•165154	2•249732	2•346148
1•1800000	2•071292	2•134903	2•210628	2•299056	2•400235
1•1899999	2•112101	2•178251	2•257176	2•349611	2•455773

$\alpha =$ •829999

Θ	K VALUES				
	•318821117	•415016431	•514599755	•613601043	•708073407
1•2000000	2•153804	2•222579	2•304823	2•401427	2•512795
1•2100000	2•196416	2•267906	2•353590	2•454530	2•571338
1•2200000	2•239955	2•314250	2•403499	2•508945	2•631434
1•2300000	2•284436	2•361630	2•454570	2•564699	2•693118
1•2400000	2•329875	2•410063	2•506823	2•621816	2•756421
1•2500000	2•376286	2•459564	2•560278	2•680318	2•821374
1•2599999	2•423682	2•510149	2•614950	2•740228	2•888005
1•2699999	2•472076	2•561830	2•670858	2•801565	2•956342
1•2799999	2•521477	2•614621	2•728013	2•864347	3•026409
1•2899999	2•571896	2•668530	2•786429	2•928590	3•098227
1•3000000	2•623338	2•723568	2•846117	2•994306	3•171816
1•3100000	2•675810	2•779739	2•907082	3•061506	3•247190
1•3200000	2•729315	2•837047	2•969330	3•130196	3•324361
1•3300000	2•783854	2•895494	3•032863	3•200380	3•403338
1•3400000	2•839425	2•955079	3•097681	3•272059	3•484122
1•3500000	2•896024	3•015797	3•163778	3•345228	3•566712
1•3600000	2•953645	3•077641	3•231147	3•419880	3•651100
1•3700000	3•012277	3•140599	3•299777	3•496001	3•737275
1•3799999	3•071906	3•204658	3•369650	3•573574	3•825217
1•3899999	3•132517	3•269799	3•440747	3•652577	3•914900
1•4000000	3•194089	3•336000	3•513044	3•732982	4•006296
1•4100000	3•256597	3•403235	3•586510	3•814754	4•099361
1•4200000	3•320015	3•471473	3•661112	3•897856	4•194053
1•4300000	3•384310	3•540679	3•736812	3•982242	4•290318
1•4400000	3•449449	3•610816	3•813564	4•067861	4•388095
1•4500000	3•515390	3•681838	3•891320	4•154657	4•487317
1•4600000	3•582091	3•753700	3•970028	4•242568	4•587908
1•4700000	3•649506	3•826350	4•049628	4•331526	4•689786
1•4800000	3•717583	3•899730	4•130056	4•421456	4•792860
1•4900000	3•786268	3•973782	4•211247	4•512280	4•897036
1•5000000	3•855504	4•048443	4•293127	4•603915	5•002210
1•5100000	3•925230	4•123645	4•375621	4•696270	5•108272
1•5200000	3•995383	4•199317	4•458648	4•789252	5•215108
1•5300000	4•065896	4•275388	4•542128	4•882764	5•322598
1•5400000	4•136701	4•351782	4•625973	4•976708	5•430620
1•5500000	4•207728	4•428421	4•710097	5•070978	5•539047
1•5600000	4•278907	4•505226	4•794411	5•165471	5•647747
1•5699999	4•350164	4•582119	4•878822	5•260079	5•756591
1•5707963	4•355839	4•588243	4•885546	5•267615	5•765261
1•5707963	4•355836	4•588240	4•885543	5•267612	5•765260

$\alpha =$ .829999

Θ	K VALUES				
	.794250555	.868696860	.928444378	.971111163	.994996249
.0000000	.000000	.000000	.000000	.000000	.000000
.0100000	.010000	.010000	.010000	.010000	.010000
.0200000	.020003	.020003	.020003	.020003	.020003
.0300000	.030011	.030011	.030011	.030011	.030011
.0400000	.040026	.040027	.040027	.040028	.040028
.0500000	.050051	.050052	.050054	.050054	.050055
.0600000	.060088	.060091	.060093	.060094	.060095
.0700000	.070140	.070144	.070148	.070150	.070152
.0800000	.080210	.080216	.080221	.080225	.080227
.0900000	.090299	.090308	.090315	.090320	.090323
.1000000	.100410	.100423	.100433	.100440	.100444
.1100000	.110547	.110563	.110577	.110586	.110592
.1200000	.120711	.120732	.120750	.120762	.120769
.1300000	.130904	.130932	.130955	.130970	.130979
.1400000	.141131	.141166	.141194	.141214	.141225
.1500000	.151393	.151436	.151470	.151495	.151509
.1600000	.161693	.161745	.161787	.161817	.161834
.1700000	.172033	.172096	.172147	.172183	.172203
.1800000	.182417	.182492	.182552	.182596	.182620
.1900000	.192848	.192936	.193007	.193058	.193086
.2000000	.203327	.203430	.203514	.203573	.203607
.2100000	.213858	.213978	.214075	.214144	.214183
.2200000	.224444	.224583	.224695	.224775	.224820
.2300000	.235087	.235247	.235375	.235467	.235519
.2400000	.245792	.245974	.246121	.246226	.246285
.2500000	.256560	.256767	.256934	.257053	.257120
.2600000	.267395	.267629	.267818	.267953	.268029
.2700000	.278300	.278564	.278776	.278929	.279014
.2800000	.289278	.289574	.289813	.289984	.290080
.2900000	.300333	.300664	.300931	.301122	.301230
.3000000	.311468	.311837	.312134	.312348	.312467
.3100000	.322686	.323096	.323426	.323664	.323797
.3200000	.333992	.334445	.334811	.335074	.335222
.3300000	.345388	.345888	.346293	.346584	.346747
.3400000	.356878	.357429	.357875	.358196	.358376
.3500000	.368465	.369072	.369562	.369915	.370113
.3600000	.380155	.380820	.381358	.381745	.381963
.3700000	.391951	.392678	.393268	.393691	.393930
.3800000	.403856	.404651	.405295	.405758	.406019
.3900000	.415875	.416742	.417444	.417950	.418234

$\alpha =$ .829999

Θ	K VALUES				
	.794250555	.868696860	.928444378	.971111163	.994996249
.4000000	.428013	.428956	.429721	.430271	.430581
.4100000	.440273	.441298	.442129	.442728	.443065
.4200000	.452660	.453772	.454675	.455325	.455692
.4300000	.465179	.466383	.467362	.468068	.468465
.4400000	.477834	.479137	.480197	.480961	.481392
.4500000	.490631	.492039	.493184	.494011	.494477
.4600000	.503574	.505093	.506330	.507223	.507727
.4700000	.516669	.518306	.519640	.520604	.521148
.4800000	.529921	.531683	.533121	.534160	.534746
.4900000	.543335	.545230	.546778	.547897	.548529
.5000000	.556917	.558954	.560617	.561822	.562502
.5100000	.570672	.572859	.574646	.575941	.576673
.5200000	.584608	.586953	.588872	.590263	.591049
.5300000	.598730	.601243	.603301	.604793	.605638
.5400000	.613044	.615735	.617940	.619541	.620447
.5500000	.627557	.630436	.632798	.634514	.635485
.5600000	.642276	.645355	.647883	.649720	.650761
.5700000	.657209	.660498	.663201	.665168	.666283
.5800000	.672361	.675873	.678762	.680866	.682060
.5900000	.687741	.691489	.694575	.696825	.698101
.6000000	.703357	.707353	.710649	.713053	.714418
.6100000	.719216	.723476	.726993	.729560	.731019
.6200000	.735327	.739865	.743617	.746358	.747916
.6300000	.751698	.756531	.760530	.763456	.765119
.6400000	.768339	.773483	.777745	.780865	.782641
.6500000	.785259	.790731	.795271	.798599	.800494
.6600000	.802466	.808286	.813121	.816667	.818689
.6700000	.819972	.826159	.831305	.835085	.837241
.6800000	.837786	.844360	.849837	.853864	.856162
.6899999	.855919	.862903	.868729	.873018	.875468
.7000000	.874381	.881798	.887995	.892562	.895173
.7100000	.893185	.901060	.907648	.912510	.915293
.7200000	.912342	.920700	.927703	.932879	.935843
.7300000	.931865	.940733	.948176	.953684	.956842
.7400000	.951765	.961172	.969082	.974943	.978307
.7500000	.972057	.982034	.990438	.996674	1.000256
.7600000	.992753	1.003333	1.012260	1.018894	1.022709
.7700000	1.013869	1.025085	1.034567	1.041624	1.045687
.7800000	1.035418	1.047307	1.057377	1.064885	1.069211
.7899999	1.057416	1.070016	1.080710	1.088696	1.093303

$\alpha =$ .829999

Θ	K VALUES				
	.794250555	.868696860	.928444378	.971111163	.994996249
.8000000	1.079879	1.093231	1.104587	1.113081	1.117987
.8100000	1.102823	1.116971	1.129027	1.138063	1.143288
.8200000	1.126265	1.141254	1.154055	1.163666	1.169232
.8300000	1.150223	1.166101	1.179693	1.189916	1.195845
.8400000	1.174716	1.191534	1.205964	1.216841	1.223156
.8500000	1.199762	1.217575	1.232896	1.244467	1.251196
.8600000	1.225381	1.244247	1.260514	1.272825	1.279995
.8700000	1.251593	1.271574	1.288845	1.301946	1.309588
.8799999	1.278420	1.299580	1.317919	1.331862	1.340009
.8899999	1.305885	1.328293	1.347767	1.362608	1.371294
.9000000	1.334009	1.357739	1.378420	1.394220	1.403483
.9100000	1.362817	1.387946	1.409911	1.426734	1.436617
.9200000	1.392333	1.418944	1.442274	1.460192	1.470737
.9300000	1.422583	1.450764	1.475548	1.494634	1.505890
.9400000	1.453593	1.483437	1.509768	1.530105	1.542124
.9500000	1.485391	1.516997	1.544976	1.566651	1.579488
.9600000	1.518005	1.551479	1.581214	1.604320	1.618037
.9699999	1.551464	1.586918	1.618524	1.643163	1.657826
.9799999	1.585800	1.623352	1.656953	1.683236	1.698915
.9899999	1.621043	1.660821	1.696548	1.724593	1.741367
1.0000000	1.657226	1.699364	1.737361	1.767295	1.785250
1.0100000	1.694383	1.739024	1.779443	1.811406	1.830632
1.0200000	1.732548	1.779845	1.822848	1.856990	1.877590
1.0300000	1.771758	1.821872	1.867636	1.904120	1.926201
1.0400000	1.812050	1.865152	1.913866	1.952867	1.976551
1.0500000	1.853460	1.909736	1.961600	2.003310	2.028728
1.0600000	1.896030	1.955672	2.010905	2.055532	2.082827
1.0699999	1.939799	2.003015	2.061850	2.109619	2.138947
1.0799999	1.984809	2.051818	2.114506	2.165662	2.197197
1.0899999	2.031102	2.102138	2.168949	2.223757	2.257689
1.1000000	2.078722	2.154034	2.225257	2.284009	2.320544
1.1100000	2.127712	2.207564	2.283511	2.346521	2.385891
1.1200000	2.178120	2.262790	2.343797	2.411410	2.453866
1.1300000	2.229990	2.319777	2.406203	2.478794	2.524615
1.1400000	2.283370	2.378589	2.470821	2.548799	2.598294
1.1500000	2.338308	2.439293	2.537749	2.621560	2.675069
1.1600000	2.394853	2.501958	2.607084	2.697217	2.755118
1.1700000	2.453052	2.566653	2.678930	2.775918	2.838631
1.1800000	2.512955	2.633450	2.753395	2.857819	2.925810
1.1899999	2.574611	2.702420	2.830587	2.943087	3.016875

$\alpha =$ .829999

Θ	K VALUES				
	.794250555	.868696860	.928444378	.971111163	.994996249
1.2000000	2.638069	2.773636	2.910622	3.031895	3.112057
1.2100000	2.703377	2.847171	2.993615	3.124425	3.211607
1.2200000	2.770585	2.923099	3.079687	3.220871	3.315795
1.2300000	2.839738	3.001494	3.168961	3.321436	3.424909
1.2400000	2.910882	3.082429	3.261561	3.426332	3.539262
1.2500000	2.984064	3.165976	3.357615	3.535784	3.659189
1.2599999	3.059324	3.252207	3.457252	3.650026	3.785054
1.2699999	3.136704	3.341189	3.560602	3.769304	3.917249
1.2799999	3.216242	3.432989	3.667794	3.893875	4.056198
1.2899999	3.297971	3.527671	3.778958	4.024007	4.202365
1.3000000	3.381924	3.625294	3.894222	4.159981	4.356251
1.3100000	3.468126	3.725912	4.013708	4.302082	4.518400
1.3200000	3.556599	3.829574	4.137539	4.450613	4.689411
1.3300000	3.647362	3.936323	4.265829	4.605882	4.869936
1.3400000	3.740424	4.046194	4.398687	4.768205	5.060691
1.3500000	3.835792	4.159214	4.536212	4.937906	5.262465
1.3600000	3.933462	4.275401	4.678491	5.115311	5.476126
1.3700000	4.033426	4.394762	4.825600	5.300748	5.702634
1.3799999	4.135667	4.517292	4.977599	5.494542	5.943055
1.3899999	4.240158	4.642976	5.134529	5.697011	6.198573
1.4000000	4.346865	4.771785	5.296414	5.908463	6.470512
1.4100000	4.455743	4.903672	5.463250	6.129178	6.760343
1.4200000	4.566739	5.038581	5.635010	6.359415	7.069723
1.4300000	4.679788	5.176436	5.811641	6.599392	7.400509
1.4400000	4.794816	5.317147	5.993055	6.849278	7.754780
1.4500000	4.911739	5.460606	6.179135	7.109177	8.134869
1.4600000	5.030462	5.606689	6.369727	7.379117	8.543376
1.4700000	5.150879	5.755253	6.564640	7.659030	8.983176
1.4800000	5.272876	5.906140	6.763647	7.948738	9.457401
1.4900000	5.396327	6.059176	6.966482	8.247935	9.969371
1.5000000	5.521099	6.214170	7.172843	8.556173	10.522453
1.5100000	5.647049	6.370916	7.382387	8.872844	11.119758
1.5200000	5.774025	6.529193	7.594741	9.197182	11.763693
1.5300000	5.901871	6.688772	7.809496	9.528253	12.455201
1.5400000	6.030424	6.849409	8.026219	9.864965	13.192773
1.5500000	6.159513	7.010853	8.244449	10.206082	13.971339
1.5600000	6.288969	7.172846	8.463709	10.550247	14.781461
1.5699999	6.418614	7.335126	8.683506	10.896021	15.609440
1.5707963	6.428941	7.348053	8.701017	10.923581	15.675660
1.5707963	6.428951	7.348045	8.701008	10.923569	15.675637

$\alpha =$ .839999

Θ	K VALUES				
	.009966711	.039469502	.087332193	.151646642	.229848846
.0000000	.000000	.000000	.000000	.000000	.000000
.0100000	.010000	.010000	.010000	.010000	.010000
.0200000	.020002	.020002	.020002	.020002	.020002
.0300000	.030007	.030007	.030007	.030008	.030008
.0400000	.040018	.040018	.040018	.040019	.040020
.0500000	.050035	.050035	.050036	.050038	.050039
.0600000	.060060	.060061	.060063	.060066	.060068
.0700000	.070096	.070098	.070101	.070104	.070109
.0800000	.080144	.080147	.080151	.080156	.080163
.0900000	.090205	.090209	.090215	.090223	.090232
.1000000	.100282	.100287	.100295	.100306	.100319
.1100000	.110376	.110382	.110393	.110407	.110425
.1200000	.120488	.120497	.120511	.120529	.120552
.1300000	.130622	.130632	.130650	.130674	.130703
.1400000	.140777	.140791	.140813	.140842	.140878
.1500000	.150957	.150973	.151001	.151037	.151082
.1600000	.161162	.161183	.161216	.161260	.161314
.1700000	.171396	.171420	.171460	.171513	.171578
.1800000	.181659	.181687	.181735	.181798	.181875
.1900000	.191953	.191987	.192042	.192117	.192208
.2000000	.202280	.202320	.202385	.202472	.202579
.2100000	.212643	.212690	.212765	.212866	.212989
.2200000	.223043	.223097	.223183	.223299	.223441
.2300000	.233482	.233543	.233642	.233775	.233938
.2400000	.243962	.244032	.244144	.244296	.244481
.2500000	.254486	.254564	.254691	.254863	.255073
.2600000	.265054	.265142	.265286	.265479	.265716
.2700000	.275669	.275768	.275929	.276147	.276412
.2800000	.286333	.286444	.286624	.286867	.287164
.2900000	.297049	.297172	.297373	.297643	.297974
.3000000	.307818	.307954	.308177	.308477	.308845
.3100000	.318642	.318793	.319039	.319372	.319778
.3200000	.329524	.329691	.329962	.330329	.330777
.3300000	.340467	.340650	.340948	.341351	.341844
.3400000	.351471	.351672	.351999	.352441	.352982
.3500000	.362541	.362760	.363118	.363601	.364194
.3600000	.373677	.373916	.374307	.374834	.375481
.3700000	.384883	.385143	.385568	.386143	.386848
.3800000	.396160	.396443	.396905	.397529	.398296
.3900000	.407513	.407819	.408319	.408997	.409828

$\alpha =$ .839999

Θ	K VALUES				
	.009966711	.039469502	.087332193	.151646642	.229848846
.4000000	.418942	.419273	.419815	.420548	.421448
.4100000	.430450	.430809	.431393	.432185	.433159
.4200000	.442041	.442427	.443058	.443912	.444963
.4300000	.453717	.454133	.454812	.455732	.456864
.4400000	.465481	.465928	.466657	.467647	.468865
.4500000	.477336	.477815	.478598	.479660	.480969
.4600000	.489284	.489797	.490636	.491776	.493180
.4700000	.501328	.501878	.502776	.503996	.505500
.4800000	.513472	.514060	.515020	.516325	.517935
.4900000	.525719	.526346	.527371	.528765	.530486
.5000000	.538072	.538740	.539834	.541321	.543158
.5100000	.550534	.551246	.552410	.553995	.555954
.5200000	.563109	.563866	.565105	.566792	.568879
.5300000	.575800	.576604	.577921	.579716	.581937
.5400000	.588610	.589464	.590862	.592769	.595130
.5500000	.601543	.602449	.603933	.605957	.608465
.5600000	.614603	.615563	.617136	.619282	.621944
.5700000	.627794	.628810	.630476	.632750	.635573
.5800000	.641119	.642194	.643957	.646365	.649355
.5900000	.654583	.655719	.657583	.660130	.663296
.6000000	.668190	.669390	.671359	.674051	.677400
.6100000	.681944	.683210	.685288	.688133	.691673
.6200000	.695849	.697183	.699376	.702379	.706118
.6300000	.709909	.711316	.713628	.716794	.720742
.6400000	.724130	.725611	.728047	.731385	.735549
.6500000	.738516	.740075	.742639	.746155	.750546
.6600000	.753072	.754711	.757409	.761111	.765737
.6700000	.767802	.769526	.772362	.776257	.781128
.6800000	.782713	.784523	.787504	.791600	.796726
.6899999	.797809	.799709	.802841	.807145	.812537
.7000000	.813095	.815090	.818377	.822898	.828567
.7100000	.828578	.830670	.834118	.838865	.844821
.7200000	.844263	.846455	.850072	.855053	.861308
.7300000	.860156	.862453	.866243	.871468	.878034
.7400000	.876263	.878668	.882639	.888116	.895006
.7500000	.892590	.895107	.899266	.905005	.912230
.7600000	.909144	.911778	.916131	.922142	.929716
.7700000	.925931	.928686	.933240	.939533	.947470
.7800000	.942958	.945838	.950601	.957187	.965501
.7899999	.960233	.963242	.968221	.975111	.983817

$\alpha =$ •839999

Θ	K VALUES				
	•009966711	•039469502	•087332193	•151646642	•229848846
•8000000	•977763	•980906	•986109	•993314	1•002425
•8100000	•995554	•998836	1•004271	1•011802	1•021336
•8200000	1•013615	1•017041	1•022716	1•030586	1•040557
•8300000	1•031954	1•035528	1•041453	1•049673	1•060099
•8400000	1•050579	1•054307	1•060489	1•069073	1•079970
•8500000	1•069498	1•073385	1•079834	1•088794	1•100180
•8600000	1•088721	1•092772	1•099496	1•108847	1•120741
•8700000	1•108255	1•112476	1•119486	1•129241	1•141661
•8799999	1•128110	1•132507	1•139813	1•149987	1•162952
•8899999	1•148296	1•152875	1•160487	1•171094	1•184625
•9000000	1•168823	1•173590	1•181518	1•192574	1•206691
•9100000	1•189700	1•194661	1•202916	1•214437	1•229162
•9200000	1•210938	1•216100	1•224693	1•236694	1•252050
•9300000	1•232547	1•237917	1•246860	1•259359	1•275367
•9400000	1•254539	1•260123	1•269428	1•282442	1•299126
•9500000	1•276924	1•282730	1•292409	1•305956	1•323341
•9600000	1•299715	1•305749	1•315815	1•329913	1•348025
•9699999	1•322923	1•329194	1•339659	1•354328	1•373191
•9799999	1•346560	1•353075	1•363953	1•379212	1•398855
•9899999	1•370639	1•377406	1•388711	1•404580	1•425030
1•0000000	1•395173	1•402201	1•413946	1•430447	1•451732
1•0100000	1•420175	1•427472	1•439673	1•456826	1•478976
1•0200000	1•445658	1•453233	1•465904	1•483732	1•506777
1•0300000	1•471637	1•479498	1•492655	1•511181	1•535153
1•0400000	1•498125	1•506282	1•519941	1•539188	1•564119
1•0500000	1•525137	1•533600	1•547777	1•567770	1•593693
1•0600000	1•552688	1•561466	1•576179	1•596941	1•623891
1•0699999	1•580792	1•589896	1•605161	1•626720	1•654732
1•0799999	1•609466	1•618905	1•634741	1•657122	1•686233
1•0899999	1•638725	1•648510	1•664935	1•688165	1•718413
1•1000000	1•668585	1•678727	1•695759	1•719867	1•751290
1•1100000	1•699061	1•709571	1•727231	1•752245	1•784882
1•1200000	1•730170	1•741060	1•759367	1•785316	1•819210
1•1300000	1•761929	1•773211	1•792184	1•819100	1•854292
1•1400000	1•794353	1•806039	1•825701	1•853614	1•890147
1•1500000	1•827461	1•839563	1•859935	1•888876	1•926795
1•1600000	1•861268	1•873798	1•894902	1•924905	1•964255
1•1700000	1•895790	1•908763	1•930621	1•961720	2•002548
1•1800000	1•931046	1•944474	1•967110	1•999337	2•041691
1•1899999	1•967050	1•980947	2•004384	2•037777	2•081706

$\alpha =$ •839999

Θ	K VALUES				
	•009966711	•039469502	•087332193	•151646642	•229848846
1•2000000	2•003821	2•018200	2•042462	2•077056	2•122610
1•2100000	2•041372	2•056248	2•081361	2•117191	2•164422
1•2200000	2•079720	2•095108	2•121095	2•158201	2•207161
1•2300000	2•118879	2•134794	2•161682	2•200100	2•250843
1•2400000	2•158865	2•175321	2•203136	2•242907	2•295486
1•2500000	2•199691	2•216703	2•245472	2•286634	2•341106
1•2599999	2•241369	2•258954	2•288703	2•331297	2•387718
1•2699999	2•283912	2•302084	2•332841	2•376908	2•435336
1•2799999	2•327330	2•346106	2•377899	2•423480	2•483972
1•2899999	2•371633	2•391029	2•423885	2•471022	2•533637
1•3000000	2•416829	2•436862	2•470810	2•519544	2•584341
1•3100000	2•462924	2•483609	2•518677	2•569052	2•636092
1•3200000	2•509922	2•531276	2•567493	2•619552	2•688893
1•3300000	2•557826	2•579866	2•617261	2•671045	2•742750
1•3400000	2•606637	2•629379	2•667980	2•723534	2•797661
1•3500000	2•656352	2•679812	2•719649	2•777015	2•853625
1•3600000	2•706968	2•731163	2•772262	2•831483	2•910638
1•3700000	2•758476	2•783422	2•825814	2•886931	2•968689
1•3799999	2•810867	2•836580	2•880292	2•943349	3•027769
1•3899999	2•864127	2•890624	2•935683	3•000720	3•087860
1•4000000	2•918241	2•945536	2•991970	3•059028	3•148946
1•4100000	2•973188	3•001297	3•049132	3•118250	3•211002
1•4200000	3•028945	3•057883	3•107144	3•178361	3•274001
1•4300000	3•085486	3•115266	3•165979	3•239333	3•337913
1•4400000	3•142779	3•173417	3•225605	3•301130	3•402701
1•4500000	3•200792	3•232300	3•285986	3•363718	3•468327
1•4600000	3•259486	3•291876	3•347083	3•427053	3•534747
1•4700000	3•318821	3•352105	3•408852	3•491090	3•601913
1•4800000	3•378751	3•412940	3•471246	3•555782	3•669773
1•4900000	3•439229	3•474332	3•534215	3•621075	3•738270
1•5000000	3•500204	3•536231	3•597706	3•686912	3•807346
1•5100000	3•561620	3•598579	3•661660	3•753235	3•876936
1•5200000	3•623421	3•661319	3•726019	3•819980	3•946975
1•5300000	3•685548	3•724391	3•790720	3•887083	4•017393
1•5400000	3•747939	3•787732	3•855698	3•954475	4•088119
1•5500000	3•810532	3•851277	3•920888	4•022089	4•159080
1•5600000	3•873260	3•914962	3•986220	4•089852	4•230199
1•5699999	3•936060	3•978719	4•051628	4•157693	4•301401
1•5707963	3•941063	3•983797	4•056837	4•163097	4•307073
1•5707963	3•941059	3•983794	4•056834	4•163093	4•307069

$\alpha =$ .839999

Θ	K VALUES				
	.318821117	.415016431	.514599755	.613601043	.708073407
.0000000	.000000	.000000	.000000	.000000	.000000
.0100000	.010000	.010000	.010000	.010000	.010000
.0200000	.020002	.020002	.020002	.020003	.020003
.0300000	.030009	.030009	.030009	.030010	.030010
.0400000	.040021	.040022	.040023	.040024	.040025
.0500000	.050041	.050043	.050045	.050047	.050049
.0600000	.060072	.060075	.060079	.060082	.060086
.0700000	.070114	.070120	.070125	.070131	.070136
.0800000	.080170	.080179	.080187	.080196	.080204
.0900000	.090243	.090255	.090267	.090279	.090291
.1000000	.100334	.100350	.100367	.100383	.100399
.1100000	.110445	.110466	.110488	.110511	.110532
.1200000	.120578	.120606	.120635	.120664	.120691
.1300000	.130735	.130771	.130808	.130845	.130880
.1400000	.140920	.140964	.141010	.141056	.141100
.1500000	.151132	.151187	.151244	.151301	.151355
.1600000	.161376	.161442	.161512	.161581	.161647
.1700000	.171652	.171732	.171815	.171898	.171978
.1800000	.181963	.182059	.182158	.182256	.182351
.1900000	.192312	.192424	.192541	.192658	.192769
.2000000	.202700	.202831	.202968	.203104	.203235
.2100000	.213130	.213282	.213441	.213599	.213751
.2200000	.223604	.223780	.223963	.224145	.224321
.2300000	.234124	.234326	.234535	.234745	.234946
.2400000	.244693	.244923	.245162	.245401	.245630
.2500000	.255313	.255574	.255845	.256116	.256377
.2600000	.265987	.266281	.266587	.266894	.267188
.2700000	.276716	.277047	.277391	.277736	.278067
.2800000	.287504	.287874	.288260	.288646	.289017
.2900000	.298353	.298765	.299196	.299627	.300041
.3000000	.309265	.309724	.310202	.310682	.311143
.3100000	.320244	.320752	.321282	.321814	.322326
.3200000	.331291	.331852	.332438	.333026	.333592
.3300000	.342410	.343028	.343674	.344322	.344947
.3400000	.353604	.354282	.354992	.355705	.356392
.3500000	.364874	.365617	.366395	.367178	.367932
.3600000	.376225	.377037	.377888	.378744	.379571
.3700000	.387658	.388544	.389473	.390408	.391312
.3800000	.399177	.400142	.401154	.402173	.403159
.3900000	.410785	.411833	.412933	.414042	.415116

$\alpha =$ .839999

Θ	K VALUES				
	.318821117	.415016431	.514599755	.613601043	.708073407
.4000000	.422485	.423622	.424816	.426020	.427187
.4100000	.434281	.435511	.436804	.438110	.439376
.4200000	.446175	.447504	.448903	.450317	.451688
.4300000	.458170	.459605	.461116	.462644	.464127
.4400000	.470271	.471817	.473446	.475095	.476697
.4500000	.482481	.484144	.485898	.487675	.489404
.4600000	.494803	.496590	.498476	.500389	.502251
.4700000	.507241	.509158	.511184	.513240	.515244
.4800000	.519798	.521853	.524026	.526234	.528388
.4900000	.532479	.534679	.537008	.539376	.541688
.5000000	.545288	.547640	.550132	.552669	.555149
.5100000	.558227	.560740	.563405	.566120	.568777
.5200000	.571303	.573984	.576830	.579734	.582578
.5300000	.584518	.587376	.590413	.593515	.596557
.5400000	.597877	.600921	.604159	.607470	.610720
.5500000	.611385	.614624	.618073	.621604	.625074
.5600000	.625045	.628490	.632161	.635923	.639625
.5700000	.638864	.642523	.646427	.650433	.654379
.5800000	.652845	.656729	.660878	.665140	.669344
.5900000	.666994	.671113	.675519	.680051	.684526
.6000000	.681316	.685682	.690357	.695172	.699933
.6100000	.695815	.700440	.705397	.710509	.715571
.6200000	.710498	.715393	.720646	.726071	.731450
.6300000	.725370	.730547	.736111	.741864	.747577
.6400000	.740436	.745909	.751798	.757896	.763960
.6500000	.755702	.761485	.767714	.774174	.780607
.6600000	.771175	.777281	.783867	.790707	.797528
.6700000	.786861	.793304	.800264	.807502	.814732
.6800000	.802765	.809561	.816912	.824568	.832228
.6899999	.818895	.826059	.833819	.841913	.850025
.7000000	.835258	.842806	.850994	.859548	.868135
.7100000	.851860	.859809	.868445	.877481	.886567
.7200000	.868708	.877076	.886180	.895722	.905333
.7300000	.885810	.894615	.904209	.914280	.924442
.7400000	.903173	.912434	.922540	.933166	.943908
.7500000	.920806	.930542	.941183	.952391	.963743
.7600000	.938716	.948948	.960148	.971965	.983957
.7700000	.956912	.967661	.979445	.991901	1.004565
.7800000	.975403	.986690	.999084	1.012209	1.025580
.7899999	.994196	1.006045	1.019076	1.032902	1.047016

$\alpha =$ •839999

Θ	K VALUES				
	•318821117	•415016431	•514599755	•613601043	•708073407
•8000000	1•013302	1•025736	1•039433	1•053993	1•068887
•8100000	1•032729	1•045772	1•060165	1•075494	1•091207
•8200000	1•052488	1•066166	1•081285	1•097419	1•113992
•8300000	1•072588	1•086927	1•102805	1•119781	1•137259
•8400000	1•093040	1•108068	1•124737	1•142596	1•161023
•8500000	1•113853	1•129599	1•147094	1•165877	1•185302
•8600000	1•135040	1•151532	1•169891	1•189640	1•210113
•8700000	1•156612	1•173881	1•193139	1•213901	1•235474
•8799999	1•178579	1•196657	1•216855	1•238677	1•261406
•8899999	1•200954	1•219874	1•241053	1•263983	1•287926
•9000000	1•223750	1•243546	1•265747	1•289838	1•315056
•9100000	1•246978	1•267686	1•290954	1•316259	1•342817
•9200000	1•270652	1•292309	1•316689	1•343266	1•371230
•9300000	1•294786	1•317429	1•342970	1•370876	1•400318
•9400000	1•319392	1•343062	1•369814	1•399111	1•430105
•9500000	1•344486	1•369223	1•397238	1•427990	1•460613
•9600000	1•370082	1•395929	1•425260	1•457534	1•491869
•9699999	1•396195	1•423196	1•453899	1•487766	1•523898
•9799999	1•422841	1•451041	1•483175	1•518707	1•556726
•9899999	1•450034	1•479482	1•513106	1•550381	1•590381
1•0000000	1•477793	1•508537	1•543715	1•582811	1•624892
1•0100000	1•506132	1•538224	1•575021	1•616021	1•660287
1•0200000	1•535070	1•568561	1•607045	1•650037	1•696597
1•0300000	1•564623	1•599569	1•639811	1•684884	1•733852
1•0400000	1•594810	1•631267	1•673340	1•720589	1•772084
1•0500000	1•625650	1•663676	1•707655	1•757178	1•811327
1•0600000	1•657159	1•696815	1•742780	1•794679	1•851612
1•0699999	1•689359	1•730707	1•778740	1•833121	1•892976
1•0799999	1•722268	1•765373	1•815557	1•872532	1•935454
1•0899999	1•755906	1•800835	1•853259	1•912942	1•979080
1•1000000	1•790293	1•837115	1•891870	1•954381	2•023894
1•1100000	1•825449	1•874235	1•931415	1•996879	2•069930
1•1200000	1•861396	1•912219	1•971921	2•040467	2•117229
1•1300000	1•898153	1•951089	2•013415	2•085177	2•165830
1•1400000	1•935743	1•990869	2•055922	2•131041	2•215770
1•1500000	1•974185	2•031583	2•099471	2•178089	2•267091
1•1600000	2•013502	2•073254	2•144087	2•226356	2•319833
1•1700000	2•053714	2•115905	2•189798	2•275871	2•374036
1•1800000	2•094842	2•159560	2•236631	2•326669	2•429740
1•1899999	2•136908	2•204243	2•284613	2•378781	2•486986

$\alpha =$ •839999

Θ	K VALUES				
	•318821117	•415016431	•514599755	•613601043	•708073407
1•2000000	2•179932	2•249975	2•333769	2•432238	2•545816
1•2100000	2•223933	2•296780	2•384126	2•487072	2•606267
1•2200000	2•268933	2•344679	2•435709	2•543313	2•668379
1•2300000	2•314949	2•393694	2•488542	2•600991	2•732192
1•2400000	2•362000	2•443846	2•542650	2•660134	2•797741
1•2500000	2•410105	2•495153	2•598055	2•720771	2•865064
1•2599999	2•459278	2•547634	2•654777	2•782927	2•934193
1•2699999	2•509535	2•601306	2•712838	2•846627	3•005162
1•2799999	2•560890	2•656184	2•772254	2•911892	3•078000
1•2899999	2•613355	2•712282	2•833041	2•978742	3•152733
1•3000000	2•666941	2•769612	2•895215	3•047196	3•229388
1•3100000	2•721654	2•828182	2•958784	3•117266	3•307982
1•3200000	2•777502	2•888000	3•023758	3•188964	3•388532
1•3300000	2•834487	2•949069	3•090141	3•262296	3•471051
1•3400000	2•892610	3•011391	3•157936	3•337267	3•555545
1•3500000	2•951870	3•074963	3•227140	3•413876	3•642017
1•3600000	3•012260	3•139779	3•297747	3•492116	3•730462
1•3700000	3•073772	3•205830	3•369748	3•571976	3•820870
1•3799999	3•136393	3•273102	3•443126	3•653441	3•913223
1•3899999	3•200106	3•341578	3•517863	3•736488	4•007499
1•4000000	3•264893	3•411236	3•593935	3•821091	4•103665
1•4100000	3•330726	3•482046	3•671309	3•907213	4•201681
1•4200000	3•397578	3•553979	3•749951	3•994814	4•301501
1•4300000	3•465415	3•626997	3•829819	4•083848	4•403067
1•4400000	3•534198	3•701059	3•910867	4•174259	4•506317
1•4500000	3•603886	3•776118	3•993042	4•265987	4•611176
1•4600000	3•674432	3•852121	4•076285	4•358964	4•717564
1•4700000	3•745782	3•929011	4•160532	4•453115	4•825390
1•4800000	3•817881	4•006728	4•245713	4•548360	4•934555
1•4900000	3•890670	4•085204	4•331753	4•644609	5•044954
1•5000000	3•964083	4•164368	4•418573	4•741771	5•156472
1•5100000	4•038051	4•244146	4•506086	4•839746	5•268987
1•5200000	4•112504	4•324457	4•594203	4•938428	5•382373
1•5300000	4•187367	4•405220	4•682832	5•037709	5•496494
1•5400000	4•262562	4•486350	4•771876	5•137477	5•611213
1•5500000	4•338010	4•567759	4•861236	5•237614	5•726388
1•5600000	4•413630	4•649357	4•950810	5•338003	5•841871
1•5699999	4•489339	4•731054	5•040496	5•438523	5•957516
1•5707963	4•495369	4•737562	5•047640	5•446530	5•966728
1•5707963	4•495366	4•737558	5•047637	5•446527	5•966727

$\alpha =$ .839999

Θ	K VALUES				
	.794250555	.868696860	.928444378	.971111163	.994996249
.0000000	.000000	.000000	.000000	.000000	.000000
.0100000	.010000	.010000	.010000	.010000	.010000
.0200000	.020003	.020003	.020003	.020003	.020003
.0300000	.030011	.030011	.030011	.030011	.030012
.0400000	.040026	.040027	.040027	.040028	.040028
.0500000	.050051	.050053	.050054	.050055	.050055
.0600000	.060089	.060091	.060094	.060095	.060096
.0700000	.070141	.070146	.070149	.070151	.070153
.0800000	.080211	.080218	.080223	.080226	.080228
.0900000	.090301	.090310	.090318	.090323	.090326
.1000000	.100414	.100426	.100436	.100443	.100447
.1100000	.110551	.110568	.110581	.110591	.110596
.1200000	.120716	.120738	.120756	.120768	.120775
.1300000	.130912	.130940	.130962	.130978	.130987
.1400000	.141140	.141175	.141203	.141223	.141234
.1500000	.151405	.151447	.151482	.151506	.151520
.1600000	.161707	.161759	.161801	.161831	.161848
.1700000	.172050	.172113	.172164	.172200	.172220
.1800000	.182438	.182512	.182573	.182616	.182640
.1900000	.192871	.192960	.193031	.193082	.193110
.2000000	.203355	.203458	.203541	.203601	.203634
.2100000	.213890	.214011	.214107	.214177	.214216
.2200000	.224481	.224620	.224732	.224812	.224857
.2300000	.235130	.235290	.235418	.235510	.235562
.2400000	.245841	.246023	.246170	.246275	.246334
.2500000	.256615	.256823	.256989	.257109	.257176
.2600000	.267458	.267692	.267881	.268016	.268092
.2700000	.278371	.278635	.278847	.279000	.279085
.2800000	.289358	.289654	.289893	.290064	.290160
.2900000	.300422	.300753	.301020	.301212	.301319
.3000000	.311567	.311936	.312234	.312447	.312567
.3100000	.322796	.323206	.323537	.323774	.323907
.3200000	.334113	.334567	.334934	.335197	.335344
.3300000	.345522	.346023	.346428	.346719	.346882
.3400000	.357026	.357578	.358024	.358345	.358525
.3500000	.368628	.369235	.369726	.370079	.370277
.3600000	.380334	.380999	.381538	.381925	.382143
.3700000	.392146	.392874	.393464	.393888	.394127
.3800000	.404069	.404865	.405509	.405973	.406234
.3900000	.416108	.416975	.417678	.418184	.418469

$\alpha =$ .839999

Θ	K VALUES				
	.794250555	.868696860	.928444378	.971111163	.994996249
.4000000	.428266	.429210	.429976	.430527	.430837
.4100000	.440548	.441574	.442406	.443006	.443344
.4200000	.452958	.454071	.454975	.455627	.455993
.4300000	.465502	.466708	.467688	.468394	.468792
.4400000	.478184	.479488	.480549	.481314	.481746
.4500000	.491009	.492418	.493565	.494393	.494860
.4600000	.503982	.505503	.506742	.507636	.508140
.4700000	.517108	.518748	.520084	.521049	.521594
.4800000	.530393	.532159	.533599	.534639	.535227
.4900000	.543843	.545742	.547292	.548413	.549046
.5000000	.557463	.559503	.561170	.562376	.563058
.5100000	.571259	.573449	.575240	.576537	.577270
.5200000	.585237	.587586	.589509	.590902	.591690
.5300000	.599404	.601922	.603984	.605479	.606325
.5400000	.613765	.616462	.618672	.620276	.621184
.5500000	.628329	.631214	.633581	.635301	.636274
.5600000	.643102	.646187	.648720	.650562	.651605
.5700000	.658090	.661387	.664097	.666068	.667186
.5800000	.673302	.676823	.679719	.681829	.683025
.5900000	.688745	.692502	.695597	.697852	.699132
.6000000	.704427	.708435	.711739	.714150	.715518
.6100000	.720357	.724629	.728156	.730731	.732193
.6200000	.736543	.741094	.744856	.747605	.749168
.6300000	.752993	.757840	.761851	.764785	.766454
.6400000	.769717	.774877	.779152	.782282	.784064
.6500000	.786724	.792214	.796769	.800107	.802009
.6600000	.804024	.809864	.814715	.818274	.820302
.6700000	.821628	.827837	.833001	.836794	.838958
.6800000	.839545	.846144	.851640	.855682	.857989
.6899999	.857788	.864798	.870646	.874952	.877411
.7000000	.876366	.883812	.890033	.894618	.897240
.7100000	.895292	.903198	.909814	.914696	.917490
.7200000	.914578	.922971	.930004	.935202	.938179
.7300000	.934236	.943143	.950620	.956152	.959324
.7400000	.954281	.963731	.971677	.977565	.980944
.7500000	.974724	.984748	.993192	.999458	1.003057
.7600000	.995581	1.006212	1.015183	1.021851	1.025685
.7700000	1.016866	1.028139	1.037670	1.044764	1.048847
.7800000	1.038594	1.050546	1.060670	1.068217	1.072567
.7899999	1.060782	1.073451	1.084204	1.092234	1.096866

$\alpha =$ •839999

Θ	K VALUES				
	•794250555	•868696860	•928444378	•971111163	•994996249
•8000000	1•083445	1•096873	1•108293	1•116836	1•121771
•8100000	1•106601	1•120831	1•132959	1•142048	1•147305
•8200000	1•130267	1•145346	1•158225	1•167896	1•173496
•8300000	1•154461	1•170439	1•184116	1•194405	1•200371
•8400000	1•179204	1•196131	1•210656	1•221604	1•227962
•8500000	1•204514	1•222447	1•237872	1•249522	1•256297
•8600000	1•230413	1•249410	1•265791	1•278190	1•285411
•8700000	1•256921	1•277045	1•294442	1•307639	1•315338
•8799999	1•284061	1•305378	1•323855	1•337905	1•346113
•8899999	1•311857	1•334437	1•354063	1•369021	1•377776
•9000000	1•340331	1•364250	1•385098	1•401026	1•410366
•9100000	1•369510	1•394846	1•416994	1•433960	1•443926
•9200000	1•399419	1•426256	1•449788	1•467862	1•478500
•9300000	1•430084	1•458513	1•483518	1•502778	1•514136
•9400000	1•461534	1•491650	1•518225	1•538752	1•550884
•9500000	1•493798	1•525702	1•553949	1•575833	1•588796
•9600000	1•526906	1•560706	1•590735	1•614073	1•627928
•9699999	1•560888	1•596699	1•628628	1•653524	1•668339
•9799999	1•595778	1•633721	1•667678	1•694242	1•710092
•9899999	1•631608	1•671814	1•707933	1•736289	1•753252
1•0000000	1•668414	1•711020	1•749447	1•779726	1•797889
1•0100000	1•706230	1•751384	1•792276	1•824619	1•844077
1•0200000	1•745095	1•792953	1•836477	1•871039	1•891895
1•0300000	1•785047	1•835775	1•882112	1•919060	1•941426
1•0400000	1•826124	1•879900	1•929244	1•968758	1•992758
1•0500000	1•868369	1•925381	1•977939	2•020217	2•045986
1•0600000	1•911823	1•972272	2•028269	2•073524	2•101208
1•0699999	1•956530	2•020629	2•080305	2•128769	2•158531
1•0799999	2•002534	2•070511	2•134125	2•186051	2•218068
1•0899999	2•049882	2•121978	2•189808	2•245471	2•279939
1•1000000	2•098621	2•175093	2•247440	2•307138	2•344272
1•1100000	2•148799	2•229920	2•307106	2•371166	2•411202
1•1200000	2•200466	2•286526	2•368898	2•437676	2•480875
1•1300000	2•253672	2•344981	2•432911	2•506795	2•553446
1•1400000	2•308469	2•405354	2•499244	2•578658	2•629081
1•1500000	2•364909	2•467718	2•568002	2•653409	2•707956
1•1600000	2•423047	2•532149	2•639291	2•731197	2•790260
1•1700000	2•482935	2•598721	2•713222	2•812182	2•876197
1•1800000	2•544628	2•667514	2•789912	2•896532	2•965982
1•1899999	2•608182	2•738607	2•869481	2•984424	3•059849

$\alpha =$ .839999

Θ	K VALUES				
	.794250555	.868696860	.928444378	.971111163	.994996249
1.2000000	2.673651	2.812079	2.952051	3.076046	3.158047
1.2100000	2.741089	2.888012	3.037750	3.171593	3.260844
1.2200000	2.810550	2.966488	3.126710	3.271275	3.368527
1.2300000	2.882090	3.047588	3.219064	3.375310	3.481407
1.2400000	2.955760	3.131395	3.314951	3.483929	3.599818
1.2500000	3.031611	3.217990	3.414510	3.597374	3.724121
1.2599999	3.109693	3.307453	3.517882	3.715900	3.854704
1.2699999	3.190053	3.399863	3.625213	3.839772	3.991990
1.2799999	3.272736	3.495294	3.736644	3.969270	4.136436
1.2899999	3.357783	3.593819	3.852321	4.104685	4.288536
1.3000000	3.445233	3.695509	3.972386	4.246322	4.448833
1.3100000	3.535117	3.800425	4.096976	4.394494	4.617909
1.3200000	3.627464	3.908626	4.226229	4.549529	4.796408
1.3300000	3.722298	4.020164	4.360275	4.711763	4.985031
1.3400000	3.819635	4.135081	4.499235	4.881542	5.184549
1.3500000	3.919485	4.253414	4.643224	5.059219	5.395807
1.3600000	4.021850	4.375185	4.792342	5.245152	5.619738
1.3700000	4.126725	4.500409	4.946678	5.439698	5.857374
1.3799999	4.234095	4.629086	5.106302	5.643215	6.109857
1.3899999	4.343935	4.761205	5.271267	5.856050	6.378457
1.4000000	4.456214	4.896738	5.441603	6.078542	6.664594
1.4100000	4.570883	5.035641	5.617313	6.310997	6.969843
1.4200000	4.687889	5.177856	5.798375	6.553702	7.295978
1.4300000	4.807164	5.323304	5.984734	6.806897	7.644983
1.4400000	4.928631	5.471890	6.176302	7.070769	8.019083
1.4500000	5.052197	5.623500	6.372955	7.345436	8.420770
1.4600000	5.177761	5.778001	6.574529	7.630932	8.852819
1.4700000	5.305209	5.935239	6.780822	7.927188	9.318299
1.4800000	5.434415	6.095042	6.991588	8.234014	9.820547
1.4900000	5.565240	6.257219	7.206540	8.551084	10.363102
1.5000000	5.697539	6.421563	7.425350	8.877917	10.949549
1.5100000	5.831152	6.587846	7.647644	9.213857	11.583200
1.5200000	5.965913	6.755826	7.873015	9.558077	12.266610
1.5300000	6.101645	6.925249	8.101019	9.909571	13.000777
1.5400000	6.238168	7.095845	8.331178	10.267159	13.784080
1.5500000	6.375292	7.267338	8.562991	10.629506	14.611103
1.5600000	6.512825	7.439439	8.795932	10.995148	15.471776
1.5699999	6.650571	7.611859	9.029463	11.362527	16.351490
1.5707963	6.661544	7.625594	9.048069	11.391809	16.421848
1.5707963	6.661551	7.625588	9.048062	11.391800	16.421830

$\alpha =$ .849999

Θ	K VALUES				
	.009966711	.039469502	.087332193	.151646642	.229848846
.0000000	.000000	.000000	.000000	.000000	.000000
.0100000	.010000	.010000	.010000	.010000	.010000
.0200000	.020002	.020002	.020002	.020002	.020002
.0300000	.030007	.030007	.030008	.030008	.030008
.0400000	.040018	.040018	.040019	.040019	.040020
.0500000	.050035	.050036	.050037	.050038	.050040
.0600000	.060061	.060062	.060064	.060066	.060069
.0700000	.070097	.070099	.070102	.070106	.070110
.0800000	.080146	.080148	.080152	.080158	.080165
.0900000	.090208	.090211	.090217	.090225	.090235
.1000000	.100285	.100290	.100298	.100309	.100322
.1100000	.110380	.110387	.110397	.110412	.110429
.1200000	.120494	.120503	.120517	.120535	.120558
.1300000	.130629	.130640	.130657	.130681	.130710
.1400000	.140786	.140800	.140822	.140852	.140888
.1500000	.150968	.150985	.151012	.151049	.151093
.1600000	.161176	.161197	.161229	.161274	.161328
.1700000	.171412	.171437	.171476	.171530	.171595
.1800000	.181678	.181707	.181755	.181818	.181895
.1900000	.191976	.192011	.192066	.192141	.192232
.2000000	.202308	.202348	.202413	.202500	.202606
.2100000	.212675	.212722	.212797	.212898	.213021
.2200000	.223080	.223133	.223220	.223336	.223478
.2300000	.233525	.233586	.233685	.233818	.233981
.2400000	.244011	.244080	.244193	.244345	.244530
.2500000	.254540	.254619	.254746	.254918	.255128
.2600000	.265116	.265204	.265348	.265542	.265778
.2700000	.275738	.275838	.275999	.276216	.276482
.2800000	.286411	.286522	.286702	.286945	.287243
.2900000	.297136	.297259	.297460	.297731	.298062
.3000000	.307915	.308051	.308274	.308575	.308942
.3100000	.318750	.318901	.319147	.319480	.319886
.3200000	.329643	.329810	.330082	.330448	.330897
.3300000	.340598	.340781	.341080	.341483	.341977
.3400000	.351616	.351816	.352144	.352586	.353128
.3500000	.362699	.362919	.363276	.363760	.364353
.3600000	.373850	.374090	.374480	.375008	.375656
.3700000	.385072	.385333	.385758	.386333	.387039
.3800000	.396367	.396650	.397112	.397737	.398504
.3900000	.407737	.408044	.408545	.409223	.410055

$\alpha =$ .849999

Θ	K VALUES				
	.009966711	.039469502	.087332193	.151646642	.229848846
.4000000	.419185	.419518	.420059	.420793	.421695
.4100000	.430715	.431073	.431659	.432452	.433426
.4200000	.442328	.442714	.443345	.444201	.445253
.4300000	.454027	.454443	.455122	.456044	.457178
.4400000	.465815	.466262	.466993	.467984	.469204
.4500000	.477696	.478176	.478960	.480024	.481334
.4600000	.489671	.490186	.491026	.492167	.493573
.4700000	.501745	.502296	.503195	.504417	.505924
.4800000	.513920	.514508	.515470	.516777	.518389
.4900000	.526200	.526828	.527854	.529250	.530974
.5000000	.538587	.539257	.540352	.541841	.543681
.5100000	.551086	.551799	.552965	.554553	.556515
.5200000	.563699	.564457	.565699	.567389	.569480
.5300000	.576430	.577236	.578556	.580354	.582579
.5400000	.589283	.590139	.591540	.593451	.595817
.5500000	.602261	.603169	.604656	.606684	.609198
.5600000	.615369	.616331	.617907	.620058	.622726
.5700000	.628610	.629628	.631298	.633577	.636406
.5800000	.641988	.643065	.644832	.647246	.650243
.5900000	.655507	.656646	.658514	.661068	.664241
.6000000	.669172	.670375	.672349	.675049	.678406
.6100000	.682987	.684256	.686341	.689192	.692742
.6200000	.696957	.698295	.700494	.703505	.707255
.6300000	.711085	.712496	.714814	.717990	.721949
.6400000	.725377	.726863	.729306	.732654	.736831
.6500000	.739838	.741402	.743974	.747501	.751905
.6600000	.754473	.756118	.758824	.762538	.767179
.6700000	.769287	.771016	.773862	.777770	.782657
.6800000	.784284	.786101	.789092	.793202	.798346
.6899999	.799472	.801379	.804522	.808842	.814253
.7000000	.814855	.816856	.820156	.824694	.830383
.7100000	.830439	.832538	.836000	.840765	.846744
.7200000	.846230	.848431	.852062	.857063	.863343
.7300000	.862234	.864540	.868347	.873593	.880186
.7400000	.878458	.880874	.884862	.890362	.897281
.7500000	.894908	.897437	.901614	.907378	.914636
.7600000	.911592	.914238	.918610	.924649	.932258
.7700000	.928515	.931282	.935858	.942181	.950156
.7800000	.945685	.948579	.953365	.959983	.968338
.7899999	.963110	.966134	.971138	.978063	.986813

$\alpha =$ .849999

Θ	K VALUES				
	.009966711	.039469502	.087332193	.151646642	.229848846
.8000000	.980797	.983956	.989187	.996429	1.005589
.8100000	.998754	1.002053	1.007518	1.015090	1.024675
.8200000	1.016989	1.020434	1.026141	1.034054	1.044082
.8300000	1.035511	1.039105	1.045064	1.053332	1.063818
.8400000	1.054328	1.058078	1.064296	1.072932	1.083894
.8500000	1.073449	1.077359	1.083848	1.092864	1.104320
.8600000	1.092884	1.096960	1.103727	1.113138	1.125108
.8700000	1.112641	1.116889	1.123946	1.133765	1.146266
.8799999	1.132730	1.137157	1.144512	1.154755	1.167809
.8899999	1.153163	1.157773	1.165438	1.176119	1.189746
.9000000	1.173948	1.178749	1.186734	1.197870	1.212090
.9100000	1.195098	1.200095	1.208412	1.220018	1.234854
.9200000	1.216622	1.221823	1.230482	1.242576	1.258051
.9300000	1.238532	1.243944	1.252958	1.265556	1.281693
.9400000	1.260840	1.266470	1.275851	1.288972	1.305795
.9500000	1.283559	1.289413	1.299173	1.312835	1.330370
.9600000	1.306700	1.312786	1.322939	1.337161	1.355433
.9699999	1.330276	1.336603	1.347162	1.361963	1.380999
.9799999	1.354301	1.360876	1.371855	1.387256	1.407083
.9899999	1.378788	1.385620	1.397032	1.413054	1.433702
1.0000000	1.403751	1.410848	1.422709	1.439373	1.460871
1.0100000	1.429205	1.436576	1.448900	1.466229	1.488607
1.0200000	1.455164	1.462818	1.475622	1.493638	1.516928
1.0300000	1.481643	1.489589	1.502889	1.521616	1.545851
1.0400000	1.508659	1.516906	1.530718	1.550180	1.575393
1.0500000	1.536226	1.544785	1.559125	1.579349	1.605575
1.0600000	1.564361	1.573242	1.588129	1.609139	1.636414
1.0699999	1.593081	1.602295	1.617746	1.639570	1.667930
1.0799999	1.622403	1.631960	1.647995	1.670659	1.700143
1.0899999	1.652344	1.662255	1.678893	1.702426	1.733073
1.1000000	1.682923	1.693199	1.710459	1.734891	1.766741
1.1100000	1.714156	1.724810	1.742712	1.768073	1.801168
1.1200000	1.746062	1.757106	1.775672	1.801992	1.836375
1.1300000	1.778660	1.790106	1.809357	1.836668	1.872384
1.1400000	1.811969	1.823829	1.843787	1.872123	1.909217
1.1500000	1.846007	1.858295	1.878983	1.908377	1.946895
1.1600000	1.880794	1.893523	1.914964	1.945451	1.985442
1.1700000	1.916348	1.929533	1.951751	1.983365	2.024879
1.1800000	1.952690	1.966344	1.989364	2.022142	2.065228
1.1899999	1.989838	2.003976	2.027822	2.061802	2.106513

$\alpha =$ .849999

Θ	K VALUES				
	.009966711	.039469502	.087332193	.151646642	.229848846
1.2000000	2.027811	2.042448	2.067146	2.102366	2.148756
1.2100000	2.066628	2.081778	2.107355	2.143855	2.191977
1.2200000	2.106307	2.121986	2.148469	2.186287	2.236199
1.2300000	2.146866	2.163091	2.190506	2.229685	2.281443
1.2400000	2.188323	2.205109	2.233486	2.274066	2.327729
1.2500000	2.230695	2.248058	2.277424	2.319449	2.375076
1.2599999	2.273997	2.291954	2.322339	2.365852	2.423504
1.2699999	2.318244	2.336813	2.368246	2.413290	2.473029
1.2799999	2.363450	2.382648	2.415159	2.461779	2.523667
1.2899999	2.409627	2.429471	2.463091	2.511333	2.575434
1.3000000	2.456788	2.477296	2.512055	2.561964	2.628342
1.3100000	2.504939	2.526129	2.562058	2.613681	2.682402
1.3200000	2.554089	2.575979	2.613110	2.666493	2.737621
1.3300000	2.604244	2.626851	2.665215	2.720405	2.794007
1.3400000	2.655404	2.678747	2.718375	2.775420	2.851562
1.3500000	2.707571	2.731668	2.772593	2.831539	2.910286
1.3600000	2.760742	2.785611	2.827863	2.888758	2.970177
1.3700000	2.814911	2.840570	2.884181	2.947071	3.031228
1.3799999	2.870069	2.896536	2.941536	3.006467	3.093428
1.3899999	2.926203	2.953496	2.999916	3.066934	3.156762
1.4000000	2.983298	3.011433	3.059304	3.128454	3.221212
1.4100000	3.041332	3.070327	3.119677	3.191003	3.286754
1.4200000	3.100281	3.130152	3.181010	3.254556	3.353360
1.4300000	3.160117	3.190880	3.243275	3.319081	3.420997
1.4400000	3.220808	3.252478	3.306436	3.384543	3.489627
1.4500000	3.282315	3.314908	3.370454	3.450900	3.559206
1.4600000	3.344599	3.378128	3.435287	3.518108	3.629688
1.4700000	3.407613	3.442091	3.500886	3.586117	3.701018
1.4800000	3.471306	3.506746	3.567198	3.654871	3.773139
1.4900000	3.535626	3.572039	3.634168	3.724312	3.845988
1.5000000	3.600515	3.637911	3.701734	3.794376	3.919498
1.5100000	3.665911	3.704299	3.769832	3.864995	3.993597
1.5200000	3.731748	3.771136	3.838394	3.936099	4.068210
1.5300000	3.797959	3.838354	3.907349	4.007613	4.143258
1.5400000	3.864474	3.905882	3.976622	4.079460	4.218659
1.5500000	3.931221	3.973645	4.046138	4.151561	4.294329
1.5600000	3.998124	4.041568	4.115818	4.223834	4.370181
1.5699999	4.065110	4.109574	4.185585	4.296197	4.446129
1.5707963	4.070445	4.114991	4.191142	4.301961	4.452178
1.5707963	4.070441	4.114987	4.191138	4.301957	4.452175

$\alpha =$ .849999

Θ	K VALUES				
	.318821117	.415016431	.514599755	.613601043	.708073407
.0000000	.000000	.000000	.000000	.000000	.000000
.0100000	.010000	.010000	.010000	.010000	.010000
.0200000	.020002	.020002	.020002	.020003	.020003
.0300000	.030009	.030009	.030009	.030010	.030010
.0400000	.040021	.040022	.040023	.040024	.040025
.0500000	.050042	.050044	.050046	.050048	.050050
.0600000	.060072	.060076	.060079	.060083	.060086
.0700000	.070115	.070121	.070126	.070132	.070137
.0800000	.080172	.080180	.080189	.080197	.080206
.0900000	.090245	.090257	.090269	.090282	.090293
.1000000	.100337	.100353	.100370	.100387	.100402
.1100000	.110449	.110471	.110493	.110515	.110536
.1200000	.120584	.120612	.120641	.120670	.120697
.1300000	.130743	.130779	.130815	.130852	.130887
.1400000	.140929	.140973	.141020	.141066	.141110
.1500000	.151144	.151199	.151255	.151312	.151366
.1600000	.161390	.161456	.161526	.161595	.161661
.1700000	.171669	.171749	.171832	.171915	.171995
.1800000	.181983	.182079	.182178	.182277	.182371
.1900000	.192335	.192448	.192565	.192681	.192793
.2000000	.202727	.202859	.202996	.203132	.203263
.2100000	.213162	.213315	.213473	.213632	.213784
.2200000	.223641	.223817	.224000	.224183	.224358
.2300000	.234166	.234368	.234578	.234788	.234989
.2400000	.244741	.244971	.245211	.245450	.245679
.2500000	.255368	.255629	.255900	.256172	.256432
.2600000	.266049	.266343	.266650	.266956	.267251
.2700000	.276786	.277117	.277461	.277806	.278138
.2800000	.287583	.287953	.288339	.288725	.289096
.2900000	.298441	.298854	.299284	.299715	.300130
.3000000	.309363	.309822	.310301	.310780	.311242
.3100000	.320353	.320861	.321391	.321923	.322435
.3200000	.331412	.331973	.332559	.333147	.333714
.3300000	.342543	.343161	.343807	.344456	.345081
.3400000	.353750	.354428	.355139	.355852	.356540
.3500000	.365034	.365778	.366557	.367340	.368095
.3600000	.376400	.377213	.378065	.378922	.379749
.3700000	.387850	.388737	.389666	.390602	.391507
.3800000	.399386	.400352	.401365	.402385	.403372
.3900000	.411013	.412062	.413163	.414273	.415348

$\alpha =$ .849999

Θ	K VALUES				
	.318821117	.415016431	.514599755	.613601043	.708073407
.4000000	.422733	.423871	.425066	.426271	.427439
.4100000	.434549	.435781	.437076	.438383	.439650
.4200000	.446466	.447797	.449197	.450613	.451985
.4300000	.458485	.459922	.461434	.462964	.464449
.4400000	.470612	.472159	.473790	.475441	.477046
.4500000	.482848	.484514	.486270	.488049	.489780
.4600000	.495199	.496988	.498877	.500792	.502657
.4700000	.507667	.509587	.511616	.513675	.515682
.4800000	.520256	.522314	.524491	.526702	.528859
.4900000	.532971	.535174	.537506	.539879	.542194
.5000000	.545815	.548171	.550668	.553209	.555693
.5100000	.558793	.561310	.563979	.566700	.569361
.5200000	.571908	.574594	.577445	.580355	.583204
.5300000	.585165	.588029	.591072	.594180	.597227
.5400000	.598569	.601619	.604864	.608182	.611438
.5500000	.612123	.615370	.618826	.622365	.625842
.5600000	.625834	.629286	.632965	.636736	.640446
.5700000	.639705	.643372	.647285	.651301	.655256
.5800000	.653741	.657634	.661793	.666066	.670280
.5900000	.667948	.672078	.676495	.681038	.685524
.6000000	.682332	.686709	.691396	.696224	.700997
.6100000	.696896	.701533	.706503	.711630	.716706
.6200000	.711647	.716555	.721824	.727264	.732658
.6300000	.726590	.731783	.737363	.743133	.748863
.6400000	.741732	.747222	.753129	.759245	.765328
.6500000	.757078	.762879	.769128	.775609	.782062
.6600000	.772635	.778760	.785368	.792231	.799075
.6700000	.788409	.794873	.801857	.809120	.816376
.6800000	.804406	.811226	.818603	.826286	.833974
.6899999	.820634	.827824	.835613	.843737	.851879
.7000000	.837100	.844677	.852896	.861483	.870103
.7100000	.853810	.861791	.870460	.879533	.888656
.7200000	.870772	.879175	.888316	.897897	.907548
.7300000	.887994	.896837	.906471	.916585	.926792
.7400000	.905484	.914786	.924935	.935609	.946400
.7500000	.923250	.933030	.943719	.954979	.966384
.7600000	.941300	.951580	.962832	.974707	.986756
.7700000	.959644	.970444	.982286	.994804	1.007531
.7800000	.978289	.989633	1.002090	1.015282	1.028722
.7899999	.997246	1.009156	1.022256	1.036155	1.050344

$\alpha =$ .849999

Θ	K VALUES				
	.318821117	.415016431	.514599755	.613601043	.708073407
.8000000	1.016523	1.029024	1.042795	1.057435	1.072412
.8100000	1.036132	1.049247	1.063721	1.079137	1.094940
.8200000	1.056081	1.069837	1.085044	1.101273	1.117945
.8300000	1.076381	1.090805	1.106778	1.123858	1.141443
.8400000	1.097043	1.112164	1.128936	1.146908	1.165452
.8500000	1.118079	1.133924	1.151532	1.170437	1.189990
.8600000	1.139500	1.156100	1.174580	1.194462	1.215075
.8700000	1.161317	1.178703	1.198094	1.219000	1.240726
.8799999	1.183544	1.201748	1.222090	1.244068	1.266963
.8899999	1.206192	1.225249	1.246582	1.269683	1.293807
.9000000	1.229275	1.249219	1.271588	1.295864	1.321280
.9100000	1.252807	1.273674	1.297124	1.322630	1.349403
.9200000	1.276800	1.298629	1.323207	1.350001	1.378199
.9300000	1.301270	1.324099	1.349854	1.377996	1.407692
.9400000	1.326230	1.350101	1.377084	1.406637	1.437907
.9500000	1.351698	1.376651	1.404915	1.435946	1.468869
.9600000	1.377687	1.403768	1.433368	1.465944	1.500606
.9699999	1.404215	1.431468	1.462462	1.496656	1.533143
.9799999	1.431297	1.459770	1.492218	1.528105	1.566510
.9899999	1.458952	1.488693	1.522657	1.560315	1.600736
1.0000000	1.487196	1.518256	1.553801	1.593313	1.635850
1.0100000	1.516048	1.548479	1.585673	1.627123	1.671885
1.0200000	1.545525	1.579383	1.618295	1.661774	1.708873
1.0300000	1.575648	1.610989	1.651692	1.697293	1.746846
1.0400000	1.606436	1.643318	1.685888	1.733708	1.785839
1.0500000	1.637909	1.676392	1.720909	1.771049	1.825887
1.0600000	1.670087	1.710235	1.756779	1.809346	1.867028
1.0699999	1.702992	1.744869	1.793526	1.848629	1.909298
1.0799999	1.736645	1.780318	1.831176	1.888931	1.952735
1.0899999	1.771067	1.816607	1.869756	1.930283	1.997379
1.1000000	1.806282	1.853760	1.909297	1.972720	2.043271
1.1100000	1.842311	1.891802	1.949824	2.016273	2.090451
1.1200000	1.879179	1.930759	1.991368	2.060978	2.138962
1.1300000	1.916908	1.970657	2.033958	2.106870	2.188847
1.1400000	1.955522	2.011522	2.077625	2.153984	2.240149
1.1500000	1.995045	2.053380	2.122398	2.202356	2.292913
1.1600000	2.035502	2.096259	2.168308	2.252021	2.347184
1.1700000	2.076916	2.140185	2.215385	2.303017	2.403006
1.1800000	2.119311	2.185185	2.263661	2.355380	2.460427
1.1899999	2.162713	2.231286	2.313166	2.409146	2.519491

$\alpha =$ .849999

Θ	K VALUES				
	.318821117	.415016431	.514599755	.613601043	.708073407
1.2000000	2.207144	2.278515	2.363931	2.464352	2.580245
1.2100000	2.252629	2.326897	2.415985	2.521034	2.642734
1.2200000	2.299190	2.376459	2.469358	2.579228	2.707003
1.2300000	2.346851	2.427226	2.524080	2.638967	2.773096
1.2400000	2.395634	2.479223	2.580179	2.700287	2.841057
1.2500000	2.445560	2.532473	2.637681	2.763220	2.910929
1.2599999	2.496648	2.586998	2.696613	2.827797	2.982751
1.2699999	2.548918	2.642820	2.756999	2.894048	3.056562
1.2799999	2.602388	2.699958	2.818862	2.962001	3.132400
1.2899999	2.657073	2.758430	2.882222	3.031680	3.210296
1.3000000	2.712988	2.818252	2.947097	3.103109	3.290282
1.3100000	2.770143	2.879435	3.013503	3.176305	3.372383
1.3200000	2.828548	2.941992	3.081452	3.251286	3.456622
1.3300000	2.888209	3.005929	3.150953	3.328063	3.543016
1.3400000	2.949131	3.071251	3.222012	3.406643	3.631578
1.3500000	3.011313	3.137958	3.294629	3.487030	3.722315
1.3600000	3.074752	3.206047	3.368801	3.569220	3.815225
1.3700000	3.139442	3.275511	3.444521	3.653206	3.910304
1.3799999	3.205370	3.346336	3.521776	3.738974	4.007535
1.3899999	3.272522	3.418507	3.600545	3.826502	4.106897
1.4000000	3.340877	3.492001	3.680807	3.915765	4.208361
1.4100000	3.410408	3.566790	3.762528	4.006725	4.311883
1.4200000	3.481088	3.642841	3.845672	4.099342	4.417418
1.4300000	3.552878	3.720115	3.930196	4.193565	4.524904
1.4400000	3.625740	3.798568	4.016049	4.289336	4.634275
1.4500000	3.699626	3.878148	4.103174	4.386590	4.745452
1.4600000	3.774485	3.958799	4.191507	4.485253	4.858345
1.4700000	3.850260	4.040457	4.280978	4.585242	4.972856
1.4800000	3.926887	4.123054	4.371508	4.686467	5.088877
1.4900000	4.004299	4.206515	4.463015	4.788832	5.206290
1.5000000	4.082425	4.290762	4.555408	4.892231	5.324967
1.5100000	4.161186	4.375708	4.648591	4.996553	5.444772
1.5200000	4.240501	4.461264	4.742463	5.101680	5.565562
1.5300000	4.320285	4.547337	4.836919	5.207488	5.687186
1.5400000	4.400451	4.633829	4.931848	5.313850	5.809488
1.5500000	4.480906	4.720641	5.027139	5.420633	5.932306
1.5600000	4.561559	4.807670	5.122674	5.527704	6.055476
1.5699999	4.642314	4.894812	5.218338	5.634923	6.178828
1.5707963	4.648746	4.901753	5.225958	5.643463	6.188654
1.5707963	4.648743	4.901750	5.225955	5.643462	6.188655

$\alpha =$ .849999

Θ	K VALUES				
	.794250555	.868696860	.928444378	.971111163	.994996249
.0000000	.000000	.000000	.000000	.000000	.000000
.0100000	.010000	.010000	.010000	.010000	.010000
.0200000	.020003	.020003	.020003	.020003	.020003
.0300000	.030011	.030011	.030011	.030012	.030012
.0400000	.040026	.040027	.040028	.040028	.040028
.0500000	.050052	.050053	.050054	.050055	.050056
.0600000	.060089	.060092	.060094	.060096	.060097
.0700000	.070142	.070147	.070150	.070153	.070154
.0800000	.080213	.080219	.080224	.080228	.080230
.0900000	.090304	.090313	.090320	.090325	.090328
.1000000	.100417	.100430	.100440	.100447	.100451
.1100000	.110556	.110572	.110586	.110595	.110601
.1200000	.120722	.120744	.120762	.120774	.120781
.1300000	.130919	.130947	.130969	.130985	.130994
.1400000	.141150	.141185	.141212	.141232	.141244
.1500000	.151416	.151459	.151493	.151518	.151532
.1600000	.161721	.161773	.161815	.161845	.161862
.1700000	.172067	.172130	.172181	.172217	.172237
.1800000	.182458	.182533	.182593	.182636	.182660
.1900000	.192895	.192984	.193055	.193106	.193134
.2000000	.203382	.203486	.203569	.203629	.203662
.2100000	.213922	.214043	.214140	.214209	.214248
.2200000	.224518	.224658	.224769	.224850	.224895
.2300000	.235173	.235333	.235461	.235553	.235605
.2400000	.245890	.246072	.246219	.246324	.246383
.2500000	.256671	.256878	.257045	.257165	.257232
.2600000	.267521	.267755	.267944	.268079	.268155
.2700000	.278442	.278706	.278919	.279071	.279157
.2800000	.289437	.289734	.289972	.290144	.290240
.2900000	.300511	.300842	.301109	.301301	.301409
.3000000	.311666	.312035	.312333	.312547	.312667
.3100000	.322906	.323316	.323647	.323885	.324018
.3200000	.334235	.334689	.335056	.335319	.335467
.3300000	.345657	.346158	.346563	.346854	.347018
.3400000	.357174	.357726	.358173	.358494	.358674
.3500000	.368791	.369399	.369890	.370243	.370441
.3600000	.380512	.381179	.381718	.382105	.382323
.3700000	.392342	.393071	.393661	.394085	.394324
.3800000	.404283	.405079	.405725	.406189	.406450
.3900000	.416341	.417209	.417913	.418419	.418704

$\alpha =$ •849999

Θ	K VALUES				
	•794250555	•868696860	•928444378	•971111163	•994996249
•4000000	•428519	•429464	•430231	•430783	•431094
•4100000	•440823	•441850	•442684	•443284	•443622
•4200000	•453257	•454372	•455277	•455929	•456296
•4300000	•465826	•467033	•468014	•468722	•469120
•4400000	•478534	•479841	•480903	•481669	•482101
•4500000	•491387	•492799	•493947	•494776	•495244
•4600000	•504390	•505914	•507154	•508050	•508555
•4700000	•517549	•519191	•520529	•521496	•522041
•4800000	•530868	•532636	•534078	•535120	•535709
•4900000	•544353	•546255	•547808	•548931	•549565
•5000000	•558011	•560055	•561725	•562933	•563616
•5100000	•571847	•574042	•575836	•577135	•577870
•5200000	•585868	•588222	•590148	•591544	•592333
•5300000	•600080	•602603	•604669	•606168	•607016
•5400000	•614490	•617192	•619407	•621014	•621924
•5500000	•629104	•631996	•634368	•636091	•637067
•5600000	•643930	•647023	•649562	•651408	•652453
•5700000	•658976	•662280	•664997	•666973	•668093
•5800000	•674248	•677777	•680681	•682795	•683994
•5900000	•689754	•693521	•696624	•698885	•700168
•6000000	•705504	•709522	•712836	•715252	•716624
•6100000	•721505	•725789	•729325	•731907	•733374
•6200000	•737765	•742330	•746103	•748860	•750428
•6300000	•754295	•759157	•763180	•766123	•767797
•6400000	•771103	•776279	•780568	•783708	•785495
•6500000	•788199	•793707	•798277	•801626	•803534
•6600000	•805593	•811452	•816320	•819891	•821927
•6700000	•823296	•829526	•834709	•838516	•840687
•6800000	•841318	•847941	•853457	•857514	•859830
•6899999	•859671	•866708	•872579	•876901	•879370
•7000000	•878366	•885842	•892087	•896691	•899323
•7100000	•897416	•905355	•911997	•916900	•919705
•7200000	•916832	•925261	•932324	•937545	•940535
•7300000	•936629	•945575	•953085	•958642	•961828
•7400000	•956819	•966312	•974295	•980211	•983605
•7500000	•977417	•987489	•995973	1•002269	1•005886
•7600000	•998437	1•009120	1•018136	1•024837	1•028690
•7700000	1•019894	1•031225	1•040804	1•047935	1•052040
•7800000	1•041805	1•053820	1•063997	1•071585	1•075959
•7899999	1•064185	1•076923	1•087735	1•095810	1•100469

$\alpha =$ .849999

Θ	K VALUES				
	.794250555	.868696860	.928444378	.971111163	.994996249
.8000000	1.087052	1.100556	1.112041	1.120634	1.125597
.8100000	1.110423	1.124737	1.136937	1.146081	1.151369
.8200000	1.134317	1.149488	1.162447	1.172177	1.177812
.8300000	1.158753	1.174831	1.188596	1.198951	1.204956
.8400000	1.183750	1.200789	1.215409	1.226431	1.232831
.8500000	1.209331	1.227385	1.242916	1.254646	1.261469
.8600000	1.235515	1.254646	1.271143	1.283630	1.290904
.8700000	1.262326	1.282596	1.300121	1.313416	1.321172
.8799999	1.289786	1.311264	1.329881	1.344038	1.352311
.8899999	1.317921	1.340677	1.360457	1.375534	1.384360
.9000000	1.346755	1.370866	1.391884	1.407944	1.417361
.9100000	1.376314	1.401861	1.424196	1.441306	1.451358
.9200000	1.406626	1.433695	1.457432	1.475666	1.486399
.9300000	1.437719	1.466401	1.491632	1.511068	1.522531
.9400000	1.469622	1.500015	1.526838	1.547560	1.559808
.9500000	1.502365	1.534573	1.563094	1.585193	1.598284
.9600000	1.535982	1.570115	1.600445	1.624020	1.638018
.9699999	1.570504	1.606680	1.638941	1.664097	1.679071
.9799999	1.605966	1.644309	1.678630	1.705484	1.721508
.9899999	1.642403	1.683047	1.719568	1.748243	1.765399
1.0000000	1.679853	1.722940	1.761809	1.792441	1.810818
1.0100000	1.718353	1.764034	1.805412	1.838146	1.857841
1.0200000	1.757944	1.806379	1.850438	1.885432	1.906551
1.0300000	1.798665	1.850026	1.896952	1.934378	1.957037
1.0400000	1.840560	1.895029	1.945022	1.985066	2.009391
1.0500000	1.883673	1.941445	1.994718	2.037582	2.063712
1.0600000	1.928049	1.989330	2.046115	2.092019	2.120106
1.0699999	1.973734	2.038746	2.099291	2.148475	2.178684
1.0799999	2.020778	2.089755	2.154327	2.207051	2.239567
1.0899999	2.069231	2.142423	2.211310	2.267857	2.302881
1.1000000	2.119143	2.196816	2.270328	2.331009	2.368762
1.1100000	2.170567	2.253005	2.331476	2.396626	2.437354
1.1200000	2.223558	2.311062	2.394851	2.464840	2.508813
1.1300000	2.278170	2.371061	2.460556	2.535786	2.583302
1.1400000	2.334461	2.433080	2.528698	2.609609	2.660999
1.1500000	2.392488	2.497198	2.599389	2.686462	2.742091
1.1600000	2.452311	2.563497	2.672745	2.766505	2.826782
1.1700000	2.513990	2.632059	2.748886	2.849911	2.915288
1.1800000	2.577584	2.702972	2.827939	2.936860	3.007840
1.1899999	2.643155	2.776322	2.910034	3.027543	3.104687

$\alpha =$ .849999

Θ	K VALUES				
	.794250555	.868696860	.928444378	.971111163	.994996249
1.2000000	2.710766	2.852198	2.995306	3.122162	3.206098
1.2100000	2.780477	2.930690	3.083894	3.220930	3.312360
1.2200000	2.852350	3.011890	3.175942	3.324073	3.423781
1.2300000	2.926447	3.095890	3.271598	3.431827	3.540696
1.2400000	3.002827	3.182780	3.371012	3.544442	3.663464
1.2500000	3.081550	3.272654	3.474341	3.662183	3.792474
1.2599999	3.162674	3.365602	3.581740	3.785325	3.928144
1.2699999	3.246253	3.461713	3.693370	3.914159	4.070930
1.2799999	3.332341	3.561073	3.809390	4.048990	4.221323
1.2899999	3.420987	3.663768	3.929961	4.190135	4.379860
1.3000000	3.512237	3.769878	4.055245	4.337929	4.547124
1.3100000	3.606132	3.879476	4.185395	4.492713	4.723745
1.3200000	3.702709	3.992631	4.320567	4.654847	4.910419
1.3300000	3.801996	4.109408	4.460908	4.824701	5.107901
1.3400000	3.904019	4.229858	4.606558	5.002654	5.317025
1.3500000	4.008794	4.354026	4.757649	5.189094	5.538703
1.3600000	4.116328	4.481946	4.914296	5.384416	5.773942
1.3700000	4.226620	4.613639	5.076605	5.589013	6.023855
1.3799999	4.339661	4.749113	5.244661	5.803279	6.289674
1.3899999	4.455428	4.888360	5.418527	6.027600	6.572769
1.4000000	4.573891	5.031360	5.598246	6.262347	6.874668
1.4100000	4.695003	5.178066	5.783828	6.507862	7.197067
1.4200000	4.818707	5.328422	5.975256	6.764462	7.541875
1.4300000	4.944935	5.482348	6.172477	7.032416	7.911224
1.4400000	5.073603	5.639744	6.375403	7.311933	8.307506
1.4500000	5.204613	5.800488	6.583903	7.603147	8.733393
1.4600000	5.337856	5.964436	6.797804	7.906101	9.191864
1.4700000	5.473206	6.131423	7.016888	8.220726	9.686206
1.4800000	5.610525	6.301262	7.240890	8.546822	10.219997
1.4900000	5.749662	6.473743	7.469498	8.884036	10.797024
1.5000000	5.890455	6.648637	7.702354	9.231851	11.421120
1.5100000	6.032724	6.825693	7.939051	9.589556	12.095826
1.5200000	6.176285	7.004643	8.179140	9.956256	12.823869
1.5300000	6.320941	7.185204	8.422133	10.330858	13.606304
1.5400000	6.466487	7.367077	8.667506	10.712082	14.441382
1.5500000	6.612712	7.549951	8.914703	11.098478	15.323294
1.5600000	6.759398	7.733506	9.163147	11.488454	16.241247
1.5699999	6.906325	7.917417	9.412243	11.880318	17.179592
1.5707963	6.918029	7.932068	9.432089	11.911552	17.254642
1.5707963	6.918040	7.932061	9.432080	11.911541	17.254621

$\alpha =$ .859999

Θ	K VALUES				
	.009966711	.039469502	.087332193	.151646642	.229848846
.0000000	.000000	.000000	.000000	.000000	.000000
.0100000	.010000	.010000	.010000	.010000	.010000
.0200000	.020002	.020002	.020002	.020002	.020002
.0300000	.030007	.030007	.030008	.030008	.030008
.0400000	.040018	.040018	.040019	.040019	.040020
.0500000	.050036	.050036	.050037	.050039	.050040
.0600000	.060062	.060063	.060065	.060067	.060070
.0700000	.070099	.070100	.070103	.070107	.070111
.0800000	.080147	.080150	.080154	.080160	.080166
.0900000	.090210	.090214	.090220	.090228	.090237
.1000000	.100289	.100294	.100302	.100312	.100326
.1100000	.110385	.110391	.110402	.110416	.110434
.1200000	.120500	.120509	.120522	.120541	.120564
.1300000	.130636	.130647	.130665	.130689	.130717
.1400000	.140796	.140809	.140831	.140861	.140897
.1500000	.150980	.150996	.151023	.151060	.151104
.1600000	.161190	.161210	.161243	.161288	.161342
.1700000	.171429	.171454	.171493	.171546	.171611
.1800000	.181698	.181727	.181775	.181838	.181915
.1900000	.192000	.192034	.192090	.192164	.192255
.2000000	.202336	.202375	.202440	.202527	.202634
.2100000	.212707	.212754	.212829	.212930	.213053
.2200000	.223117	.223170	.223257	.223373	.223516
.2300000	.233567	.233628	.233727	.233860	.234023
.2400000	.244059	.244128	.244241	.244393	.244578
.2500000	.254595	.254674	.254801	.254973	.255183
.2600000	.265178	.265266	.265410	.265604	.265840
.2700000	.275808	.275907	.276069	.276286	.276552
.2800000	.286489	.286600	.286781	.287024	.287321
.2900000	.297223	.297346	.297547	.297818	.298149
.3000000	.308012	.308148	.308371	.308672	.309040
.3100000	.318857	.319009	.319255	.319588	.319995
.3200000	.329762	.329929	.330201	.330568	.331017
.3300000	.340729	.340913	.341211	.341615	.342109
.3400000	.351760	.351961	.352289	.352731	.353273
.3500000	.362857	.363077	.363435	.363920	.364513
.3600000	.374024	.374264	.374654	.375183	.375831
.3700000	.385262	.385523	.385948	.386524	.387230
.3800000	.396573	.396857	.397319	.397945	.398713
.3900000	.407962	.408269	.408771	.409449	.410282

$\alpha =$ .859999

Θ	K VALUES				
	.009966711	.039469502	.087332193	.151646642	.229848846
.4000000	.419430	.419762	.420305	.421039	.421942
.4100000	.430980	.431339	.431925	.432719	.433694
.4200000	.442615	.443002	.443634	.444490	.445543
.4300000	.454337	.454754	.455434	.456357	.457492
.4400000	.466150	.466598	.467329	.468322	.469543
.4500000	.478057	.478538	.479323	.480388	.481700
.4600000	.490060	.490575	.491417	.492559	.493968
.4700000	.502163	.502715	.503615	.504839	.506348
.4800000	.514370	.514959	.515922	.517231	.518846
.4900000	.526682	.527311	.528339	.529738	.531464
.5000000	.539104	.539775	.540871	.542364	.544207
.5100000	.551639	.552353	.553522	.555112	.557078
.5200000	.564291	.565051	.566294	.567988	.570083
.5300000	.577063	.577870	.579193	.580994	.583224
.5400000	.589959	.590816	.592221	.594135	.596506
.5500000	.602983	.603892	.605382	.607415	.609933
.5600000	.616138	.617102	.618682	.620838	.623511
.5700000	.629429	.630450	.632123	.634408	.637244
.5800000	.642860	.643940	.645711	.648131	.651135
.5900000	.656436	.657577	.659450	.662010	.665192
.6000000	.670160	.671365	.673344	.676051	.679417
.6100000	.684037	.685309	.687399	.690258	.693817
.6200000	.698071	.699413	.701618	.704637	.708398
.6300000	.712268	.713683	.716008	.719193	.723163
.6400000	.726633	.728123	.730573	.733931	.738120
.6500000	.741169	.742738	.745318	.748856	.753274
.6600000	.755884	.757534	.760249	.763975	.768630
.6700000	.770781	.772516	.775372	.779293	.784196
.6800000	.785867	.787690	.790692	.794816	.799978
.6899999	.801147	.803061	.806215	.810551	.815981
.7000000	.816628	.818637	.821948	.826503	.832214
.7100000	.832314	.834422	.837897	.842681	.848683
.7200000	.848213	.850423	.854068	.859089	.865394
.7300000	.864330	.866646	.870468	.875736	.882357
.7400000	.880673	.883099	.887104	.892628	.899577
.7500000	.897249	.899789	.903984	.909774	.917064
.7600000	.914063	.916722	.921114	.927181	.934825
.7700000	.931125	.933905	.938503	.944856	.952869
.7800000	.948440	.951348	.956158	.962809	.971205
.7899999	.966018	.969057	.974087	.981047	.989842

$\alpha =$ .859999

Θ	K VALUES				
	.009966711	.039469502	.087332193	.151646642	.229848846
.8000000	.983865	.987041	.992299	.999579	1.008788
.8100000	1.001991	1.005308	1.010802	1.018416	1.028054
.8200000	1.020404	1.023867	1.029606	1.037565	1.047649
.8300000	1.039112	1.042727	1.048720	1.057036	1.067584
.8400000	1.058125	1.061897	1.068153	1.076840	1.087869
.8500000	1.077452	1.081387	1.087915	1.096987	1.108516
.8600000	1.097103	1.101206	1.108017	1.117487	1.129535
.8700000	1.117089	1.121365	1.128468	1.138352	1.150938
.8799999	1.137418	1.141875	1.149280	1.159593	1.172737
.8899999	1.158103	1.162746	1.170465	1.181222	1.194946
.9000000	1.179154	1.183990	1.192033	1.203250	1.217576
.9100000	1.200583	1.205618	1.213997	1.225691	1.240640
.9200000	1.222401	1.227643	1.236369	1.248557	1.264154
.9300000	1.244621	1.250076	1.259162	1.271862	1.288130
.9400000	1.267255	1.272931	1.282389	1.295619	1.312583
.9500000	1.290316	1.296220	1.306064	1.319843	1.337530
.9600000	1.313819	1.319959	1.330201	1.344549	1.362984
.9699999	1.337775	1.344160	1.354814	1.369751	1.388963
.9799999	1.362201	1.368837	1.379919	1.395466	1.415482
.9899999	1.387110	1.394008	1.405531	1.421708	1.442559
1.0000000	1.412518	1.419685	1.431665	1.448497	1.470213
1.0100000	1.438440	1.445887	1.458338	1.475847	1.498459
1.0200000	1.464893	1.472628	1.485568	1.503777	1.527319
1.0300000	1.491893	1.499925	1.513371	1.532305	1.556810
1.0400000	1.519457	1.527797	1.541765	1.561449	1.586952
1.0500000	1.547602	1.556261	1.570769	1.591230	1.617767
1.0600000	1.576347	1.585335	1.600401	1.621666	1.649274
1.0699999	1.605710	1.615038	1.630681	1.652777	1.681496
1.0799999	1.635710	1.645389	1.661629	1.684585	1.714454
1.0899999	1.666366	1.676408	1.693265	1.717111	1.748170
1.1000000	1.697699	1.708115	1.725610	1.750377	1.782669
1.1100000	1.729727	1.740530	1.758684	1.784404	1.817973
1.1200000	1.762473	1.773675	1.792510	1.819215	1.854105
1.1300000	1.795956	1.807571	1.827110	1.854833	1.891092
1.1400000	1.830198	1.842240	1.862505	1.891281	1.928957
1.1500000	1.865221	1.877703	1.898719	1.928584	1.967725
1.1600000	1.901046	1.913983	1.935775	1.966764	2.007423
1.1700000	1.937697	1.951103	1.973695	2.005847	2.048075
1.1800000	1.975194	1.989084	2.012503	2.045857	2.089707
1.1899999	2.013560	2.027949	2.052223	2.086817	2.132346

$\alpha =$ •859999

Θ	K VALUES				
	•009966711	•039469502	•087332193	•151646642	•229848846
1•2000000	2•052817	2•067722	2•092877	2•128753	2•176018
1•2100000	2•092988	2•108425	2•134489	2•171689	2•220747
1•2200000	2•134094	2•150079	2•177081	2•215648	2•266559
1•2300000	2•176157	2•192707	2•220677	2•260654	2•313480
1•2400000	2•219197	2•236330	2•265298	2•306730	2•361534
1•2500000	2•263236	2•280970	2•310966	2•353899	2•410744
1•2599999	2•308293	2•326645	2•357701	2•402182	2•461134
1•2699999	2•354386	2•373375	2•405523	2•451600	2•512726
1•2799999	2•401534	2•421179	2•454451	2•502172	2•565539
1•2899999	2•449752	2•470071	2•504501	2•553915	2•619593
1•3000000	2•499055	2•520069	2•555690	2•606847	2•674906
1•3100000	2•549456	2•571183	2•608028	2•660980	2•731490
1•3200000	2•600964	2•623425	2•661530	2•716326	2•789359
1•3300000	2•653590	2•676803	2•716202	2•772895	2•848524
1•3400000	2•707338	2•731325	2•772052	2•830693	2•908990
1•3500000	2•762212	2•786991	2•829082	2•889722	2•970761
1•3600000	2•818210	2•843803	2•887291	2•949984	3•033837
1•3700000	2•875330	2•901756	2•946677	3•011474	3•098213
1•3799999	2•933564	2•960842	3•007230	3•074182	3•163881
1•3899999	2•992900	3•021051	3•068940	3•138098	3•230828
1•4000000	3•053323	3•082365	3•131790	3•203204	3•299035
1•4100000	3•114811	3•144764	3•195756	3•269477	3•368478
1•4200000	3•177340	3•208223	3•260815	3•336889	3•439129
1•4300000	3•240880	3•272710	3•326933	3•405408	3•510952
1•4400000	3•305395	3•338190	3•394075	3•474995	3•583907
1•4500000	3•370846	3•404622	3•462197	3•545606	3•657947
1•4600000	3•437186	3•471959	3•531252	3•617192	3•733019
1•4700000	3•504365	3•540150	3•601187	3•689695	3•809065
1•4800000	3•572326	3•609138	3•671943	3•763057	3•886018
1•4900000	3•641010	3•678861	3•743456	3•837208	3•963810
1•5000000	3•710350	3•749251	3•815658	3•912079	4•042363
1•5100000	3•780276	3•820238	3•888473	3•987590	4•121595
1•5200000	3•850713	3•891745	3•961825	4•063662	4•201421
1•5300000	3•921584	3•963694	4•035632	4•140209	4•281750
1•5400000	3•992806	4•036001	4•109808	4•217141	4•362487
1•5500000	4•064298	4•108581	4•184266	4•294367	4•443536
1•5600000	4•135971	4•181346	4•258915	4•371793	4•524797
1•5699999	4•207740	4•254209	4•333663	4•449323	4•606168
1•5707963	4•213457	4•260013	4•339617	4•455499	4•612649
1•5707963	4•213453	4•260009	4•339613	4•455495	4•612645

$\alpha =$ .859999

θ	K VALUES				
	.318821117	.415016431	.514599755	.613601043	.708073407
.0000000	.000000	.000000	.000000	.000000	.000000
.0100000	.010000	.010000	.010000	.010000	.010000
.0200000	.020002	.020002	.020002	.020003	.020003
.0300000	.030009	.030009	.030010	.030010	.030010
.0400000	.040021	.040022	.040023	.040024	.040025
.0500000	.050042	.050044	.050046	.050048	.050050
.0600000	.060073	.060076	.060080	.060084	.060087
.0700000	.070116	.070122	.070128	.070133	.070139
.0800000	.080174	.080182	.080191	.080199	.080207
.0900000	.090248	.090260	.090272	.090284	.090296
.1000000	.100340	.100357	.100373	.100390	.100406
.1100000	.110454	.110475	.110497	.110520	.110541
.1200000	.120590	.120618	.120647	.120675	.120703
.1300000	.130750	.130786	.130823	.130860	.130895
.1400000	.140938	.140983	.141029	.141075	.141119
.1500000	.151155	.151210	.151267	.151324	.151378
.1600000	.161404	.161470	.161540	.161609	.161675
.1700000	.171685	.171766	.171849	.171932	.172011
.1800000	.182003	.182099	.182198	.182297	.182391
.1900000	.192359	.192472	.192588	.192705	.192817
.2000000	.202755	.202887	.203024	.203160	.203291
.2100000	.213194	.213347	.213506	.213664	.213816
.2200000	.223678	.223854	.224037	.224220	.224395
.2300000	.234209	.234411	.234621	.234831	.235032
.2400000	.244790	.245020	.245260	.245499	.245728
.2500000	.255423	.255684	.255956	.256227	.256488
.2600000	.266111	.266406	.266712	.267019	.267313
.2700000	.276856	.277187	.277532	.277877	.278208
.2800000	.287661	.288032	.288418	.288804	.289176
.2900000	.298529	.298942	.299372	.299804	.300219
.3000000	.309461	.309920	.310399	.310879	.311341
.3100000	.320461	.320970	.321500	.322033	.322545
.3200000	.331532	.332093	.332680	.333269	.333836
.3300000	.342676	.343294	.343941	.344590	.345215
.3400000	.353896	.354575	.355286	.356000	.356688
.3500000	.365195	.365939	.366718	.367502	.368258
.3600000	.376576	.377389	.378242	.379099	.379928
.3700000	.388042	.388929	.389860	.390797	.391702
.3800000	.399596	.400562	.401576	.402597	.403585
.3900000	.411241	.412291	.413393	.414505	.415580

$\alpha =$ .859999

Θ	K VALUES				
	.318821117	.415016431	.514599755	.613601043	.708073407
.4000000	.422981	.424120	.425316	.426523	.427692
.4100000	.434819	.436052	.437348	.438657	.439925
.4200000	.446758	.448090	.449492	.450909	.452284
.4300000	.458801	.460239	.461753	.463285	.464772
.4400000	.470953	.472503	.474135	.475789	.477395
.4500000	.483216	.484884	.486642	.488424	.490158
.4600000	.495595	.497387	.499279	.501197	.503064
.4700000	.508094	.510017	.512048	.514111	.516121
.4800000	.520715	.522777	.524956	.527171	.529332
.4900000	.533464	.535671	.538007	.540383	.542703
.5000000	.546344	.548705	.551205	.553751	.556239
.5100000	.559360	.561881	.564555	.567281	.569947
.5200000	.572515	.575206	.578063	.580978	.583832
.5300000	.585815	.588684	.591733	.594848	.597901
.5400000	.599263	.602320	.605571	.608896	.612159
.5500000	.612866	.616119	.619583	.623129	.626613
.5600000	.626626	.630085	.633773	.637552	.641270
.5700000	.640550	.644225	.648148	.652172	.656137
.5800000	.654642	.658544	.662713	.666996	.671220
.5900000	.668908	.673048	.677475	.682030	.686528
.6000000	.683353	.687742	.692441	.697281	.702067
.6100000	.697982	.702632	.707616	.712756	.717847
.6200000	.712802	.717724	.723008	.728463	.733873
.6300000	.727818	.733026	.738622	.744410	.750157
.6400000	.743036	.748543	.754468	.760603	.766705
.6500000	.758463	.764282	.770551	.777052	.783527
.6600000	.774104	.780250	.786880	.793765	.800632
.6700000	.789968	.796454	.803462	.810750	.818031
.6800000	.806059	.812903	.820306	.828017	.835732
.6899999	.822386	.829602	.837420	.845574	.853747
.7000000	.838956	.846562	.854812	.863433	.872087
.7100000	.855776	.863788	.872493	.881601	.890761
.7200000	.872854	.881291	.890470	.900091	.909782
.7300000	.890198	.899078	.908753	.918911	.929163
.7400000	.907816	.917158	.927353	.938075	.948914
.7500000	.925717	.935542	.946280	.957592	.969050
.7600000	.943910	.954238	.965543	.977475	.989583
.7700000	.962403	.973256	.985155	.997736	1.010528
.7800000	.981206	.992607	1.005127	1.018388	1.031898
.7899999	1.000328	1.012301	1.025470	1.039443	1.053709

$\alpha =$ .859999

Θ	K VALUES				
	.318821117	.415016431	.514599755	.613601043	.708073407
.8000000	1.019781	1.032349	1.046196	1.060917	1.075977
.8100000	1.039573	1.052762	1.067318	1.082822	1.098716
.8200000	1.059716	1.073552	1.088848	1.105173	1.121945
.8300000	1.080221	1.094732	1.110801	1.127986	1.145680
.8400000	1.101099	1.116313	1.133190	1.151276	1.169939
.8500000	1.122362	1.138308	1.156030	1.175059	1.194742
.8600000	1.144021	1.160731	1.179335	1.199352	1.220106
.8700000	1.166091	1.183595	1.203120	1.224174	1.246054
.8799999	1.188583	1.206916	1.227403	1.249541	1.272604
.8899999	1.211511	1.230706	1.252198	1.275472	1.299780
.9000000	1.234889	1.254983	1.277523	1.301988	1.327604
.9100000	1.258731	1.279761	1.303396	1.329107	1.356098
.9200000	1.283052	1.305057	1.329835	1.356852	1.385287
.9300000	1.307867	1.330887	1.356859	1.385243	1.415197
.9400000	1.333193	1.357268	1.384486	1.414302	1.445854
.9500000	1.359045	1.384220	1.412738	1.444053	1.477284
.9600000	1.385440	1.411760	1.441635	1.474520	1.509515
.9699999	1.412396	1.439907	1.471199	1.505727	1.542578
.9799999	1.439930	1.468681	1.501451	1.537701	1.576501
.9899999	1.468061	1.498102	1.532415	1.570466	1.611317
1.0000000	1.496808	1.528192	1.564114	1.604052	1.647057
1.0100000	1.526191	1.558971	1.596572	1.638485	1.683755
1.0200000	1.556229	1.590463	1.629815	1.673795	1.721446
1.0300000	1.586944	1.622690	1.663868	1.710011	1.760166
1.0400000	1.618358	1.655675	1.698759	1.747166	1.799951
1.0500000	1.650491	1.689444	1.734514	1.785290	1.840840
1.0600000	1.683366	1.724020	1.771162	1.824417	1.882872
1.0699999	1.717007	1.759429	1.808731	1.864580	1.926087
1.0799999	1.751438	1.795698	1.847251	1.905813	1.970529
1.0899999	1.786683	1.832853	1.886754	1.948153	2.016239
1.1000000	1.822766	1.870923	1.927269	1.991636	2.063263
1.1100000	1.859713	1.909934	1.968828	2.036299	2.111645
1.1200000	1.897550	1.949915	2.011465	2.082180	2.161432
1.1300000	1.936304	1.990896	2.055211	2.129318	2.212671
1.1400000	1.976000	2.032906	2.100102	2.177752	2.265411
1.1500000	2.016667	2.075976	2.146170	2.227523	2.319701
1.1600000	2.058331	2.120135	2.193451	2.278671	2.375592
1.1700000	2.101021	2.165414	2.241979	2.331238	2.433135
1.1800000	2.144764	2.211845	2.291789	2.385266	2.492381
1.1899999	2.189589	2.259458	2.342918	2.440795	2.553382

$\alpha =$ •859999

Θ	K VALUES				
	•318821117	•415016431	•514599755	•613601043	•708073407
1•2000000	2•235523	2•308284	2•395400	2•497869	2•616191
1•2100000	2•282594	2•358354	2•449270	2•556528	2•680860
1•2200000	2•330830	2•409699	2•504563	2•616814	2•747440
1•2300000	2•380258	2•462347	2•561313	2•678768	2•815983
1•2400000	2•430904	2•516330	2•619554	2•742430	2•886540
1•2500000	2•482794	2•571675	2•679320	2•807840	2•959161
1•2599999	2•535953	2•628410	2•740640	2•875034	3•033895
1•2699999	2•590405	2•686562	2•803546	2•944050	3•110786
1•2799999	2•646171	2•746154	2•868065	3•014921	3•189880
1•2899999	2•703272	2•807209	2•934225	3•087679	3•271218
1•3000000	2•761728	2•869749	3•002048	3•162353	3•354839
1•3100000	2•821552	2•933790	3•071556	3•238969	3•440774
1•3200000	2•882760	2•999349	3•142765	3•317548	3•529056
1•3300000	2•945361	3•066437	3•215691	3•398108	3•619708
1•3400000	3•009364	3•135063	3•290344	3•480663	3•712749
1•3500000	3•074772	3•205231	3•366728	3•565220	3•808193
1•3600000	3•141585	3•276941	3•444845	3•651781	3•906045
1•3700000	3•209799	3•350188	3•524690	3•740342	4•006302
1•3799999	3•279403	3•424963	3•606252	3•830892	4•108956
1•3899999	3•350385	3•501250	3•689515	3•923413	4•213985
1•4000000	3•422724	3•579028	3•774455	4•017879	4•321363
1•4100000	3•496395	3•658269	3•861040	4•114253	4•431048
1•4200000	3•571366	3•738938	3•949233	4•212494	4•542991
1•4300000	3•647601	3•820996	4•038989	4•312550	4•657131
1•4400000	3•725054	3•904393	4•130252	4•414357	4•773395
1•4500000	3•803677	3•989074	4•222963	4•517845	4•891698
1•4600000	3•883412	4•074978	4•317049	4•622934	5•011944
1•4700000	3•964195	4•162034	4•412434	4•729532	5•134025
1•4800000	4•045957	4•250165	4•509031	4•837541	5•257820
1•4900000	4•128621	4•339289	4•606745	4•946850	5•383198
1•5000000	4•212106	4•429315	4•705477	5•057343	5•510017
1•5100000	4•296323	4•520146	4•805115	5•168891	5•638121
1•5200000	4•381180	4•611680	4•905546	5•281363	5•767351
1•5300000	4•466579	4•703809	5•006648	5•394617	5•897533
1•5400000	4•552418	4•796423	5•108296	5•508507	6•028492
1•5500000	4•638592	4•889406	5•210361	5•622881	6•160041
1•5600000	4•724995	4•982640	5•312708	5•737585	6•291992
1•5699999	4•811517	5•076005	5•415202	5•852461	6•424152
1•5707963	4•818409	5•083441	5•423367	5•861611	6•434680
1•5707963	4•818405	5•083438	5•423363	5•861609	6•434679

$\alpha =$ .859999

Θ	K VALUES				
	.794250555	.868696860	.928444378	.971111163	.994996249
.0000000	.000000	.000000	.000000	.000000	.000000
.0100000	.010000	.010000	.010000	.010000	.010000
.0200000	.020003	.020003	.020003	.020003	.020003
.0300000	.030011	.030011	.030011	.030012	.030012
.0400000	.040026	.040027	.040028	.040028	.040029
.0500000	.050052	.050054	.050055	.050056	.050056
.0600000	.060090	.060093	.060095	.060097	.060097
.0700000	.070144	.070148	.070151	.070154	.070155
.0800000	.080215	.080221	.080226	.080230	.080232
.0900000	.090306	.090315	.090323	.090328	.090331
.1000000	.100420	.100433	.100443	.100450	.100454
.1100000	.110560	.110577	.110590	.110600	.110605
.1200000	.120728	.120750	.120767	.120780	.120787
.1300000	.130927	.130955	.130977	.130993	.131002
.1400000	.141159	.141194	.141222	.141242	.141253
.1500000	.151428	.151470	.151505	.151530	.151543
.1600000	.161735	.161787	.161829	.161859	.161876
.1700000	.172084	.172147	.172197	.172234	.172254
.1800000	.182478	.182553	.182613	.182656	.182680
.1900000	.192919	.193007	.193078	.193129	.193158
.2000000	.203410	.203514	.203597	.203657	.203690
.2100000	.213955	.214075	.214172	.214242	.214281
.2200000	.224556	.224695	.224807	.224887	.224932
.2300000	.235216	.235376	.235504	.235597	.235648
.2400000	.245939	.246121	.246268	.246373	.246432
.2500000	.256727	.256934	.257101	.257221	.257288
.2600000	.267584	.267818	.268007	.268143	.268219
.2700000	.278513	.278777	.278990	.279142	.279228
.2800000	.289517	.289813	.290052	.290224	.290320
.2900000	.300600	.300931	.301199	.301390	.301498
.3000000	.311765	.312135	.312433	.312646	.312766
.3100000	.323017	.323427	.323758	.323996	.324129
.3200000	.334357	.334812	.335179	.335442	.335590
.3300000	.345791	.346293	.346699	.346990	.347154
.3400000	.357322	.357875	.358322	.358644	.358824
.3500000	.368955	.369562	.370054	.370407	.370606
.3600000	.380692	.381358	.381898	.382285	.382503
.3700000	.392538	.393267	.393858	.394283	.394522
.3800000	.404497	.405294	.405940	.406405	.406666
.3900000	.416574	.417443	.418148	.418655	.418940

$\alpha =$ .859999

Θ	K VALUES				
	.794250555	.868696860	.928444378	.971111163	.994996249
.4000000	.428774	.429720	.430487	.431039	.431350
.4100000	.441100	.442128	.442962	.443563	.443902
.4200000	.453557	.454673	.455579	.456232	.456599
.4300000	.466151	.467360	.468342	.469050	.469449
.4400000	.478886	.480194	.481257	.482024	.482457
.4500000	.491767	.493181	.494331	.495161	.495629
.4600000	.504800	.506326	.507568	.508465	.508971
.4700000	.517990	.519635	.520975	.521944	.522490
.4800000	.531343	.533114	.534559	.535603	.536192
.4900000	.544865	.546770	.548325	.549450	.550085
.5000000	.558561	.560609	.562281	.563492	.564176
.5100000	.572438	.574636	.576434	.577736	.578471
.5200000	.586502	.588860	.590790	.592189	.592979
.5300000	.600759	.603287	.605358	.606859	.607709
.5400000	.615217	.617925	.620144	.621755	.622667
.5500000	.629883	.632781	.635158	.636885	.637863
.5600000	.644763	.647862	.650407	.652257	.653305
.5700000	.659866	.663178	.665901	.667882	.669004
.5800000	.675198	.678736	.681647	.683767	.684969
.5900000	.690769	.694545	.697656	.699923	.701210
.6000000	.706586	.710615	.713938	.716361	.717737
.6100000	.722659	.726955	.730501	.733090	.734561
.6200000	.738995	.743573	.747358	.750123	.751694
.6300000	.755605	.760482	.764518	.767469	.769148
.6400000	.772498	.777690	.781993	.785143	.786936
.6500000	.789683	.795210	.799795	.803155	.805069
.6600000	.807172	.813052	.817936	.821519	.823562
.6700000	.824975	.831228	.836429	.840250	.842429
.6800000	.843104	.849751	.855288	.859360	.861684
.6899999	.861569	.868633	.874526	.878865	.881343
.7000000	.880382	.887888	.894158	.898780	.901423
.7100000	.899557	.907529	.914199	.919122	.921939
.7200000	.919106	.927571	.934665	.939907	.942910
.7300000	.939043	.948028	.955572	.961154	.964355
.7400000	.959381	.968918	.976938	.982881	.986292
.7500000	.980135	.990255	.998780	1.005107	1.008741
.7600000	1.001321	1.012057	1.021118	1.027853	1.031725
.7700000	1.022953	1.034342	1.043971	1.051140	1.055266
.7800000	1.045049	1.057128	1.067360	1.074990	1.079387
.7899999	1.067625	1.080434	1.091307	1.099427	1.104112

$\alpha =$ •859999

Θ	K VALUES				
	•794250555	•868696860	•928444378	•971111163	•994996249
•8000000	1•090700	1•104281	1•115833	1•124476	1•129468
•8100000	1•114291	1•128690	1•140963	1•150162	1•155482
•8200000	1•138417	1•153681	1•166721	1•176512	1•182183
•8300000	1•163099	1•179279	1•193133	1•203555	1•209599
•8400000	1•188357	1•205508	1•220226	1•231321	1•237765
•8500000	1•214213	1•232391	1•248029	1•259841	1•266711
•8600000	1•240689	1•259955	1•276571	1•289149	1•296475
•8700000	1•267810	1•288229	1•305883	1•319278	1•327093
•8799999	1•295598	1•317239	1•335999	1•350266	1•358603
•8899999	1•324080	1•347015	1•366953	1•382151	1•391048
•9000000	1•353283	1•377590	1•398781	1•414975	1•424471
•9100000	1•383233	1•408994	1•431520	1•448778	1•458918
•9200000	1•413959	1•441263	1•465210	1•483607	1•494437
•9300000	1•445490	1•474431	1•499894	1•519509	1•531080
•9400000	1•477859	1•508536	1•535614	1•556535	1•568901
•9500000	1•511098	1•543617	1•572417	1•594736	1•607958
•9600000	1•545239	1•579713	1•610352	1•634169	1•648312
•9699999	1•580318	1•616868	1•649468	1•674893	1•690028
•9799999	1•616372	1•655125	1•689820	1•716970	1•733173
•9899999	1•653437	1•694531	1•731463	1•760466	1•777821
1•0000000	1•691554	1•735134	1•774456	1•805451	1•824048
1•0100000	1•730763	1•776985	1•818862	1•851997	1•871937
1•0200000	1•771106	1•820135	1•864745	1•900183	1•921574
1•0300000	1•812628	1•864640	1•912173	1•950091	1•973052
1•0400000	1•855374	1•910557	1•961219	2•001808	2•026469
1•0500000	1•899391	1•957946	2•011958	2•055427	2•081930
1•0600000	1•944729	2•006870	2•064469	2•111044	2•139546
1•0699999	1•991437	2•057392	2•118835	2•168763	2•199436
1•0799999	2•039569	2•109580	2•175144	2•228693	2•261726
1•0899999	2•089178	2•163506	2•233487	2•290951	2•326552
1•1000000	2•140321	2•219241	2•293961	2•355661	2•394058
1•1100000	2•193055	2•276861	2•356666	2•422950	2•464397
1•1200000	2•247439	2•336444	2•421708	2•492957	2•537735
1•1300000	2•303534	2•398072	2•489197	2•565830	2•614246
1•1400000	2•361403	2•461830	2•559249	2•641722	2•694121
1•1500000	2•421109	2•527802	2•631985	2•720797	2•777560
1•1600000	2•482718	2•596081	2•707531	2•803231	2•864779
1•1700000	2•546297	2•666756	2•786018	2•889207	2•956012
1•1800000	2•611913	2•739923	2•867585	2•978920	3•051506
1•1899999	2•679635	2•815678	2•952372	3•072577	3•151530

$\alpha =$ .859999

Θ	K VALUES				
	.794250555	.868696860	.928444378	.971111163	.994996249
1.2000000	2.749533	2.894121	3.040528	3.170397	3.256372
1.2100000	2.821675	2.975351	3.132206	3.272610	3.366340
1.2200000	2.896133	3.059471	3.227565	3.379462	3.481768
1.2300000	2.972977	3.146584	3.326766	3.491210	3.603018
1.2400000	3.052275	3.236794	3.429978	3.608128	3.730475
1.2500000	3.134096	3.330205	3.537373	3.730502	3.864562
1.2599999	3.218507	3.426920	3.649126	3.858636	4.005731
1.2699999	3.305574	3.527042	3.765413	3.992846	4.154476
1.2799999	3.395359	3.630670	3.886417	4.133468	4.311329
1.2899999	3.487922	3.737902	4.012315	4.280850	4.476871
1.3000000	3.583319	3.848833	4.143292	4.435359	4.651735
1.3100000	3.681599	3.963550	4.279522	4.597373	4.836607
1.3200000	3.782810	4.082136	4.421180	4.767288	5.032239
1.3300000	3.886991	4.204667	4.568437	4.945513	5.239454
1.3400000	3.994174	4.331209	4.721455	5.132467	5.459156
1.3500000	4.104384	4.461819	4.880383	5.328580	5.692335
1.3600000	4.217636	4.596542	5.045362	5.534289	5.940084
1.3700000	4.333937	4.735409	5.216513	5.750032	6.203612
1.3799999	4.453281	4.878438	5.393939	5.976247	6.484255
1.3899999	4.575652	5.025627	5.577723	6.213363	6.783498
1.4000000	4.701020	5.176962	5.767918	6.461794	7.102997
1.4100000	4.829341	5.332402	5.964547	6.721924	7.444588
1.4200000	4.960558	5.491889	6.167600	6.994108	7.810337
1.4300000	5.094599	5.655342	6.377029	7.278648	8.202550
1.4400000	5.231375	5.822657	6.592744	7.575781	8.623808
1.4500000	5.370784	5.993706	6.814610	7.885664	9.076999
1.4600000	5.512705	6.168332	7.042443	8.208351	9.565333
1.4700000	5.657002	6.346358	7.276009	8.543774	10.092356
1.4800000	5.803523	6.527577	7.515021	8.891721	10.661917
1.4900000	5.952099	6.711759	7.759138	9.251813	11.278092
1.5000000	6.102550	6.898651	8.007969	9.623488	11.945004
1.5100000	6.254675	7.087973	8.261063	10.005974	12.666454
1.5200000	6.408267	7.279427	8.517927	10.398295	13.445366
1.5300000	6.563102	7.472693	8.778019	10.799258	14.282862
1.5400000	6.718950	7.667438	9.040758	11.207464	15.177046
1.5500000	6.875569	7.863312	9.305528	11.621327	16.121650
1.5600000	7.032714	8.059954	9.571685	12.039107	17.105051
1.5699999	7.190132	8.256998	9.838568	12.458953	18.110402
1.5707963	7.202672	8.272695	9.859832	12.492418	18.190811
1.5707963	7.202679	8.272688	9.859823	12.492406	18.190788

$\alpha =$ .869999

Θ	K VALUES				
	.009966711	.039469502	.087332193	.151646642	.229848846
.0000000	.000000	.000000	.000000	.000000	.000000
.0100000	.010000	.010000	.010000	.010000	.010000
.0200000	.020002	.020002	.020002	.020002	.020002
.0300000	.030007	.030008	.030008	.030008	.030008
.0400000	.040018	.040019	.040019	.040020	.040021
.0500000	.050036	.050037	.050038	.050039	.050041
.0600000	.060063	.060064	.060065	.060068	.060071
.0700000	.070100	.070101	.070104	.070108	.070112
.0800000	.080149	.080152	.080156	.080161	.080168
.0900000	.090213	.090216	.090222	.090230	.090240
.1000000	.100292	.100297	.100305	.100316	.100329
.1100000	.110389	.110396	.110406	.110421	.110438
.1200000	.120506	.120514	.120528	.120547	.120570
.1300000	.130644	.130655	.130672	.130696	.130725
.1400000	.140805	.140818	.140841	.140870	.140906
.1500000	.150991	.151008	.151035	.151071	.151116
.1600000	.161204	.161224	.161257	.161302	.161356
.1700000	.171446	.171470	.171510	.171563	.171628
.1800000	.181718	.181747	.181795	.181858	.181935
.1900000	.192024	.192058	.192113	.192188	.192279
.2000000	.202363	.202403	.202468	.202555	.202661
.2100000	.212739	.212786	.212861	.212962	.213085
.2200000	.223154	.223207	.223294	.223411	.223553
.2300000	.233610	.233670	.233770	.233903	.234066
.2400000	.244108	.244177	.244290	.244441	.244627
.2500000	.254650	.254729	.254856	.255028	.255238
.2600000	.265240	.265328	.265472	.265666	.265903
.2700000	.275878	.275977	.276139	.276356	.276622
.2800000	.286568	.286678	.286859	.287102	.287400
.2900000	.297310	.297434	.297635	.297906	.298237
.3000000	.308109	.308246	.308469	.308770	.309138
.3100000	.318965	.319117	.319363	.319696	.320103
.3200000	.329882	.330049	.330320	.330688	.331137
.3300000	.340861	.341044	.341343	.341747	.342241
.3400000	.351905	.352106	.352434	.352877	.353419
.3500000	.363016	.363236	.363595	.364079	.364673
.3600000	.374198	.374438	.374829	.375358	.376006
.3700000	.385452	.385713	.386139	.386715	.387422
.3800000	.396781	.397064	.397527	.398153	.398922
.3900000	.408187	.408495	.408997	.409676	.410510

$\alpha =$ •869999

Θ	K VALUES				
	•009966711	•039469502	•087332193	•151646642	•229848846
•4000000	•419675	•420008	•420551	•421286	•422189
•4100000	•431245	•431605	•432191	•432986	•433963
•4200000	•442902	•443290	•443922	•444780	•445834
•4300000	•454648	•455065	•455747	•456670	•457807
•4400000	•466486	•466935	•467667	•468660	•469883
•4500000	•478419	•478900	•479686	•480753	•482067
•4600000	•490450	•490966	•491809	•492953	•494363
•4700000	•502583	•503135	•504037	•505263	•506774
•4800000	•514820	•515410	•516375	•517686	•519303
•4900000	•527166	•527796	•528826	•530226	•531955
•5000000	•539623	•540294	•541393	•542888	•544734
•5100000	•552195	•552910	•554081	•555674	•557644
•5200000	•564885	•565647	•566893	•568589	•570688
•5300000	•577698	•578507	•579832	•581637	•583871
•5400000	•590638	•591497	•592904	•594822	•597198
•5500000	•603707	•604618	•606112	•608148	•610673
•5600000	•616911	•617877	•619460	•621620	•624300
•5700000	•630253	•631276	•632953	•635243	•638085
•5800000	•643737	•644820	•646595	•649020	•652032
•5900000	•657369	•658513	•660391	•662957	•666146
•6000000	•671152	•672361	•674345	•677059	•680434
•6100000	•685092	•686368	•688463	•691330	•694899
•6200000	•699192	•700538	•702749	•705776	•709547
•6300000	•713458	•714877	•717209	•720403	•724385
•6400000	•727895	•729390	•731847	•735215	•739417
•6500000	•742509	•744082	•746670	•750220	•754651
•6600000	•757304	•758959	•761683	•765421	•770092
•6700000	•772286	•774027	•776892	•780826	•785746
•6800000	•787461	•789290	•792303	•796441	•801621
•6899999	•802835	•804756	•807921	•812273	•817723
•7000000	•818415	•820431	•823755	•828327	•834059
•7100000	•834205	•836320	•839809	•844611	•850637
•7200000	•850213	•852431	•856091	•861132	•867463
•7300000	•866445	•868770	•872608	•877898	•884546
•7400000	•882909	•885345	•889367	•894915	•901894
•7500000	•899611	•902162	•906376	•912192	•919515
•7600000	•916559	•919230	•923643	•929737	•937417
•7700000	•933761	•936555	•941174	•947558	•955610
•7800000	•951224	•954146	•958980	•965664	•974102
•7899999	•968957	•972012	•977067	•984063	•992903

$\alpha =$ .869999

Θ	K VALUES				
	.009966711	.039469502	.087332193	.151646642	.229848846
.8000000	.986968	.990161	.995446	1.002765	1.012023
.8100000	1.005266	1.008601	1.014125	1.021780	1.031472
.8200000	1.023859	1.027342	1.033114	1.041117	1.051259
.8300000	1.042758	1.046394	1.052422	1.060787	1.071397
.8400000	1.061971	1.065765	1.072059	1.080799	1.091896
.8500000	1.081509	1.085468	1.092037	1.101166	1.112767
.8600000	1.101382	1.105511	1.112365	1.121897	1.134024
.8700000	1.121600	1.125905	1.133056	1.143006	1.155677
.8799999	1.142176	1.146663	1.154119	1.164504	1.177740
.8899999	1.163119	1.167795	1.175569	1.186403	1.200226
.9000000	1.184443	1.189314	1.197416	1.208716	1.223149
.9100000	1.206158	1.211232	1.219674	1.231458	1.246522
.9200000	1.228279	1.233561	1.242356	1.254641	1.270361
.9300000	1.250817	1.256316	1.265476	1.278279	1.294681
.9400000	1.273787	1.279510	1.289047	1.302389	1.319497
.9500000	1.297202	1.303156	1.313085	1.326984	1.344826
.9600000	1.321077	1.327271	1.337605	1.352082	1.370684
.9699999	1.345426	1.351869	1.362622	1.377697	1.397088
.9799999	1.370266	1.376965	1.388152	1.403848	1.424058
.9899999	1.395612	1.402577	1.414213	1.430551	1.451610
1.0000000	1.421481	1.428721	1.440821	1.457825	1.479765
1.0100000	1.447889	1.455413	1.467995	1.485688	1.508541
1.0200000	1.474855	1.482673	1.495752	1.514159	1.537960
1.0300000	1.502396	1.510518	1.524113	1.543259	1.568042
1.0400000	1.530531	1.538967	1.553095	1.573008	1.598810
1.0500000	1.559280	1.568041	1.582721	1.603426	1.630285
1.0600000	1.588662	1.597759	1.613009	1.634537	1.662490
1.0699999	1.618697	1.628142	1.643983	1.666361	1.695449
1.0799999	1.649407	1.659211	1.675663	1.698922	1.729187
1.0899999	1.680813	1.690989	1.708073	1.732243	1.763729
1.1000000	1.712938	1.723498	1.741236	1.766350	1.799100
1.1100000	1.745803	1.756761	1.775175	1.801266	1.835326
1.1200000	1.779433	1.790801	1.809914	1.837017	1.872435
1.1300000	1.813850	1.825643	1.845479	1.873629	1.910453
1.1400000	1.849080	1.861311	1.881896	1.911129	1.949410
1.1500000	1.885146	1.897831	1.919189	1.949542	1.989333
1.1600000	1.922075	1.935227	1.957385	1.988898	2.030253
1.1700000	1.959890	1.973527	1.996510	2.029224	2.072197
1.1800000	1.998618	2.012755	2.036593	2.070547	2.115197
1.1899999	2.038285	2.052938	2.077659	2.112896	2.159281

$\alpha =$ .869999

Θ	K VALUES				
	.009966711	.039469502	.087332193	.151646642	.229848846
1.2000000	2.078917	2.094104	2.119736	2.156301	2.204481
1.2100000	2.120540	2.136277	2.162852	2.200788	2.250827
1.2200000	2.163179	2.179485	2.207033	2.246387	2.298348
1.2300000	2.206861	2.223754	2.252307	2.293125	2.347075
1.2400000	2.251611	2.269110	2.298700	2.341031	2.397038
1.2500000	2.297454	2.315578	2.346239	2.390133	2.448264
1.2599999	2.344414	2.363183	2.394949	2.440455	2.500783
1.2699999	2.392515	2.411948	2.444853	2.492025	2.554621
1.2799999	2.441778	2.461897	2.495977	2.544866	2.609804
1.2899999	2.492225	2.513049	2.548340	2.599002	2.666357
1.3000000	2.543875	2.565427	2.601965	2.654453	2.724302
1.3100000	2.596745	2.619045	2.656869	2.711238	2.783659
1.3200000	2.650850	2.673920	2.713067	2.769374	2.844446
1.3300000	2.706203	2.730066	2.770573	2.828875	2.906677
1.3400000	2.762815	2.787492	2.829398	2.889752	2.970364
1.3500000	2.820691	2.846204	2.889548	2.952011	3.035515
1.3600000	2.879834	2.906207	2.951027	3.015658	3.102133
1.3700000	2.940245	2.967498	3.013834	3.080690	3.170219
1.3799999	3.001918	3.030074	3.077964	3.147102	3.239765
1.3899999	3.064843	3.093925	3.143406	3.214884	3.310761
1.4000000	3.129006	3.159035	3.210146	3.284020	3.383190
1.4100000	3.194386	3.225383	3.278161	3.354487	3.457029
1.4200000	3.260958	3.292944	3.347426	3.426257	3.532247
1.4300000	3.328690	3.361686	3.417907	3.499297	3.608809
1.4400000	3.397544	3.431571	3.489564	3.573565	3.686671
1.4500000	3.467478	3.502553	3.562353	3.649013	3.765783
1.4600000	3.538440	3.574582	3.636219	3.725586	3.846085
1.4700000	3.610374	3.647599	3.711104	3.803221	3.927513
1.4800000	3.683217	3.721542	3.786942	3.881851	4.009994
1.4900000	3.756899	3.796339	3.863660	3.961400	4.093446
1.5000000	3.831347	3.871914	3.941179	4.041785	4.177785
1.5100000	3.906477	3.948184	4.019415	4.122917	4.262915
1.5200000	3.982205	4.025063	4.098276	4.204703	4.348737
1.5300000	4.058440	4.102457	4.177670	4.287044	4.435146
1.5400000	4.135088	4.180272	4.257496	4.369836	4.522033
1.5500000	4.212050	4.258406	4.337651	4.452972	4.609285
1.5600000	4.289226	4.336758	4.418031	4.536342	4.696784
1.5699999	4.366514	4.415224	4.498528	4.619834	4.784412
1.5707963	4.372670	4.421474	4.504940	4.626484	4.791392
1.5707963	4.372666	4.421470	4.504935	4.626480	4.791388

$\alpha =$ .869999

Θ	K VALUES				
	.318821117	.415016431	.514599755	.613601043	.708073407
.0000000	.000000	.000000	.000000	.000000	.000000
.0100000	.010000	.010000	.010000	.010000	.010000
.0200000	.020002	.020002	.020003	.020003	.020003
.0300000	.030009	.030009	.030010	.030010	.030011
.0400000	.040021	.040023	.040024	.040025	.040026
.0500000	.050042	.050044	.050047	.050049	.050051
.0600000	.060074	.060077	.060081	.060084	.060088
.0700000	.070117	.070123	.070129	.070134	.070140
.0800000	.080176	.080184	.080192	.080201	.080209
.0900000	.090250	.090262	.090274	.090286	.090298
.1000000	.100344	.100360	.100377	.100393	.100409
.1100000	.110458	.110480	.110502	.110524	.110545
.1200000	.120595	.120623	.120652	.120681	.120709
.1300000	.130758	.130793	.130830	.130867	.130902
.1400000	.140947	.140992	.141038	.141084	.141128
.1500000	.151167	.151222	.151279	.151335	.151389
.1600000	.161417	.161484	.161554	.161623	.161689
.1700000	.171702	.171783	.171866	.171949	.172028
.1800000	.182023	.182119	.182218	.182317	.182411
.1900000	.192383	.192495	.192612	.192729	.192840
.2000000	.202783	.202914	.203051	.203188	.203318
.2100000	.213226	.213379	.213538	.213696	.213848
.2200000	.223715	.223891	.224074	.224257	.224433
.2300000	.234252	.234454	.234664	.234873	.235075
.2400000	.244839	.245069	.245308	.245548	.245777
.2500000	.255479	.255740	.256011	.256283	.256543
.2600000	.266174	.266468	.266775	.267082	.267376
.2700000	.276927	.277258	.277603	.277948	.278279
.2800000	.287740	.288111	.288497	.288884	.289255
.2900000	.298617	.299030	.299461	.299893	.300308
.3000000	.309559	.310018	.310497	.310978	.311440
.3100000	.320570	.321079	.321610	.322143	.322655
.3200000	.331652	.332214	.332801	.333390	.333958
.3300000	.342808	.343427	.344074	.344724	.345350
.3400000	.354042	.354722	.355433	.356147	.356836
.3500000	.365355	.366100	.366880	.367664	.368421
.3600000	.376752	.377566	.378419	.379278	.380106
.3700000	.388234	.389123	.390054	.390992	.391898
.3800000	.399806	.400773	.401788	.402810	.403799
.3900000	.411470	.412521	.413624	.414737	.415813

$\alpha =$ •869999

Θ	K VALUES				
	•318821117	•415016431	•514599755	•613601043	•708073407
•4000000	•423230	•424370	•425567	•426776	•427946
•4100000	•435089	•436323	•437620	•438931	•440201
•4200000	•447050	•448384	•449788	•451206	•452583
•4300000	•459118	•460558	•462074	•463607	•465096
•4400000	•471295	•472847	•474482	•476137	•477745
•4500000	•483585	•485255	•487016	•488801	•490536
•4600000	•495993	•497788	•499682	•501603	•503473
•4700000	•508522	•510448	•512483	•514548	•516561
•4800000	•521176	•523240	•525424	•527642	•529806
•4900000	•533959	•536169	•538509	•540889	•543212
•5000000	•546875	•549240	•551744	•554295	•556787
•5100000	•559929	•562455	•565134	•567864	•570535
•5200000	•573125	•575821	•578683	•581603	•584463
•5300000	•586467	•589342	•592397	•595518	•598577
•5400000	•599961	•603024	•606282	•609613	•612883
•5500000	•613611	•616871	•620342	•623896	•627388
•5600000	•627422	•630889	•634584	•638372	•642099
•5700000	•641399	•645083	•649014	•653048	•657022
•5800000	•655547	•659459	•663638	•667931	•672166
•5900000	•669872	•674022	•678461	•683027	•687537
•6000000	•684379	•688780	•693492	•698344	•703144
•6100000	•699075	•703737	•708735	•713889	•718994
•6200000	•713964	•718900	•724199	•729670	•735096
•6300000	•729053	•734276	•739890	•745694	•751458
•6400000	•744348	•749872	•755815	•761970	•768090
•6500000	•759856	•765694	•771983	•778505	•785001
•6600000	•775584	•781749	•788402	•795310	•802200
•6700000	•791537	•798046	•805078	•812392	•819698
•6800000	•807724	•814592	•822022	•829761	•837504
•6899999	•824151	•831394	•839241	•847426	•855630
•7000000	•840827	•848462	•856744	•865398	•874086
•7100000	•857758	•865802	•874541	•883687	•892884
•7200000	•874954	•883425	•892642	•902303	•912036
•7300000	•892421	•901339	•911056	•921258	•931554
•7400000	•910169	•919553	•929793	•940563	•951451
•7500000	•928207	•938077	•948864	•960229	•971741
•7600000	•946544	•956921	•968281	•980270	•992438
•7700000	•965190	•976096	•988055	1•000698	1•013555
•7800000	•984153	•995612	1•008197	1•021526	1•035107
•7899999	1•003445	1•015480	1•028719	1•042768	1•057111

$\alpha =$ .869999

θ	K VALUES				
	.318821117	.415016431	.514599755	.613601043	.708073407
.8000000	1.023075	1.035712	1.049635	1.064438	1.079583
.8100000	1.043055	1.056319	1.070957	1.086551	1.102538
.8200000	1.063396	1.077313	1.092699	1.109121	1.125995
.8300000	1.084110	1.098708	1.114876	1.132166	1.149971
.8400000	1.105207	1.120516	1.137500	1.155701	1.174486
.8500000	1.126702	1.142751	1.160589	1.179744	1.199559
.8600000	1.148606	1.165427	1.184157	1.204311	1.225210
.8700000	1.170933	1.188559	1.208220	1.229423	1.251460
.8799999	1.193697	1.212161	1.232796	1.255096	1.278332
.8899999	1.216912	1.236249	1.257901	1.281352	1.305847
.9000000	1.240592	1.260840	1.283555	1.308211	1.334031
.9100000	1.264753	1.285950	1.309774	1.335694	1.362907
.9200000	1.289412	1.311596	1.336579	1.363822	1.392501
.9300000	1.314583	1.337796	1.363990	1.392620	1.422839
.9400000	1.340283	1.364569	1.392027	1.422110	1.453950
.9500000	1.366532	1.391933	1.420712	1.452318	1.485862
.9600000	1.393345	1.419910	1.450067	1.483268	1.518605
.9699999	1.420743	1.448518	1.480116	1.514987	1.552209
.9799999	1.448744	1.477780	1.510881	1.547502	1.586708
.9899999	1.477369	1.507718	1.542388	1.580843	1.622134
1.0000000	1.506638	1.538353	1.574662	1.615037	1.658523
1.0100000	1.536571	1.569710	1.607729	1.650116	1.695909
1.0200000	1.567192	1.601813	1.641616	1.686110	1.734331
1.0300000	1.598523	1.634685	1.676352	1.723053	1.773827
1.0400000	1.630587	1.668355	1.711966	1.760978	1.814436
1.0500000	1.663409	1.702846	1.748487	1.799919	1.856201
1.0600000	1.697013	1.738188	1.785947	1.839912	1.899164
1.0699999	1.731424	1.774409	1.824376	1.880995	1.943370
1.0799999	1.766670	1.811536	1.863809	1.923205	1.988863
1.0899999	1.802777	1.849600	1.904277	1.966580	2.035692
1.1000000	1.839773	1.888632	1.945817	2.011163	2.083905
1.1100000	1.877685	1.928663	1.988463	2.056993	2.133551
1.1200000	1.916544	1.969724	2.032251	2.104113	2.184683
1.1300000	1.956379	2.011849	2.077218	2.152566	2.237352
1.1400000	1.997220	2.055070	2.123403	2.202397	2.291612
1.1500000	2.039098	2.099423	2.170843	2.253651	2.347520
1.1600000	2.082045	2.144941	2.219579	2.306373	2.405131
1.1700000	2.126092	2.191660	2.269650	2.360612	2.464504
1.1800000	2.171271	2.239615	2.321096	2.416413	2.525695
1.1899999	2.217616	2.288842	2.373958	2.473825	2.588765

$\alpha =$ .869999

Θ	K VALUES				
	.318821117	.415016431	.514599755	.613601043	.708073407
1.2000000	2.265159	2.339378	2.428277	2.532897	2.653773
1.2100000	2.313931	2.391258	2.484094	2.593676	2.720778
1.2200000	2.363966	2.444517	2.541450	2.656211	2.789842
1.2300000	2.415297	2.499193	2.600385	2.720550	2.861024
1.2400000	2.467954	2.555320	2.660939	2.786741	2.934383
1.2500000	2.521970	2.612932	2.723153	2.854830	3.009979
1.2599999	2.577375	2.672064	2.787064	2.924863	3.087870
1.2699999	2.634197	2.732747	2.852709	2.996884	3.168109
1.2799999	2.692466	2.795013	2.920124	3.070935	3.250753
1.2899999	2.752207	2.858891	2.989341	3.147056	3.335851
1.3000000	2.813445	2.924408	3.060393	3.225285	3.423452
1.3100000	2.876200	2.991587	3.133306	3.305654	3.513598
1.3200000	2.940493	3.060451	3.208105	3.388194	3.606329
1.3300000	3.006340	3.131016	3.284811	3.472931	3.701680
1.3400000	3.073752	3.203298	3.363441	3.559883	3.799678
1.3500000	3.142739	3.277305	3.444005	3.649067	3.900344
1.3600000	3.213305	3.353042	3.526509	3.740490	4.003692
1.3700000	3.285448	3.430510	3.610954	3.834153	4.109726
1.3799999	3.359163	3.509701	3.697333	3.930051	4.218441
1.3899999	3.434438	3.590602	3.785632	4.028168	4.329824
1.4000000	3.511256	3.673195	3.875830	4.128481	4.443849
1.4100000	3.589589	3.757451	3.967895	4.230956	4.560476
1.4200000	3.669407	3.843336	4.061791	4.335549	4.679656
1.4300000	3.750672	3.930807	4.157468	4.442205	4.801327
1.4400000	3.833335	4.019814	4.254870	4.550860	4.925411
1.4500000	3.917343	4.110296	4.353931	4.661437	5.051818
1.4600000	4.002633	4.202184	4.454573	4.773848	5.180442
1.4700000	4.089134	4.295402	4.556709	4.887991	5.311164
1.4800000	4.176768	4.389863	4.660243	5.003757	5.443850
1.4900000	4.265448	4.485473	4.765069	5.121021	5.578352
1.5000000	4.355082	4.582130	4.871072	5.239652	5.714512
1.5100000	4.445568	4.679721	4.978127	5.359504	5.852152
1.5200000	4.536799	4.778131	5.086102	5.480424	5.991088
1.5300000	4.628662	4.877234	5.194857	5.602251	6.131125
1.5400000	4.721039	4.976903	5.304248	5.724815	6.272058
1.5500000	4.813809	5.077001	5.414123	5.847942	6.413674
1.5600000	4.906845	5.177393	5.524327	5.971452	6.555755
1.5699999	5.000020	5.277937	5.634703	6.095161	6.698078
1.5707963	5.007442	5.285946	5.643496	6.105016	6.709416
1.5707963	5.007438	5.285942	5.643491	6.105013	6.709414

$\alpha =$ •869999

Θ	K VALUES				
	•794250555	•868696860	•928444378	•971111163	•994996249
•0000000	•000000	•000000	•000000	•000000	•000000
•0100000	•010000	•010000	•010000	•010000	•010000
•0200000	•020003	•020003	•020003	•020003	•020003
•0300000	•030011	•030011	•030012	•030012	•030012
•0400000	•040027	•040027	•040028	•040028	•040029
•0500000	•050052	•050054	•050055	•050056	•050057
•0600000	•060091	•060094	•060096	•060097	•060098
•0700000	•070145	•070149	•070152	•070155	•070156
•0800000	•080216	•080223	•080228	•080232	•080234
•0900000	•090309	•090318	•090325	•090330	•090333
•1000000	•100424	•100436	•100446	•100454	•100458
•1100000	•110565	•110581	•110595	•110604	•110610
•1200000	•120734	•120756	•120773	•120786	•120793
•1300000	•130934	•130962	•130984	•131000	•131009
•1400000	•141168	•141203	•141231	•141251	•141262
•1500000	•151439	•151482	•151516	•151541	•151555
•1600000	•161749	•161801	•161843	•161873	•161890
•1700000	•172101	•172164	•172214	•172251	•172271
•1800000	•182498	•182573	•182633	•182676	•182700
•1900000	•192943	•193031	•193102	•193153	•193182
•2000000	•203438	•203542	•203625	•203685	•203718
•2100000	•213987	•214108	•214205	•214274	•214313
•2200000	•224593	•224732	•224844	•224925	•224970
•2300000	•235259	•235419	•235547	•235640	•235691
•2400000	•245988	•246170	•246317	•246422	•246482
•2500000	•256782	•256990	•257157	•257277	•257344
•2600000	•267647	•267881	•268070	•268206	•268282
•2700000	•278584	•278848	•279061	•279214	•279299
•2800000	•289597	•289893	•290132	•290304	•290400
•2900000	•300689	•301021	•301288	•301480	•301588
•3000000	•311865	•312234	•312532	•312746	•312866
•3100000	•323127	•323537	•323869	•324107	•324240
•3200000	•334480	•334934	•335301	•335565	•335713
•3300000	•345926	•346429	•346834	•347126	•347289
•3400000	•357471	•358025	•358472	•358793	•358974
•3500000	•369118	•369726	•370218	•370572	•370771
•3600000	•380871	•381538	•382078	•382466	•382684
•3700000	•392734	•393464	•394056	•394481	•394720
•3800000	•404712	•405510	•406156	•406621	•406882
•3900000	•416808	•417678	•418384	•418891	•419177

$\alpha =$ .869999

Θ	K VALUES				
	.794250555	.868696860	.928444378	.971111163	.994996249
.4000000	.429028	.429975	.430743	.431297	.431608
.4100000	.441376	.442406	.443241	.443843	.444181
.4200000	.453857	.454974	.455881	.456535	.456903
.4300000	.466476	.467687	.468670	.469379	.469779
.4400000	.479238	.480548	.481613	.482381	.482814
.4500000	.492148	.493563	.494715	.495546	.496015
.4600000	.505211	.506739	.507983	.508881	.509388
.4700000	.518434	.520081	.521423	.522393	.522940
.4800000	.531821	.533595	.535041	.536087	.536677
.4900000	.545378	.547287	.548844	.549971	.550607
.5000000	.559113	.561164	.562840	.564052	.564737
.5100000	.573031	.575233	.577034	.578338	.579075
.5200000	.587138	.589501	.591434	.592836	.593628
.5300000	.601441	.603974	.606049	.607553	.608404
.5400000	.615948	.618661	.620885	.622499	.623413
.5500000	.630665	.633569	.635951	.637682	.638662
.5600000	.645599	.648706	.651257	.653111	.654161
.5700000	.660760	.664080	.666809	.668795	.669920
.5800000	.676153	.679700	.682618	.684743	.685948
.5900000	.691789	.695575	.698694	.700967	.702256
.6000000	.707675	.711714	.715046	.717476	.718855
.6100000	.723819	.728127	.731684	.734280	.735755
.6200000	.740232	.744824	.748619	.751392	.752969
.6300000	.756923	.761815	.765863	.768824	.770508
.6400000	.773901	.779111	.783427	.786587	.788385
.6500000	.791178	.796722	.801322	.804694	.806614
.6600000	.808763	.814662	.819563	.823159	.825209
.6700000	.826667	.832942	.838162	.841996	.844183
.6800000	.844902	.851574	.857132	.861219	.863552
.6899999	.863481	.870572	.876488	.880844	.883332
.7000000	.882414	.889950	.896245	.900886	.903540
.7100000	.901716	.909721	.916419	.921363	.924192
.7200000	.921399	.929900	.937025	.942291	.945307
.7300000	.941478	.950504	.958081	.963689	.966904
.7400000	.961966	.971548	.979605	.985576	.989003
.7500000	.982880	.993048	1.001615	1.007973	1.011625
.7600000	1.004234	1.015024	1.024130	1.030899	1.034791
.7700000	1.026044	1.037492	1.047171	1.054377	1.058526
.7800000	1.048329	1.060472	1.070760	1.078431	1.082852
.7899999	1.071104	1.083985	1.094918	1.103084	1.107796

$\alpha =$ •869999

θ	K VALUES				
	•794250555	•868696860	•928444378	•971111163	•994996249
•8000000	1•094390	1•108050	1•119669	1•128362	1•133384
•8100000	1•118204	1•132690	1•145037	1•154292	1•159645
•8200000	1•142568	1•157927	1•171048	1•180901	1•186608
•8300000	1•167501	1•183785	1•197728	1•208219	1•214303
•8400000	1•193025	1•210289	1•225107	1•236278	1•242765
•8500000	1•219163	1•237466	1•253213	1•265109	1•272027
•8600000	1•245938	1•265342	1•282077	1•294747	1•302127
•8700000	1•273375	1•293945	1•311732	1•325228	1•333102
•8799999	1•301499	1•323305	1•342212	1•356591	1•364994
•8899999	1•330338	1•353454	1•373553	1•388875	1•397844
•9000000	1•359918	1•384425	1•405792	1•422123	1•431700
•9100000	1•390269	1•416250	1•438970	1•456379	1•466608
•9200000	1•421420	1•448966	1•473127	1•491690	1•502619
•9300000	1•453404	1•482609	1•508308	1•528107	1•539787
•9400000	1•486253	1•517220	1•544557	1•565681	1•578169
•9500000	1•520001	1•552838	1•581925	1•604468	1•617825
•9600000	1•554684	1•589507	1•620461	1•644527	1•658819
•9699999	1•590338	1•627271	1•660219	1•685919	1•701218
•9799999	1•627003	1•666177	1•701255	1•728709	1•745095
•9899999	1•664719	1•706274	1•743628	1•772968	1•790526
1•0000000	1•703527	1•747614	1•787402	1•818769	1•837592
1•0100000	1•743471	1•790249	1•832640	1•866188	1•886379
1•0200000	1•784597	1•834236	1•879412	1•915309	1•936979
1•0300000	1•826951	1•879633	1•927792	1•966217	1•989489
1•0400000	1•870583	1•926502	1•977854	2•019006	2•044013
1•0500000	1•915543	1•974907	2•029680	2•073773	2•100662
1•0600000	1•961885	2•024914	2•083354	2•130622	2•159554
1•0699999	2•009663	2•076593	2•138966	2•189663	2•220816
1•0799999	2•058934	2•130017	2•196607	2•251012	2•284581
1•0899999	2•109757	2•185262	2•256378	2•314794	2•350993
1•1000000	2•162194	2•242406	2•318381	2•381139	2•420206
1•1100000	2•216306	2•301532	2•382725	2•450187	2•492383
1•1200000	2•272158	2•362724	2•449523	2•522085	2•567702
1•1300000	2•329819	2•426073	2•518896	2•596991	2•646349
1•1400000	2•389356	2•491668	2•590968	2•675072	2•728526
1•1500000	2•450841	2•559607	2•665871	2•756504	2•814451
1•1600000	2•514347	2•629986	2•743742	2•841474	2•904355
1•1700000	2•579947	2•702908	2•824725	2•930184	2•998488
1•1800000	2•647717	2•778478	2•908969	3•022842	3•097118
1•1899999	2•717735	2•856801	2•996632	3•119675	3•200533

$\alpha =$ •869999

Θ	K VALUES				
	•794250555	•868696860	•928444378	•971111163	•994996249
1•2000000	2•790080	2•937991	3•087875	3•220920	3•309046
1•2100000	2•864830	3•022157	3•182866	3•326828	3•422989
1•2200000	2•942066	3•109415	3•281782	3•437666	3•542724
1•2300000	3•021867	3•199882	3•384802	3•553716	3•668640
1•2400000	3•104315	3•293675	3•492114	3•675277	3•801161
1•2500000	3•189488	3•390912	3•603908	3•802665	3•940741
1•2599999	3•277465	3•491713	3•720381	3•936211	4•087874
1•2699999	3•368323	3•596194	3•841733	4•076266	4•243095
1•2799999	3•462137	3•704472	3•968166	4•223199	4•406988
1•2899999	3•558979	3•816662	4•099886	4•377394	4•580183
1•3000000	3•658917	3•932874	4•237097	4•539259	4•763372
1•3100000	3•762013	4•053211	4•380001	4•709211	4•957302
1•3200000	3•868326	4•177775	4•528801	4•887692	5•162796
1•3300000	3•977906	4•306657	4•683692	5•075155	5•380753
1•3400000	4•090799	4•439941	4•844861	5•272069	5•612160
1•3500000	4•207040	4•577698	5•012486	5•478913	5•858099
1•3600000	4•326653	4•719988	5•186731	5•696177	6•119764
1•3700000	4•449655	4•866856	5•367742	5•924350	6•398476
1•3799999	4•576047	5•018331	5•555648	6•163925	6•695694
1•3899999	4•705819	5•174424	5•750548	6•415384	7•013039
1•4000000	4•838948	5•335126	5•952517	6•679194	7•352316
1•4100000	4•975390	5•500404	6•161591	6•955789	7•715530
1•4200000	5•115091	5•670203	6•377772	7•245571	8•104928
1•4300000	5•257976	5•844441	6•601019	7•548886	8•523021
1•4400000	5•403953	6•023010	6•831244	7•866006	8•972617
1•4500000	5•552911	6•205775	7•068307	8•197115	9•456852
1•4600000	5•704719	6•392568	7•312014	8•542285	9•979212
1•4700000	5•859230	6•583194	7•562113	8•901451	10•543540
1•4800000	6•016274	6•777428	7•818290	9•274388	11•154010
1•4900000	6•175663	6•975015	8•080174	9•660687	11•815033
1•5000000	6•337195	7•175673	8•347332	10•059737	12•531068
1•5100000	6•500644	7•379086	8•619265	10•470694	13•306221
1•5200000	6•665772	7•584921	8•895424	10•892485	14•143645
1•5300000	6•832328	7•792817	9•175204	11•323799	15•044539
1•5400000	7•000046	8•002395	9•457955	11•763097	16•006831
1•5500000	7•168651	8•213259	9•742987	12•208632	17•023724
1•5600000	7•337860	8•424998	10•029577	12•658485	18•082622
1•5699999	7•507384	8•637194	10•316983	13•110616	19•165282
1•5707963	7•520888	8•654098	10•339882	13•146656	19•251877
1•5707963	7•520892	8•654259	10•339873	13•146645	19•251854

$\alpha =$ .879999

Θ	K VALUES				
	.009966711	.039469502	.087332193	.151646642	.229848846
.0000000	.000000	.000000	.000000	.000000	.000000
.0100000	.010000	.010000	.010000	.010000	.010000
.0200000	.020002	.020002	.020002	.020002	.020002
.0300000	.030007	.030008	.030008	.030008	.030008
.0400000	.040018	.040019	.040019	.040020	.040021
.0500000	.050036	.050037	.050038	.050039	.050041
.0600000	.060063	.060064	.060066	.060068	.060071
.0700000	.070101	.070103	.070105	.070109	.070113
.0800000	.080151	.080153	.080158	.080163	.080170
.0900000	.090215	.090219	.090225	.090232	.090242
.1000000	.100295	.100300	.100308	.100319	.100332
.1100000	.110394	.110400	.110411	.110425	.110443
.1200000	.120512	.120520	.120534	.120553	.120575
.1300000	.130651	.130662	.130680	.130703	.130732
.1400000	.140814	.140828	.140850	.140880	.140916
.1500000	.151003	.151019	.151046	.151083	.151127
.1600000	.161218	.161238	.161271	.161316	.161370
.1700000	.171463	.171487	.171527	.171580	.171645
.1800000	.181738	.181767	.181815	.181878	.181955
.1900000	.192047	.192081	.192137	.192211	.192302
.2000000	.202391	.202431	.202495	.202583	.202689
.2100000	.212771	.212818	.212893	.212994	.213117
.2200000	.223191	.223244	.223331	.223448	.223590
.2300000	.233652	.233713	.233812	.233945	.234108
.2400000	.244156	.244225	.244338	.244490	.244675
.2500000	.254705	.254784	.254911	.255083	.255294
.2600000	.265302	.265390	.265534	.265728	.265965
.2700000	.275948	.276047	.276209	.276427	.276693
.2800000	.286646	.286757	.286937	.287181	.287478
.2900000	.297398	.297521	.297722	.297994	.298325
.3000000	.308206	.308343	.308566	.308867	.309235
.3100000	.319073	.319225	.319471	.319804	.320212
.3200000	.330001	.330168	.330440	.330807	.331257
.3300000	.340992	.341176	.341475	.341879	.342374
.3400000	.352050	.352251	.352579	.353022	.353565
.3500000	.363175	.363395	.363754	.364239	.364833
.3600000	.374372	.374612	.375003	.375533	.376182
.3700000	.385642	.385903	.386330	.386906	.387614
.3800000	.396988	.397272	.397735	.398362	.399131
.3900000	.408413	.408721	.409223	.409903	.410738

$\alpha =$ •879999

Θ	K VALUES				
	•009966711	•039469502	•087332193	•151646642	•229848846
•4000000	•419920	•420253	•420797	•421533	•422437
•4100000	•431512	•431872	•432459	•433254	•434232
•4200000	•443191	•443579	•444212	•445070	•446126
•4300000	•454960	•455378	•456060	•456984	•458122
•4400000	•466823	•467272	•468005	•469000	•470224
•4500000	•478782	•479264	•480051	•481120	•482435
•4600000	•490842	•491358	•492202	•493348	•494760
•4700000	•503004	•503557	•504460	•505687	•507201
•4800000	•515273	•515863	•516830	•518142	•519762
•4900000	•527651	•528282	•529314	•530717	•532449
•5000000	•540143	•540816	•541917	•543414	•545263
•5100000	•552752	•553469	•554642	•556238	•558211
•5200000	•565482	•566245	•567493	•569193	•571295
•5300000	•578336	•579147	•580474	•582283	•584521
•5400000	•591319	•592180	•593590	•595512	•597893
•5500000	•604435	•605348	•606844	•608885	•611415
•5600000	•617687	•618655	•620242	•622407	•625092
•5700000	•631080	•632105	•633786	•636081	•638930
•5800000	•644619	•645703	•647483	•649914	•652933
•5900000	•658307	•659454	•661336	•663909	•667106
•6000000	•672150	•673362	•675351	•678072	•681456
•6100000	•686153	•687432	•689533	•692408	•695986
•6200000	•700319	•701669	•703886	•706922	•710703
•6300000	•714655	•716078	•718417	•721620	•725614
•6400000	•729166	•730665	•733130	•736508	•740723
•6500000	•743857	•745435	•748032	•751592	•756037
•6600000	•758734	•760394	•763127	•766877	•771563
•6700000	•773802	•775548	•778423	•782371	•787308
•6800000	•789067	•790903	•793925	•798079	•803277
•6899999	•804536	•806464	•809641	•814008	•819478
•7000000	•820215	•822239	•825576	•830165	•835919
•7100000	•836111	•838235	•841737	•846558	•852607
•7200000	•852229	•854457	•858132	•863193	•869550
•7300000	•868578	•870913	•874767	•880079	•886756
•7400000	•885164	•887611	•891651	•897223	•904233
•7500000	•901996	•904558	•908791	•914633	•921989
•7600000	•919080	•921762	•926196	•932319	•940035
•7700000	•936424	•939231	•943873	•950287	•958379
•7800000	•954038	•956974	•961831	•968549	•977030
•7899999	•971928	•974999	•980080	•987112	•995999

$\alpha =$ .879999

Θ	K VALUES				
	.009966711	.039469502	.087332193	.151646642	.229848846
.8000000	.990106	.993315	.998629	1.005988	1.015295
.8100000	1.008579	1.011932	1.017487	1.025184	1.034930
.8200000	1.027357	1.030859	1.036664	1.044713	1.054914
.8300000	1.046449	1.050107	1.056170	1.064585	1.075258
.8400000	1.065867	1.069685	1.076017	1.084810	1.095975
.8500000	1.085620	1.089604	1.096214	1.105401	1.117077
.8600000	1.105720	1.109876	1.116775	1.126370	1.138576
.8700000	1.126178	1.130511	1.137710	1.147728	1.160485
.8799999	1.147005	1.151523	1.159031	1.169488	1.182818
.8899999	1.168213	1.172923	1.180752	1.191665	1.205589
.9000000	1.189817	1.194724	1.202886	1.214271	1.228812
.9100000	1.211827	1.216939	1.225446	1.237321	1.252503
.9200000	1.234258	1.239582	1.248447	1.260829	1.276677
.9300000	1.257124	1.262668	1.271903	1.284812	1.301350
.9400000	1.280439	1.286210	1.295829	1.309284	1.326539
.9500000	1.304219	1.310225	1.320241	1.334262	1.352263
.9600000	1.328478	1.334729	1.345156	1.359764	1.378537
.9699999	1.353234	1.359737	1.370590	1.385807	1.405382
.9799999	1.378502	1.385266	1.396561	1.412409	1.432817
.9899999	1.404301	1.411335	1.423087	1.439588	1.460861
1.0000000	1.430648	1.437961	1.450187	1.467366	1.489536
1.0100000	1.457561	1.465164	1.477880	1.495762	1.518862
1.0200000	1.485060	1.492963	1.506186	1.524796	1.548863
1.0300000	1.513164	1.521377	1.535126	1.554491	1.579560
1.0400000	1.541895	1.550429	1.564722	1.584870	1.610979
1.0500000	1.571273	1.580139	1.594996	1.615954	1.643143
1.0600000	1.601320	1.610530	1.625971	1.647769	1.676078
1.0699999	1.632060	1.641625	1.657671	1.680339	1.709810
1.0799999	1.663514	1.673448	1.690119	1.713690	1.744366
1.0899999	1.695708	1.706023	1.723342	1.747847	1.779773
1.1000000	1.728666	1.739375	1.757365	1.782839	1.816062
1.1100000	1.762413	1.773530	1.792214	1.818692	1.853260
1.1200000	1.796976	1.808515	1.827918	1.855435	1.891399
1.1300000	1.832382	1.844358	1.864504	1.893098	1.930509
1.1400000	1.868658	1.881085	1.902002	1.931711	1.970622
1.1500000	1.905831	1.918726	1.940440	1.971304	2.011772
1.1600000	1.943932	1.957310	1.979849	2.011910	2.053990
1.1700000	1.982989	1.996867	2.020259	2.053559	2.097312
1.1800000	2.023032	2.037427	2.061702	2.096285	2.141771
1.1899999	2.064091	2.079021	2.104210	2.140121	2.187403

$\alpha =$ .879999

Θ	K VALUES				
	.009966711	.039469502	.087332193	.151646642	.229848846
1.2000000	2.106197	2.121680	2.147814	2.185100	2.234243
1.2100000	2.149381	2.165434	2.192546	2.231255	2.282327
1.2200000	2.193672	2.210317	2.238439	2.278621	2.331690
1.2300000	2.239103	2.256358	2.285526	2.327231	2.382368
1.2400000	2.285704	2.303590	2.333838	2.377118	2.434396
1.2500000	2.333505	2.352043	2.383407	2.428317	2.487811
1.2599999	2.382536	2.401747	2.434265	2.480859	2.542646
1.2699999	2.432827	2.452733	2.486442	2.534777	2.598935
1.2799999	2.484404	2.505028	2.539967	2.590101	2.656711
1.2899999	2.537296	2.558660	2.594869	2.646860	2.716005
1.3000000	2.591528	2.613655	2.651174	2.705082	2.776846
1.3100000	2.647122	2.670035	2.708906	2.764793	2.839261
1.3200000	2.704099	2.727824	2.768087	2.826015	2.903274
1.3300000	2.762479	2.787039	2.828737	2.888769	2.968907
1.3400000	2.822275	2.847696	2.890872	2.953071	3.036178
1.3500000	2.883502	2.909807	2.954504	3.018935	3.105100
1.3600000	2.946165	2.973380	3.019642	3.086369	3.175683
1.3700000	3.010269	3.038419	3.086288	3.155376	3.247931
1.3799999	3.075812	3.104922	3.154443	3.225957	3.321842
1.3899999	3.142788	3.172883	3.224098	3.298102	3.397409
1.4000000	3.211185	3.242290	3.295242	3.371800	3.474618
1.4100000	3.280983	3.313121	3.367853	3.447029	3.553445
1.4200000	3.352156	3.385352	3.441906	3.523760	3.633863
1.4300000	3.424673	3.458950	3.517365	3.601960	3.715834
1.4400000	3.498493	3.533874	3.594191	3.681583	3.799311
1.4500000	3.573569	3.610076	3.672331	3.762579	3.884239
1.4600000	3.649846	3.687499	3.751729	3.844886	3.970556
1.4700000	3.727259	3.766079	3.832319	3.928436	4.058186
1.4800000	3.805738	3.845742	3.914024	4.013150	4.147049
1.4900000	3.885204	3.926410	3.996764	4.098942	4.237052
1.5000000	3.965570	4.007994	4.080447	4.185718	4.328096
1.5100000	4.046743	4.090398	4.164974	4.273375	4.420072
1.5200000	4.128621	4.173521	4.250241	4.361804	4.512864
1.5300000	4.211100	4.257254	4.336136	4.450888	4.606350
1.5400000	4.294067	4.341483	4.422543	4.540506	4.700400
1.5500000	4.377407	4.426093	4.509341	4.630531	4.794882
1.5600000	4.461000	4.510960	4.596405	4.720833	4.889657
1.5699999	4.544726	4.595962	4.683607	4.811281	4.984585
1.5707963	4.551396	4.602733	4.690553	4.818486	4.992147
1.5707963	4.551391	4.602729	4.690549	4.818481	4.992143

$\alpha =$ .879999

Θ	K VALUES				
	.318821117	.415016431	.514599755	.613601043	.708073407
.0000000	.000000	.000000	.000000	.000000	.000000
.0100000	.010000	.010000	.010000	.010000	.010000
.0200000	.020002	.020002	.020003	.020003	.020003
.0300000	.030009	.030009	.030010	.030010	.030011
.0400000	.040022	.040023	.040024	.040025	.040026
.0500000	.050043	.050045	.050047	.050049	.050051
.0600000	.060074	.060078	.060082	.060085	.060089
.0700000	.070119	.070124	.070130	.070135	.070141
.0800000	.080177	.080186	.080194	.080203	.080211
.0900000	.090253	.090265	.090277	.090289	.090300
.1000000	.100347	.100363	.100380	.100397	.100413
.1100000	.110463	.110484	.110506	.110529	.110550
.1200000	.120601	.120629	.120658	.120687	.120715
.1300000	.130765	.130801	.130838	.130875	.130910
.1400000	.140957	.141001	.141048	.141094	.141138
.1500000	.151178	.151233	.151290	.151347	.151401
.1600000	.161431	.161498	.161568	.161637	.161703
.1700000	.171719	.171799	.171883	.171966	.172045
.1800000	.182043	.182139	.182238	.182337	.182431
.1900000	.192406	.192519	.192636	.192753	.192864
.2000000	.202811	.202942	.203079	.203216	.203346
.2100000	.213258	.213411	.213570	.213729	.213881
.2200000	.223752	.223928	.224112	.224295	.224470
.2300000	.234294	.234496	.234706	.234916	.235118
.2400000	.244887	.245118	.245357	.245597	.245826
.2500000	.255534	.255795	.256067	.256338	.256599
.2600000	.266236	.266531	.266838	.267145	.267439
.2700000	.276997	.277328	.277673	.278019	.278350
.2800000	.287819	.288190	.288576	.288963	.289335
.2900000	.298705	.299118	.299549	.299981	.300397
.3000000	.309657	.310117	.310596	.311077	.311539
.3100000	.320679	.321188	.321719	.322252	.322766
.3200000	.331773	.332335	.332922	.333512	.334080
.3300000	.342941	.343561	.344208	.344858	.345485
.3400000	.354188	.354869	.355580	.356295	.356985
.3500000	.365516	.366262	.367042	.367827	.368584
.3600000	.376928	.377743	.378597	.379456	.380285
.3700000	.388427	.389316	.390248	.391187	.392094
.3800000	.400016	.400984	.402000	.403023	.404013
.3900000	.411699	.412751	.413855	.414969	.416047

$\alpha =$ .879999

Θ	K VALUES				
	.318821117	.415016431	.514599755	.613601043	.708073407
.4000000	.423479	.424620	.425819	.427028	.428200
.4100000	.435359	.436595	.437894	.439205	.440477
.4200000	.447343	.448679	.450084	.451504	.452882
.4300000	.459435	.460877	.462394	.463930	.465421
.4400000	.471638	.473191	.474829	.476486	.478097
.4500000	.483956	.485628	.487391	.489178	.490916
.4600000	.496392	.498189	.500086	.502010	.503883
.4700000	.508952	.510880	.512918	.514987	.517003
.4800000	.521638	.523706	.525892	.528114	.530281
.4900000	.534455	.536669	.539013	.541397	.543724
.5000000	.547408	.549776	.552285	.554840	.557337
.5100000	.560500	.563031	.565715	.568450	.571126
.5200000	.573737	.576438	.579306	.582231	.585097
.5300000	.587122	.590003	.593064	.596191	.599256
.5400000	.600661	.603731	.606995	.610334	.613610
.5500000	.614359	.617627	.621105	.624667	.628166
.5600000	.628221	.631696	.635400	.639196	.642931
.5700000	.642252	.645944	.649885	.653928	.657912
.5800000	.656456	.660378	.664567	.668871	.673116
.5900000	.670841	.675002	.679452	.684030	.688551
.6000000	.685412	.689823	.694548	.699413	.704225
.6100000	.700173	.704848	.709860	.715029	.720147
.6200000	.715133	.720083	.725396	.730884	.736325
.6300000	.730296	.735534	.741164	.746986	.752768
.6400000	.745669	.751209	.757171	.763345	.769485
.6500000	.761259	.767115	.773425	.779968	.786485
.6600000	.777073	.783259	.789934	.796865	.803779
.6700000	.793118	.799650	.806706	.814045	.821377
.6800000	.809401	.816294	.823750	.831517	.839289
.6899999	.825930	.833200	.841076	.849292	.857527
.7000000	.842713	.850377	.858691	.867379	.876101
.7100000	.859757	.867833	.876607	.885790	.895024
.7200000	.877071	.885577	.894833	.904535	.914309
.7300000	.894664	.903619	.913379	.923625	.933967
.7400000	.912544	.921969	.932255	.943074	.954013
.7500000	.930721	.940637	.951474	.962892	.974459
.7600000	.949205	.959632	.971046	.983094	.995321
.7700000	.968005	.978966	.990984	1.003691	1.016613
.7800000	.987132	.998649	1.011299	1.024698	1.038351
.7899999	1.006595	1.018695	1.032004	1.046130	1.060552

$\alpha =$ •879999

Θ	K VALUES				
	•318821117	•415016431	•514599755	•613601043	•708073407
•8000000	1•026407	1•039113	1•053114	1•068000	1•083231
•8100000	1•046579	1•059917	1•074640	1•090324	1•106406
•8200000	1•067121	1•081120	1•096598	1•113119	1•130095
•8300000	1•088048	1•102735	1•119002	1•136400	1•154318
•8400000	1•109370	1•124775	1•141868	1•160186	1•179094
•8500000	1•131101	1•147255	1•165211	1•184493	1•204443
•8600000	1•153255	1•170190	1•189047	1•209342	1•230386
•8700000	1•175846	1•193595	1•213395	1•234749	1•256947
•8799999	1•198888	1•217486	1•238272	1•260737	1•284147
•8899999	1•222397	1•241879	1•263695	1•287326	1•312011
•9000000	1•246388	1•266792	1•289684	1•314537	1•340565
•9100000	1•270878	1•292243	1•316260	1•342392	1•369832
•9200000	1•295882	1•318249	1•343441	1•370916	1•399842
•9300000	1•321419	1•344830	1•371251	1•400132	1•430622
•9400000	1•347507	1•372006	1•399710	1•430066	1•462201
•9500000	1•374164	1•399797	1•428841	1•460744	1•494609
•9600000	1•401409	1•428224	1•458670	1•492193	1•527880
•9699999	1•429264	1•457310	1•489219	1•524441	1•562045
•9799999	1•457748	1•487076	1•520515	1•557517	1•597139
•9899999	1•486884	1•517548	1•552584	1•591453	1•633197
1•0000000	1•516693	1•548750	1•585454	1•626279	1•670258
1•0100000	1•547199	1•580706	1•619153	1•662028	1•708359
1•0200000	1•578425	1•613443	1•653711	1•698735	1•747541
1•0300000	1•610397	1•646988	1•689158	1•736433	1•787844
1•0400000	1•643140	1•681370	1•725525	1•775161	1•829313
1•0500000	1•676680	1•716617	1•762846	1•814954	1•871993
1•0600000	1•711045	1•752760	1•801154	1•855854	1•915929
1•0699999	1•746263	1•789829	1•840485	1•897899	1•961171
1•0799999	1•782364	1•827856	1•880873	1•941132	2•007767
1•0899999	1•819376	1•866875	1•922356	1•985596	2•055770
1•1000000	1•857332	1•906920	1•964974	2•031335	2•105234
1•1100000	1•896262	1•948025	2•008764	2•078395	2•156213
1•1200000	1•936199	1•990225	2•053767	2•126823	2•208763
1•1300000	1•977177	2•033559	2•100026	2•176667	2•262944
1•1400000	2•019231	2•078064	2•147582	2•227977	2•318816
1•1500000	2•062395	2•123779	2•196479	2•280805	2•376441
1•1600000	2•106706	2•170743	2•246762	2•335202	2•435881
1•1700000	2•152199	2•218995	2•298477	2•391221	2•497203
1•1800000	2•198912	2•268579	2•351670	2•448917	2•560472
1•1899999	2•246883	2•319534	2•406387	2•508344	2•625755

$\alpha =$ .879999

Θ	K VALUES				
	.318821117	.415016431	.514599755	.613601043	.708073407
1.2000000	2.296151	2.371903	2.462677	2.569559	2.693121
1.2100000	2.346752	2.425728	2.520587	2.632617	2.762639
1.2200000	2.398726	2.481051	2.580165	2.697575	2.834379
1.2300000	2.452112	2.537916	2.641460	2.764490	2.908411
1.2400000	2.506947	2.596364	2.704519	2.833418	2.984805
1.2500000	2.563270	2.656437	2.769390	2.904416	3.063630
1.2599999	2.621119	2.718177	2.836119	2.977537	3.144956
1.2699999	2.680528	2.781623	2.904753	3.052837	3.228849
1.2799999	2.741534	2.846815	2.975335	3.130368	3.315375
1.2899999	2.804171	2.913788	3.047908	3.210178	3.404597
1.3000000	2.868469	2.982580	3.122511	3.292318	3.496577
1.3100000	2.934458	3.053220	3.199180	3.376828	3.591368
1.3200000	3.002164	3.125739	3.277950	3.463749	3.689022
1.3300000	3.071610	3.200162	3.358850	3.553118	3.789585
1.3400000	3.142816	3.276511	3.441903	3.644963	3.893098
1.3500000	3.215796	3.354802	3.527131	3.739309	3.999591
1.3600000	3.290561	3.435047	3.614545	3.836172	4.109088
1.3700000	3.367115	3.517250	3.704153	3.935562	4.221605
1.3799999	3.445457	3.601411	3.795953	4.037479	4.337144
1.3899999	3.525578	3.687521	3.889936	4.141913	4.455697
1.4000000	3.607464	3.775564	3.986086	4.248845	4.577246
1.4100000	3.691090	3.865513	4.084372	4.358244	4.701753
1.4200000	3.776426	3.957335	4.184758	4.470066	4.829172
1.4300000	3.863431	4.050985	4.287194	4.584257	4.959438
1.4400000	3.952056	4.146410	4.391621	4.700748	5.092470
1.4500000	4.042241	4.243545	4.497965	4.819456	5.228172
1.4600000	4.133918	4.342315	4.606144	4.940284	5.366428
1.4700000	4.227008	4.442634	4.716060	5.063123	5.507108
1.4800000	4.321423	4.544404	4.827606	5.187846	5.650061
1.4900000	4.417064	4.647519	4.940659	5.314315	5.795121
1.5000000	4.513825	4.751860	5.055091	5.442378	5.942105
1.5100000	4.611587	4.857300	5.170755	5.571868	6.090814
1.5200000	4.710227	4.963702	5.287499	5.702609	6.241035
1.5300000	4.809614	5.070922	5.405161	5.834412	6.392540
1.5400000	4.909607	5.178807	5.523571	5.967082	6.545093
1.5500000	5.010064	5.287201	5.642551	6.100412	6.698444
1.5600000	5.110837	5.395940	5.761919	6.234193	6.852340
1.5699999	5.211774	5.504860	5.881490	6.368207	7.006519
1.5707963	5.219814	5.513537	5.891015	6.378883	7.018801
1.5707963	5.219810	5.513532	5.891011	6.378880	7.018800

$\alpha =$ •879999

Θ	K VALUES				
	•794250555	•868696860	•928444378	•971111163	•994996249
•0000000	•000000	•000000	•000000	•000000	•000000
•0100000	•010000	•010000	•010000	•010000	•010000
•0200000	•020003	•020003	•020003	•020003	•020003
•0300000	•030011	•030011	•030012	•030012	•030012
•0400000	•040027	•040028	•040028	•040029	•040029
•0500000	•050053	•050054	•050056	•050056	•050057
•0600000	•060092	•060094	•060096	•060098	•060099
•0700000	•070146	•070150	•070154	•070156	•070157
•0800000	•080218	•080225	•080230	•080233	•080235
•0900000	•090311	•090320	•090327	•090333	•090336
•1000000	•100427	•100440	•100450	•100457	•100461
•1100000	•110569	•110586	•110599	•110609	•110614
•1200000	•120740	•120762	•120779	•120792	•120799
•1300000	•130942	•130970	•130992	•131008	•131017
•1400000	•141178	•141213	•141241	•141260	•141272
•1500000	•151451	•151494	•151528	•151553	•151566
•1600000	•161763	•161815	•161857	•161887	•161904
•1700000	•172118	•172181	•172231	•172267	•172288
•1800000	•182518	•182593	•182653	•182696	•182721
•1900000	•192966	•193055	•193126	•193177	•193206
•2000000	•203466	•203570	•203653	•203713	•203746
•2100000	•214020	•214140	•214237	•214307	•214346
•2200000	•224631	•224770	•224882	•224962	•225007
•2300000	•235302	•235462	•235591	•235683	•235734
•2400000	•246037	•246219	•246366	•246472	•246531
•2500000	•256838	•257046	•257213	•257333	•257400
•2600000	•267710	•267945	•268134	•268269	•268345
•2700000	•278655	•278919	•279132	•279285	•279371
•2800000	•289676	•289973	•290212	•290384	•290480
•2900000	•300778	•301110	•301378	•301570	•301677
•3000000	•311964	•312334	•312632	•312846	•312966
•3100000	•323237	•323648	•323980	•324218	•324351
•3200000	•334602	•335057	•335424	•335688	•335836
•3300000	•346062	•346564	•346970	•347262	•347426
•3400000	•357620	•358174	•358622	•358943	•359124
•3500000	•369282	•369891	•370383	•370737	•370936
•3600000	•381051	•381718	•382259	•382647	•382866
•3700000	•392931	•393662	•394254	•394679	•394919
•3800000	•404927	•405725	•406372	•406838	•407099
•3900000	•417043	•417914	•418619	•419128	•419413

$\alpha =$ .879999

Θ	K VALUES				
	.794250555	.868696860	.928444378	.971111163	.994996249
.4000000	.429284	.430232	.431000	.431554	.431866
.4100000	.441654	.442684	.443521	.444123	.444462
.4200000	.454159	.455277	.456185	.456839	.457208
.4300000	.466803	.468014	.468999	.469709	.470109
.4400000	.479591	.480903	.481969	.482738	.483172
.4500000	.492530	.493947	.495100	.495933	.496402
.4600000	.505623	.507153	.508399	.509299	.509806
.4700000	.518878	.520528	.521872	.522843	.523391
.4800000	.532300	.534076	.535525	.536573	.537164
.4900000	.545894	.547805	.549365	.550494	.551131
.5000000	.559667	.561722	.563400	.564615	.565301
.5100000	.573626	.575832	.577636	.578943	.579681
.5200000	.587776	.590144	.592081	.593485	.594279
.5300000	.602126	.604664	.606743	.608250	.609103
.5400000	.616681	.619400	.621629	.623247	.624162
.5500000	.631450	.634360	.636748	.638483	.639465
.5600000	.646440	.649553	.652110	.653968	.655021
.5700000	.661658	.664986	.667722	.669712	.670841
.5800000	.677113	.680669	.683594	.685725	.686933
.5900000	.692814	.696610	.699737	.702016	.703309
.6000000	.708769	.712819	.716160	.718596	.719980
.6100000	.724986	.729306	.732873	.735477	.736956
.6200000	.741477	.746082	.749888	.752670	.754251
.6300000	.758249	.763156	.767216	.770186	.771876
.6400000	.775314	.780540	.784870	.788040	.789844
.6500000	.792682	.798245	.802860	.806243	.808170
.6600000	.810364	.816284	.821201	.824810	.826867
.6700000	.828371	.834668	.839907	.843755	.845950
.6800000	.846715	.853411	.858990	.863092	.865434
.6899999	.865408	.872526	.878465	.882838	.885336
.7000000	.884463	.892028	.898349	.903009	.905674
.7100000	.903893	.911931	.918657	.923622	.926463
.7200000	.923713	.932250	.939406	.944695	.947724
.7300000	.943935	.953002	.960613	.966247	.969476
.7400000	.964576	.974202	.982297	.988297	.991740
.7500000	.985651	.995869	1.004477	1.010866	1.014536
.7600000	1.007176	1.018020	1.027173	1.033976	1.037888
.7700000	1.029167	1.040675	1.050405	1.057649	1.061820
.7800000	1.051643	1.063853	1.074197	1.081910	1.086355
.7899999	1.074622	1.087575	1.098570	1.106783	1.111522

$\alpha =$ •879999

Θ	K VALUES				
	•794250555	•868696860	•928444378	•971111163	•994996249
•8000000	1•098123	1•111862	1•123550	1•132295	1•137347
•8100000	1•122165	1•136738	1•149161	1•158472	1•163859
•8200000	1•146770	1•162225	1•175430	1•185345	1•191089
•8300000	1•171959	1•188350	1•202384	1•212944	1•219069
•8400000	1•197755	1•215136	1•230054	1•241301	1•247834
•8500000	1•224181	1•242612	1•258470	1•270450	1•277418
•8600000	1•251262	1•270806	1•287663	1•300426	1•307862
•8700000	1•279023	1•299747	1•317669	1•331268	1•339203
•8799999	1•307492	1•329467	1•348522	1•363014	1•371484
•8899999	1•336696	1•359998	1•380259	1•395707	1•404751
•9000000	1•366664	1•391374	1•412922	1•429391	1•439051
•9100000	1•397426	1•423631	1•446550	1•464112	1•474432
•9200000	1•429016	1•456806	1•481187	1•499920	1•510949
•9300000	1•461464	1•490939	1•516879	1•536866	1•548658
•9400000	1•494807	1•526071	1•553674	1•575005	1•587617
•9500000	1•529081	1•562243	1•591623	1•614396	1•627891
•9600000	1•564322	1•599503	1•630780	1•655101	1•669545
•9699999	1•600571	1•637897	1•671201	1•697183	1•712652
•9799999	1•637869	1•677474	1•712945	1•740712	1•757286
•9899999	1•676258	1•718287	1•756075	1•785761	1•803528
1•0000000	1•715783	1•760391	1•800657	1•832407	1•851463
1•0100000	1•756491	1•803841	1•846760	1•880733	1•901182
1•0200000	1•798429	1•848697	1•894457	1•930825	1•952783
1•0300000	1•841650	1•895023	1•943826	1•982775	2•006367
1•0400000	1•886206	1•942885	1•994949	2•036681	2•062045
1•0500000	1•932150	1•992349	2•047909	2•092648	2•119935
1•0600000	1•979542	2•043489	2•102799	2•150785	2•180162
1•0699999	2•028440	2•096379	2•159714	2•211209	2•242859
1•0799999	2•078905	2•151098	2•218753	2•274046	2•308169
1•0899999	2•131003	2•207728	2•280023	2•339427	2•376247
1•1000000	2•184800	2•266356	2•343635	2•407493	2•447256
1•1100000	2•240364	2•327068	2•409705	2•478394	2•521370
1•1200000	2•297767	2•389959	2•478358	2•552288	2•598779
1•1300000	2•357083	2•455126	2•549722	2•629345	2•679684
1•1400000	2•418388	2•522669	2•623934	2•709744	2•764302
1•1500000	2•481761	2•592694	2•701137	2•793676	2•852865
1•1600000	2•547283	2•665308	2•781481	2•881345	2•945624
1•1700000	2•615037	2•740625	2•865123	2•972967	3•042848
1•1800000	2•685108	2•818760	2•952228	3•068772	3•144827
1•1899999	2•757584	2•899833	3•042967	3•169003	3•251872

$\alpha =$ .879999

Θ	K VALUES				
	.794250555	.868696860	.928444378	.971111163	.994996249
1.2000000	2.832554	2.983968	3.137520	3.273921	3.364322
1.2100000	2.910107	3.071290	3.236074	3.383800	3.482537
1.2200000	2.990335	3.161929	3.338822	3.498934	3.606912
1.2300000	3.073332	3.256018	3.445967	3.619631	3.737871
1.2400000	3.159189	3.353690	3.557718	3.746220	3.875872
1.2500000	3.248000	3.455081	3.674287	3.879049	4.021415
1.2599999	3.339858	3.560328	3.795898	4.018486	4.175037
1.2699999	3.434853	3.669566	3.922775	4.164918	4.337327
1.2799999	3.533075	3.782932	4.055149	4.318754	4.508920
1.2899999	3.634610	3.900559	4.193252	4.480423	4.690510
1.3000000	3.739543	4.022579	4.337322	4.650378	4.882855
1.3100000	3.847951	4.149117	4.487589	4.829087	5.086778
1.3200000	3.959907	4.280293	4.644288	5.017043	5.303181
1.3300000	4.075478	4.416221	4.807646	5.214755	5.533055
1.3400000	4.194724	4.557005	4.977884	5.422750	5.777483
1.3500000	4.317693	4.702736	5.155213	5.641568	6.037659
1.3600000	4.444424	4.853493	5.339827	5.871761	6.314898
1.3700000	4.574946	5.009340	5.531906	6.113885	6.610651
1.3799999	4.709271	5.170323	5.731604	6.368497	6.926525
1.3899999	4.847398	5.336465	5.939053	6.636146	7.264302
1.4000000	4.989311	5.507772	6.154350	6.917365	7.625969
1.4100000	5.134973	5.684218	6.377551	7.212650	8.013727
1.4200000	5.284331	5.865753	6.608675	7.522464	8.430044
1.4300000	5.437309	6.052300	6.847694	7.847206	8.877675
1.4400000	5.593813	6.243747	7.094521	8.187196	9.359696
1.4500000	5.753724	6.439951	7.349017	8.542654	9.879541
1.4600000	5.916902	6.640733	7.610974	8.913674	10.441023
1.4700000	6.083182	6.845880	7.880124	9.300199	11.048342
1.4800000	6.252377	7.055143	8.156124	9.701993	11.706052
1.4900000	6.424277	7.268239	8.438564	10.118615	12.418964
1.5000000	6.598652	7.484851	8.726963	10.549394	13.191933
1.5100000	6.775245	7.704623	9.020765	10.993399	14.029428
1.5200000	6.953785	7.927175	9.319352	11.449448	14.934868
1.5300000	7.133981	8.152097	9.622045	11.916085	15.909544
1.5400000	7.315527	8.378954	9.928109	12.391602	16.951176
1.5500000	7.498104	8.607291	10.236760	12.874057	18.052338
1.5600000	7.681383	8.836637	10.547182	13.361318	19.199289
1.5699999	7.865029	9.066510	10.858530	13.851113	20.372139
1.5707963	7.879659	9.084823	10.883337	13.890157	20.465951
1.5707963	7.879662	9.084868	10.883329	13.890146	20.465929

$\alpha =$ .889999

Θ	K VALUES				
	.009966711	.039469502	.087332193	.151646642	.229848846
.0000000	.000000	.000000	.000000	.000000	.000000
.0100000	.010000	.010000	.010000	.010000	.010000
.0200000	.020002	.020002	.020002	.020002	.020002
.0300000	.030008	.030008	.030008	.030008	.030009
.0400000	.040019	.040019	.040019	.040020	.040021
.0500000	.050037	.050037	.050038	.050040	.050041
.0600000	.060064	.060065	.060067	.060069	.060072
.0700000	.070102	.070104	.070106	.070110	.070115
.0800000	.080153	.080155	.080159	.080165	.080171
.0900000	.090218	.090221	.090227	.090235	.090244
.1000000	.100299	.100304	.100312	.100323	.100336
.1100000	.110398	.110405	.110415	.110430	.110447
.1200000	.120518	.120526	.120540	.120559	.120581
.1300000	.130659	.130670	.130687	.130711	.130740
.1400000	.140824	.140837	.140859	.140889	.140925
.1500000	.151014	.151031	.151058	.151094	.151139
.1600000	.161232	.161252	.161285	.161330	.161384
.1700000	.171479	.171504	.171544	.171597	.171662
.1800000	.181758	.181787	.181835	.181898	.181975
.1900000	.192071	.192105	.192160	.192235	.192326
.2000000	.202418	.202458	.202523	.202610	.202717
.2100000	.212804	.212850	.212925	.213026	.213150
.2200000	.223228	.223282	.223368	.223485	.223627
.2300000	.233694	.233755	.233855	.233988	.234151
.2400000	.244204	.244274	.244387	.244539	.244724
.2500000	.254760	.254839	.254966	.255139	.255349
.2600000	.265364	.265452	.265596	.265791	.266028
.2700000	.276018	.276117	.276279	.276497	.276763
.2800000	.286724	.286835	.287016	.287259	.287557
.2900000	.297485	.297609	.297810	.298081	.298413
.3000000	.308303	.308441	.308664	.308965	.309333
.3100000	.319181	.319333	.319580	.319913	.320321
.3200000	.330120	.330288	.330560	.330927	.331377
.3300000	.341124	.341308	.341607	.342012	.342507
.3400000	.352195	.352396	.352724	.353168	.353711
.3500000	.363334	.363555	.363914	.364399	.364994
.3600000	.374546	.374787	.375178	.375708	.376358
.3700000	.385832	.386094	.386521	.387098	.387806
.3800000	.397196	.397480	.397944	.398571	.399341
.3900000	.408640	.408948	.409451	.410131	.410967

$\alpha =$ •889999

Θ	K VALUES				
	•009966711	•039469502	•087332193	•151646642	•229848846
•4000000	•420166	•420500	•421044	•421781	•422686
•4100000	•431779	•432139	•432727	•433523	•434502
•4200000	•443480	•443868	•444502	•445362	•446419
•4300000	•455273	•455691	•456374	•457300	•458439
•4400000	•467161	•467610	•468344	•469340	•470566
•4500000	•479147	•479629	•480417	•481487	•482805
•4600000	•491234	•491751	•492596	•493744	•495158
•4700000	•503426	•503980	•504884	•506113	•507629
•4800000	•515726	•516318	•517286	•518601	•520223
•4900000	•528138	•528770	•529803	•531209	•532943
•5000000	•540666	•541339	•542442	•543942	•545794
•5100000	•553312	•554030	•555205	•556803	•558780
•5200000	•566081	•566845	•568096	•569798	•571905
•5300000	•578977	•579789	•581119	•582931	•585174
•5400000	•592004	•592866	•594279	•596205	•598590
•5500000	•605166	•606081	•607580	•609626	•612160
•5600000	•618467	•619437	•621027	•623197	•625888
•5700000	•631911	•632939	•634624	•636924	•639779
•5800000	•645504	•646592	•648375	•650812	•653838
•5900000	•659250	•660400	•662287	•664866	•668071
•6000000	•673153	•674368	•676363	•679090	•682483
•6100000	•687219	•688502	•690609	•693491	•697079
•6200000	•701453	•702807	•705030	•708074	•711866
•6300000	•715860	•717287	•719632	•722845	•726850
•6400000	•730445	•731949	•734421	•737809	•742037
•6500000	•745214	•746797	•749402	•752973	•757433
•6600000	•760173	•761839	•764581	•768343	•773045
•6700000	•775328	•777080	•779965	•783926	•788880
•6800000	•790685	•792527	•795560	•799728	•804945
•6899999	•806250	•808185	•811373	•815756	•821247
•7000000	•822031	•824062	•827411	•832018	•837794
•7100000	•838033	•840165	•843681	•848521	•854594
•7200000	•854263	•856500	•860189	•865272	•871655
•7300000	•870730	•873075	•876945	•882280	•888985
•7400000	•887441	•889898	•893956	•899552	•906593
•7500000	•904403	•906977	•911229	•917098	•924487
•7600000	•921625	•924320	•928774	•934926	•942679
•7700000	•939114	•941935	•946599	•953045	•961176
•7800000	•956881	•959832	•964714	•971465	•979989
•7899999	•974933	•978019	•983127	•990195	•999128

$\alpha =$ .889999

Θ	K VALUES				
	.009966711	.039469502	.087332193	.151646642	.229848846
.8000000	.993280	.996506	1.001849	1.009247	1.018605
.8100000	1.011931	1.015303	1.020889	1.028629	1.038429
.8200000	1.030897	1.034420	1.040258	1.048353	1.058614
.8300000	1.050188	1.053867	1.059967	1.068431	1.079169
.8400000	1.069814	1.073655	1.080027	1.088874	1.100109
.8500000	1.089788	1.093797	1.100449	1.109695	1.121446
.8600000	1.110120	1.114302	1.121247	1.130905	1.143193
.8700000	1.130822	1.135185	1.142432	1.152519	1.165364
.8799999	1.151907	1.156457	1.164018	1.174549	1.187973
.8899999	1.173388	1.178131	1.186018	1.197010	1.211036
.9000000	1.195278	1.200222	1.208446	1.219916	1.234568
.9100000	1.217591	1.222743	1.231316	1.243284	1.258585
.9200000	1.240342	1.245708	1.254644	1.267127	1.283103
.9300000	1.263545	1.269135	1.278446	1.291463	1.308141
.9400000	1.287216	1.293037	1.302738	1.316309	1.333715
.9500000	1.311372	1.317432	1.327536	1.341683	1.359845
.9600000	1.336029	1.342336	1.352859	1.367602	1.386550
.9699999	1.361204	1.367768	1.378724	1.394086	1.413850
.9799999	1.386916	1.393746	1.405151	1.421155	1.441766
.9899999	1.413184	1.420289	1.432159	1.448829	1.470320
1.0000000	1.440026	1.447416	1.459769	1.477130	1.499535
1.0100000	1.467464	1.475149	1.488002	1.506078	1.529432
1.0200000	1.495518	1.503508	1.516879	1.535699	1.560038
1.0300000	1.524209	1.532516	1.546424	1.566014	1.591377
1.0400000	1.553561	1.562196	1.576660	1.597049	1.623475
1.0500000	1.583597	1.592572	1.607612	1.628830	1.656359
1.0600000	1.614341	1.623667	1.639304	1.661382	1.690057
1.0699999	1.645818	1.655508	1.671765	1.694734	1.724599
1.0799999	1.678054	1.688122	1.705019	1.728913	1.760013
1.0899999	1.711076	1.721534	1.739096	1.763949	1.796332
1.1000000	1.744911	1.755775	1.774026	1.799872	1.833587
1.1100000	1.779589	1.790872	1.809836	1.836714	1.871811
1.1200000	1.815139	1.826856	1.846559	1.874506	1.911038
1.1300000	1.851591	1.863757	1.884227	1.913282	1.951304
1.1400000	1.888977	1.901609	1.922872	1.953077	1.992645
1.1500000	1.927328	1.940442	1.962528	1.993925	2.035098
1.1600000	1.966679	1.980292	2.003229	2.035862	2.078701
1.1700000	2.007061	2.021191	2.045011	2.078925	2.123494
1.1800000	2.048512	2.063177	2.087911	2.123153	2.169515
1.1899999	2.091064	2.106283	2.131964	2.168583	2.216807

$\alpha =$ •889999

Θ	K VALUES				
	•009966711	•039469502	•087332193	•151646642	•229848846
1•2000000	2•134755	2•150548	2•177210	2•215255	2•265411
1•2100000	2•179621	2•196008	2•223685	2•263209	2•315367
1•2200000	2•225698	2•242699	2•271428	2•312484	2•366720
1•2300000	2•273024	2•290661	2•320479	2•363121	2•419512
1•2400000	2•321635	2•339931	2•370875	2•415161	2•473785
1•2500000	2•371569	2•390545	2•422656	2•468644	2•529583
1•2599999	2•422863	2•442543	2•475860	2•523611	2•586948
1•2699999	2•475552	2•495961	2•530526	2•580100	2•645922
1•2799999	2•529673	2•550834	2•586690	2•638151	2•706547
1•2899999	2•585259	2•607197	2•644388	2•697801	2•768861
1•3000000	2•642343	2•665086	2•703656	2•759087	2•832903
1•3100000	2•700957	2•724529	2•764524	2•822041	2•898708
1•3200000	2•761129	2•785557	2•827023	2•886696	2•966310
1•3300000	2•822884	2•848197	2•891180	2•953078	3•035739
1•3400000	2•886246	2•912470	2•957020	3•021215	3•107020
1•3500000	2•951234	2•978398	3•024561	3•091125	3•180177
1•3600000	3•017863	3•045993	3•093820	3•162826	3•255226
1•3700000	3•086141	3•115267	3•164807	3•236327	3•332179
1•3799999	3•156073	3•186224	3•237526	3•311634	3•411039
1•3899999	3•227658	3•258862	3•311974	3•388744	3•491806
1•4000000	3•300887	3•333171	3•388144	3•467649	3•574469
1•4100000	3•375743	3•409136	3•466017	3•548328	3•659009
1•4200000	3•452201	3•486731	3•545568	3•630758	3•745398
1•4300000	3•530230	3•565923	3•626764	3•714901	3•833600
1•4400000	3•609787	3•646670	3•709560	3•800713	3•923564
1•4500000	3•690822	3•728920	3•793902	3•888137	4•015234
1•4600000	3•773273	3•812610	3•879728	3•977107	4•108537
1•4700000	3•857069	3•897669	3•966962	4•067546	4•203393
1•4800000	3•942130	3•984014	4•055520	4•159364	4•299708
1•4900000	4•028365	4•071552	4•145307	4•252464	4•397378
1•5000000	4•115673	4•160184	4•236218	4•346736	4•496286
1•5100000	4•203944	4•249794	4•328137	4•442059	4•596305
1•5200000	4•293060	4•340264	4•420941	4•538304	4•697300
1•5300000	4•382896	4•431466	4•514499	4•635334	4•799125
1•5400000	4•473318	4•523264	4•608670	4•733005	4•901627
1•5500000	4•564188	4•615518	4•703310	4•831164	5•004645
1•5600000	4•655363	4•708083	4•798271	4•929657	5•108016
1•5699999	4•746698	4•800810	4•893397	5•028324	5•211571
1•5707963	4•753974	4•808196	4•900975	5•036184	5•219820
1•5707963	4•753969	4•808191	4•900970	5•036179	5•219815

$\alpha =$ .889999

Θ	K VALUES				
	.318821117	.415016431	.514599755	.613601043	.708073407
.0000000	.000000	.000000	.000000	.000000	.000000
.0100000	.010000	.010000	.010000	.010000	.010000
.0200000	.020002	.020002	.020003	.020003	.020003
.0300000	.030009	.030009	.030010	.030010	.030011
.0400000	.040022	.040023	.040024	.040025	.040026
.0500000	.050043	.050045	.050047	.050049	.050051
.0600000	.060075	.060079	.060082	.060086	.060089
.0700000	.070120	.070125	.070131	.070137	.070142
.0800000	.080179	.080187	.080196	.080204	.080212
.0900000	.090255	.090267	.090279	.090291	.090303
.1000000	.100351	.100367	.100383	.100400	.100416
.1100000	.110467	.110489	.110511	.110533	.110554
.1200000	.120607	.120635	.120664	.120693	.120720
.1300000	.130773	.130808	.130845	.130882	.130917
.1400000	.140966	.141011	.141057	.141103	.141147
.1500000	.151190	.151245	.151302	.151358	.151413
.1600000	.161445	.161512	.161582	.161651	.161717
.1700000	.171736	.171816	.171900	.171983	.172062
.1800000	.182063	.182159	.182258	.182357	.182452
.1900000	.192430	.192543	.192660	.192776	.192888
.2000000	.202838	.202970	.203107	.203243	.203374
.2100000	.213291	.213443	.213602	.213761	.213913
.2200000	.223789	.223966	.224149	.224332	.224507
.2300000	.234337	.234539	.234749	.234959	.235161
.2400000	.244936	.245166	.245406	.245646	.245875
.2500000	.255589	.255850	.256122	.256394	.256655
.2600000	.266299	.266594	.266901	.267208	.267502
.2700000	.277067	.277399	.277744	.278089	.278421
.2800000	.287898	.288269	.288655	.289043	.289415
.2900000	.298793	.299207	.299638	.300070	.300486
.3000000	.309755	.310215	.310695	.311176	.311638
.3100000	.320788	.321297	.321829	.322362	.322876
.3200000	.331893	.332456	.333044	.333634	.334202
.3300000	.343075	.343694	.344342	.344993	.345620
.3400000	.354335	.355016	.355728	.356444	.357134
.3500000	.365677	.366423	.367204	.367990	.368747
.3600000	.377104	.377920	.378775	.379635	.380465
.3700000	.388620	.389510	.390443	.391382	.392290
.3800000	.400227	.401196	.402212	.403237	.404227
.3900000	.411928	.412982	.414087	.415202	.416281

$\alpha =$ •889999

Θ	K VALUES				
	•318821117	•415016431	•514599755	•613601043	•708073407
•4000000	•423728	•424871	•426071	•427282	•428454
•4100000	•435630	•436867	•438167	•439481	•440754
•4200000	•447637	•448974	•450381	•451803	•453182
•4300000	•459753	•461196	•462716	•464253	•465746
•4400000	•471982	•473537	•475177	•476836	•478449
•4500000	•484327	•486001	•487767	•489556	•491296
•4600000	•496792	•498592	•500491	•502418	•504293
•4700000	•509383	•511314	•513355	•515427	•517446
•4800000	•522101	•524173	•526362	•528588	•530758
•4900000	•534953	•537171	•539519	•541906	•544238
•5000000	•547942	•550315	•552828	•555388	•557889
•5100000	•561073	•563609	•566297	•569038	•571718
•5200000	•574351	•577058	•579930	•582862	•585733
•5300000	•587780	•590666	•593733	•596866	•599938
•5400000	•601365	•604440	•607712	•611057	•614340
•5500000	•615111	•618385	•621872	•625441	•628948
•5600000	•629024	•632507	•636219	•640023	•643767
•5700000	•643108	•646810	•650760	•654813	•658805
•5800000	•657370	•661301	•665500	•669815	•674070
•5900000	•671815	•675987	•680448	•685038	•689570
•6000000	•686449	•690873	•695609	•700488	•705313
•6100000	•701278	•705966	•710991	•716175	•721307
•6200000	•716308	•721273	•726601	•732104	•737562
•6300000	•731546	•736800	•742447	•748286	•754085
•6400000	•746998	•752555	•758536	•764729	•770888
•6500000	•762671	•768546	•774876	•781441	•787979
•6600000	•778573	•784780	•791476	•798431	•805369
•6700000	•794710	•801264	•808345	•815710	•823068
•6800000	•811091	•818008	•825491	•833287	•841087
•6899999	•827722	•835019	•842925	•851172	•859438
•7000000	•844613	•852307	•860654	•869376	•878133
•7100000	•861772	•869880	•878690	•887910	•897183
•7200000	•879206	•887748	•897043	•906786	•916602
•7300000	•896926	•905921	•915722	•926014	•936402
•7400000	•914941	•924408	•934741	•945609	•956598
•7500000	•933260	•943221	•954109	•965581	•977203
•7600000	•951892	•962369	•973839	•985946	•998234
•7700000	•970850	•981865	•993944	1•006715	1•019704
•7800000	•990142	1•001719	1•014435	1•027905	1•041631
•7899999	1•009781	1•021945	1•035327	1•049529	1•064031

$\alpha =$ .889999

Θ	K VALUES				
	.318821117	.415016431	.514599755	.613601043	.708073407
.8000000	1.029778	1.042554	1.056633	1.071603	1.086921
.8100000	1.050144	1.063559	1.078367	1.094143	1.110320
.8200000	1.070893	1.084974	1.100545	1.117166	1.134247
.8300000	1.092036	1.106813	1.123182	1.140690	1.158722
.8400000	1.113588	1.129091	1.146293	1.164731	1.183764
.8500000	1.135561	1.151821	1.169896	1.189309	1.209395
.8600000	1.157971	1.175021	1.194008	1.214444	1.235638
.8700000	1.180832	1.198706	1.218647	1.240156	1.262517
.8799999	1.204160	1.222893	1.243832	1.266466	1.290054
.8899999	1.227970	1.247599	1.269581	1.293395	1.318275
.9000000	1.252280	1.272843	1.295916	1.320968	1.347208
.9100000	1.277106	1.298644	1.322857	1.349207	1.376878
.9200000	1.302467	1.325021	1.350426	1.378137	1.407315
.9300000	1.328381	1.351994	1.378646	1.407784	1.438549
.9400000	1.354867	1.379585	1.407539	1.438175	1.470611
.9500000	1.381945	1.407815	1.437132	1.469338	1.503532
.9600000	1.409637	1.436708	1.467449	1.501302	1.537347
.9699999	1.437964	1.466287	1.498516	1.534097	1.572092
.9799999	1.466949	1.496576	1.530361	1.567754	1.607802
.9899999	1.496614	1.527602	1.563014	1.602307	1.644516
1.0000000	1.526984	1.559391	1.596502	1.637788	1.682274
1.0100000	1.558084	1.591969	1.630858	1.674234	1.721117
1.0200000	1.589941	1.625367	1.666113	1.711681	1.761089
1.0300000	1.622580	1.659613	1.702300	1.750167	1.802235
1.0400000	1.656031	1.694738	1.739454	1.789732	1.844601
1.0500000	1.690322	1.730774	1.777610	1.830416	1.888236
1.0600000	1.725484	1.767755	1.816806	1.872264	1.933191
1.0699999	1.761547	1.805713	1.857080	1.915318	1.979518
1.0799999	1.798544	1.844686	1.898472	1.959625	2.027272
1.0899999	1.836509	1.884708	1.941023	2.005233	2.076510
1.1000000	1.875475	1.925819	1.984775	2.052190	2.127291
1.1100000	1.915479	1.968057	2.029773	2.100548	2.179675
1.1200000	1.956556	2.011463	2.076061	2.150358	2.233726
1.1300000	1.998746	2.056078	2.123687	2.201675	2.289508
1.1400000	2.042086	2.101945	2.172698	2.254556	2.347090
1.1500000	2.086618	2.149108	2.223144	2.309057	2.406540
1.1600000	2.132382	2.197611	2.275077	2.365238	2.467930
1.1700000	2.179419	2.247502	2.328547	2.423159	2.531334
1.1800000	2.227774	2.298828	2.383609	2.482882	2.596826
1.1899999	2.277490	2.351637	2.440317	2.544471	2.664484

$\alpha =$ .889999

Θ	K VALUES				
	.318821117	.415016431	.514599755	.613601043	.708073407
1.2000000	2.328612	2.405977	2.498726	2.607991	2.734386
1.2100000	2.381185	2.461899	2.558892	2.673505	2.806613
1.2200000	2.435254	2.519453	2.620872	2.741082	2.881245
1.2300000	2.490866	2.578689	2.684723	2.810788	2.958364
1.2400000	2.548068	2.639659	2.750502	2.882690	3.038054
1.2500000	2.606904	2.702413	2.818268	2.956856	3.120397
1.2599999	2.667421	2.767001	2.888076	3.033351	3.205475
1.2699999	2.729665	2.833474	2.959984	3.112243	3.293369
1.2799999	2.793679	2.901879	3.034046	3.193595	3.384161
1.2899999	2.859506	2.972264	3.110315	3.277471	3.477928
1.3000000	2.927187	3.044675	3.188843	3.363932	3.574747
1.3100000	2.996760	3.119153	3.269677	3.453033	3.674687
1.3200000	3.068262	3.195737	3.352863	3.544827	3.777815
1.3300000	3.141724	3.274464	3.438441	3.639364	3.884195
1.3400000	3.217175	3.355365	3.526447	3.736685	3.993879
1.3500000	3.294640	3.438466	3.616910	3.836828	4.106915
1.3600000	3.374135	3.523788	3.709856	3.939821	4.223341
1.3700000	3.455674	3.611345	3.805298	4.045682	4.343185
1.3799999	3.539262	3.701142	3.903246	4.154424	4.466461
1.3899999	3.624896	3.793177	4.003697	4.266044	4.593172
1.4000000	3.712568	3.887440	4.106639	4.380531	4.723308
1.4100000	3.802254	3.983907	4.212048	4.497858	4.856838
1.4200000	3.893927	4.082547	4.319888	4.617984	4.993719
1.4300000	3.987545	4.183316	4.430110	4.740854	5.133886
1.4400000	4.083057	4.286157	4.542653	4.866399	5.277257
1.4500000	4.180400	4.391002	4.657438	4.994528	5.423730
1.4600000	4.279499	4.497768	4.774374	5.125138	5.573178
1.4700000	4.380264	4.606358	4.893353	5.258105	5.725457
1.4800000	4.482597	4.716663	5.014253	5.393288	5.880399
1.4900000	4.586385	4.828561	5.136937	5.530529	6.037815
1.5000000	4.691504	4.941915	5.261252	5.669654	6.197496
1.5100000	4.797816	5.056576	5.387031	5.810468	6.359210
1.5200000	4.905175	5.172384	5.514095	5.952766	6.522709
1.5300000	5.013427	5.289167	5.642253	6.096327	6.687729
1.5400000	5.122405	5.406747	5.771302	6.240918	6.853989
1.5500000	5.231939	5.524934	5.901033	6.386295	7.021197
1.5600000	5.341851	5.643536	6.031227	6.532209	7.189050
1.5699999	5.451961	5.762354	6.161664	6.678402	7.357240
1.5707963	5.460732	5.771819	6.172055	6.690048	7.370639
1.5707963	5.460728	5.771814	6.172051	6.690045	7.370637

$\alpha =$ .889999

Θ	K VALUES				
	.794250555	.868696860	.928444378	.971111163	.994996249
.0000000	.000000	.000000	.000000	.000000	.000000
.0100000	.010000	.010000	.010000	.010000	.010000
.0200000	.020003	.020003	.020003	.020003	.020003
.0300000	.030011	.030011	.030012	.030012	.030012
.0400000	.040027	.040028	.040028	.040029	.040029
.0500000	.050053	.050055	.050056	.050057	.050057
.0600000	.060092	.060095	.060097	.060099	.060100
.0700000	.070147	.070151	.070155	.070157	.070159
.0800000	.080220	.080226	.080231	.080235	.080237
.0900000	.090313	.090323	.090330	.090335	.090338
.1000000	.100430	.100443	.100453	.100460	.100464
.1100000	.110574	.110590	.110604	.110613	.110619
.1200000	.120746	.120767	.120785	.120797	.120804
.1300000	.130949	.130977	.130999	.131015	.131024
.1400000	.141187	.141222	.141250	.141270	.141281
.1500000	.151462	.151505	.151540	.151564	.151578
.1600000	.161777	.161829	.161871	.161901	.161918
.1700000	.172135	.172198	.172248	.172284	.172305
.1800000	.182538	.182613	.182673	.182717	.182741
.1900000	.192990	.193079	.193150	.193201	.193229
.2000000	.203494	.203597	.203681	.203741	.203774
.2100000	.214052	.214173	.214270	.214339	.214378
.2200000	.224668	.224807	.224919	.225000	.225045
.2300000	.235345	.235505	.235634	.235726	.235778
.2400000	.246086	.246269	.246416	.246521	.246580
.2500000	.256894	.257102	.257269	.257389	.257456
.2600000	.267773	.268008	.268197	.268333	.268409
.2700000	.278726	.278990	.279204	.279357	.279442
.2800000	.289756	.290053	.290293	.290464	.290560
.2900000	.300868	.301200	.301467	.301659	.301767
.3000000	.312064	.312434	.312732	.312946	.313066
.3100000	.323348	.323759	.324091	.324329	.324462
.3200000	.334724	.335180	.335547	.335811	.335959
.3300000	.346197	.346700	.347106	.347398	.347562
.3400000	.357769	.358324	.358772	.359093	.359274
.3500000	.369446	.370055	.370548	.370902	.371101
.3600000	.381231	.381899	.382440	.382829	.383047
.3700000	.393128	.393859	.394452	.394878	.395117
.3800000	.405142	.405941	.406589	.407055	.407317
.3900000	.417278	.418149	.418856	.419365	.419651

$\alpha =$ .889999

Θ	K VALUES				
	.794250555	.868696860	.928444378	.971111163	.994996249
.4000000	.429539	.430488	.431258	.431812	.432124
.4100000	.441932	.442963	.443801	.444404	.444743
.4200000	.454460	.455580	.456489	.457144	.457513
.4300000	.467130	.468343	.469329	.470040	.470440
.4400000	.479945	.481258	.482326	.483096	.483530
.4500000	.492913	.494332	.495487	.496320	.496790
.4600000	.506037	.507569	.508816	.509717	.510226
.4700000	.519324	.520976	.522322	.523295	.523844
.4800000	.532780	.534559	.536011	.537060	.537652
.4900000	.546411	.548326	.549888	.551019	.551657
.5000000	.560223	.562281	.563963	.565180	.565867
.5100000	.574223	.576433	.578241	.579550	.580289
.5200000	.588417	.590789	.592730	.594137	.594932
.5300000	.602813	.605356	.607439	.608950	.609804
.5400000	.617418	.620143	.622376	.623997	.624914
.5500000	.632239	.635156	.637549	.639287	.640271
.5600000	.647284	.650404	.652967	.654830	.655885
.5700000	.662561	.665897	.668639	.670634	.671765
.5800000	.678078	.681642	.684575	.686711	.687922
.5900000	.693844	.697650	.700785	.703070	.704367
.6000000	.709869	.713930	.717280	.719723	.721110
.6100000	.726160	.730492	.734069	.736680	.738164
.6200000	.742728	.747347	.751165	.753954	.755540
.6300000	.759583	.764505	.768578	.771558	.773252
.6400000	.776736	.781978	.786322	.789502	.791313
.6500000	.794196	.799778	.804408	.807803	.809736
.6600000	.811976	.817916	.822851	.826472	.828536
.6700000	.830087	.836407	.841664	.845526	.847729
.6800000	.848540	.855262	.860861	.864979	.867330
.6899999	.867350	.874496	.880458	.884848	.887356
.7000000	.886528	.894124	.900471	.905150	.907825
.7100000	.906089	.914160	.920915	.925901	.928754
.7200000	.926046	.934621	.941808	.947120	.950163
.7300000	.946415	.955522	.963169	.968828	.972072
.7400000	.967210	.976882	.985015	.991043	.994503
.7500000	.988449	.998717	1.007367	1.013788	1.017476
.7600000	1.010148	1.021047	1.030246	1.037084	1.041017
.7700000	1.032323	1.043891	1.053673	1.060956	1.065149
.7800000	1.054994	1.067270	1.077671	1.085427	1.089897
.7899999	1.078180	1.091206	1.102264	1.110524	1.115290

$\alpha =$ .889999

Θ	K VALUES				
	.794250555	.868696860	.928444378	.971111163	.994996249
.8000000	1.101900	1.115720	1.127476	1.136273	1.141356
.8100000	1.126175	1.140836	1.153335	1.162704	1.168124
.8200000	1.151026	1.166579	1.179867	1.189847	1.195627
.8300000	1.176477	1.192974	1.207101	1.217732	1.223898
.8400000	1.202550	1.220049	1.235069	1.246394	1.252972
.8500000	1.229271	1.247831	1.263801	1.275868	1.282886
.8600000	1.256664	1.276350	1.293332	1.306190	1.313681
.8700000	1.284757	1.305637	1.323696	1.337400	1.345397
.8799999	1.313578	1.335725	1.354931	1.369540	1.378078
.8899999	1.343157	1.366648	1.387076	1.402652	1.411772
.9000000	1.373523	1.398441	1.420172	1.436784	1.446527
.9100000	1.404709	1.431142	1.454263	1.471983	1.482396
.9200000	1.436748	1.464790	1.489393	1.508300	1.519433
.9300000	1.469676	1.499426	1.525612	1.545792	1.557698
.9400000	1.503528	1.535094	1.562969	1.584514	1.597252
.9500000	1.538344	1.571840	1.601519	1.624528	1.638163
.9600000	1.574163	1.609709	1.641317	1.665898	1.680500
.9699999	1.611026	1.648754	1.682423	1.708694	1.724337
.9799999	1.648979	1.689026	1.724900	1.752988	1.769755
.9899999	1.688065	1.730581	1.768814	1.798855	1.816837
1.0000000	1.728334	1.773477	1.814235	1.846380	1.865675
1.0100000	1.769835	1.817774	1.861237	1.895647	1.916363
1.0200000	1.812620	1.863535	1.909896	1.946749	1.969004
1.0300000	1.856743	1.910829	1.960296	1.999785	2.023707
1.0400000	1.902262	1.959725	2.012524	2.054857	2.080590
1.0500000	1.949236	2.010297	2.066671	2.112076	2.139776
1.0600000	1.997726	2.062622	2.122833	2.171561	2.201398
1.0699999	2.047797	2.116782	2.181113	2.233435	2.265600
1.0799999	2.099517	2.172861	2.241620	2.297833	2.332534
1.0899999	2.152954	2.230947	2.304465	2.364896	2.402362
1.1000000	2.208184	2.291136	2.369772	2.434776	2.475263
1.1100000	2.265280	2.353522	2.437664	2.507632	2.551421
1.1200000	2.324322	2.418209	2.508277	2.583635	2.631040
1.1300000	2.385392	2.485302	2.581750	2.662970	2.714336
1.1400000	2.448573	2.554913	2.658233	2.745829	2.801544
1.1500000	2.513953	2.627156	2.737882	2.832420	2.892913
1.1600000	2.581624	2.702151	2.820861	2.922965	2.988714
1.1700000	2.651678	2.780025	2.907343	3.017697	3.089239
1.1800000	2.724212	2.860906	2.997508	3.116869	3.194801
1.1899999	2.799324	2.944928	3.091548	3.220746	3.305740

$\alpha =$ .889999

Θ	K VALUES				
	.794250555	.868696860	.928444378	.971111163	.994996249
1.2000000	2.877116	3.032230	3.189661	3.329614	3.422423
1.2100000	2.957690	3.122954	3.292054	3.443774	3.545245
1.2200000	3.041153	3.217248	3.398945	3.563549	3.674634
1.2300000	3.127611	3.315261	3.510559	3.689280	3.811055
1.2400000	3.217173	3.417147	3.627131	3.821332	3.955011
1.2500000	3.309947	3.523062	3.748903	3.960088	4.107048
1.2599999	3.406043	3.633165	3.876125	4.105959	4.267759
1.2699999	3.505569	3.747614	4.009054	4.259376	4.437790
1.2799999	3.608633	3.866569	4.147954	4.420796	4.617843
1.2899999	3.715341	3.990188	4.293092	4.590701	4.808684
1.3000000	3.825795	4.118628	4.444742	4.769598	5.011150
1.3100000	3.940091	4.252039	4.603172	4.958015	5.226150
1.3200000	4.058324	4.390570	4.768655	5.156509	5.454687
1.3300000	4.180579	4.534359	4.941461	5.365655	5.697855
1.3400000	4.306934	4.683537	5.121850	5.586052	5.956859
1.3500000	4.437459	4.838222	5.310074	5.818316	6.233022
1.3600000	4.572209	4.998518	5.506370	6.063075	6.527804
1.3700000	4.711230	5.164514	5.710957	6.320967	6.842818
1.3799999	4.854550	5.336277	5.924030	6.592631	7.179847
1.3899999	5.002182	5.513852	6.145753	6.878697	7.540870
1.4000000	5.154122	5.697262	6.376261	7.179785	7.928090
1.4100000	5.310339	5.886494	6.615637	7.496470	8.343950
1.4200000	5.470787	6.081510	6.863924	7.829291	8.791184
1.4300000	5.635394	6.282236	7.121111	8.178718	9.272843
1.4400000	5.804061	6.488563	7.387122	8.545132	9.792330
1.4500000	5.976664	6.700339	7.661817	8.928804	10.353439
1.4600000	6.153051	6.917374	7.944981	9.329859	10.960378
1.4700000	6.333042	7.139437	8.236323	9.748256	11.617777
1.4800000	6.516427	7.366251	8.535471	10.183749	12.330652
1.4900000	6.702970	7.597498	8.841969	10.635858	13.104293
1.5000000	6.892407	7.832819	9.155279	11.103846	13.944034
1.5100000	7.084443	8.071811	9.474774	11.586682	14.854775
1.5200000	7.278765	8.314036	9.799756	12.083044	15.840257
1.5300000	7.475035	8.559021	10.129450	12.591306	16.901877
1.5400000	7.672893	8.806262	10.463015	13.109551	18.037109
1.5500000	7.871967	9.055231	10.799555	13.635599	19.237769
1.5600000	8.071869	9.305378	11.138131	14.167053	20.488745
1.5699999	8.272204	9.556140	11.477772	14.701358	21.768178
1.5707963	8.288164	9.576119	11.504835	14.743951	21.870517
1.5707963	8.288167	9.576149	11.504826	14.743940	21.870495

$\alpha =$ .899999

Θ	K VALUES				
	.009966711	.039469502	.087332193	.151646642	.229848846
.0000000	.000000	.000000	.000000	.000000	.000000
.0100000	.010000	.010000	.010000	.010000	.010000
.0200000	.020002	.020002	.020002	.020002	.020002
.0300000	.030008	.030008	.030008	.030008	.030009
.0400000	.040019	.040019	.040020	.040020	.040021
.0500000	.050037	.050038	.050039	.050040	.050042
.0600000	.060065	.060066	.060068	.060070	.060073
.0700000	.070103	.070105	.070108	.070111	.070116
.0800000	.080154	.080157	.080161	.080166	.080173
.0900000	.090220	.090224	.090229	.090237	.090247
.1000000	.100302	.100307	.100315	.100326	.100339
.1100000	.110403	.110409	.110420	.110434	.110452
.1200000	.120523	.120532	.120546	.120564	.120587
.1300000	.130666	.130677	.130695	.130718	.130747
.1400000	.140833	.140846	.140868	.140898	.140934
.1500000	.151025	.151042	.151069	.151106	.151150
.1600000	.161246	.161266	.161299	.161344	.161398
.1700000	.171496	.171521	.171560	.171614	.171679
.1800000	.181778	.181807	.181855	.181918	.181995
.1900000	.192094	.192129	.192184	.192259	.192350
.2000000	.202446	.202486	.202551	.202638	.202745
.2100000	.212836	.212882	.212957	.213058	.213182
.2200000	.223265	.223319	.223405	.223522	.223664
.2300000	.233737	.233798	.233897	.234031	.234194
.2400000	.244253	.244322	.244435	.244587	.244773
.2500000	.254815	.254894	.255022	.255194	.255404
.2600000	.265426	.265515	.265659	.265853	.266090
.2700000	.276088	.276187	.276349	.276567	.276833
.2800000	.286803	.286914	.287094	.287338	.287636
.2900000	.297573	.297697	.297898	.298169	.298501
.3000000	.308401	.308538	.308761	.309063	.309431
.3100000	.319289	.319441	.319688	.320021	.320429
.3200000	.330240	.330407	.330680	.331048	.331498
.3300000	.341256	.341440	.341740	.342144	.342640
.3400000	.352340	.352542	.352870	.353314	.353858
.3500000	.363494	.363714	.364074	.364560	.365155
.3600000	.374721	.374961	.375354	.375884	.376534
.3700000	.386023	.386285	.386712	.387290	.387999
.3800000	.397404	.397689	.398153	.398781	.399551
.3900000	.408866	.409175	.409678	.410359	.411196

$\alpha =$ .899999

Θ	K VALUES				
	.009966711	.039469502	.087332193	.151646642	.229848846
.4000000	.420413	.420747	.421291	.422029	.422935
.4100000	.432046	.432407	.432995	.433793	.434773
.4200000	.443769	.444158	.444793	.445654	.446712
.4300000	.455586	.456005	.456688	.457615	.458756
.4400000	.467499	.467949	.468684	.469681	.470909
.4500000	.479512	.479995	.480784	.481855	.483175
.4600000	.491627	.492145	.492991	.494140	.495557
.4700000	.503849	.504404	.505310	.506541	.508059
.4800000	.516181	.516774	.517743	.519060	.520685
.4900000	.528627	.529260	.530295	.531702	.533440
.5000000	.541190	.541865	.542969	.544471	.546327
.5100000	.553873	.554593	.555769	.557371	.559351
.5200000	.566682	.567448	.568701	.570407	.572517
.5300000	.579620	.580434	.581766	.583582	.585829
.5400000	.592691	.593555	.594971	.596901	.599291
.5500000	.605900	.606817	.608319	.610369	.612909
.5600000	.619250	.620222	.621816	.623991	.626688
.5700000	.632746	.633776	.635465	.637771	.640633
.5800000	.646394	.647484	.649272	.651715	.654748
.5900000	.660198	.661350	.663242	.665827	.669041
.6000000	.674162	.675380	.677380	.680114	.683516
.6100000	.688292	.689578	.691691	.694581	.698179
.6200000	.702594	.703951	.706181	.709233	.713036
.6300000	.717072	.718503	.720855	.724077	.728094
.6400000	.731732	.733240	.735720	.739118	.743359
.6500000	.746580	.748168	.750781	.754364	.758837
.6600000	.761623	.763294	.766045	.769819	.774536
.6700000	.776865	.778623	.781518	.785492	.790463
.6800000	.792315	.794163	.797207	.801389	.806625
.6899999	.807977	.809919	.813119	.817518	.823029
.7000000	.823860	.825899	.829261	.833886	.839684
.7100000	.839970	.842111	.845640	.850500	.856597
.7200000	.856315	.858560	.862265	.867368	.873777
.7300000	.872902	.875256	.879143	.884500	.891233
.7400000	.889738	.892207	.896282	.901903	.908974
.7500000	.906834	.909419	.913691	.919586	.927010
.7600000	.924195	.926903	.931378	.937559	.945349
.7700000	.941833	.944667	.949354	.955831	.964002
.7800000	.959755	.962721	.967627	.974412	.982980
.7899999	.977970	.981073	.986207	.993313	1.002293

$\alpha =$ •899999

Θ	K VALUES				
	•009966711	•039469502	•087332193	•151646642	•229848846
•8000000	•996490	•999734	1•005105	1•012543	1•021953
•8100000	1•015324	1•018714	1•024331	1•032115	1•041971
•8200000	1•034481	1•038025	1•043896	1•052039	1•062359
•8300000	1•053975	1•057676	1•063812	1•072328	1•083131
•8400000	1•073815	1•077679	1•084090	1•092993	1•104298
•8500000	1•094013	1•098048	1•104743	1•114048	1•125876
•8600000	1•114582	1•118793	1•125784	1•135506	1•147876
•8700000	1•135535	1•139928	1•147225	1•157381	1•170316
•8799999	1•156885	1•161467	1•169082	1•179688	1•193209
•8899999	1•178645	1•183423	1•191367	1•202441	1•216572
•9000000	1•200830	1•205811	1•214097	1•225656	1•240420
•9100000	1•223454	1•228646	1•237287	1•249349	1•264772
•9200000	1•246533	1•251944	1•260952	1•273537	1•289645
•9300000	1•270084	1•275720	1•285110	1•298237	1•315057
•9400000	1•294123	1•299994	1•309779	1•323469	1•341028
•9500000	1•318667	1•324781	1•334976	1•349250	1•367578
•9600000	1•343734	1•350100	1•360720	1•375601	1•394728
•9699999	1•369344	1•375970	1•387031	1•402542	1•422499
•9799999	1•395515	1•402412	1•413931	1•430095	1•450914
•9899999	1•422269	1•429446	1•441439	1•458281	1•479996
1•0000000	1•449626	1•457094	1•469578	1•487124	1•509771
1•0100000	1•477609	1•485378	1•498372	1•516648	1•540263
1•0200000	1•506240	1•514321	1•527844	1•546878	1•571499
1•0300000	1•535544	1•543948	1•558019	1•577840	1•603506
1•0400000	1•565545	1•574284	1•588923	1•609561	1•636314
1•0500000	1•596268	1•605355	1•620584	1•642070	1•669951
1•0600000	1•627741	1•637188	1•653028	1•675395	1•704449
1•0699999	1•659992	1•669812	1•686287	1•709566	1•739839
1•0799999	1•693050	1•703257	1•720389	1•744616	1•776156
1•0899999	1•726944	1•737552	1•755366	1•780577	1•813434
1•1000000	1•761705	1•772729	1•791251	1•817484	1•851708
1•1100000	1•797367	1•808822	1•828077	1•855370	1•891016
1•1200000	1•833961	1•845863	1•865879	1•894273	1•931396
1•1300000	1•871523	1•883888	1•904694	1•934230	1•972889
1•1400000	1•910089	1•922934	1•944558	1•975281	2•015535
1•1500000	1•949695	1•963038	1•985512	2•017465	2•059377
1•1600000	1•990380	2•004239	2•027593	2•060824	2•104458
1•1700000	2•032182	2•046576	2•070844	2•105401	2•150825
1•1800000	2•075142	2•090091	2•115306	2•151239	2•198523
1•1899999	2•119300	2•134824	2•161022	2•198384	2•247599

$\alpha =$ •899999

Θ	K VALUES				
	•009966711	•039469502	•087332193	•151646642	•229848846
1•2000000	2•164701	2•180821	2•208038	2•246882	2•298104
1•2100000	2•211385	2•228123	2•256397	2•296779	2•350086
1•2200000	2•259398	2•276776	2•306145	2•348124	2•403596
1•2300000	2•308783	2•326825	2•357331	2•400966	2•458685
1•2400000	2•359586	2•378316	2•409999	2•455352	2•515406
1•2500000	2•411853	2•431295	2•464199	2•511333	2•573810
1•2599999	2•465628	2•485808	2•519977	2•568959	2•633950
1•2699999	2•520956	2•541901	2•577381	2•628278	2•695878
1•2799999	2•577883	2•599620	2•636457	2•689339	2•759646
1•2899999	2•636452	2•659009	2•697252	2•752191	2•825304
1•3000000	2•696707	2•720112	2•759811	2•816880	2•892903
1•3100000	2•758688	2•782970	2•824175	2•883450	2•962488
1•3200000	2•822433	2•847622	2•890386	2•951944	3•034105
1•3300000	2•887979	2•914106	2•958481	3•022402	3•107795
1•3400000	2•955359	2•982455	3•028496	3•094858	3•183597
1•3500000	3•024601	3•052698	3•100459	3•169345	3•261543
1•3600000	3•095730	3•124860	3•174396	3•245889	3•341661
1•3700000	3•168764	3•198959	3•250327	3•324510	3•423973
1•3799999	3•243716	3•275009	3•328265	3•405222	3•508494
1•3899999	3•320590	3•353014	3•408215	3•488030	3•595229
1•4000000	3•399386	3•432973	3•490175	3•572933	3•684176
1•4100000	3•480090	3•514872	3•574132	3•659916	3•775321
1•4200000	3•562682	3•598691	3•660065	3•748958	3•868640
1•4300000	3•647129	3•684398	3•747940	3•840023	3•964097
1•4400000	3•733391	3•771949	3•837713	3•933066	4•061643
1•4500000	3•821412	3•861290	3•929327	4•028027	4•161216
1•4600000	3•911125	3•952352	4•022712	4•124834	4•262738
1•4700000	4•002452	4•045054	4•117785	4•223399	4•366118
1•4800000	4•095299	4•139304	4•214450	4•323624	4•471250
1•4900000	4•189563	4•234993	4•312597	4•425392	4•578013
1•5000000	4•285126	4•332003	4•412103	4•528576	4•686272
1•5100000	4•381856	4•430202	4•512831	4•633034	4•795877
1•5200000	4•479614	4•529444	4•614634	4•738612	4•906665
1•5300000	4•578247	4•629578	4•717354	4•845145	5•018462
1•5400000	4•677597	4•730440	4•820823	4•952458	5•131083
1•5500000	4•777493	4•831857	4•924864	5•060368	5•244335
1•5600000	4•877762	4•933655	5•029296	5•168685	5•358016
1•5699999	4•978226	5•035650	5•133931	5•277214	5•471922
1•5707963	4•986230	5•043775	5•142267	5•285860	5•480996
1•5707963	4•986225	5•043770	5•142262	5•285855	5•480991

$\alpha =$ .899999

Θ	K VALUES				
	.318821117	.415016431	.514599755	.613601043	.708073407
.0000000	.000000	.000000	.000000	.000000	.000000
.0100000	.010000	.010000	.010000	.010000	.010000
.0200000	.020002	.020002	.020003	.020003	.020003
.0300000	.030009	.030009	.030010	.030010	.030011
.0400000	.040022	.040023	.040024	.040025	.040026
.0500000	.050044	.050046	.050048	.050050	.050052
.0600000	.060076	.060079	.060083	.060087	.060090
.0700000	.070121	.070126	.070132	.070138	.070143
.0800000	.080181	.080189	.080198	.080206	.080214
.0900000	.090258	.090269	.090282	.090294	.090305
.1000000	.100354	.100370	.100387	.100403	.100419
.1100000	.110472	.110493	.110515	.110538	.110559
.1200000	.120613	.120641	.120670	.120699	.120726
.1300000	.130780	.130816	.130853	.130889	.130925
.1400000	.140975	.141020	.141066	.141112	.141156
.1500000	.151201	.151256	.151313	.151370	.151424
.1600000	.161459	.161526	.161596	.161665	.161731
.1700000	.171753	.171833	.171916	.172000	.172079
.1800000	.182083	.182179	.182278	.182377	.182472
.1900000	.192454	.192566	.192683	.192800	.192912
.2000000	.202866	.202998	.203135	.203271	.203402
.2100000	.213323	.213476	.213635	.213793	.213945
.2200000	.223827	.224003	.224186	.224369	.224545
.2300000	.234380	.234582	.234792	.235002	.235203
.2400000	.244985	.245215	.245455	.245695	.245924
.2500000	.255645	.255906	.256178	.256450	.256711
.2600000	.266361	.266656	.266963	.267271	.267566
.2700000	.277138	.277469	.277815	.278160	.278492
.2800000	.287977	.288348	.288735	.289122	.289494
.2900000	.298881	.299295	.299727	.300159	.300575
.3000000	.309854	.310314	.310794	.311275	.311738
.3100000	.320897	.321407	.321939	.322473	.322986
.3200000	.332014	.332577	.333165	.333756	.334324
.3300000	.343208	.343828	.344476	.345127	.345755
.3400000	.354482	.355163	.355876	.356592	.357283
.3500000	.365838	.366585	.367367	.368153	.368911
.3600000	.377281	.378098	.378953	.379813	.380644
.3700000	.388813	.389704	.390638	.391578	.392487
.3800000	.400438	.401408	.402425	.403451	.404442
.3900000	.412158	.413213	.414319	.415435	.416515

$\alpha =$ .899999

Θ	K VALUES				
	.318821117	.415016431	.514599755	.613601043	.708073407
.4000000	.423979	.425122	.426323	.427536	.428710
.4100000	.435902	.437140	.438442	.439757	.441031
.4200000	.447932	.449270	.450679	.452103	.453484
.4300000	.460072	.461517	.463039	.464578	.466072
.4400000	.472326	.473884	.475525	.477187	.478802
.4500000	.484699	.486375	.488144	.489935	.491678
.4600000	.497194	.498996	.500898	.502827	.504705
.4700000	.509815	.511749	.513793	.515868	.517890
.4800000	.522566	.524641	.526834	.529063	.531237
.4900000	.535453	.537675	.540026	.542418	.544753
.5000000	.548479	.550856	.553373	.555937	.558443
.5100000	.561649	.564189	.566882	.569627	.572313
.5200000	.574968	.577679	.580558	.583494	.586371
.5300000	.588440	.591332	.594405	.597544	.600622
.5400000	.602071	.605153	.608431	.611783	.615074
.5500000	.615866	.619147	.622641	.626218	.629733
.5600000	.629831	.633321	.637041	.640855	.644607
.5700000	.643969	.647679	.651638	.655701	.659703
.5800000	.658289	.662229	.666439	.670764	.675030
.5900000	.672795	.676976	.681449	.686051	.690595
.6000000	.687493	.691928	.696677	.701569	.706407
.6100000	.702389	.707090	.712129	.717327	.722474
.6200000	.717491	.722469	.727813	.733332	.738806
.6300000	.732804	.738073	.743737	.749594	.755411
.6400000	.748335	.753910	.759909	.766121	.772300
.6500000	.764093	.769986	.776337	.782923	.789483
.6600000	.780083	.786310	.793030	.800008	.806969
.6700000	.796314	.802890	.809996	.817387	.824771
.6800000	.812793	.819735	.827246	.835070	.842899
.6899999	.829529	.836853	.844788	.853067	.861365
.7000000	.846529	.854253	.862633	.871389	.880181
.7100000	.863804	.871945	.880790	.890048	.899360
.7200000	.881361	.889938	.899272	.909056	.918914
.7300000	.899209	.908243	.918087	.928425	.938859
.7400000	.917360	.926870	.937250	.948167	.959207
.7500000	.935822	.945830	.956770	.968297	.979974
.7600000	.954607	.965134	.976660	.988827	1.001176
.7700000	.973724	.984794	.996934	1.009772	1.022827
.7800000	.993186	1.004823	1.017605	1.031147	1.044946
.7899999	1.013003	1.025232	1.038687	1.052967	1.067549

$\alpha =$ .899999

Θ	K VALUES				
	.318821117	.415016431	.514599755	.613601043	.708073407
.8000000	1.033188	1.046035	1.060193	1.075249	1.090655
.8100000	1.053753	1.067245	1.082140	1.098009	1.114283
.8200000	1.074711	1.088877	1.104542	1.121265	1.138452
.8300000	1.096076	1.110945	1.127416	1.145035	1.163183
.8400000	1.117862	1.133465	1.150779	1.169338	1.188497
.8500000	1.140084	1.156452	1.174648	1.194193	1.214418
.8600000	1.162755	1.179922	1.199042	1.219622	1.240968
.8700000	1.185893	1.203894	1.223979	1.245645	1.268171
.8799999	1.209513	1.228384	1.249479	1.272284	1.296054
.8899999	1.233633	1.253411	1.275563	1.299564	1.324642
.9000000	1.258270	1.278995	1.302253	1.327508	1.353964
.9100000	1.283443	1.305156	1.329570	1.356141	1.384048
.9200000	1.309170	1.331914	1.357537	1.385489	1.414925
.9300000	1.335472	1.359291	1.386179	1.415580	1.446627
.9400000	1.362369	1.387310	1.415521	1.446443	1.479186
.9500000	1.389883	1.415994	1.445589	1.478107	1.512636
.9600000	1.418036	1.445368	1.476411	1.510603	1.547014
.9699999	1.446851	1.475457	1.508014	1.543963	1.582358
.9799999	1.476353	1.506288	1.540429	1.578222	1.618706
.9899999	1.506568	1.537888	1.573685	1.613414	1.656100
1.0000000	1.537521	1.570286	1.607816	1.649576	1.694583
1.0100000	1.569239	1.603512	1.642855	1.686746	1.734198
1.0200000	1.601751	1.637597	1.678835	1.724964	1.774993
1.0300000	1.635087	1.672574	1.715794	1.764271	1.817016
1.0400000	1.669277	1.708475	1.753769	1.804710	1.860318
1.0500000	1.704353	1.745337	1.792800	1.846327	1.904952
1.0600000	1.740349	1.783195	1.832926	1.889167	1.950974
1.0699999	1.777299	1.822087	1.874190	1.933280	1.998440
1.0799999	1.815239	1.862052	1.916637	1.978716	2.047411
1.0899999	1.854206	1.903131	1.960311	2.025528	2.097949
1.1000000	1.894239	1.945368	2.005260	2.073770	2.150120
1.1100000	1.935377	1.988803	2.051534	2.123499	2.203990
1.1200000	1.977661	2.033485	2.099182	2.174773	2.259629
1.1300000	2.021136	2.079458	2.148259	2.227653	2.317110
1.1400000	2.065845	2.126773	2.198817	2.282203	2.376510
1.1500000	2.111833	2.175479	2.250914	2.338487	2.437905
1.1600000	2.159148	2.225627	2.304607	2.396573	2.501377
1.1700000	2.207839	2.277272	2.359957	2.456530	2.567008
1.1800000	2.257955	2.330467	2.417024	2.518428	2.634886
1.1899999	2.309548	2.385268	2.475872	2.582342	2.705098

$\alpha =$ .899999

Θ	K VALUES				
	.318821117	.415016431	.514599755	.613601043	.708073407
1.2000000	2.362670	2.441735	2.536566	2.648346	2.777735
1.2100000	2.417374	2.499924	2.599171	2.716517	2.852889
1.2200000	2.473714	2.559895	2.663755	2.786933	2.930656
1.2300000	2.531747	2.621709	2.730385	2.859672	3.011132
1.2400000	2.591527	2.685428	2.799130	2.934816	3.094415
1.2500000	2.653112	2.751113	2.870061	3.012446	3.180604
1.2599999	2.716556	2.818826	2.943246	3.092642	3.269797
1.2699999	2.781918	2.888628	3.018756	3.175485	3.362094
1.2799999	2.849251	2.960581	3.096658	3.261056	3.457595
1.2899999	2.918611	3.034744	3.177021	3.349434	3.556394
1.3000000	2.990051	3.111176	3.259910	3.440696	3.658590
1.3100000	3.063620	3.189931	3.345387	3.534915	3.764270
1.3200000	3.139368	3.271064	3.433513	3.632161	3.873524
1.3300000	3.217339	3.354623	3.524344	3.732500	3.986432
1.3400000	3.297575	3.440654	3.617930	3.835993	4.103071
1.3500000	3.380110	3.529195	3.714316	3.942691	4.223508
1.3600000	3.464976	3.620281	3.813539	4.052641	4.347798
1.3700000	3.552194	3.713936	3.915630	4.165876	4.475989
1.3799999	3.641781	3.810178	4.020608	4.282422	4.608113
1.3899999	3.733744	3.909014	4.128482	4.402291	4.744188
1.4000000	3.828080	4.010443	4.239250	4.525482	4.884217
1.4100000	3.924773	4.114447	4.352894	4.651974	5.028180
1.4200000	4.023799	4.220999	4.469384	4.781736	5.176040
1.4300000	4.125119	4.330058	4.588674	4.914715	5.327738
1.4400000	4.228680	4.441565	4.710700	5.050839	5.483191
1.4500000	4.334415	4.555449	4.835381	5.190015	5.642291
1.4600000	4.442242	4.671618	4.962617	5.332129	5.804903
1.4700000	4.552063	4.789967	5.092288	5.477044	5.970867
1.4800000	4.663764	4.910370	5.224256	5.624603	6.139993
1.4900000	4.777215	5.032686	5.358362	5.774622	6.312066
1.5000000	4.892272	5.156758	5.494431	5.926900	6.486843
1.5100000	5.008772	5.282407	5.632264	6.081209	6.664055
1.5200000	5.126543	5.409444	5.771649	6.237306	6.843409
1.5300000	5.245396	5.537665	5.912358	6.394926	7.024590
1.5400000	5.365133	5.666853	6.054148	6.553792	7.207264
1.5500000	5.485547	5.796780	6.196764	6.713610	7.391081
1.5600000	5.606423	5.927212	6.339945	6.874077	7.575676
1.5699999	5.727539	6.057906	6.483420	7.034884	7.760679
1.5707963	5.737187	6.068318	6.494850	7.047695	7.775417
1.5707963	5.737182	6.068313	6.494846	7.047691	7.775415

$\alpha =$ .899999

Θ	K VALUES				
	.794250555	.868696860	.928444378	.971111163	.994996249
.0000000	.000000	.000000	.000000	.000000	.000000
.0100000	.010000	.010000	.010000	.010000	.010000
.0200000	.020003	.020003	.020003	.020003	.020003
.0300000	.030011	.030012	.030012	.030012	.030012
.0400000	.040027	.040028	.040029	.040029	.040029
.0500000	.050054	.050055	.050056	.050057	.050058
.0600000	.060093	.060096	.060098	.060099	.060100
.0700000	.070148	.070152	.070156	.070158	.070160
.0800000	.080222	.080228	.080233	.080237	.080239
.0900000	.090316	.090325	.090332	.090338	.090341
.1000000	.100434	.100446	.100456	.100464	.100468
.1100000	.110578	.110595	.110608	.110618	.110623
.1200000	.120752	.120773	.120791	.120803	.120810
.1300000	.130957	.130984	.131007	.131023	.131032
.1400000	.141196	.141231	.141259	.141279	.141290
.1500000	.151474	.151517	.151551	.151576	.151590
.1600000	.161791	.161843	.161885	.161915	.161932
.1700000	.172152	.172215	.172265	.172301	.172322
.1800000	.182558	.182633	.182694	.182737	.182761
.1900000	.193014	.193103	.193174	.193225	.193253
.2000000	.203522	.203625	.203709	.203769	.203802
.2100000	.214085	.214205	.214302	.214372	.214411
.2200000	.224706	.224845	.224957	.225037	.225082
.2300000	.235388	.235548	.235677	.235769	.235821
.2400000	.246135	.246318	.246465	.246570	.246629
.2500000	.256950	.257158	.257325	.257445	.257512
.2600000	.267836	.268071	.268260	.268396	.268472
.2700000	.278797	.279062	.279275	.279428	.279514
.2800000	.289836	.290133	.290373	.290544	.290641
.2900000	.300957	.301289	.301557	.301749	.301857
.3000000	.312163	.312533	.312832	.313046	.313167
.3100000	.323459	.323870	.324202	.324440	.324574
.3200000	.334847	.335303	.335671	.335935	.336083
.3300000	.346333	.346836	.347242	.347534	.347698
.3400000	.357919	.358473	.358922	.359244	.359425
.3500000	.369610	.370220	.370713	.371067	.371267
.3600000	.381411	.382080	.382621	.383010	.383229
.3700000	.393325	.394057	.394650	.395077	.395317
.3800000	.405358	.406158	.406806	.407272	.407535
.3900000	.417513	.418386	.419093	.419602	.419888

$\alpha =$ .899999

Θ	K VALUES				
	.794250555	.868696860	.928444378	.971111163	.994996249
.4000000	.429796	.430746	.431516	.432071	.432383
.4100000	.442211	.443243	.444081	.444685	.445025
.4200000	.454763	.455884	.456794	.457450	.457819
.4300000	.467458	.468673	.469660	.470371	.470772
.4400000	.480300	.481615	.482684	.483456	.483890
.4500000	.493296	.494718	.495874	.496709	.497179
.4600000	.506451	.507986	.509235	.510137	.510646
.4700000	.519771	.521426	.522774	.523748	.524298
.4800000	.533262	.535044	.536498	.537549	.538142
.4900000	.546929	.548847	.550413	.551545	.552185
.5000000	.560781	.562843	.564527	.565746	.566435
.5100000	.574822	.577037	.578847	.580159	.580900
.5200000	.589061	.591437	.593382	.594791	.595588
.5300000	.603503	.606052	.608139	.609652	.610509
.5400000	.618157	.620888	.623126	.624751	.625670
.5500000	.633031	.635954	.638353	.640095	.641081
.5600000	.648132	.651259	.653828	.655695	.656753
.5700000	.663468	.666812	.669561	.671561	.672694
.5800000	.679047	.682621	.685561	.687702	.688916
.5900000	.694880	.698696	.701839	.704130	.705430
.6000000	.710975	.715047	.718406	.720856	.722247
.6100000	.727340	.731685	.735272	.737891	.739378
.6200000	.743987	.748620	.752449	.755247	.756837
.6300000	.760926	.765863	.769948	.772937	.774637
.6400000	.778167	.783426	.787784	.790974	.792791
.6500000	.795721	.801321	.805967	.809373	.811312
.6600000	.813599	.819560	.824513	.828146	.830218
.6700000	.831815	.838158	.843434	.847311	.849522
.6800000	.850380	.857127	.862747	.866881	.869241
.6899999	.869307	.876481	.882467	.886874	.889392
.7000000	.888610	.896237	.902609	.907307	.909994
.7100000	.908303	.916408	.923192	.928199	.931064
.7200000	.928400	.937012	.944231	.949567	.952624
.7300000	.948917	.958066	.965747	.971432	.974692
.7400000	.969870	.979586	.987759	.993816	.997292
.7500000	.991275	1.001593	1.010286	1.016739	1.020446
.7600000	1.013150	1.024105	1.033351	1.040225	1.044178
.7700000	1.035513	1.047142	1.056976	1.064298	1.068513
.7800000	1.058382	1.070725	1.081184	1.088983	1.093478
.7899999	1.081778	1.094878	1.106000	1.114308	1.119102

$\alpha =$ .899999

θ	K VALUES				
	.794250555	.868696860	.928444378	.971111163	.994996249
.8000000	1.105722	1.119623	1.131450	1.140300	1.145413
.8100000	1.130233	1.144984	1.157561	1.166989	1.172442
.8200000	1.155336	1.170988	1.184361	1.194406	1.200224
.8300000	1.181054	1.197660	1.211882	1.222584	1.228791
.8400000	1.207411	1.225029	1.240153	1.251557	1.258181
.8500000	1.234432	1.253124	1.269209	1.281363	1.288433
.8600000	1.262146	1.281977	1.299085	1.312040	1.319587
.8700000	1.290579	1.311618	1.329817	1.343628	1.351687
.8799999	1.319762	1.342084	1.361443	1.376170	1.384778
.8899999	1.349724	1.373408	1.394006	1.409713	1.418910
.9000000	1.380500	1.405630	1.427548	1.444304	1.454133
.9100000	1.412121	1.438787	1.462114	1.479994	1.490502
.9200000	1.444623	1.472921	1.497752	1.516837	1.528074
.9300000	1.478044	1.508076	1.534513	1.554889	1.566912
.9400000	1.512421	1.544297	1.572450	1.594212	1.607081
.9500000	1.547796	1.581633	1.611619	1.634869	1.648649
.9600000	1.584211	1.620133	1.652080	1.676929	1.691690
.9699999	1.621711	1.659852	1.693896	1.720463	1.736284
.9799999	1.660341	1.700844	1.737132	1.765548	1.782513
.9899999	1.700152	1.743168	1.781859	1.812265	1.830467
1.0000000	1.741193	1.786886	1.828151	1.860701	1.880242
1.0100000	1.783519	1.832063	1.876086	1.910947	1.931937
1.0200000	1.827184	1.878767	1.925748	1.963102	1.985662
1.0300000	1.872249	1.927069	1.977223	2.017268	2.041533
1.0400000	1.918774	1.977046	2.030605	2.073557	2.099672
1.0500000	1.966823	2.028776	2.085992	2.132087	2.160213
1.0600000	2.016464	2.082343	2.143487	2.192983	2.223298
1.0699999	2.067766	2.137835	2.203200	2.256379	2.289079
1.0799999	2.120804	2.195342	2.265248	2.322418	2.357718
1.0899999	2.175653	2.254963	2.329753	2.391252	2.429390
1.1000000	2.232394	2.316798	2.396847	2.463044	2.504286
1.1100000	2.291109	2.380954	2.466664	2.537966	2.582604
1.1200000	2.351886	2.447542	2.539352	2.616203	2.664562
1.1300000	2.414815	2.516678	2.615064	2.697954	2.750396
1.1400000	2.479991	2.588486	2.693961	2.783429	2.840356
1.1500000	2.547511	2.663093	2.776216	2.872853	2.934715
1.1600000	2.617476	2.740631	2.862009	2.966468	3.033765
1.1700000	2.689992	2.821242	2.951530	3.064530	3.137823
1.1800000	2.765168	2.905068	3.044979	3.167314	3.247230
1.1899999	2.843115	2.992262	3.142569	3.275112	3.362357

$\alpha =$ •899999

Θ	K VALUES				
	•794250555	•868696860	•928444378	•971111163	•994996249
1•2000000	2•923950	3•082980	3•244520	3•388240	3•483605
1•2100000	3•007791	3•177382	3•351064	3•507028	3•611405
1•2200000	3•094760	3•275636	3•462445	3•631834	3•746230
1•2300000	3•184981	3•377915	3•578917	3•763038	3•888589
1•2400000	3•278581	3•484396	3•700745	3•901043	4•039036
1•2500000	3•375688	3•595258	3•828205	4•046281	4•198175
1•2599999	3•476433	3•710687	3•961581	4•199209	4•366661
1•2699999	3•580944	3•830869	4•101169	4•360311	4•545210
1•2799999	3•689353	3•955992	4•247272	4•530102	4•734601
1•2899999	3•801788	4•086246	4•400200	4•709127	4•935685
1•3000000	3•918375	4•221819	4•560272	4•897959	5•149395
1•3100000	4•039237	4•362894	4•727803	5•097200	5•376746
1•3200000	4•164492	4•509652	4•903115	5•307482	5•618856
1•3300000	4•294251	4•662267	5•086528	5•529467	5•876952
1•3400000	4•428618	4•820904	5•278355	5•763840	6•152380
1•3500000	4•567688	4•985716	5•478902	6•011310	6•446624
1•3600000	4•711541	5•156840	5•688458	6•272603	6•761321
1•3700000	4•860245	5•334399	5•907296	6•548459	7•098278
1•3799999	5•013852	5•518490	6•135661	6•839622	7•459499
1•3899999	5•172393	5•709187	6•373770	7•146830	7•847203
1•4000000	5•335883	5•906540	6•621801	7•470808	8•263863
1•4100000	5•504306	6•110557	6•879880	7•812236	8•712217
1•4200000	5•677624	6•321216	7•148085	8•171755	9•195330
1•4300000	5•855772	6•538455	7•426429	8•549929	9•716616
1•4400000	6•038653	6•762169	7•714857	8•947223	10•279884
1•4500000	6•226137	6•992203	8•013234	9•363973	10•889373
1•4600000	6•418060	7•228355	8•321341	9•800356	11•549778
1•4700000	6•614226	7•470373	8•638864	10•256353	12•266260
1•4800000	6•814399	7•717951	8•965398	10•731714	13•044401
1•4900000	7•018310	7•970729	9•300433	11•225919	13•890081
1•5000000	7•225657	8•228299	9•643365	11•738154	14•809220
1•5100000	7•436097	8•490194	9•993479	12•267263	15•807246
1•5200000	7•649262	8•755907	10•349974	12•811757	16•888296
1•5300000	7•864754	9•024885	10•711957	13•369796	18•053892
1•5400000	8•082146	9•296536	11•078454	13•939206	19•301204
1•5500000	8•300994	9•570235	11•448423	14•517507	20•621129
1•5600000	8•520835	9•845332	11•820769	15•101969	21•996883
1•5699999	8•741195	10•121160	12•194360	15•689683	23•404205
1•5707963	8•758751	10•143137	12•224130	15•736535	23•516778
1•5707963	8•758753	10•143159	12•224119	15•736522	23•516752

$\alpha =$ .909999

Θ	K VALUES				
	.009966711	.039469502	.087332193	.151646642	.229848846
.0000000	.000000	.000000	.000000	.000000	.000000
.0100000	.010000	.010000	.010000	.010000	.010000
.0200000	.020002	.020002	.020002	.020002	.020002
.0300000	.030008	.030008	.030008	.030008	.030009
.0400000	.040019	.040019	.040020	.040021	.040021
.0500000	.050038	.050038	.050039	.050041	.050042
.0600000	.060065	.060067	.060068	.060071	.060073
.0700000	.070104	.070106	.070109	.070112	.070117
.0800000	.080156	.080159	.080163	.080168	.080175
.0900000	.090223	.090226	.090232	.090240	.090249
.1000000	.100306	.100310	.100318	.100329	.100342
.1100000	.110407	.110414	.110424	.110439	.110456
.1200000	.120529	.120538	.120552	.120570	.120593
.1300000	.130674	.130684	.130702	.130726	.130755
.1400000	.140842	.140856	.140878	.140907	.140944
.1500000	.151037	.151054	.151081	.151117	.151162
.1600000	.161260	.161280	.161313	.161358	.161412
.1700000	.171513	.171538	.171577	.171631	.171696
.1800000	.181798	.181827	.181875	.181938	.182015
.1900000	.192118	.192152	.192208	.192282	.192373
.2000000	.202474	.202514	.202578	.202666	.202772
.2100000	.212868	.212914	.212989	.213091	.213214
.2200000	.223302	.223356	.223442	.223559	.223701
.2300000	.233780	.233841	.233940	.234073	.234236
.2400000	.244301	.244371	.244484	.244636	.244822
.2500000	.254870	.254949	.255077	.255249	.255459
.2600000	.265488	.265577	.265721	.265915	.266153
.2700000	.276158	.276257	.276419	.276637	.276904
.2800000	.286881	.286992	.287173	.287417	.287715
.2900000	.297661	.297784	.297986	.298257	.298590
.3000000	.308499	.308636	.308859	.309161	.309530
.3100000	.319398	.319549	.319797	.320130	.320538
.3200000	.330360	.330527	.330800	.331168	.331619
.3300000	.341388	.341572	.341872	.342277	.342773
.3400000	.352485	.352687	.353016	.353460	.354004
.3500000	.363654	.363874	.364234	.364720	.365316
.3600000	.374896	.375137	.375529	.376060	.376711
.3700000	.386215	.386477	.386904	.387482	.388192
.3800000	.397613	.397898	.398362	.398991	.399762
.3900000	.409094	.409403	.409906	.410588	.411425

$\alpha =$ •909999

Θ	K VALUES				
	•009966711	•039469502	•087332193	•151646642	•229848846
•4000000	•420660	•420994	•421539	•422278	•423185
•4100000	•432314	•432675	•433264	•434062	•435044
•4200000	•444060	•444449	•445085	•445946	•447005
•4300000	•455900	•456319	•457004	•457932	•459074
•4400000	•467838	•468289	•469025	•470024	•471253
•4500000	•479878	•480362	•481152	•482225	•483546
•4600000	•492022	•492541	•493388	•494539	•495957
•4700000	•504274	•504829	•505737	•506969	•508490
•4800000	•516638	•517231	•518202	•519521	•521149
•4900000	•529117	•529751	•530788	•532197	•533938
•5000000	•541716	•542392	•543498	•545003	•546862
•5100000	•554437	•555158	•556337	•557941	•559925
•5200000	•567286	•568053	•569308	•571017	•573131
•5300000	•580266	•581081	•582416	•584235	•586486
•5400000	•593381	•594247	•595666	•597600	•599995
•5500000	•606637	•607556	•609062	•611116	•613661
•5600000	•620037	•621011	•622608	•624788	•627491
•5700000	•633586	•634618	•636311	•638622	•641490
•5800000	•647288	•648381	•650173	•652622	•655663
•5900000	•661150	•662306	•664202	•666794	•670016
•6000000	•675176	•676397	•678402	•681144	•684554
•6100000	•689371	•690661	•692779	•695677	•699285
•6200000	•703741	•705102	•707338	•710399	•714213
•6300000	•718291	•719726	•722085	•725317	•729346
•6400000	•733027	•734540	•737027	•740436	•744690
•6500000	•747955	•749548	•752169	•755763	•760251
•6600000	•763082	•764759	•767519	•771306	•776038
•6700000	•778413	•780178	•783082	•787070	•792058
•6800000	•793956	•795811	•798866	•803063	•808317
•6899999	•809718	•811667	•814878	•819293	•824825
•7000000	•825704	•827751	•831126	•835768	•841589
•7100000	•841924	•844073	•847617	•852495	•858617
•7200000	•858384	•860639	•864359	•869483	•875918
•7300000	•875092	•877457	•881360	•886740	•893503
•7400000	•892057	•894536	•898630	•904275	•911379
•7500000	•909288	•911885	•916176	•922099	•929556
•7600000	•926792	•929512	•934009	•940219	•948046
•7700000	•944579	•947428	•952137	•958647	•966858
•7800000	•962659	•965640	•970572	•977392	•986003
•7899999	•981042	•984161	•989322	•996465	1•005493

$\alpha =$ •909999

Θ	K VALUES				
	•009966711	•039469502	•087332193	•151646642	•229848846
•8000000	•999738	1•002999	1•008400	1•015879	1•025340
•8100000	1•018757	1•022167	1•027815	1•035643	1•045556
•8200000	1•038111	1•041674	1•047580	1•055771	1•066152
•8300000	1•057810	1•061534	1•067707	1•076275	1•087144
•8400000	1•077869	1•081757	1•088208	1•097167	1•108544
•8500000	1•098297	1•102358	1•109097	1•118462	1•130367
•8600000	1•119110	1•123348	1•130386	1•140174	1•152628
•8700000	1•140319	1•144742	1•152090	1•162317	1•175343
•8799999	1•161940	1•166555	1•174224	1•184907	1•198526
•8899999	1•183986	1•188800	1•196803	1•207959	1•222197
•9000000	1•206474	1•211493	1•219843	1•231491	1•246371
•9100000	1•229418	1•234651	1•243361	1•255519	1•271067
•9200000	1•252836	1•258291	1•267373	1•280062	1•296305
•9300000	1•276745	1•282429	1•291899	1•305138	1•322103
•9400000	1•301163	1•307085	1•316956	1•330767	1•348484
•9500000	1•326107	1•332277	1•342565	1•356970	1•375467
•9600000	1•351599	1•358024	1•368745	1•383767	1•403076
•9699999	1•377658	1•384349	1•395518	1•411181	1•431335
•9799999	1•404306	1•411272	1•422907	1•439235	1•460267
•9899999	1•431564	1•438816	1•450934	1•467953	1•489898
1•0000000	1•459457	1•467005	1•479623	1•497360	1•520255
1•0100000	1•488007	1•495862	1•509001	1•527483	1•551365
1•0200000	1•517240	1•525414	1•539092	1•558348	1•583258
1•0300000	1•547182	1•555686	1•569925	1•589985	1•615963
1•0400000	1•577861	1•586708	1•601528	1•622423	1•649512
1•0500000	1•609305	1•618507	1•633930	1•655693	1•683937
1•0600000	1•641543	1•651114	1•667164	1•689828	1•719274
1•0699999	1•674607	1•684561	1•701260	1•724861	1•755556
1•0799999	1•708528	1•718879	1•736254	1•760827	1•792823
1•0899999	1•743341	1•754104	1•772179	1•797764	1•831111
1•1000000	1•779081	1•790271	1•809074	1•835708	1•870462
1•1100000	1•815783	1•827417	1•846975	1•874700	1•910918
1•1200000	1•853486	1•865580	1•885922	1•914781	1•952520
1•1300000	1•892228	1•904800	1•925956	1•955994	1•995316
1•1400000	1•932051	1•945119	1•967120	1•998382	2•039352
1•1500000	1•972996	1•986579	2•009458	2•041993	2•084677
1•1600000	2•015109	2•029226	2•053017	2•086874	2•131341
1•1700000	2•058434	2•073105	2•097843	2•133075	2•179396
1•1800000	2•103017	2•118264	2•143985	2•180646	2•228897
1•1899999	2•148908	2•164753	2•191495	2•229640	2•279899

$\alpha =$ .909999

Θ	K VALUES				
	.009966711	.039469502	.087332193	.151646642	.229848846
1.2000000	2.196157	2.212622	2.240425	2.280113	2.332460
1.2100000	2.244814	2.261923	2.290827	2.332118	2.386638
1.2200000	2.294932	2.312709	2.342757	2.385714	2.442494
1.2300000	2.346564	2.365036	2.396271	2.440960	2.500090
1.2400000	2.399766	2.418958	2.451427	2.497914	2.559489
1.2500000	2.454593	2.474532	2.508282	2.556638	2.620755
1.2599999	2.511102	2.531816	2.566895	2.617193	2.683952
1.2699999	2.569348	2.590867	2.627326	2.679640	2.749146
1.2799999	2.629388	2.651743	2.689633	2.744041	2.816401
1.2899999	2.691279	2.714500	2.753876	2.810457	2.885783
1.3000000	2.755077	2.779196	2.820113	2.878950	2.957357
1.3100000	2.820834	2.845884	2.888400	2.949577	3.031182
1.3200000	2.888605	2.914619	2.958792	3.022396	3.107321
1.3300000	2.958437	2.985451	3.031340	3.097461	3.185830
1.3400000	3.030378	3.058427	3.106094	3.174823	3.266764
1.3500000	3.104471	3.133591	3.183099	3.254528	3.350170
1.3600000	3.180753	3.210980	3.262392	3.336617	3.436092
1.3700000	3.259255	3.290627	3.344008	3.421124	3.524567
1.3799999	3.340002	3.372557	3.427972	3.508077	3.615623
1.3899999	3.423011	3.456786	3.514302	3.597493	3.709279
1.4000000	3.508290	3.543324	3.603006	3.689381	3.805545
1.4100000	3.595833	3.632164	3.694078	3.783736	3.904414
1.4200000	3.685627	3.723293	3.787504	3.880542	4.005871
1.4300000	3.777645	3.816682	3.883256	3.979771	4.109885
1.4400000	3.871845	3.912291	3.981290	4.081376	4.216407
1.4500000	3.968170	4.010060	4.081548	4.185296	4.325374
1.4600000	4.066549	4.109918	4.183953	4.291454	4.436702
1.4700000	4.166893	4.211773	4.288414	4.399751	4.550290
1.4800000	4.269097	4.315520	4.394820	4.510075	4.666016
1.4900000	4.373038	4.421034	4.503043	4.622291	4.783740
1.5000000	4.478579	4.528174	4.612939	4.736250	4.903303
1.5100000	4.585562	4.636780	4.724343	4.851779	5.024525
1.5200000	4.693817	4.746680	4.837078	4.968694	5.147210
1.5300000	4.803159	4.857685	4.950951	5.086794	5.271145
1.5400000	4.913391	4.969595	5.065753	5.205862	5.396103
1.5500000	5.024305	5.082197	5.181269	5.325673	5.521844
1.5600000	5.135683	5.195273	5.297271	5.445991	5.648121
1.5699999	5.247305	5.308596	5.413527	5.566573	5.774677
1.5707963	5.256197	5.317624	5.422789	5.576179	5.784759
1.5707963	5.256192	5.317619	5.422784	5.576174	5.784754

$\alpha =$ .909999

Θ	K VALUES				
	.318821117	.415016431	.514599755	.613601043	.708073407
.0000000	.000000	.000000	.000000	.000000	.000000
.0100000	.010000	.010000	.010000	.010000	.010000
.0200000	.020002	.020002	.020003	.020003	.020003
.0300000	.030009	.030010	.030010	.030010	.030011
.0400000	.040022	.040023	.040024	.040025	.040027
.0500000	.050044	.050046	.050048	.050050	.050052
.0600000	.060077	.060080	.060084	.060087	.060091
.0700000	.070122	.070128	.070133	.070139	.070144
.0800000	.080182	.080191	.080199	.080208	.080216
.0900000	.090260	.090272	.090284	.090296	.090308
.1000000	.100357	.100373	.100390	.100407	.100423
.1100000	.110476	.110498	.110520	.110542	.110563
.1200000	.120619	.120647	.120676	.120705	.120732
.1300000	.130788	.130823	.130860	.130897	.130932
.1400000	.140985	.141029	.141076	.141122	.141166
.1500000	.151213	.151268	.151325	.151381	.151436
.1600000	.161473	.161540	.161610	.161679	.161745
.1700000	.171770	.171850	.171933	.172016	.172096
.1800000	.182103	.182199	.182298	.182397	.182492
.1900000	.192477	.192590	.192707	.192824	.192936
.2000000	.202894	.203026	.203162	.203299	.203430
.2100000	.213355	.213508	.213667	.213826	.213978
.2200000	.223864	.224040	.224224	.224407	.224582
.2300000	.234422	.234625	.234835	.235045	.235246
.2400000	.245034	.245264	.245504	.245744	.245974
.2500000	.255700	.255961	.256233	.256505	.256767
.2600000	.266424	.266719	.267026	.267334	.267629
.2700000	.277208	.277540	.277886	.278231	.278564
.2800000	.288056	.288427	.288814	.289202	.289574
.2900000	.298970	.299384	.299816	.300248	.300664
.3000000	.309952	.310412	.310893	.311374	.311837
.3100000	.321006	.321516	.322049	.322583	.323097
.3200000	.332135	.332698	.333287	.333878	.334447
.3300000	.343342	.343962	.344611	.345262	.345890
.3400000	.354629	.355311	.356024	.356741	.357432
.3500000	.366000	.366747	.367530	.368316	.369075
.3600000	.377458	.378275	.379131	.379993	.380824
.3700000	.389007	.389899	.390833	.391774	.392684
.3800000	.400649	.401620	.402639	.403665	.404657
.3900000	.412389	.413444	.414552	.415669	.416750

$\alpha =$ •909999

Θ	K VALUES				
	•318821117	•415016431	•514599755	•613601043	•708073407
•4000000	•424229	•425374	•426577	•427790	•428965
•4100000	•436174	•437414	•438717	•440033	•441309
•4200000	•448227	•449567	•450977	•452403	•453785
•4300000	•460391	•461838	•463362	•464903	•466399
•4400000	•472672	•474232	•475875	•477539	•479156
•4500000	•485072	•486751	•488522	•490316	•492061
•4600000	•497596	•499401	•501306	•503238	•505119
•4700000	•510248	•512186	•514233	•516311	•518336
•4800000	•523033	•525110	•527307	•529540	•531717
•4900000	•535954	•538180	•540535	•542930	•545269
•5000000	•549017	•551398	•553920	•556488	•558998
•5100000	•562226	•564771	•567469	•570219	•572910
•5200000	•575587	•578303	•581187	•584130	•587011
•5300000	•589103	•592001	•595080	•598225	•601309
•5400000	•602781	•605869	•609154	•612513	•615810
•5500000	•616625	•619913	•623414	•626999	•630521
•5600000	•630641	•634139	•637868	•641690	•645451
•5700000	•644835	•648553	•652522	•656594	•660606
•5800000	•659212	•663162	•667382	•671718	•675994
•5900000	•673779	•677971	•682456	•687069	•691625
•6000000	•688542	•692989	•697751	•702656	•707506
•6100000	•703506	•708220	•713273	•718486	•723647
•6200000	•718680	•723673	•729033	•734568	•740057
•6300000	•734069	•739355	•745036	•750910	•756745
•6400000	•749681	•755273	•761291	•767523	•773721
•6500000	•765524	•771436	•777807	•784415	•790996
•6600000	•781603	•787852	•794594	•801596	•808581
•6700000	•797929	•804528	•811659	•819076	•826487
•6800000	•814508	•821475	•829013	•836866	•844724
•6899999	•831349	•838701	•846666	•854976	•863306
•7000000	•848461	•856215	•864628	•873419	•882246
•7100000	•865853	•874027	•882909	•892205	•901555
•7200000	•883533	•892147	•901520	•911347	•921248
•7300000	•901513	•910586	•920474	•930857	•941338
•7400000	•919802	•929355	•939782	•950750	•961842
•7500000	•938410	•948465	•959456	•971038	•982773
•7600000	•957349	•967927	•979510	•991737	1•004148
•7700000	•976629	•987755	•999957	1•012860	1•025984
•7800000	•996262	1•007960	1•020810	1•034424	1•048298
•7899999	1•016261	1•028556	1•042085	1•056444	1•071108

$\alpha =$ •909999

Θ	K VALUES				
	•318821117	•415016431	•514599755	•613601043	•708073407
•8000000	1•036638	1•049557	1•063796	1•078938	1•094434
•8100000	1•057405	1•070976	1•085959	1•101923	1•118295
•8200000	1•078578	1•092829	1•108590	1•125416	1•142711
•8300000	1•100170	1•115131	1•131707	1•149438	1•167704
•8400000	1•122195	1•137898	1•155326	1•174008	1•193297
•8500000	1•144670	1•161147	1•179467	1•199147	1•219512
•8600000	1•167609	1•184895	1•204149	1•224876	1•246376
•8700000	1•191030	1•209160	1•229392	1•251218	1•273913
•8799999	1•214951	1•233962	1•255216	1•278196	1•302149
•8899999	1•239388	1•259319	1•281644	1•305834	1•331114
•9000000	1•264361	1•285252	1•308698	1•334160	1•360836
•9100000	1•289890	1•311783	1•336401	1•363197	1•391346
•9200000	1•315995	1•338933	1•364778	1•392976	1•422676
•9300000	1•342696	1•366726	1•393856	1•423525	1•454860
•9400000	1•370017	1•395187	1•423660	1•454874	1•487931
•9500000	1•397980	1•424339	1•454219	1•487055	1•521928
•9600000	1•426610	1•454211	1•485563	1•520101	1•556889
•9699999	1•455931	1•484828	1•517721	1•554047	1•592853
•9799999	1•485970	1•516220	1•550725	1•588929	1•629862
•9899999	1•516755	1•548416	1•584609	1•624785	1•667962
1•0000000	1•548313	1•581448	1•619408	1•661655	1•707197
1•0100000	1•580674	1•615347	1•655156	1•699578	1•747615
1•0200000	1•613870	1•650149	1•691893	1•738599	1•789267
1•0300000	1•647932	1•685888	1•729658	1•778763	1•832207
1•0400000	1•682895	1•722601	1•768491	1•820116	1•876488
1•0500000	1•718794	1•760326	1•808436	1•862708	1•922168
1•0600000	1•755665	1•799104	1•849538	1•906590	1•969308
1•0699999	1•793546	1•838977	1•891842	1•951815	2•017971
1•0799999	1•832478	1•879987	1•935398	1•998439	2•068222
1•0899999	1•872501	1•922180	1•980257	2•046520	2•120131
1•1000000	1•913660	1•965605	2•026471	2•096120	2•173769
1•1100000	1•955999	2•010308	2•074095	2•147300	2•229211
1•1200000	1•999564	2•056342	2•123186	2•200126	2•286535
1•1300000	2•044404	2•103760	2•173804	2•254668	2•345822
1•1400000	2•090570	2•152617	2•226011	2•310996	2•407158
1•1500000	2•138114	2•202970	2•279870	2•369184	2•470630
1•1600000	2•187090	2•254879	2•335448	2•429308	2•536329
1•1700000	2•237554	2•308404	2•392813	2•491449	2•604351
1•1800000	2•289565	2•363610	2•452038	2•555687	2•674795
1•1899999	2•343181	2•420562	2•513194	2•622108	2•747761

$\alpha =$ .909999

Θ	K VALUES				
	.318821117	.415016431	.514599755	.613601043	.708073407
1.2000000	2.398466	2.479327	2.576359	2.690800	2.823355
1.2100000	2.455481	2.539974	2.641609	2.761851	2.901685
1.2200000	2.514292	2.602575	2.709025	2.835354	2.982862
1.2300000	2.574965	2.667202	2.778687	2.911403	3.067000
1.2400000	2.637568	2.733930	2.850678	2.990095	3.154215
1.2500000	2.702170	2.802833	2.925084	3.071528	3.244626
1.2599999	2.768840	2.873988	3.001990	3.155801	3.338354
1.2699999	2.837648	2.947471	3.081481	3.243013	3.435518
1.2799999	2.908664	3.023359	3.163644	3.333264	3.536242
1.2899999	2.981957	3.101728	3.248564	3.426654	3.640645
1.3000000	3.057598	3.182654	3.336327	3.523283	3.748849
1.3100000	3.135650	3.266209	3.427014	3.623243	3.860970
1.3200000	3.216181	3.352464	3.520704	3.726629	3.977122
1.3300000	3.299252	3.441488	3.617475	3.833530	4.097415
1.3400000	3.384919	3.533343	3.717397	3.944029	4.221950
1.3500000	3.473236	3.628087	3.820534	4.058202	4.350823
1.3600000	3.564249	3.725771	3.926946	4.176117	4.484118
1.3700000	3.657998	3.826438	4.036680	4.297830	4.621907
1.3799999	3.754512	3.930121	4.149775	4.423388	4.764247
1.3899999	3.853813	4.036844	4.266257	4.552822	4.911180
1.4000000	3.955910	4.146618	4.386138	4.686148	5.062730
1.4100000	4.060798	4.259436	4.509414	4.823361	5.218893
1.4200000	4.168460	4.375281	4.636063	4.964439	5.379648
1.4300000	4.278862	4.494116	4.766046	5.109338	5.544945
1.4400000	4.391953	4.615885	4.899302	5.257988	5.714703
1.4500000	4.507664	4.740513	5.035746	5.410295	5.888814
1.4600000	4.625907	4.867903	5.175271	5.566136	6.067133
1.4700000	4.746571	4.997937	5.317746	5.725360	6.249483
1.4800000	4.869528	5.130473	5.463012	5.887788	6.435652
1.4900000	4.994627	5.265347	5.610887	6.053210	6.625391
1.5000000	5.121697	5.402373	5.761163	6.221388	6.818418
1.5100000	5.250546	5.541340	5.913605	6.392052	7.014413
1.5200000	5.380962	5.682019	6.067958	6.564911	7.213026
1.5300000	5.512719	5.824161	6.223043	6.739644	7.413878
1.5400000	5.645573	5.967500	6.381265	6.915912	7.616562
1.5500000	5.779267	6.111756	6.539610	7.093356	7.820651
1.5600000	5.913534	6.256639	6.698655	7.271602	8.025699
1.5699999	6.048101	6.401848	6.858064	7.450267	8.231247
1.5707963	6.058822	6.413417	6.870764	7.464502	8.247623
1.5707963	6.058817	6.413412	6.870759	7.464498	8.247622

$\alpha =$ .909999

Θ	K VALUES				
	.794250555	.868696860	.928444378	.971111163	.994996249
.0000000	.000000	.000000	.000000	.000000	.000000
.0100000	.010000	.010000	.010000	.010000	.010000
.0200000	.020003	.020003	.020003	.020003	.020003
.0300000	.030011	.030012	.030012	.030012	.030012
.0400000	.040027	.040028	.040029	.040029	.040030
.0500000	.050054	.050056	.050057	.050058	.050058
.0600000	.060094	.060096	.060099	.060100	.060101
.0700000	.070149	.070154	.070157	.070159	.070161
.0800000	.080223	.080230	.080235	.080238	.080241
.0900000	.090318	.090327	.090335	.090340	.090343
.1000000	.100437	.100450	.100460	.100467	.100471
.1100000	.110583	.110599	.110613	.110622	.110628
.1200000	.120757	.120779	.120797	.120809	.120816
.1300000	.130964	.130992	.131014	.131030	.131039
.1400000	.141206	.141241	.141269	.141289	.141300
.1500000	.151485	.151528	.151563	.151587	.151601
.1600000	.161805	.161857	.161899	.161930	.161946
.1700000	.172169	.172232	.172282	.172318	.172339
.1800000	.182579	.182653	.182714	.182757	.182781
.1900000	.193038	.193126	.193198	.193249	.193277
.2000000	.203550	.203653	.203737	.203796	.203830
.2100000	.214117	.214238	.214335	.214404	.214443
.2200000	.224743	.224882	.224995	.225075	.225120
.2300000	.235431	.235591	.235720	.235812	.235864
.2400000	.246184	.246367	.246514	.246620	.246679
.2500000	.257006	.257214	.257381	.257501	.257568
.2600000	.267899	.268135	.268324	.268460	.268536
.2700000	.278868	.279133	.279347	.279500	.279586
.2800000	.289916	.290213	.290453	.290625	.290721
.2900000	.301047	.301379	.301647	.301839	.301947
.3000000	.312263	.312633	.312932	.313147	.313267
.3100000	.323570	.323981	.324313	.324552	.324685
.3200000	.334970	.335426	.335794	.336058	.336207
.3300000	.346468	.346972	.347379	.347671	.347835
.3400000	.358068	.358623	.359072	.359394	.359576
.3500000	.369775	.370385	.370879	.371233	.371433
.3600000	.381591	.382261	.382803	.383192	.383411
.3700000	.393523	.394256	.394849	.395276	.395516
.3800000	.405574	.406375	.407024	.407490	.407753
.3900000	.417749	.418622	.419330	.419840	.420127

$\alpha =$ •909999

Θ	K VALUES				
	•794250555	•868696860	•928444378	•971111163	•994996249
•4000000	•430052	•431003	•431775	•432330	•432643
•4100000	•442490	•443524	•444363	•444967	•445308
•4200000	•455066	•456188	•457100	•457756	•458126
•4300000	•467787	•469003	•469991	•470704	•471105
•4400000	•480656	•481973	•483043	•483816	•484251
•4500000	•493681	•495105	•496263	•497098	•497570
•4600000	•506867	•508404	•509655	•510559	•511068
•4700000	•520220	•521877	•523227	•524203	•524754
•4800000	•533745	•535530	•536986	•538039	•538633
•4900000	•547450	•549371	•550939	•552074	•552714
•5000000	•561340	•563406	•565093	•566315	•567005
•5100000	•575424	•577642	•579456	•580770	•581513
•5200000	•589706	•592088	•594036	•595448	•596247
•5300000	•604196	•606750	•608841	•610358	•611216
•5400000	•618900	•621637	•623879	•625507	•626429
•5500000	•633827	•636757	•639160	•640906	•641895
•5600000	•648983	•652118	•654693	•656565	•657625
•5700000	•664379	•667731	•670487	•672492	•673628
•5800000	•680022	•683604	•686552	•688699	•689916
•5900000	•695921	•699747	•702899	•705196	•706499
•6000000	•712087	•716171	•719538	•721995	•723390
•6100000	•728527	•732884	•736482	•739108	•740600
•6200000	•745254	•749900	•753741	•756547	•758142
•6300000	•762277	•767229	•771327	•774325	•776030
•6400000	•779607	•784883	•789255	•792456	•794278
•6500000	•797255	•802874	•807536	•810953	•812900
•6600000	•815234	•821216	•826186	•829832	•831911
•6700000	•833556	•839922	•845218	•849108	•851327
•6800000	•852233	•859006	•864648	•868797	•871166
•6899999	•871280	•878482	•884491	•888916	•891444
•7000000	•890709	•898367	•904766	•909483	•912181
•7100000	•910535	•918675	•925488	•930516	•933394
•7200000	•930774	•939425	•946676	•952036	•955106
•7300000	•951442	•960633	•968350	•974061	•977336
•7400000	•972554	•982317	•990529	•996615	1•000108
•7500000	•994129	1•004498	1•013234	1•019719	1•023445
•7600000	1•016183	1•027194	1•036488	1•043398	1•047372
•7700000	1•038736	1•050427	1•060314	1•067676	1•071914
•7800000	1•061808	1•074219	1•084736	1•092579	1•097100
•7899999	1•085418	1•098593	1•109779	1•118136	1•122958

$\alpha =$ •909999

Θ	K VALUES				
	•794250555	•868696860	•928444378	•971111163	•994996249
•8000000	1•109589	1•123573	1•135471	1•144375	1•149519
•8100000	1•134342	1•149185	1•161840	1•171327	1•176815
•8200000	1•159702	1•175454	1•188914	1•199024	1•204880
•8300000	1•185692	1•202409	1•216726	1•227501	1•233750
•8400000	1•212339	1•230079	1•245308	1•256793	1•263464
•8500000	1•239668	1•258494	1•274696	1•286938	1•294060
•8600000	1•267709	1•287687	1•304924	1•317978	1•325583
•8700000	1•296491	1•317692	1•336033	1•349953	1•358076
•8799999	1•326044	1•348545	1•368061	1•382909	1•391588
•8899999	1•356401	1•380282	1•401053	1•416893	1•426168
•9000000	1•387597	1•412943	1•435052	1•451956	1•461872
•9100000	1•419665	1•446569	1•470108	1•488151	1•498756
•9200000	1•452644	1•481204	1•506268	1•525534	1•536879
•9300000	1•486573	1•516893	1•543588	1•564165	1•576308
•9400000	1•521492	1•553685	1•582123	1•604108	1•617109
•9500000	1•557445	1•591631	1•621932	1•645429	1•659356
•9600000	1•594477	1•630783	1•663078	1•688201	1•703126
•9699999	1•632634	1•671199	1•705627	1•732499	1•748503
•9799999	1•671968	1•712937	1•749650	1•778404	1•795573
•9899999	1•712529	1•756059	1•795221	1•826002	1•844432
1•0000000	1•754373	1•800632	1•842418	1•875386	1•895180
1•0100000	1•797557	1•846725	1•891325	1•926651	1•947923
1•0200000	1•842141	1•894411	1•942031	1•979901	2•002778
1•0300000	1•888187	1•943766	1•994628	2•035249	2•059866
1•0400000	1•935764	1•994873	2•049217	2•092810	2•119320
1•0500000	1•984939	2•047815	2•105901	2•152712	2•181280
1•0600000	2•035787	2•102684	2•164794	2•215088	2•245898
1•0699999	2•088382	2•159574	2•226013	2•280082	2•313337
1•0799999	2•142806	2•218586	2•289683	2•347848	2•383771
1•0899999	2•199143	2•279823	2•355938	2•418549	2•457387
1•1000000	2•257480	2•343398	2•424919	2•492360	2•534389
1•1100000	2•317909	2•409426	2•496774	2•569469	2•614993
1•1200000	2•380526	2•478030	2•571663	2•650075	2•699434
1•1300000	2•445432	2•549339	2•649753	2•734394	2•787964
1•1400000	2•512733	2•623487	2•731222	2•822655	2•880857
1•1500000	2•582536	2•700617	2•816259	2•915105	2•978407
1•1600000	2•654957	2•780878	2•905063	3•012005	3•080933
1•1700000	2•730115	2•864424	2•997845	3•113639	3•188781
1•1800000	2•808132	2•951420	3•094827	3•220308	3•302325
1•1899999	2•889137	3•042034	3•196245	3•332336	3•421968

$\alpha =$ •909999

Θ	K VALUES				
	•794250555	•868696860	•928444378	•971111163	•994996249
1•2000000	2•973263	3•136445	3•302347	3•450069	3•548153
1•2100000	3•060646	3•234836	3•413393	3•573876	3•681353
1•2200000	3•151428	3•337398	3•529658	3•704155	3•822090
1•2300000	3•245755	3•444332	3•651430	3•841329	3•970927
1•2400000	3•343775	3•555840	3•779011	3•985852	4•128479
1•2500000	3•445640	3•672134	3•912716	4•138206	4•295415
1•2599999	3•551506	3•793431	4•052872	4•298908	4•472467
1•2699999	3•661528	3•919951	4•199821	4•468506	4•660432
1•2799999	3•775867	4•051918	4•353915	4•647585	4•860182
1•2899999	3•894678	4•189559	4•515518	4•836763	5•072671
1•3000000	4•018121	4•333104	4•685001	5•036700	5•298949
1•3100000	4•146348	4•482776	4•862742	5•248083	5•540156
1•3200000	4•279512	4•638801	5•049124	5•471644	5•797555
1•3300000	4•417757	4•801396	5•244532	5•708146	6•072531
1•3400000	4•561221	4•970773	5•449347	5•958387	6•366607
1•3500000	4•710032	5•147130	5•663942	6•223194	6•681465
1•3600000	4•864307	5•330652	5•888680	6•503418	7•018962
1•3700000	5•024145	5•521505	6•123903	6•799929	7•381150
1•3799999	5•189629	5•719830	6•369927	7•113607	7•770305
1•3899999	5•360821	5•925745	6•627037	7•445330	8•188950
1•4000000	5•537763	6•139335	6•895475	7•795964	8•639894
1•4100000	5•720459	6•360642	7•175427	8•166330	9•126250
1•4200000	5•908893	6•589674	7•467022	8•557205	9•651501
1•4300000	6•103010	6•826387	7•770318	8•969281	10•219520
1•4400000	6•302720	7•070687	8•085289	9•403136	10•834629
1•4500000	6•507892	7•322424	8•411818	9•859207	11•501627
1•4600000	6•718354	7•581387	8•749685	10•337743	12•225829
1•4700000	6•933888	7•847302	9•098561	10•838766	13•013062
1•4800000	7•154233	8•119828	9•457999	11•362031	13•869624
1•4900000	7•379080	8•398559	9•827433	11•906977	14•802138
1•5000000	7•608076	8•683022	10•206172	12•472698	15•817257
1•5100000	7•840822	8•972676	10•593396	13•057889	16•921074
1•5200000	8•076877	9•266922	10•988172	13•660853	18•118216
1•5300000	8•315764	9•565103	11•389455	14•279479	19•410367
1•5400000	8•556970	9•866511	11•796098	14•911262	20•794316
1•5500000	8•799954	10•170395	12•206869	15•553341	22•259813
1•5600000	9•044152	10•475971	12•620469	16•202559	23•787992
1•5699999	9•288984	10•782433	13•035551	16•855544	25•351611
1•5707963	9•308491	10•806851	13•068628	16•907601	25•476693
1•5707963	9•308493	10•806872	13•068619	16•907590	25•476668

$\alpha =$ .919999

Θ	K VALUES				
	.009966711	.039469502	.087332193	.151646642	.229848846
.0000000	.000000	.000000	.000000	.000000	.000000
.0100000	.010000	.010000	.010000	.010000	.010000
.0200000	.020002	.020002	.020002	.020002	.020002
.0300000	.030008	.030008	.030008	.030008	.030009
.0400000	.040019	.040020	.040020	.040021	.040022
.0500000	.050038	.050039	.050040	.050041	.050043
.0600000	.060066	.060067	.060069	.060071	.060074
.0700000	.070105	.070107	.070110	.070114	.070118
.0800000	.080158	.080160	.080164	.080170	.080177
.0900000	.090225	.090229	.090234	.090242	.090252
.1000000	.100309	.100314	.100322	.100333	.100346
.1100000	.110412	.110418	.110429	.110443	.110461
.1200000	.120535	.120544	.120557	.120576	.120599
.1300000	.130681	.130692	.130709	.130733	.130762
.1400000	.140851	.140865	.140887	.140917	.140953
.1500000	.151048	.151065	.151092	.151129	.151173
.1600000	.161274	.161294	.161327	.161372	.161426
.1700000	.171530	.171554	.171594	.171647	.171712
.1800000	.181818	.181847	.181895	.181958	.182035
.1900000	.192142	.192176	.192231	.192306	.192397
.2000000	.202501	.202541	.202606	.202693	.202800
.2100000	.212900	.212946	.213021	.213123	.213246
.2200000	.223339	.223393	.223479	.223596	.223738
.2300000	.233822	.233883	.233982	.234116	.234279
.2400000	.244350	.244419	.244532	.244685	.244870
.2500000	.254925	.255004	.255132	.255304	.255515
.2600000	.265551	.265639	.265783	.265978	.266215
.2700000	.276228	.276327	.276489	.276708	.276974
.2800000	.286960	.287071	.287252	.287496	.287794
.2900000	.297748	.297872	.298074	.298346	.298678
.3000000	.308596	.308734	.308957	.309259	.309628
.3100000	.319506	.319658	.319905	.320239	.320648
.3200000	.330480	.330648	.330920	.331289	.331739
.3300000	.341521	.341705	.342005	.342410	.342906
.3400000	.352631	.352833	.353162	.353607	.354151
.3500000	.363814	.364035	.364394	.364881	.365477
.3600000	.375071	.375312	.375705	.376236	.376887
.3700000	.386406	.386669	.387096	.387675	.388385
.3800000	.397822	.398107	.398572	.399201	.399973
.3900000	.409321	.409631	.410135	.410817	.411655

$\alpha =$ .919999

Θ	K VALUES				
	.009966711	.039469502	.087332193	.151646642	.229848846
.4000000	.420907	.421242	.421788	.422527	.423435
.4100000	.432583	.432944	.433534	.434333	.435315
.4200000	.444351	.444741	.445377	.446239	.447300
.4300000	.456215	.456635	.457320	.458249	.459393
.4400000	.468179	.468630	.469367	.470367	.471597
.4500000	.480245	.480730	.481521	.482595	.483918
.4600000	.492418	.492937	.493786	.494938	.496358
.4700000	.504700	.505256	.506165	.507399	.508922
.4800000	.517096	.517690	.518662	.519984	.521614
.4900000	.529609	.530244	.531282	.532694	.534438
.5000000	.542243	.542921	.544029	.545536	.547398
.5100000	.555003	.555725	.556906	.558513	.560500
.5200000	.567892	.568660	.569917	.571630	.573748
.5300000	.580914	.581731	.583069	.584891	.587147
.5400000	.594074	.594942	.596364	.598301	.600701
.5500000	.607377	.608298	.609807	.611866	.614417
.5600000	.620827	.621803	.623404	.625589	.628298
.5700000	.634429	.635463	.637160	.639476	.642351
.5800000	.648187	.649282	.651079	.653533	.656582
.5900000	.662108	.663266	.665167	.667766	.670996
.6000000	.676196	.677420	.679430	.682179	.685598
.6100000	.690456	.691749	.693873	.696779	.700397
.6200000	.704895	.706260	.708502	.711572	.715397
.6300000	.719517	.720957	.723323	.726564	.730605
.6400000	.734330	.735848	.738342	.741762	.746029
.6500000	.749339	.750938	.753567	.757172	.761675
.6600000	.764551	.766234	.769003	.772802	.777551
.6700000	.779973	.781743	.784657	.788659	.793664
.6800000	.795610	.797472	.800537	.804750	.810023
.6899999	.811471	.813428	.816651	.821083	.826635
.7000000	.827564	.829618	.833006	.837666	.843509
.7100000	.843894	.846052	.849609	.854507	.860654
.7200000	.860471	.862735	.866470	.871616	.878078
.7300000	.877303	.879678	.883597	.889000	.895792
.7400000	.894398	.896888	.900999	.906670	.913806
.7500000	.911766	.914375	.918686	.924636	.932128
.7600000	.929415	.932148	.936666	.942906	.950771
.7700000	.947355	.950217	.954950	.961492	.969744
.7800000	.965596	.968592	.973549	.980404	.989060
.7899999	.984149	.987284	.992473	.999654	1.008730

$\alpha =$ .919999

Θ	K VALUES				
	.009966711	.039469502	.087332193	.151646642	.229848846
.8000000	1.003024	1.006303	1.011733	1.019254	1.028768
.8100000	1.022232	1.025661	1.031342	1.039215	1.049184
.8200000	1.041786	1.045370	1.051311	1.059550	1.069994
.8300000	1.061697	1.065443	1.071654	1.080274	1.091210
.8400000	1.081978	1.085891	1.092382	1.101399	1.112848
.8500000	1.102642	1.106729	1.113512	1.122939	1.134923
.8600000	1.123703	1.127970	1.135056	1.144910	1.157450
.8700000	1.145176	1.149630	1.157029	1.167328	1.180446
.8799999	1.167074	1.171723	1.179448	1.190209	1.203928
.8899999	1.189415	1.194264	1.202328	1.213569	1.227914
.9000000	1.212214	1.217272	1.225687	1.237426	1.252423
.9100000	1.235488	1.240763	1.249542	1.261799	1.277474
.9200000	1.259254	1.264754	1.273912	1.286707	1.303087
.9300000	1.283532	1.289265	1.298816	1.312170	1.329284
.9400000	1.308340	1.314315	1.324274	1.338210	1.356087
.9500000	1.333700	1.339925	1.350308	1.364847	1.383518
.9600000	1.359630	1.366117	1.376939	1.392106	1.411603
.9699999	1.386155	1.392912	1.404191	1.420010	1.440366
.9799999	1.413297	1.420334	1.432087	1.448583	1.469835
.9899999	1.441079	1.448407	1.460653	1.477853	1.500035
1.0000000	1.469528	1.477158	1.489915	1.507847	1.530998
1.0100000	1.498669	1.506612	1.519900	1.538593	1.562752
1.0200000	1.528529	1.536799	1.550638	1.570122	1.595329
1.0300000	1.559139	1.567746	1.582157	1.602463	1.628763
1.0400000	1.590527	1.599485	1.614491	1.635652	1.663088
1.0500000	1.622725	1.632047	1.647671	1.669720	1.698339
1.0600000	1.655767	1.665466	1.681733	1.704705	1.734556
1.0699999	1.689686	1.699778	1.716711	1.740644	1.771777
1.0799999	1.724518	1.735018	1.752644	1.777576	1.810044
1.0899999	1.760301	1.771225	1.789571	1.815542	1.849400
1.1000000	1.797076	1.808439	1.827533	1.854585	1.889890
1.1100000	1.834881	1.846701	1.866574	1.894750	1.931561
1.1200000	1.873761	1.886056	1.906737	1.936082	1.974463
1.1300000	1.913760	1.926548	1.948069	1.978631	2.018647
1.1400000	1.954924	1.968225	1.990620	2.022448	2.064167
1.1500000	1.997303	2.011137	2.034441	2.067585	2.111078
1.1600000	2.040948	2.055335	2.079584	2.114099	2.159440
1.1700000	2.085910	2.100872	2.126104	2.162046	2.209311
1.1800000	2.132245	2.147806	2.174059	2.211486	2.260757
1.1899999	2.180010	2.196193	2.223509	2.262480	2.313841

$\alpha =$ .919999

Θ	K VALUES				
	.009966711	.039469502	.087332193	.151646642	.229848846
1.2000000	2.229264	2.246093	2.274515	2.315095	2.368633
1.2100000	2.280067	2.297569	2.327141	2.369395	2.425201
1.2200000	2.332483	2.350684	2.381452	2.425449	2.483619
1.2300000	2.386577	2.405505	2.437518	2.483328	2.543960
1.2400000	2.442416	2.462100	2.495407	2.543105	2.606303
1.2500000	2.500068	2.520538	2.555191	2.604855	2.670725
1.2599999	2.559602	2.580889	2.616944	2.668652	2.737307
1.2699999	2.621091	2.643228	2.680738	2.734576	2.806130
1.2799999	2.684605	2.707625	2.746651	2.802703	2.877276
1.2899999	2.750217	2.774156	2.814756	2.873112	2.950830
1.3000000	2.818001	2.842893	2.885131	2.945884	3.026875
1.3100000	2.888026	2.913910	2.957850	3.021095	3.105492
1.3200000	2.960363	2.987277	3.032985	3.098821	3.186762
1.3300000	3.035082	3.063065	3.110610	3.179139	3.270765
1.3400000	3.112248	3.141340	3.190793	3.262118	3.357575
1.3500000	3.191922	3.222166	3.273598	3.347827	3.447264
1.3600000	3.274161	3.305600	3.359084	3.436327	3.539897
1.3700000	3.359016	3.391692	3.447306	3.527674	3.635532
1.3799999	3.446531	3.480488	3.538306	3.621914	3.734219
1.3899999	3.536737	3.572022	3.632122	3.719083	3.835997
1.4000000	3.629661	3.666317	3.728778	3.819209	3.940892
1.4100000	3.725311	3.763384	3.828283	3.922301	4.048917
1.4200000	3.823685	3.863220	3.930636	4.028357	4.160068
1.4300000	3.924763	3.965805	4.035816	4.137356	4.274323
1.4400000	4.028510	4.071103	4.143786	4.249259	4.391642
1.4500000	4.134870	4.179058	4.254488	4.364006	4.511960
1.4600000	4.243767	4.289592	4.367842	4.481513	4.635191
1.4700000	4.355105	4.402607	4.483747	4.601675	4.761223
1.4800000	4.468762	4.517980	4.602077	4.724362	4.889918
1.4900000	4.584596	4.635566	4.722683	4.849418	5.021112
1.5000000	4.702441	4.755197	4.845392	4.976663	5.154615
1.5100000	4.822108	4.876679	4.970004	5.105889	5.290208
1.5200000	4.943386	4.999800	5.096301	5.236869	5.427652
1.5300000	5.066045	5.124325	5.224042	5.369352	5.566681
1.5400000	5.189837	5.250001	5.352967	5.503068	5.707011
1.5500000	5.314499	5.376562	5.482802	5.637730	5.848339
1.5600000	5.439756	5.503726	5.613257	5.773039	5.990349
1.5699999	5.565323	5.631207	5.744038	5.908686	6.132716
1.5707963	5.575327	5.641364	5.754457	5.919493	6.144059
1.5707963	5.575321	5.641358	5.754452	5.919488	6.144053

$\alpha =$ .919999

Θ	K VALUES				
	.318821117	.415016431	.514599755	.613601043	.708073407
.0000000	.000000	.000000	.000000	.000000	.000000
.0100000	.010000	.010000	.010000	.010000	.010000
.0200000	.020002	.020003	.020003	.020003	.020003
.0300000	.030009	.030010	.030010	.030011	.030011
.0400000	.040023	.040024	.040025	.040026	.040027
.0500000	.050045	.050047	.050049	.050051	.050053
.0600000	.060077	.060081	.060084	.060088	.060091
.0700000	.070123	.070129	.070134	.070140	.070146
.0800000	.080184	.080192	.080201	.080209	.080218
.0900000	.090263	.090274	.090287	.090299	.090310
.1000000	.100361	.100377	.100394	.100410	.100426
.1100000	.110481	.110502	.110524	.110547	.110568
.1200000	.120625	.120653	.120682	.120710	.120738
.1300000	.130795	.130831	.130868	.130904	.130940
.1400000	.140994	.141039	.141085	.141131	.141175
.1500000	.151224	.151279	.151336	.151393	.151447
.1600000	.161487	.161554	.161624	.161693	.161759
.1700000	.171787	.171867	.171950	.172033	.172113
.1800000	.182124	.182219	.182318	.182417	.182512
.1900000	.192501	.192614	.192731	.192848	.192959
.2000000	.202921	.203053	.203190	.203327	.203458
.2100000	.213387	.213540	.213699	.213858	.214010
.2200000	.223901	.224078	.224261	.224444	.224620
.2300000	.234465	.234668	.234878	.235088	.235290
.2400000	.245082	.245313	.245553	.245793	.246023
.2500000	.255755	.256017	.256289	.256561	.256822
.2600000	.266487	.266782	.267089	.267397	.267692
.2700000	.277279	.277611	.277957	.278302	.278635
.2800000	.288135	.288507	.288894	.289282	.289654
.2900000	.299058	.299473	.299905	.300338	.300754
.3000000	.310051	.310511	.310992	.311474	.311937
.3100000	.321116	.321626	.322159	.322693	.323208
.3200000	.332256	.332820	.333409	.334000	.334569
.3300000	.343475	.344096	.344746	.345397	.346026
.3400000	.354776	.355459	.356172	.356890	.357581
.3500000	.366162	.366910	.367693	.368480	.369239
.3600000	.377636	.378454	.379310	.380172	.381005
.3700000	.389201	.390094	.391029	.391971	.392881
.3800000	.400861	.401833	.402853	.403880	.404873
.3900000	.412620	.413676	.414785	.415903	.416985

$\alpha =$ .919999

Θ	K VALUES				
	.318821117	.415016431	.514599755	.613601043	.708073407
.4000000	.424481	.425627	.426830	.428045	.429222
.4100000	.436447	.437688	.438993	.440310	.441588
.4200000	.448523	.449865	.451277	.452704	.454088
.4300000	.460712	.462161	.463686	.465229	.466727
.4400000	.473018	.474580	.476226	.477892	.479511
.4500000	.485446	.487127	.488900	.490697	.492444
.4600000	.498000	.499807	.501715	.503650	.505533
.4700000	.510683	.512624	.514674	.516755	.518783
.4800000	.523501	.525582	.527782	.530018	.532199
.4900000	.536457	.538686	.541045	.543445	.545788
.5000000	.549558	.551943	.554469	.557042	.559556
.5100000	.562806	.565355	.568058	.570814	.573509
.5200000	.576208	.578930	.581819	.584767	.587655
.5300000	.589769	.592672	.595757	.598909	.601999
.5400000	.603493	.606588	.609879	.613245	.616549
.5500000	.617386	.620682	.624191	.627783	.631313
.5600000	.631455	.634961	.638698	.642529	.646298
.5700000	.645704	.649431	.653409	.657491	.661512
.5800000	.660140	.664099	.668330	.672676	.676964
.5900000	.674768	.678972	.683467	.688092	.692660
.6000000	.689596	.694055	.698830	.703748	.708612
.6100000	.704630	.709357	.714424	.719651	.724827
.6200000	.719877	.724884	.730259	.735810	.741316
.6300000	.735343	.740644	.746342	.752235	.758087
.6400000	.751036	.756645	.762682	.768934	.775152
.6500000	.766964	.772896	.779288	.785917	.792521
.6600000	.783134	.789404	.796169	.803195	.810204
.6700000	.799555	.806178	.813334	.820778	.828215
.6800000	.816235	.823228	.830794	.838676	.846563
.6899999	.833183	.840563	.848558	.856901	.865263
.7000000	.850408	.858192	.866638	.875465	.884327
.7100000	.867919	.876126	.885045	.894379	.903769
.7200000	.885725	.894375	.903789	.913658	.923602
.7300000	.903838	.912951	.922882	.933312	.943841
.7400000	.922267	.931864	.942338	.953358	.964501
.7500000	.941023	.951126	.962170	.973808	.985599
.7600000	.960119	.970749	.982389	.994677	1.007151
.7700000	.979564	.990747	1.003011	1.015982	1.029175
.7800000	.999372	1.011132	1.024050	1.037738	1.051687
.7899999	1.019556	1.031919	1.045522	1.059961	1.074709

$\alpha =$ .919999

Θ	K VALUES				
	.318821117	.415016431	.514599755	.613601043	.708073407
.8000000	1.040128	1.053121	1.067441	1.082671	1.098258
.8100000	1.061103	1.074754	1.089825	1.105885	1.122356
.8200000	1.082494	1.096832	1.112690	1.129621	1.147025
.8300000	1.104317	1.119373	1.136054	1.153900	1.172286
.8400000	1.126587	1.142393	1.159936	1.178744	1.198163
.8500000	1.149321	1.165910	1.184356	1.204172	1.224681
.8600000	1.172535	1.189942	1.209333	1.230209	1.251866
.8700000	1.196247	1.214508	1.234889	1.256877	1.279744
.8799999	1.220475	1.239629	1.261045	1.284202	1.308344
.8899999	1.245238	1.265324	1.287825	1.312210	1.337695
.9000000	1.270557	1.291616	1.315253	1.340927	1.367829
.9100000	1.296452	1.318527	1.343354	1.370381	1.398776
.9200000	1.322945	1.346082	1.372154	1.400603	1.430573
.9300000	1.350059	1.374304	1.401680	1.431624	1.463253
.9400000	1.377817	1.403220	1.431962	1.463475	1.496854
.9500000	1.406245	1.432857	1.463029	1.496190	1.531416
.9600000	1.435368	1.463243	1.494912	1.529805	1.566978
.9699999	1.465213	1.494407	1.527644	1.564358	1.603585
.9799999	1.495809	1.526381	1.561260	1.599887	1.641280
.9899999	1.527185	1.559196	1.595796	1.636432	1.680112
1.0000000	1.559372	1.592887	1.631288	1.674036	1.720129
1.0100000	1.592403	1.627488	1.667777	1.712745	1.761384
1.0200000	1.626312	1.663037	1.705303	1.752604	1.803931
1.0300000	1.661133	1.699572	1.743909	1.793663	1.847827
1.0400000	1.696904	1.737134	1.783640	1.835972	1.893132
1.0500000	1.733665	1.775765	1.824544	1.879586	1.939909
1.0600000	1.771454	1.815509	1.866669	1.924561	1.988223
1.0699999	1.810315	1.856412	1.910068	1.970955	2.038144
1.0799999	1.850292	1.898523	1.954793	2.018831	2.089745
1.0899999	1.891431	1.941893	2.000902	2.068253	2.143101
1.1000000	1.933781	1.986574	2.048454	2.119288	2.198292
1.1100000	1.977393	2.032622	2.097510	2.172007	2.255400
1.1200000	2.022318	2.080093	2.148134	2.226483	2.314514
1.1300000	2.068613	2.129049	2.200394	2.282794	2.375724
1.1400000	2.116334	2.179552	2.254359	2.341019	2.439126
1.1500000	2.165543	2.231668	2.310104	2.401244	2.504820
1.1600000	2.216300	2.285465	2.367703	2.463556	2.572910
1.1700000	2.268672	2.341014	2.427237	2.528045	2.643503
1.1800000	2.322726	2.398388	2.488788	2.594807	2.716714
1.1899999	2.378531	2.457665	2.552442	2.663940	2.792659

$\alpha =$ .919999

Θ	K VALUES				
	.318821117	.415016431	.514599755	.613601043	.708073407
1.2000000	2.436162	2.518924	2.618288	2.735547	2.871462
1.2100000	2.495692	2.582247	2.686416	2.809732	2.953247
1.2200000	2.557200	2.647719	2.756923	2.886606	3.038147
1.2300000	2.620766	2.715427	2.829906	2.966281	3.126296
1.2400000	2.686472	2.785461	2.905466	3.048874	3.217834
1.2500000	2.754402	2.857914	2.983705	3.134502	3.312903
1.2599999	2.824642	2.932880	3.064729	3.223288	3.411650
1.2699999	2.897280	3.010454	3.148646	3.315355	3.514224
1.2799999	2.972405	3.090732	3.235563	3.410828	3.620775
1.2899999	3.050106	3.173813	3.325589	3.509833	3.731456
1.3000000	3.130472	3.259795	3.418835	3.612498	3.846420
1.3100000	3.213590	3.348773	3.515406	3.718946	3.965817
1.3200000	3.299548	3.440841	3.615411	3.829300	4.089798
1.3300000	3.388431	3.536094	3.718953	3.943681	4.218507
1.3400000	3.480319	3.634619	3.826131	4.062204	4.352086
1.3500000	3.575289	3.736500	3.937038	4.184978	4.490667
1.3600000	3.673411	3.841814	4.051761	4.312102	4.634373
1.3700000	3.774746	3.950627	4.170376	4.443666	4.783313
1.3799999	3.879349	4.063000	4.292949	4.579746	4.937582
1.3899999	3.987261	4.178978	4.419531	4.720403	5.097256
1.4000000	4.098511	4.298593	4.550160	4.865682	5.262393
1.4100000	4.213112	4.421858	4.684850	5.015601	5.433017
1.4200000	4.331060	4.548771	4.823600	5.170159	5.609131
1.4300000	4.452333	4.679307	4.966382	5.329325	5.790704
1.4400000	4.576886	4.813417	5.113144	5.493042	5.977668
1.4500000	4.704651	4.951028	5.263802	5.661215	6.169917
1.4600000	4.835536	5.092039	5.418245	5.833718	6.367301
1.4700000	4.969420	5.236319	5.576329	6.010387	6.569629
1.4800000	5.106155	5.383708	5.737874	6.191017	6.776661
1.4900000	5.245568	5.534014	5.902668	6.375365	6.988109
1.5000000	5.387453	5.687015	6.070465	6.563151	7.203641
1.5100000	5.531577	5.842458	6.240980	6.754049	7.422872
1.5200000	5.677683	6.000060	6.413901	6.947702	7.645378
1.5300000	5.825487	6.159514	6.588884	7.143716	7.870692
1.5400000	5.974684	6.320486	6.765559	7.341668	8.098310
1.5500000	6.124950	6.482624	6.943533	7.541107	8.327697
1.5600000	6.275947	6.645559	7.122394	7.741563	8.558293
1.5699999	6.427326	6.808910	7.301719	7.942550	8.789522
1.5707963	6.439387	6.821924	7.316006	7.958563	8.807945
1.5707963	6.439381	6.821919	7.316001	7.958559	8.807943

$\alpha =$ .919999

Θ	K VALUES				
	.794250555	.868696860	.928444378	.971111163	.994996249
.0000000	.000000	.000000	.000000	.000000	.000000
.0100000	.010000	.010000	.010000	.010000	.010000
.0200000	.020003	.020003	.020003	.020003	.020003
.0300000	.030011	.030012	.030012	.030012	.030012
.0400000	.040028	.040028	.040029	.040030	.040030
.0500000	.050054	.050056	.050057	.050058	.050059
.0600000	.060095	.060097	.060099	.060101	.060102
.0700000	.070150	.070155	.070158	.070161	.070162
.0800000	.080225	.080231	.080237	.080240	.080242
.0900000	.090321	.090330	.090337	.090342	.090345
.1000000	.100441	.100453	.100463	.100470	.100474
.1100000	.110587	.110604	.110617	.110627	.110632
.1200000	.120763	.120785	.120803	.120815	.120822
.1300000	.130972	.130999	.131022	.131038	.131047
.1400000	.141215	.141250	.141278	.141298	.141309
.1500000	.151497	.151540	.151574	.151599	.151613
.1600000	.161819	.161872	.161914	.161944	.161960
.1700000	.172186	.172248	.172299	.172335	.172356
.1800000	.182599	.182674	.182734	.182777	.182801
.1900000	.193062	.193150	.193221	.193272	.193301
.2000000	.203578	.203681	.203765	.203824	.203858
.2100000	.214149	.214270	.214367	.214437	.214476
.2200000	.224781	.224920	.225032	.225113	.225158
.2300000	.235474	.235634	.235763	.235855	.235907
.2400000	.246233	.246416	.246564	.246669	.246728
.2500000	.257062	.257270	.257437	.257557	.257624
.2600000	.267963	.268198	.268387	.268523	.268599
.2700000	.278940	.279205	.279418	.279571	.279657
.2800000	.289996	.290294	.290533	.290705	.290802
.2900000	.301136	.301469	.301737	.301929	.302037
.3000000	.312363	.312733	.313032	.313247	.313367
.3100000	.323681	.324092	.324425	.324663	.324797
.3200000	.335093	.335549	.335918	.336182	.336330
.3300000	.346604	.347108	.347515	.347808	.347972
.3400000	.358218	.358774	.359223	.359545	.359727
.3500000	.369940	.370550	.371044	.371399	.371599
.3600000	.381772	.382442	.382985	.383374	.383593
.3700000	.393721	.394455	.395049	.395476	.395716
.3800000	.405790	.406592	.407241	.407709	.407971
.3900000	.417985	.418859	.419568	.420078	.420365

$\alpha =$ .919999

Θ	K VALUES				
	.794250555	.868696860	.928444378	.971111163	.994996249
.4000000	.430310	.431262	.432034	.432590	.432903
.4100000	.442770	.443805	.444645	.445250	.445591
.4200000	.455370	.456494	.457406	.458064	.458434
.4300000	.468116	.469334	.470324	.471037	.471439
.4400000	.481013	.482332	.483404	.484177	.484613
.4500000	.494067	.495493	.496652	.497489	.497961
.4600000	.507284	.508823	.510076	.510981	.511491
.4700000	.520670	.522329	.523682	.524659	.525210
.4800000	.534230	.536018	.537476	.538531	.539126
.4900000	.547972	.549897	.551467	.552604	.553245
.5000000	.561902	.563972	.565662	.566885	.567576
.5100000	.576027	.578250	.580068	.581384	.582128
.5200000	.590355	.592741	.594693	.596108	.596908
.5300000	.604892	.607451	.609546	.611066	.611926
.5400000	.619646	.622388	.624636	.626268	.627191
.5500000	.634626	.637562	.639971	.641722	.642712
.5600000	.649839	.652981	.655562	.657438	.658501
.5700000	.665295	.668655	.671417	.673427	.674566
.5800000	.681001	.684592	.687548	.689700	.690920
.5900000	.696968	.700804	.703964	.706267	.707574
.6000000	.713205	.717300	.720677	.723141	.724539
.6100000	.729721	.734091	.737698	.740332	.741829
.6200000	.746528	.751188	.755040	.757855	.759455
.6300000	.763636	.768604	.772715	.775722	.777433
.6400000	.781056	.786349	.790735	.793947	.795775
.6500000	.798800	.804438	.809116	.812545	.814498
.6600000	.816881	.822883	.827870	.831530	.833616
.6700000	.835310	.841699	.847014	.850919	.853146
.6800000	.854101	.860899	.866562	.870728	.873106
.6899999	.873268	.880499	.886532	.890974	.893512
.7000000	.892825	.900514	.906940	.911677	.914386
.7100000	.912787	.920962	.927804	.932854	.935744
.7200000	.933170	.941859	.949143	.954526	.957610
.7300000	.953990	.963224	.970976	.976715	.980005
.7400000	.975265	.985074	.993326	.999441	1.002952
.7500000	.997011	1.007432	1.016212	1.022730	1.026474
.7600000	1.019248	1.030316	1.039658	1.046604	1.050599
.7700000	1.041994	1.053748	1.063689	1.071090	1.075352
.7800000	1.065272	1.077752	1.088328	1.096216	1.100762
.7899999	1.089100	1.102351	1.113603	1.122009	1.126859

$\alpha =$ .919999

Θ	K VALUES				
	.794250555	.868696860	.928444378	.971111163	.994996249
.8000000	1.113503	1.127571	1.139541	1.148500	1.153675
.8100000	1.138503	1.153438	1.166172	1.175720	1.181243
.8200000	1.164125	1.179978	1.193526	1.203703	1.209598
.8300000	1.190393	1.207222	1.221637	1.232485	1.238778
.8400000	1.217336	1.235199	1.250537	1.262103	1.268821
.8500000	1.244981	1.263942	1.280263	1.292596	1.299771
.8600000	1.273357	1.293485	1.310853	1.324006	1.331670
.8700000	1.302496	1.323862	1.342347	1.356378	1.364566
.8799999	1.332429	1.355111	1.374787	1.389758	1.398509
.8899999	1.363191	1.387272	1.408219	1.424196	1.433551
.9000000	1.394818	1.420385	1.442689	1.459744	1.469749
.9100000	1.427347	1.454493	1.478248	1.496458	1.507162
.9200000	1.460817	1.489644	1.514947	1.534398	1.545853
.9300000	1.495269	1.525884	1.552843	1.573625	1.585890
.9400000	1.530747	1.563265	1.591994	1.614207	1.627344
.9500000	1.567297	1.601841	1.632464	1.656215	1.670293
.9600000	1.604967	1.641668	1.674319	1.699723	1.714817
.9699999	1.643806	1.682805	1.717628	1.744812	1.761004
.9799999	1.683869	1.725317	1.762467	1.791569	1.808947
.9899999	1.725210	1.769268	1.808914	1.840082	1.858745
1.0000000	1.767889	1.814731	1.857053	1.890450	1.910506
1.0100000	1.811966	1.861777	1.906972	1.942776	1.964341
1.0200000	1.857507	1.910487	1.958766	1.997171	2.020373
1.0300000	1.904580	1.960942	2.012536	2.053751	2.078733
1.0400000	1.953256	2.013230	2.068387	2.112644	2.139562
1.0500000	2.003612	2.067443	2.126432	2.173983	2.203009
1.0600000	2.055726	2.123679	2.186792	2.237913	2.269237
1.0699999	2.109682	2.182041	2.249594	2.304588	2.338420
1.0799999	2.165567	2.242636	2.314973	2.374173	2.410745
1.0899999	2.223474	2.305581	2.383075	2.446845	2.486414
1.1000000	2.283500	2.370997	2.454053	2.522793	2.565645
1.1100000	2.345746	2.439010	2.528068	2.602220	2.648672
1.1200000	2.410318	2.509756	2.605295	2.685343	2.735749
1.1300000	2.477330	2.583377	2.685918	2.772397	2.827151
1.1400000	2.546897	2.660024	2.770133	2.863632	2.923174
1.1500000	2.619145	2.739854	2.858147	2.959318	3.024139
1.1600000	2.694200	2.823034	2.950181	3.059744	3.130395
1.1700000	2.772198	2.909739	3.046470	3.165220	3.242320
1.1800000	2.853280	3.000152	3.147263	3.276079	3.360324
1.1899999	2.937593	3.094466	3.252822	3.392681	3.484853

$\alpha =$ .919999

Θ	K VALUES				
	.794250555	.868696860	.928444378	.971111163	.994996249
1.2000000	3.025290	3.192884	3.363427	3.515411	3.616393
1.2100000	3.116528	3.295615	3.479372	3.644681	3.755471
1.2200000	3.211473	3.402882	3.600969	3.780935	3.902662
1.2300000	3.310297	3.514913	3.728547	3.924649	4.058595
1.2400000	3.413174	3.631948	3.862451	4.076334	4.223956
1.2500000	3.520288	3.754234	4.003044	4.236539	4.399493
1.2599999	3.631823	3.882027	4.150707	4.405847	4.586028
1.2699999	3.747971	4.015590	4.305837	4.584887	4.784457
1.2799999	3.868925	4.155192	4.468847	4.774327	4.995765
1.2899999	3.994880	4.301110	4.640166	4.974881	5.221033
1.3000000	4.126035	4.453623	4.820239	5.187310	5.461448
1.3100000	4.262584	4.613008	5.009515	5.412412	5.718311
1.3200000	4.404723	4.779549	5.208460	5.651041	5.993059
1.3300000	4.552641	4.953522	5.417541	5.904094	6.287277
1.3400000	4.706523	5.135199	5.637229	6.172508	6.602711
1.3500000	4.866545	5.324841	5.867991	6.457264	6.941290
1.3600000	5.032868	5.522697	6.110282	6.759375	7.305149
1.3700000	5.205642	5.728996	6.364542	7.079885	7.696653
1.3799999	5.384995	5.943942	6.631185	7.419852	8.118425
1.3899999	5.571033	6.167714	6.910591	7.780343	8.573377
1.4000000	5.763837	6.400453	7.203096	8.162415	9.064754
1.4100000	5.963451	6.642253	7.508972	8.567079	9.596152
1.4200000	6.169889	6.893167	7.828428	8.995302	10.171593
1.4300000	6.383120	7.153189	8.161590	9.447956	10.795552
1.4400000	6.603071	7.422250	8.508485	9.925786	11.473010
1.4500000	6.829618	7.700213	8.869031	10.429372	12.209503
1.4600000	7.062582	7.986864	9.243023	10.959074	13.011145
1.4700000	7.301729	8.281911	9.630121	11.514990	13.884635
1.4800000	7.546767	8.584978	10.029840	12.096896	14.837197
1.4900000	7.797339	8.895600	10.441543	12.704195	15.876417
1.5000000	8.053035	9.213229	10.864440	13.335874	17.009900
1.5100000	8.313374	9.537224	11.297572	13.990446	18.244596
1.5200000	8.577826	9.866868	11.739840	14.665947	19.585764
1.5300000	8.845808	10.201364	12.189996	15.359918	21.035297
1.5400000	9.116686	10.539850	12.646663	16.069422	22.589502
1.5500000	9.389790	10.881403	13.108352	16.791091	24.236661
1.5600000	9.664414	11.225053	13.573487	17.521201	25.955251
1.5699999	9.939835	11.569802	14.040426	18.255766	27.714220
1.5707963	9.961780	11.597273	14.077638	18.314331	27.854937
1.5707963	9.961782	11.597292	14.077630	18.314321	27.854932

$\alpha =$ •929999

Θ	K VALUES				
	•009966711	•039469502	•087332193	•151646642	•229848846
•0000000	•000000	•000000	•000000	•000000	•000000
•0100000	•010000	•010000	•010000	•010000	•010000
•0200000	•020002	•020002	•020002	•020002	•020002
•0300000	•030008	•030008	•030008	•030009	•030009
•0400000	•040019	•040020	•040020	•040021	•040022
•0500000	•050039	•050039	•050040	•050041	•050043
•0600000	•060067	•060068	•060070	•060072	•060075
•0700000	•070107	•070108	•070111	•070115	•070119
•0800000	•080159	•080162	•080166	•080172	•080178
•0900000	•090227	•090231	•090237	•090245	•090254
•1000000	•100312	•100317	•100325	•100336	•100349
•1100000	•110416	•110423	•110433	•110448	•110465
•1200000	•120541	•120549	•120563	•120582	•120605
•1300000	•130688	•130699	•130717	•130741	•130770
•1400000	•140861	•140874	•140896	•140926	•140962
•1500000	•151060	•151077	•151104	•151140	•151185
•1600000	•161288	•161308	•161341	•161386	•161440
•1700000	•171547	•171571	•171611	•171664	•171729
•1800000	•181838	•181867	•181915	•181978	•182055
•1900000	•192165	•192199	•192255	•192330	•192421
•2000000	•202529	•202569	•202634	•202721	•202828
•2100000	•212932	•212978	•213054	•213155	•213279
•2200000	•223377	•223430	•223517	•223633	•223776
•2300000	•233865	•233926	•234025	•234159	•234322
•2400000	•244399	•244468	•244581	•244733	•244919
•2500000	•254981	•255059	•255187	•255360	•255570
•2600000	•265613	•265702	•265846	•266040	•266278
•2700000	•276298	•276398	•276560	•276778	•277045
•2800000	•287039	•287150	•287331	•287575	•287873
•2900000	•297836	•297960	•298162	•298434	•298766
•3000000	•308694	•308832	•309055	•309357	•309726
•3100000	•319615	•319767	•320014	•320348	•320757
•3200000	•330600	•330768	•331041	•331409	•331860
•3300000	•341653	•341838	•342138	•342543	•343040
•3400000	•352777	•352979	•353308	•353753	•354298
•3500000	•363974	•364195	•364555	•365042	•365639
•3600000	•375247	•375488	•375881	•376413	•377064
•3700000	•386598	•386861	•387289	•387868	•388579
•3800000	•398032	•398317	•398782	•399412	•400185
•3900000	•409550	•409859	•410364	•411047	•411886

$\alpha =$ •929999

Θ	K VALUES				
	•009966711	•039469502	•087332193	•151646642	•229848846
•4000000	•421155	•421490	•422036	•422776	•423685
•4100000	•432852	•433214	•433804	•434604	•435587
•4200000	•444643	•445033	•445670	•446533	•447595
•4300000	•456531	•456951	•457637	•458568	•459712
•4400000	•468520	•468972	•469710	•470711	•471943
•4500000	•480613	•481098	•481891	•482966	•484291
•4600000	•492814	•493335	•494184	•495338	•496760
•4700000	•505127	•505684	•506594	•507831	•509355
•4800000	•517555	•518151	•519124	•520447	•522080
•4900000	•530102	•530738	•531779	•533193	•534939
•5000000	•542773	•543451	•544561	•546071	•547937
•5100000	•555571	•556294	•557477	•559087	•561078
•5200000	•568500	•569269	•570529	•572245	•574367
•5300000	•581565	•582383	•583724	•585550	•587810
•5400000	•594770	•595640	•597064	•599006	•601411
•5500000	•608121	•609044	•610556	•612619	•615175
•5600000	•621621	•622600	•624204	•626393	•629109
•5700000	•635276	•636313	•638013	•640335	•643217
•5800000	•649091	•650188	•651989	•654450	•657506
•5900000	•663070	•664232	•666138	•668743	•671981
•6000000	•677221	•678448	•680464	•683220	•686648
•6100000	•691547	•692844	•694973	•697888	•701515
•6200000	•706055	•707424	•709673	•712752	•716587
•6300000	•720752	•722195	•724568	•727819	•731872
•6400000	•735642	•737164	•739666	•743097	•747376
•6500000	•750733	•752336	•754974	•758591	•763108
•6600000	•766031	•767719	•770497	•774309	•779074
•6700000	•781543	•783319	•786244	•790259	•795282
•6800000	•797277	•799145	•802221	•806449	•811741
•6899999	•813239	•815202	•818438	•822886	•828459
•7000000	•829438	•831501	•834901	•839579	•845445
•7100000	•845881	•848047	•851619	•856537	•862708
•7200000	•862577	•864850	•868601	•873768	•880257
•7300000	•879534	•881919	•885855	•891282	•898103
•7400000	•896761	•899262	•903392	•909088	•916256
•7500000	•914268	•916889	•921220	•927198	•934725
•7600000	•932064	•934811	•939350	•945620	•953523
•7700000	•950159	•953036	•957793	•964367	•972661
•7800000	•968565	•971576	•976558	•983449	•992151
•7899999	•987290	•990442	•995659	1•002879	1•012004

$\alpha =$ •929999

θ	K VALUES				
	•009966711	•039469502	•087332193	•151646642	•229848846
•8000000	1•006348	1•009646	1•015106	1•022668	1•032236
•8100000	1•025750	1•029199	1•034912	1•042830	1•052858
•8200000	1•045508	1•049114	1•055090	1•063378	1•073884
•8300000	1•065634	1•069403	1•075652	1•084326	1•095331
•8400000	1•086143	1•090082	1•096614	1•105688	1•117212
•8500000	1•107049	1•111163	1•117990	1•127480	1•139544
•8600000	1•128365	1•132661	1•139795	1•149717	1•162344
•8700000	1•150107	1•154593	1•162044	1•172417	1•185629
•8799999	1•172291	1•176973	1•184755	1•195595	1•209417
•8899999	1•194934	1•199820	1•207945	1•219271	1•233727
•9000000	1•218053	1•223150	1•231631	1•243463	1•258580
•9100000	1•241665	1•246983	1•255834	1•268191	1•283996
•9200000	1•265791	1•271337	1•280572	1•293476	1•309996
•9300000	1•290449	1•296232	1•305866	1•319338	1•336603
•9400000	1•315661	1•321690	1•331739	1•345801	1•363842
•9500000	1•341449	1•347732	1•358212	1•372888	1•391737
•9600000	1•367834	1•374383	1•385310	1•400625	1•420314
•9699999	1•394841	1•401665	1•413058	1•429036	1•449600
•9799999	1•422495	1•429605	1•441480	1•458149	1•479625
•9899999	1•450822	1•458229	1•470606	1•487993	1•510418
1•0000000	1•479850	1•487565	1•500464	1•518597	1•542011
1•0100000	1•509607	1•517642	1•531083	1•549993	1•574436
1•0200000	1•540123	1•548490	1•562495	1•582213	1•607728
1•0300000	1•571430	1•580143	1•594733	1•615292	1•641923
1•0400000	1•603561	1•612633	1•627832	1•649266	1•677061
1•0500000	1•636551	1•645996	1•661828	1•684172	1•713179
1•0600000	1•670436	1•680269	1•696759	1•720051	1•750321
1•0699999	1•705256	1•715491	1•732666	1•756944	1•788530
1•0799999	1•741049	1•751704	1•769591	1•794895	1•827853
1•0899999	1•777859	1•788949	1•807577	1•833950	1•868337
1•1000000	1•815729	1•827272	1•846671	1•874157	1•910034
1•1100000	1•854706	1•866720	1•886921	1•915566	1•952997
1•1200000	1•894839	1•907343	1•928378	1•958230	1•997282
1•1300000	1•936179	1•949193	1•971096	2•002206	2•042947
1•1400000	1•978779	1•992323	2•015131	2•047551	2•090054
1•1500000	2•022695	2•036792	2•060541	2•094326	2•138667
1•1600000	2•067987	2•082658	2•107388	2•142595	2•188854
1•1700000	2•114716	2•129985	2•155736	2•192425	2•240685
1•1800000	2•162945	2•178837	2•205653	2•243887	2•294234
1•1899999	2•212743	2•229284	2•257207	2•297052	2•349578

$\alpha =$ .929999

Θ	K VALUES				
	.009966711	.039469502	.087332193	.151646642	.229848846
1.2000000	2.264180	2.281396	2.310474	2.351999	2.406798
1.2100000	2.317328	2.335247	2.365528	2.408805	2.465977
1.2200000	2.372264	2.390916	2.422450	2.467553	2.527203
1.2300000	2.429066	2.448481	2.481323	2.528330	2.590565
1.2400000	2.487816	2.508027	2.542230	2.591224	2.656158
1.2500000	2.548599	2.569639	2.605262	2.656327	2.724080
1.2599999	2.611503	2.633406	2.670509	2.723735	2.794429
1.2699999	2.676616	2.699419	2.738064	2.793545	2.867309
1.2799999	2.744031	2.767771	2.808024	2.865856	2.942825
1.2899999	2.813841	2.838558	2.880487	2.940770	3.021085
1.3000000	2.886141	2.911876	2.955552	3.018391	3.102197
1.3100000	2.961026	2.987821	3.033317	3.098821	3.186270
1.3200000	3.038591	3.066490	3.113882	3.182165	3.273413
1.3300000	3.118931	3.147980	3.197347	3.268525	3.363736
1.3400000	3.202139	3.232385	3.283808	3.358002	3.457344
1.3500000	3.288304	3.319795	3.373359	3.450694	3.554340
1.3600000	3.377511	3.410297	3.466088	3.546692	3.654821
1.3700000	3.469838	3.503971	3.562078	3.646082	3.758877
1.3799999	3.565358	3.600889	3.661403	3.748942	3.866591
1.3899999	3.664130	3.701114	3.764126	3.855338	3.978033
1.4000000	3.766205	3.804696	3.870301	3.965324	4.093259
1.4100000	3.871616	3.911668	3.979961	4.078937	4.212307
1.4200000	3.980381	4.022050	4.093126	4.196196	4.335200
1.4300000	4.092500	4.135840	4.209795	4.317101	4.461935
1.4400000	4.207947	4.253014	4.329942	4.441624	4.592485
1.4500000	4.326676	4.373523	4.453517	4.569715	4.726795
1.4600000	4.448611	4.497291	4.580442	4.701290	4.864780
1.4700000	4.573647	4.624210	4.710608	4.836237	5.006318
1.4800000	4.701648	4.754144	4.843872	4.974408	5.151255
1.4900000	4.832448	4.886922	4.980060	5.115621	5.299399
1.5000000	4.965846	5.022342	5.118963	5.259659	5.450521
1.5100000	5.101608	5.160164	5.260336	5.406267	5.604353
1.5200000	5.239472	5.300122	5.403905	5.555158	5.760592
1.5300000	5.379142	5.441916	5.549361	5.706014	5.918902
1.5400000	5.520299	5.585221	5.696371	5.858487	6.078916
1.5500000	5.662600	5.729690	5.844576	6.012203	6.240241
1.5600000	5.805684	5.874954	5.993600	6.166771	6.402464
1.5699999	5.949178	6.020636	6.143053	6.321785	6.565158
1.5707963	5.960612	6.032243	6.154961	6.334136	6.578121
1.5707963	5.960606	6.032237	6.154955	6.334130	6.578115

$\alpha =$ .929999

Θ	K VALUES				
	.318821117	.415016431	.514599755	.613601043	.708073407
.0000000	.000000	.000000	.000000	.000000	.000000
.0100000	.010000	.010000	.010000	.010000	.010000
.0200000	.020002	.020003	.020003	.020003	.020003
.0300000	.030009	.030010	.030010	.030011	.030011
.0400000	.040023	.040024	.040025	.040026	.040027
.0500000	.050045	.050047	.050049	.050051	.050053
.0600000	.060078	.060082	.060085	.060089	.060092
.0700000	.070124	.070130	.070136	.070141	.070147
.0800000	.080186	.080194	.080203	.080211	.080219
.0900000	.090265	.090277	.090289	.090301	.090313
.1000000	.100364	.100380	.100397	.100414	.100429
.1100000	.110485	.110507	.110529	.110551	.110572
.1200000	.120630	.120658	.120687	.120716	.120744
.1300000	.130802	.130838	.130875	.130912	.130947
.1400000	.141003	.141048	.141094	.141140	.141184
.1500000	.151236	.151291	.151348	.151404	.151459
.1600000	.161501	.161568	.161638	.161707	.161773
.1700000	.171803	.171884	.171967	.172050	.172130
.1800000	.182144	.182239	.182339	.182438	.182532
.1900000	.192525	.192638	.192755	.192871	.192983
.2000000	.202949	.203081	.203218	.203355	.203486
.2100000	.213420	.213573	.213732	.213891	.214043
.2200000	.223938	.224115	.224298	.224482	.224657
.2300000	.234508	.234710	.234921	.235131	.235333
.2400000	.245131	.245362	.245602	.245842	.246072
.2500000	.255811	.256072	.256345	.256617	.256878
.2600000	.266549	.266845	.267152	.267460	.267755
.2700000	.277350	.277682	.278028	.278374	.278706
.2800000	.288215	.288586	.288974	.289361	.289734
.2900000	.299147	.299561	.299994	.300427	.300843
.3000000	.310149	.310610	.311091	.311573	.312037
.3100000	.321225	.321736	.322269	.322804	.323318
.3200000	.332378	.332942	.333531	.334122	.334692
.3300000	.343609	.344231	.344880	.345533	.346161
.3400000	.354924	.355607	.356321	.357039	.357731
.3500000	.366324	.367072	.367856	.368644	.369404
.3600000	.377813	.378632	.379489	.380352	.381185
.3700000	.389395	.390289	.391225	.392168	.393079
.3800000	.401074	.402046	.403067	.404095	.405089
.3900000	.412851	.413909	.415019	.416138	.417221

$\alpha =$ .929999

Θ	K VALUES				
	.318821117	.415016431	.514599755	.613601043	.708073407
.4000000	.424732	.425880	.427085	.428301	.429478
.4100000	.436720	.437963	.439269	.440588	.441867
.4200000	.448819	.450163	.451576	.453005	.454391
.4300000	.461033	.462484	.464011	.465556	.467056
.4400000	.473366	.474930	.476577	.478246	.479867
.4500000	.485822	.487505	.489280	.491080	.492829
.4600000	.498405	.500214	.502125	.504063	.505949
.4700000	.511119	.513063	.515116	.517200	.519231
.4800000	.523970	.526054	.528258	.530498	.532682
.4900000	.536962	.539195	.541558	.543962	.546308
.5000000	.550100	.552489	.555020	.557597	.560116
.5100000	.563388	.565942	.568650	.571410	.574111
.5200000	.576832	.579559	.582454	.585408	.588300
.5300000	.590437	.593346	.596438	.599596	.602692
.5400000	.604208	.607309	.610608	.613981	.617292
.5500000	.618152	.621454	.624971	.628571	.632109
.5600000	.632273	.635787	.639533	.643372	.647150
.5700000	.646577	.650314	.654301	.658392	.662423
.5800000	.661072	.665041	.669282	.673640	.677938
.5900000	.675763	.679977	.684484	.689121	.693701
.6000000	.690657	.695127	.699915	.704847	.709724
.6100000	.705760	.710500	.715582	.720823	.726014
.6200000	.721080	.726102	.731493	.737060	.742582
.6300000	.736624	.741941	.747657	.753567	.759438
.6400000	.752399	.758026	.764082	.770354	.776592
.6500000	.768414	.774365	.780778	.787430	.794055
.6600000	.784676	.790967	.797755	.804805	.811839
.6700000	.801194	.807840	.815021	.822491	.829955
.6800000	.817976	.824995	.832588	.840499	.848417
.6899999	.835032	.842440	.850466	.858841	.867236
.7000000	.852371	.860186	.868666	.877528	.886426
.7100000	.870002	.878244	.887199	.896573	.906002
.7200000	.887937	.896624	.906077	.915989	.925977
.7300000	.906184	.915337	.925313	.935790	.946366
.7400000	.924755	.934396	.944920	.955990	.967186
.7500000	.943662	.953813	.964910	.976604	.988454
.7600000	.962917	.973600	.985298	.997648	1.010186
.7700000	.982531	.993771	1.006099	1.019137	1.032400
.7800000	1.002517	1.014339	1.027327	1.041088	1.055115
.7899999	1.022889	1.035320	1.048999	1.063520	1.078351

$\alpha =$ .929999

Θ	K VALUES				
	.318821117	.415016431	.514599755	.613601043	.708073407
.8000000	1.043661	1.056728	1.071131	1.086450	1.102129
.8100000	1.064846	1.078578	1.093739	1.109896	1.126469
.8200000	1.086461	1.100887	1.116843	1.133881	1.151395
.8300000	1.108520	1.123672	1.140460	1.158423	1.176929
.8400000	1.131041	1.146951	1.164611	1.183545	1.203098
.8500000	1.154040	1.170742	1.189315	1.209270	1.229925
.8600000	1.177534	1.195065	1.214595	1.235622	1.257439
.8700000	1.201544	1.219940	1.240471	1.262626	1.285667
.8799999	1.226088	1.245387	1.266969	1.290307	1.314640
.8899999	1.251186	1.271430	1.294111	1.318693	1.344388
.9000000	1.276860	1.298091	1.321924	1.347813	1.374944
.9100000	1.303132	1.325394	1.350434	1.377696	1.406343
.9200000	1.330026	1.353365	1.379669	1.408375	1.438619
.9300000	1.357564	1.382030	1.409658	1.439882	1.471812
.9400000	1.385774	1.411416	1.440432	1.472251	1.505960
.9500000	1.414682	1.441554	1.472024	1.505519	1.541105
.9600000	1.444315	1.472472	1.504466	1.539723	1.577291
.9699999	1.474703	1.504203	1.537794	1.574904	1.614563
.9799999	1.505877	1.536780	1.572044	1.611104	1.652971
.9899999	1.537868	1.570239	1.607257	1.648365	1.692563
1.0000000	1.570711	1.604615	1.643472	1.686735	1.733396
1.0100000	1.604439	1.639948	1.680731	1.726262	1.775522
1.0200000	1.639092	1.676277	1.719081	1.766995	1.819003
1.0300000	1.674707	1.713644	1.758567	1.808990	1.863899
1.0400000	1.711325	1.752095	1.799238	1.852301	1.910276
1.0500000	1.748989	1.791676	1.841148	1.896987	1.958203
1.0600000	1.787744	1.832436	1.884350	1.943111	2.007752
1.0699999	1.827637	1.874425	1.928900	1.990738	2.058999
1.0799999	1.868716	1.917698	1.974860	2.039934	2.112023
1.0899999	1.911035	1.962311	2.022291	2.090773	2.166909
1.1000000	1.954648	2.008325	2.071261	2.143330	2.223745
1.1100000	1.999611	2.055799	2.121837	2.197682	2.282624
1.1200000	2.045985	2.104801	2.174092	2.253914	2.343643
1.1300000	2.093831	2.155398	2.228104	2.312112	2.406905
1.1400000	2.143217	2.207662	2.283951	2.372369	2.472518
1.1500000	2.194210	2.261668	2.341718	2.434778	2.540595
1.1600000	2.246884	2.317496	2.401492	2.499442	2.611254
1.1700000	2.301313	2.375227	2.463364	2.566465	2.684621
1.1800000	2.357577	2.434947	2.527432	2.635957	2.760826
1.1899999	2.415758	2.496748	2.593796	2.708033	2.840004

$\alpha =$ .929999

Θ	K VALUES				
	.318821117	.415016431	.514599755	.613601043	.708073407
1.2000000	2.475943	2.560722	2.662560	2.782813	2.922299
1.2100000	2.538221	2.626967	2.733833	2.860422	3.007859
1.2200000	2.602685	2.695586	2.807728	2.940991	3.096839
1.2300000	2.669433	2.766683	2.884365	3.024655	3.189402
1.2400000	2.738565	2.840370	2.963864	3.111554	3.285713
1.2500000	2.810185	2.916758	3.046354	3.201834	3.385946
1.2599999	2.884400	2.995966	3.131963	3.295644	3.490281
1.2699999	2.961320	3.078113	3.220826	3.393138	3.598902
1.2799999	3.041059	3.163322	3.313081	3.494474	3.711996
1.2899999	3.123730	3.251718	3.408867	3.599814	3.829758
1.3000000	3.209451	3.343429	3.508326	3.709320	3.952383
1.3100000	3.298338	3.438582	3.611600	3.823155	4.080067
1.3200000	3.390508	3.537304	3.718832	3.941485	4.213007
1.3300000	3.486078	3.639724	3.830164	4.064472	4.351401
1.3400000	3.585162	3.745964	3.945734	4.192276	4.495440
1.3500000	3.687869	3.856145	4.065677	4.325051	4.645311
1.3600000	3.794303	3.970380	4.190119	4.462945	4.801191
1.3700000	3.904562	4.088776	4.319179	4.606095	4.963246
1.3799999	4.018733	4.211427	4.452964	4.754622	5.131627
1.3899999	4.136891	4.338417	4.591565	4.908635	5.306463
1.4000000	4.259098	4.469812	4.735059	5.068222	5.487862
1.4100000	4.385393	4.605657	4.883495	5.233440	5.675899
1.4200000	4.515801	4.745976	5.036902	5.404325	5.870618
1.4300000	4.650320	4.890770	5.195279	5.580876	6.072023
1.4400000	4.788921	5.040006	5.358592	5.763057	6.280073
1.4500000	4.931544	5.193620	5.526771	5.950788	6.494679
1.4600000	5.078098	5.351513	5.699705	6.143943	6.715695
1.4700000	5.228454	5.513544	5.877238	6.342348	6.942916
1.4800000	5.382447	5.679534	6.059172	6.545775	7.176077
1.4900000	5.539871	5.849260	6.245257	6.753941	7.414844
1.5000000	5.700482	6.022454	6.435199	6.966510	7.658821
1.5100000	5.863992	6.198804	6.628649	7.183085	7.907540
1.5200000	6.030078	6.377959	6.825218	7.403221	8.160474
1.5300000	6.198380	6.559526	7.024468	7.626419	8.417036
1.5400000	6.368505	6.743079	7.225926	7.852138	8.676582
1.5500000	6.540033	6.928158	7.429081	8.079797	8.938427
1.5600000	6.712522	7.114284	7.633400	8.308784	9.201844
1.5699999	6.885514	7.300957	7.838328	8.538466	9.466086
1.5707963	6.899297	7.315831	7.854656	8.556767	9.487141
1.5707963	6.899291	7.315825	7.854651	8.556763	9.487139

$\alpha =$ .929999

Θ	K VALUES				
	.794250555	.868696860	.928444378	.971111163	.994996249
.0000000	.000000	.000000	.000000	.000000	.000000
.0100000	.010000	.010000	.010000	.010000	.010000
.0200000	.020003	.020003	.020003	.020003	.020003
.0300000	.030011	.030012	.030012	.030012	.030012
.0400000	.040028	.040029	.040029	.040030	.040030
.0500000	.050055	.050056	.050058	.050059	.050059
.0600000	.060095	.060098	.060100	.060102	.060103
.0700000	.070152	.070156	.070159	.070162	.070163
.0800000	.080227	.080233	.080238	.080242	.080244
.0900000	.090323	.090332	.090340	.090345	.090348
.1000000	.100444	.100456	.100467	.100474	.100478
.1100000	.110592	.110608	.110622	.110631	.110637
.1200000	.120769	.120791	.120808	.120821	.120828
.1300000	.130979	.131007	.131029	.131045	.131054
.1400000	.141225	.141259	.141287	.141307	.141318
.1500000	.151508	.151551	.151586	.151610	.151624
.1600000	.161833	.161886	.161928	.161958	.161975
.1700000	.172202	.172265	.172316	.172352	.172373
.1800000	.182619	.182694	.182754	.182797	.182822
.1900000	.193086	.193174	.193245	.193296	.193325
.2000000	.203605	.203709	.203793	.203852	.203886
.2100000	.214182	.214303	.214400	.214469	.214508
.2200000	.224818	.224958	.225070	.225150	.225195
.2300000	.235517	.235677	.235806	.235899	.235950
.2400000	.246283	.246466	.246613	.246719	.246778
.2500000	.257118	.257326	.257493	.257613	.257681
.2600000	.268026	.268261	.268451	.268587	.268663
.2700000	.279011	.279276	.279490	.279643	.279729
.2800000	.290077	.290374	.290614	.290786	.290882
.2900000	.301226	.301558	.301827	.302019	.302127
.3000000	.312463	.312834	.313133	.313347	.313468
.3100000	.323792	.324204	.324536	.324775	.324909
.3200000	.335216	.335673	.336041	.336306	.336454
.3300000	.346740	.347245	.347652	.347945	.348109
.3400000	.358368	.358924	.359374	.359696	.359878
.3500000	.370105	.370716	.371210	.371565	.371765
.3600000	.381954	.382624	.383167	.383557	.383776
.3700000	.393920	.394654	.395248	.395676	.395916
.3800000	.406007	.406810	.407460	.407927	.408191
.3900000	.418222	.419097	.419807	.420317	.420604

$\alpha =$ .929999

Θ	K VALUES				
	.794250555	.868696860	.928444378	.971111163	.994996249
.4000000	.430568	.431521	.432294	.432850	.433164
.4100000	.443050	.444087	.444928	.445533	.445874
.4200000	.455675	.456800	.457713	.458372	.458742
.4300000	.468447	.469666	.470657	.471371	.471774
.4400000	.481371	.482691	.483765	.484539	.484975
.4500000	.494455	.495882	.497043	.497881	.498354
.4600000	.507702	.509243	.510498	.511405	.511916
.4700000	.521121	.522783	.524138	.525117	.525669
.4800000	.534717	.536508	.537968	.539024	.539620
.4900000	.548496	.550424	.551997	.553135	.553778
.5000000	.562466	.564539	.566232	.567458	.568150
.5100000	.576633	.578861	.580681	.582000	.582745
.5200000	.591006	.593396	.595352	.596770	.597572
.5300000	.605590	.608154	.610254	.611777	.612639
.5400000	.620395	.623143	.625396	.627031	.627956
.5500000	.635429	.638372	.640786	.642540	.643533
.5600000	.650699	.653849	.656435	.658315	.659381
.5700000	.666215	.669583	.672352	.674367	.675509
.5800000	.681985	.685586	.688549	.690706	.691930
.5900000	.698020	.701866	.705035	.707344	.708654
.6000000	.714329	.718436	.721822	.724292	.725695
.6100000	.730922	.735304	.738922	.741564	.743064
.6200000	.747810	.752484	.756347	.759171	.760776
.6300000	.765004	.769987	.774111	.777128	.778844
.6400000	.782515	.787825	.792226	.795448	.797282
.6500000	.800356	.806013	.810706	.814147	.816107
.6600000	.818539	.824562	.829567	.833240	.835333
.6700000	.837076	.843489	.848824	.852743	.854979
.6800000	.855983	.862807	.868492	.872673	.875060
.6899999	.875272	.882531	.888589	.893049	.895597
.7000000	.894959	.902680	.909132	.913889	.916609
.7100000	.915059	.923268	.930140	.935212	.938115
.7200000	.935588	.944315	.951631	.957039	.960137
.7300000	.956563	.965839	.973628	.979393	.982699
.7400000	.978001	.987858	.996150	1.002295	1.005823
.7500000	.999922	1.010395	1.019220	1.025771	1.029534
.7600000	1.022344	1.033470	1.042862	1.049844	1.053860
.7700000	1.045288	1.057105	1.067100	1.074542	1.078827
.7800000	1.068774	1.081325	1.091961	1.099894	1.104466
.7899999	1.092826	1.106154	1.117472	1.125927	1.130807

$\alpha =$ .929999

Θ	K VALUES				
	.794250555	.868696860	.928444378	.971111163	.994996249
.8000000	1.117465	1.131618	1.143662	1.152675	1.157883
.8100000	1.142716	1.157745	1.170560	1.180169	1.185728
.8200000	1.168605	1.184562	1.198200	1.208444	1.214379
.8300000	1.195158	1.212101	1.226614	1.237538	1.243874
.8400000	1.222404	1.240393	1.255839	1.267488	1.274256
.8500000	1.250371	1.269471	1.285912	1.298337	1.305566
.8600000	1.279091	1.299371	1.316872	1.330128	1.337851
.8700000	1.308595	1.330130	1.348762	1.362906	1.371161
.8799999	1.338919	1.361786	1.381625	1.396721	1.405546
.8899999	1.370097	1.394382	1.415509	1.431624	1.441062
.9000000	1.402168	1.427959	1.450463	1.467672	1.477768
.9100000	1.435170	1.462565	1.486539	1.504921	1.515725
.9200000	1.469146	1.498246	1.523793	1.543433	1.555001
.9300000	1.504138	1.535055	1.562263	1.583276	1.595666
.9400000	1.540194	1.573044	1.602071	1.624518	1.637795
.9500000	1.577361	1.612271	1.643225	1.667235	1.681469
.9600000	1.615691	1.652796	1.685813	1.711506	1.726773
.9699999	1.655237	1.694682	1.729910	1.757415	1.773801
.9799999	1.696056	1.737996	1.775596	1.805054	1.822649
.9899999	1.738207	1.782809	1.822953	1.854519	1.873423
1.0000000	1.781754	1.829197	1.872072	1.905912	1.926237
1.0100000	1.826763	1.877238	1.923046	1.959344	1.981209
1.0200000	1.873304	1.927016	1.975977	2.014932	2.038471
1.0300000	1.921449	1.978621	2.030972	2.072802	2.098162
1.0400000	1.971278	2.032147	2.088145	2.133089	2.160430
1.0500000	2.022872	2.087694	2.147617	2.195937	2.225438
1.0600000	2.076318	2.145366	2.209519	2.261500	2.293358
1.0699999	2.131706	2.205277	2.273988	2.329945	2.364377
1.0799999	2.189133	2.267544	2.341172	2.401450	2.438698
1.0899999	2.248700	2.332294	2.411226	2.476206	2.516536
1.1000000	2.310516	2.399660	2.484320	2.554418	2.598130
1.1100000	2.374691	2.469781	2.560630	2.636307	2.683730
1.1200000	2.441344	2.542807	2.640346	2.722109	2.773614
1.1300000	2.510602	2.618897	2.723672	2.812082	2.868080
1.1400000	2.582596	2.698216	2.810823	2.906498	2.967451
1.1500000	2.657464	2.780943	2.902030	3.005656	3.072080
1.1600000	2.735353	2.867263	2.997539	3.109872	3.182347
1.1700000	2.816415	2.957374	3.097611	3.219492	3.298670
1.1800000	2.900813	3.051484	3.202525	3.334885	3.421499
1.1899999	2.988715	3.149813	3.312577	3.456451	3.551330

$\alpha =$ .929999

Θ	K VALUES				
	.794250555	.868696860	.928444378	.971111163	.994996249
1.2000000	3.080298	3.252593	3.428085	3.584621	3.688700
1.2100000	3.175747	3.360066	3.549382	3.719857	3.834197
1.2200000	3.275256	3.472488	3.676823	3.862660	3.988463
1.2300000	3.379027	3.590128	3.810788	4.013569	4.152203
1.2400000	3.487269	3.713266	3.951675	4.173165	4.326187
1.2500000	3.600201	3.842194	4.099905	4.342072	4.511261
1.2599999	3.718048	3.977219	4.255924	4.520962	4.708351
1.2699999	3.841043	4.118656	4.420200	4.710557	4.918479
1.2799999	3.969425	4.266832	4.593221	4.911632	5.142766
1.2899999	4.103438	4.422085	4.775501	5.125017	5.382446
1.3000000	4.243333	4.584761	4.967574	5.351602	5.638883
1.3100000	4.389359	4.755209	5.169987	5.592329	5.913575
1.3200000	4.541770	4.933785	5.383310	5.848205	6.208182
1.3300000	4.700818	5.120848	5.608123	6.120298	6.524538
1.3400000	4.866750	5.316752	5.845014	6.409732	6.864675
1.3500000	5.039808	5.521844	6.094576	6.717688	7.230840
1.3600000	5.220223	5.736463	6.357396	7.045396	7.625529
1.3700000	5.408211	5.960928	6.634047	7.394132	8.051513
1.3799999	5.603970	6.195537	6.925081	7.765199	8.511870
1.3899999	5.807672	6.440556	7.231018	8.159922	9.010026
1.4000000	6.019465	6.696216	7.552331	8.579623	9.549803
1.4100000	6.239450	6.962693	7.889423	9.025587	10.135438
1.4200000	6.467695	7.240114	8.242627	9.499050	10.771676
1.4300000	6.704217	7.528537	8.612179	10.001148	11.463795
1.4400000	6.948975	7.827944	8.998199	10.532874	12.217672
1.4500000	7.201868	8.138232	9.400675	11.095026	13.039825
1.4600000	7.462723	8.459201	9.819443	11.688149	13.937454
1.4700000	7.731294	8.790551	10.254169	12.312466	14.918430
1.4800000	8.007257	9.131867	10.704337	12.967816	15.991229
1.4900000	8.290204	9.482621	11.169233	13.653581	17.164732
1.5000000	8.579645	9.842170	11.647943	14.368631	18.447826
1.5100000	8.875001	10.209745	12.139335	15.111248	19.848612
1.5200000	9.175618	10.584468	12.642084	15.879127	21.373202
1.5300000	9.480764	10.965354	13.154669	16.669341	23.023775
1.5400000	9.789639	11.351320	13.675394	17.478370	24.796003
1.5500000	10.101385	11.741201	14.202411	18.302153	26.676234
1.5600000	10.415098	12.133764	14.733749	19.136182	28.639440
1.5699999	10.729841	12.527734	15.267355	19.975622	30.649540
1.5707963	10.754921	12.559128	15.309882	20.042553	30.810360
1.5707963	10.754923	12.559145	15.310251	20.042524	30.810306

$\alpha =$ .939999

Θ	K VALUES				
	.009966711	.039469502	.087332193	.151646642	.229848846
.0000000	.000000	.000000	.000000	.000000	.000000
.0100000	.010000	.010000	.010000	.010000	.010000
.0200000	.020002	.020002	.020002	.020002	.020002
.0300000	.030008	.030008	.030008	.030009	.030009
.0400000	.040020	.040020	.040021	.040021	.040022
.0500000	.050039	.050040	.050041	.050042	.050044
.0600000	.060068	.060069	.060070	.060073	.060076
.0700000	.070108	.070109	.070112	.070116	.070120
.0800000	.080161	.080164	.080168	.080173	.080180
.0900000	.090230	.090233	.090239	.090247	.090257
.1000000	.100316	.100321	.100329	.100339	.100352
.1100000	.110421	.110427	.110438	.110452	.110470
.1200000	.120547	.120555	.120569	.120588	.120610
.1300000	.130696	.130707	.130724	.130748	.130777
.1400000	.140870	.140884	.140906	.140935	.140972
.1500000	.151071	.151088	.151115	.151152	.151196
.1600000	.161302	.161322	.161355	.161400	.161454
.1700000	.171564	.171588	.171628	.171681	.171746
.1800000	.181859	.181888	.181935	.181998	.182076
.1900000	.192189	.192223	.192279	.192353	.192445
.2000000	.202557	.202597	.202662	.202749	.202855
.2100000	.212964	.213011	.213086	.213187	.213311
.2200000	.223414	.223467	.223554	.223671	.223813
.2300000	.233907	.233968	.234068	.234201	.234364
.2400000	.244447	.244517	.244630	.244782	.244968
.2500000	.255036	.255115	.255243	.255415	.255626
.2600000	.265675	.265764	.265908	.266103	.266341
.2700000	.276368	.276468	.276630	.276848	.277115
.2800000	.287117	.287229	.287410	.287654	.287952
.2900000	.297924	.298048	.298250	.298522	.298855
.3000000	.308792	.308930	.309153	.309456	.309825
.3100000	.319723	.319875	.320123	.320457	.320866
.3200000	.330720	.330888	.331161	.331530	.331981
.3300000	.341786	.341971	.342271	.342677	.343174
.3400000	.352923	.353126	.353455	.353900	.354446
.3500000	.364134	.364356	.364716	.365203	.365801
.3600000	.375423	.375664	.376057	.376590	.377242
.3700000	.386791	.387053	.387482	.388062	.388773
.3800000	.398241	.398527	.398993	.399623	.400397
.3900000	.409778	.410088	.410593	.411277	.412117

$\alpha =$ .939999

Θ	K VALUES				
	.009966711	.039469502	.087332193	.151646642	.229848846
.4000000	.421404	.421739	.422286	.423027	.423937
.4100000	.433122	.433484	.434075	.434876	.435860
.4200000	.444935	.445326	.445964	.446828	.447891
.4300000	.456847	.457268	.457955	.458887	.460033
.4400000	.468862	.469314	.470053	.471056	.472290
.4500000	.480982	.481468	.482262	.483339	.484665
.4600000	.493212	.493733	.494584	.495740	.497164
.4700000	.505556	.506113	.507025	.508263	.509790
.4800000	.518016	.518613	.519588	.520913	.522548
.4900000	.530598	.531235	.532277	.533693	.535442
.5000000	.543304	.543984	.545096	.546609	.548477
.5100000	.556140	.556865	.558050	.559663	.561658
.5200000	.569110	.569881	.571144	.572863	.574989
.5300000	.582218	.583038	.584381	.586211	.588476
.5400000	.595469	.596341	.597768	.599714	.602123
.5500000	.608868	.609793	.611308	.613375	.615937
.5600000	.622419	.623400	.625008	.627202	.629923
.5700000	.636127	.637167	.638871	.641198	.644087
.5800000	.649998	.651099	.652904	.655371	.658434
.5900000	.664038	.665202	.667113	.669725	.672971
.6000000	.678251	.679482	.681503	.684266	.687704
.6100000	.692644	.693945	.696080	.699002	.702640
.6200000	.707223	.708596	.710851	.713938	.717785
.6300000	.721993	.723441	.725821	.729082	.733147
.6400000	.736962	.738489	.740999	.744440	.748733
.6500000	.752135	.753744	.756390	.760019	.764550
.6600000	.767521	.769214	.772002	.775827	.780607
.6700000	.783125	.784907	.787842	.791872	.796912
.6800000	.798956	.800830	.803918	.808161	.813472
.6899999	.815020	.816991	.820239	.824704	.830297
.7000000	.831327	.833398	.836812	.841508	.847397
.7100000	.847884	.850059	.853646	.858583	.864780
.7200000	.864701	.866984	.870750	.875939	.882456
.7300000	.881785	.884180	.888134	.893584	.900435
.7400000	.899146	.901659	.905807	.911529	.918729
.7500000	.916795	.919429	.923780	.929785	.937348
.7600000	.934741	.937501	.942062	.948363	.956304
.7700000	.952994	.955885	.960666	.967273	.975609
.7800000	.971566	.974594	.979602	.986528	.995276
.7899999	.990469	.993638	.998882	1.006141	1.015317

$\alpha =$ •939999

θ	K VALUES				
	•009966711	•039469502	•087332193	•151646642	•229848846
•8000000	1•009713	1•013029	1•018520	1•026124	1•035746
•8100000	1•029312	1•032781	1•038527	1•046491	1•056577
•8200000	1•049278	1•052905	1•058917	1•067256	1•077826
•8300000	1•069625	1•073417	1•079705	1•088433	1•099507
•8400000	1•090367	1•094330	1•100905	1•110038	1•121637
•8500000	1•111519	1•115660	1•122533	1•132087	1•144233
•8600000	1•133096	1•137422	1•144605	1•154597	1•167312
•8700000	1•155115	1•159633	1•167137	1•177585	1•190893
•8799999	1•177592	1•182309	1•190148	1•201069	1•214995
•8899999	1•200545	1•205469	1•213656	1•225070	1•239639
•9000000	1•223993	1•229131	1•237680	1•249606	1•264845
•9100000	1•247955	1•253316	1•262240	1•274699	1•290636
•9200000	1•272450	1•278043	1•287357	1•300372	1•317035
•9300000	1•297501	1•303335	1•313055	1•326646	1•344066
•9400000	1•323130	1•329214	1•339355	1•353547	1•371756
•9500000	1•349361	1•355704	1•366283	1•381099	1•400130
•9600000	1•376217	1•382829	1•393864	1•409331	1•429216
•9699999	1•403724	1•410617	1•422126	1•438268	1•459045
•9799999	1•431910	1•439095	1•451096	1•467942	1•489648
•9899999	1•460804	1•468291	1•480804	1•498382	1•521057
1•0000000	1•490435	1•498236	1•511282	1•529622	1•553306
1•0100000	1•520834	1•528962	1•542562	1•561696	1•586431
1•0200000	1•552034	1•560503	1•574678	1•594639	1•620470
1•0300000	1•584071	1•592894	1•607668	1•628489	1•655463
1•0400000	1•616982	1•626172	1•641570	1•663287	1•691452
1•0500000	1•650803	1•660376	1•676423	1•699073	1•728481
1•0600000	1•685577	1•695548	1•712270	1•735893	1•766597
1•0699999	1•721346	1•731730	1•749156	1•773792	1•805848
1•0799999	1•758155	1•768970	1•787128	1•812820	1•846286
1•0899999	1•796051	1•807315	1•826236	1•853027	1•887965
1•1000000	1•835085	1•846816	1•866531	1•894470	1•930944
1•1100000	1•875309	1•887526	1•908069	1•937203	1•975281
1•1200000	1•916779	1•929502	1•950907	1•981288	2•021041
1•1300000	1•959552	1•972802	1•995106	2•026789	2•068290
1•1400000	2•003691	2•017491	2•040732	2•073772	2•117098
1•1500000	2•049261	2•063634	2•087852	2•122308	2•167542
1•1600000	2•096329	2•111299	2•136536	2•172471	2•219697
1•1700000	2•144969	2•160561	2•186861	2•224339	2•273648
1•1800000	2•195255	2•211497	2•238906	2•277994	2•329480
1•1899999	2•247267	2•264186	2•292753	2•333524	2•387285

$\alpha =$ .939999

Θ	K VALUES				
	.009966711	.039469502	.087332193	.151646642	.229848846
1.2000000	2.301089	2.318715	2.348490	2.391018	2.447158
1.2100000	2.356809	2.375172	2.406208	2.450573	2.509201
1.2200000	2.414518	2.433651	2.466004	2.512288	2.573518
1.2300000	2.474314	2.494250	2.527979	2.576267	2.640219
1.2400000	2.536296	2.557072	2.592237	2.642621	2.709421
1.2500000	2.600571	2.622223	2.658889	2.711464	2.781244
1.2599999	2.667247	2.689815	2.728050	2.782915	2.855813
1.2699999	2.736439	2.759963	2.799837	2.857098	2.933258
1.2799999	2.808265	2.832788	2.874375	2.934140	3.013716
1.2899999	2.882846	2.908412	2.951790	3.014175	3.097324
1.3000000	2.960309	2.986965	3.032214	3.097338	3.184227
1.3100000	3.040778	3.068574	3.115779	3.183766	3.274570
1.3200000	3.124386	3.153372	3.202620	3.273603	3.368502
1.3300000	3.211263	3.241492	3.292876	3.366989	3.466174
1.3400000	3.301540	3.333067	3.386683	3.464068	3.567734
1.3500000	3.395347	3.428230	3.484176	3.564980	3.673333
1.3600000	3.492811	3.527110	3.585489	3.669864	3.783115
1.3700000	3.594054	3.629829	3.690748	3.778852	3.897220
1.3799999	3.699190	3.736505	3.800073	3.892068	4.015778
1.3899999	3.808325	3.847245	3.913573	4.009627	4.138911
1.4000000	3.921551	3.962142	4.031347	4.131629	4.266725
1.4100000	4.038942	4.081272	4.153470	4.258153	4.399304
1.4200000	4.160555	4.204692	4.280002	4.389263	4.536712
1.4300000	4.286421	4.332435	4.410976	4.524993	4.678987
1.4400000	4.416545	4.464505	4.546397	4.665346	4.826133
1.4500000	4.550898	4.600872	4.686234	4.810293	4.978119
1.4600000	4.689416	4.741473	4.830422	4.959763	5.134869
1.4700000	4.831994	4.886199	4.978849	5.113643	5.296265
1.4800000	4.978484	5.034900	5.131362	5.271771	5.462137
1.4900000	5.128690	5.187378	5.287756	5.433935	5.632261
1.5000000	5.282371	5.343388	5.447778	5.599874	5.806360
1.5100000	5.439232	5.502629	5.611123	5.769266	5.984099
1.5200000	5.598935	5.664758	5.777434	5.941744	6.165089
1.5300000	5.761094	5.829383	5.946311	6.116890	6.348889
1.5400000	5.925282	5.996070	6.117307	6.294240	6.535011
1.5500000	6.091036	6.164349	6.289939	6.473291	6.722925
1.5600000	6.257866	6.333721	6.463694	6.653510	6.912070
1.5699999	6.425260	6.503666	6.638038	6.834342	7.101860
1.5707963	6.438599	6.517208	6.651931	6.848751	7.116984
1.5707963	6.438592	6.517201	6.651924	6.848745	7.116977

$\alpha =$ .939999

Θ	K VALUES				
	.318821117	.415016431	.514599755	.613601043	.708073407
.0000000	.000000	.000000	.000000	.000000	.000000
.0100000	.010000	.010000	.010000	.010000	.010000
.0200000	.020002	.020003	.020003	.020003	.020003
.0300000	.030009	.030010	.030010	.030011	.030011
.0400000	.040023	.040024	.040025	.040026	.040027
.0500000	.050045	.050047	.050049	.050052	.050054
.0600000	.060079	.060082	.060086	.060089	.060093
.0700000	.070125	.070131	.070137	.070142	.070148
.0800000	.080188	.080196	.080204	.080213	.080221
.0900000	.090268	.090279	.090291	.090304	.090315
.1000000	.100367	.100384	.100400	.100417	.100433
.1100000	.110490	.110511	.110533	.110556	.110577
.1200000	.120636	.120664	.120693	.120722	.120750
.1300000	.130810	.130846	.130883	.130919	.130954
.1400000	.141013	.141057	.141104	.141150	.141194
.1500000	.151247	.151302	.151359	.151416	.151470
.1600000	.161516	.161582	.161652	.161721	.161787
.1700000	.171820	.171901	.171984	.172067	.172147
.1800000	.182164	.182259	.182359	.182458	.182552
.1900000	.192549	.192661	.192778	.192895	.193007
.2000000	.202977	.203109	.203246	.203383	.203514
.2100000	.213452	.213605	.213764	.213923	.214075
.2200000	.223976	.224152	.224336	.224519	.224695
.2300000	.234551	.234753	.234964	.235174	.235376
.2400000	.245180	.245411	.245651	.245891	.246121
.2500000	.255866	.256128	.256401	.256673	.256934
.2600000	.266612	.266908	.267215	.267523	.267819
.2700000	.277420	.277753	.278099	.278445	.278777
.2800000	.288294	.288666	.289053	.289441	.289814
.2900000	.299236	.299650	.300083	.300516	.300933
.3000000	.310248	.310709	.311190	.311673	.312137
.3100000	.321335	.321846	.322379	.322914	.323429
.3200000	.332499	.333063	.333653	.334245	.334815
.3300000	.343743	.344365	.345015	.345668	.346297
.3400000	.355071	.355755	.356470	.357188	.357881
.3500000	.366486	.367235	.368020	.368808	.369569
.3600000	.377991	.378811	.379669	.380532	.381366
.3700000	.389590	.390484	.391421	.392365	.393277
.3800000	.401286	.402260	.403281	.404310	.405306
.3900000	.413083	.414142	.415253	.416373	.417457

$\alpha =$ .939999

Θ	K VALUES				
	.318821117	.415016431	.514599755	.613601043	.708073407
.4000000	.424985	.426133	.427339	.428557	.429736
.4100000	.436995	.438238	.439546	.440867	.442147
.4200000	.449117	.450462	.451877	.453307	.454695
.4300000	.461355	.462808	.464337	.465884	.467385
.4400000	.473714	.475280	.476930	.478600	.480224
.4500000	.486198	.487884	.489661	.491463	.493215
.4600000	.498811	.500623	.502536	.504477	.506366
.4700000	.511557	.513503	.515559	.517647	.519681
.4800000	.524441	.526529	.528736	.530979	.533167
.4900000	.537469	.539705	.542072	.544480	.546830
.5000000	.550644	.553037	.555572	.558154	.560677
.5100000	.563972	.566530	.569243	.572009	.574714
.5200000	.577458	.580190	.583091	.586050	.588949
.5300000	.591108	.594023	.597121	.600285	.603387
.5400000	.604927	.608034	.611339	.614720	.618038
.5500000	.618920	.622230	.625754	.629362	.632908
.5600000	.633094	.636616	.640371	.644219	.648006
.5700000	.647455	.651200	.655197	.659298	.663339
.5800000	.662009	.665988	.670240	.674608	.678917
.5900000	.676763	.680988	.685507	.690156	.694748
.6000000	.691723	.696206	.701006	.705951	.710842
.6100000	.706897	.711650	.716746	.722002	.727208
.6200000	.722291	.727327	.732734	.738318	.743856
.6300000	.737913	.743247	.748979	.754908	.760797
.6400000	.753772	.759416	.765491	.771783	.778041
.6500000	.769874	.775845	.782279	.788952	.795600
.6600000	.786229	.792541	.799352	.806427	.813485
.6700000	.802844	.809514	.816721	.824218	.831709
.6800000	.819730	.826774	.834396	.842337	.850284
.6899999	.836896	.844332	.852389	.860796	.869224
.7000000	.854350	.862196	.870710	.879608	.888543
.7100000	.872104	.880379	.889372	.898785	.908254
.7200000	.890167	.898892	.908386	.918341	.928373
.7300000	.908552	.917745	.927766	.938291	.948915
.7400000	.927268	.936953	.947526	.958648	.969898
.7500000	.946328	.956527	.967678	.979429	.991337
.7600000	.965744	.976480	.988237	1.000650	1.013252
.7700000	.985529	.996828	1.009220	1.022327	1.035660
.7800000	1.005697	1.017583	1.030641	1.044477	1.058581
.7899999	1.026261	1.038761	1.052516	1.067120	1.082036

$\alpha =$ •939999

θ	K VALUES				
	•318821117	•415016431	•514599755	•613601043	•708073407
•8000000	1•047236	1•060378	1•074865	1•090274	1•106047
•8100000	1•068637	1•082450	1•097703	1•113959	1•130634
•8200000	1•090479	1•104994	1•121050	1•138196	1•155823
•8300000	1•112780	1•128029	1•144926	1•163007	1•181637
•8400000	1•135557	1•151573	1•169352	1•188415	1•208103
•8500000	1•158827	1•175645	1•194348	1•214444	1•235247
•8600000	1•182610	1•200265	1•219937	1•241118	1•263098
•8700000	1•206924	1•225456	1•246142	1•268465	1•291685
•8799999	1•231792	1•251240	1•272990	1•296512	1•321040
•8899999	1•257235	1•277640	1•300504	1•325287	1•351196
•9000000	1•283274	1•304680	1•328713	1•354822	1•382187
•9100000	1•309934	1•332387	1•357644	1•385147	1•414050
•9200000	1•337240	1•360787	1•387327	1•416296	1•446821
•9300000	1•365218	1•389908	1•417794	1•448305	1•480543
•9400000	1•393894	1•419781	1•449078	1•481209	1•515256
•9500000	1•423298	1•450436	1•481212	1•515048	1•551004
•9600000	1•453460	1•481905	1•514232	1•549863	1•587836
•9699999	1•484411	1•514224	1•548178	1•585696	1•625799
•9799999	1•516185	1•547429	1•583088	1•622592	1•664945
•9899999	1•548816	1•581556	1•619004	1•660599	1•705330
1•0000000	1•582341	1•616647	1•655971	1•699766	1•747010
1•0100000	1•616798	1•652742	1•694035	1•740146	1•790046
1•0200000	1•652228	1•689886	1•733245	1•781793	1•834502
1•0300000	1•688673	1•728125	1•773652	1•824767	1•880446
1•0400000	1•726179	1•767509	1•815310	1•869128	1•927947
1•0500000	1•764793	1•808087	1•858276	1•914941	1•977083
1•0600000	1•804564	1•849915	1•902610	1•962274	2•027931
1•0699999	1•845544	1•893050	1•948376	2•011199	2•080575
1•0799999	1•887790	1•937550	1•995639	2•061792	2•135103
1•0899999	1•931358	1•983481	2•044471	2•114131	2•191609
1•1000000	1•976311	2•030908	2•094945	2•168303	2•250192
1•1100000	2•022712	2•079901	2•147139	2•224394	2•310954
1•1200000	2•070630	2•130535	2•201135	2•282499	2•374005
1•1300000	2•120136	2•182886	2•257020	2•342716	2•439462
1•1400000	2•171305	2•237039	2•314884	2•405149	2•507445
1•1500000	2•224218	2•293078	2•374826	2•469908	2•578085
1•1600000	2•278958	2•351096	2•436945	2•537109	2•651517
1•1700000	2•335613	2•411188	2•501348	2•606872	2•727884
1•1800000	2•394276	2•473454	2•568147	2•679327	2•807337
1•1899999	2•455044	2•538002	2•637461	2•754607	2•890036

$\alpha =$ •939999

θ	K VALUES				
	•318821117	•415016431	•514599755	•613601043	•708073407
1•2000000	2•518020	2•604944	2•709414	2•832856	2•976148
1•2100000	2•583312	2•674394	2•784136	2•914221	3•065848
1•2200000	2•651031	2•746477	2•861763	2•998857	3•159321
1•2300000	2•721296	2•821322	2•942438	3•086930	3•256761
1•2400000	2•794231	2•899062	3•026311	3•178610	3•358371
1•2500000	2•869965	2•979839	3•113539	3•274075	3•464362
1•2599999	2•948632	3•063797	3•204283	3•373512	3•574955
1•2699999	3•030371	3•151090	3•298713	3•477114	3•690380
1•2799999	3•115326	3•241874	3•397004	3•585081	3•810875
1•2899999	3•203648	3•336312	3•499336	3•697620	3•936685
1•3000000	3•295489	3•434571	3•605897	3•814945	4•068065
1•3100000	3•391005	3•536820	3•716873	3•937270	4•205271
1•3200000	3•490356	3•643233	3•832459	4•064817	4•348568
1•3300000	3•593702	3•753985	3•952849	4•197811	4•498222
1•3400000	3•701203	3•869252	4•078238	4•336473	4•654498
1•3500000	3•813019	3•989205	4•208818	4•481025	4•817662
1•3600000	3•929306	4•114014	4•344779	4•631683	4•987971
1•3700000	4•050212	4•243843	4•486302	4•788655	5•165676
1•3799999	4•175878	4•378844	4•633557	4•952138	5•351010
1•3899999	4•306432	4•519156	4•786699	5•122309	5•544189
1•4000000	4•441989	4•664905	4•945869	5•299329	5•745405
1•4100000	4•582638	4•816188	5•111174	5•483324	5•954812
1•4200000	4•728450	4•973083	5•282702	5•674394	6•172531
1•4300000	4•879463	5•135630	5•460499	5•872594	6•398632
1•4400000	5•035683	5•303838	5•644573	6•077934	6•633131
1•4500000	5•197075	5•477667	5•834884	6•290370	6•875979
1•4600000	5•363561	5•657034	6•031337	6•509796	7•127054
1•4700000	5•535013	5•841799	6•233779	6•736037	7•386155
1•4800000	5•711248	6•031764	6•441991	6•968847	7•652993
1•4900000	5•892029	6•226672	6•655685	7•207898	7•927186
1•5000000	6•077060	6•426199	6•874507	7•452787	8•208258
1•5100000	6•265981	6•629956	7•098021	7•703020	8•495631
1•5200000	6•458377	6•837492	7•325729	7•958028	8•788634
1•5300000	6•653778	7•048294	7•557062	8•217165	9•086505
1•5400000	6•851661	7•261794	7•791389	8•479712	9•388399
1•5500000	7•051459	7•477378	8•028028	8•744892	9•693400
1•5600000	7•252573	7•694392	8•266255	9•011881	10•000533
1•5699999	7•454377	7•912156	8•505313	9•279817	10•308784
1•5707963	7•470458	7•929509	8•524363	9•301168	10•333348
1•5707963	7•470452	7•929503	8•524357	9•301164	10•333346

$\alpha =$ .939999

θ	K VALUES				
	.794250555	.868696860	.928444378	.971111163	.994996249
.0000000	.000000	.000000	.000000	.000000	.000000
.0100000	.010000	.010000	.010000	.010000	.010000
.0200000	.020003	.020003	.020003	.020003	.020003
.0300000	.030012	.030012	.030012	.030012	.030012
.0400000	.040028	.040029	.040030	.040030	.040030
.0500000	.050055	.050057	.050058	.050059	.050059
.0600000	.060096	.060099	.060101	.060102	.060103
.0700000	.070153	.070157	.070160	.070163	.070164
.0800000	.080228	.080235	.080240	.080244	.080246
.0900000	.090326	.090335	.090342	.090347	.090350
.1000000	.100447	.100460	.100470	.100477	.100481
.1100000	.110596	.110613	.110626	.110636	.110641
.1200000	.120775	.120797	.120814	.120827	.120834
.1300000	.130987	.131014	.131037	.131053	.131062
.1400000	.141234	.141269	.141297	.141317	.141328
.1500000	.151520	.151563	.151597	.151622	.151636
.1600000	.161847	.161900	.161942	.161972	.161989
.1700000	.172219	.172282	.172333	.172369	.172389
.1800000	.182639	.182714	.182774	.182818	.182842
.1900000	.193109	.193198	.193269	.193320	.193349
.2000000	.203633	.203737	.203821	.203880	.203914
.2100000	.214214	.214335	.214432	.214502	.214541
.2200000	.224856	.224995	.225107	.225188	.225233
.2300000	.235560	.235721	.235850	.235942	.235994
.2400000	.246332	.246515	.246662	.246768	.246827
.2500000	.257174	.257382	.257550	.257670	.257737
.2600000	.268090	.268325	.268515	.268651	.268727
.2700000	.279083	.279348	.279562	.279715	.279801
.2800000	.290157	.290454	.290694	.290866	.290963
.2900000	.301316	.301648	.301917	.302109	.302218
.3000000	.312563	.312934	.313233	.313448	.313569
.3100000	.323903	.324315	.324648	.324887	.325021
.3200000	.335340	.335796	.336165	.336430	.336579
.3300000	.346877	.347381	.347789	.348082	.348246
.3400000	.358519	.359075	.359525	.359848	.360029
.3500000	.370270	.370882	.371376	.371732	.371932
.3600000	.382135	.382806	.383349	.383740	.383959
.3700000	.394118	.394853	.395448	.395876	.396117
.3800000	.406225	.407028	.407679	.408147	.408410
.3900000	.418459	.419335	.420045	.420557	.420844

$\alpha =$ .939999

Θ	K VALUES				
	.794250555	.868696860	.928444378	.971111163	.994996249
.4000000	.430826	.431780	.432554	.433111	.433425
.4100000	.443332	.444369	.445211	.445817	.446159
.4200000	.455980	.457106	.458021	.458680	.459051
.4300000	.468778	.469999	.470991	.471706	.472109
.4400000	.481730	.483052	.484127	.484902	.485339
.4500000	.494843	.496272	.497435	.498274	.498747
.4600000	.508122	.509665	.510922	.511829	.512341
.4700000	.521574	.523238	.524595	.525575	.526128
.4800000	.535205	.536999	.538462	.539519	.540116
.4900000	.549022	.550953	.552529	.553669	.554313
.5000000	.563032	.565108	.566805	.568033	.568726
.5100000	.577242	.579473	.581297	.582618	.583365
.5200000	.591659	.594054	.596014	.597435	.598238
.5300000	.606292	.608861	.610965	.612491	.613355
.5400000	.621148	.623902	.626159	.627797	.628725
.5500000	.636235	.639185	.641605	.643363	.644358
.5600000	.651563	.654720	.657312	.659197	.660265
.5700000	.667140	.670516	.673292	.675312	.676457
.5800000	.682975	.686584	.689555	.691718	.692944
.5900000	.699078	.702934	.706111	.708427	.709740
.6000000	.715460	.719577	.722973	.725451	.726857
.6100000	.732130	.736525	.740153	.742802	.744307
.6200000	.749100	.753788	.757663	.760495	.762105
.6300000	.766380	.771379	.775516	.778542	.780264
.6400000	.783983	.789311	.793726	.796959	.798799
.6500000	.801922	.807598	.812308	.815760	.817727
.6600000	.820208	.826253	.831276	.834962	.837063
.6700000	.838856	.845292	.850647	.854581	.856825
.6800000	.857879	.864729	.870436	.874634	.877030
.6899999	.877292	.884581	.890662	.895140	.897699
.7000000	.897110	.904863	.911342	.916119	.918851
.7100000	.917350	.925595	.932496	.937590	.940506
.7200000	.938027	.946793	.954143	.959575	.962688
.7300000	.959159	.968478	.976304	.982097	.985418
.7400000	.980765	.990670	.999001	1.005177	1.008722
.7500000	1.002863	1.013389	1.022258	1.028843	1.032626
.7600000	1.025474	1.036657	1.046099	1.053119	1.057156
.7700000	1.048618	1.060499	1.070549	1.078033	1.082341
.7800000	1.072317	1.084939	1.095635	1.103614	1.108213
.7899999	1.096595	1.110002	1.121387	1.129893	1.134802

$\alpha =$ .939999

θ	K VALUES				
	.794250555	.868696860	.928444378	.971111163	.994996249
.8000000	1.121475	1.135715	1.147833	1.156902	1.162142
.8100000	1.146983	1.162107	1.175004	1.184675	1.190270
.8200000	1.173145	1.189207	1.202936	1.213249	1.219223
.8300000	1.199989	1.217048	1.231661	1.242661	1.249042
.8400000	1.227544	1.245661	1.261218	1.272952	1.279769
.8500000	1.255842	1.275083	1.291646	1.304165	1.311449
.8600000	1.284913	1.305349	1.322986	1.336345	1.344130
.8700000	1.314793	1.336499	1.355281	1.369540	1.377863
.8799999	1.345517	1.368574	1.388578	1.403802	1.412702
.8899999	1.377123	1.401616	1.422927	1.439184	1.448705
.9000000	1.409650	1.435671	1.458378	1.475744	1.485933
.9100000	1.443140	1.470788	1.494987	1.513543	1.524451
.9200000	1.477636	1.507017	1.532812	1.552647	1.564330
.9300000	1.513186	1.544412	1.571915	1.593124	1.605642
.9400000	1.549838	1.583029	1.612362	1.635048	1.648468
.9500000	1.587644	1.622930	1.654222	1.678499	1.692892
.9600000	1.626657	1.664178	1.697570	1.723559	1.739005
.9699999	1.666936	1.706840	1.742485	1.770320	1.786903
.9799999	1.708541	1.750987	1.789049	1.818876	1.836692
.9899999	1.751535	1.796697	1.837354	1.869329	1.888481
1.0000000	1.795987	1.844048	1.887493	1.921790	1.942392
1.0100000	1.841967	1.893126	1.939567	1.976376	1.998552
1.0200000	1.889552	1.944022	1.993686	2.033211	2.057098
1.0300000	1.938820	1.996830	2.049963	2.092430	2.118181
1.0400000	1.989857	2.051654	2.108523	2.154179	2.181959
1.0500000	2.042752	2.108601	2.169495	2.218611	2.248606
1.0600000	2.097599	2.167785	2.233019	2.285894	2.318307
1.0699999	2.154498	2.229330	2.299247	2.356206	2.391263
1.0799999	2.213554	2.293364	2.368337	2.429739	2.467692
1.0899999	2.274880	2.360025	2.440459	2.506702	2.547829
1.1000000	2.338595	2.429461	2.515799	2.587318	2.631929
1.1100000	2.404823	2.501825	2.594550	2.671826	2.720268
1.1200000	2.473696	2.577283	2.676921	2.760486	2.813146
1.1300000	2.545356	2.656012	2.763137	2.853579	2.910888
1.1400000	2.619951	2.738197	2.853437	2.951407	3.013850
1.1500000	2.697637	2.824038	2.948077	3.054297	3.122417
1.1600000	2.778582	2.913744	3.047333	3.162603	3.237011
1.1700000	2.862959	3.007540	3.151497	3.276705	3.358090
1.1800000	2.950955	3.105663	3.260885	3.397018	3.486157
1.1899999	3.042766	3.208364	3.375831	3.523990	3.621760

$\alpha =$ .939999

Θ	K VALUES				
	.794250555	.868696860	.928444378	.971111163	.994996249
1.2000000	3.138597	3.315911	3.496696	3.658104	3.765502
1.2100000	3.238664	3.428584	3.623861	3.799884	3.918039
1.2200000	3.343198	3.546683	3.757738	3.949898	4.080095
1.2300000	3.452437	3.670523	3.898763	4.108761	4.252465
1.2400000	3.566634	3.800435	4.047401	4.277137	4.436021
1.2500000	3.686053	3.936770	4.204146	4.455746	4.631727
1.2599999	3.810969	4.079894	4.369524	4.645367	4.840641
1.2699999	3.941669	4.230191	4.544091	4.846841	5.063933
1.2799999	4.078451	4.388063	4.728434	5.061074	5.302896
1.2899999	4.221624	4.553927	4.923173	5.289044	5.558960
1.3000000	4.371508	4.728218	5.128960	5.531808	5.833708
1.3100000	4.528424	4.911378	5.346470	5.790489	6.128888
1.3200000	4.692708	5.103867	5.576411	6.066300	6.446448
1.3300000	4.864696	5.306149	5.819516	6.360532	6.788547
1.3400000	5.044726	5.518697	6.076535	6.674558	7.157584
1.3500000	5.233134	5.741981	6.348233	7.009831	7.556231
1.3600000	5.430249	5.976466	6.635381	7.367876	7.987460
1.3700000	5.636390	6.222607	6.938748	7.750290	8.454584
1.3799999	5.851859	6.480838	7.259087	8.158722	8.961298
1.3899999	6.076934	6.751564	7.597122	8.594860	9.511726
1.4000000	6.311863	7.035154	7.953538	9.060415	10.110478
1.4100000	6.556850	7.331917	8.328943	9.557068	10.762682
1.4200000	6.812056	7.642107	8.723869	10.086460	11.474084
1.4300000	7.077580	7.965896	9.138737	10.650130	12.251084
1.4400000	7.353453	8.303366	9.573831	11.249456	13.100812
1.4500000	7.639626	8.654488	10.029274	11.885592	14.031177
1.4600000	7.935958	9.019112	10.504998	12.559388	15.050907
1.4700000	8.242211	9.396950	11.000718	13.271302	16.169537
1.4800000	8.558033	9.787566	11.515909	14.021315	17.397314
1.4900000	8.882961	10.190362	12.049783	14.808832	18.744954
1.5000000	9.216410	10.604579	12.601279	15.632605	20.223161
1.5100000	9.557668	11.029279	13.169038	16.490636	21.841669
1.5200000	9.905907	11.463364	13.751432	17.380162	23.607803
1.5300000	10.260186	11.905578	14.346551	18.297613	25.524161
1.5400000	10.619457	12.354519	14.952238	19.238644	27.585561
1.5500000	10.982585	12.808658	15.566115	20.198201	29.775696
1.5600000	11.348360	13.266369	16.185631	21.170641	32.064707
1.5699999	11.715523	13.725955	16.808109	22.149890	34.409591
1.5707963	11.744783	13.762582	16.857725	22.227977	34.597214
1.5707963	11.744787	13.762602	16.857859	22.227950	34.597162

$\alpha =$ .949999

Θ	K VALUES				
	.009966711	.039469502	.087332193	.151646642	.229848846
.0000000	.000000	.000000	.000000	.000000	.000000
.0100000	.010000	.010000	.010000	.010000	.010000
.0200000	.020002	.020002	.020002	.020002	.020002
.0300000	.030008	.030008	.030008	.030009	.030009
.0400000	.040020	.040020	.040021	.040021	.040022
.0500000	.050039	.050040	.050041	.050042	.050044
.0600000	.060068	.060069	.060071	.060073	.060076
.0700000	.070109	.070111	.070113	.070117	.070122
.0800000	.080163	.080165	.080170	.080175	.080182
.0900000	.090232	.090236	.090242	.090250	.090259
.1000000	.100319	.100324	.100332	.100343	.100356
.1100000	.110425	.110432	.110442	.110457	.110474
.1200000	.120553	.120561	.120575	.120594	.120616
.1300000	.130703	.130714	.130732	.130756	.130784
.1400000	.140879	.140893	.140915	.140945	.140981
.1500000	.151083	.151100	.151127	.151163	.151208
.1600000	.161316	.161336	.161369	.161414	.161468
.1700000	.171580	.171605	.171644	.171698	.171763
.1800000	.181879	.181908	.181955	.182018	.182096
.1900000	.192213	.192247	.192302	.192377	.192468
.2000000	.202584	.202624	.202689	.202777	.202883
.2100000	.212996	.213043	.213118	.213219	.213343
.2200000	.223451	.223504	.223591	.223708	.223850
.2300000	.233950	.234011	.234110	.234244	.234407
.2400000	.244496	.244565	.244678	.244831	.245017
.2500000	.255091	.255170	.255298	.255470	.255681
.2600000	.265738	.265827	.265971	.266166	.266403
.2700000	.276439	.276538	.276700	.276919	.277186
.2800000	.287196	.287307	.287489	.287733	.288032
.2900000	.298012	.298136	.298338	.298610	.298943
.3000000	.308890	.309028	.309252	.309554	.309924
.3100000	.319832	.319984	.320232	.320567	.320976
.3200000	.330841	.331009	.331282	.331651	.332103
.3300000	.341919	.342104	.342404	.342810	.343307
.3400000	.353070	.353272	.353602	.354047	.354593
.3500000	.364295	.364517	.364877	.365365	.365963
.3600000	.375599	.375840	.376234	.376767	.377420
.3700000	.386983	.387246	.387675	.388255	.388967
.3800000	.398452	.398738	.399204	.399835	.400609
.3900000	.410007	.410317	.410823	.411508	.412348

$\alpha =$ .949999

Θ	K VALUES				
	.009966711	.039469502	.087332193	.151646642	.229848846
.4000000	.421653	.421989	.422536	.423278	.424188
.4100000	.433392	.433755	.434347	.435148	.436134
.4200000	.445228	.445619	.446258	.447123	.448188
.4300000	.457165	.457586	.458274	.459207	.460354
.4400000	.469205	.469658	.470398	.471401	.472637
.4500000	.481353	.481839	.482634	.483712	.485041
.4600000	.493612	.494133	.494985	.496143	.497569
.4700000	.505986	.506544	.507457	.508697	.510226
.4800000	.518479	.519076	.520052	.521380	.523018
.4900000	.531095	.531733	.532776	.534195	.535947
.5000000	.543838	.544519	.545632	.547148	.549019
.5100000	.556712	.557438	.558626	.560242	.562240
.5200000	.569723	.570496	.571760	.573483	.575613
.5300000	.582875	.583696	.585042	.586875	.589144
.5400000	.596171	.597044	.598474	.600424	.602839
.5500000	.609618	.610545	.612064	.614135	.616703
.5600000	.623220	.624203	.625815	.628014	.630741
.5700000	.636983	.638024	.639733	.642066	.644961
.5800000	.650911	.652014	.653824	.656296	.659367
.5900000	.665011	.666178	.668094	.670712	.673966
.6000000	.679288	.680522	.682548	.685319	.688765
.6100000	.693748	.695052	.697193	.700123	.703771
.6200000	.708398	.709774	.712036	.715132	.718990
.6300000	.723243	.724695	.727082	.730353	.734430
.6400000	.738291	.739822	.742340	.745792	.750098
.6500000	.753548	.755161	.757816	.761456	.766003
.6600000	.769021	.770720	.773517	.777355	.782152
.6700000	.784718	.786507	.789452	.793495	.798553
.6800000	.800647	.802529	.805628	.809886	.815217
.6899999	.816816	.818794	.822054	.826536	.832151
.7000000	.833232	.835311	.838738	.843453	.849365
.7100000	.849905	.852089	.855690	.860647	.866869
.7200000	.866844	.869136	.872918	.878129	.884674
.7300000	.884057	.886463	.890433	.895907	.902789
.7400000	.901555	.904078	.908245	.913994	.921226
.7500000	.919347	.921993	.926365	.932398	.939998
.7600000	.937445	.940219	.944802	.951133	.959114
.7700000	.955860	.958765	.963570	.970211	.978589
.7800000	.974602	.977645	.982679	.989642	.998436
.7899999	.993684	.996870	1.002143	1.009442	1.018667

$\alpha =$ .949999

Θ	K VALUES				
	.009966711	.039469502	.087332193	.151646642	.229848846
.8000000	1.013118	1.016453	1.021974	1.029622	1.039298
.8100000	1.032918	1.036407	1.042187	1.050198	1.060344
.8200000	1.053097	1.056746	1.062795	1.071184	1.081819
.8300000	1.073669	1.077485	1.083813	1.092595	1.103740
.8400000	1.094650	1.098639	1.105257	1.114449	1.126124
.8500000	1.116055	1.120223	1.127143	1.136761	1.148990
.8600000	1.137900	1.142255	1.149488	1.159550	1.172355
.8700000	1.160202	1.164752	1.172311	1.182834	1.196240
.8799999	1.182980	1.187731	1.195630	1.206633	1.220665
.8899999	1.206252	1.211213	1.219464	1.230967	1.245651
.9000000	1.230038	1.235217	1.243835	1.255858	1.271221
.9100000	1.254359	1.259765	1.268763	1.281327	1.297399
.9200000	1.279236	1.284877	1.294272	1.307400	1.324209
.9300000	1.304693	1.310578	1.320385	1.334099	1.351678
.9400000	1.330753	1.336893	1.347128	1.361453	1.379833
.9500000	1.357442	1.363845	1.374527	1.389487	1.408703
.9600000	1.384785	1.391464	1.402609	1.418230	1.438318
.9699999	1.412812	1.419776	1.431404	1.447714	1.468710
.9799999	1.441552	1.448813	1.460942	1.477970	1.499913
.9899999	1.471035	1.478605	1.491257	1.509032	1.531963
1.0000000	1.501294	1.509185	1.522381	1.540935	1.564896
1.0100000	1.532364	1.540589	1.554351	1.573716	1.598752
1.0200000	1.564281	1.572854	1.587205	1.607415	1.633572
1.0300000	1.597083	1.606018	1.620983	1.642074	1.669401
1.0400000	1.630810	1.640123	1.655726	1.677736	1.706284
1.0500000	1.665507	1.675211	1.691481	1.714448	1.744271
1.0600000	1.701217	1.711330	1.728294	1.752259	1.783413
1.0699999	1.737989	1.748527	1.766214	1.791220	1.823764
1.0799999	1.775872	1.786854	1.805295	1.831388	1.865383
1.0899999	1.814922	1.826366	1.845592	1.872818	1.908331
1.1000000	1.855193	1.867119	1.887164	1.915574	1.952672
1.1100000	1.896746	1.909174	1.930074	1.959720	1.998474
1.1200000	1.939644	1.952596	1.974388	2.005324	2.045810
1.1300000	1.983954	1.997453	2.020176	2.052460	2.094756
1.1400000	2.029748	2.043816	2.067512	2.101204	2.145395
1.1500000	2.077100	2.091764	2.116475	2.151638	2.197811
1.1600000	2.126091	2.141376	2.167147	2.203849	2.252096
1.1700000	2.176804	2.192738	2.219618	2.257929	2.308347
1.1800000	2.229329	2.245942	2.273980	2.313974	2.366666
1.1899999	2.283762	2.301083	2.330333	2.372087	2.427160

$\alpha =$ .949999

Θ	K VALUES				
	.009966711	.039469502	.087332193	.151646642	.229848846
1.2000000	2.340202	2.358264	2.388780	2.432378	2.489946
1.2100000	2.398754	2.417591	2.449434	2.494960	2.555143
1.2200000	2.459532	2.479180	2.512409	2.559957	2.622880
1.2300000	2.522654	2.543150	2.577832	2.627496	2.693292
1.2400000	2.588245	2.609629	2.645831	2.697713	2.766523
1.2500000	2.656437	2.678751	2.716545	2.770751	2.842722
1.2599999	2.727368	2.750655	2.790119	2.846762	2.922050
1.2699999	2.801184	2.825492	2.866704	2.925902	3.004671
1.2799999	2.878039	2.903415	2.946460	3.008338	3.090762
1.2899999	2.958092	2.984588	3.029555	3.094244	3.180504
1.3000000	3.041510	3.069180	3.116162	3.183801	3.274089
1.3100000	3.128464	3.157366	3.206461	3.277195	3.371713
1.3200000	3.219135	3.249328	3.300640	3.374621	3.473580
1.3300000	3.313707	3.345253	3.398889	3.476279	3.579902
1.3400000	3.412366	3.445331	3.501406	3.582371	3.690893
1.3500000	3.515303	3.549756	3.608388	3.693106	3.806769
1.3600000	3.622710	3.658722	3.720036	3.808689	3.927750
1.3700000	3.734774	3.772421	3.836545	3.929326	4.054051
1.3799999	3.851681	3.891041	3.958110	4.055218	4.185884
1.3899999	3.973608	4.014761	4.084915	4.186556	4.323450
1.4000000	4.100721	4.143749	4.217133	4.323520	4.466939
1.4100000	4.233165	4.278155	4.354915	4.466269	4.616518
1.4200000	4.371066	4.418106	4.498395	4.614940	4.772331
1.4300000	4.514523	4.563702	4.647674	4.769639	4.934490
1.4400000	4.663599	4.715006	4.802818	4.930434	5.103067
1.4500000	4.818313	4.872040	4.963847	5.097347	5.278085
1.4600000	4.978636	5.034773	5.130732	5.270346	5.459511
1.4700000	5.144483	5.203119	5.303383	5.449339	5.647247
1.4800000	5.315704	5.376925	5.481644	5.634163	5.841122
1.4900000	5.492080	5.555968	5.665285	5.824581	6.040885
1.5000000	5.673317	5.739951	5.854001	6.020273	6.246202
1.5100000	5.859042	5.928494	6.047402	6.220835	6.456646
1.5200000	6.048807	6.121142	6.245020	6.425780	6.671705
1.5300000	6.242086	6.317361	6.446307	6.634539	6.890779
1.5400000	6.438286	6.516548	6.650642	6.846467	7.113190
1.5500000	6.636751	6.718035	6.857342	7.060853	7.338188
1.5600000	6.836776	6.921108	7.065670	7.276931	7.564968
1.5699999	7.037620	7.125013	7.274853	7.493898	7.792684
1.5707963	7.053627	7.141264	7.291525	7.511190	7.810832
1.5707963	7.053620	7.141257	7.291517	7.511183	7.810825

$\alpha =$ .949999

Θ	K VALUES				
	.318821117	.415016431	.514599755	.613601043	.708073407
.0000000	.000000	.000000	.000000	.000000	.000000
.0100000	.010000	.010000	.010000	.010000	.010000
.0200000	.020002	.020003	.020003	.020003	.020003
.0300000	.030010	.030010	.030010	.030011	.030011
.0400000	.040023	.040024	.040025	.040026	.040027
.0500000	.050046	.050048	.050050	.050052	.050054
.0600000	.060080	.060083	.060087	.060090	.060094
.0700000	.070127	.070132	.070138	.070144	.070149
.0800000	.080189	.080198	.080206	.080215	.080223
.0900000	.090270	.090282	.090294	.090306	.090318
.1000000	.100371	.100387	.100404	.100420	.100436
.1100000	.110494	.110516	.110538	.110560	.110581
.1200000	.120642	.120670	.120699	.120728	.120756
.1300000	.130817	.130853	.130890	.130927	.130962
.1400000	.141022	.141067	.141113	.141159	.141203
.1500000	.151259	.151314	.151371	.151427	.151482
.1600000	.161530	.161596	.161666	.161735	.161801
.1700000	.171837	.171917	.172001	.172084	.172164
.1800000	.182184	.182280	.182379	.182478	.182573
.1900000	.192572	.192685	.192802	.192919	.193031
.2000000	.203005	.203137	.203274	.203411	.203541
.2100000	.213484	.213637	.213797	.213955	.214108
.2200000	.224013	.224190	.224373	.224557	.224732
.2300000	.234594	.234796	.235007	.235217	.235419
.2400000	.245229	.245460	.245700	.245940	.246170
.2500000	.255922	.256184	.256456	.256729	.256990
.2600000	.266675	.266971	.267278	.267586	.267882
.2700000	.277491	.277824	.278170	.278516	.278849
.2800000	.288373	.288745	.289133	.289521	.289894
.2900000	.299324	.299739	.300172	.300606	.301023
.3000000	.310347	.310808	.311290	.311772	.312237
.3100000	.321445	.321956	.322490	.323025	.323540
.3200000	.332621	.333185	.333776	.334368	.334938
.3300000	.343878	.344500	.345151	.345804	.346434
.3400000	.355219	.355903	.356619	.357337	.358031
.3500000	.366649	.367399	.368183	.368972	.369734
.3600000	.378170	.378990	.379849	.380713	.381547
.3700000	.389785	.390680	.391618	.392563	.393475
.3800000	.401499	.402474	.403496	.404526	.405523
.3900000	.413316	.414375	.415487	.416609	.417694

$\alpha =$ .949999

Θ	K VALUES				
	.318821117	.415016431	.514599755	.613601043	.708073407
.4000000	.425237	.426387	.427595	.428813	.429994
.4100000	.437269	.438515	.439824	.441146	.442427
.4200000	.449415	.450761	.452178	.453610	.454999
.4300000	.461678	.463132	.464663	.466212	.467716
.4400000	.474063	.475631	.477283	.478956	.480581
.4500000	.486575	.488263	.490044	.491848	.493602
.4600000	.499218	.501033	.502949	.504892	.506784
.4700000	.511996	.513945	.516004	.518095	.520132
.4800000	.524914	.527005	.529215	.531462	.533654
.4900000	.537977	.540217	.542588	.545000	.547354
.5000000	.551190	.553587	.556127	.558713	.561241
.5100000	.564558	.567121	.569839	.572610	.575320
.5200000	.578087	.580824	.583730	.586695	.589599
.5300000	.591782	.594703	.597806	.600977	.604086
.5400000	.605648	.608762	.612074	.615462	.618787
.5500000	.619692	.623009	.626541	.630157	.633711
.5600000	.633920	.637450	.641213	.645070	.648865
.5700000	.648337	.652091	.656097	.660209	.664259
.5800000	.662951	.666940	.671202	.675581	.679901
.5900000	.677768	.682004	.686535	.691196	.695800
.6000000	.692795	.697290	.702103	.707062	.711966
.6100000	.708040	.712806	.717916	.723188	.728408
.6200000	.723509	.728560	.733982	.739583	.745137
.6300000	.739210	.744560	.750310	.756257	.762164
.6400000	.755153	.760815	.766909	.773221	.779500
.6500000	.771344	.777334	.783790	.790485	.797155
.6600000	.787792	.794126	.800961	.808060	.815143
.6700000	.804507	.811201	.818433	.825957	.833476
.6800000	.821498	.828568	.836218	.844189	.852166
.6899999	.838774	.846239	.854327	.862767	.871229
.7000000	.856346	.864223	.872772	.881705	.890677
.7100000	.874224	.882533	.891564	.901016	.910526
.7200000	.892418	.901180	.910716	.920715	.930791
.7300000	.910941	.920176	.930243	.940815	.951489
.7400000	.929805	.939535	.950157	.961332	.972636
.7500000	.949020	.959268	.970473	.982283	.994250
.7600000	.968601	.979391	.991207	1.003683	1.016351
.7700000	.988561	.999918	1.012375	1.025551	1.038956
.7800000	1.008913	1.020863	1.033992	1.047905	1.062087
.7899999	1.029672	1.042242	1.056076	1.070763	1.085765

$\alpha =$ •949999

Θ	K VALUES				
	•318821117	•415016431	•514599755	•613601043	•708073407
•8000000	1•050855	1•064073	1•078645	1•094145	1•110013
•8100000	1•072475	1•086372	1•101717	1•118074	1•134853
•8200000	1•094550	1•109156	1•125314	1•142569	1•160310
•8300000	1•117098	1•132446	1•149454	1•167655	1•186410
•8400000	1•140137	1•156260	1•174160	1•193355	1•213180
•8500000	1•163685	1•180620	1•199454	1•219694	1•240648
•8600000	1•187762	1•205546	1•225361	1•246700	1•268844
•8700000	1•212391	1•231061	1•251904	1•274399	1•297800
•8799999	1•237591	1•257190	1•279111	1•302821	1•327548
•8899999	1•263387	1•283957	1•307008	1•331996	1•358123
•9000000	1•289803	1•311388	1•335624	1•361957	1•389562
•9100000	1•316863	1•339510	1•364989	1•392737	1•421902
•9200000	1•344594	1•368352	1•395135	1•424372	1•455184
•9300000	1•373024	1•397945	1•426095	1•456898	1•489452
•9400000	1•402183	1•428320	1•457904	1•490356	1•524748
•9500000	1•432101	1•459510	1•490600	1•524787	1•561122
•9600000	1•462811	1•491552	1•524220	1•560234	1•598622
•9699999	1•494346	1•524481	1•558806	1•596743	1•637302
•9799999	1•526743	1•558337	1•594401	1•634363	1•677216
•9899999	1•560040	1•593160	1•631051	1•673145	1•718425
1•0000000	1•594276	1•628996	1•668802	1•713143	1•760989
1•0100000	1•629493	1•665887	1•707706	1•754414	1•804975
1•0200000	1•665736	1•703884	1•747816	1•797018	1•850452
1•0300000	1•703052	1•743036	1•789187	1•841018	1•897492
1•0400000	1•741490	1•783398	1•831880	1•886481	1•946174
1•0500000	1•781102	1•825026	1•875958	1•933479	1•996580
1•0600000	1•821944	1•867980	1•921486	1•982087	2•048797
1•0699999	1•864073	1•912324	1•968534	2•032383	2•102917
1•0799999	1•907552	1•958124	2•017178	2•084453	2•159038
1•0899999	1•952446	2•005452	2•067495	2•138385	2•217263
1•1000000	1•998824	2•054382	2•119569	2•194274	2•277703
1•1100000	2•046758	2•104994	2•173487	2•252218	2•340473
1•1200000	2•096327	2•157372	2•229344	2•312325	2•405696
1•1300000	2•147612	2•211605	2•287236	2•374705	2•473505
1•1400000	2•200700	2•267787	2•347270	2•439479	2•544036
1•1500000	2•255682	2•326019	2•409556	2•506771	2•617439
1•1600000	2•312657	2•386406	2•474212	2•576716	2•693869
1•1700000	2•371728	2•449059	2•541361	2•649454	2•773493
1•1800000	2•433003	2•514099	2•611135	2•725135	2•856484
1•1899999	2•496599	2•581651	2•683674	2•803919	2•943031

$\alpha =$ •949999

Θ	K VALUES				
	•318821117	•415016431	•514599755	•613601043	•708073407
1•2000000	2•562638	2•651848	2•759127	2•885973	3•033331
1•2100000	2•631249	2•724830	2•837648	2•971474	3•127592
1•2200000	2•702569	2•800746	2•919402	3•060612	3•226036
1•2300000	2•776744	2•879754	3•004566	3•153584	3•328897
1•2400000	2•853925	2•962020	3•093322	3•250602	3•436422
1•2500000	2•934274	3•047719	3•185865	3•351885	3•548873
1•2599999	3•017960	3•137035	3•282400	3•457667	3•666523
1•2699999	3•105162	3•230162	3•383141	3•568193	3•789662
1•2799999	3•196066	3•327302	3•488314	3•683719	3•918593
1•2899999	3•290867	3•428668	3•598154	3•804514	4•053634
1•3000000	3•389770	3•534482	3•712907	3•930860	4•195116
1•3100000	3•492984	3•644972	3•832827	4•063043	4•343380
1•3200000	3•600728	3•760375	3•958178	4•201367	4•498783
1•3300000	3•713227	3•880937	4•089231	4•346139	4•661691
1•3400000	3•830709	4•006905	4•226262	4•497676	4•832478
1•3500000	3•953409	4•138533	4•369553	4•656297	5•011523
1•3600000	4•081558	4•276075	4•519383	4•822324	5•199206
1•3700000	4•215387	4•419780	4•676033	4•996075	5•395905
1•3799999	4•355122	4•569896	4•839774	5•177861	5•601989
1•3899999	4•500980	4•726655	5•010867	5•367979	5•817811
1•4000000	4•653162	4•890279	5•189558	5•566710	6•043706
1•4100000	4•811846	5•060961	5•376060	5•774299	6•279965
1•4200000	4•977188	5•238870	5•570563	5•990960	6•526846
1•4300000	5•149307	5•424136	5•773209	6•216861	6•784547
1•4400000	5•328279	5•616841	5•984092	6•452108	7•053199
1•4500000	5•514130	5•817014	6•203244	6•696737	7•332850
1•4600000	5•706824	6•024616	6•430622	6•950705	7•623449
1•4700000	5•906256	6•239535	6•666102	7•213869	7•924836
1•4800000	6•112245	6•461571	6•909466	7•485983	8•236723
1•4900000	6•324522	6•690436	7•160391	7•766683	8•558687
1•5000000	6•542730	6•925741	7•418450	8•055483	8•890158
1•5100000	6•766414	7•166991	7•683093	8•351761	9•230410
1•5200000	6•995027	7•413592	7•953663	8•654771	9•578567
1•5300000	7•227928	7•664850	8•229392	8•963639	9•933604
1•5400000	7•464392	7•919977	8•509407	9•277376	10•294359
1•5500000	7•703620	8•178105	8•792745	9•594888	10•659550
1•5600000	7•944750	8•438299	9•078372	9•915000	11•027794
1•5699999	8•186881	8•699579	9•365203	10•236479	11•397644
1•5707963	8•206178	8•720403	9•388062	10•262100	11•427121
1•5707963	8•206171	8•720396	9•388056	10•262096	11•427119

$\alpha =$ .949999

Θ	K VALUES				
	.794250555	.868696860	.928444378	.971111163	.994996249
.0000000	.000000	.000000	.000000	.000000	.000000
.0100000	.010000	.010000	.010000	.010000	.010000
.0200000	.020003	.020003	.020003	.020003	.020003
.0300000	.030012	.030012	.030012	.030012	.030013
.0400000	.040028	.040029	.040030	.040030	.040030
.0500000	.050056	.050057	.050059	.050059	.050060
.0600000	.060097	.060099	.060102	.060103	.060104
.0700000	.070154	.070158	.070162	.070164	.070165
.0800000	.080230	.080237	.080242	.080245	.080247
.0900000	.090328	.090337	.090345	.090350	.090353
.1000000	.100451	.100463	.100473	.100481	.100485
.1100000	.110601	.110617	.110631	.110640	.110646
.1200000	.120781	.120803	.120820	.120833	.120840
.1300000	.130994	.131022	.131044	.131060	.131069
.1400000	.141243	.141278	.141306	.141326	.141337
.1500000	.151531	.151574	.151609	.151634	.151647
.1600000	.161861	.161914	.161956	.161986	.162003
.1700000	.172236	.172299	.172350	.172386	.172406
.1800000	.182659	.182734	.182795	.182838	.182862
.1900000	.193133	.193222	.193293	.193344	.193373
.2000000	.203661	.203765	.203849	.203908	.203942
.2100000	.214247	.214368	.214465	.214534	.214573
.2200000	.224893	.225033	.225145	.225226	.225271
.2300000	.235604	.235764	.235893	.235985	.236037
.2400000	.246381	.246564	.246712	.246817	.246877
.2500000	.257230	.257438	.257606	.257726	.257793
.2600000	.268153	.268389	.268578	.268714	.268791
.2700000	.279154	.279420	.279633	.279787	.279873
.2800000	.290237	.290535	.290775	.290947	.291044
.2900000	.301406	.301738	.302007	.302200	.302308
.3000000	.312663	.313034	.313334	.313549	.313669
.3100000	.324014	.324427	.324760	.324999	.325133
.3200000	.335463	.335920	.336289	.336554	.336703
.3300000	.347013	.347518	.347926	.348219	.348384
.3400000	.358669	.359226	.359676	.359999	.360181
.3500000	.370436	.371048	.371543	.371899	.372099
.3600000	.382317	.382989	.383532	.383923	.384143
.3700000	.394318	.395053	.395649	.396077	.396318
.3800000	.406443	.407246	.407898	.408366	.408630
.3900000	.418697	.419574	.420285	.420796	.421084

$\alpha =$ .949999

Θ	K VALUES				
	.794250555	.868696860	.928444378	.971111163	.994996249
.4000000	.431085	.432040	.432815	.433373	.433687
.4100000	.443613	.444652	.445495	.446102	.446444
.4200000	.456286	.457414	.458330	.458990	.459361
.4300000	.469110	.470332	.471326	.472042	.472445
.4400000	.482090	.483413	.484489	.485266	.485703
.4500000	.495232	.496663	.497828	.498668	.499142
.4600000	.508542	.510088	.511347	.512256	.512768
.4700000	.522028	.523695	.525054	.526036	.526590
.4800000	.535695	.537491	.538957	.540016	.540614
.4900000	.549549	.551484	.553062	.554204	.554849
.5000000	.563600	.565680	.567379	.568609	.569304
.5100000	.577852	.580088	.581915	.583239	.583987
.5200000	.592315	.594715	.596679	.598102	.598907
.5300000	.606996	.609571	.611679	.613208	.614073
.5400000	.621903	.624663	.626925	.628567	.629496
.5500000	.637045	.640001	.642427	.644189	.645186
.5600000	.652431	.655595	.658194	.660083	.661153
.5700000	.668069	.671454	.674236	.676261	.677409
.5800000	.683969	.687588	.690566	.692735	.693964
.5900000	.700142	.704008	.707194	.709515	.710832
.6000000	.716597	.720726	.724131	.726615	.728026
.6100000	.733345	.737752	.741391	.744048	.745558
.6200000	.750397	.755099	.758986	.761827	.763442
.6300000	.767765	.772780	.776930	.779966	.781693
.6400000	.785462	.790807	.795236	.798480	.800326
.6500000	.803499	.809194	.813920	.817384	.819358
.6600000	.821890	.827957	.832997	.836696	.838805
.6700000	.840649	.847109	.852483	.856432	.858685
.6800000	.859790	.866666	.872396	.876610	.879016
.6899999	.879328	.886646	.892752	.897249	.899818
.7000000	.899280	.907065	.913572	.918369	.921112
.7100000	.919661	.927942	.934873	.939990	.942919
.7200000	.940488	.949294	.956677	.962135	.965261
.7300000	.961780	.971143	.979006	.984826	.988163
.7400000	.983555	.993509	1.001881	1.008088	1.011650
.7500000	1.005834	1.016413	1.025328	1.031946	1.035749
.7600000	1.028636	1.039879	1.049371	1.056428	1.060487
.7700000	1.051984	1.063931	1.074036	1.081562	1.085895
.7800000	1.075901	1.088594	1.099352	1.107377	1.112003
.7899999	1.100409	1.113896	1.125349	1.133906	1.138844

$\alpha =$ .949999

Θ	K VALUES				
	.794250555	.868696860	.928444378	.971111163	.994996249
.8000000	1.125536	1.139863	1.152056	1.161182	1.166455
.8100000	1.151305	1.166526	1.179506	1.189240	1.194872
.8200000	1.177746	1.193915	1.207735	1.218118	1.224134
.8300000	1.204887	1.222063	1.236779	1.247856	1.254282
.8400000	1.232759	1.251006	1.266676	1.278496	1.285362
.8500000	1.261394	1.280779	1.297467	1.310081	1.317421
.8600000	1.290827	1.311421	1.329196	1.342660	1.350507
.8700000	1.321091	1.342972	1.361907	1.376283	1.384675
.8799999	1.352227	1.375476	1.395650	1.411003	1.419980
.8899999	1.384271	1.408977	1.430476	1.446877	1.456483
.9000000	1.417268	1.443524	1.466439	1.483965	1.494249
.9100000	1.451260	1.479167	1.503597	1.522331	1.533345
.9200000	1.486294	1.515961	1.542011	1.562044	1.573845
.9300000	1.522420	1.553961	1.581747	1.603176	1.615826
.9400000	1.559688	1.593228	1.622874	1.645806	1.659372
.9500000	1.598155	1.633826	1.665466	1.690016	1.704572
.9600000	1.637877	1.675823	1.709601	1.735895	1.751523
.9699999	1.678916	1.719291	1.755364	1.783538	1.800326
.9799999	1.721337	1.764305	1.802842	1.833047	1.851091
.9899999	1.765208	1.810946	1.852132	1.884530	1.903937
1.0000000	1.810603	1.859302	1.903335	1.938104	1.958992
1.0100000	1.857598	1.909463	1.956559	1.993894	2.016391
1.0200000	1.906275	1.961527	2.011919	2.052033	2.076281
1.0300000	1.956720	2.015597	2.069541	2.112667	2.138822
1.0400000	2.009025	2.071783	2.129555	2.175950	2.204185
1.0500000	2.063288	2.130202	2.192104	2.242049	2.272556
1.0600000	2.119611	2.190980	2.257339	2.311143	2.344133
1.0699999	2.178105	2.254251	2.325423	2.383426	2.419135
1.0799999	2.238886	2.320154	2.396530	2.459107	2.497796
1.0899999	2.302078	2.388844	2.470848	2.538411	2.580371
1.1000000	2.367813	2.460481	2.548576	2.621582	2.667138
1.1100000	2.436229	2.535236	2.629928	2.708883	2.758395
1.1200000	2.507475	2.613294	2.715138	2.800598	2.854473
1.1300000	2.581710	2.694851	2.804451	2.897036	2.955727
1.1400000	2.659101	2.780118	2.898136	2.998531	3.062549
1.1500000	2.739826	2.869316	2.996479	3.105446	3.175363
1.1600000	2.824076	2.962686	3.099788	3.218174	3.294636
1.1700000	2.912051	3.060481	3.208394	3.337142	3.420879
1.1800000	3.003966	3.162974	3.322652	3.462814	3.554649
1.1899999	3.100048	3.270454	3.442947	3.595694	3.696563

$\alpha =$ .949999

Θ	K VALUES				
	.794250555	.868696860	.928444378	.971111163	.994996249
1.2000000	3.200540	3.383231	3.569691	3.736331	3.847296
1.2100000	3.305696	3.501634	3.703323	3.885321	4.007590
1.2200000	3.415788	3.626013	3.844319	4.043312	4.178264
1.2300000	3.531105	3.756742	3.993190	4.211013	4.360224
1.2400000	3.651951	3.894218	4.150482	4.389193	4.554468
1.2500000	3.778647	4.038861	4.316780	4.578688	4.762101
1.2599999	3.911534	4.191118	4.492711	4.780410	4.984347
1.2699999	4.050970	4.351461	4.678946	4.995349	5.222564
1.2799999	4.197329	4.520386	4.876196	5.224583	5.478260
1.2899999	4.351006	4.698420	5.085223	5.469280	5.753112
1.3000000	4.512413	4.886112	5.306833	5.730710	6.048987
1.3100000	4.681977	5.084034	5.541873	6.010241	6.367959
1.3200000	4.860140	5.292785	5.791242	6.309356	6.712351
1.3300000	5.047361	5.512984	6.055880	6.629650	7.084753
1.3400000	5.244107	5.745268	6.336765	6.972837	7.488061
1.3500000	5.450853	5.990284	6.634908	7.340744	7.925514
1.3600000	5.668077	6.248690	6.951350	7.735318	8.400739
1.3700000	5.896252	6.521142	7.287145	8.158611	8.917801
1.3799999	6.135845	6.808285	7.643351	8.612775	9.481256
1.3899999	6.387302	7.110745	8.021012	9.100041	10.096214
1.4000000	6.651045	7.429117	8.421143	9.622700	10.768412
1.4100000	6.927447	7.763934	8.844687	10.183043	11.504262
1.4200000	7.216836	8.115673	9.292513	10.783351	12.310968
1.4300000	7.519470	8.484717	9.765365	11.425806	13.196582
1.4400000	7.835522	8.871337	10.263831	12.112428	14.170090
1.4500000	8.165064	9.275671	10.788297	12.844975	15.241475
1.4600000	8.508045	9.697695	11.338911	13.624847	16.421760
1.4700000	8.864278	10.137197	11.915536	14.452955	17.722984
1.4800000	9.233421	10.593760	12.517707	15.329598	19.158079
1.4900000	9.614959	11.066734	13.144595	16.254325	20.740549
1.5000000	10.008199	11.555225	13.794982	17.225816	22.483855
1.5100000	10.412251	12.058073	14.467216	18.241738	24.400224
1.5200000	10.826042	12.573869	15.159238	19.298710	26.498848
1.5300000	11.248312	13.100952	15.868571	20.392239	28.783020
1.5400000	11.677632	13.637423	16.592350	21.516747	31.246362
1.5500000	12.112419	14.181184	17.327373	22.665667	33.868720
1.5600000	12.550974	14.729968	18.070157	23.831598	36.613194
1.5699999	12.991509	15.281393	18.817026	25.006533	39.426663
1.5707963	13.026621	15.325346	18.876565	25.100236	39.651810
1.5707963	13.026624	15.325363	18.876652	25.100220	39.651776

$\alpha =$ .959999

Θ	K VALUES				
	.009966711	.039469502	.087332193	.151646642	.229848846
.0000000	.000000	.000000	.000000	.000000	.000000
.0100000	.010000	.010000	.010000	.010000	.010000
.0200000	.020002	.020002	.020002	.020002	.020002
.0300000	.030008	.030008	.030009	.030009	.030009
.0400000	.040020	.040020	.040021	.040022	.040022
.0500000	.050040	.050040	.050041	.050043	.050044
.0600000	.060069	.060070	.060072	.060074	.060077
.0700000	.070110	.070112	.070115	.070118	.070123
.0800000	.080165	.080167	.080171	.080177	.080183
.0900000	.090235	.090238	.090244	.090252	.090262
.1000000	.100322	.100327	.100335	.100346	.100359
.1100000	.110430	.110436	.110447	.110461	.110479
.1200000	.120558	.120567	.120581	.120599	.120622
.1300000	.130711	.130722	.130739	.130763	.130792
.1400000	.140889	.140902	.140924	.140954	.140990
.1500000	.151094	.151111	.151138	.151175	.151219
.1600000	.161330	.161350	.161383	.161428	.161482
.1700000	.171597	.171622	.171661	.171715	.171780
.1800000	.181899	.181928	.181975	.182038	.182116
.1900000	.192236	.192270	.192326	.192401	.192492
.2000000	.202612	.202652	.202717	.202804	.202911
.2100000	.213029	.213075	.213150	.213252	.213375
.2200000	.223488	.223541	.223628	.223745	.223888
.2300000	.233993	.234054	.234153	.234287	.234450
.2400000	.244545	.244614	.244727	.244880	.245066
.2500000	.255146	.255225	.255353	.255526	.255737
.2600000	.265800	.265889	.266034	.266228	.266466
.2700000	.276509	.276609	.276771	.276990	.277257
.2800000	.287275	.287386	.287568	.287812	.288111
.2900000	.298101	.298225	.298427	.298699	.299032
.3000000	.308988	.309126	.309350	.309653	.310022
.3100000	.319941	.320093	.320341	.320676	.321086
.3200000	.330962	.331130	.331403	.331772	.332224
.3300000	.342052	.342237	.342538	.342944	.343442
.3400000	.353216	.353419	.353749	.354195	.354741
.3500000	.364456	.364678	.365039	.365527	.366125
.3600000	.375775	.376017	.376411	.376944	.377598
.3700000	.387176	.387440	.387869	.388450	.389162
.3800000	.398662	.398949	.399415	.400047	.400822
.3900000	.410237	.410547	.411053	.411739	.412580

$\alpha =$ •959999

Θ	K VALUES				
	•009966711	•039469502	•087332193	•151646642	•229848846
•4000000	•421902	•422238	•422787	•423529	•424441
•4100000	•433663	•434026	•434619	•435421	•436408
•4200000	•445522	•445914	•446553	•447419	•448485
•4300000	•457483	•457905	•458593	•459527	•460676
•4400000	•469549	•470002	•470743	•471748	•472985
•4500000	•481724	•482211	•483007	•484087	•485417
•4600000	•494012	•494534	•495388	•496547	•497975
•4700000	•506417	•506976	•507890	•509132	•510664
•4800000	•518942	•519541	•520519	•521848	•523489
•4900000	•531593	•532232	•533277	•534699	•536454
•5000000	•544373	•545055	•546171	•547688	•549564
•5100000	•557287	•558013	•559203	•560822	•562824
•5200000	•570338	•571112	•572379	•574105	•576239
•5300000	•583533	•584357	•585705	•587542	•589815
•5400000	•596876	•597751	•599184	•601138	•603558
•5500000	•610371	•611300	•612823	•614899	•617472
•5600000	•624025	•625010	•626626	•628830	•631564
•5700000	•637842	•638886	•640599	•642937	•645839
•5800000	•651828	•652934	•654748	•657226	•660305
•5900000	•665989	•667159	•669079	•671704	•674967
•6000000	•680330	•681567	•683599	•686377	•689833
•6100000	•694858	•696165	•698313	•701251	•704909
•6200000	•709579	•710960	•713228	•716333	•720202
•6300000	•724500	•725957	•728351	•731631	•735721
•6400000	•739628	•741164	•743690	•747152	•751472
•6500000	•754969	•756588	•759251	•762904	•767465
•6600000	•770532	•772237	•775043	•778894	•783707
•6700000	•786324	•788118	•791073	•795131	•800207
•6800000	•802352	•804240	•807351	•811624	•816974
•6899999	•818626	•820611	•823883	•828382	•834018
•7000000	•835153	•837240	•840681	•845414	•851349
•7100000	•851943	•854136	•857752	•862729	•868977
•7200000	•869006	•871308	•875106	•880339	•886911
•7300000	•886350	•888766	•892755	•898253	•905165
•7400000	•903986	•906521	•910707	•916482	•923748
•7500000	•921925	•924584	•928976	•935038	•942674
•7600000	•940178	•942965	•947571	•953933	•961954
•7700000	•958756	•961676	•966505	•973180	•981602
•7800000	•977671	•980731	•985791	•992791	1•001632
•7899999	•996937	1•000140	1•005442	1•012781	1•022058

$\alpha =$ .959999

Θ	K VALUES				
	.009966711	.039469502	.087332193	.151646642	.229848846
.8000000	1.016565	1.019918	1.025471	1.033163	1.042895
.8100000	1.036570	1.040080	1.045893	1.053952	1.064158
.8200000	1.056966	1.060638	1.066723	1.075164	1.085864
.8300000	1.077769	1.081609	1.087977	1.096815	1.108031
.8400000	1.098994	1.103009	1.109670	1.118923	1.130676
.8500000	1.120657	1.124854	1.131821	1.141505	1.153818
.8600000	1.142776	1.147163	1.154447	1.164580	1.177477
.8700000	1.165370	1.169953	1.177567	1.188168	1.201673
.8799999	1.188457	1.193244	1.201202	1.212290	1.226429
.8899999	1.212057	1.217057	1.225373	1.236967	1.251768
.9000000	1.236191	1.241413	1.250100	1.262222	1.277712
.9100000	1.260883	1.266334	1.275408	1.288079	1.304289
.9200000	1.286154	1.291844	1.301321	1.314564	1.331523
.9300000	1.312029	1.317968	1.327864	1.341703	1.359444
.9400000	1.338535	1.344732	1.355064	1.369524	1.388081
.9500000	1.365698	1.372164	1.382950	1.398057	1.417464
.9600000	1.393548	1.400294	1.411552	1.427332	1.447627
.9699999	1.422114	1.429151	1.440901	1.457384	1.478604
.9799999	1.451429	1.458768	1.471030	1.488245	1.510432
.9899999	1.481526	1.489181	1.501976	1.519954	1.543148
1.0000000	1.512441	1.520424	1.533775	1.552548	1.576795
1.0100000	1.544212	1.552537	1.566466	1.586069	1.611415
1.0200000	1.576878	1.585559	1.600092	1.620560	1.647054
1.0300000	1.610483	1.619535	1.634696	1.656066	1.683759
1.0400000	1.645070	1.654508	1.670325	1.692637	1.721582
1.0500000	1.680688	1.690529	1.707029	1.730324	1.760577
1.0600000	1.717386	1.727647	1.744860	1.769181	1.800802
1.0699999	1.755218	1.765917	1.783874	1.809266	1.842317
1.0799999	1.794241	1.805397	1.824130	1.850642	1.885188
1.0899999	1.834516	1.846148	1.865692	1.893372	1.929483
1.1000000	1.876106	1.888235	1.908625	1.937528	1.975276
1.1100000	1.919078	1.931728	1.953002	1.983182	2.022643
1.1200000	1.963507	1.976699	1.998897	2.030414	2.071668
1.1300000	2.009469	2.023227	2.046391	2.079306	2.122439
1.1400000	2.057046	2.071397	2.095571	2.129948	2.175050
1.1500000	2.106326	2.121296	2.146527	2.182436	2.229600
1.1600000	2.157402	2.173020	2.199356	2.236870	2.286196
1.1700000	2.210373	2.226670	2.254164	2.293358	2.344952
1.1800000	2.265347	2.282353	2.311060	2.352015	2.405989
1.1899999	2.322436	2.340185	2.370162	2.412964	2.469436

$\alpha =$ .959999

Θ	K VALUES				
	.009966711	.039469502	.087332193	.151646642	.229848846
1.2000000	2.381761	2.400289	2.431598	2.476337	2.535431
1.2100000	2.443450	2.462795	2.495500	2.542272	2.604120
1.2200000	2.507642	2.527843	2.562013	2.610919	2.675662
1.2300000	2.574483	2.595582	2.631290	2.682437	2.750222
1.2400000	2.644128	2.666170	2.703492	2.756995	2.827980
1.2500000	2.716745	2.739777	2.778796	2.834773	2.909124
1.2599999	2.792511	2.816583	2.857384	2.915964	2.993859
1.2699999	2.871614	2.896780	2.939454	3.000773	3.082398
1.2799999	2.954255	2.980570	3.025215	3.089415	3.174970
1.2899999	3.040646	3.068169	3.114889	3.182123	3.271817
1.3000000	3.131012	3.159807	3.208710	3.279139	3.373197
1.3100000	3.225589	3.255724	3.306925	3.380720	3.479378
1.3200000	3.324627	3.356172	3.409794	3.487137	3.590647
1.3300000	3.428389	3.461418	3.517591	3.598673	3.707301
1.3400000	3.537146	3.571740	3.630601	3.715625	3.829652
1.3500000	3.651183	3.687425	3.749119	3.838300	3.958023
1.3600000	3.770791	3.808770	3.873450	3.967013	4.092747
1.3700000	3.896268	3.936077	4.003904	4.102089	4.234165
1.3799999	4.027915	4.069652	4.140796	4.243853	4.382619
1.3899999	4.166032	4.209800	4.284438	4.392631	4.538452
1.4000000	4.310914	4.356821	4.435139	4.548742	4.702000
1.4100000	4.462840	4.510997	4.593189	4.712489	4.873581
1.4200000	4.622070	4.672594	4.758860	4.884154	5.053493
1.4300000	4.788835	4.841845	4.932393	5.063987	5.241999
1.4400000	4.963324	5.018943	5.113985	5.252194	5.439315
1.4500000	5.145673	5.204026	5.303778	5.448921	5.645595
1.4600000	5.335951	5.397164	5.501843	5.654243	5.860918
1.4700000	5.534144	5.598343	5.708167	5.868146	6.085269
1.4800000	5.740145	5.807454	5.922637	6.090513	6.318525
1.4900000	5.953733	6.024273	6.145024	6.321105	6.560435
1.5000000	6.174569	6.248455	6.374974	6.559555	6.810613
1.5100000	6.402177	6.479516	6.611988	6.805345	7.068514
1.5200000	6.635946	6.716837	6.855431	7.057815	7.333442
1.5300000	6.875129	6.959657	7.104523	7.316154	7.604546
1.5400000	7.118848	7.207086	7.358348	7.579410	7.880824
1.5500000	7.366108	7.458112	7.615867	7.846505	8.161140
1.5600000	7.615819	7.711628	7.875944	8.116257	8.444252
1.5699999	7.866821	7.966456	8.137368	8.387410	8.728838
1.5707963	7.886830	7.986769	8.158207	8.409024	8.751523
1.5707963	7.886822	7.986761	8.158199	8.409017	8.751515

$\alpha =$ .959999

Θ	K VALUES				
	.318821117	.415016431	.514599755	.613601043	.708073407
.0000000	.000000	.000000	.000000	.000000	.000000
.0100000	.010000	.010000	.010000	.010000	.010000
.0200000	.020002	.020003	.020003	.020003	.020003
.0300000	.030010	.030010	.030010	.030011	.030011
.0400000	.040023	.040024	.040026	.040027	.040028
.0500000	.050046	.050048	.050050	.050052	.050054
.0600000	.060080	.060084	.060087	.060091	.060094
.0700000	.070128	.070133	.070139	.070145	.070150
.0800000	.080191	.080199	.080208	.080216	.080224
.0900000	.090272	.090284	.090296	.090308	.090320
.1000000	.100374	.100390	.100407	.100424	.100440
.1100000	.110499	.110520	.110542	.110565	.110586
.1200000	.120648	.120676	.120705	.120734	.120761
.1300000	.130825	.130860	.130897	.130934	.130969
.1400000	.141031	.141076	.141122	.141168	.141212
.1500000	.151270	.151325	.151382	.151439	.151493
.1600000	.161544	.161610	.161680	.161749	.161815
.1700000	.171854	.171934	.172018	.172101	.172181
.1800000	.182204	.182300	.182399	.182498	.182593
.1900000	.192596	.192709	.192826	.192943	.193055
.2000000	.203033	.203165	.203302	.203438	.203569
.2100000	.213517	.213670	.213829	.213988	.214140
.2200000	.224050	.224227	.224411	.224594	.224770
.2300000	.234637	.234839	.235050	.235260	.235462
.2400000	.245278	.245509	.245749	.245989	.246220
.2500000	.255978	.256240	.256512	.256785	.257046
.2600000	.266738	.267034	.267342	.267650	.267945
.2700000	.277562	.277895	.278241	.278587	.278920
.2800000	.288453	.288825	.289213	.289601	.289975
.2900000	.299413	.299828	.300261	.300695	.301112
.3000000	.310446	.310908	.311389	.311872	.312337
.3100000	.321555	.322066	.322600	.323136	.323652
.3200000	.332742	.333308	.333898	.334491	.335061
.3300000	.344012	.344635	.345286	.345940	.346570
.3400000	.355368	.356052	.356768	.357487	.358181
.3500000	.366812	.367562	.368347	.369137	.369899
.3600000	.378348	.379169	.380029	.380893	.381729
.3700000	.389981	.390877	.391815	.392761	.393674
.3800000	.401713	.402689	.403712	.404743	.405740
.3900000	.413548	.414609	.415722	.416845	.417931

$\alpha =$ .959999

Θ	K VALUES				
	.318821117	.415016431	.514599755	.613601043	.708073407
.4000000	.425491	.426642	.427851	.429071	.430252
.4100000	.437545	.438791	.440102	.441425	.442708
.4200000	.449713	.451062	.452480	.453914	.455305
.4300000	.462002	.463458	.464991	.466541	.468047
.4400000	.474414	.475984	.477638	.479313	.480940
.4500000	.486954	.488644	.490427	.492233	.493990
.4600000	.499626	.501444	.503362	.505309	.507203
.4700000	.512436	.514388	.516451	.518544	.520585
.4800000	.525388	.527482	.529696	.531947	.534142
.4900000	.538487	.540730	.543105	.545521	.547880
.5000000	.551738	.554139	.556684	.559274	.561806
.5100000	.565146	.567714	.570437	.573213	.575928
.5200000	.578718	.581461	.584372	.587343	.590253
.5300000	.592458	.595385	.598495	.601672	.604787
.5400000	.606372	.609493	.612812	.616207	.619539
.5500000	.620467	.623791	.627331	.630955	.634517
.5600000	.634749	.638287	.642059	.645925	.649729
.5700000	.649223	.652986	.657002	.661123	.665184
.5800000	.663898	.667897	.672169	.676559	.680890
.5900000	.678779	.683025	.687568	.692241	.696858
.6000000	.693873	.698380	.703207	.708179	.713096
.6100000	.709189	.713969	.719094	.724380	.729616
.6200000	.724734	.729800	.735239	.740856	.746427
.6300000	.740516	.745882	.751650	.757615	.763540
.6400000	.756543	.762223	.768337	.774669	.780968
.6500000	.772823	.778834	.785311	.792029	.798721
.6600000	.789367	.795722	.802581	.809705	.816813
.6700000	.806182	.812899	.820158	.827710	.835256
.6800000	.823279	.830375	.838054	.846055	.854063
.6899999	.840667	.848161	.856281	.864754	.873249
.7000000	.858358	.866267	.874850	.883820	.892829
.7100000	.876362	.884706	.893774	.903267	.912818
.7200000	.894690	.903489	.913067	.923110	.933231
.7300000	.913354	.922630	.932742	.943363	.954086
.7400000	.932366	.942142	.952814	.964043	.975401
.7500000	.951740	.962038	.973298	.985166	.997193
.7600000	.971488	.982333	.994209	1.006749	1.019483
.7700000	.991625	1.003041	1.015565	1.028812	1.042289
.7800000	1.012165	1.024180	1.037381	1.051372	1.065634
.7899999	1.033124	1.045765	1.059677	1.074449	1.089539

$\alpha =$ •959999

Θ	K VALUES				
	•318821117	•415016431	•514599755	•613601043	•708073407
•8000000	1•054518	1•067813	1•082471	1•098065	1•114029
•8100000	1•076362	1•090343	1•105783	1•122241	1•139126
•8200000	1•098676	1•113374	1•129634	1•147001	1•164858
•8300000	1•121476	1•136924	1•154044	1•172367	1•191250
•8400000	1•144782	1•161015	1•179038	1•198366	1•218331
•8500000	1•168615	1•185669	1•204638	1•225024	1•246131
•8600000	1•192995	1•210908	1•230870	1•252369	1•274682
•8700000	1•217945	1•236757	1•257760	1•280430	1•304015
•8799999	1•243487	1•263240	1•285335	1•309237	1•334167
•8899999	1•269646	1•290384	1•313625	1•338824	1•365173
•9000000	1•296449	1•318217	1•342660	1•369223	1•397072
•9100000	1•323921	1•346767	1•372473	1•400472	1•429905
•9200000	1•352091	1•376066	1•403096	1•432607	1•463714
•9300000	1•380989	1•406145	1•434565	1•465669	1•498545
•9400000	1•410647	1•437040	1•466919	1•499699	1•534445
•9500000	1•441097	1•468785	1•500196	1•534742	1•571466
•9600000	1•472375	1•501419	1•534438	1•570845	1•609660
•9699999	1•504517	1•534982	1•569690	1•608057	1•649084
•9799999	1•537562	1•569516	1•605997	1•646430	1•689797
•9899999	1•571552	1•605065	1•643410	1•686020	1•731864
1•0000000	1•606531	1•641676	1•681980	1•726885	1•775351
1•0100000	1•642543	1•679400	1•721761	1•769087	1•820329
1•0200000	1•679637	1•718290	1•762813	1•812691	1•866874
1•0300000	1•717866	1•758400	1•805197	1•857767	1•915065
1•0400000	1•757283	1•799790	1•848978	1•904389	1•964988
1•0500000	1•797947	1•842523	1•894225	1•952635	2•016732
1•0600000	1•839919	1•886666	1•941013	2•002587	2•070394
1•0699999	1•883263	1•932289	1•989419	2•054335	2•126075
1•0799999	1•928050	1•979467	2•039525	2•107971	2•183884
1•0899999	1•974352	2•028279	2•091421	2•163595	2•243936
1•1000000	2•022249	2•078812	2•145200	2•221313	2•306355
1•1100000	2•071821	2•131153	2•200961	2•281238	2•371269
1•1200000	2•123158	2•185400	2•258810	2•343489	2•438820
1•1300000	2•176355	2•241654	2•318861	2•408195	2•509156
1•1400000	2•231510	2•300024	2•381233	2•475491	2•582434
1•1500000	2•288731	2•360627	2•446055	2•545523	2•658826
1•1600000	2•348132	2•423584	2•513462	2•618445	2•738509
1•1700000	2•409833	2•489028	2•583602	2•694422	2•821679
1•1800000	2•473964	2•557099	2•656629	2•773631	2•908539
1•1899999	2•540663	2•627948	2•732708	2•856260	2•999309

$\alpha =$ .959999

Θ	K VALUES				
	.318821117	.415016431	.514599755	.613601043	.708073407
1.2000000	2.610078	2.701733	2.812018	2.942509	3.094226
1.2100000	2.682365	2.778625	2.894745	3.032591	3.193536
1.2200000	2.757691	2.858805	2.981091	3.126735	3.297510
1.2300000	2.836235	2.942467	3.071272	3.225184	3.406430
1.2400000	2.918187	3.029819	3.165515	3.328199	3.520603
1.2500000	3.003751	3.121080	3.264064	3.436055	3.640351
1.2599999	3.093141	3.216484	3.367179	3.549048	3.766021
1.2699999	3.186589	3.316280	3.475135	3.667490	3.897979
1.2799999	3.284336	3.420734	3.588226	3.791714	4.036617
1.2899999	3.386643	3.530126	3.706762	3.922073	4.182350
1.3000000	3.493784	3.644753	3.831074	4.058942	4.335616
1.3100000	3.606045	3.764928	3.961506	4.202713	4.496877
1.3200000	3.723733	3.890981	4.098425	4.353801	4.666622
1.3300000	3.847164	4.023259	4.242213	4.512643	4.845362
1.3400000	3.976672	4.162121	4.393271	4.679691	5.033630
1.3500000	4.112602	4.307942	4.552012	4.855416	5.231981
1.3600000	4.255309	4.461109	4.718863	5.040304	5.440985
1.3700000	4.405155	4.622014	4.894262	5.234851	5.661226
1.3799999	4.562509	4.791056	5.078648	5.439556	5.893294
1.3899999	4.727734	4.968631	5.272460	5.654919	6.137775
1.4000000	4.901190	5.155129	5.476131	5.881432	6.395249
1.4100000	5.083216	5.350917	5.690067	6.119556	6.666262
1.4200000	5.274131	5.556343	5.914652	6.369728	6.951327
1.4300000	5.474215	5.771709	6.150223	6.632332	7.250898
1.4400000	5.683697	5.997266	6.397057	6.907683	7.565350
1.4500000	5.902745	6.233194	6.655354	7.196009	7.894952
1.4600000	6.131441	6.479584	6.925215	7.497427	8.239846
1.4700000	6.369770	6.736420	7.206623	7.811918	8.600015
1.4800000	6.617600	7.003558	7.499420	8.139306	8.975255
1.4900000	6.874665	7.280710	7.803287	8.479230	9.365149
1.5000000	7.140551	7.567427	8.117729	8.831131	9.769045
1.5100000	7.414677	7.863081	8.442052	9.194222	10.186026
1.5200000	7.696302	8.166867	8.775365	9.567497	10.614917
1.5300000	7.984517	8.477798	9.116579	9.949721	11.054276
1.5400000	8.278252	8.794716	9.464411	10.339443	11.502404
1.5500000	8.576296	9.116307	9.817412	10.735020	11.957381
1.5600000	8.877324	9.441134	10.173989	11.134648	12.417098
1.5699999	9.179924	9.767665	10.532452	11.536412	12.879314
1.5707963	9.204045	9.793695	10.561027	11.568439	12.916160
1.5707963	9.204037	9.793688	10.561020	11.568434	12.916158

$\alpha =$ •959999

Θ	K VALUES				
	•794250555	•868696860	•928444378	•971111163	•994996249
•0000000	•000000	•000000	•000000	•000000	•000000
•0100000	•010000	•010000	•010000	•010000	•010000
•0200000	•020003	•020003	•020003	•020003	•020003
•0300000	•030012	•030012	•030012	•030013	•030013
•0400000	•040028	•040029	•040030	•040030	•040031
•0500000	•050056	•050058	•050059	•050060	•050060
•0600000	•060097	•060100	•060102	•060104	•060105
•0700000	•070155	•070159	•070163	•070165	•070167
•0800000	•080232	•080238	•080243	•080247	•080249
•0900000	•090331	•090340	•090347	•090352	•090355
•1000000	•100454	•100467	•100477	•100484	•100488
•1100000	•110605	•110622	•110635	•110645	•110650
•1200000	•120787	•120808	•120826	•120838	•120845
•1300000	•131002	•131029	•131052	•131068	•131077
•1400000	•141253	•141287	•141315	•141335	•141347
•1500000	•151543	•151586	•151620	•151645	•151659
•1600000	•161876	•161928	•161970	•162000	•162017
•1700000	•172253	•172316	•172367	•172403	•172423
•1800000	•182679	•182755	•182815	•182858	•182882
•1900000	•193157	•193246	•193317	•193368	•193397
•2000000	•203689	•203793	•203877	•203937	•203970
•2100000	•214279	•214400	•214498	•214567	•214606
•2200000	•224931	•225070	•225183	•225263	•225308
•2300000	•235647	•235807	•235936	•236029	•236080
•2400000	•246431	•246614	•246761	•246867	•246926
•2500000	•257286	•257494	•257662	•257782	•257850
•2600000	•268217	•268452	•268642	•268778	•268854
•2700000	•279226	•279491	•279705	•279859	•279945
•2800000	•290318	•290615	•290856	•291028	•291125
•2900000	•301495	•301829	•302097	•302290	•302398
•3000000	•312764	•313135	•313435	•313650	•313770
•3100000	•324126	•324539	•324872	•325111	•325245
•3200000	•335587	•336044	•336413	•336678	•336827
•3300000	•347150	•347655	•348064	•348357	•348522
•3400000	•358820	•359377	•359827	•360151	•360333
•3500000	•370602	•371214	•371710	•372066	•372266
•3600000	•382499	•383171	•383715	•384106	•384326
•3700000	•394517	•395253	•395850	•396278	•396519
•3800000	•406661	•407465	•408117	•408586	•408850
•3900000	•418935	•419813	•420525	•421037	•421325

$\alpha =$ .959999

Θ	K VALUES				
	.794250555	.868696860	.928444378	.971111163	.994996249
.4000000	.431345	.432301	.433077	.433635	.433949
.4100000	.443896	.444936	.445779	.446387	.446729
.4200000	.456593	.457722	.458639	.459300	.459672
.4300000	.469443	.470667	.471661	.472379	.472783
.4400000	.482451	.483776	.484853	.485631	.486069
.4500000	.495622	.497055	.498222	.499063	.499538
.4600000	.508964	.510512	.511773	.512683	.513196
.4700000	.522483	.524153	.525514	.526497	.527052
.4800000	.536186	.537985	.539453	.540514	.541113
.4900000	.550079	.552016	.553598	.554742	.555388
.5000000	.564169	.566253	.567956	.569188	.569884
.5100000	.578465	.580705	.582536	.583862	.584611
.5200000	.592974	.595378	.597346	.598772	.599579
.5300000	.607703	.610283	.612396	.613928	.614795
.5400000	.622662	.625428	.627695	.629340	.630272
.5500000	.637859	.640822	.643252	.645018	.646018
.5600000	.653303	.656474	.659079	.660973	.662046
.5700000	.669003	.672396	.675185	.677215	.678365
.5800000	.684969	.688597	.691582	.693757	.694990
.5900000	.701211	.705088	.708282	.710610	.711930
.6000000	.717740	.721881	.725296	.727787	.729201
.6100000	.734566	.738987	.742636	.745301	.746815
.6200000	.751702	.756419	.760317	.763167	.764787
.6300000	.769159	.774189	.778353	.781398	.783131
.6400000	.786950	.792312	.796756	.800011	.801863
.6500000	.805087	.810802	.815544	.819020	.821000
.6600000	.823584	.829672	.834731	.838443	.840559
.6700000	.842455	.848939	.854334	.858297	.860558
.6800000	.861716	.868619	.874371	.878601	.881017
.6899999	.881381	.888729	.894860	.899375	.901954
.7000000	.901468	.909286	.915820	.920637	.923392
.7100000	.921992	.930309	.937271	.942411	.945352
.7200000	.942972	.951818	.959235	.964717	.967858
.7300000	.964426	.973833	.981733	.987581	.990935
.7400000	.986373	.996376	1.004790	1.011027	1.014608
.7500000	1.008835	1.019468	1.028429	1.035082	1.038905
.7600000	1.031833	1.043135	1.052678	1.059773	1.063854
.7700000	1.055388	1.067401	1.077563	1.085130	1.089488
.7800000	1.079526	1.092292	1.103113	1.111184	1.115837
.7899999	1.104270	1.117836	1.129358	1.137968	1.142937

$\alpha =$ .959999

Θ	K VALUES				
	.794250555	.868696860	.928444378	.971111163	.994996249
.8000000	1.129647	1.144063	1.156332	1.165516	1.170823
.8100000	1.155683	1.171002	1.184068	1.193865	1.199534
.8200000	1.182409	1.198686	1.212601	1.223055	1.229111
.8300000	1.209854	1.227150	1.241970	1.253125	1.259597
.8400000	1.238050	1.256429	1.272214	1.284121	1.291039
.8500000	1.267032	1.286562	1.303378	1.316089	1.323485
.8600000	1.296834	1.317589	1.335505	1.349077	1.356987
.8700000	1.327494	1.349552	1.368643	1.383139	1.391600
.8799999	1.359051	1.382496	1.402843	1.418330	1.427385
.8899999	1.391547	1.416470	1.438160	1.454709	1.464402
.9000000	1.425027	1.451523	1.474650	1.492340	1.502721
.9100000	1.459537	1.487709	1.512374	1.531290	1.542413
.9200000	1.495126	1.525085	1.551396	1.571632	1.583553
.9300000	1.531845	1.563710	1.591786	1.613441	1.626225
.9400000	1.569751	1.603649	1.633616	1.656799	1.670516
.9500000	1.608902	1.644969	1.676966	1.701796	1.716520
.9600000	1.649359	1.687743	1.721918	1.748524	1.764339
.9699999	1.691188	1.732047	1.768560	1.797084	1.814081
.9799999	1.734458	1.777962	1.816989	1.847583	1.865863
.9899999	1.779243	1.825575	1.867306	1.900139	1.919810
1.0000000	1.825622	1.874979	1.919619	1.954874	1.976058
1.0100000	1.873677	1.926272	1.974043	2.011923	2.034752
1.0200000	1.923498	1.979559	2.030704	2.071428	2.096049
1.0300000	1.975177	2.034951	2.089735	2.133545	2.160120
1.0400000	2.028815	2.092569	2.151279	2.198441	2.227149
1.0500000	2.084518	2.152539	2.215488	2.266294	2.297334
1.0600000	2.142400	2.214999	2.282529	2.337300	2.370893
1.0699999	2.202581	2.280095	2.352577	2.411669	2.448058
1.0799999	2.265190	2.347981	2.425823	2.489626	2.529085
1.0899999	2.330365	2.418825	2.502472	2.571418	2.614251
1.1000000	2.398252	2.492808	2.582745	2.657313	2.703858
1.1100000	2.469006	2.570117	2.666878	2.747597	2.798235
1.1200000	2.542794	2.650961	2.755127	2.842585	2.897741
1.1300000	2.619796	2.735558	2.847770	2.942617	3.002770
1.1400000	2.700201	2.824145	2.945104	3.048066	3.113751
1.1500000	2.784213	2.916975	3.047450	3.159333	3.231159
1.1600000	2.872049	3.014319	3.155157	3.276860	3.355510
1.1700000	2.963942	3.116470	3.268600	3.401127	3.487375
1.1800000	3.060142	3.223740	3.388185	3.532657	3.627381
1.1899999	3.160913	3.336466	3.514351	3.672022	3.776221

$\alpha =$ .959999

Θ	K VALUES				
	.794250555	.868696860	.928444378	.971111163	.994996249
1.2000000	3.266542	3.455009	3.647574	3.819849	3.934660
1.2100000	3.377331	3.579755	3.788365	3.976821	4.103542
1.2200000	3.493607	3.711120	3.937281	4.143687	4.283803
1.2300000	3.615718	3.849551	4.094922	4.321268	4.476484
1.2400000	3.744034	3.995526	4.261938	4.510463	4.682736
1.2500000	3.878953	4.149556	4.439029	4.712257	4.903845
1.2599999	4.020898	4.312192	4.626953	4.927730	5.141242
1.2699999	4.170320	4.484018	4.826526	5.158065	5.396523
1.2799999	4.327699	4.665663	5.038629	5.404558	5.671472
1.2899999	4.493543	4.857792	5.264206	5.668631	5.968087
1.3000000	4.668395	5.061118	5.504275	5.951839	6.288610
1.3100000	4.852823	5.276391	5.759921	6.255876	6.635547
1.3200000	5.047428	5.504407	6.032304	6.582597	7.011725
1.3300000	5.252844	5.746006	6.322661	6.934021	7.420323
1.3400000	5.469729	6.002066	6.632298	7.312338	7.864918
1.3500000	5.698768	6.273503	6.962592	7.719921	8.349548
1.3600000	5.940669	6.561266	7.314985	8.159324	8.878769
1.3700000	6.196155	6.866328	7.690972	8.633285	9.457727
1.3799999	6.465956	7.189675	8.092092	9.144717	10.092236
1.3899999	6.750804	7.532299	8.519904	9.696693	10.788868
1.4000000	7.051417	7.895179	8.975974	10.292425	11.555055
1.4100000	7.368477	8.279249	9.461824	10.935203	12.399168
1.4200000	7.702626	8.685391	9.978918	11.628368	13.330670
1.4300000	8.054431	9.114396	10.528600	12.375217	14.360205
1.4400000	8.424364	9.566929	11.112047	13.178904	15.499711
1.4500000	8.812770	10.043488	11.730199	14.042314	16.762512
1.4600000	9.219833	10.544362	12.383692	14.967908	18.163367
1.4700000	9.645546	11.069586	13.072785	15.957543	19.718436
1.4800000	10.089672	11.618891	13.797277	17.012268	21.445100
1.4900000	10.551709	12.191656	14.556434	18.132113	23.361519
1.5000000	11.030870	12.786880	15.348929	19.315880	25.485798
1.5100000	11.526039	13.403126	16.172760	20.560911	27.834399
1.5200000	12.035785	14.038531	17.025257	21.862994	30.419745
1.5300000	12.558344	14.690795	17.903057	23.216239	33.246464
1.5400000	13.091643	15.357197	18.802133	24.613102	36.306464
1.5500000	13.633329	16.034649	19.717870	26.044501	39.573592
1.5600000	14.180821	16.719751	20.645162	27.500051	42.999809
1.5699999	14.731374	17.408889	21.578554	28.968413	46.515911
1.5707963	14.775264	17.463829	21.652977	29.085542	46.797344
1.5707963	14.775267	17.463849	21.653058	29.085509	46.797284

$\alpha =$ .969999

Θ	K VALUES				
	.009966711	.039469502	.087332193	.151646642	.229848846
.0000000	.000000	.000000	.000000	.000000	.000000
.0100000	.010000	.010000	.010000	.010000	.010000
.0200000	.020002	.020002	.020002	.020002	.020002
.0300000	.030008	.030008	.030009	.030009	.030009
.0400000	.040020	.040021	.040021	.040022	.040023
.0500000	.050040	.050041	.050042	.050043	.050045
.0600000	.060070	.060071	.060073	.060075	.060078
.0700000	.070111	.070113	.070116	.070119	.070124
.0800000	.080166	.080169	.080173	.080178	.080185
.0900000	.090237	.090241	.090247	.090254	.090264
.1000000	.100326	.100331	.100339	.100349	.100363
.1100000	.110434	.110441	.110451	.110466	.110483
.1200000	.120564	.120573	.120587	.120605	.120628
.1300000	.130718	.130729	.130747	.130770	.130799
.1400000	.140898	.140912	.140934	.140963	.141000
.1500000	.151106	.151123	.151150	.151186	.151231
.1600000	.161344	.161364	.161397	.161442	.161496
.1700000	.171614	.171638	.171678	.171732	.171797
.1800000	.181919	.181948	.181995	.182058	.182136
.1900000	.192260	.192294	.192350	.192424	.192516
.2000000	.202640	.202680	.202745	.202832	.202939
.2100000	.213061	.213107	.213183	.213284	.213408
.2200000	.223525	.223579	.223665	.223782	.223925
.2300000	.234035	.234096	.234196	.234330	.234493
.2400000	.244593	.244663	.244776	.244928	.245115
.2500000	.255202	.255281	.255409	.255581	.255792
.2600000	.265863	.265952	.266096	.266291	.266529
.2700000	.276580	.276679	.276842	.277060	.277327
.2800000	.287354	.287466	.287647	.287891	.288190
.2900000	.298189	.298313	.298515	.298788	.299121
.3000000	.309087	.309224	.309449	.309751	.310121
.3100000	.320050	.320203	.320451	.320786	.321195
.3200000	.331082	.331250	.331524	.331894	.332346
.3300000	.342186	.342370	.342671	.343078	.343576
.3400000	.353363	.353566	.353896	.354342	.354889
.3500000	.364618	.364839	.365201	.365689	.366288
.3600000	.375952	.376194	.376588	.377122	.377776
.3700000	.387370	.387633	.388063	.388644	.389357
.3800000	.398873	.399160	.399627	.400259	.401035
.3900000	.410467	.410777	.411284	.411970	.412812

$\alpha =$ .969999

Θ	K VALUES				
	.009966711	.039469502	.087332193	.151646642	.229848846
.4000000	.422153	.422489	.423038	.423781	.424694
.4100000	.433935	.434298	.434891	.435695	.436683
.4200000	.445817	.446209	.446849	.447716	.448783
.4300000	.457802	.458224	.458914	.459849	.460999
.4400000	.469894	.470348	.471090	.472096	.473335
.4500000	.482096	.482584	.483381	.484462	.485794
.4600000	.494413	.494937	.495791	.496952	.498382
.4700000	.506849	.507409	.508325	.509569	.511103
.4800000	.519408	.520007	.520987	.522318	.523961
.4900000	.532093	.532733	.533780	.535204	.536962
.5000000	.544910	.545593	.546711	.548231	.550110
.5100000	.557863	.558591	.559783	.561405	.563410
.5200000	.570956	.571732	.573001	.574730	.576868
.5300000	.584195	.585020	.586371	.588211	.590489
.5400000	.597584	.598461	.599897	.601854	.604279
.5500000	.611128	.612059	.613585	.615665	.618244
.5600000	.624834	.625821	.627440	.629649	.632389
.5700000	.638706	.639752	.641469	.643813	.646722
.5800000	.652750	.653858	.655677	.658161	.661247
.5900000	.666972	.668145	.670070	.672702	.675973
.6000000	.681378	.682618	.684655	.687441	.690906
.6100000	.695974	.697285	.699439	.702385	.706053
.6200000	.710768	.712152	.714427	.717542	.721422
.6300000	.725765	.727226	.729628	.732918	.737020
.6400000	.740974	.742515	.745049	.748522	.752856
.6500000	.756401	.758025	.760697	.764361	.768937
.6600000	.772054	.773764	.776580	.780444	.785273
.6700000	.787941	.789742	.792707	.796779	.801873
.6800000	.804070	.805965	.809087	.813376	.818746
.6899999	.820450	.822443	.825727	.830243	.835901
.7000000	.837090	.839185	.842639	.847391	.853350
.7100000	.853999	.856201	.859831	.864829	.871103
.7200000	.871187	.873499	.877314	.882569	.889170
.7300000	.888665	.891092	.895097	.900620	.907563
.7400000	.906442	.908988	.913194	.918995	.926295
.7500000	.924529	.927201	.931613	.937705	.945377
.7600000	.942940	.945740	.950369	.956763	.964824
.7700000	.961684	.964620	.969473	.976182	.984648
.7800000	.980776	.983851	.988939	.995977	1.004865
.7899999	1.000228	1.003449	1.008780	1.016160	1.025488

$\alpha =$ .969999

Θ	K VALUES				
	.009966711	.039469502	.087332193	.151646642	.229848846
.8000000	1.020054	1.023427	1.029011	1.036747	1.046535
.8100000	1.040269	1.043799	1.049647	1.057754	1.068022
.8200000	1.060887	1.064581	1.070704	1.079197	1.089964
.8300000	1.081926	1.085790	1.092198	1.101094	1.112382
.8400000	1.103400	1.107442	1.114147	1.123461	1.135293
.8500000	1.125328	1.129554	1.136569	1.146320	1.158719
.8600000	1.147729	1.152147	1.159483	1.169688	1.182678
.8700000	1.170621	1.175238	1.182909	1.193588	1.207195
.8799999	1.194025	1.198850	1.206869	1.218042	1.232291
.8899999	1.217963	1.223003	1.231385	1.243071	1.257992
.9000000	1.242456	1.247721	1.256480	1.268702	1.284322
.9100000	1.267529	1.273027	1.282179	1.294959	1.311309
.9200000	1.293207	1.298947	1.308508	1.321870	1.338982
.9300000	1.319515	1.325508	1.335495	1.349463	1.367370
.9400000	1.346482	1.352738	1.363169	1.377768	1.396505
.9500000	1.374137	1.380667	1.391560	1.406818	1.426420
.9600000	1.402512	1.409327	1.420701	1.436645	1.457151
.9699999	1.431638	1.438750	1.450625	1.467286	1.488736
.9799999	1.461552	1.468973	1.481370	1.498778	1.521214
.9899999	1.492289	1.500032	1.512974	1.531161	1.554627
1.0000000	1.523889	1.531968	1.545478	1.564477	1.589019
1.0100000	1.556393	1.564821	1.578924	1.598772	1.624438
1.0200000	1.589846	1.598638	1.613358	1.634092	1.660934
1.0300000	1.624293	1.633466	1.648830	1.670489	1.698559
1.0400000	1.659785	1.669354	1.685391	1.708016	1.737372
1.0500000	1.696374	1.706357	1.723096	1.746730	1.777430
1.0600000	1.734116	1.744531	1.762003	1.786693	1.818800
1.0699999	1.773072	1.783938	1.802176	1.827969	1.861548
1.0799999	1.813305	1.824642	1.843681	1.870628	1.905749
1.0899999	1.854884	1.866713	1.886588	1.914743	1.951479
1.1000000	1.897882	1.910225	1.930975	1.960393	1.998821
1.1100000	1.942375	1.955256	1.976922	2.007663	2.047864
1.1200000	1.988448	2.001891	2.024515	2.056642	2.098703
1.1300000	2.036189	2.050221	2.073848	2.107427	2.151440
1.1400000	2.085694	2.100342	2.125021	2.160121	2.206182
1.1500000	2.137065	2.152359	2.178139	2.214836	2.263047
1.1600000	2.190412	2.206383	2.233318	2.271690	2.322160
1.1700000	2.245853	2.262534	2.290680	2.330811	2.383655
1.1800000	2.303514	2.320939	2.350357	2.392336	2.447676
1.1899999	2.363532	2.381739	2.412492	2.456413	2.514378

$\alpha =$ .969999

Θ	K VALUES				
	.009966711	.039469502	.087332193	.151646642	.229848846
1.2000000	2.426053	2.445081	2.477238	2.523200	2.583929
1.2100000	2.491235	2.511125	2.544758	2.592867	2.656506
1.2200000	2.559246	2.580044	2.615228	2.665599	2.732305
1.2300000	2.630271	2.652023	2.688841	2.741594	2.811533
1.2400000	2.704506	2.727262	2.765802	2.821065	2.894414
1.2500000	2.782163	2.805978	2.846331	2.904241	2.981190
1.2599999	2.863471	2.888402	2.930668	2.991371	3.072123
1.2699999	2.948676	2.974786	3.019070	3.082723	3.167493
1.2799999	3.038046	3.065398	3.111814	3.178583	3.267602
1.2899999	3.131865	3.160529	3.209198	3.279261	3.372776
1.3000000	3.230442	3.260494	3.311544	3.385093	3.483368
1.3100000	3.334106	3.365626	3.419196	3.496435	3.599752
1.3200000	3.443214	3.476287	3.532524	3.613671	3.722333
1.3300000	3.558145	3.592863	3.651925	3.737213	3.851544
1.3400000	3.679304	3.715765	3.777822	3.867502	3.987847
1.3500000	3.807124	3.845433	3.910665	4.005003	4.131735
1.3600000	3.942062	3.982330	4.050931	4.150214	4.283727
1.3700000	4.084600	4.126946	4.199122	4.303655	4.444372
1.3799999	4.235241	4.279793	4.355764	4.465873	4.614245
1.3899999	4.394507	4.441402	4.521402	4.637433	4.793940
1.4000000	4.562936	4.612317	4.696596	4.818916	4.984069
1.4100000	4.741065	4.793085	4.881905	5.010905	5.185244
1.4200000	4.929431	4.984250	5.077891	5.213981	5.398076
1.4300000	5.128550	5.186338	5.285090	5.428704	5.623153
1.4400000	5.338902	5.399835	5.504005	5.655592	5.861023
1.4500000	5.560908	5.625170	5.735074	5.895104	6.112165
1.4600000	5.794908	5.862688	5.978651	6.147605	6.376965
1.4700000	6.041126	6.112615	6.234970	6.413340	6.655680
1.4800000	6.299640	6.375032	6.504112	6.692392	6.948397
1.4900000	6.570346	6.649833	6.785970	6.984650	7.255000
1.5000000	6.852927	6.936695	7.080212	7.289769	7.575126
1.5100000	7.146810	7.235037	7.386241	7.607129	7.908123
1.5200000	7.451156	7.544006	7.703182	7.935822	8.253036
1.5300000	7.764840	7.862461	8.029861	8.274628	8.608583
1.5400000	8.086452	8.188969	8.364809	8.622022	8.973160
1.5500000	8.414324	8.521835	8.706286	8.976196	9.344866
1.5600000	8.746564	8.859137	9.052317	9.335100	9.721546
1.5699999	9.081118	9.198790	9.400762	9.696511	10.100861
1.5707963	9.107795	9.225874	9.428547	9.725330	10.131108
1.5707963	9.107787	9.225865	9.428538	9.725321	10.131099

$\alpha =$ .969999

Θ	K VALUES				
	.318821117	.415016431	.514599755	.613601043	.708073407
.0000000	.000000	.000000	.000000	.000000	.000000
.0100000	.010000	.010000	.010000	.010000	.010000
.0200000	.020003	.020003	.020003	.020003	.020003
.0300000	.030010	.030010	.030011	.030011	.030011
.0400000	.040024	.040025	.040026	.040027	.040028
.0500000	.050047	.050049	.050051	.050053	.050055
.0600000	.060081	.060084	.060088	.060092	.060095
.0700000	.070129	.070134	.070140	.070146	.070151
.0800000	.080193	.080201	.080210	.080218	.080226
.0900000	.090275	.090287	.090299	.090311	.090323
.1000000	.100377	.100394	.100410	.100427	.100443
.1100000	.110503	.110525	.110547	.110569	.110590
.1200000	.120654	.120682	.120711	.120740	.120767
.1300000	.130832	.130868	.130905	.130942	.130977
.1400000	.141041	.141085	.141132	.141178	.141222
.1500000	.151282	.151337	.151394	.151451	.151505
.1600000	.161558	.161624	.161694	.161763	.161829
.1700000	.171871	.171951	.172035	.172118	.172198
.1800000	.182224	.182320	.182419	.182518	.182613
.1900000	.192620	.192733	.192850	.192967	.193079
.2000000	.203060	.203192	.203330	.203466	.203597
.2100000	.213549	.213702	.213861	.214020	.214173
.2200000	.224088	.224264	.224448	.224632	.224807
.2300000	.234679	.234882	.235093	.235303	.235505
.2400000	.245327	.245558	.245798	.246039	.246269
.2500000	.256033	.256295	.256568	.256841	.257102
.2600000	.266801	.267097	.267405	.267713	.268009
.2700000	.277633	.277966	.278312	.278659	.278992
.2800000	.288532	.288905	.289293	.289682	.290055
.2900000	.299502	.299918	.300351	.300785	.301202
.3000000	.310545	.311007	.311489	.311972	.312437
.3100000	.321665	.322177	.322711	.323247	.323763
.3200000	.332864	.333430	.334021	.334614	.335185
.3300000	.344147	.344770	.345422	.346076	.346706
.3400000	.355516	.356201	.356917	.357637	.358331
.3500000	.366975	.367726	.368512	.369302	.370065
.3600000	.378527	.379349	.380209	.381075	.381910
.3700000	.390177	.391073	.392013	.392959	.393873
.3800000	.401927	.402903	.403928	.404960	.405958
.3900000	.413782	.414843	.415958	.417081	.418169

$\alpha =$ .969999

Θ	K VALUES				
	.318821117	.415016431	.514599755	.613601043	.708073407
.4000000	.425745	.426897	.428107	.429328	.430511
.4100000	.437821	.439069	.440381	.441706	.442990
.4200000	.450013	.451363	.452783	.454218	.455611
.4300000	.462326	.463784	.465319	.466871	.468379
.4400000	.474765	.476337	.477993	.479670	.481300
.4500000	.487333	.489026	.490811	.492620	.494379
.4600000	.500036	.501856	.503777	.505726	.507624
.4700000	.512877	.514833	.516898	.518995	.521039
.4800000	.525863	.527961	.530179	.532433	.534631
.4900000	.538998	.541246	.543625	.546045	.548407
.5000000	.552288	.554694	.557242	.559838	.562374
.5100000	.565737	.568309	.571037	.573818	.576539
.5200000	.579352	.582100	.585017	.587993	.590909
.5300000	.593137	.596070	.599186	.602370	.605491
.5400000	.607100	.610227	.613553	.616955	.620295
.5500000	.621246	.624578	.628125	.631757	.635327
.5600000	.635582	.639128	.642908	.646784	.650597
.5700000	.650114	.653886	.657911	.662042	.666113
.5800000	.664849	.668858	.673141	.677543	.681884
.5900000	.679794	.684052	.688607	.693293	.697921
.6000000	.694958	.699477	.704316	.709302	.714233
.6100000	.710346	.715139	.720278	.725580	.730831
.6200000	.725967	.731048	.736502	.742136	.747724
.6300000	.741830	.747212	.752998	.758982	.764926
.6400000	.757942	.763641	.769774	.776127	.782446
.6500000	.774313	.780343	.786842	.793583	.800298
.6600000	.790953	.797330	.804212	.811362	.818495
.6700000	.807869	.814611	.821896	.829475	.837049
.6800000	.825074	.832197	.839905	.847936	.855974
.6899999	.842576	.850099	.858251	.866757	.875286
.7000000	.860387	.868328	.876946	.885953	.894999
.7100000	.878518	.886898	.896005	.905538	.915130
.7200000	.896981	.905820	.915440	.925527	.935694
.7300000	.915789	.925107	.935266	.945936	.956709
.7400000	.934953	.944774	.955498	.966780	.978193
.7500000	.954487	.964835	.976151	.988079	1.000166
.7600000	.974406	.985305	.997243	1.009848	1.022648
.7700000	.994724	1.006200	1.018790	1.032108	1.045659
.7800000	1.015455	1.027536	1.040810	1.054879	1.069222
.7899999	1.036617	1.049330	1.063322	1.078180	1.093359

$\alpha =$ .969999

Θ	K VALUES				
	.318821117	.415016431	.514599755	.613601043	.708073407
.8000000	1.058226	1.071601	1.086346	1.102034	1.118095
.8100000	1.080300	1.094367	1.109902	1.126463	1.143456
.8200000	1.102856	1.117648	1.134013	1.151493	1.169467
.8300000	1.125915	1.141465	1.158700	1.177146	1.196158
.8400000	1.149495	1.165839	1.183987	1.203451	1.223558
.8500000	1.173620	1.190795	1.209901	1.230436	1.251699
.8600000	1.198310	1.216355	1.236466	1.258128	1.280612
.8700000	1.223589	1.242546	1.263712	1.286560	1.310334
.8799999	1.249483	1.269393	1.291666	1.315763	1.340900
.8899999	1.276016	1.296925	1.320360	1.345773	1.372349
.9000000	1.303217	1.325171	1.349827	1.376624	1.404723
.9100000	1.331114	1.354163	1.380100	1.408356	1.438063
.9200000	1.359737	1.383933	1.411216	1.441008	1.472416
.9300000	1.389119	1.414516	1.443212	1.474623	1.507829
.9400000	1.419292	1.445948	1.476128	1.509245	1.544354
.9500000	1.450294	1.478268	1.510008	1.544923	1.582045
.9600000	1.482161	1.511517	1.544896	1.581706	1.620959
.9699999	1.514934	1.545738	1.580839	1.619648	1.661157
.9799999	1.548654	1.580977	1.617888	1.658805	1.702702
.9899999	1.583367	1.617283	1.656097	1.699237	1.745663
1.0000000	1.619121	1.654706	1.695521	1.741007	1.790114
1.0100000	1.655964	1.693300	1.736221	1.784183	1.836130
1.0200000	1.693951	1.733125	1.778260	1.828837	1.883795
1.0300000	1.733138	1.774241	1.821707	1.875043	1.933195
1.0400000	1.773586	1.816714	1.866633	1.922884	1.984423
1.0500000	1.815359	1.860612	1.913114	1.972446	2.037578
1.0600000	1.858525	1.906011	1.961233	2.023820	2.092767
1.0699999	1.903157	1.952989	2.011077	2.077104	2.150102
1.0799999	1.949333	2.001630	2.062737	2.132404	2.209704
1.0899999	1.997135	2.052024	2.116314	2.189830	2.271701
1.1000000	2.046652	2.104267	2.171914	2.249502	2.336232
1.1100000	2.097979	2.158460	2.229647	2.311547	2.403444
1.1200000	2.151216	2.214714	2.289637	2.376101	2.473494
1.1300000	2.206471	2.273146	2.352012	2.443312	2.546553
1.1400000	2.263862	2.333882	2.416912	2.513335	2.622801
1.1500000	2.323511	2.397056	2.484484	2.586339	2.702434
1.1600000	2.385553	2.462812	2.554889	2.662503	2.785661
1.1700000	2.450130	2.531307	2.628298	2.742022	2.872707
1.1800000	2.517397	2.602706	2.704895	2.825104	2.963814
1.1899999	2.587518	2.677190	2.784878	2.911972	3.059242

$\alpha =$ .969999

Θ	K VALUES				
	.318821117	.415016431	.514599755	.613601043	.708073407
1.2000000	2.660673	2.754950	2.868461	3.002868	3.159272
1.2100000	2.737051	2.836194	2.955871	3.098049	3.264204
1.2200000	2.816860	2.921146	3.047356	3.197795	3.374365
1.2300000	2.900321	3.010046	3.143182	3.302408	3.490104
1.2400000	2.987673	3.103153	3.243634	3.412211	3.611800
1.2500000	3.079175	3.200748	3.349023	3.527553	3.739859
1.2599999	3.175105	3.303131	3.459681	3.648810	3.874722
1.2699999	3.275761	3.410626	3.575966	3.776390	4.016861
1.2799999	3.381467	3.523585	3.698265	3.910728	4.166787
1.2899999	3.492571	3.642382	3.826994	4.052297	4.325050
1.3000000	3.609447	3.767426	3.962601	4.201603	4.492244
1.3100000	3.732495	3.899148	4.105566	4.359188	4.669000
1.3200000	3.862148	4.038017	4.256405	4.525638	4.856003
1.3300000	3.998865	4.184533	4.415671	4.701577	5.053983
1.3400000	4.143142	4.339230	4.583955	4.887675	5.263721
1.3500000	4.295501	4.502677	4.761882	5.084640	5.486046
1.3600000	4.456499	4.675475	4.950120	5.293225	5.721839
1.3700000	4.626719	4.858258	5.149366	5.514224	5.972026
1.3799999	4.806775	5.051688	5.360355	5.748464	6.237577
1.3899999	4.997301	5.256455	5.583846	5.996806	6.519496
1.4000000	5.198948	5.473264	5.820618	6.260133	6.818816
1.4100000	5.412370	5.702822	6.071454	6.539329	7.136573
1.4200000	5.638218	5.945836	6.337133	6.835277	7.473800
1.4300000	5.877119	6.202985	6.618407	7.148828	7.831491
1.4400000	6.129657	6.474901	6.915973	7.480773	8.210572
1.4500000	6.396344	6.762139	7.230445	7.831805	8.611858
1.4600000	6.677590	7.065145	7.562316	8.202484	9.036004
1.4700000	6.973669	7.384215	7.911912	8.593180	9.483446
1.4800000	7.284676	7.719452	8.279349	9.004026	9.954343
1.4900000	7.610486	8.070721	8.664477	9.434853	10.448504
1.5000000	7.950711	8.437602	9.066836	9.885144	10.965328
1.5100000	8.304659	8.819345	9.485595	10.353961	11.503727
1.5200000	8.671309	9.214846	9.919539	10.839931	12.062105
1.5300000	9.049296	9.622627	10.367034	11.341211	12.638314
1.5400000	9.436911	10.040833	10.826036	11.855491	13.229668
1.5500000	9.832124	10.467271	11.294122	12.380033	13.832977
1.5600000	10.232641	10.899452	11.768548	12.911738	14.444629
1.5699999	10.635967	11.334676	12.246332	13.447237	15.060702
1.5707963	10.668128	11.369381	12.284431	13.489939	15.109830
1.5707963	10.668120	11.369373	12.284424	13.489933	15.109827

$\alpha =$ .969999

Θ	K VALUES				
	.794250555	.868696860	.928444378	.971111163	.994996249
.0000000	.000000	.000000	.000000	.000000	.000000
.0100000	.010000	.010000	.010000	.010000	.010000
.0200000	.020003	.020003	.020003	.020003	.020003
.0300000	.030012	.030012	.030012	.030013	.030013
.0400000	.040029	.040030	.040030	.040031	.040031
.0500000	.050057	.050058	.050059	.050060	.050061
.0600000	.060098	.060101	.060103	.060105	.060105
.0700000	.070156	.070160	.070164	.070166	.070168
.0800000	.080234	.080240	.080245	.080249	.080251
.0900000	.090333	.090342	.090350	.090355	.090358
.1000000	.100457	.100470	.100480	.100487	.100491
.1100000	.110610	.110626	.110640	.110649	.110655
.1200000	.120793	.120814	.120832	.120844	.120851
.1300000	.131009	.131037	.131059	.131075	.131084
.1400000	.141262	.141297	.141325	.141345	.141356
.1500000	.151555	.151597	.151632	.151657	.151671
.1600000	.161890	.161942	.161984	.162014	.162031
.1700000	.172270	.172333	.172384	.172420	.172440
.1800000	.182700	.182775	.182835	.182878	.182903
.1900000	.193181	.193270	.193341	.193392	.193421
.2000000	.203717	.203821	.203905	.203965	.203998
.2100000	.214312	.214433	.214530	.214600	.214639
.2200000	.224968	.225108	.225221	.225301	.225346
.2300000	.235690	.235850	.235980	.236072	.236124
.2400000	.246480	.246663	.246811	.246917	.246976
.2500000	.257342	.257551	.257718	.257839	.257906
.2600000	.268280	.268516	.268706	.268842	.268918
.2700000	.279298	.279563	.279777	.279931	.280017
.2800000	.290398	.290696	.290936	.291109	.291205
.2900000	.301586	.301919	.302188	.302381	.302489
.3000000	.312864	.313236	.313536	.313751	.313871
.3100000	.324238	.324651	.324984	.325223	.325358
.3200000	.335710	.336168	.336538	.336803	.336952
.3300000	.347287	.347792	.348201	.348495	.348659
.3400000	.358971	.359528	.359979	.360303	.360485
.3500000	.370768	.371381	.371877	.372233	.372433
.3600000	.382681	.383354	.383899	.384290	.384510
.3700000	.394717	.395454	.396051	.396480	.396721
.3800000	.406879	.407685	.408337	.408807	.409071
.3900000	.419174	.420053	.420765	.421278	.421566

$\alpha =$ .969999

Θ	K VALUES				
	.794250555	.868696860	.928444378	.971111163	.994996249
.4000000	.431605	.432562	.433339	.433898	.434212
.4100000	.444179	.445220	.446065	.446673	.447016
.4200000	.456901	.458031	.458949	.459610	.459983
.4300000	.469777	.471002	.471998	.472716	.473121
.4400000	.482812	.484139	.485218	.485997	.486435
.4500000	.496014	.497449	.498617	.499459	.499935
.4600000	.509388	.510938	.512200	.513112	.513626
.4700000	.522940	.524613	.525976	.526961	.527516
.4800000	.536679	.538481	.539951	.541014	.541614
.4900000	.550610	.552551	.554135	.555281	.555928
.5000000	.564741	.566829	.568534	.569769	.570466
.5100000	.579080	.581324	.583158	.584487	.585238
.5200000	.593635	.596044	.598016	.599445	.600253
.5300000	.608414	.610999	.613116	.614651	.615520
.5400000	.623424	.626196	.628468	.630117	.631050
.5500000	.638676	.641646	.644082	.645852	.646854
.5600000	.654179	.657358	.659969	.661867	.662942
.5700000	.669941	.673343	.676139	.678174	.679327
.5800000	.685973	.689611	.692604	.694784	.696020
.5900000	.702286	.706173	.709376	.711710	.713034
.6000000	.718890	.723042	.726466	.728965	.730383
.6100000	.735795	.740229	.743889	.746562	.748080
.6200000	.753015	.757746	.761657	.764515	.766140
.6300000	.770562	.775608	.779785	.782840	.784578
.6400000	.788447	.793828	.798287	.801552	.803411
.6500000	.806685	.812420	.817179	.820667	.822654
.6600000	.825290	.831400	.836477	.840203	.842327
.6700000	.844275	.850783	.856199	.860177	.862447
.6800000	.863657	.870587	.876361	.880609	.883034
.6899999	.883451	.890828	.896984	.901518	.904108
.7000000	.903674	.911526	.918087	.922925	.925692
.7100000	.924344	.932698	.939690	.944853	.947808
.7200000	.945478	.954365	.961816	.967324	.970480
.7300000	.967097	.976549	.984487	.990363	.993733
.7400000	.989220	.999271	1.007728	1.013997	1.017595
.7500000	1.011868	1.022556	1.031563	1.038251	1.042093
.7600000	1.035064	1.046427	1.056021	1.063155	1.067258
.7700000	1.058831	1.070910	1.081129	1.088739	1.093122
.7800000	1.083193	1.096034	1.106917	1.115036	1.119717
.7899999	1.108177	1.121825	1.133417	1.142079	1.147079

$\alpha =$ .969999

Θ	K VALUES				
	.794250555	.868696860	.928444378	.971111163	.994996249
.8000000	1.133810	1.148316	1.160663	1.169905	1.175246
.8100000	1.160119	1.175538	1.188689	1.198552	1.204258
.8200000	1.187136	1.203523	1.217533	1.228059	1.234157
.8300000	1.214892	1.232310	1.247234	1.258470	1.264989
.8400000	1.243420	1.261933	1.277835	1.289831	1.296801
.8500000	1.272756	1.292435	1.309380	1.322189	1.329643
.8600000	1.302937	1.323856	1.341915	1.355597	1.363571
.8700000	1.334002	1.356242	1.375492	1.390110	1.398643
.8799999	1.365993	1.389639	1.410162	1.425784	1.434919
.8899999	1.398955	1.424098	1.445984	1.462684	1.472466
.9000000	1.432932	1.459673	1.483016	1.500874	1.511355
.9100000	1.467975	1.496418	1.521323	1.540427	1.551660
.9200000	1.504136	1.534395	1.560973	1.581417	1.593462
.9300000	1.541470	1.573666	1.602039	1.623925	1.636847
.9400000	1.580036	1.614301	1.644597	1.668039	1.681909
.9500000	1.619896	1.656369	1.688732	1.713850	1.728747
.9600000	1.661115	1.699949	1.734531	1.761458	1.777467
.9699999	1.703764	1.745122	1.782089	1.810971	1.828185
.9799999	1.747918	1.791975	1.831507	1.862502	1.881024
.9899999	1.793656	1.840601	1.882894	1.916176	1.936119
1.0000000	1.841063	1.891100	1.936366	1.972124	1.993613
1.0100000	1.890228	1.943577	1.992046	2.030489	2.053662
1.0200000	1.941246	1.998145	2.050071	2.091426	2.116434
1.0300000	1.994221	2.054927	2.110582	2.155101	2.182112
1.0400000	2.049262	2.114051	2.173735	2.221694	2.250893
1.0500000	2.106484	2.175657	2.239696	2.291398	2.322993
1.0600000	2.166014	2.239895	2.308644	2.364425	2.398645
1.0699999	2.227982	2.306923	2.380773	2.441002	2.478102
1.0799999	2.292533	2.376915	2.456290	2.521377	2.561642
1.0899999	2.359819	2.450055	2.535422	2.605819	2.649567
1.1000000	2.430003	2.526541	2.618412	2.694621	2.742207
1.1100000	2.503261	2.606586	2.705522	2.788099	2.839923
1.1200000	2.579780	2.690421	2.797037	2.886602	2.943111
1.1300000	2.659763	2.778294	2.893267	2.990508	3.052206
1.1400000	2.743426	2.870470	2.994545	3.100229	3.167686
1.1500000	2.831003	2.967240	3.101235	3.216219	3.290076
1.1600000	2.922745	3.068913	3.213731	3.338972	3.419957
1.1700000	3.018922	3.175825	3.332462	3.469032	3.557969
1.1800000	3.119825	3.288340	3.457894	3.606992	3.704820
1.1899999	3.225767	3.406850	3.590534	3.753509	3.861298

$\alpha =$ .969999

Θ	K VALUES				
	.794250555	.868696860	.928444378	.971111163	.994996249
1.2000000	3.337087	3.531780	3.730934	3.909301	4.028274
1.2100000	3.454147	3.663587	3.879696	4.075159	4.206716
1.2200000	3.577343	3.802770	4.037474	4.251956	4.397706
1.2300000	3.707097	3.949867	4.204984	4.440654	4.602449
1.2400000	3.843869	4.105461	4.383006	4.642317	4.822294
1.2500000	3.988152	4.270182	4.572389	4.858118	5.058750
1.2599999	4.140481	4.444715	4.774060	5.089353	5.313515
1.2699999	4.301431	4.629798	4.989031	5.337460	5.588492
1.2799999	4.471623	4.826233	5.218403	5.604025	5.885830
1.2899999	4.651728	5.034883	5.463378	5.890806	6.207953
1.3000000	4.842469	5.256685	5.725264	6.199751	6.557605
1.3100000	5.044618	5.492643	6.005474	6.533005	6.937883
1.3200000	5.259010	5.743843	6.305553	6.892947	7.352314
1.3300000	5.486537	6.011450	6.627167	7.282204	7.804901
1.3400000	5.728155	6.296711	6.972116	7.703669	8.300205
1.3500000	5.984879	6.600958	7.342336	8.160521	8.843422
1.3600000	6.257785	6.925605	7.739898	8.656250	9.440487
1.3700000	6.548009	7.272146	8.167011	9.194662	10.098180
1.3799999	6.856739	7.642148	8.626008	9.779893	10.824255
1.3899999	7.185205	8.037240	9.119335	10.416403	11.627584
1.4000000	7.534677	8.459100	9.649534	11.108970	12.518326
1.4100000	7.906425	8.909415	10.219188	11.862627	13.508064
1.4200000	8.301716	9.389875	10.830905	12.682644	14.610055
1.4300000	8.721776	9.902114	11.487238	13.574407	15.839380
1.4400000	9.167743	10.447659	12.190608	14.543297	17.213151
1.4500000	9.640621	11.027864	12.943205	15.594507	18.750665
1.4600000	10.141222	11.643834	13.746868	16.732811	20.473501
1.4700000	10.670092	12.296330	14.602944	17.962272	22.405488
1.4800000	11.227436	12.985666	15.512132	19.285896	24.572434
1.4900000	11.813034	13.711605	16.474312	20.705238	27.001481
1.5000000	12.426166	14.473252	17.488390	22.220003	29.719844
1.5100000	13.065521	15.268940	18.552112	23.827588	32.752469
1.5200000	13.729164	16.096182	19.661991	25.522798	36.118502
1.5300000	14.414490	16.951613	20.813210	27.297566	39.825820
1.5400000	15.118235	17.831003	21.999639	29.140885	43.863920
1.5500000	15.836522	18.729318	23.213927	31.038955	48.196269
1.5600000	16.564959	19.640846	24.447688	32.975563	52.754871
1.5699999	17.298774	20.559376	25.691777	34.932697	57.441380
1.5707963	17.357293	20.632630	25.791008	35.088869	57.816624
1.5707963	17.357296	20.632647	25.791075	35.088846	57.816577

$\alpha =$ .979999

Θ	K VALUES				
	.009966711	.039469502	.087332193	.151646642	.229848846
.0000000	.000000	.000000	.000000	.000000	.000000
.0100000	.010000	.010000	.010000	.010000	.010000
.0200000	.020002	.020002	.020002	.020002	.020002
.0300000	.030008	.030009	.030009	.030009	.030009
.0400000	.040021	.040021	.040021	.040022	.040023
.0500000	.050041	.050041	.050042	.050044	.050045
.0600000	.060071	.060072	.060073	.060076	.060078
.0700000	.070112	.070114	.070117	.070120	.070125
.0800000	.080168	.080171	.080175	.080180	.080187
.0900000	.090240	.090243	.090249	.090257	.090266
.1000000	.100329	.100334	.100342	.100353	.100366
.1100000	.110439	.110445	.110456	.110470	.110488
.1200000	.120570	.120579	.120592	.120611	.120634
.1300000	.130726	.130736	.130754	.130778	.130807
.1400000	.140907	.140921	.140943	.140973	.141009
.1500000	.151117	.151134	.151161	.151198	.151242
.1600000	.161358	.161378	.161411	.161456	.161510
.1700000	.171631	.171655	.171695	.171748	.171814
.1800000	.181939	.181968	.182015	.182079	.182156
.1900000	.192284	.192318	.192373	.192448	.192539
.2000000	.202668	.202708	.202772	.202860	.202967
.2100000	.213093	.213139	.213215	.213316	.213440
.2200000	.223562	.223616	.223703	.223820	.223962
.2300000	.234078	.234139	.234239	.234372	.234536
.2400000	.244642	.244712	.244825	.244977	.245163
.2500000	.255257	.255336	.255464	.255637	.255848
.2600000	.265926	.266015	.266159	.266354	.266592
.2700000	.276650	.276750	.276912	.277131	.277398
.2800000	.287433	.287545	.287726	.287971	.288270
.2900000	.298277	.298401	.298604	.298876	.299210
.3000000	.309185	.309323	.309547	.309850	.310220
.3100000	.320160	.320312	.320560	.320895	.321305
.3200000	.331203	.331371	.331645	.332015	.332468
.3300000	.342319	.342504	.342805	.343212	.343710
.3400000	.353510	.353713	.354043	.354490	.355037
.3500000	.364779	.365001	.365363	.365851	.366450
.3600000	.376129	.376371	.376766	.377300	.377955
.3700000	.387563	.387827	.388257	.388839	.389553
.3800000	.399085	.399372	.399839	.400472	.401248
.3900000	.410697	.411008	.411515	.412202	.413045

α = .979999

K VALUES			
.415016431	.514599755	.613601043	.708073407
.000000	.000000	.000000	.000000
.010000	.010000	.010000	.010000
.020003	.020003	.020003	.020003
.030010	.030011	.030011	.030012
.040025	.040026	.040027	.040028
.050049	.050051	.050053	.050055
.060085	.060089	.060092	.060096
.070136	.070141	.070147	.070152
.080203	.080211	.080220	.080228
.090289	.090301	.090313	.090325
.100397	.100414	.100430	.100446
.110529	.110551	.110574	.110595
.120688	.120717	.120746	.120773
.130875	.130912	.130949	.130984
.141095	.141141	.141187	.141231
.151348	.151405	.151462	.151516
.161639	.161708	.161777	.161843
.171968	.172052	.172135	.172214
.182340	.182439	.182538	.182633
.192756	.192874	.192991	.193102
.203220	.203357	.203494	.203625
.213735	.213894	.214053	.21420
.224302	.224486	.224669	.22484
.234925	.235136	.235346	.23554
.245607	.245848	.246088	.24631
.256351	.256624	.256897	.25715
.267160	.267468	.267776	.26807
.278037	.278383	.278730	.27906
.288985	.289373	.289762	.2901
.300007	.300440	.300875	.3012
.311107	.311589	.312072	.3125
.322287	.322822	.323358	.3238
.333552	.334144	.334737	.3353
.344905	.345557	.346212	.3468
.356350	.357067	.357787	.3584
.367890	.368676	.369467	.3702
.379529	.380390	.381256	.3820
.391270	.392211	.393158	.3940
.403119	.404144	.405177	.406
.415078	.416194	.417318	.418

α = .979999

Θ	K VALUES				
	.009966711	.039469502	.087332193	.151646642	.229848846
.4000000	.422403	.422740	.423289	.424033	.424947
.4100000	.434207	.434571	.435165	.435969	.436958
.4200000	.446112	.446504	.447145	.448014	.449082
.4300000	.458121	.458544	.459235	.460171	.461323
.4400000	.470239	.470694	.471437	.472444	.473685
.4500000	.482470	.482958	.483756	.484839	.486173
.4600000	.494816	.495340	.496196	.497358	.498790
.4700000	.507283	.507844	.508761	.510007	.511543
.4800000	.519875	.520475	.521456	.522790	.524435
.4900000	.532595	.533236	.534285	.535711	.537472
.5000000	.545449	.546133	.547253	.548776	.550658
.5100000	.558441	.559171	.560365	.561990	.563999
.5200000	.571576	.572353	.573625	.575357	.577499
.5300000	.584859	.585685	.587039	.588883	.591166
.5400000	.598295	.599173	.600612	.602574	.605004
.5500000	.611889	.612822	.614350	.616435	.619020
.5600000	.625646	.626636	.628259	.630473	.633219
.5700000	.639574	.640623	.642343	.644693	.647609
.5800000	.653676	.654787	.656610	.659101	.662195
.5900000	.667960	.669136	.671066	.673705	.676984
.6000000	.682431	.683675	.685718	.688511	.691985
.6100000	.697097	.698412	.700571	.703526	.707204
.6200000	.711964	.713352	.715634	.718757	.722649
.6300000	.727039	.728504	.730913	.734213	.738327
.6400000	.742329	.743874	.746416	.749900	.754248
.6500000	.757842	.759471	.762152	.765828	.770419
.6600000	.773586	.775303	.778128	.782005	.786851
.6700000	.789570	.791377	.794353	.798440	.803551
.6800000	.805801	.807703	.810836	.815141	.820531
.6899999	.822289	.824290	.827587	.832120	.837800
.7000000	.839043	.841147	.844614	.849385	.855368
.7100000	.856073	.858283	.861929	.866948	.873247
.7200000	.873389	.875710	.879541	.884819	.891448
.7300000	.891001	.893439	.897463	.903010	.909984
.7400000	.908921	.911479	.915704	.921532	.928866
.7500000	.927160	.929844	.934278	.940399	.948108
.7600000	.945731	.948545	.953197	.959623	.967724
.7700000	.964645	.967595	.972474	.979218	.987728
.7800000	.983916	.987008	.992123	.999198	1.008135
.7899999	1.003559	1.006798	1.012158	1.019579	1.028960

$\alpha =$ .979999

Θ	K VALUES				
	.009966711	.039469502	.087332193	.151646642	.229848846
.8000000	1.023587	1.026979	1.032596	1.040376	1.050222
.8100000	1.044016	1.047567	1.053450	1.061606	1.071935
.8200000	1.064861	1.068578	1.074739	1.083285	1.094120
.8300000	1.086140	1.090029	1.096479	1.105432	1.116794
.8400000	1.107870	1.111939	1.118689	1.128066	1.139978
.8500000	1.130070	1.134326	1.141388	1.151208	1.163694
.8600000	1.152760	1.157209	1.164598	1.174877	1.187962
.8700000	1.175959	1.180610	1.188338	1.199098	1.212807
.8799999	1.199689	1.204551	1.212632	1.223892	1.238253
.8899999	1.223974	1.229054	1.237503	1.249284	1.264327
.9000000	1.248837	1.254145	1.262977	1.275302	1.291055
.9100000	1.274303	1.279848	1.289080	1.301972	1.318466
.9200000	1.300400	1.306192	1.315839	1.329322	1.346590
.9300000	1.327156	1.333205	1.343285	1.357384	1.375461
.9400000	1.354601	1.360918	1.371449	1.386191	1.405112
.9500000	1.382766	1.389362	1.400364	1.415776	1.435579
.9600000	1.411686	1.418572	1.430064	1.446176	1.466901
.9699999	1.441395	1.448584	1.460588	1.477430	1.499118
.9799999	1.471932	1.479437	1.491974	1.509579	1.532273
.9899999	1.503338	1.511171	1.524265	1.542666	1.566412
1.0000000	1.535654	1.543830	1.557505	1.576737	1.601583
1.0100000	1.568926	1.577460	1.591741	1.611842	1.637839
1.0200000	1.603203	1.612111	1.627024	1.648033	1.675234
1.0300000	1.638536	1.647834	1.663409	1.685366	1.713828
1.0400000	1.674981	1.684686	1.700951	1.723901	1.753682
1.0500000	1.712596	1.722726	1.739713	1.763701	1.794864
1.0600000	1.751444	1.762018	1.779760	1.804834	1.837445
1.0699999	1.791592	1.802632	1.821163	1.847374	1.881502
1.0799999	1.833113	1.844639	1.863996	1.891398	1.927117
1.0899999	1.876084	1.888118	1.908340	1.936989	1.974378
1.1000000	1.920588	1.933154	1.954282	1.984239	2.023379
1.1100000	1.966713	1.979837	2.001913	2.033242	2.074221
1.1200000	2.014556	2.028264	2.051336	2.084103	2.127014
1.1300000	2.064220	2.078540	2.102655	2.136933	2.181874
1.1400000	2.115816	2.130778	2.155989	2.191854	2.238928
1.1500000	2.169464	2.185101	2.211461	2.248993	2.298314
1.1600000	2.225293	2.241638	2.269208	2.308493	2.360177
1.1700000	2.283445	2.300534	2.329375	2.370505	2.424679
1.1800000	2.344070	2.361942	2.392120	2.435192	2.491990
1.1899999	2.407334	2.426030	2.457615	2.502734	2.562300

Θ	
	.009966711
1.2000000	2.473415
1.2100000	2.542508
1.2200000	2.614823
1.2300000	2.690590
1.2400000	2.770062
1.2500000	2.853510
1.2599999	2.941236
1.2699999	3.033565
1.2799999	3.130856
1.2899999	3.233501
1.3000000	3.341931
1.3100000	3.456616
1.3200000	3.578072
1.3300000	3.706868
1.3400000	3.843623
1.3500000	3.989018
1.3600000	4.143795
1.3700000	4.308764
1.3799999	4.484806
1.3899999	4.672874
1.4000000	4.873993
1.4100000	5.089253
1.4200000	5.319810
1.4300000	5.566865
1.4400000	5.831642
1.4500000	6.115360
1.4600000	6.419180
1.4700000	6.744151
1.4800000	7.091126
1.4900000	7.460665
1.5000000	7.852931
1.5100000	8.267554
1.5200000	8.703534
1.5300000	9.159134
1.5400000	9.631827
1.5500000	10.118304
1.5600000	10.614554
1.5699999	11.116035
1.5707963	11.156051
1.5707963	11.156042

Θ	
	.318821117
.0000000	.000000
.0100000	.010000
.0200000	.020003
.0300000	.030010
.0400000	.040024
.0500000	.050047
.0600000	.060082
.0700000	.070130
.0800000	.080195
.0900000	.090277
.1000000	.100381
.1100000	.110508
.1200000	.120660
.1300000	.130840
.1400000	.141050
.1500000	.151293
.1600000	.161572
.1700000	.171888
.1800000	.182244
.1900000	.192644
.2000000	.203088
.2100000	.213581
.2200000	.224125
.2300000	.234722
.2400000	.245376
.2500000	.256089
.2600000	.266864
.2700000	.277704
.2800000	.288612
.2900000	.29959
.3000000	.31064
.3100000	.32177
.3200000	.33298
.3300000	.34428
.3400000	.35566
.3500000	.36713
.3600000	.37870
.3700000	.39037
.3800000	.40214
.3900000	.41401

$\alpha =$ .979999

Θ	K VALUES				
	.009966711	.039469502	.087332193	.151646642	.229848846
.4000000	.422403	.422740	.423289	.424033	.424947
.4100000	.434207	.434571	.435165	.435969	.436958
.4200000	.446112	.446504	.447145	.448014	.449082
.4300000	.458121	.458544	.459235	.460171	.461323
.4400000	.470239	.470694	.471437	.472444	.473685
.4500000	.482470	.482958	.483756	.484839	.486173
.4600000	.494816	.495340	.496196	.497358	.498790
.4700000	.507283	.507844	.508761	.510007	.511543
.4800000	.519875	.520475	.521456	.522790	.524435
.4900000	.532595	.533236	.534285	.535711	.537472
.5000000	.545449	.546133	.547253	.548776	.550658
.5100000	.558441	.559171	.560365	.561990	.563999
.5200000	.571576	.572353	.573625	.575357	.577499
.5300000	.584859	.585685	.587039	.588883	.591166
.5400000	.598295	.599173	.600612	.602574	.605004
.5500000	.611889	.612822	.614350	.616435	.619020
.5600000	.625646	.626636	.628259	.630473	.633219
.5700000	.639574	.640623	.642343	.644693	.647609
.5800000	.653676	.654787	.656610	.659101	.662195
.5900000	.667960	.669136	.671066	.673705	.676984
.6000000	.682431	.683675	.685718	.688511	.691985
.6100000	.697097	.698412	.700571	.703526	.707204
.6200000	.711964	.713352	.715634	.718757	.722649
.6300000	.727039	.728504	.730913	.734213	.738327
.6400000	.742329	.743874	.746416	.749900	.754248
.6500000	.757842	.759471	.762152	.765828	.770419
.6600000	.773586	.775303	.778128	.782005	.786851
.6700000	.789570	.791377	.794353	.798440	.803551
.6800000	.805801	.807703	.810836	.815141	.820531
.6899999	.822289	.824290	.827587	.832120	.837800
.7000000	.839043	.841147	.844614	.849385	.855368
.7100000	.856073	.858283	.861929	.866948	.873247
.7200000	.873389	.875710	.879541	.884819	.891448
.7300000	.891001	.893439	.897463	.903010	.909984
.7400000	.908921	.911479	.915704	.921532	.928866
.7500000	.927160	.929844	.934278	.940399	.948108
.7600000	.945731	.948545	.953197	.959623	.967724
.7700000	.964645	.967595	.972474	.979218	.987728
.7800000	.983916	.987008	.992123	.999198	1.008135
.7899999	1.003559	1.006798	1.012158	1.019579	1.028960

$\alpha =$ .979999

Θ	K VALUES				
	.009966711	.039469502	.087332193	.151646642	.229848846
.8000000	1.023587	1.026979	1.032596	1.040376	1.050222
.8100000	1.044016	1.047567	1.053450	1.061606	1.071935
.8200000	1.064861	1.068578	1.074739	1.083285	1.094120
.8300000	1.086140	1.090029	1.096479	1.105432	1.116794
.8400000	1.107870	1.111939	1.118689	1.128066	1.139978
.8500000	1.130070	1.134326	1.141388	1.151208	1.163694
.8600000	1.152760	1.157209	1.164598	1.174877	1.187962
.8700000	1.175959	1.180610	1.188338	1.199098	1.212807
.8799999	1.199689	1.204551	1.212632	1.223892	1.238253
.8899999	1.223974	1.229054	1.237503	1.249284	1.264327
.9000000	1.248837	1.254145	1.262977	1.275302	1.291055
.9100000	1.274303	1.279848	1.289080	1.301972	1.318466
.9200000	1.300400	1.306192	1.315839	1.329322	1.346590
.9300000	1.327156	1.333205	1.343285	1.357384	1.375461
.9400000	1.354601	1.360918	1.371449	1.386191	1.405112
.9500000	1.382766	1.389362	1.400364	1.415776	1.435579
.9600000	1.411686	1.418572	1.430064	1.446176	1.466901
.9699999	1.441395	1.448584	1.460588	1.477430	1.499118
.9799999	1.471932	1.479437	1.491974	1.509579	1.532273
.9899999	1.503338	1.511171	1.524265	1.542666	1.566412
1.0000000	1.535654	1.543830	1.557505	1.576737	1.601583
1.0100000	1.568926	1.577460	1.591741	1.611842	1.637839
1.0200000	1.603203	1.612111	1.627024	1.648033	1.675234
1.0300000	1.638536	1.647834	1.663409	1.685366	1.713828
1.0400000	1.674981	1.684686	1.700951	1.723901	1.753682
1.0500000	1.712596	1.722726	1.739713	1.763701	1.794864
1.0600000	1.751444	1.762018	1.779760	1.804834	1.837445
1.0699999	1.791592	1.802632	1.821163	1.847374	1.881502
1.0799999	1.833113	1.844639	1.863996	1.891398	1.927117
1.0899999	1.876084	1.888118	1.908340	1.936989	1.974378
1.1000000	1.920588	1.933154	1.954282	1.984239	2.023379
1.1100000	1.966713	1.979837	2.001913	2.033242	2.074221
1.1200000	2.014556	2.028264	2.051336	2.084103	2.127014
1.1300000	2.064220	2.078540	2.102655	2.136933	2.181874
1.1400000	2.115816	2.130778	2.155989	2.191854	2.238928
1.1500000	2.169464	2.185101	2.211461	2.248993	2.298314
1.1600000	2.225293	2.241638	2.269208	2.308493	2.360177
1.1700000	2.283445	2.300534	2.329375	2.370505	2.424679
1.1800000	2.344070	2.361942	2.392120	2.435192	2.491990
1.1899999	2.407334	2.426030	2.457615	2.502734	2.562300

$\alpha =$ .979999

Θ	K VALUES				
	.009966711	.039469502	.087332193	.151646642	.229848846
1.2000000	2.473415	2.492979	2.526048	2.573325	2.635811
1.2100000	2.542508	2.562986	2.597619	2.647172	2.712744
1.2200000	2.614823	2.636266	2.672549	2.724506	2.793339
1.2300000	2.690590	2.713052	2.751078	2.805576	2.877857
1.2400000	2.770062	2.793599	2.833467	2.890653	2.966585
1.2500000	2.853510	2.878185	2.920002	2.980033	3.059834
1.2599999	2.941236	2.967115	3.010996	3.074040	3.157943
1.2699999	3.033565	3.060720	3.106788	3.173028	3.261286
1.2799999	3.130856	3.159364	3.207752	3.277385	3.370269
1.2899999	3.233501	3.263445	3.314298	3.387535	3.485338
1.3000000	3.341931	3.373402	3.426874	3.503945	3.606984
1.3100000	3.456616	3.489710	3.545970	3.627123	3.735740
1.3200000	3.578072	3.612896	3.672125	3.757628	3.872195
1.3300000	3.706868	3.743534	3.805929	3.896074	4.016993
1.3400000	3.843623	3.882257	3.948032	4.043133	4.170842
1.3500000	3.989018	4.029753	4.099140	4.199541	4.334513
1.3600000	4.143795	4.186777	4.260028	4.366101	4.508851
1.3700000	4.308764	4.354153	4.431542	4.543690	4.694778
1.3799999	4.484806	4.532773	4.614597	4.733262	4.893295
1.3899999	4.672874	4.723606	4.810188	4.935845	5.105486
1.4000000	4.873993	4.927694	5.019385	5.152552	5.332517
1.4100000	5.089253	5.146143	5.243322	5.384562	5.575627
1.4200000	5.319810	5.380127	5.483206	5.633124	5.836130
1.4300000	5.566865	5.630864	5.740286	5.899539	6.115393
1.4400000	5.831642	5.899601	6.015842	6.185132	6.414808
1.4500000	6.115360	6.187573	6.311141	6.491220	6.735760
1.4600000	6.419180	6.495960	6.627396	6.819063	7.079571
1.4700000	6.744151	6.825827	6.965700	7.169794	7.447433
1.4800000	7.091126	7.178040	7.326940	7.544335	7.840316
1.4900000	7.460665	7.553169	7.711702	7.943293	8.258857
1.5000000	7.852931	7.951378	8.120156	8.366846	8.703241
1.5100000	8.267554	8.372292	8.551915	8.814591	9.173048
1.5200000	8.703534	8.814896	9.005937	9.285448	9.667141
1.5300000	9.159134	9.277425	9.480412	9.777537	10.183545
1.5400000	9.631827	9.757313	9.972706	10.288123	10.719385
1.5500000	10.118304	10.251199	10.479367	10.813624	11.270900
1.5600000	10.614554	10.755010	10.996217	11.349702	11.833528
1.5699999	11.116035	11.264135	11.518520	11.891441	12.402105
1.5707963	11.156051	11.304761	11.560198	11.934669	12.447475
1.5707963	11.156042	11.304751	11.560188	11.934660	12.447466

$\alpha =$ .979999

Θ	K VALUES				
	.318821117	.415016431	.514599755	.613601043	.708073407
.0000000	.000000	.000000	.000000	.000000	.000000
.0100000	.010000	.010000	.010000	.010000	.010000
.0200000	.020003	.020003	.020003	.020003	.020003
.0300000	.030010	.030010	.030011	.030011	.030012
.0400000	.040024	.040025	.040026	.040027	.040028
.0500000	.050047	.050049	.050051	.050053	.050055
.0600000	.060082	.060085	.060089	.060092	.060096
.0700000	.070130	.070136	.070141	.070147	.070152
.0800000	.080195	.080203	.080211	.080220	.080228
.0900000	.090277	.090289	.090301	.090313	.090325
.1000000	.100381	.100397	.100414	.100430	.100446
.1100000	.110508	.110529	.110551	.110574	.110595
.1200000	.120660	.120688	.120717	.120746	.120773
.1300000	.130840	.130875	.130912	.130949	.130984
.1400000	.141050	.141095	.141141	.141187	.141231
.1500000	.151293	.151348	.151405	.151462	.151516
.1600000	.161572	.161639	.161708	.161777	.161843
.1700000	.171888	.171968	.172052	.172135	.172214
.1800000	.182244	.182340	.182439	.182538	.182633
.1900000	.192644	.192756	.192874	.192991	.193102
.2000000	.203088	.203220	.203357	.203494	.203625
.2100000	.213581	.213735	.213894	.214053	.214205
.2200000	.224125	.224302	.224486	.224669	.224845
.2300000	.234722	.234925	.235136	.235346	.235548
.2400000	.245376	.245607	.245848	.246088	.246318
.2500000	.256089	.256351	.256624	.256897	.257159
.2600000	.266864	.267160	.267468	.267776	.268072
.2700000	.277704	.278037	.278383	.278730	.279063
.2800000	.288612	.288985	.289373	.289762	.290135
.2900000	.299591	.300007	.300440	.300875	.301292
.3000000	.310644	.311107	.311589	.312072	.312537
.3100000	.321775	.322287	.322822	.323358	.323875
.3200000	.332987	.333552	.334144	.334737	.335309
.3300000	.344282	.344905	.345557	.346212	.346843
.3400000	.355665	.356350	.357067	.357787	.358482
.3500000	.367138	.367890	.368676	.369467	.370231
.3600000	.378707	.379529	.380390	.381256	.382093
.3700000	.390373	.391270	.392211	.393158	.394073
.3800000	.402141	.403119	.404144	.405177	.406176
.3900000	.414015	.415078	.416194	.417318	.418407

$\alpha =$ .979999

Θ	K VALUES				
	.318821117	.415016431	.514599755	.613601043	.708073407
.4000000	.425999	.427153	.428364	.429587	.430771
.4100000	.438097	.439347	.440660	.441987	.443272
.4200000	.450313	.451665	.453086	.454524	.455918
.4300000	.462652	.464111	.465648	.467202	.468712
.4400000	.475117	.476691	.478349	.480029	.481661
.4500000	.487713	.489409	.491196	.493008	.494770
.4600000	.500446	.502269	.504194	.506145	.508046
.4700000	.513320	.515279	.517347	.519448	.521494
.4800000	.526340	.528441	.530663	.532920	.535122
.4900000	.539512	.541763	.544146	.546570	.548936
.5000000	.552840	.555250	.557803	.560403	.562944
.5100000	.566330	.568907	.571640	.574426	.577151
.5200000	.579988	.582741	.585664	.588646	.591567
.5300000	.593819	.596758	.599881	.603070	.606198
.5400000	.607831	.610964	.614298	.617707	.621053
.5500000	.622029	.625367	.628923	.632563	.636140
.5600000	.636419	.639973	.643762	.647646	.651468
.5700000	.651009	.654790	.658825	.662966	.667046
.5800000	.665805	.669824	.674119	.678531	.682884
.5900000	.680816	.685085	.689651	.694349	.698990
.6000000	.696048	.700579	.705432	.710431	.715376
.6100000	.711509	.716316	.721470	.726786	.732052
.6200000	.727207	.732303	.737774	.743425	.749030
.6300000	.743152	.748551	.754354	.760357	.766319
.6400000	.759351	.765067	.771221	.777594	.783934
.6500000	.775813	.781864	.788384	.795148	.801886
.6600000	.792550	.798949	.805856	.813030	.820189
.6700000	.809569	.816335	.823647	.831254	.838856
.6800000	.826882	.834032	.841770	.849831	.857901
.6899999	.844500	.852052	.860236	.868777	.877340
.7000000	.862434	.870407	.879060	.888105	.897188
.7100000	.880694	.889109	.898254	.907829	.917462
.7200000	.899294	.908171	.917834	.927966	.938179
.7300000	.918247	.927608	.937813	.948533	.959357
.7400000	.937565	.947433	.958208	.969545	.981014
.7500000	.957263	.967662	.979034	.991021	1.003171
.7600000	.977355	.988310	1.000309	1.012981	1.025848
.7700000	.997856	1.009394	1.022051	1.035442	1.049067
.7800000	1.018783	1.030931	1.044279	1.058427	1.072852
.7899999	1.040153	1.052938	1.067011	1.081956	1.097225

$\alpha =$ .979999

Θ	K VALUES				
	.318821117	.415016431	.514599755	.613601043	.708073407
.8000000	1.061982	1.075436	1.090270	1.106053	1.122213
.8100000	1.084289	1.098442	1.114075	1.130741	1.147842
.8200000	1.107093	1.121980	1.138451	1.156046	1.174140
.8300000	1.130416	1.146070	1.163421	1.181994	1.201137
.8400000	1.154277	1.170735	1.189010	1.208612	1.228864
.8500000	1.178701	1.195999	1.215244	1.235930	1.257352
.8600000	1.203709	1.221889	1.242152	1.263980	1.286639
.8700000	1.229327	1.248430	1.269762	1.292792	1.316758
.8799999	1.255582	1.275652	1.298107	1.322403	1.347751
.8899999	1.282500	1.303583	1.327217	1.352847	1.379656
.9000000	1.310111	1.332256	1.357129	1.384165	1.412518
.9100000	1.338446	1.361703	1.387877	1.416395	1.446382
.9200000	1.367537	1.391959	1.419501	1.449580	1.481296
.9300000	1.397418	1.423062	1.452041	1.483767	1.517312
.9400000	1.428127	1.455051	1.485541	1.519003	1.554484
.9500000	1.459700	1.487968	1.520046	1.555338	1.592870
.9600000	1.492179	1.521855	1.555603	1.592828	1.632531
.9699999	1.525608	1.556761	1.592266	1.631529	1.673533
.9799999	1.560032	1.592735	1.630088	1.671503	1.715945
.9899999	1.595499	1.629829	1.669126	1.712813	1.759840
1.0000000	1.632062	1.668100	1.709444	1.755530	1.805298
1.0100000	1.669776	1.707607	1.751106	1.799727	1.852402
1.0200000	1.708699	1.748413	1.794181	1.845481	1.901241
1.0300000	1.748895	1.790587	1.838745	1.892876	1.951911
1.0400000	1.790429	1.834200	1.884877	1.942001	2.004515
1.0500000	1.833373	1.879329	1.932662	1.992953	2.059161
1.0600000	1.877803	1.926058	1.982191	2.045831	2.115966
1.0699999	1.923802	1.974474	2.033560	2.100747	2.175056
1.0799999	1.971455	2.024672	2.086874	2.157816	2.236566
1.0899999	2.020857	2.076752	2.142245	2.217164	2.300639
1.1000000	2.072110	2.130826	2.199792	2.278927	2.367431
1.1100000	2.125319	2.187007	2.259643	2.343248	2.437108
1.1200000	2.180601	2.245422	2.321938	2.410283	2.509850
1.1300000	2.238082	2.306208	2.386826	2.480200	2.585850
1.1400000	2.297896	2.369508	2.454466	2.553181	2.665319
1.1500000	2.360189	2.435482	2.525033	2.629420	2.748482
1.1600000	2.425118	2.504299	2.598715	2.709129	2.835582
1.1700000	2.492853	2.576142	2.675713	2.792536	2.926884
1.1800000	2.563577	2.651212	2.756247	2.879889	3.022674
1.1899999	2.637491	2.729724	2.840556	2.971455	3.123263

$\alpha =$ .979999

Θ	K VALUES				
	.318821117	.415016431	.514599755	.613601043	.708073407
1.2000000	2.714812	2.811912	2.928898	3.067526	3.228989
1.2100000	2.795773	2.898031	3.021553	3.168419	3.340218
1.2200000	2.880631	2.988358	3.118827	3.274477	3.457349
1.2300000	2.969666	3.083195	3.221052	3.386076	3.580818
1.2400000	3.063180	3.182871	3.328591	3.503624	3.711098
1.2500000	3.161507	3.287744	3.441840	3.627569	3.848709
1.2599999	3.265007	3.398207	3.561231	3.758397	3.994216
1.2699999	3.374079	3.514690	3.687238	3.896643	4.148238
1.2799999	3.489155	3.637661	3.820378	4.042889	4.311454
1.2899999	3.610711	3.767634	3.961217	4.197776	4.484607
1.3000000	3.739269	3.905176	4.110379	4.362006	4.668512
1.3100000	3.875398	4.050901	4.268542	4.536343	4.864059
1.3200000	4.019725	4.205488	4.436453	4.721633	5.072227
1.3300000	4.172936	4.369679	4.614933	4.918797	5.294092
1.3400000	4.335784	4.544290	4.804878	5.128850	5.530828
1.3500000	4.509092	4.730210	5.007270	5.352897	5.783723
1.3600000	4.693760	4.928413	5.223183	5.592150	6.054184
1.3700000	4.890769	5.139962	5.453787	5.847929	6.343745
1.3799999	5.101187	5.366009	5.700354	6.121668	6.654074
1.3899999	5.326166	5.607805	5.964259	6.414919	6.986975
1.4000000	5.566951	5.866694	6.246987	6.729355	7.344392
1.4100000	5.824861	6.144104	6.550110	7.066751	7.728387
1.4200000	6.101296	6.441550	6.875299	7.428988	8.141149
1.4300000	6.397711	6.760605	7.224287	7.818025	8.584952
1.4400000	6.715589	7.102876	7.598845	8.235856	9.062117
1.4500000	7.056406	7.469958	8.000731	8.684466	9.574950
1.4600000	7.421571	7.863375	8.431625	9.165748	10.125653
1.4700000	7.812352	8.284501	8.893042	9.681411	10.716214
1.4800000	8.229782	8.734453	9.386212	10.232845	11.348248
1.4900000	8.674543	9.213967	9.911948	10.820965	12.022825
1.5000000	9.146829	9.723256	10.470484	11.446039	12.740258
1.5100000	9.646193	10.261836	11.061289	12.107468	13.499858
1.5200000	10.171426	10.828398	11.682921	12.803628	14.299743
1.5300000	10.720422	11.420666	12.332871	13.531697	15.136642
1.5400000	11.290122	12.035329	13.007494	14.287564	16.005789
1.5500000	11.876515	12.668051	13.702012	15.065849	16.900942
1.5600000	12.474747	13.313578	14.410637	15.860030	17.814538
1.5699999	13.079315	13.965960	15.126814	16.662719	18.738004
1.5707963	13.127557	14.018018	15.183964	16.726773	18.811696
1.5707963	13.127548	14.018009	15.183956	16.726767	18.811695

$\alpha =$ .979999

θ	K VALUES				
	.794250555	.868696860	.928444378	.971111163	.994996249
.0000000	.000000	.000000	.000000	.000000	.000000
.0100000	.010000	.010000	.010000	.010000	.010000
.0200000	.020003	.020003	.020003	.020003	.020003
.0300000	.030012	.030012	.030013	.030013	.030013
.0400000	.040029	.040030	.040030	.040031	.040031
.0500000	.050057	.050059	.050060	.050061	.050061
.0600000	.060099	.060102	.060104	.060105	.060106
.0700000	.070157	.070162	.070165	.070168	.070169
.0800000	.080235	.080242	.080247	.080251	.080253
.0900000	.090336	.090345	.090352	.090357	.090360
.1000000	.100461	.100473	.100483	.100491	.100495
.1100000	.110614	.110631	.110644	.110654	.110659
.1200000	.120798	.120820	.120838	.120850	.120857
.1300000	.131016	.131044	.131067	.131083	.131091
.1400000	.141271	.141306	.141334	.141354	.141365
.1500000	.151566	.151609	.151644	.151668	.151682
.1600000	.161904	.161956	.161998	.162028	.162045
.1700000	.172287	.172350	.172401	.172437	.172457
.1800000	.182720	.182795	.182855	.182899	.182923
.1900000	.193205	.193294	.193365	.193416	.193445
.2000000	.203745	.203849	.203933	.203993	.204026
.2100000	.214345	.214465	.214563	.214632	.214671
.2200000	.225006	.225146	.225258	.225339	.225384
.2300000	.235733	.235894	.236023	.236115	.236167
.2400000	.246530	.246713	.246860	.246966	.247025
.2500000	.257399	.257607	.257775	.257895	.257962
.2600000	.268344	.268580	.268770	.268906	.268982
.2700000	.279369	.279635	.279849	.280003	.280089
.2800000	.290479	.290777	.291017	.291190	.291286
.2900000	.301676	.302009	.302278	.302471	.302580
.3000000	.312965	.313336	.313636	.313852	.313973
.3100000	.324349	.324763	.325096	.325336	.325470
.3200000	.335834	.336292	.336662	.336928	.337077
.3300000	.347424	.347930	.348339	.348633	.348797
.3400000	.359122	.359680	.360131	.360455	.360637
.3500000	.370934	.371548	.372044	.372401	.372601
.3600000	.382864	.383538	.384083	.384474	.384695
.3700000	.394917	.395655	.396252	.396682	.396923
.3800000	.407099	.407905	.408558	.409028	.409292
.3900000	.419413	.420293	.421006	.421519	.421808

$\alpha =$ .979999

Θ	K VALUES				
	.794250555	.868696860	.928444378	.971111163	.994996249
.4000000	.431866	.432824	.433601	.434161	.434476
.4100000	.444463	.445505	.446351	.446960	.447303
.4200000	.457209	.458341	.459260	.459922	.460295
.4300000	.470111	.471338	.472335	.473054	.473459
.4400000	.483175	.484504	.485584	.486364	.486803
.4500000	.496406	.497843	.499013	.499857	.500333
.4600000	.509812	.511364	.512629	.513541	.514056
.4700000	.523399	.525074	.526439	.527425	.527982
.4800000	.537173	.538979	.540451	.541516	.542117
.4900000	.551143	.553087	.554674	.555822	.556470
.5000000	.565315	.567407	.569115	.570352	.571051
.5100000	.579698	.581946	.583784	.585115	.585867
.5200000	.594299	.596713	.598688	.600120	.600930
.5300000	.609127	.611717	.613838	.615377	.616248
.5400000	.624190	.626967	.629244	.630897	.631832
.5500000	.639497	.642474	.644915	.646689	.647694
.5600000	.655059	.658246	.660863	.662765	.663843
.5700000	.670884	.674294	.677097	.679137	.680293
.5800000	.686983	.690630	.693631	.695817	.697056
.5900000	.703367	.707264	.710476	.712816	.714144
.6000000	.720046	.724210	.727644	.730149	.731572
.6100000	.737032	.741478	.745149	.747830	.749352
.6200000	.754337	.759082	.763005	.765872	.767502
.6300000	.771974	.777036	.781226	.784291	.786035
.6400000	.789955	.795354	.799827	.803104	.804968
.6500000	.808295	.814050	.818825	.822326	.824320
.6600000	.827008	.833140	.838236	.841975	.844107
.6700000	.846109	.852642	.858077	.862071	.864349
.6800000	.865613	.872571	.878368	.882632	.885066
.6899999	.885538	.892945	.899126	.903679	.906280
.7000000	.905900	.913784	.920374	.925233	.928011
.7100000	.926717	.935108	.942131	.947317	.950285
.7200000	.948008	.956936	.964421	.969955	.973125
.7300000	.969794	.979291	.987268	.993173	.996559
.7400000	.992095	1.002196	1.010695	1.016996	1.020612
.7500000	1.014932	1.025676	1.034730	1.041453	1.045316
.7600000	1.038330	1.049754	1.059401	1.066574	1.070700
.7700000	1.062312	1.074460	1.084736	1.092390	1.096797
.7800000	1.086904	1.099819	1.110767	1.118934	1.123642
.7899999	1.112132	1.125864	1.137527	1.146242	1.151273

$\alpha =$ •979999

Θ	K VALUES				
	•794250555	•868696860	•928444378	•971111163	•994996249
•8000000	1•138026	1•152624	1•165050	1•174351	1•179727
•8100000	1•164614	1•180134	1•193372	1•203301	1•209046
•8200000	1•191928	1•208428	1•222534	1•233133	1•239274
•8300000	1•220002	1•237543	1•252575	1•263893	1•270459
•8400000	1•248870	1•267520	1•283541	1•295627	1•302649
•8500000	1•278569	1•298399	1•315476	1•328386	1•335899
•8600000	1•309139	1•330226	1•348431	1•362225	1•370264
•8700000	1•340621	1•363045	1•382457	1•397199	1•405806
•8799999	1•373058	1•396908	1•417611	1•433371	1•442588
•8899999	1•406497	1•431867	1•453952	1•470806	1•480679
•9000000	1•440988	1•467978	1•491544	1•509573	1•520155
•9100000	1•476581	1•505301	1•530452	1•549747	1•561093
•9200000	1•513333	1•543898	1•570750	1•591406	1•603578
•9300000	1•551302	1•583838	1•612514	1•634638	1•647702
•9400000	1•590551	1•625192	1•655827	1•679533	1•693562
•9500000	1•631146	1•668036	1•700775	1•726189	1•741263
•9600000	1•673157	1•712453	1•747454	1•774712	1•790919
•9699999	1•716660	1•758530	1•795964	1•825216	1•842652
•9799999	1•761734	1•806360	1•846412	1•877822	1•896593
•9899999	1•808466	1•856043	1•898916	1•932661	1•952885
1•0000000	1•856947	1•907686	1•953599	1•989877	2•011682
1•0100000	1•907273	1•961403	2•010596	2•049622	2•073150
1•0200000	1•959550	2•017316	2•070050	2•112061	2•137469
1•0300000	2•013888	2•075559	2•132118	2•177374	2•204837
1•0400000	2•070406	2•136270	2•196967	2•245754	2•275465
1•0500000	2•129233	2•199604	2•264777	2•317413	2•349587
1•0600000	2•190506	2•265723	2•335745	2•392579	2•427454
1•0699999	2•254372	2•334804	2•410082	2•471500	2•509344
1•0799999	2•320988	2•407036	2•488017	2•554448	2•595558
1•0899999	2•390527	2•482623	2•569798	2•641717	2•686426
1•1000000	2•463170	2•561790	2•655695	2•733630	2•782313
1•1100000	2•539115	2•644771	2•746000	2•830538	2•883613
1•1200000	2•618574	2•731827	2•841032	2•932825	2•990766
1•1300000	2•701778	2•823239	2•941137	3•040916	3•104255
1•1400000	2•788975	2•919309	3•046693	3•155272	3•224612
1•1500000	2•880433	3•020367	3•158112	3•276403	3•352427
1•1600000	2•976445	3•126772	3•275843	3•404869	3•488352
1•1700000	3•077324	3•238912	3•400380	3•541287	3•633112
1•1800000	3•183414	3•357211	3•532259	3•686340	3•787514
1•1899999	3•295086	3•482130	3•672073	3•840781	3•952455

$\alpha =$ .979999

Θ	K VALUES				
	.794250555	.868696860	.928444378	.971111163	.994996249
1.2000000	3.412745	3.614174	3.820470	4.005446	4.128940
1.2100000	3.536830	3.753891	3.978157	4.181256	4.318090
1.2200000	3.667821	3.901881	4.145920	4.369241	4.521166
1.2300000	3.806241	4.058802	4.324618	4.570543	4.739584
1.2400000	3.952661	4.225372	4.515198	4.786433	4.974939
1.2500000	4.107706	4.402379	4.718707	5.018330	5.229034
1.2599999	4.272058	4.590688	4.936296	5.267818	5.503908
1.2699999	4.446463	4.791245	5.169240	5.536669	5.801877
1.2799999	4.631742	5.005092	5.418946	5.826865	6.125575
1.2899999	4.828792	5.233373	5.686969	6.140629	6.478008
1.3000000	5.038598	5.477347	5.975033	6.480457	6.862613
1.3100000	5.262237	5.738389	6.285034	6.849142	7.283324
1.3200000	5.500895	6.018022	6.619080	7.249829	7.744670
1.3300000	5.755872	6.317914	6.979496	7.686051	8.251866
1.3400000	6.028592	6.639896	7.368851	8.161774	8.810939
1.3500000	6.320616	6.985978	7.789978	8.681452	9.428862
1.3600000	6.633647	7.358359	8.245998	9.250076	10.113730
1.3700000	6.969547	7.759440	8.740334	9.873234	10.874952
1.3799999	7.330336	8.191836	9.276735	10.557164	11.723491
1.3899999	7.718204	8.658378	9.859281	11.308796	12.672129
1.4000000	8.135506	9.162120	10.492395	12.135805	13.735802
1.4100000	8.584747	9.706310	11.180805	13.046590	14.931916
1.4200000	9.068582	10.294392	11.929551	14.050310	16.280815
1.4300000	9.589769	10.929954	12.743903	15.156792	17.806185
1.4400000	10.151127	11.616657	13.629275	16.376411	19.535522
1.4500000	10.755454	12.358148	14.591087	17.719871	21.500569
1.4600000	11.405428	13.157918	15.634564	19.197874	23.737652
1.4700000	12.103462	14.019124	16.764477	20.820638	26.287817
1.4800000	12.851526	14.944351	17.984797	22.597252	29.196543
1.4900000	13.650924	15.935331	19.298280	24.534848	32.512738
1.5000000	14.502051	16.992623	20.705996	26.637638	36.286611
1.5100000	15.404084	18.115221	22.206759	28.905748	40.565569
1.5200000	16.354765	19.300262	23.796690	31.334212	45.387863
1.5300000	17.350148	20.542712	25.468754	33.911960	50.772818
1.5400000	18.384484	21.835205	27.212525	36.621221	56.708149
1.5500000	19.450235	23.168071	29.014215	39.437477	63.136417
1.5600000	20.538266	24.529576	30.857025	42.330098	69.945466
1.5699999	21.638222	25.906412	32.721858	45.263758	76.970350
1.5707963	21.726001	26.016293	32.870705	45.498015	77.533213
1.5707963	21.726007	26.016317	32.870780	45.498457	77.533197

$\alpha =$ .989999

Θ	K VALUES				
	.009966711	.039469502	.087332193	.151646642	.229848846
.0000000	.000000	.000000	.000000	.000000	.000000
.0100000	.010000	.010000	.010000	.010000	.010000
.0200000	.020002	.020002	.020002	.020002	.020002
.0300000	.030008	.030009	.030009	.030009	.030009
.0400000	.040021	.040021	.040022	.040022	.040023
.0500000	.050041	.050042	.050043	.050044	.050046
.0600000	.060071	.060072	.060074	.060076	.060079
.0700000	.070114	.070115	.070118	.070122	.070126
.0800000	.080170	.080172	.080176	.080182	.080189
.0900000	.090242	.090246	.090252	.090259	.090269
.1000000	.100332	.100337	.100345	.100356	.100369
.1100000	.110443	.110450	.110460	.110475	.110492
.1200000	.120576	.120584	.120598	.120617	.120640
.1300000	.130733	.130744	.130762	.130785	.130814
.1400000	.140917	.140930	.140952	.140982	.141018
.1500000	.151129	.151146	.151173	.151209	.151254
.1600000	.161372	.161392	.161425	.161470	.161524
.1700000	.171648	.171672	.171712	.171765	.171830
.1800000	.181959	.181988	.182035	.182099	.182176
.1900000	.192307	.192341	.192397	.192472	.192563
.2000000	.202695	.202735	.202800	.202888	.202994
.2100000	.213125	.213172	.213247	.213349	.213472
.2200000	.223600	.223653	.223740	.223857	.224000
.2300000	.234121	.234182	.234281	.234415	.234579
.2400000	.244691	.244761	.244874	.245026	.245212
.2500000	.255313	.255391	.255520	.255693	.255904
.2600000	.265988	.266077	.266222	.266417	.266655
.2700000	.276721	.276821	.276983	.277202	.277469
.2800000	.287512	.287624	.287805	.288050	.288349
.2900000	.298366	.298490	.298692	.298965	.299298
.3000000	.309284	.309422	.309646	.309949	.310319
.3100000	.320269	.320422	.320670	.321005	.321415
.3200000	.331324	.331493	.331767	.332137	.332590
.3300000	.342453	.342638	.342939	.343347	.343845
.3400000	.353657	.353860	.354191	.354638	.355185
.3500000	.364941	.365163	.365525	.366014	.366614
.3600000	.376306	.376549	.376944	.377478	.378133
.3700000	.387757	.388021	.388452	.389034	.389748
.3800000	.399297	.399584	.400052	.400685	.401462
.3900000	.410928	.411239	.411747	.412434	.413278

$\alpha =$ .989999

Θ	K VALUES				
	.009966711	.039469502	.087332193	.151646642	.229848846
.4000000	.422655	.422992	.423541	.424286	.425201
.4100000	.434480	.434844	.435439	.436244	.437234
.4200000	.446408	.446801	.447442	.448312	.449381
.4300000	.458442	.458865	.459556	.460494	.461647
.4400000	.470586	.471041	.471785	.472794	.474036
.4500000	.482844	.483333	.484132	.485216	.486552
.4600000	.495220	.495745	.496602	.497766	.499200
.4700000	.507718	.508280	.509199	.510446	.511985
.4800000	.520343	.520944	.521927	.523263	.524911
.4900000	.533099	.533741	.534792	.536220	.537983
.5000000	.545990	.546676	.547797	.549323	.551208
.5100000	.559022	.559753	.560949	.562577	.564589
.5200000	.572199	.572977	.574251	.575987	.578133
.5300000	.585526	.586354	.587710	.589558	.591846
.5400000	.599009	.599889	.601331	.603297	.605732
.5500000	.612652	.613587	.615119	.617209	.619799
.5600000	.626463	.627455	.629081	.631300	.634053
.5700000	.640446	.641497	.643222	.645577	.648500
.5800000	.654607	.655721	.657549	.660046	.663147
.5900000	.668953	.670133	.672068	.674713	.678001
.6000000	.683491	.684738	.686786	.689587	.693070
.6100000	.698226	.699545	.701710	.704673	.708362
.6200000	.713167	.714559	.716847	.719980	.723883
.6300000	.728320	.729790	.732206	.735516	.739643
.6400000	.743693	.745243	.747793	.751288	.755649
.6500000	.759293	.760928	.763617	.767306	.771912
.6600000	.775130	.776852	.779687	.783577	.788440
.6700000	.791211	.793025	.796011	.800112	.805243
.6800000	.807545	.809454	.812599	.816920	.822330
.6899999	.824143	.826151	.829461	.834011	.839713
.7000000	.841013	.843124	.846606	.851396	.857403
.7100000	.858165	.860384	.864045	.869085	.875411
.7200000	.875610	.877942	.881789	.887090	.893748
.7300000	.893360	.895808	.899850	.905422	.912428
.7400000	.911425	.913995	.918240	.924095	.931463
.7500000	.929818	.932515	.936970	.943121	.950868
.7600000	.948551	.951380	.956055	.962514	.970656
.7700000	.967638	.970604	.975508	.982288	.990842
.7800000	.987093	.990201	.995344	1.002458	1.011443
.7899999	1.006930	1.010187	1.015578	1.023040	1.032475

$\alpha =$ .989999

Θ	K VALUES				
	.009966711	.039469502	.087332193	.151646642	.229848846
.8000000	1.027164	1.030575	1.036225	1.044051	1.053955
.8100000	1.047811	1.051384	1.057303	1.065508	1.075901
.8200000	1.068889	1.072629	1.078828	1.087428	1.098332
.8300000	1.090414	1.094329	1.100820	1.109832	1.121269
.8400000	1.112406	1.116502	1.123298	1.132739	1.144733
.8500000	1.134885	1.139170	1.146282	1.156171	1.168745
.8600000	1.157870	1.162352	1.169794	1.180149	1.193331
.8700000	1.181384	1.186071	1.193857	1.204699	1.218513
.8799999	1.205450	1.210350	1.218494	1.229843	1.244319
.8899999	1.230092	1.235214	1.243732	1.255610	1.270776
.9000000	1.255336	1.260689	1.269596	1.282026	1.297914
.9100000	1.281209	1.286803	1.296115	1.309121	1.325762
.9200000	1.307740	1.313584	1.323319	1.336926	1.354354
.9300000	1.334959	1.341065	1.351240	1.365474	1.383724
.9400000	1.362898	1.369277	1.379912	1.394800	1.413910
.9500000	1.391593	1.398255	1.409370	1.424941	1.444950
.9600000	1.421079	1.428037	1.439652	1.455937	1.476885
.9699999	1.451395	1.458662	1.470799	1.487829	1.509759
.9799999	1.482582	1.490172	1.502854	1.520662	1.543620
.9899999	1.514685	1.522611	1.535862	1.554484	1.578518
1.0000000	1.547751	1.556028	1.569872	1.589345	1.614505
1.0100000	1.581828	1.590472	1.604937	1.625300	1.651638
1.0200000	1.616971	1.625998	1.641112	1.662405	1.689979
1.0300000	1.653237	1.662664	1.678457	1.700724	1.729591
1.0400000	1.690687	1.700533	1.717035	1.740322	1.770545
1.0500000	1.729387	1.739670	1.756915	1.781270	1.812915
1.0600000	1.769408	1.780149	1.798171	1.823644	1.856781
1.0699999	1.810824	1.822044	1.840881	1.867527	1.902229
1.0799999	1.853718	1.865440	1.885130	1.913007	1.949352
1.0899999	1.898177	1.910425	1.931010	1.960177	1.998250
1.1000000	1.944297	1.957097	1.978620	2.009142	2.049030
1.1100000	1.992178	2.005557	2.028065	2.060012	2.101808
1.1200000	2.041933	2.055919	2.079462	2.112905	2.156710
1.1300000	2.093681	2.108305	2.132936	2.167952	2.213873
1.1400000	2.147552	2.162847	2.188621	2.225294	2.273443
1.1500000	2.203688	2.219688	2.246666	2.285084	2.335582
1.1600000	2.262242	2.278986	2.307231	2.347488	2.400465
1.1700000	2.323383	2.340909	2.370491	2.412687	2.468282
1.1800000	2.387293	2.405645	2.436636	2.480880	2.539242
1.1899999	2.454175	2.473397	2.505877	2.552284	2.613572

$\alpha =$ •989999

Θ	K VALUES				
	•009966711	•039469502	•087332193	•151646642	•229848846
1•2000000	2•524246	2•544389	2•578441	2•627137	2•691522
1•2100000	2•597749	2•618864	2•654581	2•705699	2•773365
1•2200000	2•674949	2•697094	2•734572	2•788257	2•859404
1•2300000	2•756139	2•779375	2•818721	2•875128	2•949972
1•2400000	2•841642	2•866036	2•907364	2•966662	3•045434
1•2500000	2•931816	2•957440	3•000874	3•063246	3•146198
1•2599999	3•027059	3•053990	3•099664	3•165308	3•252715
1•2699999	3•127811	3•156134	3•204196	3•273327	3•365485
1•2799999	3•234566	3•264373	3•314981	3•387835	3•485068
1•2899999	3•347871	3•379264	3•432592	3•509425	3•612088
1•3000000	3•468343	3•501432	3•557670	3•638763	3•747244
1•3100000	3•596670	3•631576	3•690933	3•776594	3•891316
1•3200000	3•733630	3•770485	3•833190	3•923756	4•045189
1•3300000	3•880096	3•919047	3•985353	4•081197	4•209853
1•3400000	4•037057	4•078266	4•148452	4•249985	4•386433
1•3500000	4•205632	4•249278	4•323651	4•431329	4•576199
1•3600000	4•387091	4•433372	4•512275	4•626603	4•780592
1•3700000	4•582876	4•632012	4•715826	4•837365	5•001249
1•3799999	4•794629	4•846867	4•936016	5•065392	5•240037
1•3899999	5•024221	5•079835	5•174793	5•312705	5•499078
1•4000000	5•273786	5•333084	5•434381	5•581613	5•780797
1•4100000	5•545748	5•609074	5•717305	5•874736	6•087944
1•4200000	5•842870	5•910612	6•026446	6•195061	6•423659
1•4300000	6•168281	6•240875	6•365064	6•545973	6•791494
1•4400000	6•525508	6•603443	6•736832	6•931284	7•195453
1•4500000	6•918490	7•002317	7•145856	7•355252	7•640009
1•4600000	7•351566	7•441904	7•596658	7•822571	8•130090
1•4700000	7•829424	7•926961	8•094120	8•338307	8•671018
1•4800000	8•356970	8•462471	8•643356	8•907766	9•268363
1•4900000	8•939100	9•053406	9•249466	9•536240	9•927685
1•5000000	9•580327	9•704349	9•917155	10•228611	10•654110
1•5100000	10•284205	10•418907	10•650124	10•988720	11•451671
1•5200000	11•052594	11•198970	11•450312	11•818578	12•322481
1•5300000	11•884731	12•043762	12•316923	12•717360	13•265673
1•5400000	12•776288	12•948890	13•245449	13•680387	14•276335
1•5500000	13•718652	13•905606	14•226913	14•698347	15•344684
1•5600000	14•698733	14•900621	15•247678	15•757086	16•455860
1•5699999	15•699610	15•916753	16•290112	16•838310	17•590649
1•5707963	15•779642	15•998004	16•373466	16•924767	17•681388
1•5707963	15•779633	15•997995	16•373458	16•924758	17•681381

$\alpha =$ .989999

θ	K VALUES				
	.318821117	.415016431	.514599755	.613601043	.708073407
.0000000	.000000	.000000	.000000	.000000	.000000
.0100000	.010000	.010000	.010000	.010000	.010000
.0200000	.020003	.020003	.020003	.020003	.020003
.0300000	.030010	.030010	.030011	.030011	.030012
.0400000	.040024	.040025	.040026	.040027	.040028
.0500000	.050047	.050049	.050052	.050054	.050056
.0600000	.060082	.060086	.060089	.060093	.060096
.0700000	.070131	.070137	.070142	.070148	.070154
.0800000	.080196	.080204	.080213	.080222	.080230
.0900000	.090280	.090292	.090304	.090316	.090327
.1000000	.100384	.100400	.100417	.100434	.100450
.1100000	.110512	.110534	.110556	.110578	.110599
.1200000	.120666	.120694	.120723	.120751	.120779
.1300000	.130847	.130883	.130920	.130957	.130992
.1400000	.141059	.141104	.141150	.141196	.141240
.1500000	.151305	.151360	.151417	.151474	.151528
.1600000	.161586	.161653	.161722	.161791	.161857
.1700000	.171905	.171985	.172069	.172152	.172231
.1800000	.182264	.182360	.182459	.182559	.182653
.1900000	.192667	.192780	.192897	.193014	.193126
.2000000	.203116	.203248	.203385	.203522	.203653
.2100000	.213614	.213767	.213926	.214085	.214238
.2200000	.224162	.224339	.224523	.224707	.224883
.2300000	.234765	.234968	.235179	.235390	.235592
.2400000	.245425	.245656	.245897	.246137	.246368
.2500000	.256145	.256407	.256680	.256953	.257215
.2600000	.266927	.267223	.267532	.267840	.268136
.2700000	.277775	.278108	.278455	.278802	.279135
.2800000	.288692	.289065	.289453	.289842	.290216
.2900000	.299680	.300096	.300530	.300964	.301382
.3000000	.310744	.311206	.311689	.312172	.312638
.3100000	.321886	.322398	.322933	.323470	.323986
.3200000	.333109	.333675	.334267	.334860	.335432
.3300000	.344417	.345041	.345693	.346349	.346980
.3400000	.355814	.356499	.357217	.357938	.358633
.3500000	.367302	.368054	.368841	.369633	.370397
.3600000	.378886	.379709	.380571	.381438	.382275
.3700000	.390569	.391468	.392409	.393357	.394273
.3800000	.402356	.403334	.404361	.405395	.406394
.3900000	.414250	.415313	.416430	.417556	.418645

$\alpha =$ .989999

Θ	K VALUES				
	.318821117	.415016431	.514599755	.613601043	.708073407
.4000000	.426254	.427409	.428622	.429845	.431031
.4100000	.438374	.439625	.440940	.442268	.443555
.4200000	.450614	.451967	.453391	.454829	.456225
.4300000	.462978	.464439	.465978	.467534	.469045
.4400000	.475470	.477046	.478707	.480388	.482022
.4500000	.488095	.489792	.491583	.493397	.495161
.4600000	.500858	.502684	.504611	.506566	.508469
.4700000	.513765	.515726	.517798	.519901	.521951
.4800000	.526819	.528923	.531148	.533410	.535615
.4900000	.540027	.542282	.544669	.547097	.549468
.5000000	.553394	.555808	.558365	.560970	.563516
.5100000	.566925	.569507	.572245	.575036	.577767
.5200000	.580626	.583385	.586313	.589301	.592228
.5300000	.594504	.597449	.600578	.603774	.606908
.5400000	.608565	.611705	.615045	.618462	.621815
.5500000	.622814	.626160	.629724	.633372	.636958
.5600000	.637260	.640822	.644620	.648513	.652344
.5700000	.651908	.655698	.659743	.663895	.667985
.5800000	.666767	.670796	.675101	.679524	.683888
.5900000	.681843	.686123	.690701	.695412	.700065
.6000000	.697144	.701688	.706554	.711567	.716526
.6100000	.712679	.717499	.722668	.728000	.733281
.6200000	.728455	.733566	.739053	.744721	.750343
.6300000	.744482	.749898	.755719	.761741	.767722
.6400000	.760769	.766504	.772677	.779071	.785432
.6500000	.777324	.783395	.789937	.796724	.803485
.6600000	.794158	.800581	.807511	.814711	.821895
.6700000	.811282	.818073	.825411	.833046	.840676
.6800000	.828706	.835882	.843649	.851742	.859843
.6899999	.846440	.854022	.862238	.870813	.879411
.7000000	.864497	.872503	.881192	.890274	.899396
.7100000	.882889	.891340	.900524	.910141	.919816
.7200000	.901628	.910545	.920250	.930429	.940687
.7300000	.920729	.930133	.940385	.951155	.962030
.7400000	.940203	.950119	.960945	.972338	.983863
.7500000	.960067	.970518	.981947	.993995	1.006207
.7600000	.980336	.991348	1.003409	1.016147	1.029083
.7700000	1.001024	1.012624	1.025350	1.038814	1.052514
.7800000	1.022150	1.034365	1.047788	1.062017	1.076525
.7899999	1.043731	1.056590	1.070746	1.085779	1.101139

$\alpha =$ .989999

Θ	K VALUES				
	.318821117	.415016431	.514599755	.613601043	.708073407
.8000000	1.065784	1.079319	1.094243	1.110124	1.126385
.8100000	1.088330	1.102572	1.118304	1.135076	1.152288
.8200000	1.111389	1.126372	1.142951	1.160662	1.178879
.8300000	1.134981	1.150741	1.168210	1.186911	1.206188
.8400000	1.159131	1.175703	1.194107	1.213850	1.234249
.8500000	1.183860	1.201284	1.220670	1.241511	1.263095
.8600000	1.209195	1.227512	1.247929	1.269926	1.292763
.8700000	1.235161	1.254414	1.275915	1.299130	1.323292
.8799999	1.261787	1.282020	1.304660	1.329160	1.354723
.8899999	1.289101	1.310362	1.334199	1.360052	1.387097
.9000000	1.317136	1.339474	1.364569	1.391849	1.420463
.9100000	1.345923	1.369391	1.395808	1.424593	1.454867
.9200000	1.375497	1.400150	1.427957	1.458330	1.490361
.9300000	1.405895	1.431792	1.461061	1.493109	1.527001
.9400000	1.437157	1.464358	1.495164	1.528980	1.564843
.9500000	1.469324	1.497892	1.530317	1.565998	1.603950
.9600000	1.502439	1.532444	1.566572	1.604222	1.644389
.9699999	1.536550	1.568063	1.603983	1.643714	1.686228
.9799999	1.571707	1.604803	1.642610	1.684539	1.729543
.9899999	1.607963	1.642721	1.682516	1.726767	1.774413
1.0000000	1.645374	1.681879	1.723768	1.770474	1.820925
1.0100000	1.684000	1.722342	1.766438	1.815740	1.869168
1.0200000	1.723907	1.764179	1.810602	1.862650	1.919242
1.0300000	1.765163	1.807466	1.856343	1.911297	1.971250
1.0400000	1.807844	1.852283	1.903748	1.961778	2.025305
1.0500000	1.852026	1.898714	1.952911	2.014199	2.081527
1.0600000	1.897798	1.946853	2.003934	2.068673	2.140047
1.0699999	1.945248	1.996798	2.056926	2.125323	2.201003
1.0799999	1.994478	2.048655	2.112002	2.184279	2.264546
1.0899999	2.045591	2.102540	2.169291	2.245683	2.330838
1.1000000	2.098704	2.158576	2.228927	2.309688	2.400055
1.1100000	2.153939	2.216896	2.291058	2.376458	2.472385
1.1200000	2.211431	2.277646	2.355842	2.446172	2.548034
1.1300000	2.271324	2.340982	2.423452	2.519024	2.627224
1.1400000	2.333776	2.407075	2.494076	2.595223	2.710198
1.1500000	2.398957	2.476108	2.567916	2.674997	2.797217
1.1600000	2.467055	2.548283	2.645193	2.758597	2.888568
1.1700000	2.538272	2.623820	2.726149	2.846291	2.984563
1.1800000	2.612829	2.702958	2.811048	2.938378	3.085545
1.1899999	2.690969	2.785959	2.900177	3.035179	3.191886

$\alpha =$ .989999

Θ	K VALUES				
	.318821117	.415016431	.514599755	.613601043	.708073407
1.2000000	2.772959	2.873110	2.993854	3.137052	3.303996
1.2100000	2.859088	2.964727	3.092424	3.244385	3.422325
1.2200000	2.949679	3.061155	3.196268	3.357608	3.547369
1.2300000	3.045085	3.162779	3.305809	3.477193	3.679674
1.2400000	3.145697	3.270020	3.421511	3.603664	3.819843
1.2500000	3.251948	3.383346	3.543887	3.737598	3.968544
1.2599999	3.364318	3.503275	3.673510	3.879638	4.126520
1.2699999	3.483340	3.630384	3.811012	4.030496	4.294595
1.2799999	3.609610	3.765316	3.957102	4.190967	4.473687
1.2899999	3.743790	3.908789	4.112568	4.361940	4.664823
1.3000000	3.886626	4.061606	4.278296	4.544409	4.869153
1.3100000	4.038948	4.224666	4.455274	4.739486	5.087962
1.3200000	4.201697	4.398984	4.644618	4.948426	5.322702
1.3300000	4.375928	4.585703	4.847586	5.172642	5.575007
1.3400000	4.562838	4.786113	5.065596	5.413731	5.846723
1.3500000	4.763777	5.001675	5.300256	5.673499	6.139938
1.3600000	4.980280	5.234046	5.553391	5.953998	6.457025
1.3700000	5.214090	5.485112	5.827071	6.257556	6.800677
1.3799999	5.467192	5.757015	6.123655	6.586825	7.173960
1.3899999	5.741846	6.052199	6.445831	6.944827	7.580366
1.4000000	6.040632	6.373450	6.796664	7.335006	8.023880
1.4100000	6.366478	6.723932	7.179633	7.761276	8.509025
1.4200000	6.722724	7.107255	7.598709	8.228098	9.040960
1.4300000	7.113151	7.527504	8.058384	8.740525	9.625526
1.4400000	7.542020	7.989283	8.563724	9.304249	10.269302
1.4500000	8.014092	8.497735	9.120385	9.925627	10.979639
1.4600000	8.534611	9.058527	9.734599	10.611667	11.764637
1.4700000	9.109241	9.677777	10.413096	11.369933	12.633039
1.4800000	9.743910	10.361893	11.162923	12.208346	13.594001
1.4900000	10.444535	11.117266	11.991109	13.134807	14.656659
1.5000000	11.216571	11.949790	12.904138	14.156605	15.829437
1.5100000	12.064310	12.864104	13.907111	15.279473	17.118965
1.5200000	12.990002	13.862637	15.002701	16.506417	18.528721
1.5300000	13.992724	14.944393	16.189813	17.836210	20.057290
1.5400000	15.067247	16.103723	17.462235	19.261870	21.696612
1.5500000	16.203162	17.329382	18.807600	20.769503	23.430634
1.5600000	17.384654	18.604281	20.207118	22.337989	25.234961
1.5699999	18.591276	19.906331	21.636493	23.940030	27.078053
1.5707963	18.687759	20.010446	21.750790	24.068135	27.225436
1.5707963	18.687752	20.010440	21.750786	24.068135	27.225442

$\alpha =$ .989999

Θ	K VALUES				
	.794250555	.868696860	.928444378	.971111163	.994996249
.0000000	.000000	.000000	.000000	.000000	.000000
.0100000	.010000	.010000	.010000	.010000	.010000
.0200000	.020003	.020003	.020003	.020003	.020003
.0300000	.030012	.030012	.030013	.030013	.030013
.0400000	.040029	.040030	.040031	.040031	.040031
.0500000	.050057	.050059	.050060	.050061	.050062
.0600000	.060100	.060102	.060104	.060106	.060107
.0700000	.070159	.070163	.070166	.070169	.070170
.0800000	.080237	.080243	.080249	.080252	.080254
.0900000	.090338	.090347	.090354	.090360	.090363
.1000000	.100464	.100477	.100487	.100494	.100498
.1100000	.110619	.110635	.110649	.110658	.110664
.1200000	.120804	.120826	.120844	.120856	.120863
.1300000	.131024	.131052	.131074	.131090	.131099
.1400000	.141281	.141316	.141344	.141364	.141375
.1500000	.151578	.151621	.151655	.151680	.151694
.1600000	.161918	.161970	.162012	.162042	.162059
.1700000	.172304	.172367	.172418	.172454	.172474
.1800000	.182740	.182815	.182876	.182919	.182943
.1900000	.193229	.193317	.193389	.193440	.193468
.2000000	.203773	.203877	.203961	.204021	.204054
.2100000	.214377	.214498	.214595	.214665	.214704
.2200000	.225044	.225184	.225296	.225376	.225422
.2300000	.235777	.235937	.236066	.236159	.236211
.2400000	.246579	.246762	.246910	.247016	.247075
.2500000	.257455	.257663	.257831	.257951	.258019
.2600000	.268408	.268643	.268834	.268970	.269046
.2700000	.279441	.279707	.279921	.280075	.280161
.2800000	.290559	.290858	.291098	.291271	.291368
.2900000	.301766	.302100	.302369	.302562	.302670
.3000000	.313065	.313437	.313738	.313953	.314074
.3100000	.324461	.324875	.325209	.325448	.325583
.3200000	.335959	.336417	.336787	.337053	.337202
.3300000	.347561	.348068	.348477	.348771	.348936
.3400000	.359274	.359832	.360283	.360608	.360790
.3500000	.371101	.371715	.372212	.372569	.372769
.3600000	.383047	.383721	.384267	.384659	.384879
.3700000	.395118	.395856	.396454	.396884	.397126
.3800000	.407318	.408125	.408779	.409249	.409514
.3900000	.419653	.420533	.421247	.421761	.422050

$\alpha =$ .989999

Θ	K VALUES				
	.794250555	.868696860	.928444378	.971111163	.994996249
.4000000	.432127	.433086	.433864	.434425	.434740
.4100000	.444747	.445790	.446637	.447247	.447590
.4200000	.457518	.458651	.459571	.460234	.460608
.4300000	.470447	.471675	.472674	.473394	.473799
.4400000	.483539	.484869	.485951	.486732	.487171
.4500000	.496800	.498239	.499410	.500255	.500732
.4600000	.510238	.511792	.513058	.513973	.514488
.4700000	.523858	.525536	.526903	.527891	.528449
.4800000	.537669	.539478	.540953	.542019	.542621
.4900000	.551678	.553625	.555215	.556365	.557014
.5000000	.565891	.567986	.569698	.570937	.571637
.5100000	.580318	.582570	.584411	.585745	.586499
.5200000	.594965	.597384	.599363	.600798	.601609
.5300000	.609843	.612438	.614564	.616106	.616979
.5400000	.624959	.627742	.630024	.631680	.632618
.5500000	.640322	.643305	.645752	.647530	.648537
.5600000	.655943	.659138	.661761	.663668	.664749
.5700000	.671832	.675250	.678061	.680105	.681264
.5800000	.687998	.691654	.694663	.696855	.698097
.5900000	.704453	.708362	.711582	.713928	.715260
.6000000	.721208	.725384	.728828	.731341	.732767
.6100000	.738275	.742735	.746417	.749105	.750632
.6200000	.755666	.760426	.764361	.767237	.768872
.6300000	.773394	.778473	.782676	.785752	.787501
.6400000	.791473	.796889	.801378	.804666	.806537
.6500000	.809916	.815691	.820483	.823996	.825997
.6600000	.828739	.834894	.840008	.843761	.845900
.6700000	.847957	.854514	.859970	.863979	.866266
.6800000	.867585	.874570	.880390	.884671	.887115
.6899999	.887642	.895080	.901286	.905857	.908469
.7000000	.908144	.916063	.922681	.927560	.930351
.7100000	.929111	.937539	.944594	.949803	.952785
.7200000	.950562	.959531	.967051	.972611	.975796
.7300000	.972517	.982060	.990075	.996009	.999412
.7400000	.994999	1.005151	1.013693	1.020025	1.023661
.7500000	1.018029	1.028828	1.037931	1.044689	1.048572
.7600000	1.041632	1.053119	1.062818	1.070030	1.074179
.7700000	1.065833	1.078049	1.088384	1.096082	1.100515
.7800000	1.090659	1.103650	1.114663	1.122879	1.127615
.7899999	1.116137	1.129952	1.141687	1.150457	1.155519

$\alpha =$ .989999

Θ	K VALUES				
	.794250555	.868696860	.928444378	.971111163	.994996249
.8000000	1.142297	1.156988	1.169493	1.178855	1.184266
.8100000	1.169169	1.184792	1.198119	1.208115	1.213899
.8200000	1.196788	1.213401	1.227605	1.238279	1.244464
.8300000	1.225186	1.242854	1.257995	1.269395	1.276009
.8400000	1.254402	1.273192	1.289333	1.301511	1.308588
.8500000	1.284474	1.304458	1.321669	1.334682	1.342255
.8600000	1.315443	1.336700	1.355054	1.368962	1.377068
.8700000	1.347352	1.369965	1.389543	1.404412	1.413092
.8799999	1.380248	1.404307	1.425194	1.441095	1.450394
.8899999	1.414179	1.439781	1.462069	1.479081	1.489047
.9000000	1.449198	1.476445	1.500237	1.518442	1.529127
.9100000	1.485360	1.514363	1.539766	1.559256	1.570718
.9200000	1.522722	1.553602	1.580734	1.601608	1.613909
.9300000	1.561349	1.594233	1.623221	1.645588	1.658797
.9400000	1.601305	1.636332	1.667314	1.691292	1.705484
.9500000	1.642663	1.679982	1.713107	1.738825	1.754081
.9600000	1.685497	1.725269	1.760700	1.788299	1.804710
.9699999	1.729888	1.772287	1.810200	1.839834	1.857499
.9799999	1.775922	1.821135	1.861723	1.893560	1.912590
.9899999	1.823693	1.871922	1.915393	1.949618	1.970132
1.0000000	1.873297	1.924762	1.971345	2.008161	2.030292
1.0100000	1.924842	1.979779	2.029721	2.069351	2.093247
1.0200000	1.978439	2.037106	2.090678	2.133368	2.159192
1.0300000	2.034211	2.096885	2.154384	2.200405	2.228338
1.0400000	2.092289	2.159272	2.221022	2.270673	2.300916
1.0500000	2.152813	2.224433	2.290789	2.344399	2.377176
1.0600000	2.215935	2.292547	2.363898	2.421833	2.457393
1.0699999	2.281818	2.363809	2.440583	2.503246	2.541869
1.0799999	2.350637	2.438430	2.521094	2.588937	2.630933
1.0899999	2.422584	2.516636	2.605708	2.679229	2.724949
1.1000000	2.497865	2.598676	2.694724	2.774479	2.824317
1.1100000	2.576701	2.684817	2.788468	2.875077	2.929475
1.1200000	2.659336	2.775353	2.887298	2.981452	3.040910
1.1300000	2.746032	2.870600	2.991604	3.094079	3.159162
1.1400000	2.837074	2.970907	3.101815	3.213478	3.284827
1.1500000	2.932774	3.076652	3.218401	3.340227	3.418570
1.1600000	3.033471	3.188250	3.341879	3.474963	3.561130
1.1700000	3.139537	3.306155	3.472817	3.618395	3.713332
1.1800000	3.251376	3.430865	3.611844	3.771309	3.876101
1.1899999	3.369433	3.562927	3.759653	3.934582	4.050474

$\alpha =$ •989999

Θ	K VALUES				
	•794250555	•868696860	•928444378	•971111163	•994996249
1•2000000	3•494197	3•702945	3•917011	4•109190	4•237618
1•2100000	3•626203	3•851581	4•084765	4•296225	4•438844
1•2200000	3•766043	4•009569	4•263861	4•496910	4•655640
1•2300000	3•914370	4•177720	4•455348	4•712618	4•889690
1•2400000	4•071904	4•356933	4•660395	4•944896	5•142911
1•2500000	4•239445	4•548208	4•880306	5•195485	5•417487
1•2599999	4•417881	4•752654	5•116543	5•466355	5•715919
1•2699999	4•608198	4•971509	5•370741	5•759737	6•041077
1•2799999	4•811499	5•206158	5•644737	6•078163	6•396265
1•2899999	5•029014	5•458148	5•940598	6•424516	6•785305
1•3000000	5•262122	5•729219	6•260657	6•802091	7•212633
1•3100000	5•512366	6•021317	6•607539	7•214641	7•683401
1•3200000	5•781488	6•336644	6•984227	7•666480	8•203644
1•3300000	6•071449	6•677683	7•394096	8•162560	8•780443
1•3400000	6•384466	7•047243	7•840986	8•708585	9•422140
1•3500000	6•723050	7•448505	8•329262	9•311130	10•138605
1•3600000	7•090047	7•885085	8•863903	9•977796	10•941569
1•3700000	7•488694	8•361092	9•450590	10•717381	11•845026
1•3799999	7•922675	8•881207	10•095815	11•540076	12•865748
1•3899999	8•396185	9•450767	10•807000	12•457699	14•023912
1•4000000	8•914013	10•075860	11•592638	13•483961	15•343895
1•4100000	9•481593	10•763403	12•462402	14•634705	16•855194
1•4200000	10•105122	11•521284	13•427345	15•928276	18•593696
1•4300000	10•791618	12•358435	14•500010	17•385772	20•603069
1•4400000	11•548987	13•284924	15•694554	19•031329	22•936502
1•4500000	12•386059	14•311993	17•026816	20•892294	25•658693
1•4600000	13•312564	15•452033	18•514271	22•999231	28•848005
1•4700000	14•339007	16•718424	20•175818	25•385609	32•598580
1•4800000	15•476388	18•125179	22•031273	28•086992	37•021910
1•4900000	16•735682	19•686282	24•100447	31•139472	42•246955
1•5000000	18•127010	21•414638	26•401672	34•577082	48•417371
1•5100000	19•658345	23•320424	28•949483	38•427736	55•683082
1•5200000	21•333874	25•409011	31•751701	42•707980	64•183869
1•5300000	23•151913	27•678318	34•805714	47•416334	74•021086
1•5400000	25•102803	30•116133	38•094717	52•526478	85•217420
1•5500000	27•167296	32•698065	41•584832	57•981997	97•670849
1•5600000	29•316129	35•387004	45•224340	63•694886	111•119047
1•5699999	31•511468	38•134951	48•946254	69•550010	125•139679
1•5707963	31•687024	38•354710	49•243943	70•018520	126•265395
1•5707963	31•687040	38•354751	49•244046	70•018897	126•265460

MATHEMATICAL TABLES

by Herbert B. Dwight

This set of tables is unique in English mathematical literature for its coverage, in one handy inexpensive volume, of almost every function of importance in applied mathematics, engineering, and the physical sceinces. Statisticians, electrical, civil, mechanical, nuclear engineers, aero- and hydronamicists, physicists, chemists, astrophysicists, meteorologists, biochemists, biomathematicians, geologists—everyone concerned with the evaluation of mathematical formulae used in various branches of science will find this book a gold-mine of information otherwise difficult or impossible to obtain in one volume.

In addition to extremely fine tables of the 3 trigonometric functions sine, cosine and tangent, and their inverse functions to thousandths of radians, natural and common logarithms, squares, cubes, square and cube roots, reciprocals, and the exponential functions e^x and e^{-x}, Mr Dwight hs included tables of the hyperbolic functions and the inverse hyperbolic functions, (a^2+b^2) exp. 1/2a, complete elliptic integrals of the firist and second kind, the sine and cosine integrals, the exponential integrals Ei(x) and Ei(—x), binomial coefficients, factorials to 250, Gregory-Newton interpolation coefficients, Lagrangean interpolation coefficients (3, 5, and 7 tabulated values), surface zonal Harmonics and first derivatives, Bernoulli and Euler numbers and their logarithms to the base 10, the Gamma functions, the normal probability integral, the error function, over 60 pages of Bessel functions, roots of Bessel function equations, and the Riemann Zeta function. Each table is followed by a short note giving the formulae generally used in connection with the table, sources of more extensive tables, interpolation data, etc. Over half of the tables are provided with columns of differences to facilitate interpolation.

Revised and corrected new edition. Introduction. Index. viii + 231pp. 5⅜ x 8.

S445 Paperbound **$1.75**

DICTIONARY OF CONFORMAL REPRESENTATIONS

by H. Kober

Developed for the British Admiralty during World War II, this unique book enables its users to solve Laplace's Equation in Two Dimensions for many boundary conditions. It contains scores of geometrical forms and their transformations for use in checking against specific problems.

Kober's DICTIONARY OF CONFORMAL REPRESENTATIONS is especially helpful in hydrodynamics, gas dynamics, free streamline theory, heat flow, magnetic field problems, soil mechanics, electrostatics, map projection, etc. It contains the following specific features for workers in different fields: Linear and bilinear transformations for electrical engineers — Joukowski aerofoil for aerodynamists — Transcendental functions for physicists and engineers — Schwartz-Christophel transformations for hydrodynamicists and electrical engineers — Borda's mouthpiece for researchers in hydraulics and jet propulsion. The book is classified according to the analytic functions describing the transformations; it gives instant access to time-saving set-ups and eliminates much of the work involved in deriving a particular configuration.

"Of great value to workers in such fields as electricity, hydrodynamics, aerodynamics and heat flow," BRITISH JOURNAL OF APPLIED PHYSICS. "Useful to engineers and physicists as well as to mathematicians," JOURNAL OF ROYAL NAVAL SCIENTIFIC SERVICE. "May well remain the standard work for many years," MATHEMATICAL GAZETTE.

Bibliography. Glossary. Topological index. 447 diagrams. xvi + 208pp. 6⅛ x 9¼.

S160 Paperbound **$1.85**

NUMERICAL SOLUTIONS OF DIFFERENTIAL EQUATIONS

by H. Levy and E. A. Baggott

The primary emphasis in this time-saving volume is on methods of solving ordinary differential equations of the first and higher orders. Most of the familiar methods and many new ones are presented, all subject to two basic requirements — 1) they must be easy to grasp and practical; and 2) they must offer more rapid solutions than ordinary school methods.

Beginning with geometrical properties useful in the application of graphical methods, the authors proceed to the numerical solution of differential equations. They discuss the methods of Frobenius involving power series; those of Euler, Runge and Kutta expressing values of y corresponding to tabulated values of x; and numerous others, both classical and modern. One chapter is devoted to forward integration methods of first order equations; another discusses simultaneous equations and equations of second and higher orders. The final chapter treats special methods applicable to linear differential equations. Numerous illustrative examples are worked out in careful detail, and over eighty typical problems are offered for the reader's solution.

"Fulfills a great need in this field . . . extremely useful," SCIENCE. "Should be in the hands of all those who are in research in applied mathematics and of all who are interested in the improvement of mathematical teaching," NATURE (London).

21 figures. viii + 238pp. 5⅜ x 8.

S168 Paperbound **$1.75**

ALMOST PERIODIC FUNCTIONS

by A. S. Besicovitch

This important summary by a well-known mathematician covers the theory of almost periodic functions created by Harold Bohr. It examines Bohr's own work, as well as newer, shorter, and more elementary proofs than Bohr's, and also demonstrates extensions of the theory beyond the class of uniformly continuous functions to which Bohr's work was limited. The contributions of Wiener, Weyl, de la Vallée Poussin, Stepanoff, and Bochner are examined, while the author's own work on the piecewise continuous case is also included.

The first portion of this book establishes basic theorems of uniformly a.p. functions, including Bohr's original work, and de la Vallée Poussin's ingenious short proof based on classical theory of purely periodic functions. It considers such matters as summation of Fourier series of u.a.p. functions by partial sums, the Bochner-Fejer summation of u.a.p. functions, particular cases of Fourier series, and u.a.p. functions of two variables.

The second portion of this work covers generalizations and extensions of the original theory, discussing relaxation of continuity restrictions, auxiliary theorems and formulae, the Parseval equation and the Riesc-Fischer theorem, and similar matters. The third chapter discusses analytic a.p. functions, including results in the location of singularities, behavior at infinity, and convergence of series. It opens a way to study a wide class of trigonometric series of the general type and of exponential series (Dirichlet series).

"For those interested in the concrete and calculational aspects of theory," APPLIED MECHANICS REVIEW. "A clear, concise, reasonably self-contained treatment of theory fundamentals," DESIGN NEWS.

Bibliography. xiii + 180pp. 5 3/8 x 8.

S18 Paperbound **$1.75**

MATHEMATICAL FOUNDATIONS OF STATISTICAL MECHANICS

by A. I. Khinchin

The translation of this important book brings to the English-speaking mathematician and mathematical physicist a thoroughly up to date introduction to statistical mechanics.

It offers a precise and mathematically rigorous formulation of the problems of statictical mechanics, as opposed to the non-rigorous discussion presented in most other works. It provides analytical tools needed to replace many of the cumbersome concepts and devices commonly used for establishing basic formulae, and it furnishes the mathematician with a logical step-by-step introduction, which will enable him to master the elements of statictical mechanics in the shortest possible time.

After a historical sketch the author discusses the geometry and kinematics of the phase space, with the theorems of Liouville and Birkhoff; the ergodic problem (in the sense of replacing time averages by phase averages); the theory of probability, central limit theorem, ideal monatomic gas; foundation of thermodynamics, and dispersion and distribution of sum functions.

"An excellent introduction to the difficult and important discipline of Statistical Mechanics. It is clear, concise, and rigorous. There is a very good chapter on the ergodic theorem, (with a complete proof!) and . . . a highly lucid chapter on statistical foundations of thermodynamics . . . useful to teachers . . . and to mathematicians," M. Kac, QUARTERLY OF APPLIED MATHEMATICS.

Index. Key to notations. viii + 179pp. 5⅜ x 8.

S147 Paperbound **$1.35**

ASYMPTOTIC EXPANSIONS

by A. Erdelyi

This is an unabridged republication of a monograph prepared for the office of Naval Research. Unavailable for some time, it presents new and recent methods based on research done for the U. S. Navy. It is an introduction to various methods for the asymptotical evaluation of integrals containing a large parameter and to the study of solutions of ordinary linear differential equations by means of asymptotical expansions.

The only modern work available in English on this important topic, Erdelyi's ASYMPTOTIC EXPANSIONS presents a large number of subjects carefully developed. After an introduction to the theory of asymptotic series, the author proceeds to the most important methods for asymptotic expansion of functions defined by integrals. The remainder of the book concerns solutions of ordinary linear differential equations.

PARTIAL CONTENTS: **Asymptotic Series.** Sequence, expansions. Linear operations, power series, summation. **Integrals.** Integration by parts. Laplace integrals. Critical points. Laplace's method. Steepest descents. Airy's integral. Fourier integral. Stationary phase. **Singularities of Differential Equations.** Classification. Normal solutions. Integral equation, solution. Expansions. Complex variable. Stokes' phenomenon. Bessel functions of order zero. **Differential Equations with a Large Parameter.** Liouville's problems. Formal solutions. Asymptotic solutions. Application to Bessel functions. Transition points. Airy functions. Asymptotic solutions valid in transposition region. Uniform asymptotic representations of Bessel functions.

Bibliography. vi + 108pp. 5⅜ x 8.

S318 Paperbound **$1.35**

ELLIPTIC INTEGRALS

by Harris Hancock

While elementary calculus methods are adequate for integrating any expression in which a quadratic in one variable appears under a square root sign, a more advanced calculus is necessary to integrate similar expressions where cubics and quartics occur under the root sign. ELLIPTIC INTEGRALS is a rigorous exposition of this branch of advanced calculus according to the Legendre-Jacobi theory, and deals with the integration of elliptic integrals of the first and second kinds.

ELLIPTIC INTEGRALS shows the student, mathematician, geometer, physicist, or engineer whose work involves differential equations containing cubics or quartics under the root sign, as in electrical theory, theory of the potential, resistance and elastica problems, how these integrals may be transformed into standard normal forms. 5-place tables of these normal forms are included, so that the integrals may be calculated to any degree of exactness required without the need of referring to another book. Another valuable feature of ELLIPTIC INTEGRALS is that it contains an account of the elliptic functions associated with elliptic integrals, with emphasis on their doubly periodic properties.

CONTENTS: Introduction. Chapter I: Elliptic Integrals of the First, Second, and Third Kinds. The Legendre Transformations. Chapter II: The Elliptic Functions. Chapter III: Elliptic Integrals of the First Kind Reduced to Legendre's Normal Form. Chapter IV: Numerical Computation of the Elliptic Integrals of the First and Second Kinds. Landen's Transformations. Chapter V: Miscellaneous Examples and Problems. Chapter VI: Five-Place Tables. Index.

20 figures. Five-place tables. Index. 104pp. 5⅜ x 8.

Paperbound **$1.25**